To Henry!
My Love and Best Wishes
to you Always. Live long,
be Positive and Happy.
You Are My Friend
Always.

Love
Peggy December
1990

Webster's Illustrated Dictionary Encyclopedia

First published in 1984 by Grisewood & Dempsey Ltd.

This 1989 edition published by Crescent Books distributed by Crown Publishers, Inc., 225 Park Avenue South, New York, New York 10003

Printed and bound in Italy

Library of Congress Cataloguing-in-Publication Data
Webster's illustrated dictionary encyclopedia.
p. cm.
ISBN 0-517-68835-2
1. Encyclopedias and dictionaries.
AG5.W384 1989
031–dc20
89–1480 CIF

h g f e d c b a

Webster's Illustrated Dictionary Encyclopedia

CRESCENT BOOKS
NEW YORK

INTRODUCTION

This work, combining as it does a really useful dictionary with an up-to-date, fully illustrated encyclopedia, fulfills a need for easily accessible information on a huge and varied range of subjects within a single, manageable volume. Take, for instance: **submarine** *n.* a kind of boat that can move under the water instead of on the surface. This bald dictionary entry is followed by an arrowhead ▶ which tells us to read on. In reading on we learn, with accompanying illustrations, how a submarine works and something of its history. And so it is with hundreds more otherwise purely dictionary entries, from abacus to taste, from trees to zinc. The arrowheads are the signposts which direct us in our pursuit for further information. And to help in this pursuit, there are cross-references within the articles to other related articles. These are printed in SMALL CAPITALS. So, in the article following the arrowhead under the dictionary entry "religion" there are cross-references to BUDDHA, CHRISTIANITY, HINDUS, ISLAM and JUDAISM.

There are also hundreds of entries which are not usually found in a dictionary – they are the names of people and places. These articles are placed in the normal alphabetical order with all the other entries. But the headword is printed on a separate line in capital and small letters, for example **Roman Empire** or **Rubens, Peter Paul**. Every entry on an independent country has a location map with names of surrounding countries.

An important feature of this work is the specialized vocabularies which accompany certain of the articles. Thus, for example, under the entry **computer** there is a list of some of the more important computer terms from analogue to VDU and word processor; and so it is with, for example, **geology**, **horses**, **mathematics**, music and so on.

May we therefore recommend this work to you as an important and more useful family reference book, a source of highly interesting, accurate and up-to-date information on a vast spectrum of subjects, as well as a sound, modern dictionary.

D 200

How to use this Dictionary

Alphabetical order
All the entries in this Illustrated Reference Dictionary are listed in the order of the alphabet. The words entered under each letter of the alphabet are themselves in the alphabetical order of the second, third, etc. letter of that word. So, for example, under the F entries, fabric follows fable: since the first three letters, "f", "a" and "b" are the same, you must look to the fourth letter, and "l" comes before "r."

Entries
A word with all its information is called an *entry*. All entries in this book are in bold black type. So are other forms of the same word. For example, **abduct** is an entry word in bold black type and the other forms of the word, **abduction** and **abductor,** are also in bold black type. If the entry is an encyclopedic one only – usually the name of a place or person – the type appears as big and small letters (also in bold black) and on a separate line, for example, **North Carolina,** or **Van Gogh, Vincent.**

Arrowheads ► ►
Arrowheads following a dictionary entry mean that you should read on to find out more about the subject. The dictionary entry for aardvark for example tells us that it is a noun (*n.*) and that it is an African mammal that resembles an anteater. The short article following the arrowhead describes the aardvark in greater detail.

Pronunciation
Sometimes an entry is followed by a pronunciation guide: the part of the word to be stressed is in bold letters, the rest is in sloping or italic type. For example in the pronunciation guide for aborigines, (*abo*-**rij**-*in-ees*), the part of the word to be stressed is **rij.**

Parts of speech
After either the entry or the pronunciation comes the word's part of speech, printed in italics and in an abbreviated form. For example, *n.* stands for noun and *vb.* stands for verb. The parts of speech are also given after other forms of the same word.

Helpful sentences
Some words are easier to understand if you see them in a sentence. Many words in this dictionary have a sentence to help you understand their meaning. These sentences are printed in italics, like this: *John, vase and cats are all nouns.*

Which words do I need?
Some words are spelled the same, but have more than one meaning. If a word has two or more separate meanings, each meaning is numbered with the part of speech following the number. For example, **abrasive** 1. *adj.* — 2. *adj.* — 3. *n.* —. If a word has separate meanings but both meanings are the same part of speech, the part of speech goes before the number. For example, **abdomen** *n.* 1. — 2. —

Adjectival forms
Many of the encyclopedic entries, printed in bold type, have the adjectival form of the word in brackets and printed in ordinary type. For example, **Belgium** (Belgian); **Norway** (Norwegian); **Wales** (Welsh) and so on.

Abbreviations used

abbrev.	abbreviation
adj.	adjective
adv.	adverb
Austral.	Australian
conj.	conjunction
e.g.	for example
etc.	etcetera
i.e.	*id est* (Latin) that is.
interj.	interjection
n.	noun
pl.n.	plural noun
past part.	past participle
pron.	pronoun
Sc.	Scottish
U.S.A.	United States of America
vb.	verb

A

The Pont du Gard aqueduct in France is perhaps the most splendid of all Roman aqueducts.

a, an the indefinite article, used before a noun. *A person. An apple.*
aardvark *n.* an African mammal that resembles an anteater.
► The aardvark is an animal that eats TERMITES. When it has broken open a termites' nest with its powerful claws, it pokes in its long, sticky tongue and pulls it out covered with the insects. The aardvark lives in central and southern Africa. It has large ears like a donkey and is an expert burrower. If caught away from its home, it can dig a hole for itself at astonishing speed. The word "aardvark" is Dutch for "earth pig." These shy animals can be over 6 ft. (2 meters) long and nearly 3 feet high.

aardwolf *n.* a burrowing animal from Africa that looks like a small hyena.
ab- abs- *prefix* meaning away from, without, e.g. **abnormal** different from what is normal.
abacus *n.* a frame with sliding beads, used for counting.
► The abacus was first used by the ancient Greeks and Romans. It consists of rows of beads strung on wires; those on the first wire count as ones, those on the second wire count as tens, on the third wire they count as hundreds, and so on. The abacus is still used in Eastern countries such as China and Japan, and experts on the abacus can calculate more quickly than most westerners can do with pencil and paper. The Romans sometimes used small stones as counters. They called these counters *calculi* and it is from this that we get our word "calculate."

abandon *vb.* 1. stop doing something. *They had to abandon the game.* 2. leave and not return. *They had to abandon the ship.*
abbey *n.* church and other buildings where monks or nuns live; a great church.
► An abbey is a MONASTERY or convent, the home of monks or nuns, headed by an abbot or abbess. During the MIDDLE AGES many abbeys were built all over Europe. Some of them had beautiful churches attached to them. WESTMINSTER ABBEY in London, for example, is part of an abbey begun by EDWARD the Confessor, though most of the other abbey buildings have been destroyed.

The abbey often included an open space, or great court; cloisters where the monks walked, studied and thought; and a dormitory where they slept. There were also kitchens, stables, storehouses, a guest-house and vegetable gardens within the abbey walls. The monks ate their meals in a *refectory*, or dining hall.

The monks did all the work in the abbey, including cleaning, cooking, carpentry, farming and beekeeping. Some abbeys became famous for making wine and spirits; others are well known for their honey, their medicines and their cheeses. Monks were one of the few groups of educated people, and their beautiful handwritten books were famous.

Between 1524 and 1540 all the abbeys in England were closed down by HENRY VIII and their lands and possessions confiscated.

abbot *n.* the man in charge of the monks in an abbey.
abbreviation *n.* a short way of

COMMON ABBREVIATIONS
A.A. Alcoholics Anonymous
A.A.A. American Automobile Association
ABC American Broadcasting Company
AC alternating current
A.D. *anno Domini* in the year of our Lord
ad lib. *ad libitum* as one pleases
B.C. before Christ
C carbon; celsius; centigrade
c. *circa* about
CBS Columbia Broadcasting System
cf. *confer* compare
CIA Central Intelligence Agency
cont. continued
cwt. hundredweight(s)
CB Citizen's Band radio
D.A. district attorney
DNA deoxyribonucleic acid
Do. *ditto* the same
DDR *Deutsche Democratische Republik* German Democratic Republic
e.g. *exempli gratia* for example
EEC European Economic Community
E.T.A. estimated time of arrival
etc. *et cetera* and so on
F Fahrenheit
FBI Federal Bureau of Investigation
FM frequency modulation
ft. feet; foot
h.p. horsepower
H.Q. headquarters
i.e. *id est* that is
I.Q. intelligence quotient
Jr. junior
kc kilocycle
kg kilogram
km kilometer
mss. manuscripts
NASA National Aeronautics and Space Administration
NATO North Atlantic Treaty Organization
n.b. *nota bene* note well
NCO noncommissioned officer
percent *per centum* by the hundred
pro tem *pro tempore* for the time being
P.T.A. Parent/Teacher Association
R.I.P. *requiescat in pace* rest in peace
rpm revolutions per minute
R.S.V.P. *répondez s'il vous plait* answer if you please
viz. *videlicet* namely

A

writing either a word or a group of words. *Tom is an abbreviation of Thomas.*

abdicate *vb.* give up a position of power, usually that of king or queen. **abdication** *n.*

abdomen *n.* 1. the stomach (in people). 2. the rear part of the body (in insects).

abduct *vb.* kidnap, carry off. **abduction** *n.* **abductor** *n.* a person who abducts.

Aberdeen

An ancient university city in north-eastern SCOTLAND, Aberdeen was formerly important mainly as a fishing port. Today, it has become prosperous as a result of North Sea oil.

abhor *vb.* detest, feel hatred for. **abhorrence** *n.*

abject *adj.* miserable, degraded.

able *adj.* having the power or strength to do something. *Are you able to help me?* **ability** *n.*

aboard *adv.* on a ship, aircraft, or train. *They went aboard the ship.*

abolish *vb.* stop or put an end to something, e.g. slavery.

abolitionists *n.* the name given to people in the 17th and 18th centuries who worked for the abolition of slavery.

► In the United States, the Northern states had almost done away with slavery before the word "abolitionist" came into use. The abolitionists had two main aims: first, to put an end to the slave trade – to make it illegal for slavers to capture people and sell them as slaves; and, second, to set free all those who were already slaves. In 1794, the United States prohibited slave trading with foreign countries, and in 1807 forbade the importing of slaves. Slavery was finally abolished after the Civil War by Amendment 13 to the United States Constitution.

In England, a court decided in 1772 that no person could legally be held as a slave. In 1807, Parliament finally prohibited dealings in slaves.

abominable *adj.* disgusting, unpleasant.

aborigines (*abo*-**rij**-*in-ees*) *pl. n.* the first people who lived in a country, especially the first Australians.

An Aborigine boomerang and shield.

► The Aborigines of AUSTRALIA are slim people with broad noses and black wavy hair. They came to Australia thousands of years ago from southeastern Asia. In Australia they had no permanent homes but wandered about the desert hunting or gathering their food. Their chief weapons were the BOOMERANG and the throwing spear.

The Aborigines were very badly treated by the white men who came to Australia.

abort *vb.* cause to miscarry; put an end to, e.g. spacecraft mission.

abortion *n.* operation to remove fetus from womb.

about 1. *adv.* more or less; roughly. *About an hour ago.* 2. *prep.* around; nearby. *She wandered about.*

above *prep.* overhead, higher than something.

Abraham

Abraham was a patriarch (ruler of a tribe) who lived about 4,000 years ago in Mesopotamia. At the command of God, he took his family to Canaan (modern Israel). He is regarded as the founder of God's chosen people, the Jewish race. The Bible tells the story of Abraham in the Book of Genesis.

abrasive 1. *adj.* having the property of grinding or smoothing down. 2. *adj.* (of a person) rude; upsetting people. 3. *n.* a substance that grinds or smooths.

abreast *adv.* side by side. *Keep abreast of me.*

abridge *vb.* shorten, condense.

abroad *adv.* in another country.

abrupt *adj.* sudden; hasty.

abscess *n.* a boil; a collection of pus.

absent *adj.* not there.

absolute *adj.* complete.

absolve *vb.* free someone from blame.

absorb *vb.* take in water or some other liquid. *A sponge absorbs water.* **absorbent** *adj.* & *n.*

abstain *vb.* hold back or restrain oneself from doing something, e.g. eating, voting, etc. **abstinence** *n.*

absurd *adj.* something that is ridiculous or comical.

abundance *n.* a plentiful quantity of something. **abundant** *adj.*

abuse *vb.* 1. use something wrongly. 2. be rude to someone. **abusive** *adj.*

abyss (*a*-**biss**) *n.* deep pit or gorge. **abysmal** *adj.* bottomless.

academy *n.* a higher or specialized school; society for art, science, etc. **academic** *adj.* scholarly; theoretical.

accelerate (*ack*-**sel**-*erate*) *vb.* go faster. **acceleration** *n.* **accelerator** *n.* device, e.g. gas pedal, for increasing speed.

► We use the term acceleration to describe an increase in speed. To a scientist, acceleration means much more than this. The scientist defines acceleration as the rate of change of VELOCITY, and this term involves direction as well as speed. Therefore, when a body moving at constant speed changes direction, it accelerates in the new direction. For example, if you are walking north and then turn left, you have accelerated in a westerly direction. You have also undergone deceleration (a loss of acceleration) in a northerly direction.

accent (**ack**-*sent*) 1. *n.* local way of pronouncing a language 2. *vb.* emphasize; stress.

accept (*ack*-**sept**) *vb.* receive or take something which is offered to you; agree to; believe.

access *n.* entrance, approach. **accessible** *adj.* that can be easily approached or reached.

accident (**ack**-*sident*) *n.* something that happens and is not expected, usually something bad; a mishap.

acclaim *vb.* praise; welcome.

accommodate *vb.* provide someone with a place in which to live. **accommodation** *n.* lodging.

accompany *vb.* 1. go along with someone or something, perhaps on a journey. 2. play a musical instrument alongside another instrument or voice. **accompaniment** *n.*

accomplice *n.* helper, partner (particularly in crime).

accomplish *vb.* achieve, carry out. **accomplished** *adj.* skilled, talented. *She is an accomplished violinist.*

accord *vb.* agree, be consistent with.

according *adv.* (with, to) asserted by. *According to him the report is true.*

accordion *n.* musical instrument carried by means of a strap over the shoulder, played by pumping air from bellows, and fitted with keys like a piano.

account 1. *n.* a record of money owed, received, or paid. 2. *n.* a description or report of an event. 3. *vb.* explain, give reasons for.

accumulate *vb.* collect; pile up; continue to gradually increase. **accumulation** *n.*

accurate *adj.* correct and exact. **accuracy** *n.*

accuse *vb.* charge someone with wrongdoing.

accustom *vb.* make used to, familiar with.

ace *n.* 1. the name for "one" in cards. *The ace of spades.* 2. someone of great skill, such as an aircraft fighter pilot. 3. a successful unreturned serve in tennis.

ache (rhymes with *cake*) *n.* a pain that goes on for a long time, like a toothache.

achieve *vb.* succeed; reach a goal or target. **achievement** *n.*

Achilles

Achilles was the Greek hero of the siege of Troy in HOMER's poem the

Iliad. Achilles' father was human but his mother was a goddess. She tried to make him immortal like herself by dipping him in the Styx River. Unfortunately the heel she held him by stayed dry and unprotected. After killing the Trojan hero HECTOR, and just as Troy was about to fall, Achilles was killed by an arrow which hit him in his heel.

acid (**as**-*id*) *n*. a substance which tastes sour, like vinegar. *Strong acids can burn you*. **acidic** *adj*.

▶ An acid is a liquid chemical COMPOUND that has a sour taste. Some acids, such as sulfuric acid, nitric acid and hydrochloric acid, are very strong and can corrode, or eat away, even the strongest metals. Other acids are harmless. These include the citric acid that gives lemons and oranges their sharp taste, and the acetic acid in vinegar. Lactic acid is produced when milk goes sour. Some acids are, in fact, essential to life. The digestive juice in the stomach contains acid that enables us to digest (break down) proteins in our food. From these proteins are formed various amino acids, without which we could not live. The body uses them to build up other types of protein. All acids turn a special sort of paper called litmus from blue to red.

acknowledge *vb*. admit to; recognize; accept something as one's own. **acknowledgment** *n*.

acme *n*. highest point or stage.

acne *n*. red spots on the skin, common among young people.

Aconcagua

An extinct volcano in the ANDES, on the border between ARGENTINA and CHILE. It is considered to be the highest peak in the Americas. Aconcagua is 22,834 ft. (6,960 meters) high, and was first climbed in 1897.

acorn *n*. the fruit or nut of an oak tree.

acoustics *n*. 1. the science of sound. 2. the effect of a building on sounds, particularly music, produced inside it. *The acoustics were so bad that I could not hear the orchestra properly*.

▶ In designing a concert hall, or theater, the architect must carefully consider the acoustics (quality of sound) of the building. Will the full range of sound waves reach every seat in the auditorium? Will there be too much reflection, or is too much sound going to be absorbed by the walls and ceiling?

Sound waves travel in straight lines and will go out from their source in all directions. But in much the same way as with light, sound waves can be reflected or absorbed by surfaces they strike.

The quality of the sound depends largely on the proportion of those waves reaching the listener directly and those which are reflected.

acquaintance (*ack*-**wain**-*tance*) *n*. person who is known, but who is not a close friend. **acquaint** *vb*. make aware or familiar. *Let me acquaint you with the facts*.

acquit *vb*. (in law) declare not guilty; set free.

acre (**a**-*ker*) *n*. a measure of land (4,840 sq. yards or 4,047 sq. meters). *A football field has an area of about one and a half acres*.

acrobat *n*. a person who does balancing tricks, often in a circus. **acrobatics** *pl.n*.

acronym *n*. a word formed from the initial letters of other words, e.g. NATO, which stands for North Atlantic Treaty Organization.

Acropolis

Acropolis is a Greek word for the high central part of many ancient Greek cities. The most famous acropolis is in ATHENS, the capital of modern Greece. On top of the Acropolis are the ruins of ancient temples built in the 400s B.C. when Athens was a rich and powerful city. The PARTHENON, the largest and most important of these, was built to honor the goddess Athena, the patron goddess of Athens.

across *prep*. from one side to the other. *Kate walked across the road*.

acrostic *n*. a set of words, often in the form of a poem, where the first letters of each line spell a word.

act 1. *n*. a thing done. *There are some acts you do every day*. 2. *vb*. behave; play a part or pretend. *He acts the part of a pirate in our play*. **acting** *n*. art of performing. 3. *n*. part of a stage play.

action *n*. 1. a deed. 2. a gesture. 3. a lawsuit.

active *adj*. busy, full of energy. **activity** *n*.

actor *n*. person who acts in plays, in films or on TV.

actress *n*. woman who acts in a play or film or on TV.

actual *adj*. existing in fact; real.

acupuncture *n*. kind of medical treatment in which thin needles are used to puncture various parts of the body. Developed by the Chinese about 5,000 years ago, it is still in use today.

acute *adj*. 1. sharp, penetrating. *He had an acute pain in his shoulder*. 2. coming to a crisis. *The situation is acute*.

A.D. *abbr*. short for *anno Domini* (Latin for "in the year of Our Lord") used with dates after the birth of Christ.

ad- *prefix* (also **ac-** before c, **aff-**, **all-**) meaning to, toward.

Adams, John

John Adams (1735–1826) was the second President of the United States. He was a member of the committee that drew up the Declaration of Independence and succeeded George Washington as President in 1796. In the election of 1800 he was defeated by Thomas Jefferson.

Adams, John Quincy

John Quincy Adams (1767–1848) was the sixth President of the United States and the son of John Adams. His term as President was uneventful. He was defeated by Andrew Jackson in 1828 and later elected to the House of Representatives, where he served until his death.

adapt *vb*. change something to make it more suitable for the purpose. **adaptation** *n*.

add *vb*. put things together to make more. *Colin added all the numbers together to find the total*. **addition** *n*.

adder *n*. a small poisonous snake found in northern countries; a viper.

addict *n*. a person who is obsessed with a habit – especially drugs – almost beyond cure.

address *n*. 1. the place where a person lives and to which letters are sent. 2. a speech.

adenoids *pl.n*. small lumps at the back of the nose that help to prevent infection. When enlarged, they can make breathing through the nose difficult.

adequate *adj*. enough; sufficient.

adhere *vb*. stick to something. **adherence** *n*.

adhesive *adj*. sticky; able to stick to things. *Adhesive tape*. *n*. a substance that sticks things together; glue.

adjective *n*. a word that describes what something or somebody is like. *The black cat*. "Black" is an adjective. *The water is cold*. "Cold" is an adjective. Most adjectives can be "compared," e.g. cold, colder, coldest.

adjourn (*ad*-**jern**) *vb*. postpone (a meeting), suspend, move elsewhere. **adjournment** *n*.

adjust *vb*. arrange; put in order. **adjustment** *n*.

administer *vb*. govern; run something. **administration** *n*.

admiral *n*. very senior officer in the navy.

admire *vb*. think well of something or somebody. **admiration** *n*. **admirable** *adj*. worthy of admiration; excellent.

admit *vb*. 1. allow to enter. 2. confess; own up as true. *He admits his mistake*. **admission** *n*. being allowed into somewhere; the money you pay to go in. **admissible** *adj*. what may be admitted or allowed.

admonish *vb*. warn, usually mildly.

ado (*a*-**do**) *n.* unnecessary fuss.
adobe (*ad*-**doh**-*be*) *n.* sun-dried brick; also building made of adobe.
adolescence *n.* the period of life when a person moves from childhood to adulthood.
► Adolescence usually starts at the beginning of puberty, at age 12 or 13, when the sex organs become capable of functioning. At this time boys' voices break, girls' breasts fill out, and pubic hair grows on both girls and boys. Adolescence is for many children a time of physical and emotional upheaval, as they move from being totally dependent on their parents to becoming independent adults.

Adonis
In Greek mythology, a young man famous for his beauty and loved by the goddess Aphrodite (VENUS).

adopt *vb.* 1. accept somebody else's child as a child of your own family. *The couple decided to adopt the boy.* 2. take up, accept (an idea etc.).
adore *vb.* worship; think highly of someone or something; love.
adorn *vb.* cover with ornaments. **adornment** *n.*

Adriatic Sea
An arm of the MEDITERRANEAN SEA, between Italy, Yugoslavia and Albania. Covering 60,000 sq. miles (155,400 sq. km), it is a tourist area.

adult 1. *adj.* grown-up. *An adult person.* 2. *n.* a grown-up.
advance *vb.* move forward, proceed. *n.* a movement forward; a loan of money.
advantage *n.* gain; a better condition or circumstance.
advent *n.* the coming or arrival. *Ice cream sales increased with the advent of warmer weather.*
adventure *n.* exciting happening or experience.
adverb *n.* a word that tells us how, when or where something happens. Most adverbs have the ending *-ly*. *They walked home slowly.* "Slowly" is an adverb.
adversary *n.* opponent. **adverse** *adj.* hostile; unfavorable.
adverse *adj.* unfavorable.
advertise *vb.* tell people about something you want to sell. *People advertise in newspapers, on television, or by sticking up posters.*
advertisement *n.* a printed notice in a newspaper or a message about goods or services on radio or television.
advice *n.* something said to you to help you decide what to do. *We took our teacher's advice and borrowed the book from the library.*
advise *vb.* tell someone what you think he should do. *What do you advise me to do?*

Aegean Sea
The Mediterranean between Greece and Turkey.

aerial *n.* something through which radio and television signals are sent out or received.
aero- *prefix* meaning of air, aircraft, e.g. **aerobatics** stunts in aircraft.
aeronautics *pl.n.* the science of flight.
► An aircraft flies because of the lift generated by the movement of the wings through the air. The wing of an aircraft has a special shape called an airfoil. It is flat at the bottom and curved at the top. When air passes over the top surface it has to travel faster than the air beneath the wing, because it has farther to go. This means that the air pressure above the wing is less than the pressure below it. The suction produced in this way lifts the wing, and the higher the speed, the greater the lift.

There are four forces which act on an aircraft. The first is lift, and to produce lift the wings must move through the air at a high enough speed. So the aircraft needs a second force, thrust, to push it forward. This thrust comes from either a propeller or a jet.

As thrust drives the aircraft forward another force, drag, tries to hold it back. Drag is caused by the resistance of the air. The fourth force acting on an aircraft in flight is its weight. The aircraft would fall to the ground were it not for the lift produced by the wings.

aerosol *n.* substance which can be sprayed under pressure from a container.

Aesop
The Ancient Greek writer Aesop probably lived around 600 B.C. He wrote short stories called fables, usually about animals, but which teach particular lessons about the way people behave. Perhaps Aesop's best known fable is the story of the tortoise and the hare. Historians think that Aesop was a slave who was freed because he told stories.

affair *n.* business; that which has to be done. **affairs** *pl.n.* business in general. *The affairs of state.*
affect *vb.* make someone or something different in some way. *The hot weather affects her health.* **affectation** *n.* insincere, pretentious manner.
affection *n.* a great liking.
affinity *n.* an attraction.
affirm *vb.* state positively, formally or confidently.

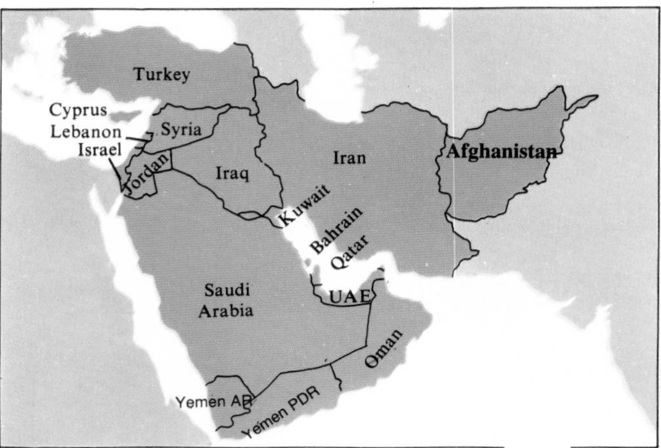

affix *vb.* attach; fasten to.
afflict *vb.* cause pain of body or mind. **affliction** *n.*
affluence *n.* wealth.
afford *vb.* have enough money to buy something. *He can't afford that car.*

Afghanistan (Afghan)
Afghanistan is a country in ASIA. It is a mountainous land sandwiched between U.S.S.R., Pakistan and Iran. Nearly all the people are Muslim farmers or nomadic herdsmen. In 1978 the government was overthrown by rebels friendly to Russia, but Muslim bands continued to fight against the new government. In 1979 Russian troops moved in to take over the country, an act which caused world-wide opposition.
AREA: 250,014 SQ. MILES (647,497 SQ. KM)
POPULATION: 16,024,000
CAPITAL: KABUL
CURRENCY: AFGHANI
OFFICIAL LANGUAGES: PUSHTU, DARI (PERSIAN)

afraid *adj.* 1. frightened. 2. sorry. *I am afraid this shop is closed.*

Africa (African)
Africa is the world's second largest continent after ASIA. It covers an area of 11,706,000 sq. miles (30,319,000 sq. km), one fifth of the world's land. Africa stretches from the Mediterranean Sea in the north to the Cape of Good Hope at its tip in the south. Large parts of Africa are empty wasteland. The burning SAHARA spreads over much of the

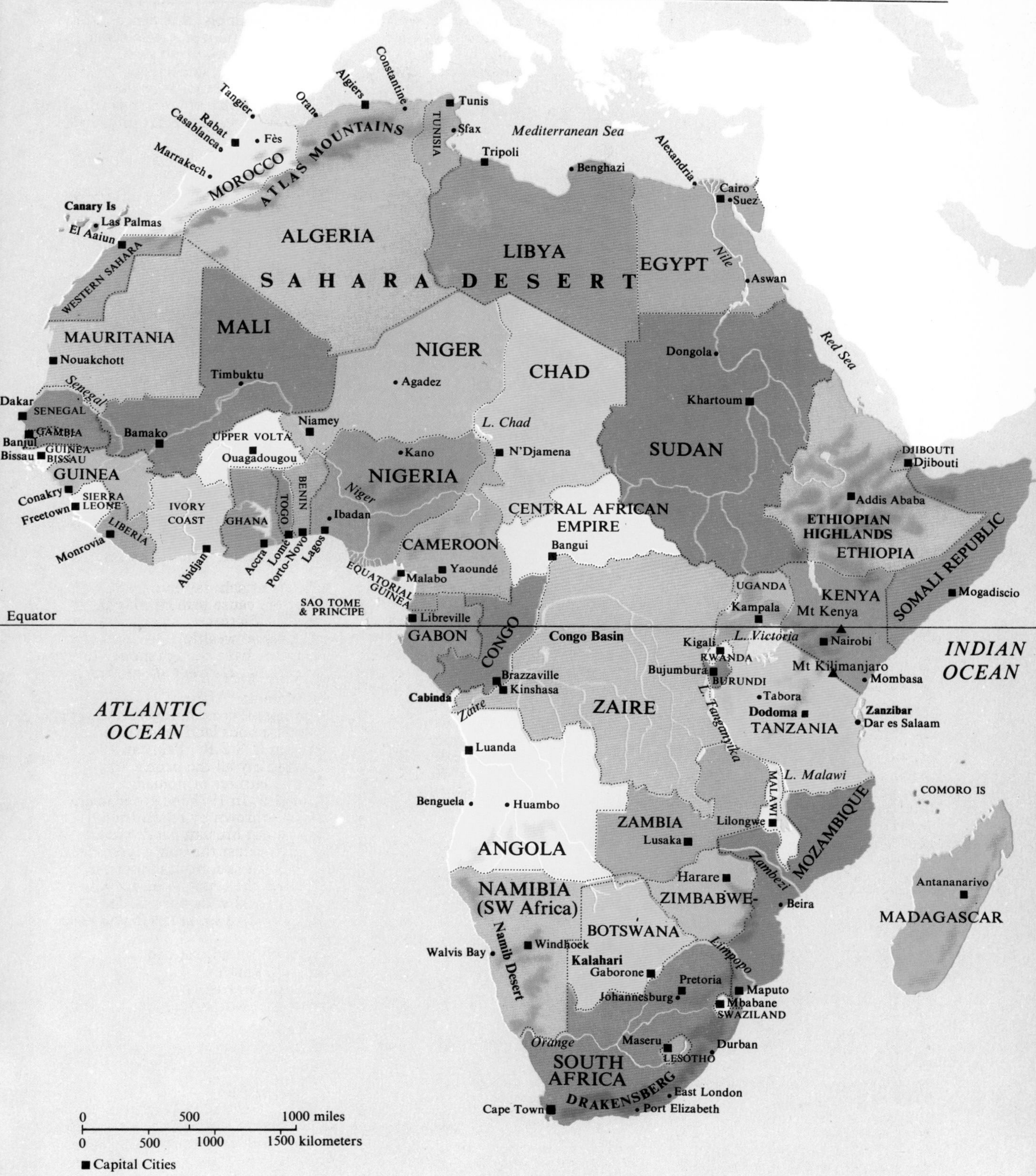
Mediterranean Sea
Tangier
Rabat
Casablanca
Fès
Marrakech
Oran
Algiers
Constantine
Tunis
Sfax
TUNISIA
Tripoli
Benghazi
Alexandria
Cairo
Suez
MOROCCO
ATLAS MOUNTAINS
Canary Is
Las Palmas
El Aaiun
WESTERN SAHARA
ALGERIA
LIBYA
EGYPT
Nile
Aswan
SAHARA DESERT
MAURITANIA
Nouakchott
MALI
NIGER
CHAD
Red Sea
Dongola
Timbuktu
Agadez
Senegal
Dakar
SENEGAL
GAMBIA
Banjul
GUINEA-BISSAU
Bissau
Bamako
UPPER VOLTA
Ouagadougou
Niamey
L. Chad
N'Djamena
Khartoum
SUDAN
Kano
NIGERIA
GUINEA
Conakry
SIERRA LEONE
Freetown
LIBERIA
Monrovia
IVORY COAST
Abidjan
GHANA
Accra
TOGO
Lomé
BENIN
Porto-Novo
Lagos
Ibadan
Niger
DJIBOUTI
Djibouti
Addis Ababa
ETHIOPIAN HIGHLANDS
ETHIOPIA
CENTRAL AFRICAN EMPIRE
Bangui
CAMEROON
Yaoundé
EQUATORIAL GUINEA
Malabo
SAO TOME & PRINCIPE
SOMALI REPUBLIC
Mogadiscio
UGANDA
Kampala
KENYA
Mt Kenya
Equator
Libreville
GABON
CONGO
Congo Basin
Kigali
RWANDA
L. Victoria
Nairobi
INDIAN OCEAN
Bujumbura
BURUNDI
Mt Kilimanjaro
Mombasa
Brazzaville
Kinshasa
Cabinda
Zaire
ZAIRE
Tabora
Dodoma
TANZANIA
Zanzibar
Dar es Salaam
ATLANTIC OCEAN
L. Tanganyika
Luanda
MALAWI
L. Malawi
COMORO IS
Benguela
Huambo
ZAMBIA
Lusaka
Lilongwe
MOZAMBIQUE
ANGOLA
Zambezi
Harare
ZIMBABWE
Beira
NAMIBIA (SW Africa)
Antananarivo
MADAGASCAR
BOTSWANA
Namib Desert
Windhoek
Walvis Bay
Kalahari
Gaborone
Limpopo
Pretoria
Johannesburg
Maputo
Mbabane
SWAZILAND
Orange
Maseru
LESOTHO
Durban
SOUTH AFRICA
DRAKENSBERG
East London
Cape Town
Port Elizabeth
0 500 1000 miles
0 500 1000 1500 kilometers
Capital Cities

northern part of the continent. Near the equator, which runs through the center of Africa, are thick rain forests. There the trees grow so close together that their leaves blot out the sunlight.

More than a third of Africa is a high, flat plain, or plateau, much of which is covered in grassland called savanna. Great herds of grazing animals roam the savanna. They include zebras, giraffes, wildebeest and impala. Other animals, such as lions, cheetahs and hyenas, prey upon the grazing animals. In the past, many animals were killed by hunters, but today special reserves have been set up to protect them.

Mt. Kilimanjaro, the highest mountain in Africa, rises 19,340 ft. (5,895 meters) in Tanzania. Africa's largest lake, Lake Victoria, lies between Kenya and Tanzania. The continent's great rivers are the NILE, ZAIRE (once called the Congo), Niger and Zambezi.

Many different types of people live in Africa. In North Africa are ARABS and Berbers, who mostly follow the Muslim religion. So-called "Black Africa" lies south of the Sahara. The Negroid peoples who live there make up three-fourths of Africa's population. People with European and Asian ancestors make up the rest of the population.

A finely carved ivory mask from West Africa.

Most Africans are farmers, growing crops such as cocoa, coffee, cotton, sisal and tea. Africa produces nearly three-fourths of the world's palm oil and palm kernels, which are used to make things like soap and margarine. The continent has valuable mineral resources, too, including gold and diamonds, copper, tin and bauxite for making aluminum.

For centuries Africa was called the "Dark Continent" because Europeans knew little about it or its people. The Phoenicians and Romans had built trading centers along the north coast and they knew of the great early civilization in Egypt. But the lands to the south remained a mystery.

The first Europeans to learn more about this huge unexplored continent were the Portuguese who were the first to find a sea route to India by sailing around the southern tip of Africa. They hugged the coast, fearing to sail out of sight of land. Soon the African coastline was charted. But it was still a long time before people became interested in exploring inland. From the 1400s, European sailors began to ship slaves from Africa. About 14 million slaves were taken to the Americas between 1500 and the 1800s. Usually these slaves were bought from tribes that lived along the African coast. So Europeans did not need to travel into the interior of the great continent.

By the 1800s the countries of Europe were becoming interested in setting up colonies in Africa. Brave explorers such as David LIVINGSTONE, Mungo Park and Henry Stanley traveled into the interior and soon the continent was carved up between the European powers. The Europeans brought new ways of life to Africa. Missionaries brought the Christian religion and set up schools.

After some years many Africans began to resent being ruled by foreigners. During the 1950s and 1960s most former colonies became independent African countries. The boundaries of most African countries are still the ones fixed by Europeans 100 years ago. Many are poor and some have had bloody civil wars as different rulers fought for power. But today the countries are working together to help one another and to develop industry and their natural resources.

Afrikaans *n.* dialect of Dutch spoken in South Africa.
aft *adj.* toward the stern of a ship or back of an aircraft.
after 1. *adv.* behind. *They followed after.* 2. *conj.* later in time. *After they left.* 3. used with other verbs: *Look after my bags* (take care of them). *He takes after his father* (he is like his father).
aftermath *n.* period following a disastrous event; the outcome.
afternoon *n.* the part of the day between morning and evening.
afterward *adv.* later. *We watched TV and afterward went out to a play.*
again *adv.* once more; another time.
against *prep.* 1. next to; resting on. *Put it up against the wall.* 2. in opposition to; versus. *Which team are we playing against?*

Agamemnon
According to Greek legend, Agamemnon was the king of Mycenae who led the Greeks in the Trojan War. Stories about him are told in HOMER's *Iliad.*

agate *n.* a semiprecious stone marked by bands of color.
age *n.* 1. length of time a person has lived. 2. a length of time in history, such as the Stone Age and Bronze Age.
aged 1. *adj.* (**aj**-*id*) very old. 2. *vb.* to become older. *He has aged a lot since I saw him last.*
agenda *n.* list of things to be done at a meeting.
agent *n.* 1. someone working on behalf of someone else. 2. a spy. A double agent is a spy who tries to serve both sides. 3. the representative of a musician, artist, actor, etc. *His agent has found him a wonderful part in a new play.*
aggravate *vb.* make worse; annoy. **aggravation** *n.* annoyance.
aggression *n.* an attack without cause or provocation. **aggressive** *adj.* eager to attack; great energy. **aggressor** *n.*
aghast *adj.* shocked, amazed.
agile *adj.* nimble, quick. **agility** *n.*

Agincourt, Battle of
One of the most famous battles of the HUNDRED YEARS WAR. On October 25, 1415, an English army led by HENRY V defeated the French. The heavily armored French knights fell under a hail of arrows from the longbows of the English archers.

agitate *vb.* disturb, shake up; make nervous, stir up unrest. **agitation** *n.* **agitator** *n.*
agnostic *n.* a person who believes that nothing can be known about the existence of God.
ago *adj.* & *adv.* in the past; previously. *Ten years ago.*
agony *n.* great pain or suffering. **agonizing** *adj.*
agrarian *adj.* relating to farming and land management.
agree *vb.* say yes to; consent. *If you agree, I will come, too.*
agriculture *n.* farming.
aground *adv.* (of ships) stranded on the bottom of shallow water. *The ship ran aground.*
ahead *adv.* in front. *Dad went ahead to get seats for us.*
aid *vb.* help. *n.* the help that is given.
aim 1. *vb.* point a weapon at something. 2. *n.* something you try to do. *Jane's aim was to learn French.*
air *n.* the mixture of gases we breathe. *vb.* expose to the air (to dry); make known. *They aired their views at the meeting.*
► Air is all around us – it surrounds the earth in a layer we call the

atmosphere. All living things must have air in order to live. Air is colorless and has no smell, yet it is really a mixture of a number of different gases. We can feel air when the wind blows, and we know air has weight. Air carries sounds — without it we would not be able to hear, because sounds cannot travel in a VACUUM.

The chief gas in air is nitrogen, which makes up nearly four-fifths of the air. About one-fifth of the air is made up of OXYGEN. Air also holds some water in very fine particles called vapor. When we talk about the degree of HUMIDITY in the air, it is the amount of water in the air.

The air that surrounds the earth gets thinner the higher you go. All high-flying aircraft have to keep the air in their cabins at ground-level pressure so that passengers can breathe normally. In the same way, mountaineers carry their own air supply because the air at the top of high mountains is too thin to breathe properly.

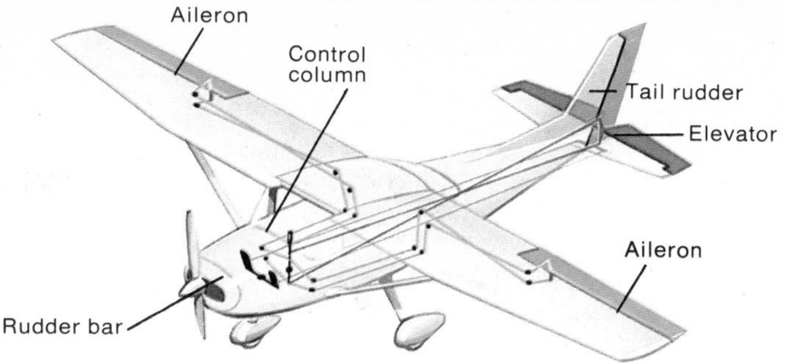

Above: The main controls of an airplane. The control column lifts or lowers the elevators causing the plane to climb or dive. It also makes the plane bank for a safe turn. The rudder bar turns the tail rudder left or right and so steers the plane's nose to the left or right.

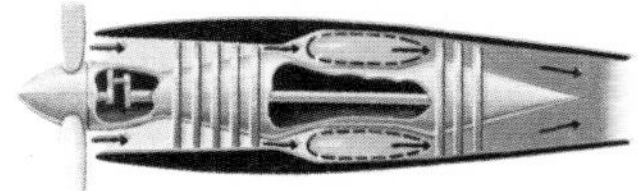

In a turboprop engine the hot exhaust gases drive a propeller.

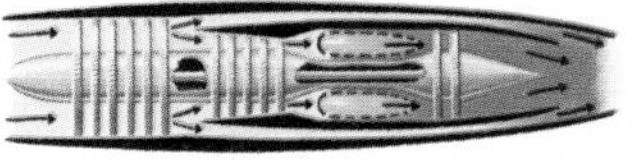

A bypass turbofan sucks in more air, giving more power.

A turbojet sucks in air and shoots out hot gases which drive the plane forward.

A simple ramjet. It has no moving parts and works best at high speeds.

air-conditioning *n.* system for cooling and cleaning the air in a building.

aircraft *n.* airplane, airship or helicopter, etc.

airline *n.* organization that owns and flies aircraft.

airplane *n.* a flying machine driven by an engine or engines.

► People have always dreamed of being able to fly like birds. At first, they attached artificial "wings" to their arms and tried to flap them. Their muscles were not strong enough to keep them in the air.

In the 1800s, the British scientist Sir George Cayley suggested that a vehicle could be built that was designed like a bird but with fixed wings. Many people tried to build such a machine, and some built gliders. But these could only fly short distances and were difficult to control.

In 1903 two American brothers, Orville and Wilbur WRIGHT, built the *Flyer*, a flimsy-looking machine with a gasoline engine at the back. They were successful. The first powered flight in the world took place at Kitty Hawk, North Carolina, on December 17, 1903. The new means of transport did not catch on immediately. But by 1908, after the Wright brothers had demonstrated their planes all over Europe, the development of aircraft was rapid. In 1909 Louis BLERIOT flew the English Channel. During WORLD WAR I, aircraft were used for watching enemy movements, and later for fighting.

The war proved that aircraft were not only useful, but a necessity. In 1919 John Alcock and Arthur Whitten Brown made the first Atlantic crossing; Charles LINDBERGH made the first solo crossing in 1927. In 1936 the *Douglas DC-3*, or *Dakota*, went into service, and proved itself the most successful airliner ever built. WORLD WAR II saw the development of fast fighter aircraft and heavy bombers, and by the end of the war jet aircraft had appeared.

The first aircraft to fly faster than the speed of sound (supersonic speed) was tested in 1947. Today, military fighter aircraft and some airliners such as *Concorde* are designed for supersonic speeds. Others, like the "jumbo" jets, can carry almost 500 people and big freight loads.

To fly, an aircraft must have lift to raise it against the pull of the earth's GRAVITY. This lift is produced by the movement of air over the aircraft's wings, which have a special shape called an airfoil. The force (thrust) needed to push the aircraft forward comes either from propellers or from a jet engine. The tail on the aircraft steadies it and helps to control its flight. The rudder and elevators on the tail and the ailerons on the wings all help the pilot to control the craft. A modern airliner also has a wide variety of controls to help the pilot keep a check on all the aircraft's systems and to navigate on course.

airport *n.* place where aircraft land and take off.

► Airports have three main jobs; they must handle passengers, mail and freight; they must be sure that all aircraft take off and land safely and on time; and they must provide hangars and workshops so that planes can be checked regularly.

The center of operations at the airport is the air-traffic control tower, where controllers organize the landing and takeoff of each airplane. With complicated electronic aids, including computers and radar, the ground controller guides the pilot of the airplane from a height of 5 or 6 miles (6 to 8 km) onto a concrete runway about 2 miles (3 km) long and 200 ft. (60 meters) wide. The runways are usually parallel and in line with the prevailing wind, so that aircraft can land against the wind, which is always safer. As soon as an airplane has landed, it moves along, or taxis, to an area called an apron. Here trucks are waiting, ready to carry baggage to the terminal. Fuel tankers move in to refill the airliner's fuel tanks. Cleaners and caterers arrive to empty the cabin and load on food for the next flight.

airscrew *n.* propeller of an aircraft, etc.

airship *n.* a lighter-than-air craft that is powered and can be steered by its pilot. Airships are sometimes called "dirigibles" from a French word meaning "to steer."

► The first airship was flown by the French engineer Henri Giffard in 1852. It was 144 ft. (44 meters) long and was propelled by a 3-horsepower steam engine. But the most famous name in airship history is that of the German Count Ferdinand von Zeppelin (1838-1917). He built his first airship in 1900 and this provided the pattern for over a hundred other Zeppelins that flew thousands of kilometers in peace and war.

After World War I the British *R34* was the first to cross the Atlantic Ocean, in 1919. In 1926 Roald Amundsen flew over the North Pole in an airship piloted by Captain Umberto Nobile. The British *R101* crashed into a hill in France in 1930. The great Zeppelin *Hindenburg* was destroyed by fire in New Jersey in 1937. She had been inflated with highly explosive HYDROGEN gas. HELIUM gas does not have quite as much lift as hydrogen but is safer.

airtight *adj*. so tightly shut that air cannot get in or out.

aisle *n*. side of church nave, separated by pillars from main nave.

ajar *adv*. partly open. *The door was ajar*.

akin *adj*. related, similar to.

Alabama (*abbrev*: **Ala.**)

A state in the southeast United States. Its main river, the Mobile, flows south through a narrow coastal strip into the Gulf of Mexico. In the north, Alabama has valuable coal and iron deposits in the Appalachian Highlands. Birmingham, the largest city, is an important industrial center. The state capital is Montgomery. The state is heavily forested. Cotton and maize (Indian corn) are two important crops.

Alabama became the 22nd state in 1819. During the Civil War, it was one of the original six Confederate States. It returned to the Union in 1868.

alabaster *n*. a stone similar to marble.

alarm 1. *n*. a warning sound or signal. 2. *vb*. frighten; arouse to sense of danger.

Alaska (*abbrev*: **Alas.**)

Alaska is the largest state in the USA, covering an area of 586,400 sq. miles (1,518,800 sq. km). It is separated from the rest of the United States by the province of British Columbia in Canada.

Much of Alaska is north of the Arctic Circle. For most of the year it is covered in snow and ice. Alaska has large reserves of oil, and is connected to the rest of the U.S.A. by an oil pipeline. The main river is the Yukon. Mt McKinley, at 20,322 ft. (6,194 meters) high, is the highest peak in North America.

The U.S.A. purchased Alaska from Russia in 1867 for $7,200,00. In 1959 Alaska became the 49th state of the United States of America.

Albania (Albanian)

Albania is a small, rugged country that lies between Yugoslavia and

Greece on the eastern shore of the Adriatic Sea. Most Albanians live in small, remote mountain villages. Albanian farmers grow wheat, barley, tobacco and cotton. Beneath the ground there are deposits of chrome, copper, iron, oil and natural gas. Albania was ruled by Turkey for over 400 years. After World War II it became a Communist state.

AREA: 11,100 SQ. MILES (28,748 SQ. KM)
POPULATION: 2,873,000
CAPITAL: TIRANE
CURRENCY: LEK
OFFICIAL LANGUAGE: ALBANIAN

albatross *n*. a large seabird that spends most of its time in the air over the oceans.

Alberta

Alberta is a province of western Canada that consists mainly of prairie. The west of the province includes part of the Rocky Mountains. BANFF is the best-known of Alberta's national parks.

Wheat is grown on the high plains, where there are also vast cattle ranches. Two of the most important mineral resources are oil and natural gas. Irrigation has turned most of Alberta into good agricultural land. The main cities are Edmonton, the capital, and Calgary, famous for its Stampede (rodeo).

In 1870, the Canadian government bought the area from the Hudson Bay Company. In 1882 it was named after one of Queen Victoria's daughters, Princess Louise Alberta. It became a Canadian province in 1905.

albino *n*. & *adj*. a person or animal without natural coloring matter (pigmentation) in skin, hair and eyes.

album *n*. 1. a blank book for keeping photographs, stamps, etc. 2. a collection of songs (on a long-playing record).

alchemy *n*. a medieval form of chemistry. **alchemist** *n*.

► Alchemy centered around attempts to change ordinary metals into gold and the search for the "Philosopher's Stone" which it was thought would have the power to make this change. Alchemy was practiced as early as 100 B.C. in Alexandria in Egypt. It was popular in Europe during the Middle Ages.

alcohol *n*. 1. the name of a group of chemical substances, mostly liquids. 2. strong drinks, such as beer, wine and spirits. **alcoholic** *n*. person addicted to drinking alcohol.

alcove *n*. a recess in a wall.

alder *n*. a tree belonging to the birch family.

ale *n*. a kind of beer.

alert 1. *adj*. paying attention. 2. *vb*. attract someone's attention. 3. *n*. watchfulness. *Be on the alert*.

Alexander the Great

Alexander the Great (356-323 B.C.) was a ruler of GREECE and one of the greatest generals that ever lived. The son of Philip of Macedon, Alexander conquered the Greek city-states after he became king when Philip died in 336 B.C. He then marched east to conquer Persia, which was at that time the greatest empire in the world. By 327 Alexander's empire stretched from Greece to India. When his armies reached India they were worn out from marching and fighting. Alexander had to turn back. When he reached BABYLON he became ill with a fever and died. He was still only 33. Alexander's body was taken back to Alexandria, the great city he founded in EGYPT. There it was placed in a magnificent tomb.

A bronze statue which is thought to be of Alexander the Great. Alexander was a brilliant commander who set a standard of military leadership which has not been surpassed.

Alfalfa
Alfalfa is one of the most widely grown hay crops. It contains large amounts of protein, which makes it a valuable fodder for milk- and meat-producing animals. Farmers in every state and in most Canadian provinces grow more alfalfa each year than any other hay crop. Alfalfa adapts well to many different soils and climates. It flourishes where other crops fail because of its long roots, which can extend for as much as 30 feet (9 meters). Unlike some other crops, alfalfa improves the soil by restoring nitrogen to it. This is why farmers plant alfalfa in fields that have been used for wheat and corn. These plants use up the nitrogen which alfalfa replaces. Alfalfa does not have to be replanted every year. It will go on yielding abundantly for many years.

algae *pl.n.* a group of plants that includes seaweeds and other water plants.

algebra *n.* a branch of mathematics in which letters are used to represent quantities.

Algeria (Algerian)
Algeria is a large Arab republic in north Africa. The southern part of the country lies in the Sahara. Most of the people live on the coastal strip bordering the southern Mediterranean. The Atlas Mountains form a barrier between the coast and the interior.

Algeria is an oil-rich country. Natural gas and oil account for 90 percent of exports. From 1848 to 1962 Algeria was ruled by France. It achieved independence only after many years of bitter guerrilla war. Most of the one million French settlers left the country after independence.

AREA: 919,646 SQ. MILES (2,381,471 SQ. KM)
POPULATION: 20,042,000
CAPITAL: ALGIERS
CURRENCY: ALGERIAN DINAR
OFFICIAL LANGUAGE: ARABIC

alias *n.* an assumed name.

alibi *n.* a term used in law when a person or persons accused of a crime says that they were somewhere else at the time it was committed.

alien 1. *adj.* strange; foreign. 2. *n.* a stranger; a foreigner. **alienate** *vb.* turn away; make a stranger of.

align (*al-ine*) *vb.* bring into line. **alignment** *n.*

alike *adj.* 1. looking or acting the same. *People say my sister and I are very much alike.* 2. in the same way. *We were always treated alike.*

alive *adj.* living; not dead.

alkali *n.* the name of a number of chemical substances, such as ammonia, which have the property of dissolving other substances, but which are distinct from acids.

all *adj.* each, every; the whole of something.

Allah *n.* the name for God among Muslims.

allegory *n.* story with a deeper meaning than the literal one.

allergy *n.* a bodily reaction to some normally harmless substance. *She has an allergy to eggs.* **allergic** *adj.*

alleviate *vb.* make easier, relieve. *The pill quickly alleviated the pain.*

alley *n.* a short narrow passage between buildings.

alliance *n.* a union, especially of states, political parties, etc.

alligator *n.* a reptile like a crocodile that lives in parts of the Americas and in China.

► The alligator is a large reptile that belongs to the same family as the CROCODILE. There are two species: one is the American alligator of the southeastern U.S.A.; the other is the smaller Chinese alligator that lives in the YANGTZE river. Alligators look very like crocodiles, but have broader, flatter heads with rounded snouts.

alliteration *n.* the same sound frequently repeated in a poem or sentence. *Peter Piper picked a peck of pickled peppers.*

allot *vb.* share out. **allotment** *n.* a share.

allow *vb.* let someone do something, permit. *He allows us to play in his garden.* **allowance** *n.* fixed sum (of money) allowed.

alloy *n.* a mixture of metals. *vb.* mix metals together.

► In an alloy the mixture is usually more useful than each metal on its own. For example, a soft metal such as COPPER can be strengthened by adding ZINC to it to form BRASS, or TIN to form BRONZE, both of which are strong metals. Iron is the main substance in the most frequently used alloys – called *ferrous alloys*. A large number of these are steels.

allude *vb.* refer to briefly or indirectly. **allusion** *n.*

allure *n.* & *vb.* charm, have the power to attract.

alluvium *n.* sand, soil, gravel, etc., washed down by a river.

ally (*al-eye*) *n.* a friend, or a country that helps another.

almond *n.* a tree cultivated in warm climates for its edible nuts (almonds).

almost *adj.* very nearly; not quite.

alone *adj.* by itself; with no one else.

along *prep.* the length of something; from end to end. *Jill walked along the path.*

aloud *adv.* in a voice that can be heard.

alpha (*al-fa*) *n.* the first letter of the Greek alphabet: A.

alphabet *n.* all the letters of a language arranged in order. **alphabetical** *adj.*

► An alphabet is a group of letters, or symbols, used to write down a language. The word "alphabet" comes from the names of the first two letters in the Greek alphabet: alpha and beta. The 26 letters in the English alphabet come from the Roman alphabet of 2,500 years ago. Other alphabets in common use today include the Greek, Arabic, Hebrew, and Russian or Cyrillic alphabets. Most contain symbols for vowels (soft sounds like "a" and "e")

Alligators were once hunted for their hide. Now they are being killed off by water pollution.

Greek

Letter	Name	Transliteration
Α α	alpha	a
Β β	beta	b
Γ γ	gamma	g
Δ δ	delta	d
Ε ϵ	epsilon	e
Ζ ζ	zeta	z
Η η	eta	ē
Θ θ	theta	th
Ι ι	iota	i
Κ κ	kappa	k
Λ λ	lambda	l
Μ μ	mu	m
Ν ν	nu	n
Ξ ξ	xi	x (ks)
Ο ο	omicron	o
Π π	pi	p
Ρ ρ	rho	r
Σ σ,s*	sigma	s
Τ τ	tau	t
Υ υ	upsilon	u, y
Φ φ	phi	ph
Χ χ	chi	kh, ch
Ψ ψ	psi	ps
Ω ω	omega	o

Russian

Letter		Transliteration
А	а	a
Б	б	b
В	в	v
Г	г	g
Д	д	d
Е	е	e, ye
Ж	ж	zh
З	з	z
И	и	i
Й	й	i
К	к	k
Л	л	l
М	м	m
Н	н	n
О	о	o
П	п	p
Р	р	r
С	с	s
Т	т	t
У	у	u
Ф	ф	f
Х	х	kh
Ц	ц	ts
Ч	ч	ch
Ш	ш	sh
Щ	щ	shch
	ы	i
	ь	'
Э	э	e
Ю	ю	yu
Я	я	ya

The 24-letter Greek alphabet (left) and the Cyrillic alphabet which is derived from it. The people of Yugoslavia speak Serbo-Croatian, the Serbs write it with the Cyrillic alphabet and the Croats write it with the Roman alphabet.

and consonants (hard sounds like "t" and "s"). But the Arabic and Hebrew alphabets have consonants only.

Alps (Alpine)
The Alps are the greatest mountain range in EUROPE. They are centered in SWITZERLAND, but they stretch from France all the way to Yugoslavia. Mont Blanc, 15,771 ft. (4,807 meters) high, is the highest peak in Europe. There are many lakes in the valleys; the largest is Lake Geneva.

The Alps attract many tourists. They go to ski and climb, and to admire the magnificent scenery.

already *adv*. by this time; previously. *Have you finished your work already?*
also *adv*. as well as; in addition to something.
although *conj*. even if. *Although he was ill, he went to work.*
altar *n*. the table with a cross on it in a church. Communion table.
alter *vb*. change something. *You should alter the dress to make it fit.*
alternate *vb*. happen by turn, one after the other.
alternative *adj*. & *n*. a choice between two things.
altitude *n*. height above the sea level. *The aircraft flew at a very high altitude.*
alto *n*. second highest of the four voice parts.
altogether *adv*. completely, utterly.
aluminum *n*. a silvery metal which weighs less than most other metals. *Aluminum is used to make cooking pots and aircraft.*
► Aluminum (symbol – *Al*) is the most common of all the metals found in the earth's crust. It is found mainly in an ore called bauxite. Aluminum is a good conductor of heat and electricity.

Aluminum does not rust and can be made into strong alloys, so it is used in the building of airplanes and ships. It is also made into thin "tin" foil for bottle tops and "silver" paper.

always *adv*. at all times; all the time.
a.m. *abbr*. the hours between midnight and noon from the Latin *ante meridiem* meaning "before noon." *Nine a.m. is nine o'clock in the morning.*
amalgamate *vb*. combine, mix. **amalgamation** *n*.
amass *vb*. gather together; accumulate.
amateur *n*. a person who is keenly interested in sport, music or some other activity for pleasure, not for payment; unprofessional. **amateurish** *adj*. inexpert.
amaze *vb*. astonish, astound. **amazement** *n*.

Amazon River
The Amazon is the mightiest river in South America, and, at a length of 4,000 miles (6,448 kilometers) is the second longest in the world.

ambassador *n*. a person who represents one country in another country.
amber *n*. a golden-yellow fossil resin from prehistoric trees; the color of amber, used for the lights between green and red in traffic lights.
ambi- *prefix* meaning both, e.g. **ambidextrous** able to use both hands equally well.
ambition *n*. strong desire to succeed; the object of such desire. *Her ambition was to be a vet.* **ambitious** *adj*.
amble *vb*. walk at an easy pace.
ambulance *n*. a vehicle for carrying people who are ill or injured.
ambush *vb*. hide and wait for someone so that you can take him by surprise. *n*. a hiding place for a surprise attack.
amen *n*. an expression used to show agreement, especially at the end of a prayer.
amend *vb*. correct, make improvements.

America (American)
The word "America" is often used to mean the United States. Originally, however, it covered a much larger area that today is more properly called the Americas. The Americas include North America, Central America and South America, and the islands of the Caribbean and northern Canada. Despite their vast size, the Americas have fewer people than Europe. The Americas were named after the Italian navigator Amerigo Vespucci, who explored part of the South American coast in the 1400s, about the same time as Christopher COLUMBUS.

American Indians
American Indians are the native peoples of the Americas – that is, the first people to live there. They are known as Indians because when Christopher Columbus reached America in 1492 he thought he had arrived in India.

The Indians of the Americas are thought to have crossed to the North American continent from Asia about 20,000 years ago. Very gradually, over the centuries, they spread through North America and down into what is now Central and South America. They developed different ways of life according to where they lived. "American Indians" now usually refers to the Indians of North America.

There, in the eastern woodlands, the Iroquois and Algonquin tribes built domed wigwams of wood and bark and hunted deer and other game. On the Great Plains, tribes such as the Sioux and Cheyenne lived off the huge herds of bison, which they hunted, first on foot, and then on horses brought to the New World by the Spaniards. In the deserts of the southwest, the Acoma and Hopi tribes built villages of adobe (dried mud bricks). Along the coast of the Pacific northwest, tribes such as the Haida and Kwakiutl built huge totem poles of elaborately carved wood.

When Europeans began to settle in America, conflict broke out as they invaded the Indians' hunting grounds. Many Indians were killed or forced to move farther west. By the late 1800s almost all the tribes had been given land on special

The North American Indian village of Pomeiooc. This painting was done around 1585 by an Englishman, John White.

reservations by the U.S. government. Today many Indians are working to gain equal opportunities for themselves as American citizens.

amethyst *n.* a semiprecious stone; a purple variety of quartz.
amicable *adj.* kindly, friendly.
ammonia *n.* a strong chemical, often used for cleaning purposes.
ammunition (*am-mu-***ni***-shun*) *n.* bullets and other projectiles that are fired from guns.
amnesia *n.* loss of memory.
amnesty *n.* general pardon, especially of prisoners.
amoeba *n.* a one-celled animal that moves about by changing its body shape.
among *prep.* in the middle of; together with a group.
amorphous (*am-***or***-fuss*) *adj.* shapeless.
amoral *adj.* neither moral nor immoral; without a sense of morality.
amount *n.* the total sum; a quantity. *He needed a large amount of money to buy the car.*
ampere *n.* a unit for measuring the strength of an electrical current.
ampersand *n.* the sign (&) which means *and.*
amphibian *n.* an animal that lives both in water and on land. *A frog is an amphibian.*
► Amphibians are animals such as FROGS, TOADS, SALAMANDERS and NEWTS that can live in water or on land. Most amphibians start their lives in water. Amphibians are cold-blooded creatures. They do not drink like other animals but absorb water directly through their skins. For this reason they must keep their skins moist. Amphibians were one of the earliest groups of animals on earth. They crawled out of the water and onto the land about 400 million years ago.

All amphibians have backbones. Nearly all of them lay their eggs in water, in a layer of jelly which protects them. When the young amphibians hatch, they feed on algae (tiny water plants). A young frog at this stage is called a tadpole. It breathes the oxygen dissolved in water through GILLS. After two or three months the tadpole begins to change into an adult. Its tail gradually disappears, and its gills turn into LUNGS. Hind legs and then front legs appear. The little frog leaves the water and spends the rest of its life as an air-breathing adult. But it must return to the water to mate and lay its eggs.

A Fire salamander and, below it, a Marine toad – both of which belong to a group of cold-blooded animals called amphibians. Amphibians were one of the earliest groups of animals on earth.

amphitheater *n.* in Roman times an arena surrounded by tiers of seats, used for sporting events.
amphora *n.* (plural **amphorae, am**-*for-eye*) a Greek jar with two handles.
ample *adj.* enough, plenty.
amplifier *n.* electrical equipment used to make sounds louder.
amputate *vb.* (surgical) cut off a limb. **amputation** *n.*

Amsterdam
Amsterdam is the capital and biggest city in the NETHERLANDS. It is, with Venice, one of the most beautiful canal cities in Europe. Amsterdam was one of the world's greatest trading centers in the 1600s. Today it is still an important commercial city.

Amundsen, Roald
Roald Amundsen (1872–1928) was a Norwegian explorer. In 1910 he set out to be the first to reach the North Pole, but was beaten by the American, Robert Peary. Amundsen then decided to go for the undiscovered South Pole, which he reached on December 14, 1911, the first ever to do so.

amuse *vb.* make someone smile or laugh. **amusement** *n.* **amusing** *adj.*
anachronism *n.* a person, event or thing that is historically/chronologically out of place. *Napoleon rode to Waterloo in a jeep.*
anaconda *n.* the longest and heaviest snake in the world. Some have reached 30 feet in length.
► The anaconda lives on the banks of slow-running rivers in South America, catching fish and lying in wait for animals that come to the water to drink. The anaconda is not poisonous. Once it has a victim in its coils, the anaconda kills it by drowning it or by squeezing it until it suffocates. Like many snakes, anacondas can unhinge their jaws to swallow prey larger than themselves.

anagram *n.* a word or phrase made up with the letters of another in a different order. *Alps is an anagram of slap.*
analyze *vb.* examine in detail. **analysis** (plural **analyses**) *n.*
anarchy *n.* without government; disorder.
anatomy *n.* the science of the structure of the body, learned by dissection (cutting up) of dead bodies.
ancestor *n.* forefather, a person now dead, from whom one is descended. *His ancestors lived in this house for hundreds of years.* **ancestral** *adj.* **ancestry** *n.*

A

anchor *n.* a heavy iron hook on a long chain. *An anchor is dropped into the water to stop a boat from moving.* *vb.* secure a ship with an anchor.
anchovy *n.* small fish of the herring family, with a strong flavor.
ancient (**ayn**-shent) *adj.* very old or very long ago.
and *conj.* a link word expressing addition to what has gone before.

Andersen, Hans Christian
Hans Christian Andersen (1805–75) was a Danish storyteller whose fairy tales, such as *The Little Mermaid* and *The Ugly Duckling*, are still popular all over the world.

Andes
The Andes is the name of the great range of mountains that runs over about 4,500 miles (7,000 km) down the western coast of South America. There are dozens of peaks that are more than 20,000 ft. (6,100 meters) high. Among them is Aconcagua, 22,835 ft. (6,960 meters), the highest mountain in the Western Hemisphere.

Andorra
Andorra is a tiny country in the Pyrenees – the mountains between France and Spain. It is ruled jointly by the President of France and the Bishop of Urgel in Spain. Andorra enjoys tax-free status. Its principal industry is tourism.
AREA: 175 SQ. MILES (453 SQ. KM)
POPULATION: 32,700
CAPITAL: ANDORRE-LA-VIELLE (ANDORRA LA VELLA)
OFFICIAL LANGUAGE: CATALAN

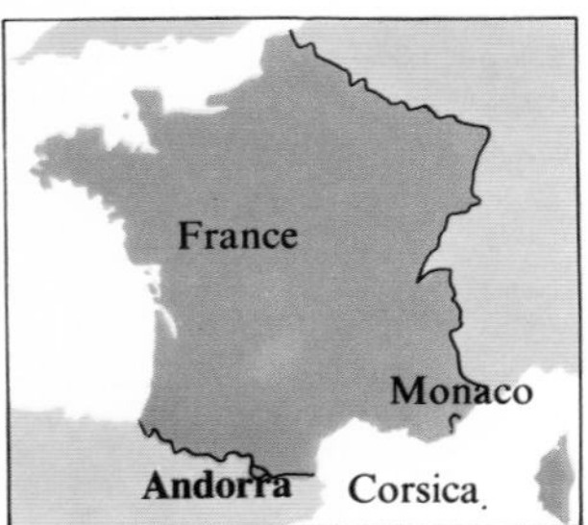

anecdote *n.* a very short story, account of an amazing or amusing nature.
anemia *n.* a lack of red blood cells. **anemic** *adj.*
anemometer *n.* instrument used to measure air speed or pressure.
anemone (*an*-**em**-*on-ee*) *n.* cultivated or woodland flower of which there are many species.
anesthetic *n.* a drug used so that people do not feel pain during an operation.
angel *n.* a messenger from God. **angelic** *adj.*
anger *n.* bad temper, fury, rage. **angry** *adj.*

angle *n.* the space between two straight lines or surfaces that meet.
► The size of all angles is measured in degrees (°). The angle that forms the corner of a square is called a "right" angle and has 90°. An acute angle is less than 90°; an obtuse angle is between 90° and 180°.

The three types of angle. A right angle (top) as made by the hands of a clock at 3 o'clock, i.e. 90°; an acute angle (less than 90°) and an obtuse angle (more than 90°).

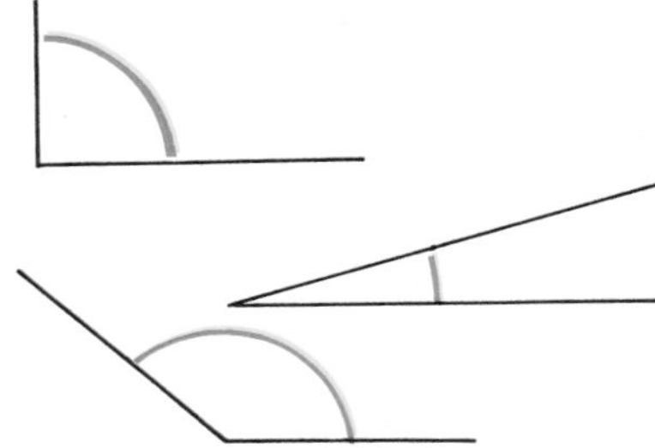

Anglican *n.* member of the Church of England or an episcopal church in communion with it.
Anglo- *prefix* meaning English, e.g. **Anglo-French Treaty**.

Anglo-Saxons
Anglo-Saxon is the name given to the group of Germanic tribes who settled in Britain during the A.D. 400s and 500s: These tribes were the Angles, Saxons and Jutes. They gradually occupied all of England, driving the original Celtic people of Britain into Wales and Cornwall. By the 700s there were seven main Anglo-Saxon kingdoms – Wessex, Sussex, Kent, Essex, East Anglia, Mercia and Northumbria. The Anglo-Saxon language is one of the two main ingredients of modern English.

Angola (Angolan)
Angola is a republic in westcentral AFRICA. Much of the country is grassland, with forests in the south and northeast. Most of the people speak Bantu languages. About two-thirds of them are farmers. The main food crops are cassava and corn.
Angola was once a colony of Portugal. In 1961, nationalists began a war against the Portuguese. Angola achieved independence in 1975, but the power struggle between rival groups continued.
AREA: 481,380 SQ. MILES (1,246,700 SQ. KM)
POPULATION: 7,414,000
CAPITAL: LUANDA
CURRENCY: KWANZA
OFFICIAL LANGUAGE: PORTUGUESE

Animals without backbones – invertebrates – form a huge group which includes earthworms, starfish and crabs as well as insects and spiders.

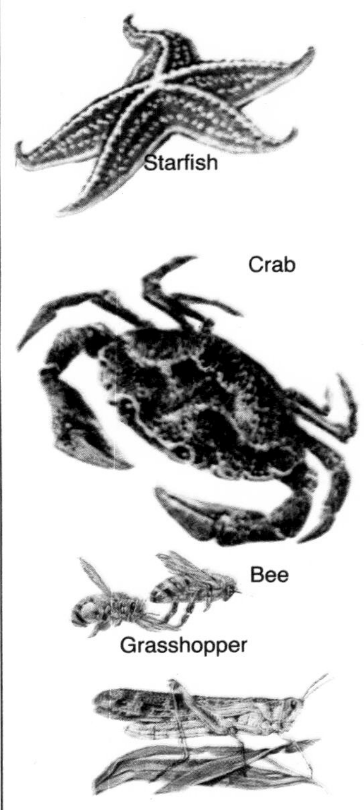

anguish *n.* extreme distress.
animal *n.* any living thing that is not a plant.
► No one knows how many different kinds of animals there are on earth; hundreds of new kinds are

discovered every year. The biggest difference between animals and plants is in the way they get their food. Animals eat plants or other animals. Plants make their food out of substances taken in through their roots or leaves. Animals can also, unlike plants, move about.
Some animals such as the tiny

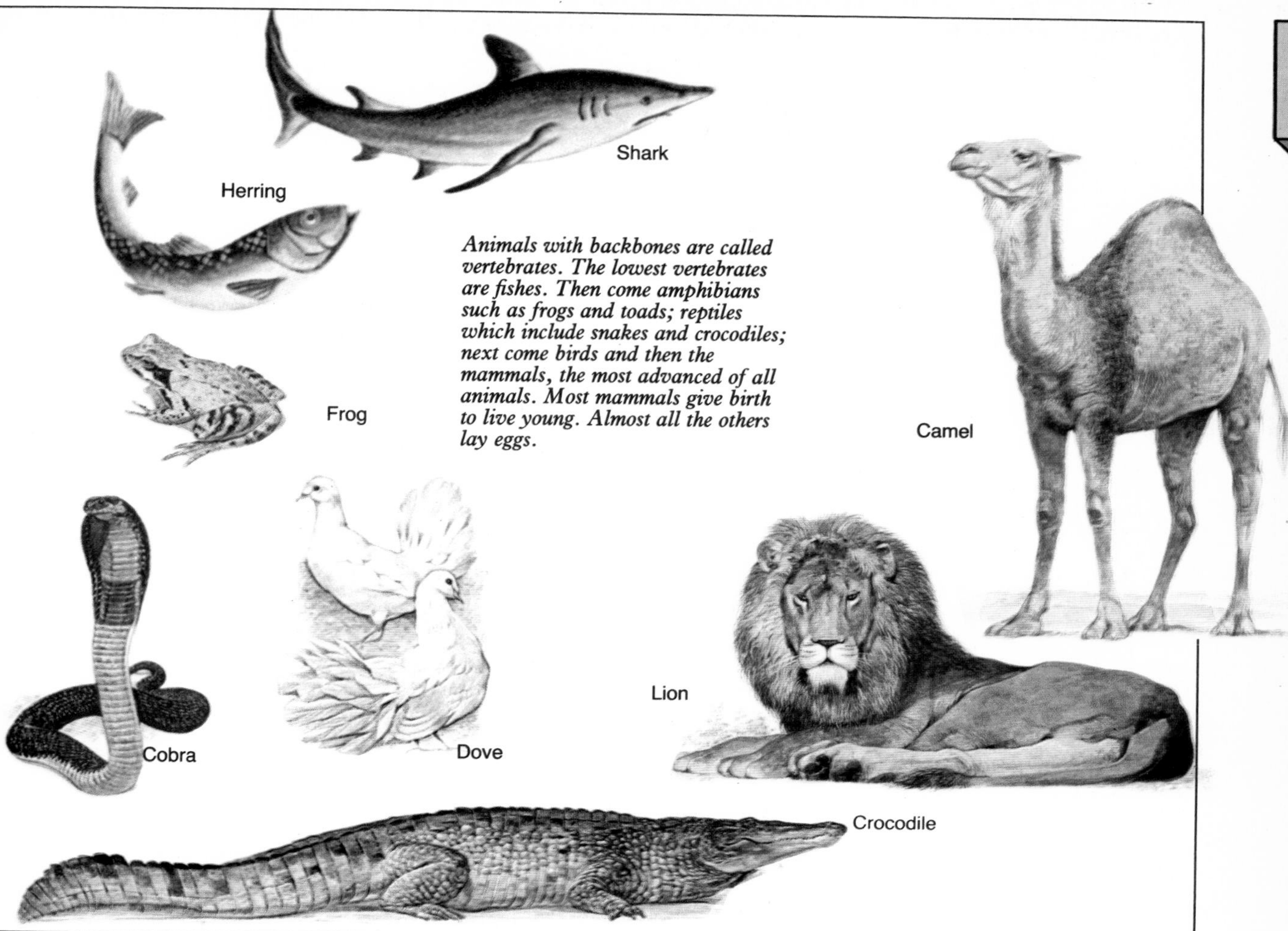

Animals with backbones are called vertebrates. The lowest vertebrates are fishes. Then come amphibians such as frogs and toads; reptiles which include snakes and crocodiles; next come birds and then the mammals, the most advanced of all animals. Most mammals give birth to live young. Almost all the others lay eggs.

amoeba reproduce by just splitting in two. In most other animals, the female produces eggs which are fertilized by the male. Creatures such as the cod produce millions of eggs, of which only a very few ever hatch, and even fewer reach maturity. These animals never see or care for their young. Other animals such as elephants and human beings develop the fertilized egg inside their bodies, and the mother feeds and cares for her infant for months or years.

animosity *n.* extreme dislike, hatred.

Ankara
Ankara has been the capital of TURKEY since 1923. It is the second largest city in Turkey, after ISTANBUL. Although built on an ancient site, it is a spacious, modern city. Ankara used to be called Angora, a name still used for the local breed of long-haired goats.

ankle *n.* the joint between the leg and the foot.

Anne, Queen
Anne was queen of Great Britain and Ireland from 1702–14. She was born in 1665. During her reign the Duke of Marlborough won several victories over the French. His wife, Sarah Churchill, was one of Anne's favorites. Anne's husband, Prince George of Denmark, and her 17 children, all died before her. One of the most important events of her reign was the Act of Union with Scotland (1707).

annex *vb.* seize, take possession of (territory). **annex** *n.* additional building.
annihilate *vb.* destroy completely.
anniversary *n.* a day on which an event is remembered each year, like the anniversary of a wedding.
announce *vb.* tell; declare; make known; present (a person or event). *She announced that she was leaving at once.* **announcement** *n.* **announcer** *n.* (especially in radio) a person who reads the news.
annoy *vb.* make someone cross or angry, irritate.
annual 1. *adj.* happening every year. *Christmas is an annual event.* 2. *n.* a plant that lives for one year only.
annul *vb.* abolish, cancel.
anoint *vb.* smear with oil, especially in a religious ceremony.
anomaly *n.* exceptional or irregular condition.
anonymous *adj.* without (the person's) name. *The author of this poem is anonymous.*
anorak *n.* a waterproof jacket, now usually made of plastic material, with a hood; parka.
anorexia *n.* a chronic lack of appetite for food.
another *adj.* one more; a different one. *Have another glass of lemonade. That is quite another thing.*
answer 1. *n.* & *vb.* reply to a question. 2. *n.* the solution to a problem.
ant *n.* a small insect that lives with many other ants.
► Ants live in all but the coldest parts of the world. There are about 7,000 species and nearly all are social insects: they live in colonies which may contain as few as a dozen ants or as many as 200,000. The colony consists of a mated female – the queen – a number of males and many sterile wingless females – workers – who find food, build the nest, often underground, and care for the young. In many species, workers

A

have stings as a defense; others squirt acid at their enemies. Ants get food in three ways: some species hunt small insects; others collect seeds, nectar and honeydew – the sticky liquid given out by aphids; while some South American ants actually produce their own food by growing FUNGI on beds of chewed leaves in their nests.

antagonism *n.* hostility, dislike. **antagonist** *n.* opponent. **antagonize** *vb.* cause dislike, hostility.
Antarctic *adj.* & *n.* (of) the south polar regions.

Antarctic
The Antarctic is the continent that surrounds the SOUTH POLE. It is a vast region of cold wasteland, with very little animal or plant life. Nearly all of the Antarctic is covered by an ice cap, broken only by a few mountain ranges. This ice cap averages 8,200 ft. (2,500 meters) in thickness, but is as much as 15,400 ft. (4,700 meters) thick in places.

ante- *prefix* meaning before, e.g. **antenatal** before birth, **anteroom** a room leading into another room.
anteater *n.* a toothless mammal of South America.
► The anteater is a curious creature with a long, tapering snout. This snout is specially shaped to extract ants, termites and grubs from their nests. It catches the insects with its long, whiplike tongue. An anteater may measure over 7 ft. (2 meters) from the tip of its tail to its snout. It uses its strong front claws to tear open ant and termite nests. Another kind of anteater, the pangolin, lives in Africa and Asia. It has scaly armor like an armadillo.

Anteaters, which are found in South America, live entirely on ants and termites. Anteaters, together with armadillos and sloths, make up the mammal order known as edentates which means "without teeth".

antelope *n.* an animal like a deer with upward-pointing horns.
► Antelopes are a family of grazing animals with horns and hoofs. They look like DEER, but are actually related to the goat and the ox. Most antelopes live on the African plains. They are fast runners and often live in large herds, fleeing suddenly at any hint of danger. Some of the best known are the impala, the waterbuck, the hartebeest, the gnu, the eland and the little dikdik, hardly bigger than a rabbit.

antenna (plural **antennae** *an*-**ten**-*ee*) *n.* 1. one of a pair of feelers on an insect's or a lobster's head. 2. an aerial.
anthropology *n.* the study of all aspects of people.
anti- *prefix* meaning against or opposed to, e.g. **anticlimax**, **anticlockwise**.
antibiotic *n.* a drug which helps destroy harmful bacteria. *Penicillin is an antibiotic.*
anticipate *vb.* 1. expect. *We did not anticipate that you would get here so quickly.* 2. do something first. *Do not anticipate the question before I have finished asking it.* **anticipation** *n.*
antifreeze *n.* a substance used to lower the freezing point of water in car engines.
antique (*ant*-**eek**) 1. *adj.* very old. 2. *n.* a very old object. *Antiques are often valuable.*
antiseptic *n.* & *adj.* a substance, such as chlorine, that kills certain kinds of germs. *The doctor cleaned the child's cut knee with an antiseptic.*
► A British surgeon called Joseph LISTER introduced antiseptics to SURGERY in the 1860s. He applied a dressing soaked in carbolic acid to a patient's wounded leg. The acid prevented the wound from becoming infected, and it healed rapidly. Many antiseptics are now used in surgery.

antithesis *n.* the opposite of something or contrast of ideas.
antler *n.* the branched horn of a deer.
antonym *n.* a word which has the opposite meaning to another, e.g. long, short.
anvil *n.* a block on which a blacksmith hammers metal into shape.
anxiety *n.* uneasy feeling of uncertainty. **anxious** *adj.*
any *adj.* some. *I haven't got any money.*
anybody *n.* (also **anyone**) any person; no matter who. *Can anybody tell me the time?*
Anzac *n.* & *adj.* Australian and New Zealand Army Corps in the First World War.
apart *adv.* away from each other; distant. *Our houses are two miles apart.*
apartheid *n.* in South Africa the political system of total separation of Europeans from other races.
apartment *n.* a set of rooms used for dwelling in a building.
apathy *n.* lack of interest, indifference.

ape *n.* 1. a large monkeylike animal with no tail. 2. *vb.* imitate, mimic.
► Apes are humans' closest animal relatives. We share the same kind of skeleton and have the same kind and number of teeth. We also have the same kind of blood and catch many similar diseases. Apes have large brains, but even the gorilla's brain is only half the size of a human being's. Unlike monkeys, apes have no tails. There are four kinds of ape: the GORILLA and CHIMPANZEE are African; ORANGUTANS live in Borneo and Sumatra; gibbons live in Southeast Asia.

aperture *n.* opening or gap.
aphid *n.* tiny soft-bodied insect which does great harm to plants.

Apollo
After ZEUS, Apollo was the most important god in Greek mythology. He was always pictured as young, strong and handsome and was a symbol of wisdom, truth and justice. Apollo was also the god of prophecy, of shepherds, of music and of healing. Later he became the Sun god.

Apollo Space Program
The Apollo Space Program was launched as part of the "space race" between the U.S.A. and Russia to be first to reach the MOON with a manned SPACECRAFT. For several years the United States experimented with spacecraft that orbited the earth; finally, in 1968, it launched a manned spacecraft that circled the moon and returned to earth. The climax of the program came on July 20, 1969, when astronaut Neil Armstrong became the first person to step onto the moon's surface.

apologize *vb.* express regret for doing something wrong. **apology** *n.*
apostle *n.* any of the 12 chosen by Jesus Christ to preach the Gospel.
► The apostles were the 12 followers of JESUS Christ, chosen to spread his

teachings throughout the world. Jesus knew he did not have much time on earth and concentrated on telling them exactly what his message meant. One of the apostles, Judas Iscariot, betrayed Jesus to his enemies, and Jesus was put to death. Later Judas killed himself. The other apostles, together with followers such as St. Paul, went on preaching the message of Jesus. CHRISTIANITY gradually spread through the Roman world and eventually through the entire world. The Bible does not tell us much about the apostles but we know that some of them were simple and uneducated. They laid the foundations for the success of Christianity.

apostrophe (*a-pos-trofee*) *n.* a punctuation mark, like this ('). It is used when letters are left out (*don't* means *do not*) or when "s" is added to a word to show ownership. *That is John's bicycle.*

appall *vb.* horrify or shock greatly. *She was appalled by his rude behavior.*

Appalachians

The Appalachians are the most important mountain range in eastern North America. They stretch 1,500 miles (2,400 km) from Quebec Province in Canada to Alabama in the southern United States. The Appalachians are heavily forested and contain important coalfields.

apparatus *n.* equipment designed for a particular use.

apparent *adj.* obvious, clear.

apparition *n.* unusual or unexpected sight; a ghost.

appeal *vb.* 1. call for, make an earnest request. *The police appealed for witnesses to the crime.* 2. be attractive. *The idea appeals to me.*

appear *vb.* 1. come into sight. *A man appeared through the mist.* 2. seem to be. *A microscope makes things appear larger.* **appearance** *n.*

appease *vb.* calm, soothe.

appendicitis *n.* painful inflammation of the appendix.

appendix *n.* 1. part of the intestines. 2. addition to a book, at the end.

appetite *n.* the desire for food; hunger.

applaud *vb.* clap one's hands as a sign of enjoying something; praise. **applause** *n.*

apple *n.* the edible fruit of the apple tree.

► All apple trees are descended from wild crab apple trees, and are members of the ROSE family. Apples were cultivated in prehistoric times, probably as early as the beginning of the Stone Age. By the A.D. 300s a Roman writer named 37 varieties of apple, and today there are thousands of different varieties. Apples are grown in places with mild climates, and enormous quantities are produced.

appliance *n.* a piece of equipment for a special purpose, e.g. an attachment to a vacuum cleaner for cleaning difficult corners.

apply *vb.* 1. ask for something. *He applied for a job in the local factory.* 2. be relevant. *That rule does not apply in this case.*

appoint *vb.* choose someone to do a particular job.

appointment *n.* a time agreed for a meeting.

appreciate *vb.* value highly, think much of; rise in value. *Paintings appreciate rather than depreciate in value the longer you keep them.* **appreciative** *adj.* showing gratitude.

apprentice *n.* a person learning a craft or trade from an employer. **apprenticeship** *n.*

approach 1. *vb.* go near. *They approached the house.* 2. *n.* access; the means of getting to a place. *The approach to the house was through a forest.*

approve *vb.* express a good opinion of.

approximate *adj.* nearly correct. *I can give you the approximate cost.*

apricot *n.* an orange-yellow fruit with a big, hard seed.

► Apricots look like small peaches, but they are actually fruits of the plum family. They grow best in warm climates, as they are easily damaged by frost. Apricots can be eaten fresh but are often canned or dried. At one time people believed that apricots originally came from America, but they are now thought to be native to China.

April *n.* the fourth month of the year.

apron *n.* a piece of cloth or plastic worn in front of and over clothes to keep them clean.

apse *n.* a semi-circular end to a church.

apt *adj.* suitable.

aptitude *n.* talent or ability.

aqualung *n.* breathing apparatus for swimming under water.

aquarium *n.* a place where fish and other water animals and plants are kept and studied. **Aqua** is the Latin name for water.

► Many large public aquariums have become famous for their expertly trained performing animals, such as DOLPHINS and WHALES. A home aquarium is usually made of glass or has a glass side through which its contents can easily be seen. Many people keep tropical fish in aquariums that are specially heated to keep the water warm. These fish need very special care and attention.

aquatic *adj.* growing or living in water; taking place in or on water.

aqueduct *n.* a channel or pipe for carrying water, often a bridge, across a valley.

► Many aqueducts were built in the past, but today most water is piped underground. The Egyptians, Babylonians, Assyrians and Greeks built aqueducts, but the Romans were the greatest aqueduct builders of all time. These early engineers had to solve the problem of how to carry water from lakes to their fortified hilltop towns. This almost always meant that a valley had to be crossed. The Romans built high, bridge-like spans supported by huge ARCHES to take the water across.

Most aqueducts, such as that built in ancient Jerusalem by Hezekiah, King of Judah, were fairly short, but some Roman aqueducts were very long. The longest was in Carthage in North Africa, covering 87 miles (140 km) and carrying 6.5 million gallons (30 million liters) of water every day.

The Roman aqueduct at Nimes in France, which can still be seen today, is 157 ft. (48 meters) high. It is unique in that it consists of no fewer than three separate tiers of arches built on top of one another. Another famous Roman aqueduct, at Segovia in Spain, is 2,950 ft. (900 meters) long.

Arab (Arabic)

Arabs were originally those people who lived in Arabia. But from the A.D.600s Arabian Arabs, inspired by their new faith, ISLAM, swept through western Asia and North Africa, conquering and settling a huge area. They taught the inhabitants the Arabic language and their Islamic religion. Today an Arab is anyone whose mother tongue is Arabic. This includes Arabic-speaking peoples from countries such as Algeria, Syria, Iraq and Libya. Muslims in Iran, India and Pakistan pray in Arabic, but do not use it in everyday speech, so are not considered Arabs.

The Arabs ruled North Africa and southwest Asia for 900 years, until they were defeated by the Turks in the 1500s. They lived under Turkish rule until World War I. After World War II many Arab countries became rich from the production of huge quantities of valuable OIL. There have been several attempts to unify the Arab nations, though in recent years conflict with the state of Israel has caused a split in the Arab ranks. The oil-producing countries hold great political power in the world because of their control of important oil resources.

Arabia (Arabian)

Arabia is a large, mainly desert, region in the Middle East. For many centuries it formed part of the Ottoman (Turkish) Empire. Today Arabia consists of several Arab

A clay seal with a form of writing on it, a buried statue, a fragment of mosaic, an ancient pot – these are all clues which help the archaeologist piece together a picture of the past.

countries of which by far the largest is Saudi Arabia. Ancient Roman writers referred to *Arabia Felix* ("Happy Arabia" – the coastal areas) and *Arabia Deserta* ("Empty Arabia").

arc *n.* a curved line; part of a circle.
arcade *n.* row of arches supported by columns.
arch *n.* a curved structure of stones that can support a load, used to cover an opening such as a doorway or the ceiling of a church.
► An arch consists of a series of wedge-shaped stones arranged in a curve so that they not only support each other but are strong enough to support a heavy weight. The arch was one of the earliest important advances in building, and was first used in ancient BABYLON and ASSYRIA. The Romans built many structures with round arches, as,

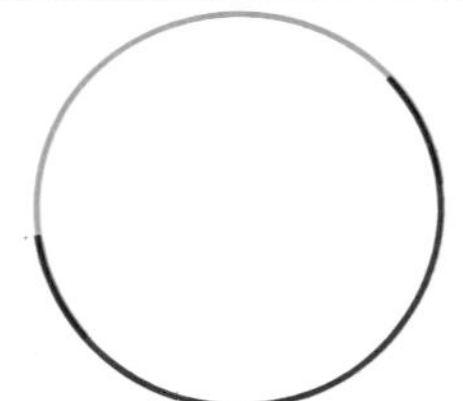

later, did the Normans. Pointed arches were a feature of Gothic architecture in the MIDDLE AGES.

arch- *prefix* meaning chief, principal, e.g. **archbishop, archvillain**.
archaeology (**ark**-*i*-*ology*) *n.* the study of history through the things that people have made and built. **archaeologist** *n.*
► Archaeologists study all things, from the greatest of monuments to the tiniest pin. Modern archaeology began during the RENAISSANCE, when people became interested in the culture of ancient GREECE and ROME. At first archaeological sites were ransacked for the treasures they contained. But by the early 1800s archaeologists had begun to uncover sites carefully, noting all they found and where they found it. Many exciting and important discoveries were made, including the remains of ancient TROY (1871); the early Greek civilization at Mycenae (1876); and the tomb of TUTANKHAMEN (1922).

Today, science helps the archaeologist in his work. Radiocarbon dating and dendrochronology (dating by tree rings) help tell us when particular objects were made. Infrared and X-RAY photography can show up designs under the rotted surface of a bronze bowl. Archaeology has even gone under the sea. With modern diving equipment, archaeologists can explore sunken wrecks and other long-lost remains of the past. Archaeologists are not only interested in ancient civilizations and buried sites. Industrial archaeology is the study of old factories and machinery.

archaeopteryx *n.* a prehistoric bird about the size of a crow, with teeth like a lizard.
archaic (*ar*-**kay**-*ik*) *adj.* ancient, no longer in use, antiquated.
archer *n.* a person who shoots with a bow and arrow.
archery *n.* the sport of shooting with a bow.
►Archery is the use of the bow and arrow, once for hunting and warfare, now mostly for sport. No one knows when bows and arrows were first used, but prehistoric people certainly used them to shoot animals for food and to protect themselves. Until the discovery of GUNPOWDER, the army with the best archers usually won.

Today, archery is a popular sport. In target shooting the target is 4 ft. (1.2 meters) across. The length of the arrow is about 28 in. (71 cm) for men and slightly shorter for women. Bows are usually made of laminated wood or fiberglass.

Archimedes
Archimedes (282–212 B.C.) was a Greek scientist who lived in Sicily. Among many other things he discovered Archimedes' Principle which tells us that if we weigh an object in the air and then weigh it again submerged in a liquid, it will lose weight equal to the weight of the liquid it displaces. Archimedes is supposed to have discovered this when he stepped into a bath full to the brim, and water spilled onto the floor.
archipelago (*ark-i*-**pel**-*ago*) *n.* a group of islands; an area of sea containing many islands.

Three types of arch (from the left): Semi-circular arch (Roman); horseshoe arch (Moorish); and lancet arch (medieval).

architecture *n.* style of buildings. **architectural** *adj.*
► Architecture as we know it began about 7,000 years ago in ancient EGYPT. The Egyptians built huge pyramids as tombs for their kings, and many of these pyramids still stand.

Greek architecture began to take shape about 600 B.C. and developed into the beautiful styles we can see today on the ACROPOLIS at ATHENS.

When the Romans conquered GREECE they copied Greek architecture. But they soon discovered how to make an ARCH, so they could build larger, stronger buildings. They also began to make DOMES for the first time.

About A.D. 800 the Romanesque period of architecture began. Romanesque architecture at first imitated the style of ancient Rome, but soon took on a style of its own – a style that was strong and heavy. This style was followed by the Gothic. Many of the fine old cathedrals are in the Gothic style. They have graceful pointed arches over doors, window, and often in the roof as well. The roof of a Gothic cathedral is usually made of a series of crisscross arches which take the weight of the ceiling. Roofs like this are called vaulted roofs.

In about 1400 a new style of architecture began in Italy. This was called the RENAISSANCE (the word means rebirth) and it spread all over Europe. Renaissance architects paid almost as much attention to public buildings and people's houses as they did to building fine churches and cathedrals.

Later, many famous architects changed the building styles to fit the times in which they lived. Christopher WREN (1632–1723) designed buildings such as St. Paul's Cathedral in London and Hampton Court.

Today people still build with brick and stone, but they also have new materials which have changed the way in which buildings are constructed. Concrete and steel, glass and plastic are shaping the new world in which we live. Architects are designing offices, factories and sports arenas so as to make the best use of these new materials. They even have the opportunity sometimes to design whole new cities.

archives (**ark**-*ives*) *pl. n.* public records; place where the records are kept. **archivist** *n.* person who keeps the records.

Arctic *adj.* & *n.* (of) the North Polar region.

Arctic

The Arctic is the region around the NORTH POLE. At the actual North Pole there is no land, only a huge area of frozen sea. The land in the Arctic region is frozen solid for most of the year. In the short summer the surface soil thaws and some plants can grow, even brightly colored flowers. There are now more people in the Arctic than there used to be, because valuable minerals and oil have been found there.

It is cold near the North Pole because the sun never rises high in the sky. In winter there are days when it does not rise at all and in summer there are days when it can be seen all day and night.

Arctic animals include seals, polar bears, foxes, owls, weasels, musk oxen and reindeer. The only people native to the Arctic are the Eskimos.

Corinthian

Doric

Ionic

The three orders or styles of ancient Greek columns which became standard models for later architects.

ardor *n.* enthusiasm, warmth. **ardent** *adj.*

arduous *adj.* difficult to do.

area *n.* 1. the size of a surface. Areas are measured in units such as square feet, square yards and acres. *A football field is about 5300 square yards in area.* 2. part of a country or the world. *They come from the Detroit area.*

arena *n.* a sports stadium; originally the enclosed space in which the Ancient Roman games took place.

Argentina (Argentinian)

Argentina is the second largest country in SOUTH AMERICA. Most of the country's population are farmers and ranchers, for much of Argentina's wealth comes from livestock and crops. Argentina is one of the world's top producers of beef and veal, fruit, wheat, millet and sorghum, and wool. The chief farming region is on the pampas, a Spanish word meaning "plains." Vast farms on the pampas raise millions of cattle and sheep, which graze on the rich pasture. Northern Argentina is an area of tropical forests, and is little developed. In the far south, near the tip of South America, is Patagonia, a desert waste. The western part of the country is dry, and the land rises to the Andes Mountains, including ACONCAGUA, at 22,834 ft. (6,960 meters) the highest peak in the Americas. Argentina was ruled by Spain from 1535 to 1810. Today, most Argentinians are descended from Europeans, though there are still about 20,000 native Indians.

Argentina has always laid claim to the British Crown Colony of the FALKLAND ISLANDS. In 1982 Argentinian forces invaded the Falklands. However, the British sent a naval task force and the Argentinians were forced to withdraw.

AREA: 1,068,360 SQ. MILES (2,766,889 SQ. KM)
POPULATION: 27,796,000
CAPITAL: BUENOS AIRES
CURRENCY: PESO
OFFICIAL LANGUAGE: SPANISH

argue (**arg**-*yoo*) *vb.* dispute; give reasons why you support something. *They argue their case well.* **argument** *n.* reason put forward. **argumentative** *adj.* fond of arguing.

arid *adj.* dry; parched with heat.

arise *vb.* get up; come up for consideration.

aristocracy *n.* nobility.

Aristotle

Aristotle (384–322 B.C.) was a Greek philosopher and a student of another famous Greek philosopher, PLATO. At the age of 17 Aristotle went to Athens to become Plato's pupil. He worked there for 20 years and then became tutor to ALEXANDER THE GREAT. Aristotle invented the method of thinking called logic. His writings cover many areas, including nature and politics.

arithmetic *n.* sums; the science of numbers.
► Arithmetic is the branch of MATHEMATICS that deals with counting and calculating, using numbers. The four principal operations in arithmetic are addition, subtraction, multiplication and division.

Arizona (*abbrev.* **Ariz.**)

Arizona is a state in the southwest of

A

the U.S.A. bordering on Mexico. Arizona contains many national parks and monuments including the Grand Canyon, through which the Colorado River flows, the Painted Desert and the Petrified Forest.

Arizona is one of the largest states, but it has a population of only 2 million. It is rich in minerals, particularly copper. Manufacturing and agriculture are also important sources of income. Today, most of the population live in Phoenix, the state capital, and Tucson.

Arizona, once a part of Mexico, became a U.S. territory after the Mexican War of 1848. Arizona became a state in 1912.

ark *n.* 1. ship or large boat, particularly Noah's Ark. 2. the wooden chest in which the Jewish Tablets of the Law were kept (the Ark of the Covenant).

A carving (1 century A.D.*) of the Ark of the Covenant found in the ruins of Capernaum Synagogue.*

Arkansas (*abbrev.* **Ark.**)
Arkansas (pronounced ***Ark****-en-saw*) is a state in the south central part of the U.S.A. The main river is the Arkansas, which drains into the Mississippi. The largest city is the state capital, Little Rock.

Arkansas is largely an agricultural state, producing cotton, soybeans, rice and other crops. Bauxite is mined and processed into aluminum, and there is an important chemical industry.

Arkansas was bought from France in the Louisiana Purchase of 1803. It became the 25th state in 1836. During the American Civil War, Arkansas was one of the Confederate States.

Arkwright, Richard
Richard Arkwright (1732–92) was an English inventor best known for his spinning frame, which made factory production of cotton cloth possible. Arkwright patented his spinning machine in 1769, after which he built his first spinning mill. He became the pioneer of the modern factory system. His great success laid the groundwork for the INDUSTRIAL REVOLUTION.

arm 1. *vb.* give weapons to. *They will arm the soldiers with the latest weapons.* 2. *n.* part of the body from the shoulder to the hand.
► The upper arm contains one large bone, the *humerus*. Two smaller bones, the *ulna* and *radius*, make up the forearm. Nineteen muscles attached to these bones move the hand and fingers.

armada *n.* a Spanish word for a great fleet of armed ships.
► The most famous armada was the Spanish fleet that tried to invade England in 1588. The 130 Spanish ships were large, clumsy and heavily armed. The English ships were faster and easier to maneuver, and were manned by more skillful seamen. The English sent fireships toward the Spanish fleet, which retreated out to sea. Later, several Spanish ships were sunk and many damaged in battle. The Armada was forced to flee around the northern tip of Britain. Only 67 of the original 130 ships reached Spain.

armadillo *n.* a small South American mammal protected by a shield of bony scales.
► Some kinds of armadillo can roll themselves into a ball when attacked, giving them complete protection. They have strong claws which they use for digging burrows and tearing open termite nests to find food. There are 10 different kinds of armadillo, the biggest being about 4 ft. (1.2 meters) long.

armed forces *pl. n.* the army, navy and air force of a country.
armistice *n.* a truce, an agreement to stop fighting.
armor *n.* a covering, usually made of metal, that protects the body in battle.
► Armor goes back at least 5,000 years and was originally made of tough leather. Then men made metal breastplates, helmets and shields. But the rest of the body was still protected by leather or mail, many small iron rings linked together to form a flexible metal coat. In the MIDDLE AGES, knights rode into battle encased from head to toe in plate armor which weighed up to 70 lb. (30 kg). When firearms were invented, armor was no longer worn, except for the helmet. The weight of metal needed to stop a bullet was too great.

Today, tough light metals and plastics are being used in armored jackets worn by soldiers and the police.

army (plural **armies**) *n.* a large number of soldiers.
► Most armies today are made up of combat troops, service troops, and staff officers. The combat troops include the infantry, armed mostly with rifles and grenades; armored troops, who use tanks and other armored vehicles; artillery, who fire the heavy guns; and paratroopers, who are dropped into battle by parachute.

Service troops are vital to the modern army. They provide the ammunition, food, fuel and other supplies needed by the combat troops. They include doctors and medical staff, and engineers who lay mines, build bridges and prepare landing strips for aircraft.

The staff is made up of headquarters officers who plan army operations and control all the combat and service troops. Should atomic weapons ever be used, the role of the modern army would have to change overnight.

aroma *n.* a smell – usually pleasant or belonging to something in particular.
arose past of **arise**.
around 1. *adv.* on all sides. *She looked around but could see nobody.* 2. *prep.* in a circle; in all directions. *We walked around the old town.*
arouse *vb.* wake up, stir to action.
arrange *vb.* fix or organize something; put things in order. **arrangement** *n.*
array *n.* arrangement, display. *There was a lovely array of flowers on the table.*
arrest *vb.* take a suspected criminal into custody.
arrive *vb.* reach a place. *The train arrived at the station.* **arrival** *n.* reaching a place.

A Norman knight wearing a long mail tunic and a helmet with a distinctive nasal *(metal bar over the nose to protect the face).*

Two distinctive styles of art – one western, the other eastern: Leonardo da Vinci's Virgin of the Rocks *(left) and* The Emperor Kuang-Wu fording a river.

arrogant *adj*. exaggerating one's own importance; conceited.

arrow *n*. a pointed stick that is shot from a bow.

arsenal *n*. a place where weapons and ammunition are stored or made.

arsenic *n*. a chemical element, a form of which (white arsenic) is extremely poisonous.

arson *n*. a name used in law for the crime of deliberately setting fire to property.

art *n*. drawing, painting and modeling, and the things that are made that way.

► Since the very earliest times people have painted and made sculptured objects. We can still admire cave paintings that were drawn over 20,000 years ago. Beautiful wall paintings and sculptures from ancient EGYPT, GREECE and ROME still survive.

The Christian religion had a great influence on art. During the MIDDLE AGES painters worked on religious scenes, often in a rather stiff way. But when the RENAISSANCE came in the 1300s art began to flower and painters such as LEONARDO DA VINCI and MICHELANGELO began to make their subjects more lifelike. Great Dutch painters like REMBRANDT painted everyday scenes. In the 1700s and 1800s many artists went back to making their work look something like early Greek and Roman art.

Later, painting became more real looking, but by the 1870s a new style called Impressionism was starting. Artists such as Monet (1840–1926) and Renoir (1841–1919) painted with little dabs of color, making soft, misty outlines. Painting in the 1900s became even freer. Styles included Abstract Art and Cubism, with painters such as Cézanne (1839–1906) and PICASSO.

The oldest pieces of sculpture we know were made by STONE AGE people about 20,000 years ago. The ancient Egyptians made very fine sculptures between 2,000 and 4,000 years ago. Many of them were huge statues of kings and queens. Some of the world's most beautiful carving was done by the sculptors of ancient Greece and Rome, in what is known as the Classical period. During the Renaissance, especially in Italy, the art of sculpture advanced by leaps and bounds. Michelangelo carved superb statues such as his *David*, which can be seen in Florence.

Modern sculptors often carve sculptures in which the general shape is more important than showing the likeness of a figure.

artery *n*. one of the tubes that carries blood from the heart to all parts of the body.

► Arteries have thick, elastic walls. The largest is the *aorta*, which is connected directly to the heart. The word artery comes from Greek words meaning "air carrier." Because dead bodies have little or no blood in the arteries, the ancient Greek doctors who dissected them came to the conclusion that arteries carried air around the body. Veins carry blood back to the heart.

arthritis *n*. painful inflammation of a body joint causing severe stiffness.

arthropod *n*. group of animals which includes insects, spiders and crabs.

Arthur, King
King Arthur was a legendary British ruler of the A.D. 500s. His kingdom was supposed to have been in the west of Britain. Many stories grew up around King Arthur's court and his Knights of the Round Table. These stories were first collected by Sir Thomas Malory in the 1400s.

artichoke *n*. name applied to two different plants: (Jerusalem) plant with edible tuber; (globe) thistle-like plant, the flowerhead of which is eaten.

article *n*. 1. any object. 2. a passage in a newspaper, encyclopedia, etc. 3. the words "a, an" (indefinite article) and "the" (definite article).

articulate *adj*. 1. clear and distinct of speech. *vb*. speak clearly. 2. having joints. *An articulated truck*. *vb*. connect by joints.

artificial (*art-i-***fish***-el*) *adj*. not natural, made by people and machines; not grown. *Natural rubber comes from the juice of a tree, but artificial rubber is made from coal.*

artillery *n*. the big guns used by an army.

artist *n*. a person who draws, paints, or carves. **artistic** *adj*.

as 1. *adv*. to the same extent. *Please do it as soon as possible*. (Also used in proverbial phrases. *The baby was as good as gold*.) 2. *conj*. because. *As she is sick, you will have to go.*

asbestos *n*. the name given to a

ARCTIC OCEAN
USSR
URAL MOUNTAINS
Yenisey
Lena
Ob
Omsk
Novosibirsk
Irkutsk
L. Baikal
Amur
Black Sea
Izmir
Ankara
TURKEY
CAUCASUS
Caspian Sea
Aral Sea
Syr Darya
Amu Darya
L. Balkhash
Ulan Bator
MONGOLIA
CYPRUS
Nicosia
Aleppo
LEBANON
Beirut
SYRIA
Damascus
Jerusalem
ISRAEL
Amman
JORDAN
IRAQ
Baghdad
Euphrates
Tigris
Tehran
Isfahan
Basra
Abadan
Kuwait
KUWAIT
IRAN
TIEN SHAN
Hwang Ho
Beijing (Peking)
Gobi Desert
Tianjin (Tients
Lanchow
Xian (Sian)
AFGHANISTAN
Kabul
Islamabad
Lahore
Kashmir
Tibet
CHINA
Wuhan
Medina
Riyadh
BAHRAIN
QATAR
Doha
Jidda
Mecca
UAE
Arabian Desert
Red Sea
SAUDI ARABIA
OMAN
Muscat
PAKISTAN
Indus
Karachi
Hyderabad
Delhi
New Delhi
HIMALAYAS
Lhasa
Mt Everest
NEPAL
Katmandu
Thimphu
BHUTAN
Brahmaputra
Chengdu
Yangtze-Kiang
Chungking
Kunming
Si-Kiang
MACA
Kanpur
Lucknow
Varanasi
Ganges
Dacca
BURMA
Mandalay
Hanoi
Ahmadabad
INDIA
Calcutta
BANGLADESH
Irrawaddy
Salween
LAOS
Vientiane
VIETNAM
Mekong
San'a
Yemen AR
Aden
Nagpur
Godavari
Bombay
Hyderabad
Rangoon
THAILAND
Bangkok
KAMPUCHEA
Phnom Penh
Saigon (Ho Chi Minh City
Bangalore
Madras
SRI LANKA
Colombo
Equator
MALDIVE IS
Malé
Penang
MALAYSIA
Kuala Lumpur
SINGAPORE
ASIA
INDIAN OCEAN
0 400 800 1200 miles
0 400 800 1200 1600 kilometers
Capital Cities
Sumatra
INI
Djakarta
Java

group of minerals that occur naturally as fibers. Because asbestos does not burn, it is used for fireproof materials.

ascent *n.* the act of going up a slope or hill.

ascertain (*ass-sur-***tane**) *vb.* find out, make sure.

ash *n.* 1. the powder that is left after something has been burned. 2. a tall tree with grayish bark and tough white wood.

ashamed *adj.* feeling guilty or disgraced.

ashen *adj.* pale, ash-colored.

Ash Wednesday first day of Lent in the Christian Church.

Asia (Asiatic, Asian)

Asia is the largest of all the continents. It also has more people (2,693,000,000) than any other continent. Places such as the GANGES-Brahmaputra delta, the river valleys of CHINA and the island of Java are among the most thickly populated places in the world.

Northern Asia is a cold, desolate tundra region. In contrast, the islands of INDONESIA are in the steamy tropics. The world's highest mountain range, the HIMALAYAS, is in Asia, and so is the lowest point on land, the shores of the Dead Sea. Asia's people belong to the three main races: Caucasoids live in the southwest and northern INDIA; Mongoloids, including the Chinese and Japanese, live in the east; a few Negroids are found in the southeast. And all the world's great religions began in Asia.

Most Asians are farmers, and many are very poor. The chief food crops are wheat and rice. Other crops are exported: they include tea, cotton, jute, rubber, citrus fruits and tobacco. Many nations such as China are developing their industries, but JAPAN is the only truly industrialized nation.

Asia was the birthplace of civilization, and was the home of many great civilizations, including those of Mesopotamia, BABYLON, China and the Indus Valley in what is now Pakistan. Europeans began to visit Asia in the 1400s and trade quickly grew up between the two continents. Later, for several centuries, China and Japan closed their doors to trade with Europe. By the late 1800s most of the rest of Asia was ruled by European powers. But after World War II, during which Japan occupied parts of east Asia, most European colonies became independent. In 1949 the Chinese Communists took control of mainland China. In 1975 Communists took over VIETNAM, Laos and Cambodia (now Kampuchea) after a seven-year war for control, fought mainly in Vietnam.

aside *adv.* apart; on one side. *I shall put this book aside for you.*

ask *vb.* put a question, enquire; make a request. *She asked her boss for more pay.*

asleep *adj.* & *adv.* the state of sleeping; not awake. *They were all asleep in bed when the phone rang.*

asp *n.* a small poisonous snake.

aspect *n.* a view, a look; the direction in which a house faces.

asphalt *n.* a brown or black tarry substance, used for surfacing roads.

aspidistra *n.* indoor plant with broad pointed leaves.

aspiration *n.* ambition. **aspire** *vb.* aim high.

aspirin *n.* a drug used to reduce pain.

ass *n.* a donkey, especially a wild one.

assassinate *vb.* murder a public figure. **assassin** *n.*

assault *vb.* attack someone. *n.* an attack.

assemble *vb.* collect together a number of people or things; put the parts of something together to make a whole. **assembly** *n.*

assent *vb.* agree. *n.* formal consent.

assert *vb.* declare, maintain.

assign *vb.* appoint; give someone a share. **assignment** *n.* a task.

assist *vb.* help someone. **assistance** *n.*

association *n.* a group of people or organizations that works together. **associate** *vb.* join, connect.

assorted *adj.* mixed, various.

assume *vb.* 1. take for granted as true. *We assume the facts are correct.* 2. take upon oneself. *She has assumed far too much responsibility.* **assumption** *n.*

assure *vb.* promise, make certain. *She assured me that she had posted the letter.*

Assyrians

The Assyrians were a warlike people in the ancient world. They lived in Mesopotamia in the Middle East. Their name comes from their chief city of Ashur (Assur). The Assyrian Empire began over 4,000 years ago. Periods of expansion alternated with periods of decline. The golden age of the Empire lasted from the 1000s to the 800s B.C.. In the 600s B.C. the empire was conquered by the Babylonians. It finally became part of the Persian Empire.

Scholars have learned much about the Assyrians from their sculptures and writings. The kings of Assyria lived in great luxury. The vast armies consisted mainly of paid mercenaries, who fought with great skill in war chariots. Assyria's main god was Assur, the god of war.

asterisk *n.* a star-shaped mark (*), often used in books to refer to footnotes.

astern *n.* at or behind the stern, or rear, of a boat.

asthma *n.* a medical condition which causes wheezing and difficulty in breathing.
astonish *vb.* amaze; surprise.
astound *vb.* surprise, shock.
astray *adv.* in the wrong direction; lost. *My notes seem to have gone astray.*
astrology *n.* the study of the stars in order to predict the future.
► Ancient peoples believed that the heavenly bodies influenced people and their affairs. This led to the growth of a priesthood of astrologers, men who claimed to be able to read the future in the heavens. Throughout history, kings, generals and other powerful people have listened to their advice. Today many people still follow the predictions of astrologers.

astronaut *n.* a traveler in space.
astronautics *n.* the science of space travel.
► The first man-made object in space was the Russian satellite *Sputnik I*, launched on October 4, 1957. The first man in space was the Russian, Yuri Gagarin, on April 12, 1961. The only woman in space was Valentina Tereshkova, in 1963. The first moon landing was made by the unmanned Russian *Lunik* on September 14, 1959. The first man on the moon was Neil Armstrong, who stepped off the lunar module of *Apollo 11* on July 20, 1969.

astronomy *n.* the study of the sun, planets, moon and stars. **astronomer** *n.* a student or expert in astronomy.
► Astronomy is the oldest of all the sciences. Early observations enabled people to divide the year into months, weeks, and days, based on the movements of the SUN, EARTH and MOON. The development of the CALENDAR helped early astronomers to forecast the appearance of COMETS and the dates of ECLIPSES. For many centuries people believed that the earth was the center of the UNIVERSE, until, in the 1540s, Nicolaus COPERNICUS revived the idea that the sun was at the center of the SOLAR SYSTEM. In 1608 Hans Lippershey invented the TELESCOPE, an important new tool for astronomers. Today, big telescopes are aided by radio telescopes, which collect radio waves emitted by objects in space, such as pulsars and quasars.

astute *adj.* shrewd, crafty.
asylum *n.* refuge, shelter. Once a place for treating people with mental illness.

Ataturk, Kemal
Kemal Ataturk (1881–1938) was born Mustafa Kemal. In 1934 he was given the name Ataturk, which means "father of the Turks." He made his name during World War I, when he showed great courage and ability in organizing the defenses of Gallipoli against the Allied invasion. After the war, he expelled the Greeks from Turkey. He proclaimed the Turkish Republic in 1923. In the same year he was elected President.
Ataturk introduced major changes into the Turkish way of life. Under his guidance, Turkey adopted the Roman alphabet, and women were given the vote. He is regarded as the founder of modern Turkey.

ate *vb.* past of **eat**.

Athabaska, Lake
This large lake in the Canadian mid-west covers an area of 3,100 sq. miles (8,000 sq. km). It straddles the provinces of Alberta and Saskatchewan. Uranium and other minerals are mined in the surrounding area.

atheist *n.* a person who does not believe that there is a God. **atheism** *n.* disbelief in God.

Athens
Athens is the capital of GREECE, but it was once the center of the world's civilization and learning. It was already an important city when its citizens took a leading part in driving the powerful Persians from Europe in 479 B.C. After this, Athens quickly rose to become the most important state in Greece under a leader called Pericles (490–429 B.C). Pericles built many magnificent buildings, especially on the hill called the ACROPOLIS. Even after the Romans conquered Greece, Athens remained famous as a center of culture.

athlete *n.* someone who is good at sports or games that need strength or speed. **athletic** *adj.*

Atlantic Ocean
The Atlantic Ocean is the second largest ocean in the world, after the PACIFIC OCEAN. It lies between Europe and Africa in the east and the Americas in the west. Its average depth is more than 6,000 ft. (1,800 meters and it covers 41,000,000 sq. miles (106,000,000 sq. km). There are a number of strong currents in the Atlantic. The best known is the GULF STREAM which carries warm water towards the coasts of Europe. It is this current which keeps Europe comparatively warm in the winter months.

atlas *n.* a book of maps.

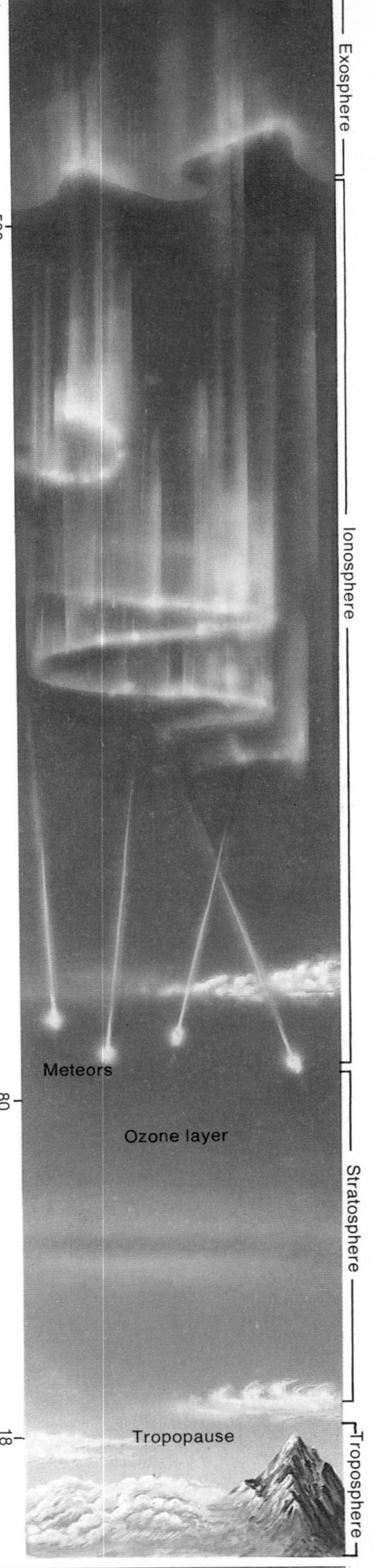

The Earth's atmosphere can be divided into four layers: the troposphere which contains 80% of the atmosphere; the stratosphere where the ozone layer filters out some of the sun's harmful ultraviolet rays; the stratosphere where meteroids burn up; and the exosphere.

atmosphere *n.* the air around the earth.
atoll *n.* a coral island with a central lagoon, or lake.

atom *n.* the smallest particle of a chemical element.
► Everything is made of atoms. Things you can see, like the wood in a table; things you cannot see, like the air, are all made of atoms. People and animals are made of atoms, too. If the atoms in something are packed closely together, that something is a solid. If the atoms in something are not so tightly packed – if they move about more – that something is a liquid, like water. And if the atoms move about a great deal, we have a gas, like air.

It is difficult to imagine how small an atom is. Look at the period at the end of this sentence. It has in it about 250 billion atoms! But even atoms are made up of smaller pieces. The simplest atom is that of the light gas HYDROGEN. The center is a tiny body called a proton. Around it spins an electron. Other atoms are much more complicated than the hydrogen atom. The carbon atom, for example, has at its center six protons and six other particles called neutrons. Round these spin six electrons.

►► **Atomic energy** An atomic bomb produces an enormous amount of heat in a fraction of a second. Atomic energy is produced in an atomic reactor in a similar way, but the energy is controlled. Heat is produced much more slowly and safely.

To make useful power from the atom scientists use a metal called URANIUM. The atoms in uranium are always breaking up and making heat. To control the amount of heat, the uranium is made into long rods. The rods are put into a reactor core and are separated by other rods made of CARBON. With the right number of uranium rods and carbon rods, the reactor goes on making a lot of safe heat.

Water flows around inside the reactor. This water boils and the steam is made to drive turbines. The turbines drive generators which make ELECTRICITY. This electricity is fed into the ordinary grid system, just like electricity from power stations which run on oil or coal.

atrocious *adj.* cruel, wicked; very bad. **atrocity** (*at-tross-ity*) *n.* wicked act; (*casual*) ugly object.
attach *vb.* fasten or join one thing to another.
attack *vb.* try to hurt a person or capture a place. *The soldiers planned to attack the castle.*
attain *vb.* reach, arrive at, accomplish. **attainment** *n.* accomplishment.

attempt *vb.* try to do something. *Jack will attempt the climb tomorrow.*
attend 1. *vb.* be present. **attendance** *n.* 2. *vb.* give thought to. *Please attend to what I am saying.* **attention** *n.*
attic *n.* a room just below the roof.
attire *n.* clothes, costume. *vb.* to clothe.
attitude *n.* way of thinking, opinion.
attorney *n.* 1. lawyer. 2. person authorized to act on behalf of someone else in legal matters.

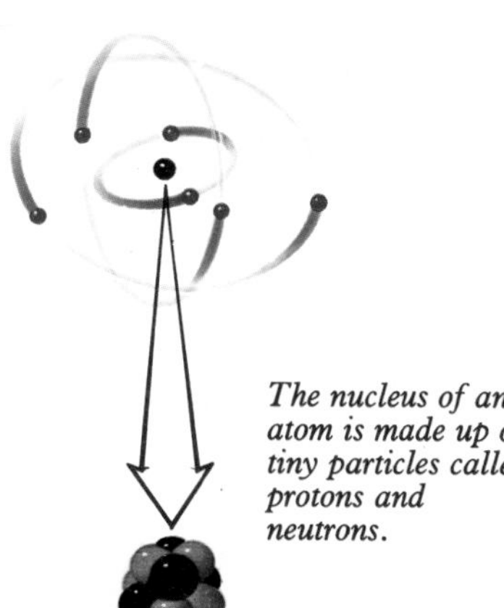

The nucleus of an atom is made up of tiny particles called protons and neutrons.

Electron
Proton
Neutron

attract *vb.* pull toward; have an appeal for. **attraction** *n.* **attractive** *adj.*
auburn *n.* a reddish-brown color. *She had auburn hair.*

Auckland
Auckland is the largest city in New Zealand, and the country's chief port. It is also New Zealand's main naval base.

auction *n.* a public sale at which the asking price is raised until a buyer is found. *vb.* sell by auction. **auctioneer** *n.*
audible *adj.* loud enough to be heard.
audience *n.* people who watch a play or listen to music together; a formal interview.
audition *n.* trial hearing of a musician, actor, etc.
auditorium *n.* part of concert hall or theater where audience sits.
August *n.* the eighth month of the year.
aunt *n.* the sister of your mother or father. Also your uncle's wife.
austere *adj.* stern; without luxury; severe. **austerity** *n.*

Australia (Australian)
Australia is one of the world's seven CONTINENTS. It is a huge island about three-quarters the size of the whole of Europe, but the population is only about 15 million compared to Europe's 695 million. The heart of Australia is a region of forbidding desert, with very few people. Ringing the coasts on the east of the country are a long chain of low-lying mountains. But Australia is a flat land with few high mountains.

Australia was almost unknown until 1770, when the explorer Captain James COOK landed in Botany Bay and claimed the great land for Britain. The only people living there were the ABORIGINES.

Today Australia is one of the world's richest lands, with great wealth in minerals and farmland. The country exports large quantities of wool, meat and wheat.

Australia has a federal form of government, something like that of the United States of America. Each of the Australian states – New South Wales, Queensland, South Australia, Tasmania, Victoria, and Western Australia – has its own parliament. But they all come under the central government, together with two territories – Northern Australia and Australian Capital Territory.

AREA: 2,968,081 SQ. MILES (7,686,849 SQ. KM)
POPULATION: 15,066,000
CAPITAL: CANBERRA
CURRENCY: AUSTRALIAN DOLLAR
OFFICIAL LANGUAGE: ENGLISH

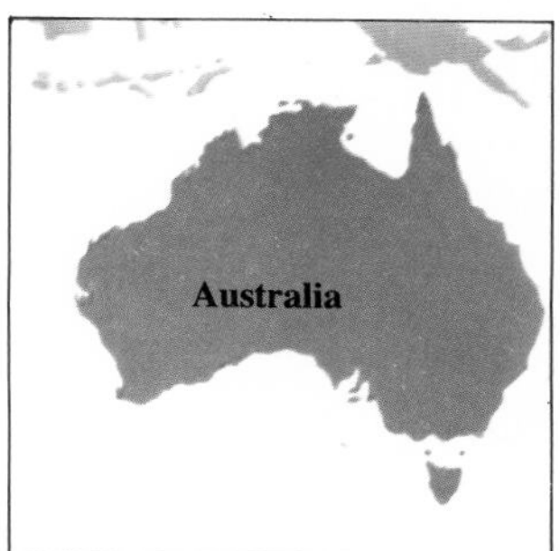

Austria (Austrian)
Today, this small country is hardly much bigger than Ireland. But once it was one of the largest and most powerful nations in Europe.

For more than 700 years, from 1278 to 1918, Austria was ruled by a dynasty of kings and queens called the HABSBURGS. Their lands covered most of Central Europe. They included Hungary, Czechoslovakia, large parts of Italy, Yugoslavia, Poland, Germany, Spain and the Netherlands.

The Austrian Empire collapsed after World War I. But there are many relics of the rich court life of the Habsburg emperors. Vienna, the

Changing shape of the automobile:
1. An early hand-built car.
2. Modern streamlined design.
3. American car (1950s).

capital city where over 1½ million Austrians live, is filled with castles, beautiful buildings and churches, statues and royal parks.
AREA: 32,376 SQ. MILES (83,849 SQ. KM)
POPULATION: 7,526,000
CAPITAL: VIENNA
CURRENCY: SCHILLING
OFFICIAL LANGUAGE: GERMAN

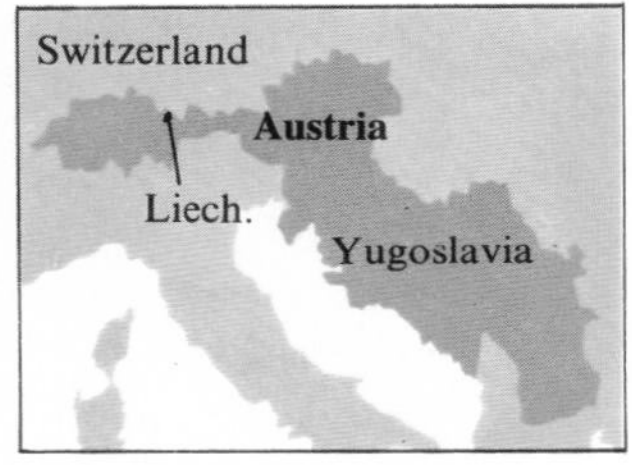

authentic *adj*. genuine, reliable.
author (**aw**-*ther*) *n*. a person who writes a book or a play.
authority *n*. 1. power over others. 2. an expert. *She was an authority on Shakespeare*.
auto- *prefix* meaning self, e.g. **automobile** (self-moving).
autobiography *n*. the story of a person's life written by that person.
autograph *n*. someone's name written in their own handwriting. *Georgia collected the autographs of famous authors*.
automatic *adj*. working without being looked after, like an automatic washing machine.
automation *n*. the control by machine of the process of manufacturing goods.
automobile *n*. a passenger car.
► In 1885, two German engineers, working independently, produced vehicles which can be considered the forerunners of today's cars. These men, Karl BENZ and Gottlieb DAIMLER, used INTERNAL COMBUSTION ENGINES fueled by gasoline. In 1913 Henry FORD in the United States introduced the first successful way of producing cars quickly and cheaply. The cars moved down a line of workers who each assembled a certain part. Cars are still made in this way.

The power for the car comes from an internal combustion engine which burns a mixture of gasoline and air in cylinders. Most engines have four or six cylinders. Inside the cylinders are pistons which are forced down by the burning gases and turn a crankshaft. At one end of the crankshaft is a heavy flywheel which smooths out the motion of the engine. From the crankshaft, the power goes through a clutch, a device for disconnecting the engine from the propeller shaft, which takes the drive, to the wheels. (The wheels that are driven can be either at the front or the back.) The driver uses GEARS to make the car go faster or slower for the same engine speed, and to reverse. Some cars have automatic transmission that changes gear automatically. All cars need a BATTERY, which is charged from the engine. The battery provides power for the starter motor, the lights, the horn and the windshield wipers.

autopsy *n*. post-mortem, examination of a body after death.
autumn *n*. the season of the year between summer and winter. **autumnal** *adj*.
avail *vb*. help, benefit.
available *adj*. obtainable, ready to be used.
avalanche *n*. a great mass of snow and rocks sliding down a mountain.
avarice *n*. greed for wealth or gain.
avenge *vb*. take vengeance; get satisfaction for a wrong by punishing the wrongdoer.
avenue *n*. a road with trees on both sides; a broad street in a town.
average 1. *adj*. normal; usual. 2. *n*. a mathematical word. To find the average of 2, 4 and 6 you add them together and divide by 3. The answer is 4.
averse *adj*. opposed to; unwilling.
aviary *n*. a place in which birds are kept, often a large cage or a building containing cages.
aviation *n*. (science of) flying in a powered plane.
avid *adj*. eager, greedy.
avocado *n*. a pulpy green fruit with a large stone which grows on several kinds of tropical trees.
avoid *vb*. keep out of the way of someone or something; fail to do something. *He decided that she was deliberately avoiding him*.
await *vb*. wait for someone or something.
awake *adv*. not sleeping.
award *vb*. give someone a prize or distinction. *n*. a prize.
aware *adj*. conscious; knowing. *Aware of dangers*.
away *adv*. 1. at a distance; far off. *Do not throw anything away*. 2. continuously. *Sing away*.
awe *n*. respect mixed with fear. *The soldier stood in awe of the general*.
awful *adj*. terrible; dreadful; nasty.
awkward *adj*. clumsy; uncomfortable; difficult.
awning *n*. covering, often of canvas, to protect against weather.
ax *n*. a tool for chopping wood.
axle *n*. the rod on which a wheel turns.
ayatollah *n*. a Moslem religious leader.

Ayers Rock
The world's largest rock, in central Australia. It is about 6 miles (9 km) around its base and 1,100 ft (335 metres) high.

Azores
Nine Portuguese islands 750 miles (12,000 km) west of Portugal in the Atlantic. The Azores gained partial independence in 1976. The capital is Ponta Delgada.

Aztecs
The empire of the Aztecs was a great Indian civilization in Mexico and Central America when Spanish soldiers discovered it. A Spanish commander by the name of Hernando CORTES landed with 600 men on their shores in 1519. Within two years he had smashed the Aztec empire forever.

Montezuma, the last ruler of the Aztecs, was captured by Spanish soldiers soon after a small army of them arrived in his capital city. By holding him hostage, they were able to control his subjects even though they were greatly outnumbered.

The Aztecs were famous for their grim religious practices. One of their gods regularly had human beings sacrificed to him in front of his temple.

azure *n*. & *adj*. the unclouded sky; sky-blue.

B

A scene from the ballet Swan Lake *the music for which was composed by Tchaikovsky.*

Babel
The story of the Tower of Babel is told in the Book of Genesis in the Bible. According to Genesis, the inhabitants of Babel tried to build a tower that would reach up to heaven. For their pride, they were cursed by being made to speak in many different languages. From this we get the word "babble" meaning nonsense.

babble *vb*. chatter, prattle.

baboon *n*. a large kind of monkey.
► Baboons are the largest members of the monkey family. A fully grown male can reach the size of a large German shepherd. Their coats are short-haired, usually yellow-brown in color, and their rumps are a bright red-pink. They have long snouts that give their faces a doglike look.

Baboons spend most of their time on the ground and can run quickly on all fours. They can also climb well and often escape from their enemies, such as lions, by running up tall trees.

Baboons live in Africa and Arabia. They move about in troops of 10 to more than 100 animals. Their homes are in high, rocky places that are easy to guard. They are aggressive and will bark loudly and bare their great daggerlike teeth at intruders.

Baboons feed on seeds, fruits, roots, insects, birds' eggs, lizards and small mammals.

baby *n*. a very young child. also **babe**.

Babylon (Babylonians)
Babylonia was one of the great civilizations of the ancient world. It rivaled EGYPT in its splendor. Babylonia, meaning "gate of god", lay between the fertile valleys of the Tigris and Euphrates rivers in a region that is today called IRAQ.

The first signs of civilization appeared about 3,000 B.C. At first Babylonia was a collection of small cities, each with its own ruler. Then the city of Babylon grew more powerful and began to dominate its neighbors. Under the rule of its great king Hammurabi it became the capital of Babylonia in the 1700s B.C. Hammurabi was a scholar and a poet. He drew up fair laws for his people, including some that set out the rights of women and children.

When Hammurabi died, other tribes raided and lived in Babylon. A new king called Nebuchadnezzar built magnificent temples and palaces as well as the Hanging Gardens of Babylon, one of the Seven Wonders of the ancient world.

baby-sitter *n*. a person who is paid to look after a child or children while the parent(s) are out.

Bacchus
Roman god of wine and fertility, similar to the Greek god Dionysius. His festival, Bacchanalia, developed into a drunken orgy.

Bach, Johann Sebastian
Johann Sebastian Bach (1685–1750), one of the greatest composers of all time, was born in Eisenach, Germany, to a family of musicians. His composing life can be divided into three parts. The first began in 1708 when he was appointed organist at the court of Weimar. There he composed much of his great organ music. The second period was spent at the court of Cöthen (1717–23) where he composed most of his orchestral music, including the Brandenburg concertos. In the third period from 1723 he composed most of his choral masterpieces, the three *Passions* and the great *B Minor Mass*. Almost a hundred years passed before his genius was appreciated.

bachelor *n*. an unmarried person; someone who has taken first university degree – *B.A.*, *B.S.* (Bachelor of Arts, Bachelor of Science), etc.

backdrop *n*. part of stage scenery hung across the rear of a stage.

back 1. *n*. the part of the body from the neck to the buttocks. 2. *n*. the side opposite the front. 3. *vb*. move backward. *Ask her to back up the car*. 4. *vb*. support. *I back your decision*. 5. *vb*. bet on. *She backed a loser*.

backbone *n*. the bones that run down the back of a skeleton; the spine.

backer *n*. a supporter.

backgammon *n*. a game for two people played on a board with 15 light and 15 dark pieces which are moved according to the fall of dice.

background *n*. the part of a scene or picture that is behind all the rest or in the distance; a person's education, etc.

backstage *adv*. behind the scenes at the theater.

backward *adv*. toward the back, opposite of forward. *adj*. directed backward; slow in learning.

bacon *n*. smoked or salted meat from a pig.

Bacon, Francis
Francis Bacon (1561–1626) was an English scholar who set about his studies by making long lists of all the facts he knew. For example, if

studying wood he might list everything he knew about it as a plant, then as a building material and then as a fuel. He then compared the lists of facts and drew his conclusions.

At the age of 12 Bacon went to Cambridge University, and when only 15 he went to France with the English ambassador. At 23 he became a member of Parliament. He was knighted in 1603 and in 1618 he became Lord High Chancellor of England. Bacon was then accused of taking bribes and was imprisoned for a few days. His last years were spent writing books. Francis Bacon was one of the first people to experiment with the process of refrigerating food. In 1626 he tried to preserve a chicken by stuffing the bird with snow. But he caught a chill during the experiment and died soon afterward.

Bacon, Roger
Roger Bacon (1214–94) was an English Franciscan friar, scholar and scientist. He taught that it is better to see and try things for yourself than accepting without question what other people tell you. His scientific studies were a great success. He invented the magnifying glass, and described how it might be used in both microscopes and telescopes, although neither had yet been invented.

bacteria *pl. n.* tiny living things that can only be seen with a powerful microscope.

► Bacteria are some of the simplest kinds of life. They are more like plants than animals and come in various shapes and sizes. Under a good MICROSCOPE it is possible to see that some are rodlike, some spiraled and others round in shape.

There are thousands of different kinds of bacteria. They are found in huge numbers almost everywhere. Some live in the soil. They help break down animal and vegetable matter and thus make the soil rich. Bacteria also take the gas nitrogen from the air and turn it into forms that help plants to grow. Some bacteria even live inside human bodies. They help with the digestion of food.

Although most bacteria are quite harmless, some can cause diseases. These are known as GERMS. Pimples and boils are caused by bacteria. A few are even deadly once they get inside the human body.

Bacteria multiply very quickly. Some of them can divide in two every 20 minutes. From a single bacterium there can be 16 million in only a few hours.

We now have drugs which kill bacteria. Sulfonamides are chemicals which stop bacteria from growing. Antibiotics such as PENICILLIN destroy bacteria. But because bacteria multiply so quickly, they soon develop new kinds which are not affected by the drugs that once killed them. Then new drugs have to be made to kill the new kinds of bacteria.

The French chemist Louis PASTEUR was the first to study bacteria. He found out that it was bacteria that made food go bad. However, we also use bacteria to make pleasant food flavors. Cheeses and some meats are improved by "ripening." Harmless bacteria live in them for a while and make, for example, the green or blue parts in certain cheeses.

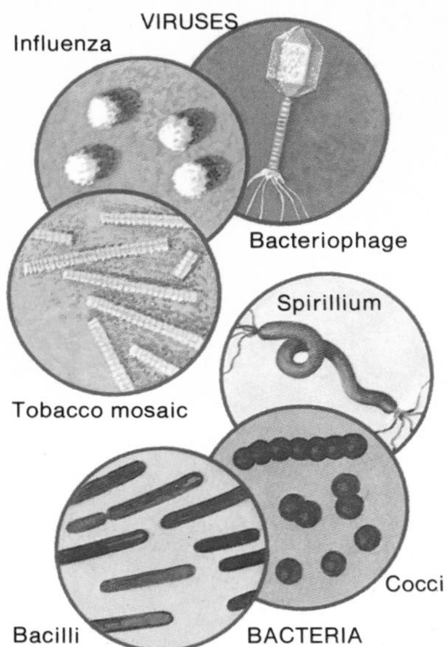

Bacteria and viruses are the smallest living things. Viruses have no cell walls and can only work properly inside the cells of other living organisms. Bacteria, which are larger than viruses, can live by themselves.

bad *adj.* not good; faulty; wicked.

Baden-Powell, Lord
Robert Stephenson Smythe Baden-Powell (1857–1941) began his career in the British Army, where he rose to the rank of major general. He fought in the Boer War in South Africa, and organized the defense of Mafeking. Baden-Powell founded the Boy Scout movement in 1908. His sister Agnes started the Girl Guides two years later.

badge *n.* something worn by a person, usually with a picture or message on it; an emblem. *Badges often show that a person belongs to a school or club.*

badger *n.* a burrowing nocturnal mammal with a white mark on its forehead.

► Badgers are common in North America, Europe and Asia. They have thickset bodies, long blunt claws used for digging, sharp teeth and powerful jaws. A fully grown adult badger measures about 29 in. (75 cm) from nose to tail and stands almost 12 in. (30 cm) high. After sunset badgers emerge from their underground dens to begin feeding. They browse on plant roots and hunt mice, rats and voles, insects, frogs and other small animals.

Badgers build elaborate underground burrows called sets. A set has several entrances, a system of long tunnels and a number of rooms. Here a badger couple makes a home and raises from two to four young at a time. Badgers are quite peaceful animals but can fight fiercely if attacked.

badly *adv.* incorrectly; to a serious extent. *The house badly needs repairing.*

badminton *n.* a game that is played with rackets like tennis, but with a shuttlecock instead of a ball.

Baffin Bay
Baffin Bay is an arm of the Atlantic Ocean, dividing Greenland and Baffin Island. The bay is about 600 miles (over 1000 km) long. It is frozen over for most of the year. Both Baffin Bay and Baffin Island were named after the British navigator William Baffin (1584–1622).

baffle *vb.* bewilder, mystify.

bag *n.* a sack or pouch; a handbag; the animals or birds a sportsman has shot. *vb.* capture, seize.

bagel *n.* a hard glazed doughnut-shaped roll.

baggy *adj.* hanging loosely.

Baghdad
This ancient city, since 1921 the capital of IRAQ, was founded in A.D. 762. It stands on the River Tigris and is the commercial and industrial center of the country. For many centuries it was a major center of Islamic culture. It was part of the Ottoman Empire, until occupied by the British after World War I.

bagpipes *n.pl.* a musical instrument with a windbag and pipes.

► Bagpipes are made from a leather bag and pipes. One pipe is used to blow air into the bag. The other pipes are played to make the music. Different kinds of bagpipes were used for centuries in European countries and parts of Asia and North Africa.

The Highland bagpipes from Scotland are now played all over the world. They are used in military bands and to play Scottish music for dancing.

Bahamas
The Bahamas are a group of 14 large and about 700 small islands off the southeast coast of Florida. There are also over a thousand uninhabited cays (islets). Nassau, the capital, lies on the island of New Providence.

Tourism is the main industry. Tourists are attracted by the warm climate and beautiful scenery. The islands export fruit, vegetables, and fish, notably the crawfish or spiny lobster.

In 1492, Christopher COLUMBUS became the first European to set foot on the islands. The islands were a British colony from 1717 to 1964. The Bahamas achieved full independence within the Commonwealth in 1973.

AREA: 5,381 SQ. MILES (13,935 SQ. KM)
POPULATION: 237,000
CAPITAL: NASSAU
CURRENCY: BAHAMIAN DOLLAR
OFFICIAL LANGUAGE: ENGLISH

Bahrain
Bahrain is a small Arab country consisting of some islands in the Persian Gulf. The capital, Manama, is on the largest island, also called Bahrain. The country was a British protectorate from 1861 until independence in 1971. Almost the whole of Bahrain's income comes from oil.

AREA: 240 SQ. MILES (622 SQ. KM)
POPULATION: 467,000
CAPITAL: MANAMA
CURRENCY: DINAR
OFFICIAL LANGUAGE: ARABIC

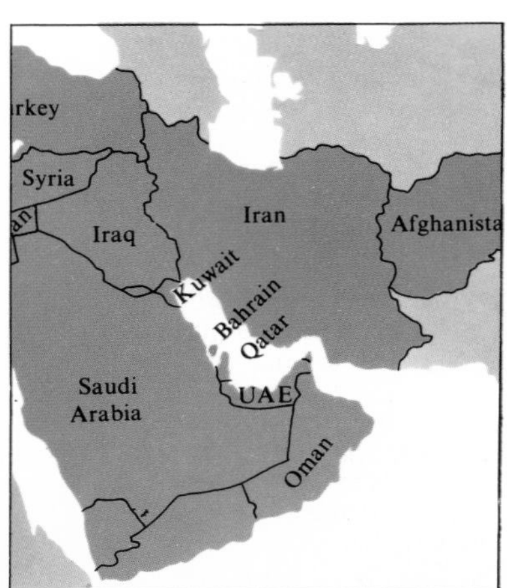

Baikal, Lake
The world's deepest freshwater lake. It is in central SIBERIA, U.S.S.R., and is fed by 300 streams. The maximum depth is 5,712 ft. (1,741 meters) and it is 390 miles (627 km) long. Lake Baikal abounds in sturgeon, salmon, seals and herring.

bail 1. *n.* money or other security given to free an accused person before trial. *He was released on bail of $1000. vb.* (out) secure temporary release of; drop from aircraft by parachute. 2. *vb.* scoop water out of a boat.

Baird, John Logie
John Logie Baird (1883–1946) was a Scottish engineer who in 1925 invented a mechanical television system which was used experimentally by the British Broadcasting Company in 1929.

bait *n.* food used to attract fish or animals so that they can be caught. *vb.* set a trap; tease.

baize *n.* woolen cloth, often green, used to cover a table.

bake *vb.* cook in the oven.

baker *n.* a person who makes cakes and bread and sells them. **bakery** *n.* a place where bread is baked and may be sold.

baking powder *n.* a white powder used in cooking to make cakes light and spongy.

► Baking powder is a mixture of bicarbonate of soda and some weak acid. When baking powder is added to a cake mixture, or batter, the liquid in the batter makes the baking powder produce thousands of tiny bubbles like those in a fizzy drink. In the oven these bubbles grow bigger and spread all through the cake. There are different kinds of baking powders. Some of them act quickly, others act more slowly.

balalaika *n.* triangular stringed instrument.

balance 1. *vb.* keep steady. *Roger balanced the book on his head.* 2. *n.* an instrument for weighing.

► The ancient Egyptians and Romans used balances but the measurements were not very accurate. The first balances that were accurate enough to be used by scientists in laboratories were made in the 1700s. They were known as knife-edge balances and work as follows. Two pans are hung from a rigid cross-beam. One pan holds the weight. The other holds the object being measured. The cross-beam balances on a knife-edge in exactly the same way as a see-saw balances on a bar. At the center of the beam is a scale that reads off the weight.

Balboa, Vasco Nuñez de
Balboa (1475–1519) was a Spanish adventurer and explorer. In 1513 he and his men crossed the Isthmus of Darien. Balboa became the first European to set eyes on the Pacific Ocean, which he claimed on behalf of Spain.

Balboa sailed from Spain in 1501. After an unsuccessful period as a farmer on the island of Hispaniola, Balboa joined a ship taking supplies to a Spanish colony in Colombia. Finding the colony almost deserted, the expedition went on to Panama, where Balboa founded the colony of Darien.

Balboa was made Captain-General of the South Sea (Pacific) but he fell foul of Avila, the new Governor of Darien. Balboa was beheaded in 1519 on a trumped-up charge of treason.

The Spanish adventurer and explorer, Vasco Nuñež de Balboa.

balcony *n.* a platform or gallery attached to an outside wall.

bald (rhymes with *called*) *adj.* without hair. **baldness** *n.*

bale *n.* a large bundle. *vb.* pack into bundles.

Balearic Islands
The Balearics are a group of islands in the Mediterranean that belong to Spain. They cover an area of about 2,000 sq. miles (5,000 sq. km). The main islands are Majorca (Mallorca), Minorca (Menorca), Ibiza, Formentera and Cabrera. Together

B

they form a Spanish province (Baleares) of which the capital is Palma on Majorca.

The islands are famous as a tourist resort, and have several million visitors every year. Many of the people work in fishing and agriculture. Several kinds of fruit are grown, and wine and olive oil are produced. The local population is 558,300.

Bali
Bali is a small island in INDONESIA, just to the east of JAVA. Bali is noted for its traditional native culture. It is also beautiful and is therefore a popular tourist resort. The capital is Denpasar.

Balkans
The Balkan peninsula is a mountainous region of southeastern EUROPE. It includes GREECE, ALBANIA, and parts of TURKEY, YUGOSLAVIA, BULGARIA and ROMANIA.

The Turks ruled much of this region for 500 years, from the 1300s to the 1800s. In the 1800s the Balkan countries were in great turmoil and fought the Turks for their independence.

It was in the Balkans that Archduke Ferdinand of Austria was assassinated in 1914. This event triggered off WORLD WAR I.

ball *n.* 1. a round object, often used in games. 2. a dance.
ballad *n.* a simple poem or song that tells a story.
ballast *n.* a heavy material, such as sand or water, used to fill the storage areas of an empty cargo ship.
ballerina *n.* a female ballet dancer.
ballet (**bal**-*ay*) *n.* a stage show that usually tells a story with dance and music.

► A kind of ballet first appeared in Italy in the 1400s, but ballet as it is danced today began in France. During the reign of King LOUIS XIV, in the 1600s, it was officially recognized as a form of art. The French Royal Academy of Dance was founded in 1661 to promote ballet.

Traditional, or classical, ballet follows strict rules and traditions. There are standard positions for the arms, legs and hands, and special movements that make the dance flow smoothly.

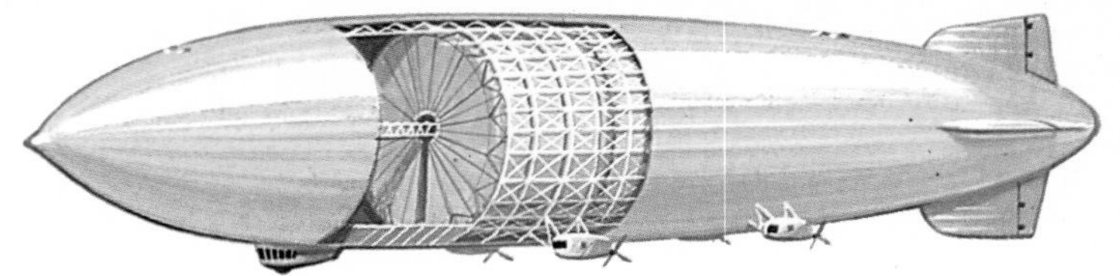

Right: A hot air baloon and (above) an airship wich has a rigid framework and can be streed. (*see* AIRSHIP)

Classical ballet uses orchestras, elaborate scenery and splendid costumes. Many ballets tell a story. But the dancers do not speak any words. They mime (act out) the story, using their bodies. The person who arranges the dance movements is called the choreographer.

Some ballets are very famous and have been danced for many years. *Giselle*, a story of a tragic young village girl who dies in love-stricken grief, was first performed in 1841. Two other long-time favorites, which are as famous for their music as for their dancing, are *Swan Lake* and *Sleeping Beauty*.

Modern ballets often look very different from classical ones. They include freer, less traditional dance steps. Sometimes, instead of telling a story, they dwell on certain moods or themes. Special effects may be produced with lighting, rather than scenery.

ballistics *pl. n.* the study of the movement of bullets, shells, and other projectiles.
balloon *n.* a bag of thin material filled with air or gas.

► Balloons and airships use lighter-than-air gases to fly. Balloons can only drift in the wind, but airships can be flown and steered.

The first manned balloon was a hot air craft launched in 1783. It was built by two French brothers, the Montgolfiers. Their balloon was an open-ended bag. A fire burned under the opening to keep it filled with hot air. The biggest problem the Montgolfiers had was to keep the balloon from bursting into flames. It had to be drenched with water throughout the flight.

In the same year, the first gas-filled balloon took to the air. The gas used was HYDROGEN, and it was a simpler craft to fly. To go down, one simply opened a valve and let some gas escape.

In the 1800s, manned balloons were used by the military for observations. Today, most balloons are used to study the weather.

Most **airships** are much bigger than balloons. The simplest sort looks like a huge cigar-shaped bag under which is slung a cabin and the

The five basic positions in classical ballet.

engines. More advanced kinds of airships have a rigid skeleton covered with fabric. Inside the skeleton are a number of large gas bags that give the airship its lift.

The first successful airship flew in 1852. It was powered by a steam engine and could manage a speed of 5 mph (8 km/h). During World War I, airships were used to bomb cities. In 1919, the British-built *R34* made the first Atlantic crossing. In 1929 the famous *Graf Zeppelin* of Germany flew around the world. But a series of disasters brought the building of airships to an end. They were simply not safe enough for regular passenger use.

ballot *n.* a method of voting secretly.
► Voting by ballot is popular in many countries because each voter can make his or her choice in secret. When the voter has marked the ballot paper, he or she drops it into a sealed box. After the voting has been completed, the box is opened and the ballots are counted. Automatic voting machines are now used in many countries.

Voting by secret ballot is quite a recent way of holding ELECTIONS. Before then, voting took place at open meetings, often by a show of hands.

ballpoint *adj.* & *n.* a kind of pen with a ball in place of a nib.
balm *n.* a healing ointment; a soothing influence. **balmy** *adj.* mild.

Baltic Sea
The Baltic is an arm of the Atlantic Ocean. It is almost entirely enclosed by land. Sweden, Finland, Russia, Poland, the two Germanies and Denmark all have coastlines on the Baltic. Because of its low salt content, the northern part of the Baltic freezes over in winter.

Balzac, Honore de
This French novelist (1799–1850) wrote a series of 90 realistic studies about everyday life in France called the Human Comedy. The best known include *Old Goriot* and *Cousin Bette*.

Baltimore
Baltimore, MARYLAND, is one of the chief ports of the U.S.A. It lies near the head of the Chesapeake Bay, on the eastern seaboard. Founded in 1729, Baltimore was an important shipping and supply port during both world wars. It is now a great industrial city, well known for its food processing, sugar, oil, chemical, steel and aircraft industries.

bamboo *n.* giant, woody tropical grass.
► Bamboo is a grass, but it often grows so tall that it looks more like a tree. Over 200 different kinds of bamboo grow in tropical regions all over the world. Bamboo grows in such thick clumps that a forest of bamboo is almost impossible to walk through.

Bamboo stems are woody. They are long and thin, and are hollow on the inside and smooth to touch. The stems of the giant bamboos may grow as high as 120 ft. (36 meters) above the forest floor and measure anything up to 3 ft (one meter) around in the steaming monsoon jungles of southern Asia.

Bamboo has hundreds of uses. Young shoots are tender enough to be eaten. Even slightly larger plants are soft enough to weave into mats and baskets, and to make fences and thatched roofs. Larger bamboo trunks may be sawn up to make furniture, water pipes, or planks for building. In the Far East, fluid found in the stem joints of bamboo is also used in preparing certain kinds of medicine.

ban 1. *n.* a prohibition; something that is forbidden. 2. *vb.* forbid; outlaw. *Cars are banned in the park.*
banal *adj.* commonplace, trite. **banality** *n.*
banana *n.* a long, thin tropical fruit with a yellow skin when ripe.
► The banana is grown on plantations in many places, though the largest ones are in Central and South America. The original home of the banana is the East Indies and Malaya.

Banana plants grow into "trees" that are as much as 20 ft. (6 meters) tall. A single bunch of fruit forms at the crown of each plant. When the bunch is four months old it is ready to be cut. At this time it weighs anything from 45 to 143 lb. (20 to 65 kg). There may be as many as 150 individual bananas on it. Each banana is known as a "finger". The fingers grow in clusters of 10 to 20, each of which is called a "hand".

Bananas are always harvested while they are still green and not quite ripe. They are transported to other countries in fast, refrigerated ships, so that they do not ripen too quickly.

band *n.* 1. a thin strip of material for fastening things together. 2. a group of people who do things together. 3. a group of musicians.
► The word "band" is usually used to describe a group of musicians that play percussion instruments, brasses, woodwinds and electric instruments.

Marching bands may either be military or civilian. They usually have drums, cymbals, flutes and fifes, tubas, trombones, horns and trumpets.

Dance bands have many of the same instruments, but also include clarinets, saxophones and even pianos. Their sound is much smoother and gentler.

Modern pop bands usually include electric instruments such as guitars and keyboards.

bandage *n.* a strip of material for covering a wound. *vb.* tie up with a bandage.
bandicoot *n.* a rat-like marsupial of Australia and New Guinea.
► Like kangaroos, bandicoots belong to a group of animals called MARSUPIALS. These creatures all have pouches of loose skin in which they carry their young.

Bandicoots have gray-brown fur and are similar in size and shape to rats. They make their nests in underground burrows and feed on insects, worms and roots.

bandit *n.* a robber, often working in a group or band.
bandy 1. *adj.* having curved legs. 2. *vb.* hurl from one person to another.

Banff National Park
Banff is a magnificent national park in southwest ALBERTA, Canada, covering 2,564 sq. miles (6,640 sq. km). The national park, a favorite tourist resort, includes some of the highest peaks in the Canadian Rockies, as well as a number of lakes. The wildlife, which is protected, includes mountain goats, bears, deer and sheep. Established in 1885, Banff is the oldest of Canada's national parks.

bang 1. *vb.* beat violently. 2. *n.* a sudden loud noise.

Bangkok
Bangkok is the capital of THAILAND. It is also the headquarters of SEATO (Southeast Asia Treaty Organization), the eastern equivalent of NATO. Many visitors stop at Bangkok on their way to Hong Kong and other Far Eastern destinations.

Bangladesh (Bangladeshi)
Bangladesh is a small, heavily populated country in southern Asia on the Bay of Bengal. Two great rivers, the GANGES and Brahmaputra, flow through the country, which is mainly flat and fertile. These rivers often flood. Most of the people are Muslims.

When India was partitioned by the British in 1947, Bangladesh became East PAKISTAN. In 1971 there was a war between East and West Pakistan.

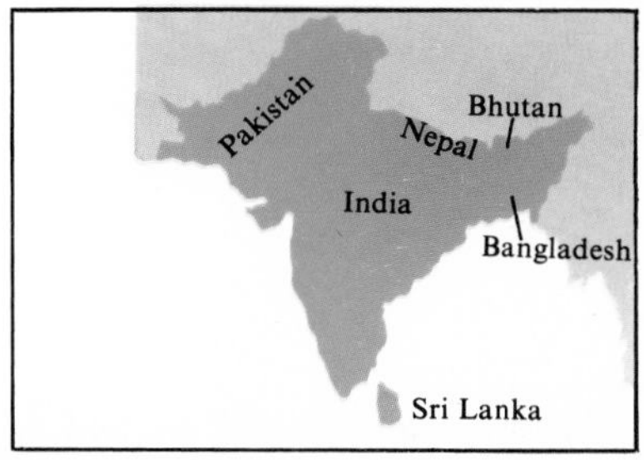

B

India helped East Pakistan, which became the People's Republic of Bangladesh.
AREA: 55,601 SQ. MILES (143,998 SQ. KM)
POPULATION: 94,472,000
CAPITAL: DACCA
CURRENCY: TAKA
OFFICIAL LANGUAGE: BENGALI

banish *vb.* send away from (a country); exile. **banishment** *n.*
banister(s) *n.* rail(s) up the sides of staircases.
banjo *n.* a stringed musical instrument with a long and round body.
bank *n.* 1. sloping ground. 2. land along the side of a river. 3. a place where people keep money; a business that specializes in money. **banker** *n.* someone in the business of banking.
► Banks are companies that take people's money for safekeeping. When someone's money is first put in a bank, this is called "opening an account." Every time you put more money in, you make a deposit. If you wish to take some out, you make a withdrawal.
Banks do not only hold money in safety. They also make loans to people and provide other ways of making saving and spending easier.

bankrupt *n.* & *adj.* (someone) unable to pay debts. *vb.* make bankrupt.
banner *n.* a flag.

banns *pl. n.* official announcement of an intended forthcoming marriage read aloud in church.
banquet (**bang**-*kwet*) *n.* a feast or official dinner with speeches.

Bantu
A group of people living in central and southern Africa who all speak one of the Bantu languages. There are about 70 million Bantus of many different tribes, and hundreds of Bantu languages, including Swahili and Zulu.

Banyan tree
The banyan is a remarkable tree of tropical Asia. Each tree can look like an entire grove of trees. The seeds sprout in the branches of another tree where birds have dropped them. The young plants put out roots that bend down to the ground and take root. The host tree is killed as the banyan spreads, making more and more trunks. One huge Indian banyan had 3,000 trunks.

baptism *n.* the Christian ceremony of christening someone, usually a child, by pouring water on their forehead. **baptize** *vb.* give baptism.

Baptists
The Baptists are a large Protestant religious group. Most Baptists live in the United States. The Baptist faith began in the 1600s with English Puritanism. Many Baptists do not believe in baptizing babies. They think that before people are baptized they should be old enough to make up their own minds about their religion.

bar 1. *n.* a long piece of hard material. 2. *n.* counter at which refreshments are served; a room with a bar serving drinks. 3. *vb.* to stop someone going through. *The man tried to bar our way into the park.*

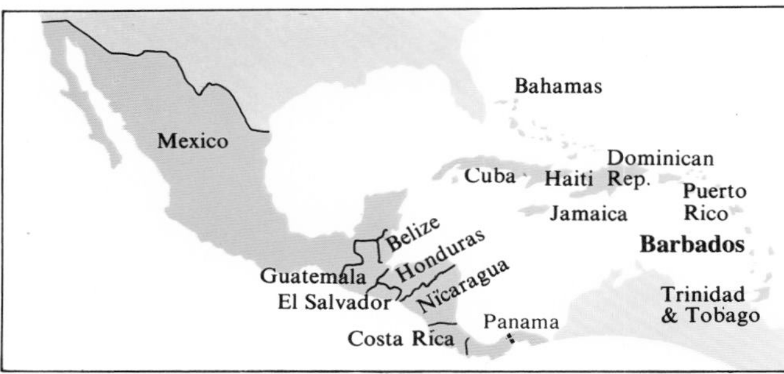

Barbados
An island in the West Indies. Part of the Commonwealth of Nations, it became independent in 1966. Its economy is based on sugar cane and tourism. Capital: Bridgetown.

barbarian *n.* a rough, uncivilized person. (In the Ancient World a barbarian meant anyone who was neither Greek nor Roman). **barbaric** *adj.* cruel. **barbarity** *n.* savage cruelty.
barbecue *n.* a frame for roasting meat, etc.; an outdoor party at which such food is cooked and served. *vb.* roast food on a barbecue.
barber *n.* a person who cuts men's hair.

Barcelona
Barcelona is a seaport in the Spanish province of Catalonia. It was founded by the Carthaginians, and was an important trading center in the Middle Ages. The university dates from 1450. Today, Barcelona is a major industrial city.

bare 1. *adj.* naked; not covered. 2. *vb.* expose. *The dog bared its teeth.* 3. *adj.* empty. *The room looked bare without its furniture.* **barely** *adv.* only just, scarcely.
bargain 1. *n.* something bought cheap. 2. *vb.* haggle; argue over the price.
barge 1. *n.* a flat-bottomed boat used on canals and rivers. 2. *vb.* knock into.
baritone *n.* & *adj.* male singing voice between tenor and bass.
bark 1. *n.* & *vb.* the sharp noise made by a dog. 2. *n.* outer covering of a tree.
► The outer layer of WOOD on the trunk and branches of a TREE is the bark. Bark is dead wood. It is tough and waterproof and protects the living wood underneath. In this way it has the same purpose as the outer layers of skin on our bodies.
As trees grow, they form layers, or rings, of new wood and become thicker. When this new wood is formed inside a tree it pushes against the dead bark and makes it crack and peel off.
The most useful bark is probably cork, which comes from the cork oak, a tree found in southern Europe. The cork is carefully removed from the tree and used for many different purposes. Other types of bark are used for tanning and dyeing and in making medicines.

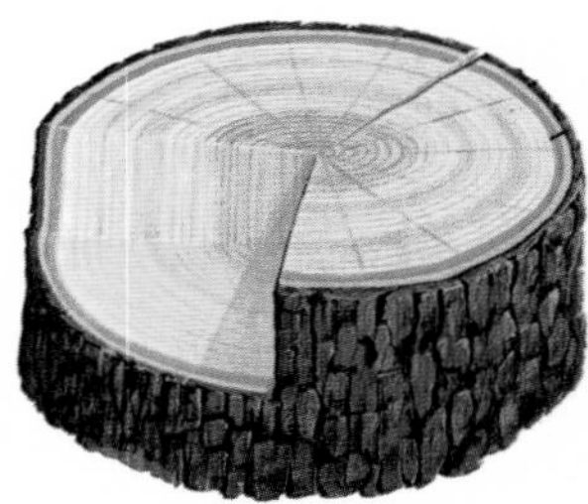
Each year a tree adds a new growth ring of cells round the solid core or heartwood. The bark is dead wood.

barley *n.* a cereal plant.
► Barley is a CEREAL plant. Most is grown as animal feed and to provide the malt used in brewing beer. It is hardy and can grow in thin soils and cold climates. Barley was first harvested over 7,000 years ago.
bar mitzvah *n.* Jewish boy of 13; the religious ceremony for the boy.
barn *n.* a farm building for animals or for storing grain or hay.
barnacle *n.* a small sea creature with a soft body surrounded by hard, bony plates.
► Barnacles belong to a group of animals called CRUSTACEANS. Barnacles fasten themselves to the hulls of ships, to piers and to rocks. Every so often, ships must have their

bottoms scraped to get rid of barnacles which slow down the ship.

barometer *n*. an instrument for measuring air pressure.

► Put simply, high air pressure is a sign of good weather. Low air pressure is a sign of changing and bad weather. The barometer is used to measure such changes.

There are two kinds of barometer, the aneroid and the mercury. The aneroid is more widely used. Inside it is a flat metal box. The air inside the box is at very low pressure. The metal walls of the box are so thin they will bend very easily. They do not collapse because a spring keeps them apart.

As air pressure drops, the spring pushes the sides of the box apart. As it rises, the sides of the box are squeezed together. These movements are picked up by levers and gears that move a pointer around.

A 13-year old Jewish boy reading from a scroll bearing the Torah, the Jewish Law, during his bar mitzvah ceremony. He now takes on the religious duties of an adult.

baron *n*. a lord; a peer. (In Britain a baron is the lowest rank of the peerage.) **baroness** *n*. female peer in her own right or the wife of a baron.

baroque *n*. & *adj*. a heavily decorated European style of architecture about 1600 to 1750.

barrack *n*. a building where soldiers live.

barracuda *n*. large West Indian fish.

barrage *n*. dam built across a river.

barrel *n*. 1. a container with curved sides. 2. the tube of a gun.

barren *adj*. bare, sterile; unable to bear offspring.

barricade *n*. a hastily built fortification across the road. *vb*. fortify in haste.

barrier *n*. a fence or rail; an obstacle.

barrister *n*. a lawyer who can plead in the English courts.

barrow *n*. 1. a small cart, usually with one wheel, used in gardening. 2. a prehistoric burial mound.

barter *vb*. exchange goods for other goods without using money; swap.

Bartok, Bela

1881–1945, Hungarian composer and violinist who was strongly influenced by the folk music of his country.

base 1. *n*. the part of an object on which it stands. 2. *n*. a headquarters. 3. *vb*. establish, found.

baseball *n*. an American game played with a ball and bat by two teams of nine players each, who compete to score the greatest number of runs in nine innings.

basement *n*. a floor of a building below the ground.

bash *vb*. strike violently, smash.

bashful *adj*. shy.

basic *adj*. fundamental, forming the base.

basil *n*. an aromatic herb.

basilica *n*. a church in the form of a long oblong hall with apse at one end and two colonnades; a Roman Catholic church with special privileges.

basin *n*. 1. a container for holding water or other liquid; a bowl for washing one's hands. 2. (in geography) the land drained by a river.

basis *n*. (plural **bases**) foundation; principle.

basket *n*. a container, often made from cane. *Some baskets are used for carrying shopping, while others are used for wastepaper.*

basketball *n*. a game in which two teams of five players each attempt to score points by throwing a ball through one of two metal rings placed above each end of a rectangular court.

bas mitzvah *n*. Jewish girl of about 13; the religious ceremony for the girl.

Basque

The Basque people live on both the French and the Spanish sides of the Pyrenees. They speak a tongue which is not related to any other European language. Many Basque nationalists wish to create a separate Basque state.

bass 1. *n*. (rhymes with *case*) lowest male singing voice. 2. *n*. (rhymes with *mass*) a sea fish.

bassoon *n*. a large musical wind instrument that makes low notes.

bastard *n*. an illegitimate child.

baste *vb*. 1. pour fat over roasting meat. 2. to sew with long loose stitches.

Bastille

The Bastille was the name of a former fortress prison in Paris. The storming of the Bastille by the mob on July 14, 1789, marked the beginning of the French Revolution. The governor was killed and the prisoners (there were only seven) were set free. The building was then destroyed. The place where it stood is now marked by a column.

Bastille Day on July 14 is an important public holiday in France.

bat 1. *n*. a small mouse-like flying animal. 2. *n*. a piece of wood for hitting a ball. *vb*. hit a ball with a bat.

► Bats fly like birds, yet in fact they are MAMMALS. They are the only mammals that can truly be said to fly. Their wings do not have feathers but are made of a thin sheet of skin stretched between the long "finger" bones. In most bats the wings are also joined to the legs and tail.

There are more than 2,000 different kinds of bat, most of which live in

Bats do not need good eyesight for flying at night. They find their way around by a method called echolocation. They produce high-pitched shrieks which no human can hear and use the echoes bouncing back from objects to tell where those objects are.

MAJOR BATTLES

GREEKS AND ROMANS

Marathon 490B.C. Force of 10,000 Athenians and allies defeated 50,000 Persian troops.

Salamis 480B.C. Greek fleet of 360 ships defeated Persian fleet of 1,000 ships.

Actium 31B.C. Roman fleet under Octavian (later Emperor Augustus) defeated the combined fleet of Mark Antony and Cleopatra.

EARLY EUROPE

Tours 732 The Franks under Charles Martel defeated the Saracens.

Hastings 1066 William of Normandy defeated Saxon King Harold II. England soon came under Norman rule.

Crècy 1346 Invading army of 10,000 English defeated 20,000 French.

Agincourt 1415 Henry V of England with 10,000 troops defeated 30,000 Frenchmen and recaptured Normandy.

Siege of Orléans 1428–1429 English troops began siege in October 1428 but in April 1429 Joan of Arc forced the besiegers to withdraw.

Siege of Constantinople 1453 Ottoman Turkish army of more than 100,000 captured the city, held by 10,000 men.

WARS OF FAITH AND SUCCESSION

Lepanto 1571 Allied Christian fleet of 208 galleys defeated Ali Pasha's Turkish fleet of 230 galleys.

Armada 1588 Spanish invasion fleet defeated by the English.

Boyne 1690 William III of England routed his rival, James II.

Blenheim 1704 A British-Austrian army led by Duke of Marlborough and Prince Eugène defeated the French and Bavarians.

COLONIAL STRUGGLES

Plassey 1757 Robert Clive with an Anglo-Indian army defeated the Nawab of Bengal's army of 60,000.

Quebec 1759 British troops under James Wolfe defeated the French forces under the Marquis de Montcalm. Montcalm and Wolfe were killed.

Yorktown 1781 British troops surrendered to George Washington. American War of Independence ended.

AGE OF NAPOLEON

Trafalgar 1805 British fleet of 27 ships under Nelson shattered Franco-Spanish fleet of 33 ships. Nelson was killed.

Austerlitz 1805 Emperor Napoleon I with 65,000 French troops defeated an 83,000-strong Austro-Russian army under the Austrian and Russian Emperors.

Waterloo 1815 A British, Dutch and Belgian force fought off French troops under Napoleon I until the arrival of Blücher's Prussian army.

FIRST WORLD WAR

Marne 1914 French and British armies halted German forces invading France.

Verdun 1916 In a six-month struggle French forces held off a major attack by German armies. French losses were 348,000; German losses 328,000.

Jutland 1916 British Grand Fleet fought German High Seas Fleet.

Somme 1916 In a 141-day battle following Verdun, the British and French captured 125sq. miles (320sq. km) of ground, losing 600,000 men. The German defenders lost almost 500,000 men.

Passchendaele 1917 British forces launched eight attacks over 102 days through thick mud. They gained 5 miles (8 km) and lost 400,000 men.

SECOND WORLD WAR

Britain 1940 A German air force launched an attack lasting 14 days to try to win air supremacy over Britain. The smaller Royal Air Force defeated the attack.

Midway 1942 A fleet of 100 Japanese ships was defeated in the Pacific by an American fleet half the size.

El Alamein 1942 Montgomery's British Eighth Army drove Rommel's German Afrika Korps out of Egypt.

Stalingrad 1942–1943 Twenty-one German divisions tried to capture Stalingrad (now Volgograd) but the siege was broken and 100,000 German troops surrendered.

Normandy 1944 Allied forces under Eisenhower invaded German-held northern France in biggest-ever seaborne attack.

the tropics and warm parts of the world.

The biggest of all bats are the fruit-eaters or flying foxes. One, the kalong, has a wing-span of 5 ft. (1.5 meters). The insect-eaters are usually smaller, their wing-span being rarely as much as 12 in. (30 cm). They live in most parts of the world. Where winters are cold, they HIBERNATE.

The vampire bat of South America has a very unusual way of feeding. It bites animals with its teeth and drinks their blood.

Most bats are nocturnal. Scientists have shown in experiments that bats do not need good eyesight for flying. They find their way in the dark by using a "sonar" system. They make high-pitched shrieks that no human ear can hear, and use the echoes bouncing off objects to tell where they are.

batch *n.* a number of cakes or loaves baked together; a group of things that come together. *We must answer this batch of letters.*

bath *n.* a large basin for washing the whole body.

bathe *vb.* swim or wash. **bather** *n.*

bathroom *n.* a room containing a bath, for washing.

bathyscaphe *n.* an underwater vessel for exploring the ocean depths.

► On average, the floor of the ocean lies under 13,124 ft. (4,000 meters) of water. At that depth, the pressure of the water would crush an ordinary SUBMARINE like an eggshell.

A special craft, the bathyscaphe, is needed to dive to the bottom of the sea safely. The first such machine was the *Trieste*. It was built by a Swiss, Auguste Piccard, and dived for the first time in 1948.

Piccard's bathyscaphe is, quite simply, a huge diving tank with an observation chamber slung beneath. The tank is filled with gasoline, which is lighter than water. At either end there are air chambers. When they are flooded, the craft dives. To surface again a load of steel pellets is released. The light gasoline buoys the bathyscaphe to the surface.

The *Trieste* is steered by two propellers turned by electric motors. The round observation chamber under the diving tank is tiny, barely more than 6 ft. (2 meters) across. A crew of up to three can squeeze into it. Its walls are 3.5 in. (9 cm) thick.

In January 1960, the *Trieste* dived to a depth of 6.8 miles (11 km) in the Pacific Ocean. This is over 1 mile (2 km) deeper than Mount Everest is high.

batik *n.* an Eastern method of producing designs on cloth with the use of wax and dyes.

baton *n.* the stick a conductor uses to beat time for an orchestra.

batter 1. *vb.* hit very hard. 2. *n.* a mixture of flour, eggs and milk cooked to make pancakes etc.

battery (plural **batteries**) *n.* 1. a container for storing electricity. 2. *n.* two to six guns which work together.

► Batteries make ELECTRICITY from chemicals stored inside them. The chemicals change into other chemicals and produce an electric current. Dry batteries, used in transistor radios, make electricity for only a limited time. Others, such as car batteries, can be recharged and used again.

battle *n.* a fight between two armies. *vb.* fight, struggle. *The wind was so strong, we had to battle against it.*
battleship *n.* a large, heavily armored naval ship with batteries of guns.
bauxite *n.* a clay which is the chief source of the metal aluminum.
bay 1. *n.* part of the seashore that makes a wide curve inward. 2. *n.* a kind of laurel. 3. *n.* a recess, e.g. a bay window. 4. *vb.* cry made by hounds. 5. *n.* & *adj.* reddish-brown horse.

Bayeux Tapestry
After WILLIAM THE CONQUEROR invaded England in 1066, one of his relations had a tapestry embroidered to record the conquest. This is known as the Bayeux Tapestry. It is a piece of linen 230 ft. (70 meters) long. There are 72 colorful scenes on it telling the story of William's victory. Latin text explains what is happening in the pictures. It is a kind of early strip cartoon.

bayonet *n.* a blade which can be attached to the end of a rifle.
bazaar (*be-***zar**) *n.* 1. a market in Eastern countries. 2. a sale to raise money.
B.C. *abbr.* time before Jesus Christ was born.
be *vb.* have some quality; exist. *When will you be free?*
beach *n.* the shore between the high and low tide marks; the edge of the sea or lake.
beacon *n.* a warning or signal light or fire.
bead *n.* a small piece of wood, glass or other material with a hole through it. *Beads are threaded on string to make necklaces and other jewelry.*
beagle *n.* small hound used in hunting hares.
beak *n.* the hard outer part of a bird's mouth.
beaker *n.* a large cup with no handle; a glass vessel used in chemistry.
beam 1. *n.* a big heavy bar used as a support in a building or in a ship. 2. *n.* a ray of light, like *the beam of a torch*. 3. *vb.* smile widely.
bean *n.* the fruit or seed of certain plants, eaten as food, and related to peas. *Broad beans; green beans; French beans, etc.*
► Beans belong to a family of plants called pulses. They are grown all over the world. There is evidence that beans were being eaten over 10,000 years ago by prehistoric people in Switzerland.
Beans are one of the cheapest and most widely eaten foods of all. They are rich in PROTEINS. Some kinds are used for animal fodder.
There are hundreds of different kinds of bean. Some, such as SOYBEANS, are used to make vegetable oil. They are also used in making soaps and varnishes.

bear 1. *n.* a large kind of furry mammal. 2. *vb.* tolerate, support or put up with something. *I can't bear the thought of it.* 3. *vb.* give birth to.
► Bears are found in most parts of the world except for Australia and Africa. They are some of the biggest meat-eaters on earth.
The largest of all bears are the brown bears of Alaska. These can reach a weight of over 1,653 lb. (750 kg). Other giants include the polar bear of the Arctic and the grizzly bear of western North America.
The only bear that lives in South America is the small spectacled bear, a name which comes from the ring-like markings around its eyes.
The smallest bear in the world is the sun bear of the jungles of Southeast Asia. It weighs no more than 143 lb. (65 kg). Sloth bears, found in India and Sri Lanka, have enormously long tongues for lapping up insects, which are an important part of their diet.
Bears are slow, lumbering beasts. They have short, powerful limbs and heavy, broad heads with powerful jaws. They also have long, dangerous claws which they use for digging and tearing.
Bears eat almost anything. They browse on leaves, roots, berries, fruit and nuts. They enjoy eating honey and ants and often attack beehives and anthills.
Bears are usually shy, but if they are disturbed and cornered they will attack fiercely.

The sun bear (above) of Southeast Asia is so fond of honey that it is often called the honey bear. The spectacled bear (above right) is the only bear from South America.

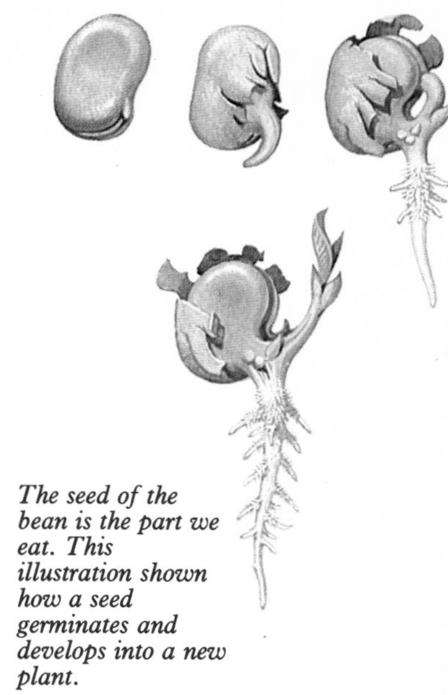

The seed of the bean is the part we eat. This illustration shown how a seed germinates and develops into a new plant.

beard *n.* hair that grows on the lower part of a man's face.
bearing *n.* 1. way a person acts or moves. 2. relative position. 3. part of a machine that supports moving parts and reduces friction.
beast *n.* an animal.

beat 1. *vb.* hit hard and often. *The cruel man beat the boy. n.* throb, pulse, rhythm. 2. *vb.* conquer or defeat. *John beat me at table tennis.*

Beatles, The
The Beatles were one of the most successful POP MUSIC groups ever. They were well known in Liverpool, England, before making their first record *I Want to Hold Your Hand* in 1963. This was a great success and they became world famous.

beauty *n.* good looks, loveliness. *She was famous for her beauty.* **beautiful** *adj.* **beautify** *vb.*

A beaver's lodge is an island home with an underwater entrance.

beaver *n.* a furry, flat-tailed mammal that lives on land and in the water.
► Beavers are big RODENTS more than 1 yd. (a meter) long, including the tail, and weigh more than 55 lb. (25 kg). They live in woods by the side of lakes and rivers and are good swimmers. Beavers are able to stay under water for up to 15 minutes. They have a broad, flat tail covered in scaly skin which is used for steering when they swim.

Beavers need pools to build their homes in, and often block up, or dam, streams with mud and sticks to make one.

They build a home of mud and sticks by the side of the pool. This home has an underwater entrance and an escape hole. Inside, there is a nest above water for the young beavers.

Beavers live in many parts of North America where, for hundreds of years, hunters have trapped them for their fur. They are now protected by law.

Beavers were once common in Asia and Europe too, but they were over-hunted and are now found only in a few places.

became *vb.* past of **become**.
because *conj.* as a result of; for the reason that. *Do it because I say so.*

Becket, Thomas à
Thomas à Becket (1118–70) was an Archbishop of Canterbury who angered King Henry II by demanding special rights for the Church. He was exiled but returned later and once more quarreled with the King. Four knights mistakenly thought the King wanted Becket killed, and murdered him in Canterbury Cathedral. He was canonized (made a saint) in 1173.

beckon *vb.* call by signs, make a silent signal.
become *vb.* grow to be. *He has become a strong athlete.*

Becquerel, Antoine Henri
Henri Becquerel (1852–1908) was a French physicist. In 1896 he discovered the radioactive properties of uranium. He shared the 1903 Nobel prize for physics with Pierre and Marie Curie for his work on radioactivity.

bed *n.* 1. something to sleep on. 2. a place where flowers are planted. 3. bottom of the sea or river.
bedding *n.* sheets, blankets, etc.; straw, etc., for cattle to lie on.
bedeck *vb.* decorate, adorn.
bedouin *n.* a wandering desert tribe of Arabs.
► The Bedouin are an Arab people who live in the deserts of the Middle East. They are nomads, constantly moving their herds of camels, goats and sheep in search of grazing. Traditionally living in tents, they are a fierce but hospitable people. Today, many Bedouin have moved to the towns.

bedroom *n.* a room with a bed or beds.
bee *n.* an insect that makes honey. *People keep bees in a beehive.*
► There are many different kinds of bee, but the best known kind is the honey bee. Honey bees live in hives or colonies of about 50,000 worker bees. Worker bees are female but they do not breed. Each colony also has a queen bee which breeds, and a few hundred stingless drones which are male.

The worker bee's life is very short, usually about four weeks, so the queen has to lay many eggs to provide enough bees. She can lay up to 1,500 eggs in one day. From time to time a new queen is born. The old queen then leaves the hive with a swarm of about half the workers to seek another home.

The workers collect POLLEN and nectar from flowers. The nectar is made into honey. It is stored in the hive to feed the bees in winter.

There are other types of bee which do not live in large colonies. These are called solitary bees. They produce a small family of a few hundred bees which die each winter. The queen hibernates and produces a new family the following year.

beech *n.* a smooth, silvery-barked, glossy-leaved tree.
beef *n.* the meat of cattle. **beefy** *adj.* thickset, strong.
beehive *n.* a small box where bees are kept.
been *vb.* past participle of **be**.
beer *n.* alcoholic drink made from malted barley, flavored with hops. *Ale and lager are both kinds of beer.*

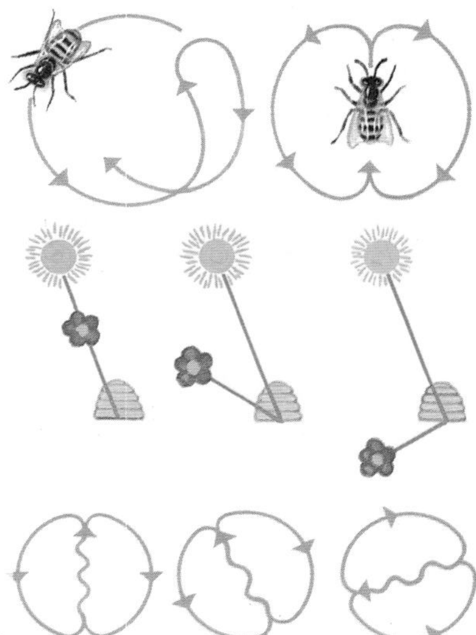

When a bee finds a source of nectar (bee's food) it returns to its hive and performs a dance on the surface of one of the combs. This tells the other bees where the nectar is.

beet *n.* a plant with an edible root, a variety of which is used to make sugar.
► Beet is an important food plant. The garden beet is grown for its fleshy root, which is deep red and 4 to 6 inches (10 to 15 cm) in diameter. The sugar beet is much more important commercially. About one-third of all the world's sugar is made from it. It has a large whitish or yellowish root which can be about 25 percent sugar. Beets are biennials that flourish in a cool climate. Sugar is obtained by pressing and grinding the beet pulp, then boiling the juice. The juice is put in vacuum cookers, where it makes sugar crystals.

Beethoven, Ludwig van
Ludwig van Beethoven (1770–1827) was a German musician who composed some of the world's greatest music. This included nine symphonies, six concertos, plus choral and chamber music. When he was young, Beethoven was well-known as a pianist. He began to go deaf at the age of 30 but continued to compose music even when he was totally deaf.

beetle *n.* an insect with hard wing covers.
► There are over 300,000 species of beetle known.
Some beetles are as small as a pin head. Others are very large. The giant African goliath beetle measures up to 4 in. (10 cm) long and can weigh 3.5 oz. (100 g).
Beetles start their lives as eggs which hatch into grubs, or larvae. The larvae then turn into chrysalises, or pupae, before the adult beetles emerge.
Many beetles and their larvae are destructive pests. Woodworms, weevils, wireworms, cockroaches, Colorado and flea beetles do great damage to crops, trees and buildings.
Some beetles can be very useful. Ladybugs are small beetles which eat harmful insects such as aphids. Dung beetles and burying beetles clear away dung and dead animals.

before 1. *prep.* in front of. *Age before beauty.* 2. *conj.* at an earlier time; previous to. *They ran away before I could stop them.*
beg *vb.* ask earnestly for help, especially for money. **beggar** *n.* someone who begs.
began *vb.* past of **begin**.
begin *vb.* (past **began**; past part. **begun**) start doing something; commence. **beginning** *n.* **beginner** *n.*
behave *vb.* act in a particular way. *Sue behaved very badly at the party.* act well. *Try to behave.* **behavior** *n.*
behead *vb.* cut someone's head off; execute someone in this way.
behind 1. *adv.* somewhere else; at the rear. *I left my book behind.* 2. *prep.* on the other side of something. *The burglar was hiding behind the curtain.*
beige *n.* & *adj.* a light brown color.
being 1. *n.* a person. *A human being.* 2. *vb. part.* in a certain state or situation. *Stop being so difficult.*

Beijing see **Peking**
Beirut
Beirut is the capital of LEBANON, on the east coast of the Mediterranean. The city is built on a Phoenician site. Since then it has belonged in turn to the Romans, Arabs and Turks. Until 1975 it was a prosperous banking and commercial center. Then civil war broke out and many people were killed. In the 1970s, the Palestinian Liberation Organization (PLO) chose Beirut for its headquarters. In 1982, Israel invaded Lebanon in order to force the Palestinians to leave. Much of Beirut was destroyed in the fighting.

belch *vb.* let out wind from the stomach through the mouth; throw out smoke from a volcano.

Belfast
Belfast is the capital city of Northern Ireland. It is situated on the mouth of the River Lagan in Belfast Lough. Belfast was founded in 1177 and became a city in 1888. It contains an important shipyard, and is the center of Irish linen manufacture. Queen's University, Belfast, was founded in 1845.
Belfast has been the scene of much violence as a result of longstanding and bitter differences between the Protestant and Catholic communities. In the late 1970s and 1980s it has suffered badly from unemployment.

belfry *n.* bell tower.

Belgium (Belgian)
Belgium is a small country sandwiched between France, Germany and Holland. It is a constitutional monarchy. Belgium's population is made up of two main groups: the Germanic Flemings of the north, and the French-speaking Walloons of the south. Because of its

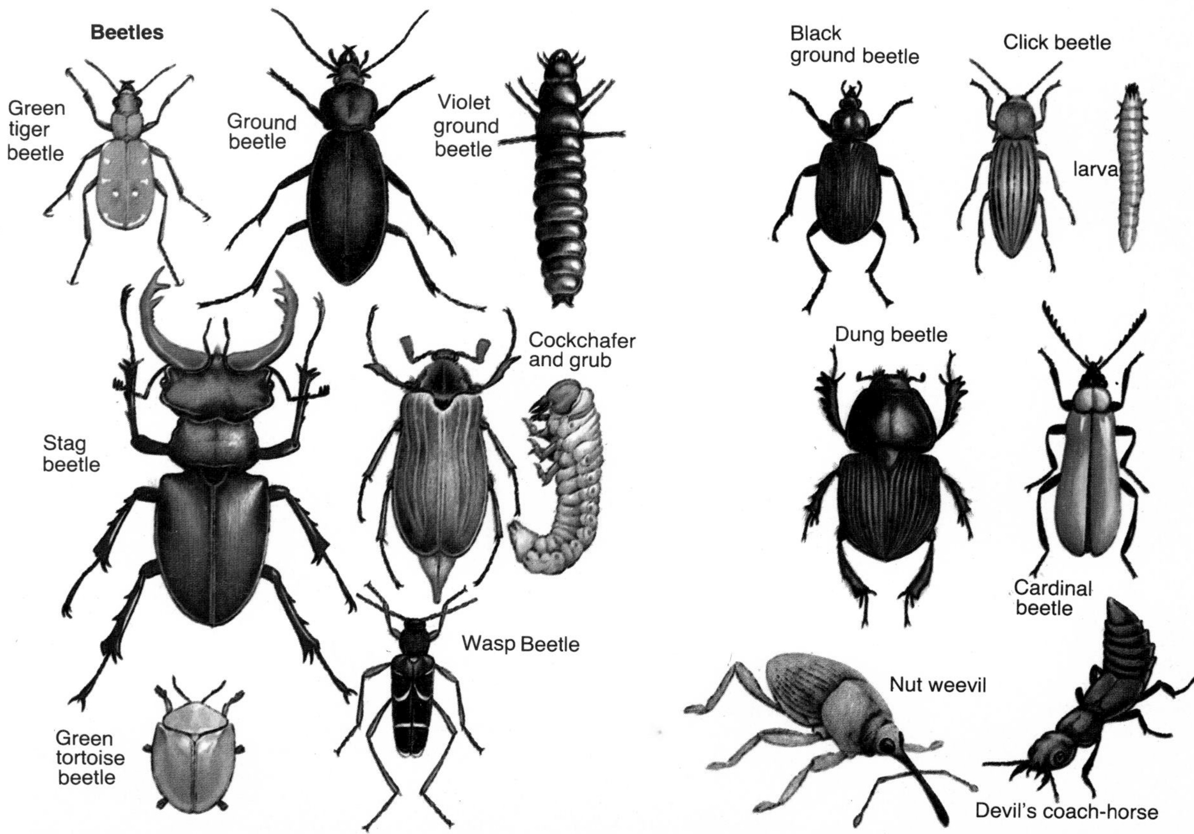

central and strategic position, Belgium has been invaded and fought over throughout the course of European history. Today Belgium is an international center. Its chief port is Antwerp. The headquarters of the EUROPEAN ECONOMIC COMMUNITY (EEC) and NATO are both in Brussels, the capital.

AREA: 11,782 SQ. MILES (30,513 SQ. KM)
POPULATION: 941,000
CURRENCY: BELGIAN FRANC
CAPITAL: BRUSSELS
OFFICIAL LANGUAGES: DUTCH, FRENCH, GERMAN

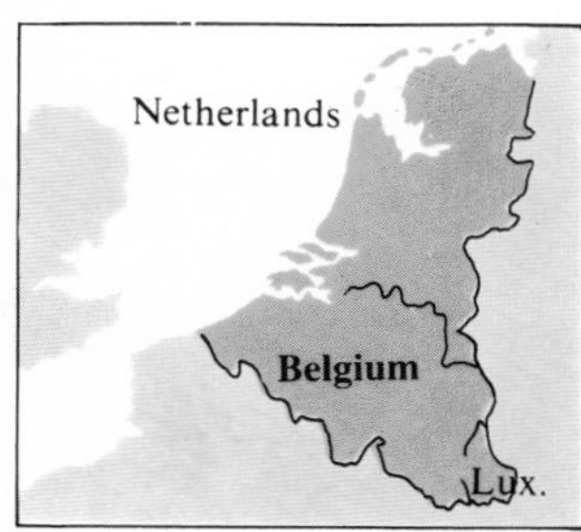

Belgrade
Belgrade is the capital city of YUGOSLAVIA. It stands at the junction of the Sava and Danube rivers. Before the creation of Yugoslavia, Belgrade was the capital of Serbia. It was occupied by the German Army in World War II and partly destroyed. It has since been rebuilt and is a major center of industry and culture.

believe *vb*. feel sure about the truth of something. **belief** *n*.

Belize
Belize is a small country in Central America. Much of the country is covered in tropical forest. The chief crop is sugar cane. Belize was a British colony from 1862 until it became fully independent in 1981. Belize is claimed by its neighbor Guatemala.

AREA: 8,867 SQ. MILES (22,965 SQ. KM)
POPULATION: 135,000
CAPITAL: BELMOPAN
CURRENCY: DOLLAR
OFFICIAL LANGUAGES: ENGLISH, SPANISH

bell *n*. a hollow object which makes a musical sound when struck.
► Bells have been used for thousands of years to attract attention and signal events. Nearly all bells are made of metal and they vary in size from tiny hand bells weighing a few ounces to the mighty Kolokol bell in Moscow, which weighs 196 tons. For centuries bells have signaled the births and deaths of rulers, the end of wars, and victory or defeat in battle. They have also performed many everyday tasks, from sounding fire alarms to being hung around the necks of sheep and cattle. Perhaps the best known are the bells which are rung in church towers.

Bell, Alexander Graham
Alexander Graham Bell (1847–1922) is remembered as the inventor of the TELEPHONE. Bell was the son of a Scottish teacher who went to Canada with his family in 1870. Two years later Alexander set up a school for teachers of the deaf in Boston, Massachusetts. Through his work with devices to help the deaf, Bell became interested in sending voices over long distances. On March 10, 1876, the first sentence was transmitted by telephone. The historic words were spoken by Bell to his assistant: "Mr Watson, come here; I want you."

Bellini, Giovanni
A leading painter of the Italian RENAISSANCE (*c*.1430–1516), one of a famous family of artists. Bellini painted many fine religious works. TITIAN was one of his pupils.

bellow *vb*. shout or roar. *n*. the noise made by a bull.
bellows *pl. n*. hand instrument for pumping air into a fire, etc.
belly *n*. the stomach.
belong *vb*. be someone's property; be owned by someone. *Does this watch belong to you?*
belongings *pl.n*. possessions, one's property.
below *prep*. & *adv*. underneath; lower than; beneath.
belt *n*. a strap of leather or other material worn around the waist; strap connecting wheels of machinery. *vb*. thrash, beat with a belt.

Benares
Benares is the most holy city of the Hindus in India. It lies on the banks of the Ganges River, about 430 miles (690 km) northwest of Calcutta. Millions of pilgrims visit the shrines and bathe in the Ganges, whose waters are thought to be purifying. It is believed that any Hindu who dies in Benares goes at once to Paradise. The most venerated Hindu shrine is the small Golden Temple. Benares is also an important trading center.

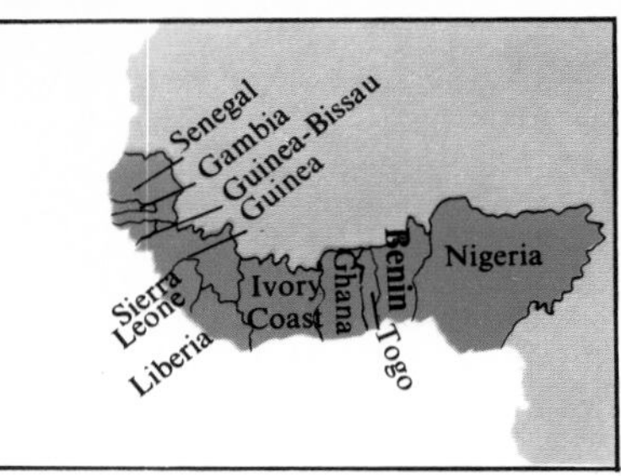

bench *n*. a long wooden seat, often without a back.
bend 1. *n*. a curve; not straight. 2. *vb*. curve over; lean over from upright.
bene- *prefix* meaning well.
benefit *n*. advantage. *She speaks perfect French because she has the benefit of living in France*. profit; pension, allowance. *vb*. do good for.

Benin
Benin is a small country with a narrow coastline in West Africa, bordering NIGERIA. It was formerly the French protectorate of Dahomey. It achieved full independence in 1960. The name was changed to Benin in 1975.

Benin is also the name of a former kingdom (and present large town) in western Nigeria. The great period of Benin was the 1500s and 1600s A.D. The Benin civilization has become famous for its sculptures and carvings in wood and ivory.

The black African population is divided into 50 groups, the largest being the Fon, Adja, Bariba and Yoruba.

AREA: 43,486 SQ. MILES (112,622 SQ. KM)
POPULATION: 3,734,000
CAPITAL: PORTO NOVO
CURRENCY: FRANC
OFFICIAL LANGUAGE: FRENCH

bent *vb*. past of **bend**.

Benz, Karl
German engineer and automobile pioneer (1844–1929) who produced the first gasoline-powered AUTOMOBILE in 1885.

bequeath *vb*. leave in a will. **bequest** *n*. what has been bequeathed.

Berbers
Berbers are the original inhabitants of North Africa. Some are farmers. Others, such as the Tuareg, are nomads, and roam the desert with their herds. Most Berbers are Muslims.

beret (*ber*-**ray**) *n*. a round flat hat, commonly worn in France and Spain.

Bering, Vitus
Vitus Bering (1680–1741) was a Danish navigator who explored on behalf of the Tsar of Russia. The

Bering Sea and Strait are named after him.

Berlin
Berlin is the largest city in GERMANY and, before World War II, was the capital of all of Germany. Today it is divided into West Berlin, a part of West Germany, and East Berlin, the capital of communist East Germany. In 1945, when Germany was divided into two countries, East and West, Berlin was divided into four zones between the Americans, British, French and Russians. In 1948 the Russians quarreled with the other allies and blockaded the city by cutting its road and rail links with West Germany. But Britain and the U.S.A. flew in supplies to keep the city going. After a year the Russians gave up and reopened the roads and railroads. Berlin was largely destroyed by bombing during World War II, but at the end of the war rebuilding was rapid. Today West and East Berlin are almost completely rebuilt. The Berlin Wall, built by the communists in 1961, divides the Eastern part of the city from the West.

Berlioz, Hector
Berlioz (1803–69) was one of the greatest of the French Romantic composers. He experimented with pieces for large orchestras. Among his best-known works are *Symphonie Fantastique* and *The Damnation of Faust*.

Bermuda
Bermuda is a British island colony in the North Atlantic. It is about 572 miles (920 km) from the U.S.A. The climate is mild and tourism is the most important industry. Bermuda has had its own government since 1968.
AREA: 20 SQ. MILES (53 SQ. KM)
POPULATION: 54,670
CAPITAL: HAMILTON
OFFICIAL LANGUAGE: ENGLISH

Berne
Berne (or Bern) is the capital of SWITZERLAND. Surrounded on three sides by the River Aar, Berne is from an architectural point of view one of the most impressive cities in Europe.

berry *n.* a small fruit with lots of seeds.

Left: Haws or hawthorn berries, and blackberries.

berserk *adj.* in a violent frenzy.
berth *n.* 1. a bunk or bed in a ship or train. 2. the place where a ship docks. *The ship was tied up at her berth.*
beside *prep.* at the side of, close to.
besides *adv.* as well; in addition.
besiege (*bi-***seej**) *vb.* to surround with armed forces.

Bessemer process
A STEEL-making process developed by Sir Henry Bessemer (1813–98). The process consists simply of blasting air through molten pig iron to remove impurities. Measured quantities of carbon and other substances are then added to produce the particular type of steel required.

best *adj.* of the finest quality; very good; excellent. *vb.* defeat; outwit.
bestial *adj.* like a beast; rude; cruel.
bet *vb.* & *n.* wager; put money on (a horse); assume something to be the case. *I bet you can't climb that garden wall.*
beta *n.* second letter of the Greek alphabet: β

Bethlehem
Bethlehem is a small town on a hillside about 5 miles (8 km) south of Jerusalem in Israel. It is famous as the birthplace of JESUS. In Old Testament times it was also the birthplace of King David. Although Bethlehem was largely destroyed by the Roman Emperor Hadrian, its fame as the birthplace of Jesus grew. Today thousands of Christian pilgrims visit it every year.

betray *vb.* give someone up, or let them down; deceive. *The spy was betrayed to the enemy.* **betrayal** *n.*
better *adj.* improved; more suitable, recovering or having recovered health; *vb.* make better.
between *prep.* in the middle of. *The player kicked the ball straight between the goalposts.*
beverage *n.* any kind of drink. *Orangeade and beer are both beverages.*
beware *vb.* be warned. *The sign said: "Beware of the dog."*
bewilder *vb.* confuse, puzzle, mystify. **bewildering** *adj.*
beyond *prep.* on the far side of. *Julia's house is beyond the church.*

Bhutan
Bhutan is a mountainous country on the border between India and China. Most of the people work on the land: many are very poor. The head of state is the king, but the country is governed by a National Assembly.
AREA: 18,148 SQ. MILES (47,000 SQ. KM)
POPULATION: 1,352,000
CAPITAL: THIMPHU
CURRENCY: NGULTRUM
OFFICIAL LANGUAGES: DZONGKHA, NEPALI, ENGLISH

bi- *prefix* meaning twice or double; appearing or occurring once in every two, e.g. **bilateral** with two sides; **bilingual** speaking two languages; **biped** two-footed animal.
bias *n.* a leaning toward, inclination; prejudice.
bib *n.* cloth or plastic shield placed under a child's chin to protect clothing.
Bible *n.* the sacred book of the Christian religion.
► The Bible is in two parts. The Old Testament records the history of the Jewish people and the teachings of their prophets before the birth of JESUS. The second part, the New Testament, records the life and sayings of Jesus and his disciples.

bicycle *n.* a two-wheeled vehicle powered by its rider.

The dandyhorse or draisine of 1817. It looked like a bicycle but had no pedals.

► The earliest bicycles, called "dandy-horses", were invented in the 1700s. They were simply two wheels joined by a rod, with a seat on top, and the rider pushed it along the ground with his feet.

The first bicycle with pedals did not appear until 1865. These machines were known as "bone-shakers" because the seats had no springs. The next important development was the "penny farthing", which had an enormous front wheel and a tiny rear wheel. The modern style of bicycle appeared in the 1880s. It had a chain-driven rear wheel and air-filled tires, and this basic style has changed very little since then.

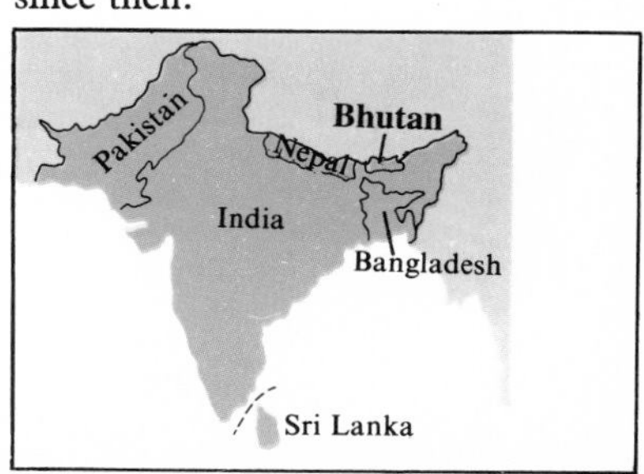

B

bicker *vb*. quarrel in a pointless way.
bid 1. *vb*. offer to pay a price at an auction. 2. *n*. call (in card games). 3. *vb*. command.
bidet (*bee*-**day**) *n*. a low basin on which one sits to wash the lower part of the body. The word is French for "pony."
big *adj*. large; important.
bigot *n*. a person who obstinately sticks to a belief or opinion.
bikini *n*. a scanty two-piece bathing suit.
bill *n*. 1. a paper showing how much you owe for something you have bought. 2. a bird's beak.
billboard *n*. 1. a flat surface on which bills are posted. 2. the spot on the bow of a ship where the anchor rests.
billiards *n*. a game in which balls are struck by a cue into pockets at the edge of a flat table.
billion *n*. one thousand million (1,000,000,000). Sometimes still used in Britain to mean one million million (1,000,000,000,000).
billow *n*. wave. *vb*. to rise or roll in waves, to bulge or swell out.
billygoat *n*. a male goat.
bin *n*. a storage container, such as a breadbin or dustbin.
binary *adj*. made up of two parts or units. In the binary arithmetic system only two numbers are used, 0 and 1.
bind *vb*. tie; make fast.
binding 1. *n*. book cover. 2. *adj*. obligatory.
bingo *n*. a numbers game, usually with many players.
binoculars *n*. field glasses; an instrument to make things far away look closer. *You look through a pair of binoculars with both eyes*.
bio- *prefix* meaning life or of life.
biography *n*. the written story of a person's life.
biology *n*. the study of living things. **biologist** *n*.
► Biology is the study of living things, from the tiniest amoeba, which consists of just one CELL, to a mighty oak tree or a human being. That part of biology that deals with the PLANT world is called BOTANY. The study of ANIMALS is called zoology. One of the earliest biologists was the ancient Greek thinker ARISTOTLE, who was the first to dissect, or cut open, and classify animals.

There was little interest in biology for more than a thousand years, until the RENAISSANCE, when scholars and artists such as LEONARDO DA VINCI tried to discover how living things grew and worked. At first the study of the human body by dissection was frowned upon by the Church. But this changed after the 1500s, and William HARVEY was able to show how the BLOOD travels around the body, and other people were able to compare the structure of various animals with that of humans.

The invention of the MICROSCOPE in the 1600s opened up whole new areas of study for biologists. They were able to learn more about the animal and plant cells that are the building blocks of life. The study of other microscopic organisms, such as BACTERIA, helped men like LOUIS PASTEUR understand more about disease and how to prevent it.

In the 1800s the English naturalist Charles DARWIN revolutionized biology with his theory of EVOLUTION. Today biology is divided into dozens of separate sciences. Biologists can spend their entire careers studying one tiny part of living matter.

biplane *n*. an aircraft with two sets of wings.
birch *n*. a tree with a slim trunk and branches, and a smooth bark.
bird *n*. the only feathered member of the animal kingdom, with front

This French fighter aircraft of World War I was a biplane

The parts of a bird.

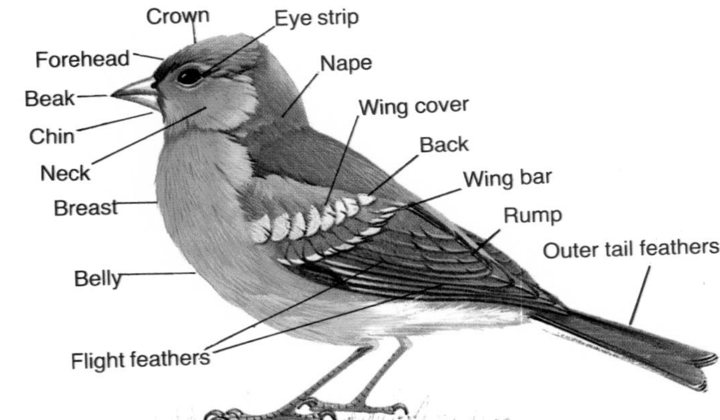

Birds' beaks have many different shapes. They are used for catching moths, cracking nuts, eating seeds and insects and tearing up prey or for probing for food in mud.

Birds' claws also tell us about their way of life. The osprey's hooked claws, for example, are for grasping food.

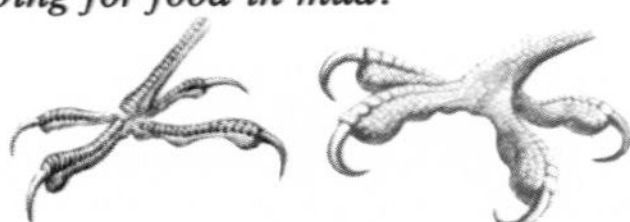

limbs adapted as wings.
► Some birds can fly thousands of miles. Others, such as the OSTRICH and the PENGUIN, cannot fly at all. The ostrich is the largest bird. It can weigh more than 330 lb. (150 kg). The smallest bird, a HUMMINGBIRD, weighs less than 0.07 oz. (2 gm).

Birds developed from scaly REPTILES that lived about 180,000,000 years ago. Their scales changed over millions of years into feathers, and their front legs became wings. Birds have hollow bones for lightness in the air and strong breast muscles for working their wings. Large birds can flap their wings slowly and float, or hover, on air currents. Small birds need to flap their wings fast to stay in the air.

All birds lay EGGS. Most birds are busy parents who work hard to rear their young. Some, like the CUCKOO, lay their eggs in other birds' nests for foster parents to rear. Other birds bury their eggs in warm places and leave them. Most birds are wild but some, such as chickens, PIGEONS and CANARIES, have been tamed or domesticated. Many birds are bred on farms for their eggs and meat.

Birds' beaks have many different shapes. Sparrowhawks have hooked beaks for tearing up their prey. Blue-tits have short beaks for eating small nuts, seeds and insects. The nuthatch has a powerful, pointed beak for breaking open nuts.

Blackbirds have sharp beaks for digging up worms and slugs. The strange-looking crossbill has a crossed beak for tearing open pine cones to reach the kernels inside. Nightjars have short, wide beaks for snapping up moths and other night-flying insects.

Wading birds, such as the oyster-catcher, have long, thin beaks for probing in the mud. Many birds have beaks adapted for one kind of food only, but others such as the sparrow and the thrush thrive on a mixed diet.

Birmingham, U.K.
Birmingham is the second largest city in the United Kingdom. Situated in the West Midlands, it is an important industrial and manufacturing center. It has two universities (Birmingham and Aston) and has always encouraged the arts.

Birmingham, U.S.A.
Birmingham is the largest city in the state of ALABAMA. It began as a railway junction in the 1870s. Birmingham lies at the center of an area rich in minerals. Iron and steel manufacture is a major industry.

birth *n.* coming into life; emergence of a child or animal from the body of its mother.
birth control *n.* contraception, the prevention of pregnancy.
birthday *n.* the day or anniversary of a person's birth.
biscuit *n.* a small, flat, thin roll.
bisect *vb.* divide into two equal parts.
bishop *n.* 1. a priest in charge of a diocese, or group of parishes. 2. a piece in chess.

Bismark, Prince Otto von
Otto von Bismark (1815–98) was Chancellor (prime minister) of Germany from 1867 to 1890. Perhaps the greatest statesman of his day, he helped to make Germany one of the most powerful nations in the world.

bison *n.* an American buffalo.
► The bison is a large animal of the cattle family. Its head and humped shoulders are covered in shaggy hair.

There are two kinds of bison, the American and the European. There used to be great herds of bison in America. At one time there were probably as many as 50 million of the creatures. The Indians were the first people to hunt them. When Europeans went to America they killed great numbers of bison until, by 1889, there were only about 500 left. Today, there are no bison living in the wild in America and Europe. Those that survive all live in parks and zoos.

bit *n.* 1. a small piece. 2. a metal bar that goes in a horse's mouth: part of the bridle. 3. single unit of information expressed in binary numbers, especially for computers.
bitch *n.* a female dog, fox or wolf.
bite *n.* & *vb.* take a piece of something, usually food, with the teeth.
bitter *adj.* sharp, unpleasant taste; not sweet. **bitterness** *n.*
black 1. *n.* the darkest of all colors; the opposite of white. 2. *adj.* & *n.* belonging to a dark-skinned race.
blackball *vb.* vote against, such as to exclude a candidate by putting a black ball in a ballot box.
blackberry *n.* the fruit of the bramble.
blackbird *n.* songbird related to the thrush.
blackboard *n.* a board, usually painted black, which can be written on with chalk and is used for teaching.
black box *n.* electronic equipment on an aircraft which records details of the flight.
blackcurrant *n.* the small black fruit of a garden plant, much used to make drinks.

Black Death
The Black Death was a terrible disease which was at its worst during the MIDDLE AGES. In one outburst in the 1300s, 25 million people died of the disease. About a third of all the people in Europe were killed by it. The Black Death is now known as bubonic plague. It is carried by the fleas on rats. The fleas suck the blood of a rat with the disease. When the fleas next bite another rat or a person, the disease is passed on.

black hole *n.* an area in space where the pull of gravity is so strong that nothing can escape, not even light.
blacklist *vb.* to boycott or punish someone.
black magic *n.* evil magic; witchcraft.
blackmail *n.* & *vb.* the crime of demanding money from someone in return for keeping something secret. *The man said that if I gave him $5 he would keep quiet about the window I broke. This was blackmail.* **blackmailer** *n.*
blackout *n.* temporary loss of consciousness or light.

Black Sea
The Black Sea is an enormous inland sea between Europe and Asia. It covers 180,000 sq. miles (475,800 sq. km). Russia lies to the north, Turkey to the south, and Romania and Bulgaria to the west.

The Black Sea is connected to the MEDITERRANEAN SEA in three ways, through a channel called the Bosporus, the Sea of Marmara and another channel called the Dardanelles. The Black Sea is less salty than the Mediterranean because many large rivers flow into it. It is more than 7,000 feet (2,130 meters) deep.

black sheep *n.* scoundrel; member of a family who is a good-for-nothing.
blacksmith *n.* a person who works with iron and makes shoes for horses.
bladder *n.* the part of the body where liquid wastes gather before they are passed out.
blade *n.* the sharp cutting edge of a knife, razor, sword, etc.

Blake, William
William Blake (1757–1827) was an English poet and painter. He worked as an engraver, and illustrated many of his own books of verse. In 1789 he published *Songs of Innocence*. Blake illustrated *The Book of Job*, Milton's *Paradise Lost* and Dante's *Divine Comedy*. His paintings are strange and disturbing images of unearthly visions. Two of his most famous poems are *The Tiger* and *Jerusalem*.

blame *vb.* say that it was the fault of something or someone that something went wrong. *n.* responsibility for bad happening.
blanche *vb.* take the color out of.
bland *adj.* smooth; gentle, mild; dull.
blank *adj.* empty; with nothing written on it.

blanket *n*. a sheet of (usually thick) cloth used as a bed covering.
blare *vb*. make a loud noise; shout. *I can't hear what you are saying with that radio blaring*.
blaspheme *vb*. speak irreverently about God. **blasphemy** *n*.
blast *n*. a strong wind; the shock waves of an explosion.
blast furnace *n*. an enormous oven for producing iron from ore.
► A modern furnace can be over 131 ft. (40 meters) high. It is thickly lined with material which can withstand very high temperatures.
A mixture of iron ore, coke and limestone is fed into the top. Very hot air is blasted in at the side.
At a temperature of about 2,764°F (1,500°C) the heavy iron melts and sinks to the bottom of the furnace. The lighter mixture of waste ore, coke ash and limestone floats to the top. The molten iron can then be taken out at the bottom. The lighter waste, or slag, is drawn off from higher up the furnace.

blast-off *n*. the moment when a rocket is launched into space.
blatant *adj*. noisy; obvious and obtrusive.
blaze *n*. a bright flame or fire.
blazer *n*. colored jacket, often part of a uniform.
bleach *n*. & *vb*. make white.
► Bleaching is whitening a substance by taking away its natural color. Cloth, paper, and sometimes sugar and flour are bleached to make them white.
Cloth is soaked in chemicals for between 2 and 12 hours to make it white. Then the bleaching chemical has to be washed out by other chemicals to stop the bleach harming the cloth.
The oldest way of bleaching cloth is to soak it and lay it out in the sun. If the cloth is frequently sprinkled with water, the sun takes away the natural color of the cloth. This method of getting clothes white is still used in some countries.

bleak *adj*. exposed, barren and often windswept.
bleat *vb*. & *n*. the cry of a sheep or goat.
bleed *vb*. lose blood.
blemish *vb*. mark, spoil. *n*. stain; fault.
blend *vb*. mix two or more substances together; go well with something.

Blériot, Louis
Louis Blériot (1872–1936) was a French airman and a pioneer of aviation who designed and built a number of early airplanes. On July 25, 1909, he took off from Calais in one of his own planes. Twenty-seven minutes later he touched down at Dover, becoming the first man to cross the English Channel by air. In doing so he won a prize of £1000 offered by the London *Daily Mail* newspaper. Blériot went on to design other airplanes and became the owner of a large aircraft company.

bless *vb*. ask God to protect someone or something. **blessing** *n*.
blew *vb*. past of **blow**.

Bligh, William
William Bligh (1754–1817) was a British naval officer. He was a fine seaman but a strict disciplinarian. During the famous voyage of the *Bounty*, his crew mutinied. Bligh survived an epic journey of 45 days in an open boat. He was later the victim of another mutiny while Governor of New South Wales in Australia. Despite everything, he ended his career as a vice admiral.

blight *n*. plant disease caused by fungus or insects.
blind 1. *adj*. not able to see. **blindness** *n*. 2. *n*. window cover.
blindfold *adj*. & *adv*. having the eyes covered with a handkerchief etc. *vb*. cover eyes.
blink *vb*. shut and open eyes rapidly.
blinker *n*. flap on a bridle to prevent a horse from seeing to the side.

bliss *n*. greatest happiness. **blissful** *adj*.
blister *n*. a swelling like a bubble on the skin, filled with a watery fluid.
blitz *n*. & *vb*. attack, usually sudden, from the air.
blizzard *n*. a snowstorm with very strong winds.
bloated *adj*. swollen, puffy.
blob *n*. a drop; small round mass.
bloc *n*. a combination of nations or parties.
block 1. *n*. a large, solid piece of something, e.g. wood or stone. 2. *n*. a large building divided into separate units. 3. *vb*. get in the way of. *A fallen tree can block a road*.
blockade *vb*. & *n*. cutting off of supplies to an enemy.
blood *n*. the red liquid that is pumped around our bodies by the heart.

► Blood is the fluid that nourishes our bodies and removes waste products. It takes in food from the DIGESTIVE SYSTEM, and oxygen from the LUNGS, and carries them to all the CELLS in the body. Each cell takes exactly what it needs from the blood and the blood carries away cell waste, including water and carbon dioxide. Blood also carries special body chemicals

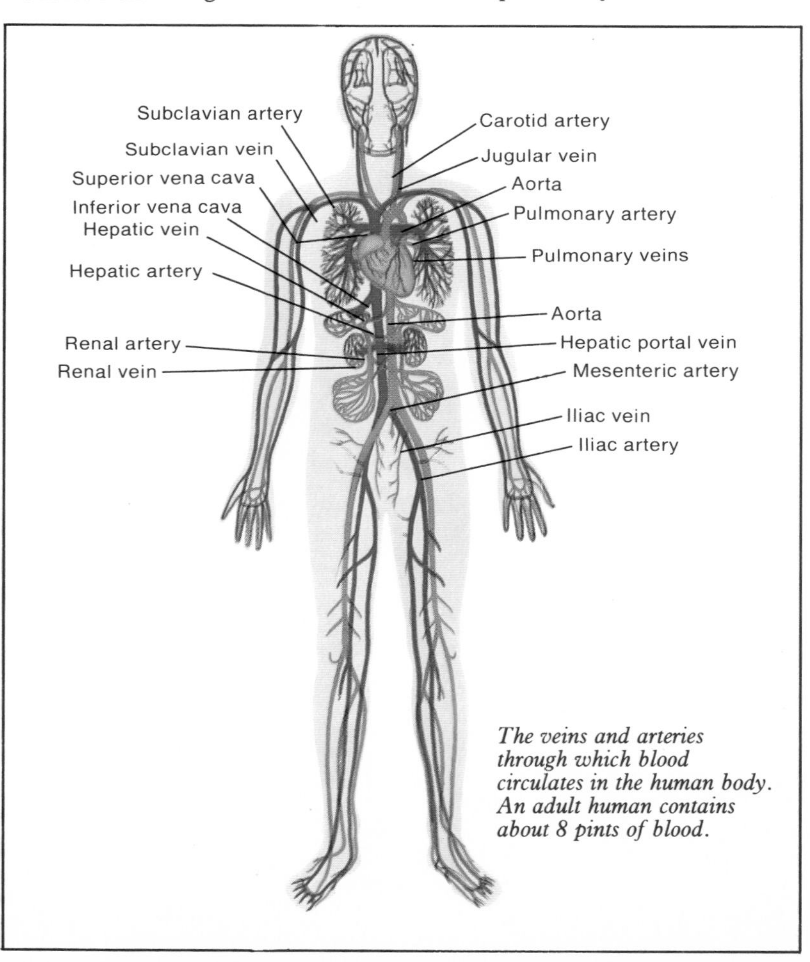

The veins and arteries through which blood circulates in the human body. An adult human contains about 8 pints of blood.

to where they are needed. It also kills germs and keeps the body at the right temperature. Many organs work to keep the blood functioning. The heart, lungs, kidneys, liver and intestines all play their part.

Blood is made in the marrow of the bones. The adult human body contains about eight pints (five liters) of blood. This blood is made up of a pale liquid called plasma, and millions of cells, or corpuscles. Corpuscles are tiny red disks that give the blood its color. The blood also contains white corpuscles. There are about 5 million red corpuscles and between 80 and 160 million white corpuscles in every cubic inch of blood.

White corpuscles attack GERMS that enter the body by absorbing them. Often many white corpuscles are killed in the fight against disease or infection. Large numbers of dead white corpuscles collect as pus. Other blood particles, called platelets, help our blood to clot when we bleed. This clotting helps scratches and other wounds to heal more quickly.

We can all be classified into blood groups A, B, AB, or O, according to the type of blood we have. Blood groups are important when hospital patients are given blood transfusions. Transfusions are given either to replace diseased blood, or blood that has been lost through an injury. The blood a person is given is generally the same blood type as his or her own.

bloom *n.* flower; first freshness or beauty. *In the bloom of youth.* *vb.* bear blooms; flourish.
blossom *n.* flower or mass of flowers, especially on fruit trees.
blot *n.* an inky stain; a smudge or mark. *vb.* make a blot on.
blouse *n.* a kind of loose shirt, usually worn by women.
blow 1. *n.* a hard knock. 2. *vb.* (past **blew**) make the air move. *The wind blows from the west.*
blubber 1. *n.* whale fat. 2. *vb.* weep excessively.
blue *n.* the color of the sky.
bluebell *n.* a name given to two different kinds of wild flowers: the wild hyacinth and the harebell.
bluebottle *n.* a name given to several species of large fly, having a blue abdomen, and particularly attracted to rotting meat.
bluff 1. *vb.* deceive, make pretense. 2. *adj.* outspoken, blunt.
blunder *n.* & *vb.* (make) a stupid mistake. *John made a blunder when he wrote 10 instead of 100.*
blunt *adj.* not sharp.
blur *n.* smudge; indistinct impression. *vb.* blot, obscure.
blurb *n.* publisher's description of a book usually printed on the jacket.
blush *vb.* become red in the face because you are ashamed or shy.
boa 1. *n.* a family of large snakes, mainly from South America, which kill their prey by crushing it to death. 2. *n.* a long, tube-shaped scarf, made of fur or feathers, once worn by women.

boar (rhymes with *sore*) *n.* a male pig; wild pig.
board 1. *n.* a long, flat piece of wood; a plank. 2. a flat piece of wood or card used for a special purpose. *A chess board is used for the game of chess.* 3. *n.* an authorized group of people, e.g. board of directors. 4. *vb.* get onto a ship, train or aircraft. *We must board the plane now.*
boast *vb.* talk about how good you think you are, brag.
boat *n.* a small or medium-sized vessel used for traveling on water. (The term "ship" is used for larger vessels such as liners and warships.)
► The first boats date back to prehistoric times, and were simply floating logs or driftwood paddled with the hands. The first real boats appeared later. One was the dugout canoe, which was a log hollowed out by fire or stone tools. Another was a raft made of logs or bundles of reeds tied together. When there were no logs or reeds, boats were made of skins stretched over a light framework. Small round boats called coracles and Eskimo kayaks were made in this way.

After a while the dugout and the raft were built up with sides of wooden planks to make them drier and sturdier. A keel was added at the bottom to make the boat more seaworthy. Different types and shapes of sails were fitted so as to catch as much wind as possible. Until the 1800s, all boats were driven by sails, oars or poles, but the invention of the STEAM ENGINE made paddle wheels and PROPELLERS possible. Today, motorboats, sailing boats, kayaks and row boats are used by people in all parts of the world.

boater *n.* hard, flat straw hat.
boatswain (**bo**-*sun*) *n.* a senior seaman who controls the work of other seamen.

Bobolink
The bobolink is a North American bird named after its musical song. It is about 7 inches (18 cm) long, yellow-brown in color, with dark stripes on its head. In summer the male is black with white and yellow markings. Bobolinks fly south to South America for the winter. In the spring and summer they return as far north as Canada. They eat insects and seeds, and are considered an enemy of the rice crop.

body *n.* 1. the visible part of a person or animal. 2. a group of people. 3. the main part of something. 4. an astronomical object. *A star is sometimes called a heavenly body.* **bodily** *adj.* of the body.
bodyguard *n.* person employed to protect someone.

Boer War
The Boer War (1899–1902) was fought in SOUTH AFRICA between the Boers – settlers of Dutch descent – and the British. The slow and badly led British troops were no match for the fast and lightly armed Boers in the early days of the war. But in the end Britain's overwhelming strength won. There were about 450,000 soldiers in the British armies during the Boer War, and only about 60,000 Boers.

Dugout canoe (*c.* 6000 BC) Egyptian boat with sail (*c.* 1500 BC)

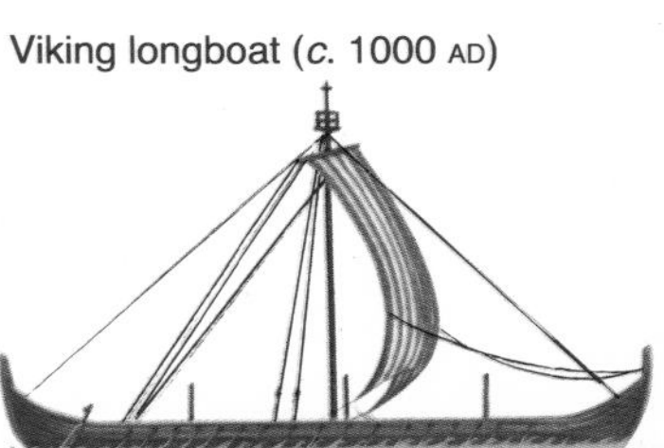
Viking longboat (*c.* 1000 AD)

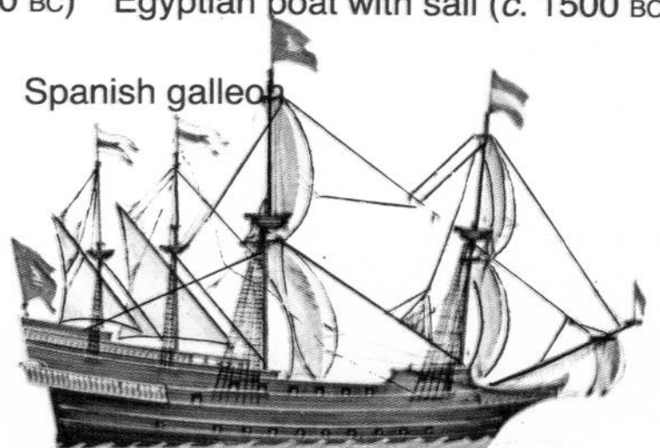
Spanish galleon

The first boats were probably no more than some logs fastened together. The Egyptians had sails which grew in complexity throughout the centuries until the 19th century when steam was used to drive ships

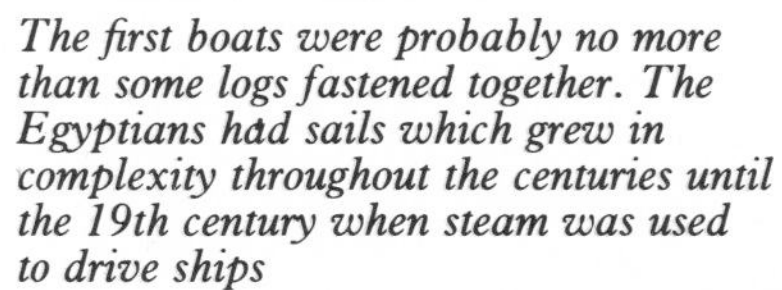

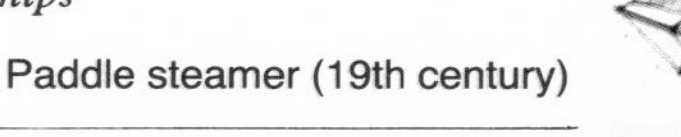

Paddle steamer (19th century)

B

bog *n*. spongy ground, a marsh.

Bogotá
Capital and largest city of COLOMBIA in South America originally settled by the Spanish in 1538.

bog down *vb*. overwhelm with work.
bogus *adj*. false, sham.

Bohr, Niels
Niels Bohr (1885–1962) was a Danish physicist. In 1922, he was awarded the Nobel Prize for physics for his work on explaining the structure of the atom. Later, he went to the U.S.A. as an adviser on atomic weapons.

boil 1. *vb*. heat a liquid until it bubbles and steams. 2. *n*. painful, infected swelling on the body.
boisterous *adj*. noisy, lively.
bold *adj*. showing no fear.

Boleyn, Anne
The second of the six wives of HENRY VIII of England and mother of ELIZABETH I.

Bolivar, Simon
Simon Bolivar (1783–1830) was a South American hero. He became known as the "Liberator" because he won independence for Colombia, Bolivia, Ecuador, Venezuela and Peru. These countries were colonies of Spain, but they became independent countries because of Bolivar's efforts.

Simon Bolivar was born in Caracas, Venezuela, and went to Europe as a young man to study. During a visit to Rome in 1805 he vowed to dedicate his life to Venezuela's freedom. When he returned to Venezuela he joined a group of patriots who were plotting against Spain. He captured Caracas in 1813 and became dictator of Venezuela.

Bolivia
Bolivia is a landlocked country in central SOUTH AMERICA, west of Brazil. Most of Bolivia is an enormous plain stretching from the Brazilian border to the eastern foothills of the Andes Mountains. High in the Andes lies the great Bolivian plateau, over 13,000 ft. (4,000 meters) high. Two-thirds of Bolivia's people live here. The capital, La Paz, is the highest capital in the world, and Lake Titicaca, at 12,507 ft. (3,812 meters) above sea level, is one of the highest lakes.

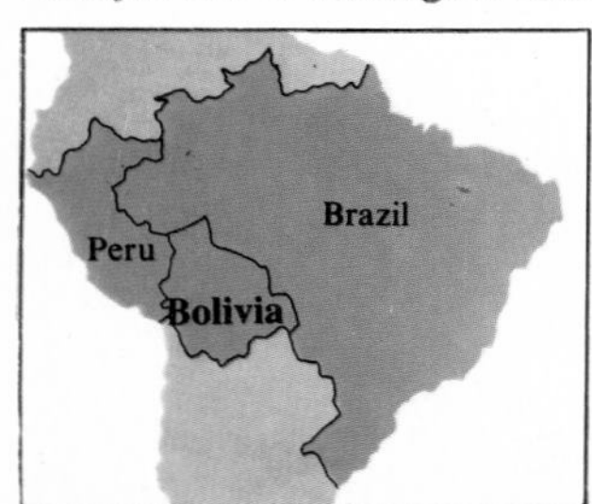

Spain ruled Bolivia from 1532 until 1825. It gained freedom from Spain with the help of Simon BOLIVAR, a Venzuelan general, after whom Bolivia is named. More than half the people are Indians, a third are mestizos (people who are part European, part Indian) and the rest are direct descendants of Europeans. Bolivia is the world's second largest producer of tin, and mining is the country's most valuable industry.

AREA: 424,188 SQ. MILES (1,098,581 SQ. KM)
POPULATION: 5,897,000
CAPITAL: LA PAZ
CURRENCY: PESO
OFFICIAL LANGUAGE: SPANISH

Bolshevik *n*. a member of the Russian revolutionary party that seized power in 1917. **Bolshevism** *n*.
► In the early 1900s, the Russian revolutionary socialist movement split into two groups. These were the Bolsheviks ("the majority") and the Mensheviks ("the minority"). V.I. Lenin was the leader of the Bolsheviks.

After the Russian Revolution of 1917, Lenin and the Bolsheviks seized control of the country. Russia then became involved in a civil war. The Bolshevik Red Army fought the Tsarist (royalist) White Army. The Bolsheviks (now renamed the Communists) finally won. The Communists were now in full control of U.S.S.R., which has remained under Communist rule ever since.

bolt 1. *n*. a metal fastening on a door or window. 2. *n*. a metal pin with a screw at one end that goes into a nut to fasten things. 3. *vb*. run away quickly. 4. *vb*. fasten with bolts.
bomb *n*. a container filled with explosive. *vb*. attack with bombs. **bomber** *n*. aircraft using bombs.
bombard *vb*. attack with gunfire; abuse.

Bombay
Bombay is one of the largest cities in INDIA. Situated on an island in the west coast of the country, it is also a major port. Bombay is a university city and the center of the Indian film industry. It was founded by the Portuguese in the 1500s, and later passed into British ownership.

Bonaparte, Napoleon, see **Napoleon**
bond *n*. 1. something that links or connects. *The close bond of friendship*. 2. a written promise to pay a sum or carry out a contract.
bone *n*. the hard framework that supports the flesh and organs of all vertebrates (animals with backbones). *vb*. remove bones from. *She boned the fish*.
► All bones are made up of the same thing, mostly calcium. Bones are hard on the outside but soft on the inside. Bone marrow, in the hollow center of the bone, is where new red BLOOD cells are made.

The human skeleton has four kinds of bones: long bones, such as arm and leg bones; flat bones such as the skull; short bones, including ankle and wrist bones; and irregular bones, such as those that make up the backbone. If bones are broken they will knit together again if they are rejoined or set properly. The cells in the broken ends of the bone produce a substance that helps the ends to grow together again so that the mended bone is as strong as it ever was. But, as human beings get older, their bones become more brittle and will break more easily. Children's bones, on the other hand, are able to bend a little and are not so easily broken or injured.

bonfire *n*. a big fire made in the open air.

Bonn
Bonn is the capital of the German Federal Republic (*see* GERMANY, WEST). It is the birthplace of the composer Beethoven and has a university. The Münster cathedral dates from the 12th century. Much of the city was destroyed in the World War II, but today it is a busy metropolitan center.

bonnet 1. *n*. a woman's or baby's headdress tied on by strings.
bonny *adj*. pleasant, healthy-looking.

Bonnie Prince Charlie
Prince Charles Edward Stuart (1720–88) is better known as "Bonnie

HAND BOOKBINDING

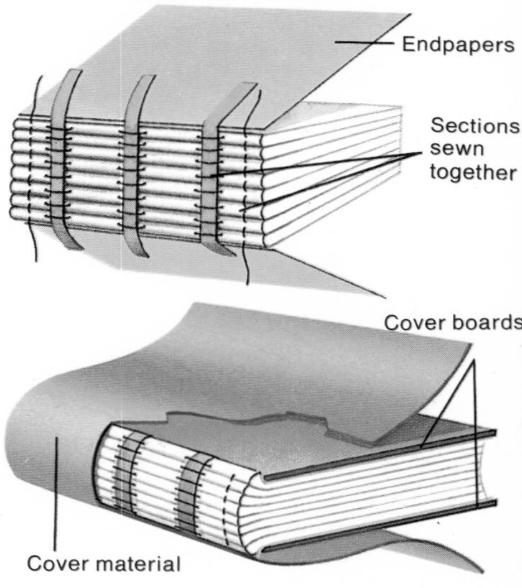

The pages of a book come in sections like thin books. These are placed in order and sewn together. The cover is then glued onto the sides and back.

Prince Charlie." He is also called the "Young Pretender" (claimant), because he claimed the English Throne. His grandfather, JAMES II, had been forced to abdicate because he was a Roman Catholic.

Charles landed in Scotland in 1745. His supporters, known as Jacobites, joined him with an army. The Jacobites beat the English at Prestonpans, and began to march on London. However, many of Charles' soldiers deserted, and his army retreated. The Jacobite army was massacred at Culloden in 1746. Charles was forced into hiding, but finally managed to escape to France. He died in Rome, disillusioned and a drunkard.

bonsai (*bon*-**sigh**) *n.* dwarf tree grown in a pot; an art which was developed in Japan.

bonus *n.* something extra; money paid in addition to wages or dividends.

book 1. *n.* pages of – usually – printed paper bound together in a cover. 2. *vb.* reserve a ticket or place.

▶ The history of books goes back to 3,000 B.C. when books were written on rolls of PAPYRUS in Egypt. By the period of the Roman Empire both papyrus and PARCHMENT (made from sheepskin) were used as writing materials.

After the fall of Rome the making of books was kept alive in the monasteries of Europe. Handwritten books with elaborate and richly colored decorations appeared. These are known as illuminated manuscripts. PAPER was introduced in Europe by the Moors, though it had originated in China. But the greatest revolution in PRINTING was the invention of movable type by Johann GUTENBERG, who printed his famous Bible between 1452 and 1456. Today, book production is highly automated – huge four color presses can produce thousands of copies of a book in an hour. Bookbinding is the process by which printed sheets are made into the completed book. Though hand bookbinding is still a fine art, most books today are bound by machine.

bookkeeper *n.* a person who looks after business accounts and keeps them in order.

bookmaker *n.* someone who makes a living by taking bets on horse races, etc.

bookworm *n.* 1. an avid reader. 2. a grub that eats holes in books.

boom 1. *n.* & *vb.* deep, hollow sound. 2. *n.* period of great commercial activity. 3. *n.* a spar or pole attached at one end to a mast to stretch the foot of a sail.

boomerang *n.* a throwing stick used by Australian aborigines for hunting. *vb.* recoil like a boomerang.

▶ The boomerang is a wooden throwing stick used mainly by the Australian Aborigines. There are two kinds. One, the hunting boomerang, is very heavy and is thrown straight at the target. The other is lighter. It is shaped in a special way so that when it is skillfully thrown it is possible to make it return to the thrower.

boon *n.* benefit, blessing.

boost *vb.* help on (by shoving); raise voltage. **booster** *n.* auxiliary motor in a rocket.

boot *n.* a sort of shoe that also covers the ankle and sometimes the leg. *vb.* kick.

booty *n.* plunder, spoils.

Bordeaux

Bordeaux, which is a major French port, lies on the estuary of the River Gironde. It is one of the main centers of French wine production. The French government moved to Bordeaux from Paris in both world wars.

border *n.* 1. the part near the edge of something. 2. the land near the line dividing two countries.

bore 1. *vb.* drill out; make a hole in. 2. *vb.* make someone weary with uninteresting conversation. *n.* a boring person; someone who does not know when he or she is not wanted. **boredom** *n.* 3. *n.* inside diameter of a gun barrel.

Borneo

Borneo, in Southeast Asia, is the third largest island in the world. Kalimantan State, which occupies the southern 70 percent of Borneo, belongs to INDONESIA. It was formerly part of the Dutch East Indies. Sabah State and Sarawak State in the north and west are part of Malaysia. Brunei, in the north-west, a small former British protectorate, is an independent monarchy.

Much of the interior of Borneo is mountainous and densely forested. There is a variety of animal life but few people. Most of the inhabitants are Dyaks, many of whom live in long houses built on stilts. Malays and Chinese make up the remainder of the population.

borrow *vb.* get something from someone else which you use and then give back. The other person *lends* it to you.

bosom *n.* breast. **bosom friend**. intimate friend.

Bosporus

The Bosporus is the name of the narrow strip of water which joins the Black Sea to the Sea of Marmara in Turkey. The great city of ISTANBUL lies near the Bosporus, which is 19 miles (30 km) long. The Bosporus divides Europe from Asia.

boss *n.* 1. the chief person in an organization; the person you work for. 2. a stud or ornament in the center of a shield.

Boston

Boston is the capital of MASSACHUSETTS, and the largest city in New England. Puritan colonists settled in Boston in 1630. Before the war of INDEPENDENCE Boston became an important port. It was a leading center for opposition to British rule. The Boston Massacre (1770) and the Boston Tea Party (1773) took place there.

The Boston area has many important educational institutions, including Massachusetts Institute of Technology (MIT) and Harvard University.

Boston Tea Party

On December 16, 1773, a band of American colonists disguised as Indians boarded a British ship in Boston harbor and dumped overboard the cargo of tea. The Boston Tea Party was one of the events leading up to the war of INDEPENDENCE.

Tea being dumped overboard during the Boston Tea Party of 1773.

B

The colonists were furious when Britain decided to send extra tea to America and make the colonists pay a tax on it. The British governor of Boston was asked to send all ships carrying tea back to England. But he refused.

So Boston's citizens banded together and the Boston Tea Pary took place. This act of rebellion caused great anger in London. The port of Boston was closed until the cost of the tea was paid. Anger built up, and soon there was revolution.

botany *n.* the study of plants and how they grow. **botanist** *n.*

► There are more than 300,000 different kinds of plants. They vary from tiny algae that can only be seen with a microscope, to giant redwood trees nearly 300 ft. (100 meters) high.

Without plants there would be no animals, because animals depend on plants for all their food.

By studying the way in which the qualities of one generation of plants are passed on to the next generation, scientists are able to grow bigger and better crops. They can breed varieties that fight plant disease better.

In 1753 Carolus Linnaeus, a Swedish botanist, invented the first real system for naming plants. He gave every plant a name made up of two Latin words.

Botany Bay
Botany Bay is a large inlet of the sea near Sydney in southeastern AUSTRALIA. It was here that Captain COOK landed in 1770. The name was given to the bay because of the large number of new plants found by Cook's party. Botany Bay was later the name of the British prison colony at Port Jackson.

botch *vb.* patch badly, make a bungle of something.
both *adj.* & *pron.* the two together. *She invited both of us to her party.*
bother 1. *vb.* worry, annoy. *n.* a nuisance. 2. *vb.* take the trouble. *Why should I bother to telephone?*

Botswana
Botswana is a land-locked republic in southern AFRICA. The Kalahari, a semidesert region, covers most of the country. Only small numbers of Bushmen live in the Kalahari. Most of the people work in farming even though very little of the land is suitable for agriculture. In the 1960s, valuable deposits of diamonds and other minerals were discovered. These are now the country's main source of income.

Botswana used to be called Bechuanaland. It became a British protectorate in 1885. In 1966 Botswana became fully independent within the Commonwealth of Nations.

AREA: 231,818 SQ. MILES (600,372 SQ. KM)
POPULATION: 820,600
CAPITAL: GABORONE
CURRENCY: PULA
OFFICIAL LANGUAGES: ENGLISH, SETSWANA

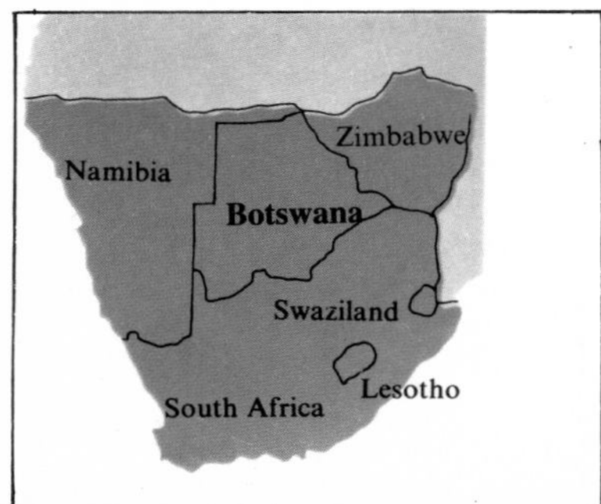

Botticelli, Sandro
Botticelli was the nickname of Alessandro di Mariano dei Filipepi (*c.* 1445–1510). He was one of the greatest painters of his time. The Medici family of Florence, in Italy, acted as his patrons. Botticelli's graceful paintings illustrate scenes both from the Bible and from classical mythology.

bottle *n.* a container, usually made of glass, in which liquid is kept. *vb.* put in bottles.
bottom 1. *n.* the lowest part of something. *adj.* lowest, last. *Bottom drawer.* 2. *n.* a person's seat or backside.
bough *n.* the branch of a tree.
bought *vb.* past of **buy**.
boulder *n.* a large rock rounded by action of water, etc.
bounce *vb.* spring up again like a ball that is dropped on the ground.
bound *vb.* past of **bind**.
boundary *n.* 1. the border or frontier of a country; a line separating one place from another. 2. the edge of a field.
bounty *n.* gift, bonus.
bout (*bowt*) *n.* turn, attack, fit (of illness).
bovine *adj.* oxlike; stupid.
bow (rhymes with *low*) *n.* 1. a piece of wood curved by a tight string. *A bow is used for shooting arrows.* 2. a knot with loops. 3. a stick with long hairs attached to it, which is used for playing musical instruments like violins.

► The bow and arrow is one of the earliest weapons ever invented by man. It was used by armies in Egypt 4,000 years ago. During the MIDDLE AGES longbows and crossbows were popular, but were soon replaced by guns.

bow (rhymes with *cow*) 1. *n.* the front of a ship. 2. *vb.* & *n.* bend at the waist to greet an important person.
bowels *pl. n.* the part of the body where solid wastes gather; intestines.
bower *n.* dwelling, retreat, shelter.

Bower bird
A bird native to Australia and New Guinea.

Bower birds have a type of courtship that is different from all other birds. When bower birds are ready to mate, the male builds a little room, or bower, of sticks to attract the female. He even decorates it with flowers, shells and small bones.

bowl 1. *n.* a deep dish or basin. 2. *vb.* roll a ball in the game of bowling.
bowler *n.* 1. person bowling. 2. hard hat with round crown.
bowling *n.* any of several games in which balls are rolled on a green or down an alley at an object or group of objects.

► Ten-pin bowling is the most popular type in the United States. In this sport the player bowls a ball not more than 27 inches (68.5 cm) around. It weighs from 10 to 16 pounds (4.5 to 7 kg). The lane is about 42 inches (107 cm) wide.

box 1. *n.* a hollow, container, often made of wood or cardboard. *vb.* put in a box. 2. *vb.* fight with the fists. 3. *n.* a small evergreen tree or shrub which has hard yellowish wood.
boxer *n.* 1. a person who fights with the fists; one who boxes. 2. a kind of dog related to the bulldog.
boxing *n.* sport of fighting with fists.
boy *n.* a young male person.
boycott *vb.* refuse to speak to someone; have nothing to do with. *n.* the act of boycotting someone or something.
boyhood *n.* time of being a boy.

Boyle, Robert
Irish chemist and physicist (1627–91), often called the "father of

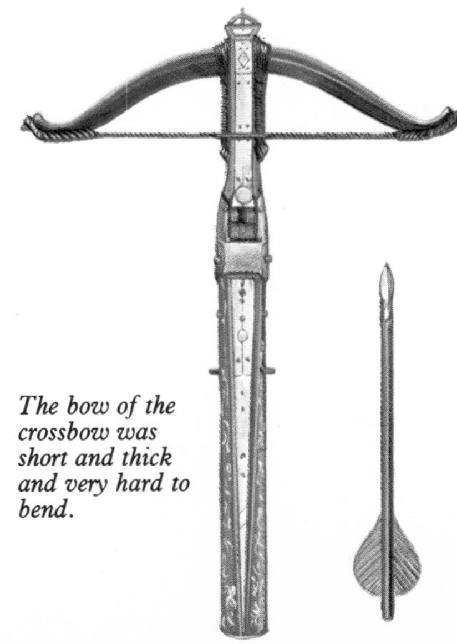

The bow of the crossbow was short and thick and very hard to bend.

modern chemistry", who formulated Boyle's Law on the properties of gases. He invented the compressed air pump. He was a pioneer of fresh attitudes to scientific method.

Boy Scouts
The Boy Scouts is a worldwide organization for boys that was founded in Britain in 1908 by Robert BADEN-POWELL. Today it has over 10 million members in 100 countries.

brace 1. *n.* a carpenter's tool. 2. *n.* a pair or couple, especially of game. 3. *vb.* tighten, support, make firm.
bracelet *n.* a band worn around the arm or wrist.
bracing *adj.* invigorating.
bracken *n.* a kind of fern.
bracket *n.* 1. a support to hold a shelf. 2. one of a pair of marks [ ] used to enclose words or mathematical symbols. *vb.* enclose with brackets.
bradawl *n.* small tool used for boring.
brae (*Sc*) *n.* a hill.
braid *vb.* plait, interlace.
braille (rhymes with *sail*) *n.* raised letters that a blind person can read by touching them.
► Braille is an ALPHABET for the blind. It is made up of raised dots which the reader can feel with his fingertips. Many books have been translated into braille for blind readers. Special braille typewriters make it easy to write braille. The system was invented by a Frenchman, Louis Braille, in the 1800s.

brain *n.* the gray matter in the head which controls the work of the body, and with which you think; the intellect itself. **brainy** *adj.* clever.
► The brain controls all the other parts of the body. In some tiny insects it is no bigger than a speck of dust. Even in some mighty dinosaurs it was no bigger than a walnut. But MAMMALS have big brains in relation to their size, and human beings have the biggest brains of all. The human brain is largely made up of gray and white matter. Gray matter is NERVE cells, and white matter is the nerve fibers that carry messages from the nerve cells to the body. These nerve fibers leave the brain in large bundles like telephone cables and reach out to all parts of the body. Messages from the body travel back along the fibers to the brain all the time.

The brain consists of the *cortex*, or *cerebrum* (the largest part), the *cerebellum*, the midbrain, the *pons* and the *medulla oblongata*, which connects it with the spinal cord. The brain is also divided into various lobes, or sections. The frontal lobes control movements of the body – the left half controls the right half of the body, and vice versa. These lobes also have important speech, intellectual and emotional functions. The parietal lobes receive nerve messages from all parts of the body by way of the spinal cord. Hearing is centered on the parietal and *temporal* lobes. The *occipital* lobes are responsible for sight.

Although the brain makes up only 2 percent of the body's weight, it uses about 20 percent of the energy produced in our body. The energy comes from glucose and oxygen in the blood. When your blood sugar level is too low, at first you feel hungry. Then your brain partly shuts down. You become weak and faint.

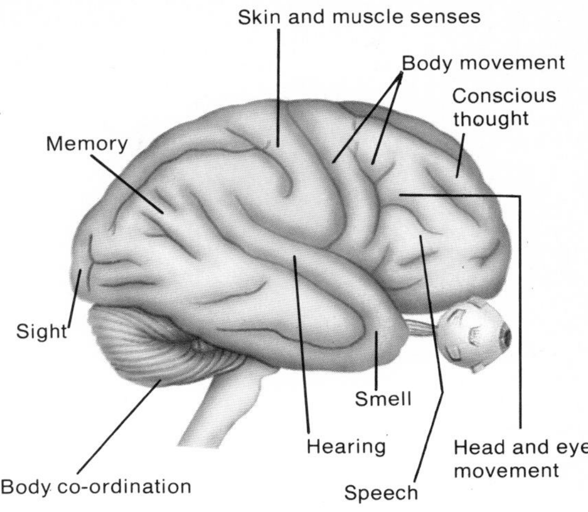

The main parts of the brain. Different parts have different functions. The largest part of the brain is the cerebral cortex. Different parts of the body are linked to different areas of the cortex.

braise *vb.* stew in a covered pan.
brake *n.* something that is pressed against a wheel to stop it turning. *vb.* apply the brake.
bramble *n.* a blackberry bush.
branch *n.* 1. one of the arm-like parts of a tree growing out of the trunk. 2. a division of a large business or service organization, family, etc.
brand 1. *vb.* to burn the owner's symbol on the hide of cattle with a hot iron. 2. *n.* a make of goods. 3. *n.* a poetic word for a sword.
brandish *vb.* wave about, especially a weapon.
brandy *n.* an alcoholic drink distilled from wine.

Brasilia
Brasilia is the capital of BRAZIL, in South America. It was built in the 1950s, and in 1960 replaced Rio de Janeiro as the capital. The purpose of moving the capital inland was to develop the vast interior of Brazil.

brass *n.* a bright, yellowish metal made by mixing copper and zinc.
► Brass is an ALLOY of ZINC and COPPER. Small amounts of other metals may sometimes be added for special uses. Brass is often used for plumbing and electrical fixtures and for making delicate instruments.

The amount of copper in brass may vary from 50 percent to more than 95 percent. Brass with a large amount of copper in it is quite soft and is a reddish-yellow color. Brass with a small amount of tin added is used for many of the fittings on boats and ships, as it does not rust.

brave 1. *adj.* fearless. *vb.* meet boldly without fear. **bravery** *n.* 2. *n.* an American Indian warrior.
brawl *n.* a rowdy quarrel. *vb.* quarrel noisily.
brawn *n.* muscular strength.

Brazil (Brazilian)
Brazil is by far the largest country in SOUTH AMERICA and the fifth largest country in the world. Much of Brazil is low-lying, and contains the huge basin of the AMAZON river and the world's largest rain forest. Until recently, only tribes of Indians lived here. Today, the government is trying to open up the Amazon region.

Over half of Brazil's people live in cities that include Rio de Janeiro, São Paulo, Belo Horizonte and Recife. BRASILIA, a specially built modern city, has been the capital of Brazil since 1960.

Brazil was ruled by Portugal from the early 1500s until 1822, and most people speak Portuguese. About three-fourths of the people are descended from Europeans; most of the rest are of mixed European, Indian and African ancestry. There are some pure Indians and Negroes. Most Brazilians work on farms. The country leads the world in producing

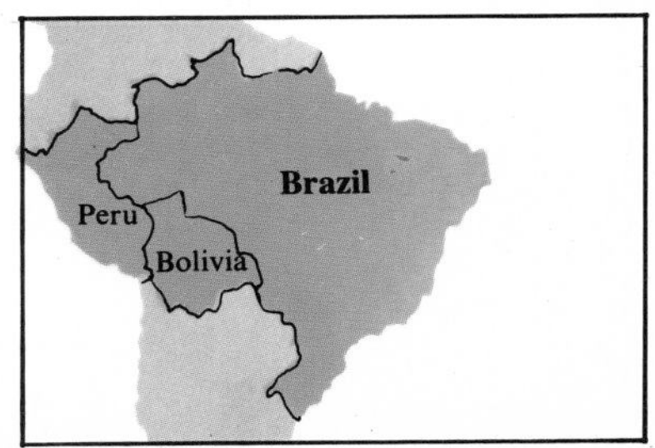

B

coffee, and oil is becoming more and more important. Brazil is also one of the biggest producers of beef, cocoa, cotton, corn, sugar cane and tobacco. Most of Brazil's great mineral wealth is still undeveloped.
AREA: 3,286,668 SQ. MILES (8,511,965 SQ. KM)
POPULATION: 113,882,000
CAPITAL: BRASILIA
CURRENCY: CRUZEIRO
OFFICIAL LANGUAGE: PORTUGUESE

bread *n.* a food made from flour and baked in an oven.
▶ Bread is one of the oldest foods, dating back to at least 2000 B.C. It may be made from wheat, corn, oats, barley, or rye FLOUR. At first bread was flat, but the Egyptians added YEAST to make the dough rise. Today most bread is baked with yeast.

breadth *n.* width, broadness, distance from side to side.
break 1. *vb.* smash. 2. *n.* a rest. *When she had finished her work, she took a break.* 3. *n.* in pool or billiards, a series of scoring strokes.
break down 1. *vb.* (of a piece of machinery) to stop working. 2. separate something into the parts it is made up of. *It's quite a big job, but if we break it down sensibly, we can do it.*
breaker *n.* heavy ocean wave which breaks on rocks or shore.

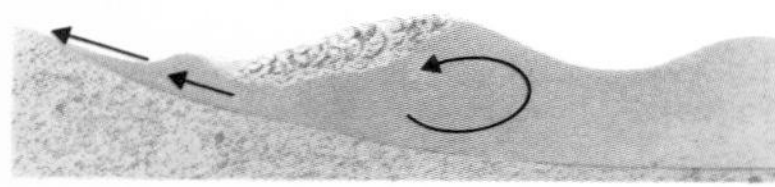

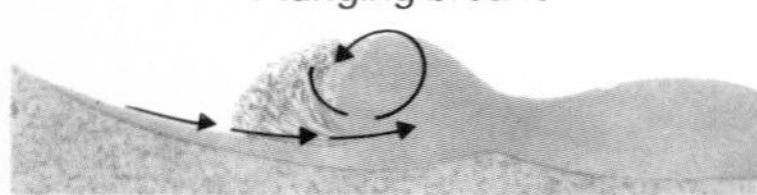

breakfast *n.* the first meal of the day, usually eaten in the early morning.
breakthrough *n.* major advance in science, etc.
breakwater *n.* a structure built in the sea, usually near a harbor, to break the force of the waves.
bream *n.* a freshwater or sea fish.
breast (rhymes with *rest*) *n.* the milk-secreting organ in mammals; the chest of a person or an animal.
breathalyser *n.* device for measuring the amount of alcohol in the blood.
breathe (*breeth*) *vb.* take air into the lungs and let it out again. **breath** (*breth*) *n.* air drawn in and expelled by lungs.
▶ Breathing is something we rarely have to think about. As soon as a baby is born, it starts to breathe, and we go on breathing all our lives. It is the OXYGEN in the air that we need. Like all other animals, we must have oxygen to stay alive. The oxygen is used with the food we eat to give us energy to move about and keep our bodies going.

Air is drawn into the LUNGS. From there it goes through tiny tubes which allow the oxygen to pass into the BLOOD vessels. So oxygen goes all round the body in the blood. We breathe out another type of gas called carbon dioxide.

An adult normally breathes in and out about 20 times a minute (children usually breathe faster than this).

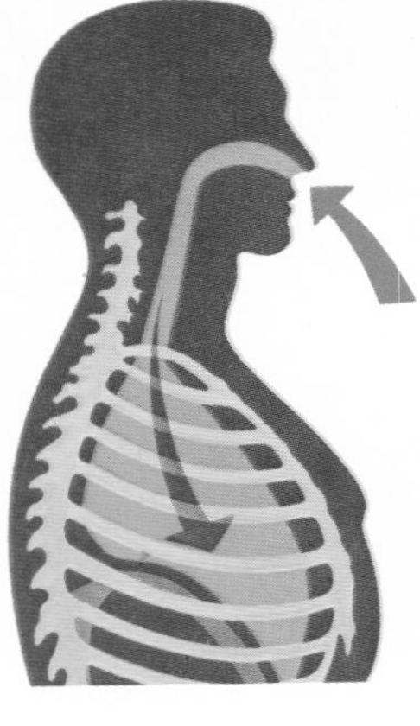

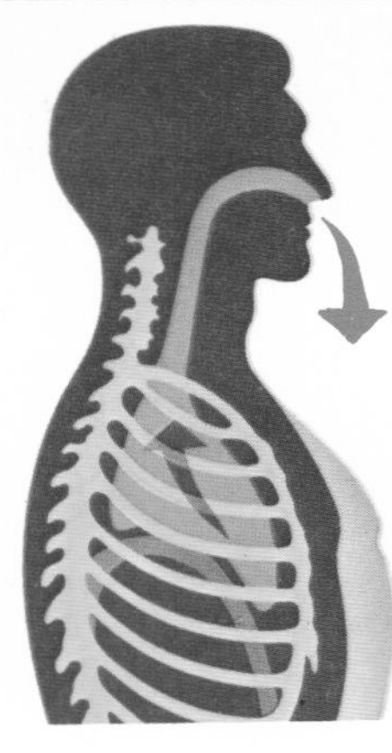

Oxygen reaches the body through the lungs. When we breathe, our chest expands and air rushes in through the nose. When our chest muscles relax, the lungs are squeezed and air is pushed out.

breed 1. *n.* animals that produce others of exactly the same kind. *The Labrador is a breed of dog.* 2. *vb.* produce young ones.
breeze *n.* a gentle wind.
brevity *n.* briefness, shortness in speech or writing. *Brevity is the soul of wit.*
brewery *n.* a place where beer is brewed, or made. **brew** *vb.* make beer.
bribe *n.* money or something else offered to obtain some services – usually dishonest or illegal. *vb.* offer a bribe.
brick *n.* a block of hardened clay used in building.
▶ Bricks have been used for more than 5,000 years and are the oldest manmade building material. Some of the earliest types of bricks that were made can still be seen today.

Ancient brickmakers discovered that rectangular bricks were the easiest to build with. Today, bricks are still rectangular in shape. The first bricks were left to dry in the sun and the clay had to be mixed with straw to stop the bricks crumbling. Later on, it was discovered that if bricks were heated in a furnace they became much harder and the straw was not needed. Modern bricks are shaped by machine.

Good bricklaying is skilled work. Often ornamental designs are worked into brick walls.

bride *n.* a woman who is about to be married or who has just been married. **bridal** *adj.* of a bride or wedding.
bridegroom *n.* a man who is about to be married or who has just been married.
bridesmaid *n.* a girl who helps a bride at her wedding.
bridge 1. *n.* a structure that enables people or vehicles to cross a road, river or other obstacle. *vb.* span a space with a bridge. 2. *n.* platform on a ship for navigating, etc. 3. *n.* the name of a card game for four players.
▶ The first simple bridges were probably fallen tree trunks placed across a river or small valley. Later, they may have been supported underneath by stones or logs. Another kind of simple bridge is the rope bridge made from long pieces of rope slung across a river.

The Romans were among the first great bridge builders. Some of their stone bridges are still standing today. In the MIDDLE AGES bridges in towns often had shops and houses built on top of them.

There are three main kinds of bridge: the beam, the arch and the suspension bridge.

A modern beam bridge works in the same way as a simple tree trunk bridge. It is made of strong girders, or beams, which stretch from one bank to the other. Sometimes the middle of the bridge rests on pillars.

An arch bridge may have one arch or more. In the past, it was usually built from stone, but today some are made of steel, like the Sydney Harbour bridge in Australia. It has a span (the distance from one side to the other) of 1,650 ft. (503 meters).

Suspension bridges are hung by strong steel cables from tall towers. The towers also have cables fixed to the ground.

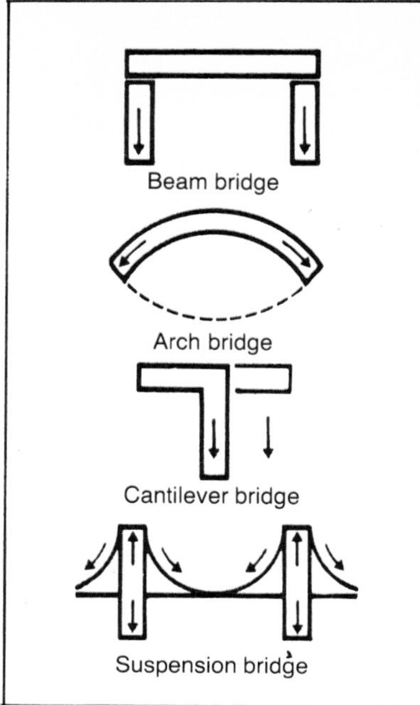

Four types of bridge.

Some beam bridges over rivers can be moved to let ships pass through. Tower Bridge in London is a bascule bridge. Both sides of the bridge can be lifted up in the middle, like drawbridges. Swing bridges are on pivots and can be swung sideways.

Modern bridge building began with iron bridges in the 1700s. Later, many of these were built for the railroads. The first modern suspension bridge was built by Thomas Telford at Menai in North Wales.

By the end of the 1800s, steel was being used. The Brooklyn Bridge in New York, finished in 1883, was one of the first steel suspension bridges. One of the longest bridges in the world is the Verrazano Narrows suspension bridge, also in New York. It was opened in 1964 and its main span is 4,260 ft. (1,298 meters).

In the 1900s many concrete bridges have been built. The Gladesville Bridge in Australia is one of the longest concrete bridges in the world. Its arch spans 1,000 ft. (305 meters).

bridle *n.* the harness that goes on a horse's head, including the reins.
brief 1. *adj.* lasting for a short time only. *The meeting was a brief one.* 2. *n.* an instruction, particularly to a lawyer.
brigand *n.* a robber.
bright (rhymes with *bite*) *adj.* 1. shiny, cheerful. 2. clever. **brightness** *n.*
brilliant 1. *adj.* very bright. *A brilliant star shone between the clouds.* 2. *adj.* very clever. **brilliance** *n.*
brim *n.* 1. the edge of a cup or container. *The bucket was full to the brim.* 2. the projecting edge of a hat.
bring *vb.* fetch or carry.
bring up *vb.* care for a child as it grows.
brink *n.* the edge of something, such as a river or precipice.
brisk *adj.* lively, alert.
bristle 1. *n.* a short stiff hair. 2. *vb.* become angry.

Bristol
Bristol is a major British seaport, located near the mouth of the River Avon. In 1497 John Cabot set out from Bristol on his famous voyage to Canada. Much of the city was rebuilt after bomb damage in World War II. Bristol has a cathedral and a university.

Brisbane
Brisbane is the third biggest city in AUSTRALIA after Sydney and Melbourne. It has 959,000 people and is the capital of the state of QUEENSLAND.

Bristlecone pine
The bristlecone pine is a tree that sometimes grows as a shrub. Bristlecones grow in Nevada, California and Arizona and they are believed to be the oldest living things in the world. The oldest bristlecone still alive is about 4,600 years old. It had been growing in the White Mountains of eastern California for more than 2,000 years when Jesus Christ was born.

The bristlecone gets its name from its slender, prickly cones.

British Columbia
British Columbia is the most westerly province of CANADA, lying mostly between the Rocky Mountains and the Pacific Ocean. Nearly half the people of the province live in or near the city of Vancouver. The capital, Victoria, is on Vancouver Island.

Much of British Columbia is covered with thick forests. The province provides more than half of Canada's lumber, and there are many pulp and paper mills. Mining ranks second in importance to the forest industries. British Columbia is also Canada's leading fishing province. The most valuable fish is salmon. Many tourists come to British Columbia.

The province has grown very rapidly since World War II. Additional jobs, mostly in the forest industries, hydroelectric power, and manufacturing, have tripled the population since 1941. The population today is over 2½ million.

In 1871 British Columbia agreed to join the Dominion of Canada, provided a railroad was built from eastern Canada to the Pacific coast. This was a huge task, and the railroad did not reach the Pacific until 1885.

British Isles
The British Isles contain two large nations, the United Kingdom of Great Britain and Northern Ireland (comprising ENGLAND, Northern IRELAND, SCOTLAND and WALES) and the Republic of Ireland, and two small British dependencies, the Isle of Man and the Channel Islands. Separated from mainland Europe by the North Sea, the Strait of Dover and the English Channel, the British Isles have a combined population of over 59 million.

Despite their northerly position the British Isles have a mostly mild and moist climate, because the prevailing southwest winds are warmed by the offshore North Atlantic Drift, an ocean current which originates in the Caribbean Sea. The weather is changeable, partly because of the depressions, or "lows", which come from the Atlantic Ocean.

The highest peak is Ben Nevis in Scotland at 4,406 ft. (1,343 meters) above sea level. The longest river is the Shannon in the Republic of Ireland. It is 240 miles (386 km) long. The United Kingdom of Great Britain and Northern Ireland is a leading trading and manufacturing nation. Farming is the chief industry in the Republic of Ireland.

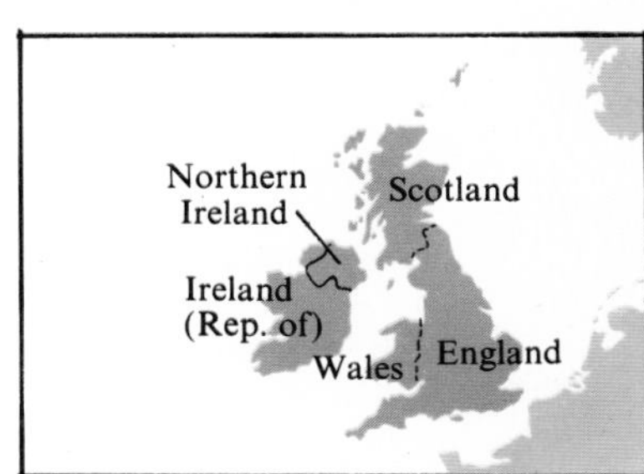

Britten, Benjamin
Benjamin Britten (1913–76) is one of the most important British composers of this century. Much of his work, such as *The Young Person's Guide to the Orchestra*, is meant for children. His operas include *Peter Grimes* and *Billy Budd*. Lord Britten – he was created a life peer in 1976 – also started the annual Aldeburgh music festival in 1948.

brittle *adj.* easily snapped or broken.
broad *adj.* wide, a long way across.
broadcast 1. *vb.* & *n.* send out in all directions, particularly by radio or television. 2. *vb.* scatter seed.
broaden *vb.* make or become broader.
broccoli *n.* hardy variety of cauliflower.
brochure *n.* pamphlet or booklet.
brock *n.* a badger.
broke, broken *vb.* past and past part. of **break**.

bronchitis *n.* inflammation of the windpipe, resulting in coughing, wheezing and shortness of breath.

Brontë Sisters
Charlotte (1816–55), Emily (1818–48), and Anne Brontë (1820–49) were three sisters who are all famous as writers. They lived in Haworth in Yorkshire, England. Emily's only novel is *Wuthering Heights*. Charlotte's *Jane Eyre* was an instant success. Anne's best known book is probably *The Tenant of Wildfell Hall*.

brontosaurus *n.* a giant dinosaur which lived 150 million years ago.
► Now most commonly known as apatosaurus, brontosaurus was one of the largest animals that ever lived. Fully grown it was more than 65 ft. (20 meters) long and weighed more than 35 tons.

Brontosaurus fed on plants. It had a long neck with a small head and a very long tail. Its brain was very small. It walked on four legs and probably lived in small herds. In this way they would have been able to give each other some protection from the fierce meat-eating dinosaurs which may have attacked them.

People once thought that the brontosaurus lived in swamps and rivers but now it is thought that it lived on dry land. It used its long neck to reach up and pull leaves off the treetops to eat. Because brontosaurus was so big it must have eaten about 1,102 lb. (500 kg) of food a day.

bronze *n.* a reddish-brown metal made from mixing copper and tin.
► Bronze can be hammered or shaped into many things. Early craftsmen of the BRONZE AGE used it to make swords and tools which were much sharper and stronger than the flints they replaced. Bronze Age people also made pots, armor and jewelry from bronze.

Because bronze is so hard and longlasting it is also used to make coins. The Greeks and Romans were among the first people to make bronze coins.

Bronze is also used to make statues. It may be beaten into shape or cast by heating it until it melts and pouring it into a mold. Bronze statues which are kept in the open air often become green. This coating stops the bronze from rusting and the statues may last a long time.

Bells are usually cast from bronze. They have a much better sound than bells made from other metals. Guns used to be made from gun metal, which is bronze with zinc added.

Very strong kinds of bronze are used in modern engineering and electrical industries. One type of bronze used is phosphor bronze, made with tiny amounts of phosphorus.

A bronze horse bit from Luristan, in the Zagros mountains of Iran. It probably dates from between the 10th and 7th century B.C. Bronze still has a number of practical applications–very strong kinds of bronze are, for instance, used in modern engineering and electrical industries.

Bronze Age the time between the Stone Age and the Iron Age when people made weapons and tools of bronze.
► Bronze was first made in the countries at the eastern end of the Mediterranean in about 3000 B.C. It took another thousand years to reach Europe.

Bronze changed the lives of the STONE AGE people in Europe, for with bronze they could make better tools and weapons much more quickly.

The Bronze Age people used their new tools to make other objects more quickly from bronze. These included pots, shields, helmets and ornaments. Soon, Stone Age huts were replaced by towns and people began to build palaces and temples.

The Bronze Age lasted until about 800 B.C. when iron – an even more useful metal – started to be used in Europe. But bronze was still used in England 400 years later, and for hundreds of years after this in Scotland and Ireland.

brooch (rhymes with *coach*) *n.* a piece of jewelry that is pinned onto clothing.
brood *n.* birds hatched at the same time. *vb.* sit on eggs; meditate deeply; worry about.
brook *n.* a small stream.
broom *n.* 1. a brush with a long handle. 2. yellow-flowered shrub.
broth *n.* a thin soup.
brother *n.* a son of the same parents as someone; member of a religious order, trade union, etc.
brought *vb.* past of **bring**.
brow *n.* the forehead; top of a hill in a road. **browbeat** *vb.* bully.
brown *n.* & *adj.* the name of a dark color between black and orange; the color of earth.
brownie *n.* 1. a small friendly elf. 2. a junior Girl Scout.

Brown, John
John Brown (1800–1859) was an abolitionist whose attempts to free the slaves helped to start the Civil War. His home in Pennsylvania was a station in the "underground railroad," a secret network of people who helped escaped slaves fleeing to Canada.

In an attempt to start a slave rebellion in Virginia, he and 18 followers raided a government arsenal at Harper's Ferry in October 1859. Brown was captured and sent to trial. He was convicted and hanged in December 1859. He is commemorated in the song "John Brown's Body."

Bruce, Robert
Robert Bruce (1274–1329) was crowned Robert I of Scotland in 1306. He defeated the army of Edward II at the Battle of BANNOCKBURN in 1314, thus gaining complete control of Scotland from the English. There is a story that Bruce once received encouragement from watching the efforts of a spider to climb up its thread.

Brueghel
This is the name of a family of Flemish painters of the 1500s and 1600s. The best known is Pieter Brueghel the Elder (1525–69) whose superb series of pictures of the seasons shows his skill as a fine landscape painter. He also painted scenes of country life.

bruise (*brooze*) *n.* a blue-black mark on the skin caused by an injury, a fall, etc. *vb.* inflict bruises.

Brunel, Isambard Kingdom
I.K. Brunel (1806–59) was probably the greatest British engineer of the last century. He built several famous bridges and much of the Great Western Railway. Brunel also built three great passenger liners: the *Great Western*, the *Great Britain* (the first large ship to be built entirely of iron) and the *Great Eastern*.

brush 1. *n.* implement with bristles for sweeping, smoothing hair, cleaning teeth, etc. *vb.* use a brush. 2. *n.* fox's tail.

Brussels
Brussels is the capital of BELGIUM. It is also the headquarters of the European Economic Community (EEC). Brussels has many fine old buildings, museums and art galleries which include the church of St.

Gudule and the Grand Place, a market square in the center of the city.

brute *n.* an animal; unkind person. **brutal** *adj.* inhuman; unfeeling; merciless.

bubble *n.* a thin skin of liquid filled with a gas.

buccaneer *n.* a pirate who plundered Spanish ships in America in the 17th and 18th centuries.

► Buccaneers were sailors who roamed the east coast of the Americas and the CARIBBEAN Sea, then called the Spanish Main, in the 1600s and early 1700s. At that time the Spanish ruled much of America. They took gold and treasure back to Spain in GALLEONS. The pirate ships lay hidden in small island shelters waiting for treasure ships to sail past. These buccaneers also raided towns on shore and people lived in dread of them.

Buchanan, James

James Buchanan (1791–1868) was Democratic President from 1857 to 1861. He had a moderate policy on the slavery issue, but his efforts to make peace between the North and the South were unsuccessful.

Bucharest

Bucharest is the capital of ROMANIA. Situated on the River Dimbovita, it was founded in the 1300s. Bucharest, which today is largely a modern city, was occupied by Germany in both world wars.

buck 1. *n.* a male deer or rabbit. 2. *vb.* (of a horse) kick up the heels.

bucket *n.* an open container with a handle, often used for carrying water.

Buckingham Palace

The London residence of the British royal family, at the west end of St. James's Park, originally built as Buckingham House in 1703–5.

buckle *n.* & *vb.* a fastener, usually on a belt or strap; to fasten with a buckle.

bud *n.* a young flower or leaf before it opens. *vb.* sprout buds.

► A bud is an undeveloped shoot of a PLANT. There are two kinds of bud: flower buds and leaf buds. If the covering of the bud is peeled off, the tightly packed flowers or leaves can be seen inside. Some buds are eaten as food. These include asparagus, brussels sprouts and globe artichokes.

Budapest

Budapest is the capital of HUNGARY. It consists of the two towns of Buda and Pest on opposite banks of the Danube River. They were united to form a single city in 1873.

Budapest once formed part of the Turkish Empire. It then became one of the two capitals of Austria-Hungary. Much of the old city was destroyed in World War II (1939–45). In 1956, Russian troops moved in to put down an uprising against the Communist rulers of the country.

Buddha (Buddhism *n.* Buddhist *n.* & *adj.*)

The word Buddha means "Enlightened One". This name is given to great teachers of the Buddhist religion.

The first Buddha was Siddhartha Gautama. He was born about 563 B.C. in northern India. For most of his life he traveled round India teaching people. Buddha taught his followers that the only way to true happiness was to be peaceful and kind to other people and animals, and avoid evil.

Like the HINDUS, Buddhists believe that after they die they are born again as an animal or human being. If they are very good, they are not born again but live in a kind of heaven called Nirvana.

Saffron-robed Buddhist monks chant before a reclining statue of the Buddha in a temple in Thailand.

budge *vb.* move slightly; shift.

budgerigar *n.* a brightly colored Australian bird, similar to a small parrot.

► Budgerigars fly together in large flocks and eat mainly grass seeds. People in Australia often keep budgerigars as pets in cages. Many budgerigars can be taught to speak, though, of course, they do not understand what they are saying!

budget *n.* financial statement or forecast of revenue and expenditure for a specific period. *vb.* (for) allow for in a budget.

Buenos Aires

Buenos Aires is the capital of ARGENTINA. With a population of 9 million, it has more people than any other city in South America. Buenos Aires is a very modern city and one of the leading ports in the Americas. Its name means "fair winds" in Spanish. Buenos Aires was named by the Spanish navigators who entered the harbor in the 1500s and called it after their patron saint of fair winds.

Although Buenos Aires is the chief port of Argentina, it is 125 miles (200 km) from the sea on the estuary of the Plate river. The broad harbor has been dug out, or dredged, to make it deep enough for seagoing ships. The port sends grain, wool, meat, leather and livestock all over the world.

buffalo *n.* in Asia, a kind of wild ox; in North America, a bison.

► The buffalo is a large relative of the COW. The Asian buffalo originally came from India where it has been used as a work animal for many centuries. Today the buffalo is used to plow and pull loads all over the Far East and also in Syria, Turkey, Hungary and the Balkans. It is often called the water buffalo because it loves to wallow in the mud by the side of rivers, or at water holes. The water keeps off flies and keeps the animal cool.

Another kind of buffalo lives by the swamps and rivers of central and southern Africa. It is wild and has never been tamed by man. This buffalo can be very dangerous and will charge without warning. The North American BISON is often called a buffalo but it is not really a close relative.

buffet (*buff*-**fay**) 1. *n.* refreshment bar; meal set out on a table from which people help themselves. 2. *vb.* & *n.* (**buff**-*ut*) strike, knock about.

bug *n.* one of a group of insects with a mouth that can prick and suck.

bugle *n.* a musical instrument, usually made of brass or copper, similar to a trumpet but without the stops, and mainly used for military calls or signals.

build (rhymes with *milled*) *vb.* make something by putting different parts together. *This bird builds its nest from twigs and feathers.* **building** *n.* a structure with roof and walls.

► Early people built with the materials they found around them – stones, branches, mud and turf. In Europe, poor people usually lived in houses made of wattle and daub. Wattle was a wickerwork of branches, and this was plastered over with a "daub" of wet mud. When this hardened it made quite a strong wall.

Because in some areas certain materials were easily available, buildings look quite different in different places. Where there was plenty of clay, people built with bricks; where there was plenty of limestone or sandstone, people built their houses with those.

Today, houses being built everywhere look very much the same. Large buildings have a framework of steel girders or reinforced CONCRETE which takes all the weight of the building. The walls can be light and there can be plenty of windows.

A Chinese house of about 3000 B.C. It is made of earthen walls and clay and a straw-covered roof supported inside by wooden pillars.

building site *n.* the place where a building is being built.

built *vb.* past of **build**.

bulb *n.* 1. an electric lamp. 2. the roundish underground stem of some plants, like onions.

► Many plants, such as tulips, daffodils and onions, grow from bulbs. The bulb is the underground part of the plant where food is stored during the winter months. When the plant has finished flowering, the bulb begins to grow under the ground. Then the leaves above the ground wither away, leaving only the bulb. It is made up of fleshy scales packed tightly together. The scales feed the bud as it grows.

Bulgaria (Bulgarian)
Bulgaria is a country in Eastern Europe. It belongs to a group of countries which are all Communist. In these countries much of the land and most industries are owned by the government.

In the north are the Balkan Mountains. To the east is the BLACK SEA, a favorite vacation resort. In the center of Bulgaria is a big valley with many farms. The farmers grow fruit, flowers, vegetables, grain and tobacco. There are also many factories and mines in Bulgaria.

AREA: 42,826 SQ. MILES (110,912 SQ. KM)
POPULATION: 8,880,000
CAPITAL: SOFIA
OFFICIAL LANGUAGE: BULGARIAN

bulky *adj.* large and clumsy.

bull *n.* a male of the cattle family or a male elephant.

bulldog *n.* a breed of muscular, short-haired English dog.

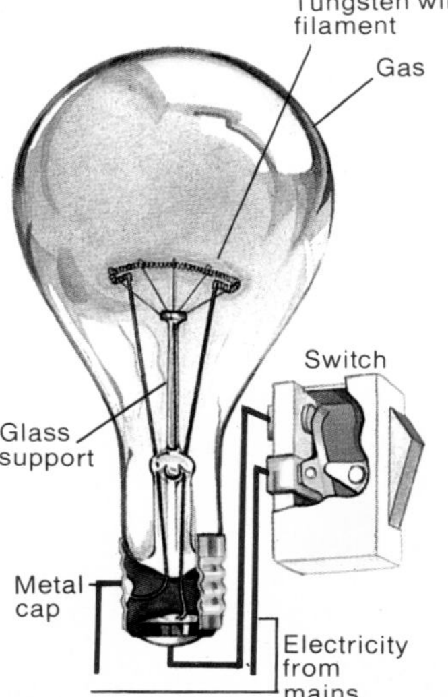

When electricity reaches the filament in an electric light bulb, it makes it so hot that it glows with light.

bulldozer *n.* a heavy tractor for clearing land.

bullet *n.* a piece of shaped metal made to be shot from a handgun.

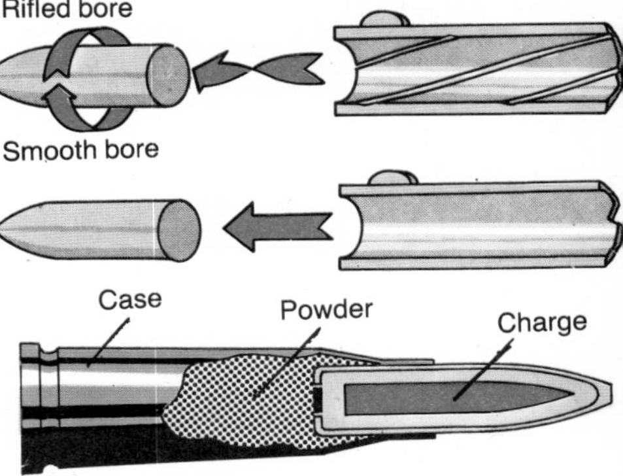

Rifling (spiral grooves) around the inside of a barrel causes a bullet to spin as it leaves the gun and helps the bullet to fly more directly.

bullion *n.* bars of gold or silver before being turned into coins, medals, etc.

bullock *n.* castrated bull.

bully *vb.* & *n.* a person who uses his or her strength to frighten other, weaker people.

bulrush *n.* a tall plant that grows near water.

bumblebee *n.* a large hairy bee that hums noisily.

bump 1. *vb.* knock into something. *n.* a collision, a jolt. 2. *n.* a lump or swelling.

bumper 1. *adj.* large or abundant. *A bumper crop of wheat.* 2. *n.* the bars or fenders that protect the front and back of a car.

bun *n.* a kind of small round cake or bread roll.

bunch *n.* a number of things of the same kind together, like a *bunch of grapes*. *vb.* make into a bunch.

bundle *n.* a number of things wrapped up together. *vb.* tie into a bundle.

bungalow *n.* a house with all its rooms on the ground floor.

bungle *vb.* blunder; do something awkwardly.

bunion *n.* a lump or inflamed swelling on the big toe.

bunk *n.* a narrow bed fixed to the wall, often one above the other.

Bunyan, John
John Bunyan (1628–88) was an English writer and preacher. His most famous book, *The Pilgrim's Progress*, is an allegory and tells the story of one man's journey in search of God. Bunyan fought in the English Civil War. He was put in prison twice for expressing his religious views. While in prison he wrote *Grace Abounding*.

Buoys come in many different shapes, sizes and colors. They also have different lights and sounds.

buoy (**boo**-*ee*) *n.* an anchored float marking a channel or a reef for ships. **buoyant** *adj.* apt to float; cheerful.

► Buoys are floating signposts for sailors and are used for NAVIGATION. Buoys are anchored in the sea, especially near land or in places where there are many ships.

Some buoys show sailors the channels where the water is safe for ships to pass through; others show where there are hidden rocks, sandbanks or wrecks under the water.

Most buoys have flashing lights so they can be seen at night. They may also have whistles or bells to warn ships in fog.

burden *n.* & *vb.* a load; difficulty to bear.

burglar *n.* a person who breaks into a house to steal. **burglary** *n.* **burgle** *vb.*

burial *n.* burying of a dead body; a funeral.

buried *vb.* past of **bury**.

Burke and Wills

Robert O'Hara Burke (1820–61) and William John Wills (1834–61) were the leaders of an expedition which set out in 1860 to cross Australia from south to north. They succeeded, but died on the way back from a combination of poor organization and bad luck.

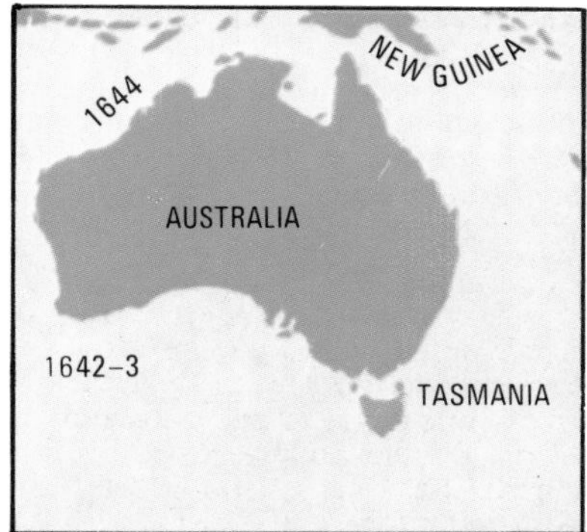

Burkina Faso *see* **Upper Volta**

Burma (Burmese)

Burma is a country in Southeast ASIA. It has mountains, forests and rivers. The biggest river is the Irrawaddy which is 1,290 miles (2,080 km) long. Most of the people are farmers. They grow rice, teak, rubber and jute. Most Burmese follow the Buddhist religion. Britain took Burma between 1823 and 1855, making it a province of India. It became independent in 1948.

AREA: 261,232 SQ. MILES (676,552 SQ. KM)
POPULATION: 35,211,000
CAPITAL: RANGOON
CURRENCY: KYAT
OFFICIAL LANGUAGE: BURMESE

burly *adj.* large and sturdy.

burn 1. *vb.* (past and past part. **burnt, burned**) destroy or damage something by fire. *n.* injury or mark caused by burning. 2. *n.* (*Sc.*) a brook; stream.

Burns, Robert

Robert Burns (1759–96) was the most famous Scottish poet. He came from a poor farming family. Burns wrote many well-known poems and songs in the Scottish dialect or speech. They include *Auld Lang Syne*, *Holy Willie's Prayer*, *The Cotter's Saturday Night*, *To a Mouse*.

burrow *n.* a hole made in the ground by an animal as a home. *vb.* make or live in a burrow.

burst *vb.* break apart suddenly, or explode. *The balloon burst with a loud bang.*

burst in or **into** *vb.* rush in. *Jane burst into the room.*

Burundi

Burundi is a small, landlocked republic in east central AFRICA.

However it has a large population for its size. Bounded on the west by Lake Tanganyika, most of the country is high, grassy plateau. Most of the people work on the land. First a German and then a Belgian colony, Burundi became a republic in 1966.

AREA: 10,747 SQ. MILES (27,834 SQ. KM)
POPULATION: 4,293,000
CAPITAL: BUJUMBURA
CURRENCY: BURUNDI FRANC
OFFICIAL LANGUAGES: FRENCH, KIRUNDI

bury *vb.* put something in the ground; hide away.

bus *n.* a motor vehicle for carrying large numbers of people (short for "omnibus" – a Latin word meaning "for all").

bush *n.* a shrub; a small thick tree.

bushman *n.* a native of the southern African deserts.

► Long ago Bushmen lived in many parts of Africa. They were pushed into the deserts when other Africans and Europeans spread into southern Africa.

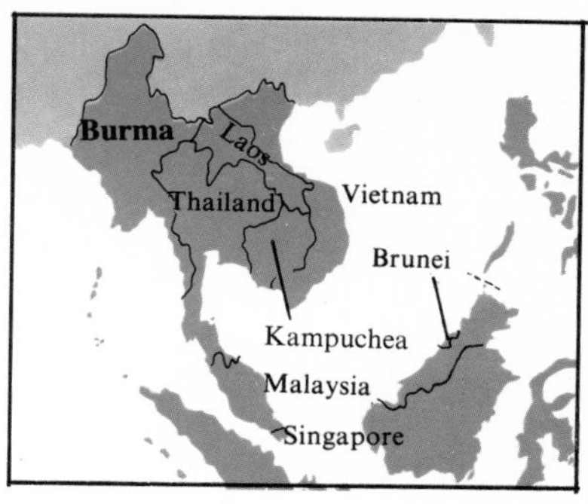

Bushmen are small, gentle people. They live together in groups, or bands, of families. These bands travel around the desert looking for food and water. Often they stop and camp, building small houses of branches and grass.

Bushmen live by hunting and by picking wild vegetables, nuts and fruit. Sometimes they have to walk a long way before they find food, water and wood for their fires. Bushmen children do not go to school. They are taught by their parents and other people in their band. Bushmen have their own religions and languages.

business (**biz**-*ness*) 1. *n.* a shop or organization. 2. *n.* a person's work or occupation. *My father's business is running a bookshop.*

bust *n.* 1. a statue of a person's head and shoulders. 2. a woman's breast. 3. *adj.* (*slang*) bankrupt; penniless. *They all lost their jobs when their company went bust.*

bustle *vb.* hurry (or make others hurry) about. *n.* excited activity.

busy (*bizzy*) *adj.* having a lot to do.

but *conj.* however; on the other hand.

butcher *n.* a person who kills or cuts up animals to sell their meat.

butler *n.* head manservant in a household.

butt *vb.* to hit with the head.

butter *n.* a soft, yellow food made from fats contained in cream. *vb.* spread butter.

► Butter is a fat made from cream. Cream from MILK is first cooled and then the germs are killed by pasteurizing it (see PASTEUR). The

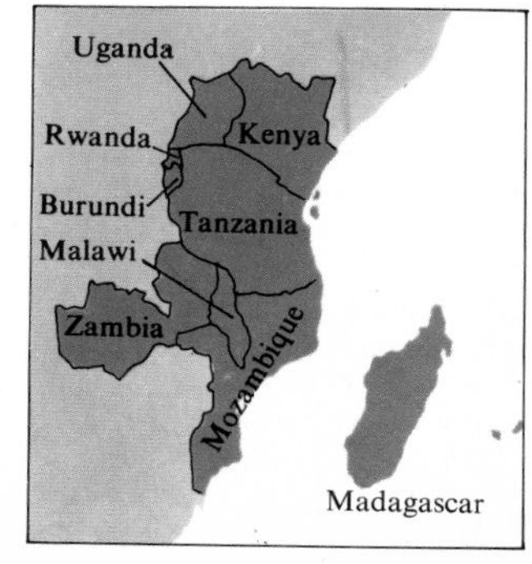

An ivory carving which may be of the Bzyantine empress Irene (752–803). The Byzantine empire was at its greatest under the emperor Justinian (527–565). His general Belisarius conquered Sicily, Italy and parts of North Africa.

cream is then put into a machine called a churn which moves the cream about until it turns into butter. In some countries such as India the butter is nearly liquid. Indian butter is called ghee.

buttercup *n.* a small wild flower with yellow petals.

butterfly *n.* an insect with large colorful wings. Unlike the moth, it flies during the daytime.

► Butterflies are flying INSECTS. There are about 12,000 kinds of butterfly. They are related to MOTHS. They live in most parts of the world. They are found even as far north as the Arctic circle.

Butterflies have many colors and sizes. One of the smallest, the dwarf blue of South Africa, has a wingspan of only 0.5 in. (14 mm). The largest, the Queen Alexandra birdwing, has a wing-span of 11 in. (28 cm).

All butterflies begin their lives as CATERPILLARS which hatch from eggs. The caterpillars spend their lives eating the plant they were hatched on. They change their skins several times as they grow. When a caterpillar is fully grown it changes into a chrysalis with a hard skin, inside which it changes into an adult butterfly. When it is ready, the butterfly breaks out and flies away to find a mate and lay eggs of its own.

Some butterflies migrate. They fly from one part of the world to another at certain times of the year. One of the most famous migrating butterflies is the monarch butterfly of North America. In the summer it lives all over the United States, Canada and Alaska. In the fall, the butterflies gather together in groups. They fly south to Mexico, Florida and southern California for the winter. Sometimes thousands of monarchs are seen flying together. In spring, they can be seen flying north again.

buttock *n.* one of the two fleshy parts of the bottom or backside.

button *n.* a small round object, made of plastic, leather, horn, etc., which is used for fastening clothes.

buttress *n.* a prop or support built against a wall. *vb.* support, strengthen.

buy *vb.* (past **bought**) purchase something; obtain goods in exchange for money.

buzz *vb.* make a noise like a bee.

buzzard *n.* the name of a family of birds of prey related to the falcon.

by *prep.* along; through; during; as a result of. *Little by little. By the way. By force.*

by-election *n.* an election held to fill a vacancy caused by death or resignation.

bystander *n.* a spectator.

byre *n.* cow shed.

Byron, Lord

Lord Byron (1788–1824) was an English Romantic poet who wrote several long narrative poems. The finest is *Don Juan*, a lighthearted criticism of society of the time. Byron left England in 1816 to help the Greeks rebel against the Turks. Byron died in Greece.

Byzantine Empire

In A.D. 330 Constantine the Great moved the capital of the Roman Empire from Rome to Byzantium (modern ISTANBUL). He renamed the city Constantinople. In A.D. 395, the Empire collapsed, but the Eastern, or Byzantine, Empire survived. During the reign of Justinian I, the general Belsarius temporarily reconquered much of Italy. In 1453, Constantinople was finally captured by the Turks.

The Byzantine Empire was a great center of learning and culture. It is famous for its architecture and art, particularly its MOSAICS. The most famous building is the beautiful church of Santa Sophia.

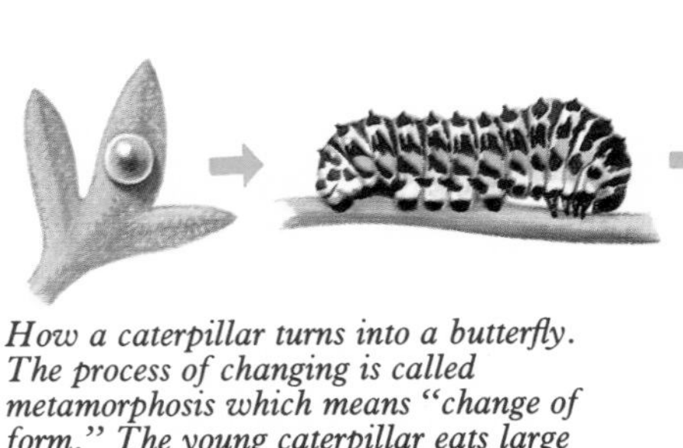

How a caterpillar turns into a butterfly. The process of changing is called metamorphosis which means "change of form." The young caterpillar eats large amounts of plant material. From time to time it sheds it skin to show a larger shape underneath. Eventually the new skin has a different shape and hardens into the case of a pupa or chrysalis. Inside the pupa the butterfly develops, appears, and flies away.

Inveraray Castle – home of the Dukes of Argyll.

cab *n*. 1. a taxi. 2. the part of a truck or locomotive in which the driver sits.

cabbage *n*. a vegetable with thick green leaves growing very close together.

► Cabbage leaves can be eaten raw, pickled or cooked. There are many varieties, and they may be green, white, or red. They grow in cool moist climates. Some ripen in spring and summer. Others are only ready to be eaten in winter.

cabin *n*. 1. a room in a ship or aircraft. 2. a hut; a simple house.

cabinet *n*. 1. a cupboard or similar piece of furniture. 2. the senior members of a government.

cable *n*. 1. a strong wire or rope; a bundle of telegraph wires. 2. an overseas telegram. *vb*. send a message by cable.

cackle *vb*. & *n*. noise made by a hen; silly talk; foolish laughter.

cactus *n*. (plural **cacti**) a prickly desert plant with a thick green stem.

► Although there are dozens of different cacti, they all have one thing in common: they are able to grow in hot desert climates. Cacti can do this because they store water in their fleshy stems. They are covered with prickly spines instead of leaves. The spines protect the plant's store of water from the desert animals.

caddie *n*. a person who carries clubs for a golfer.

caddy *n*. a small tea container.

cadet *n*. a young person studying to become a member of the armed forces or the police.

cadge *vb*. beg; take advantage of someone's generosity.

Caesar, Julius see **Julius Caesar**.

café (*caf*-**fay**) *n*. a place where food and drink is sold; a small restaurant.

cage *n*. a box with bars in which birds or animals are kept. *vb*. keep in a cage.

Cairo

Cairo is the capital of EGYPT. One of the biggest cities in Africa, it lies on the banks of the NILE. Nearby are the PYRAMIDS and the great statue of the SPHINX. The site of modern Cairo is thought to have originally been a town founded by settlers who came from ancient BABYLON.

cake *n*. a sweet kind of food made from flour, butter, eggs, sugar, etc., and baked in an oven; a hard mass (of soap, etc.).

calamity *n*. a disaster, terrible misfortune.

A barrel cactus

calcium *n*. a metallic chemical element (symbol – *Ca*) present in many rocks and minerals such as limestone and gypsum. Calcium is also present in teeth and bones.

calculate *vb*. work out with math, reckon. **calculation** *n*. **calculator** *n*. an electronic machine for doing mathematics.

► Modern electronic calculators work at very high speeds. In a few seconds they can do as much as a mechanical calculator could do in a year. The first ever mechanical calculator was built in 1642 by a French scientist called Pascal.

Calcutta

Calcutta is the state capital of West Bengal, in northeastern INDIA. Situated on the Hooghly River, it is India's chief port. Calcutta contains many parks and fine buildings, but there is also much overcrowding and terrible poverty. Calcutta and its suburbs have a population of 9,165,600, which makes it one of the world's largest cities. Calcutta was founded in 1687 by the East India Company. It was the capital of British India from 1772 until the headquarters was moved to DELHI in 1912.

calendar *n*. a list of the days, weeks and months of the year.

► Calendars were first used in ancient Babylon. There have been many different ways of keeping track of the days, months and seasons of the year. The one we use today is called the Gregorian calendar, named after Pope Gregory XIII who introduced it in 1582. It divides the year into 365 days, with every fourth year (the "leap year") having 366 days.

C

calf (rhymes with *half*) (plural **calves**) *n.* 1. a young cow, seal, elephant or whale. 2. the fleshy back part of the leg below the knee.

Calgary
Calgary is the oil center of Canada. It is in Alberta in the foothills of the Rockies and is an important transportation and cattle center. It is famous for the annual Calgary Stampede, which has rodeo events, horse racing and livestock shows. Calgary was founded in 1883.

California (*abbrev.* **Calif.**)
California has more people than any other state of the U.S.A. In 1950 it had just over 10 million people. Today its population is more than 22 million. The state grew so quickly because people kept pouring into it from other states to work in industries such as electronics and aircraft. They also arrived because of the warm southern Californian winters.

California is a big state. The eastern wall of the state is the Sierra Nevada Mountains. California's largest cities are LOS ANGELES, San Diego, SAN FRANCISCO, and San Jose. The capital is Sacramento.

The first group of American settlers came to California in 1841, when it still belonged to Mexico. The United States and Mexico went to war in 1846, and when peace was declared in 1848 Mexico agreed to hand over California to the U.S. In 1850 California became the 31st state of the U.S.A.

call *n.* & *vb.* 1. shout, cry out; summon. 2. speak to on the telephone. 3. name. 4. pay a short visit. **caller** *n.*
call for *vb.* 1. demand. *The committee called for reforms.* 2. go and fetch. *I shall call for you on my way to the match.*
calligraphy (*kal*-**ig**-*raf-ee*) *n.* handwriting as an art.
calling *n.* profession; occupation.
call off *vb.* decide not to do something that has been arranged. *The game was called off because the field was flooded.*
calm (rhymes with *palm*) *adj.* quiet, smooth. *vb.* soothe, make or become calm. *n.* stillness.
calorie *n.* a unit of heat. Calories are also used as a measure of the energy produced by food and drink. A person on a diet may need to count the calories in his or her food intake.
calve *vb.* give birth to a calf.

Calvin, John (Calvinism. Calvinist *n.*)
Johannes Calvinus is the Latin form of the name of Jean Chauvin (1509–64). Brought up in France as a Roman Catholic, Calvin became a Protestant. He moved to Geneva in Switzerland, and developed a strict set of rules for living. Followers of Calvin are called Calvinists. In Scotland they are known as Presbyterians.
calypso *n.* West Indian song.
Cambodia see **Kampuchea**

Cambridge, U.K.
The City of Cambridge is a university town in eastern England. The exact date of the founding of the university is disputed, but it was probably about A.D. 1200. Peterhouse, the oldest college, was founded in 1284. Cambridge is a small but attractive city, with many fine college buildings on the banks of the River Cam, or Granta.

Cambridge, U.S.A.
Cambridge is a city in eastern MASSACHUSETTS. It is now a suburb of BOSTON. Situated on the Charles River, Cambridge is the home of Harvard University and the Massachusetts Institute of Technology.

came *vb.* past of **come**.
camel *n.* an animal with a long neck and one hump or two on its back.

► Camels are one of the few creatures that can stand up to extreme heat and still do work carrying heavy loads. They are ideally suited for the job of making long journeys across deserts. Their wide padded feet grip well on loose sandy ground. They are powerful and swift and can go for days without eating or drinking, living off the fat stored in their humps. Camels will eat almost anything. Besides eating the thorny shrubs and thistles found in the desert, they will chew their way through tent cloth, mats and even baskets.

camellia *n.* evergreen shrub with beautiful rose-like flowers.
camera *n.* an instrument for taking photographs.
► Modern cameras work in much the same way as the box cameras of a hundred years ago. A shutter opens for a fraction of a second – just long enough to let light from the scene being photographed pass through the glass LENS to fall on the film. The light forms a reversed image of the scene on the film. The film is then treated with chemicals (developed). The image on the piece of developed film is printed onto a special type of paper. The result is a photograph.

Today, most cameras have a lot of different parts to help us to take photographs in many kinds of light, close up or far away.

Cameroon
Cameroon is a republic in west-central AFRICA. The south of the country is covered by tropical rain forest. The north has open grassland. Most people work on the land, but there is also some mining. The first Europeans to reach Cameroon were the Portuguese. The country later became a German colony. After the World War II, it was divided between Britain and France. Cameroon became independent in 1961.

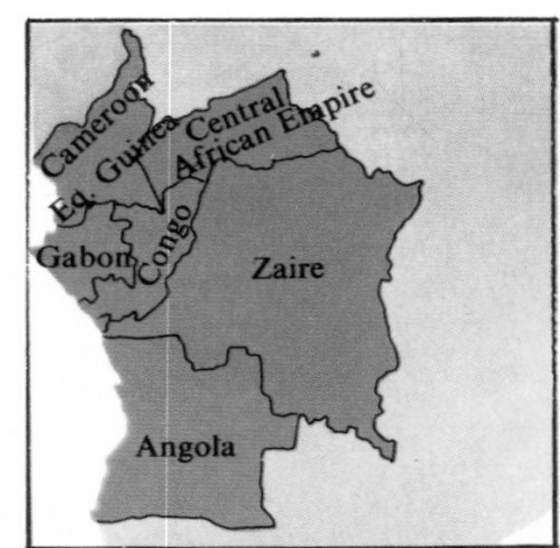

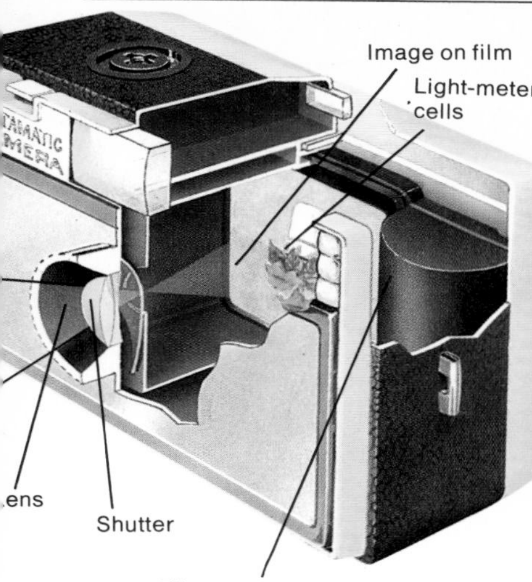

AREA: 183,579 SQ. MILES (475,422 SQ. KM
POPULATION: 8,804,000
CAPITAL: YAOUNDÉ
CURRENCY: FRANC CFA
OFFICIAL LANGUAGES: FRENCH, ENGLISH

camouflage *vb.* & *n.* disguise of guns, ships, aircraft, and so on with paint, tree branches, or nets so that they cannot easily be seen.
camp *n.* a place where people stay in tents or huts. *vb.* to live in a tent.
campaign *vb.* & *n.* a series of military or political operations, an organized program.
campus *n.* grounds of a college or university.
can 1. *vb.* be able to. *Can you run faster than me?* 2. *vb.* be allowed to. *You can come and go as you like.* 3. *n.* a metal container; a tin.

Canada (Canadian)
The second biggest country in the world, Canada covers an area of nearly 4 million sq. miles (almost 10 million sq. km).

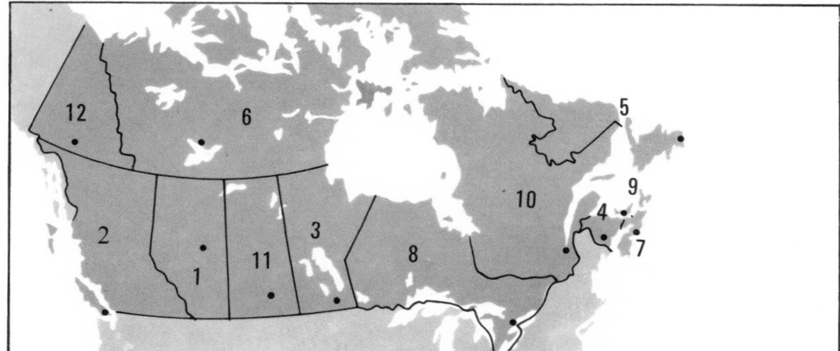

In the ARCTIC, Canada reaches almost as far north as Greenland. To the south, it extends to the same LATITUDE as southern France. The distance from the Pacific coast in the west to the Atlantic in the east is farther than from North America to Europe. But, in spite of its size, two-thirds of the population of Canada live in a narrow belt of land no more than 120 miles (about 200 km) from the United States border. Most Canadians speak English, but many speak French (Quebec is almost entirely French-speaking).
Canada is a country of many different kinds of land. The west of the country is mountainous. The highest peak in the ROCKY MOUNTAINS soars to almost 20,000 ft. (6000 meters). By contrast, much of the northern part of the country is covered with endless forests and dotted with lakes. The great central plains are given over to pasture land and wheat farming. Farther east are the GREAT LAKES, five huge inland seas that empty into the St. Lawrence river. Many people live along its fertile valley, and the great cities of Toronto and Montreal are found here. The federal parliament consists of a Senate and a House of Commons. The Head of State is Queen Elizabeth II.
AREA: 3,852,019 SQ. MILES (9,976,139 SQ. KM)
POPULATION: 23,673,00
CAPITAL: OTTAWA
CURRENCY: DOLLAR
OFFICIAL LANGUAGES: ENGLISH, FRENCH

PROVINCES AND TERRITORIES

	Province or territory	Capital
1	Alberta	Edmonton
2	British Columbia	Victoria
3	Manitoba	Winnipeg
4	New Brunswick	Fredericton
5	Newfoundland	St John's
6	Northwest territories	Yellowknife
7	Nova Scotia	Halifax
8	Ontario	Toronto
9	Prince Edward Is.	Charlottetown
10	Quebec	Quebec
11	Saskatchewan	Regina
12	Yukon Territory	Whitehorse

canal *n.* a man-made waterway for barges or for taking water to fields.
► Canals have been in use for thousands of years. In ancient Egypt and Babylon they were used to irrigate farmland. One of the oldest canals still in use is the Grand Canal of China. It was opened in the A.D. 600s.
Until the 1500s, canals could only be built across flat country. With the invention of canal locks, they could be built across high ground too. The locks allowed boats to sail over hills by lifting them in a series of steps from one level to another.
Early canals could only be used by narrow, shallow-bottomed boats. These boats were pulled along by horses that walked on tow paths running alongside the canal. Modern canals like the SUEZ CANAL and the PANAMA CANAL are big enough to let ocean liners pass through them.

canary *n.* a small yellow, singing bird which is often kept in a cage as a pet. *adj.* color of a canary.
► In the wild, the canary is a native of the Canary Islands in the Atlantic Ocean. Its original color is a yellow-green, but there are now many breeds, with widely different colors and markings.
Canaries are among the most popular of all caged birds. Their lively, cheerful song and their ability to copy tunes and words make them ideal pets. In the past, canaries were taken down into mines to detect poison gases. They are very sensitive to gas. Even small amounts cause them to become groggy and fall off their perches.

Canary Islands
The Canaries are a group of mountainous islands off the north-west coast of AFRICA. They belong to SPAIN. The main ports are Santa Cruz de Tenerife and Las Palmas de Gran Canaria. Two of the most important industries are tourism and fishing.

canasta *n.* a card game of the rummy family.

Canberra
Canberra is the capital of AUSTRALIA. It is a small city whose main, and almost sole, activity is government.
Canberra was founded in 1908 by an act of the Australian parliament. At this time, Australia was governed from Melbourne. A site for the new city was chosen in New South Wales, and it was built from nothing soon after World War I. All the major departments of government have their headquarters here. There is also a university.

cancel *vb.* cross out; bring to an end; call off. *The football game was canceled.* **cancellation** *n.*
cancer *n.* a name given to a variety of serious diseases; a disease of the body cells; a growth or tumor.

C

candid *adj*. outspoken, sincere, frank. **candor** *n*.
candidate *n*. a person who seeks election or appointment; a person who takes any examination.
candle *n*. a stick of wax with a string or wick through the middle.
► In ancient Egypt, candles were made by dipping a wick made of reeds or vegetable fiber into melted animal fat or beeswax. Beeswax and animal fat were used for thousands of years, until the 1800s when candles made from paraffin wax and *stearine*, a manufactured fat, became common. The flame from these candles was much less smoky and they gave a far brighter light.

candlestick *n*. a holder for a candle.
candy *n*. crystallized sugar; sweets.
cane *n*. the hollow, jointed stem of large reeds and grasses such as bamboo, used to make walking sticks and furniture; walking stick. *vb*. beat with a cane.
canine *n*. of or belonging to a dog.
canister *n*. small box for holding dry products such as tea.
cannibal *n*. a human being who eats human flesh.
canning *n*. a way of preserving food by heating and sealing it in airtight containers. The heat kills any germs in the food. The airtight containers keep out bacteria that make it spoil.
► Canning was invented in 1810 by a French cook, Nicolas Appert. He won a prize for finding a way to keep meat and vegetables fresh and tasty for months.

Today, canning is the most widely used way of keeping food. Billions of glass, metal and plastic containers are made every year to hold everything from drinks to baby food, meat and fish.

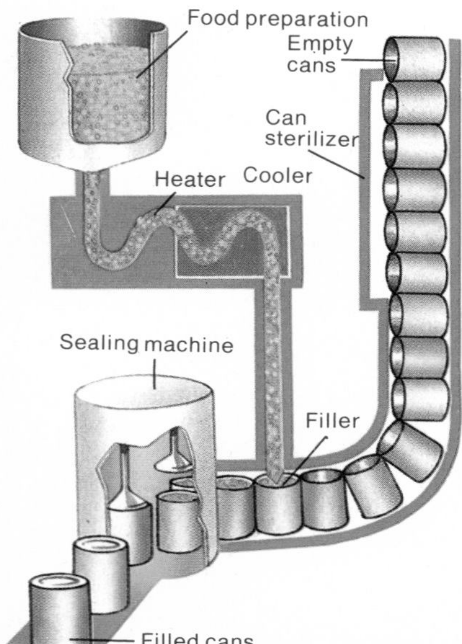

How food is packed in cans.

Cannons were first used at the Siege of Metz in 1324. At first firearms were often a greater danger to the users than their targets.

cannon *n*. a big, heavy gun.
canny *adj*. shrewd.
canoe (*can*-**oo**) *n*. a light boat that is paddled through the water.
► Canoes have been in use since the STONE AGE. The earliest type of canoe was made from a hollowed-out log. The Indians of North America made their canoes from the bark of trees. They were light enough to be carried on land by one man, but strong enough to support a heavy load in water. The Eskimos made canoes from animal skins stretched over a frame of bone or wood. Modern canoes have a wooden frame covered with water-proofed canvas. They are also made of light metal or fiberglass.

canon *n*. 1. a church dignitary. 2. a church decree, rule.
canopy *n*. a covering over a throne, bed, etc.
canteen *n*. restaurant in factory or office.
canter *vb*. & *n*. an easy gallop on horseback.
cantor *n*. a choir leader, often of the Jewish faith.

Canterbury
Canterbury is a cathedral and university city in Kent, in south-eastern England. The present cathedral replaced earlier buildings and was completed in about A.D. 1500. The Archbishop of Canterbury is the senior priest of the Church of England. A former archbishop, Thomas à Becket, was murdered in the cathedral in 1170.

canvas *n*. a coarse cloth used for tents and sails. Artists paint on it.
canvass *vb*. go to people and ask them to vote for your political party, etc. *We shall canvass for John Smith.*

canyon *n*. a deep gorge, usually cut through rock by a river.
cap *n*. 1. a soft hat with a peak at the front. 2. a lid.
capable *adj*. able; competent.
capacity *n*. ability; the amount that can be held in something.
cape *n*. 1. a coat with no sleeves, worn over the shoulders. 2. a piece of land that juts out into the sea.

Cape Horn
Cape Horn, on Horn Island, is the southern tip of South America. It was probably sighted by Drake in 1578, and was named by a Dutch expedition in 1616. Cape Horn is noted for severe storms, and "rounding the Horn" has always been a dangerous undertaking in sailing ships.

Cape Town
The port of Cape Town is the capital of Cape Province, SOUTH AFRICA. It is South Africa's legislative (law-making) capital, and contains the Union Parliament. Situated at the foot of Table Mountain, the city was founded as a supply base by the Dutch in the 1600s.

capital *n*. 1. the city where the government of a country works. 2. letters written like this: A, M, R, Z. 3. money with which business is started; accumulated wealth in stocks or shares, etc.
capsize *vb*. overturn, especially in a boat.
capstan *n*. apparatus for winding in cables, etc.
capsule *n*. 1. a small cylindrical case containing medicine. 2. part of a spacecraft.
captain *n*. 1. the officer in charge of a ship. 2. an army officer below a major and above a lieutenant.
caption *n*. the words near a picture which explain what it is.
captivate *vb*. fascinate, charm.
captive *n*. a prisoner.
capture *vb*. take someone prisoner.

Capybara
The capybara is the largest of all the RODENTS. It lives on South American river banks and can be up to 4 feet (1.2 meters) long. It looks like a large guinea pig.

car *n*. a motor vehicle.
caramel *n*. burnt sugar used as a flavoring; a kind of toffee.
carat *n*. a measure of weight for precious stones; also used as a measure of the purity of gold.
caravan *n*. 1. a home on wheels, pulled by a car or horse. 2. a group of people traveling together across a desert.
carbon *n*. a nonmetallic element that is found in all living things, both plant and animal. (symbol – *C*).
► Carbon occurs naturally as soot, charcoal, graphite and diamond. These *allotropes* – physically different

forms – all have the same chemical properties. Soot and charcoal are known as *amorphous* carbon. This means that they have no definite shape or form. Amorphous carbon consists of tiny fragments of graphite crystals. Graphite is soft because its atoms are joined together by weak bonds. The strong bonds between the carbon atoms of diamond make it the hardest substance known. There are more compounds of carbon than of all the other elements put together. The study of carbon compounds forms the branch of CHEMISTRY described as *organic*.

carbon dioxide *n.* a gas (symbol – CO_2) that occurs in small quantities in the atmosphere. People and animals breathe in oxygen and breathe out mainly carbon dioxide.
carbon monoxide *n.* a very poisonous gas (symbol – *CO*) with no smell, which is present in car exhaust fumes.
carburetor *n.* apparatus in internal-combustion engines for mixing air with gas vapor for combustion.
carcass *n.* dead body of an animal.
cardboard *n.* extra-thick card or paper.

Card games
Playing cards probably originated in China. They seem to have reached Europe in the 1300s. There are numerous card games, including Solitaire (for one player), Whist and Bridge (for four players) and Poker. Tarot cards are different from ordinary playing cards, and are used for fortune-telling.

cardiac *adj.* of the heart.

Cardiff
Cardiff (Caerdedd) has been the capital of Wales since 1955. During the 1800s it was the main port of the South Wales coal industry. Cardiff is the home of the University College of South Wales. Cardiff Castle is built on the site of a Roman fort.

cardigan *n.* a knitted woolen jacket.
cardinal *n.* 1. a senior priest in the Roman Catholic Church. 2. a red American songbird.
care *n.* anxiety, concern, serious attention. *vb.* feel concern, anxiety; affection for.
career 1. *vb.* go fast and perhaps dangerously. 2. *n.* the series of jobs or positions that people have during their working life. *He has spent his whole career as a teacher.*
care for *vb.* look after someone; love someone.
careless *adj.* not thinking about what one does.
caret *n.* mark (λ) showing where missing word should be placed in writing.
cargo *n.* (plural **cargoes**) goods carried by ship or aircraft.

Caribbean
The Caribbean Sea is part of the ATLANTIC OCEAN. It is bounded by the West Indies, Central America and South America. The Caribbean was named after the CARIB INDIANS.

Carib Indians
The Carib Indians were living in the CARIBBEAN area when CHRISTOPHER COLUMBUS landed. They had moved to the islands from the mainland of South America. They almost died out after the arrival of the Europeans, and only a handful survive today. The word "cannibal" comes from the Spanish name of this people, who ate their victims.

caribou *n.* wild reindeer of North America.
caricature *n.* an exaggerated or distorted drawing of someone which makes them appear ridiculous or absurd. *Many political cartoons contain caricatures.*
caries (rhymes with **bear**-*ease*) *n.* decay of tooth.
carnation *n.* a large, brightly colored flower, related to the garden pink.

Carnegie, Andrew
Andrew Carnegie (1835–1919) was a Scottish-born industrialist. He made his fortune in the United States as a steel manufacturer. He used his great wealth to found libraries and for many other educational, artistic and peaceful purposes.

carnival *n.* a public occasion for making merry. *In New Orleans there is a famous carnival called Mardi Gras.*
carnivore *n.* an animal that eats meat.
► Carnivores are a group of MAMMALS that feed mainly on the flesh of other animals. They do not, however, include birds of prey or people.

Although carnivores mostly live on meat, they will sometimes eat insects and plants. But what they all have in common is a set of very powerful jaws for chopping up their food, deadly curved claws for tearing, and long sharp teeth for seizing, stabbing and killing their victims.

Carnivores include CATS, DOGS, BEARS, RACCOONS, WEASELS and HYENAS. All have good eyesight, smell and hearing and are fast, intelligent and skilled at hunting down other animals. Some carnivores, such as wild dogs and hyenas, hunt in packs. In this way they can kill animals much larger than themselves. Other carnivores, such as the LEOPARD and the JAGUAR, hunt alone.

carol *n.* a kind of song, usually religious, and sung at Christmas.
carp 1. *n.* large freshwater fish. 2. *vb.* find fault.

carpenter *n.* a person who makes things from wood.
carpet *n.* heavy floor covering of woven or knotted material.
► As long as 2,000 years ago, handwoven woolen carpets were being made in Turkey and the Middle East. But until the 1500s, they were very rare in Europe. In those days people put their carpets on walls and over tables rather than on the floor.

Today, most carpets are machine-made of wool, cotton or synthetic fibers. One type of carpet WEAVING is called Wilton – the pattern is woven separately with loops of wool onto the main weave of the carpet. Another type is Tufted – the pile is sewn into a woven backing. The loops are then cut in order to make a soft pile.

carriage *n.* vehicle, usually with four wheels, pulled by horses; a coach for passengers on a train.
carrion *n.* the decaying flesh of a dead body.

Carroll, Lewis
Lewis Carroll (1832–98) is the pen-name of an English writer, Charles Dodgson. Dodgson was a mathematics professor at Oxford University, but he is best known for his children's stories. The most famous is *Alice's Adventures in Wonderland* (1865). The story was written for the daughter of a fellow professor at the university. He also wrote *Through the Looking Glass* (1872).

carrot *n.* a plant with an orange-red root which is used as a vegetable.
carry on *vb.* continue doing something.
cart *n.* a two-wheeled vehicle pulled by a horse, ox or other animal.

Carthage
A great Phoenician trading center founded in the 700s B.C. on the north coast of Africa near present day Tunis. Carthage dominated the western Mediterranean in the 600s B.C. but eventually clashed with the growing power of Rome. The three Punic Wars were fought between Rome and Carthage, resulting in the final destruction of Carthage in 146 B.C.. It was during the Second Punic War that Hannibal, the Carthaginian general, made his famous crossing of the Alps with his elephants and marched on Rome.

Cartier, Jacques
Jacques Cartier (1491–1557) was a French explorer. He made three voyages to CANADA in search of the NORTHWEST PASSAGE. In 1535 he sailed up the St. Lawrence River as far as the site of modern Montreal. Later French claims to Canada were largely based on Cartier's explorations.

C

cartilage (**car**-*till-ij*) *n.* a material in the body similar to bone but lighter and more flexible. *You have pads of cartilage in your knee joints.*
cartography *n.* art of making maps or charts.
carton *n.* cardboard box.
cartoon *n.* a funny drawing, often of people in politics. **cartoonist** *n.*
► A cartoon is a drawing that makes its own point, often humorous, and is often accompanied by a caption. The word cartoon also refers to a film made up of a number of drawings to provide animation. Perhaps the most famous cartoon animator was Walt DISNEY, who revolutionized the cartoon film technique. His cartoon characters Mickey Mouse and Donald Duck became popular all over the world.

cartridge *n.* the case holding the explosive that fires a bullet.
carve *vb.* 1. shape a piece of wood or stone. 2. cut up meat to serve at a meal.
cascade *n.* waterfall. *vb.* fall like a cascade.
case *n.* 1. a box for carrying things or storing them. 2. an example; an instance. *There was a case of whooping cough in the class.* 3. a trial in a law court. *The man and woman in the case were found guilty.*
cash *n.* money in paper notes and coins. *vb.* exchange a check for money.
cashier *n.* the person who takes in and pays out money in a shop, hotel or other business.
cashmere *n.* wool from goats of Kashmir.
casino (*ka*-**seen**-*o*) *n.* public building for gambling.
cask *n.* a wooden barrel, often used for wines or spirits.
casket *n.* small case for jewels; coffin.

Caspian Sea
The Caspian Sea is the world's largest inland body of water. Most of it lies within the U.S.S.R. The southern shore is the northern border of IRAN. The Volga is the most important river flowing into the Caspian. There is no outlet. Because of the loss of water through evaporation, the sea is shrinking.

casserole *n.* vessel in which food is both cooked and served.
cassette *n.* a container for holding magnetic tape used for recording.
cassock *n.* long robe, usually black, worn by clergymen.
cassowary *n.* a large flightless bird of New Guinea and Australia related to the ostrich and emu.
cast 1. *vb.* throw or fling. 2. *vb.* give parts in a play. 3. *n.* an impression or mold, generally done in plaster. *The police made a cast of the footprint.* **casting** *n.*
► Casting is a way of making different shapes out of metal, plastic and plaster. In the "lost wax" method, a model of the shape is first made in wax. Then it is covered with wet clay. When the clay is heated, the wax melts and runs out through a drain hole. Now the molten metal is poured into the mold. When the metal is cool and hard, the clay mold is broken and the metal casting is taken out.

castanets *pl. n.* small wooden instruments held in the hand and clicked as accompaniment to dance.
castaway *n.* a person left on a distant land, often after the ship has been wrecked.
castle *n.* a large building with thick walls, fortified against attack.
► One of the few places where kings and lords in the MIDDLE AGES could feel safe was behind the thick stone walls of their castles. There, they and their men could fight off attacks by roving bandits and sit out long sieges by invading armies.
As castles developed they became larger and more comfortable. Instead of having all the living quarters crowded into the main keep, small "villages" of huts and buildings sprang up inside the castle walls.
Castles had high, thick stone walls. A wall-walk ran right around the top, and through each tower. Soldiers could run from one point of attack to another without ever showing themselves to their enemies.
The rounded towers could stand up to battering rams and hurled rocks much better than square ones. The towers also jutted out from the main wall. This let the defenders fire on the attackers from three sides and stopped them from reaching the foot of the castle walls.

For hundreds of years – until the coming of gunpowder – a castle was the safest place in time of war.

castrate *vb.* remove the testicles so that a mammal cannot mate and reproduce.

Castro, Fidel
Fidel Castro (1927—) became prime minister of CUBA in 1959. Previously he had been leader of the guerrilla force that overthrew President Batista. Under Castro, Cuba became a Communist country, and relies on help from the U.S.S.R.

casual *adj.* accidental, by chance. *A casual meeting.* informal. *Casual manners.*
casualty *n.* a person who is ill or injured. In warfare, casualties are soldiers who have been killed or wounded.

The tiger, cheetah and domestic cat are all members of the same family.

cat *n.* a small furry domestic animal; any member of the cat family.
► A cat belongs to a group of MAMMALS called the feline family (*felidae*). Although the cat family range in size from domestic breeds to TIGERS, they all have many things in common. Cats have short, rounded heads, long face whiskers, sharp teeth that serve as deadly weapons for grabbing and biting their prey to death, and powerful claws. All cats except the CHEETAH can pull their claws back into a sheath of skin when they are not in use. Their long tails help them balance and make them superb at jumping and climbing. LIONS and cheetahs live in families. All other cats live mostly alone.

catacombs *pl. n.* underground cemeteries containing passageways and crypts for burial of the dead.

catalog (**cat**-*a-log*) *n.* a list of things, such as the pictures in an exhibition or the books in a library.

catalyst (**cat**-*a-list*) *n.* a substance that speeds up a chemical reaction but is left unchanged and so can be used several times for the process of catalysis.

catamaran *n.* a boat with two hulls joined together.

catapult *n.* 1. a Y-shaped stick with a piece of elastic fixed to it. *A catapult is used for throwing small stones.* 2. an ancient weapon for throwing large stones. 3. a device for launching aircraft from an aircraft carrier.

cataract *n.* 1. a waterfall. 2. a condition of the eye, affecting vision.

A medieval catapult which shot a huge stone with enormous force.

catarrh *n.* a runny nose; a cold in the head.

catastrophe *n.* a sudden and widespread disaster.

catch 1. *n.* the lock or fastening of a door. 2. *vb.* get hold of something or someone, perhaps after a chase. 3. *vb.* get a disease or illness. *I hope you don't catch my cold.*

category *n.* class or order of something.

caterpillar *n.* the larva stage in the growth of a butterfly or moth.
► When a butterfly or moth egg hatches, a small caterpillar crawls out and starts to eat. The caterpillar soon grows too big for its skin, which bursts open and the caterpillar wriggles out, wearing a new skin. The wormlike creature has several new skins before it changes into a *pupa*. Some caterpillars live for only a few days before they begin to change into a butterfly or moth, but most stay in this form throughout the warm season.

cathedral *n.* the main church of an area (diocese) in which a bishop or archbishop has his *cathedra* (Latin for "chair").

catkin *n.* the hanging, fluffy flower of the hazel, willow and some other trees.
► Many trees have FLOWERS. On some broad-leaved kinds the flowers take the shape of small green or brownish tails. These are called catkins. Birch, oak and willow trees all have catkins.

Catkins hang in clusters. They appear early in the year before all the leaves are out. This is important. It allows the wind to spread their POLLEN before the leaves get in the way.

There are male and female catkins. The males carry pollen and the females carry SEEDS. Male catkins are usually bigger than the females and they are coated with yellowish pollen. The wind blows it onto the females to fertilize their seeds.

cattle *pl. n.* heavily built grass-eating mammals which include all oxen and cows.
► Wild cattle are all horned and include the BISON, BUFFALO and YAK. Domestic cattle are descended from the *auroch*, a wild species that once lived in Europe but is now extinct. Cattle were first domesticated some 6,000 years ago. They have become indispensable to us and are kept all over the world for their meat and milk, and other products including leather, glue and soap. Cattle eat about 150 lb. (68 kg) of grass a day and digest it in an odd way. Their stomachs have four parts: the grass is swallowed whole and stored in the first part; next, it goes into the second part to be softened and turned into balls called cud; the cud is sent to the mouth for chewing, then goes back to the third part and is finally digested in the fourth.

Caucasus
This mountain range in the U.S.S.R. extends about 745 miles (1,200 km) between the Black and Caspian seas, forming a boundary between Asia and Europe.

caught *vb.* past of **catch**.

cauliflower *n.* a kind of cabbage, whose tightly bunched flowers form whitish heads.

cause (rhymes with *saws*) 1. *vb.* make something happen. *My dog was the cause of the accident.* 2. *n.* a principle or ideal to which a person or group of persons is devoted. *Freedom is a noble cause.*

causeway *n.* a raised path through marshland or water.

caution 1. *n.* care; carefulness. *Proceed with caution.* 2. *vb.* warn (especially of the police).

cavalry *n.* soldiers who fight on horseback.

cave *n.* an open chamber in the side of a hill or under the ground.
► A cave is formed when slightly ACID waters flow or seep through LIMESTONE rocks. The water dissolves the rock, sometimes leaving behind a whole network of caves, like a huge decaying cavity in the earth.

After a cave has been formed, water may go on dripping through the walls and ceiling. This often results in odd-shaped deposits known as STALACTITES and STALAGMITES.

caveman *n.* a prehistoric human who lived in caves.
► What we usually mean by cavemen are people who were the ancestors of modern people. Caves are natural places for shelter from the weather and from wild animals. They were some of the first dwelling places used by human beings.

The mouth of a cave is often dry and it is possible to build a fire inside when the weather is cold. In hot weather, caves give shelter from the sun. Also, with walls all around them, the cavemen could fight off dangerous animals from the cave mouth. The remains of ancient cave dwellers have been found in sites all around the world – in China, southern Asia, Europe and Africa. Here, bits and pieces of their tools and weapons have been dug up along with bones of the animals they hunted. Remains of their fires have also been found. Deep toward the back of the caves, graves of cave people have been unearthed. From all these things, archaeologists have been able to piece together a great deal about the way of life of these people of long ago.

caviar *n.* the eggs, or roe, of certain species of fish, especially the

C

sturgeon, prized as a delicacy.
cavity *n.* hole, space within a solid body.

Caxton, William
In the 1400s, PRINTING was just becoming known in Europe. William Caxton (*c.* 1421–91) was the man who brought the new invention to Britain.

Caxton learned the art of printing in Belgium and Germany. In 1476 he set up a wooden press in England and the next year produced the first printed book there. In all, Caxton printed about 100 books, of which about a third can still be seen today. These include editions of the work of CHAUCER.

cease *vb.* stop.
cedar *n.* a large, spreading, evergreen coniferous tree.
cede (*seed*) *vb.* surrender, give up.
ceiling (*seeling*) *n.* the roof of a room.
celebrate *vb.* hold a party or other festivity in honor of an important event. **celebration** *n.*
celebrity *n.* famous, celebrated person.
celery *n.* a vegetable plant. It is the crisp stalk-like leaves that are eaten.
cell *n.* 1. a small room in a monastery, convent, or prison.
2. a very small unit of living matter in animals and plants.
► A single living cell can be seen only under a MICROSCOPE. Even a tiny bit of human skin contains millions of them.

Cells are usually round in shape. A few are spiraled and some, like nerve cells, have sprawling treelike branches.

In 1665, a scientist called Robert Hooke looked at a piece of cork under a microscope and saw that it was made up of many tiny compartments. He named them cells and this term has been used ever since.

cellar *n.* an underground room for storing things.
cello (*chello*) *n.* a stringed instrument like a large violin. **cellist** *n.*

A cello – a member of the violin family.

cellulose *n.* the substance that gives plants their rigidity or stiffness.
► Cellulose is found particularly in such substances as cotton, straw and wood. Cellulose forms the basis of textiles and paper, and is used in plastics and explosives.

Celsius *adj.* another name for centigrade scale on a thermometer, named after its inventor, Anders Celsius.

Celts (Celtic)
The Celts were an ancient people of northwestern Europe. At one time, over 2,000 years ago, they lived all over Britain, France and part of Spain and Germany. In about 400 B.C. they even crossed into Italy and attacked Rome.

The Celts were tall, fair and very warlike. They lived in tribes made up of a chief, nobles, free men and slaves. The tribes often fought each other. They were good metalworkers and liked to decorate their weapons and armor with bright designs and curious creatures. And they were gifted musicians and poets. The Celtic religion was known as Druidism, and their priests were called DRUIDS.

When the armies of the Roman empire spread out, many Celts fled to remote regions. In the lands they had once conquered the Celtic way of life was soon lost. It was only in the far-off corners of Europe that their language and way of life survived.

Celtic speech was very common in Ireland, Cornwall, Wales, Scotland and Brittany until a few hundred years ago. Today, although less common, Celtic speech can still be heard. Irish and Scottish Gaelic and Welsh are Celtic languages. The Celtic people of Scotland were known to the Romans as the Picts.

cement *n.* a gray powder that, when mixed with water, becomes hard.
► Cement is a very important building material. It is the ingredient which binds CONCRETE. Cement is made by roasting a mixture composed largely of limestone and clay, and then crushing it to a fine, gray powder. When water is added it forms a sludge-like mass which quickly sets rock hard.

Cement is seldom used by itself. Mixed with sand it forms the mortar used to bind one brick to another. Mixed with sand and larger pieces of stone it forms the concrete used to build skyscrapers, bridges and dams.

Cement has been used since ancient times. The Greeks and Romans used a kind of mortar which was stronger than the mortar used in the Middle Ages. The most common type of modern cement is called Portland cement. It was invented in the early 1800s.

cemetery *n.* a place (not a churchyard) where people are buried.
cenotaph *n.* monument to persons buried elsewhere.
census *n.* a counting of all the people in a country.
► Most countries hold a census regularly. The United States has one every 10 years. Among the facts that a census finds out are how many men and women live in the country, what ages they are, where they live and what they earn.

The taking of a census is a very complex affair. Usually every household in a country has to fill in a census form, and computers sort out the results. Governments use the results of censuses to help them decide future policies.

cent *n.* an American, Australian, Canadian or New Zealand coin. *There are 100 cents in a dollar.*
centaur *n.* an imaginary creature, half man and half horse.
► In Greek mythology there were a number of creatures that were part human and part animal. Along with the mermaids, the best known were the centaurs.

From the waist up, centaurs had the bodies of men. Below, they had the body and legs of horses. They were fierce, cruel and warlike. The most famous of the centaurs was Chiron. He was known for his skill with weapons, but he was also a great healer.

centenary *n.* a hundredth anniversary. *It was the centenary of the great writer's birth.*
center (rhymes with *enter*) *n.* the middle part or point of something.
centi- *prefix* meaning 100 or one hundredth.
centigrade scale *n.* a temperature scale on which water freezes at 0° and boils at 100° (symbol – **C**).
► This scale for measuring the temperature of things was invented by a Swedish scientist, Anders Celsius, in 1742. (It is often called the Celsius Scale, after its inventor.) It is a very simple system and is the most widely used. The centigrade scale is divided into 100 degrees. Zero degrees is the temperature at which water freezes. One hundred degrees is the boiling point of water.
centimeter *n.* a metric measure of length. *There are 100 centimeters in a meter.*

This line is 3 centimeters long.

centipede *n.* a wormlike creature with a long body and many legs.
► Centipedes are long wormlike creatures. Their bodies are made of many parts, or sections. Under each section they have a pair of clawed

A centipede.

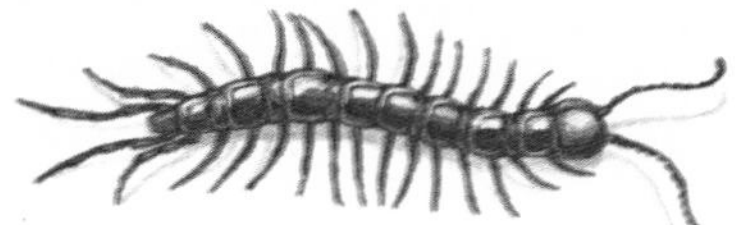

legs. The head has long feelers, powerful jaws, and two stinging claws that are able to inject poison into their prey. Centipedes are found all over the world. They feed mainly on worms, insects and snails.

Millipedes have two pairs of legs under each section. They eat plants and are harmless to humans although they may cause damage to crops.

central *adj*. at or near the center. *Andy lives in central Birmingham.*

Central African Republic
The Central African Republic is a land-locked country lying just north of the equator. Most of the people are farmers. Formerly part of the French Equatorial Africa, it became independent in 1960.
AREA: 240,549 SQ. MILES (622,984 SQ. KM)
POPULATION: 2,086,000
CAPITAL: BANGUI
CURRENCY: FRANC CFA
OFFICIAL LANGUAGE: FRENCH

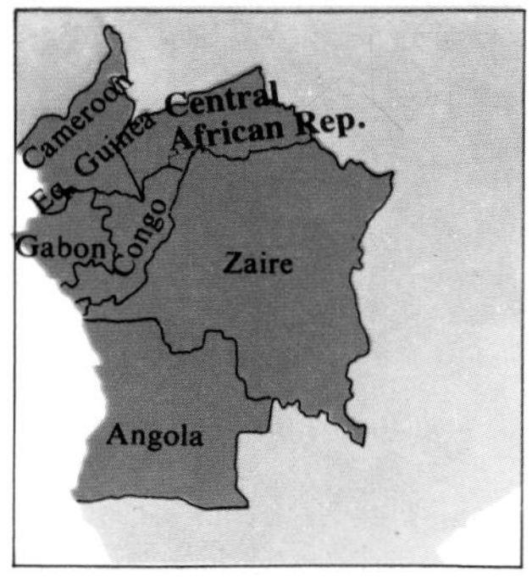

Central America
Central America is the name of the neck of land between MEXICO and COLOMBIA that joins North and South America. It is divided into seven small countries: GUATEMALA, BELIZE, HONDURAS, EL SALVADOR, NICARAGUA, COSTA RICA and PANAMA.
THE PANAMA CANAL, which links the Atlantic and Pacific oceans, is controlled by the U.S.A. There are plans for a Pan-American Highway through Central America. This road system, when completed, will link the U.S.A. and CANADA to the countries of South America. The region's greatest wealth comes from its mines, and plantations.

centrifugal force *n*. an outward force produced by a body rotating in a circle.
► If you swing a ball around you on the end of a string, the ball feels as if it is trying to fly off. If it is not securely tied, it *will* fly off. The force acting on it is called *centrifugal* force. The force of the string in preventing it flying off is called *centripetal* force.

A centrifuge is a machine that can separate heavier liquids from lighter. The heavier a liquid, the stronger the centrifugal force that operates it. When the mixture is spun around, the heavier liquid is thrown to the outside of the container. This principle has many uses, for example, separating cream from milk.

centurion *n*. a Roman soldier in command of a *century* (100 men).

A Roman centurion.

century *n*. 1. 100 years. 2. a company of soldiers in ancient Roman army. 3. a group of 100 like things.
ceramic *n*. & *adj*. concerning pottery or **ceramics** *pl.n.*
cereal *n*. grain crops such as corn, rice or wheat used for food; breakfast food made from grain.
► Cereals are the seeds of a group of plants that belong to the GRASS family. Throughout history they have been the most important of all types of food. In ancient times, cereals were collected from wild plants. Later, when they began to be grown on farms, they became the most important food of early civilizations.

Some cereals, such as RICE and corn, are eaten in their natural form. Others, such as WHEAT and rye, are ground into flour before being baked or cooked. Cereals are also used to make alcoholic drinks and to feed farm animals.

ceremony *n*. a dignified occasion; religious rite. *The wedding ceremony took place in an old church.* **ceremonial** *adj*. with ceremony, formal.
certain *adj*. 1. sure. *I am certain they will come soon.* 2. some. *Certain people are color blind.* **certainty** *n*.
certificate *n*. a piece of paper that is proof of something. *Nicola was given a certificate to show she had swum five lengths of the pool.*
certify *vb*. declare officially.

Cervantes, Miguel de
Miguel de Cervantes (1547–1616) was a Spanish writer. He is best known for his novel *Don Quixote de la Mancha* (pronounced Don *Ke-ho-tay*). This book tells the story of an elderly knight who lives in a fantasy world of giants and castles. He is accompanied by Sancho Panza, his faithful servant. Cervantes uses the story to make fun of some of the romantic books of his time.

Cervantes himself had an adventurous life, and suffered many misfortunes. He served as a soldier, and was wounded in the great sea battle of Lepanto in 1571. He was later captured by pirates and sold into slavery. He was imprisoned several times. He dictated part of *Don Quixote* to a fellow prisoner.

Ceylon see **Sri Lanka**

Cézanne, Paul
Paul Cézanne (1839–1906) was a French painter who created still-lifes, landscapes and portraits in which he tried to show the solid shape of objects by the use of colors and tones.

Chad
Chad is a country in northcentral AFRICA. It gets its name from Lake Chad in the west. Chad was formerly a French colony. It achieved full independence in 1960. Since then there has been much fighting between rival political groups.
AREA: 495,782 SQ. MILES (1,284,000 SQ. KM)
POPULATION: 4,714,000
CAPITAL: N'DJAMENA
CURRENCY: FRANC CFA
OFFICIAL LANGUAGE: FRENCH

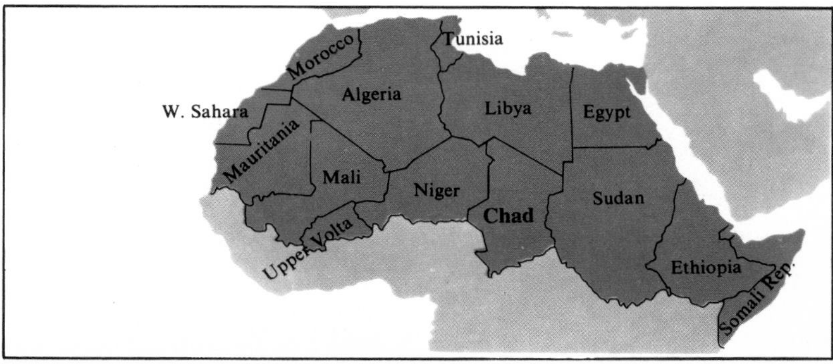

C

chaff 1. *n.* husks of corn which need to be separated from the grain. 2. *vb.* make fun of someone (now slightly old-fashioned).

chaffinch *n.* small songbird.

chain *n.* a line of rings joined together. *The rings in a chain are called "links."*

chair *n.* a piece of furniture for sitting on.

chairman *n.* a person who presides over a meeting. Also **chairwoman** and **chairperson**.

chalet (*shall*-**lay**) *n.* Swiss house of wood with overhanging roof.

chalk *n.* a kind of soft white rock; white material used for writing on a blackboard.

► Chalk is a pure white, soft and crumbly form of LIMESTONE. Land that is rich in chalk is found in parts of North America, the south of England, and in France.

Most chalk was formed between 135 and 65 million years ago. It is made up of the crushed shells of countless tiny sea creatures. When these creatures died their shells built up in thick layers at the bottom of warm, shallow seas. As the shape of the earth's surface changed, these layers were lifted out of the seas.

We usually think of chalk as something that we use to write with, but it is also used in many other ways. Mixed with other things, chalk is used to make paints, medicines, rubber, paper, ink and toothpaste.

challenge *n.* & *vb.* question, as a sentry; question truth of; invite to fight.

chameleon ("*ch*" spoken like *k*) *n.* type of tree lizard living mainly in tropical Africa.

► Chameleons have narrow bodies with a crest along the back, and helmeted or horned heads. The most unusual thing about a chameleon is that it can change the color of its skin to blend in with its background.

Chameleons live in trees. They move very slowly and will sit on branches for hours, as still as a statue, waiting until insects come close to them. They catch insects with a long sticky tongue, which shoots out with such speed that the insects seem to vanish without trace.

A chameleon catapulting out its long sticky tongue to seize its prey.

champagne (*sham*-**pain**) *n.* sparkling white wine.

champion *n.* the overall winner. *vb.* defend, uphold.

championship *n.* a competition to find the best person or team.

chance *n.* a possibility of something happening. *Leroy has a good chance of becoming champion, but Eric has no chance at all.*

chancel *n.* part of church near the altar used by choir and clergy.

chancy *adj.* risky.

change 1. *vb.* make something different. *The girls changed their hairstyles.* 2. *n.* the money given back when you give too much money for something you are buying. *I bought a loaf of bread and the assistant gave me change for my dollar.*

channel *n.* 1. a narrow strip of water joining two seas. 2. a narrow passage, natural or artificial, for water to run through.

chant *n.* & *vb.* recite in a half-singing style; intone.

chaos (**kay**-*oss*) *n.* utter confusion. **chaotic** *adj.*

chapel *n.* a small church, or part of a large church.

chaperon (**shap**-*er-own*) *vb.* & *n.* an older person in charge of a child at parties, etc.

chaplain *n.* clergyman attached to an institution or the armed forces.

Chaplin, Charles

Charlie Chaplin (1889–1977) was one of the most famous comic CINEMA actors of all time. He was best known for his role as the gentle, well-meaning tramp who was always making mistakes and getting into trouble.

Chaplin was born in London, but he spent most of his working life in the United States. He started as an actor on stage, but he became famous for the parts he played in silent films in HOLLYWOOD. He also wrote, directed and produced the films that he made in later years.

Charlie Chaplin – the cinema's comic tramp.

chapter *n.* one section of a book.

char 1. *vb.* to scorch. 2. *n.* a cleaning lady (short for charwoman). 3. *n.* a charred substance.

character *n.* 1. the things that make you the person you are. *Margaret's character was so pleasant that everyone liked her.* 2. one of the people in a book or play. *Little Red Riding Hood is a character in a children's story.*

charade (*sha*-**raid**) *n.* game in which syllables of a word are acted out separately, the whole word being guessed at by the audience.

charcoal *n.* a form of carbon made by heating wood with little air present.

charge 1. *vb.* rush forward and attack. 2. *vb.* ask a certain price for something. 3. *n.* manage, be responsible for. *Simon was left in charge of the department while the manager was out.*

chariot *n.* a horse-drawn vehicle used for fighting and racing long ago. **charioteer** *n.* driver of a chariot.

► Chariots were light, horse-drawn carts. They were used long ago for traveling, hunting and fighting in battles.

The people of ancient Babylon, Egypt and Rome all used two-wheeled chariots that were drawn by teams of two or four horses. Next to the driver rode a heavily armed warrior who was ready to fight with a bow and arrows, a spear, an ax, or a javelin and shield.

charity *n.* help and kindness given to others.

Charlemagne

Charlemagne (A.D. 742–814) was a great military leader. In the A.D. 700s he founded an empire that covered most of western Europe.

In the year A.D. 768, Charlemagne became the king of the Franks, a people who lived in the country we now call France. Through his skill in war he soon took over northern Spain, Italy and Germany. He fought for the Church in Rome, and in return, the POPE crowned him Holy Roman Emperor on Christmas Day, in the year A.D. 800.

Charlemagne wanted to build another ROMAN EMPIRE, but after his death his sons fought among themselves and his empire broke up.

Charles I

Charles I (reigned 1625–1649) is the only British king to have caused his people to rebel and execute their king. Charles believed that he ruled by divine right – that God had appointed him and his family before him to rule. His reign became a struggle with Parliament, principally over money and religion. In 1642 this rift resulted in CIVIL WAR. The King's army was defeated by Oliver Cromwell's New Model Army. In 1649 Charles was tried by a special court, which sentenced him to death for treason and tyranny. He was publicly beheaded in London. Until 1660 the country was a republican Commonwealth, and later became a Protectorate, with Cromwell as Lord Protector.

Charles II
As King of Britain, Charles II (reigned 1660–85) was liked as much as his father was hated. He spent most of his youth in exile in Europe, while CHARLES I fought to save his crown and his life, and lost both.

In 1660, after being ruled by Oliver CROMWELL for 10 years, the English invited Charles II to return and take back the crown. His return marked the start of a period called the Restoration. He was a wise ruler and he was very careful in the way he treated his people and PARLIAMENT.

charm *n.* something that has magic power. *He carried a rabbit's foot charm.* **charming** *adj.* very attractive; delightful.
chart *n.* 1. a sea map for sailors, showing the sea depth, the position of buoys, rocks, etc. 2. information shown by a diagram or graph.
chase *vb.* run after and try to catch.
chasm ("*ch*" spoken like *k*) *n.* wide hollow, gap.
chat *vb.* & *n.* talk in a friendly way. **chatty** *adj.*
château (*sha*-**tow**) *n.* the French word for castle.
chatter *vb.* 1. talk nonstop about unimportant things. 2. (of teeth) rattling together from fear or cold.

Chaucer, Geoffrey
Geoffrey Chaucer (1345–1400) was a great English poet. He was one of the first people to write in English rather than in Latin. His best known work is the *Canterbury Tales*. It is a collection of stories told by an imaginary group of pilgrims as they traveled to Canterbury Cathedral.

chauffeur (*show*-**fur**) *n.* someone paid to drive an employer's car.
chauvinism *n.* exaggerated and blind patriotism; passionate support for a cause.
cheap *adj.* not expensive; low in price (and therefore with a suggestion of poor quality). **cheapen** *vb.* make or become cheap.
cheat *vb.* act dishonestly in order to help oneself. *n.* someone who cheats.
check *vb.* 1. make sure that something is right. *Did you check if all the windows were closed?* 2. stop or hold back for a short time. *He was checked in the goal area, but still managed to shoot. n.* 3. a piece of paper which, when filled in and signed, tells a bank to pay money to someone.
checkers *pl. n.* (U.S.) the game of draughts.
cheek *n.* 1. the fleshy part of your face on either side of your mouth. 2. impudence. **cheeky** *adj.*
cheer *vb.* 1. make happy; comfort. 2. shout joyfully.
cheerful *adj.* looking and feeling happy.
cheese *n.* a food made from milk.
► Most cheese is made from cows' MILK, but it can be made from the milk of goats, sheep, buffalo and even reindeer. To make cheese, the milk is turned sour so that it will *curdle*.

The solid bits, called the *curds*, are taken away from the liquid, or *whey*, and are pressed into a more solid form and dried. The cheese is then left to ripen.

cheetah *n.* a spotted, feline animal found mostly in East Africa. It is the world's fastest mammal.
chef (*sheff*) *n.* a head cook who is in charge of a large kitchen.

Chekhov, Anton
Russian dramatist and short story writer (1860–1904). His four most famous plays are *Uncle Vanya, Three Sisters, The Seagull*, and *The Cherry Orchard*.

chemical (**kem**-*ical*) *n.* a substance used in chemistry.
chemist (**kem**-ist) *n.* a person who is trained in chemistry.
chemistry *n.* a branch of science that is about what substances are made of and how they work together.
► Chemistry is the study of materials – solids, liquids and gases. A chemist finds out what things are made of and how they are joined together. If a piece of wood is burned in a fire, this is a *chemical reaction*. The wood turns to ash and, at the same time, heat and light are given off. It took chemists a long time to find out that burning is the joining together of the wood with the gas oxygen from the air. There are a great many chemical reactions.

The true science of chemistry as we know it began only in the 1600s. Chemists at this time began to find out how chemicals really work. Then they discovered the *elements*, simple substances which make up all the millions of different substances on earth. There are only about a hundred elements, each of them made up of tiny ATOMS. The atoms of elements often join together to make different substances. The salt you put on your food is made up of atoms of the elements sodium and chlorine. An atom of sodium joins with an atom of chlorine to make a *molecule* of salt.

Chemistry is today a very important science, and chemists are employed in a vast number of industries.

cherish *vb.* value highly, treat with affection.
cherry *n.* the small round fruit of the cherry tree.
► The cherry is one of the most favored of all trees. When it blooms it produces a mass of beautiful pink and white blossoms. The cherry belongs to the rose family. There are three main groups of cherry – the sweet, the sour and the Duke, which is a hybrid of the first two.

Sweet cherries need a mild climate, without frost or extreme heat. The fruit can be black, yellow or red, and is sweet when ripe. A good sweet cherry tree can produce hundreds of pounds of fruit each season.

Sour cherry trees are smaller than the sweet trees. They thrive in moderate, rather cool climates. Most of the crop is canned or frozen.

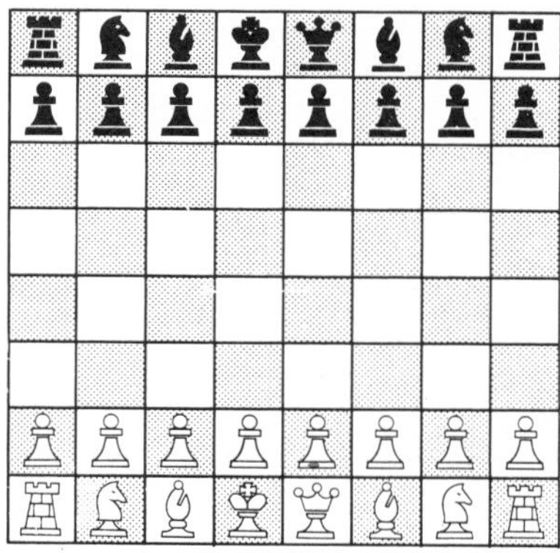

How chess pieces are arranged at the start of a game.

The cherry is sacred to the Japanese. They cultivate the trees for their blossoms alone, and hold festivals when the trees bloom.

chess *n.* a game for two people, each with 16 pieces (chessmen), played on a board of 64 squares.
► Chess is a game that has been played for hundreds of years. Each of the two players has 16 pieces which they line up on either side of the board. Every piece can only be moved around the board in a special way. They are used to attack, retreat, to defend each other, and can be captured and taken out of play. The most important piece for each player

C

is the "king." The game is won when one player manages to capture the other player's king.

chest *n.* 1. a large, strong box with a lid. 2. the upper part of the front of one's body.

chestnut *n.* a large tree with prickly fruits containing shiny, red-brown nuts (chestnuts).

▶ There are two quite different kinds of chestnut trees. We eat the nuts of the sweet chestnut either boiled or roasted, or preserved in sugar as *marrons glacés*. The "nuts" of the horse chestnut are not really nuts but large round seeds.

chew *vb.* crush food in your mouth with your teeth.

chic (*sheek*) *adj.* elegant, very smart.

Chicago

Chicago, ILLINOIS, is the second largest city in the United States. Situated on Lake Michigan, it is the most important of the Great Lakes ports. Its O'Hare International Airport is the busiest in the world.

The arrival of the railroads made Chicago one of the world's largest railroad terminals. People from all over the world came to live and work in the city. The first skyscraper was built here in 1883.

Chicago produces steel, electrical machinery and plastics. The city and its suburbs have a population of over 7 million.

chick *n.* a baby bird.

chicken *n.* a young hen. *adj.* (*slang*) cowardly.

chicken pox *n.* a disease that causes red itchy spots on the skin.

chief 1. *n.* a ruler or leader. 2. *adj.* most important; main. *Farming is the chief industry in many countries of the world.*

chilblain *n.* a painful swelling that sometimes forms on people's hands and feet in cold weather.

child *n.* young person (plural **children**).

Chile (Chilean)

Chile is a long, narrow country in South America. The ANDES mountains divide Chile from ARGENTINA. In the north of the country are hot deserts. Most Chileans live in the milder central zone. The forested south is cool and wet.

Chile was a Spanish colony for about 300 years. It became independent in 1818. It gained its mineral-rich northern provinces in a war with PERU and BOLIVIA in 1879–83. In 1973 a military government came to power.

AREA: 292,274 SQ. MILES (756,945 SQ. KM)
POPULATION: 11,478,000
CAPITAL: SANTIAGO
CURRENCY: PESO
OFFICIAL LANGUAGE: SPANISH

chill 1. *vb.* cool. 2. *n.* a cold or fever. **chilly**. *adj.*

chime *vb.* & *n.* set of tuned bells.

chimney *n.* a structure in a building that allows the smoke from a fire to escape.

chimpanzee *n.* an African ape.

▶ Chimpanzees are the most human-looking of all the APES. Fully grown, they are about 5 ft. tall (1.3 meters) tall and are able to walk upright, although they often use their hands to help push themselves along the ground. Chimpanzees come from the jungles of Africa. They live in family groups and are very fond of their young and take good care of them. They are playful and intelligent animals. Tame chimpanzees have been taught to behave like humans in many ways. They can even learn to talk in sign language.

chin *n.* the lowest part of the face, below the mouth.

china *n.* fine clay baked and glazed, made into plates, cups and so on.

The emperor Kuang-wu, who ruled China in the 1st century A.D.

The Chinese developed the art of making fine porcelain long before anyone else (above right).

China (Chinese)

China is the third biggest nation in the world, and it has a population larger than that of any other country. A fifth of all the people on earth are Chinese – over 1 billion.

To the north and west, China is cut off from the rest of ASIA by great deserts and by the HIMALAYAS. To the east lies the Pacific Ocean and Japan. The Chinese have ruled within this area almost without a break for the past 3,500 years.

The first great Chinese civilization grew up in the large river valleys of the Hwang Ho in the north and the YANGTZE in the south. Today, more Chinese live crowded close to these rivers than in any other part of the country. By far the greatest number of Chinese are farmers. In modern China, the farmers do not own their farms. Each village or commune owns its own land. Everyone works

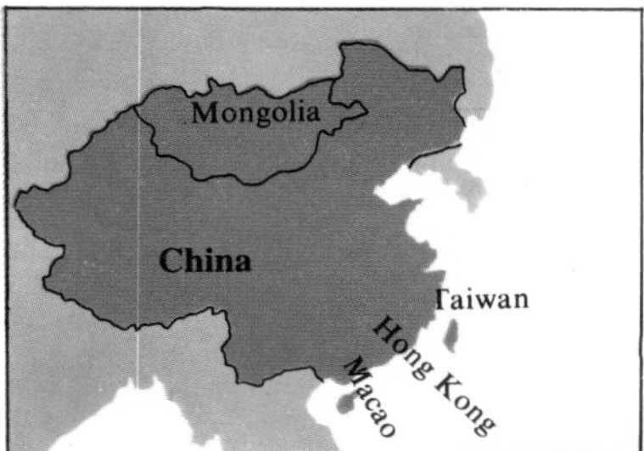

on it together and the harvest is shared out between them.

Hot summers and cool or cold winters with plenty of rainfall all year make the heart of China a very good farming region. But much of China cannot be farmed, and growing enough food for the many people who live there is still a great problem. The main crops that are grown are RICE in the south and WHEAT and millet in the north. Silk, tea and COTTON are also important and there is a large fishing industry.

The biggest cities of China are the great port of Shanghai – near the mouth of the Yangtze – and the Tientsin. The capital is PEKING, a fine old city. For centuries the

Chinese emperors lived in great splendor in the Forbidden City in the center of Peking.

In 1949, China was greatly changed when the civil war which had been raging since the 1920s came to an end. The Communist Party led by MAO TSE-TUNG came into power. Mao Tse-tung persuaded the Chinese people to give up many of their old ways of life. He set out to make China an important industrial center, and today China is as powerful as the other large nations.

AREA: 3,705,610 SQ. MILES (9,596,961 SQ. KM)
POPULATION: 1,008,176,000
CAPITAL: PEKING
CURRENCY: YUAN
OFFICIAL LANGUAGE: CHINESE

Chinchilla
Chinchillas are small RODENTS with soft, gray fur. Most of them are found high in the Andes of South America. The chinchilla is about half the size of a rabbit, with a bushy tail. Its pelts are valued for the luxurious coats they make. About 130 pelts are needed for one coat.

chink 1. *n.* narrow opening, gap. 2. *n.* & *vb.* sound of glasses or coins hitting together.
chintz *n.* glazed cotton cloth printed with flower patterns.
chip *n.* 1. a small piece broken off something. 2. a tiny electronic device, usually made of silicon, that holds a circuit with thousands of transistors.
chipmunk *n.* a small member of the squirrel family.
► Chipmunks are not more than 12 in. (30 cm) in length and they have light and dark colored stripes on their backs. They live in the forests of North America and Asia. They make their homes in holes, or burrows, which they dig under tree roots or rocks. They feed on nuts, seeds and berries.

chipolata *n.* small sausage.
chips *pl. n.* slices of fried potato.
chiropodist (*ki*-**rop**-*o-dist*) *n.* person who treats feet, e.g corns and toenails.
chisel *n.* a sharp tool used for shaping wood, stone, etc. *vb.* cut or shape with a chisel.
chivalry (**shiv**-*al-ree*) *n.* medieval system of knighthood; gallantry, courage, etc.
chive *n.* herb related to the onion.
chlorine *n.* a yellow-green, poisonous, choking gas used in the manufacture of bleach, hydrochloric acid; small quantities are used to kill germs in drinking water (symbol – *Cl*).
chlorophyll ("*ch*" spoken as *k*) *n.* green coloring matter found in plant cells.
► Chlorophyll is found inside plant CELLS in tiny bodies called *chloroplasts*.

Plants need chlorophyll to make their food. Sunlight, falling on the leaves, acts with the chlorophyll to turn carbon dioxide from the air, and water, which the plant's roots suck up from the soil, into food made up of SUGARS and STARCHES. At the same time, the plant's leaves give out OXYGEN. This whole process is called *photosynthesis*.

It is a very important part of life on our earth, as all living things need oxygen in order to breathe.

Plants can produce chlorophyll only when they are grown in the light. Plants kept in darkness often turn white or yellow.

chocolate *n.* food or drink made from the ground and roasted beans from the cacao tree.
► The beans of the cacao tree grow inside pods, which hang from the trunk and the branches of the tree.

To make chocolate, the beans are first roasted, then ground up to give an oily liquid called "chocolate liquor." Other things may then be added to the liquor. The milk chocolate we buy in stores has milk and sugar added to it.

choice *n.* the act of choosing; the thing chosen.
choir (*kwire*) *n.* a group of people trained to sing together.
choke 1. *vb.* not able to breathe because of something in your throat or lungs. 2. *vb.* block something up. 3. *n.* a control on a car that helps it start when the engine is cold.
choose *vb.* decide between two or more possibilities; to come to a decision.
chop 1. *vb.* cut into pieces, often with an ax. 2. *n.* a thick slice of meat with a bit of bone in it.

Chopin, Frédéric
Chopin (1810–49) was a Polish composer. In 1831 he settled in Paris. Most of Chopin's works are for the solo piano. Some of them were influenced by Polish folk music. Chopin was a close friend of the French woman novelist George Sand.

chopsticks *pl. n.* a pair of sticks held in one hand and used in Oriental countries for eating.
chord (*kord*) *n.* group of musical notes sounded together.
chore *n.* job about the house; dull, unenjoyable work.
choreography (*ko-ree*-**og**-*rafee*) *n.* the art of arranging the steps and movements of a dance. **choreographer** *n.*
chorus (**kore**-*rus*) *n.* choir, band of singers; part of a song that everyone sings after a solo part. **choral** *adj.* of, sung by, a choir or chorus.
christen *vb.* give a name to and receive into the Christian Church; baptize. *Our baby was christened Angela by the priest.* **christening** *n.*

Christian *n.* a believer in and follower of the teachings of Jesus Christ.
Christianity *n.* the religion that was started by Jesus Christ.
► Christianity is one of the world's great RELIGIONS. More than 1 billion people call themselves Christians. These are people who follow the teachings of JESUS, and who believe that he is the son of God who came to earth in human form.

Christianity is almost 2,000 years old. In fact, we date our calendar from the year in which it is believed that Jesus was born. Christians accept the BIBLE as their holy book and Sunday is their holy day, when they go to church, pray and observe other religious traditions. The most important festivals are Christmas, which marks the birth of Jesus, and Easter, which marks his death and rise to heaven.

In some ways Christianity grew out of the Jewish religion of JUDAISM. But the teachings of Jesus upset the Jewish and Roman leaders of the time, and in A.D. 29 he was crucified. After his death, the followers of Jesus, the disciples, spread his teachings far and wide. Today, there are many different forms of Christianity.

The cross is a symbol of the Christian religion. It appears in architecture, in heraldry and in church decoration. Stone crosses were often erected at holy places.

A bishop of the Eastern Orthodox Church, a branch of the Christian church which separated from the Roman church in the 11th century.

Christmas *n.* the festival on December 25 celebrating the birth of Jesus.
► It is not known if Jesus was actually born on this date. In fact, the first mention of a festival of Christmas comes from a Roman calendar over 300 years after his death. However, there were a number of Roman and pagan festivals that were held on this day, and early Christians may have thought that by celebrating the birthday of Jesus on the same day as the others, it would show that this festival was just as important.

C

chromium *n.* a hard white metal that does not rust (symbol – *Cr*).
► Chromium was first discovered in 1797. Mixed with steel it forms a very tough ALLOY known as stainless steel. This is used to make kitchenware. It does not rust or go dull, but keeps its shiny bright finish and is tough enough to stand up to constant use.

chromosome *n.* a tiny threadlike structure, several of which occur in a cell nucleus and contain genes (hereditary instructions).
chronic *adj.* (of diseases) lasting, recurring; (*casual*) bad, boring.
chronicle (**kron**-*ic-al*) *n.* record of events in the order they happened. *vb.* write a chronicle.
chronometer *n.* a very accurate clock used as a navigational instrument to determine longitude at sea or in the air.
chrysalis *n.* a stage in the development of an insect between caterpillar and adult. *The caterpillar turned into a chrysalis, and then it became a butterfly.*
chunk *n.* thick lump or block.
church *n.* a building used by Christians for worship (from a Greek word meaning "belonging to the Lord").
► Christian churches are as varied as the countries in which they are found. They come in all shapes and sizes – from tents and tiny wooden huts to towering stone cathedrals. But all churches are used for the same purposes. They serve as places of prayer, as settings for holding religious services and as places that house all kinds of religious objects.
Larger churches, especially traditional Catholic ones, were usually built in the shape of a cross. In most, the altar is built at the east end. It is found at the end farthest away from the main door. Throughout the ages, churches have been built in many different styles of ARCHITECTURE, depending on the period of history and which country they were built in. Many churches adopted the Romanesque style of architecture known as *Byzantine*. They all had wide, rounded arches and low round DOMES. In the Middle Ages, in western Europe, a style known as *Gothic* appeared. After the 1000s, cathedrals with pointed spires, narrow soaring arches, richly stained glass windows and lots of stone carvings became very popular. These churches were cool and dark on the inside. The huge space inside them helped to give churchgoers a sense of awe and wonder at being in the presence of God.
Most cathedrals were laid out in the same way on the inside. The worshipers sat in the center, in a section called the *nave*. They faced toward the altar and the place where the choir sang. On either side were the wings, called *transepts*, which gave the church its cross shape. Sometimes, a number of small chapels were placed inside the transepts.

Churchill, Winston
Sir Winston Churchill (1874–1965) was a great British Prime Minister, war leader, and writer. Although he was a senior minister in PARLIAMENT before and during World War I, he was not very powerful. But in 1940, when WORLD WAR II threatened Britain the country chose him as their Prime Minister. As a leader during wartime he showed great courage and determination. His rousing speeches helped the people of Britain to fight on when they stood alone against Germany and its allies.
Churchill was also a great writer. He wrote clearly and vividly as a historian and war reporter.
Churchill's father was Lord Randolph Churchill, a brilliant politician. His mother was Jennie Jerome, who came from an old New York family.
During his long life, Churchill was awarded the Order of the Garter, he won the Nobel Prize for literature, and in 1963 he was made an honorary citizen of the United States.
He died in London on January 24, 1965, at the age of 90, and was given the unforgettable funeral of a hero.

churchyard *n.* the land surrounding a church, usually used as a burial ground.
churn *n.* vessel for making butter. *vb.* stir or agitate violently.
chutney *n.* flavoring for food, usually made from mangos, chillies, and other ingredients.
cider *n.* the juice of fruit; as in apple cider.
cigar *n.* tobacco rolled in a tobacco leaf for smoking.
cigarette *n.* a small roll of tobacco in thin paper for smoking.

Cincinnati
Cincinnati is the third largest city in Ohio. Located on the Ohio River, Cincinnati is a major manufacturing center and a leading producer of machine tools, soaps and playing cards. Automobiles, jet engines and cosmetics are also important.
The first settlers arrived in 1788 and named the village Losantiville. In 1790 it was renamed Cincinnati for the Society of the Cincinatti, which was formed by Continental Army Officers at the end of the American Revolution.
Cincinnati was chartered as a city in 1819.

cinder *n.* piece of partly burned coal or wood.
cinema *n.* a theater where moving pictures are shown.
cinnamon *n.* a spice from the bark of the Ceylon laurel tree; light yellow-brown color of cinnamon.
cipher see **code**.

The church of St Mary and All Saints at Fotheringhay, Northamptonshire.

circa *prep.* a Latin word meaning about and used mainly with dates. It is usually abbreviated to *c.*, e.g. *c.* 1782.

circle *n.* a round flat shape, the line about this shape.

circuit *n.* 1. a circular journey. 2. the path of electric current.

circular 1. *adj.* in the shape of a circle; round. 2. *n.* a letter or other document sent to a number of people.

circulate *vb.* move or send around.

circulation *n.* 1. movement of blood around the body. 2. number of copies of a newspaper sold.

circum- (*sur-come*) *prefix* meaning round, about, e.g. **circumnavigate** sail around; **circumstance** everything surrounding an act, event, etc.

circumcision *n.* the cutting away of the foreskin of the penis. This is practiced by many religions, but is especially important to the Jews.

circumference *n.* the distance around the outside of a circle.

circus *n.* a traveling show with clowns, animals and acrobats, usually held in a tent.

► The Romans first used the word "circus" to describe a large open-air space where exciting displays of horsemanship, acrobatics, chariot racing and wrestling were held. The modern type of circus began in the 1700s, and circus events today include jugglers, clowns, acrobats and all sorts of trained animals.

The first American circus opened in Philadelphia in 1793. In the 1800s, circus people became wanderers. They went from town to town in horse-drawn wagons. When they reached town they paraded down the main street with the band blaring to tell everyone that the circus had come to town.

The great age of the circus was between 1880 and 1920, with great names like Barnum and Bailey, and the Ringling Brothers. Barnum and Bailey's "big top" had five rings and could hold 12,000 spectators. It was called the "Greatest Show on Earth." The Ringling Brothers circus employed more than 1,000 people. It traveled on a special train that had over 60 railroad cars.

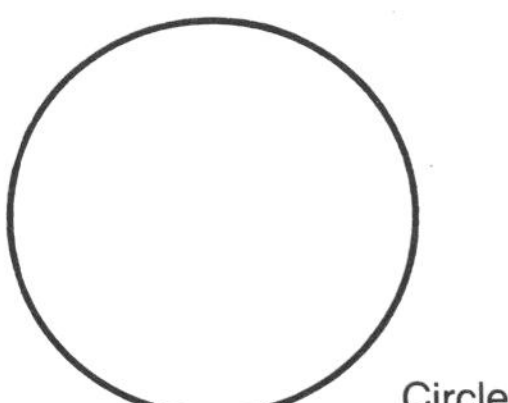

Circle

The circus is seldom seen in big tents any more. But it is still very much the same as it always was.

citadel *n.* fortress protecting a city.

citizen *n.* 1. a person who lives in a town or city. 2. a person who has every right to live in a particular country. *She was an American citizen.*

city *n.* a large or important town.

civil engineering *n.* the branch of engineering that deals with man-made structures.

► Civil engineering includes the building of homes, offices and factories as well as roads, bridges, harbors, airports, tunnels and many other constructions. A civil engineer needs to have all kinds of specialized knowledge. This includes knowing about the properties of building materials, and different kinds of rock and soil. Today's civil engineers are able to make use of many kinds of modern building and earth-moving equipment.

civilian *adj.* & *n.* a person who is not in one of the fighting services.

civility *n.* politeness, kindness.

civilization *n.* a group of people in an advanced stage of development. **civilize** *vb.* make cultured, enlighten. **civilized** *adj.* living in a well-organized way.

Civil War

The American Civil War (1861–1865) was a war fought between the Northern and Southern states. For many years before the war, the Northern and Southern states had opposed each other. When Abraham Lincoln was elected president in 1860, the Southern states thought that he would abolish slavery in all the South. This meant that the cotton plantations would be ruined. Nearly all the labor on these plantations was done by 4 million Black slaves.

In 1861, 11 Southern states broke away from the Union. They chose Jefferson DAVIS as their president and formed the Confederate States of America. War began when the Confederates attacked and captured Fort Sumter in the harbor of Charleston in April 1861. The Confederate army was led by two brilliant generals, Robert E. Lee and "Stonewall" Jackson. General Lee won the South's first victory at the Battle of Bull Run in July 1861.

In 1863 Lee marched into Pennsylvania. He fought a bloody battle at the little town of Gettysburg and was beaten. This battle crippled the Southern army. In 1864 General Ulysses S. Grant was put in charge of the Northern armies. In April 1865, Richmond, the Southern capital, was captured. General Lee surrendered to General Grant, and the Civil War was over.

More than 600,000 people died because of the war. The South lost because it had fewer factories for making guns and other munitions. All slaves were freed and the Southern states again became part of the United States. But the war gave rise to many new problems that took many years to settle.

Civil War (English)

The civil war in England lasted from 1642 to 1648. It was fought between the king, CHARLES I, and PARLIAMENT. In 1629, Charles got rid of Parliament and ruled without it, taxing the people whenever he needed money. In 1640, Charles was forced to recall Parliament because he needed more money. Instead of giving him money, Parliament argued with the King and said he could not rule on his own. In 1642 the King called his friends to arm themselves. They were called Royalists. The Parliamentary army, called Roundheads, was commanded by Oliver CROMWELL.

After several battles, the Royalist force lost the war and the King was captured. Charles was put on trial and executed in 1649. Parliament began to rule without a king, with Cromwell as its leader. This period (1649–60) was known as the Commonwealth.

claim *vb.* 1. say that something is yours. *You should claim your prize.* 2. say that something is a fact. *He claims that he can lift great weights.*

clammy *adj.* damp and sticky.

clamor *vb.* & *n.* (make) loud demand, noisy outcry.

clamp 1. *n.* a metal object for holding things in place. 2. *vb.* fasten with a clamp.

clan *n.* a group of families who claim to share the same ancestor.

► A clan's ancestor is sometimes real but often legendary because no one knows whether he ever really existed. Each clan shares the same surname or family name.

In Scotland the clan name often begins with "Mac". This means "son of," so Macdonald means "the son of Donald". In Ireland "O" also means "son of," so O'Neil means "son of Neill."

Scottish clans often lived in the same valley or glen where they kept cattle. They defended these fiercely against all strangers and enemies. Cattle-stealing raids were common between clans. These sometimes caused quarrels, or feuds, that often lasted for generations.

clap *vb.* applaud by smacking one's hands together.

clapper *n.* tongue or striker of bell.

claret *n.* a red wine from Bordeaux. Also its color.

clarify *vb.* make clear, explain.

clarinet *n.* a musical wind instrument with a single reed.

C

clarity *n.* clearness.
clash 1. *n.* a loud noise; the noise made by banging cymbals. 2. *vb.* (of colors) go badly together.
clasp 1. *n.* a fastening, such as a buckle or brooch. 2. *vb.* hold tightly. *They clasped hands.*
class *n.* a group of the same kind of people, e.g. children who are taught together. *I go to the class at the ballet school.*
classic *adj.* & *n.* 1. established quality of excellence, especially in art. 2. of ancient Greece and Rome and their cultures. **classical** *adj.* of ancient Greece or Rome.
clause (*klawz*) *n.* 1. part of a sentence. 2. section in a document.
claustrophobia (*klaws-tro-***foab***-ia*) *n.* fear of being in enclosed spaces.
claw *n.* a pointed nail on an animal's foot.
clay *n.* a soft kind of earth that gets hard when baked.

► Clay is rock which has been broken down by millions of years of weathering. It is made of tiny particles that make a thick, sticky paste.

Clay particles are so small and closely packed together that a layer of them is waterproof. When a thick layer of clay lies underground, rain that seeps down through the soil cannot go through it. The water forms an underground pool, or *reservoir*. People can get the water out by digging wells. London lies over a layer of clay like this and still gets some of its water supply from wells.

Clay is easy to mold and can be baked hard in an oven, or *kiln*. People began making pots from clay in prehistoric times. Today even the finest porcelain is made from clay. Clay is also used to make bricks for houses and other buildings.

clean *adj.* not dirty; bright. *vb.* remove dirt from something.
clear *adj.* easy to see through. *The glass was clear.* easy to understand. *The meaning of the word was quite clear.* free from obstacles. *Before you cross, see that the road is clear. vb.* make or become clear.
clematis *n.* a climbing shrub.
clement *adj.* showing mercy; gentle, mild, soft. **clemency** *n.*

Cleopatra
Cleopatra (69-30 B.C.) was a queen of Egypt. She was made ruler with her brother at the age of 17, but her brother's supporters soon drove her from the throne. When JULIUS CAESAR visited Egypt he fell in love with Cleopatra and helped her to become queen again. Cleopatra followed Caesar back to Rome and lived in his house until he was murdered in 44 B.C. After this she went back to Egypt.

Three years later Cleopatra met Mark Antony, who ruled the Roman Empire with Octavian. Antony also fell in love with Cleopatra and left his wife, the sister of Octavian, to live with her. Octavian did not trust Cleopatra or Antony and started a war with them. He defeated them in a naval battle at Actium in Greece in 31 B.C.

Cleopatra and Antony fled to Alexandria in Egypt. They were followed by Octavian and his army. Cleopatra began to realize that she could never beat the Romans. She and Antony decided to kill themselves. Antony stabbed himself first and died in Cleopatra's arms. Cleopatra then died from a poisonous snake bite.

clerk (rhymes with *jerk*) *n.* a person who works in an office writing things down.

Cleveland
Cleveland is the largest city in OHIO. It lies at the mouth of the Cuyahoga River on Lake Erie. Cleveland is one of the leading industrial centers of the United States. Its industries include iron and steel, chemicals and oil refining.

Cleveland, Grover
Grover Cleveland (1837–1908), served two terms as President of the United States. He was the first Democratic President elected after the Civil War. Cleveland worked hard for honest and well-run government.

clever *adj.* bright; intelligent.
cliché (*klee-***shay**) *n.* commonplace, unoriginal expression, idea, etc.
cliff *n.* a very steep, high bank, especially by the sea.
climate *n.* the usual weather of a place over a long period.

► The sun has the greatest influence on the climate. It heats the land, the sea and the air. Countries near the equator get more of the sun's rays and usually have a hotter climate than places farther north or south. The sun's rays do not get to the ARCTIC and the ANTARCTIC easily. They have very cold climates.

When the sun heats the air it causes wind which can make the climate hotter or colder. The winds may also carry rain or dry air which can make the climate wet or dry.

Together with the winds, the sun's heat makes ocean currents. The Gulf Stream is a current which travels from Mexico to northwestern Europe. In winter the warmth from its water makes the climate of northwest Europe milder.

climax *n.* the high point of a piece of music, drama, expedition, holiday, etc. *The climb to the top of the castle walls formed the climax of the school visit.*
climb *n.* & *vb.* go up, sometimes using both hands and feet to hold on.

► Mountain climbing is a popular sport, though it can be difficult and dangerous. Climbers must be strong and healthy and have the right equipment in order to climb safely. In difficult areas, climbers often rope themselves together so that they can stop one climber from falling if he should slip.

Climbers' equipment often includes rope, ice axes, strong boots, and *crampons* – special frames with spikes that they can strap on to their boots for climbing on hard ice or snow. If the climb is going to last more than a day, they must carry food and tents for shelter. A first aid kit is also very important. At the top of high mountains the air is often very thin, and climbers sometimes wear breathing equipment.

cling *vb.* hang on to something.

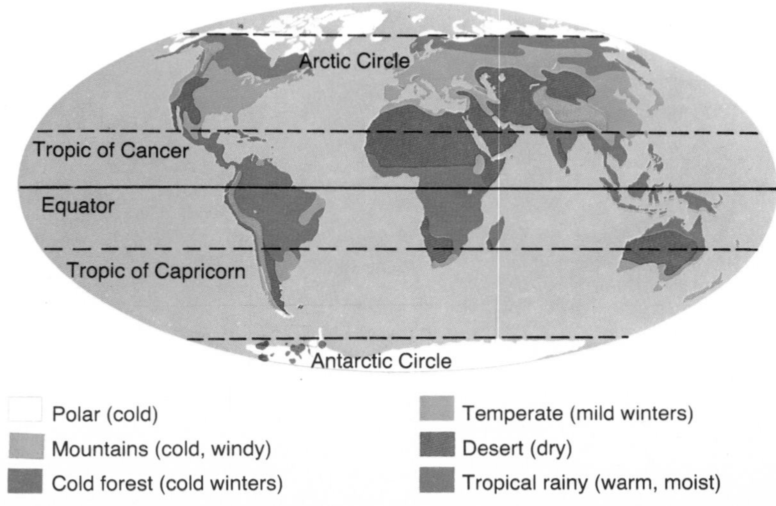

clinic *n.* a small hospital, for outpatients.
clip 1. *vb.* & *n.* a fastener or device for holding things together. 2. *vb.* cut with scissors, cut short.
clipper *n.* a fast sailing ship of the mid-1800s.
► Clippers were specially built for speed. They were very long and slim and had many large sails. Because they were slender they could not carry as large a cargo as other ships, so they had to carry valuable cargoes, like tea, grain or wood, instead. Most clippers had three masts on which five or six square sails were rigged. A good captain with a trained crew could set these sails to catch every bit of wind. Some clippers set records for speed. One, called *Lightning*, once sailed 502 miles (808 km) in a day, a record that even steamships could not beat for many years.

A clipper – the fastest ever sailing ship.

Clippers were first built in the United States in the 1830s, but a few years later they were also being built in England and Scotland. When the tea trade between China and the West began, the first ship home with this valuable cargo made the most money. Many famous races took place. The most famous clipper ship of all, the *Cutty Sark*, spent many years in the tea and wool trade. Later she was fully restored, and today she can be visited in dry dock at Greenwich in London.

Clive, Robert
Robert Clive (1725–74), founder of the British Empire in India, won notable victories against French troops and the armies of various Indian rulers. His greatest success was at Plassey in 1757.

cloak (rhymes with *poke*) *n.* a loose coat with no sleeves; a long cape.
cloakroom *n.* a place to leave your coat.
clock *n.* a machine for telling the time.
► Long ago people measured TIME by putting a stick in the ground and watching its shadow move with the sun. SUNDIALS work in the same way. Sun-clocks work only when the sun is shining, so people began to measure time by watching how long it took a candle to burn or a tank of water to empty.

The first mechanical clocks were made in Europe in the 1200s, although the Chinese probably had clocks as early as the 600s. European clocks were first used in churches and abbeys to mark the time of services.

Early clocks like these were bad timekeepers and could lose or gain an hour a day. In 1581 the great astronomer Galileo discovered that the PENDULUM could be used to measure time. This helped people to make much more accurate clocks. From then on improvements were made and ordinary clocks are now accurate to within a few minutes a year.

Today's scientists need very accurate clocks. They invented first the electric and then the quartz crystal clock. The most accurate clock today is at the United States Naval Research Laboratory in Washington, D.C. It is an atomic hydrogen maser clock and is accurate to one second in 1,700,000 years.

clockwise *adj.* going around in the same direction as the hands of a clock. **counterclockwise** going around in the opposite direction to a clock.
clockwork *n.* worked by a spring that is wound up.
clod *n.* 1. lump of earth. 2. lout, blockhead.
clog 1. *vb.* choke, fill up or obstruct. 2. *n.* a wooden shoe, especially in the Netherlands.
cloister *n.* covered way (arcade) open on one side and overlooking a quadrangle.
close 1. *adj.* (rhymes with *dose*) nearby; narrow. 2. *vb.* (rhymes with *nose*) shut; bring to an end.
cloth *n.* a material made by weaving fibers such as wool, linen or nylon.
► No one knows when cloth was first woven but it was certainly made in prehistoric times. Fabric from as far back as 6000 B.C. has been found. Once the secret of weaving had been discovered it spread around the world. Only a few people, such as the African Bushmen, do not weave cloth.

Cloth was probably first used instead of animal skins to protect people from the weather. From early times cloth has been colored and decorated. This can be done by dyeing the fibers before they are woven. Or the cloth can be decorated with dyes or paints after it is woven. An even more important discovery was that different colored threads could be woven together to make patterns or pictures. Tapestries and patterned rugs and carpets are made in this way. Cloth was first woven by hand. Even today much fine cloth is handwoven, but in many parts of the world it is woven by machines in factories.

Cloth is used to make many useful and beautiful things, from carpets and curtains to tents and sails. It is also very important for making clothes. Synthetic or manmade fibers are now used in many cloths. They are often more hard-wearing and cheaper than cloth made from natural fibers. Modern cloths are often treated to make them easier to wash and care for.

clothes *pl. n.* things to wear.
clotheshorse frame to dry clothes on.
► Most people in the world wear some sort of clothing. What they wear depends on things like climate and how civilized they are. Because clothes decorate us as well as protect us, styles of clothing change with fashion.

The earliest clothes were animal skins. In the ancient world people wore loose, draped tunics. By the MIDDLE AGES the dress of poorer people remained simple and crude, but the wealthy dressed in fine silks and damasks from the East. The new wealth and interest in art during the RENAISSANCE made rich, colorful fabrics popular. In the 1700s costume became very grand to match the grand buildings of the period. People wore huge wigs and wide, stiffened skirts, often beautifully embroidered. By the 1900s fashions had become more practical, especially for women. Today western dress is worn by many people throughout the world. How styles change from year to year is decided by fashion designers.

cloud *n.* great clusters of tiny water droplets in the air.
► A cloud may float more than 30,000 ft. (10,000 meters) up, or

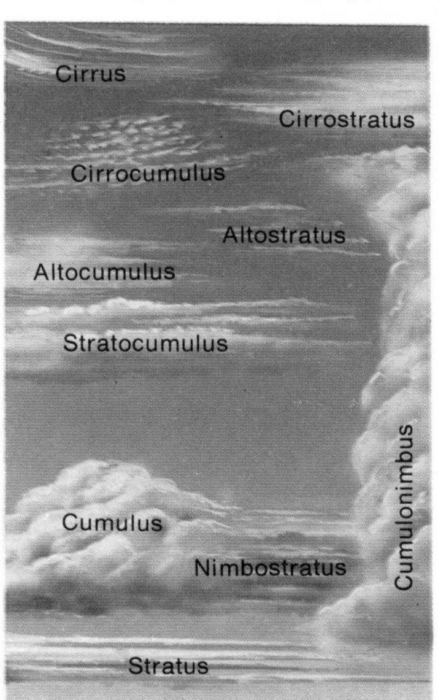

C

drift so low that it touches the ground, when it is known as mist or fog. There is always a certain amount of water *vapor* in the air. It is made up of tiny specks of water. Warm air that contains water vapor often rises and cools. Since cool air cannot hold as much water as warm air, the vapor particles start to form droplets (*condense*) around bits of dust, pollen and salt that the wind has carried into the sky.

As more water vapor condenses, the droplets grow in size and clouds begin to form. At first they are white and gauzy and then become thick and gray. Finally the droplets become so heavy that they clump together and fall to the earth. If the temperature is high enough they come down as rain. Otherwise they land as hail or snow.

Most clouds form along the boundaries between cold and warm air masses. By watching how they build and move it is possible to tell what sort of weather is coming. Different types of clouds tell weather forecasters different things. Clouds are one of the best ways we have of predicting the WEATHER.

cloudburst *n.* torrential rainstorm.
clout *n.* heavy swinging blow with the hand; to have power.
clove *n.* the dried bud of the clove tree, used as a spice.
cloven *adj.* divided.
clover *n.* a small green plant, usually with three leaves, which often grows in fields. The flowers are usually red or white. Widely cultivated as animal fodder.
clown *n.* a person who does funny things, especially in a circus.
club *n.* 1. a heavy stick with which to hit things. 2. a group that people can join to do things together. *We have a chess club in our school.*
cluck *vb.* & *n.* sound made by a hen.
clue *n.* something that helps you to solve a puzzle.
clumsy *adj.* heavy and awkward.
clung *vb.* past of **cling**.
cluster *vb.* & *n.* number of things growing closely together; a group or bunch.
clutch 1. *vb.* seize or grab eagerly. *n.* a firm hold. 2. *n.*device for engaging and disengaging gears, etc. 3. *n.* nest of eggs.
coach 1. *n.* a four-wheeled horse-drawn carriage; a single-decker bus. 2. *vb.* teach someone, especially a sport. *n.* someone who helps others to prepare for examinations.
coal *n.* a black mineral that burns slowly and gives out heat.
► Coal is a FUEL which is found in layers, or *seams*, under the ground. It is known as a *fossil* fuel because it was made millions of years ago from dead plants. Coal is used for heating and in making electricity, gas and chemicals. It is also made into another fuel called coke.

coarse *adj.* rough; not fine.
coast *n.* land along the edge of the sea.
coat *n.* 1. an article of clothing with sleeves that covers the top half of the body; an overcoat. 2. a covering. *That door needs another coat of paint.*
coax *vb.* persuade gently.
cobbler *n.* a person who mends shoes.
cobra *n.* a poisonous snake that can expand its neck into a hood.
cobweb *n.* a fine web made by a spider.
cock *n.* a male bird, especially a farmyard fowl.
cockatoo *n.* a crested parrot.
cockerel *n.* a young cock bird.
cockle *n.* a kind of shellfish.
cockney *n.* a person from the East End of London.
cockpit *n.* the area where the pilot sits in an aircraft; the driver's seat in a racing car. (Originally an enclosed space for contests between fighting cocks.)
cocoa *n.* chocolate powder made from the seeds, or beans, of the cacao tree of South America and West Africa.
coconut *n.* large oval, hard-shelled fruit of the coconut palm.
► The inside of a coconut is white and sweet. It can be eaten fresh or dried into copra. Copra is made into coconut oil and is used in soap, margarine and other things. The hairy husk near the outside is made into coir for weaving mats and rope.

cocoon *n.* covering made by a caterpillar to protect itself during the chrysalis stage.
cod *n.* a large sea fish eaten as a food.
► The cod is one of the most important food fishes. It is found in the colder parts of the Atlantic and Pacfic oceans. The Atlantic cod is usually between 2 and 4 feet (.6 and 1.2 meters) long and weighs from 10 to 35 pounds (4.5 to 16 kg). Specimens have been caught which weighed over 200 pounds (90 kg).

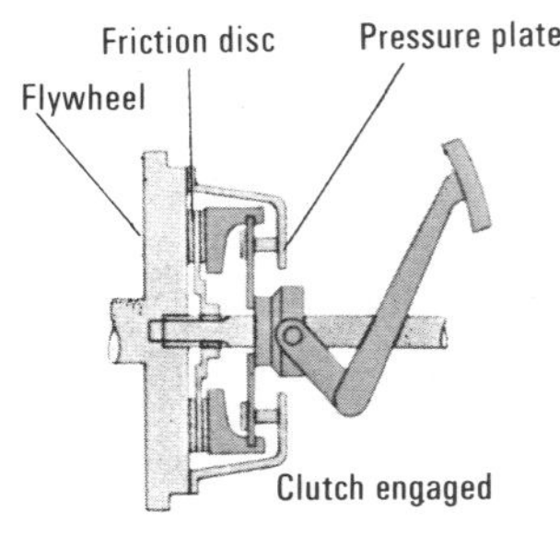

Clutch engaged

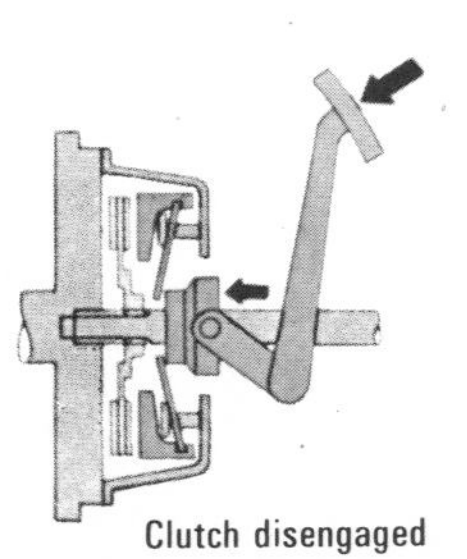
Clutch disengaged

code *n.* 1. a secret system of writing; cipher. 2. a set of rules. *We should all learn the Highway Code.* 3. a signal system. *Bob learned the Morse code.*
► Ciphers and codes are ways of sending information secretly. They are most often used in wartime. Messages are coded so that they cannot be understood if they fall into the hands of the enemy.

In many codes, the letters of the alphabet are replaced by other letters according to a definite plan. For example, a simple code would be to substitute A for Z, B for Y, and so on. A person who breaks codes would have little difficulty with this code. But many codes have very complex *keys*. As well as substituting letters, the order of the letters can be rearranged in many ways. Sometimes ciphers can be broken because experts know that some letters of the alphabet occur more often than others. In English the letters E, T, A, and O are the most common letters.

Instead of using letters, a coded message might consist of a series of numbers. The key to the cipher might be the page of a book, the numbers giving a certain line down the page and the number of a letter in that line.

coeducation *n.* education of boys and girls together.

Coelacanth
The coelacanth (*see-la-kanth*) is a strange, bony fish. Scientists once thought that it had been extinct for 60 million years. Then, in 1938, a coelacanth was caught off the coast of South Africa. Since then, a number of other specimens have been caught.

coffee *n.* a drink made from the roasted and ground beans of the coffee plant.

Coffee

coffer *n.* box or chest for storing money, etc.
coffin *n.* a box in which a dead person is buried or cremated.
cog *n.* one of the teeth around the rim of a gear wheel.
coil *vb.* & *n.* wind something in circles or spirals. *The old electric heater had two coils of wire that gave off heat.*
coin *n.* a piece of metal, usually of a uniform size and design, used as money.
► Coins may be made of a variety of metals including gold, silver, brass, bronze, aluminum and nickel. Coins were first used in Asia Minor in the 600s B.C. The Greeks and Romans used silver and gold coins. Today governments control the type and number of coins minted as part of their control of the national money supply. Most coins are made of the cheaper metals, and are used for fraction parts of the basic monetary unit, such as the dollar in the USA or the pound in Britain.

Top: Early Chinese coin shaped like a sword. Above: A coin of Constantine, the first Christian Roman emperor.

coincide *vb.* happen at the same time; agree exactly. **coincidence** *n.* combination of events happening by chance at the same time.
coke *n.* what is left of coal after the gases have been removed by heating.
cold 1. *adj.* not hot. 2. *n.* a kind of illness which gives people a runny nose and causes sneezing and a sore throat.

Coleridge, Samuel Taylor
Samuel Taylor Coleridge (1772–1834) was an English Romantic poet who wrote the famous poem *The Rime of the Ancient Mariner*. His other outstanding poems include *Christabel* and *Kubla Khan*.

The three primary light colors are red, green and blue. Any other color can be made by mixing them. The colors in a television set are made from these three colors. The three primary paint colors are red, blue and yellow.

collaborate *vb.* work together (with), cooperate. **collaboration** *n.*
collage (*koll*-**adge**) *n.* a picture made up of pieces of cloth, paper or other materials.
collapse *vb.* fall down; fall to pieces; *n.* breakdown. **collapsible** *adj.* folding.
collar *n.* part of a shirt or other clothing that goes around the neck; a leather band around an animal's neck.
collect *vb.* gather or bring together. *We collect coins.* gather from a number of people. *They went to the houses to collect money for charity.*
college *n.* a place where people go to study after high school; part of a university.
collide *vb.* bump into something by mistake. **collision** *n.*
collie *n.* a long-haired breed of sheepdog, originally from Scotland.
collier *n.* a coal miner; a ship that carries coal.

Colombia (Colombian)
Colombia is a republic in the north-east of South America. It has coast-lines on both the Atlantic and Pacific Oceans. Most of the people live in

the high, fertile valleys. Colombia once formed part of the Spanish colony of New Granada.
AREA: 439,761 SQ. MILES (1,138,914 SQ. KM)
POPULATION: 27,966,000
CAPITAL: BOGOTA
CURRENCY: PESO
OFFICIAL LANGUAGE: SPANISH

colon *n.* 1. the large intestine. 2. punctuation mark (:).
colonel (**kern**-el) *n.* a senior rank in the army, below brigadier and above lieutenant-colonel.
colony *n.* 1. a group of settlers in a new country who are still governed by their mother country; the country where the settlers live. *Hong Kong is still a British colony.* 2. a group of people or animals that live together. *He came upon a large colony of bees.* **colonial** *adj.* **colonize** *vb.*

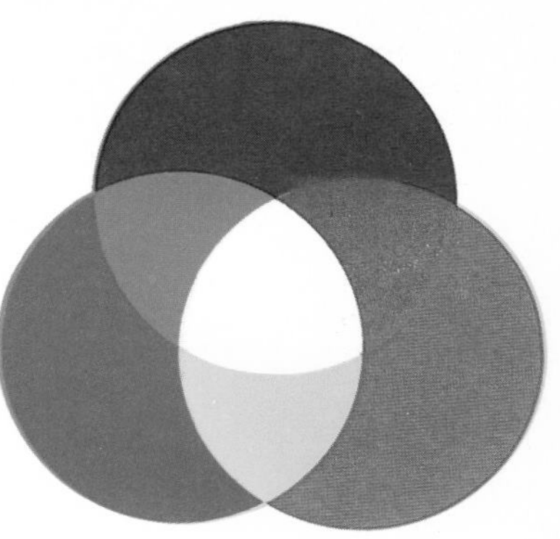

color *n.* red, blue, green, etc. *vb.* the act of applying color.

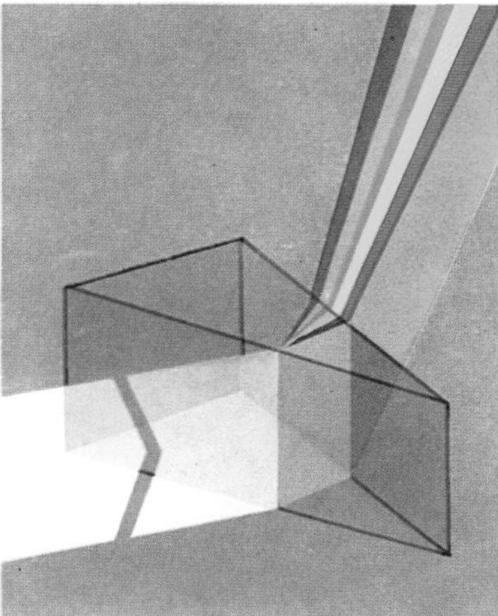

► The first person to find out about colored light was Isaac NEWTON. He shone sunlight through a piece of glass called a *prism*. The light that came out of the prism was broken up into all the colors of the rainbow – red, orange, yellow, green, blue, indigo and violet. Newton had found out that ordinary white light is made up of many colors added together.

When sunlight falls on rain or spray from a garden hose, we sometimes see a rainbow. Rainbows are caused by the drops of water behaving like tiny prisms. They break up the sun's light into colors. The colors are always in the same order, from red to violet.

A red flower is red because it takes in all the other colors and throws back only red. A white flower gives back to our eyes all the colors of light. We know that all the colors added together make white.

Colorado (*abbrev.* **Col.**)
Colorado is one of the Rocky Mountain states. It has more high peaks than any other state, and it covers an area of about 104,000 sq. miles (about 270,000 sq. km).

Food and machinery are the state's main industries. Denver, the capital and largest city, is an important commercial and financial center. Other cities are Colorado Springs, Lakewood and Aurora.

Many metals are mined in Colorado's mountains. The most important is a metal called molybdenum. It is used to harden steel and in the making of rockets.

Colorado became a state on August 1, 1876. It is called the Centennial State because it entered the Union 100 years after the signing of the Declaration of Independence.

Colorado is the state where Buffalo Bill rode the Pony Express and Kit Carson fought the Indians.

Colosseum
The Colosseum of Rome was a giant sports stadium which could hold more than 50,000 people and was the largest building of its kind in the Roman Empire. It still stands in the center of Rome but is partly in ruins.

The Colosseum was started in A.D. 72, during the rule of the Emperor Vespasian, and finished in A.D. 79. It covers an area of about 6 acres (2.5 hectares). The seats were built on three levels, or *tiers*, with rows at the very top for people to stand. A sheet, or *awning*, could be put up over the audience to protect it from the sun or bad weather.

The floor, or *arena*, was used for GLADIATOR combats, battles between men and animals and fights between different kinds of animals. It was also used for showing rare wild creatures. The floor could also be flooded so that sea battles could be fought on it. Underneath the arena were pens in which to keep the wild beasts.

colt *n*. a young male horse.

Colt, Samuel
Samuel Colt (1814–62) was an American gunsmith who in 1836 patented his design for a revolver. This was a pistol with a rotating cylinder which could hold six bullets.

Colt's most famous revolver is the Colt '45, first produced in 1873. This gun was the famous six-shooter of the Wild West.

Columbus, Christopher
Christopher Columbus (1451–1506) was a sailor and explorer. He discovered America for Spain in 1492. Although Columbus returned to America three more times, he died believing that the land he had reached was Asia.

Like many people of his time, Columbus knew that the earth was not flat but round. Sailors from Europe used to sail east to the "Indies" (Asia). They brought back rich cargoes of gold, spices and treasure. Columbus thought that if he sailed west instead he could reach the Indies quicker. The Queen and King of Spain gave him ships and money to make this voyage.

In 1492 Columbus sailed west with three small ships, the *Santa Maria*, the *Pinta* and the *Niña*. The ships sailed for three weeks without seeing any land and the crew become afraid. Then, on 12 October, they reached an island near America. Columbus named it San Salvador. When he returned to Spain Columbus had a hero's welcome.

Columbus thought he had sailed to the Indies. This is why the people he met in America were called Indians. The islands he first reached are still known as the West Indies.

column *n*. a tall round pillar composed of a base, a shaft and a capital top. The capital is often decorated.
comb *n*. & *vb*. a small object with "teeth" used by people for making their hair tidy.
combat *n*. & *vb*. fight; battle.
combine *vb*. join together.
combine harvester *n*. a large farm machine that cuts grain and threshes it.
combustion *n*. another word for burning, a chemical reaction that produces light and heat. **combustible** *adj*.
come *vb*. arrive; draw near. *"Come" is the opposite of "go."*
come about *vb*. happen. *It came about that we all met at the beach.*
come across *vb*. find something when you do not expect to. *I came across your letter when I was tidying my desk.*
comedy *n*. a funny play. **comedian** *n*. a stage or TV entertainer who tells jokes or plays comic roles.
comet *n*. a body of (probably) ice and gas, which looks like a star but moves around our sun.

► Comets travel around the SOLAR SYSTEM in paths, or orbits. Sometimes they pass close to the sun. At other times they move far beyond the path of Pluto, the outermost planet. A complete orbit by a comet is called its period. Encke's Comet has the shortest period of all. It is three-and-a-half years. Others have periods of centuries or even thousands of years.

Comets are clouds of frozen gases, ice, dust and rock. The biggest are only a few miles across, but their bright tails may be millions of miles long.

Most of the time comets cannot be seen, even through the biggest telescopes. But whenever their orbits bring them back into the middle of the solar system they flare up and look very bright.

As a comet travels toward the sun, the sun's rays knock particles out of the comet and push them away to make a long tail. The tail is made of glowing gas and dust. But the tail is so fine that a rocket passing through it would not be harmed. The earth has passed through the tails of several comets. One of the most famous comets is named after the British astronomer Edmund Halley. In 1682 he studied the path of a bright comet and accurately forecast when it would return.

come to *vb*. 1. total cost of several things. *When it is all added together it will come to $17.43*. 2. recover consciousness. *He has just come to after his operation.*
comfort *vb*. help someone who is unhappy. *Sandra comforted the little girl until her mother arrived.* **comfortable** *adj*.
comic 1. *adj*. funny. 2. *n*. humorous illustrated strip or cartoon.
comma *n*. a punctuation mark like this (,) that is used to show a pause or separation in writing.
command 1. *vb*. order someone to do something. 2. *n*. be in charge of. *Napoleon took command of the whole army*.
commence *vb*. begin. **commencement** *n*.
comment *n*. & *vb*. a remark made about someone or something; an observation. **commentary** *n*. continuous comments on some happening, especially when it is taking place, e.g. a football commentary.
commerce *n*. trade. **commercial** *adj*. concerned with trade. *n*. broadcast advertisement.
commit *vb*. 1. do, carry out. 2. hand over, entrust.
committee *n*. a small group of people who are appointed by a larger group of people to run the larger group's affairs. *Our club's committee meets once a month*.
common *adj*. usual, normal; often seen. *A thrush is a very common bird.*
common sense *n*. good, ordinary, sensible thinking.

Commonwealth
A commonwealth is a group of countries or people who are friendly and help each other. The Commonwealth of Nations is made up from most of the countries that were once ruled by Britain. Most of these countries now have their own governments and laws but many of them still have the reigning monarch of Britain as their Head of State.

The Commonwealth came into being at a meeting held in 1926. Commonwealth countries share some of the same beliefs and trade with each other. The heads of Commonwealth countries that have their own governments meet together often. They talk about their problems and try to help each other. Commonwealth countries also take part in sports meetings called the Commonwealth Games.

The anniversary of the Russian Communist Revolution of 1917 is celebrated in Red Square, Moscow, with huge parades.

communicate *vb*. pass on information or feelings to other people. **communication** *n*. the passing of information from one person to another.

communion *n*. 1. an act of sharing; fellowship; 2. Christian celebration of the Lord's supper.

communiqué (*kom-mune-ik*-**aye**) *n*. an official announcement.

Communism *n*. a political system which holds that all property should be held in common.

► Communism is a set of ideas about the way a country should be run. The main idea of Communism is that people should share or own together all wealth and property. This makes people more equal because nobody is very rich or very poor. In most Communist countries the people own the factories and farms but it is usually the government which runs them. People who believe in Communism are often called Marxists. This is because they follow the ideas of Karl MARX, a thinker, or *philosopher*, of the 1800s.

Many countries have become Communist in the 1900s. They include U.S.S.R., China and Cuba, and some countries in Eastern Europe and the Far East. LENIN and MAO TSE-TUNG were among the great Communist leaders of this century.

community *n*. all the people who live in a place.

commuter *n*. a person who travels some distance daily to and from work. **commute** *vb*.

compact (*kom*-**pact**) *adj*. packed closely together; easy to handle.

companion *n*. a friend; someone who goes with you.

company *n*. 1. an organization in business to make, buy or sell things. 2. visitors in your house.

compare *vb*. look at things to see how alike or unlike they are. *Roger compared the two chairs and decided to buy the larger one*. **comparison** *n*.

compartment *n*. marked off division of an enclosed space (box, railway carriage, etc).

compass *n*. 1. an instrument that shows direction, used for finding the way. 2. an instrument for drawing circles or for measuring.

► A magnetic compass always points to the earth's magnetic poles, which are close to the North and South poles. The magnetic compass has been used for centuries by sailors and explorers to find the right direction.

A magnetic compass works by MAGNETISM. It has a magnetic needle fixed to a pivot so that it is free to swing around. The needle always points north and south when it is at rest. With a compass showing where north and south are, it is easy to travel in a straight line in any direction you wish to go.

The needle always points north and south because the earth itself is a big magnet. The compass lines up parallel with the earth's magnetic field.

► A pair of compasses is quite different from the magnetic, or mariner's, COMPASS. It is a mathematical instrument consisting of two legs, joined by a hinge. At the end of one leg is a sharp point. At the end of the other is a pencil. Compasses are used both for drawing circles and arcs (parts of circles) and for measuring distances on maps.

compassion *n*. having pity or sorrow for the sufferings of another. **compassionate** *adj*.

compel *vb*. force, make or urge someone to do something.

compensate *vb*. make up for (the loss of). **compensation** *n*. something given to make up for.

compete *vb*. take part in a contest. *All the girls will compete in the race*.

competition *n*. a contest in which a number of people take part to see who is the best.

competent *adj*. able, efficient, qualified. **competence** *n*.

complain *vb*. say that you are not pleased with something. **complaint** *n*. a grievance, protest; bodily illness.

complement *n*. something that fills up, completes, or makes perfect.

complete 1. *adj*. whole; the full number. *When the party was complete, it numbered 16 boys*. 2. *vb*. finish. *It will take three months to complete the new school*.

complex *adj*. complicated, difficult to understand. **complexity** *n*.

complexion *n*. color and appearance of the skin, especially of the face.

complicated *adj*. made up of many different parts; difficult to understand. **complicate** *vb*. make complicated, entangle. **complication** *n*. complicated state; new illness developing in the course of another.

compliment *n*. & *vb*. praise, flattery, formal greeting.

comply *vb*. do as asked or commanded.

compose *vb*. write a story or make up a piece of music. **composer** *n*. a person who makes up music.

compound *n*. something made up of separate parts or elements. *vb*. mix or combine into a whole.

► Compounds are formed when elements come together and make a new thing which is completely different from the elements. Water is a compound of the gas elements hydrogen and oxygen, and it is very different from either of them. Salt is a compound made up of the elements sodium and chlorine.

There are millions of compounds in the world. They can be very simple, like water (with three ATOMS), or complex like some plastics with hundreds of atoms.

comprehend *vb*. understand; include. **comprehensible** *adj*. intelligible. **comprehensive** *adj*. all-inclusive.

comprise *vb*. include, consist of.

compromise *vb*. & *n*. a settlement of differences by meeting halfway, each side giving up part of its claim.

C

COMPUTER TERMS

analogue something that varies continuously; the opposite of digital
binary numbers a number coded in a series of 0 and 1 digits, in which the value of each digit is twice the value of the digit to its right.
bit a single digit of a binary number. Eight bits are together known as byte.
BASIC stands for Beginner's All Purpose Symbolic Instruction Code. It is language most widely used by microcomputers.
byte the "chunk" of memory which a computer uses to store one letter or number. Eight bits make a byte.
CPU stands for Central Processing Unit. This is the "brain" of the Computer. It reads instructions put into the computer and passes them on to other parts; it sorts out information and does calculations; and it sends the results to the input device.
floppy disk a circular piece of thin plastic, coated with a thin layer of the magnetic material used in recording tape. It can be used to store large quantities of binary information.
data the information which is given to a computer for processing. Large stores of data for computers are known as databanks.
debug remove mistakes, or bugs from a program.
digital something that is separated in units; the opposite of analogue.
input is the data fed into the computer through devices such as keyboards, sensors, cameras, etc.
inteface a device placed between the computer and equipment connected to it, which translates input into a code of electronic pulses, and which translates the computer's results from the pulse code into a form the output device can act on.
hardware means the computer itself and devices connected to it.
output is the result of the computer's processing. It might be displayed on a screen, printed as words or pictures or cause the movement of a robot's arm.
program the set of instructions for the computer either stored in its permanent memory or fed into it.
RAM stands for Random Access Memory. This is the part of the computer's memory which temporarily stores information fed into it.
ROM stands for Read Only Memory. It is the part of the computer's memory which contains instructions the computer always needs to help it work.
software is the term given to computer programs.
VDU stands for Visual Display Unit. This is the screen, on which information from the computer is shown.
word processor a specialized typewriter with a VDU used for producing letters in an office.

computer *n.* an electronic calculating machine that stores information and works with enormous speed.
► Computers do not think for themselves. They have to be "fed" or programmed with information by people. The information is usually on a tape or disk. Computers can work out problems that would take people months to solve because they work faster than the human brain. They can also store a lot of information.

Computers are used for many things, including airline bookings, working machines in factories and helping to make weather forecasts.

One of the first modern computers was built in 1946 in the U.S.A. It was known as ENIAC and was so big it filled a large room. Since then, scientists have invented new ways of making computers and they are now much smaller and work faster.

comrade *n.* a friend; a companion.
concave *adj.* a surface that curves inward, like the inside of a saucer.
conceal *vb.* hide.
concede (*con*-**seed**) *vb.* give up; grant; allow.
conceive (*con*-**seeve**) *vb.* become pregnant; think of.
concentrate *vb.* bring together, compress; focus attention on.
concentration *n.* the act of concentrating or giving one's attention to.
conception *n.* 1. becoming pregnant. 2. idea.
concern *vb.* have to do with; cause a feeling of responsibility. *I am concerned about your bad tooth.* *n.* what one is interested in; a business.
concerning *prep.* about, with regard to.
concert *n.* a musical entertainment.
concise *adj.* made shorter; abbreviated. *A concise encyclopedia.*
conclude *vb.* bring to an end; come to an opinion. *He concluded she was right.* **conclusion** *n.* ending; final opinion. **conclusive** *adj.* convincing.
concrete *n.* a hard building material made of cement, sand, gravel and water. see **cement**
condemn *vb.* pronounce someone or something guilty or unfit for use. *The judge condemned the criminal to five years in prison.*
condense *vb.* 1. make something more solid; shorten. *She condensed the story by cutting out some unnecessary sentences.* 2. change from a gas into a liquid. *The steam condensed into water.*
condition *n.* 1. state of being, health. *She is in no fit condition to go dancing.* 2. provision, specification. *You may go on condition you finish your homework first.*
conduct 1. *vb.* (*kon*-**duct**) lead, manage; direct a performance, orchestra, etc. 2. *n.* (**kon**-*duct*) direction, behavior. *His conduct was terrible.*
conductor *n.* 1. a person who leads a group of singers or musicians; a person who collects fares on a bus or train. 2. any material that allows electricity to pass through it is called a conductor. Metals are good conductors, the best being silver and copper. Substances that do not conduct electricity are called insulators.
cone *n.* 1. solid body with a round bottom and a pointed top. 2. the fruit of a fir or pine tree.
confess *vb.* admit to doing wrong; own up. **confession** *n.*
confetti *pl. n.* tiny pieces of colored paper tossed at gala events such as parties and weddings.
confidence *n.* 1. feeling of certainty; a trust in one's own abilities. 2. thing told as a secret. **confident** *adj.*
confidential *adj.* private, secret.
confine *vb.* shut up, imprison; keep within limits. **confinement** *n.*
confirm *vb.* 1. establish more firmly; ratify. 2. admit to full membership of the Christian church. **confirmation** *n.*
conflict 1. *n.* a war or fighting; an argument. 2. *vb.* differ; disagree.
conform *vb.* follow the accepted customs and rules, comply.
confront *vb.* face, oppose.

Confucius
Confucius (551–479 B.C.) lived nearly 2,500 years ago in China. He was a very great thinker who taught people how to live and behave in a good way. The Chinese people followed his teaching for centuries.

The most important rule made by Confucius was that people should think of others, and not do to others anything that they would not like done to themselves.

Confucius came from a poor family of nobles. When he was young he had a school where he learned many things and talked to other people about his ideas. When Confucius died he was not well-known but his followers spread his ideas.

confuse *vb.* mix up, throw into disorder; mistake one thing for another. **confusion** *n.*

Congo (Congolese)
The Congo is a country in the west of central AFRICA. It used to be enormous, about the size of western Europe. Now it is much smaller. It is a little bigger than New Mexico.

The Congo is a hot, wet country. It has great forests and swamps, and a low grassy plain on the coast. It produces a lot of timber, but it also has diamonds, sugar, oil, cocoa and coffee.

When the Congo was a larger country, the river that ran through it was called the Congo River. Now most of the river runs along the Congo's border with ZAIRE. The Congo River is now called the Zaire River. It is 2,700 miles (4,828 km) long: one of the longest in the world. Many other rivers flow into it. It is used for travel, but only small boats can go any distance on it. Waterfalls block the way for big ships.

AREA: 132,054 SQ. MILES (342,000 SQ. KM)
POPULATION: 1,613,000
CAPITAL: BRAZZAVILLE
CURRENCY: FRANC CFA
OFFICIAL LANGUAGE: FRENCH

Congo River see **Zaire River**
congratulate *vb.* tell someone you are glad that they have done well.
congregate *vb.* gather together in a crowd, or **congregation** *n.*
Congress *n.* the U.S. House of Representatives and Senate.
► Congress is made up of two chambers: the House of Representatives and the Senate. Representatives are elected for two years and senators for six years.
To make a new law, a "bill" is introduced by a member into one of the chambers. It is discussed by groups, or *committees*, and then voted on by the members of the chamber. The bill then goes to the other chamber. When the bill has been passed by both chambers, the President signs it and it becomes law.

conifer *n.* an evergreen tree with cones for fruit.
► Conifers have cones instead of flowers for making pollen and seeds. There are about 600 different kinds of conifer. Many of them are found in the cool parts of the world. Some even grow north of the Arctic Circle.
Conifers include pines, firs, spruces, larches, and cedars. Most have needlelike leaves which they do not lose in winter.

Two types of conifers; a Gingko (left) and a Scots pine.

conjuror *n.* a person who performs tricks that look like magic. **conjure** *vb.*
connect *vb.* join things together. *This road connects our town to the main highway.* **connection** *n.*
connoisseur *n.* well-informed person in matters of taste, etc.

Connecticut (*abbrev.* **Conn.**)
Connecticut is one of the smaller states. It has busy cities and beautiful New England countryside. The state's main products are food, machinery, electrical and electronic equipment, chemicals and lumber. It is the nation's leader in the use of nuclear power to make electricity. The capital and largest city is Hartford.
The first Europeans came to Connecticut in the early 1600s. By 1637, the colonists had won a war against the Pequot Indians and the Connecticut Colony was formed. It became the fifth state when it approved the United States Constitution in 1788.

conquer (**con**-ker) *vb.* defeat an enemy, overcome. **conquest** *n.*
conquistador *n.* Spanish soldier-explorer of the 1500s.
conscience (**kon**-*shunz*) *n.* sense of right and wrong.
conscious (**kon**-*shuss*) *adj.* awake, alert, active.
consecrate *vb.* set apart; make holy; devote. *He consecrated all his time to music.*
consent *vb.* agree to. *n.* permission. *You took the book without my consent.*
consequence *n.* outcome, result of something. *The consequence of his actions.*
conserve *vb.* keep something as it was without changing it.
conservation *n.* looking after things so they are not spoiled or destroyed.
conservative *adj.* opposed to great change; cautious.
consider *vb.* think about. *Did you consider buying a new belt?*
consideration *n.* quality of being thoughtful esp. of other people.
considerate *adj.*
consist *vb.* be composed of.
consonant *n.* any letter of the alphabet except A, E, I, O, U, which are vowels.
conspiracy *n.* a secret plot, often with an evil purpose. **conspire** *vb.* plot secretly for an evil purpose.
constable *n.* a policeman. (Formerly a senior officer of a royal household, e.g. *Lord High Constable of England*).

Constable, John
John Constable (1776–1837) was a British landscape painter who painted his scenes outdoors directly from nature and so succeeded in giving them realistic color and light. His most famous pictures include *The Hay Wain* and *View on the Stour.*

constant *adj.* all the time.

A Spanish conquistador. The conquistadors conquered South and Central America.

Constantinople
Constantinople is the old name of the city of ISTANBUL, in Turkey. It lies between Asia and Europe.
Constantinople was the most important city in the western world for more than a thousand years. It was named after the Roman emperor Constantine. In A.D. 330 Constantine started the city in a place where there had once been the ancient Greek town of Byzantium. He divided the Roman Empire into two to make it easier to manage. Constantinople was the capital of the eastern half, the BYZANTINE EMPIRE.
After the last Roman emperor was overthrown in A.D. 476, Constantinople and the Byzantine Empire continued to be powerful. The city was a great center of Christianity, trade and western

C

learning until it was invaded by the Ottoman Turks in 1453.

The Byzantines built many beautiful buildings. One of these is the famous Cathedral of Saint Sophia which was begun in the reign of Constantine. It was first a Christian church and then a Muslim church, or *mosque*. Today it is a museum containing fine pieces of Byzantine art.

constellation *n*. a group of stars which make a recognizable shape in the sky.
constitution *n*. 1. laws or rules by which a country, society, etc., is governed. 2. a person's physical condition. *He has a strong constitution.*
constrict *vb*. make narrow, compress. **constriction** *n*.
construct *vb*. build, fit together. **construction** *n*. **constructive** *adj*. creative, helpful.
consult *vb*. try to get advice or help from someone or from a book. *When we do not know the meaning of a word we consult a dictionary.* **consultation** *n*.
consume *vb*. eat or drink; devour; destroy. *Fire consumed the building.*
contact *vb*. meet; join; get in touch with someone. *n*. a link; an electrical connection; a person you can get in touch with. *I have a good contact working in TV.*
contain *vb*. hold something. *This box contains my belongings.* **container** *n*.
contempt *n*. 1. the act of despising. 2. disobedience to or open disrespect of a court or judge.
contented *adj*. peaceful and satisfied.
contents 1. *n*. the things that are in something. *The contents of Rudolph's pockets were a penknife, a rubber band, and two candy bars.*
contest *n*. a competition; a fight.
continent *n*. one of the seven main land masses of the world: North America, South America, Asia, Africa, Europe, Australia and Antarctica.

► The continents are not fixed. They are made of lighter rock than the rock on the ocean floor. The great heat in the center of the earth has made the surface rocks break into huge pieces called *plates*. When the plates move they move the continents with them. This movement is very slow – only about an inch in one century.

A few hundred years ago some people saw that the shapes of America, Europe and Africa looked like jigsaw pieces that would fit closely if they were pushed together. This gave them the idea that the continents used to be one big piece of land which broke up. This idea is called continental drift. Today people who study GEOLOGY believe this idea is true.

Geologists think that the movements of the continents pushed up some pieces of land to make mountains such as the Alps and the Himalayas.

continental shelf This is a gently sloping shelf of land under the sea which rings each of the continents. The continental shelf sometimes stretches for hundreds of miles from the shore and reaches a maximum depth of about 600 ft. Beyond the continental shelf is the deep ocean floor.

In the past, the sea level was lower and much of the continental shelf was dry land. Rivers flowed through it to the sea and made valleys or canyons. These canyons are still there, but today they are under the sea.

THE CONTINENTS

AFRICA
AREA: 11,707,000 sq. miles (30,319,000 sq. km).
POPULATION: 484,000,000.
INDEPENDENT COUNTRIES (1982): 53. (including island nations).
HIGHEST PEAK: Mt Kilimanjaro, 19,341 ft. (5,895 m).
LOWEST POINT: Lake Assal (Djibouti), 509 ft. (155 m.) below see level.
LARGEST LAKE: Victoria, 26,828 sq. miles (69,484 sq. km) in Kenya, Tanzania and Uganda.
LONGEST RIVERS: Nile, Zaire, Niger, Zambezi.

ASIA
AREA: 17,139,000 sq. miles (44,387,000 sq. km), including 75 percent of the USSR (east of the Urals and Caspian Sea) and 97 percent of Turkey.
POPULATION: 2,693,000,000.
INDEPENDENT COUNTRIES (1982): 40.
HIGHEST PEAK: Mt. Everest, 29,028 ft. (8,848 m).
LOWEST POINT: Shore of Dead Sea, 1,289 ft. (393 m) below sea level.
LARGEST LAKE: Caspian Sea, 169,390 sq. miles (438,695 sq. km).
LONGEST RIVERS: Yangtze, lena, Yenisey, Hwang Ho Ob, Mekong, Amur.

NORTH AMERICA
AREA: 9,363,000 sq. miles (24,249,000 sq. km) including Mexico, Central America, the West Indies and Greenland, a self-governing county of Denmark.
POPULATION: 382,000,000.
INDEPENDENT COUNTRIES (1982): 22.
HIGHEST PEAK: Mt. McKinley (Alaska), 20,322 ft. (6,194 m).
LOWEST POINT: Death Valley (California), 282 ft. (86 m) below sea level.
LARGEST LAKE: Lake Superior, 31,820 sq. miles (82,409 sq. km).
LONGEST RIVERS: Mississippi-Missouri-Red Rock.

SOUTH AMERICA
AREA: 6,885,000 sq. miles (17,832,000 sq. km).
POPULATION: 262,000,000.
INDEPENDENT COUNTRIES (1982): 12.
HIGHEST PEAK: Mt. Aconcagua, 22,835 ft. (6,960 m).
LARGEST LAKE: Maracaibo (Venezuela), 8,296 sq. miles (21,485 sq. m).
LONGEST RIVER: Amazon.
HIGHEST WATERFALL: Angel Falls in Venezuela (the world's highest), 3,212 ft. (979 m).

EUROPE
AREA: 4,066,000 sq. miles (10,531,000 sq. km), including 25 percent of the USSR (west of the Urals and Caspian Sea) and 3 percent of Turkey.
POPULATION: 695,000,000, Europe is the most densely populated continent.
INDEPENDENT COUNTRIES: 32 (not including the USSR and Turkey).
HIGHEST POINT: Mt. Elbruz 18,481 ft. (5,633 m).
LARGEST LAKE: Caspian Sea on Europe-Asia border, 169,390 sq. miles (438,695 sq. km).
LONGEST RIVERS: Volga, Danube.

OCEANIA
AREA: 3,286,000 sq. miles (8,510,000 sq. km) of which Australia and New Zealand make up 93.5 percent.
POPULATION: 24,500,000.
INDEPENDENT COUNTRIES: 11.
HIGHEST PEAK: Mt. Wilhelm (Papua New Guinea), 15,400 ft. (4,694 m).
LOWEST POINT: Lake Eyre (Australia), 39 ft. (12 m) below sea level.
LONGEST RIVERS: (Australia): Murray, 1,600 miles (2,575 km) and its tributary, the Darling, 1,702 miles (2,740 km).

ANTARCTICA
AREA: 5,100,000 sq miles (13,209,000 sq. km).
POPULATION: there is no permanent population.
HIGHEST POINT: 16,860 ft. (5,139 m) in the Vinson Massif.
ICE SHEET: Antarctica contains the world's largest ice sheet; the average thickness of the ice is 6,560–12,470 ft. (2,000–3,800 m).

Most sea life is found on the continental shelf. Sunlight shines through the water, helping plants, fish and other animals to grow.

continue *vb.* go on being or doing. *We will continue collecting stamps.* **continual** *adj.* unceasing. **continuous** *adj.* uninterrupted, unbroken.

contour *n.* an outline; line on a map joining points of equal height.

contraception *n.* birth control. **contraceptive** *n.* device or drug which prevents conception.

contract 1. *n.* an agreement. *The butcher had a contract to deliver meat to the school.* 2. *vb.* grow smaller. *A heated metal bar contracts as it becomes colder.* **contraction** *n.* tightening of the muscles.

contradict *vb.* go against a person in what he or she says; deny, oppose. **contradiction** *n.* denial, inconsistency.

contrast *vb.* compare different things and notice the differences. *n.* the difference shown by comparing things.

contribute *vb.* give (money etc.). *She's contributed to a number of charities.* **contribution** *n.*

control *vb.* 1. be in charge of. 2. operate machinery. *n.* a lever, wheel or knob which is used to control machinery.

controversy *n.* dispute, argument.

convalescent *n.* & *adj.* regaining health after illness. **convalesce** *vb.*

convene *vb.* call a meeting, meet. **convention** *n.* formal assembly to discuss business, etc.

convenient *adj.* suitable, handy. *Our new house is only two minutes from school. It is very convenient.*

convent *n.* a place where nuns live and work.

converge *vb.* come nearer together. *The two boats were converging rapidly and were in danger of colliding.*

conversation *n.* talk. **converse** *vb.*

convex *adj.* a surface that curves outward, like an upturned saucer.

convey *vb.* carry from one place to another; transmit sound, etc.; lead.

convict 1. *n.* (**kon**-*vikt*) a criminal who has been sent to prison. 2. *vb.* (*kon*-**vict**) prove someone guilty of a crime.

convoy *n.* a group of merchant ships sailing together under naval escort for protection.

cook *vb.* prepare food for table. *n.* a person who cooks.

Cook, James

James Cook (1728–79) was a British sea captain and explorer. His expeditions took him round the world and all over the Pacific Ocean. Cook's discoveries led to Australia, New Zealand and many South Pacific islands becoming British colonies. He was killed in Hawaii in a scuffle with natives.

cooking *n.* a way of making meals by heating food.

Cook Islands

A group of 15 widely scattered islands in the south Pacific Ocean, self-governing in free association with New Zealand. About half the islands' population lives on Raratonga, the seat of government.
LAND AREA: 92 SQ. MILES (238 SQ. KM)
POPULATION: 21,317.

Cook, Mount

Mt Cook is the highest peak in New Zealand. It rises to 12,349 ft. (3,760 meters) in the Southern Alps in the South Island, and was named after the explorer James Cook. The mountain's name in Maori is *Aorangi*, meaning "cloud-piercer." Today it forms part of Mount Cook National Park.

cool *adj.* rather cold; the opposite of warm.

Coolidge, John Calvin

Calvin Coolidge (1872–1933) was the 30th President of the United States. He was elected Vice-President in 1920 and became President when President Harding died in 1923. In 1924 he was elected to a full four-year term of office. He was a popular President and he would probably have been re-elected had he not decided to retire after one term. Coolidge strongly disapproved of government interference in business. He reduced taxes on businesses and cut government spending.

Coolidge was born in Plymouth, Vermont. He studied at Amherst College and became a lawyer in 1897. He was mayor of Northampton, Massachusetts, then state senator and governor of the state.

Coolidge was not very interested in foreign affairs. At that time isolationism was popular and he did not support the League of Nations. In 1919 he called in the State Guard to deal with rioters and looters during a Boston police strike. In 1927 he handed newspapermen a note saying, "I do not choose to run for President in 1928." He was succeeded by Herbert Hoover.

Cooper, James Fenimore

James Fenimore Cooper (1789–1851) was the first writer to tell stories about American Indians and the excitement of early America. His best known books are *The Last of the Mohicans, The Deerslayers, The Pathfinder* and *The Prairie*.

cooperate *vb.* work with others to do something. *If we cooperate we will finish the job sooner.* **cooperation** *n.* **cooperative** *adj.* willing to help.

Copenhagen

Copenhagen is the capital and largest city of DENMARK. It is also one of the oldest and most beautiful cities in Europe. Some of the buildings date back to the 1500s.

It is the principal port and the busiest center of trade between Scandinavia and other countries. A quarter of all the people in Denmark live in Copenhagen.

The city has a large trade in butter, wool, grain and metals. It is famous for its fine porcelain ware.

The most famous of Copenhagen's many statues is that of the *Little Mermaid*, a character in one of Hans Christian ANDERSEN'S fairy tales.

Copernicus, Nicolaus

Nicolaus Copernicus (1473–1543) was a Polish scientist. He is sometimes called the father of modern ASTRONOMY.

Copernicus showed that the earth is not the center of the UNIVERSE, as people used to believe. Instead, the earth and PLANETS revolve around the sun. Copernicus also showed that the earth itself moves round, or *rotates*, each day, and stars do not.

copper *n.* a reddish-brown metal (symbol – *Cu*).

► Copper was probably one of the first metals that people used. About 7,000 years ago the ancient Egyptians and people in Iraq began to use copper for their tools and weapons. They also made copper ornaments. At first they used pure copper which they found in the ground. But most copper is found with other metals and minerals in a mixture called ore. People began to heat, or *smelt*, copper ores so that the pure copper melted and flowed out.

Copper is very soft when it is pure. But if it is mixed with other metals it makes ALLOYS such as BRASS and BRONZE, which are harder and better for making tools. Copper can be beaten into sheets or pulled out into wire. It lets heat and electricity pass through it very easily, so it is often used for making pots and pans and electric wires.

copy *vb.* make something look exactly like something else. *n.* exact reproduction.

copyright *n.* the ownership of a piece of writing or other art form.

coral *n.* hard pink or white material made mainly in warm, shallow seas from the skeletons of tiny animals.

► Coral is made by tiny animals, called coral polyps, that build limestone "shells" around themselves for protection. Most coral polyps live in groups, or colonies. These may take many shapes, from lacy fans to stubby branches, all in beautiful colors. Other colonies form thick underwater walls known as reefs.

Along some reefs waves may throw up bits of sand and coral which gradually build up on top of the reef

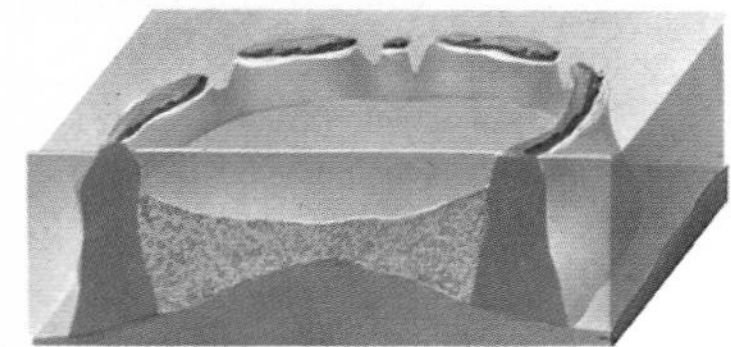

A coral reef of atoll.

until it is above water. The reef then becomes an island. One kind of coral island is the *atoll*, a ringed reef that encloses a central lagoon.

cord *n.* a thin rope or stout length of string.
corduroy *n.* a cotton velvet fabric with ridges or "wales" in the pile.
core *n.* the center of, the middle part. *Our dog likes to eat the core of my apple.*
corgi *n.* a small Welsh breed of dog.
cork *n.* the light tough bark of the cork-oak tree; a bottle stopper made from cork.
► The cork used to make bottle-stoppers comes from the smooth bark of the cork oak tree of the Mediterranean. It is a light, spongy material that forms a thick layer about 1.5 in. (3 cm) deep around the trunk of the tree.

Cork is stripped from cork oaks once very nine or 10 years until the trees are about 150 years old.

A cork oak must be about 20 years old before its bark is thick enough to be stripped. The best cork comes after the second stripping. When the cork is carefully stripped off, the inner layer continues to produce more cork. Cork will never grow on a spot where the inner layer of the bark has been cut by the stripper's hatchet.

corkscrew *n.* a tool for taking corks out of bottles.
corm *n.* a bulblike underground swelling on the stem of a plant. *A crocus grows from a corm.*
cormorant *n.* a sea bird.
► The cormorant is found in most parts of the world. It has a curved bill, black plumage, and webbed feet. An excellent swimmer, it is used to catch fish by people in some eastern countries.

corn *n.* the seeds of wheat, oats, rye and barley; the ears or kernels of corncob corn.
corner *n.* a point where two sides meet. *The front door is near the corner of the building.*
cornet *n.* a brass instrument similar to the trumpet.
cornflour *n.* finely ground maize, rice, etc.

coronation *n.* the ceremony when a king or queen is crowned.
corpse *n.* dead human body.
correct *adj.* right; true; with no mistakes. *All my work was correct today. vb.* put right any mistakes. *Our teacher corrects our work every day.* **correction** *n.*
correspond *vb.* 1. be similar to. 2. exchange letters. **correspondence** *n.*
corridor *n.* a long passage in a building.
corroborate *vb.* support something with more evidence. *The witness will corroborate my story.*
corrode *vb.* wear away by the action of rust, etc. **corrosion** *n.*
corrupt *vb.* spoil, influence badly. *adj.* evil, rotten. **corruption** *n.*

Corsica
Corsica is an island in the MEDITERRANEAN Sea. It is a department (county) of FRANCE. Corsica has been under French control since the 1700s, except for a brief period when it was ruled by Britain. The capital is Ajaccio (*A-jax-io*). NAPOLEON BONAPARTE was born on the island.

Cortes, Hernando
Hernando Cortes (1485–1547) was a Spanish soldier and explorer who in 1519 landed on the coast of Mexico. With a force of only 600 men and a handful of horses he conquered the great AZTEC empire. Cortes' horses and guns helped convince the Aztecs he was a god. He marched on their capital, captured the Aztec emperor Montezuma, and by 1521 had taken control of Mexico.

Cortez spent the next few years taking other cities and districts for Spain. In 1536, he commanded an expedition that founded the first settlement in Lower California.

After a while, Cortez fell out of favor with the Spanish king. He returned to Spain to plead his cause but was unsuccessful.

cosmetics *n.* beauty preparations for hair, skin, etc. **cosmetic** *adj.*
► Cosmetics have been used since prehistoric times when cave people decorated their dead with dyes and paints. Lipsticks, eye-shadow, nail polish, rouge and hair dyes were used widely by the ancient Egyptians. The Greeks and Romans bathed with many kinds of scented oil and wore perfumes to make their bodies and clothing smell sweet.

Today cosmetics are big business. Modern cosmetics are used for cleaning the skin and for coloring and decorating the face and body in countless ways.

cosmic rays *pl. n.* tiny particles that crash into the earth's atmosphere from outer space.
► Like other kinds of RADIOACTIVITY, cosmic rays carry an electric charge.

When cosmic rays reach the upper layers of the atmosphere they collide with atoms of air. Showers of new particles, known as "secondary rays", are formed. These weaker rays are the ones that finally reach the ground.

cosmonaut *n.* (usually) a Soviet astronaut.
cost 1. *n.* the amount one has to pay for something. 2. *vb.* cause the loss of. *His attempt to save the boy cost him his life.* **costly** *adj.* expensive.

From left: Barley, corn, rice, rye, oats and wheat.

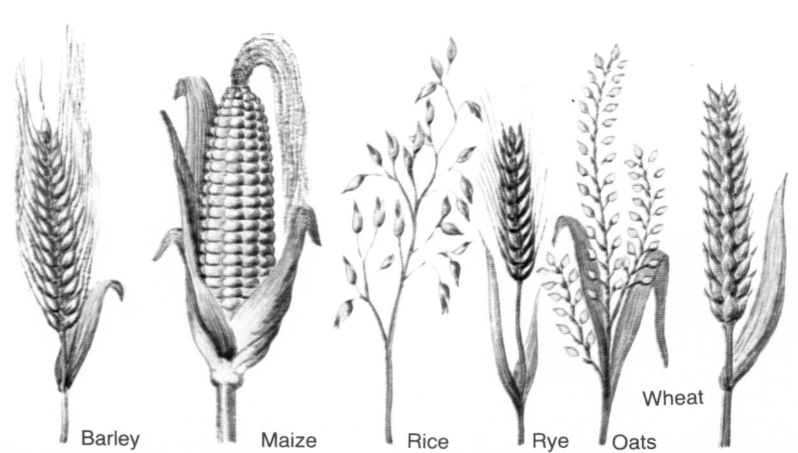

Costa Rica (Costa Rican)
Costa Rica (Spanish for "Rich Coast") is a mountainous republic in Central America. Costa Rica is a comparatively prosperous country. Its main cash crop is coffee. Costa Rica became independent in 1821.
AREA: 19,576 SQ. MILES (50,700 SQ. KM)
POPULATION: 2,329,000
CAPITAL: SAN JOSÉ
CURRENCY: COLON
OFFICIAL LANGUAGE: SPANISH

costume *n.* clothes, especially the clothes worn by actors.

► Costumes in the ancient world were based on the tunic, which developed into the soft folds of the Greek *chiton* and the Roman *toga*. The influence of the East through the BYZANTINE EMPIRE brought rich colors and patterns to clothing that was of finer materials and often decorated with jewels. Throughout the MIDDLE AGES in Europe, the dress of ordinary people remained crude, but the wealthly dressed in fine silks and damasks from the East. The new wealth and reawakening of art during the RENAISSANCE brought with it a taste for sumptuous fabrics and often exaggerated styles.

Outrageous styles reached their peak in the 18th century. The reaction to these resulted in the simpler fashions of the early 19th century. Costume remained sober, though often elaborate, throughout the 1800s. The 20th century saw a social revolution in clothing styles, with more practical fashions for women and a uniformity of modern dress that has spread to most parts of the world.

cot *n.* a small bed. (Formerly a naval officer's swinging bed).
cottage *n.* a small house usually in the country.
cotton *n.* fiber from the seeds of the cotton plant.
► Cotton grows in warm and tropical places all around the world. It is one of the most important plants grown by people; its fibers and seeds are both used. The fibers are made into cloth and the seeds are used for oil and cattle food. The oil is used in soaps, paints and cosmetics.

Cotton has green fruits called bolls. When they are ripe, the bolls split open. Inside them is a mass of white fibers and seeds. The bolls are harvested and the fibers are separated from the seeds. The fibers are spun into yarn and then woven into cloth.
couch *n.* a long, soft seat.
cougar *n.* another name for the puma, or mountain lion, a large member of the cat family native to the Americas.
cough (koff) *n.* & *vb.* a sudden and noisy rush of air from the lungs.
council *n.* a group of people who meet to make decisions.
counsel *vb.* & *n.* advice. *He gave Tom some wise counsel.* an adviser in law.
count 1. *vb.* add up. *Have you started to count the money yet?* 2. *n.* a European nobleman.
counter 1. *n.* a table or flat surface in a shop. 2. *n.* a small piece used in a board game. 3. *prefix* meaning against, opposing, opposite, rival, e.g. **counteract** act in opposition to; **counterbalance** act against in equal strength; **counterattraction** rival attraction.
countess *n.* wife of an earl.
country *n.* the whole land where people live. *France is the country of the French.* the land outside towns. *We like to walk in the country on weekends.*
county *n.* a part of the country with its own local government.
couple *n.* two; a pair.
coupon *n.* detachable ticket which can be exchanged for something or used to apply for something.
courage *n.* bravery.
courier (**koo**-*ree-er*) *n.* messenger; often someone in the diplomatic service.
course *n.* 1. the direction in which something goes. *We followed the course of the river to its mouth.* 2. one of successive parts of a meal. *The dessert course.*
court *n.* 1. the place where trials are held. 2. the place where a king or queen lives, and the people who live there. 3. an area marked out for certain outdoor games, as a tennis court or squash court.
courteous (**kur**-*tee-us*) *adj.* polite, well-mannered. **courtesy** *n.*
cousin *n.* the child of your aunt or uncle.
cover *vb.* put something over something else.
covering *n.* something that covers something. *Bark is the covering of a tree trunk.*
cow *n.* 1. a farm animal kept for its milk. 2. a female of the ox family or a female elephant, whale or seal.
coward *n.* a person who cannot hide fear and who lacks courage.
cowardice *n.* cowardly conduct.
cowardly *adj.*
cowboy *n.* a person who looks after cattle on the American prairies.
► There are still many people in the American West who ride horses and herd cows, but the great days of the cowboys lasted only 40 years, from the 1860s to 1900.

At that time, there were open grasslands stretching from Texas to Canada. Cattle were grazed there and then driven in great herds by cowboys to the railroad stations.

A cowboy's life was simple and hard. Out on the grassland, or *range*, he was his own boss. He often stayed in the wild for many months.

Because of the roaming life they led, cowboys traveled light. Usually they owned nothing more than their horse, saddle, bedroll and the clothes they wore. Although many cowboys had guns, they never carried pistols when they worked. They were too heavy and got in the way.

cowslip *n.* a plant of the primrose family.
coy *adj.* excessively shy.
coyote (*koy*-**oh**-*ti*) *n.* the wild dog of North America, resembling a small wolf.
coypu *n.* South American aquatic rodent whose fur is highly valued.
crab *n.* a marine animal with a hard shell and 10 legs, two of which have large claws.
► Most people think that crabs live only in the sea. But there are some kinds that live in fresh water (rivers or lakes) and some tropical kinds that make their home on land.

Crabs belong to a group of animals called CRUSTACEANS. They have hard, thick shells that cover their flat bodies. They also have long, spidery legs for walking under water, swimming and burrowing. The first pair of legs have pincers which are used for attacking and holding prey. Crabs have their eyes on the end of short stalks. These can be pulled into the shell for safety.

crack 1. *vb.* split; break. *Jack cracked a nut.* **cracked** *adj.* split, broken. 2. *n.* a sharp noise. 3. *n.* a split or small opening. *There is a crack in the cup.*
cracker *n.* 1. a small party favor

enclosed in a cylinder of colored paper which snaps when the ends are pulled. 2. a crisp biscuit or wafer.

cradle *n.* a bed for a small baby, usually on rockers.

craft *n.* 1. skilled work with the hands. 2. a boat; an aircraft.

craftsman *n.* a skilled person who works at a craft.

cram *vb.* stuff into a small space.

cramp *n.* 1. sudden painful contraction of the muscles. 2. restrict; write too small.

crane (bird) *n.* a large water bird with long legs.

► Cranes are tall birds that live in marshlands all around the world. They are 3 to 4 ft. (more than a meter) high and have long legs like stilts. Their necks are slender and they have pointed beaks.

The feathers, or *plumage*, of cranes vary from white to brown and gray in color.

Cranes wade through the shallow waters of their home searching for frogs, insects and other prey which they snatch up with their long beaks.

They are famous for their unusual mating, or courtship, dances. The birds leap and turn and sometimes the males and females dance in circles around each other.

crane (machine) *n.* a machine that lifts and moves heavy things.

► A crane usually has a long arm, or *jib*. Cranes may be fixed in one place, like the tower cranes on top of tall buildings. Sometimes they are mounted on special wheels, railroad wagons, or the backs of trucks, so they can be moved around.

Modern jib-cranes have a powerful motor which hoists up the hook, raises and lowers the crane's arm, and also moves the driver's cab around. Instead of a hook, some cranes have a big electromagnet for lifting scrap metal. To drop the load the driver switches off the electric current.

Some of the biggest cranes are traveling ones. The hook hangs from an overhead arm which can move back and forth along a set of rails. These cranes can lift hundreds of tons at a time.

crash *n.* & *vb.* 1. a loud noise. 2. a collision. *Several cars were involved in the crash.*

crass *adj.* ignorant and stupid.

crate *n.* a large box made from thin pieces of wood.

crater *n.* 1. mouth of a volcano. 2. a hole in the ground made by the explosion of a bomb or shell.

crave *vb.* have a great desire for. **craving** *n.*

crawl 1. *vb.* move on all fours like a baby. 2. *n.* an overarm stroke in swimming.

crayon *n.* a stick of colored chalk or wax for drawing.

craze *n.* a general but passing fashion.

crazy *adj.* foolish, mad; eager for.

creak *n.* & *vb.* (make) harsh, squeaky sound.

cream *n.* the fatty part of milk. *n* & *adj.* the color of cream (yellowish white).

crease *n.* 1. a mark or line made in folding cloth, paper, etc.

create *vb.* make something; bring something into existence. *Authors create characters for their stories.* **creation** *n.* the thing made or created.

creator *n.* 1. a person who creates. 2. the God who created the universe.

creature *n.* any living being.

creek *n.* a small stream, often a tributary to a river.

creep *vb.* move along close to the ground; crawl; move stealthily.

creeper *n.* a plant that creeps along the ground or up a wall.

cremate *vb.* burn to ashes (especially dead bodies).

Creole *n.* & *adj.* person of European descent born in West Indies or Latin America; person of mixed French or Spanish and Negro descent.

crêpe paper (crêpe rhymes with *grape*) *n.* a special sort of crinkly paper.

crept *vb.* past of **creep**.

crescent *n.* the moon when less than one-quarter of it is visible; any object with one side concave and the other convex.

cress *n.* a family of plants, such as watercress, some of which are eaten in salads.

crest *n.* 1. tuft of hair or feathers on the head of certain birds and animals. 2. emblem on a coat of arms. 3. highest point.

Crete (Cretan)

Crete is a mountainous island in the Mediterranean. It lies to the south of GREECE. Today it is a poor land, the home of half-a-million people who are mostly Greek and live mainly by farming. About 5,000 years ago a great civilization began in Crete. It lasted for over a thousand years.

This civilization was forgotten about until 1900 when Arthur Evans, a British archaeologist, rediscovered it. He began digging, or *excavating*, the ruins of a palace at Knossos.

Soon Evans found more remains which told him about the old civilization. It had busy towns and traded with ancient EGYPT. The people had well-built homes and some of the houses had beautiful wall paintings, or *frescoes*. Evans called this civilization Minoan, after a legendary king of Crete called Minos. The Minoans also had an alphabet and could write.

Suddenly, in about 1400 B.C., many of the palaces and cities were destroyed. This may have been caused by an earthquake.

crew *n.* workers on a ship or aircraft.

crib *n.* 1. a baby's bed. 2. rack for animal fodder. 3. a literal translation of something in a foreign language. 4. a note used for cheating in an examination.

cribbage *n.* a card game.

crick *n.* cramp or stiffness in the back of the neck.

cricket *n.* 1. a small insect like a grasshopper that leaps and makes a chirping noise. 2. an outdoor summer game played with bats and a ball by teams of 11 players.

► Cricket is a very old game. It was probably first played in the 1300s in England. The early bats were curved, and there were no wickets. But by the early 1800s the game was very much as it is now. The pitch is 22 yards (20 meters) from wicket to wicket; the three stumps are 28 inches (71.1 cm) high and 9 inches (22.9 cm) wide. The ball must weigh between 5½ and 5¾ ounces (156 and 163 gm); the bat must not be more than 4¼ inches (10.8 cm) wide.

cried *vb.* past of **cry**.

crime *n.* something done that is against the law.

Crimean War

The Crimean War (1854–56) was a struggle between Russia on one side and Turkey, FRANCE and GREAT BRITAIN on the other. At that time the Turkish Empire was very weak. Russia hoped to make its power greater in the eastern Mediterranean by taking CONSTANTINOPLE.

The British, French and Turks pushed the Russian army back into the Crimean peninsula, where the war was fought. There was much misery and suffering.

For the first time, newspaper reporters and photographers went to the battlegrounds. They reported the terrible conditions of the soldiers to the newspapers.

Part of the ruins of the Palace of Knossos in Crete.

criminal *n.* someone who is guilty of a crime.
crimson *n.* & *adj.* a deep red color.
cringe *vb.* shrink in fear.
cripple *n.* someone whose body is so badly hurt or deformed as to be lame or unable to do things easily. *vb.* disable, maim.
crisis *n.* a decisive point; a difficult time.
crisp *adj.* dry and hard, but easy to break.
criticize (**krit**-*is-ize*) *vb.* express judgment on (work of art, etc.); analyze; find fault with. **critic** *n.* person who criticizes, reviews a work of art, etc. **critical** *adj.* fault-finding; concerning a crisis or risk. *A critical operation.*
croak *vb.* & *n.* (make) a harsh, hoarse sound of a frog, raven, etc.
crochet (*kro*-**shay**) *n.* kind of knitting done with a hooked needle.
crockery *n.* earthenware or china vessels, e.g. cups, plates, etc.

Crockett, David
Davy Crockett (1786–1836) was an American frontiersman. In 1813 he became a scout in General Andrew Jackson's army which was fighting the Creek Indians.

During the Texas Revolution, when the Texans were fighting against the Mexicans, Crockett became a national hero. He joined a group of American soldiers trapped in the Alamo, a Spanish fort that now stands in the center of San Antonio, Texas. The Americans were outnumbered by the Mexican army and Davy Crockett died in fierce hand-to-hand fighting.

Crockett's bravery and simple humor made him a legendary figure in American history. There are many stories about him, his long-barreled rifle "Betsy" and his famous coonskin cap.

crocodile *n.* a fierce, long reptile that lives in rivers.
► Crocodiles and their relatives, the ALLIGATORS, caymans and gavials are the largest of the living REPTILES. They live in swamps and rivers in warm parts of the world.

A crocodile (above) shows its fourth tooth in its lower jaw. In alligators the tooth is hidden.

Crocodiles have heavy bodies covered with bony scales. Their tails are long and powerful, and they wave them from side to side when swimming. Their jaws have sharp teeth.

Crocodiles hunt fish, turtles, birds and water mammals. They usually attack from under the water. Sometimes crocodiles eat land mammals. They float in the water with only the tops of their heads showing. When an animal comes to the river bank to drink, the crocodile swims quickly towards it underwater. The crocodile then pulls the animal into the water with its strong jaws and drowns it.

Crocodiles lay white eggs in nests or holes in the ground. As soon as the young hatch out of the eggs they are able to run and catch their own food. Many kinds of crocodile are becoming extinct because people hunt them for their skins.

crocus *n.* a small garden flower of the iris family.

Cromwell, Oliver
Oliver Cromwell (1599–1658) was the only ruler of Britain who was not a king or queen. He came to power after the CIVIL WAR of the 1640s. Cromwell was a member of PARLIAMENT. He fought against CHARLES I with the army of Parliament and became its leader.

After Charles I was beheaded, Cromwell became the head of the country but he never made himself king. He was called the "Lord Protector." After Cromwell died, the monarchy was restored.

crook 1. *n.* stick with a hooked top, used by shepherds. 2. *n.* a cheat, swindler. *vb.* bend, cheat.
crooked *adj.* 1. not straight. 2. dishonest.
croon *vb.* sing softly. **crooner** *n.*
crop 1. *n.* the plants that are gathered each year from a farm. 2. *vb.* cut short.
croquet (*krow*-**kay**) *n.* game played on a lawn in which balls are hit with a mallet through a series of hoops.
cross *n.* 1. the mark (X). 2. the wooden frame on which Jesus was crucified; the sign of the cross (+) as the symbol of the Christian faith.
crossbow *n.* spring-operated medieval weapon which fired an iron bolt.
crossing *n.* a place where people can go to the other side of the street. *It is safer to walk at the crossing.*
crossroads *n.* a place where two roads intersect.
crosswind *n.* blowing from the side.
crow 1. *n.* a large, black bird with a harsh cry. 2. *vb.* give a shrill cry like a cock. 3. *vb.* boast.
► Crows belong to a family of birds which may reach 20 in. (50 cm) in length when fully grown. Most are dark gray or a shiny black color. They feed on almost anything: grain, eggs and young birds, insects and dead animals. Their nests are big and untidy and built in tall trees.

Crows are clever birds and are easy to tame. They can be taught to copy human speech.

crowbar *n.* bar of iron used as a lever.
crowd *n.* a lot of people gathered together.
crown *n.* the headdress of a king or queen.

Crown Jewels
The Crown Jewels belong to the kings and queens of Great Britain and are kept in the Tower of London. Some of the Crown Jewels are worn by the monarch when he or she is being crowned.

The Crown Jewels include crowns, scepters, staffs, spurs, swords and bracelets. They are made of gold and precious stones. The Imperial State Crown, made for Queen VICTORIA, has in it a huge ruby, called the Black Prince's Ruby.

crucial *adj.* critical, decisive.
crucifix *n.* a figure or picture of Christ on the cross.
crude *adj.* rough, unfinished, raw in natural state. **crudeness**, *n.* **crudity** *n.*
cruel *adj.* liking to give pain to others. **cruelty** *n.*
cruise *vb.* sail about for pleasure. **cruiser** *n.* warship designed for speed.

An archer winding back the cord of his crossbow.

crumb *n.* a small scrap of bread or other food.
crumble *vb.* fall or break into small pieces.
crumpet *n.* soft round cake which is toasted and buttered.
crumple *vb.* crease carelessly; crush into a ball.
crunch *vb.* crush, grind noisily with the teeth; tread underfoot making noise of grinding gravel.
crusade *n.* & *vb.* a campaign or movement or undertaking to further a cause.
► The Crusades were wars between Christians and Muslims in the MIDDLE AGES. They took place in Palestine, the Holy Land. In 1087, the Turks captured the city of Jerusalem in Palestine. The Turks were Muslims and they stopped Christians from visiting the holy places in Palestine.

The Christian rulers in Europe were angered by this. A few years later, the Byzantine emperor in Constantinople asked the Pope to help him drive the Turks from the Holy Land. The Pope started the first Crusade. He said that the sins of all the people who went and fought in the Holy Land would be forgiven.

The armies of the first Crusade were successful. They took Jerusalem from the Turks in 1099. The Crusaders set up Christian kingdoms along the coast of Palestine and Syria and built strong fortresses to defend their new lands.

There were seven more Crusades. Many failed because the Crusaders quarreled with each other. The Turks took back much of the Holy Land from the Christians. When the Turks took Jerusalem in 1187, the third Crusade set off from Europe. When they got to the Holy Land the Crusaders were defeated by the Turks who had a new general called Saladin.

Later, the Crusaders forgot that they were fighting for their religion. Many of them went to Palestine hoping to take the land and become rich. By 1291, the Turks took the last remaining Christian city at Acre.

During the Crusades European people learned more about the eastern parts of the world. When they returned to Europe they took back with them many new things such as foods, spices, silk clothes and paper. They learned about medicine, mathematics and astronomy from the Arabs of the east, and trade between east and west began to grow.

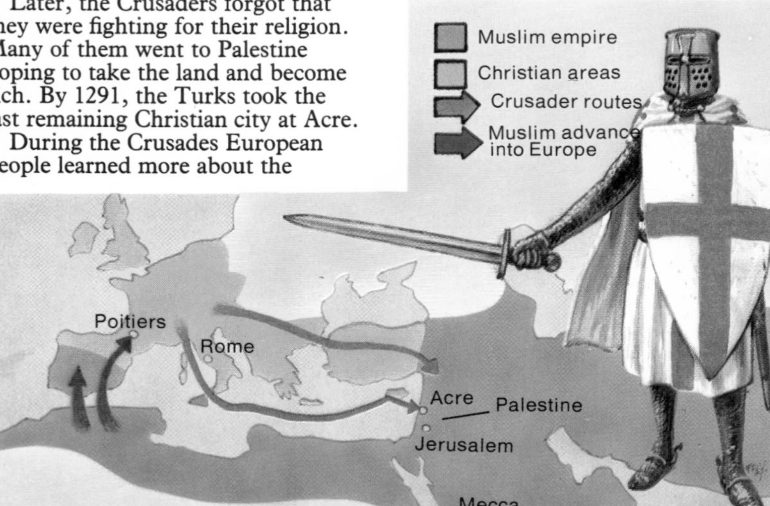

crush *vb.* 1. press on and break into pieces. *If you sit on the crackers you will crush them.* 2. defeat. *Napoleon went on to crush all his enemies.*
crust *n.* a hard, outer layer, like a crust of bread. **crusty** *adj.* having much crust; irritable.
crustacean *n.* one of a group of animals, most of which have a hard, chalky shell and live in the sea.
► Crustaceans are a large group of about 10,000 animals. They include sandhoppers, wood lice, water fleas, BARNACLES, crayfish, shrimps, prawns, CRABS and LOBSTERS. All have hard jointed bodies and jointed legs. Most crustaceans live in the sea.

Crustaceans are *invertebrates* (animals with no backbones). Most have SHELLS around their bodies. This keeps their soft bodies safe. Many have a set of claws, or pincers, on their front legs. They use these to defend themselves and to grab their prey.

Crustaceans are born as eggs. These hatch into tiny *larvae* which make up much of the floating PLANKTON which other sea animals eat. As each larva grows, it sheds its shell and grows a new one which is bigger. This is called *molting*. When the larva becomes an adult, it continues to grow and molt.

The best-known crustaceans are the large shellfish such as lobsters, shrimps, crabs and crayfish. They all have 10 legs, including one pair with pincers. Except for crayfish, they all live in the sea. Many of them are very good to eat.

Many crustaceans live on the seashore in rock pools. Lobsters have two very big claws, or pincers, on their front legs. They use these to grab and crush their prey before they eat it. They have long feelers on the front of their head to help them find food.

There are many kinds of crab, including the one that we usually eat. The smallest is the pea crab which lives inside mussels. Hermit crabs live inside the empty shells of other sea animals. The sea spider is a tiny crab with long legs like a spider.

Barnacles live on rocks, on pieces of wood and often on the bottom of boats. They open their shells and put out long, feathery hairs which trap food floating in the water.

crutch *n.* something that helps a lame person to walk.
cry *vb.* make a loud noise; weep or sob.
crypt *n.* the basement of a church; an underground place of worship.
cryptogram *n.* a message written in code.
crystal 1. *n.* a hard glasslike mineral. 2. *adj.* the shape which tiny pieces of many chemicals, such as salt, always take. 3. *n.* a kind of good quality, very clear glass.
► If you look closely at sugar through a magnifying glass, you will see that it is made up of thousands of tiny glassy pieces with flat sides. They are sugar crystals. SNOW is made up of tiny crystals of frozen water.

All crystals have a definite shape. They have smooth, flat sides that meet in sharp edges. The shape of any one type of crystal never changes, but there are many different crystal shapes. The differences between them are caused by the arrangements of the ATOMS in the crystals.

For example, the salt you eat is made up of two different kinds of

All the crystals that make up a substance are always the same. Snowflakes are made up of tiny crystals of water and are always six-sided.

atoms – sodium and chlorine atoms. The tiny sodium and chlorine atoms are arranged in cube patterns. If you look at salt grains through a magnifying glass, you will see that most of them are little cubes. All salt crystals are built in the same way.

cub *n.* 1. a young bear, lion, fox, tiger, or some other animal. 2. a junior Boy Scout.

Cuba (Cuban)
Cuba is an island in the Caribbean Sea. It is part of the WEST INDIES. Much of the island is hilly, with high mountains on the southeast. In the center are large cedar and mahogany forests. Cuba has big sugar cane plantations and tobacco farms.

The climate is warm and pleasant, but Cuba lies in the path of hurricanes which come blowing through the West Indies every year. Hurricanes are very strong winds which travel fast and often damage buildings and farms.

Cuba was ruled by Spain after Christopher Columbus went there in 1492. The United States took Cuba from Spain in 1898. In 1902 the island became independent. Cuba became a Communist country in 1959 under its leader Fidel Castro.

AREA: 44,220 SQ. MILES (114,524 SQ. KM)
POPULATION: 10,346,000
CAPITAL: HAVANA
CURRENCY: PESO
OFFICIAL LANGUAGE: SPANISH

cube *n.* a solid object with six equal sides. **cubic** *adj.* cube shaped.

► The space a cube fills is called its volume. You can find the volume of a cube by multiplying the length of a side by itself and then by itself again. If the length of a side is 3 in. the volume of the cube is $3 \times 3 \times 3 = 27$ cubic inches.

Many kinds of CRYSTAL have a cube shape. This is because of the way their ATOMS are arranged.

cuckoo *n.* a family of birds that lay their eggs in the nests of other birds.
► The European cuckoo is a large bird about 12 in. (30 cm) long. It is blue-gray in color with stripes underneath. It eats mainly insects. The call of the European cuckoo sounds just like its name.

European cuckoos do not build nests. They lay their eggs in the nests of other birds such as warblers and sparrows. The female cuckoo watches while the other birds build their nests and lay their eggs. When they leave the nest to find food the cuckoo pulls one of the eggs out of the nest, then lays her own egg in its place and flies away. After about two weeks the young cuckoo hatches. It pushes the other eggs or baby birds out of the nest. The foster parents feed and take care of the cuckoo.

Two American cuckoos, the black-billed cuckoo and the yellow-billed cuckoo, are very different from the European kind. They are shy birds which live in trees and eat caterpillars. These birds do not have the same call as the European cuckoo and they usually build their own nests and take care of their young.

cucumber *n.* the long, narrow, green fruit of a kind of vine, eaten in salads.
cud *n.* food that cows and other ruminants bring back from their first stomach to chew again.
cuddle *vb.* hug, **cuddly** *adj.* pleasant to hug, like soft toys.

cue *n.* 1. a long rod for playing billiards, pool, etc. 2. signal for an actor to enter stage or start a speech; hint.
cuff 1. *n.* the end of the sleeve. 2. *n.* & *vb.* hit someone with the open hand.
culprit *n.* a guilty person.
cultivate *vb.* help plants to grow by preparing the soil well and looking after them.
culture *n.* type of civilization. **cultured** *adj.* well educated.

Cuneiform
Cuneiform is the earliest known kind of writing. It was used from about 3300 B.C. to about A.D. 75 by people living in Mesopotamia and surrounding countries. Cuneiform means "wedge-shaped." It was written on soft clay tablets with a broad-headed stylus which made wedge-shaped marks.

cunning *adj.* crafty; artful. *The fox is a cunning animal.*
cup *n.* an open, bowl-shaped vessel for drinking beverages.
cupboard (**cub**-*erd*) *n.* a closet with shelves for storing things.
curate *n.* assistant to a parish priest.
curb 1. *vb.* & *n.* part of a bridle used to check or restrain a horse; a restraint. 2. *n.* the stone edge of a pavement.
cure *vb.* 1. make well. 2. preserve some substances such as leather, tobacco and some meats by drying, smoking or salting them.

Curie, Marie and Pierre
Marie Curie (1867–1934) and Pierre Curie (1859–1906) were scientists who worked together. They studied RADIOACTIVITY and discovered the elements RADIUM and polonium. They married each other in 1895.

Because of their work on radioactivity and their discovery of radium in 1898, they were given the NOBEL PRIZE for physics in 1903. When Pierre was killed three years later, Marie took over his job as professor at the Sorbonne University in Paris. In 1911 she was given a second Nobel Prize, this time for chemistry.

curious *adj.* 1. odd; strange. *Jane was wearing a very curious hat.* 2. wanting to find out about something. *I am very curious as to why she is wearing that hat.*
curlew *n.* wading bird with a long curved bill.
curly *adj.* something that is twisted into shape like a spiral or coil, especially hair. **curl** *n.* & *vb.*
currant *n.* a small, seedless dried grape.
currency *n.* the money that is used in a country.
current *n.* air or water running in one direction.
current (electric) *n.* the movement or flow of electricity.

C

▶ Current must always be flowing before electricity can work. Electricity is made in a GENERATOR at a power station. From there the current travels through wires to your home. Before it reaches your home, a *transformer* reduces its force, or *voltage*, so that it does not burn up the wires and electric equipment in your house.

The current flows out of the sockets in the walls of your house and through the equipment you are using. Then it returns to the generator in the power station through another set of wires.

Electricity in houses flows in one direction and then in the opposite direction. It is called *alternating* current. Each movement back and forth happens very quickly (about 60 times a second). This is too fast for us to notice that the lights are flickering.

Electricity from BATTERIES flows in only one direction. It is called *direct* current.

curry *n.* a hot, spicy food, originally made in India and Pakistan.
curse *n.* asking that evil or punishment fall on a person. *vb.* swear.
curtail *vb.* shorten, reduce.
curtain *n.* a piece of cloth used as a screen, particularly as a covering for windows. *The Iron Curtain is the name given to the frontier between the communist countries of Eastern Europe and the democratic countries of Western Europe.*
curtsy *vb.* & *n.* old-fashioned gesture of respect made by women by bending the knees.
curve *n.* & *vb.* bend; a line that is not straight.
cushion *n.* an object like a small pillow, used for making a chair more comfortable. *vb.* protect (as if with cushions).
custard *n.* sauce made with milk and eggs or cornflour.

Custer, George Armstrong
George Custer was an American army officer who, after the Civil War, won fame as he fought the Indians in the southwest and in the Montana and Dakota territories. He and his regiment were ordered to capture Cheyenne and Sioux Indians and resettle them in reservations.

In 1876, while marching into Montana, Custer came upon a Sioux village on the Little Bighorn River. Custer believed that there were only about 1,000 Indians in the village, but there were really about 3,000. Custer ordered an attack. In fierce fighting, the Sioux, led by Chief Sitting Bull, killed Custer and his men. The battle became known as "Custer's Last Stand."

custody *n.* the state of being detained, often in jail, while awaiting trial. **custodian** *n.* guardian, keeper.
custom *n.* the usual way of doing something. *It is the custom in some countries to kiss people on both cheeks when you meet them.* **customary** *adj.* usual.
customer *n.* a person who buys things from a shop or business, sometimes regularly.
cut *vb.* slice with a knife or other sharp objects. *Can I have a bandage? I've just cut my knee.*
cutlery *n.* knives, fork, spoons, etc., used at table.
cycle 1. *vb.* ride a bicycle. 2. *n.* a series of changes. *These pictures illustrate the life cycle of a frog.*
cyclone *n.* a violent storm with strong winds.

▶ Cyclones are winds which blow inward in a circle, or spiral. In hot, or *tropical* parts of the world cyclones can be very strong and cause great damage. The wind speed can be as fast as 150 mph (240 k/h). These strong cyclones are known by different names such as hurricanes, TORNADOES and, in eastern Asia, typhoons.

Cyclones usually come with storms. The winds bring black clouds and heavy, driving rain, and sometimes thunder and lightning.

Cyclones often start at sea. When they move over land they cause terrible damage. They destroy houses, overturn cars and can even pull up trees.

cygnet *n.* a young swan.
cylinder *n.* 1. a solid or hollow tube-shaped object. 2. the part of an engine in which the piston moves.

Cymbals belong to the percussion section of an orchestra.

cymbals *n. pl.* a metal musical instrument consisting of two brass plates that are struck against each other to make a clashing sound.
cynic (**sin**-*ik*) *n.* a person who sees no good in anything. **cynical** *adj.* sneering; disbelieving good in anything.
cypress (**sigh**-*press*) *n.* tall, evergreen conifer with dark foliage.

Cyprus (Cypriot)
Cyprus is a large, mountainous island in the eastern Mediterranean. It has a warm climate and the farmers grow grapes, lemons, oranges and olives.

Cyprus was ruled by Turkey for 300 years until 1878, when Britain took it over. It became independent

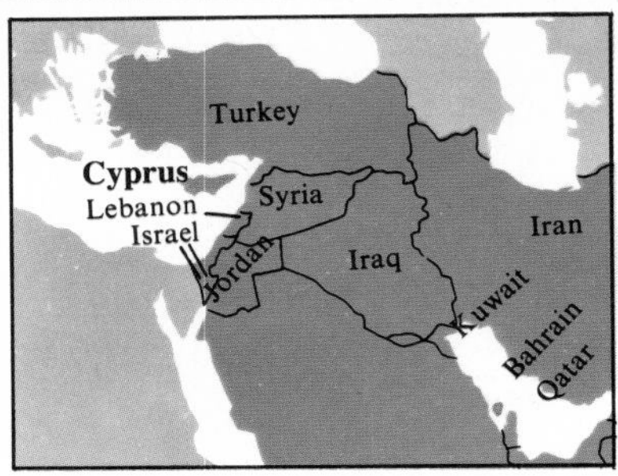

in 1960. The people are Greek Cypriots who are Christian, and Turkish Cypriots who are Muslim. These two groups often quarreled with each other and in the 1960s there was a civil war. Today, Cyprus is split into two parts, one part for the Greek Cypriots and one part for the Turkish Cypriots (the "Turkish Cypriot Federated State")
AREA: 3,572 SQ. MILES (9,251 SQ. KM)
POPULATION: 665,500
CAPITAL: NICOSIA
CURRENCY: GREEK AND TURKISH POUND
OFFICIAL LANGUAGES: GREEK, TURKISH

czar (**tzar**) (*zar*) *n.* title of the former rulers of Russia.

Czechoslovakia (Czechoslovak)
Czechoslovakia is a country in eastern EUROPE. It is surrounded by Germany, Poland, Russia, Hungary and Austria.

Much of Czechoslovakia is covered in hills and mountains, and there are some big forests. Many of the people are farmers. Czechoslovakia also has coal and iron and an important steel industry.

The capital of Czechoslovakia, Prague, is a medieval town, filled with churches and old buildings. Most of the people speak either Czech or Slovak, the two main languages of the country. The government has been communist since 1948. Demands for more freedom in 1968 led to an invasion by

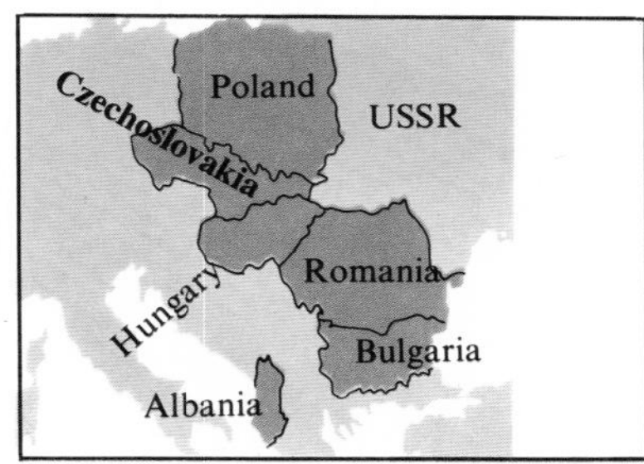

Soviet troops.
AREA: 49,373 SQ. MILES (127,869 SQ. KM)
POPULATION: 15,556,000
CAPITAL: PRAGUE
CURRENCY: KORUNA
OFFICIAL LANGUAGES: CZECH, SLOVAK

D

Sources of Middle Eastern wealth old style and new: sheep and oil.

dab 1. *vb.* press repeatedly. *She dabbed at her eyes with a handkerchief to dry them.* 2. *n.* a kind of flatfish.
dabble *vb.* 1. splash about. 2. undertake in an amateurish way.
dachshund *n.* a small dog with a long body and short legs once used in Germany for hunting badgers.
daddy *n.* a word for "father" used by children.
daffodil *n.* a tall yellow flowering bulb that grows in the spring.
daft *adj.* silly, foolish, crazy.
dagger *n.* a short, two-edged knife used as a weapon.

Daggers (from top): Rondel dagger; Holbein dagger; left-handed dagger.

Daguerre, Louis Jacques
Louis Jacques Daguerre (1789–1851) was a French inventor who in the 1830s developed the daguerreotype photographic process, using metal plates, from which no copies could be made. In Daguerre's process, the sensitive plate had to be exposed for about twenty minutes. When portraits were taken, the subject's head was fixed in a wooden frame to prevent it moving.

dahlia *n.* a brightly colored family of garden flowers related to the daisy.
daily 1. *adj.* something that happens every day. 2. *adv.* every day. 3. *n.* a newspaper that is published every weekday.
dainty *adj.* small, neat and elegant; fastidious.
dairy *n.* a place where milk is kept and butter and cheese are made.
daisy *n.* a small wild flower with a yellow center surrounded by white petals.
dale *n.* valley.

Dalton, John
John Dalton (1766–1844) was an English chemist. He did valuable work on the theory of the atom, and prepared the first table of atomic weights. In physics, Dalton's Law concerns the pressure exerted by gases.

dam *n.* a thick wall of earth, rock or concrete for holding back water. *vb.* restrain with a dam.
► Dams are used for IRRIGATION, to make electricity, or to provide water for towns. Dams are particularly useful in places where there is not much rain. They store the rainwater in large lakes and release it steadily over the whole year. Some dams are made of enormous quantities of earth and rock. Others are made of concrete and stone. Dam-bursts are water breaks through the wall of the dam. The severe flooding that may follow can cause great disasters.

damage *vb.* injure or do harm to something. *You will damage the gate if you swing on it.* *n.* harm, injury. *Little damage was done.*

Damascus
Damascus has been the capital of SYRIA since 1941. The inhabitants believe that it is the oldest continuously inhabited city in the world. It lies on the Plain of Damascus, about 60 miles (100 km) inland from the port of BEIRUT in LEBANON.

damn *vb.* condemn.
damp *adj.* rather wet; soggy; not dry. *n.* moisture. *vb.* moisten; smother.
damson *n.* a small, dark-red kind of plum.
dance *vb.* & *n.* move the feet and body in a rhythmical way, especially to music. **dancer** *n.* one who dances.
► All through the ages dance has been important to people. Early prehistoric cave paintings show men dancing. And today Australian Aborigines still paint dancing figures

D

on their sacred rocks. Archaeologists think that the earliest dances were about the hunt. People used to dress up as animals and make rhythmical movements. They believed this would attract the animals they needed for food and fur. These ancient ritual dances eventually developed into religious ceremonies. People danced to please their gods. They asked them for rain or for a good harvest. Sometimes they asked for success in the hunt or in battle. Dances like these still exist in many parts of the world. But some of them, like the rain dance of the American Indian or the Bolivian temple dance, are now more a tourist attraction than a religious ceremony.

In the Western world the religious meaning of dances disappeared many years ago. Today people dance only for pleasure or entertainment. In the 1920s and 1930s there were hundreds of dance halls. Dances like the foxtrot, quickstep and waltz were popular. Some people still enjoy ballroom dancing and competitions are often shown on television. But young people today prefer a freer form of dance. In modern discotheques where rock and reggae music is played, they make up the dance steps as they go along.

Another kind of dance is the traditional folkdance. Most countries have their own typical dances. In England, Morris dancing is popular and in Spain, the flamenco.

The other main kind of dance is classical BALLET. This graceful dance obeys certain rules of posture and motion. To become a successful ballet dancer needs years of training.

dandelion *n.* a wild flower with bright yellow petals.

dandruff *n.* scurf on skin of skull.

danger *n.* something that is likely to do harm to you. *The ice on the step is a danger to everyone.* **dangerous** *adj.*

Dante

Dante Alighieri (1265–1321) is the greatest poet of ITALY and one of the greatest in the world. His most famous work is the *Divine Comedy*, which consists of three parts (*Inferno, Purgatorio* and *Paradiso*).

As a young man, Dante wrote many poems in praise of Beatrice Portinari (the "Blessed Beatrice"). He became a magistrate of his native Florence in 1300, but was exiled soon afterwards. Dante died in poverty in Ravenna.

Danube River

The Danube is the second longest river in Europe. Only the Volga is longer. The Danube rises as a small stream in the Black Forest in Germany. It flows for more than 1,740 miles (2,800 km) through Germany, Austria, Czechoslovakia, Romania and Bulgaria to the Black Sea. Ships can sail up the Danube for three-quarters of its length.

dare *vb.* 1. be brave enough to do something, venture. *I wouldn't dare cross that road at night.* 2. ask someone to show how brave they are, defy. *I dare you to jump over the stream.* **daring** *adj.* & *n.*

dark 1. *n.* & *adj.* without light; nighttime; gloomy. *I should go home before it gets dark.* 2. *adj.* not light in color. 3. *adj.* having black or brown hair or skin. **darken** *vb.* make or become dark. **darkness** *n.* absence of light.

Dark Ages

Early scholars gave the name Dark Ages to the period in Europe after the fall of the great Roman Empire in the A.D. 400s. During this period barbarian Goths, Vandals and Huns swept down on Europe from the north. They destroyed many fine buildings and works of art that had existed during Roman times. This is why the time was called the Dark Ages. It lasted for about 500 years during the early MIDDLE AGES.

During the Dark Ages, knowledge survived only in monasteries, and there were very few schools. Many of the old arts and crafts were lost.

At this time, however, people were still writing and thinking and making fine works of art in other parts of the world. The eastern Roman Empire was not conquered by the barbarians. There the arts still flourished. And in China and India great civilizations grew and spread.

In the A.D. 1000s Europe began slowly to recover from her artistic darkness. The lost knowledge of the ancient Greeks and Romans was found again. The richer life of the Middle Ages began.

darling *n.* & *adj.* a dearly loved person; a pet.

darn *n.* & *vb.* mend a hole in cloth by sewing threads across it.

dart 1. *vb.* move forward suddenly. 2. *n.* a small sharp-pointed arrow; a game in which darts are thrown.

Darwin, Charles

Charles Darwin (1809–82) was an English biologist. In 1859 he published his great book *The Origin of Species*. Before this, almost everyone believed that the world was created by God exactly as the Bible described. Darwin put forward the theory that all living things evolved from earlier forms. They were alive because they had won the struggle to survive.

Within any species of living thing there would be small variations in shape, size or habit. Some of these variations would increase the living thing's chance of survival. For example, a giraffe with a long neck could reach leaves a giraffe with a shorter neck could not. In times of famine, the taller giraffe would survive while the shorter one would die. The taller giraffe that survived would, in time, replace the variety with the shorter neck. Darwin's theory is known as the theory of EVOLUTION.

dash 1. *vb.* rush; run quickly. 2. *n.* the punctuation mark (—). 3. *n.* a sprinkling. *A dash of sauce.*

dashing *adj.* showy.

data *n.* a fact or thing known used as basis for calculating, reasoning, etc. *There is little data to go on.*

date 1. *n.* the day, the month, the year, or all three together. *The date today is July 13.* *vb.* mark with a date; become out-of-date, old-fashioned. **dateless** *adj.* timeless. 2. *n.* the sweet, sticky fruit that grows on a date palm.

daub *vb.* smear, paint badly.

daughter *n.* a person's female child. **daughter-in-law** *n.* wife of a person's son.

daunt *vb.* lessen the courage of, intimidate.

David

The story of David is told in the Book of Samuel in the Old Testament. David was a skilled harpist, who killed the Philistine giant Goliath. After a period of conflict, he succeeded Saul as the king of Israel.

Davis, Jefferson

Jefferson Davis (1808–1889) was president of the Confederate States of America during the Civil War. As the war turned against the South, Davis became unpopular. He was finally captured by U.S. troops and imprisoned. His sufferings in prison aroused the sympathy of the Southern people and he became a martyr. He was released after two years.

Davis retired in 1878 to write his book "The Rise and Fall of the Confederate Government."

Davy, Humphry

Humphry Davy (1778–1829) was an English scientist. He is best remembered for his invention of the miner's safety lamp. Before this, miners used naked candle flames or oil lamps to light the mine. These caused many fatal gas explosions. Davy's lamp had wire gauze around the flame. This gauze let in air to keep the flame burning, but it also absorbed much of the flame's heat. So the gas in the mine never became hot enough to explode.

dawdle *vb.* move slowly, waste time.

dawn *n.* sunrise, daybreak. *vb.* begin to grow light.

day *n.* the time from midnight to the next midnight; also the part of the day from sunrise to sunset.

▶ The earth turns on its own axis as it moves around the sun. So the part of the earth facing the sun is light while the part facing away from the sun is dark. The lighted part is "day" and the dark part "night." Because the earth turns around, day and night follow each other continually.

Scientists have another way of describing a "day." They say it is the time the earth takes to complete one full turn on its axis. This takes exactly 24 hours.

The length of time that any particular part of the earth is in daylight varies depending on where it is on the globe. This is because the axis of the earth is tilted at an angle to its path around the sun. This also means that some parts of the earth have different amounts of day and night at certain times of the year. For instance, in June in the Arctic it is always daylight. In the Antarctic it is always night. In December it is the other way around – dark all the time in the Arctic and light all the time in the Antarctic.

Because the earth turns all the time it is always day in one place when it is night somewhere else. There is no single time such as "noon" for the whole world. "Noon" occurs with twelve hours difference at opposite sides of the globe. When it is noon in London it is midnight in New Zealand.

To make a clear difference between one day and the next, an imaginary line was drawn from the North to the South Pole. On one side would be one day, and on the other side the day following. This line, known as the "dateline," runs through the Pacific Ocean. It has a strange effect: if you cross the dateline going eastward you gain a day, while those traveling westward miss a day.

The earth rotates on its axis from west to east. As we travel eastward on the revolving earth we pass into sunlight. We see the sun first in the east in the morning. In the evening the sun disappears (sets) in the west.

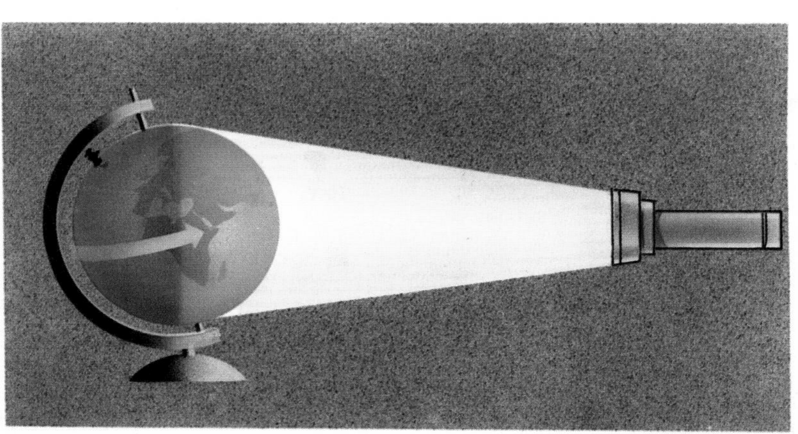

daytime *n.* the time when it is light; the opposite of nighttime.
daze *vb.* bewilder; confuse.
dazzle *vb.* shine very brightly; blind for a moment with a bright light. *It can be difficult to drive a car when the sun dazzles you.*
de- *prefix* meaning down, away, off, from, not, e.g. **decode**, **deduce**, **deform**, **degrade**.
deacon *n.* minor priest. **deaconess** (fem).
dead *adj.* no longer alive.
dead heat *n.* a race in which two or more competitors finish at exactly the same time.
deadlock *n.* inaction, the result of two sides being equally powerful.
deadly *adj.* causing death. *Deadly nightshade is a fatally poisonous plant.*

Dead Sea

The Dead Sea is an enormous salt water lake between Israel and Jordan. It is 50 miles (80 km) long and 10 miles (16 km) wide. Its surface is over 1,292 ft. (394 meters) below sea level. The Dead Sea is six times saltier than the open sea. Nothing can live in it. It is so salty that people who swim in it cannot sink.

Dead Sea Scrolls

The Dead Sea Scrolls is the name given to a number of ancient manuscripts found in caves around Qumran, near the DEAD SEA. The scrolls, which date from around 100 B.C. to A.D. 50, contain much information of value to scholars. They include parts of the Old Testament and many other works. The first scrolls were discovered by accident in 1947.

deaf *adj.* not able to hear well or at all. **deafen** *vb.* **deafness** *n.*
▶ Some people are born deaf. Others go deaf through illness or accident. Deafness and dumbness often go together. In the 1600s a French priest called de L'Epée worked out a language of hand signs. This language has enabled deaf people to communicate with each other. They can also "talk" to people with good hearing who understand the hand signs. Scientists have discovered that many people previously thought to be totally deaf do have some hearing left. Today we have machines that can enable these people to hear and speak properly.

deal *vb.* 1. tell about. *The book deals with butterflies and moths.* 2. give out. *It is your turn to deal the cards.*
deal in *vb.* buy and sell. *The butcher deals in meat.* **dealer** *n.* a person who buys and sells.
deal with *vb.* do whatever has to be done. *You tidy this room and I'll deal with the kitchen.*
dean *n.* head of a cathedral administration (chapter); head of a college or university. **deanery** *n.* dean's house; group of parishes under a dean.
dear *adj.* 1. greatly loved. 2. costing a lot of money; expensive.
dearth *n.* scarcity, lack of (especially of food).
death *n.* end of life; destruction. **deathly** *adj.* like death.
debase *vb.* lower the quality or value.
debate *vb.* discuss or argue in public. *n.* a formal discussion. **debatable** *adj.* something that can be disputed.
debris (*day*-**bree**) *n.* wreckage, broken pieces left after an accident.
debt (rhymes with *yet*) *n.* something that you owe someone.
decade *n.* a 10-year period.
decapitate *vb.* cut off the head.
decathlon *n.* an Olympic sport, consisting of 10 events.
decay *vb.* rot, go bad.
decease *vb.* die. **deceased** *n.* & *adj.* dead (person).
deceive (*de*-**seeve**) *vb.* make someone believe something that you know is not true; cheat. **deceit** *n.* trick. **deceitful** *adj.*
December *n.* the 12th month of the year.
decent *adj.* modest; fairly good; kindly and tolerant.
decibel *n.* a unit of measurement of the intensity of sound.
decide *vb.* make up your mind about something.
deciduous *adj.* trees such as maples and poplars, that lose all their leaves in winter.
decimal *adj.* & *n.* a way of writing fractions by using tens and tenths. Each place to the right of the decimal point stands for one tenth of the value of the place on its left; so 2.1 = 2 units + 1 tenth; 2.14 = 2 units + 1 tenth + 4 hundredths; 3.276 = 3 units + 2 tenths + 7 hundredths + 6 thousandths.

D

deck 1. *n.* the floor of a ship on which you walk. 2. *vb.* dress up; decorate.

declare *vb.* make known publicly. *When we have all made an attempt, the teacher will declare the winner.* **declaration** *n.* a formal announcement.

Declaration of Independence
The Declaration of Independence was one of the most important documents ever written. It declared the 13 American colonies free from Great Britain for all time. The first draft was written by Thomas Jefferson and Congress made a few changes before it was adopted on July 4 1776. On July 8, the Declaration was read outside the State House in Philadelphia to the ringing of the Liberty Bell. Though the old bell is now cracked, it remains the symbol of American Independence. The Declaration of Independence is now in the National Archives Building, Washington, D.C.

decline *vb.* get smaller. *Many theaters are suffering from declining audiences.* go down (in quality). *n.* gradual decrease.

decorate *vb.* 1. make more attractive by ornamenting. 2. give someone a medal.

decoy (**dee**-*koy*) *n.* a model or other device to act as a trap for game birds, etc. *vb.* (di-**koy**) entice, snare.

decrease *vb.* make something grow less.

decree *n.* an official order. *vb.* order.

deduce *vb.* arrive at a conclusion from the facts given.

deed *n.* something which is done, usually good or bad or brave.

deep *adj.* 1. going a long way down. *The river is very deep near the bridge.* 2. wide. *The shelf was not deep enough.* 3. dark. *The dress was a deep red.* **deepen** *vb.* make or to become deeper.

deer *n.* quick, graceful animals belonging to the cow or antelope families.

► Deer are different from their relatives because they have antlers rather than permanent horns. Male deer grow new antlers every year. Female deer, except for reindeer, do not grow antlers.

Every year in early spring, a lot of blood starts to flow into two bony lumps on the male deer's forehead. The blood carries a substance that makes the antlers grow quite rapidly. At first they are covered with a soft, hairy skin known as velvet. In early summer the antlers are fully grown. The blood supply is then cut off and the velvet dies. The male deer rubs off the velvet until his antlers are hard and shiny. Some antlers can be very big indeed. One Red deer's antlers have weighed as much as 77 lb. (35 kg).

In the fall male deer become very aggressive. They fight each other over groups of females which they guard very jealously.

Deer vary enormously in size. The biggest is the Alaskan moose which stands up to 7½ ft. (2.3 meters) at the shoulder and weighs over 1,764 lb. (800 kg). The smallest is the Pudu of Chile which can measure as little as 13 in. (33 cm) at the shoulder and weigh as little as 17½lb. (8 kg).

deface *vb.* spoil something by writing on it or in some other way disfigure.

defeat *vb.* beat someone at a game or in battle. *n.* a lost battle or contest.

defect 1. *n.* (**dee**-*fekt*) fault, blemish. 2. *vb.* (*di*-**fect**) desert. **defector** *n.*

defend *vb.* guard or make safe. **defense** *n.* resistance against attack; military fortifications, armaments. *A castle wall is a defense.* (in law) a defendant's case.

defer *vb.* 1. put off, postpone. 2. give in to another's opinion.

defiant *adj.* rebellious. **defy** *vb.* challenge. *I defy you to prove it.* **defiance** *n.* open rebellion.

deficient (*di*-**fish**-*ent*) *adj.* incomplete, insufficient.

define *vb.* explain the meaning of words; mark out limits. **definition** *n.*

definite *adj.* certain, without doubt.

definitive *adj.* decisive, final.

Defoe, Daniel
Daniel Defoe (1660–1731) was an English writer. His most famous book was *Robinson Crusoe*, a novel based on the true-life story of a shipwrecked sailor, Alexander Selkirk.

deform *vb.* spoil the shape of.

defunct *adj.* dead, no longer existing.

De Gaulle, Charles
Charles de Gaulle (1890–1970) was a French general and statesman. He went to the Military Academy at St.

There are about 53 species in the deer family. Nearly all species have antlers which are grown each year and shed after the rut or breeding season.

Right: Sika deer originally came from Asia.

Below: A Roe deer which is common in woodland.

Above: A Red deer.

Left: A Fallow deer.

Cyr and fought in World War I in which he was badly wounded. After the war he continued his army career. When World War II broke out in 1939 he was put in command of a tank division. After Hitler occupied France in 1940 De Gaulle went to Britain and formed the Free French Movement which fought very bravely.

In 1944 he returned to France as Head of Government. But two years later he resigned when the political parties could not agree. By 1958 France was in desperate political trouble. The French settlers in Algiers and the French army were rebelling. De Gaulle became President of France in 1959 and settled the Algerian problem. He stayed in office until 1969.

defy *vb.* challenge, confront, resist.
degree *n.* 1. a unit of measurement for temperature or angles. It is often written like this: 10° means 10 degrees. 2. a title given by a university to someone who has passed an examination.
dehydrate (*dee-**hi**-drate*) *vb.* dry out the water from something. *Powdered milk is dehydrated.*
deity *n.* a god.

Delaware (*abbrev.* **Del.**)
Delaware is a small state on the East Coast of the U.S.A. Most people work in industry, but about half the total area is farmland. Dover is the capital, but Wilmington is the only large town. Delaware was one of the original 13 states.

delay *vb.* make late or slow down; put off.
delegate *n.* a representative to a meeting, etc. *vb.* send as a representative or assign responsibility to someone.
delete *vb.* cross out, erase.

Delhi
The city of Delhi, in northern INDIA, has two parts. New Delhi, the capital, is a spacious modern city. Designed by British architects, it was built a short distance away from the ancient walled city of Old Delhi. Old Delhi contains many historic buildings.

deliberate *adj.* something that is done on purpose. *That was a deliberate foul.*
delicacy *n.* choice kind of food.
delicate *adj.* soft and not strong; dainty.
delicious *adj.* delightful to eat.
delightful *adj.* very pleasant.
deliver *vb.* 1. take things to a place where they are needed. *The boy delivers our newspapers every morning.* 2. give a speech. 3. help at the birth of a baby. *The doctor arrived in time to deliver the baby.* **delivery** *n.*
delta *n.* the triangle of sand and soil deposited at the mouth of some rivers; fourth letter of the Greek alphabet: Δ.

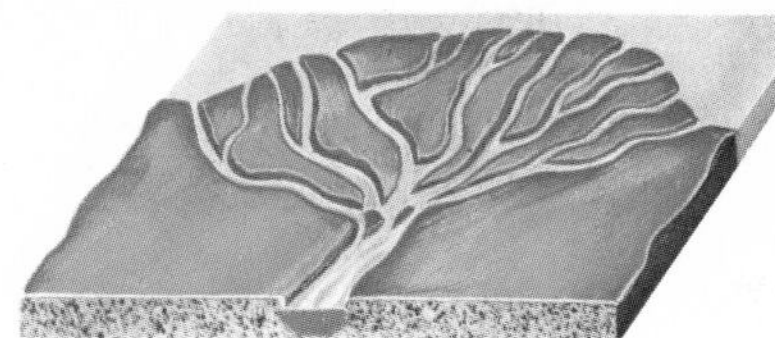
The delta of the Nile River forms many smaller rivers.

► When a river flows across a flat plain into the sea, it flows very slowly. On its way it deposits soil and sand on the plain. In time this sediment begins to form mudbanks. The river flows through these in many channels, often changing direction. This wide, blocked-up mouth with many channels is called a delta. This is because its shape is often like the Greek letter *delta* Δ.

deluge *n.* a heavy rainstorm; a downpour. *vb.* flood.
demand *vb.* ask for something that you think is due to you. *I shall demand payment of the money now. n.* a request, urgent claim.
democracy *n.* a country in which the government is chosen by all the adult electors; this kind of government. *Denmark is a democracy.*
► Representatives of different political parties stand for election and people vote for the one they prefer. The people can also dismiss their government if they want to. In a democracy people can say and read what they like. They cannot be put into prison without a proper trial.

There are many different kinds of democracy. The British form is a monarchy with an elected PARLIAMENT. The American form is a republic with an elected president and an elected CONGRESS. There is no one perfect democracy in the world.

demolish *vb.* tear down. *They are demolishing the office building at the end of our street.* **demolition** *n.*
demon *n.* devil or evil spirit.
demonstrate *vb.* 1. show or explain something to others. 2. take part in a protest march or similar political activity.
den *n.* the hidden home of an animal.
denarius (plural **denarii**) *n.* ancient Roman silver coin.
denied *vb.* past of **deny**.
denim *n.* durable twilled fabric.

Denmark (Danish; Dane)
Denmark is a small Scandinavian country in the north of EUROPE. It consists mainly of a peninsula called Jutland surrounded by 600 islands. In the west is the North Sea, to the east is the Baltic Sea, and to the south is West Germany.

Denmark is a flat country whose soil and climate is ideal for agriculture. Dairy and pig farming are especially important. Denmark is a member of the EUROPEAN ECONOMIC COMMUNITY. It exports a lot of butter and bacon. The Danes also make and export lager beer. There is little heavy industry. The Danes prefer to concentrate on high quality goods such as china, furniture and textiles.

AREA: 16,630 SQ. MILES (45,069 SQ. KM)
POPULATION: 5,175,000
CAPITAL: COPENHAGEN

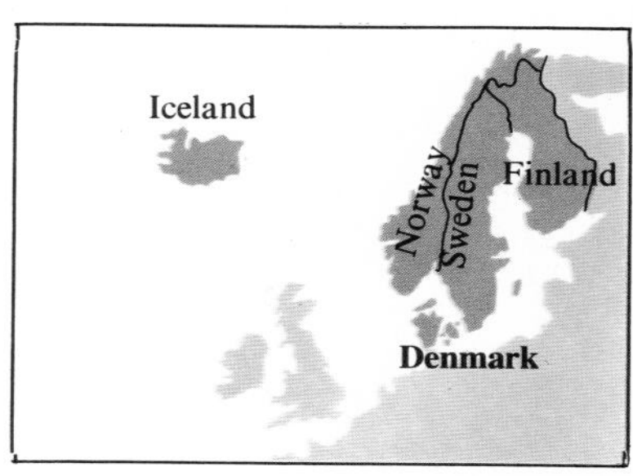

CURRENCY: KRONE
OFFICIAL LANGUAGE: DANISH

denounce *vb.* speak critically or violently against.
dense *adj.* thick. **density** *n.*
dent *vb.* & *n.* a mark or hole. *He dented the side of his car. That car has a dent in its side.*
dental *adj.* of teeth or dentistry.
dentist *n.* a person who takes care of and treats teeth. **dentistry** *n.*
► Until the mid-1700s there were no dentists. Before then tooth-pulling was done by barbers and traveling medicine-sellers. People used to suffer a great deal from toothaches and tooth-pulling. When anesthetics were introduced scientific dentistry was made possible.

Today, dentists are skilled professionals. They now concentrate on keeping teeth healthy rather than taking them out. They drill away the bad parts and fill the holes with metal and other special materials. Dentists encourage people to look after their teeth by keeping them clean and by eating the right foods.

denture *n.* a set of false teeth.
deny (*den-**eye***) *vb.* say that something is not true. **denial** *n.*
deodorant *n.* a substance that gets rid of smells.
depart *vb.* leave; go away. **departure** *n.*
department *n.* a separate part of a whole, e.g. a branch of government or business.
depend on *vb.* rely on someone for money or other things. *The child depends on us for all his or her needs.*
depict *vb.* describe, draw.

deplore *vb.* regret greatly, grieve. **deplorable** *adj.* regrettable, shocking.
deport *vb.* send out of the country; exile.
deposit *n.* a sum of money put down in advance of a larger payment. *They have put down a deposit on the trip and will pay the rest before they go away. vb.* place, put a deposit down.
depot (**deep**-*owe*) *n.* a storehouse or railroad station.
depreciate *vb.* fall in value. *The car depreciated by 20 percent in three months.*
deprive *vb.* prevent from use or enjoyment; take away.
depth *n.* the distance from the top downward (how deep something is) or from the front to the back. *The depth of the shelf is just right.*

Depression, Great
The Great Depression was the worst business slump in the history of the United States. It lasted from 1929 to 1934, beginning with the Wall Street "crash" of October 1929. Prices of stocks and shares fell sharply and thousands of businesses were ruined. By 1932, 12 million people were unemployed in the U.S. The situation began to improve when Franklin D. Rossevelt introduced his "New Deal" policies in 1934. European nations were also badly affected.

derrick *n.* 1. framework over a bore hole, e.g. an oil well. 2. a kind of crane, especially for unloading ships.

Descartes, René
René Descartes (1596–1650) was a French philosopher and mathematician. He attempted to unify the different branches of science under one heading, that of geometry. His "analytical geometry" was a way of doing geometry by using algebra. Descartes summed up the basis of his philosophy in the Latin phrase *cogito, ergo sum* ("I think, therefore I am").

descend (*de*-**send**) *vb.* 1. go down. 2. come from, be derived from.
describe *vb.* say what something or somebody is like. *We can describe the man exactly.* **description** *n.* detailed account. **descriptive** *adj.*
desert (**dez**-*ert*) *n.* a large dry area of land where there is little water or rain.
► Not all deserts are hot and sandy. Some are cold, and some are rocky. But all of them are very dry. Some scientists say that a desert is any area where less than 3 in. (8 cm) of rain falls in a year.
Many big deserts are in the tropics, often deep inside large continents where rain-bearing winds cannot reach them.

This map show the world's deserts, about a third of the world's surface.

DESERTS

	sq. miles
Sahara	3,240,000
Australian Desert	600,000
Arabian Desert	500,000
Gobi	400,000
Kalahari	200,000

Plants which have adapted to the desert. Many of them store water in their stems and leaves.

There are three main types of desert. The first is rocky, where any soil is blown away by the wind. The second has large areas of gravel. The third is made up of great sand dunes, burning hot by day and bitterly cold at night.
It is difficult for plants and animals to live in such conditions. Some plants, like the CACTUS, store moisture in their fleshy stems. Others have seeds that lie apparently lifeless in the ground for long periods. When a shower of rain falls they burst into life and can flower and produce new seeds within weeks. Many desert animals shelter from the sun by day and come out only at night. Some never drink but get all the moisture they need from their food.
The world's largest desert is the SAHARA in Africa. The driest desert is the Atacama in South America where it may not rain for several years. There are also cold deserts. These include Antarctica and a large part of the Arctic.

desert (*dez*-**ert**) *vb.* abandon; leave behind. *Why did you desert us when we most needed you?*
deserve *vb.* be worthy of something. *You deserve the prize because of all your hard work.*
desiccate *vb.* dry up; preserve food by drying.
design (rhymes with *line*) *vb.* make a plan or pattern for something. *n.* plan. **designer** *n.*
designate *vb.* appoint; specify.
designedly *adv.* intentionally.
desire *vb.* want something very much. *n.* wish, longing. **desirable** *adj.* worth wanting; advisable.
desk *n.* a piece of furniture, like a table, for writing on.
despair *n.* & *vb.* give up hope.
despise *vb.* look down on; think oneself superior. **despicable** *adj.* contemptible, unworthy.
dessert (*dez*-**ert**) *n.* the last course of a meal, usually sweet.
destiny *n.* fate, predetermined future.
destitute *adj.* & *n.* absolute poverty.
destroy *vb.* break up; make something useless. **destruction** *n.* **destructive** *adj.*
detach *vb.* remove something that was previously attached to something else.
detain *n.* hold someone up; make a person late.
detect *vb.* discover, find out. **detection** *n.*
detective *n.* a person who follows clues to find a criminal. *adj.* concerned with detection or detectives.
deter (*di*-**ter**) discourage, hinder. **deterrent** *n.* something that deters, as, for example, bug spray.

detergent *n.* a substance which removes dirt; a kind of washing powder.
► The word *detergent* means any substance that will clean things. SOAP is a detergent. But today the word detergent is usually used to mean synthetic, or man-made, detergents, such as most washing powders. Detergents are similar to soaps. But soaps leave filmy deposits behind, such as the familiar bathtub ring. Detergents can reach soiled areas better than soaps, and do not leave deposits.

deteriorate *vb.* become worse in condition or quality. *Her health began to deteriorate after the accident.*
determined *vb.* past of **determine.** *adj.* with your mind firmly made up.
detest *vb.* hate someone or something; loathe.
detonate *vb.* set off an explosion. **detonator** *n.* device for setting off an explosion.
detour *n.* roundabout way temporarily replacing a more direct route.
detract *vb.* (from) lessen the credit due to; belittle.

Detroit
Detroit is the largest city in Michigan and one of the most important automobile manufacturing centers in the world. The city lies along the Detroit River and has access to the Great Lakes and the St. Lawrence Seaway. It is one of the world's busiest inland ports.
Detroit was ceded to the British in 1763. It was turned over to the United States in 1796 and destroyed by fire in 1805. It was rebuilt, and occupied by the British for a year during the War of 1812.
Detroit became an important commercial center after the opening of the Erie Canal in 1825. In 1899, the first automobile manufacturing plant was built, and the city soon became the "Motor Capital of the World." American Motors, Ford and Chrysler all have their headquarters in or near the city. Detroit also produces steel, paints, chemicals and business machines. The city has many museums, including the Detroit Institute of Arts, and several universities.

De Valera, Eamon
Eamon de Valera (1882–1975) was an Irish revolutionary and statesman. He was born in New York, but educated in Ireland. He took part in the Easter Rebellion in 1916 and was sentenced to death, but released the following year. He became the Irish Prime Minister in 1932 and remained so for most of the period up to 1959. In that year he became President of the Republic of Ireland. He retired in 1973.

devastate *vb.* lay waste, destroy completely. **devastation** *n.*
develop *vb.* grow gradually. *A tadpole develops into a frog.* **development** *n.*
deviate *vb.* turn aside from main course.
device (*di-***vise**) *n.* something made to do a particular thing.
devil *n.* an evil spirit; a demon. **devilish** *adj.* cruel; wicked.
devise (*di-***vize**) *vb.* plan.
devote *vb.* set aside; give up. *Monks and nuns devote a large part of each day to prayer.* **devoted** *adj.* loyal, very affectionate. **devotion** *n.* great loyalty; love; (plural) prayers.
devour *vb.* eat something up whole. *The lions quickly devoured the antelope.*
devout *adj.* religious; pious; reverential.
dew *n.* the tiny drops of water that form on cool surfaces at night outdoors. **dewy** *adj.*
dexterity *n.* skill. **dextrous** *adj.*
diabetes *n.* a disorder in which too much glucose builds up in the blood.
diagnose *vb.* decide what illness someone is suffering from. *The doctor diagnosed measles.* **diagnosis** *n.*
diagonal *adj.* a straight line across a rectangular area from one corner to the opposite corner. *n.* an oblique line.
diagram *n.* a drawing that explains something. *The word "diagonal" is explained here with a diagram.*
dial *n.* the face of a clock, watch or instrument; the numbered part of a telephone. *vb.* use the dial of a telephone.
dialect *n.* a form of a language which is slightly different from the usual one.
dialogue *n.* conversation in speech; the spoken part of a play; argument and exchange of views. *The dialogue between America and the USSR continues.*
diameter *n.* a line right across a circle passing through the center.
diamond *n.* 1. a very hard, brilliant precious stone. 2. a four-sided figure with equal sides but no right angles.
► Diamonds are CRYSTALS. They are harder than anything else in the world. They are formed by great heat and pressure deep beneath the surface of the earth. Diamonds are made of pure CARBON, the same mineral that is found in ordinary coal. They are usually colorless and have to be cut in a special way to catch the light and "sparkle."
A diamond cutter is very skilled and uses tools tipped with diamonds, for only another diamond is hard enough to cut a diamond. Diamonds and diamond dust are used in industry for drilling and cutting many other materials.

diaper *n.* a baby's absorbent towel or underpants.
diary *n.* a book in which someone writes down what happens each day. **diarist**. *n.* a person who keeps a diary, or notes down future engagements.

Dias, Bartholomeu
Bartholomeu Dias (or Bartholomew Diaz) (1450–1500) was a Portuguese explorer and navigator. Dias was the first European to sail around the Cape of Good Hope, at the southern tip of AFRICA. He later accompanied Vasco da GAMA on one of his voyages to try to find a sea route to the Indies by way of the Cape of Good Hope. He was drowned in a storm while sailing with the expedition that discovered BRAZIL.

dice *pl.n.* (singular **die**) small cubes with one to six dots on each side, used in games. *vb.* play with dice; cut into small cubes. *The cook diced the carrots.*

Dickens, Charles
Charles Dickens (1812–70) was a great English writer. His books give us a vivid picture of life in Victorian England in the mid-1800s. Many of his stories are about children, especially poor children and orphans. Dickens tried to improve the lives of the poor by making their sufferings more widely known through his books. He also created some of the liveliest and best-known characters in English literature. Some of his most famous books are *Oliver Twist*, *David Copperfield*, *Great Expectations* and *A Christmas Carol*.

dictate *vb.* speak or read aloud something to be written down. *She dictated letters to her secretary.*
dictator *n.* absolute ruler; a tyrant.
diction *n.* correctness and clearness of speech.
dictionary *n.* a book containing an alphabetical list of words with an explanation of their meaning or a translation of the words into another language.
did *vb.* past of **do**.
didactic *adj.* meant to instruct.
die 1. *vb.* stop living; become dead. 2. *n.* the singular form of "dice."
diesel engine *n.* an internal combustion engine that burns a certain kind of oil to supply power.
► Diesel engines are named after their inventor, Rudolf Diesel, a German born in Paris. He built his first successful engine in 1897 to replace the steam engine. Diesel engines use a cruder, heavier fuel oil than gasoline. They are cheaper to run than gasoline engines, but they are heavier and more difficult to start, so they are not widely used in automobiles. They are more often used to drive heavy machines such as trains, cranes, tractors, ships, buses and trucks.

D

A diesel engine is very like a gasoline engine. But, instead of using a spark from a spark plug to ignite (set fire to) the fuel, the diesel engine uses heat that is made by squeezing air in a cylinder. When air is very tightly compressed, or pushed into a much smaller space than it filled before, it gets very hot. This heat sets fire to the diesel oil, which burns instantly, like a small explosion, as soon as it is pumped into the cylinder. The burning oil heats the air and forces it to expand again to push the piston and thus drive the engine.

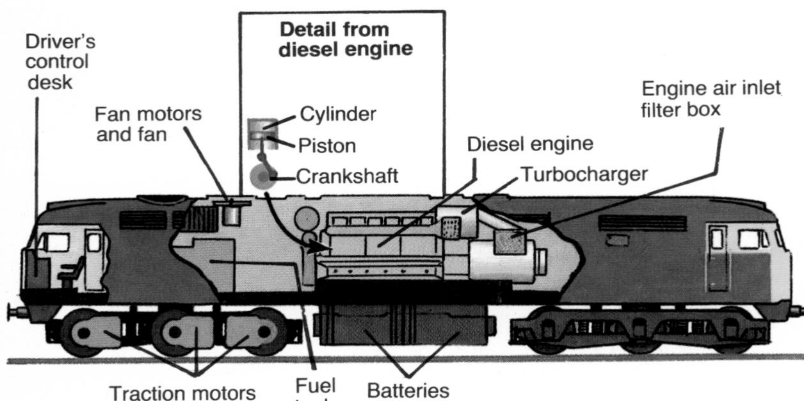

Left: How a diesel locomotive works. A piston inside each of the cylinders (from four to 16) is joined to a crankshaft. The crankshaft is connected to generators which make electricity when they turn. The electricity from the main generator goes to the traction motors which drive the locomotive.

Many RAILROADS began using diesel engines after World War II. Railroads in need of repair after the war took the opportunity to modernize their engines and replaced the old steam LOCOMOTIVES with diesel engines. But diesel engines were first used regularly on the railroads of the United States and Denmark in the 1930s. Today, diesel-electric engines are in use all over the world. In these engines the diesel motor is used to make electricity. The electricity then drives the train.

diet (**di**-*et*) *vb*. & *n*. the food you usually eat; special meals that some people have to make them healthy, and others have to help them lose weight.
dif- *prefix* see **dis-**.
differ *vb*. be unlike; disagree. **difference** *n*. amount of unlikeness; a disagreement.
different *adj*. separate; not the same, unlike.
difficult *adj*. hard; not easy. **difficulty** *n*. hard to overcome; an obstacle.
diffidence *n*. shyness; disinterest.
diffuse (*di*-**fyuze**) *vb*. disperse; spread around.
dig *vb*. (past **dug**) make a hole in the ground; turn over the earth, usually with a spade.
digest 1. *vb*. change the food you have eaten in such a way that your body can use it. **digestion** *n*. 2. *n*. summary.
► Digestion takes place in the digestive tract or *alimentary canal*, a long tube that runs from the mouth to the anus. Digestion starts in the mouth, where the teeth and special chemicals in the saliva help to break down the food. The food then passes down a tube called the *esophagus*. Muscles in the esophagus push and squeeze the food down into the STOMACH. There, acids and more chemicals help to turn the food into a creamy liquid. Then a muscle at the lower end of the stomach opens from time to time to release food into the small intestine.
Inside the small intestine, bile from the LIVER and juice from the pancreas help to break down the food still further. Much of it passes through the thin walls of the intestine into the bloodstream. The remainder passes on into the large intestine. There, liquids are absorbed until only solid material is left. BACTERIA in the large intestine digest any remaining food. The final waste is passed out of the body as *feces*.

digit *n*. 1. a finger or toe. 2. a figure or number. *The number 100 contains three digits*.
digital *adj*. having figures or numbers. *A digital watch does not have hands, but shows the time in figures*.
digitalis *n*. a drug made from leaves of foxgloves, often used for heart problems.
dignity *n*. a quality of worthy, estimable behavior. **dignify** *vb*. do honor to.
dike *n*. a ditch; a wall to keep the sea out of the surrounding land (especially in the Netherlands).
dilate (**dye**-*late*) *vb*. widen, expand, enlarge. *The pupils of the eyes dilate in the dark*.
dilemma *n*. a choice involving one of two unsatisfactory alternatives; having to choose the lesser of two evils.
dilute *vb*. water down, reduce strength of.
dim *adj*. not bright. *vb*. make or become darker.
dime *n*. a coin worth 10 cents.
dimension *n*. size, extent.
diminish *vb*. make or become less.
din *n*. a loud, ugly noise.
dinar *n*. currency of Yugoslavia.
dinghy *n*. a small, open boat.
dingo *n*. the wild dog of Australia.
dining room *n*. the room in which meals are eaten.
dinner *n*. the main meal of the day, usually eaten in the evening. **dine**. *vb*.

dinosaur *n*. one of a large group of prehistoric reptiles that became extinct millions of years ago.
► The word *dinosaur* means "terrible lizard." These creatures lived between 65 and 225 million years ago. They developed from primitive REPTILES. Dinosaurs included the largest and most ferocious animals ever to live on earth.
There were two main groups of dinosaurs, the *Saurischians* and the *Ornithischians*. The Ornithischian dinosaurs were all plant-eaters and most of them went about on all fours. Some of these, like *Stegosaurus* and *Triceratops*, were large and lumbering, but had bony armor and horns to protect them from the teeth and claws of the great meat-eating dinosaurs.
The second of the two main groups, the Saurischians, contained both plant-eaters and meat-eaters. The plant-eaters included the largest dinosaurs, the biggest of which was the *Brachiosaurus*. This huge creature was 80 ft. (24 meters) long and weighed about 50 tons. *Brachiosaurus* had a long neck and a tiny head, a long tapering tail and a thick body. *Brachiosaurus* and other similar dinosaurs such as *Apatosaurus* (BRONTOSAURUS) and *Diplodocus* ate the leaves at the tops of trees.
Perhaps the most famous of the Saurischian dinosaurs are the great carnivores, or meat-eaters. TYRANNOSAURUS, which was up to 47 ft. (14 meters) from snout to tail, stood on its hind legs. Its forward pointing toes bore claws as long as carving knives. Saber-like teeth – some nearly the length of a human's hand – lined the jaws. No flesh-eating beasts that ever lived on land were larger or more menacing than these monsters.

A scene from over 100 million years ago. The fierce dinosaur Tyrannosaurus attacks a plant-eating Corythosaurus.

D

About 65 million years ago the dinosaurs suddenly, and mysteriously, died out. What killed them remains one of the great puzzles of the past. Many scientists think that as the earth's climate grew colder, these great animals found it impossible to hold their body heat, and eventually froze to death.

diocese (**di**-*oss-ese*) *n.* district under control of a bishop.
dip *vb.* put something into a liquid.
diphtheria *n.* dangerous infectious disease of the throat.
diplomacy *n.* the art of keeping good relations between countries; the use of charm or tact in relationships between people. **diplomat** *n.* official representative in diplomacy; skilled negotiator. **diplomatic** *adj.* tactful.
direct 1. *vb.* show or tell someone how to do something or go

Dinosaurs and other creatures that came from animals like Euparkeria.

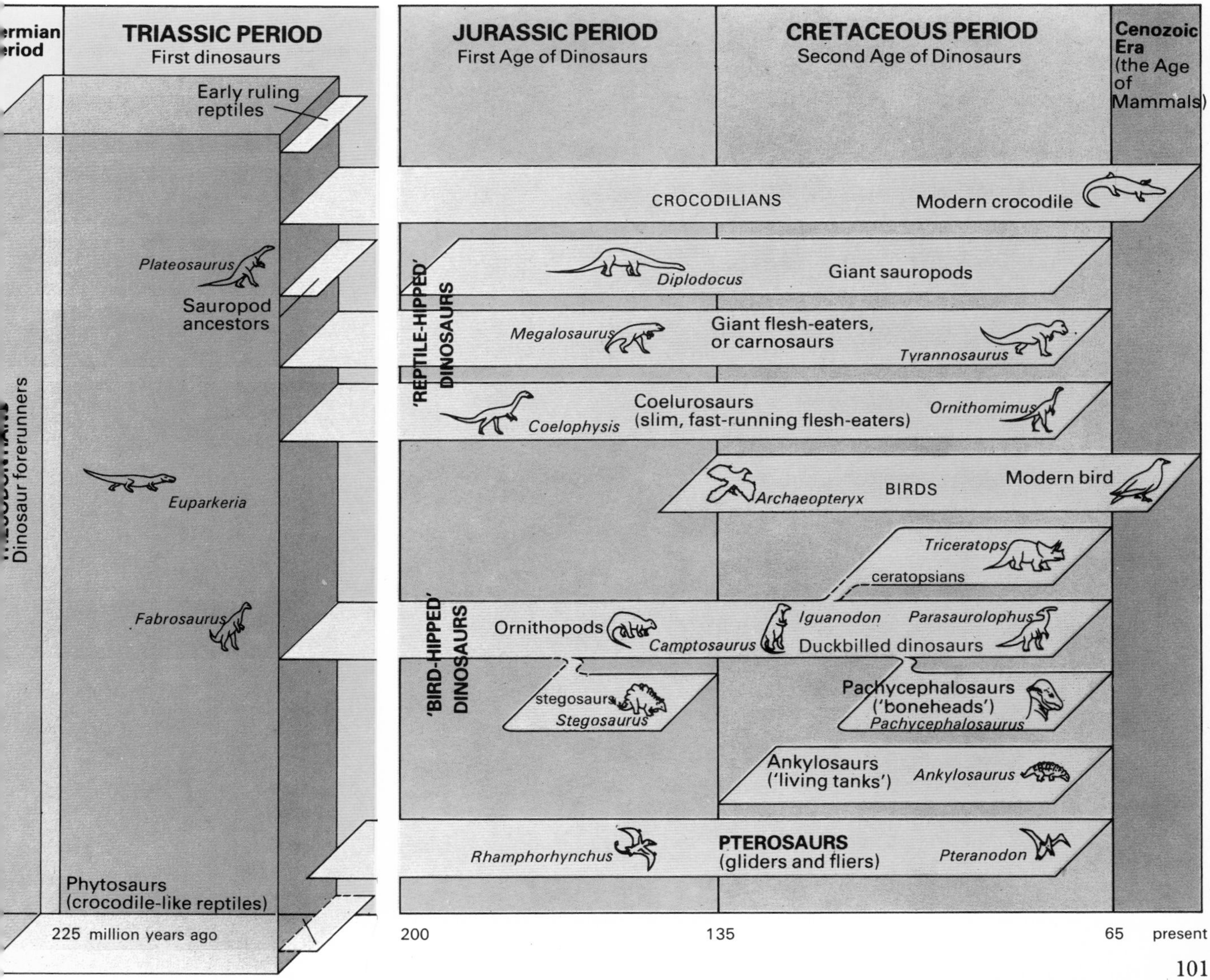

ermian
eriod

TRIASSIC PERIOD
First dinosaurs

JURASSIC PERIOD
First Age of Dinosaurs

CRETACEOUS PERIOD
Second Age of Dinosaurs

Cenozoic Era
(the Age of Mammals)

Early ruling reptiles

CROCODILIANS
Modern crocodile

Plateosaurus
Sauropod ancestors

'REPTILE-HIPPED' DINOSAURS

Diplodocus
Giant sauropods

Megalosaurus
Giant flesh-eaters, or carnosaurs
Tyrannosaurus

Coelophysis
Coelurosaurs (slim, fast-running flesh-eaters)
Ornithomimus

Dinosaur forerunners

Euparkeria

Archaeopteryx
BIRDS
Modern bird

Triceratops
ceratopsians

Fabrosaurus

'BIRD-HIPPED' DINOSAURS

Ornithopods
Camptosaurus
Iguanodon
Parasaurolophus
Duckbilled dinosaurs

stegosaurs
Stegosaurus

Pachycephalosaurs ('boneheads')
Pachycephalosaurus

Ankylosaurs ('living tanks')
Ankylosaurus

Rhamphorhynchus
PTEROSAURS (gliders and fliers)
Pteranodon

Phytosaurs (crocodile-like reptiles)

225 million years ago
200
135
65
present

somewhere. 2. *adv*. the quickest way from one point to another. *This train goes direct to New York*.
direction *n*. the way from one place to another.
directly *adv*. very soon; in a direct way.
dirty *adj*. not clean; covered by **dirt** *n*.
dis- *prefix* that turns the main word into its opposite, usually negative, e.g. **disband, disbelieve, discolor, disconnect, discontinue, discourage**.
disable (*diss*-**ay**-*ball*) *vb*. make incapable through injury, cripple.
disagree *vb*. 1. have different ideas about something. 2. have a bad effect. *I cannot eat onions; they disagree with me*. **disagreeable** *adj*. unpleasant.
disappear *vb*. vanish; be seen no more. **disappearance** *n*.
disappoint *vb*. make someone sad by not doing what was hoped for; fail to fulfill expectations.
disarray *n*. lack of order, confusion.
disaster *n*. a terrible accident. *Fifty people were killed in the disaster*. **disastrous** *adj*.
discern *vb*. see clearly with the mind. **discerning** *adj*.
disciple *n*. a follower. *Jesus left his disciples to carry on his work*.
discotheque (**disco**) *n*. a place where people dance to recorded music.
discover *vb*. find out something new.
discriminate *vb*. make or see differences between; make a distinction and single out, often for unfair treatment.
discus *n*. disk used in hurling competitions; a discus-throwing contest.
► The discus is a wooden plate with a metal rim. Athletes take turns to stand in a circle and throw the discus as far as they can.

discuss *vb*. talk about something with other people. **discussion** *n*.
disease *n*. illness.
disgrace *n*. shame; downfall. *vb*. bring shame upon.
disguise *n*. & *vb*. change what someone or something looks like. *His disguise was a mask and black cloak. He disguised himself*.
disgust *n*. strong loathing for **disgusting** *adj*.
dish *n*. a plate; a particular kind of food.
dishonest *adj*. lying or cheating; not honest.
disinfect *vb*. make something free from germs and disease. **disinfectant** *n*.
disk *n*. a flat circle, like a stereo record.
dislike *vb*. unfavorable feeling.
dismal *adj*. gloomy; feeble. *The players gave a dismal performance of the piece*.
dismay *vb*. & *n*. upset; fill with fear, despair.
dismiss *vb*. send away; order someone to leave a job; disregard. **dismissal** *n*.

Disney, Walt
Walter Elias ("Walt") Disney (1901–66) is still probably the most famous producer of cartoon films. Disney introduced the cartoon character Mickey Mouse in a film called *Steamboat Willie* in 1928. This was the first cartoon film to make use of sound. *Snow White and the Seven Dwarfs* (1938) was the first full-length animated cartoon. Disney's other world-famous characters include Donald Duck. Disney later made "straight" adventure films, such as *Davy Crockett*, and nature films like *The Living Desert*.

disobedient *adj*. refusing to obey. *The girl did not do what her teacher told her. She was disobedient*. **disobedience** *n*. **disobey** *vb*.
display *vb*. show something off. *n*. an exhibition; show.
dispute (*dis*-**pyoot**) *vb*. quarrel, argue; call in question.
disregard *vb*. pay no attention to.
dissect *vb*. cut up a plant or dead animal in order to examine it scientifically.
dissident *n*. a person who disagrees with or opposes authority.
dissolve *vb*. mix something in a liquid so that it becomes part of the liquid. *Salt dissolves easily in water*.
distance *n*. the length between two points.
distant *adj*. far away.
distill *vb*. turn into steam or other vapor and then condense back into a liquid. *Brandy is made by the distillation of wine*.
► When water is boiled it turns into a gas called *water vapor*. The clear space near the spout of a boiling kettle is filled with *steam*. The cloud which we call "steam" is really tiny drops of water that form when the steam cools. The cloud is *condensed* steam. Condensed steam can be collected in a cold vessel. It is then *distilled* water that contains no impurities. The impurities are left behind because they do not evaporate at the boiling point of water.
Alcoholic drinks such as whisky, rum and brandy are made by distilling grain "mash", sugar juices or wine.

distinct *adj*. clear; separate; different in kind.
distinguish *vb*. see differences between; make a distinction between; separate into classes. **distinguished** *adj*. famous, eminent.
distract *vb*. draw attention away; bewilder. **distraction** *n*. relaxation, amusement; mental confusion.
distress *vb*. cause unhappiness. *n*. great trouble, grief.
distribute *vb*. give each of a number of people a share of something. *Please distribute these books to the class*.
district *n*. part of a city or country.
disturb *vb*. interrupt or annoy someone; move something from its usual position. **disturbance** *n*.
ditch *n*. a narrow channel for water.
ditto *n*. the same; repeat statement.
dive *vb*. plunge into water headfirst.
diver *n*. someone who dives; someone who goes deep into water for long periods by carrying an air supply or having air pumped down from the surface.
► People have been diving underwater for thousands of years. The first divers just held their breath. This meant they could make only short, shallow dives.
Modern inventions allow divers to dive deeper and stay down longer. Scuba divers carry their own air supply with them. They wear rubber foot fins and they can swim about freely. Helmeted divers breathe air pumped down through a tube. Heavy weights allow them to work on the seabed without bobbing up. All divers see through glass face masks and wear special suits to stay warm.

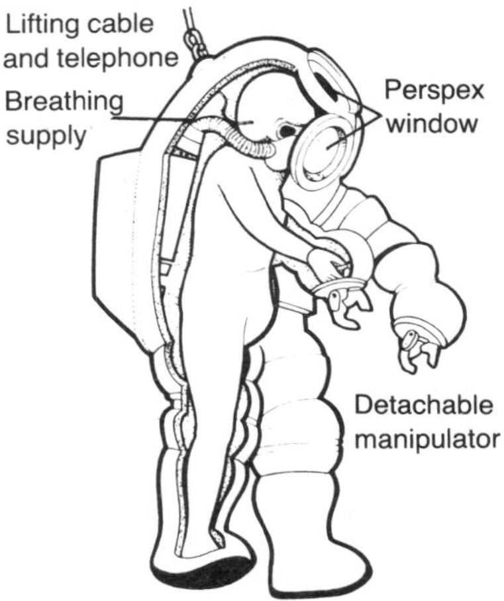

A cutaway drawing of JIM *– a pressure-proof diving suit. Inside this metal monster a diver can breathe air (at atmospheric pressure 1,300ft (400 meters) below the surface*.

Today's divers can study water life, build harbors, and search for sunken treasure.
divert *vb*. turn aside from; amuse.
divide *vb*. 1. separate, cut into parts; share. 2. find out how many times one number goes into another.
divine *adj*. of or like God or a god.
divorce *n*. & *vb*. the legal ending of a marriage.
Djakarta see **Jakarta**
do *vb*. (past **did**) carry out an action.
docile *adj*. easily led, teachable.
dock 1. *n*. a place in a harbor where ships are loaded and unloaded. *vb*. bring ships into dock. 2. *n*. the

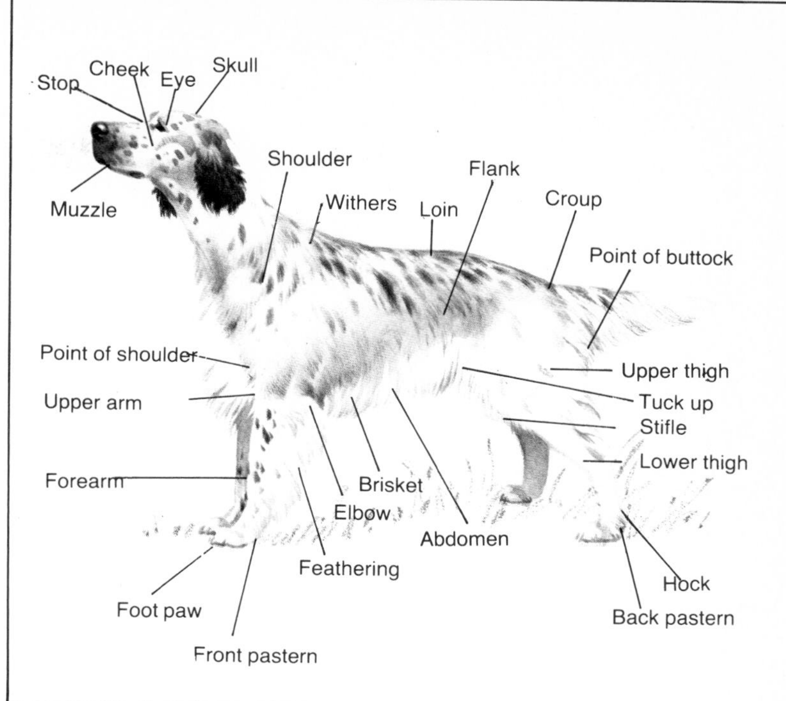

place in a law court where the prisoner stands.
▶ Docks are man-made basins where people load and unload ships or repair them. There are wet docks and dry docks. Both kinds have gates that can be closed to shut out the sea. In a wet dock, a ship floats on water that stays at the same level although the sea level outside the gates rises and falls with the tide. Wet docks make it easy to load and unload cargo and passengers.

In a dry dock, a ship settles on the bottom as water is pumped out of the dock. Workers can then stand on dry land to mend those parts of the ship that are usually under water. After the ship has been repaired it is refloated.

doctor *n.* a person who treats sick people; also a graduate holding a degree. *vb.* treat medically; falsify.
▶ Doctors are people who have been given a degree by a university. Doctors of MEDICINE have an M.D. degree. Many scientists and other scholars have a Ph.D. degree. Ph.D. stands for doctor of PHILOSOPHY. Most doctors have to pass difficult examinations to gain their degrees.

How a dry dock works. Water is let in from a harbor (1). Steel gates open and a ship sails into the dock (2). The gates close and water is pumped out of the dock (3). When the ship is repaired water flows back in to refloat the vessel.

doctrine *n.* religious or political beliefs or dogma.
document *n.* written information.
dodge *vb.* get quickly out of the way; duck. *The little boy neatly dodged the snowball.*
dodo *n.* a now extinct, giant flightless bird with stumpy legs.
▶ About 400 years ago a Dutch ship landed explorers on Mauritius, a lonely island in the Indian Ocean. They found doves, fish, and large flocks of birds as big and fat as turkeys. These birds had no proper wings and could not fly. In time people called them "dodos," from the Portuguese word *doudo*. This means "simpleton" or stupid person.

Sailors quickly learned that dodos were good to eat. Ships that visited Mauritius sailed off with larders full of salted dodo meat. Meanwhile rats and dogs that came from the ships started eating dodo eggs and chicks.

By the 1690s all the dodos were dead. Only drawings, bones and one stuffed bird remained.

doe *n.* a female deer or rabbit.
dog *n.* one of a family of mammals which includes wolves, jackals and foxes.
▶ The first dog was probably descended from a WOLF and looked much like one. Today, there are more than 100 breeds of dog of many colors, shapes, and sizes. The St. Bernard is the largest breed. A St. Bernard may weigh nearly twice as much as a person. The Yorkshire terrier is one of the smallest dogs. A full-grown Yorkshire terrier may weigh less than a pound.

Different breeds were developed to be good at special kinds of work. Airedales and terriers make fine rat hunters. Labrador retrievers bring back ducks shot by hunters. Collies round up sheep. Dachshunds were used for hunting badgers. Setters find animals for hunters to shoot. Dobermanns are ferocious guard dogs.

All puppies are born blind and helpless, and at first feed only on their mother's milk. But small dogs are fully grown in a year or so. Most kinds of dog live for about 12 years.

dogma *n.* a system of beliefs; authoritative doctrine. **dogmatic** *adj.* intolerant.
dole *n.* money paid to unemployed people.
doll *n.* a small model of a person, usually for a child to play with.
▶ Dolls may be made of wood, china, plastic or many other substances. The very first doll may have just been a forked twig that looked a bit like a human being. Homemade dolls can cost nothing. But doll collectors will pay a lot of money for rare old dolls.

D

dollar *n.* a banknote or coin used in many countries, including Australia, Canada, Hong Kong, the U.S.A. and New Zealand.
► The word "dollar" comes from the name of an old Bohemian coin called the *Joachimsthaler*, which was shortened to *thaler*. The dollar became the basic United States money unit in 1792 and the first silver dollars were made in 1794. These coins were made until 1935, when minting stopped. Dollar coins came into circulation again in 1971, but the new coins had no silver in them. U.S. gold dollar pieces were issued from 1849 through 1889. They were taken out of circulation in 1933.

dolphin *n.* a small type of whale.
► Dolphins are small, toothed WHALES, with a long snout rather like a beak. The largest dolphins are twice as long as a human being and five times as heavy. Most kinds live in the sea but two kinds live in rivers. Dolphins swim in groups called schools. They signal to each other by making whistling sounds.
Dolphins are playful and intelligent. Tame dolphins can learn many tricks. They will jump through hoops and snatch fish from a trainer's mouth. Dolphins can also learn to "walk" across water on their tails.

dome *n.* a rounded roof like an upsidedown bowl.
► Some domes are made from bricks or stones. Other domes are made of concrete, steel, or plastic. Domed roofs cover famous religious buildings, such as St. Sophia in Istanbul, St. Peter's in Rome, and St. Paul's Cathedral in London. The world's largest dome is the Louisiana Superdome in the American city of New Orleans. It is as wide as two football pitches placed end to end.

Domesday Book
The Domesday Book is really two volumes of records. It was ordered by William the Conqueror in 1085, and completed a year later. It is a remarkably detailed account of the ownership of land and wealth in the England of the time. As such, it has been of great use to historians, who think its original purpose was to act as a basis for taxation.

domestic *adj.* to do with the home.
domesticated *adj.* word describing an animal that is used to living with people.
dominate *vb.* overshadow; exert control over.

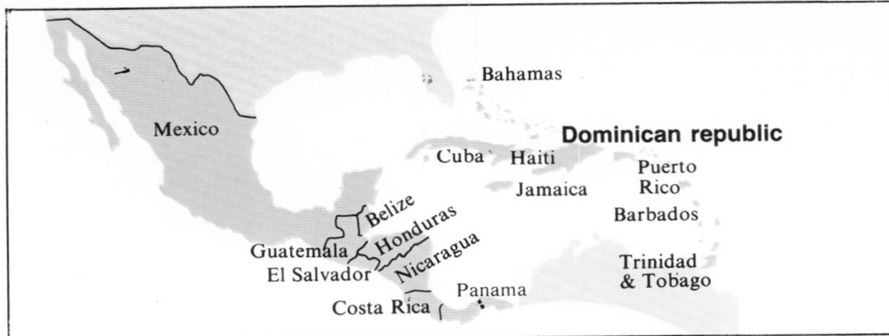

Dominican Republic
The Dominican Republic occupies the eastern two-thirds of the island of Hispaniola, in the CARIBBEAN Sea. (Haiti makes up the rest of the island.) The main industries are agriculture and tourism.
Christopher COLUMBUS discovered the island in 1492. The country became an independent republic in 1844.
AREA: 18,817 SQ. MILES (48,734 SQ. KM)
POPULATION: 5,776,000
CURRENCY: PESO
CAPITAL: SANTO DOMINGO
OFFICIAL LANGUAGE: SPANISH

domino *n.* (plural **dominoes**) one of 28 pieces marked with dots (or blank) used in a game of dominoes.
don *n.* fellow or tutor in a college or university.
donate *vb.* make a **donation**, e.g. gift of money.

Donatello
Donatello (1386?–1466) was an Italian sculptor of the RENAISSANCE who influenced many later artists. His sculptures include noble figures, such as David, and fine reliefs for several churches.

done *vb.* past part. of **do**.
donkey *n.* an ass; an animal of the horse family with long ears.
► You see many a hard-working donkey in poor parts of southern Europe, northern Africa, and southwest Asia. A donkey carries heavy loads over rough ground yet needs less good food than its much larger cousin the HORSE. A donkey has long ears, a large head, and its tail ends in a tuft of hair. Donkeys are descended from the wild asses of Africa. Other wild asses live in dry parts of Asia.

Don Quixote (*Don Ke-**ho**-tay*)
Some people think that this long Spanish tale is one of the world's best books. The story describes the adventures of a crazy old man called Don Quixote. He makes absurd mistakes because he tries to behave like a fairytale knight. Miguel de CERVANTES wrote *Don Quixote* in the early 1600s.

don't *vb.* contraction of **do not**.
doodle *vb.* draw in an absentminded way. *n.* a drawing done in this way.
doom *n.* destiny or fate *vb.* condemn.
door *n.* a movable panel (usually of wood or glass) which opens or closes the entrance to a room or building.
dormitory *n.* a bedroom for several people, especially in a school or monastery.
dormouse *n.* a small gnawing rodent.
dose *n.* amount of medicine to be taken at regular times. *vb.* give medicine to.

Dostoyevsky, Fyodor Mikhailovich
Dostoyevsky (1821–81) is one of the greatest Russian novelists. He studied at a military school, and was an army officer from 1841 to 1844. A few years later he was condemned to death for revolutionary activities. He was pardoned at the last minute but was sent to a prison camp in Siberia, where he stayed for four years.
Not surprisingly, most of Dostoyevsky's work is gloomy and somber. Two of his greatest novels are *Crime and Punishment* and *The Brothers Karamazov*.

dot *n.* small spot or point. *vb.* mark with a dot. *Dot the i's.*
double 1. *adj.* twice the amount. 2. *vb.* make twice as great. 3. *n.* a person exactly like someone else.
double-cross *vb.* betray.
doubt (rhymes with *out*) *vb.* feel unsure about something. *I doubt whether you are right. n.* feeling of uncertainty.
dough (rhymes with *go*) *n.* a mixture of flour and water for making bread or pastry.
doughnut *n.* a sweet doughy cake fried in fat. *Doughnuts are usually round and may be ring-shaped.*
dove *n.* a bird related to the pigeon.
dowager *n.* widow of a titled person.
dowdy *adj.* drab, badly dressed.
down 1. *prep.* toward somewhere lower. *She went down the hill.* 2. *n.* very soft feathers.

downward *adv.* toward a lower level.
doze *vb.* be half asleep.
dozen *n.* twelve.
drab *adj.* dull light brown; colorless.
drachma *n.* unit of Greek money.
draft (rhymes with *raft*) 1. *n.* a flow of air, especially coming through a narrow gap in a door or window. 2. *n.* the first plan or rough sketch of something. 3. *n.* & *vb.* call up for military service.
drag *vb.* pull roughly along the ground.
dragon *n.* a fierce legendary creature that breathed fire.
► Dragons are storybook monsters, but many people once believed that they really lived. Artists showed them as huge snakes or lizards with wings of skin and terrifying claws. They were supposed to breathe fire and swallow people, cows, and horses whole.

Fighting dragons called for great bravery. Legends tell how HERCULES, St. George and other heroes killed these evil monsters.

Not everyone thought dragons wicked. The Chinese looked upon the creatures as gods.

dragonfly *n.* a brightly colored insect with long wings that lives near water.
► These insects hatch from eggs laid in pools and rivers. The young are called nymphs. Dragonfly nymphs live in water for up to five years. Meanwhile they may shed their skin 11 times. At last they crawl out of the water, grow wings, and fly away.

drain *n.* a pipe that takes waste water away. *vb.* to take water away through pipes and ditches; empty. *When he gives a toast, they will all drain their glasses.*
drake *n.* a male duck.

Drake, Francis
Sir Francis Drake (*c.*1540–96) was a sea captain who helped to make England a great sea power. In the 1570s he led sea raids against Spanish ships and ports in and near the Caribbean Sea. He also became the first Englishman to sail around the world. In 1588 he helped to destroy the Spanish ARMADA and so saved England from invasion.

drama *n.* an acted story; a play; the art of the theater. **dramatic** *adj.* **dramatist** *n.* a person who writes plays.
► There are several kinds of drama. *Tragedy* is a story of how someone's life is ruined, often by some slight mistake he or she makes. *Comedy* is amusing and has a happy ending. *Farce* is comedy with absurd people and crazy situations.

Drama began thousands of years ago. Stone Age hunters probably acted out a hunt. They thought that this would help them in the real hunt. This acting was a kind of magic.

Later, the Greeks used music and MIME to tell stories in honor of a god. The oldest tragedies we know were written down in Greece more than 2,400 years ago. Dramas of the kind we see today began only in the 1500s, in the time of SHAKESPEARE.

Early dramas took place in the open. In the Middle Ages actors performed plays on carts in streets. People began building covered THEATERS about 500 years ago.

drank *vb.* past of **drink**.
draper *n.* a person who deals in cloth.
drastic *adj.* severe.
draw *vb.* 1. make a picture or diagram with pen, pencil or crayon but not with paint. 2. the result of a game in which neither team nor player wins. 3. pull. *They draw water from the well.*
drawback *n.* a disadvantage.
drawbridge *n.* a bridge across a moat that could be pulled up when a castle was being attacked.
drawer *n.* a box-shaped part of a chest or cupboard that can be pulled open.
dread *vb.* fear terribly, especially before an event.
dreadful *adj.* terrible; unpleasant. (originally "inspiring dread.") **dread** *n.* fear.
dreadlocks *pl. n.* long ringlets of hair worn notably by Rastafarians.
dream *n.* something that you think is happening during sleep. *vb.* experience a dream.
dreary *adj.* gloomy, tedious.
dredge *vb.* clear away sand and mud from under water.
► Sand and mud slowly pile up on the bottom of many rivers and harbors. Dredging is the work of carrying the sand and mud away. This keeps the water deep and wide enough for ships to use. But dredging is also a way of collecting sand and gravel from the seabed. Much of the sand and gravel used by builders is obtained by special dredging ships (dredges).

Dipper dredges scoop up material in a huge mechanical shovel. Hydraulic dredges are like giant vacuum cleaners, sucking up sand and mud through pipes.

drench *vb.* soak, make entirely wet.

Dresden
Dresden is a city in East GERMANY, on the Elbe River. It used to be considered one of the most beautiful cities in Europe. However, it was destroyed by Allied bombing during the World War II (1939–45). It has since been rebuilt.

The world-famous "Dresden china" is not in fact made in Dresden but in nearby Meissen.

dress 1. *n.* a single piece of clothing covering the body from the shoulders to the legs, worn by women and girls. 2. *vb.* put on clothes. 3. *vb.* clean and trim wool, cloth, poultry, etc.
► The word "dress" means something slightly different from the word "clothing." People wear clothes to keep themselves warm or because they are useful in some other way. They dress to look smart or to appear in the fashion of the time. The way people dress in various parts of the world has been affected by many different things. But the most important influences have been climate and the materials that people had in any place. The ancient Egyptians could weave cotton and linen. So both men and women dressed in garments made from these materials. Eskimos dress in caribou skin and sealskin because they live in a cold climate and many of these animals live around them.

dresser *n.* a chest of drawers or bureau with a mirror.
drew *vb.* past of **draw**.
dribble *vb.*1. let saliva (spit) fall from corner of the mouth. 2. in basketball, to work the ball forward with short bounces.
dried *vb.* past of **dry**.
drift *vb.* be carried slowly along by wind or water. *Without its engine, the ship will drift onto the rocks.*
drill *n.* 1. a pointed tool that is turned to bore holes. 2. exercises that are part of a soldier's training.
drink 1. *vb.* (past **drank**) swallow water or other liquid. 2. *n.* any liquid that is swallowed.
drip *vb.* fall in drops.
dripping *n.* fat melted from roasting meat.
drive 1. *vb.* (past **drove**) steer a car or other vehicle. 2. *vb.* strike a golf ball. 3. *n.* a road from the street to the front of a house (driveway).
drivel *n.* nonsensical talk. *vb.* talk foolishly.
driver *n.* the person who steers a car or other vehicle.
drizzle *n.* & *vb.* fine dense rain.
dromedary *n.* a fast camel with one hump.
drone *n.* a male bee or ant that does no work.
droop *vb.* hang down limply, wilt.
drop 1. *n.* a small amount of liquid, a raindrop. 2. *vb.* let something fall.
drop in *vb.* visit someone without telling them you are coming.
drought (rhymes with *out*) *n.* a long period of dry weather.
drove *vb.* past of **drive**.
drown *vb.* die by suffocation in water; drench.
drowsy *adj.* sleepy, not fully awake.
drug *n.* a medicine; a substance that takes away anxiety or pain. *vb.* to stupefy with drugs; add drugs to food etc.
► Drugs are chemicals that affect

D

the way the body works. Doctors give drugs to patients to help them fight disease. Antibiotics attack certain kinds of GERMS. These drugs help to cure people suffering from pneumonia and other illnesses. Drugs like aspirin help to deaden pain. The strongest painkillers are called anesthetics. Some people need drugs containing VITAMINS or other substances their bodies must have, but cannot get from food.

Certain drugs come from plants or animals. For instance, the foxglove gives us a drug called digitalis. This makes weak hearts beat more strongly. Many other drugs are made from MINERALS.

Some people take drugs such as cocaine, cannabis or alcohol just because these give a pleasant feeling. These drugs can be very dangerous.

Druids

These were the priests of the ancient CELTS of Britain, Ireland and France. What we know about them was largely written down by their enemies, the Romans. Druids seem to have worshiped the same type of gods as the Romans. But they believed that oak and mistletoe were sacred, and they killed animals and human beings as sacrifices.

The Celtic people looked on Druids as wise men. Druids judged law cases. They also tried to see into the future.

drum *n.* a round, hollow musical instrument with a skin stretched over a frame. *vb.* play a drum.
► Drums are the most important of those MUSICAL INSTRUMENTS that are played by being struck. The sound is made by hitting a tightly stretched sheet of skin or plastic called a drumhead. A kettledrum has one drumhead stretched over a metal basin. A bass drum or a side drum has two drumheads, one across each end of a large open "can."

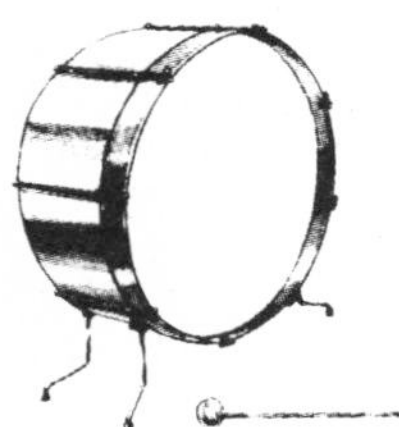

drunk 1. *adj.* having drunk too much alcohol. *People who drive when they are drunk are responsible for too many accidents.* 2. *n.* a person who habitually drinks too much. 3. *vb.* past part. of **drink**.
drupe *n.* fruit such as a plum with a stone contained in fleshy pulp.
dry *adj.* not wet; without water.

dual *adj.* making a pair, double. *Dual exhausts.*
dubious (**dew**-*bius*) *adj.* doubtful, open to question.

Dublin

The city of Dublin is the capital of the Republic of IRELAND. It lies at the mouth of the Liffey River, on the east coast of Ireland. The city has many fine Georgian buildings. It is the seat of the Irish Parliament **dail** (rhymes with *oil*). The Viking's established the city in the 800s.

duck 1. *n.* a web-footed water bird with a broad beak. 2. *vb.* bend down quickly to get out of the way of something.

► The two main groups of ducks are dabbling ducks and diving ducks. Dabbling ducks feed at the surface of the water. They may put most of their body under the water, but they do not dive. Dabbling ducks include the mallards that swim in ponds and rivers in the northern half of the world. (Farmyard ducks were bred from mallards). Other dabbling ducks include teal and wigeon, and the pretty mandarin and Carolina ducks.

Diving ducks dive completely under water in their hunt for food. Most diving ducks live out at sea. These ducks include the eider duck from which we get eiderdown. Sawbills are also diving ducks. Their long, slim beaks have inside edges like the teeth of a saw. Sawbills are good at grasping fish. The long-tailed duck is a diving duck that can fly at 70 mph (112 k/h).

The two sexes of ducks have different plumage although in later summer the drakes (males) molt and for a time resemble the ducks (females).

duckling *n.* a young duck.
due *adj.* owing; merited; expected. *The plane is due at ten o'clock.*
duet *n.* a piece of music for two performers.
dug *vb.* past of **dig**.
duke *n.* an important nobleman, next to a prince in rank. *A duke's wife is called a duchess.*
dull *adj.* not bright; not sharp; not interesting. *It is never dull when Mrs. Perfect teaches our class.*

Dumas, Alexandre

Alexandre Dumas (1802–70) was a French writer. His best-known books are *The Three Musketeers* and *The Count of Monte Cristo.* Although he made a great deal of money from his writing, he died poor. He is usually called Dumas *père* (father) to distinguish him from his son, also called Alexandre Dumas (1824–95) who is known as Dumas *fils* (son). The younger Dumas wrote a number of novels and plays, including *The Lady of the Camellias,* which provided Verdi with the story for his opera *La Traviata.*

dumb *adj*. 1. not able to speak. 2. (*slang*) stupid.
dummy *n*. model of a human figure.
dump *vb*. put in a heap. *n*. rubbish collection spot; (*casual*) a dull place.
dumpling *n*. small piece of steamed or boiled dough.
dunce *n*. a person slow at learning.
dune *n*. a low hill of sand.
► If the wind blows steadily from one direction it may move huge quantities of sand. The sand grains blow along just above the ground. They cannot rise to cross an obstacle. So where the sand grains reach a rock or a plant they just pile up against it. In this way sand forms mounds called dunes.

Dunes form wherever the wind keeps blowing sand in one direction. Many dunes form behind sandy beaches. The wind blows sand up the beach from the sea. Grasses trap the sand and in time low dunes cover the grasses. But these grow up through the dunes. More sand collects around the plants, so the dunes grow taller still. Some Spanish dunes have grown as high as skyscrapers.

The world's tallest dunes stand inland, not beside the sea. These dunes rise in the SAHARA and look like giant waves of sand. Just one of them can measure 1,410 ft. (430 meters) high and stretch 3 miles (5 km) from front to back.

A "barchan" type sand dune. It has ends curved by the wind blowing from left to right.

Desert dunes sometimes cover an OASIS. Each year the Sahara dunes cover trees and crops. Farmers try to halt the dunes by growing special plants in the sands. The plant roots help to hold the sand still.

dung *n*. farmyard manure.
dungeon (**dun**-*jun*) *n*. an underground prison.
duplicate *vb*. make exact copy of.
durable *adj*. strong and long lasting.

Durban
Durban is the main port of SOUTH AFRICA. It is a leading manufacturing center, and the home of the University of Natal. Originally called Port Natal, it was renamed after Sir Benjamin D'Urban, the governor of Cape Colony.

Dürer, Albrecht
Albrecht Dürer (1471–1528) was a German artist. He worked in oils and water colors, but today he is best known as an engraver in wood and copper. Probably his most famous print is *The Knight, Death, and the Devil*. He was a friend of Martin Luther.

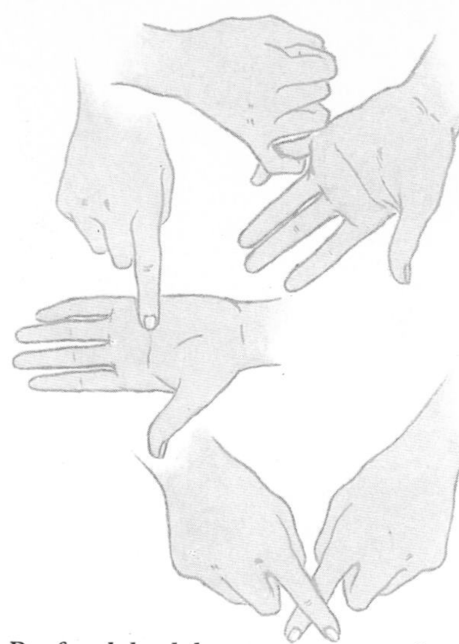

Deaf and dumb language – a way of communicating with the hands and fingers.

during *prep*. 1. throughout. *The old man slept during the entire speech*. 2. at some time in. *They arrived during the afternoon*.
dusk *n*. the time of evening when it is starting to get dark; twilight.
dust *n*. tiny grains of dirt.
dustbin *n*. a container for household rubbish.
dust bowl *n*. a dry area (especially in the western Great Plains of the USA) which has many dust storms.
duty *n*. something that you must do. *The policeman's duty is to arrest the burglar*.
dwarf *n*. a person, animal, or plant that does not grow to full size.
► Any unusually small kind of adult plant, animal or human being is called a dwarf. Dwarf fruit trees, Shetland ponies, and PYGMIES are all dwarfs.

Some dwarfs happen naturally. Some can be produced by breeding. Others had too little nourishment to make them grow.

There are three kinds of human dwarf. One looks like a tiny normal person. Another has short arms and legs. The third kind has a strangely shaped body.

dwell *vb*. 1. live somewhere. 2. write or speak about at great length.
dwindle *vb*. steadily become smaller, grow less.

Dyaks
Dyaks (or Dayaks) are a people who live in the island of BORNEO. At one time, Dyaks practiced head-hunting and cannibalism. Today, many work on plantations or in factories. Some live in large family groups in longhouses built on stilts. Their religion involves the worship of ancestors. They use elaborately carved masks and shields in their ceremonials.

dye (rhymes with *lie*) *vb*. change color of something by putting in a special liquid called a **dye** (*n*.).
► Dyes are substances that people use to color TEXTILES and other materials. Some dyes come from plants. Most dyes are made from chemicals. To dye an object you dip it in water containing dissolved dye. If the dye is *fast* the object will keep its dyed color however much you wash it afterwards.

The dyes used before the mid-1800s were all natural dyes. These were made from a wide range of plants such as indigo, madder, walnut, henna, etc. Most dyes used today are synthetic. They are cheaper than natural dyes and longer lasting. Most synthetic dyes come from coal tar and more than 5,000 different colors have been produced.

The first synthetic dye was discovered by an English chemist, William Perkin. In 1856, when he was only 18, Perkin accidentally produced a dye while he was trying to make synthetic quinine. He called the dye *mauve*. Because Perkin's first dye was made from aniline oil, all synthetic dyes were, for a long time, called "aniline dyes."

Until the start of World War I, Germany produced most of the world's dyes. The war cut off this supply to the Allies, so they had to start making their own. Today, the United States is one of the main manufacturers of dyes.

dyke see **dike**.
dynamic *adj*. very active; filled with energy.
dynamite *n*. a powerful explosive used for blasting.
► Dynamite was invented in the 1860s by the Swedish chemist Alfred Nobel. Its main ingredient is nitroglycerin. Dynamite is packed in paper tubes. Then someone a safe distance away sends an electric current through a wire to explode the charge. Engineers use dynamite to blast holes in mines, quarries, and building sites. There are many kinds of dynamite.

Nobel's invention earned him a fortune. He used much of it to set up the NOBEL PRIZES.

dynasty *n*. a historical line of kings or queens.
dysentery (**dis**-*en-ter-ee*) *n*. serious disease of the bowels.
dyslexia *n*. word blindness, inability to read easily.
dyspepsia *n*. indigestion, especially when chronic. **dyspeptic** *adj*.

E

Benjamin Franklin demonstrating (in 1852) the electrical nature of lightning by flying a kite in a thunderstorm.

each *adj.* every member of a group thought of separately. *He held a gun in each hand.*

eager *adj.* keen; enthusiastic. **eagerness** *n.*

eagle *n.* a large bird of prey.

► Most eagles hunt small mammals and birds. Some catch fish or reptiles. The harpy eagle and the monkey-eating eagle catch monkeys. Each of these great birds measures more than 7 ft. (2 meters) across its outspread wings. These eagles are the largest in the world.

Many eagles soar high above the ground. Others perch on a tree or rock. When an eagle sees its prey it swoops suddenly and pounces. The eagle seizes its prey with its sharp claws, and tears off chunks of flesh with its strong, hooked beak.

ear *n.* 1. the organ, or part of the body, with which we hear. 2. the sense of hearing.

► Our ears help us to hear and to keep our balance. Each ear has three main parts: the outer ear, middle ear and inner ear.

The outer ear is the part we can see, and the tube leading from it into the head. Sounds reach the outer ear as vibrations, or waves, in the air. The cup-like shape of the ear collects these sound waves and sends them into the tube.

Next, the sound waves reach the middle ear. Here, the waves make the eardrum move to and fro. This is a thin "skin" across the entrance of the middle ear. The moving eardrum sets tiny bones vibrating in the middle ear.

The vibrations travel on into the inner ear. Here they set liquid moving in the *cochlea*. This looks like a snail's shell. The nerves inside it turn vibrations into messages that travel to the brain. The inner ear also has three hollow loops containing liquid. These loops send signals to the brain to help you keep your balance.

Ears are delicate and easily damaged. Hitting or poking into an ear can sometimes cause an injury that leads to deafness.

earache (**ear**-*ayk*) *n.* a pain in the ear.

earl *n.* the middle rank of the British peerage, between marquis and viscount. *The wife of an earl is called a countess.* **earldom** *n.*

early *adv.* & *adj.* soon; at the beginning (of the day). *She is an early riser.*

earn *vb.* 1. get something by working for it. 2. deserve. *She earns everyone's respect.*

earnest *adj.* serious; keen, but lacking in humor.

earnings *pl. n.* money earned.

Earp, Wyatt
Wyatt Earp (1848–1929) was a lawman in the days of the "Wild West." After a variety of jobs, he worked as an armed guard for the Wells Fargo company in Tombstone, Arizona. Earp has become a symbol of the tough American lawman.

earrings *pl. n.* ornaments worn in the ears.

earshot *n.* within hearing distance.

earth 1. *n.* the planet on which we live. 2. *n.* soil. **earthy** *adj.* of earth or soil; coarse. 3. *n.* hole of a burrowing animal.

► The earth is the fifth largest of the PLANETS that move around the sun. Seen from space the earth looks like a giant ball. Land and WATER cover the surface, and AIR surrounds the earth. The earth has three main layers. The top layer is a thin *crust* of hard rock which floats on a thicker layer of rock called the *mantle*. This is so hot that its rocks are at least partly melted. Below the mantle lies the *core*. Much of this is made of iron so hot that it is liquid.

All living things live on and just above the crust. (GEOLOGY tells us much about past life on earth). Earth is the only planet in the SOLAR SYSTEM to have living things. Other planets are too hot or cold or are surrounded by poisonous gases.

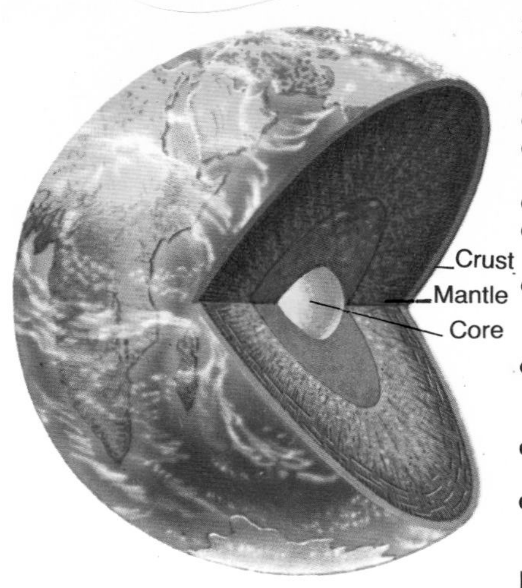

The earth spins as it speeds through space. It takes a DAY and NIGHT to spin around once and a year to travel around the sun. The earth spins in a tilted position. This causes the different SEASONS of the year.

earthquake *n.* a shaking movement of the surface of the earth.
► About half-a-million earthquakes happen every year. Most are so weak that only special instruments called *seismographs* show that they have happened. Only one earthquake in 500 does any damage. But some earthquakes can cause terrible damage and suffering. Three-quarters of a million people are thought to have died when an earthquake hit the Chinese city of Tangshan in 1976.
Small tremors can happen when VOLCANOES erupt, when there is a landslide, or when the roof of an underground cave falls in. The largest earthquakes occur when one huge piece of the earth's crust slips suddenly against another piece. This slipping may take place deep underground. But the shock travels up through the crust and sets the surface quaking.
A seabed earthquake may set off a huge ocean wave called a TIDAL WAVE.

earthwork *n.* a mound of earth used as a fortification.
earwig *n.* insect with pincers at the end of its abdomen.
ease *n.* comfort; freedom from pain. *vb.* make easier; relieve from pain; relax.
easel *n.* a frame to hold up a picture or blackboard.
east *n.* & *adj.* the direction in which the sun rises. *East winds blow from the east.* **eastward** *adv.* **eastern** *adj.*
Easter *n.* the day on which Christians remember the Resurrection of Jesus Christ.
► Most Christians celebrate Easter on the Sunday following the first full moon after the first day of spring in the northern half of the world.

easy *adj.* simple; not difficult.
easygoing *adj.* tolerant, not fussy.
eat *vb.* (past **ate** past part. **eaten**) chew and swallow food.
eat away *vb.* destroy gradually.
ebb *vb.* & *n.* the tide flowing back from land to sea.
ebony *n.* the name of various kinds of hard, black wood. *adj.* the color of ebony; black.
eccentric *adj.* odd, peculiar. *n.* a person with unusual habits or behavior.
ecclesiastical *adj.* of or concerning the church and clergy.
echo (**ek**-*o*) *n.* & *vb.* a sound that is heard again when it bounces back or is reflected off something.
► Sound travels at a known, fixed speed, so we can use echoes to find how far off some objects are. A ship's SONAR uses echoes to find the depth of the sea. Echoes help BATS to fly in the dark. RADAR depends on echoes from radio signals.

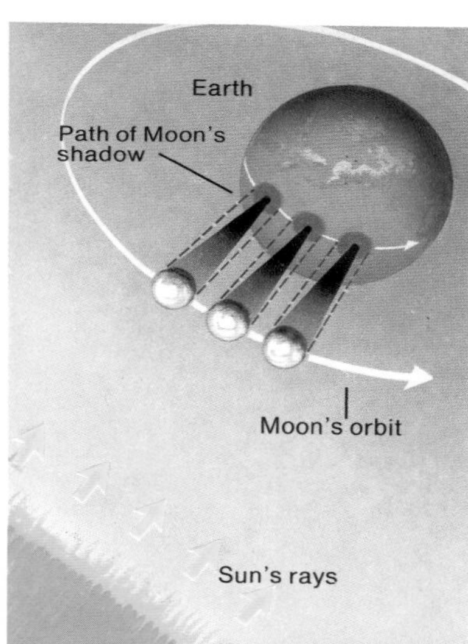

How eclipses of the sun occur.

eclipse *n.* & *vb.* a time when the sun's light is cut off because the moon passes between the earth and the sun (an eclipse of the sun); a time when the moon's light is cut off because the earth passes between the sun and the moon (an eclipse of the moon).
ecology *n.* the study of the habits of living things, the places where they live and how they depend on each other. **ecological** *adj.* **ecologist** *n.*
► Scientists called ecologists try to find out how living things and their surroundings affect each other. Ecology shows us that most plants and animals can live only in a special set of surroundings like a pond, field, forest or desert. Within each place live plants that are suited to a certain soil, temperature, and so on. All the animals living there eat the plants or one another. So the plants and animals are linked in what ecologists call a food web. If some kinds die out, those that eat them lose their food and may die too.

economy *n.* 1. the management of a country's wealth. 2. a saving. *He is always trying to make false economies in our housekeeping.* **economical** *adj.* thrifty **economize** *vb.* avoid expense.

Ecuador
Ecuador is one of the smaller countries of South America. It is so called because it lies on the equator. Much of the country, including the capital Quito, lies high up in the ANDES mountains. About half the people work on the land. Some oil is produced.
The Incas ruled the area from about 1470 until the Spaniards conquered it in 1533. Ecuador became independent in 1830. Since then it has lost territory to stronger neighboring countries. It has had a succession of military governments, but elections were held in 1979.
AREA: 109,489 SQ. MILES (283,561 SQ. KM)
POPULATION: 8,893,000
CAPITAL: QUITO
CURRENCY: SUCRE
OFFICIAL LANGUAGE: SPANISH

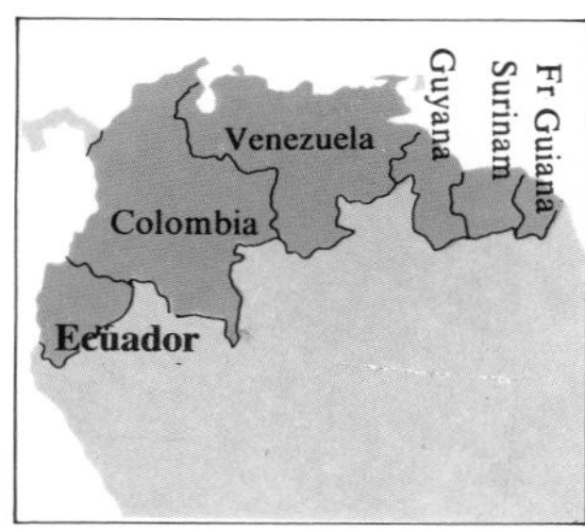

eczema (**ek**-*suh-muh*) *n.* a disease of the skin.
edge *n.* the part along the side or end of something. *The path ran around the edge of the field.*
edible *adj.* fit to be eaten.
edifice *n.* large building such as a church, etc.
edify *vb.* teach and improve mentally.

Edinburgh
Edinburgh is the capital of SCOTLAND and its second largest city. It is more than 800 years old. Edinburgh stands south of the great sea inlet called the Firth of Forth. Edinburgh Castle is perched on an extinct volcano in the city center. Each year people from all over the world come to the Edinburgh Festival of plays, films and music.

E

Edison, Thomas
Thomas Alva Edison (1847–1931) was an American inventor. As a boy he spent only three months at school, and his teacher thought him stupid. But he went on to produce over 1,000 inventions. The most famous were the electric light and the phonograph for RECORDING and playing back sounds.

edit *vb.* prepare a piece of writing for publication in a book, newspaper or magazine. **editor** *n.* a person who edits.
edition *n.* copies of a book or periodical printed at one time.

Edmonton
Edmonton is the capital and largest city of the western Canadian province of ALBERTA. It lies on the North Saskatchewan River. Edmonton's industries include oil refining, meat packing and the manufacture of chemicals.

educate *vb.* teach or train. **education** *n.* **educational** *adj.*

Edward (Kings)
Nine kings of England were called Edward. Edward "The Confessor" (reigned 1042–66) founded WESTMINSTER ABBEY. Edward I (reigned 1272–1307) brought Wales under English rule. Edward II (1307–27) was the first English Prince of Wales. Edward III (1327–77) began the HUNDRED YEARS WAR. Edward IV (1467–83) took the crown from Henry VI in the War of the Roses. Edward V (1483) was murdered in the Tower of London. Edward VI (1547–53) reigned as a boy king for only six years. Edward VII (1901–1910) was Prince of Wales for 60 years. Edward VIII, who died in 1972, gave up the throne in 1936 to marry Mrs. Simpson, a divorced American.

Edwardian *adj.* belonging to the reign of Edward VII (1901–10).
eel *n.* a long slim fish with fins like narrow ribbons.
► European and American freshwater eels swim thousands of miles and spawn far out in the Atlantic Ocean. Then they die. The tiny, transparent young that hatch look nothing like their parents. These babies find their way all the way back to their parents' homes in America and Europe. There, they travel up rivers and streams. The young eels grow up in fresh water and stay there until they are ready for their long journey back across the Atlantic.

effect *n.* result or consequence of our action.
effeminate *adj.* womanish behavior in a man.
efficient *adj.* capable, competent.
effigy *n.* image or likeness of a person.
effort *n.* hard work.
e.g. stands for two Latin words, **exempli gratia**, meaning "for example."
egg *n.* one of the roundish objects that young birds, insects, fish and reptiles live inside before they are born; an important kind of food. **egg on** *vb.* encourage.
► An egg is a female CELL that will grow into a new young plant or animal. Most eggs grow only if they are joined with, or fertilized by, male cells. In most MAMMALS the fertilized eggs grow inside the mother's body. But birds and most reptiles and fish lay eggs that contain enough food to help the developing young grow inside the egg.

egocentric *adj.* concerned with oneself; self-centered.
egoism *n.* selfishness.

Egypt (Egyptian)
About 5,000 years ago the ancient Egyptians began to build one of the world's first great civilizations. For the next 2,500 years, ancient Egypt was one of the strongest, richest nations on Earth.
The people who made Egypt great were short, slim, dark-skinned men and women with black hair. They probably numbered no more than six million. Scarcely any of them lived in the hot sand and rock deserts that cover most of Egypt. Almost all the people settled by the NILE RIVER that runs from south to north across the land.
Each year the river overflowed and left rich mud on nearby fields. Farmers learned to dig and plow the fields. They could grow two crops a year in the warm, fertile soil. The farmers grew more than enough grain, fruit and vegetables to feed themselves. The rest of the food helped to feed Egyptian craftsmen, miners, merchants, priests, noble families, and the PHARAOHS who

An Egyptian wall painting showing scenes of harvest time along the Nile River.

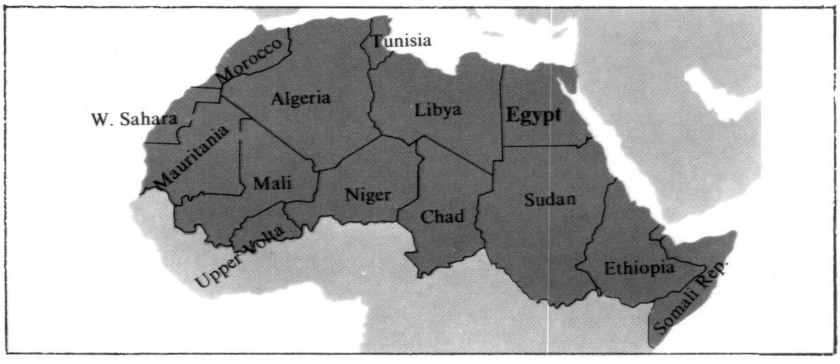

ruled over the entire land.

Most Egyptians were poor and lived in mudbrick huts with palmleaf roofs. Rich Egyptians lived in large, well-furnished houses. They wore fine clothes and jewels.

The most splendid buildings were tombs and temples. Thousands of workers toiled for years to build the PYRAMIDS. In each such tomb, Egyptians would place the MUMMY of a pharaoh. They believed the dead went on living. So they buried food and furniture beside each mummy. Thieves later emptied almost all the tombs. But TUTANKHAMEN'S tomb shows us what royal burials were like.

The dry Egyptian air has preserved HIEROGLYPHICS written in fragile paper made from the papyrus plant. Paintings and hieroglyphics tell us a great deal about how the ancient Egyptians lived.

In time, foreign armies using iron weapons defeated the Egyptians. Their land fell under foreign rule after 525 B.C.

Modern Egypt dates from A.D. 642 when Egypt was conquered by Muslim soldiers from Arabia. Egypt is now a Muslim, mainly Arab, country. No other African city is as large as CAIRO, Egypt's capital. But Egyptians still depend upon the waters of the river that made old Egypt great.

AREA: 386,683 SQ. MILES (1,001,449 SQ. KM)
POPULATION: 43,611,000
CAPITAL: CAIRO
CURRENCY: EGYPTIAN POUND
OFFICIAL LANGUAGE: ARABIC

eider *n.* a large sea duck, the soft down of which is used in eiderdowns (quilts).

Eiffel Tower
The Eiffel Tower rises more than 985 ft. (300 meters) above Paris. The tower is really four open, wrought-iron towers that curve inwards and join. Crisscross bars give the tower its strength. The metal in it weighs about 7,000 tons. People can reach the top by lifts and stairs. The French engineer Gustave Eiffel designed the tower for a Paris exhibition of 1889. For the next 40 years the Eiffel Tower was the tallest man-made structure in the world.

Einstein, Albert
Albert Einstein (1879–1955) was a scientist who was born in Germany. His theory of relativity was a new way of looking into time, space, matter and ENERGY. Einstein showed that a small amount of matter could be changed into a vast amount of energy. This made it possible for us to use ATOMIC ENERGY. Einstein won the Nobel Prize for Physics in 1921.

Eisenhower, Dwight David
Dwight D. Eisenhower (1890–1969) was a general who became a Republican President of the United States. Eisenhower distinguished himself in WORLD WAR II, becoming Supreme Commander of Western Europe in 1944. He served two terms as the 34th President, from 1953–61.

Eisenhower suffered three serious illnesses during his terms as President, but he lived to be, at the age of 70, one of the oldest Presidents in American history.

either *adj.* & *pron.* one or the other; one of two. *He can take either road to get there.*
eject *vb.* remove; send out, expel. **ejection** *n.* **ejector** *n.*
elaborate *adj.* done in great detail.
elastic *n.* & *adj.* a material that stretches out and then goes back to the same size. *A rubber band is made of elastic.*
elbow *n.* the joint between the upper and lower arm. *vb.* thrust, jostle.
elder 1. *adj.* older. *My elder brother was born before I was.* **elderly** *adj.* becoming old; past middle age. 2. *n.* an official of certain churches.
eldest *adj.* child of the greatest age. *My eldest brother was born before my elder brother.*
election *n.* a time when people can choose, by voting, the men and women who will govern their town or country, society or club. **elect** *vb.* choose by voting. **elector** *n.* a person entitled to vote. **electorate** *n.* the mass or body of electors.
electric *adj.* worked by electricity.
electrician *n.* a person who works with electricity or electrical equipment.
electricity *n.* energy that is used to make heat and light and is used to drive some machines. Electricity moves along wires from generating stations to where it is needed. **electrify** *vb.* charge with electricity; change to working by electricity. *The railroads will be electrified.*

► The electricity that we use flows through wires as electric CURRENT. Current flows when tiny particles called electrons jump between the ATOMS that make up the metal in the wire. Current can flow only if a wire makes a complete loop called a circuit. If a gap is made in the circuit, the current stops flowing. Switches are simply devices that open and close gaps in circuits.

BATTERIES produce electric current that can be used to start cars, light flashlights and work radios. But most of the electricity we use is produced in POWER STATIONS. In a power station GENERATOR, coils of wire are made to rotate between powerful magnets. This makes electric current flow through the coils of wire. This current then flows through other long wires to our homes.

electrocute *vb.* execute by using a powerful electric current.
electrode *n.* metal rod or plate through which an electric current enters or leaves a battery, etc.
electron *n.* small negatively charged subatomic particle.
electronics *pl. n.* the science that deals with things like television, radio and other pieces of apparatus that have devices such as transistors.

► Electronics involves the use of electrical circuits including *cathode-ray* tubes, TRANSISTORS or other semiconductor devices. William Crookes built a simple cathode-ray tube in 1879. The modern tubes used in TELEVISION and RADAR equipment work in the same basic way. Early RADIO equipment had limited range because no amplifying devices were available to strengthen the weak signals. Amplification became possible in 1907 with Lee De Forest's invention of the triode tube. This made possible great improvements in radio equipment and led to the development of a practical television system. The first electronic COMPUTERS, built in the 1940s, consisted of massive banks of equipment with thousands of tubes. But the development of the transistor in 1948 enabled later computers to be drastically reduced in size. Further enormous reductions in the size and cost of electronic circuits have since been made possible with the introduction of microcircuits.

elegance *n.* refinement in taste; grace. **elegant** *adj.* tasteful.
elegy *n.* sad poem or song written usually for the dead.
element *n.* a substance that cannot be divided into simpler substances.

► **Elements and compounds.** Everything in the universe is made up from fundamental materials called elements. Some substances, for example, pure COPPER or CARBON, contain just one element. The air contains a *mixture* of various gaseous elements, mainly NITROGEN and OXYGEN. In a mixture, the elements exist separately and retain their own individual properties. *Compounds* consist of two or more elements chemically combined. Most substances found on earth are compounds. Water, for example, is a compound of hydrogen and oxygen. The physical and chemical properties of a compound are quite different from those of the elements it contains.

Each element contains ATOMS with a specific atomic number. Elements with atomic numbers from 1 to 92 occur naturally. Other elements can be made artificially in nuclear reactions (*see* CHEMISTRY).

elementary *adj*. simple; introductory.

elephant *n*. the world's largest land mammal, characterized by a long trunk and curved tusks made of ivory.

► Elephants are found in Africa and southern Asia. The elephant's unique characteristic is its long trunk used for carrying food and water to the mouth, spraying water over the body, lifting things and for smelling. Elephants feed off grass, leaves, and fruit, and usually live in herds. There are two species: the Indian elephant, widely used as a work animal, and the larger, fiercer African elephant.

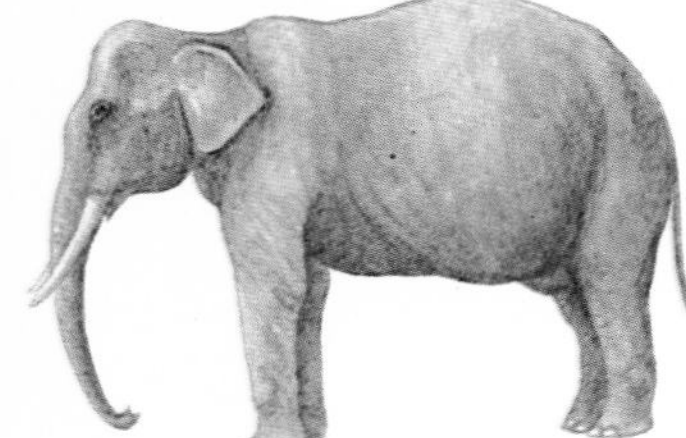

An Indian (above) and African elephant.

elevate *vb*. lift up, raise. **elevator** *n*. a conveyance in buildings.

elf *n*. (plural **elves**) in storybooks, a small fairy.

elite (*ay*-**leet**) *n*. a select, privileged group; the best.

Elizabeth I
One of the best known of all English monarchs (born 1533) she ruled from 1558 to 1603. Hers was a reign of peace. She strengthened the position of the Anglican Church but soothed differences between Protestants and Catholics. She beat off a Spanish invasion attempt in 1588 (*see* ARMADA), yet kept out of long, costly wars. During her reign, the country emerged as a leading world power and with a strong foothold in the New World (*see* DRAKE, SIR FRANCIS).

Elizabeth II
The name of the reigning queen of Great Britain (born 1926). She came to the throne in 1952 after the death of her father, King GEORGE VI. She represents Britain to the world and upholds the dignity and traditions of the throne. She also takes an active interest in government affairs. Queen Elizabeth is also the head of state of a number of Commonwealth countries, including Australia, Canada, Jamaica and New Zealand and is the head of the Commonwealth.

Elizabethan *adj*. belonging to the reign of Elizabeth I (1533-1603).

elk *n*. the name for two large kinds of deer. The European elk is known as a moose in North America. The second kind is the American elk.

elm *n*. a broad-leaved tree, the leaves having zigzag edges like the teeth of a saw.

► Elms shed their leaves in the fall. The seeds have little "wings" and drift off in the wind. Elms have tough, hard wood used for making furniture. Some kinds of elm have smooth bark, others have rough bark. An elm tree may live more than 200 years. The elm is a large tree, reaching a height of 75 to 100 feet (22 to 30 meters). Small greenish flowers appear in early spring.

Many elms have been killed by Dutch elm disease. This is caused by a FUNGUS spread by a beetle that flies from tree to tree.

elongate *vb*. stretch out, make longer.

elope *vb*. run away with a lover to get married without parental permission. *n*. **elopement**.

El Salvador
El Salvador is a small but densely-populated republic on the Pacific coast of CENTRAL AMERICA. It became independent from Spain in 1821, but did not become an independent republic until 1841. The country has long been politically unstable. In 1979 a war began between the U.S.-backed military government and left-wing guerrillas.

AREA: 8,124 SQ. MILES (21,041 SQ. KM)
POPULATION: 4,820,000
CAPITAL: SAN SALVADOR
CURRENCY: COLON
OFFICIAL LANGUAGE: SPANISH

em- *prefix* see **en-**.

emancipate *vb*. set free from control of another, e.g. social restraint, slavery.

embankment *n*. the built-up bank of a river or lake; a bank so constructed to carry a road or a railway.

embargo *n*. a ban on trading for a time.

embark *vb*. get on board ship.

embarrass *vb*. make someone feel uncomfortable or ill at ease. **embarrassment** *n*.

embassy *n*. the building used by an ambassador and his staff.

embezzle *vb*. take property, money, etc., that is not one's own but which has been put in one's charge.

emblem *n*. a badge, symbol.

embrace *vb*. take into the arms; accept; adopt (a cause).

embroidery *n*. decoration of cloth made by sewing a pattern of colored stitches. **embroider** *vb*.

► People usually make embroideries on such materials as canvas, cotton, wool or silk. They often embroider with colored threads of cotton, linen, silk, or wool. People can even stitch patterns made up of beads, pearls, or jewels.

The oldest embroidery was made over 2,300 years ago. One of the longest embroideries is the BAYEUX TAPESTRY which is a kind of historic strip cartoon.

embryo (**em**-*bree-yo*) *n*. an animal in an early stage before it is born. **embryonic** *adj*.

emend *vb*. correct, remove errors. **emendation** *n*.

emerald *n*. a precious green stone.

emerge *vb*. come out; come to notice.

emergency *n*. a sudden happening that needs quick action.

Emerson, Ralph Waldo
Ralph Waldo Emerson (1803–82) was an American philosopher, writer and poet. He visited Europe and met a number of influential men of letters. He believed that America had a great future, and should not be unduly influenced by European ideas.

emigrate *vb*. go away from your own country to live. **emigration** *n*.

eminent *adj*. distinguished; standing above others because of some special quality.

emit *vb*. give out, send out. **emission** *n*.

emotion *n*. strong feeling (of love, hate, etc.). **emotional** *adj*. agitated in feeling; easily moved by feelings.

emperor *n.* the male ruler of an empire. A female ruler is an **empress**.

emphasis (**em**-*fa-sis*) *n.* stress, e.g. on words, to show importance. **emphasize** *vb.* stress, underline; state strongly.

empire *n.* a group of countries under one ruler. *The Roman Empire spread all around the Mediterranean Sea.*

employ *vb.* 1. pay people to work. **employee** *n.* a person who works for wages. **employer** *n.* a person who employs others. **employment** *n.* 2. use. *I employ a fine pen to fill in the details.*

emporium *n.* a large shop (rather old-fashioned).

empty *adj.* having nothing inside; unoccupied. *vb.* remove contents of. **emptiness** *n.*

emu *n.* a large Australian flightless bird.

► Only the ostrich is larger than an emu. An emu is as tall as a man but not so heavy. Emu feathers are thick and dark. Its wings are small and an emu cannot fly. But it can run as fast as a horse on its long, strong legs.

Emus eat leaves and insects. Big herds of emus sometimes attack farm crops. Each female lays up to 10 green eggs in a nest on the ground. The male sits on the eggs and later guards the chicks. Emus are related to the cassowary.

en- prefix meaning to put into, on, effect, e.g. **enrage, enclose**. Before B, P and M, **en-** becomes **em-**.

enable *vb.* make able.

enamel *n.* a very hard, shiny paint; a hard, glass-like coating on metal pots and pottery or glass.

► Enamel is made from powdered glass and other substances. This powder is put on to an object that is then heated. The powder melts and forms enamel.

enchant *vb.* 1. put a magic spell on someone. 2. be very attractive to someone.

enclose *vb.* shut in on all sides. **enclosure** *n.* enclosed land.

encore (**on**-*kor*) *inter.* & *n.* shout of applause meaning *Again*! repetition of a song, etc.

encounter *vb.* meet someone. *n.* a casual meeting.

encourage *vb.* make someone feel able to do something; urge someone on. **encouragement** *n.*

encyclopedia *n.* a book or set of books that give you information about many subjects, usually alphabetically arranged.

► Some encyclopedias try to say something about nearly everything. Others cover just one subject, like plants or animals. In this book, all the entries are in alphabetical order. In some encyclopedias articles about one subject are grouped together in the same part of the encyclopedia.

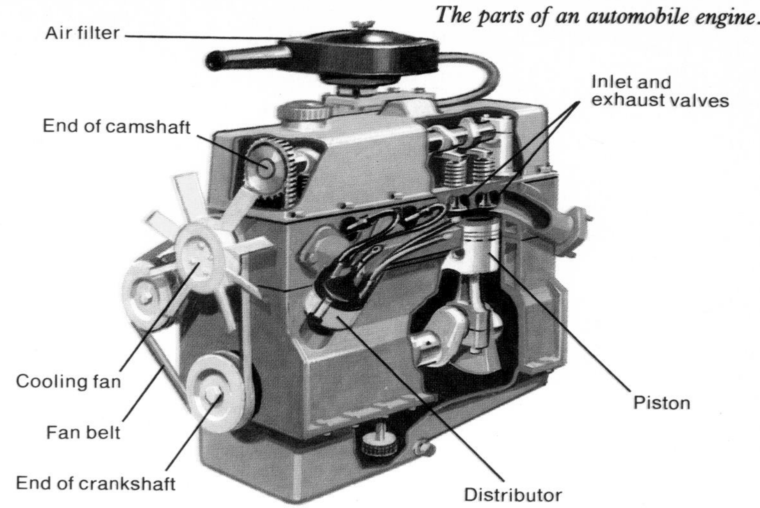

The parts of an automobile engine.

end *n.* the place where something stops; the edge or side of something. *vb.* to put a stop to. **endless** *adj.* without ending; incessant.

endeavor (*en*-**dev**-*er*) *vb.* try hard to do. *n.* an attempt.

endure *vb.* continue unchanged; tolerate suffering. **endurance** *n.* permanence; ability to withstand hardship.

enemy *n.* the people that one fights in time of war.

energy *n.* the strength or power to do work; vigor; activity. *Machines have energy. The food we eat gives us energy.* **energetic** *adj.*

► Energy occurs in many forms – mechanical, chemical, electrical, nuclear and radiant. A wound-up clock spring has a store of mechanical energy. As the coiled spring slowly unwinds, it does useful WORK in turning the mechanism to drive the hands. The water behind a dam also has stored mechanical energy. The water can turn TURBINES linked to generators to make electricity. Stored mechanical energy is termed *potential* energy. Mechanical energy occurs also as *kinetic* energy – energy of movement, as in a falling object. Chemical energy is released in certain chemical reactions – for example, when a fuel is burned. Electrical energy is produced in cells and BATTERIES, or by GENERATORS. ATOMIC ENERGY, mainly in the form of heat, is produced in nuclear reactions. Radiant energy includes heat, light and other forms of electromagnetic radiation.

engage *vb.* 1. bind by promise. 2. hire. 3. (in) take part in. 4. begin fighting. 5. interlock. *He engaged the gear.*

engine *n.* a machine which changes energy into power or movement.

engineer *n.* 1. a person who plans and builds bridges, roads, machines and big buildings. 2. a person who looks after or works with engines.

► Engineers do a great many different types of jobs. Mining engineers find useful minerals and take them from the ground. Metallurgical engineers separate metals from unwanted substances and make them usable. Chemical engineers use chemicals to make such things as explosives, paint, plastics, and soap. Civil engineers build bridges, tunnels, roads, railroads, ports, airports, and so on. Mechanical engineers make and use machines. Such people design jet engines and factory machinery. Electrical engineers work with devices that produce and use electricity. Some specialize in building a particular type of generator. Others work in ELECTRONICS. Most of the main kinds of engineering fall into one or the other of these groups.

England (English)
Part of the United Kingdom of GREAT BRITAIN and Northern IRELAND.

England's main wealth comes from manufacturing and international commerce and trade. Manufacturing began during the INDUSTRIAL REVOLUTION which started in the late 1700s. It was based on abundant local supplies of coal and iron ore.

Farming in England, with its rich soils and mild, moist climate, is scientific and highly productive. But comparatively few people work on farms and much food is imported.

England is the most densely-populated part of the BRITISH ISLES and most people live in cities and towns. The chief cities are LONDON, Birmingham, Leeds, Sheffield, LIVERPOOL and Manchester. The

E

English are a blend of many peoples, including conquerors and settlers, such as the Romans, Angles, Saxons, Jutes, VIKINGS, Danes and NORMANS. Some later immigrants, such as the French Huguenots and Jews, settled in England to escape persecution. Most recently, people from the Commonwealth have made their homes in England. England united with WALES in 1536 and with SCOTLAND in 1707.

▶ **English language** More people speak English than any other language except Chinese. English is the main language spoken in the United Kingdom, Ireland, Australia, New Zealand, Canada, the United States, and many other countries. Altogether more than 370 million people speak English as their everyday language. Another 100 million or more speak at least some English. Most English words come from old Anglo-Saxon, French, or Latin words.

▶ **English literature** No other nation has equaled Great Britain in the achievements of its written word. The first works in English were long poems, such as *Beowulf*, written over 1,000 years ago in Anglo-Saxon. In the 1300s Geoffrey Chaucer began to write in English. During the reign of Elizabeth I, poets such as Edmund Spenser and the playwrights William Shakespeare and Ben Jonson wrote some of the finest works in the English language. In the following centuries came works such as John Milton's *Paradise Lost* and John Bunyan's *Pilgrim's Progress*, followed by the writings of Alexander Pope and William Congreve. In the 1700s and early 1800s came a spate of great novelists and poets — Daniel Defoe, Coleridge, Byron, Shelley, Keats, Browning, Tennyson, Dickens, the Brontë sisters and many others. Later, the list continued with people such as W.B. Yeats, T.S. Eliot, James Joyce, G.B. Shaw, D.H. Lawrence and W.H. Auden.

engrave *vb.* cut a picture or writing into wood, steel or other hard substance. **engraving** *n.* a print made by this method.

enigma *n.* a mystery, a riddle. **enigmatic** (-**al**) *adj.*

enjoy *vb.* get pleasure from. *I always enjoy going to the ballet.* **enjoyable** *adj.* **enjoyment** *n.*

enlarge *vb.* make or become bigger. **enlargement** *n.*

enlist *vb.* engage, take on (especially as a soldier).

enormous *adj.* very big.

enough *adj.* sufficient. *Have you had enough to eat?*

ensign *n.* a flag or badge.

ensue *vb.* happen afterward.

ensure *vb.* make safe or certain. *Please ensure the door is locked at night.*

enter *vb.* go into a place; record something (in a book); take part in a competition.

enterprise *n.* project or undertaking; an aptitude for taking on a project. *She showed great enterprise.*

entertain *vb.* 1. amuse people with a show. 2. have people as guests in your home. **entertainment** *n.* hospitality; public performance, e.g. in a theater. **entertainer** *n.* professional singer, dancer, etc.

enthusiasm *n.* great interest, zeal. **enthusiast** *n.* someone who is full of enthusiasm; a keen person.

entire *adj.* whole; complete.

entrance *n.* the place through which one enters or goes in.

entreat *vb.* beg, plead.

entry *n.* entrance; something entered in a book, etc.; a competitor in a race, etc.

envelope *n.* a paper covering for a letter; a wrapper.

environment *n.* surroundings; the place or kind of life surrounding an animal.

envoy *n.* a diplomat lower in rank than an ambassador.

envy *n.* & *vb.* a feeling of wanting what someone else has; jealousy. **envious** *adj.* full of envy. **enviable** *adj.* exciting envy; desirable.

epic *n.* 1. a long poem that tells a story, such as Homer's *Odyssey*. 2. an historical film made at great expense with large numbers of actors.

epidemic *n.* a disease which a large number of people have at the same time.

epigram *n.* a short witty remark or poem.

epilepsy *n.* a nervous disease marked by repeated fits and loss of consciousness.

epiphany (*i*-**pif**-*anee*) *n.* Christian feast (January 6) marking the visit of the Magi to Jesus.

episode *n.* one event in a series of events; one part of a film or other serial. **episodic** *adj.*

epistle *n.* a letter (especially in the New Testament).

epoch *n.* an era, period marked by historic events.

equal *adj.* the same in size or number, etc.; a person of same rank. **equality** *n.* being equal.

equalize *vb.* make even or equal.

equate *vb.* regard as equal.

equator *n.* an imaginary line around the middle of the earth that is drawn on maps. **equatorial** *adj.* of, at, or near the equator.

▶ The equator is half way between the NORTH POLE and the SOUTH POLE. A journey around the equator covers 24,902 miles (40,076 km).

The word "equator" comes from an old Latin word meaning "equalizer." The equator divides the world into two equal halves. The half north of the equator is called the Northern Hemisphere. The half south of the equator is the Southern Hemisphere. Distances north and south of the equator are measured in degrees of latitude. The equator itself has a latitude of 0 degrees. (See also LATITUDE AND LONGITUDE).

On the equator, nights are always as long as days. At midday the sun shines from directly or almost directly overhead. So all places on the equator except high mountains are warm all through the year.

Equatorial Guinea

This republic in westcentral Africa consists of two islands, Bioko (formerly Fernando Póo) and Pagalu and an area of mainland called Rio Muni. Most people are farmers and the main crop is coffee. Independence from Spain was achieved in 1968.

AREA: 10,831 SQ. MILES (28,051 SQ. KM)
POPULATION: 378,000
CAPITAL: MALABO
CURRENCY: EKUELE
OFFICIAL LANGUAGE: SPANISH

equine *n.* of or like a horse.

equinox *n.* the time of year in spring and autumn when the day and night are of equal length all over the world. The equinoxes happen about March 21 and September 23.

equipment *n.* things needed to do something. **equip** *vb.* provide with things necessary, e.g. for fighting, playing games, etc.

equivalent *adj.* the same or equal in force, value or meaning. *In 1984, British £1.00 was the equivalent of about U.S. $1.40.*

era *n.* period of time, particularly of history.

eradicate *vb.* uproot, destroy, wipe out, abolish.

erase *vb.* rub out; wipe off.

Erasmus, Desiderius

Erasmus (*c.* 1466–1536) was a Dutch priest and teacher. He traveled widely in Europe, and spent some time in England. He sympathized with some of the aims of the first Protestants, but did not join them. The works of Erasmus include a Greek translation of the New Testament.

erect *vb.* raise up, build. *adj.* upright. **erection** *n.* building.

ermine *n.* the white winter fur of a species of weasel.

erosion *n.* the slow wearing away of the land by wind, water and other means. **erode** *vb.* gradually wear away.

erotic *adj.* arousing sexual desire, passion.

err *vb.* make a mistake; sin.

errand *n.* short journey to carry messages etc.

error *n.* mistake; something that is done wrongly.

erupt *vb.* burst out violently, shoot out suddenly (as lava etc.).

eruption *n.* volcanic outbreak etc.
escalate *vb.* go up, increase by degrees.
escalator *n.* a moving staircase.
► The steps of an escalator are fixed to an endless, moving belt. When steps reach the top or bottom, they form a platform level with the floor. This makes it easy to step on or off. An escalator can carry several thousand people up or down each hour. Some airports also have lengths of level moving walkway.

escape 1. *vb.* get away from or get free. *The lion escaped from its cage in the zoo.* 2. *n.* a leakage. *There was an escape of gas.*
escapement *n.* part of the works of a watch or clock.
escort *vb.* accompany for protection.

Eskimo *n.* (plural **Eskimos**) native people of the Arctic Circle.
► Eskimos have slanting eyes, a wide, flat face, and a short, thick body with short arms and legs. This shape helps to keep them warm in the cold, Arctic climate. Eskimos wear fur clothes. Some live in tents in summer and build snow homes called igloos for the winter. All Eskimos once killed for food. They used bows and arrows and harpoons, and hunted seals, whales, fish, seabirds and deer. Eskimos paddled skin boats. Dogs pulled their sledges overland.

Many Eskimos no longer lead this kind of life. They now live and work in towns.

especially *adj.* chiefly; more than normally. *I like raspberries, especially with cream.*
Esperanto *n.* an artificial international language invented by L.L. Zamenhof in 1887.
espionage *n.* spying.
esquire (es-*kwire*) *n.* polite title added to a man's name when addressing a letter: *J.P. Jones, Esq.*
essay *n.* a short piece of writing. *You may have to write essays in school.*
essence *n.* the main quality of something.
essential *adj.* very important; cannot do without.
establish *vb.* settle or organize; set up. *The expedition established a camp at the foot of the mountains.* **establishment** *n.*
estate *n.* an area of land that someone owns.
estimate *vb.* guess the size, weight or cost of something. *Can you estimate how tall that giraffe is?*

Estonia (Estonian)
Today, Estonia is one of the smaller Russian republics. It is situated on the Gulf of Finland, in the BALTIC Sea. The capital is Tallinn. In the past, Estonia has belonged to several different countries. It became independent in 1919, but was taken over by Russia during World War II.

estuary *n.* the mouth of a large river.
et cetera *n.* (abbrev. **etc.**) and so on; and other things. *Cats, cows, horses, etc., are domestic animals.*
etch *vb.* draw on metal or glass by cutting lines with acid.
eternal *adj.* having no beginning or end; lasting forever. **eternity** *n.* infinite time; the afterlife.
ether (ee-*ther*) *n.* a liquid chemical, formerly used as an anesthetic, whose industrial uses include refrigeration.

Ethiopia (Ethiopian)
Much of Ethiopia consists of high, cool tablelands. Here, dark-skinned Ethiopians grow grain and coffee. Herdsmen wander over the hot deserts of the north and south. The RED SEA coast in the north is one of the hottest places on earth.

Ethiopia is Black Africa's oldest state and the deposed royal line which was ousted in 1974 claimed descent from the son of Solomon and the Queen of Sheba.

AREA: 471,804 SQ. MILES (1,221,900 SQ. KM)
POPULATION: 34,244,000
CAPITAL: ADDIS ABABA
CURRENCY: ETHIOPIAN DOLLAR
OFFICIAL LANGUAGE: AMHARIC

Tunisia
Libya
Egypt
Niger
Chad
Sudan
Ethiopia
Somali Rep.

ethnic *adj.* of race (people).
► Ethnic groups are groups of people who have ties of culture, nationality, language, race, religion, or some combination of these characteristics. Many ethnic groups are minority groups inside larger societies. The word *ethnic* comes from a Greek word *ethnikos*, meaning "belonging to a national group."

Etna, Mount
Mount Etna is an active VOLCANO in Sicily. It is the highest active volcano in Europe. Early eruptions have been described by classical writers. The last major eruption was in 1971.

Etruscans
The Etruscans were a mysterious people who lived in western Italy long ago. They called themselves *Rasenna*. But the Romans called them *Etrusci* and named their land *Etruria*.(Today we call it *Tuscany*.) Most experts think that the Etruscans sailed in from southwest Asia about 3,000 years ago. The Etruscans won lands by war and became masters of the local people. They built ports and towns and ruled ROME as it grew into a city.

Etruscan craftsmen worked with clay and metals. They made splendid jewelry, mirrors, statues, lamps, and painted pots. Artists painted lively scenes on the rock walls of underground burial rooms. Many of these tombs are hidden under the soil. But scientists have peeped inside through special tubes pushed down into the ground.

Etruscans built temples for their gods. Their wise men tried to see into the future by watching birds fly.

The Romans defeated the Etruscans in the 200s B.C. Later, Etruria became a part of the ROMAN EMPIRE.

eucalyptus *n.* an Australian gum tree.
► Eucalyptus trees get their name from Greek words that mean "well covered." This describes the "cap" that covers each flower bud. People also call them gum trees. When the leaves first appear, they are broad and clasp the stems. Older leaves are long, thin, and tough. Gum trees are evergreen. They grow fast and some grow very tall. One measured 375 ft. (114 meters). Probably no other kind of tree can grow that high.

Gum trees provide useful oil and wood and their leaves are the staple food of koalas.

Euclid
Euclid was a Greek mathematician who lived and worked about 300 B.C. Most of his work he recorded in a 13-volume book of geometry and other mathematics. Euclid's great contribution is his method of solving problems by stating the known facts and arguing with logical statements to the end.

Eucharist (yoo-*kar-ist*) *n.* Christian service of Holy Communion.
eulogize *vb.* praise highly.
euphemism (yoo-*fem-izm*) *n.* the use of a mild or indirect word or expression in place of a harder, correct or true one. *He would not say "dead" but always used the euphemism "passed away."*

Euphrates
The Euphrates River flows for 2,235 miles (3,598 km) from Turkey until it joins the Tigris River near the Persian Gulf. It has always been important for irrigation. In ancient times the land between the two rivers was called Mesopotamia. This was the home of the great civilizations of Sumeria, Babylon and Assyria.

ARCTIC OCEAN
Reykjavik
ICELAND
Murmansk
Narvik
KJOLEN MOUNTAINS
Arkhangelsk
NORWEGIAN SEA
FINLAND
Faroe Is
Trondheim
L. Onega
Sundsvall
Tampere
L. Ladoga
Shetland Is
NORWAY
SWEDEN
Vyborg
Bergen
Helsinki
Leningrad
Orkney Is
Oslo
Stavanger
Vänern
Stockholm
Yaroslavl
Aberdeen
Vättern
Glasgow
Gothenburg
Edinburgh
Moscow
Riga
NORTH SEA
BALTIC SEA
Belfast
Dvina
IRELAND
UNITED KINGDOM
DENMARK
Copenhagen
Malmö
Dublin
Manchester
Smolensk
Liverpool
Sheffield
Cork
Kaliningrad
ATLANTIC OCEAN
Birmingham
NETHERLANDS
Minsk
Hamburg
Bremen
Vistula
Cardiff
Amsterdam
Elbe
POLAND
UNION OF SOVIET SOCIALIST REPUBLIC
Thames
London
Hannover
Berlin
Plymouth
Rotterdam
EAST GERMANY
Poznań
Warsaw
Southampton
Antwerp
Brussels
Cologne
Łódz
Kharkov
English Channel
BELGIUM
Bonn
Wroclaw
Kiev
Dnepr
Brest
Le Havre
Frankfurt
Rhine
LUXEMBOURG
Prague
Kraków
Paris
Dnepropetrovsk
WEST GERMANY
CZECHOSLOVAKIA
Seine
Stuttgart
Dnestr
Nantes
Loire
Strasbourg
Munich
Vienna
Linz
Basel
CARPATHIANS
Prut
Zürich
AUSTRIA
Budapest
Odessa
FRANCE
Saône
Bern
SWITZERLAND
LIECH
Geneva
ALPS
HUNGARY
La Coruña
Lyon
Bordeaux
ROMANIA
Po
Milan
Trieste
Zagreb
Santander
Turin
Venice
YUGOSLAVIA
Bilbao
Ebro
Toulouse
Genoa
Belgrade
Bucharest
BLACK SEA
Oporto
Douro
PYRENEES
Rhône
SAN MARINO
Danube
Valladolid
Marseille
MONACO
Nice
Florence
ITALY
PORTUGAL
ANDORRA
Toulon
APENNINES
Sofia
Lisbon
Zaragoza
Tagus
Madrid
Barcelona
Corsica
Dubrovnik
ALBANIA
BULGARIA
Ajaccio
Rome
TURKEY
Istanbul
Guadiana
SPAIN
Tirana
Valencia
Naples
Bari
Thessaloniki
Sardinia
Taranto
Sevilla
Balearic Is
Cagliari
GREECE
Cádiz
Málaga
Cartagena
GIBRALTAR
MEDITERRANEAN SEA
Athens
Palermo
Messina
Sicily
MALTA
Crete
EUROPE
0 100 200 300 400 miles
0 200 400 600 kilometers
Capital Cities

Europe (European)
Europe is a peninsula poking out from the western end of Asia. Other small peninsulas jut from the main one and there are many offshore islands. Australia is the only continent smaller than Europe, but Europe has a greater population than any continent except Asia.

Europeans have settled in the Americas, Australia, New Zealand, South Africa, and Siberia. European ideas and inventions helped shape the way of life of many people in lands all around the world.

Mountains cross the countries of southern Europe. From west to east there are the Pyrenees, Alps, Apennines, Balkans, Carpathians, Caucasus, and other ranges. The Caucasus has Mt. Elbrus, Europe's highest peak.

In northern Europe low mountains cover much of Iceland, Ireland, Scotland, Wales, Norway, and Sweden. Between the mountains of the north and south lies a great plain. Here flow Europe's longest rivers. The Volga in the U.S.S.R. is the longest of them all.

All Europe lies north of the hot tropics and most of it lies south of the cold Arctic. So most of Europe has a temperate climate. But Mediterranean lands have hot summers, and countries in the north and east have long, cold winters.

Shrubs and flowering plants grow in the far north. Next come the great northern forests of CONIFERS. Farther south lie most of Europe's farms and cities. Much of Europe's wealth comes from factories, farms, and mines.

European Economic Community (EEC)
This is a group of Western European nations that was formed to organize industries on an international basis, to abolish economic barriers and create a single economic community. The countries work together to help goods, people, and money travel between countries in the community. Its members are Belgium, Denmark, France, Ireland, Italy, Great Britain, Greece, Luxembourg, the Netherlands and West Germany. People also call the community the European Common Market.

evacuate *vb*. 1. empty. 2. withdraw from a dangerous place. **evacuee** *n*. a person who is removed.

evade *vb*. escape, get away; avoid something or someone on purpose. *She evaded the question.*

evangelist *n*. a writer of one of the Gospels (Matthew, Mark, Luke or John); a preacher. **evangelism** *n*. the preaching of the gospel.

evaporate *vb*. turn from a liquid into a vapor or gas, usually because of heat. **evaporation** *n*.

► Some liquids evaporate in air. Water evaporates quite quickly in warm, dry, moving air. This is why windy days are good for drying damp clothes. Huge amounts of water evaporate from the sea, land, and plants.

even 1. *adv*. a word used to strengthen a statement. *He hasn't even read the book*. 2. *adj*. smooth; equal. 3. *adj*. divisible by two. *Even numbers are the opposite of odd numbers*.

evening *n*. the time between afternoon and night.

event *n*. an important happening. **eventful** *adj*. full of incident.

eventually *adv*. in the end, at last.

ever *adv*. always; at all times. *They lived happily ever after*.

Everest, Mount
Mount Everest is the world's highest peak. It rises 29,028 ft. (8,848 meters) above sea level. The mountain stands in the HIMALAYAS on the borders of Nepal and Tibet. Everest is named after Sir George Everest, a British surveyor. Many climbers tried to reach the top before two finally succeeded, in 1953. They were the New Zealander, Edmund Hillary, and Tenzing Norgay, a Nepalese Sherpa tribesman.

evergreen *n*. & *adj*. a tree whose leaves are green all year.

every *adj*. each one, every individual member of a group thought of as making up the whole group.

everybody, everyone *pron*. each person; all the people.

everything *pron*. all things; each thing.

everywhere *adv*. in every place.

evict *vb*. turn out from, expel. **eviction** *n*.

evidence *n*. proof; particularly in a trial.

evil *n*. & *adj*. very bad, wicked.

evolution *n*. the process by which animals and plants develop and change over millions of years.

► Evolution means gradual change. Scientists use the word "evolution" to describe the gradual changes that give rise to all living plants and animals, including human beings. Charles DARWIN developed this idea more than a hundred years ago.

Some of the first living things were very tiny organisms made up of a single CELL. By chance some cells grew in a slightly different way from the rest. Most of the new cells were misfits and soon died. But others survived. Through HEREDITY these passed on their shapes to their descendants. The new kinds of cell may have found food more easily than the first kind, and they probably took it all. This meant that the first kind just starved to death and disappeared.

From one new kind of cell could come another. This happened time and time again over 3 billion years and more. Eventually, tiny one-celled organisms gave rise to larger plants and animals made up of many cells. From simple plants related to the seaweed came more complicated kinds like mosses, ferns, and flowering plants. From simple animals without a backbone came fishes, amphibians, reptiles, birds, and mammals.

The less successful kinds died out. But PREHISTORIC ANIMALS and plants left FOSSILS. These show that evolution happened.

ewe (rhymes with *new*) *n*. a female sheep.

ex- *prefix* meaning out, from, beyond; formerly (**ef-** before F; **e** before many consonants).

exact *adj*. just right, perfectly correct.

exaggerate *vb*. make something sound bigger or smaller, or more or less important than it really is. **exaggeration** *n*.

exalt *vb*. praise. **exalted** *adj*. highly placed. *She has an exalted position in the government*.

exam, examination *n*. 1. an important test to find out how much you know. 2. a close look at something.

examine *vb*. look at something very carefully; inquire into; interrogate. **examiner** *n*.

example *n*. 1. something which shows what something else is like or how it works. *This cake is a good example of my cooking*. 2. a model; a warning to others.

exasperate *vb*. irritate, annoy, rouse to anger. **exasperation** *n*.

excavate *vb*. uncover by digging, unearth. **excavation** *n*.

exceed *vb*. go beyond. *It is dangerous to exceed the stated dose of this medicine*.

excellent *adj*. very good.

except *prep*. not included, omitting. *Everyone is here except John*. **exceptional** *adj*. out of the ordinary, outstanding.

exchange *vb*. change one thing for another; swap.

excite *vb*. make someone look forward to something; thrill. **excitement** *n*.

exclude *vb*. shut out, keep out from. *He was excluded from the meeting*.

excursion *n*. short journey, pleasure trip.

excuse 1. *n*. an apology; a reason for not doing something, or for doing wrong. 2. *vb*. let someone off. *She was excused from choir practice, as she has a cold*.

execute *vb*. put someone to death legally as a punishment.

exercise *vb*. & *n*. 1. work that helps to make the body strong and healthy. 2. drill.

E

EXPLORATION AND DISCOVERY

Place	Achievement	Explorer or discoverer	Date
World	circumnaviated	Ferdinand Magellan (Portugal for Spain)	1519–21
Pacific Ocean	discovered	Vasco Núñez de Balboa (Sp.)	1515
Africa			
River Congo (mouth)	discovered	Diogo Cão (Port.)	c. 1483
Cape of Good Hope	sailed round	Bartolomeu Dias (Port.)	1488
River Niger	explored	Mungo Park (Scotland)	1795
River Zambezi	discovered	David Livingstone (Scot.)	1851
Sudan	explored	Heinrich Barth (Germany for Great Britain)	1852–5
Victoria Falls	discovered	Livingstone	1855
Lake Tanganyika	discovered	Richard Burton & John Speke (GB)	1858
River Congo	traced	Sir Henry Stanley (GB)	1877
Asia			
China	visited	Marco Polo (Italy)	c. 1272
India (Cape route)	visited	St. Francis Xavier (Sp.)	1549
China	explored	Ferdinand Richthofen (Germ.)	1868
North America North America	discovered	Leif Ericson (Norse)	c. 1000
West Indies	discovered	Christopher Columbus (Ital. for Sp.)	1492
Newfoundland	discovered	John Cabot (Ital. for Eng.)	1497
Mexico	conquered	Hernando Cortès (Sp.)	1519–21
St. Lawrence River	explored	Jacques Cartier (France)	1534–6
Mississippi River	discovered	Hernando de Soto (Sp.)	1541
Canadian interior	explored	Samuel de Champlain (Fr.)	1603–9
Hudson Bay	discovered	Henry Hudson (Eng.)	1610
Alaska	discovered	Vitus Bering (Denmark for Russia)	1728
Mackenzie River	discovered	Sir Alexander Mackenzie (Scot.)	1789
South America South America	visited	Columbus	1498
Venezuela	explored	Alonso de Ojeda (Sp.)	1499
Brazil	discovered	Pedro Alvares Cabral (Port.)	1500
Rio de la Plata	discovered	Juan de Solis (Sp.)	1516
Tierra del Fuego	discovered	Magellan	1520
Peru	explored	Francisco Pizarro (Sp.)	1530–8
River Amazon	explored	Francisco de Orellana (Sp.)	1541
Cape Horn	discovered	Willem Schouten (Dutch)	1616
Australasia, Polar regions, etc.			
Greenland	visited	Eric the Red (Norse)	c. 982
Australia	discovered	unknown	1500s
Spitsbergen	discovered	Willem Barents (Dut.)	1596
Australia	visited	Abel Tasman (Dut.)	1642
New Zealand	sighted	Tasman	1642
New Zealand	visited	James Cook (GB)	1769
Antarctica	sighted	Nathaniel Palmer (USA)	1820
Antarctica	circumnavigated	Fabian von Bellingshausen (Russ.)	1819–21
Australian interior	explored	Charles Sturt (GB)	1828
Antarctica	explored	Charles Wilkes (USA)	1838–42
Australia	crossed (S–N)	Robert Burke (Ir.) & William Wills (Eng.)	1860–1
Greenland	explored	Fridtjof Nansen (Norway)	1888
Arctic	explored	Abruzzi, Duke of the (Ital.)	1900
North Pole	reached	Robert Peary (USA)	1909
South Pole	reached	Roald Amundsen (Nor.)	1911
Antarctica	crossed	Sir Vivian Fuchs (GB)	1957–8

exert *vb*. bring into action; apply. **exertion** *n*. effort.

exhale *vb*. breathe out.

exhaust (*ex*-**awst**) 1. *vb*. use up completely; make very tired. 2. *n*. the part of an engine that lets out burned gases; the burned gases.

exhaustive *adj*. thorough, complete. *The police made exhaustive inquiries*.

exhibit *vb*. show something in public. *n*. the thing that is shown.

exhibition (*eks-i*-**bish**-*un*) *n*. a place or event where things are shown to the public, such as an art exhibition.

exile *n*. & *vb*. a person who has been forbidden by law to live in his or her own country. *He spent 10 years in exile*.

exist *vb*. be or live. **existence** *n*.

exit *vb*. go out; leave. *n*. the place through which you go out; a direction in a play which tells an actor to leave the stage.

exodus *n*. the departure of a large group of people. *The Book of Exodus in the Bible deals with the departure of the Israelites from Egypt*.

exotic *adj*. brought in from abroad; unusual.

expand *vb*. get larger.

expanse *n*. a broad area. *An expanse of sky*.

expect *vb*. think that something will happen; look forward to. *I expect they will be here soon*.

expedition *n*. a journey for a specific purpose, such as climbing a mountain; a group making such a journey.

expel *vb*. drive out, compel to leave.

expensive *adj*. costing a lot of money.

experience 1. *n*. something that happens to you, and from which you may learn. *Going to camp is a great experience*. 2. *vb*. feel; meet with. *They will experience great heat in the center of Africa*. **experienced** *adj*.

experiment *n*. a test; a trial. *vb*. carry out a test.

expert *n*. someone who has special knowledge about something.

expire *vb*. breathe out air; breathe one's last breath, die.

expiration *n*. coming to an end; close.

explain *vb*. show or make the meaning clear. **explanation** *n*. statement or fact that explains something, makes it clear. *So that is the explanation of the conjuring trick*.

explode *vb*. burst with a loud bang and, usually, great damage.

exploit 1. *n*. an adventure. 2. *vb*. develop or use profitably. *You must exploit your talent*.

explore *vb*. look carefully around a place where you have not been before; examine, discuss a possibility, etc. **exploration** *n*.

explorer *n*. a person who travels to

find out about places where people have not been before.

► There have always been explorers. The Stone Age men and women who wandered across continents were in a way explorers. Phoenician seamen sailed the Mediterranean about 2,600 years ago. In the Middle Ages MARCO POLO reached China from Europe. But the great age of exploration began in the 1400s. Sailors like Vasco da GAMA, Christopher COLUMBUS, Ferdinand MAGELLAN, and James COOK discovered the shape, size, and position of continents and oceans. Later, men like David LIVINGSTONE and Roald AMUNDSEN explored wild, untamed continents. SPACE EXPLORATION now takes people beyond the earth.

explosion (*ex*-**plo**-*shun*) *n.* a loud noise when something explodes.
► Explosions happen when people heat or strike certain solid or liquid substances. These suddenly turn into hot GASES. They fill more space than the solids or liquids, so they rush violently outward. High explosives like DYNAMITE explode faster and do more damage than low explosives like GUNPOWDER. Engineers use explosives to break up rocks and old buildings. Armies use explosives to destroy vehicles and cities.

explosive *n.* anything, such as dynamite, used to make things explode or blow up.
exponent *n.* someone who explains or interprets.
export (**eks**-*port*) *vb.* sell goods to another country.
exports (**eks**-*ports*) *pl. n.* the goods that are exported.
expose *vb.* uncover; leave unprotected. *The troops were exposed to gunfire.* make public a villainy.
exposure *n.* 1. the act of exposing, leaving unprotected. 2. period of time light is allowed to fall on a sensitive emulsion in photography.
express 1. *vb.* explain something in words. *He has difficulty in expressing his meaning.* 2. *adj.* fast. *An express train.*
expression *n.* 1. an often-used word or words. 2. the look on a person's face.
extant *adj.* still living, existing.
extend *vb.* stretch out, lengthen; prolong.
exterior *n.* the outside part or surface.
exterminate *vb.* destroy completely.
external *adj.* outside, outer.
extinct *adj.* a thing which was living is extinct when none of its kind is alive any more. *Dinosaurs have been extinct for millions of years.*

► Some animals died out through the process of EVOLUTION. The most dramatic example of this process was when the great dinosaurs died out about 65 million years ago. No one knows why this happened. Usually, animals that become extinct are replaced by other creatures that are better adapted for survival.
Human beings have caused the extinction of many animals. They have done this sometimes by hunting the animal, and sometimes by destroying its environment. Animals that have been hunted to extinction range from the quagga of southern Africa to the passenger pigeon of North America. Many other animals, such as several species of whales, are today threatened with extinction.

extinguish *vb.* put out, cause to stop. *The firemen extinguished the blaze.*
extra *adj.* more than usual. *You will need extra clothes because it's so cold.*
extraordinary *adj.* very unusual.
extravagant *adj.* exceeding limits of necessity; spending too much.
extreme *adj.* very great or very far.
extremist *n.* a person who holds strong, uncompromising (political) views.
eye *n.* the organ, or part of the body, we use for seeing.

► A human eye is much larger than the part you can see. The eye is a ball bigger than a marble. It works much like a camera. Both bend LIGHT rays to form a picture of the object that the rays come from.
Light rays enter the eye through a layer of transparent skin called the *conjunctiva*. The rays pass through a hard, transparent layer called the *cornea*. This bends the rays. The LENS brings them into focus on the *retina* at the back of the eye. But you do not see the picture formed here until light-sensitive nerve endings on the retina send the brain a message along the *optic nerve*.
To be able to see properly, all the parts of the eye have to work correctly. For instance, the *iris* (the colored part of the eye) can open and close to let more or less light through the *pupil*. This is the dark opening in front of the lens.
People and some other animals have *binocular* (two-eyed) vision. Because the eyes are about two inches apart, they each see an object from a slightly different angle. And each eye swivels as it focuses on an object. These two factors enable us to see objects in depth and to judge their distance. Animals with their eyes at the sides of their heads, such as cattle, cannot see the same object with both eyes, and do not see things in depth.

eyebrow *n.* the curve of hair above the eye.
eyelashes *pl.n.* the fringes of hair on the eyelids.
eyelid *n.* the flap of skin that covers the eye when it is closed.
eye-opener *n.* something which suddenly surprises you or makes you suddenly understand.
eyesight *n.* the ability to see.
eyewitness *n.* someone who sees an event happening.

Eyre, Lake
Lake Eyre lies in South Australia. It is Australia's largest salt water lake. It is also the continent's lowest point, being about 40 ft. (about 12 meters) below sea level. Lake Eyre was discovered by the explorer Edward Eyre in 1840.

Animals that have become extinct: the mamoth (right) and saber-toothed tiger in prehistoric times and the dodo in the late 17th century.

F

Fishes photograhed in their natural habitat – under water.

fable *n.* a story that tries to teach us something. The characters are usually animals that talk.

► Some of the most famous fables are those of AESOP, an ancient Greek storyteller. His fables of the fox and the crow, and of the grasshopper and the ant, are told to this day.

fabric *n.* cloth.
fabulous *adj.* in a fable; marvelous, incredible.
façade (*fass*-**sahd**) *n.* the front of a building; appearance given to other people.
face *n.* the front part of the head. *vb.* meet confidently and without fear.
facet *n.* one side of a cut gem.
facility *n.* ease; no difficulty in doing, learning, etc.
facsimile (*fak*-**sim**-*ilee*) *n.* exact copy.
fact *n.* something that really happened, so people know that it is true. *It is a fact that William the Conqueror invaded England in 1066.*
factory *n.* a building where people and machines work together to make things.
factual *adj.* concerned with or containing fact.
fad *n.* a craze, passing enthusiasm.
fade *vb.* 1. lose color. *Our curtains have faded in the sun.* 2. wither. *The flowers faded.* 3. disappear slowly. *The ship faded from sight in the mist.*
Fahrenheit (**fa**-*ren-hite*) *n.* a thermometer scale in which the freezing point of water is 32° and the boiling point is 212°. It was invented by a German, Gabriel Daniel Fahrenheit (1686–1736).
fail *vb.* be unsuccessful.
failing *n.* weakness, defect, shortcoming.
failure *n.* lack of success; omission. *Failure in duty.*
faint 1. *adj.* weak; not clear. *We could hear a faint sound when we listened carefully.* 2. *vb.* become dizzy, with everything going black, so you may fall down; become unconscious.
fair 1. *adj.* acting in a just way, that is seen to be right. *Everyone should have a fair share of the cake.* 2. *adj.* light colored. *Mary has fair hair and blue eyes.* 3. *adj.* (of weather) good. 4. *n.* a group of outdoor amusements, with sideshows and merry-go-rounds.
fairly *adv.* moderately. *I know him fairly well.*
fairy *n.* an imaginary small creature with magic powers.
faith *n.* 1. a strong belief; trust. *I have complete faith in her.* 2. religion.
faithful *adj.* honest; trustworthy.
fake *n.* & *adj.* something that looks real but is not.
falcon *n.* a bird of prey related to the eagle.

► Falcons are found all over the world. They can be recognized by the dark markings around their eyes and by their pointed wings. Falcons use their large, hooked beaks for tearing flesh. But they kill their prey with their sharp claws. Falcons swoop down on their victims from above, hitting them with their claws. This act is called "stooping." It is used to kill smaller birds in mid-flight and also to take rodents and other small animals on the ground.

The biggest falcon is the gyr falcon of the Arctic. It may reach over 2 ft. (60 cm) in size. The smallest is the pygmy falcon of southern Asia. It is less than 6 in. (15 cm) long and feeds mainly on insects.

The peregrine falcon is one of the fastest flyers in the world. In a fast dive, it can reach 175 mph (280 km/h).

Falkland Islands
The Falklands are a group of islands in the South Atlantic Ocean. The two largest islands are East Falkland and West Falkland. The capital is Port Stanley. Traditionally, the main occupation has been sheep farming.

The Falklands were discovered by a British ship in 1592. They then became a French colony, the "Iles Malouines." Later, the French sold the islands to Spain. In 1833 the British took over the islands by force. Since then, the islands have remained almost continuously in British hands.

Argentina has always claimed the Falklands for herself. In 1982, Argentinian troops unexpectedly invaded the islands. The British sent a naval task force, and the Argentinians were forced to surrender and leave.

fall 1. *vb.* drop to the ground. *n.* drop. 2. *n.* autumn.
fall behind *vb.* fail to keep up with. *He has no money, so he will fall behind with his rent.*
fall out 1. *vb.* quarrel. 2. *n.* **fallout** radioactive dust settling after nuclear explosion.
fall through *vb.* fail to take place.
false *adj.* not true; not real.
falsetto *n* & *adj.* male voice which is made artificially high.
falter *vb.* hesitate, stumble; lose courage.
fame *n.* outstanding reputation. *Her fame is worldwide.*
familiar *adj.* well-known.
family *n.* a group of people who are all related to each other.
famine *n.* a time when there is very little food in an area and people go hungry.
famous *adj.* widely known. *He is a famous musician.*
fan *n.* 1. a device that circulates air to another area. 2. a person who greatly admires someone famous; a supporter.
fancy *vb.* imagine, picture to oneself; take a liking to, *have a fancy for*; be under a delusion. *He fancies he can fly.*
fanfare *n.* a flourish played on a trumpet, usually to introduce an important person.
fang *n.* a long, sharp tooth, especially the poisonous tooth of snakes such as vipers and cobras.
fantasy *n.* something, usually pleasant, that you imagine or dream about, but is not real.
far *adj.* a long way off.

Faraday, Michael
Michael Faraday (1791–1867) was an English scientist who is best known for his experiments with ELECTRICITY. He showed that it could be made to flow in a wire when the wire was passed between a set of magnets (electro-magnetic induction). Today this is how most electricity is produced in big generators.

farce *n.* an amusing kind of play, full of misunderstandings; an absurd situation.
fare *n.* 1. the price of traveling on a bus, train, etc. 2. food and drink (now old-fashioned).
farewell *inter., n.* & *adj.* good-bye. *A farewell speech.*
farm *n.* land and buildings where crops are grown and animals reared. *vb.* use land to grow crops or rear animals. **farmer** *n.*
► Farming is the human race's most important activity. More people work at it than any other job. And, in all, about a third of the land on our planet is farmed.

Farmers grow hundreds of different kinds of crops. But a few, such as WHEAT, RICE and BARLEY, and BEANS and peas, are by far the most important.

The kinds of crops that are grown in one region depends on several things. The climate, altitude (the height of the land above sea level), and the fertility of the soil are the most important. For example, RICE, ORANGES, and COCONUTS all need a warm, tropical climate in which to grow. COFFEE needs warmth, but does best at a high altitude. Rye, on the other hand, can stand cool climates right up to the Arctic Circle.

Farmers do not only grow our food. They also grow crops such as hay and clover to feed animals. Some plant TOBACCO, COTTON or SUGAR cane. Others raise animals for meat.

Modern farmers use machines to plow, plant and harvest. FERTILIZERS and pesticides (pest-killing sprays) improve harvests.

About five out of every 100 persons in the United States live on farms. Each American farmer produces enough foood for about 50 people.

Faroes
The Faroes are a group of islands in the North Atlantic. The Faroes belong to Denmark, but are largely self-governing and have their own parliament. The capital, Thorshavn, is situated on the island of Stromso. The main industries are fishing and local crafts.

farrago (*fa*-**rah**-*go*) *n.* a mixture.
farrow *n.* litter of pigs. *vb.* give birth to pigs.
farther *adj.* (**further**) more distant.
farthest *adj.* (**furthest**) the most distant.
farthing *n.* former British coin worth a quarter of the former penny.
fascinate *vb.* attract, charm. **fascination** *n.*
Fascism *n.* a political belief and form of government in which a country has only one political party, and is ruled by a dictator.
► Fascism was founded in Italy in the 1920s by Benito MUSSOLINI. Mussolini seized power in 1922 as dictator of Italy and head of the Italian Fascist Party. Fascism takes its name from the Roman *fasces*, the bundle of rods and the axe that were the symbol of authority in ancient Rome.

Fascist political ideas include the belief that the government of a country should be all powerful. Its citizens must work hard and obey the government for the good of the nation. Fascists believe in strict discipline and training for all people.

Anybody opposed to the government is made an outlaw. In Fascist Italy, many people were jailed, exiled or put to death because they did not agree with the Fascists. All the other political parties were made illegal.

fashion *n.* a way of dressing or doing things that most people like to copy at a certain time. *Huge sweaters were in fashion last year.*
► Fashionable CLOTHES are those which are the most popular at the moment. But fashion styles change all the time. Some styles are created by fashion designers, and sold the world over. Many of these are often imitations of styles that were fashionable 20, 30, or even 100 years ago.

Fashion also describes popular styles in other things we make or use, from cars and furniture to movies and the kinds of foods we eat. It can also be used to describe beliefs and manners that are popular at a particular time. For example, the stiff and formal politeness people used 100 years ago would seem strange today.

fast 1. *adj.* very quick. 2. *adv.* firmly fixed. *My boot was stuck fast in the mud.* 3. *vb.* eat no food for a time.
fasten *vb.* tie; fix firmly. **fastener** *n.* **fastening** *n.*
fat 1. *adj.* plump, fleshy and round. 2. *n.* the soft, oily part of the body of a person or an animal.
► Fat is an important food for both animals and plants. The tissues of these living things contain fat. Fat in the pure state can take the form of a liquid, such as vegetable oil, or a solid, such as butter or lard.

Fat is a store of ENERGY. A unit of fat contains twice as much energy as the same amount of PROTEIN or STARCH. Fats play an important part in our diet. We get most vegetable fats from the seeds and fruits of plants, where it is stored. In animals and human beings fat is stored in tiny "droplets" in a layer under the

F

skin and in the CELLS of the body. Pigs and cattle are our main sources of animal fats. Fats are also important in making soaps, perfumes and polishes.

fatal *adj*. causing death or disaster. *A fatal accident.*
fate *n*. power which some believe determines events; destiny.
father *n*. a person's male parent.
fathom 1. *n*. a nautical term used to measure the depth of water. A fathom equals six feet. 2. *vb*. measure the depth of water with a sounding line; get to the bottom of, understand.
fatigue *n*. weariness; weakness in a metal. *vb*. tire.
fatty *adj*. containing fat.
fault (rhymes with *salt*) *n*. an imperfection; a mistake.
fauna (**fawn**-*a*) *n*. animal life of a district.
favor 1. *n*. an act of kindness or help. *Can you do me a favor by picking up my dress?* 2. *vb*. like one person or thing more than another.
favorite *adj*. & *n*. the best-liked person or thing.

Fawkes, Guy
Guy Fawkes (1570–1606) and his group of Roman Catholic plotters sought to kill King JAMES I of England by blowing up the House of Lords with gunpowder. They were protesting against laws which tried to control the rights of Roman Catholics. The plot failed. Fawkes was arrested on November 5 1606, in the cellars of the House of Lords and, with the other conspirators, was executed.

fawn 1. *n*. a young deer. *adj*. fawn-colored, yellowish brown. 2. *vb*. grovel, cringe (like a dog).
fear *vb*. feel frightened. *n*. the feeling of being frightened.
fearless *adj*. brave; without fear.
feast *n*. 1. a very grand meal. 2. a religious festival.
feat (*feet*) *n*. act or deed, especially showing strength or courage.
feather *n*. one of the many light coverings that grow on a bird's body.

Two main kinds of feathers: strong contour feathers covering the outer part of the bird; and soft down feathers.

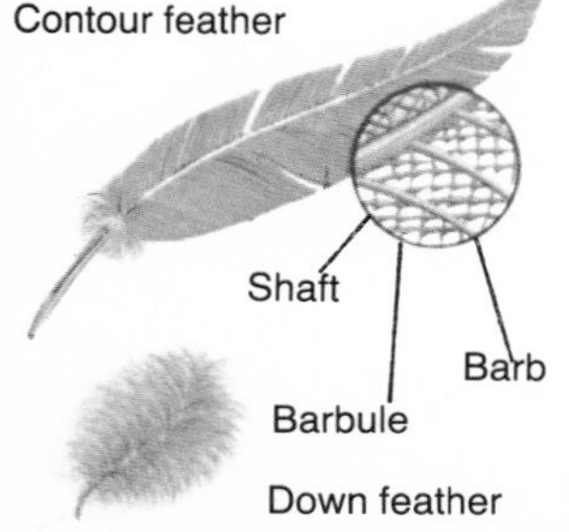

► Feathers protect birds and keep them warm. They give their bodies a smooth, streamlined shape. Feathers also form the broad surface area of the wing that allows birds to fly.

Feathers are replaced once or twice a year. This process is called molting. Old feathers that are worn and broken fall out. New ones grow in their place.

feature *n*. 1. one of the parts of the face. *Your nose is one of your features.* 2. an important part of something.
February *n*. The second month of the year.
fed 1. *vb*. past tense and past part. of **feed**. 2. *adj*. **fed up** (*casual*) bored. *She was fed up with her job.*
fee *n*. a payment made to someone for a professional service.
feeble *adj*. weak; indistinct.
feed *vb*. give food to a person or animal.
feel *vb*. be aware of something by touch; be conscious of; experience.
feeler *n*. the antenna of an insect, with which it touches or feels things.
feeling *n*. a sensation; an emotion; something that you know inside yourself, like knowing that you dislike someone. *A feeling of pain.*
feet *pl. n*. more than one foot.
feline *adj*. of cats or the cat family.
fell *vb*. past of **fall**. *Jack fell down and broke his crown.*
fellow *n*. a male person; a member of a learned society. *adj*. of the same class or kind. *A fellow countryman.*
felony *n*. serious crime such as murder.
felt 1. *vb*. past of **feel** 2. *n*. a kind of cloth made from bits of wool pressed together rather than woven.
female *n*. a woman; a girl; any animal that is not a male.
feminine *adj*. belonging to or characteristic of women. **feminist** *n*. supporter of women's rights.
fen *n*. low-lying marshland or bog.
fence 1. *n*. a wooden or metal barrier. 2. *vb*. fight with special swords.
► Fencing can be described as the sport of "friendly dueling." Fencers wear a special glove, pads and face masks. They fight with blunted swords. The winner is the one who scores the most points by touching his opponent with his sword. There are three types of sword: the foil, the epée, and the saber.

Today, fencing is a popular sport and an OLYMPIC GAMES event. But in the past it was a form of sword practice for real duels.

fender *n*. 1. protective frame around an open fireplace; fireguard. 2. a car's bumper.
fennec *n*. North American fox.
fennel *n*. a yellow-flowered herb.
ferment *vb*. 1. undergo fermentation. 2. be in a state of agitation.
► Milk goes sour, bread dough rises, grape juice turns into wine. All these are examples of fermentation. Fermentation is caused by the work of very tiny living BACTERIA, YEASTS and MOLDS. These tiny things break up substances into simpler forms. People have been using fermentation since the earliest times to make bread, beer, wine and cheese. But it was not until the 1800s that the French scientist Louis PASTEUR found out how fermentation works.

Fermi, Enrico
Enrico Fermi (1901–54) was an Italian scientist. His studies of the ATOM were rewarded by the NOBEL PRIZE in 1938.

In 1942, during World War II, Fermi built the first atomic reactor. He constructed it in an empty squash court under a football stadium in Chicago. Here he set off the first man-made nuclear chain reaction. Later, Fermi helped to develop the atom bomb.

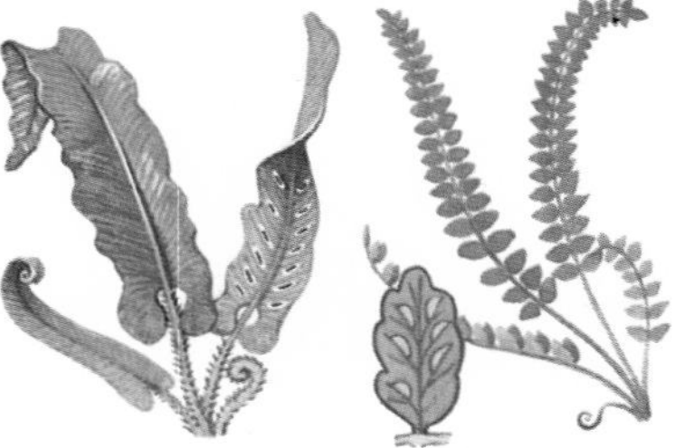

Sometimes the fronds of ferns have simple shapes, like the hart's tongue fern. But more often the fronds are divided into leaflets known as pinnae.

fern *n*. a plant with feathery leaves which does not produce flowers.
► The primitive ferns were some of the earliest land plants. Today their delicate, feathery leaves look much the same as they did millions of years ago.

About 10,000 different kinds of ferns live on the earth today. They are found all over the world, usually in damp, shady places. In the tropics, giant tree-ferns grow to over 50 ft (15 meters) high.

Ferns do not have flowers or seeds. Instead, they form spores from which new ferns develop.

ferocious *adj*. fierce, cruel, savage.
ferret *n*. a small animal that can be trained to hunt rabbits and rats. *vb*. hunt with ferrets; rummage.
ferry *n*. a boat that carries people for short distances. *We crossed the river by the ferry.*
fertile *adj*. able to produce a lot of good crops. *The Nile valley is very fertile.*

fertilize *vb.* make fruitful or productive.
► Fertilizers are substances dug into the soil to nourish it. In this way fertilizers give plants the chemical "foods" they need to grow. The most important fertilizers are calcium, phosphorus, potassium and sulfur.
Fertilizers are usually added to soils that do not contain enough nutrients. This can happen if the same crops have been planted in the soil year after year, or if the rain has washed all the nutrients out.
Organic fertilizers include animal manure and bone meal.

fervent *adj.* ardent, intense. **fervor** *n.* zeal.
fester *vb.* become sore and filled with pus.
festival *n.* a time for celebration – dancing, music, and feasting.
fetch *vb.* collect something or bring it back.
fête (rhymes with *late*) *n.* a kind of open-air party where there are games and things to buy. *A fête is usually organized to collect money for charity.*
fetus (**feet**-*us*) *n.* the developing offspring (baby) in its mother's womb.

Feudal System
In the MIDDLE AGES, all power came from the king. The king gave land to the nobles in exchange for their support in wartime. The nobles in turn granted land to the peasants, in return for a similar agreement. The feudal system was very rigid, but everyone had a place in it.

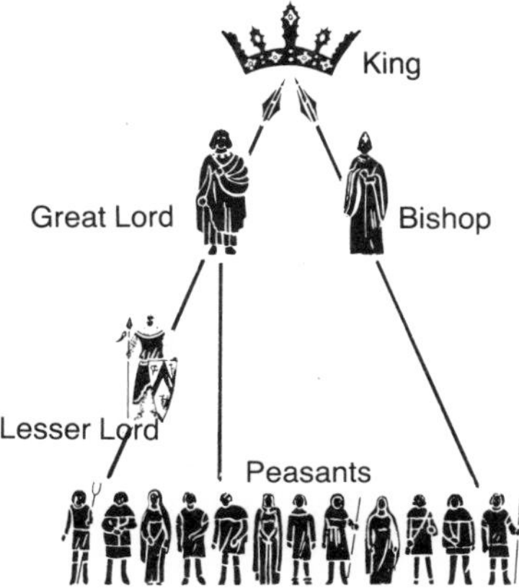

The basis of the feudal system was the granting of land by a powerful person to a less powerful person in return for service. The system began at the top with the king.

fever *n.* body temperature that is above normal. **feverish** *adj.*
► The normal temperature of the human body is 98.4°F (37°C). If a disorder makes it rise above this, the person is said to have a fever. Fever is not an illness itself; it is caused by injuries and infections

few *adj.* not many, a small number. *He has few friends.*
fez *n.* brimless red felt hat worn by Muslims.
fiancé (*fi*-**on**-*say*) *n.* person to whom a woman is engaged to be married. (feminine: **fiancée**).
fiasco (*fee*-**ass**-*koh*) *n.* complete breakdown; mess.
fib *n.* small lie.
fiber (**fie**-*ber*) *n.* 1. a very fine thread. 2. material made from fibers.
fibula *n.* outer and smaller bone of the lower part of the leg.
fickle *adj.* changeable (especially in affections).
fiction *n.* a story that has been made up, that is not about real people or events.
fiddle 1. *n.* violin. *vb.* play a violin. 2. *n.* & *vb.* putter; meddle.
fidget *vb.* move about restlessly.
field *n.* a piece of ground, often used for growing crops or keeping animals, and usually surrounded by a hedge or fence.
fierce *adj.* cruel and angry.
fiery *adj.* like fire, flaming; quick-tempered.
fiesta *n.* Spanish word for "feast-day." All Latin American countries hold fiestas, celebrating either religious or political events.
fig *n.* the soft, sweet fruit of a small-sized tree of the same name, which has large leaves.
fight *n.* a violent contest, either in battle or in some kinds of sports, e.g. boxing. *vb.* take part in a fight.
fighter *n.* boxer; soldier. aircraft designed for combat.
figure *n.* 1. a sign for a number, such as 5 or 9. 2. a diagram in a book. 3. the shape of the body. *The athletes have good figures.*
figurehead *n.* statue on a ship's bow.

Fiji (Figian)
Fiji is a country made up of a group of islands in the southcentral Pacific. Most of the people live on two big islands, Viti Levu and Vanua Levu. About half the population is of Indian descent. The other half are Pacific Islanders. A former British colony, Fiji became independent in 1970.
AREA: 7,056 SQ. MILES (18,274 SQ. KM)
POPULATION: 656,000
CURRENCY: FIJI DOLLAR
CAPITAL: SUVA

filament *n.* fine wire used in an electric light bulb.
file 1. *vb.* put papers in order. 2. *n.* holder for keeping papers in order. 3. *n.* a metal tool with roughened sides for smoothing surfaces.
fill *vb.* make something full. *Please fill the kettle.* occupy all the space.
filly *n.* a young female horse.
film 1. *n.* a thin covering. 2. *n.* a coated roll of plastic that can be placed in a camera and used to take photographs. 3. *n.* moving pictures. 4. *vb.* take moving pictures.
filter *vb.* strain a liquid through a fine mesh to remove impurities. *n.* a device for straining liquid.
filthy *adj.* offensively dirty.
fin *n.* part of a fish. *The fin helps the fish to swim and balance.*
final *adj.* the last.
finale (*fin*-**ah**-*lay*) *n.* final movement of instrumental musical composition or a public performance.
finally *adv.* at last.
finance *n.* the management of money matters. *vb.* provide money for. *He financed the play.*
finch *n.* a small bird belonging to a very large family of birds found almost everywhere except Australia.
► Finches rarely grow larger than 8 in. (20 cm) in length. Their short, thick bills are used for cracking and eating seeds. Finches' bills are amazingly strong. A hawfinch can crack olive and cherry stones with ease.

find *vb.* discover or locate something.
find out *vb.* come to know something, discover. *Can you find out where he has gone?*
fine 1. *adj.* very thin or delicate. 2. *adj.* (of weather) good and clear. 3. *n.* money paid as a punishment.
finger *n.* one of the end parts, or digits, of the hand, including the thumb. *vb.* touch with the fingers.
fingerprint *n.* the mark left on something by the tip of your finger.
► Everybody has patterns of lines and swirls on their fingers. But each person's fingerprints are different from everybody else's. Because of this, police use fingerprints to help identify criminals. They keep files of millions of different prints. By comparing those on file with those found at the scene of a crime, they can often trace the guilty person.

The six most common kinds of fingerprint patterns are shown in these illustrations. But no two people have the same fingerprints – not even identical twins.

F

F

finish *vb.* & *n.* end something; complete a task.

Finland (Finnish: Finn)
Finland is a country in northern EUROPE tucked between Scandinavia and Russia. Northern Finland stretches north of the Arctic Circle.

The thousands of lakes and rivers that dot the Finnish landscape form a great inland waterway. About three-fourths of the land is covered by thick forests of spruce, pine and larch trees. The main industries of Finland are logging and the making of wood products such as paper.
AREA: 130,127 SQ. MILES (337,009 SQ. KM)
POPULATION: 4,829,000
CAPITAL: HELSINKI
CURRENCY: MARKKA
OFFICIAL LANGUAGES: FINNISH, SWEDISH

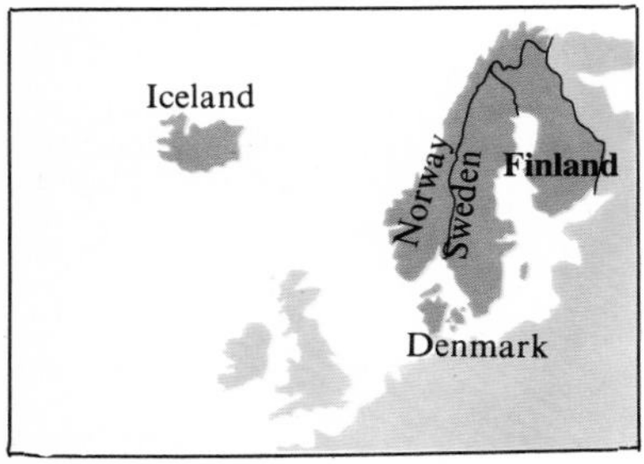

fiord *n.* a long, narrow valley with steep sides along the coast, especially of Norway and Greenland.
► Fiords were formed when the great GLACIERS of the ICE AGES gouged out valleys as they flowed to the sea. When the ice melted, the sea flooded the valleys. Fiords are very deep and make perfect shelters for large oceangoing ships.

fir *n.* an evergreen tree with flat needle-like leaves and erect cones.
► Firs are mostly found in cool climates. Forests of fir trees grow all over northern Asia, Europe and America.

The leaves of fir trees are short, thin and needlelike. They grow separately along the twigs, unlike PINE needles, which grow in clusters. The fruit of the fir tree is a scaly cone. The tall Douglas "Fir" is not really a fir – it belongs to a different group of evergreens.

fire 1. *n.* the bright light and heat that comes when something is burned. 2. *vb.* shoot a gun.
► The ability to make and use fire is one of the great advantages people have over the animals. Primitive people found fire frightening, just as animals do. But once they learned to make and control fires, they became a necessary part of life. Fires kept out the cold, lit up the dark, cooked food, and kept away wild animals. But even today fires that get out of control cause terrible damage and suffering.

fire engine *n.* a vehicle used to carry hoses, ladders and equipment to put out fires.
fire escape *n.* a way out of a burning building.
fireman *n.* a person whose job it is to put out fires. *A fireman goes to a fire in a fire engine.*
fireplace *n.* an area in a room to hold an open fire.
fire station *n.* a fireman's head-quarters, where fire engines are kept.
firewood *n.* small pieces of wood to fuel a fire.
fireworks *pl. n.* devices that burn with noise or striking colors, such as a rocket or a sparkler.
► Fireworks are devices that produce spectacular displays of lights, colors, smoke and noise in the night sky. They were invented in China centuries ago, but only became known in Europe in the 1300s.

Fireworks are often launched in rockets. They are shot into the air and made to explode by a black powder called GUNPOWDER. The brilliant colors of fireworks come from burning different chemicals.

firm 1. *adj.* solid, hard, steady. 2. *n.* a business, company.
firmament *n.* the whole expanse of the sky with its stars and clouds.
first *adj.* & *adv.* number one in order; at the beginning.
first aid *n.* on-the-spot care of the victims of accidents or sudden illnesses.
► The most essential rules in first aid are to be sure the victims are out of further harm and to keep them calm and resting while you send for professional medical help.

First aid techniques are easy to learn and use. They will help you to care for people who have suffered cuts and burns; wounds such as broken bones and sprains; animal bites and stings, and also to deal with electrical shocks and poisoning. Many people keep a first aid kit around the house filled with bandages, dressings, salves and scissors.

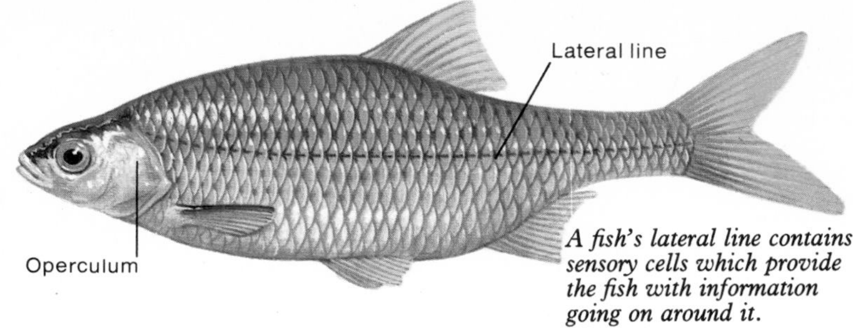

A fish's lateral line contains sensory cells which provide the fish with information going on around it.

fish 1. *n.* a cold-blooded vertebrate (backboned) animal that lives in water and breathes through gills. 2. *vb.* try to catch fish. **fishy** *adj.* of fish; smell of fish; suspicious.
► There are about 30,000 different kinds of fish – more than all the other backboned animals put together. Fish are also the oldest backboned animals. The ancestors of modern fish first appeared on earth over 500 million years ago.

Fish range in size from tiny gobies less than ½ in. (12 mm) long to the great whale SHARKS, up to 49 ft. (15 meters) long. Their shapes vary from the snake-like EELS to the flatfish that lie on their "sides" on the seabed. The SEAHORSE, another fish, looks nothing like a fish at all. And a few fishlike creatures are not fish. WHALES and DOLPHINS are really mammals – they give birth to live young and feed them milk.

Fish are cold-blooded. They live in fresh and salt water, and are found everywhere from the tropics to the poles. They breathe through gills, and move by bending their bodies from side to side. Their fins and tails help them to swim well. Over short distances, fish can swim with surprising speed. The record is 44 mph (70 k/h) for the bluefin tuna.

Most fish lay eggs in the water. This is called *spawning*. A few, such as some shark rays, give birth to live young. Egg-laying fish release millions of eggs into the water. But only a few of them will survive to become adults. Some fish, such as bass, SALMON and sticklebacks, protect their eggs by building nests. Because more eggs will survive, fewer are laid. Male seahorses and pipefish have a pouch into which the female lays her eggs. The male carries them until they hatch.

fisherman *n.* a person who catches fish.
► **Fishing** is one of the most important activities in the world. In one year, about 60 million tons of fish are taken from the seas, rivers and lakes.

Although fish are a good source of food, much of the catch ends up as animal feed, FERTILIZER, or oil used to make SOAPS or for tanning, turning animal skins into leather.

Often, the catch is made far away from home port. The fish must be preserved or they will quickly spoil. In the past fish were often dried, smoked or salted, because there were no refrigerators. Today they are packed on ice or frozen. Some fishing fleets include large factory ships which take fresh fish straight from the other ships, and can them or package them on the spot.

The best places to fish at sea are where the sloping sea bottom is no more than about 600 ft. (180 meters) deep. Here, fish can be found feeding in huge numbers. The Grand Banks off the coast of NEWFOUNDLAND is one such region.

fishmonger *n.* a person who sells fish.

fission *n.* splitting or dividing into parts; the splitting of an atomic nucleus.

fist *n.* the tightly closed hand.

fit 1. *adj.* in good health or physical condition. 2. *vb.* be suitable, the right size. *Are you sure that shoe fits you?* 3. *n.* a sudden, violent convulsion.

fix 1. *vb.* mend something. 2. *vb.* decide. *We will fix a date for the match.* 3. *n.* a difficult position. *We are in a fix.*

fixture *n.* anything fixed firmly in position, within a house, store, building, etc.

flabbergast *vb.* astonish.

flabby *adj.* hanging loosely (especially of flesh); limp.

flaccid (**flak**-*sid*) *adj.* flabby, hanging loosely.

flag 1. *n.* a piece of colored cloth with a pattern on it as a symbol of the country or organization to which it belongs.

► Flags have been used as emblems since the time of the ancient Egyptians. Their flags were flown on long poles as battle standards, held by "standard-bearers." Flying high in the air, flags helped soldiers to find their companions quickly as they plunged into battle. And they showed which soldiers belonged to which king or general.

Today, national flags are flown as a symbol of a country's history, its power and its importance. They are also a symbol of people's loyalty to one nation and one government.

Flags are also used for signaling. Since 1857 there has been an

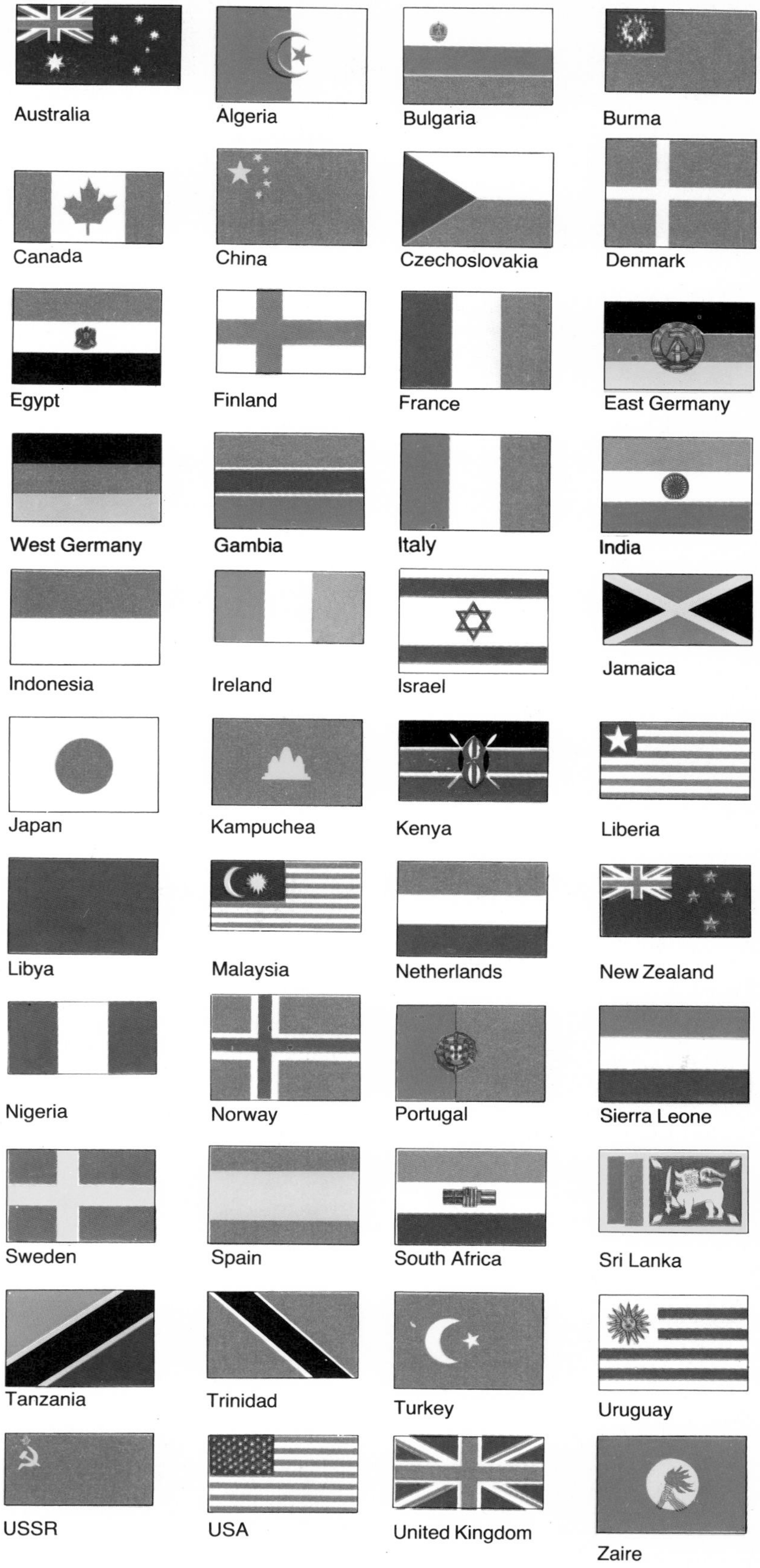

Australia

Algeria

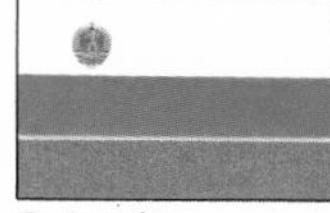
Bulgaria

Burma

Canada

China

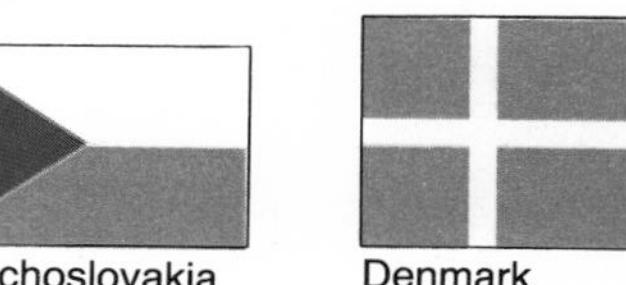
Czechoslovakia

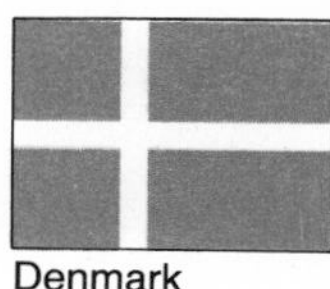
Denmark

Egypt

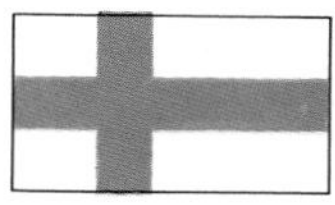
Finland

France

East Germany

West Germany

Gambia

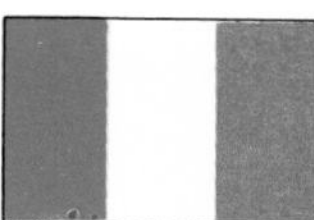
Italy

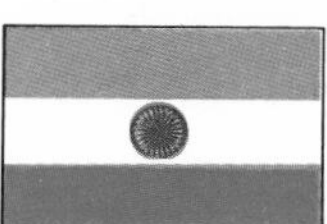
India

Indonesia

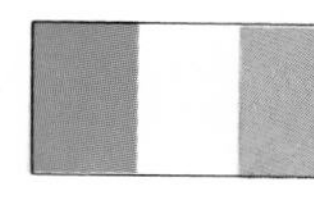
Ireland

Israel

Jamaica

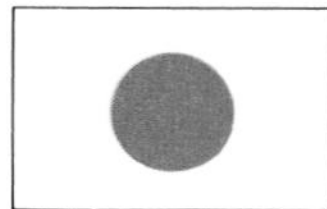
Japan

Kampuchea

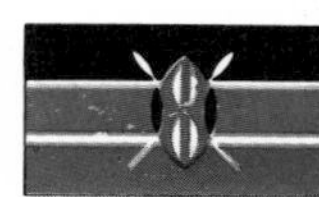
Kenya

Liberia

Libya

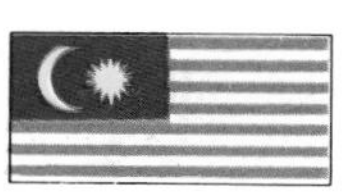
Malaysia

Netherlands

New Zealand

Nigeria

Norway

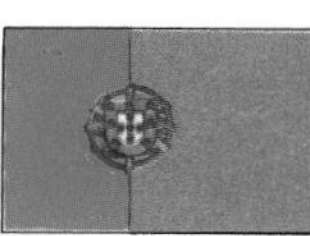
Portugal

Sierra Leone

Sweden

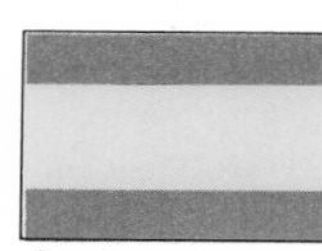
Spain

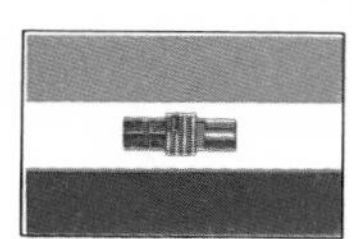
South Africa

Sri Lanka

Tanzania

Trinidad

Turkey

Uruguay

USSR

USA

United Kingdom

Zaire

A selection of national flags. Although they show a great variety of design all flags seem to conform to certain basic shapes and patterns. Various kinds of crosses form the basic design of flags of many countries with a Christian history.

F

international code for flag signals. It is used by ships. A yellow flag, for instance, means that a ship is in quarantine because of illness on board. A blue flag with a white rectangle, known as the "Blue Peter", means that a ship is about to sail. For thousands of years flags have been important as a way of identifying ships at sea. Ships from countries that were enemies could therefore avoid or challenge each other.

Other well-known signals are a white flag – a sign of truce – and a flag raised to half-mast – a sign that people are mourning someone's death.

flagon *n*. a large, round, short-necked bottle (old-fashioned).
flagstone *n*. flat slab of stone for paving.
flair *n*. natural talent. *She has a flair for writing*.
flake *n*. a small, loose, flat piece of something, such as snow.
flamboyant *adj*. ornate, showy.
flame *n*. the burning gas from a fire.
► When something is heated enough to make it burn, it will also often burst into flames. These flames are gases that are given off during burning. Bright flames that give off plenty of light, such as those of candles, wood or coal, have tiny CARBON particles in them that glow brightly. Flames are not all equally hot. Wood fires burn at about 1830°F (1000°C). The flames of acetylene WELDING torches are about 5450°F (3000°C).

flamingo *n*. a tropical bird, pink in color, with long legs and neck.
► Flamingos are found in huge flocks in many parts of the world. Flamingos live in marshes and shallow lakes, wading on their stilt-like legs.

The flamingo's body is not much bigger than that of a goose. But its long legs and neck can make it up to 6 ft. (1.8 meters) tall. These elegant birds feed on tiny plants and animals that are found in shallow waters. When feeding, they tuck their heads right under the water and use their broad hooked beaks like sieves to filter their food from the water and mud.

flan *n*. an open tart.
flange *n*. projecting rim that strengthens or guides.
flank *n*. the side of certain things, especially animals, or a formation. *vb*. stand at the side of.
flannel *n*. soft woolen cloth.
flap 1. *n*. a piece of material that hangs down over an opening. 2. *vb*. make something move up and down. *The wind flapped the clothes on the line*.
flare 1. *vb*. blaze up (of fire or light). *n*. bright light. 2. *vb*. spread outward, e.g. a skirt.
flash *n*. a sudden burst of light. *vb*. reflect light.
flask *n*. a stoppered bottle, particularly one for carrying liquor.
flat 1. *adj*. level and smooth. 2. *n*. a musical note one half step lower than the specified tone.
flatter *vb*. please someone by praising them more than they deserve.
flatulence *n*. gas in the stomach or bowels.
flaunt *vb*. show off, make a great display of.
flautist *n*. flute player; flutist.
flavor *n*. the taste and smell of food. *vb*. give flavor to; season.
flaw *n*. a defect or imperfection in something. *There is a flaw in your argument*.
flax *n*. a slender-stemmed plant with blue flowers. **flaxen** *adj*.
► Flax is grown all over the world. One kind is grown for its fibers, the other for its seeds. When the seeds are ripe, the flax is harvested.

Flax fibers are used to make linen. Linen thread is stronger than cotton and is made into canvas, cloth and paper. Flax seeds are used to make linseed oil. Linseed oil is important in the mixing of PAINTS.

Flax has been used for many thousands of years. Bundles of flax have been found in the remains of STONE AGE lake dwellers in Switzerland. These people used flax to make cord for fishing. The ancient Egyptians used linen to wrap the mummies of their pharaohs. Roman emperors wore linen clothes.

flea *n*. a small, jumping insect that feeds on blood.
► Fleas are wingless insects less than $\frac{1}{8}$ in. (3 mm) long. They live on the bodies of birds, animals and human beings. Fleas are parasites, and feed on their hosts by biting through the skin and sucking the blood. Fleas can carry germs from one host to another. Rat fleas, for example, can give bubonic plague to people.

fleck *n*. speck of color, light, etc. *vb*. mark with flecks.
fledgling *n*. a young bird that is just able to fly.
flee *vb*. run away from.
fleece *n*. a sheep's wooly covering.
fleet *n*. a number of ships under one leader.
fleeting *adj*. passing by quickly. *A fleeting moment*.

Fleming, Alexander
Sir Alexander Fleming (1881–1955) was a British doctor who discovered the antibiotic drug penicillin. It is one of the most important drugs known. Penicillin fights infections caused by many kinds of GERMS and BACTERIA. Although the drug fights the infection it does not usually harm the body. Penicillin has saved thousands of lives.

Fleming discovered the drug by accident in 1928. He found an unknown kind of MOLD growing in his laboratory, but he did not isolate the antibiotic. This was achieved by Howard Florey and Ernst Chain.

flesh *n*. the soft part of the body covering the bones.
flew *vb*. past of **fly**.
flex *v*. to bend, usually repeatedly.
flexible *adj*. easily bent this way and that.
flicker *vb*. shine or burn, now bright, now faint.
flight (rhymes with *bite*) *n*. 1. the act of flying. 2. a journey in an aircraft. 3. running away from danger.
flimsy *adj*. light and frail.
fling *n*. & *vb*. throw forcefully, hurl.
flint *n*. a glassy hard mineral that is a form of quartz.
► Flint is found in beds of chalk and limestone. A lump of flint is dull white on the outside and shiny gray to black on the inside.

Flint is very hard, but it can be easily chipped into sharp-edged flakes. In ancient times people made tools and weapons out of flint. Because it will give off a spark when struck against iron, it can be used for starting a fire. A spark from a flint also ignited the powder in a flintlock gun.

flippant *adj*. to treat serious matters lightly.
flipper *n*. an arm like part used by seals and other water animals to swim.
flirt (*flurt*) *vb*. play at courting a person.
float 1. *vb*. be held up in air or in water. 2. *n*. a piece of cork or wood on a fishing line or net.
flock *n*. a large group of animals, particularly sheep or birds.
flog *vb*. whip, thrash with a stick, etc.
flood (*flud*) *n*. a lot of water that spreads over usually dry land. *vb*. cover with a flood.
floor *n*. 1. the part of the room on which one walks. 2. a level or story of a building. *Nick lives on the second floor*.
flop 1. *vb*. throw oneself down clumsily or loosely. 2. *n*. utter failure. *The musical flopped*.
flora *n*. plant life of a particular district.

Florence (Florentine)
Florence, called Firenze in Italian, is a city in central Italy, on the Arno River. It is the capital of the province of Tuscany. In the Middle Ages, Florence was a powerful city state. Under the rule of the Medici family in the 1200s and 1300s, it became the main artistic center of Western Europe. Today, many tourists visit

the cathedral, and admire the works of art in the Uffizi Gallery and the Pitti Palace.

Florida (*abbrev.* **Fla.**)
The state of Florida is a low-lying peninsula in the southeastern United States, facing the Atlantic Ocean on the east and the Gulf of Mexico on the west.

Most of the state's income comes from tourism. Beautiful beaches and a warm, sunny climate attract more and more visitors to resorts such as Miami Beach, Palm Beach and Daytona Beach. Other attractions include the famous Everglades National Park and Disney World.

Florida is one of the fastest-growing states. The largest cities are Jacksonville, Miami and Tampa. The capital is Tallahassee. Cape Canaveral is the place from which America's space launches are made.

florist *n.* a person or shop that sells flowers.
flounder 1. *n.* small flat fish. 2. *vb.* stumble, thrash about as if helpless in water; make a mess of things.
flour *n.* a powder made from grain and used in cooking. *Bread is made from flour.*
► Flour is made from the finely ground kernels of grain such as wheat or corn. It can also be made from potatoes or beans, but this is much less usual. Every year, over 125 million tons of flour are milled from grain. By far the greatest amount comes from wheat. Wheat flour contains many of the things the body needs, such as STARCH, PROTEINS, FATS, MINERALS and some VITAMINS.

Flour is used for all kinds of cooking and baking. Most breads, cakes and pies are made from wheat flour. Flour is also used for making pasta such as macaroni and spaghetti. Bread flours are made from soft-grain wheat, and paste flours (pasta) from hard-grain or *durum* wheat.

flourish *vb.* prosper, thrive, be healthy. *The shop is flourishing.*
flow *vb.* move along as water does in a river. *n.* process of flowing.
flower *n.* the colored part of a plant that produces seeds. *vb.* blossom.
► There are about 250,000 different kinds of flowering plants in the world. Their flowers come in a dazzling array of colors, sizes and shapes. Some grow singly. Some grow in tight clusters. Many have showy colors, a strong scent and produce a sweet nectar. Others are quite drab and plain-smelling.

Flowers all have the same part to play in the life of the plant. They help plants to reproduce themselves. Inside a flower are male parts, called *stamens*, and female parts, known as *pistils*. The stamens contain hundreds of powdery grains of POLLEN. These fertilize the pistil. Then a FRUIT begins to form and grow. Inside the fruit are the SEEDS for a new generation of plants. The seeds are scattered in different ways. They may be blown by the wind, or carried off by birds and animals.

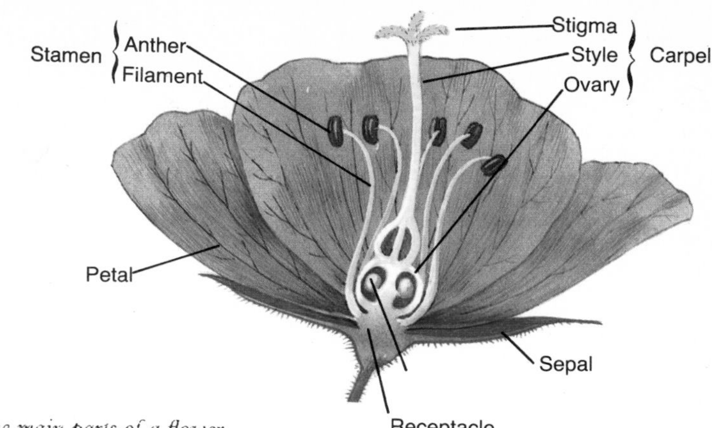

The main parts of a flower.

flown *vb.* past part. of **fly**.
flu abbreviation of influenza.
flue *n.* smoke channel in a chimney.
fluff *n.* soft down, hair, etc.
fluid *n.* any liquid or gas that can flow easily.
flung *vb.* past of **fling**.
flush *vb.* 1. blush. 2. clear out with sudden rush of water.
fluster *vb.* make confused or nervous; agitate.
flute *n.* a wind instrument with holes in the side. **flutist** *n.* flute player.
flutter *vb.* flap wings quickly and irregularly without flying.
fly 1. *vb.* move through the air; travel in an aircraft; depart suddenly. 2. *n.* one of a large group of winged insects.
► Flies have two pairs of wings, one pair for flying and another set of small wings behind the main pair to help them to balance in flight.

Many flies are dangerous. They spread diseases such as cholera and dysentery. They pick up germs from manure and rotting food and carry them into homes where they leave them on fresh food.

Some flies bite and feed on the blood of animals. Hornflies and gadflies attack cattle and horses in great swarms. Tsetse flies, which live in the tropics, spread sleeping sickness among humans. Blowflies lay their eggs in open wounds on the skin of animals. The maggots that hatch eat into the flesh and cause great harm.

Flying fish
Flying fish live in warm seas. They do not really "fly." They shoot themselves out of the water by beating their strong tails. In the air, the fish spreads large fins which act as wings to help it glide for 150 to 1,000 feet (45 to 300 meters). The California flying fish can be as much as 18 inches (45 cm) in length. The fish is considered a delicacy by some people in tropical lands.

foal *n.* a young horse.
foam *n.* a white mass of small bubbles; froth.
focus *vb.* adjust the lens of a camera, telescope, etc., in order to get a clear picture or view. *n.* distance from a lens at which the image is clear.
fodder *n.* food for cattle.
foe *n.* an enemy.

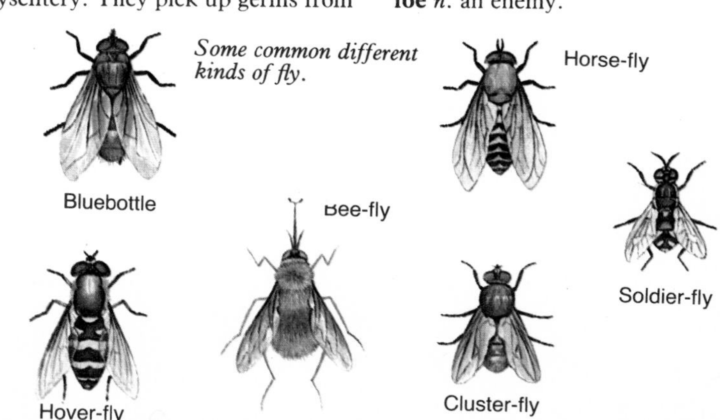

Some common different kinds of fly.

fog *n.* a thick mist that it is difficult to see through.
► Fog is a low-lying bank of cloud. Fog forms when warm, moist air comes into contact with cold ground. As the air cools, the moisture it contains forms the tiny droplets that make up any cloud.
Fog may form when warm air currents blow across chilled water or land. This kind is common around the coast. Another kind occurs on still, clear winter nights when the cold ground chills the air above it and there is no wind to blow the resulting fog away. By international standards, fog occurs when the visibility is reduced to about ½ mile (less than 1 kilometer).

foil 1. *n.* metal sheet rolled or beaten very thin. 2. *vb.* defeat; beat off attacks.
fold 1. *vb.* bend part of a thing back over itself. 2. *n.* part of material that is folded; a crease.
folder *n.* file, holder for papers.
foliage *n.* the leaves of plants.
folk (rhymes with *smoke*) *n.* people.
folklore *n.* popular beliefs, legends and customs.
► Folklore is usually handed down by word of mouth as songs, stories, poems and remedies; weather lore ("red sky at night, shepherd's delight"), and the casting of hexes and superstitions ("black cats are bad luck").

follow *vb.* go after a person or thing; pursue. **follower** *n.*
folly *n.* foolishness, a stupid action.
fondle *vb.* caress, pet.
font *n.* a (usually stone) basin for holding baptismal water.
food *n.* what is eaten. **feed** *vb.*
► Food is needed by all living things for life and growth. Food contains CARBOHYDRATES and FAT for energy, PROTEIN for growth and tissue repair, and MINERALS and VITAMINS for the proper functioning of the various organs. Plants, through PHOTOSYNTHESIS, make their own food, but animals have to rely on ready-made food: plants or other animals that have themselves eaten plants. Many animals eat only plants or flesh – they are herbivores or CARNIVORES – but humans generally eat some plant foods such as cereals, vegetables and fruit, and some animal products. These include meat, eggs, butter, cheese and milk.

foolish *adj.* without much sense; silly.
foot 1. *n.* the part of the leg on which we stand, below the ankle. 2. *n.* the bottom of something. *The foot of the page.* 3. *n.* a measurement of length (12 inches).
football *n.* a game played between two teams; the ball used to play football.
► There are several kinds of football. They differ in the shape of the ball, the size of the teams and the rules.
American Football is the chief sport in most universities and colleges and in thousands of schools. It is also played by professional teams.
The football field is 300 feet long by 160 feet wide, with end zones extending 30 feet behind each goal line. The goalposts are 30 feet behind the goal line. The oval ball weighs from 14 to 15 ounces. The field is sometimes called a *gridiron.* Yard lines run across the field every 5 yards. Playing time is 60 minutes divided into four quarters.
The game is played by teams of 11 players and is started by a kickoff from the kicker's 40-yard line. When a receiver catches the ball he tries to run as far as he can upfield without being tackled. His teammates form *interference* to prevent the opponents from tackling him. The ball carrier is *downed* if touched by an opponent while any part of his body other than his feet and one hand touches the ground. The teams then take up positions facing each other across the line of *scrimmage* where the ball carrier has been downed. The team with the ball has four downs in which to advance the ball at least 10 yards. If they advance 10 yards they have a *first down.* The defending team gains possession by holding the offensive team to less than 10 yards in four downs.
The object of the game is to carry the ball over the opponents' goal line. This is a touchdown, worth six points. A *field goal* (three points) can be scored from a scrimmage by kicking the ball over the goalpost crossbar from any part of the field.
Association Football or "soccer" was born in Britain and is the most widely played and watched game in the world. It is played by two teams of 11 players with a round ball. Players use their feet, head or any other part of their body, except their arms and hands, to propel the ball toward their opponents' goal. Only the goalkeeper may handle the ball within his own penalty area.
Rugby Union Football is a game in which the emphasis is in handling the oval-shaped ball. It bears some resemblance to American Football, but only the player with the ball can be tackled.

footlights *pl. n.* lights along the front of a theater stage.
footnote *n.* note at the bottom of a printed page.
footprint *n.* the mark left by a foot on a surface.
footsteps *pl. n.* the sound of someone walking; footfalls. *I can hear footsteps on the stairs.*
for *prep.* 1. showing goal or direction. *He left for home.* 2. length of time or space. *She waited for an hour.* 3. showing preparation, purpose. *You must get ready for school.* 4. showing cause or reason. *He couldn't eat for laughing.*
forbid *vb.* (past **forbade**) prevent; prohibit. *I forbid you to tell lies.*
force 1. *vb.* make people do something they do not want to. 2. *n.* power; strength. 3. *n.* a group of people who work together, such as the *police force.*
ford *n.* a shallow place where a river can be crossed by walking across it.

Ford, Henry
Henry Ford (1863–1947) was a pioneer automobile maker. He was the first to use assembly lines. By building his cars out of standard parts he was able to turn out hundreds a day. His cars were designed so that many people could afford to buy them. Ford's biggest success was the Model-T. His

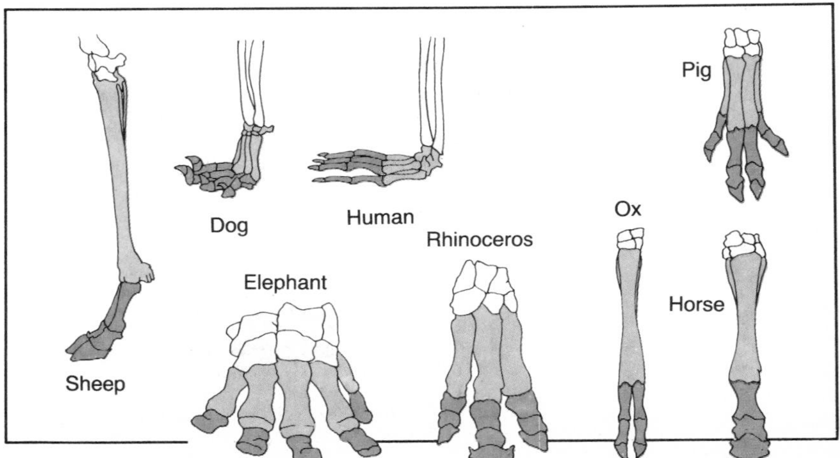

Skeletons of mammals' feet showing how the number of toes varies.

Detroit factories turned out 15 million Model-Ts during the 19 years it was in production.

fore- *prefix* meaning in front, beforehand, earlier, e.g. **foreleg, forefather, foreshadow**.
forecast *vb*. say what is likely to happen before it does. *n*. what is forecast. *Every morning we listen to the weather forecast on the radio.*
forehead *n*. the part of the face above the eyebrows.
foreign (**for**-*rin*) *adj*. from or of another country. **foreigner** *n*. a person from another country.

Foreign Legion
The Foreign Legion is a special unit of the French army. Men from any country can join it, with no questions asked about their past. The Legion was set up in 1831. It gained a name for attracting tough, hard men. Until 1962 the Legion was based in North Africa. Since then it has been based in France.

forest *n*. a large area of land covered thickly with trees.
► Tropical rain forests are found near the equator. In their hot and steamy climate many kinds of tree and plant grow very quickly. In some places the trees grow so closely together that the sunlight cannot reach the dark, bare forest floor. The trees include such valuable species as mahogany, teak and ebony.
Coniferous forests are nearly always found in cold northern lands. These forests are mostly made up of one kind of tree, such as spruce, fir or pine. Few other plants grow there. In temperate regions such as Europe and the cooler parts of Australia and Africa, there are deciduous forests with trees like oak and beech.
Trees cover about a third of the United States – 800 million acres. Canada has more than 1 billion acres of forest.

forfeit (**for**-*fit*) *n*., *adj*. & *vb*. thing lost through crime; penalty for crime or neglect.
forge *vb*. work metals by heating them, then hammering and rolling.
forgave *vb*. past of **forgive**.
forgery *n*. writing or a picture that is made to look as if someone else has done it; a false copy.
forget *vb*. (past **forgot**) fail to remember something.
forgive *vb*. (past **forgave**) stop being angry with someone for something they have done to you; pardon. **forgiveness** *n*.
fork *n*. 1. a tool with two or more points for lifting food to the mouth. 2. a large pronged tool for digging earth. 3. a place where something divides. *Go on until you reach the fork in the road, and then keep to the left.*
form 1. *n*. the shape something has. 2. *n*. a printed paper with spaces where answers have to be filled in. 3. *vb*. make or turn into. *Water forms ice when it freezes.*
formal *adj*. following the rules, stiff, conventional.
format *n*. shape, size and style of a book, etc.
formerly *adv*. in past times.
formidable *adj*. hard to cope with; to be dreaded.
formula *n*. 1. a rule or fact in sciences written in signs or numbers. *The chemical formula for water is H_2O.* 2. set of instructions for making up medicines etc.
forsake *vb*. desert, give up, abandon.
fort *n*. a strong building that can be defended.
forte (**for**-*tay*) *n*. a person's strong point. *Common sense is his forte.*
fortify *vb*. make something strong or enduring.
fortnight *n*. a period of two weeks.
fortress *n*. a stronghold, fort.
fortunate *adj*. lucky, having or bringing good luck.
fortune *n*. 1. luck, fate. 2. a lot of money. *James inherited a fortune from his great-uncle.*
forward 1. *adj*. in front of; at the front. 2. *n*. a player position in football and other games.
fossil *n*. the remains of a prehistoric animal or plant that have turned to stone.
► A fossil may be a shell, a bone, a tooth, a leaf, a skeleton or even sometimes an entire animal.
Most fossils have been found in areas that were once in or near the sea. When the plant or creature died its body sank to the seabed. The soft parts usually rotted away but the hard skeleton became buried in the mud.
Over millions of years more and more mud settled on top of the skeleton. Eventually these layers of mud hardened into rock, and the skeleton became part of that rock. Water seeping through the rock slowly dissolved away the original skeleton. It was replaced by stony MINERALS which formed exactly the same shape.
These fossils lay buried until movements in the earth's crust pushed up the seabed and it became dry land. In time water, ice and wind wear away the rock and the fossil comes to the surface.

foster *vb*. bring up; encourage, promote.
foster-mother *n*. a woman who takes a child into her own home when the real parents cannot look after it. also **foster-father, foster-parent**.
fought *vb*. past of **fight**.
foul *adj*. dirty, disgusting, bad. *He has a foul temper.*
found *vb*. 1. past of **find**. 2. establish, originate. **founder** *n*. person who starts a firm, institution, etc.
foundation *n*. the strong base of a building, usually below ground.
foundry *n*. a place where metals or glass are melted and molded.
fountain *n*. an artificial structure with jets and basins of water; a spring of water.
► Some fountains are only a simple gush of water into a basin in a garden. Others are complicated arrangements of great jets of water in a public square. One of the earliest simple fountains was made in BABYLON in about 3000 B.C. and still works. The most powerful fountain today is in Arizona. It shoots up a jet of water 560 ft. (170 meters) high. This column of water weighs 8 tons. The tradition of throwing coins into fountains comes from the old habit of making offerings to the water gods.

fowl *n*. any bird, but particularly those kept for their eggs or meat.
fox *n*. a wild animal of the dog family with red-brown fur and a bushy tail. *vb*. deceive by outwitting.
► The most common kind of fox is the red fox, which is found in Europe, North Africa, North America and parts of Asia. It eats small birds, animals and insects, and occasionally poultry or lambs.

Two well-preserved fossils.

Foxes are seldom seen because they are shy and only come out at night. They live in holes called "earths" which they either dig themselves or take over from rabbits or badgers. Recently, some foxes have been found in cities. They live under the floors of buildings or in any hidden place they can find. They eat scraps from the trashcans.

Foxes are very cunning animals. Sometimes they catch rabbits and other prey by chasing their own tails very fast. This fascinates the rabbit who watches without realizing that the fox is gradually getting nearer and nearer. When the fox gets close enough it suddenly straightens out and grabs its prey.

foxglove *n.* a tall plant with purple or white flowers; source of the drug digitalis.
foyer (**foi**-*er*) *n.* entrance hall of a hotel, theater, etc.; lobby.
fraction (**frack**-*shun*). *n.* 1. a number that is less than a whole number. *½ (one half) and ¼ (one quarter) are fractions.* 2. a small part of something. *We only got a fraction of what we expected.*
fracture *vb.* & *n.* break; crack.
fragile *adj.* delicate; easily damaged.
fragment *n.* a small piece.
fragrant *adj.* sweet-smelling. **fragrance** *n.*
frail *adj.* feeble; weak, fragile. **frailty** *n.*
frame *n.* 1. a number of pieces that fit together to give something its shape. *The frame of our tent is made up of two posts with a pole going across between them.* 2. structure that holds a picture, window, etc.
franc *n.* unit of currency in France, Belgium, Switzerland, etc.

France (French: Frenchman; Frenchwoman)
France is the largest country in Western EUROPE. In ancient times France was inhabited by CELTS, but Julius CAESAR conquered it and for 500 years it was part of the Roman Empire. The Franks, from whom the country got its name, invaded in the A.D. 400s. Since then France has remained one country.

France is a very varied and beautiful country with large plains to the north and west, a big central plateau and mountains to the east and south. It has a temperate climate and is very fertile. Farmland covers about half the country and many of the people are employed in farming, fishing or forestry work. France produces a lot of grain, fruit and vegetable, and it is famous for its WINES.

The history of France is long and turbulent. For centuries the French and English were enemies and fought many wars. The French people had their own troubles too. For many years they suffered under the rule of greedy kings and nobles. Then in 1789 the people started the FRENCH REVOLUTION. They overthrew their king and made France a republic.

But the country was soon taken over by NAPOLEON who made himself Emperor. He went to war and conquered most of the countries of Europe before he was finally defeated at Waterloo in 1815. Since then France has fought several wars.

Today, France is one of the wealthiest nations in Europe. It was one of the first members of the EUROPEAN ECONOMIC COMMUNITY. It has many beautiful historical buildings and palaces and it is famous for the number of writers, artists and musicians who have been born there. The capital city of PARIS is visited by thousands of people every year.

AREA: 211,219 SQ. MILES (547,026 SQ. KM)
POPULATION: 54,414,000
CAPITAL: PARIS
CURRENCY: FRANC
OFFICIAL LANGUAGE: FRENCH

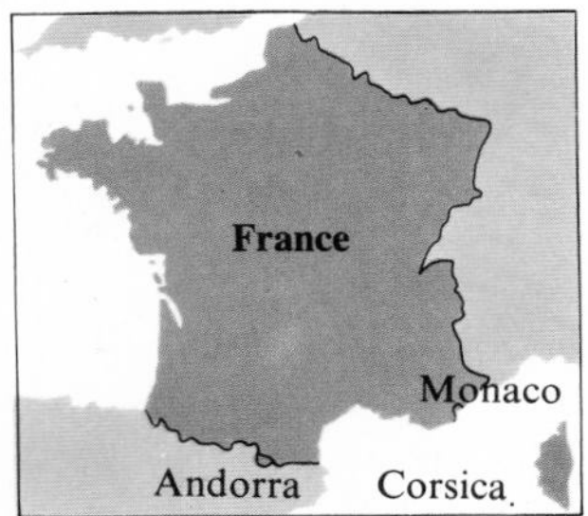

franchise *n.* right to vote.

Francis of Assisi
St. Francis (1182–1226) was born in Assisi in central Italy. When he was 22 he suffered a severe illness. Afterwards he decided to devote his life to the service of God. He gave up all his worldly goods to live in poverty. He gathered around him a band of friars who became known as the Franciscans. St. Francis was very fond of birds and animals which he called his brothers and sisters.

frank *adj.* open and honest. **frankly** *adv.* **frankness** *n.*

Frankenstein
The original Frankenstein was a character in a novel written by Mary Shelley in 1818. Dr. Frankenstein created an imitation human being that looked like an ordinary man, only bigger. This creature finally killed his creator and disappeared into the night. Since then there have been many films and stories about this man-made monster.

frankincense *n.* sweet-smelling resin burnt as incense.

Franklin, Benjamin
Benjamin Franklin (1706–90) was an American politician and scientist. He was born in Boston, the youngest of 17 children. Franklin became a printer and then went on to publish a yearly almanac which made his fortune.

He became involved in the War of Independence, which brought America freedom from British rule. He helped draw up the peace treaty at the end of the war and was one of the men who signed the Declaration of Independence.

His scientific inventions included bifocal glasses, and the lightning rod.

Franklin spent a large part of his life in Europe. He was in London for more than 16 years, during which time he tried to keep good relations with Britian. At the age of 70 he was appointed minister to France, where he became very popular and obtained French aid for the Revolutionary War. When he died in 1790, the world knew that he was a true friend of liberty.

frantic *adj.* frenzied; excited with grief, pain, worry, etc.
fraud *n.* 1. a confidence trick or other crime that involves taking money by deceit. 2. a person who is not what he seems; a swindler.
freckle *n.* a small brown mark on the skin.
free 1. *adj.* costing no money. 2. *adj.* able to do what you want. *vb.* set at liberty, release.
freedom *n.* the state of being free, liberty; independence.
freeze *vb.* turn from a liquid to a solid by lowering the liquid's temperature to below its freezing point. *As water freezes it turns into ice.* **frozen** *adj.*
freezer *n.* a box or compartment kept very cold.
freight (rhymes with *late*) *n.* cargo, goods that are carried from one place to another.
freighter (rhymes with *later*) *n.* a ship or aircraft that carries freight.

French Guiana
French Guiana, in northeastern South America, has been an overseas department of France since 1946. At one time, the area was used by the French as a place to send convicts. The best known convict settlement,

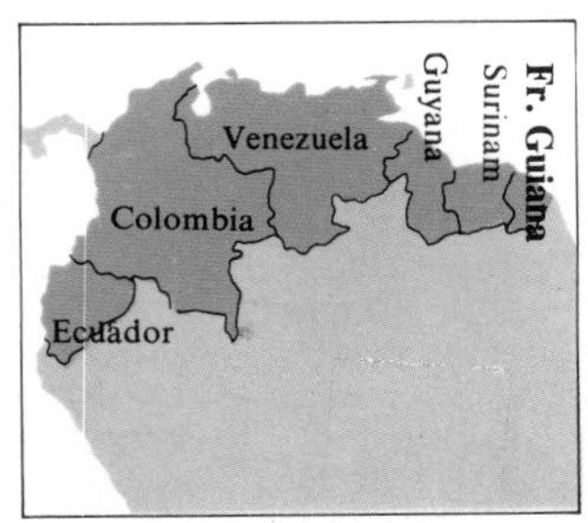

Devil's Island, was closed in 1945.

French Revolution
For many centuries the poor people of FRANCE suffered under the rule of their kings and nobles. By 1789 France was deeply in debt because of expensive wars, and badly governed by an élite of the nobility, who lived in luxury while many poor people starved. Faced with national bankruptcy, the King, Louis XVI, decided to summon the Estates General, a national parliament which had not met since 1614. It consisted of three "Estates" – 300 noblemen, 300 clergy, and 600 commoners. Each Estate had one vote, which meant that the nobility and the clergy could outvote the commoners. So the commoners formed a national Constituent Assembly, pledged to make a new constitution for France. Louis planned to dismiss the Assembly. This aroused the fury of the Paris mob, which stormed the fortress prison of the Bastille on July 14, 1789. Louis had to give way, and the Assembly proceeded to bring in many reforms.

The Republic: Louis conspired with his allies in Austria and Prussia, and in June 1791 tried to flee the country. He was captured and taken back to Paris. War with Austria and Prussia followed in April 1792. In August the Paris mob attacked the King in the Palace of the Tuileries, butchering his guards and imprisoning him. French victory against the Prussians in the battle of Valmy encouraged the revolutionaries. A new assembly, the National Convention, declared the monarchy abolished and set up a republic on September 21.

Death and Terror: Power in the Convention passed to a political group called the Girondins, who had Louis tried for treason and executed. But during 1793 a more extremist group, the Jacobins, gained power. The Girondins were executed, and a Committee of Public Safety ruled the country, headed by Maximilien Robespierre. Under his influence anyone suspected of opposing the new regime was executed, in a bloodbath known as the "Reign of Terror". In July 1794 Robespierre himself was accused and guillotined. In 1795 a new two-chamber assembly was elected, and order was restored.

frenzy *n*. violent rage, excitement.
frequency *n*. 1. repeated occurrence. 2. number of vibrations, waves, cycles per second.
frequent (**free**-*kwent*) *adj*. happening often. *vb*. (free-**kwent**) visit often.
fresco *n*. a painting made on freshly laid, still wet plaster. The greatest time of fresco painting was during the Renaissance in Italy.
fresh *adj*. new. *Start on a fresh page*. not stale; not preserved. *Fresh fruit and vegetables*.
fret 1. *n*. cut or sawn ornamental pattern in wood. 2. *n*. bar across fingerboard on a guitar etc. 3. *vb*. worry, grieve.

Freud, Sigmund
Known as the "father of modern psychiatry", Freud (1856–1939) was a Viennese doctor when he began his revolutionary theories on human nature. He was baffled by the side of human behavior that seemed to make no sense. He held that there was a deep unexplored part of the human mind called the unconscious. Tensions and forces within this shadowy world often led people to act in ways they could not explain. The science of psychiatry was a way to explore and treat problems that arose from the unconscious.

friction *n*. rubbing of two things together; the resistance something meets with when it rubs against something else.
► Friction makes it harder to move something across a surface. Smooth objects cause much less friction than rough objects, so when things need to go fast we try to reduce friction. This is why the rails and wheels of railroads are smooth. When we want things to slow down we add friction, like putting on the brakes in cars. If two things rub together at great speed the friction produces heat. If you rub your hand very fast against your leg you can feel the heat made by the friction.

To reduce friction, engineers use ball-bearings and oil. These make parts of machinery slide easily over one another.

Friday *n*. the name of the sixth day of the week, between Thursday and Saturday; named after Frigg, Norse goddess.
fridge *n*. abbreviation for refrigerator.
friend *n*. a person you know well and like. **friendship** *n*.
frieze *n*. ornamental band along the top of a wall.
frigate *n*. originally a sailing warship of the mid-18th century, today, large guided-missile destroyer.
frighten *vb*. make afraid.
frill *n*. pleated edging on clothing; unnecessary extravagance.
fringe 1. *n*. ornamental border of loose threads. 2. *n*. hair brushed down on forehead and cut straight, bangs. 3. *adj*. not central, so less important.
fritter *vb*. waste time, money, etc.
frivolous *adj*. silly, not serious. **frivolity** *n*.
frock *n*. a woman's or girl's dress (now rather old-fashioned).
frog *n*. a small, tailless, web-footed amphibian.
► Frogs are found all over the world except in very cold lands that are always frozen. There are hundreds of different kinds. The biggest is the Goliath frog of Central Africa. This frog can be over 31 in. (80 cm) long and weigh over 6½ lb. (3 kg). The smallest is a tree frog from the United States which is less than ¾ in. (2 cm) long.

Frogs breathe through their skins as well as their lungs. It is important that a frog keep its skin wet because if the skin became too dry it could not breathe and the frog would die. This is why you will never find a frog very far away from water, and why they like to stay in the shade.

Common frogs feed on insects, grubs and slugs. They catch their food with the long sticky tongue which is attached to the front of their mouths. A frog can flick its tongue in and out in a fraction of a second.

from *prep*. showing place or person where something starts. *That letter's from my sister*.
front *n*. the part of something that faces forward.
frontier *n*. part of a country touching another country.
frost *n*. the powdery ice that covers everything when it is very cold.
► There are three kinds of frost. Hoarfrost forms when tiny drops of water in the air freezes as they touch cold objects. Hoarfrost makes lacy patterns on windowpanes. Glazed frost forms when rain falls on a cold road and covers the surface with a glassy coat. Rime frost is white ice that forms when cold fog or drizzle freezes on surfaces like aircraft wings.

froth *n*. foam; a collection of bubbles on the top of a liquid.
frown *vb*. & *n*. pull the eyebrows together when you are cross or thinking hard.
froze *vb*. past of **freeze**.
fruit (rhymes with *boot*) *n*. that part of a plant which has seeds in it and which is often eaten.
► To most of us "fruit" means juicy foods which grow on certain plants and trees. Apples, oranges, and pears are three examples. These fruits taste good and are important in our diet. They give us mineral salts, sugar and VITAMINS. The water, skins and seeds of fruit help our DIGESTION.

To scientists who study plants, fruits are the ripe seed cases of any flowering plant. The fruits protect the seeds as they develop and help spread them when they are ripe. Some fruits scatter seeds. Others are eaten by birds and animals that spread the seeds.

fry *vb*. cook food in hot fat or oil.
fudge (*fuj*) *n*. a soft creamy candy.

F

All these fungi are good to eat. ***But never eat any fungus that you cannot identify for certain.***

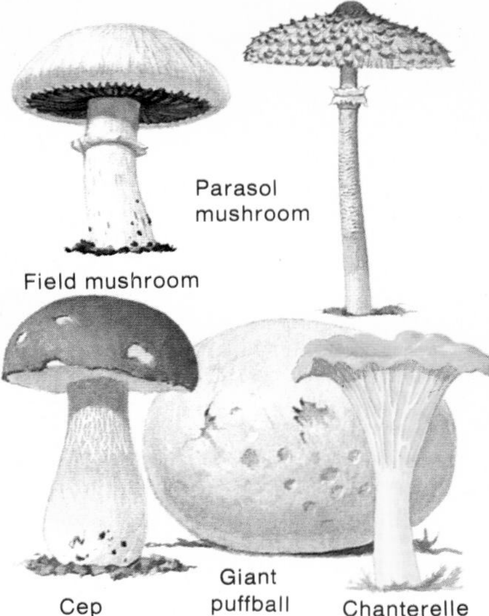

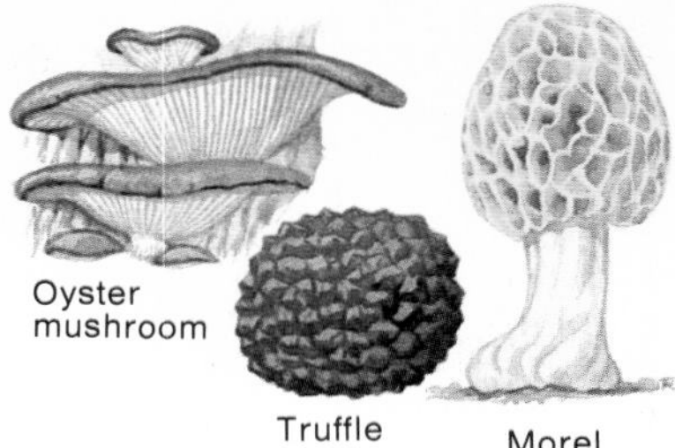

Fry, Elizabeth
Elizabeth Fry (1780–1845) was a British Quaker who became interested in prison reform. On a visit to Newgate Prison in London, she was shocked by the conditions in which the prisoners had to live. She devoted the rest of her life to campaigning for improvements in these conditions. She was asked by the King of France to report on French prisons, and she made similar visits to other countries.

fuel *n.* anything that is burned to make heat or to give energy, such as coal, oil, gas or wood.
► Fuels provide most of the ENERGY we use for heating, cooking, powering ships, planes, cars and machines, and producing electricity.
The most important fuels are COAL, OIL, and NATURAL GAS. These were formed underground from the remains of prehistoric plants or animals. They are often called fossil fuels.
Some fuels give out more heat than others. A ton of coal gives nearly three times as much heat as a ton of wood. Oil gives nearly four times as much, and HYDROGEN gas 10 times as much. But URANIUM can give more than half-a-million times as much heat as hydrogen.
As fossil fuels are used up we may have to make more use of atomic energy, solar energy, wind and water power.

fulcrum *n.* the support on which a lever moves.
full *adj.* without space for more; the opposite of "empty."
fulmar *n.* a gull-like arctic sea bird.

Fulton, Robert
Robert Fulton (1765–1815) was an American inventor and engineer. He developed torpedoes and other naval weapons, and built a submarine, the *Nautilus*. In 1807 he launched a steamboat, the *Clermont*, which did much to popularize the use of steam power in ships.

fumble *vb.* grope, use hands clumsily.
fumes *pl. n.* strong-smelling smoke.
fun *n.* amusement; a good time.
function (**funk**-*shun*) 1. *n.* the special work of a person or thing. *A hammer's function is to knock in nails.* 2. *vb.* do something. *This tool functions as a drill and as a screwdriver.*
fund *n.* sum of money used for a charity or other purpose.
fundamental *adj.* basic, essential.
funeral *n.* the ceremony when someone who has died is buried.
fungus (plural **fungi**) *n.* a small plant with no leaves, flowers or green coloring (chlorophyll), such as a mushroom.
► Fungi do not have the CHLOROPHYLL that helps green plants to make food. So fungi have to find a ready-made supply of food. Some feed as parasites on living plants or animals. Others feed on animal and plant remains.
There are more than 50,000 kinds of fungi. Some have only one CELL. Other fungi are chains of cells. These produce tiny threadlike growths that spread through the substance they feed on. Many fungi grow a large fruiting body which sheds spores that produce new fungus plants. The mushrooms we eat are the fruiting bodies of a fungus.

funk *n.* paralyzing fear; coward. *vb.* try to get out of because of fear.
funnel *n.* a tube with a wide top and narrow bottom. *A funnel is used to pour liquid into a container with a narrow opening. vb.* use a funnel.
funny *adj.* 1. amusing; comical. *She read me a funny story.* 2. peculiar; odd. *He gave me a funny look.*
fur *n.* the soft, thick, hairy covering on some mammals. **furry** *adj.*
► There are two kinds of fur fiber. Short soft fur grows close to the skin. Longer, stiffer hairs cover this underfur and prevents the fur from becoming matted.
Fur keeps in body heat. Mammals with thick fur stay warm even in the coldest weather. Animals with very thick fur live in the coldest parts of the world.
Since STONE AGE times people have worn furs to keep them warm. Wearing furs today is a sign of luxury. Some of the best furs come from the chinchilla, fur seals, mink, muskrat, silver fox and ermine (the white winter coat of the stoat).

furious *adj.* raging, very angry.
furnace *n.* an enclosed fireplace producing great heat.
furniture *n.* chairs, tables, beds, desks and other similar things. **furnish** *vb.*
► The first pieces of furniture were simple slabs of stone and chunks of wood. In time, people tried to make furniture that was beautiful as well as useful.
Wealthy Egyptians carved and painted beds, chairs and tables 4,000 years ago. The Romans used bronze and marble, and made tables with legs carved in animal shapes. From the end of the Middle Ages onwards many different styles of furniture have been made.
More recently, people have tried using new materials and machines to make furniture with clean, simple shapes. Today you can buy metal or plastic furniture.

furrow *n.* a straight, narrow cut made in the ground by a plow.
fury *n.* violent anger.
fuse 1. *n.* a safety device in an electric circuit. 2. *n.* a device that sets off explosions. 3. *vb.* join together by heat.
► One kind of fuse is a safety device in an electric circuit. Fuse wire is made so that it will melt at a low temperature. If too much ELECTRICITY flows through the circuit the wire "fuses", or melts. This breaks the circuit and stops the flow of electric current.
In this way, an electric fuse stops the wire in the circuit from becoming too hot and possibly setting fire to nearby objects. Electric current must pass through fuse wire to get from the main power line to the electric wiring in a house. Inside the house, each electric plug also has a fuse.
The other kind of fuse is a device that sets off explosions. A safety fuse burns slowly until the flame reaches the explosive. A detonating fuse explodes itself and this explosion sets off a much larger amount of DYNAMITE.

fuselage (**fyoo**-*se-lazh*) *n.* the body of an aircraft.
fuss *n.* nervous excitement, bustle, bother. *vb.* worry, complain.
future *n.* the time yet to come.

G

The Grand Canyon in Arizona and Nevada

gabardine *n.* a fine durable cloth used for clothes.

gable *n.* triangular part of outer house wall between the sloping sides of the roof.

Gabon
Gabon is a republic on the equator in westcentral AFRICA. Most of the country is covered in rain forests. About 70 percent of the population works on the land, but most of the Gabon's wealth comes from oil and other minerals. Before it became independent, Gabon was part of French Equatorial Africa.
AREA: 103,352 SQ. MILES (267,667 SQ. KM)
POPULATION: 667,000
CAPITAL: LIBREVILLE
CURRENCY: FRANC
OFFICIAL LANGUAGE: FRENCH

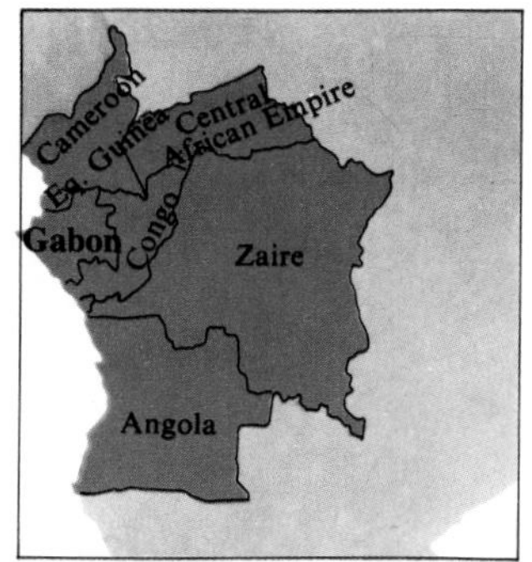

gadget *n.* a small thing made to do a particular job. *A can opener is a gadget.*

Gaelic *n.* one of the ancient languages of the Celts. It reached Ireland from Europe, and spread to Scotland and the Isle of Man. In Eire (Ireland) it is an official language, but only five percent of the people still use it regularly. "Clan" and "loch" are Gaelic words.

gag 1. *n.* something tied around someone's mouth to stop speech. 2. *n.* a joke, funny story. *vb.* make gags. 3. *vb.* retch, choke.

gaga *adj.* crazy or foolish.

gaggle *n.* a flock of geese.

gaiety *n.* cheerfulness, merrymaking.

Gagarin, Yuri
A Russian astronaut (1934–68). In 1961 he orbited the Earth in *Vostok I*, becoming the first man in space.

gain (rhymes with *lane*) *vb.* win or reach. *Eric is sure to gain the prize. n.* addition, increase. *A gain in weight.*

Gainsborough, Thomas
An English portrait painter (1727–88). Largely self-taught, he painted over 500 of the fashionable people of his day, including King GEORGE III, Benjamin FRANKLIN and Samuel JOHNSON. But his best-known work is called *The Blue Boy*. He was a founder of the Royal Academy.

gainsay *vb.* contradict, deny.

gala *n.* festivity.

Galapagos
An island group in the Pacific Ocean, about 650 miles (1,050 km) west of ECUADOR, which governs it. These volcanic islands cover a total of 3,029 sq. miles (7,844 sq. km) and there are about 4,000 people. The islands contain many strange animals and some plants, which are found only there. A study of these animals helped Charles DARWIN to arrive at his theory of EVOLUTION.

galaxy *n.* a very large group of stars in outer space. *The Milky Way is a galaxy.*
► The sun is just one of about 1 billion stars in a vast spiral arrangement of stars that we call our galaxy. In some parts of the night sky there are so many stars that they form the white band of light we call the MILKY WAY. Outside this great system of stars to which we and the sun belong there are billions of other vast galaxies, some spiral in shape, others elliptical, and still others of no distinctive form.

gale *n.* a very strong wind.

Galileo, Galilei
An Italian scientist (1564–1642) who lived in an age when very few people had any knowledge of science. At the age of 18 he made his first great discovery. Sitting in Pisa Cathedral he watched the swinging of a lamp suspended by a long chain. Common sense told him that wider swings would take a longer time than short swings, but when he timed the swings against the beat of his pulse he found that this was not so. All swings, large and small, took the same time (see PENDULUM). Later he

carried out his famous experiment of dropping balls of different weights from the top of the Leaning Tower of Pisa. They all took the same time to reach the ground, showing that the weight of objects made no difference to their rate of fall. Galileo made himself one of the first TELESCOPES, through which he saw the craters of the moon, and in 1610 he discovered the moons of JUPITER revolving around their parent planet. He also discovered the phases of VENUS and said that Venus therefore revolved around the sun. This supported the ideas of COPERNICUS, who had said that the sun was the center of the solar system. But it clashed with the ideas of the Church, and Galileo was made to renounce his Copernican ideas. In his lifetime Galileo had lain the foundations of modern science.

gallant *adj*. brave, daring, courteous – especially to women.

galleon *n*. a large ancient Spanish sailing ship with a high stern.
► A type of large, square-rigged sailing ship, built from the 1500s to the 1700s, especially by the Spanish, who used a heavy, cumbersome version for warfare and for trade with their American colonies.

gallery *n*. 1. a building where pictures or other works of art are shown. 2. the highest part of a theater or church where people sit.

galley *n*. 1. an open, seagoing vessel powered mainly by oars and used by Mediterranean nations from ancient times until the 1700s. 2. a ship's kitchen.

Gallic *adj*. relating to the Gauls; French.

gallon *n*. a liquid measure. *There are eight pints in a gallon.*

gallop *n*. & *vb*. the fastest pace of a horse.

gallows *n*. wooden framework on which criminals used to be hanged.

galore *adv*. plenty. *At the party there was food and drink galore.*

Galvani, Luigi
Luigi Galvani (1737–98) was an Italian physician from whose name many terms in electricity, such as "galvanising" and "galvanometer" are derived. Galvani was the professor of anatomy at the university of Bologna. During one of his experiments on muscles and nerves, he noticed that a frog's legs twitched when touched with charged metal. Galvani made an arc of two metals, which also made the legs twitch, and wrongly explained it as electricity in the muscle. Volta, another Italian, disagreed and correctly attributed the electricity to the arc.

galvanize *vb*. 1. reduce the corrosion (rust) of iron and steel by coating it with a thin layer of zinc. 2. shock someone into doing something.

Gama, Vasco Da
Vasco da Gama (*c*. 1469–1524) discovered a sea route from Europe to India by way of southern Africa. This Portuguese navigator left Lisbon with four ships in July 1497. In East Africa he found a guide who showed him how to sail across the Indian Ocean. Da Gama reached Calicut in southern India in May 1498. But Arab traders who were jealous of the Portuguese tried to stop him from trading with the Indians. On the journey home, 30 of his 90 crewmen died of scurvy, and only two of the four ships got back to Lisbon.
But da Gama had found a way to reach the spice-rich lands of the East. Portuguese traders and empire builders were soon sailing out to India along the route he pioneered.

Gambia (Gambian)
Gambia is a tiny country in West Africa. It is almost entirely surrounded by SENEGAL. Most of the people work on the land, and the main export is peanuts. Gambia is rapidly expanding its tourist industry. A former British colony, Gambia became independent in 1965.
AREA: 4,361 SQ. MILES (11,295 SQ. KM)
POPULATION: 642,000
CAPITAL: BANJUL
CURRENCY: DALASI
OFFICIAL LANGUAGE: ENGLISH

gambit *n*. opening moves in a game of chess.

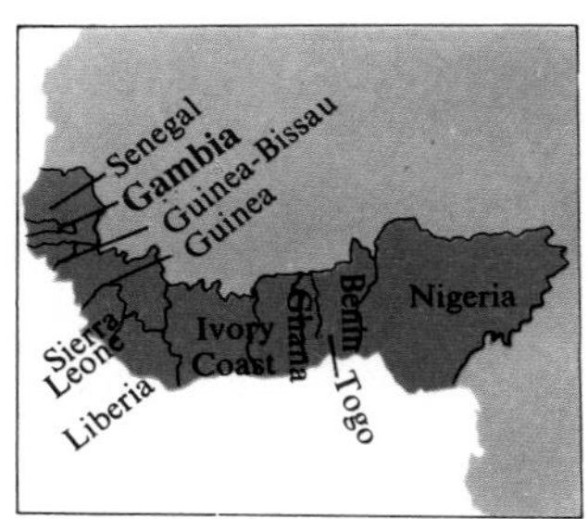

gamble *vb*. risk money in the hope of gaining more. **gambler** *n*. a person who gambles. **gambling** *n*.

game 1. *n*. a form of indoor or outdoor play, usually with rules. 2. *n*. wild animals that are hunted for food or for sport. 3. *adj*. ready; spirited.

gamma *n*. third letter of the Greek alphabet: γ.

gamma rays *adj*. & *pl.n*. high-frequency electromagnetic rays similar to, but more powerful than, X-rays. They can pass through iron one foot thick and are used in medicine against cancer.

gander *n*. a male goose.

Gandhi, Mohandas
Mohandas Karamchand Gandhi (1869–1948) is sometimes called the "father of modern India." This frail-looking Hindu lawyer helped to free INDIA from British rule by showing Indians peaceful ways of disobeying British laws. From 1893 to 1915 he lived in South Africa, where he tried to win equal rights for Indians under British and local rule.
In 1915 Gandhi moved back to India. He became the leader of those who wanted Indian, not British, rule in India. When the British passed a law against this movement he called the people out on strike. In 1920 he told the Indians to spin cloth for their own clothes instead of buying it from Britain. In 1930 he broke a British law by making salt from seawater instead of buying salt from the government.
People admired Gandhi's beliefs, his kindness to all men, and his simple way of life. But he spent seven years in prisons for disobeying British laws. In 1947 Britain gave India independence. Soon after, one of his fellow HINDUS shot Gandhi for preaching peace to Muslims.

gang *n*. a group of people working together.

Ganges River
One of the greatest rivers of INDIA and BANGLADESH, the Ganges is sacred to Hindus. It flows about 1,540 miles (2,480 km) from its source in the HIMALAYAS to its mouth in the Bay of Bengal.

gangster *n*. a member of a gang of criminals.

gangway *n*. 1. a movable bridge between a ship and the shore. 2. an opening for boarding a ship.

gannet *n*. large white seabird.

gap *n*. 1. an opening; a space. 2. a space of time. *There was a long gap in the conversation.*

gape *vb*. stare, open mouth wide, be wide open.

garage *n*. a place where cars are kept or repaired. *vb*. put or keep in a garage.

Ghandi was a leader in the Indian independence movement. He stressed the importance of nonviolence.

garbage *n*. rubbish, refuse, trash.
garden *n*. a piece of land for growing flowers, fruit or vegetables. *vb*. to work in a garden. **gardener** *n*. a person who looks after a garden.
► There were gardens in Egypt 4,500 years ago. BABYLON was later famous for its hanging gardens. RENAISSANCE Italy had gardens with fountains, pools, terraces and steps.
In the 1700s English landscape gardeners placed natural-looking lawns and trees around big houses. In the 1800s cities laid out gardens where anyone might walk.

Garfield, James Abram
James Garfield (1831–1881) was the 20th President of the United States. He was assassinated only a few months after his inauguration. He lay near death for 80 days before he died in Elberon, New Jersey, on September 19th, 1881.

Giuseppe Garibaldi

gardenia *n*. one of a large group of tropical plants with fragrant white or yellow flowers.
gargle *vb*. wash the throat by bubbling liquid about in it. n. liquid used to gargle with.
gargoyle *n*. rainspout of a gutter carved with grotesque figures.

Garibaldi, Giuseppe
Giuseppe Garibaldi (1807–82) was an Italian soldier and patriot. He helped to turn ITALY from a collection of small states into an independent state. After two periods of exile in the U.S., Garibaldi led his "thousand Redshirts" against the Austrians who then controlled Italy. In 1860 he gained control of the Kingdom of the Two Sicilies (Sicily and southern Italy). This formed the basis of a united Italy, although Garibaldi twice failed to capture Rome. A heroic and romantic figure, Garibaldi retired in 1871.

garlic *n*. plant grown for its strong-tasting bulb, used as flavoring in cooking.
garment *n*. a piece of clothing.
garret *n*. room immediately below the roof of a house; an attic.
garrison *n*. body of troops stationed in a town or fortress. *vb*. occupy as a garrison.
garter *n*. 1. strap or band used to support a stocking. 2. the highest order of knighthood in the United Kingdom.
gas *n*. 1. any substance like air. *They filled balloons with helium gas because it is lighter than air*. 2. various mixtures used for fuel. *We cook with gas in our house*. 3. gasoline.
► Gas is one of the three states in which matter exists, the others being liquid and solid. The particles in a gas move about freely and spread out as widely as possible. If a quantity of gas is placed in a container, the gas spreads out until it fills the whole container. If the temperature of a gas is lowered, the particles in it move more slowly and stay closer together and the gas will become a liquid. If the temperature is lowered still further the liquid becomes a solid.

gash *vb*. & *n*. a deep cut.
gasoline *n*. a liquid fuel made from oil and used to power motor vehicles.
gasp *n*. & *vb*. struggle to breathe; breathe in short, quick breaths.
gastric *adj*. concerning the stomach.
gastronomy *n*. the art of good eating and cooking.

Gas Turbine
An efficient type of engine perfected in the 1930s and used largely in aircraft.
A gas turbine usually has a single shaft which carries a series of fans, divided into two groups – the compressor and the turbine. Air is drawn in by the compressor fans and its pressure increased. The compressed air is mixed with fuel. This mixture is ignited and the expanding hot gases are forced against fans to drive the compressor and then against the power-producing turbine blades, where the mixture passes out as exhaust. In jet aircraft this exhaust is used to thrust the plane forward. Gas turbine engines are becoming more important in industry because they are compact and efficient. (*see* JET PROPULSION TURBINE).

gate *n*. an outside door, often in a wall or fence.
gate-crasher *n*. one who attends a party etc. without having been invited.
gather *vb*. bring or come together, collect, pick. *Marian gathered a bunch of roses*.
gaucho *n*. the South American cowboy of the pampas.

gauge (rhymes with *rage*) 1. *n*. an instrument for measuring. 2. *n*. the distance between a pair of railway lines; a standard measure. 3. *vb*. measure exactly; judge, reckon.

Gauguin, Paul
A French artist (1848–1903) who was influenced by VAN GOGH. He developed a simple, colorful style of painting, and used it to depict the unspoiled life of the South Pacific.

gaunt *adj*. lean, haggard.
gauze *n*. thin fabric of open texture.
gave *vb*. past of **give**
gay *adj*. cheerful and full of fun.
gaze *vb*. look at something for a long time. *n*. a fixed look.
gazelle *n*. slender, graceful, swift antelope found on dry grasslands in Africa and parts of Asia.
gazette *n*. a newspaper.
gear *n*. 1. a set of toothed wheels working together in a machine. 2. tackle; apparatus. 3. (*casual*) clothes.
► A gear is a wheel with teeth along its rim. These teeth can fit into the teeth of other gear wheels. Metal rods, or axles, are fitted into the center of each gear. If one axle is turned, its gear turns and makes the second axle turn too.

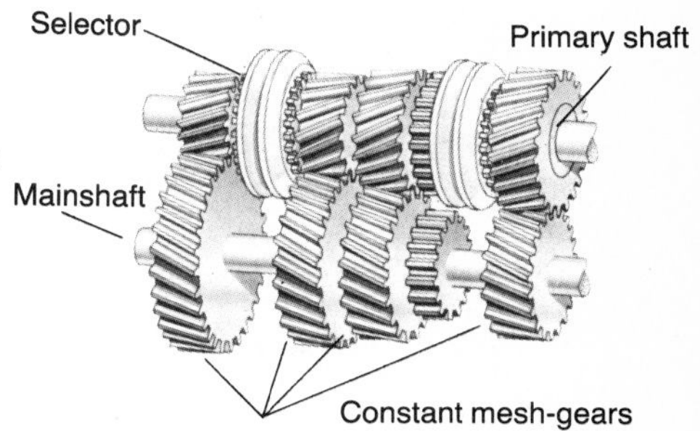

Gears are used to increase or decrease the speed at which wheels turn. They are also used to increase or decrease the turning power of wheels.
Let us imagine a large gear wheel which has four times as many teeth as a small wheel. If the small wheel is turned by a machine, the big wheel will turn at only a quarter the speed of the small wheel. And the big wheel will turn in the opposite direction to the small wheel. But the big wheel will have four times the turning power of the small wheel. When a motor car is in low gear, this is what happens. The car goes quite slowly, but it has plenty of power for starting or going up steep hills.
If our imaginary big gear wheel is made to turn by an engine, the small gear wheel will spin round four times as fast as the big wheel. But the small wheel will only have a quarter the turning power of the big wheel.

G

geese *pl. n.* more than one goose.
geisha *n.* Japanese girl trained to entertain men.
gelatin (jell-*a-tin*) *n.* substance obtained from animal skins and bones. Gelatin is hard, transparent and tasteless, and consists mostly of protein; it forms a stiff jelly when dissolved in water. It is used in cooking, medicine, and photography.
gelignite *n.* explosive used for blasting.
gem *(jem)* *n.* a jewel or precious stone.
► The most valuable gems are DIAMONDS and EMERALDS, followed by RUBIES and SAPPHIRES. Many others are "semi-precious" (PEARLS are also valuable, but are not stones). The value of a gem depends on its size, color and lack of flaws. Most types are cut into special shapes, to catch the light more brilliantly. Poor-quality gems can often be used in industry, and many of these are now made synthetically.

Several varieties of the mineral beryl are shown in this picture.

gender *n.* sex.
gene *n.* basic part of each cell that transmits heredity characteristics.
► A living organism inherits genes from its parents. Each gene causes the development of a certain characteristic such as the shape of a leaf, hair color or height. There are hundreds, sometimes thousands, of genes in every cell; they exist in the nucleus where they are arranged along minute strands called chromosomes.

genealogy *n.* a history of descent of persons and families from ancestors; pedigree.
general 1. *adj.* to do with most people or things. *There is a general feeling that dogs should be kept on leashes in the street.* 2. *n.* a senior officer in the army.
generate *vb.* make, produce, especially electricity.
generation *n.* all the people of about the same age. *I get along well with people of my mother's generation.*
generator *n.* a machine that produces electricity.
► In a generator, mechanical energy is turned into electricity. The mechanical energy comes from some kind of engine or TURBINE, usually powered by oil or coal. A generator works because an electric current flows in a loop of wire when it is rotated between the poles of a magnet. Usually there are many loops of wire (the armature) which rotate on a shaft between electromagnets. The electromagnets create magnetic fields when current passes through them. The current generated in the rotating coils is collected by carbon "brushes" which press against copper rings at the end of the shaft.

generous *adj.* ready to give freely and happily.
genesis *n.* origin, formation; the first book of the Old Testament.

Geneva
Geneva is a city in SWITZERLAND, at the southern end of Lake Geneva. It contains the European headquarters of the UNITED NATIONS, and is the center of many other international organizations.

Genghis Khan
Genghis Khan (1167–1227) was a Mongol chief who cruelly attacked many Asian peoples and won a mighty empire. His real name was Temujin ("Ironsmith").

At 13 he took his dead father's place as chief of a small Mongol tribe of NOMADS. He soon won power over nearby tribes as well. In 1206 he became known as Genghis Khan, "Very Mighty King." Genghis Khan formed a huge army of tough, hard-riding nomads on the great grasslands of central Asia. Then he set off to conquer the lands around him. His troops pushed southeast to Peking in China, and south into Tibet and what are now Pakistan and Afghanistan. In the southwest they invaded Iran and southern Russia.

No city could drive off the fierce Mongol archers. Genghis Khan forced prisoners of war to lead his army. He punished cities that resisted him by killing most of the people.

After Genghis Khan died, other Mongol rulers won more land and made the empire even larger.

genius (jean-*ius*) *n.* a particularly clever, intelligent person.
gentile *n.* a person who is not a Jew.
gentle *adj.* quiet, mild or kind.
genuflect *vb.* bend the knee, especially in worship. **genuflexion** *n.*
genuine *adj.* real and true; authentic, not a sham.
genus *n.* (plural **genera**) a biological grouping of similar plants or animals. In the Latin name of a species, the first word is the name of the genus. For example, the dingo of Australia is called *Canis dingo*. *Canis* is the name of the genus (the dog family). *Dingo* is the name of the species.
geo- *prefix* meaning earth, e.g. **geography**.
geography *n.* the study of the earth and what happens on it.
► Geography has various branches. Physical geography deals with land forms and scenery, and how they have evolved. Climatology studies weather and CLIMATE. Some geographers study SOILS, while others are concerned with how climate and soils interact with plants and animals.

Human geography deals with the interaction of people and their environments. Economic geography deals with natural resources, food production, the location of minerals and fuels and the distribution of industry. Urban geography is concerned with the location and growth of cities, and historical geography is the study of the geography of periods in the past. Because geographers are especially interested in the distribution of features on the earth's surface, their chief tool is the map.

geology *n.* the study of the earth's history as shown in the rocks. **geological** *adj.* **geologist** *n.*
► Two of the main branches of geology are petrology, the study of rocks, and mineralogy, the study of minerals. The earth has been in existence for billions of years and has undergone many changes. The result of these changes can be seen in the shape of the earth's surface, its mountains, valleys, oceans and rivers: in the fossilized remains of extinct animals, and in the presence of minerals such as coal, which is the compressed remains of primeval forests. All these things are studied by the geologist.
(*See* EARTH; EARTHQUAKE; FOSSIL; MINERALS; ROCKS).

geometry *n.* the mathematical study of lines, surfaces, angles and solids. **geometric** *adj.*
► Plane geometry deals with figures lying entirely in one plane (two-dimensional). Solid geometry deals with three-dimensional bodies, while spherical geometry deals with figures drawn on a spherical surface.

George, St.
An early Christian martyred in Palestine in A.D. 303. The old Greek

King George V delivering his Christmas broadcast – the first British monarch to do so – and starting a tradition which has continued to this day.

myth of dragon-killing is linked with him. Crusaders brought his story back to England, and he was made patron saint of England in 1350.

George (Kings of Great Britain)
Six British kings were called George.

George I (1660–1727) was a German ruler who inherited the British throne. JAMES I was his great grandfather.

George II (1683–1760) was the last British king to lead troops into battle. He reigned when Britain was winning Canada and India.

George III (1738–1820). His reign saw such decisive events as the American WAR OF INDEPENDENCE, the Napoleonic Wars, and the INDUSTRIAL REVOLUTION. But, though a dedicated ruler, George III suffered from attacks of madness, and from 1811 his son had to rule as Regent.

George IV (1762–1830) was important as a patron of art and architecture, but his lack of interest in government, and scandals in his private life, greatly lowered royal prestige.

George V (1865–1936) was a naval officer before he was king. He reigned during WORLD WAR I.

George VI (1895–1952) became king unexpectedly, on the abdication of his brother Edward VIII in 1936. But he proved dedicated and well-intentioned, a good national leader through the crises of WORLD WAR II, Indian independence and rapid social change at home.

GEOLOGICAL TERMS

caldera very large volcanic crater formed when the top of a volcano collapses.
core the innermost region of the earth.
crust the outer skin of the earth.
epicenter the point on the surface of the earth directly above the focus of an earthquake.
fault a crack in the crust of the earth caused by the movement of large masses of rock.
lava molten rock that flows from a volcano.
mantle the layer of the earth between the crust and the core.
Richter Scale scale used for measuring the strength of an earthquake.
tectonics the study of the structure of the earth.
volcano a hill or mountain formed when lava bursts through the surface of the earth.

Georgia (*abbrev.* **Ga.**)
Georgia is the largest state of the U.S.A. east of the Mississippi river. For many years the state depended on its cotton crop, grown on large plantations, with slave labor. During the American Civil War, Georgia was Confederate, and much of the state was destroyed by Union troops.

Today, Georgia is a thriving agricultural and industrial state. It is the nation's biggest supplier of poultry and peanuts. It makes textiles and produces lumber, cotton, tobacco and peaches. Atlanta is the capital and biggest city.

The eastern border of Georgia lies along the Atlantic Ocean. The northern part of the state is covered by the Appalachian Mountains.

The state was first explored by Spanish adventurers. Spain first claimed the area, but the English later made it a colony.

Georgian *adj.* belonging to the reigns of King George I-VI.
geranium *n.* popular name for two groups of plants. One group, found wild in woodlands and also cultivated in gardens, has pink, purple or blue flowers. The other group, with scarlet, pink or white flowers, is often grown indoors or in greenhouses.
gerbil *n.* a small rodent (gnawing animal), also known as a desert rat, and popular as a pet.
geriatrics *n.* branch of medicine concerned with the health of the aged.
germ *n.* a microbe, especially one that makes people ill.
► Many diseases are caused by living things so tiny that you can only see them through a microscope. These living things are germs. Germs include certain BACTERIA, VIRUSES, and some kinds of FUNGUS. Some germs get into the body with breathed-in air. Others can get in through a cut that is not clean.

Germany, East and **West** (German)
In 1945, Germany was occupied and divided into four zones under the Americans, British, French and Russians. BERLIN, the capital, was also split into four sectors. By 1948 the American, British and French zones had been joined together to form West Germany (German Federal Republic). But the Russian zone remained separate, with a Communist government. West Berlin, although surrounded by East Germany, became part of West Germany. But the Russian sector of East Berlin became the capital of East Germany (German Democratic Republic (DDR).

The northern part of Germany consists mostly of a broad plain, with generally infertile soils. The chief crops are potatoes and rye. The land rises in the south of both countries, although West Germany has a much larger area of uplands, including part of the ALPS in the far south. The uplands are warmer and often fertile and a great variety of crops are grown.

West Germany is chiefly an industrial nation and it has become western Europe's leading manufacturing country. The main industrial region was the Ruhr coalfield; the Ruhr is a tributary of the River RHINE. But today, many cities throughout West Germany have become major industrial centers. Before 1945, East Germany's economy was primarily agricultural. Since then, with Russian help, it has now become a leading industrial nation.

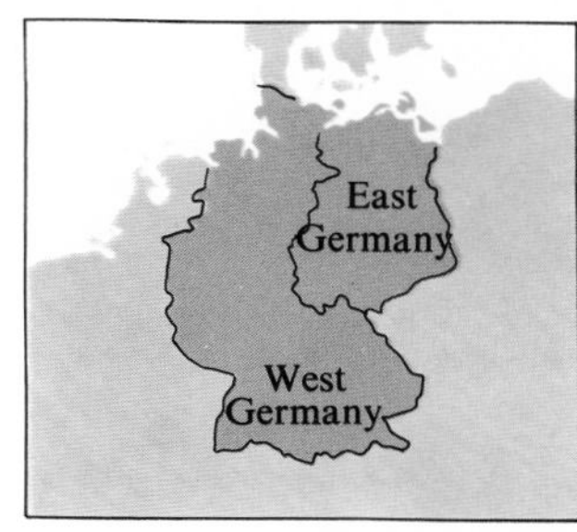

Germany, East
AREA: 41,770 SQ. MILES (108,178 SQ. KM)
POPULATION: 16,748,000
CAPITAL: EAST BERLIN
CURRENCY: DDR MARK
OFFICAL LANGUAGE: GERMAN

Germany, West
AREA: 95,981 SQ. MILES (248,577 SQ. KM)
POPULATION: 61,382,000
CAPITAL: BONN
CURRENCY: DEUTSCHMARK
OFFICIAL LANGUAGE: GERMAN

germinate *vb.* start to grow, especially of plants.

gesture *vb.* move the hand or head to show someone something. *She gestured toward the gate and everyone ran out. n.* an expressive movement.
get (past **got**, past part. **gotten**). *vb.* 1. gain, become or achieve something. *What will you do if you get rich?* 2. go. *Get out of my sight.*
get away with *vb.* avoid the result of something you have done or not done. *I did my work badly, but I will get away with it.*
get on *vb.* make progress.
get one's back up *vb.* to become angry.
get over *vb.* recover. *Penny was getting over the loss of her cat.*
get rid of *vb.* throw away, shake off, discard.
get-together *n.* a meeting, especially for special reasons.

Gettysburg, Battle of
The battle of Gettysburg was the most important battle of the Civil War. It was fought at the little town of Gettysburg, Pa. on July 1–3, 1863. The defeat of General Lee's Southern army was a turning point in the war. The Confederate forces lost 28,000 dead, wounded and missing; the Union forces lost about 23,000.
Today, the town of Gettysburg has many memorials to the battle. At the dedication of a national cemetery there in 1863, President Lincoln delivered his famous Gettysburg Address.

geyser (**guy**-*zer*) *n.* a natural hot spring from which hot water and steam erupt, often at regular intervals.

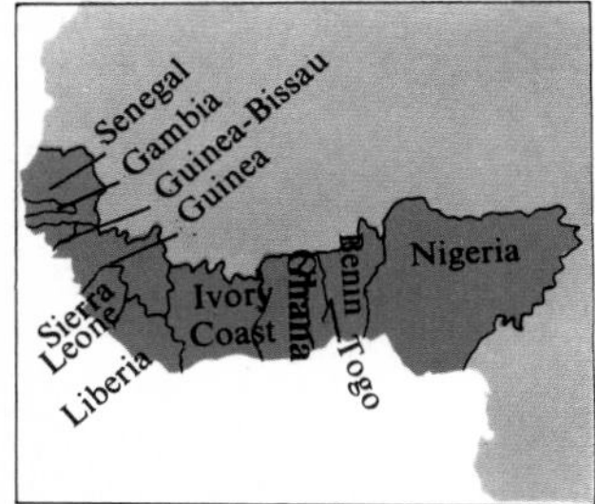

► Geysers occur in places where there has been recent volcanic activity and where there are very hot rocks not far from the surface. Often the passage through the rock is something like a long narrow tube where water collects. The water at the bottom becomes steam and rushes up the tube, forcing out the water above it. A spectacular jet of steam spouts into the air. When the pressure is relieved, the tube refills and the process is repeated. Geysers are found in Yellowstone National Park, Greenland and New Zealand.

Ghana (Ghanian)
Ghana is a republic in West Africa. Formerly called the Gold Coast, the country became independent from Britain, as Ghana, in 1957. Most people are farmers and Ghana is one of the world's main producers of COCOA.
AREA: 92,105 SQ. MILES (238,537 SQ. KM)
POPULATION: 12,413,000
CAPITAL: ACCRA
CURRENCY: CEDI
OFFICIAL LANGUAGE: ENGLISH

ghastly *adj.* horrible, terrifying.
ghetto *n.* once the Jewish quarter of a city; part of a city – especially slums – lived in by a particular group of people.
ghost *n.* the spirit of a dead person that some people believe walks at night.
giant *n.* a huge animal or plant.

Giant's Causeway
The Giant's Causeway is the name of a stretch of coast in County Antrim, Northern Ireland. It consists of thousands of hexagonal (six-sided) columns of a volcanic rock called basalt. It extends for about 3 miles (5 km) and is a great tourist attraction.

gibbon *n.* a long-armed, tailless ape.
giblets *pl. n.* liver, gizzard, etc., of poultry.

Gibraltar
Gibraltar is a British territory on a rocky peninsula in southern Spain. It is an important fortress and tourist center, the Barbary apes being a special attraction. Gibraltar has about 30,000 people and an area of 2½ sq. miles (6½ sq. km). Spain claims that it should take over Gibraltar.

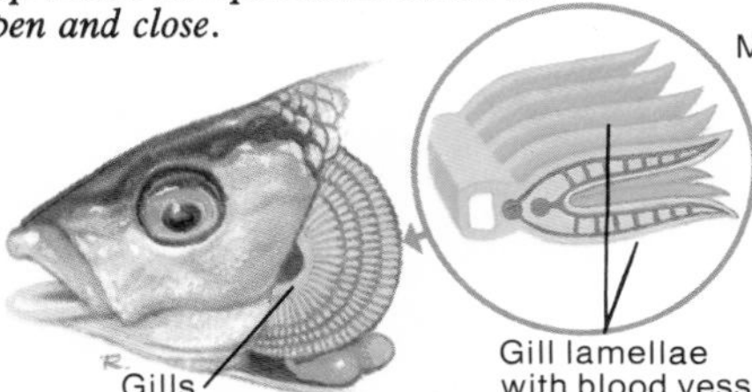

Gills lead from the back of the mouth cavity to the outside. Each of the openings to the outside is covered by a flap called the operculum which can open and close.

giddy *adj.* dizzy; thoughtless.
gift *n.* a present, something that is given to someone. **gifted** *adj.* talented.
gig ("g" as in *give*) *n.* 1. light, two wheeled horse-drawn carriage. 2. public jazz, pop or rock performance.
gigantic (jye-**gan**-*tic*) *adj.* very large indeed.
giggle *n.* & *vb.* laugh in a silly way.

Gilbert and Sullivan
Gilbert and Sullivan were the creators of England's most famous comic OPERAS, including *HMS Pinnafore* (1878), *The Pirates of Penzance* (1879) and *The Mikado* (1885). Sir William Gilbert (1836–1911) wrote the stories and lyrics. Sir Arthur Sullivan (1842–1900) composed the music.

gill ("g" as in *give*) *n.* a part on each side of a fish through which it breathes.
► FISH, CRABS and many other water animals breathe by forcing water past gills. Gills are flat or feathery pieces of thin "skin". They take oxygen from water and give out carbon dioxide waste. Many fish have hard gill covers to protect their soft gills.

gild *v.* put on a thin coating of gold.
gimmick *n.* new and showy device. *Her kitchen was fitted with all the latest gimmicks.* method of attracting attention, especially for publicity purposes.
gin *n.* 1. snare, trap (for animals). 2. colorless alcoholic beverage made from grain flavored with juniper.
ginger 1. *adj.* & *n.* a reddish-brown color. *She has ginger hair.* 2. *n.* the hot-tasting root of a plant, used as flavoring for ginger ale, gingerbread, etc.
gingerly *adj.* delicately, timidly.
gingham ("g" as in *give*) *n.* cotton cloth with checked or striped pattern.
giraffe *n.* an African animal with very long legs and neck.
► The giraffe is the world's tallest animal. With its immensely long neck and legs, it stands over 16 ft. (5 meters) high. It has a dark-spotted orange-red skin and a long tufted tail which acts as a fly whisk. Giraffes live on the dry African plains and feed on tree leaves, especially acacia leaves. They defend themselves by kicking powerfully.

girder *n.* beam, usually of steel.
girl *n.* a female child; a young woman. **girlish** *adj.*

gist (*jist*) *n.* general meaning of a subject.
give *vb.* hand something over to someone else without payment.
give back *vb.* return something to someone.
give in *vb.* agree to something unwillingly. *Bill kept asking for another ice cream, and at last his father gave in.*

give out *vb*. announce, distribute. *Can you give out the programs?*
give up *vb*. stop doing something. *My uncle will give up smoking on New Year's Day*.
gizzard *n*. a bird's second stomach used for grinding food.
glacier *n*. body of ice that moves down valleys under the force of gravity. (Ice sheets are even larger bodies of ice). *Glaciers have carved much of the world's most impressive mountain scenery*.
glad *adj*. pleased, happy.
gladiator *n*. a man who fought, often to the death, for the entertainment of spectators in ancient Rome.
► Many gladiators were criminals, prisoners of war or slaves. Some fought with a sword and shield. Others had a three-pronged spear and a net. Most fights ended when one gladiator killed the other. The winner would spare the loser's life if the crowd waved handkerchiefs.

glamour *n*. alluring charm, often of a false kind.
glance *vb*. look briefly at something. *He glanced at the newspaper and then put it aside*. *n*. a brief look.
gland *n*. an organ in the body which makes and secretes substances needed by the body.
► There are two types of gland: *exocrine* and *endocrine*. Exocrine glands release their product through ducts (tubes) either into the intestines or on to the body's surface: tear, saliva, and sweat glands are all examples of exocrine glands. Endocrine glands discharge their substances, called HORMONES, directly into the blood-stream. Hormones influence the growth and development of the body. One important endocrine gland is the THYROID; its hormone controls the rate at which the body uses oxygen and food.

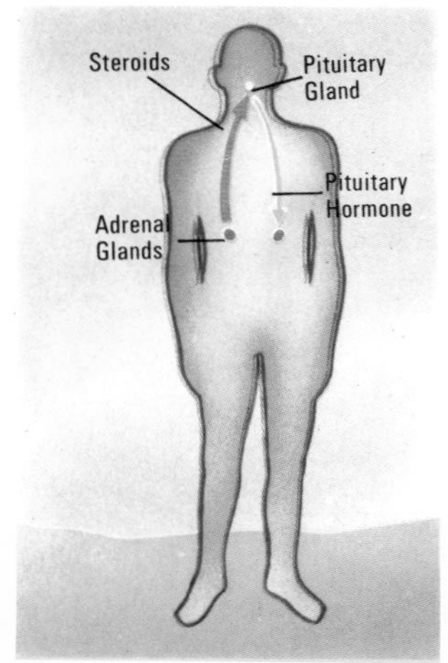

glare 1. *vb*. look angrily at someone. 2. *n*. a strong continuous light.

Glasgow
This is Scotland's largest city. Nearly 800,000 people live in it. Glasgow stands on the River Clyde in southern SCOTLAND. The city makes ships, iron, steel, whisky and chemicals. Big ships sail in and out along the river.

glass *n*. 1. a hard, brittle material which can usually be seen through. 2. anything made of glass, such as a tumbler. 3. a mirror.
► Glass is one of the most useful materials of all, giving us not only windows, mirrors and containers, but also glasses, scientific LENSES, ornaments and, in fiberglass, a material strong enough for the hulls of boats. It is made from sand, soda and lime, fused together at great heat. Shapes such as bottles are made by blowing air into tubes of hot glass. Decorative glass can be etched, engraved, or stamped with color.
Window glass is made by drawing a thin film of glass vertically from the furnace. Polished *plate* glass for high-quality work such as store fronts can be made in two ways. One is by rolling a continuous ribbon of molten glass horizontally and then grinding and polishing it smooth. The other is by floating the molten glass on a flat bed of molten tin.
After all the shaping processes, the glass is carefully repeated and cooled slowly. This *annealing* process strengthens the glass.

glasses *pl. n*. spectacles; lenses in frames to help you see better.
glaze 1. *n*. a mixture coated on pottery to give it a shiny surface. 2. *vb*. fit with glass or windows; coat pottery with glaze. **glazier** *n*. a person who glazes windows.
glean *vb*. gather corn left by harvesters; pick up facts here and there.
glen *n*. (*Sc*) valley.

Glenn, John Herschel
John Glenn (1921–) was the first American to orbit the earth. On February 20, 1962, he became a national hero when he circled the earth three times in *Friendship* 7. The flight lasted 4 hours 46 minutes and gave a great boost to American space development, leading up to the eventual landing on the moon.
Glenn later entered Democratic politics.

glide *vb*. move very smoothly.
glider *n*. an aircraft that flies without an engine.
► Gliding AIRCRAFT slide down through air like sleds sliding down a snowy slope. If the air is rising as fast as the craft is falling, the glider may stay at the same level above the ground. If the air is rising at a faster rate, the aircraft may actually climb.
Gliders called sailplanes have long narrow wings. The upper side of each wing bulges slightly upwards. The wing's lower side is almost flat. As the sailplane moves forward, air rushing over the wing must travel farther than air rushing under the wing. So the air above gets more thinly spread than the air below. The wing is sucked up into the thin air above, and pushed up by the "thick" air below. This gives the glider "lift". Some sailplanes gain so much lift that they sink through still air more slowly than thistledown or soap bubbles.
glimmer *vb*. & *n*. faint flickering light.
glitter *vb*. shine brightly and reflect light.
global *adj*. worldwide; general.
globe *n*. an object shaped like a ball, especially a map of the world shaped that way.
gloom *n*. dark, dismal; depression of the spirits. *The news filled him with gloom*. **gloomy** *adj*. dark, sullen.
glory *n*. splendor, fame; happiness of heaven. **glorious** *adj*. majestic; delightful.
gloss *n*. 1. smooth shining coating. *Gloss paint*. **glossy** *adj*. 2. *vb*. to cover up (an error, fault, etc.).
glossary *n*. a list, like a short dictionary, of special words used in a book.
glove *n*. a covering for the hand.
glow *vb*. shine with a bright, steady light.
glowworm *n*. a beetle whose wingless female emits a greenish light.
► The male glowworm has wings and looks like an ordinary beetle. The female has no wings and looks like a beetle grub. It is the females which produce special chemicals that glow with a cold, green light. At night this guides the flying males to the females, which crawl on the ground. Young glowworms live in or on the soil and feed by sucking blood from snails and slugs. A fully grown glowworm may never eat.

glucose *n*. a sweet substance that occurs widely in nature.
glue *n*. & *vb*. a sticky substance used for joining (gluing) things together.
► People make glue from the skins or bones of animals, or the skins, scales, bones and heads of fish. First, they wash the ingredients, then they cook them in water. Cooking breaks down the PROTEINS in the ingredients and turns them into glue. All substances used for sticking things together are called adhesives. The most powerful include a plastic "glue" called epoxy resin.
glum *adj*. gloomy, morose.
glut *n*. too great a supply.
glutton *n*. a very greedy person. **gluttony** *n*.

glycerine *n.* colorless, odorless, liquid alcohol, used in the making of perfume, cosmetics, explosives, antifreeze mixtures, and in medicine.
gnat (*nat*) *n.* a general name for any small, thin, two-winged insect with long delicate legs, such as the mosquito.
gnaw(*naw*) *vb.* chew at. *Dogs love to gnaw bones.*
gnome (*nome*) *n.* a small goblin that lives under the ground.
gnu (*new*) *n.* a large African oxlike antelope.
► Antelopes are generally graceful, but the gnu, or wildebeest, with its thick neck, long face, small eyes and heavy horns, often appears ugly and awkward.

go (past **went**) *vb.* move from one place to another, travel, depart, turn, work, function, etc.
goal (rhymes with *hole*) *n.* 1. the posts between which a ball must be sent in some games; points scored by doing this. 2. something you are trying to achieve or some place you are trying to reach.
goat *n.* an animal with horns, related to sheep.
► Its beard and strong smell distinguish the male goat from a sheep. Wild goats, found in the Middle East and central Asia, are agile, surefooted creatures. They live in herds and eat grass and leaves. Domestic goats are descended from a Persian species.

gobble *n.* & *vb.* 1. eat rapidly and greedily. 2. make the noise of a turkey.

Gobi
The Gobi is a large desert in central ASIA. It occupies most of Mongolia and part of northern China. It is almost uninhabited apart from a few wandering Mongolian tribes. The Gobi Desert has hot summers and cold winters.

goblin *n.* a legendary ugly and usually evil spirit or fairy.
god *n.* a supreme being that is worshipped because people believe that it has control over their lives.
► The ancient Egyptians, Babylonians, and others believed that whole families of gods controlled the world. Hindus, ancient Greeks, Romans and Celts believed in the same kinds of gods, but gave them different names. They also believed that one god was more powerful than the rest. The chief god of the Greeks was Zeus. The Romans called him Jupiter.
Meanwhile some people began believing that there was just one god. This idea gave rise to the great RELIGIONS of JUDAISM, CHRISTIANITY, and ISLAM.
Ancient peoples believed that gods punished people they disliked and rewarded those who worshiped them and offered presents. Cruel people like the AZTECS believed that only sacrifices of human lives kept the sun rising day after day. People made special buildings called temples in honor of different gods. Each temple had its priests who served the temple god.

godchild (**goddaughter, godson**). *n.* one for whom one acts as sponsor at a baptism, the sponsor being a **godparent** (**godmother** or **godfather**).
goddess *n.* a female god.
godly *adj.* pious.

Goethe, Johann Wolfgang Von
A German writer (1749–1832), Goethe was a novelist, poet and playwright, as well as an artist, statesman and scientist. His masterpiece was *Faust*: the story of a man who sells his soul to the Devil. His work began the Romantic movement.

go for *vb.* attack (usually animals).
goggles *pl. n.* large glasses that protect the eyes from water, wind or at work.

The domestic goat.

Gogh, Vincent van, see **Van Gogh**
gold *n.* a precious, shiny yellow metal used for coinage, jewelry, etc. (symbol – *Au*). **golden** *adj.*
► Gold is a beautiful yellow metal that never goes rusty. It is so soft that you can beat it into thin sheets, or pull it out into a wire.
Thin veins of gold can be found in cracks in certain rocks. It was left there by hot gases and liquids rising from deep underground. If water washes out the gold, lumps called nuggets may collect in the beds of streams and rivers. Half of the world's gold is mined in just one part of South Africa. Much of the rest comes from the U.S.S.R.
Because gold is beautiful and scarce, it is also very valuable. Most of the world's gold is kept in brick-shaped bars in banks. People make jewelry from gold mixed with other substances to make it harder. But gold is useful too. Dentists sometimes put gold fillings in people's teeth.

An Inca gold puma.

golden *adj.* the color of gold.

Golden Fleece
In Greek legend, this was a golden sheepskin which hung on a tree in Colchis, a land by the Black Sea. A fierce dragon guarded the tree. JASON and his crew of Argonauts sailed in the ship Argo to win the fleece. First Jason had to fight soldiers who sprang up from the dragon's teeth where they had been thrown on the ground. Princess Medea of Colchis then put the dragon to sleep so that Jason could take the fleece.

golden wedding *n.* 50th wedding anniversary.
goldfish *n.* an ornamental fish descended from a type of carp in China.

Gold Rush
In the 1800s, the discovery of GOLD often brought a flood of prospectors into undeveloped territory; towns sometimes sprang up overnight. The gold rushes of California (1849) and the Yukon (1897) were the most famous.

golf *n.* a game in which a small ball is driven by a club (stick) from hole to hole. **golfer** *n.*
► Each player uses golf clubs to hit a small, hard ball around a course

peppered with sandy patches or other obstacles. The course has nine or 18 holes in well-mown grass areas called greens. The golfer hits his ball into each hole in turn. The object of the game is to complete each hole in the fewest number of strkes.

Goliath
Goliath of Gath was a giant in the Bible. He was a champion of the Philistines, and challenged the Israelites to send a warrior against him in single combat. DAVID took up the challenge, and felled Goliath with a stone from his sling. The story of David and Goliath is told in the Book of Samuel.

gondola *n.* a narrow boat, with curved prow and stern, used on the canals in Venice. **gondolier** *n.*
gone *vb.* past part. of **go**.
gong *n.* metal disk giving a ringing note when struck.
good (**better, best**) *adj.* 1. of high quality. *I'm reading a very good book.* 2. well-behaved. *Be a good girl.*
good-bye *interj.* farewell; an expression of good wishes on parting.
Good Friday *n.* the Friday before Easter, observed as the anniversary of the Crucifixion of Jesus.
goodness *n.* being good, virtue, excellence.
goods *pl. n.* 1. things that are bought and sold. 2. things that are carried on trains or trucks. *They took the goods off the truck and put them on the train.*
goose *n.* (plural **geese**) a large, web-footed water bird of the duck family.
► Geese usually live in flocks and spend much of their time on land, feeding off grass and other plants. There are two main groups: gray geese and black geese, both found in cold northern zones. The domestic goose comes from a gray species, the Gray Lag.

gooseberry *n.* the edible fruit of the gooseberry bush.
gopher *n.* burrowing rodent (gnawing animal) of North America.
gore *vb.* pierce or wound with horns.
gorge 1. *n.* deep narrow valley. 2. *vb.* eat greedily; stuff to capacity.
gorgeous *adj.* magnificent, splendid; marvelous. *Gorgeous gown.*
gorilla *n.* the largest of the apes.
► Gorillas are found in the forests of equatorial Africa. Gorillas, up to 6 ft. (180 cm) tall, walk on all fours; they live in family groups and spend most of their time on the ground looking for food such as roots, leaves and fruit. At night, they sleep in nests, built of branches or undergrowth. In spite of their massive size, gorillas are peaceful and will attack only if provoked.

gosling *n.* a young goose.
gospel *n.* one of the four books of the New Testament containing accounts of the life and teachings of Jesus.
gossip *vb.* chatter about other people and what they are doing. *n.* idle talk.
got *vb.* past and past part. of **get**.

Gothic Art and **Architecture**
Gothic ARCHITECTURE was the main church style in Western Europe throughout the later MIDDLE AGES. It started in Normandy and Burgundy, and its typical features were tall pillars and spires, pointed arches, flying buttresses and rib vaulting. Chartres Cathedral is a famous example. In England the style lasted from 1200–1575, but there was also a "Gothic Revival" in the 1800s, when it was used for many public buildings. Gothic ART was mainly concerned with the decoration of the Gothic churches, with stone carvings, tapestries, wall paintings and decorative iron work.

go through *vb.* examine carefully.

Goths
The Goths were a Germanic people, probably from southern Sweden, who invaded the Roman Empire after A.D. 200. Pushed west by the HUNS, one branch (Visigoths) sacked Rome in A.D. 410, and finally set up a kingdom in Spain which lasted until the Arab conquest of A.D. 711. The others (Ostrogoths) reached Italy later, and were absorbed into the existing population.
► Gothic is a style of architecture which developed in France in the 12th century and was the main style until the 16th century. Gothic architecture used pointed arches, vaulted roofs and flying buttresses. Famous examples are Notre Dame, Chartres and Rheims cathedrals in France, Westminster Abbey and Canterbury Cathedral in England.

FORMS OF GOVERNMENT

System	Rule by
anarchy	harmony, without law
aristocracy	a privileged order
autocracy	one man, absolutely
bureaucracy	officials
democracy	the people
diarchy	two rulers or authorities
ergatocracy	the workers
ethnocracy	race or ethnic group
gerontocracy	old men
matriarchy	a mother (or mothers)
meritocracy	those in power on ability
monarchy	hereditary head of state
oligarchy	small exclusive class
patriarchy	male head of family
plutocracy	the wealthy
technocracy	technical experts
theocracy	divine guidance

gotten *vb.* past part. of **get**.
goulash *n.* highly seasoned Hungarian stew.
gourd *n.* large fleshy fruit of the cucumber family.
govern *vb.* rule, control people or a country.
government *n.* the people who rule or govern a country.
gown *n.* a woman's dress; a long flowing garment.

Goya
Francisco de Goya (1746–1828) was a Spanish painter and engraver. His work made sharp criticisms of life in Spain at that time. His portraits of royalty barely hide his contempt of Spain's ruling family.

grab *vb.* seize quickly and roughly. *n.* an attempt to seize.
graceful *adj.* pleasing movement or shape.
grade *vb.* arrange according to quality etc. *n.* rank, class, division.
gradient *n.* slope of a road, railway, etc.
gradual *adj.* happening slowly. *The change was so gradual we hardly noticed it.*
graduate *vb.* get a degree or diploma. *n.* holder of a degree.
graffito *n.* (plural **graffiti** *graf-**fee**-tee*) words or drawings scribbled on a wall.
graft *vb.* cut part of one plant and join it to another so that it grows. *n.* (surgical) transplant.
grain *n.* 1. the small, hard seeds of all plants like wheat, rice and maize. 2. the natural pattern in wood.
gram (or **gramme**) *n.* a small unit for measuring weight. *There are 1000 grams in a kilogram.*
grammar *n.* the rules for using words and putting them together.
granary *n.* a building where grain is stored.
grand *adj.* important, splendid.

Grand Canyon
The Colorado River carved this deep gash in the earth's surface. The canyon crosses a desert in Arizona. The canyon is about 217 miles (350 km) long. It is up to 13 miles (20 km) across, and more than 1 mile (2 km) deep. This is the deepest gorge anywhere on land.

grandchild (**grand-daughter son**) *n.* the child of one's own child.
grandfather *n.* the father of a mother or father, also **granddad, grandpa**.
grandmother *n.* the mother of a mother or father. also **grandma, granny**.

grandstand *n.* rows of seats at a sports ground, usually roofed.

granite *n.* a hard rock made largely of crystals of quartz and feldspar.
► Quartz is transparent, like glass. Feldspar is pink, white or gray. Granite also has specks of dark minerals in it.

Granite was once a mass of hot, melted rock underground. As the rock cooled it hardened. Then movements of the earth's crust forced it up to the surface. The weather very slowly breaks down granite into sand and clay.

Builders use granite when they need a hard, strong stone. People also use granite to make polished stone monuments because they last longer than those made of LIMESTONE.

grant *vb.* allow, give. *He was granted a pension. n.* something granted, especially money.

Grant, Ulysses Simpson
Ulysses Simpson Grant (1822–85) was the 18th president of the United States. He became famous as a successful Union general in the Civil War. At first Grant's troops suffered heavy casualties, but they were finally able to push back the Confederate army. On April 9, 1865, General Robert E. Lee surrendered to Grant at Appomattox Courthouse.

grape *n.* a green or purple berry that grows in bunches on a vine.
► Most grapes are used to make wine but some are cultivated as dessert fruit and some are dried and turned into currants, RAISINS and sultanas. Grapes mostly grow in warm temperate lands such as the Mediterranean zone, California, South Africa and Australia and South America.

grapefruit *n.* a large yellow citrus fruit, often eaten at breakfast.

Vines are grown in warm places such as California and around the Mediterranean. The grapes are hand picked.

graph (rhymes with **laugh**) *n.* a diagram used to show how numbers and amounts compare.
► A pie graph shows the amounts of different things as different sized slices cut in a pie. Bar graphs show different amounts as long and short bars. Line graphs show temperature and other changes by a line that rises and falls.

grapple 1. *n.* a clutching instrument. 2. *vb.* seize, grip, fight.

grasp *vb.* hold tightly; understand. **grasping** *adj.* greedy.

grass *n.* a plant with thin green leaves grown on lawns and in fields.
► Grass is a common flowering plant found all over the world. Grasses have long narrow leaves and dull flowers with no petals, bright color or scent; their stems are nearly always soft and hollow. There are about 5,000 species of grass. Some are vital to man: for example, all cereals such as wheat, rice and oats are cultivated grasses.

grasshopper *n.* a small jumping insect which chirps.
► The grasshopper is related to the CRICKET. Grasshoppers live among grass and flowers near the ground and feed entirely on plants. Although most species can fly, they usually move by jumping and their hind legs are long and powerful. Many grasshoppers have a distinctive song, made by rubbing their back legs against their wings.

grass roots *n.* (in politics) at the local level. *States often pass new tax laws that start at the grass roots.*

grate 1. *n.* iron frame in a fireplace. 2. *vb.* produce harsh noise by rubbing something on a rough surface.

grateful *adj.* feeling of thanks for something. *She was very grateful to the nurses who looked after her in the hospital.*

grave 1. *n.* a hole in the ground in which a dead body is buried. 2. *adj.* serious, solemn.

gravel *n.* small stones used in the making of roads and paths.

graveyard *n.* a place where people are buried, near a church.

gravity *n.* 1. solemnity. 2. the force that pulls things together. *Gravity makes things fall.*
► The force of gravitation applies to everything in the universe. NEWTON's law of gravitation says that any two objects are pulled toward each other with a force that is directly proportional to the product of their masses and inversely proportional to the square of the distance between them. In other words, the bigger their masses and the closer they are, the more strongly they are pulled together. This is why the earth pulls us and everything on it with a strong force. To escape from this pull we need to build up a very high speed with powerful rockets about 25,000 mph (40,000 km/h). But spacecraft can be sent into orbit around the earth at speeds less than this. The speed necessary to keep the craft in orbit depends on the height of the orbit. The higher the orbit, the less the craft is influenced by gravity, and therefore the lower the speed needed to counter gravity. In the same way, the moon is held in its

Grass snakes live in damp places including river banks and ditches.

Grasses have thin, wiry roots. The flowers are arranged in groups called spikelets.

Gravity keeps our earth circling the sun, and the moon circling the earth.

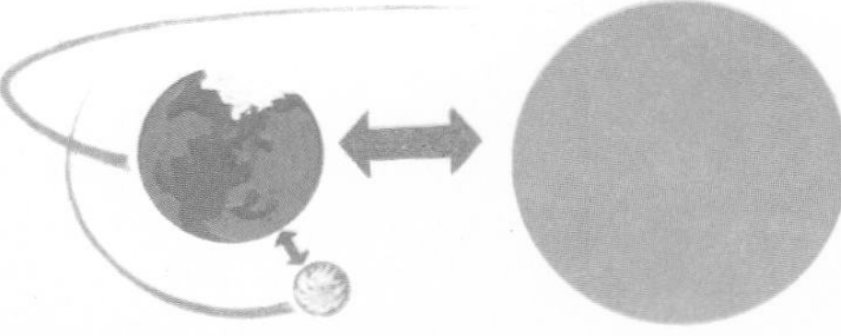

orbit around the earth by gravity. And it is gravitation that keeps the planets in their orbits around the sun.

gravy *n.* hot sauce made with meat juices.

gray *n.* & *adj.* color midway between black and white.

graze 1. *vb.* eat growing grass; put out to pasture. 2. *n.* & *vb.* scrape lightly in passing.

grease *n.* any thick oil substance. *vb.* lubricate.

great *adj.* 1. large or heavy. *That's a great deal of money.* 2. important or famous. *He was a truly great man.*

Great Barrier Reef
This is the longest CORAL reef in the world. It measures about 1,250 miles (about 2,000 km) from end to end. The reef stands in the sea off the northeast coast of Australia. Most of the top of the reef lies just under water and is a danger to ships.

The Great Barrier Reef is built of hard limy stone. Most of it was produced by millions of tiny, soft-bodied creatures related to the sea anemone. In the 1960s, part of the reef was destroyed by crown-of-thorns starfish. These feed on the little reef builders.

Great Bear *n.* a constellation (*Ursa Major*) in the northern sky, made up of seven stars, "the Plough."

Great Bear Lake
Canada's biggest fresh-water lake, it covers an area of 12,275 sq. miles (31,080 sq. km) in the Northwest Territory. It is frozen for about nine months of the year. Bears inhabit the surrounding woods.

Great Britain (British)
The largest island in the BRITISH ISLES, Great Britain comprises the mainland of ENGLAND, SCOTLAND and WALES, together with their offshore islands. The term, Great Britain, does not usually include the Channel Islands and the Isle of Man, because these islands have their own governments.

Great Britain (or simply Britain) is also sometimes used as the name for the larger United Kingdom of Great Britain and Northern Ireland. In this case, the Channel Islands and the Isle of Man are included. The capital of the United Kingdom is LONDON, but regional capitals include Belfast (Northern Ireland), CARDIFF (Wales) and EDINBURGH (Scotland).

Great Dane *n.* large, strong dog of German origin, despite its name. It is quiet and good-tempered but can be very fierce and so makes a good guard dog.

Great Dividing Range
A mountain range extending throughout eastern Australia. The mountains of TASMANIA are also part of the range. The highest peak is Mount Kosciusko at 7,316 ft. (2,230 meters).

The Greeks were famous for their pottery, which they decorated with scenes from myths and everyday life.

Great Lakes
This is the world's largest group of freshwater lakes. They are a bit larger than the state of Oregon. Lake Michigan lies in the UNITED STATES. Lakes Superior, Erie, Huron and Ontario are shared by the United States and CANADA. The largest lake of all is Superior. The lakes were formed when a huge sheet of ice melted 18,000 years ago.

Rivers and canals connect the lakes to each other and to the Atlantic Ocean. Ships can reach the sea from lake ports that lie 1,000 miles (1,600 km) inland. Lots of factories are built around the lakes to take advantage of the water supply. Most of the goods that the factories produce are taken to other parts of the country by ship.

Great Wall of China
More than 2,000 years ago the first emperor of CHINA, Ch'in Shi Huang Ti, built this wall to keep out China's enemies from the north. The Great Wall is the longest wall in the world. It stretches for 2,130 miles (3,460 km) from the Yellow Sea in the east to Asia in the west. It is the only man-made structure on earth that is visible from space.

The wall is made from earth and stone. Watchtowers were built every 200 yds. (180 meters) along it. Chinese sentries sent warning signals from the towers if anyone attacked the wall. The signal was smoke by day and a fire at night.

Grecian *adj.* & *n.* Greek.

Greco, El
The nickname of Domenico Theotokopoulos (1541–1614), a famous artist. Born on Crete, he worked mainly in Spain, and is best known for his religious paintings. His style involves vivid colors, and twisted, elongated shapes.

Greece, Ancient
Greece is the birthplace of Western civilization but it was never united under one ruler until it was conquered in its decline. The earliest Greek civilization was the MYCENAEAN, a tribal Bronze Age culture which had links with the MINOAN CIVILIZATION of Crete. It flourished from 1600 to 1200 B.C., but was destroyed by waves of invaders. A "dark age" followed, lasting to about 800 B.C.

During this "dark age" period many people from the mainland set up cities on the coast of Asia Minor, and on the mainland the great "city states" emerged (ATHENS, SPARTA, Thebes). But the mountainous terrain prevented any movement towards national unity. Instead the Greeks took to the sea, and from about 750 B.C. became a great trading people, with an economy based on olives, grapes and imported grain. Colonies grew up at trading points throughout the MEDITERRANEAN and the Black Sea. Some of them became very rich and important.

All these Greek cities were linked by their common language, beliefs and traditions, but they often fought with one another. The earliest city states were ruled by kings. But in many of them the growth of wealth spread political power wider; first to rich landowners and merchants, and then to the people as a whole. This DEMOCRACY was possible because of the small size of the "states": everyone could meet in one place to debate public affairs.

Greek culture reached its peak after 600 B.C., with a flourishing Greek literature and the beginnings of European science and philosophy. The threat of Persian conquest was beaten off, after 500 B.C., with famous victories at Marathon, Salamis and Platea. Later, quarrels between the city states led to Greek decline. In long struggles, the power of Athens was destroyed by Sparta, then Sparta's by Thebes, until Macedonia (the country to the north) was able to extend her power over all Greece (under her Greek-speaking ruler Philip II and his son ALEXANDER THE GREAT). Finally, in 146 B.C., Greece was annexed by ROME; although Greek culture survived and in fact dominated the later Roman Empire.

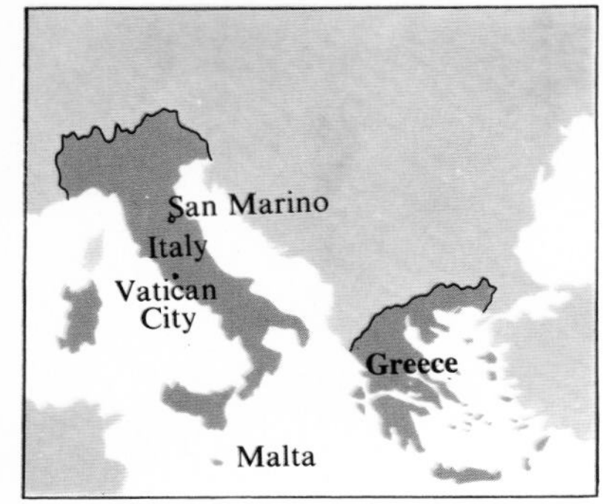

Greece (Greek)
Greece is a republic in southeastern Europe which attracts over 2 million visitors every year. Many go to the country to see the magnificent ruins of ancient Greece. They can also enjoy the hot dry summers and mild winters, while traveling on the mainland or around the many beautiful islands in the MEDITERRANEAN SEA. The largest island is CRETE.

Agriculture employs more than half of the working population. But two-thirds of the land is mountainous and many soils are thin and infertile. Processing farm products and manufacturing are now important in the cities and towns, including ATHENS, Piraeus and Salonika. Greece also obtains much revenue from its large merchant navy.

From 1453 to 1822 Greece was part of the Turkish Ottoman empire. After defeating Turkey in the Greek war of independence, Greece became a monarchy in 1830. Apart from two breaks (1924–35 and 1941–44), it remained a constitutional monarchy until 1973, when it became a republic.
AREA: 50,947 SQ. MILES (113,944 SQ. KM)
POPULATION: 9,665,000
CAPITAL: ATHENS
CURRENCY: DRACHMA
OFFICIAL LANGUAGE: GREEK

greedy *adj*. selfishly fond of food, money or other things. **greed** *n*.
green 1. *n*. & *adj*. a color like that of grass or leaves. 2. *n*. an open, grassy area.
greenbelt *n*. area of countryside around a town where building is restricted.
greenhorn *n*. someone without much experience.
greenhouse *n*. a building with a glass roof and glass walls in which plants are grown.

Greenland
The world's largest island, Greenland, in the North Atlantic Ocean, covers 840,000 sq. miles (2,175,600 sq. km). Administratively, Greenland is a county of Denmark. About 85 percent of Greenland is buried by a vast ice sheet, which is up to 10,000 ft. (3,050 meters) thick.
AREA: 840,050 SQ. MILES (2,175,600 SQ. KM)
POPULATION: 50,000
CAPITAL: GODTHAAB
CURRENCY: DANISH KRONE
OFFICIAL LANGUAGES: DANISH, GREENLANDIC.

Greenwich
Greenwich is a borough in southeast London, on the south bank of the Thames. It is the site of the Royal Naval College and the Royal Greenwich Observatory. The Prime Meridian (0° of longitude) passes through the Observatory. Greenwich Mean Time (GMT) is used to calculate the exact time all over the world.

greet *vb*. welcome. *She always greets me with a kiss*. **greeting** *n*.
grenade *n*. small explosive shell thrown by hand.
grew *vb*. past of **grow**.
greyhound *n*. fast-running dog with a slender body and long powerful legs. Greyhounds are used for hunting game and for racing. In a greyhound race, the dogs chase a mechanical hare around an oval track.
grief (rhymes with *reef*) *n*. great sadness. **grieve** *vb*.

Grieg, Edvard
A major Norwegian composer (1843–1907), often inspired by country songs and dances. He won fame in 1876 with his music for the play *Peer Gynt*.

grim *adj*. severe, without joy.
grime *n*. dirt; squalor.

Grimm, Brothers
Jakob Ludwig Grimm (1785–1863) and Wilhelm Karl Grimm (1786–1859) became famous for their book of *Grimm's Fairy Tales*. These were tales the brothers heard German parents tell their children.

Two of the most famous stories are *Hansel and Gretel* and *Cinderella*.

grin *n*. & *vb*. wide smile.
grind *vb*. 1. crush to a powder. *They grind wheat into flour at the mill*. 2. sharpen.
grip *vb*. & *n*. hold firmly.
grit *n*. 1. tiny pieces of stone or sand. 2. courage; staying power.
grizzly bear *n*. large bear from North America.
► The grizzly bear gets its name from the *grizzled* (gray) tips on its dark fur. Grizzly bears eat both plants and animals, including fish. Once common, the grizzly is now comparatively rare.

groan *vb*. make a deep sound of pain or sorrow. *n*. groaning sound.
grocer *n*. a person who sells meats, produce, household supplies, etc.
groom 1. *vb*. & *n*. brush and clean a horse; a person who looks after a horse for someone else. 2. *n*. a bridegroom.
groove *n*. a long, narrow cut in a surface.
grope *vb*. feel one's way by touch, fumble.
gross 1. *adj*. large; fat; disgusting. 2. *adj*. (of prices, weights, etc.) including all items. 3. *n*. 12 dozen (144).
grotesque *adj*. distorted style of decorative art using fantastic human and animal shapes.
grotto *n*. cave, often artificial.
ground 1. *n*. the surface of the earth. 2. *vb*. past of **grind**.
group *n*. a number of people or things gathered together or belonging together. *vb*. form or fall into a group.
grouse 1. *n*. large game bird from the Northern Hemisphere which usually nests on the ground. There are about 30 species, mostly gray,

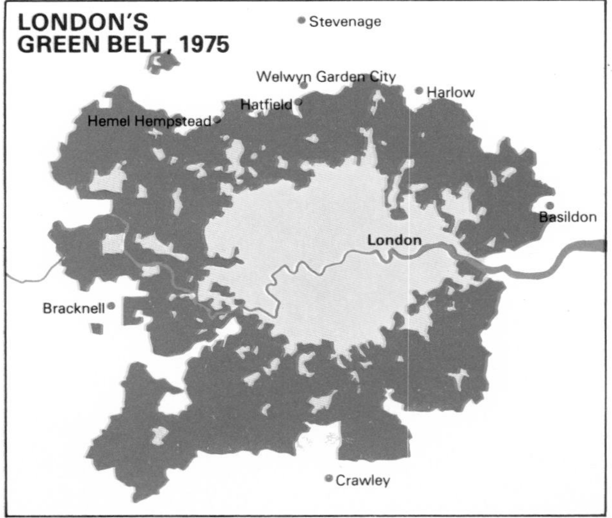

brown or black in color. 2. *vb.* grumble.

grow (past **grew** past part. **grown**) *vb.* 1. become larger or taller. 2. live (of plants). 3. become. *They are growing old gracefully.*

growl *n.* & *vb.* a low, angry noise, as made by a dog.

grown-up *n.* an[illegible]rson who is an adult.

growth *n.* 1. the act of growing. 2. an abnormal tumor in the body.

grow up *vb.* stop being a child, attain maturity, become adult.

grub *n.* 1. the larva stage of an insect. 2. (*slang*) food. **grubby** *adj.* dirty.

grudge *vb.* envy, agree to do something unwillingly. *She grudged paying for it.*

grumble *vb.* complain in a cross way, protest. *n.* murmur, complaint.

grunt *vb.* & *n.* (make) a low noise like a pig.

guano *n.* rich manure composed of the dung of seabirds.

guarantee *n.* a promise to do something, especially to mend or replace something which goes wrong after it has been bought. *vb.* promise, answer for, secure.

guard *vb.* protect someone or something. *The police will guard the exhibition of jewels. n.* a person who guards things.

Guatemala (Guatemalan)
Guatemala is a republic in CENTRAL AMERICA. This tropical country produces coffee. The people are mostly Indians or they are of mixed Indian and Spanish descent.
AREA: 42,042 SQ. MILES (108,889 SQ. KM)
POPULATION: 7,436,000
CAPITAL: GUATEMALA CITY
CURRENCY: QUETZAL
OFFICIAL LANGUAGE: SPANISH

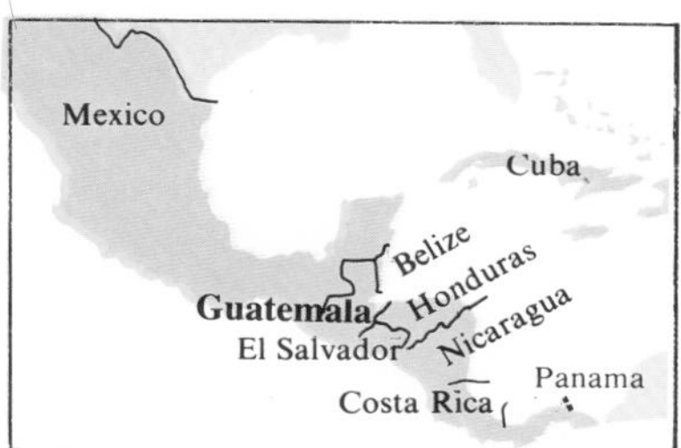

guerrilla *n.* a fighter who does not belong to a country's organized army.

guess *vb.* & *n.* form an opinion without really knowing the facts. *He didn't know how to spell the word, so he made a guess.*

guest *n.* a person who is visiting another person's house or who stays in a hotel.

guide *vb.* show someone the way. *n.* a person who guides other people.

guided missile *n.* a rocket- or jet-propelled missile with an explosive warhead.
► A guided missile is controlled in flight by radio or an automatic guidance system. Such missiles were developed by the Germans during World War II (the V-1 and V-2). Since then, advances in electronics have increased accuracy of missiles such as the American *Polaris* and *Minuteman* which can home in on targets over thousands of miles.

guilder *n.* the main unit of Dutch currency.

guillotine *n.* an instrument for beheading people, named after a Dr. Guillotin, first used in the French Revolution. *vb.* execute with a guillotine.

guilty *adj.* having done something wrong. *The dog looked very guilty when we found the meat was gone.* **guilt** *n.*

Guinea
Guinea is a poor republic in West AFRICA. Formerly a French colony, it gained its independence in 1958. Its chief resource is bauxite, but most people work on the land.
AREA: 94,970 SQ. MILES (245,957 SQ. KM)
POPULATION: 5,741,000
CAPITAL: CONAKRY
CURRENCY: SYLI
OFFICIAL LANGUAGE: FRENCH.

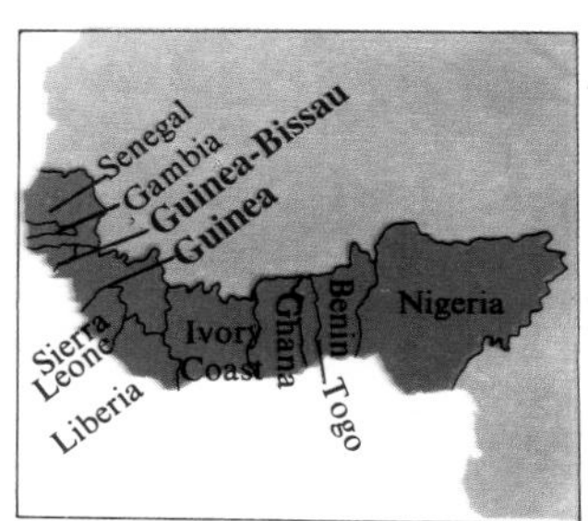

Guinea-Bissau
Guinea-Bissau is a republic in West AFRICA. Formerly a Portuguese colony, it gained its independence in 1974. Its main cash crop is groundnuts.
AREA: 13,050 SQ. MILES (36,125 SQ. KM)
POPULATION: 817,000
CAPITAL: BISSAU
CURRENCY: ESCUDO
OFFICIAL LANGUAGE: PORTUGUESE

guinea pig *n.* small tailless animal belonging to a family of South American rodents called cavies.

guitar *n.* a musical instrument with six strings which are plucked with the fingers. **guitarist** *n.* a guitar player.

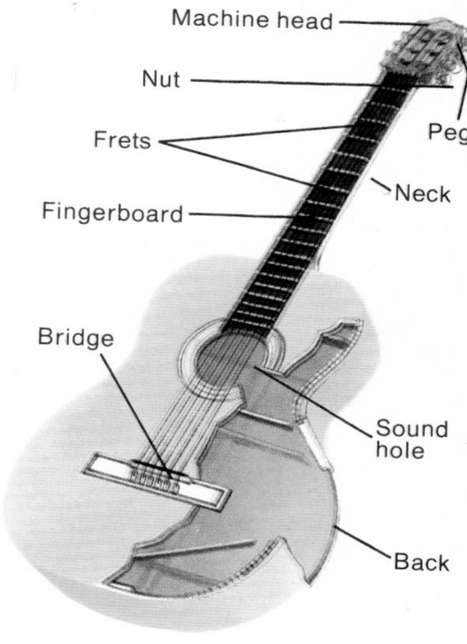

gulf *n.* a large area of the sea almost surrounded by land.

Gulf Stream
This ocean current is like a giant river flowing through the sea. It carries warm water from the Gulf of Mexico northward along the eastern coast of the United States. The Gulf Stream is up to 40 miles (60 km) wide and 2,000 ft. (600 meters) deep. The current divides. One branch crosses the ATLANTIC OCEAN and brings warm water to the British Isles and Norway.

gull *n.* a kind of large seabird.
► Gulls are seabirds with long wings, web feet, mainly white plumage and a harsh cry. Found over much of the world, they are strong swimmers and fliers. Gulls feed off fish and floating refuse and usually nest in colonies on cliff ledges or the ground.

gullet *n.* food passage through the throat.

gulp *vb.* & *n.* swallow noisily and quickly.

gum *n.* 1. the pink flesh in which the teeth are set. 2. glue. 3. chewing gum.
► Gum is a sticky substance made from the sap of certain trees such as cherry, acacia and eucalyptus. Gums harden when dry but are soluble in water. They are used in dyeing, medicine and ink-making.

gun *n.* a weapon that fires bullets or some other missile from a long tube open at one end; a firearm.
► Guns were probably invented in the 1200s. By the 1300s, guns were firing missiles that could pierce armor and break down castle walls.
Early guns were large weapons, far too heavy for one man to carry. The first gun was a big bucket with a small hole in the bottom. Soldiers

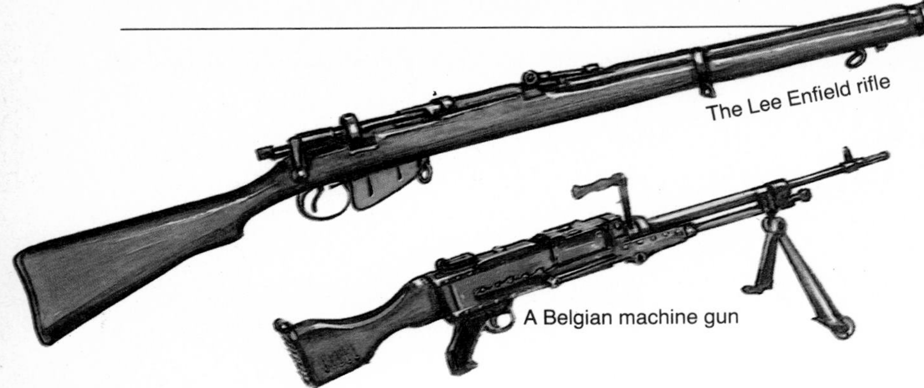

put GUNPOWDER in the bucket. Then they piled stones on top. They lit the gunpowder through the hole. When the gunpowder exploded the stones flew out. The large, long guns called cannons were first used about 1350. Cannons fired metal cannonballs. In the 1800s came guns which fired pointed shells that exploded when they hit their target. A spiral groove cut in the gun barrel made the shells spin as they flew through the air. Soldiers could fire such shells farther and hit their targets more often than with cannonballs.

Troops first used small arms in the 1300s. Small arms are guns that one man can carry. Inventors developed short-barreled pistols and revolvers for firing at nearby targets. They developed MUSKETS, RIFLES, and machine guns for long-distance shooting. In modern guns a hammer sets off an explosion that drives a shell or bullet from the barrel.

gunpowder *n.* an explosive made by mixing special amounts of charcoal, sulphur and saltpeter.

► Gunpowder is believed to have been invented in China about the 800s, and did not reach Europe until the 1300s. Gunpowder revolutionized warfare but is now seldom used except in fireworks.

gunsmith *n.* maker of guns.
gurgle *vb.* & *n.* bubbling sound.
guru *n.* religious teacher, especially in the Hindu religion.
gush *vb.* flow out suddenly. *Water gushed through the door.*
gust *n.* sudden rush of wind.
gusto *n.* zest.

Gustavus 11 Adolphus
Gustavus Adolphus (1594–1632), king of Sweden, called "the Lion of the North". A Protestant champion in the religious wars, he was the greatest soldier of his age.

Gutenberg, Johannes
Johannes Gutenberg (*c.* 1395–1468) was a German goldsmith who is sometimes called the father of PRINTING. In his day, people slowly copied books by hand or printed them from wooden blocks where each letter of every page had to be carved separately. About 1440, Gutenberg learned to make metal letters called type. He could pick them up and place them in rows to build pages of type. Each page was held together by a frame. Gutenberg fixed the frame to a press, and quickly pressed the inked surface of his type onto sheets of paper. Gutenberg's movable type helped him to make copies of a book faster and more cheaply than ever before.

guts *pl. n.* 1. the intestines. 2. (*casual*) courage.
gutter *n.* a small channel for carrying off rainwater.
guttural *adj.* & *n.* sound formed in the throat; harsh, grating.
guy (rhymes with *lie*) *n.* 1. (*casual*) a man or boy. 2. a rope or chain used to secure a tent, sail, etc.

Guyana
Guyana is a republic in northwestern SOUTH AMERICA. Sugar cane, diamonds, gold and bauxite are the chief products. Forests cover large areas with grass on the highest mountains.
AREA: 83,005 SQ. MILES (214,969 SQ. KM)
POPULATION: 887,000
CAPITAL: GEORGETOWN
CURRENCY: GUYANESE DOLLAR
OFFICIAL LANGUAGE: ENGLISH

guzzle *vb.* drink greedily.
gym or **gymnasium** *n.* a room for sports and training.
gymkhana *n.* a competition for horses and ponies and their riders.
gymnast *n.* a person who does exercises as a sport.
gymnastics *pl. n.* special exercises that develop fitness and coordination.

► The word gymnastics comes from a Greek word for "naked", because the ancient Greeks did their gymnastic exercises with no clothes.

The OLYMPIC GAMES have separate gymnastic exercises for men and women. Women perform graceful steps, runs, jumps, turns and somersaults on a narrow wooden beam. They hang from a high bar and swing to and fro between it and a lower one. They leap over a vaulting horse.

Women also perform floor exercises on a big mat, to music. They do handsprings, somersaults, cartwheels, jumps and other movements in a graceful flowing way, without stepping off the mat.

The men's Olympic exercises are different. They hang from a high bar and swing up and down, to and fro, and over and over in giant circles. Using two raised, level bars they swing, vault and do handstands. They grip hoops that jut up from a leather-covered pommel "horse", and swing their legs and body this way and that without touching the horse. They leap over a vaulting horse. They hang and swing from two rings slung from ropes. They also perform floor exercises.

gynecology (guy-na-**kol**-*ojee*) *n.* branch of medicine treating diseases of women.
gypsy *n.* a member of a dark-haired group of wandering people.

► Gypsies are found in small groups throughout Europe, America and Asia. In the past they called themselves *Roma* and spoke a language known as Romany. It is thought that they originally came from India. Gypsies trade in cars and horses and make metalwork or tell people's fortunes. They are famous for their songs and dances.

Gypsies have always been treated with suspicion and many were killed in Germany during World War II. They live in caravans, many of the vehicles being very picturesque and colorfully decorated. The women are more important in the group than the men. Children once took the mother's name, not that of the father, but this is no longer the rule.

gyroscope ("g" as in *giant*) *n.* a rapidly spinning wheel set in a frame which only touches another surface at one point.

► When a gyroscope's wheel is spun, its support may be turned in any direction without altering the wheel's original plane of motion. A spinning gyroscope will balance on the tip of a pencil without toppling, until the wheel begins to slow down. Then it will begin to wobble like a dying top. The gyrocompass and other navigational aids are based on the gyroscope.

H

A mare and her foal. A typical attitude of maternal affection.

habit *n.* 1. something that a person or animal does so often as to not think about it. 2. a monk's robe.
habitat *n.* the place where an animal or plant normally lives.
hacienda *n.* large estate or farm in Spanish-speaking countries.
hack 1. *vb.* chop roughly. 2. *vb.* cough harshly. 3. *n.* hired riding horse. 4. *n.* dull tedious work or person.
had *vb.* past of **have**.
haddock *n.* a fish, related to the cod, and important as food.

Hades
In Greek myths, Hades was the god of the underworld. (The Romans called him Pluto). In his underground kingdom, Hades ruled sternly over the dead. In time, people gave his name to the underworld itself. Christians came to use Hades as another name for Hell, the home of the devil, where wicked people who died were supposed to be punished for ever.

Hadrian
Hadrian was a Roman emperor (born A.D. 76, ruled A.D. 117–138). He halted Roman expansion and concentrated on making government, law and communication more efficient. Hadrian's Wall was built in northern Britain on Hadrian's orders between A.D. 122 and 136. It marked the northern frontier of the Roman Empire. It was about 73 miles (118 km) long, with many stone forts along its length. Parts of the wall can still be seen today.

hag *n.* a witch, ugly old woman.
haggard *adj.* gaunt and hollow-eyed.

The Hague
The Hague ('s-Gravenhage) is a city in the NETHERLANDS, and the country's administrative center. The Dutch Supreme Court is situated at the Hague, which is also the seat of the International Court of Justice.

ha-ha 1. *inter.* expressing laughter or derision. 2. *n.* boundary fence sunk in ditch.
haiku (**hye**-*koo*) *n.* three-line Japanese poem of 17 syllables.
hail 1. *n.* frozen rain. *vb.* fall as hail. 2. *vb.* greet someone by calling out to him or her.
hair *n.* a threadlike substance growing out of the skin of mammals.
► Hair gives warmth and protection. There are many different kinds. The fur of cats, rabbits and bears is hair. So are the bristles of pigs, the wool of sheep and the quills of porcupines.
hairdresser *n.* someone who cuts and looks after other people's hair.
hairy *adj.* covered in hair; similar to hair.

Haiti (Haitian)
Haiti is a republic on the western part of the island of Hispaniola in the West Indies. (The DOMINICAN REPUBLIC occupies the rest of the island). Haiti is a poor country. Most of the people are of black African descent, and work as subsistence farmers. Once a French colony, Haiti became independent in 1804 following a successful slave revolt.
AREA: 10,715 SQ. MILES (27,750 SQ. KM)
POPULATION: 5,220,000
CAPITAL: PORT-AU-PRINCE
CURRENCY: GOURDE
OFFICIAL LANGUAGE: FRENCH

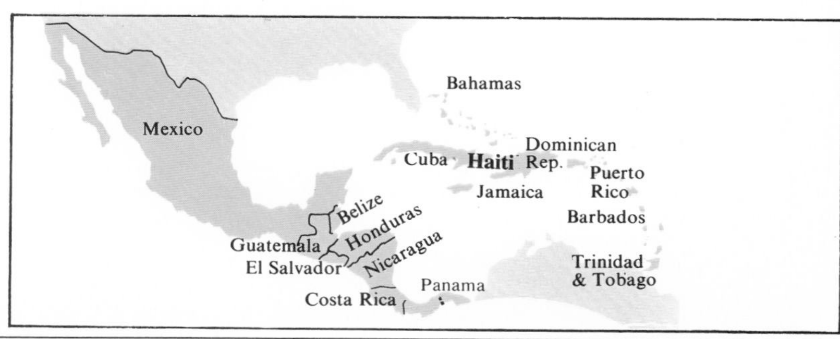

H

hake *n.* a fish, related to the cod, and eaten as food.
half *n.* (plural **halves**) one of the two equal parts of something.
half time *n.* the intermission that takes place after completing half of a game, e.g. football.
halibut *n.* a large flatfish of the North Atlantic and North Pacific.

Halifax, Nova Scotia
Halifax, the capital and commercial center of the province of Nova Scotia, Canada, was founded by the British in 1749. Its busy port is usually ice-free during winter.

halitosis *n.* foul-smelling breath.
hall *n.* 1. the entrance room of a house. 2. a large room for meetings, plays and other activities.
hallmark *n.* mark on gold or silver showing place of origin.
Halloween *n.* a festival held on October 31, the day before All Saints' Day. (Halloween roughly means "holy evening.") People once believed that ghosts, demons and witches roamed about on Halloween night.
halo (**hay**-*low*) *n.* a circle of light around something.
halt *vb.* & *n.* stop.
halter *n.* 1. rope with headstall for leading a horse. 2. a blouse with bare arms, shoulder, and midriff.
halve *vb.* divide into two equal parts.
ham *n.* 1. salted or smoked meat from a pig's thigh. 2. (*slang*) inexpert but showy performer.

Hamburg
Hamburg is a prosperous port in the north of West GERMANY. One of the country's largest cities, it is a major commercial industrial and cultural center. Hamburg is situated on the River Elbe, over 70 miles (100 km) from the North Sea. It was badly damaged in WORLD WAR II, but rebuilt soon afterwards.

hamburger *n.* a round cake of chopped beef, eaten hot, in a bun.
hamlet *n.* small village, usually without a church.
hammer *n.* a tool for driving in nails or breaking things. *vb.* strike with a hammer.
hammock *n.* a kind of bed, made of canvas or other cloth, and hung from cords at both ends. *In the days of sailing ships, sailors usually slept in hammocks.*

hamster *n.* a small, roundish rodent, often kept as a pet.
hand 1. *n.* the part of the arm beyond the wrist with five fingers (one of which is the thumb). 2. *vb.* give something with the hand. *Please hand me a glass of milk.*
handbag *n.* a small bag or purse, usually carried by women; pocketbook.
handcuffs *pl. n.* a pair of bracelets for locking a prisoner's hands together.

Handel, George Frederick
George Frederick Handel (1685–1759) was a German-born composer who settled in London and became a British subject. He is famous for the *Water Music* (1715) and for his oratorio the *Messiah* (1742).

handicap *n.* anything that makes it more difficult to do things. *In golf, good players have low handicaps.*
handicapped *adj.* having a physical, mental, or learning disability. *Blind people and deaf people are handicapped.*
handicraft *n.* a craft, skill or trade; a piece of work made by a craftsman or craftswoman.
handkerchief (**hang**-*ker-chief*) *n.* (plural **-chieves**) a piece of cloth or paper, carried in a pocket or handbag, used for wiping the nose.
handle 1. *n.* part of an object designed to be grasped. 2. *vb.* feel something with the hands.
handlebar *n.* the bar with which a bicycle or motorcycle is steered.
hand over *vb.* give something to someone else, often when you do not want to. *The thief made us hand over the money.*
handsome *adj.* good looking, usually applied to men.
handwriting *n.* writing done with a pen or pencil, not typed or printed. *She has very clear handwriting.* **handwritten** *adj.*
hang *vb.* 1. hold from above so that the lower part is free. *Ripe cherries hang from that tree.* 2. execute a person by hanging from the neck. past **hanged**
hang around *vb.* wait.
hangar *n.* a large building where aircraft are kept.
hang-glider *n.* frame on which a person can glide through the air.

Hannibal
Hannibal (247–182 B.C.) was a general of CARTHAGE in her struggle against Rome. He crossed the Alps with his war elephants and invaded Italy, beating the Romans at Cannae (216 B.C.). Later, he was defeated, exiled and driven to suicide.

happen *vb.* take place. *The sales happen every year in January.* take place by chance. *My friend and I happen to share the same birthday.* **happening** *n.* something that happens; an event.
happiness *n.* the state of being happy or contented.
happy *adj.* contented; cheerful; pleased.

Hapsburgs (or **Habsburgs**)
The Hapsburgs were a European royal family who were rulers of Austria and often emperors of the HOLY ROMAN EMPIRE. With Charles V of Spain (1500–58), their rule also covered Spain and its empire, the Netherlands and Burgundy. The Hapsburgs held thrones almost continuously from 1273 to 1918.

harangue *vb.* & *n.* a ranting, rousing speech.
harass *vb.* worry, trouble by repeated attacks. **harassment** *n.*
harbor *n.* a shelter for ships. *vb.* give shelter.
hard 1. *adj.* solid or firm; not soft. *The ground was too hard to dig.* 2. *adj.* difficult. *This problem is too hard for me to do.* 3. *adv.* with great effort. *She tried hard to win the match.* 4. *adj.* tough. *You're a hard man.*
hardback *n.* book bound in a hard, long-lasting cover.

Harding, Warren Gamaliel
Warren Harding (1865–1923) was the 29th President of the United States. He was elected after Woodrow WILSON, who was President during World War I. Harding's term in office is known for its inefficiency and corruption. This was the period of prohibition and bootlegging. He died in office.

hardly *adv.* only just. *She had hardly reached home when the telephone rang.*
hardware *n.* electronic parts of a computer.
hardy *adj.* strong, able to face difficulties.

hare *n.* an animal like a large rabbit with long ears and a short tail.
► The hare is noted for its acute hearing and fast running. Hares, unlike rabbits, live above ground in nests, called *forms*. They are found in all parts of the world except Antarctica.

harm *vb.* & *n.* hurt, damage.
harmless *adj.* safe; not dangerous.
harmonica *n.* a mouth organ.
harmony *n.* 1. agreeable arrangement of parts. 2. a secondary tune that blends with the main melody. **harmonize** *vb.*
harness *n.* all the leather straps and other equipment by which a horse is controlled.

Harold, King
Harold II (*c.* 1022–66) was the last of the ANGLO-SAXONS to rule England. In 1053 he became Earl of Wessex. In 1064 he was shipwrecked off France and caught by his cousin William of Normandy (WILLIAM THE CONQUEROR). Harold was freed when he promised to help William become King of England. But the English nobles chose Harold as king. He was killed at the Battle of HASTINGS, where William's Norman invaders defeated the English.

harp *n.* a large musical instrument played by plucking strings with the fingers of both hands.

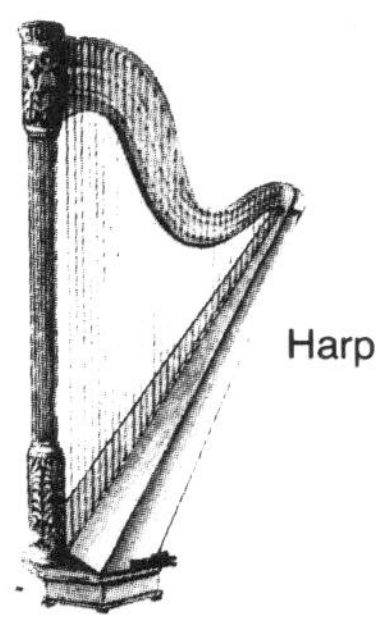
Harp

► This musical instrument has long and short strings stretched over a tall frame that stands on the floor. One side of the frame is hollow. This helps to give the harp its special sound. A harpist plays by plucking the strings with fingers and thumbs. Harps are the oldest stringed instruments. People made harps in IRAQ more than 4,000 years ago.

harpoon *n.* a spear on a rope for catching whales and large fish. *A harpoon is thrown or fired and can then be pulled back. vb.* strike with a harpoon.
harpsichord *n.* a stringed instrument with a keyboard similar to a piano.
► A harpsichord looks rather like a harp laid on its side and put in a box on legs. The first successful ones date from the 1500s. A harpsichord player plays a keyboard like a piano. Each key lifts a piece of wood called a jack. A quill or a bit of leather fixed to the jack plucks a string. Other members of the harpsichord family include the virginal and the spinet.

Harrison, Benjamin
Benjamin Harrison (1833–1901) was the 23rd President of the United States. He was the grandson of President William Henry HARRISON. Harrison defeated Grover CLEVELAND in the election of 1888, and four years later lost to the same man.

Harrison, William Henry
William Harrison (1773–1841) was the 9th President of the United States. One month after his inauguration he died from pneumonia, the first president to die while in office.

harrow *n.* a device to break up the soil after plowing. Disk harrows contain sharp rotating disks mounted on a shaft. *vb.* 1. draw a harrow over. 2. distress.
harsh *adj.* rough, unkind; hard to the feelings; coarse to touch.
harvest *n.* the time for cutting and bringing in grain and other crops; the crops brought in at harvest time. *vb.* gather in the harvest.

Harvey, William
William Harvey (1578–1657) was an English doctor who showed that blood flows around the body in an endless stream. Harvey proved that a beating heart squeezes blood through arteries and flaps in the heart, and that veins stop the blood flowing back. He worked out that the amount of blood pumped by a heart in an hour weighs three times more than a person.

hassle 1. *n.* heated disagreement 2. *vb.* harass.
haste *n.* hurry, quickness of movement. **hasten** *vb.*

Hastings, Battle of
In 1066 this battle made Norman invaders from France the masters of England.
WILLIAM THE CONQUEROR sailed with 7,000 Norman troops and some war-horses from France to England in about 450 open boats. Meanwhile, ANGLO-SAXONS under King HAROLD were defeating Norse invaders in northern England.
Harold quickly marched south. He met William at Senlac near Hastings. The battle lasted all day. Then the Normans pretended to run away. When some Anglo-Saxons followed, Norman cavalry cut them down. Then the Normans showered arrows on the rest and attacked once more. By evening, Harold was dead and his army beaten.

hat *n.* a covering worn on the head.
hatch 1. *vb.* come out of an egg. 2. *n.* movable covering over an opening.
hatchback *n.* car with a back door hinged at the top.
hatchet *n.* a chopper; a small ax. *"To bury the hatchet" was an American Indian expression meaning "to make peace."*
hate *vb.* & *n.* loathe; dislike someone or something very much. **hatred** *n.* active dislike, intense loathing.
haul (rhymes with *ball*) *vb.* pull a heavy load.
haunt *vb.* (of a ghost) to visit a place often.

have *vb.* own or possess something.
havoc *n.* ruin, chaos, destruction.

Hawaii (*abbrev.* **Hi.**)
A group of tropical islands in the Pacific Ocean, Hawaii covers 6,450 sq, miles (16,705 sq. km). The capital is Honolulu. Hawaii became the 50th state of the U.S.A. in 1959.
The main crops are pineapples and sugar, and tourists bring in much of Hawaii's wealth.

The biggest island is also called Hawaii. It has a greater area than all the other islands put together. It has five volcanoes, two of them still active. Mauna Loa is the largest volcano on earth and throws out more lava than any other.

hawk *n.* 1. a bird of prey. 2. someone who supports a warlike policy.
► The best-known hawks are the small bluish-gray Sparrowhawk and the larger gray-brown Goshawk. Both are active by day when they hunt birds and small animals. They usually nest in trees.
hawthorn *n.* a spiny shrub related to the rose and often found in hedges.
hay *n.* dried grass used to feed animals.

Haydn, Franz Joseph
Franz Joseph Haydn (1732–1809) was an Austrian composer known as the "father of the symphony." He wrote 104 symphonies. Many of them used an ORCHESTRA in a powerful new way. He also wrote fine pieces for the piano and for four stringed instruments. MOZART and BEETHOVEN both studied Haydn's music.

hay fever *n.* an allergy; people who suffer from hay fever react to the pollen in the air by sneezing.
haystack *n.* a large pile of hay.
hazard *vb.* risk, venture on. *Hazard a guess.*
hazel 1. *n.* a small nut tree. 2. *n.* & *adj.* the brownish-green color of some people's eyes.
H-bomb *n.* hydrogen bomb.
head *n.* 1. the top part of the body, above the neck. 2. the chief person, e.g. the head teacher in a school. *vb.* lead (a strike, etc.).

headache (rhymes with **bake**) *n.* a pain in the head.
headlight *n.* one of the main lights at the front of a vehicle.
headline *n.* a very brief summary in larger print at the top of a story in a newspaper.
headquarters *n.* the main office of an organization; an army base.
headway *n.* progress.
headwind *n.* blowing directly from in front.
heal *vb.* make better, particularly of a wound.
health (*helth*) *n.* how well or ill the body and mind are.
healthy *adj.* well and strong.
heap *n.* a pile of things. *vb.* pile things on, load.
hear *vb.* listen; notice a sound or noise. **hearing** *n.*
hearing aid *n.* a device worn by a person with impaired hearing to amplify sounds.
hearse *n.* vehicle for carrying a coffin to the grave.
heart *n.* the organ or part of the body which pumps blood around the body.
► All but the simplest animals have some sort of heart. In most cases, this consists of a muscular bag divided into two or more chambers. Mammals, including man, have a four-chambered heart: two upper chambers, or *auricles*, and two lower chambers, or *ventricles*. Pure blood, carrying oxygen, is sent from the left ventricle to the various parts of the body and comes back, carrying CARBON DIOXIDE, to the right auricle. From the right auricle, the blood is driven back into the right ventricle, and from there to the LUNGS where it gives up carbon dioxide and collects fresh oxygen. The pure blood returns to the left auricle, then into the left ventricle, ready for another journey around the body. The tubes taking blood away from the heart are called ARTERIES and those bringing it back are called VEINS.

Superior vena vava
Aorta
Right auricle
Left auricle
Valve
Right ventricle
Left Ventricle

heartless *adj.* without feeling or pity.
heartbreak *n.* great sorrow. **heart-breaking** *adj.*
hearth *n.* the floor or surroundings of a fireplace.
heat 1. *n.* hotness. 2. *vb.* make hot. *We heated the milk.*
► Heat is a form of energy. It comes from the movement of atoms which are always in motion, constantly bumping into each other. But when a body has plenty of heat energy, the bumping movements of its atoms are fiercer and the body gets warm. The study of how heat works is called *thermodynamics*.
Heat travels in three ways: by *conduction* through solids; mostly by *convection* in liquids and gases, where the hotter parts rise above the cooler parts and cause currents; and by *radiation* through space. The heat from a fire reaches us as waves which travel at the same speed as light. The SI Unit in heat is the Joule.

heater *n.* something that produces heat. *The heater in my car takes a long time to warm up.*
heath *n.* a piece of unused land, usually with poor soil and drainage.
heave *vb.* shift, raise up with effort.
heaven (**heh**-*ven*) *n.* the home of God. **heavens** *pl.n.* firmament.
heavy *adj.* having considerable weight; dull, boring.
Hebrew *n.* an ancient language now in common use in Israel.
► Hebrew is the language of the JEWS, both in the Old Testament and modern times. It uses an alphabet of 22 consonants, with added marks for vowels. Spoken since 2000 B.C., it is one of the oldest of living languages.

Hebrews
In the early days of their history, the Jewish people were known as the Hebrews or Israelites. There were 12 tribes, descended from Abraham. The greatest Hebrew leader was Moses, who led his people out of slavery in Egypt to the Promised Land of Canaan.

Hector
Hector was a Trojan hero, the son of King Priam of Troy and his wife Hecuba. Hector killed the Greek Patroclus, the friend of Achilles, in battle. Achilles killed Hector in revenge, and dragged his body around the walls of Troy. Priam paid in gold for his son's body, and gave Hector a magnificent funeral. The story of Hector is told in HOMER's *Iliad*.

hedge *n.* a row of bushes making a fence around a field or garden. *vb.* surround with a fence; give an evasive answer.

A hedgehog.

hedgehog *n.* a small animal that is covered by prickles. It defends itself by rolling into a ball.
► The hedgehog is an animal of Europe, Asia and Africa. It is about 10 inches long, with very short legs, a small tail and a long snout. It is useful in gardens because it feeds on insects and snails.

heel *n.* the back part of the foot; part of sock etc. that covers or supports the heel.
hegira *n.* the flight of Muhammed from Mecca to Medina in 522 AD.
heifer (rhymes with *deafer*) *n.* a young cow that has not had a calf.
height (rhymes with *bite*) *n.* the measurement from the bottom to the top of something. **heighten** *vb.* raise, make higher.
heir/heiress (*air*/**air**-*ess*) *n.* the person who will inherit somebody's property or position. *Prince Charles is heir to the British throne.*

Helen of Troy
Helen of Troy was said by the ancient Greeks to be the most beautiful woman in the world. She was the wife of Menelaus, King of Sparta, but ran away with Paris, Prince of Troy. Menelaus followed with a great army, and so began the TROJAN WAR. The story is told by the poet HOMER.

helicopter *n.* an aircraft with a horizontal rotor which acts as both propeller and wings.

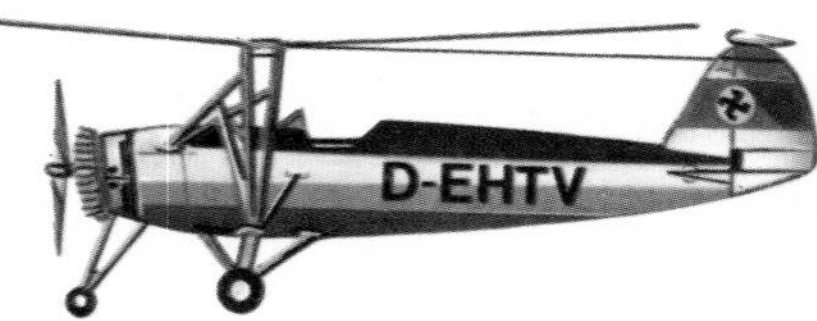

The German FW-61 (above) had two rotors fixed side by side. It was the first successful helicopter. The American Boeing-Vertol 107–11 (below) has a rotor at each end of the fuselage.

► The rotor allows the helicopter to take off and land vertically, move forward, backward or sideways as the rotor is tilted, and even to hang stationary in the air. A small tail rotor prevents the body spinning (or there can be two main rotors, turning opposite ways). Uses for helicopters include passenger and troop transport, firefighting and life-saving. The idea of a helicopter is not new. Leonardo da Vinci sketched a simple one in about 1500. But the first man-carrying craft were not built until the early 1900s. In 1907 Paul Cornu and Louis Bréguet built helicopters which rose slightly in the air.

helium *n.* a very light gas (symbol – *He*).
► Helium is the second most abundant chemical ELEMENT in the universe, but it is rare on earth. Used to lift balloons and airships, it is preferred to hydrogen because it is nonflammable.

hell *n.* the home of the devil, place of punishment.
helm *n.* tiller, wheel, steering gear of a ship.
helmet *n.* a strong covering that protects the head. *The motorcyclist wore a crash helmet.*

help *vb.* & *n.* aid someone; come to someone's assistance.
helpful *adj.* useful; providing help. *Thank you for being so helpful.*
helping 1. *adj.* giving help or assistance. *Can I give you a helping hand with the cleaning?* 2. *n.* a portion of food.
helpless *adj.* not able to look after yourself. *A baby bird is helpless if it falls out of the nest.*

Helsinki
Helsinki has been the capital of FINLAND since 1812. A seaport, it is situated on the Gulf of Finland in the BALTIC Sea. Helsinki contains many fine buildings, including a university and the Cathedral of St. Nicolas. The city was badly damaged by Russian bombing during WORLD WAR II.

hem *n.* the edge of cloth or clothing that is turned under and sewn.
hemisphere *n.* half a sphere; half the earth. *America is in the Western Hemisphere.*
hemlock *n.* poisonous herb.
hen *n.* any female bird, but especially a farmyard chicken.

Henry, Joseph
Joseph Henry (1797–1878) was an American scientist who is famous for his discoveries in electricity. He did early work on electromagnets and devised a working telegraph system.

Henry (Kings)
Eight English kings have been named Henry.

Henry I (1068–1135) was the youngest son of WILLIAM THE CONQUEROR. Henry II (1133–89) was the first of the Plantagenet line of kings. He restored order after the civil wars of Stephen and Matilda, and his marriage extended English claims in France. But his attack on the church law courts ended in the murder of Thomas à BECKET, Archbishop of Canterbury. His grandson, Henry III (1207–72) was a weak king, ruled by the barons.

During the WAR OF THE ROSES, the families of York and Lancaster fought for the English throne. Three Lancastrian kings were called Henry: Henry IV, or Henry Bolingbroke (1367–1413), Henry V (1387–1422), and Henry VI (1421–71). Henry V, son of Henry IV, a brilliant soldier, claimed the French throne, thus reopening the HUNDRED YEARS WAR. He defeated the French at AGINCOURT (1415), conquered Normandy, and married Catherine of Valois. Henry VI was a weak and sometimes insane ruler. His reign saw the loss of England's lands in France, a popular uprising (1450) and the outbreak of the WARS OF THE ROSES. He was deposed and finally imprisoned and murdered in 1471.

The first of the Tudor kings was Henry VII (1457–1509), who restored peace. His son, Henry VIII (1491–1547) was a clever, popular but ruthless king. He had six wives, and three of his children reigned after him: EDWARD VI, Mary I and ELIZABETH I. To divorce his first wife, Catherine of Aragon, he broke with the ROMAN CATHOLIC CHURCH. This and his dissolution of the monasteries set England on the road to Protestantism. His reign also saw a great increase in the strength of the state and of the English navy.

Henry The Navigator
Prince Henry ("the Navigator") (1394–1460) was the third son of King John I of Portugal. A man of great learning, he gave much encouragement to Portuguese explorers. He established an observatory and a school of navigation at Sagres, in southern Portugal.

Henry financed many expeditions to map the west coast of AFRICA. After his death Bartolomeu DIAS and Vasco da GAMA explored the southern and western coasts.

Henry's shipbuilders designed a new kind of ship for long ocean voyages. It was called a *caravel.* However, he himself never went on any of his expeditions.

her *pron.* the female possessive pronoun. *It is her birthday today.*
heraldry *n.* the study of coats of arms.
► Heraldry was first used in medieval times to identify knights in battle. Later coats of arms were linked with families rather than knights alone. As well as a shield, designs often included a crest (helmet), motto, and even supporters (such as the lion and unicorn in the British Royal Arms). Complex rules govern the designs.

Heraldic shield partitions. The coats-of-arms devised by court heralds in medieval times were drawn up according to strict rules.

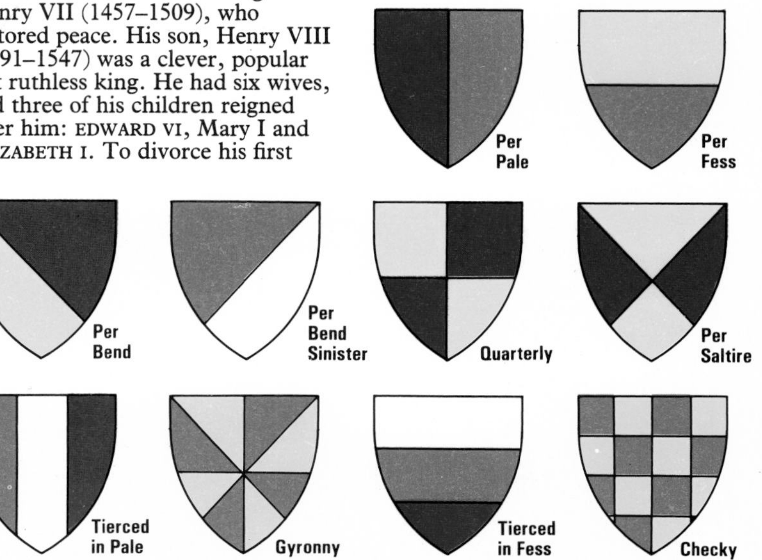

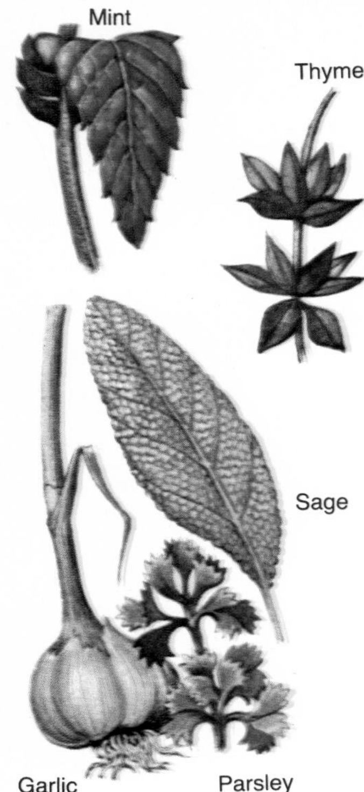

herb *n.* a plant whose leaves are used for flavoring, medicine, or scent.
► Herbs are plants with soft, rather than woody, stems. But the name "herbs" is also given to certain plants which are added to food during cooking. They are valued for their scent and flavor.

Common herbs used in cooking include sage, thyme, parsley, garlic, chervil, rosemary, basil, fennel and chives. Most can be grown quite easily.

Herbs can be used fresh from the garden, or they can be cut and dried for storage. People have grown herbs for hundreds of years. In the days before modern medicine, herbs were used to treat many illnesses. Even today some herbs are still used in this way.

herbivore *n.* an animal that eats plants, especially grass. **herbivorous** *adj*.
► The two main groups of herbivorous mammals are the *rodents* – the gnawing animals such as mice and squirrels – and the *ungulates* or hoofed mammals. These hoofed mammals include the largest land animals – elephants, rhinos and hippos – as well as horses and antelopes. The group also includes farm animals such as sheep, goats and cattle.

Hercules
Hercules was a famous hero of ancient stories told by the Greeks and Romans. He was the son of the god Jupiter and a mortal princess. He was amazingly strong. As a baby he strangled two snakes sent by Jupiter's jealous wife to kill him.

Later, Hercules went mad and killed his wife and children. To make amends, he had to perform 12 tasks, or labors. These included killing the Nemean lion and the many-headed Hydra, and washing clean the stables of King Augeas, where 3,000 oxen lived. In the end, Hercules was killed when he put on a poisoned shirt.

herd *n.* a group of animals grazing or moving together.
here *adv.* in or at this place. *Come here*.
heredity *n.* the physical characteristics passed on from parents to offspring.
► Heredity applies to all living things, and works through the cells that make them up. In the nucleus of each cell are thousands of tiny CHROMOSOMES, looking like chopped-up bits of string. On the chromosomes are the GENES, made of segments of an acid called DNA. The genes carry all the information that controls how the cells work. For example, one gene will decide what color the cells in hair become; red, black, brown or blond. In fact, everyone inherits two genes for every characteristic; one from the father and one from the mother. But one gene will always be more powerful than the other one. This *dominant* gene decides the characteristic; the other gene is called *recessive*. This is why children can have, for example, hair that is a different color from that of both their parents. They can inherit a gene that was recessive in their parents, but becomes dominant in them. (*see* MENDEL, GREGOR).

heresy *n.* opinion against what is generally accepted or officially declared. **heretic** *n.* person who supports heresy.
hermit *n.* a person who chooses to live alone, especially for religious reasons.
hero (plural **heroes**) *n.* 1. a man admired for his bravery. 2. the most important male character in a play, film or story. **heroic** *adj.* **heroism** *n.* heroic conduct, behavior worthy of a hero or heroine.
heroin *n.* a powerful, pain-killing but highly addictive drug made from morphine.
► Like morphine, heroin relieves pain. But it is stronger and more habit-forming than morphine and is not used for medical purposes. The drug is banned in the United States but some people obtain it illegally. Heroin addicts inject the drug under their skin or into a vein and soon become entirely dependent on it. Many turn to crime to pay for the drug. The treatment of heroin drug users is a very difficult problem.

heroine *n.* 1. a woman admired for her bravery. 2. the most important female character in a play, film or story.
heron *n.* a long-legged wading bird.
herring *n.* a small sea fish. When smoked it is called a kipper.
► Herrings swim in huge groups or shoals, and appear off the coasts at certain times of the year. Because fishermen have caught too many, the number of herrings has been greatly reduced and far fewer are now caught.

Herring

Hertz, Heinrich Rudolph
Heinrich Hertz (1857–1894) was a German scientist who paved the way for radio. He showed that light is a form of electromagnetic radiation and used oscillating electric sparks to cause similar electrical oscillations in a distant loop of wire.

The hertz (Hz) is now the unit of frequency of electromagnetic waves. One hertz is one cycle per second.

hesitate *vb.* stop briefly; show indecision. **hesitation** *n.* **hesitant** *adj*.
hexagon *n.* a figure with six equal sides.

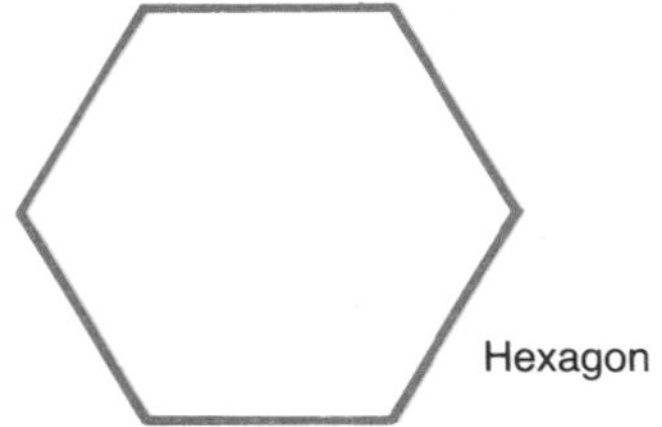
Hexagon

heyday *n.* peak, bloom (of youth, success, etc).
hibernate *vb.* spend the winter asleep. **hibernation** *n.*
► Snakes, squirrels, frogs, snails and earwigs hibernate. At the start of winter they find a sheltered place, often underground, where they can sleep through the cold weather. Hibernating animals appear lifeless and their breathing rate and heartbeats are much slower than normal. During hibernation they do not feed but live off body fat stored during the summer.

hidden *vb.* past of **hide**.
hide 1. *vb.* put something where others cannot find it; go into a place where you cannot be seen. 2. *n.* the skin of a large animal.
hideous *adj.* dreadfully ugly.

hieroglyphics *pl.n.* an ancient form of picture writing.

► Our alphabet has 26 letters. But 5,000 years ago the ancient Egyptians used picture-signs instead of letters. Later, these signs became hieroglyphics, marks which stood for things, people and ideas.

Hieroglyphic writing was very difficult and only a few people knew how to do it. When the Egyptian empire died out, the secret of reading it was lost. No one could understand the hieroglyphs carved on stones and written on papyrus scrolls. Then, in 1799, a Frenchman found the "Rosetta Stone," which is now in the British Museum in London. On it was writing in two known languages, and also in hieroglyphics. By comparing the known languages with the hieroglyphics experts were at last able to understand what the signs meant.

hi-fi *n.* & *adj.* short for high fidelity; apparatus to give good quality reproduction of recorded sound.
high *adj.* tall. *The mountain is two miles high.*
highbrow *n.* & *adj.* (person) of very intellectual interests.
highway *n.* a main road.
highwayman *n.* a robber on horseback.

► Highwaymen lay in wait for travelers on lonely roads. Many highwaymen did not hesitate to murder their victims. Famous highwaymen were romantic outlaws such as Pancho Villa, Robin Hood and Zorro. Jesse James was a highwayman who robbed stagecoaches and trains. Highwaymen ceased to trouble travelers in the 1800s, when proper police forces were set up.

hijack *vb.* (seize) control of a vehicle or aircraft during a journey by threat of violence.
hike *vb.* & *n.* go for a long country walk. **hitchhike** *vb.* get free rides from passing motorists.
hill *n.* a steep place; a slope; a small mountain. **hilly** *adj.*

Hillary, Edmund
A New Zealand mountaineer and explorer (born 1919) who in 1953, with Tensing Norgay, was the first man to reach the summit of Mount EVEREST.

hilt *n.* the handle of a sword.

Himalayas
The highest range of mountains in the world is the mighty Himalayas. The name means "land of snow." The Himalayas form a great barrier range across Asia, dividing India in the south from Tibet (part of China) in the north. Many of Asia's greatest rivers rise among the Himalayas, fed by the melting snows.

Until aircraft were invented few outsiders had ever been in the Himalayas. There are no roads or railroads. The only way to travel is on foot, over steep mountain tracks. Horses, YAKS, goats and even sheep are used to carry loads.

The highest mountain in the world lies in the Himalayas. This is Mount EVEREST, which is 29,028 feet (8,848 meters) high.

hinder *vb.* prevent, delay.
Hindu *n.* follower of the Hindu religion; someone from India.

Hinduism
Hinduism is the religion and customs of the Hindus of INDIA. Hinduism had no single founder; it developed over many centuries, and is the world's oldest living religion. Its sacred books include the *Vedas* and the *Bhagavad-Gita*. Hindus believe in *reincarnation*: the rebirth of the soul in a succession of earthly lives, with our actions in past lives affecting our future fates. Popular Hinduism includes temples and festivals to countless gods (especially Vishnu the preserver and Shiva the destroyer). But to the educated these are all just aspects of one Supreme Spirit. Worship is mainly a family matter. Even weddings are held at home.

A Hindu carving showing the four-armed god Siva.

hinge *n.* a joint on which a door or gate swings when it is opened or shut.
hint *vb.* suggest something without really saying it. *Carol hinted that she would like a new dress for her birthday.* *n.* disguised suggestion.
hip *n.* the joint where the leg joins the trunk of the body.

Hippocrates
Hippocrates (*c.* 460–357 B.C.) was an ancient Greek doctor. He is often called the "father of medicine" for his emphasis on scientific observation and reason. His Hippocratic Oath is still the basis of the oath taken by medical graduates. It includes rules governing the relationship between doctors and their patients.

hippodrome *n.* oval arena for horse races and chariot races in ancient Greece.
hippopotamus *n.* a large African animal that lives in and near lakes and rivers.

► The name hippopotamus means "river horse," but in fact the hippo is related to the pig, not the horse. Of all the land animals, only the elephant is bigger. An adult hippo can weigh over four tons.

Hippos spend most of their time in the water and are good swimmers. In spite of its fearsome-looking jaws, the hippo eats only plant food. It browses on water weeds and grasses, and at night often comes ashore to feed. A herd of hungry hippos can ruin a farmer's crops in a single night.

Hippos are not usually dangerous if left alone. But they can inflict serious wounds with slashes from the tusks in their lower jaws.

hire *vb.* rent; pay for the use of something. *We hired a car for a week when we went to Florida.*

Hiroshima
A Japanese city on Honshu island, Hiroshima was the target of the first ATOMIC BOMB, which was dropped on August 6, 1945, killing about 70,000 people. The population is now about 853,000.

hiss *vb.* & *n.* (make) a long S sound like a snake to express anger, disapproval, etc.
history *n.* the study and written account of past events. **historian** *n.* a person who studies and writes about the past. **historic** *adj.* famous in history. *The battle of Gettysburg was an historic event.*

► History is the story of the past. The people who write down history are called historians. They usually write about important events such as wars, revolutions and governments, because these affect nations. However, historians are also interested in the lives of ordinary people and in what they did and thought.

Nowadays, we think of history as being written down in history books. But, in earlier times, before books and printing, history was passed on by word of mouth. People told stories about their kings, their wars, their adventures, and also about their own families. It was in this way that the stories of ancient Greece were collected by the poet HOMER to form the *Iliad* and the *Odyssey*. Some early stories such as these were made up in verse, and sung to music.

In ancient Egypt, scholars recorded the reigns of the PHARAOHS, and listed the victories they won in battle. Often these accounts were written in HIEROGLYPHICS on stone tablets. The Chinese, Greeks and Romans were also very interested in history. They wrote of how their civilizations rose to power. During the MIDDLE AGES in Europe, it was the priests and monks who preserved ancient books and kept the official records and documents. These records include the DOMESDAY BOOK, which tells us much of what we know about Norman England. History became an important branch of study in the 1700s and 1800s. Famous historians were Edward Gibbon (1737–94) and Lord Macaulay (1800–59).

Historians get their information from hidden remains such as things found buried in old graves, as well as from old books. The study of hidden remains is called ARCHAEOLOGY. But history is not just concerned with the long distant past. After all history is *our* story. What is news today will be history tomorrow. So modern historians are also interested in recording the present. They talk to old people about the things they remember, and they keep records on film and tape of the events of today.

Historians get their information in many ways: by digging for it, by reading about it in old books and manuscripts and by listening to people talking. Above: A cave-painting at Lascaux, France dating from 16,000 to 10,000 B.C. showing a hunting scene. Left: A Chinese bronze chariot mounting of c.*400 B.C. Below: A relief showing Hammurabi, the law maker of Babylon. The stone slab on which it appears is inscribed with 282 laws (*c.*1800 B.C.).*

hit 1. *vb.* & *n.* strike or knock something; a blow. 2. *n.* a success, especially a record or show.

hitch 1. *n.* a setback, hold-up. 2. *vb.* fasten with a loop. 3. *vb.* thumb a ride (**hitchhike**).

Hitler, Adolf

Adolf Hitler (1889–1945) was the "Fuhrer", or leader, of GERMANY during WORLD WAR II. An ex-soldier, born in Vienna, AUSTRIA, he became leader of the Nazi Party which came to power in Germany in 1933.

Once in power, Hitler quickly ended the German republic. He had his political foes killed and began a ruthless campaign to wipe out the Jews. He also speeded up the rearmament of Germany.

Germany was still weak after its defeat in WORLD WAR I. The Nazis promised to avenge this defeat and create a new German empire. In 1939 Hitler led Germany into World War II. German armies conquered most of Europe. Millions of people were killed in special death camps set up by the Nazis. But by 1945 Britain, the U.S.A., Russia and the other Allies had defeated Germany. Hitler killed himself in the ruins of Berlin to avoid capture.

hive *n.* 1. colony of bees. (or **beehive**) 2. a place for bees to live in.

hoard (*hord*) *n.* & *vb.* store away secretly, especially money.

hoarding *n.* temporary fence of boards around a building and often covered with posters.

hoarse *adj.* of the voice, rough or croaking.

hoax *vb.* & *n.* a trick or practical joke.

hobble *vb.* limp, stumble along.

hobby *n.* something a person likes doing when not working. *Nick's hobby is collecting stamps.*

hock 1. *n.* joint in hind leg of horse, dog, etc. 2. *vb.* pawn something.

hockey *n.* a game played with curved wooden sticks and a puck between two teams of players. (see **ice hockey**).

hoe *n.* a tool for loosening the earth and digging out weeds. *vb.* use a hoe.

hog *n.* large pig.

hold 1. *vb.* keep firmly in the hand. 2. *n.* part of the hull of a ship where cargo is stored. 3. *vb.* contain. *This can holds a gallon.*

hold on *vb.* wait (especially on the telephone).

hold up *vb.* 1. delay. *I hope I haven't held you up.* 2. rob with a gun.

hole *n.* a hollow place; a pit, space or burrow.

holiday *n.* a day off work or school; a vacation. *We're going to France for our holiday this year.*

Holland see **Netherlands**
hollow 1. *adj.* not solid; empty inside. *The squirrels lived in a hollow tree.* 2. *vb.* to make hollow. 3. *n.* a hollow place or small valley.
holly *n.* an evergreen tree with glossy prickly leaves and red berries.
hollyhock *n.* tall flowering plant.

Hollywood
Hollywood is the "capital" of the film world. Until the early 1900s it was a sleepy suburb of Los Angeles in California. But by the 1930s Hollywood was famous. Wherever there were movies, people watched films made in Hollywood.

Its warm sunny climate and beautiful scenery made Hollywood a good place to make films. The first "movies" were silent, until the "talking picture" appeared in 1927. Inside huge studios, the film makers could build sets that looked like ancient Rome, an African jungle, or the surface of the moon. Hollywood stars became household names. However, in the 1950s television began to take over from the MOVIES, and today the Hollywood studios mostly make TV programs.

Holmes, Sherlock
Sherlock Holmes, the world's most famous detective, appears in 60 stories by Sir Arthur Conan Doyle (1859–1930). Helped by his friend Dr. Watson, the tall pipe-smoking private detective solves many baffling mysteries. In 1893 Conan Doyle wrote a "final" Holmes story, in which the detective died. But by public demand, Holmes "returned to life" in 1905.

holography *n.* a way of producing three-dimensional images.
► Light from a LASER is split into beams. One beam falls directly onto a glass photographic plate. The other half of the beam shines on the subject to be reproduced and then recombines with the first beam on the plate. There it makes a pattern called a *hologram*. When a laser beam passes through a hologram a three-dimensional image is seen – an image that appears solid; as you walk around the image its perspective changes.

holy *adj.* having religious significance; connected with God. *The Bible is the holy book of Christianity.*

Holy Roman Empire
The Holy Roman Empire is the name given to the German empire founded by Otto I in A.D. 962. (It was seen as a revival of the old Roman Empire). At its height it united Germany and most of Italy under one ruler. The empire continued in name until 1806; but it had lost most of Italy by 1300, while in Germany local rulers took over real power. After 1438 the position of Emperor was almost always held by a HAPSBURG.

home *n.* the place where you live.

Homer
Homer was a Greek poet and storyteller. He probably lived around 800 B.C., but we know nothing else about him. All we have are two great poems said to be by Homer: the *Iliad* and the *Odyssey*. These poems tell us much of what we know about ancient Greek history and legend. The *Iliad* tells the story of the TROJAN WAR. The *Odyssey* tells of the adventures of Odysseus as he returned to Greece after the war.

homesick *adj.* sad at being away from your home.
homework *n.* schoolwork that is done at home.
homicide (**hahm**-*mi-side*) *n.* killing of a human being.

Honduras (Honduran)
Honduras is a mountainous, thinly populated republic in CENTRAL AMERICA. The people are mostly of mixed Indian and Spanish descent. Bananas are the chief product.
AREA: 43,280 SQ. MILES (112,088 SQ. KM)
POPULATION: 3,941,000
CAPITAL: TEGUCIGALPA
CURRENCY: LEMPIRA
OFFICIAL LANGUAGE: SPANISH

honest (**on**-*est*) *adj.* truthful, not likely to cheat. **honesty** *n.*

honey *n.* the sweet substance made by bees from the nectar of flowers.
honeycomb *n.* the wax container made by bees in which to store their honey.
honeymoon *n.* a holiday for a newly married couple. *vb.* go on a honeymoon.
honeysuckle *n.* climbing plant with sweet-smelling flowers; woodbine.

Hong Kong
Hong Kong is a tiny British colony off the coast of China. Part of it is a small island, and the rest is a narrow strip of land called the New Territories which is actually part of mainland China. Hong Kong has been governed by Britain since 1842, but the lease from China expires in 1997.

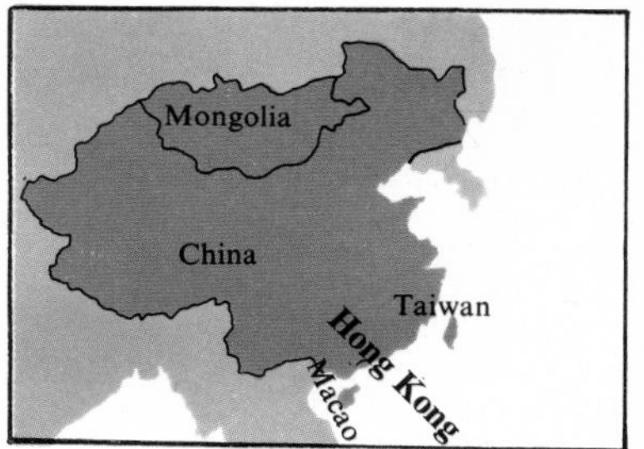

Hong Kong has a fine harbor surrounded by mountains. The capital is Victoria and another busy city is Kowloon. Hong Kong is a fascinating mixture of East and West. The people live by trade, fishing and farming. Tall apartment buildings have been built to house them, but there is still not enough room for all of the people who crowd this small island.
AREA: 403 SQ. MILES (1045 SQ. KM)
POPULATION: 4,957,000
CAPITAL: VICTORIA
CURRENCY: HONG KONG DOLLAR
OFFICIAL LANGUAGES: CHINESE, ENGLISH

honor *n.* respect, high regard, esteem.
hood *n.* a covering for the head and neck; a covering for the motor of a car.
hoodwink *vb.* trick or mislead.
hoof (plural **hoofs** or **hooves**) *n.* the hard part of the foot of a horse, and of some other animals.
► A hoof is the hard covering of horn. Animals with hoofs are divided into two main groups, those with an even number of toes and those with an odd number. The animals with an even number of toes include deer, goats, camels and sheep. All these animals have either two or four toes. Animals with only one toe include HORSES and ZEBRAS. Tame horses have their hooves cut and trimmed, and wear horseshoes.

hook *n.* a bent piece of metal, such as a fishhook. *vb.* catch or fasten with a hook. **hooked** *adj.*
hooligan *n.* ruffian, member of a gang of hoodlums.
hoop *n.* ring of metal or wood for binding casks; a child's plaything; a metal arch used in the game of croquet.
hoot *vb.* & *n.* (make) a sound of mockery; sound of a car's horn, etc.; sound of an owl.
hop 1. *vb.* & *n.* jump on one leg, or (of a bird) with both feet together. 2. *n.* a plant belonging to the mulberry family used to make beer.
► The hop plant is a tall vine which climbs up poles and wires. Fields of hops are grown for their yellow

female flowers, which give beer a bitter taste. The hops are picked, dried and ground to a powder before being taken to the brewery and mixed with water and malt to make beer.

hope *vb.* & *n.* wish for something pleasant to happen. *I hope I pass the exam.*
hopeful *adj.* having hope.
hopefully 1. *adv.* in a hopeful way. 2. (*casual*) it is hoped. *Hopefully the weather will be warm.*
hopeless *adj.* without hope.
horizon *n.* the line where the land and the sky seem to meet.
horizontal *adj.* flat; level with the horizon.
hormone (**hoar**-*moan*) *n.* chemical substance which regulates the body's activities.
► Hormones, mostly produced by GLANDS, make sure that cells, tissues and organs function properly. Two well-known hormones are *insulin,* which controls the amount of sugar in the blood (see DIABETES), and *adrenalin,* which gives the body extra strength and energy to fight – or run away – when danger threatens. Plants also have hormonelike substances, called *auxins*; these govern such processes as upward growth in stems and downward growth in roots.

horn 1. *n.* one of the long, pointed growths on the head of some animals. 2. *n.* a brass musical instrument that is blown.
► Many animals have horns, antlers or tusks. Horn is a special kind of hard SKIN. Finger and toe nails are made of horn. So are the feathers and beaks of birds, and the scales of reptiles.
Cattle, sheep, goats and most antelopes have curved horns. These are bony growths covered with a layer of horn, and they are fixed to the animal's skull. Deer have branched antlers, made of bone covered with skin. Every year the antlers fall off and the deer grows a new set.
Horned animals use their horns to defend themselves against enemies and as weapons for fighting during the mating season.
►► All kinds of *brass instruments* are called horns. They are all made of a metal tube with a wide opening at one end and a mouthpiece at the other. The player puts his lips to the mouthpiece and blows to make his lips vibrate. The vibrations caused by the lips are made louder inside the horn and are turned into a musical tone. When musicians talk about a horn, they mean the French horn used in ORCHESTRAS. It is a fine coiled instrument. If the tube was straightened out it would stretch for about 16 ft. (5 meters).

Horn, Cape
Cape Horn is the tip of land at the southern end of SOUTH AMERICA. To cross from the Atlantic Ocean into the Pacific Ocean, a ship had to go through the stormy seas off Cape Horn. In the days of sailing, this was a perilous adventure and many ships were wrecked on the rocky coast. Today, ships can take a short cut through the PANAMA CANAL.

hornet *n.* large insect of wasp family.
horoscope *n.* a prediction about someone's future, based on the sign of the zodiac under which one was born; fortune-telling.
horrible *adj.* unpleasant, frightening or ugly.
horror *n.* fright. *He watched in horror as his boat drifted out to sea.*
horse *n.* a four-legged animal with hooves, long mane and tail, used for riding, or carrying a load.
► The horse was one of the first wild animals to be tamed by man. Today there are very few wild horses left. Many "wild" horses are actually descended from domestic horses that ran wild.
The horse is valued for its speed and strength. But the first horse was a small, rather doglike creature, with a way of life quite unlike that of modern horses. Called *Eohippus,* or "dawn horse," it lived millions of years ago. It had four toes on its front feet and three toes on its back feet, and it probably hid from its enemies in the undergrowth.
Later, horses came out to live on the wide grassy plains. There was no undergrowth to hide in, so they escaped from enemies by running away. Gradually, their legs grew longer, and they lost all their toes

The horns of cattle and antelope (above) are permanent hollow outgrowths of a special kind of hard skin. Fingernails and toenails are made of horn. The antlers of deer are bony outgrowths, shed each year. On the right are the antlers of a Red deer; with each year extra tines or points are added.

EQUESTRIAN TERMS
aids the signals used by a rider to convey instructions to the horse. The *natural* aids are those produced by use of the body, legs, hands and voice; *artificial* aids include the use of spurs, whips, etc.
bit the metal or rubber device, attached to the bridle and placed in the horse's mouth to give the rider control over the pace and direction.
Blood horse an English thoroughbred.
bridle the part of the saddle that is placed over the horse's head, to which are attached the bit and reins.
colt an ungelded male horse which is under four years of age.
dam the female parent of a foal.
eventing a three-part competition (dressage, cross-country and show-jumping); all three can take place on the same day, but at advanced levels they are spread over two or three days.
dressage schooling a horse to achieve perfect obedience and supplesness.
filly a female foal.
foal a horse or pony up to one year old.
gait the movement or pace of a horse. There are four basic gaits or paces: the walk, trot, canter and gallop.
gelding a male horse that has been castrated.
hand the measurement equaling four inches (10 cm) used when giving the height of a horse.
hacking riding for pleasure.
mare a female horse or pony that is over four years of age.
near side the left side. It is usual to mount and tack up a horse from the near side.
numnah a pad worn under the saddle, made of sheepskin.
off side the right side of a horse.
stallion a male horse over four years of age, used for breeding.

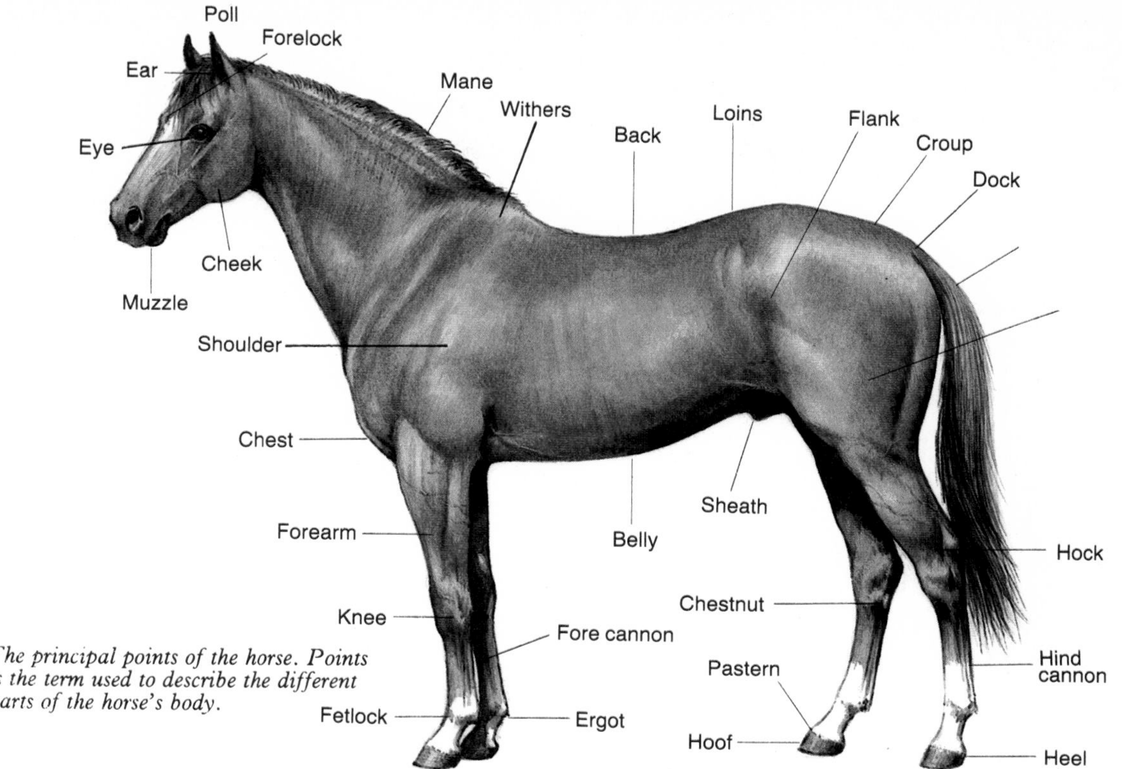

The principal points of the horse. Points is the term used to describe the different parts of the horse's body.

except one. Finally, after millions of years of EVOLUTION, there appeared the modern horse which has only one toe. In fact, it runs on tiptoe! Its toe has become a HOOF.

In the wild, horses live in herds. The leader of the herd is the strongest male, or stallion. He defends the females, or mares, and their young foals. Horses can usually outrun their enemies (such as wolves), but they can also kick and bite. They are grazing animals, feeding almost entirely on grass – although tame horses are given extra food, such as bran and oats.

Early people hunted wild horses for food. No one knows when horses were first tamed. But horses were being used for riding and for pulling CHARIOTS and carts in Egypt more than 5,000 years ago. Until the 1800s the horse was the fastest form of transport and our strongest helpmate. Horses did all kinds of jobs, in towns and in the country, until the steam railroad and the automobile replaced them.

In war, cavalry (mounted soldiers) were used right up until WORLD WAR II. In the MIDDLE AGES, knights on horseback galloped into battle on heavy chargers (war-horses). The descendants of these great horses became the hardworking Shire horses.

The Mongols of Asia were expert horsemen. It was riders from the East who first brought stirrups to Europe.

The true wild horse looks rather like a shaggy-haired mule. The ZEBRA is an African wild horse which has never been successfully tamed.

Horses are measured from the ground to the shoulder in *hands*. A hand equals 4 in. (10 cm). The tiny Shetland pony is often only 8 hands tall, while the great Shire horse may stand more than 17 hands and weigh 2,200 lb. (1,000 kg).

1. Eohippus – the earliest ancestor of the horse. It had four toes on its forefeet and was about the size of a fox.

2. Mesohippus lived between 40 and 25 million years ago. Its legs were three-toed.

3. Merychippus of between 25 and five million years ago carried its weight on its central toes.

4. Pliohippus of two million years ago was the model from which modern Equus was to develop.

5. The modern horse has entirely lost its toes and has properly formed hooves. Its teeth are better adapted for grazing.

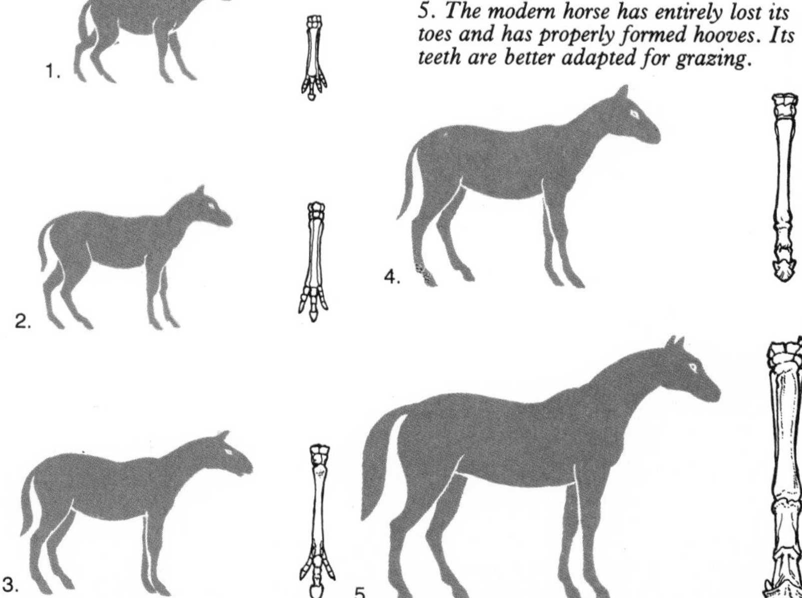

H

horsepower *n.* a unit for measuring the power of engines.
horseshoe *n.* a U-shaped piece of iron used to protect a horse's hoof.
horticulture *n.* the art of gardening.
hose *n.* a long, flexible tube through which water and other liquids can pass. *vb.* wash down with a hose.
hospital *n.* a building where sick or injured people are taken care of. **hospitalize** *vb.*

► Some hospitals treat only certain kinds of conditions. There are hospitals for children, and maternity hospitals where women have their babies. There are those that deal only with ear, nose and throat complaints, or only eye troubles. General hospitals are ones that handle everything; from traffic accidents and injuries to infectious diseases.

Certain hospitals are also teaching schools. Young doctors go there to study. They visit the wards and examine the patients. They gain experience in dealing with real illnesses, as well as the cases they learn about in medical books.

Hospitals date from ancient times. The first ones were linked with temples devoted to the gods of healing. Part of the temple was set aside for the sick to come to pray and be cared for. The Romans had both military and civilian hospitals. But toward the end of the Roman Empire, more and more hospitals became attached to monasteries. Caring for the sick was thought to be a religious study.

Until well into the 1700s, religious orders in monasteries ran most hospitals. Since then, nonreligious hospitals have grown to be the most common kind. Some are run as businesses that make money and others as charities. Today, more and more are run by governments who try to provide free or cheap medical care for all their people.

Modern hospitals have come a long way from their dirty and crowded ancestors. They are well-staffed and filled with all kinds of equipment for treating the sick and caring for them as they get better. There are operating rooms in which everything and everybody must be spotlessly clean. In X-ray rooms, experts called *radiologists* help the doctor to find out what is wrong with patients. In hospital laboratories other experts can examine samples of patients' blood and tissues to find out more about their condition.

hospitality *n.* generous, friendly entertainment of guests.
host *n.* 1. a person who has guests in his house. 2. a huge crowd. 3. bread used in the Holy Communion or mass.
hostage (**hoss**-*tij*) *n.* a person who is held prisoner and threatened until certain demands are agreed to.
hostel *n.* lodging for students, etc.
hostess *n.* 1. a woman who has guests in her house. 2. a woman who looks after travelers on an aircraft (stewardess).
hostile *adj.* unfriendly.
hot *adj.* having high temperature. *It was so hot you could fry an egg on the sidewalk.*
hot dog *n.* a heated frankfurter in a roll.
hotel *n.* a building where travelers pay to sleep and have meals.
hotfoot *adv.* in great haste.
hound *n.* a name for various kinds of dogs, especially those used in hunting. *vb.* hunt with hounds.
hour *n.* a period of 60 minutes. *There are 24 hours in a day.* **hourly** *adj.* & *adv.* occurring once every hour.
house *n.* a building in which people live, a home.

► Modern houses are airy, light and comfortable. They are built to keep out the cold and wet and to stay warm. Large windows, electricity, hot and cold running water and good heating systems make them comfortable to live in.

Houses date back to prehistoric times. Some of the first are found in the Middle East. They were simple little boxes with flat roofs. Often doors and windows were simply open spaces to let in air. Built of sun-dried bricks, their main purpose was to keep off rain and to stay cool in the hot summer sun.

Houses in Greek and Roman times could be quite large. In towns they might be apartment "blocks," perhaps five stories high. Wealthy Romans built themselves splendid villas that were even fitted with running water and heating systems.

In the MIDDLE AGES houses were mostly crude wooden affairs. They had just one or two rooms on a single level and everyone, including the animals, crowded into them to live, sleep and eat. Nobles' homes were more elaborate. They were often made of stone, and had several floors and many rooms, each for a different purpose.

As towns and cities grew in size, thousands of cheap apartments or small cheap houses were built to house workers. Today, houses are built from a wide variety of different materials, and in many shapes and sizes. Tall apartment buildings are mostly built of steel and concrete, while small suburban houses are usually made of bricks or wood.

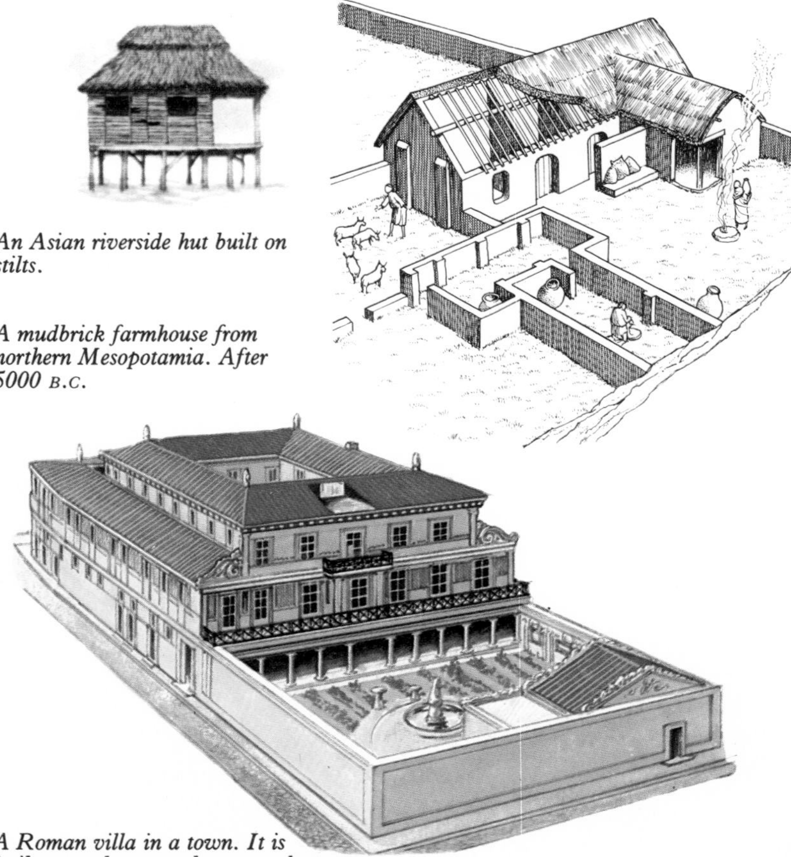

An Asian riverside hut built on stilts.

A mudbrick farmhouse from northern Mesopotamia. After 5000 B.C.

A Roman villa in a town. It is built around a central courtyard. Rooms on the ground floor looked out on the courtyard or the garden.

houseboat *n.* a boat on which people live.
household *n.* all the people who live together in a house. *Our household consists of my mother, my brother and me.* **householder** *n.* head of a household.
housekeeper *n.* a person who is paid to look after a home.

Houses of Parliament
The Houses of Parliament form the main bodies of the British PARLIAMENT, the House of Commons and the House of Lords.

The House of Commons was set up during the reign of HENRY III, and it is the more important. The members of the Commons – MPs – are chosen by the people of the country during public ELECTIONS. The political party which has the most members elected to sit in the Commons has the right to form the government and to choose the PRIME MINISTER. There are 650 members of the Commons, and only commoners (people who do not have certain titles) can become MPs.

After a bill has been approved by both Houses, it goes to the monarch for royal approval.

House of Representatives
The House of Representatives is the larger of the two Houses in the United States Congress. It helps the Senate to make the country's laws. There are at present 435 representatives, each representing about 500,000 people. A representative must have been a citizen of the United States for at least seven years and be at least 25 years old. He must also be living in the state he represents. Representatives are elected for two-year terms.

Only the House of Representatives can originate bills for raising revenue, although the Senate can propose amendments. The House chooses its chairman, the Speaker. He is usually the leader of the majority party in the House. Speeches in the House are restricted to one hour.

The House has 20 *standing committees*, membership of which varies from seven to 50. Each party is represented in standing committees in proportion to its strength in the House. The Rules Committee is a powerful committee that controls the order in which bills are acted upon. The Ways and Means Committee introduces all tax bills.

housewife *n.* a married women who looks after the home.
housework *n.* work such as cleaning and washing done in the house.

Houston, Texas
Houston, Texas, is a busy port on the Houston Ship Canal, 50 miles (80 km) from the Gulf of Mexico.

Houston is in an area that is rich in oil, gas, salt, sulfur and timber. It produces more petroleum than any other city in the United States.

Near Houston is the Lyndon B. Johnson Space Center, where astronauts are trained and the flights of Skylab and the Space Shuttle are controlled.

hovel *n.* a small, very poor house or cottage.
hover *n.* stay in the air in one place. *A dragonfly hovers over the water.*
hovercraft *n.* an air-cushion vehicle designed to skim over the surface of water or land.
► A cushion of air is maintained between the craft and the surface by driving air at pressure under the hovercraft. This cushion supports the weight of the craft and keeps it clear of the surface. The hovercraft's air cushion is like a leaking tire, in principle. Air must be pumped in continuously to maintain the necessary lift. Most craft are fitted with flexible skirts which contain the cushion of air.

how *adv.* in what way. *How do you spell this word?*
however *adv.* & *conj.* by whatever means. *However hard you try.* but. *I'd like to go; however, I can't afford it.*
howl *vb.* & *n.* (make) a long, sad noise like a dog makes when it is hurt.

hub *n.* central part of a wheel from which the spokes radiate.

Hudson Bay
Hudson Bay is a huge sea in north-central Canada. It is connected to the Atlantic and Arctic oceans and its area is about 44,175 sq. miles (114,930 sq. km). It was explored by Henry HUDSON in 1610.

Hudson, Henry
Henry Hudson (*c.* 1550–1611) was a British explorer and navigator. During the 1500s and 1600s, many attempts were made to find a sea route around the top of North America (see NORTHWEST PASSAGE). Hudson led several expeditions to North America in search of this route. He sailed up what is now called the Hudson River. On his last voyage he discovered the inland sea now called Hudson Bay. His crew mutinied and set Hudson and a few loyal men adrift in an open boat. They were never heard of again.

The hovercraft rides on a cushion of air that is forced down under the vessel. The hovercraft was invented by Sir Christopher Cockerell in 1955.

A simplified diagram showing how a bill becomes law in the U.S. Congress. Congress is made up of two chambers: the House of Representatives and the Senate.

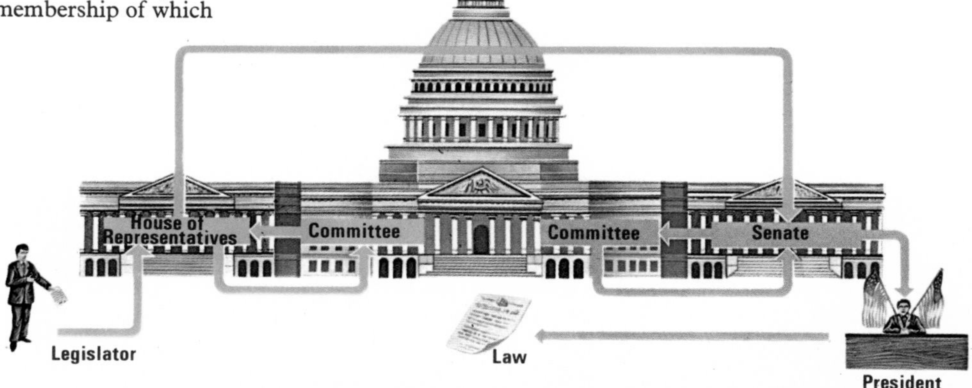

H

hue *n.* color, tint.
huff 1. *n.* fit of crossness. *He walked off in a huff.*
hug *vb.* embrace someone by clasping them tightly with your arms. *n.* a tight embrace.
huge *adj.* vast; enormous.

Hugo, Victor Marie
Victor Hugo (1802–1885) was a French writer who created characters such as the hunchback of Notre Dame and Jean Valjean. Although he was well-known as a poet and a writer of plays, his greatest works were the novels *Les Misérables* and *The Hunchback of Notre Dame*. Among his plays are *Lucrezia Borgia* and *Le roi s'amuse* on which Verdi later based his opera *Rigoletto*.
Victor Hugo was a great champion of the common man.

Huguenot (**hew**-*ge-no*) *n.* French Protestant in the 1700s.
hull *n.* the body of a ship.
hum 1. *n.* a low murmuring noise. 2. *vb.* sing with the mouth closed. *He always hums while he is working.*
human *adj.* & *n.* behaving or looking like people. *n.* human being.
humane *adj.* kind, gentle; merciful.
humanity *n.* the human race as a whole.
humble *adj.* 1. not vain or proud. *He was always very humble.* 2. of poor quality or little importance. *Be it ever so humble, there's no place like home.*

Humboldt, Baron Alexander von
Alexander von Humboldt (1769–1859) was a German scientist and explorer. He led an expedition to Central and South America, where he studied plant life, volcanoes and other natural phenomena. In 1829, Humboldt went to Siberia to study its climate and mineral wealth on behalf of the Russian government. A cold ocean current off the west coast of South America is named the Humboldt Current after him.

humbug *n.* 1. fraud; nonsense. *The speech was a lot of humbug.*
humdrum *adj.* dull, uneventful.
humidity *n.* the amount of moisture in the atmosphere. This moisture consists of tiny water particles moving about freely in the air. **humid** *adj.*
► When we say a place is humid, we mean there is too much water vapor in the air. Hot, humid weather makes us feel hot and sticky. We may feel pleasantly warm at 80°F if the humidity is low, but far too hot if the humidity is high. Air conditioning makes rooms cooler and less humid.

humiliate *vb.* offend, make a person look ridiculous or ashamed.
hummingbird *n.* a small brightly colored bird whose wings flap so quickly that they make a humming sound.
► Hummingbirds are among the smallest birds in the world. They are found only from Canada to the tip of South America. The tiniest of the 320 known kinds lives in Cuba. It is less than 2 in. (5 cm) when fully grown; hardly bigger than a large bumblebee.
The feathers of hummingbirds are colored in brilliant metallic hues of blue, green, red and yellow. The colors flash in the sun so that they look like glittering jewels on the wing.
Hummingbirds can beat their wings up to 70 times a second. This is what causes their distinctive humming sound. It also lets them hover in midair and fly backward and sideways like a helicopter. In this way, they dart from flower to flower and feed while flying. They take nectar and tiny insects from deep within the cups of flowers.

A hummingbird.

humor *n.* a mood. *She is in a bad humor.* an ability to be amused by or to laugh at funny sayings, drawings or stories. *Dominic has a very good sense of humor.* **humorous** *adj.*
► No one knows why we laugh at certain things. The idea of a fat lady slipping on a banana skin makes us laugh. But if we slipped on the banana ourselves we would not think it at all funny. Humor can be quite cruel. It often pokes fun at people's weaknesses and habits.
There are different kinds of humor. *Slapstick* and *farce*, for example, are very simple kinds. If we see a film in which someone slaps a custard pie in someone else's face, we are watching slapstick. The better dressed and the more dignified the person who receives the pie, the more we laugh.
Puns are plays on words that have similar or the same sounds, but different meanings – we say one word when we really mean another:
"A cannonball took off his legs, so he laid down his arms."
There are not very many really funny books, probably because humor is quite difficult to write. But some people have mastered it. Among those was Edward Lear who wrote nonsense verse such as:

There was an old man in a barge,
Whose nose was exceedingly large,
But in fishing by night, it
supported a light
Which helped the old man in a
barge.

When people are able to laugh at themselves, we say that they have a "sense of humor."

hump *n.* a round lump like that on a camel's back.
hundred *n.* the figure 100; 10 times 10.

Hundred Years War
The struggle between England and France (1337–1453), over England's claim to the French throne. England's two main campaigns, under Edward III and HENRY V, brought victories at Sluys, Crécy, Poitiers and AGINCOURT. But England's resources of men and money were only a third of France's, and from 1429, JOAN OF ARC led a successful French revival. By 1453 only Calais was left in English hands.

hung *vb.* past of **hang**.

Hungary (Hungarian)
A Communist republic in eastern EUROPE, Hungary is a mostly low-lying country, drained by the River DANUBE and its tributaries. There is much fertile farmland and grapes, corn, potatoes, rye, sugar beet and wheat are important products. But manufacturing is now the most valuable activity, employing about 36 percent of the working population, as opposed to 25 percent in agriculture.
Before WORLD WAR I, Hungary, with AUSTRIA, formed part of the great Austro-Hungarian empire.

Hungary became a separate country in 1919 and, in WORLD WAR II, it was one of the Axis powers. Soviet troops invaded Hungary in 1944–5 and a Communist regime was established in 1947.

AREA: 35,921 SQ. MILES (93,030 SQ. KM)
POPULATION: 10,850,000
CAPITAL: BUDAPEST
CURRENCY: FORINT
OFFICIAL LANGUAGE: MAGYAR (HUNGARIAN)

hunger *n.* the feeling of needing food. **hungry** *adj.*
hunk *n.* a large slice (of bread, etc.).

Huns
These were a group of fierce wandering warriors who swept into Europe around 400 A.D. from the plains of Central Asia. They conquered large parts of Germany and France. Their famous general, Attila, attacked Rome and nearly destroyed the Empire. However, the Huns' power declined after his death in A.D. 453.

hunt 1. *vb.* go after, and often kill, animals for sport or food. *n.* people hunting with a pack. 2. *vb.* look for something.
► In prehistoric times, hunting was the main way by which people lived. Nowadays most hunting is for sport or to keep down pests.
Big game hunting is the sport of tracking, stalking and killing large wild animals. It takes a great deal of skill and nerve to catch animals such as elephants, bears or mountain goats. Another kind of hunting is with packs of hounds. The hunters may follow on foot or by horse as the dogs chase deer, foxes or hares through the countryside. All states in the United States have game laws which regulate the amount and kind of game that can be hunted.

hunter *n.* a person who hunts animals.
hurdling *n.* a foot race in which barriers called hurdles have to be jumped.
► The hurdles are set up around the track at regular intervals of 10 yards (9 meters). The shortest men's hurdle race is 120 yards (110 meters). There are others at 240 yards (200 meters) and 480 yards (400 meters). In the shortest race there are 10 hurdles to jump. Each hurdle is 3 ft. 6 in. (1.07 meters) high. A runner may knock over some hurdles without being disqualified from the race.

hurl *vb.* throw with great force. *n.* a violent throw.
hurricane *n.* a windy violent storm.
hurry *vb.* move quickly. *You'll be late if you don't hurry. n.* great haste; eagerness or urgency.
hurt *vb.* cause pain. *He's hurt his leg.*
husband *n.* a married man.
hush *vb.* make or become silent. **hush up** *vb.* keep secret. **hush-hush** *adj.* very secret.
husky 1. *adj.* having a hoarse, whispering voice. 2. *n.* a heavy-coated dog, bred to pull sleds in the far north of America.
hut *n.* a small building, often made of wood and used as a temporary shelter. *The children made a hut out of branches.*
hutch *n.* a cage or box for rabbits or other small animals.

Hwang Ho
The Hwang Ho, or Yellow River, is the second longest river in CHINA. It is about 2,700 miles (4,345 km) long. The river gets its name from the yellow silt (mud) it carries down from the north. The silt sometimes causes serious floods, and *levees*, or banks, have been built to prevent the flooding. However, the silt left behind after flooding has made the surrounding land very fertile.

hyacinth *n.* a garden flower, often blue or purple in color.
hybrid *n.* plant or animal produced by parents of different species, e.g. a mule (male donkey and female horse).
hydrant *n.* above-ground pipe that supplies water for firefighting.
hydraulic power *n.* a form of power based on the pressure of water or other liquids which are forced through pipes.
hydro- *prefix* meaning water.
hydroelectric *adj.* producing electricity from the power of falling water.
hydrofoil *n.* a boat which, at speed, rises out of the water supported on wing-like struts, or *foils*, that project from the lower hull.
hydrogen *n.* a colorless, odorless, tasteless gas that is lighter than air (symbol – *H*).
► A colorless, odorless, tasteless GAS, hydrogen is the lightest of all the ELEMENTS. Its symbol is H. Although hydrogen makes up less than one percent of the earth's crust, it is believed to be the most abundant element in the universe, making up a large part of the material in the stars. It is used in the manufacture of ammonia and margarine.

hyena *n.* a savage, doglike creature that hunts in packs at night and feeds mostly on dead animals. Found mostly in India and parts of Africa.
hygiene *n.* the science of health and cleanliness. **hygienic** *adj.*
hymn (rhymes with *rim*) *n.* a religious song praising and glorifying God.
hyphen *n.* a mark like this (-) showing where a word has been divided at the end of a line, or where two words have been joined to make one, e.g. self-respect. **hyphenate** *vb.*
hypnosis *n.* a condition like deep sleep in which someone's actions can be controlled by another person. **hypnotize** *vb.*
hypochondria (*high-po-***kon***-dree-a*) *n.* a fear of becoming ill. **hypochondriac** *n.* & *adj.*
hypocrisy (*hip-***pok***-kra-see*) *n.* pretending to be good.
hypodermic syringe (*high-po-***dur***-mik*) *n.* an instrument with a hollow needle for injecting drugs under the skin.
hypotenuse (*high-***pot***-i-noose*) *n.* side of right-angled triangle opposite the right angle.
hysterical *adj.* in a state of wild excitement. **hysteria** *n.*

In prehistoric times big game hunters usually followed their food supply.

I

Perfect poise of ice-skating champion John Curry.

I *pron.* first person singular; the speaker or writer.

ibex (plural **ibexes**) a species of wild goat living in the mountains of Europe, Asia and Africa. It has broader horns than the true wild goat.

ibis *n.* storklike bird with a long curved beak, found worldwide in warm regions, usually near water.

ice *n.* frozen water. *vb.* freeze; cover with icing (frosting).

► Pure water freezes or ice melts at 32°F (0°C). Unlike most liquids, water increases in volume and so decreases in density as it freezes to a solid. So ice floats, with about seven-eighths of its volume below the surface.

Ice Ages

The Ice Ages were times when vast sheets of ice covered parts of the earth. Each period lasted for thousands of years. In between were warmer periods. The last Ice Age ended about 20,000 years ago but the ice might return again.

During the Ice Ages the weather was very cold. Endless snow fell and GLACIERS grew and spread. At times the glaciers covered much of North America and Asia, and Europe as far south as London. In some places the ice piled up nearly a mile high. This made the sea level lower than it is today. A land bridge was formed between Asia and North America. The first people in America came across this land bridge from Asia.

iceberg *n.* a floating mass of ice.

► Icebergs are parts of GLACIERS and ice shelves that have broken away and float in the sea. They are found in the waters of the ARCTIC and the ANTARCTIC.

Icebergs can be very big. Some weigh millions of tons. Most of an iceberg is hidden under the surface of the sea. Some icebergs may be 90 miles (145 km) long. They can be 400 ft. (120 meters) high above water. An iceberg this high would be about another 3,200 ft. (960 meters) deep under water.

Icebergs are dangerous to ships. Some icebergs float south from the Arctic into the Atlantic Ocean. In 1912, a ship called *Titanic* hit an iceberg in the Atlantic. It sank and 1,500 people on it were drowned.

ice cream *n.* a kind of soft, frozen sweet, sometimes eaten in sugar cones.

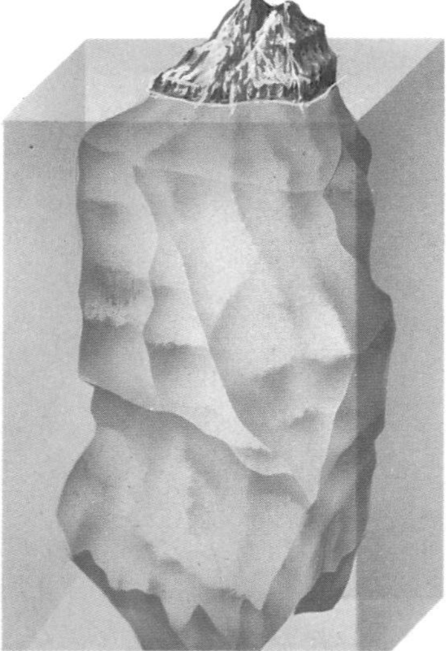

Only about a ninth of an iceberg shows above the surface of the water.

ice hockey *n.* a game played on ice between two teams, using hockey sticks to hit a rubber puck with the aim of scoring goals. Each team has six players and a goalkeeper.

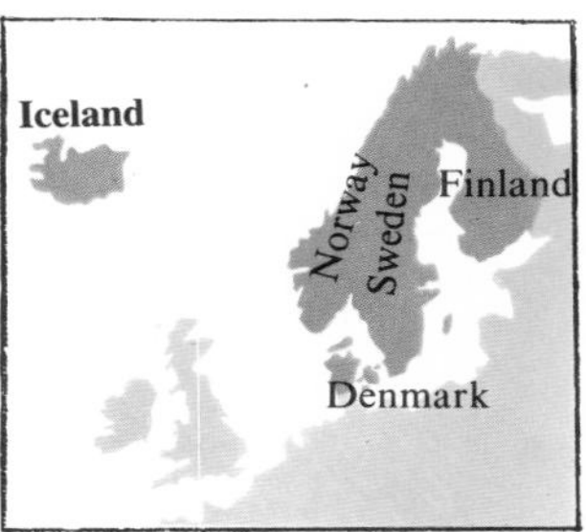

Iceland (Icelandic; Icelander)
Iceland is a small mountainous island. It was first discovered by VIKINGS in A.D. 874. The island lies just south of the Arctic in the North Atlantic between Greenland and Norway. Warm waters from the GULF STREAM keep most of the harbors free of ice all year.

Iceland has many VOLCANOES. About 25 of its volcanoes have erupted. There are many hot water springs too. Some are used to heat homes. The north of Iceland is covered by GLACIERS and a desert of stone and lava. Most of the people are farmers and fishermen. They live in the south and east where the land is lower.

AREA: 39,771 SQ. MILES (103,000 SQ. KM)
POPULATION: 234,000
CAPITAL: REYKJAVIK
CURRENCY: KRONA
OFFICIAL LANGUAGE: ICELANDIC

ice skate *n.* a boot with a blade underneath for skating (sliding rapidly) on ice. **ice-skate** *vb.*
icicle *n.* a hanging pointed piece of ice. *An icicle is made of dripping water that freezes.*
icing 1. *n.* a sweet covering for cakes, frosting. 2. *vb.* (**up**) formation of ice on an aircraft's wings.
icon *n.* the name in the Eastern Orthodox Church for any picture or image of Christ, the Virgin Mary, an angel or a saint. Usually it is a painting on wood showing the human form in a flat, stylized way.

Idaho (*abbrev.* **Id.**)
Idaho is a Rocky Mountain state on the Canadian border. It has many rivers and lakes which give the state a large supply of water for irrigation and hydroelectric power.

Agriculture is Idaho's main industry. The chief crops are potatoes, wheat, corn, apples and barley. In recent years, large areas of new land have been brought under cultivation by irrigation.

About half of Idaho's people live in cities. The largest city and state capital is Boise. But the state's population is low. There are less than half a million people in all Idaho.

Mining is important. Idaho produces more silver, cobalt and garnets than any other state.

idea *n.* a thought, a plan in the mind.
ideal *adj.* perfection, just what you want. *We thought that the plans for the holiday were ideal. n.* perfection.
identical *adj.* exactly the same.
identify *vb.* establish identity of. *He identified the star at once.*
identity *n.* individuality; distinguishing character.
idiot *n.* a person who is so weak-minded that others have to look after him or her. **idiotic** *adj.* foolish.
idle 1. *adj.* lazy; unoccupied. 2. *vb.* turn around slowly (of a car engine).
idol *n.* object of worship; fake god. **idolize** *vb.* worship, love greatly.
if *conj.* in the event that; on condition that; whether.
igloo *n.* an Eskimo hut made of blocks of snow.
igneous *adj.* formed by great heat or volcanic action.
ignite *vb.* set fire to.

An Eskimo igloo or snow house is quickly built and makes a warm shelter.

ignorant *adj.* knowing very little; uneducated. **ignorance** *n.*
ignore *vb.* take no notice of something or somebody. *The man ignored us and walked straight past.*
iguana *n.* large lizard found in tropical America, Madagascar and Polynesia.
► Iguanas may reach almost 6 ft. (2 meters) in length. About two-thirds of their length is tail.

Iguanas spend most of their time in trees, often near rivers and lakes. They feed on fruit, leaves and flowers. Iguanas are good swimmers and dive into the water to escape from danger.

il- *prefix* before L indicates negation, against, e.g. **illegal** *adj.* against the law. **illogical** *adj.* not logical.
ill *adj.* unwell, sick. **illness** *n.*
illegal *adj.* against the law.

Illinois (*abbrev.* **Ill.**)
Illinois is a state of rolling plains with fertile soil. It is one of the U.S.A.'s main agricultural states. More than half of the people in Illinois live in CHICAGO, the second largest city in the United States. Chicago lies on Lake Michigan and is one of America's great industrial, railroad, shipping and air travel centers.

Farms cover more than three-fourths of Illinois. Its rich natural resources also include coal and oil

The Illinois state capital is Springfield, where Abraham Lincoln is buried. Illinois became the 21st state in 1818. More people live in Illinois than in any other state in the Midwest.

illiterate *adj.* unable to read. **illiteracy** *n.*
illuminate *vb.* light up; make clear. **illumination** *n.*
illustrate *vb.* explain with pictures. **illustration** *n.* a picture in a book or magazine.
► The earliest illustrations in printed books were woodcuts. Today the illustration may have started life as a photograph, PAINTING, drawing, or ENGRAVING, before being printed in some way, either in black and white or color. Common uses of illustration include advertisements, posters, maps, newspapers and magazines.

im- *prefix* form of **in-** used before words beginning with b, m, and p meaning against, without, or not, e.g. **immature** *adj.* not mature. **impaired** *adj.* made worse. **immoral** *adj.* without morals.
imaginary *adj.* not real; existing only in a person's mind. *David has made up an imaginary friend called Little David.*
imagine *vb.* make up a picture in the mind. **imaginative** *adj.* using imagination. **imagination** *n.* fancy; creative power of the mind.

imitate *vb.* copy another person or thing. **imitation** *n.*
immediately *adv.* now; without losing time. *I must run down to the shops immediately before they close.*
immense *adj.* vast, huge, enormous.
immigrate *vb.* come to a country to live.
immigrant *n.* someone who comes to live in a country that is not his or her own.
imminent *adj.* about to happen. *Disaster is imminent.*
immunize *vb.* make safe from an illness. **immunization** *n.*
imp *n.* (in stories) a little devil.
impair *vb.* weaken. *The climate impaired his health.*
impala *n.* reddish-brown African antelope that lives in great herds.
impatient *adj.* not patient; not wanting to wait for others. **impatience.** *n.*
impede *vb.* get in the way of, hinder.
impersonate *vb.* pretend to be someone else.
impertinent *adj.* irrelevant; insolent.
implement 1. *n.* a tool or instrument. 2. *vb.* carry out, do.
import *vb.* (*im-***port**) bring goods into your country.
important *adj.* something that matters a great deal. *I have to go to a very important meeting this evening.* **importance** *n.*
impose *vb.* inflict on.
impossible *adj.* not possible; something that cannot be.
impresario *n.* manager of a musical company, etc.
impress *vb.* fix firmly in the mind; affect strongly. *His work impressed me.* **impressive** *adj.* creating a deep impression on the mind.
impromptu *adv.* & *adj.* without preparation.
improve *vb.* make or become better. **improvement** *n.*
in- *prefix* meaning negation, e.g. **inaccurate** *adj.* not accurate. **inactive** *adj.* not active. In most cases words beginning with this are the exact opposite of the main word, so it is generally only necessary to look up that definition to discover the contrary meaning, e.g. **adequate, inadequate**.

Incas
The Incas were a South American ruling tribe whose empire lasted from about 1200 until its destruction by Spanish CONQUISTADORS in 1532. Centered on modern Peru, their rule extended at its height from Ecuador to southern Chile. They formed a strict, ruthlessly efficient society, headed by a godlike emperor. Though writing and the wheel were unknown, architecture, metalwork and even surgery were well advanced. But the empire fell to Spanish firearms, cavalry and steel armor.

I

incense *n.* a substance, sometimes used in religious ceremonies, that gives off a sweet smell when burned.
incentive *n.* & *adj.* stimulus, something that encourages. *A raise can be an incentive to work harder.*
incessant *adj.* continual, unceasing.
inch *n.* a unit of measurement equal to 2.54 cm. *There are 12 inches in one foot.*
incident *n.* an event, a minor happening. *It was only an incident in the story.*
incite *vb.* stir up, rouse, urge on.
incline *vb.* lean, slope toward. **inclination** *n.* leaning; preference.
include *vb.* contain as part of the whole; take into account.
incognito *adj.*, *n.* & *adv.* (passing under) an assumed or false identity. *Traveling incognito.*
income *n.* pay; money received for work and from other sources during a period. *Income tax.*
incorporate *vb.* include and make part of.
increase (*in*-**crease**) *vb.* make greater in size or amount. *The number of pupils in our class has greatly increased.* (**in**-*crease*) *n.* growth, enlargement.
incredible *adj.* something that cannot be believed.
incubate *vb.* keep eggs warm in order to hatch them.
incur *vb.* (past **incurred**) bring upon oneself.
indeed *adv.* really; in truth. *It was a very big dog indeed.*

Independence, American War of
The War of Independence was fought between Britain and her 13 American colonies from 1775 to 1783. The colonies won their independence from Britain and became a new nation, the United States of America.

For many years before the war Britain and the American colonies had disagreed about a number of things, chief of which was taxes. The British tried to force the colonies to pay taxes, but would not allow the colonies any representation in the British Parliament. The colonies insisted on "no taxation without representation."

The first shot in the war was fired at Lexington, Massachusetts on April 19, 1775. In July, George WASHINGTON was made commander of the American forces. On July 4, 1776, the colonies adopted the Declaration of Independence, written by Thomas JEFFERSON.

At first the war went badly for the Americans. But in October 1777, the British were defeated at the Battle of Saratoga, in New York. This was the turning point of the war. The victory helped to bring France into the war on the side of the Americans. On October 19, 1781, the British army under Lord Cornwallis surrendered to Washington. The final peace treaty, the Treaty of Paris, was signed in 1783.

independent *adj.* free; not controlled by others. **independence** *n.*
index *n.* a list at the end of a book, giving all the subjects in the book in alphabetical order and the pages on which they appear.

India (Indian)
The world's seventh largest country, the Republic of India is the second most populous. The population is increasing rapidly. Every year there are several million more people to feed, a major problem in a land where famines often occur. The diversity of languages and religions makes national unity difficult to achieve. More than 800 languages and dialects are spoken in India, although only Hindi and English are official languages. The chief religion, HINDUISM, is followed by 83 percent of the people. Another 10 percent are MUSLIMS and there are sizeable groups of Christians, Sikhs, Buddhists and Jains.

There are three main land regions. The Himalayan mountain system extends along India's northern borders. The fertile northern plains, the most thickly populated region, are drained by the Ganges and Brahmaputra rivers. The third region is the Deccan plateau in the south. Most Indians are farmers. Rice is the main food crop. Cotton, jute, millet, sugar cane, tea and wheat are other important products. Mining is underdeveloped, but manufacturing is increasing. The largest cities are Calcutta, Bombay, Delhi and Madras.

India, with PAKISTAN and BANGLADESH, was once part of the British Empire. But in 1947, the country split into two independent nations, the mostly Hindu India, and the Muslim Pakistan. War between these two nations over Kashmir ended in 1949, with India taking over two-thirds of the disputed area.
AREA: 1,269,415 SQ. MILES (3,287,590 SQ. KM)
POPULATION: 698,632,000
CAPITAL: NEW DELHI
CURRENCY: RUPEE
OFFICIAL LANGUAGES: ENGLISH, HINDI

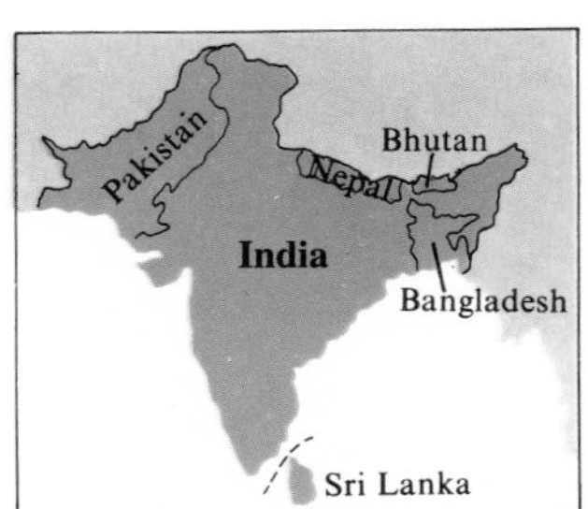

When Christopher Columbus reached America in 1492, he thought he had arrived in India. That is why the native people of the Americas are known as Indians. This illustration shows an American Indian chief, probably in ceremonial attire, drawn in about 1586.

Indian *n.* a person from India; one of the original people of the Americas.

Indiana (*abbrev.* **Ind.**)
Indiana is a small state in the Midwest. The fertile plains in the center of the state produce an abundance of grain crops. There are big oil refineries and steel mills along the shores of Lake Michigan. Coal and oil are mined in large quantities.

The state capital and largest city is Indianapolis, a great transportation and industrial center. Each year on Memorial Day people come from all over the United States to watch the Indianapolis 500 automobile race.

Indiana got its name from the many Indians who once lived there. It was first a French colony, which became British in 1763. Indiana Territory was created in 1800. It included the present states of Indiana, Wisconsin and Illinois, with parts of Minnesota and Michigan. When Illinois and Michigan became separate territories, Indiana was left almost as it is today. Indiana became the 19th state in 1816.

Indian Ocean
The world's third largest ocean, the Indian Ocean covers 28,000,000 sq. miles (73,490,000 sq. km). It lies between Africa, Asia, Australia and Antarctica. The average depth is 13,000 ft. (3,960 meters).

indicate *vb.* point to; be a sign of. **indication** *n.*

indifference *n.* lack of concern, absence of feeling. **indifferent** *adj. He was indifferent to her feelings.*

indigenous (*in*-**dij**-*e-nus*) *adj.* native, belonging from the beginning. *Kangaroos are indigenous to Australia.*

indigestion *n.* difficulty in digesting food. **indigestible** *adj.*

indignant *adj.* angry, scornful, especially at injustices, cruelty, etc.

individual 1. *adj.* of or for one person only. *We each had an individual parcel of food.* 2. *n.* a person. *He's a strange individual.*

Indonesia (Indonesian)
Indonesia is a republic in Southeast ASIA. It consists of a chain of about 3,000 islands around the equator. The islands stretch for a distance of about 3,000 miles (nearly 5,000 km). The largest regions include part of BORNEO, Sumatra and Java. Jakarta, the capital, lies on the island of Java.

Most Indonesians are farmers. Their crops include rice, tea, rubber and tobacco. Forestry is important, and Indonesia is the leading oil producer in the Far East.

The territory was ruled by the Dutch from the 1600s until World War II. Indonesia became an independent republic in 1945. East (formerly Portuguese) Timor was incorporated into Indonesia in 1976.

AREA: 782,705 SQ. MILES (2,027,087 SQ. KM)
POPULATION: 146,527,000
CAPITAL: JAKARTA
CURRENCY: RUPIAH
OFFICIAL LANGUAGE: BAHASA INDONESIA

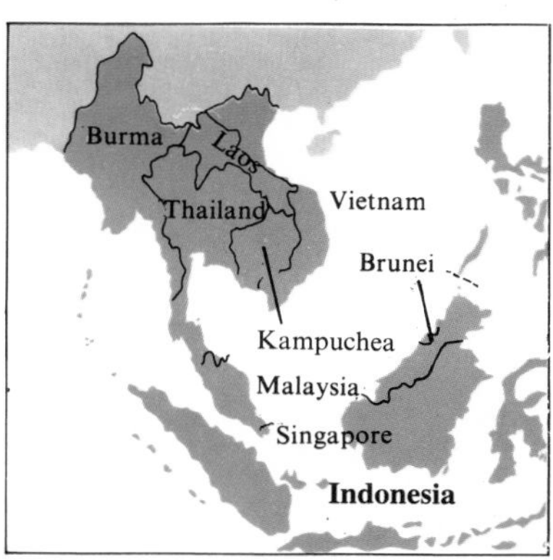

indoors *adv.* inside a building.

indulge *vb.* take pleasure in, gratify, desire. **indulgent** *adj.* too lenient.

Indus
The Indus is a river that flows through INDIA and PAKISTAN to the Arabian Sea. It is important as a source of water for irrigation and hydroelectric power. It is nearly 2,000 miles (about 3,000 km) long.

The Indus valley was the site of one of the world's earliest civilizations (*see* MOHENJO DARO).

Women and children worked long hours in the new factories of the Industrial Revolution.

Industrial Revolution
The Industrial Revolution is the name given to the sudden breakthrough in technical development and the use of MACHINE TOOLS in Europe (especially England) from 1750 to 1850 and the effect this had on people's lives. It reached North America in the early 1800s. The main inventions were STEAM power, textile machinery and improvements in metal processing. The results were factories and RAILROADS, creating large industrial towns with new classes of owners and workers. Other results included an expanding population, more banks and financial institutions and greater overseas trade.

industry *n.* 1. work done in factories. 2. a trade or business. *Steel-making is an important industry.* **industrial** *adj.* to do with manufacturing. **industrious** *adj.* hard-working.

inertia *n.* lack of energy; (in physics) property of an object that makes it resist being moved or changing its motion.

infant *n.* a baby or child under about two years of age. **infantile** *adj.* childish.

infantry *n.* soldiers who fight on foot, the main combat forces in most armies.

infection *n.* an illness that can be spread by harmful germs.

inferior *adj.* lower in rank or quality.

infinity *n.* a time or space without end; too big to be imagined.

infirmary *n.* a hospital (especially in schools).

inhabitant *n.* a person who lives in or **inhabits** (*vb.*) a place or country. *The Indians were the first inhabitants of America.*

inhale *vb.* breathe in.

inherit *vb.* receive money or property from someone who has died. **inheritance** *n.*

initial (*in*-**ish**-*al*) 1. *adj.* at the beginning. 2. *n.* the first letter in a name. *Simon Powell's initials are S.P.* *vb.* sign with initials.

injection *n.* medicine given with a hypodermic syringe. **inject** *vb.*

injure *vb.* hurt or damage. **injury** *n.* damage or harm, particularly to the body. *The unfortunate man died of his injuries.*

ink *n.* a colored fluid used for writing, drawing or printing.

► Ink has been used since ancient times. The Egyptians were making it 5,000 years ago. They made it from CARBON and GUM. To make colored inks they used DYES.

The Chinese also used ink from early times. They wrote with a brush dipped in ink. People in Europe first used pens made from long feathers, or quills. Many people now use ballpoint pens which have the ink already inside them.

inkling *n.* hint, suspicion. *She had no inkling I would turn up today.*

inland *adj.* away from the sea. *Chicago is an inland city.*

inn *n.* a public house where food and drink are sold and people can stay.

innate *adj.* inborn, natural.

innings *n.* a team's turn at bat in baseball.

innocent *adj.* not guilty; doing no harm. **innocence** *n.*

inoculate *vb.* give a mild form of a disease in order to protect a person from the disease. **inoculation** *n.*

► Inoculation is also called vaccination. By giving people a very weak dose of a disease, the body learns to fight the GERMS which cause the disease. In this way the body becomes protected, or immune, from the disease.

Immunity from a disease may last from a few months to many years, depending on the kind of disease and vaccine. There are many kinds of inoculation. They are used against diseases such as typhoid, cholera,

The four-stage growth cycle or "metamorphosis" of a bee. The adult lays eggs which hatch into larvae. Each larvae turns into a pupa or chrysalis from which emerges a fully formed bee.

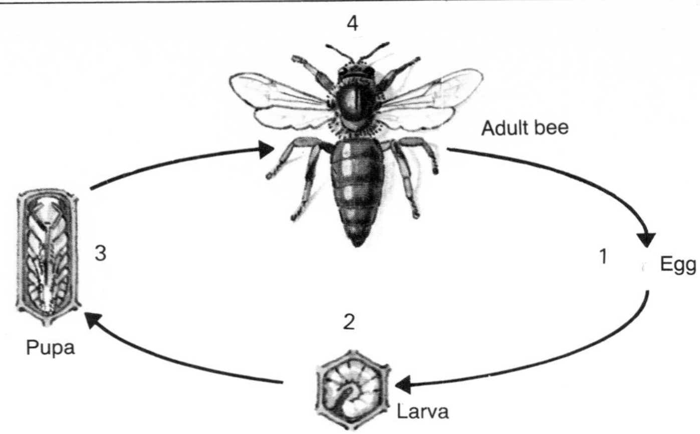

measles and polio. Many people are saved from dying every year through inoculation.

inquest *n.* (*in-kwest*) official inquiry, especially into cause of death.
inquire *vb.* ask about something or someone. **inquiry** *n.* investigation. also **enquire, enquiry**.
inquisitive *adj.* wanting to find out about things, curious.
insanity *n.* madness; utter foolishness. **insane** *adj.*
► Insanity is a legal term covering various illnesses of the mind. In law insane persons are considered incapable of doing certain acts, such as making a will, and are not held responsible for their actions.
insect *n.* a small creature with six legs and no backbone.
► There are about 35 million different kinds of insect in the world. Every year, hundreds of new kinds are found. Insects are called invertebrates (they do not have backbones). Insects live everywhere except in the sea. Some insects live in hot, volcanic pools. Others live in the cold Antarctic. They can feed on almost anything: plants, animals, plastic and even chemicals. Some insects are very small. Tiny wasps called fairy flies are only about 1/100 in. (0.25 mm) long. Some insects grow very big. Giant stick insects may be 12 in. (30 cm) long.

The bodies of insects have three parts: the *head*, the *thorax* and the *abdomen*. The head has eyes and a pair of feelers, or *antennae*. It also has a mouth for biting or sucking. The thorax has three parts, each with a pair of legs. The thorax often has two pairs of wings as well. Inside the abdomen lies the gut.

Insects breathe through tiny holes in the sides of their bodies. These are called *spiracles*. Tubes from the spiracles take air to all the cells of the body.

Many insects are pests. They damage crops and spread diseases. Some MOSQUITOES carry MALARIA. The tsetse fly spreads sleeping sickness. Flies and FLEAS also pass on diseases. Swarms of LOCUSTS can destroy tons of crops in a few hours. Some insects are useful. They eat harmful insects or lay their eggs inside them. Many insects help plants. They take POLLEN from one flower to another, like the honeybee.

Many insects go through four stages in their lives. At each stage they are different. The insect is born as an egg. The egg hatches into a grub, or *larva*. After a while the larva stops eating and turns into a *chrysalis*, or *pupa*. The adult insect grows inside the pupa and breaks out of it when it is fully formed.

Adult insects do not live long. Most live for a few weeks. Adult mayflies live only a few hours. Some insects live longer. A queen bee may live for seven years. TERMITE queens live even longer.

insecticide *n.* a poisonous mixture used to kill insects.
insert *vb.* put in, place in between. *n.* thing inserted.
inside *adj.* within. *The heart is inside the body.*
insignia *n.* badge of office, authority, etc.
insipid *adj.* without flavor; dull.
insist *vb.* press for, speak emphatically, demand.
insomnia *adj.* inability to sleep.
inspect *vb.* examine carefully. **inspection** *n.*
inspire *vb.* encourage someone to do something, influence. **inspiration** *n.* creative influence, a sudden idea.
installment *n.* a part of something, especially a story or payment.
instant *n.* a moment; a very short time. **instantly** *adv.* at once.
instead *adv.* in place of. *She is teaching the class instead of our usual teacher, who is ill.*

Insects range in size from tiny fleas to goliath beetles as big as a human hand.

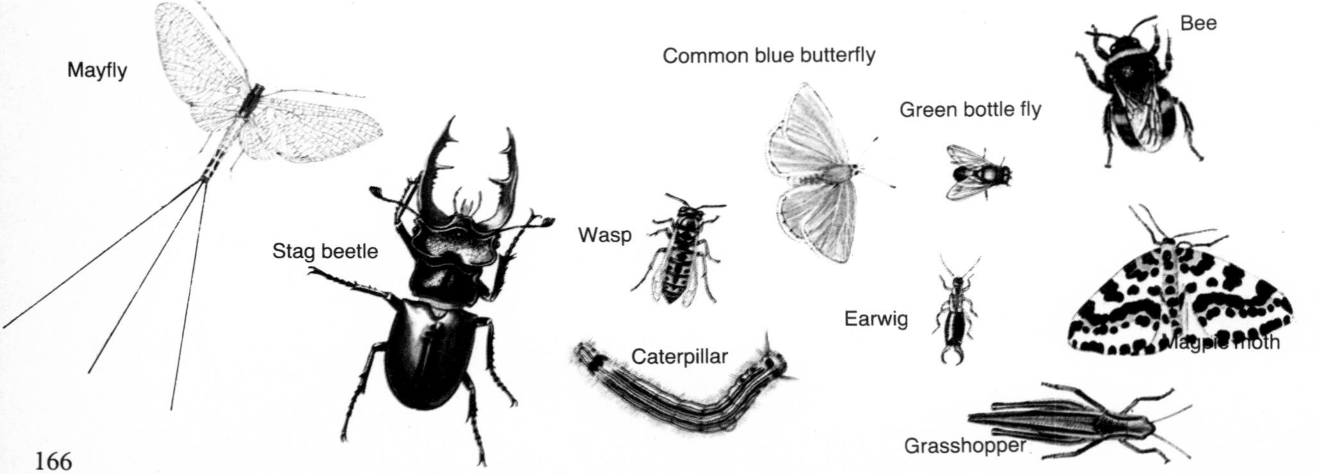

instinct *n.* something that makes animals do things that they have not learned to do, inborn behavior.
▶ Instinct plays an important part in the life of all animals. Spiders, for instance, are not taught to make webs, nor are beavers shown how to fell trees and build dams: they do these things by instinct. Instincts are inherited and control many animal activities such as self-defense, feeding habits, courtship, rearing of young, MIGRATION and HIBERNATION.

insult (*in*-**sult**) *vb.* be rude to someone. (**in**-*sult*) *n.* a rude remark. *It was an insult to call Bill a stupid, lazy fellow.*
institute *vb.* set up, establish. *n.* organization or establishment for a special purpose.
instruct *vb.* teach, direct. **instruction** *n.* teaching, orders.
instrument *n.* 1. a delicate tool or implement for a special purpose. 2. something used for making musical sounds. *A musical instrument.*
insulate *vb.* isolate, prevent passage of electricity etc. **insulator** *n.*
▶ In ELECTRICITY, a substance such as rubber, plastic, porcelain or glass that is a poor conductor is an insulator. Most nonmetals are insulators, and we use insulators to prevent electricity from leaking. The opposite of an insulator is a conductor.
Many materials give insulation against heat and cold. Our clothes insulate us against the weather. Homes can be insulated to save fuel.

insulin *n.* a hormone secreted by the pancreas used in treating diabetes.
insurance *n.* a method of protecting against loss through such risks as fire or theft, accident or death. **insure** *vb.*
▶ The idea of insurance is that many people pay small amounts of money (contributions) to an insurance company each year, so there is enough money to compensate (pay back) those who do lose. The insurance companies assess the various risks, and set the contributions (premiums) high enough to cover the likely loss and leave themselves a profit.

integrate *vb.* combine into one.
▶ Integrated circuit – tiny electronic circuit which can contain transistors and other components, formed on a single silicon chip.

integrity *n.* honesty, purity, soundness.
intelligent *adj.* clever and able to understand easily.
intelligence *n.* the ability to reason and understand.
▶ Most animal behavior is governed by reflexes (automatic responses to a stimulus such as heat or light) and by INSTINCT. Many human actions are similarly controlled: for example, a person jumps if someone sticks a pin in his arm. This is a reflex action, done without thinking. But human beings are able to think and are therefore able to act using reason and understanding: they have intelligence. The large APES, such as the chimpanzee and the gorilla, are also capable of intelligent behavior, but their intelligence is far inferior to ours. Intelligence is linked with the size of the BRAIN and although an ape has a larger brain than all other creatures, it is still only half the size of the human brain.

intend *vb.* mean to, have in mind to. *I intend to finish the weeding.* **intention** *n.* purpose, object.
intense *adj.* earnest; very strong. **intensity** *n.* **intensive** *adj.* concentrated. *The intensive care unit.*
inter- *prefix* meaning among, between, etc., e.g. **intercontinental**.
interest *n.* 1. enthusiasm, being keen on something. *He takes a great interest in my work.* 2. money paid (by or to a bank, etc.) on a loan. *I have just been paid the interest on my savings account.*
interested *adj.* wanting to know and learn about. *Robert is very interested in ships and borrowed three books about them.*
interfere *vb.* 1. meddle in other people's affairs. 2. get in the way of something.
interior *adj.* inside, inland. *n.* the inside of anything.
internal *adj.* belonging to the inside.
internal combustion engine *n.* type of engine that works by the combustion (burning) of a fuel-and-air mixture within the cylinders of the engine.
▶ There are two main types of **internal combustion engine**, the gasoline engine and the **diesel** engine. In the gasoline engine the fuel, a mixture of gasoline and air, is ignited by an electric spark. The explosion in the top of the cylinder forces the piston downwards. The piston helps to turn a crankshaft. This kind of engine is used mostly in automobiles and there are usually four, six or eight cylinders firing one after the other.
In the diesel engine air is drawn into the cylinder and compressed to make in hot. This hot air ignites the fuel oil injected into the cylinder. There is no spark. (*See* AUTOMOBILE: MOTORCYCLE).

international *adj.* affecting or involving two or more nations. *The UN is an international organization.*
interpret *vb.* 1. judge the meaning to be. *He interpreted the signs as meaning that it would rain.* 2. translate from one language to another.
interrupt *vb.* disturb someone who is doing something. **interruption** *n.*
interview *n.* & *vb.* question someone to find information or to discover suitability for a job, etc.
intestines *pl. n.* the tubes through which our food passes after it has been through the stomach.
intimate *adj.* close, familiar. *An intimate friend.*
into *prep.* put or go inside something. *Come into the kitchen.*
intoxicate *vb.* make drunk.
intricate *adj.* complicated and involved.
introduce *vb.* 1. make people known to each other. *Edward introduced me to his mother.* 2. bring into use.
introduction *n.* introducing; the first part of a book, which tells you what the book is about.
invade *vb.* go into another country or place to fight against the people. **invasion** *n.*
invalid *n.* an ill or disabled person.
invent *vb.* make something for the first time, devise, fabricate (a false story). **invention** (*in*-**ven**-*shun*) *n.* something that has been invented or made after study or experiment.
▶ A discovery is something that always existed, but was not known before. An invention is something new, thought up – from flint tools, the plow and the WHEEL, to TRANSISTORS, LASERS and COMPUTERS. People are the only animals to invent things, and they do so for three main reasons: to make life better, to make money, and to make war. Inventions in power and machinery brought the INDUSTRIAL REVOLUTION. Those in products (record players, washing machines) have brought a revolution in comfort and enjoyment. Those in communications (cars, televisions, telephones), a revolution in how society organizes itself. Those in medicine (hypodermic needles, X-ray machines), a revolution in health. Before about 1900, most inventions were the work of individuals, acting alone. Now, most are the work of research teams of scientists and engineers.
Of course, not all inventions are completely good. Some are simply new ways of killing people. Others, though useful, bring problems with them – such as the pollution caused by cars and trucks. But most inventions make life easier and happier for many people.

inventor *n.* someone who invents.
invertebrate *n.* an animal with no backbone, such as an insect, a worm, or snail. *adj.* without a backbone.
▶ There are more than a million species of invertebrates, many more than there are species of *vertebrates* – animals with backbones.
invisible *adj.* unseen; cannot be seen. *The hem was sewn so neatly that it was invisible.* **invisibility** *n.*

invite *vb*. ask someone to come somewhere. *Susan's aunt may invite her to go to India next year.*
invitation *n*. spoken or written words that ask you or invite you to come.

invoice *n*. a list of goods sent, with their prices.

iodine *n*. a gray-black crystal element which when heated gives off a violet vapor. Iodine is found in seaweed and is essential for the proper working of the thyroid gland.

ion *n*. an atom or group of atoms that is electrically charged because it has gained or lost electrons.

ionosphere *n*. a layer of the Earth's atmosphere starting at about 50 miles up and ending about 300 miles above sea level.
▶ The ionosphere is so called because the air at that level is highly ionized (*See* ION) by the sun's ultraviolet radiation. The ionosphere is important because it reflects radio waves back to earth which would otherwise be lost in space.

Iowa (*abbrev*. **IA.**)
Iowa is a great farming state. It is made up mostly of gentle rolling plains, covered with soil that is perhaps the finest in all America. The state is bordered by the Mississippi River on the east and by the Missouri River on the west. These great rivers give Iowa plenty of water and good transportation routes.

Even though 95 percent of Iowa is farmland, more than half of the state's people live in cities. The largest is the capital, Des Moines.

The state became part of the United States in 1803 as part of the Louisiana Purchase. In 1838 Congress created the Territory of Iowa, and in 1846 it became the 29th state.

Iran (Iranian)
Iran is a country in ASIA. It lies between the Caspian Sea in the north and the Persian Gulf in the south. The country is nearly seven times larger than Great Britain but it has fewer people. Deserts, snowy mountains and green valleys cover most of the land. Much of Iran has hot summers and cold winters.

Iranians speak Persian (Persia is the old name for Iran). Their religion is ISLAM. Many Iranians are NOMADS who travel around with flocks of sheep or goats. Each time they camp, the women set up simple looms and weave beautiful rugs by hand. Some Persian rugs and carpets take years to make. They are bought by people in many countries. Iran's most important product is oil. The country is one of the world's biggest oil producers.

Iran has a long history. In about 550 B.C. the Persians had a leader called Cyrus. Cyrus and his army made an empire that stretched from Greece and Egypt to India. The Persian empire was then the largest in the world.

ALEXANDER THE GREAT conquered Persia in about 330 B.C. Later, the country was ruled by ARABS and MONGOLS. During this century Iran was ruled by emperors or shahs. However, following a revolution, the Shah was forced to leave the country in 1979. A religious leader, Ayatollah Khomeini, returned from exile, and Iran became an Islamic Republic. War broke out between Iran and IRAQ in 1980.
AREA: 636,331 SQ. MILES (1,648,000 SQ. KM)
POPULATION: 40,288,000
CAPITAL: TEHRAN
CURRENCY: RIAL
OFFICIAL LANGUAGE: FARSI (PERSIAN)

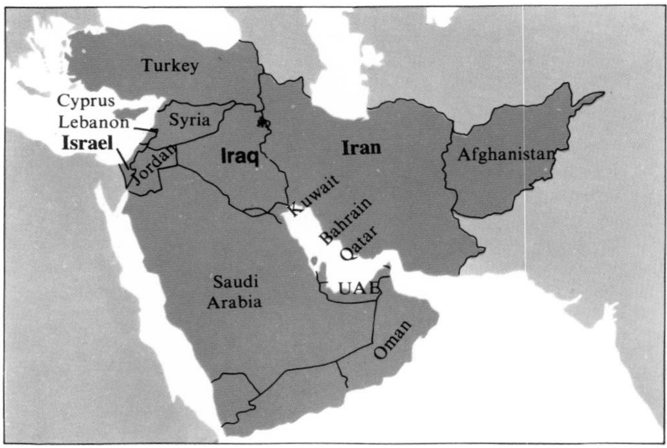

Iraq (Iraqi)
Iraq is an ARAB country in southwest ASIA. Much of Iraq is a dry, sandy and stony plain. It is cool in winter and very hot in summer. The Tigris and Euphrates rivers flow through the plain to the Persian Gulf. Their water helps the farmers to grow rice, cotton, wheat and dates. Iraq is also one of the biggest oil producers in the world. Pipelines carry the oil from the north of the country across the desert to ports in Syria and the Lebanon.

Many Iraqis are NOMADS. They live in the deserts with their sheep and goats.

Some of the first cities in the world were built near Iraq's big rivers. Ur was one of the earliest cities. It was built by a BRONZE AGE people called the Sumerians. The Bible says that Ur was also the home of Abraham. Later, the Babylonians built their famous city, BABYLON, in Iraq. The ruins of Babylon can still be seen.

War broke out between Iraq and IRAN in 1980.
AREA: 167,924 SQ. MILES (434,924 SQ. KM)
POPULATION: 13,977,000
CAPITAL: BAGHDAD
CURRENCY: IRAQI DINAR
OFFICIAL LANGUAGE: ARABIC

Ireland (Irish)
The second largest island in the BRITISH ISLES, Ireland is divided into two parts — the Republic of Ireland, which has been independent since 1921, and Northern Ireland. It lacks resources and many people have emigrated in the last 140 years. But it is a beautiful country, where farming is the chief occupation.

Northern Ireland is part of the United Kingdom of Great Britain and Northern Ireland. Protestants, who oppose unification with the mainly Roman Catholic Republic, form the majority. Since the late 1960s animosity between Protestants and Roman Catholics has led to civil disturbances.

Ireland, Republic of (Eire)
AREA: 27,138 SQ. MILES (70,283 SQ. KM)
POPULATION: 3,366,000
CAPITAL: DUBLIN
CURRENCY: IRISH POUND (PUNT)
OFFICIAL LANGUAGES: IRISH, ENGLISH

iris *n*. 1. rainbow. 2. a perennial flower with pointed leaves. 3. the colored part of the eye.

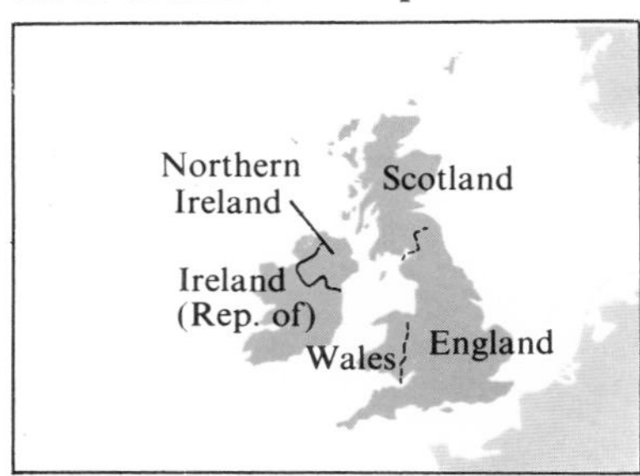

irk *vb*. trouble, bother.

iron 1. *n*. a heavy, common metal (symbol – *Fe*). 2. *n*. a tool for pressing clothes. 3. *vb*. press wrinkles out of clothes.
▶ Iron is the cheapest and most useful of all METALS. Much of our food, clothes, homes, cars, and

machines are made with machines and tools that are made from iron.

Iron is mined or quarried as iron ore, or MINERALS. The ore is melted down, or smelted, in a blast furnace. The iron is then made into cast iron, wrought iron or different kinds of steel.

Cast iron is hard but not as strong as steel. Molten cast iron is poured into molds to make such things as engine blocks. Wrought iron is soft but tough. It is used for chains and gates. Steel is hard and strong. Steel ALLOYS are used to make many different things, from bridges to nails.

Iron Curtain
A term used in the Western world to describe the barriers which have limited communications, trade and travel between the West and the Communist countries of Eastern EUROPE. It came into popular use when Winston CHURCHILL stated in a speech in 1946 that "an iron curtain has descended across the continent."

iron lung *n.* a respirator or machine to aid breathing, used when the chest muscles are paralyzed.

irregular *n.* merchandise that is not regular, often costing less to buy. *My mom bought an irregular coat and saved $50.*

irrigate *vb.* bring water to dry land in order to help crops to grow. **irrigation** *n.*

► Farmers and gardeners who water plants are irrigating them. Farmers in China, Egypt and Iraq have been irrigating large areas of land for thousands of years.

Many countries store water in lakes made by building DAMS across rivers. CANALS take water from lakes to farms. One irrigation canal in Russia is about 350 miles long (850 km). Ditches or pipes carry water from each canal to the fields. In each field the water flows between the rows of plants. Sometimes it spurts up from holes in the pipes. It sprinkles the plants like a shower of rain.

irritate *vb.* make angry, annoy. **irritable** *adj.* easily annoyed.

Irving, Washington
Washington Irving (1783–1859) was the first American writer to gain fame outside the United States. His best-known stories are *Rip Van Winkle* and *The Legend of Sleepy Hollow*. He is also remembered for his essays, travel books and biographies.

Islam *n.* the religion revealed through the prophet Muhammed. **Islamic** *adj.*

► Islam is one of the major world religions, also called Muhammedanism after its founder MUHAMMED (A.D. 570–632). Its creed says there is no God but Allah and Muhammed is his Prophet. Its holy book is the *Koran* and its basic duties are prayer, fasting, giving of alms, and pilgrimage to MECCA. Islam accepts much of the Bible but emphasizes the oneness of God and opposes the worship of saints and images. It inspired the ARAB conquests and today there are about 430 million followers (called Muslims or Moslems) worldwide.

island *n.* land area surrounded by water. **islander** *n.* someone who lives on an island.

► The largest island is GREENLAND, Australia being regarded as a continent. Some islands are parts of the CONTINENTAL SHELF around continents. Others are volcanoes which rise steeply from the ocean depths.

isobar *n.* line on a weather map which connects places that have the same atmospheric pressure.

isolate *vb.* place alone, set apart.

isotope *n.* the form of an element that has neutrons added to or taken away from the nucleus of its atoms.

► Certain isotopes are radioactive. These are very useful, as their radioactivity allows them to be followed in various industrial processes. Isotopes are also used in medicine to track down and destroy diseased cells in the body.

Israel
A republic in the eastern Mediterranean (opposite page), Israel contains about one-fifth of the world's JEWS. About 20 percent of the population are ARABS. Israel, once part of PALESTINE, was established as a Jewish homeland in 1948, despite strong Arab opposition. Short Arab-Israeli wars occurred in 1948, 1956, 1967 and 1973, during which Israel took parts of Egypt, Jordan and Syria. In 1977 Israel and Egypt sought a peace treaty, despite criticism from various Arab leaders. This resulted in the gradual return of the Sinai region to Egypt. In 1982, Israel invaded LEBANON and attacked the forces of the Palestine Liberation Organization.

Israel is a prosperous country. The people have reclaimed desert and set up thriving mining and manufacturing industries. Cut diamonds, textiles, fruits and vegetables, chemicals, machinery and fertilizers are exported.

AREA: 8,020 SQ. MILES (20,770 SQ. KM)
POPULATION: 4,093,000
CAPITAL: JERUSALEM
CURRENCY: SHEKEL
OFFICIAL LANGUAGES: HEBREW, ARABIC

The Dome of the Rock in Jerusalem encloses the 'Sacred Book' from which, according to legend, Muhammad, the founder of Islam, ascended to heaven in AD 632.

issue *vb.* & *n.* going or flowing out; offspring (children); putting into circulation money, books, etc.

Istanbul
Istanbul is a seaport which is also the largest city of Turkey. It lies on both sides of the BOSPORUS, a strip of water which separates EUROPE and ASIA. The Golden Horn is an inlet from the Bosporus which forms a natural harbor.

Istanbul was originally called Byzantium. In A.D. 330, the Roman emperor Constantine chose the city as his new capital. He renamed it CONSTANTINOPLE. When the Turkish capital was moved to Ankara, the city's name was changed again to Istanbul.

isthmus *n.* a strip of land joining two larger areas of land.
italics *pl. n.* words that are printed at a slope *like this*.

Italy (Italian)
A southern European republic, Italy is noted for its beauty, the impressive ruins of the ROMAN EMPIRE, VATICAN CITY in Rome, and magnificent medieval cities such as Florence and VENICE. Italy is also famed for its great achievements in the arts. It was the birthplace of the RENAISSANCE and home of such great artists as LEONARDO DA VINCI and MICHELANGELO. Opera was born in Italy in the 1600s. Leading Italian composers of opera include Claudio Monteverdi (1567–1643), Gioacchino Rossini (1792–1868), Giuseppe Verdi (1813–1901) and Giacomo Puccini (1858–1924). La Scala, in Milan, is one of the world's great opera houses.

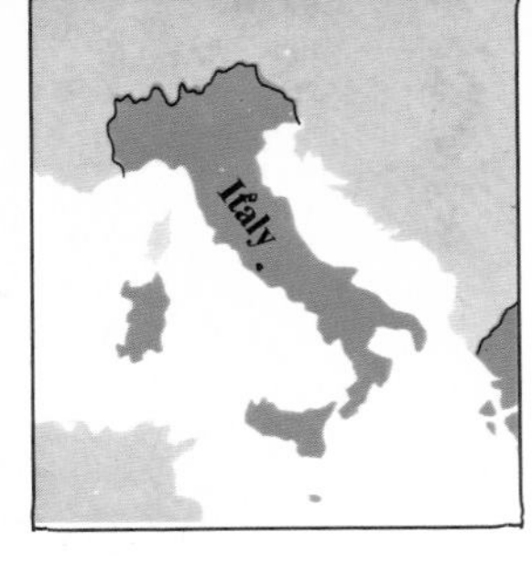

Between the Alps in the north and the Italian peninsula which juts into the Mediterranean Sea is the broad Lombardy plain, an agricultural region drained by the River Po. The Apennine Mountains form the backbone of the peninsula, but there are also fertile basins, valleys and coastal plains. The southern part of the peninsula is relatively underdeveloped, as are the islands of SICILY and Sardinia. Active volcanoes in the south include VESUVIUS, near Naples, Etna on Sicily and Stromboli in the Lipari Islands. Much of Italy has hot, dry summers and mild, moist winters, and about two-thirds of the country is farmland. But manufacturing is the most valuable industry, especially in the cities such as Rome, Milan, Naples and Turin. Manufactured products include textiles, especially silk and wool; chemicals, electrical goods and motor vehicles.
AREA: 116,310 SQ. MILES (301,225 SQ. KM)
POPULATION: 58,189,000
CAPITAL: ROME
CURRENCY: LIRA
OFFICIAL LANGUAGE: ITALIAN

Part of the walls of Constantinople (modern Instanbul), built in A.D. 439, as they appear today.

itch *n.* an uncomfortable feeling in the skin which makes you want to scratch. **itchy** *adj.*
item *n.* a single unit on a list. *How many items of furniture should there be?*
itinerary *n.* plan or record of a journey.
it's short for it is. *It's late.*
its *pron.* the possessive form of it. *The cat was washing its face.*

Ivan the Terrible
Ivan the Terrible (Ivan IV) was the first tsar (emperor) of Russia (born 1530, reigned 1533–84). Gaining effective power at 14, he had himself crowned tsar in 1547. His rule extended Russian territory and reduced the power of the nobles. But from about 1560 he grew into a ferocious tyrant.

ivory *n.* the white, bone-like material of which elephants' tusks are made.
► Walrus and narwhal tusks and hippopotamus teeth are also made of ivory. Larger pieces of ivory come from ELEPHANT and MAMMOTH tusks. Mammoths died out thousands of years ago, yet Russians still find their tusks in Siberia.

Elephant ivory bends and can be cut and polished. People use it to make ornaments, piano keys and jewelry.

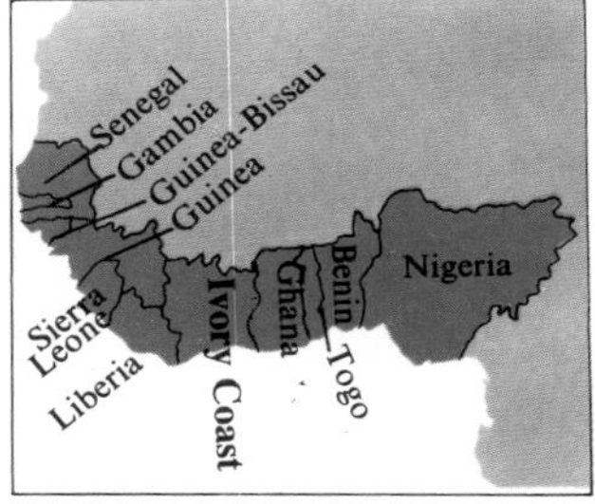

Ivory Coast
The Ivory Coast is a republic in West AFRICA. Formerly a French territory, it became independent in 1960. Farming is the most important industry, with coffee and cocoa the main products, accounting for over half the country's exports.
AREA: 124,510 SQ. MILES (322,463 SQ. KM)
POPULATION: 9,564,000
CAPITAL: ABIDJAN
CURRENCY: FIONE
OFFICIAL LANGUAGE: FRENCH

ivy *n.* a climbing evergreen vine with shiny, dark-green leaves.
► Ivy uses tiny roots, growing from its stem, to cling to walls and trees. Although the plant does not feed off any supporting tree, it does weaken and can even kill it. Since early times, ivy has been considered lucky and is often used for decoration, particularly at Christmas.

J

Japan – the three boats festival.

jab *vb.* & *n.* poke, stab. *In his anger, he jabbed at me with the end of his umbrella.*

jack *n.* 1. a tool for raising heavy weights off the ground. 2. a knave in a pack of cards.

jackal *n.* a kind of wild dog.

► Some jackals are brown or grayish and live in eastern Europe, Asia and North Africa. Africa has other kinds too. Jackals hide in bushes by day. At night they hunt small animals and find food in rubbish heaps.

jackboot *n.* long boot reaching above the knee, worn in the 17th and 18th centuries.

jackdaw *n.* a bird of the crow family.

jacket *n.* a short long-sleeved coat, sometimes part of a suit.

jackpot *n.* top prize in a slot machine.

jackrabbit *n.* a large hare found in western North America with long ears and long hind legs.

jade *n.* a hard green, blackish-green, or white stone.

► Jade is a kind of mineral. It can be carved and polished to make delicate ornaments and jewelry. The Chinese have been making jade carvings for more than 3,000 years.

jagged *adj.* rough or having sharply uneven edges. *The ship was wrecked on the jagged rocks.*

jaguar *n.* a large yellow wildat with black spots like a leopard.

► No other American wildcat is as heavy or as dangerous as the jaguar. From nose to tail a jaguar is longer than a man and may be nearly twice his weight. Jaguars live in the hot wet forests of Central and South America. They leap from trees onto wild pigs and deer. They also hunt turtles, fishes and alligators.

jail *n.* prison. *vb.* put in prison.

Jakarta
Jakarta, the capital city of INDONESIA, lies on the northwest coast of the island of Java. During the 1600s, the Dutch built a trading post on the site, which they called Batavia. Batavia became the headquarters of the Dutch East India Company. There are still a number of Dutch colonial buildings in the old part of the city, but the new part is modern.

jam 1. *vb.* push things together tightly. *He jammed his clothes into his suitcase.* 2. *vb.* cause interference on the radio. 3. *n.* food made by boiling fruit and sugar together.

► Jam and jellies are made by boiling fruit until it is soft. You can make jam from whole berries such as strawberries, but you have to chop up larger fruits, such as oranges. You may have to add pectin to make the jam 'jell."

Jamaica (Jamaican)
Jamaica is a scenic mountainous island in the WEST INDIES. It became independent in 1962, with the British monarch as head of state. The country produces bauxite and various farm products. Tourism is an important industry.

AREA: 4,244 SQ. MILES (10,990 SQ. KM)
POPULATION: 2,299,000
CAPITAL: KINGSTON
CURRENCY: JAMAICAN DOLLAR
OFFICIAL LANGUAGE: ENGLISH

jamboree (*jam-bu-***ree**) *n.* rally of scouts; a large festive gathering.

James I
James I was king of England and (as James VI) of Scotland. Born in 1566, the son of Mary, Queen of Scots, he gained the Scottish throne upon her abdication in 1567, and the English throne on the death of ELIZABETH I in 1603. But in England he upset Parliament and the Puritans with his attitudes on religion and royal authority. He died in 1625.

James II
James II (born 1633, reigned 1685–89) was king of England and Scotland. He succeeded his brother Charles II, but was distrusted for his Roman Catholicism and use of royal power. In 1688 Parliamentary leaders

J

invited William of Orange to take the throne. James fled to France, led an unsuccessful uprising in Ireland, and died in exile in 1701.

jangle *n.* & *vb.* sound harshly; out of tune.

January *n.* the first month of the year.

Japan (Japanese)
Japan is a prosperous island monarchy in eastern Asia. It is highly industrialized, with a variety of light and heavy industries, producing such things as chemicals, electrical appliances and electronic machinery, food products, iron and steel, paper, ships and textiles. Japan has been the world's leading builder of ships since 1955 and, in 1974, it accounted for just over half of the world's launchings. It has a large iron and steel industry, and specializes in producing televisions, videos and other electronic goods.

Over 70 percent of the people live in urban areas. The largest city is TOKYO. Farming is intensive on the 15 percent of the land which can be cultivated. Rice is the chief food crop. The main animal food is fish.

Japan consists of four main islands, Hokkaido, Honshu, Shikoku and Kyushu. There are also about 3,000 small islands. Much of the land is mountainous. There are many volcanoes, and earthquakes are common.

Until the mid-1800s, Japan was an isolated feudal state. In the late 1800s, the country was rapidly modernized and industrialized. During WORLD WAR II, Japan became one of the Axis powers, but it surrendered in 1945. United States troops occupied Japan and introduced democratic institutions. The emperor declared that he was not "divine" and became a constitutional monarch.

AREA: 143,759 SQ. MILES (372,313 SQ. KM)
POPULATION: 120,055,000
CAPITAL: TOKYO
CURRENCY: YEN
OFFICIAL LANGUAGE: JAPANESE

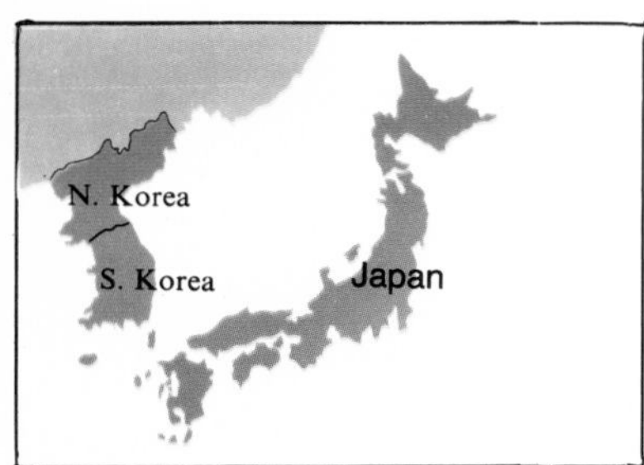

jar 1. *n.* pot, often made of glass, for jam and other things. 2. *vb.* make a harsh, grating noise. **jarring** *adj.*

jargon *n.* the special or technical language of a group of people.

jasmine *n.* a shrub with white or yellow flowers and which yields oils that are used in perfume.

Jason
Jason is the hero of an ancient Greek story. He tried to get back a kingdom stolen from his father by Pelias, Jason's uncle. Pelias let Jason have the kingdom in return for the GOLDEN FLEECE. Jason married a princess called Medea who helped him to steal the fleece.

jaundice *n.* a disease in which there is a yellowing of the skin caused by too much yellow bile pigment in the blood.

jaunt *n.* short trip, especially for pleasure.

Java (Javanese)
Java is a densely populated island in Southeast Asia. It contains nearly two-thirds of the population of INDONESIA, including the capital and largest city, Jakarta. This narrow mountainous island has rich soil, and rice is the main food crop.

javelin *n.* a short, light throwing spear.
► The javelin throw is an OLYMPIC sport. The javelin is a thin, lightweight spear. It is thrown for a maximum distance, overhand, after a run up. For a good throw, it must land point first and within a marked area.

jaw *n.* the bones of the mouth. *Your teeth are set in your jaw.*

jay *n.* a bird belonging to the crow family.

jazz *n.* a type of popular American folk music.
► Jazz began among the Blacks of New Orleans in the late 1800s, and included memories of African tribal music. There have since been many styles, but jazz usually has strong rhythms and a simple structure, and emphasizes improvisation. It has greatly influenced other music. Famous jazzmen include Louis Armstrong, Duke Ellington and Charlie Parker.

jealous (**jel**-us) *adj.* being unhappy because you want what others have. **jealousy** *n.*

jeans *pl. n.* tight-fitting, casual trousers made of a tough, blue material called denim.

jeep *n.* a kind of car originally used by the U.S. Army for going over rough ground.

jeer *n.* & *vb.* mock, make fun of, scoff. *n.*

Jefferson, Thomas
Thomas Jefferson (1743–1826) was the chief author of the Declaration of Independence and a great president of the U.S.A. During his time as President, the United States bought from France (in 1803) a huge piece of territory stretching from the Mississippi valley to the northern Pacific border. This was called the Louisiana Purchase.

jelly *n.* a soft, wobbly kind of food, usually brightly colored and flavored with fruit.

jellyfish *n.* an invertebrate sea animal with a round, semitransparent soft body fringed with stinging tentacles.

Jenner, Edward
Edward Jenner (1749–1823) was a British doctor. He inoculated a boy with cowpox germs. Cowpox is like smallpox but is far less dangerous. The boy did not catch smallpox because Jenner's inoculation made the boy's body strong and immune to smallpox.

jenny *n.* female donkey.

jeopardy (**jep**-*ur-dee*) *n.* danger, peril. **jeopardize** *vb.* put in danger.

jerboa *n.* jumping rodent of Africa with long back legs.

Jericho
An ancient city of the Jordan valley. Archaeologists have uncovered 17 layers of settlement, dating from 5000 B.C. or earlier. The Bible relates that it was the first Canaanite town captured by the Israelites, and that its walls fell to a blast of their trumpets.

jerk 1. *n.* a sudden rush or movement. 2. *vb.* move abruptly.

jersey (plural **jerseys**) *n.* a knitted woolen upper garment.

Jerusalem
Jerusalem is the capital of ISRAEL. It is a holy city of the Jews, Christians and Muslims. David, Jesus and other famous people in the Bible lived or died there.

Jerusalem stands high up in hilly country. It has many old religious buildings. Huge walls surround the city's oldest part. In 1948 Jerusalem was divided between Israel and Jordan. But Israel took the whole city during a war in 1967.

Jesuits
The largest religious order in the Roman Catholic Church. Called the Society of Jesus, it was founded by St. Ignatius of Loyola, with educational and missionary aims. The order was expelled from France,

Spain and Portugal in the 1700s, suppressed by Pope Clement XIV in 1773, and revived as a worldwide order in 1814.

Jesus Christ
Jesus Christ was a Jewish religious teacher (about 4 B.C. to about A.D. 29), born in Bethlehem to Mary, and baptized by John the Baptist in A.D. 26 or 27. His message is summed up in the Sermon on the Mount. He entered Jerusalem in triumph in A.D. 29, acclaimed by some as the Messiah; but was arrested, condemned and crucified. His apostles believed that he rose from the dead and ascended to heaven. This led to the foundation of CHRISTIANITY, in which he is seen as the Son of God.

jet *n.* 1. a fast stream of liquid or gas. 2. an aircraft with an engine that sucks in air at the front and expels it at the back, pushing the aircraft forward. 3. a hard, black mineral often used in jewelry.
▶ A swimmer swims forward by pushing water backward. A **jet engine** works in a similar way. It drives an AIRPLANE forward by pushing gases backward. Engines that work like this are called reaction engines. Rockets are also reaction engines. The main difference between jets and rockets is that jets take in oxygen from the air to burn their fuel, but rockets have their own supply of oxygen.

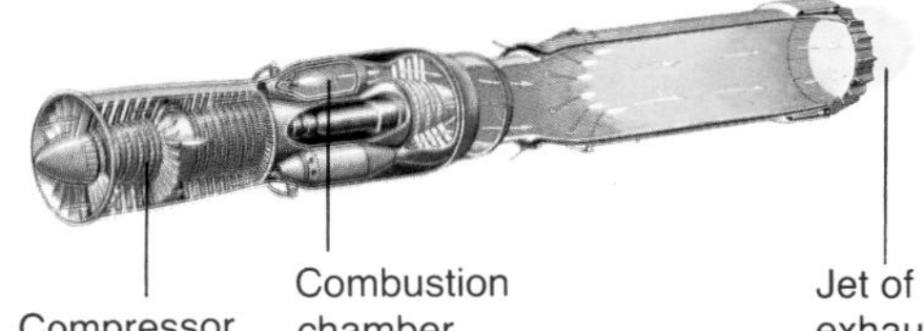

There are four main kinds of jet engine. These are turbojets, turboprops, turbofans and ramjets.
Jet engines have replaced propeller-driven piston engines in many kinds of plane. There are many reasons for this. Jet engines weigh less than piston engines. They also go wrong less often. Their moving parts spin instead of moving to and fro. This stops the plane from shaking about. Jet engines burn cheap kerosene instead of costly gasoline. Jet engines can also carry planes faster and higher than piston engines can. Some jet fighters can travel at 2,100 mph (3,400 km/h). Others can climb to about 100,000 ft. (30,500 meters).

jetsam *n.* cargo from a ship thrown overboard and then washed ashore.
jettison *vb.* throw overboard to lighten load in a time of disaster.
jetty *n.* a pier; a landing stage.
Jew *n.* a person of the Hebrew race or religion (Judaism). **Jewish** *adj.* **Jewry** *n.* Jews collectively.
▶The Jews are a Semitic people who came to Palestine from MESOPOTAMIA in about 2,000 B.C. Some became slaves in Egypt, and were led out by MOSES, who formalized their religion, JUDAISM. They conquered all of Palestine by about 1,000 B.C., but split into two kingdoms and became dominated by a succession of outside empires, from Assyria to Rome. Finally, revolts against the Romans from A.D. 66 led to the destruction of the Temple at Jerusalem and the complete dispersal of the people.
Jews in medieval Europe were persecuted as the "killers of Christ" (*see* JESUS CHRIST), and isolated in ghettos. In 1939–45 the Germans under HITLER murdered over six million Jews. In 1948 the foundation of Israel gave the Jews a homeland in Palestine, and about four million now live there.
jewel *n.* a precious stone.
jeweler *n.* a person who makes or sells jewelry.
jewelry *n.* objects with jewels or other decorations worn as adornment.

jiffy *n.* a moment. *I'll be there in a jiffy.*
jig *n.* & *vb.* a lively dance.
jigsaw *n.* & *vb.* a special kind of saw for cutting small pieces of wood very accurately. *A jigsaw puzzle is a mounted picture which has been jigsawed into pieces that fit back together.*
jingle *vb.* & *n.* (make) a tinkling noise; a clinking sound; a catchy tune or rhyme. *Many TV ads have clever jingles.*
jittery *adj.* nervous.

Joan of Arc
Joan of Arc was a French heroine (1412–31) in the HUNDRED YEARS WAR. Believing herself inspired by God, she led a French army against the English. Captured by the English, she was burned for witchcraft and heresy. She was made a saint by the Roman Catholic Church in 1920.

job *n.* a person's work.
jockey *n.* a person who rides in horse races, usually for wages.
jodhpurs (**jod**-*purrs*) *pl. n.* riding breeches that are loose-fitting around the hips but close-fitting from knee to ankle.
jog 1. *vb.* run at a slow, steady pace. 2. *n.* nudge (memory).

Johannesburg
Johannesburg is the largest city in SOUTH AFRICA. It is a great mining, manufacturing and financial center, lying on the mineral-rich Witwatersrand ridge.

John Bull *n.* a character who is a personification or caricature of the English nation.
John Doe *n.* someone involved in a legal action whose real name is not known.

John, King
John was king of England from 1199 to 1216. He became king after the death of his brother, Richard I. During his reign, the English lost most of their possessions in France. John also had to back down after a quarrel with the Pope. In 1215 the barons forced John to sign the MAGNA CARTA (the Great Charter). This limited the power of the king.

Johnson, Samuel
Samuel Johnson (1709–84) was an English writer. He is famous for his *Dictionary* and his *Lives of the Poets*. But he is best remembered for his conversation and opinions, as recorded by his friend James Boswell in his *Life of Johnson*.

join *vb.* put together, unite; take part in; become a member of.
joiner *n.* a person who works with wood; a carpenter; someone who joins.
joint 1. *n.* a point where two parts join. *The knee is the joint between the upper and lower bones of the leg.* 2. *adj.* shared, common. *They have a joint bank account.*
join up *vb.* enlist in the army, navy or air force.
joist *n.* a beam supporting a floor or ceiling in a building.
joke *n.* a funny story or remark. *vb.* tell a joke or do something to amuse.
joker *n.* 1. a person who jokes. 2. a 53rd card in a pack of cards, used in some games.

Joliot, Louis
Louis Joliot (1645–1700) was a French-Canadian explorer. In 1672, he was sent to explore the MISSISSIPPI River. He and his party descended the river by canoe and discovered that it flowed into the Gulf of Mexico. Joliot later explored many other parts of North America.

jolly *adj.* cheerful; merry. *Santa Claus is usually pictured as a jolly old gentleman with a white beard.*
jolt *vb.* move or shake with sudden jerks. *n.* a shock or sudden jerk. *The train came to a stop with a jolt.*

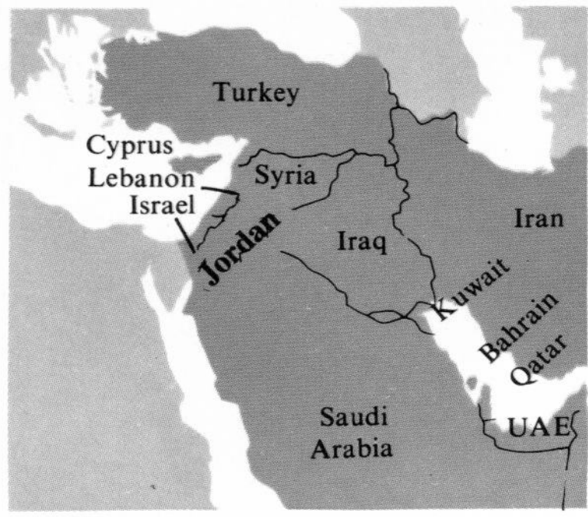

Jordan (Jordanian)
Jordan is an Arab kingdom in the Middle East. Most of the land is desert, but farmland exists in the moister uplands. The main export is phosphates. Potash is found in the DEAD SEA area. Tourism is important.
AREA: 37,740 SQ. MILES (97,740 SQ. KM)
POPULATION: 3,403,000
CAPITAL: AMMAN
CURRENCY: JORDANIAN DINAR
OFFICIAL LANGUAGE: ARABIC

jostle *vb*. shove; push against.
jot *vb*. make a note; write down briefly. *Let me jot down your telephone number*.
journalist *n*. a person who writes about or edits the news in magazines and newspapers.
journey *n*. a distance traveled. *vb*. travel.
joust *n*. & *vb*. a combat between mounted knights in a tournament; to fight in a tournament.
joy *n*. happiness.
jubilee *n*. a festival or celebration, usually of an anniversary. *Queen Victoria celebrated her Diamond Jubilee after she had reigned for 60 years*.

Judaism
Judaism is the religion of the JEWS, formalized by MOSES. It teaches that there is only one God, and that the Jews are his special people, chosen to carry out his wishes. These wishes are summed up in the law of Moses, and set out in the *Torah*, or holy book. Jewish religious life is divided between home and SYNAGOGUE. Observances include circumcision, the Sabbath as a day of rest, and the holy days of Yom Kippur, Passover, Pentecost and Tabernacles.

judge 1. *vb*. decide what is right or best out of a number of people or things. 2. *n*. a person who judges, particularly in a law court or a competition. **judgment** *n*. decision of a court; opinion; estimate.
judo *n*. a fighting sport, developed in Japan as a form of self-defense.
► Judo involves many throws, holds, and locks as well as the art of falling correctly. Various colored belts are worn to indicate the standard attained. Experts wear the sought-after black belt.
Judo developed from *ju-jitsu*, a form of unarmed combat used by Japanese *samurai* warriors.

jug *n*. an object for holding liquids, with a handle and a narrow mouth.
juggler *n*. an entertainer who tosses things in the air, catches and throws them up again. **juggle** *vb*.
juice (rhymes with *loose*) *n*. the liquid part of fruit or other food. **juicy** *adj*.

Julius Caesar
Julius Caesar (*c*. 102–44 B.C.) was a great leader of the ROMAN EMPIRE. He is most famous for his part in turning the Roman Republic into an empire ruled by one man.
Caesar first became powerful when he commanded an army that conquered what is today France, the Netherlands and Germany. In 55 B.C., he crossed the Channel and invaded Britain. He rebelled against the Roman Senate (the government), when he led his victorious armies into Italy itself. He captured Rome without a struggle, and in 48 B.C. he defeated Pompey, his main rival for power. Caesar then became the sole ruler of Rome.
Caesar made many enemies who hated what he was doing to the Republic. A group of them plotted to kill him. On the "Ides of March" (the 15th of the month) 44 B.C., they stabbed him to death in the Roman forum.

July *n*. the seventh month of the year.
jumble *vb*. & *n*. a muddle; a disorder. *She jumbled the papers together*.
jumbo *adj*. (originally the name of a circus elephant) a massive person, animal or thing, e.g. jumbo jet.

jump *vb*. & *n*. leap, spring. **jumpy** *adj*. nervous.
jump at *vb*. accept enthusiastically. *Jane jumped at the chance for a ride to the horse show*.
jumper *n*. a sleeveless one-piece dress often worn with a blouse.
junction *n*. a join or place or meetings, especially where several roads or railway lines meet.
June *n*. the sixth month of the year.
jungle *n*. thick vegetation in tropical countries.
junior *adj*. younger; lower in rank.
juniper *n*. evergreen shrub or tree with purple leaves.
junk *n*. 1. rubbish. 2. a Chinese sailing boat.

Jupiter (God)
Jupiter was the chief god of the ancient Romans. Also called Jove, he was the god of the sky and of battle, and reigned in Olympus as lord of heaven.

Jupiter (Planet)
Jupiter is the largest planet in the SOLAR SYSTEM. Its orbit lies between those of MARS and SATURN. Around the giant planet is an atmosphere made up mainly of hydrogen. The main feature of Jupiter's atmosphere is its Great Red Spot, a huge oval mark thought to consist of a swirling mass of gases in a never-ending storm.

jury *n*. people who are chosen to decide whether an accused person is guilty or not guilty in a law court.
just 1. *adv*. exactly. *That color is just right*. 2. *adv*. a moment ago. *I have only just arrived*. 3. *adj*. fair, honest. *That is a just law*.
justice *n*. 1. the law; fairness. 2. a judge. *A justice of the peace is a local magistrate*.
justify *vb*. show or prove to be right.
jut *vb*. stick out, project.
jute *n*. a coarse fiber used to make sacking, burlap, and twine.
juvenile *n*. a young person.

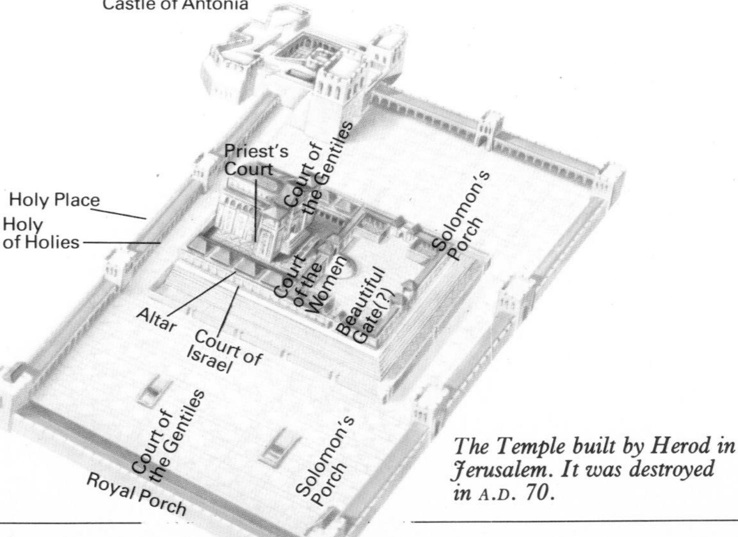

The Temple built by Herod in Jerusalem. It was destroyed in A.D. 70.

K

Knight jousting.

kaleidoscope *n.* a device made with mirrors which creates repeated colors and patterns.

Kampuchea (Kampuchean)
Kampuchea (officially Democratic Kampuchea) is a country in Southeast ASIA. It was formerly called Cambodia, and then, briefly, the Khmer Republic.

Much of Kampuchea is covered in dense forest. The economy is based on agriculture. A large part of the cultivated land is used for growing rice.

Formerly a French colony, Kampuchea became involved in the Vietnam War in the 1970s. In 1979, Phnom Penh was captured by the Vietnamese. Fighting between the Vietnamese and Kampuchean guerrillas continued into the 1980s.
AREA: 69,902 SQ. MILES (181,035 SQ. KM)
POPULATION: 8,559,000
CAPITAL: PHNOM PENH
CURRENCY: RIEL
OFFICIAL LANGUAGE: KHMER

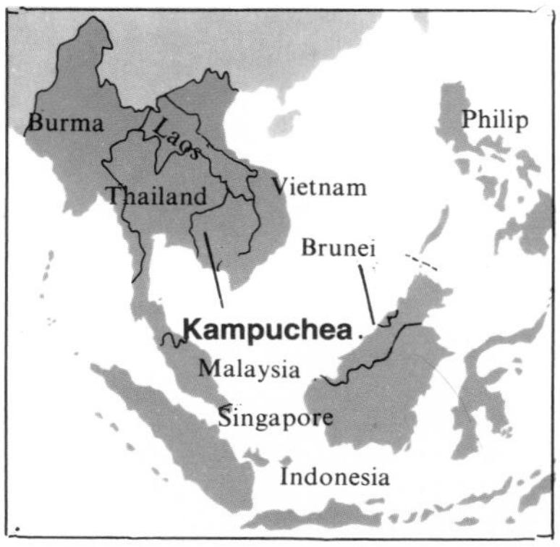

kangaroo *n.* an Australian animal with strong back legs. The female has a pouch in which she carries her baby, called a joey.
► The kangaroo is a marsupial (pouched mammal) which is native to Australia, Tasmania and New Guinea. Kangaroos have strong hind legs with elongated feet, short front legs, a thick muscular tail and a small head. The females have a pouch in which the young are carried. The kangaroo moves by taking enormous leaps with its hind legs; it only uses its front legs for grazing. When it is not moving the animal sits up on its back legs, balanced by its tail. Kangaroos eat grass and other green plants. There are many different species ranging from the rabbit-sized rat kangaroo to the man-sized red kangaroo.

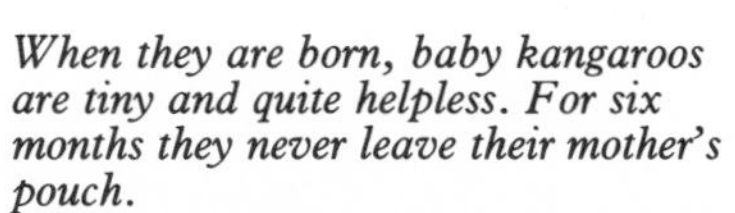
When they are born, baby kangaroos are tiny and quite helpless. For six months they never leave their mother's pouch.

Kansas (*abbrev.* **Kan.**)
The state of Kansas lies right in the center of the United States. Although most of the state's people live in rural areas or in small towns, Kansas has some quite large cities. The largest are Wichita, Kansas City and Topeka, the capital.

Kansas grows more wheat than any other state. It is also an important cattle and mining state. A main industry is manufacturing transportation equipment.

In 1803, the United States bought the Louisiana Territory from France. This territory included nearly all Kansas. But Kansas did not become a state until 1861.

K

Masters of karate wear black belts.

karate (*ka*-**raht**-*tay*) *n*. an oriental style of unarmed combat, using kicks and punches. As a sport, it involves both mock fights and formal examinations for the various grades of skill.
kayak (**kye**-*ack*) *n*. an Eskimo canoe made of skins.

Keats, John
Perhaps the greatest of the English Romantic poets (1795–1821), Keats is most famous for his *Odes*, all written in 1819: *To a Nightingale*; *To Autumn*; *On a Grecian Urn*; *On Melancholy*. He died in Rome of tuberculosis.

keel *n*. the heavy strip of metal or wood running along the bottom of a ship. *vb*. (over) capsize.
keen *adj*. eager; enthusiastic.
keep 1. *vb*. have something and not give it to anyone else. 2. *vb*. look after something for somebody. *Keep the book until I see you again*. 3. *n*. a strong tower in a castle.
keeper *n*. one who looks after people or things, particularly animals in a zoo. *He had been the elephant keeper for 20 years*.
keep on *vb*. continue doing something. *Stan keeps on talking, even when the teacher tells him not to*.
keepsake *n*. memento; something treasured because of the giver.
keep up with *vb*. not to lag behind. *He managed to keep up with the others in the race*.
keg *n*. a small barrel.

kelp *n*. kind of large brown seaweed.

Kennedy, John F.
John Fitzgerald Kennedy (1917–63) was the 35th American president. In the 1960 elections he became the youngest President ever, and the first Roman Catholic one. He dealt successfully with the Cuban crisis, forcing the Soviet Union to withdraw its nuclear weapons from Cuba.

During his term of office, Kennedy set up the Peace Corps, reduced tariffs, increased overseas aid, forced higher minimum wages and extended welfare programs. But many of his policies, including the civil rights law, were opposed by Congress. Some of these policies were achieved under Kennedy's successor, Lyndon Johnson.

In November 1963, John Kennedy visited Texas and was assassinated as he rode through Dallas in an open car. Lee Harvey Oswald was arrested and accused of the crime. But Oswald was shot dead by Jack Ruby while being held by the police.

Robert Kennedy, John Kennedy's brother, was also assassinated in Los Angeles in June 1968, while campaigning for the Democratic nomination for President.

Edward Kennedy, another brother, has been a member of the United States Senate since 1962.

kennel *n*. a shelter for a dog. *vb*. keep a dog in a kennel.

Kentucky (*abbrev*. **Ky**.)
Kentucky is a state that lies west of the Allegheny Mountains. Its long northern border is formed by the Ohio River.

Kentucky is famous for its thoroughbred horses and its tobacco. The horses graze on the rich grass of the Bluegrass region. The state produces large quantities of coal and whiskey. The largest cities are Louisville and Lexington. The capital is Frankfort.

Kentucky was caught in the middle of the American Civil War. It was invaded by troops from both sides. Two Kentuckians, Abraham Lincoln and Jefferson Davis, were the opposing presidents during the war.

Kenya (Kenyan)
Kenya is a republic in East AFRICA. A beautiful country, it has magnificent national parks, and tourism is growing quickly. Formerly a British colony, Kenya became independent in 1963. Only 12 percent of the land can be farmed. The rest is too dry. But farming is the chief industry, especially coffee and tea. Mombassa is the biggest port.
AREA: 224,973 SQ. MILES (582,646 SQ. KM)
POPULATION: 16,922,000
CAPITAL: NAIROBI
CURRENCY: KENYA SHILLING
OFFICIAL LANGUAGE: SWAHILI

kept *vb*. past of **keep**.
kernel *n*. the soft inner part of a nut, seed, or cereal, which can be eaten.
kerosene *n*. an oil used for burning in heaters and lamps.
kestrel *n*. a kind of small hawk.
ketchup *n*. a sauce made from tomatoes and spices. also called catsup.
kettle *n*. a kind of pot with a lid, handle and spout, used for boiling liquids.
key (rhymes with *me*). 1. *n*. a metal device to turn a lock or wind a clock. 2. *n*. solution, explanation, code. 3. *n*. part of a machine or instrument pressed with the fingers. *The piano keys were made of ivory*. 4. one of the systems of notes in music. 5. *adj*. of vital importance.
keystone *n*. central stone supporting an arch.
khaki *adj*. a dull, yellow-green color.
kibbutz *n*. (plural **kibbutzim**) agricultural center in Israel.
kick *vb*. hit something, such as a ball, with your foot. **kickoff** *n*. kick of a ball which starts a game.
kid 1. *n*. a young goat. 2. *n*. a child. 3. *vb*. tease.
kidnap *vb*. steal someone, often to get money as a ransom. **kidnapper** *n*.
kidney *n*. (plural **kidneys**) one of a pair of bean-shaped organs of the body that remove waste matter from the blood.
► Vertebrate (backboned) animals have two kidneys; each one consists of thousands of little tubes which filter the incoming blood. Useful substances are returned to the blood and re-enter the body's bloodstream, but unwanted substances, including excess water, are kept back by the kidney. This waste matter, called *urine*, goes through a large tube, the *ureter*, to be stored in the *bladder*. From the bladder, urine passes out of the body. Together, a human's kidneys filter about 40 gallons (190 liters) of blood a day. As well as producing urine, kidneys secrete a hormone which controls the production of red blood cells; the kidneys also maintain the body's blood pressure.

Kilimanjaro
Mt. Kilimanjaro is an extinct VOLCANO in TANZANIA, near the border with KENYA. At 19,341 feet (5,895 meters) it is the highest mountain in AFRICA. Coffee and other crops are grown on its lower slopes. Kilimanjaro was first climbed in 1889.

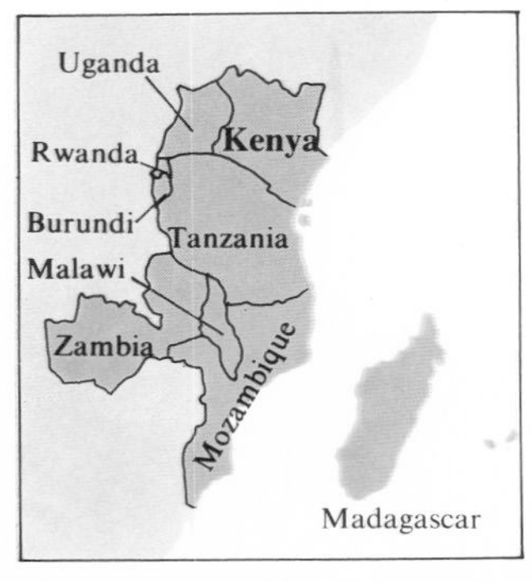

kill *vb*. put to death; take the life of someone or something.

kiln *n*. an oven or furnace for baking bricks or pottery to make them hard.

kilo- *prefix* a Greek word for 1,000. **kilowatt**. **kilogram**.

kilogram *n*. a measure of weight, often shortened to kg. *There are 1,000 grams in one kilogram.*

kilometer *n*. a measure of length, often shortened to km. *There are 1,000 meters in a kilometer.*

kilt *n*. a skirt often made of tartan cloth. *Kilts are worn by men and women in Scotland and some other countries.*

kimono (*ki*-**moan**-*oh*) *n*. a loose gown with wide sleeves worn in Japan.

kin *n*. relatives.

kind 1. *adj*. pleasant or gentle. 2. *n*. type or sort. *What kind of tree is that?* **kindness** *n*. the act of being kind, or treating someone well. *Thank you for all your kindness to me.*

kindergarten *n*. a school for very young children.

king *n*. a male ruler; a monarch.

King, Martin Luther
Martin Luther King (1929–68) was an American civil rights leader who devoted his life to fighting for equal rights for all people. He believed in fair and equal laws for everyone, no matter what their race or religion. Like the Indian leader GANDHI, whose ideas influenced him, King believed that deprived people did not have to use violence to win equality.

Under King's leadership, peaceful resistance achieved great success. Congress passed the Civil Rights Act in 1954 and the Voting Rights Act in 1965.

King received the Nobel Peace Prize in 1964 for leading the struggle for equality. In 1968 he was assassinated in Memphis, Tennessee.

kingdom *n*. a country ruled by a king or a queen.

kingfisher *n*. a small, brightly colored bird with a large head and a beak like a dagger.

► Birds of the kingfisher family live in many lands, but most live in the tropics. Kingfishers nest in burrows in river banks or in holes in trees. The nest is made of fish bones, so it is very smelly. Not all kingfishers fish for their food. One New Guinea kingfisher eats worms. Australia's KOOKABURRA eats lizards, snakes, insects and even other birds.

Kingston, Jamaica
Kingston is the capital and chief port of the island nation of JAMAICA in the WEST INDIES. It is in the heart of a rich agricultural region. Industries include food processing and clothing manufacturing.

kiosk (**key**-*ossk*) *n*. a small hut or stall, used for selling newspapers, candy, etc.

Kipling, Rudyard
Rudyard Kipling (1865–1936) was an English writer of adventure stories and poems. Many were about India and the British Empire. His best-remembered tales were stories for children. *Kim* is a story of an orphan boy's secret service adventures in India. *The Jungle Book* is about Mowgli, a boy brought up by wolves and taught by a bear, a python and a panther. *The Just So Stories* are all about animals.

Different patterns of a Scottish kilt represent different clans. Traditional Irish kilts are plain saffron color.

kipper *n*. a smoked herring.

kiss *vb*. & *n*. touch with the lips as a sign of love or friendship.

kitchen *n*. a room in a house where the cooking is done. **kitchenette** *n*. a small kitchen.

kite *n*. 1. a bird of prey related to the falcon family, noted for its long wings, deeply forked tail and graceful flight. 2. a frame of wood covered with light material which can be made to fly.

kitten *n*. a young cat. **kittenish** *adj*.

kittiwake *n*. kind of seagull.

kiwi (**kee**-*wee*) *n*. a New Zealand bird that cannot fly.

► This strange bird gets its name from the shrill cries made by the male. The kiwi is a stocky brown bird as big as a chicken. It has tiny wings but cannot fly. Instead it runs on short, thick, strong legs. Kiwi feathers look very much like hair.

Kiwis are shy birds that live in forests. By day they sleep in burrows and at night, they hunt for worms and grubs. Kiwis can hardly see. They smell out their food with the help of nostrils at the tip of their long, thin beaks. The female lays very large eggs but it is the male who sits on them and waits for them to hatch.

Klondike
The Klondike is a region of the Yukon Territory in northeastern CANADA. It lies around the Klondike River, east of the border with ALASKA.

In 1896 GOLD was discovered and thousands of prospectors descended on the area in the Klondike GOLD RUSH. Most of the easily accessible gold was exhausted by 1904, but some gold is still mined today, as well as SILVER and other metals.

knack (*nack*) *n*. skill or ability.

knave (*nave*) *n*. 1. rascal, cheat. 2. the jack in a pack of cards.

knead (*need*) *vb*. work dough or clay with the hands.

knee (*nee*) *n*. the hinged joint in the middle of the leg. **kneecap** *n*. the bone at the front of the knee; the patella.

kneel (*neel*) *vb*. go down on your knees, especially in prayer.

knew (*new*) *vb*. past of **know**.

knickers (*nickers*) *pl. n*. short pants that are loose-fitting but gathered around the knees.

knife (*nife*) *n*. a sharp-bladed cutting tool with a handle. *vb*. (past **knifed**) stab with knife.

► In the STONE AGE, people made knives by chipping lumps of FLINT into sharp-edged shapes. Modern knives are made from long, thin strips of steel cut up into lengths. Each length is heated. One end is hammered out into a blade. The other end may be shaped into a slim prong called a tang. Next the blade is heated and cooled in ways that make it hard and tough. Then the blade is sharpened on a grinder. A cutler now fits the tang with a handle made of wood, plastic or bone.

knight (*nite*) *n*. in the Middle Ages a mounted nobleman who served his king; today, the lowest British rank of a titled person with the title "Sir"; a chess piece.

► In the MIDDLE AGES, knights were soldiers on horseback who fought for a king or a prince. In peacetime they served their master in his household.

At first, anybody could become a knight. Then horses and ARMOR became so expensive that only the rich could buy them. Knighthood became an honor usually given to the rich. Boys trained for it from the age of seven.

Knights lost their usefulness in war when GUNS changed fighting methods. The British monarch still knights men as a reward for special service to the country.

A kiwi.

K

knit (*nit*) *vb*. make clothing out of wool or other fiber, using knitting needles.

▶ Knitted fabrics are more elastic than woven ones. This makes them very useful for close fitting clothes. When you pull on knitted stockings or socks, they stretch to fit your foot. But if you break one stitch, you break the chain to which it belonged. This makes a straggly run.

Hand-knitting is usually done with woolen thread and two needles. You make a row of loops on one needle. Then, using the second needle, you make a new row of loops through the first row, slipping them off the first needle and on to the second. Knitting machines do the same thing, but much faster.

knob (*nob*) *n*. a round handle.

knock (*nock*) *n*. & *vb*. hit or strike something. *Was that a knock at the door?*

knock down *vb*. force to the ground with a blow.

knocker *n*. an ornamental hammer on a door.

knock off *vb*. stop work for the day.

knot (*not*) 1. *n*. string or rope tied in such a way that it cannot come undone. *vb*. form knots. 2. *n*. hard mass in wood where a branch joins the trunk. 3. *n*. a unit of speed (nautical miles per hour) used for ships. A nautical mile is 6000 feet. **knotty** *adj*. full of knots; puzzling.

▶ Knots have many uses. STONE AGE hunters used knots to tie arrowheads to shafts. Guides and scouts learn how to tie many types of knots. Everyone needs to tie a knot at some time.

There are many ways of twisting flexible material to fasten things together. Not all such fastenings are properly called knots. Experts use the word knot to describe the fastenings you use to make a noose in a rope, to join two small cords or to hold a bundle together.

There are three other kinds of fastening that most people think of as knots. A *bend* is what you use to tie the ends of two ropes together. A *splice* is made by weaving together the strands of two rope ends to make one rope. A *hitch* is what you use to tie a rope to some other kind of object such as a post or ring.

know (past **knew**) *vb*. 1. be sure of something; be in possession of the facts. *Do you know which is the longest river in the world?* 2. be familiar with, or recognize someone or something. *I'll know him when I see him.*

know-how *n*. practical knowledge.

knowledge (**noll**-*edge*) *n*. understanding; information in the mind. **knowledgeable** *adj*.

knuckle (*nuckle*) *n*. the bones at the finger joint, especially at the root of the finger.

koala *n*. a small, furry Australian animal that lives in trees.

▶ The koala is a tubby tree-living MAMMAL from eastern Australia. Although koalas, with their thick gray fur and bushy ears, look like bears, they are not bears. They are MARSUPIALS: the young koala is reared in its mother's pouch which, unlike the KANGAROO's pouch, opens backwards. Koalas live on eucalyptus leaves and shoots.

kookaburra *n*. an Australian bird related to the kingfisher. It is also known as the "laughing jackass" because of its loud, laughter-like call.

▶ Kookaburras live in forests. They lay their eggs in holes in trees. They eat insects, snakes and other small animals.

Koran *n*. the sacred book of Islam.

▶ The Koran is said to have been revealed to the prophet MUHAMMED through the angel Gabriel. Its themes build on those of the Old Testament (*see* BIBLE), and its style has had a great influence on Arab literature. The Koran consists of verses grouped into 114 chapters. It is written in rhymed Arabic.

Korea (Korean)

Korea is a PENINSULA which juts out from CHINA into the Sea of Japan. The land has many mountains and small valleys. Forests cover most of the country. Korean farms produce much rice and silk. Korean factories make steel and many more products.

In 1948, Korea was divided into two countries. North Korea is a republic with a Communist government. South Korea is a republic which has been aided by the United States. In 1950 North Korea invaded South Korea. The North Korean forces were driven out by the U.S. army with the help of a United Nations force of British, Australian, Canadian and other troops. In 1951, Chinese forces came to the aid of the North Koreans and the following year the war ended in stalemate.

Korea, North

AREA: 46,543 SQ. MILES (120,538 SQ. KM)
POPULATION: 181,908,000
CAPITAL: PYONGYANG
CURRENCY: WON
OFFICIAL LANGUAGE: KOREAN

Korea, South

AREA: 38,027 SQ. MILES (98,484 SQ. KM)
POPULATION: 39,546,000
CAPITAL: SEOUL
CURRENCY: WON
OFFICIAL LANGUAGE: KOREAN

kosher *adj*. food that has been prepared in accordance with Jewish law.

Krakatoa

Krakatoa is an island VOLCANO which erupted with extraordinary violence in 1883 destroying two-thirds of the original island.

Kremlin

This is the oldest part of MOSCOW. It was once the fortress home of RUSSIA's tsars. Inside the high wall that surrounds it stand old palaces and cathedrals crowned by golden domes shaped like giant onions.

Kuala Lumpur

Kuala Lumpur is the largest city and capital of MALAYSIA. Most of the inhabitants are Chinese, the rest are Indians and Malays. Kuala Lumpur is a commercial and communications center. Its main industries are tin and rubber processing.

Kublai Khan

Kublai Khan was a Mongol ruler (1216–94) and the grandson of the great GENGHIS KHAN. Under his rule, the Mongol empire reached its peak of power. Kublai Khan established his capital at Cambaluc, modern Peking, and encouraged art and trade. Among his visitors was MARCO POLO.

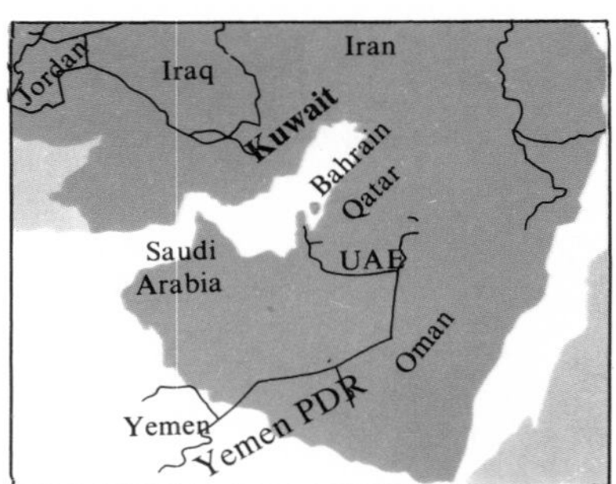

Kuwait

Kuwait is a small country, ruled by a sheikh, in northeast Arabia, on the Persian Gulf. It is hot and dry and consists mainly of desert. There is a little agriculture in the irrigated areas, but the main source of wealth is oil. Kuwait is one of the world's major oil producers.

AREA: 6,880 SQ. MILES (17,818 SQ. KM)
POPULATION: 1,516,000
CAPITAL: KUWAIT
CURRENCY: KUWAIT DINAR
OFFICIAL LANGUAGE: ARABIC

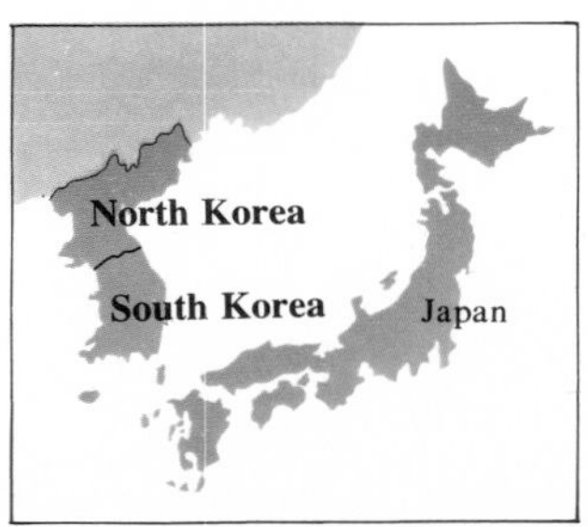

L

Lionesses lazing in the treetops.

label *n.* a piece of paper or card with writing on it attached to something. The label may say what the thing is or where it is going. *vb.* attach a label.
labor *n.* work; people who work. *vb.* work hard.
laboratory *n.* a place equipped for scientific experiments.
Labrador retriever *n.* a sporting dog originally from Newfoundland with a short black or golden coat.
labyrinth *n.* a maze, a tangle of intricate ways and connections.
lace 1. *n.* a delicate fabric made with patterns of thread. 2. *n.* cord for fastening a shoe, dress, etc. *vb.* fasten with laces. 3. *vb.* add alcohol to other drinks.
► People make collars, shawls, scarves and tablecloths from lace. Lace is made from threads of cotton, linen, nylon or silk, and sometimes gold or silver. Lacemakers twist, knot or loop the threads in special ways. Lace made by hand is expensive. Much lace is now made on machines.

laceration *n.* a cut that is torn and ragged. *It took 10 stitches to close the laceration.*
lack *n.* & *vb.* need, be without, be missing. **lacking** *adj.*
lacquer *n.* a hard, shiny varnish; a substance sprayed on the hair to keep it in place. *vb.* coat with lacquer.
lacrosse *n.* a team game played with a racket that has a net to catch and throw the ball with.
lad *n.* a boy.
ladder *n.* two lengths of wood or other material fastened with cross-bars (called rungs). *A ladder is used for climbing up and down walls.*
ladle *n.* a large deep spoon used for serving soup. *vb.* transfer with a ladle.
lady *n.* 1. a female person. 2. a woman's title. *Lady Smith is the wife of Sir John Smith.*
ladybug *n.* a small flying beetle with bright spots.
► Ladybugs were named after the Virgin Mary. From above, ladybugs look nearly round. They have shiny wing covers. The wing covers are usually red or yellow with black spots. Young ladybug grubs, or larvae, are quite different. They have long, soft bodies. Ladybugs eat aphids and other pests.

lager (**lah**-*gur*) *n.* a light-colored beer.
lagoon *n.* a shallow saltwater lake separated from the sea by a sand bank.
laid *vb.* past and past part. of **lay**.
lair *n.* a wild animal's den.
lake *n.* a large area of water surrounded by land.
► The world's largest lake is the salty Caspian Sea, 169,390 sq. miles (438,695 sq. km). It lies in the Soviet Union and Iran. The largest freshwater lake is Lake Superior, one of the GREAT LAKES.
Many lakes were formed in the ICE AGES. They began in valleys made by GLACIERS. When the glaciers melted they left behind mud and stones that formed DAMS. The melted water from the glaciers piled up behind the dams.

LARGEST LAKES

	sq. miles
Caspian Sea (USSR/Iran)	169,390
Superior (USA/Canada)	31,820
Victoria Nyanza (Africa)	26,828
Aral (USSR)	26,166
Huron (USA/Canada)	23,000
Michigan (USA)	22,400
Baykal (USSR)	13,192
Tanganyika (Africa)	12,355
Great Bear (Canada)	12,200
Malawi* (Africa)	11,000

*Also called Lake Nyasa

lamb *n.* a young sheep; the meat of a young sheep. *vb.* give birth (to lambs).
lame *adj.* not able to walk properly.
lament *vb.* mourn. *n.* elegy, sorrowful song. **lamentable** *adj.* sad; pitiful; deplorable.
lamp *n.* a light, often portable.
lamplighter *n.* someone who lights a lamp.

lance 1. *n.* a kind of spear that was used by knights and cavalry. 2. *vb.* (in surgery) to pierce or cut open.
land 1. *n.* all those parts of the earth's surface which are not sea. 2. *n.* the area owned by someone. *Farmer Green's land goes as far as the river.* 3. *vb.* come to land from the sea or the air. *Our plane should land early.*
landing *n.* 1. bringing in to ground; bringing in to shore. 2. level part at the top of a flight of stairs.
landlady, landlord *n.* a person who owns a house or other property and rents it out to others; keeper of an inn. *I must pay the rent to my landlady tomorrow.*
landmark *n.* something that can be seen from a distance and which helps you find the way. *A church steeple is often used as a landmark.*
landscape *n.* what you see when you look across a large area of land; a picture of a landscape.
lane *n.* 1. a narrow road, or pathway. 2. one of the divisions of a highway. *He drove all the way in the inside lane.*
language *n.* the words we use to talk or write to each other. *Many different languages are spoken in Africa.*
► We do not know how languages originated, although there are several possibilities. The earliest languages which we know of already have complicated grammatical systems and large vocabularies. All languages seem to find it easier to add new words and to change pronunciation than to add new grammar. But all three parts do develop and change. Such development includes new words and new meanings for old words, but new meanings for grammatical features come very much more slowly. There are now about 2,800 spoken languages, not including dialects, which are local forms of a language. The world's major languages, in terms of the number of native speakers, are Chinese, English, Russian, Hindi, Spanish and German. But English is the chief commercial or business language, followed by Chinese, French, Russian, Spanish and German.

lank *adj.* drooping, limp, thin. **lanky** *adj.*
lantern *n.* a case with glass sides for holding a light so that it does not blow out.

Laos (Laotian)
Laos is a Communist republic in Southeast ASIA. The land is mountainous, and there are few towns. Farming, particularly rice-growing, is the main occupation. Timber and coffee are the principal exports.
Formerly a French protectorate, Laos became fully independent in 1954. From 1953 onward, there was a war between the Royal Laos government and the Communist forces. The Communists took over the country in 1975.
AREA: 91,434 SQ. MILES (236,800 SQ. KM)
POPULATION: 3,611,000
CAPITAL: VIENTIANE
CURRENCY: RIEL
OFFICIAL LANGUAGE: LAO

lap 1. *n.* your upper legs when you are sitting. 2. *vb.* drink with the tongue like an animal. 3. *n.* one circuit of a racetrack.
lapel *n.* folded-back part of the front of a coat.

Lapland see **Lapps**

Lapps
Lapps are a people who live in Lapland, in the ARCTIC. It lies in the far north of Sweden, Norway, Finland and Russia. Lapps are short people. Many have straight, black hair and yellowish skin. They keep warm by wearing clothes made from wool and reindeer skins.
Some Lapps are NOMADS who travel the land with herds of REINDEER who sleep in tents and eat reindeer meat. Other Lapps are fishermen or farmers who live in small huts in villages.

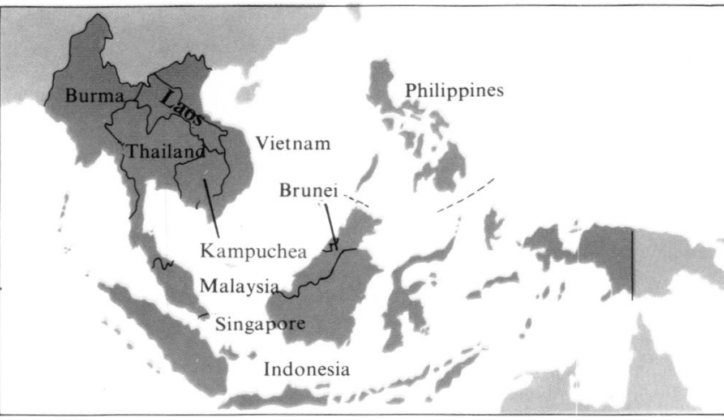

lapse *vb.* & *n.* falling back, fall into disuse; a mistake.
lapwing *n.* bird of the plover family.
larch *n.* a cone-bearing tree that loses its leaves in winter.
lard *n.* fat of a pig prepared for cooking.
larder *n.* a room where food is kept cool; pantry.
large *adj.* big, broad, or great.
lark 1. *n.* a small brown bird famous for its beautiful song. 2. *n.* & *vb.* a frolic, mischief.
larva (plural **larvae**) *n.* an insect in the first stage when it comes from its egg.
► Larvae do not resemble adult insects. For example, caterpillars are the larvae of butterflies and moths; maggots are the larvae of flies. The larva usually changes into a *pupa* and the adult develops from the pupa.
Eels have transparent, ribbon-shaped larvae called tadpoles.

larynx *n.* the cavity in the upper windpipe (air passage in the throat) where sounds are produced, also called the voice box.
laser *n.* a device for sending out enormously strong light waves.
► A laser is something that strengthens light and makes it shine in a very narrow beam. Many lasers have a ruby CRYSTAL or gas inside them. Bright light, radio waves or electricity are fed into the laser. This makes the ATOMS of the crystal or gas jump around violently. The atoms give off strong light.
The light of lasers can be used for many things. Doctors use small laser beams to burn away tiny areas of disease in the body. They also repair damaged eyes with laser beams. Dentists can use lasers to drill holes in teeth. Some lasers are so strong they can cut through diamonds. Lasers are used in factories to cut metal and join tiny metal parts together.
Lasers can also be used to measure distance. The laser beam is aimed at objects far away. The distance is measured by counting the time it takes for the light to get there and back. Laser beams can also carry radio and television signals. One laser beam can send many television programs and telephone calls at once without mixing them up.

lash *vb.* make rapid movements (of tail etc.); thrash or fasten with a rope. *n.* whip.
lass *n.* a girl.
lasso (**lass**-*oo*) *n.* a long rope with a loop used by cowboys to catch cattle and horses. *vb.* (*lass*-**oo**) use a lasso.
last 1. *adj.* coming at the end. *I came last in the race.* 2. *vb.* stay or continue. *Have we enough food to*

last the week? 3. *n.* a model of a foot used by shoemakers.

late *adj.* 1. tardy; past the correct time. *They were late for the class.* 2. previous; no longer alive. *He knew the late king.*

lately *adv.* not long ago.

latex *n.* milky juice of some trees, especially rubber trees.

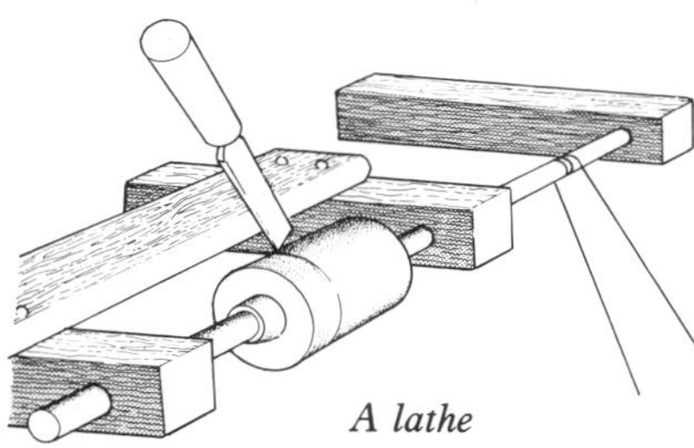

A lathe

lathe *n.* a machine for holding and turning wood or metal while it is being shaped.

lather (rhymes with *rather*) *n.* froth that is formed by mixing soap with water. *vb.* to spread lather.

Latin *n.* language of ancient Rome. *adj.* concerning countries where languages are descended from Latin.

Latin America
Latin America accounts for about 14 percent of the world's area. It includes Mexico, Central America and South America. It is called Latin America because nearly all the Europeans who settled there came from Spain, Portugal and France. All these people have a language that grew out of the Latin language. The population of Latin America is about 8 percent of the world's total. Most Latin American countries have banded together in the OAS, the Organization of American states. The rich mineral deposits and farmlands of Latin America have only been partly developed.

latitude *n.* 1. a distance measured in degrees north or south of the equator. 2. freedom of movement, scope.
► Every place on earth has a latitude and a longitude. Lines of latitude and longitude are drawn on MAPS. Lines, or parallels, of latitude show how far north or south of the EQUATOR a place is. They are measured in degrees (written as °). The equator is at 0° latitude. The North Pole has a latitude of 90° north, and the South Pole is 90° south.
Lines, or meridians, of longitude show how far east or west a place is. They are also measured in degrees. Greenwich, in London, is at 0° longitude. A place halfway around the world from Greenwich is at 180° longitude.

latter *adj.* & *n.* the more recent, the second one mentioned of two. *Romulus and Remus were brothers: the latter (Remus) was younger than the former (Romulus).*

Latvia (Latvian)
A republic of the U.S.S.R., Latvia borders the Baltic Sea. It has an area of 24,711 sq. miles (64,000 sq. km). The capital is Riga. Russia ruled Latvia from the 1700s. A brief period of independence (1918–40) ended when Soviet troops occupied the country.

laugh *vb.* the sound you make when you think something is funny. **laughter** *n.*

To make a holographic image – a three dimensional picture – laser light is used. Here two people are looking at a hologram. The images they see (known as virtual images, because the light rays do not actually come from them) are different views of the object and appear to have depth as well as width and height.

launch (*lawnch*) 1. *n.* a sort of power-boat. 2. *vb.* put a boat into water. 3. *vb.* send something off. *The rocket was launched from Cape Canaveral.*

launderette *n.* a shop with washing machines and dryers where people pay to do their laundry.

laundry *n.* a place where clothes are washed; the clothes that have to be washed.

laurel *n.* sweet bay tree, whose leaves the ancient Greeks and Romans made into wreaths, emblems of victory.

lava *n.* hot liquid rock that is expelled from an active volcano.

lavatory *n.* a wash basin; a room with a sink and toilet in it.

lavender *n.* a small Mediterranean shrub with fragrant narrow leaves and pale purple flowers, cultivated on a large scale for use in the perfume industry.

Lavoisier, Antoine Laurent
Antoine Laurent Lavoisier was a French chemist (1743–94), the founder of modern CHEMISTRY. He investigated the processes of COMBUSTION and proved that AIR is a mixture of oxygen and nitrogen. He was executed during the FRENCH REVOLUTION.

law *n.* (a set of) rules, usually made by a government, that people have to obey. **lawful** *adj.* permitted by law.
► Laws are made to help people live together in peace. They control many of the things people do. The laws of each country are often different. Some countries have very strict laws about things which other countries do not. Every country has judges and POLICE. They help to make sure that people obey the law. When people break the law they are often punished. They may have to pay money (fines) or go to prison. Sometimes people are put to death for breaking laws.
The people of BABYLON had written laws over 3,000 years ago. The ancient Greeks and Romans also made laws. In Europe, many important laws were made by kings, the Church and governments.

lawn *n.* 1. an area of short cut grass. 2. a fine sheer cloth used for nightgowns, blouses and other clothes.

lawn mower *n.* a machine for cutting grass.

lawyer *n.* a person who works in the law.

lax *adj.* careless, not strict.

lay 1. *vb.* past of **lie**. *We lay down on the lawn.* 2. *vb.* (past **laid**) of a bird, lay (produce) eggs. 3. *vb.* (past **laid**) put down; prepare a table. 4. *n.* as distinct from clergy, laity; non-professional.

L

lay away *vb.* to put something away that you will use or buy at a later time.

layer *n.* something that is spread over a surface of something else. *A thick layer of clay had washed over the river bank.*

lazy *adj.* not wanting to do much work; idle. **laze** *vb.* relax.

lead (rhymes with *bed*) *n.* a soft, heavy, blue-gray metal.

► Lead's chemical symbol is Pb. It does not rust. Lead is used for many things including water pipes and roofs. Lead shields protect ATOMIC ENERGY workers from dangerous radiation. Lead is mixed with TIN to make such things as pewter mugs. ALLOYS of tin and lead are also used in solder for joining pieces of METAL. Many things are now made without lead because lead can become poisonous when it is mixed with certain other things.

lead (rhymes with *reed*). 1. *vb.* go in front to guide others. 2. *n.* the first place. *Chris had the lead in the school play last year.* 3. *n.* a leather strap. for leading a dog (also called a leash).

leader *n.* a person who leads.

leaf (plural **leaves**) *n.* 1. one of the flat green parts of a plant growing from the stems of a branch. 2. a sheet of paper or metal foil.

► The leaf is the main food-producing part of a plant. In the presence of green chlorophyll and sunlight, a leaf makes food from carbon dioxide and water (see PHOTOSYNTHESIS). Most leaves consist of a blade and a stalk. The blade, full of green food-making cells, is usually broad and flat; underneath, it has tiny breathing holes, called *stomata*, which take in carbon dioxide and let out oxygen. The blade is supported by a skeleton of veins, carrying water to all parts of the leaf. The leaf stalk, linking the blade to the plant stem, is made up of tiny tubes which supply the veins with water from the roots and take food made by the leaf to other parts of the plant. Leaves generally grow in such a way as to trap the greatest possible amount of sunlight.

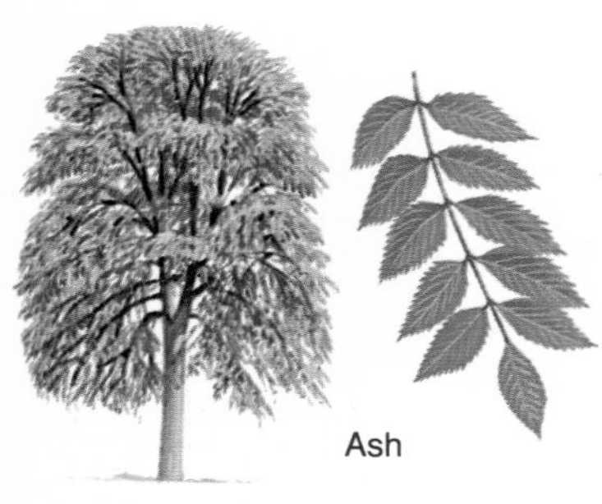
Ash

Maple

Leaf shapes are the most useful characteristic for identifying a tree. Leaves of conifers are narrow, often sharp-pointed. Broad-leaved trees have much more varied shapes.

league (*leeg*) *n.* 1. a group of sports clubs that play matches against each other. 2. an alliance; nations that agree to help each other.

leak *vb.* & *n.* a hole through which liquid or gas can escape.

lean 1. *vb.* be or put in a sloping position. *The ladder is leaning against the house.* 2. *adj.* thin, having little fat.

leap *vb.* & *n.* jump high or far. **leaped** *vb.* past of **leap**.

Leap Year
A year of 366 days which occurs when the year can be divided evenly by four. The extra day is February 29. Leap years are necessary because the CALENDAR year (365 days) is slightly shorter than the solar year. Century years are leap years only when they can be evenly divided by 400.

Lear, Edward
Edward Lear (1812–88) was an English painter and writer. He wrote funny little poems called limericks. He also wrote nonsense verse such as *The Owl and the Pussy Cat.* Lear often drew pictures for his verse. He was also a fine painter. Lear painted birds and animals. He also made drawings and paintings of the countries he visited.

learn *vb.* (past **learned**) get knowledge or information, find out. *Did you learn French at school?* **learned** (**lern**-*id*) *adj.* having much knowledge. **learner** *n.* a person learning.

lease *n.* legal document renting land, a house, etc., for a stated period and on certain conditions. *vb.* grant or take on a lease. **leaseholder** *n.*

least *adj.* the smallest in size or quantity.

leather (**leth**-*er*) *n.* material made from the skin or hide of animals. *Shoes are made of leather.*

► Factories called tanneries make leather. They use mainly hides from cattle.

First the hides are dried or salted. Then the hair and meat are taken off. Next, the hides are tanned, or made into leather, in baths of chemicals. The chemical used is often tannin, which comes from plants. Tanned hides are then dried and made soft with oil.

leave 1. *vb.* (past **left**) go away. *I leave for Paris tomorrow.* 2. *vb.* part with something; to lose it. *Did you leave your case at home?* 3. *vb.* not to use something. *Do you always leave so much of your food?* 4. *n.* permission to be absent; a holiday. *He was given a month's leave from his job.*

leaves *pl. n.* more than one **leaf**.

Lebanon (Lebanese)
Lebanon is a mountainous country in the Middle East. Most people are ARABS, but only about 60 percent are Muslims. The rest of the population are Christians. Lebanon has long been a financial and commercial center. In normal times, it has had an important tourist industry. In 1975 civil war broke out between Muslim and Christian forces. In 1978 and 1982, Israeli troops invaded Lebanon to attack Palestinian forces. During the second invasion, a large part of BEIRUT, the capital, was destroyed.

FRANCE ruled Lebanon from 1918 until independence in 1946.

AREA: 4,016 SQ. MILES (10,400 SQ. KM)
POPULATION: 3,325,000
CAPITAL: BEIRUT
CURRENCY: LEBANESE POUND
OFFICIAL LANGUAGE: ARABIC

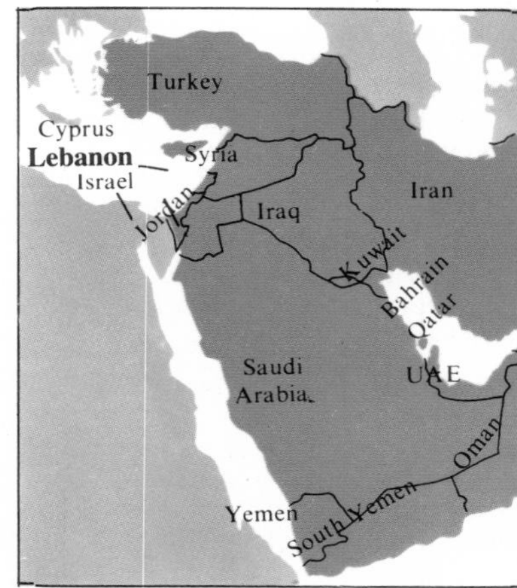

lecture *n.* a lesson or period of instruction. *vb.* deliver a lecture; tell off, reprimand. **lecturer** *n.*

led *vb.* past of **lead**.

ledge *n.* a narrow shelf on a wall or cliff.

ledger *n.* a (large) book, particularly one used for keeping accounts.

Lee, Robert Edward
Robert E. Lee (1807–1870) was a famous general who commanded the Confederate Army during the Civil War. Lee grew up in Virginia and in 1825 went to West Point. When war broke out between North and South, Lee was offered the command of the United States Army, but he refused, saying that he could not fight against his native state. He took up the defense of Richmond, Virginia.

For Lee, an encounter with the enemy was a skillful game in which a small number of soldiers had to be used in the best possible way against a more powerful foe. He won victories at the Battle of Bull Run and the Battle of Fredericksburg, but was finally defeated at Gettysburg, Pennsylvania, on July 3, 1863. Lee finally surrendered to General Grant at Appomattox Courthouse on April 9, 1865.

leek *n.* a vegetable with a thick, white stem and broad, flat leaves; it is related to the onion.
left 1. *vb.* past of **leave**. 2. *n.* & *adj.* the side opposite to right. *In Britain, people drive on the left.*
leg *n.* one of the two lower limbs of the human body. *Most animals have four or more legs.*
legal (**lee**-*gal*) *adj.* to do with the law; correct by the law. *Is it legal to ride a bicycle on the pavement?* **legalize** *vb.* make lawful.
legend (**ledge**-*end*) *n.* an old story. **legendary** *adj.* told about in old stories.
legion *n.* a division of the Roman army of between 3,000 and 6,000 men; any large force; an association.
legislate *vb.* make laws.

Leipzig
Leipzig is a city in East GERMANY. It became an important trading center during the MIDDLE AGES. It was also a cultural center, but today it is best known for its manufacturing industry and trade fairs.

NAPOLEON was heavily defeated at the Battle of Leipzig in 1813. The result of the battle was the withdrawal of the French from Germany.

leisure (**lee**-*sure*) *adj.* & *n.* rest, time free from work.
lemming *n.* a small Arctic rodent.
► There are several kinds of lemming. All have short tails. Most have brown or gray fur. They live in northern forests and in the cold lands of the ARCTIC. They feed on leaves, stems, roots and berries. In winter, lemmings keep warm by living in tunnels underneath the snow. In some summers lemmings breed very fast. They eat up all the food. Huge numbers of lemmings leave home to find more food. Many drown trying to cross rivers.

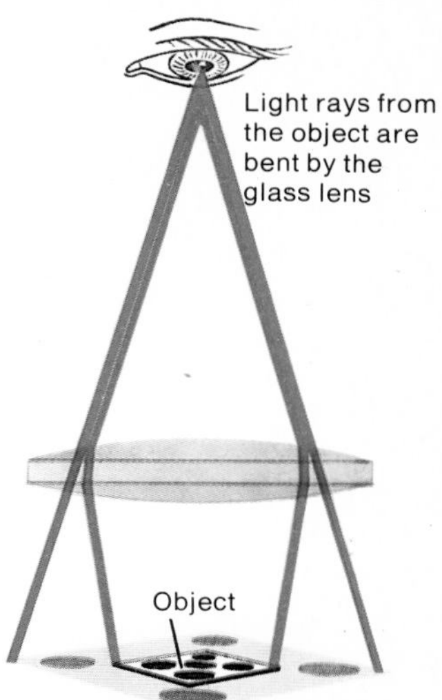

The convex lens of a magnifying glass bends light rays from all points on the object toward each other. This causes an enlarged image of the object to appear behind the glass.

lemon *n.* a small oval citrus fruit with a yellow skin and acid juice. Lemon trees are widely cultivated in southern Europe and the Middle East.
lemonade *n.* a lemon-flavored drink.
lend *vb.* give something to someone for a time, expecting to get it back. The other person borrows it.
length *n.* from one end to the other in distance or time. **lengthen** *vb.* make or become longer.

Lenin, Vladimir
Vladimir Ilyich Lenin (1870–1924) helped to make RUSSIA the first Communist country in the world. Before his time, Russia was ruled by emperors, or tsars. Like Karl MARX, Lenin believed in COMMUNISM. He wanted every country run by the workers. For many years Lenin lived outside Russia. He wrote books, and for Communist newspapers. In 1917 he returned to Russia and became the leader of a group of Communists called Bolsheviks. The Bolsheviks overthrew the government and Lenin ruled the country until he died.

Leningrad
Leningrad is the second largest city in the U.S.S.R.. The city was originally called St. Petersburg after Peter the Great, who founded it in 1703. It was laid out on a grand scale, and is still one of the most impressive cities in the world. In 1924, it was renamed Leningrad after the Russian revolutionary leader LENIN.

Leningrad, which lies on the Gulf of Finland in the BALTIC sea, is also a major seaport. It has a university and many fine schools, libraries and museums.

lens *n.* (plural **lenses**) a piece of glass with one or two curved surfaces, used in cameras, glasses, telescopes and microscopes.
► Lenses are used to make things look bigger or smaller. They are usually made of glass or plastic. The lens inside the eye is made of PROTEIN. Sometimes eye lenses do not work properly. Then people cannot see clearly. The lenses in eyeglasses improve the eyesight. Lenses are used for many other things. The lenses in MICROSCOPES, binoculars and TELESCOPES make distant things or small things seem much larger.

Each lens has two smooth sides. Both sides may be curved, or one may be curved and the other flat. There are two main kinds of lens. Lenses where the edges are thicker than the middle are called *concave* lenses. Concave means "hollowed out." When LIGHT rays pass through a concave lens, they diverge, "spread" out. Something looked at through a concave lens looks smaller than it really is.

Lenses where the middle is thicker than the edges are called *convex* lenses. Convex means rounded, like the outside of a circle.

Lent *n.* the 40 days that Christians observe as a preparation for Easter. It begins on Ash Wednesday.
lent *vb.* past of **lend**.
lentil *n.* the seed of a food plant of the pea family that grows in hot countries.

Leonardo da Vinci
Leonardo da Vinci (1452–1519) was an Italian artist and inventor. He lived during the RENAISSANCE. One of his most famous paintings is the Mona Lisa, a picture of a woman who is smiling mysteriously. Leonardo made thousands of drawings of human bodies, water, plants and animals and wrote many notes on the things he drew.

Leonardo worked as an engineer for Italian nobles and for the French king. He designed forts and canals. The canals had locks so that boats could travel up and down hills. Leonardo also drew ideas for things long before they were invented. His drawings include a helicopter, a flying machine and a machine gun.

Leonardo was interested in many other things, including music and architecture.

leopard (**lep**-*ard*) *n.* large African animal belonging to the cat family with black spots on a yellowish coat. In India leopards are called panthers.
leotard (**lee**-*o-tard*) *n.* a close-fitting one-piece garment worn for gymnastics, dance, and other sports.
leprechaun (**lep**-*ri-cawn*) *n.* a mischievous Irish elf.
leprosy *n.* a disease of the skin causing loss of feeling and a gradual eating away of the skin.

Lesotho
Lesotho is a mountainous, landlocked monarchy in southern AFRICA. Most of the people work on the land. There are large flocks of sheep and goats, and wool is exported. Lesotho became a British protectorate in 1884. It was called Basutoland until independence in 1966. Lesotho is entirely surrounded by SOUTH AFRICA, on which it is economically dependent.
AREA: 11,721 SQ. MILES (30,355 SQ. KM)
POPULATION: 1,406,000
CAPITAL: MASERU
CURRENCY: LOTI

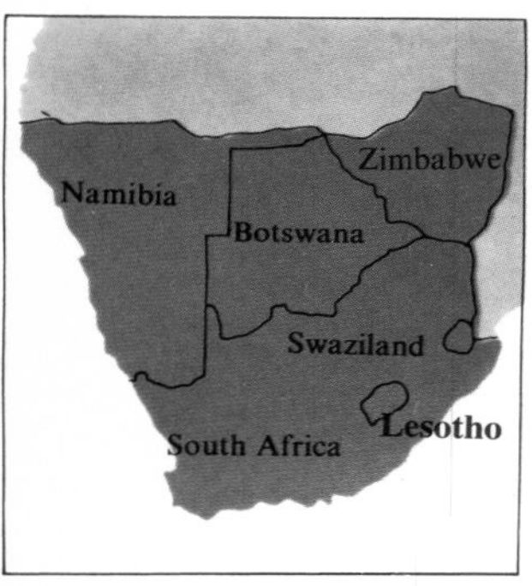

OFFICIAL LANGUAGES: ENGLISH, SESOTHO

less *adj.* a smaller amount. **lessen** *vb.* make less; reduce.
lesser *adj.* not so great as, smaller of two. *The lesser of two evils.*
lesson *n.* an exercise or assignment to be studied by a pupil; a warning, an example.
lest *conj.* for fear that, in order to avoid.
let *vb.* allow someone to do something. *Bob let us see his scar.*
let down *vb.* fail to do something that somebody expected you to do. *The workers promised to repair our roof, but they let us down, and the rain came in.*
let off *vb.* 1. free someone who has done wrong. *Our teacher let us off the hook when she saw all the extra work we had done.* 2. cause a firework to explode.
lethal *adj.* causing death.

Letter boxes from different lands.

letter *n.* 1. a part of the alphabet. *Our alphabet contains 26 letters.* 2. a written message, usually sent by mail.
letter carrier *n.* another word for a mail carrier.
lettering *n.* (the style) of letters used in an inscription, etc.
lettuce *n.* a salad vegetable that grows close to the ground on a very short stem; it has large green leaves.
level 1. *adj.* horizontal; even. *The surface of the table is perfectly level. vb.* make flat. 2. *n.* the base from which a height is measured. *The height of mountains is measured from sea level.* 3. *n.* the height to which a liquid rises in a container. *Please check the water level in the radiator.*
lever *n.* a tool used to lift something heavy or force it open. *vb.* use a lever; raise with a lever.
leveret *n.* a young hare.
levy *vb.* raise or collect taxes. *n.* the tax raised.
lexicon *n.* a dictionary.
liar *n.* someone who does not tell the truth.
liberal *adj.* abundant, free, generous; tolerant.
liberate *vb.* set free, release.

Liberia (Liberian)
Liberia is a republic in West AFRICA. Americans established the country in the 1800s as a home for freed slaves. Today, Liberia has a large merchant navy. Many foreign ships register in

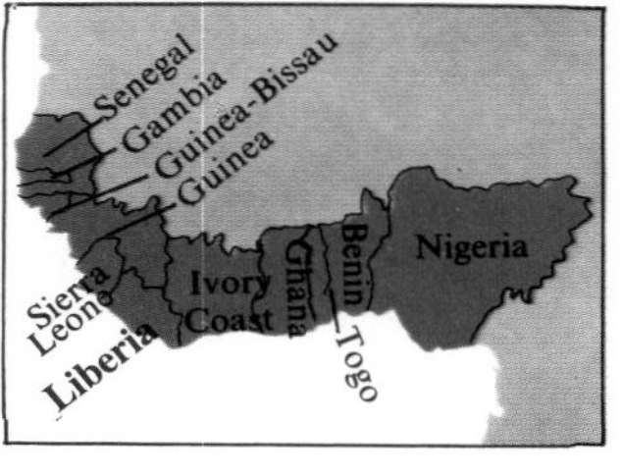

Liberia for low fees under the "flag of convenience" system.
AREA: 43,002 SQ. MILES (111,369 SQ. KM)
POPULATION: 1,992,000
CAPITAL: MONROVIA
CURRENCY: LIBERIAN DOLLAR
OFFICIAL LANGUAGE: ENGLISH

liberty *n.* freedom; the right to do what one wants.

Liberty Bell
The Liberty Bell hangs in the Tower Room of Independence Hall, Philadelphia. It was rung on July 8, 1776, to announce the Declaration of Independence, and on July 8 every year after that until it cracked in 1835.

library *n.* a building or room where books are kept and, usually, borrowed from. **librarian** *n.* a person trained to work in a library.
► In a public library the books are sorted out into sections so that they are easy to find. All the books on one subject are kept together. For instance, all stories are grouped in a section called fiction. Inside each section the books are arranged in alphabetical order according to the names of the authors.
You can find out if the library has a book without looking for it on the shelves. All the books are listed in a catalog. The simplest kind of catalog is a card index. Each book's title, author and subject are written on cards. These are kept in alphabetical order. Most libraries have an author index and a subject index.

Libya (Libyan)
Libya is a large country in North AFRICA. It is more than three times

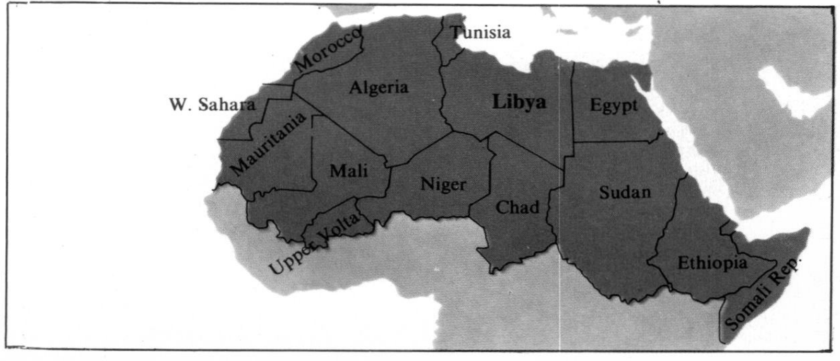

the size of France, but very few people live there. This is because most of Libya lies in the SAHARA.

Most Libyans are ARABS who farm the land. Libya is also rich in oil.
AREA: 697,399 SQ. MILES (1,759,540 SQ. KM)
POPULATION: 3,244,000
CAPITAL: TRIPOLI
CURRENCY: LIBYAN DINAR
OFFICIAL LANGUAGE: ARABIC

lice *n.* plural of **louse**.
license *n.* a permit to do something. *He has a license to drive a car. vb.* to give a license; authorize.
lichen (**lie**-*ken*) *n.* a small dry-looking plant that grows on rocks or trees.
► Lichen is a plant organism in which special types of fungus and alga (a very simple plant) live and work together. The tiny algae, bound up in the fungus threads, make food by PHOTOSYNTHESIS for themselves and the fungus. In turn, the fungus provides the algae with water, which it absorbs from the air, and mineral salts, obtained from the rocks on which it grows. Lichens are yellow or gray and spread over rocks, walls, tree trunks and poor soil.

lick *vb.* & *n.* touch something with the tongue.
lid *n.* the top covering of something, such as a pot.
lie 1. *vb.* & *n.* (say) something that is not true. 2. *vb.* put yourself down flat. *If you lie on the floor, you can see the crack.* 3. *vb.* (of places) be in a certain place. *The small islands lie just off the coast.*

Liechtenstein
Liechtenstein is a small principality between AUSTRIA and SWITZERLAND. Light industry has become important as are tourism and the sale of postage stamps. Liechtenstein has strong links with Switzerland, and uses Swiss money.
AREA: 61 SQ. MILES (157 SQ. KM)
POPULATION: 26,200
CAPITAL: VADUZ
CURRENCY: SWISS FRANC
OFFICIAL LANGUAGE: GERMAN

life *n.* (plural **lives**) 1. all living things. *When did life begin on earth?* 2. the time between birth and death. 3. liveliness; energy. *The young children were full of life.*
lifeboat *n.* a boat for rescuing people at sea.
lift 1. *vb.* raise up; take up. 2. *n.* a ride in a vehicle given to a walker.
lift-off *n.* the takeoff of a rocket.
light 1. *n.* something that shines brightly so that we can see things; illumination. 2. *vb.* set on fire. 3. *adj.* not heavy. 4. *adj.* not dark in color. *A light-blue suit.*
► Light is a form of ENERGY, as heat and sound are. We see things because light is reflected from them. Light is produced when an object gets extremely hot. The sun is a fiery ball of incandescent gas. According to the wave theory, light radiates from its source as a series of waves rather like the ripples on the surface of a pool caused by a stone's splash. The distance between any two successive crests (or troughs) is called the *wavelength* of the light. These wavelengths are very small – only a few millionths of an inch. The number of waves passing a point in space every second is the *frequency* of the light. And light travels at an enormously high speed about 186,000 miles (300,000 km) per second.
The wavelength of light also determines its color. For example, red light has a longer wavelength than blue light. When white light from the sun, which consists of a mixture of many wavelengths, is passed through a glass prism, each wavelength is refracted to a slightly different extent. As a result, a prism can split white light into its component colors, or *spectrum*. A rainbow is made up of the colors of the sun's spectrum.

According to modern theory, all forms of radiation consist of tiny "packets" of energy called QUANTA, which travel as waves. A quantum of light is called a PHOTON.

lighten *vb.* 1. make or become lighter; make easier to bear. 2. make or grow bright.
lighter 1. *n.* device for lighting cigarettes. 2. *n.* flat-bottomed boat used for unloading goods from a ship. 3. *adj.* comparative of "light:" not so heavy; not so dark.
lighthouse *n.* a tower with a flashing light in it that warns ships away from dangerous rocks.
► The Egyptians built lighthouses beside the Mediterranean Sea more than 2,000 years ago. One lighthouse, the Pharos of Alexandria, was one of the SEVEN WONDERS OF THE WORLD.

The lights in early lighthouses were fires burning in metal baskets. Modern lighthouses have powerful electric lamps and a set of glass reflectors which bend the light into powerful beams that sweep over the sea. Sailors can tell which lighthouse they are near by the pattern of its light beams, for each lighthouse has its own pattern. Many lighthouses are equipped with fog signals.

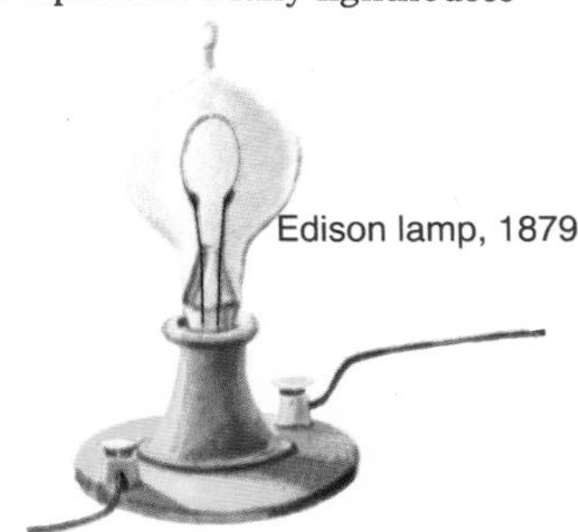
Edison lamp, 1879

lighting *n.* artificial light such as candles or lamps.
► For thousands of years, people depended on fire for light. At first they burned lumps of wood to make torches. Later they learned how to make wax candles and oil lamps. Early oil lamps were just wicks floating in dishes of oil. By the 1800s people had brighter, safer oil lamps. The flame burned inside a curved glass chimney. There were also lamps which burned coal gas. A century ago, Thomas EDISON

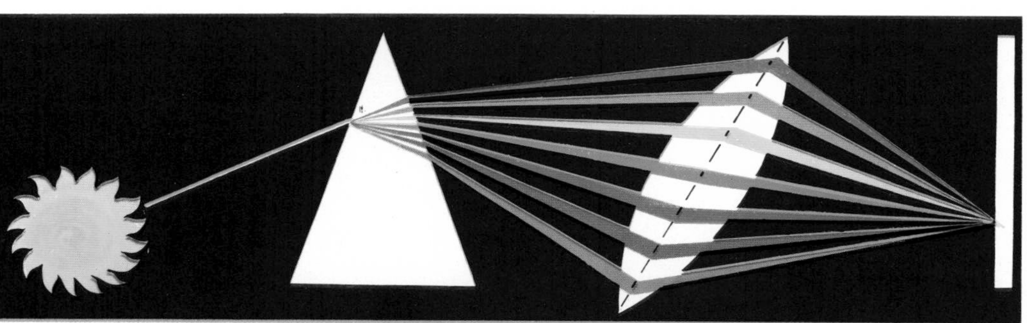
The spectrum of light. Sunlight splits up into the colors of the rainbow when it is passed through a glass prism.

L

invented the electric light bulb – a glass bulb with a thin wire inside. When an electric current passes through the wire it glows. Today, most lighting is electric.

lightning *n.* a flash of light in the sky during a thunderstorm.

► Lightning is electricity that you can see. It is a sudden flow of electric current between two clouds, between a cloud and the ground, or between two parts of the cloud. There are three types of lightning. Streak lightning flashes in a single line from cloud to earth. Forked lightning happens when the lightning divides to find the quickest way to earth. Sheet lightning happens inside a cloud and lights up the sky, like the flash bulb on a camera.

like 1. *vb.* think well of someone or something. 2. *vb.* enjoy doing something. 3. *adj.* similar to. *She looks like her sister.*

likely *adv.* expected to happen, probable. *It is likely to rain this afternoon.*

lilac *n.* a shrub grown in many parts of the world for its fragrant white or purple flowers.

lilt *vb.* sing rhythmically.

lily *n.* a plant growing from a bulb, with showy flowers. The lily family includes onions, asparagus and tulips.

limb *n.* a leg or an arm.

lime *n.* 1. a substance obtained from heating limestone, and used in making cement. 2. the small, green, lemon-like fruit of a tropical tree. 3. a deciduous tree also called the linden.

limerick *n.* a funny five-line poem with this form:

There was a young man from Nepal
Who went to a fancy dress ball;
He thought he would risk it
And go as a biscuit,
But a dog ate him up in the hall.

limestone *n.* a rock containing the chemical substance calcium carbonate.

► Most limestone was made from the limy plants and the skeletons of millions of tiny animals that lived in prehistoric seas. Dead plants and animals piled up on the seabed and were pressed together until they hardened into rock. Their FOSSILS can be seen in some types of limestone.

Water wears away limestone. It trickles through small cracks in the rock and widens them. This is how rivers eat out underground caves in limestone rock.

People quarry limestone because it is very useful. Builders use it in blocks. Burned limestone becomes lime which is used to make cement and fertilizer. It is also used in steel and glass making.

limit 1. *n.* a line or point that you cannot or should not go beyond. *The speed limit in the town is 30 miles an hour.* 2. *vb.* restrict something. *You should limit her to three candies before dinner.*

limp 1. *adj.* not stiff. *The skirt became very limp after she washed it.* 2. *vb.* walk unevenly.

limpet *n.* a kind of shellfish that clings to rocks.

Lincoln, Abraham
Abraham Lincoln (1809–65) was the 16th President of the United States. Few men have had a greater influence on American history. He grew up in a log cabin on his father's farm in Kentucky.

He was elected to Congress in 1847. In 1860 the Republican Party nominated him for President. He won the election easily. The CIVIL WAR broke out in 1861 and Lincoln tried hard to preserve the Union. He issued his Emancipation Proclamation in 1863. This said that all slaves in the rebellious states should be freed.

Lincoln began his second term as president in 1865 as the war was ending. He wanted the Southern states to take their place once more in the Union. But Lincoln did not live to see his plans carried out. On April 14, 1865, while attending a play at Ford's Theater in Washington, he was shot in the head by John Wilkes Booth, who had sympathized with the Southern states.

Lincoln was the first President who belonged to the Republican Party. After his assassination he was succeeded by his Vice-President, Andrew Johnson.

Lincoln's best-remembered words were spoken in the Gettysburg Address: "Government of the people, by the people, for the people, shall not perish from the earth."

Lindbergh, Charles
Charles Augustus Lindbergh (1902–74), was an American pilot who became the first man to fly the Atlantic Ocean alone. His single-engine airplane, *Spirit of St. Louis*, left New York on May 20, 1927. He landed in Paris, France on May 21, 33½ hours later, after flying about 3,600 miles (5,800 km) nonstop. Lindbergh's flight showed people that air travel was possible.

line 1. *n.* a long, thin mark. 2. *n.* a piece of rope or string. 3. *n.* a row of people or things. *We stand in line for dinner.* 4. *n.* a transport system. *There goes a green line bus.* 5. *vb.* put a lining into something.

linen *n.* cloth made from the fibers of the flax plant.

► Flax stems are first soaked in water and beaten to separate the strands. These are combed smooth and then spun into yarn. The yarn is very strong and soaks up water easily. It is used to make sheets, tablecloths, handkerchiefs and towels.

Ancient Egyptians grew flax and made linen more than 4,000 years ago. Today, Russia is the world's largest producer of flax.

liner *n.* a big passenger ship.

linger *vb.* wait about, be slow to go, delay.

linguist *n.* 1. a person who speaks several languages. 2. a person who makes a scientific study of how language works.

lining *n.* a layer of material inside something. *Her coat has a purple silk lining.*

link 1. *n.* one loop of a chain. 2. *vb.* connect things together.

linoleum *n.* a floor covering.

linseed *n.* seed of flax.

lion *n.* a large member of the cat family.

► Lions are large, tawny colored wildcats. An adult male weighs about 400 lb. (180 kg) and measures about 9 ft. (2.7 meters) from nose to tail.

A limestone cave is probably formed by water seeping through cracks in the surface of the limestone rock. The acid in the water gradually widens the vertical cracks and reaches a horizontal crack, which it enlarges into passageways and caverns.

Females (lionesses) are slightly smaller and have no mane.

Lions usually live in family groups called prides. A pride has one male, one or two females and all their cubs. Lions often hunt together. No other big cats seem to do this. They hunt mainly antelope and zebra, creeping up on their victims through the long grass. One lion may leap out to scare the prey into another lion's path. Lionesses do most of the hunting, as they have to feed their cubs as well as themselves.

Lions at one time roamed wild over southern Europe, India and Africa. Now they live only in South and East Africa and a tiny part of India. Most lions today lead protected lives in nature reserves. Hundreds of captive lions live in ZOOS all over the world.

lioness *n.* a female lion. **lionize** *vb.* treat as a celebrity.

lip *n.* 1. one of the top or bottom edges of the mouth. 2. the specially shaped part of a jug from which the liquid is poured.

liquid *n.* a substance like water that flows. *A liquid is not a gas or a solid. adj.* in a fluid state. **liquefy** *vb.* make or become liquid.

Lisbon

Lisbon is the capital of PORTUGAL. This ancient city is a major seaport on the estuary of the Tagus River. The old city attracts many tourists. Lisbon is an important industrial and commercial center.

lisp *vb.* speak using a "th" sound for "s" and "z."

list 1. *n.* a number of names or things written down one above the other. *Did you put bread on the shopping list? vb.* enter on list. 2. *n.* & *vb.* leaning of ship to one side.

listen *vb.* pay attention to sound. *Listen to this.*

Lister, Joseph

Joseph Lister (1827–1912) was an English surgeon who founded antiseptic SURGERY. He was the first to use carbolic acid to prevent infection in operating rooms, and he discovered that instruments could be sterilized by heat.

listless *adj.* without much desire to be active. *Mary felt listless after her illness.*

lit *vb.* past and past part. of **light**.

liter (rhymes with *heater*) *n.* a liquid measure (about one quart).

literate *adj.* able to read and write; educated.

literature *n.* books and writing, in general of a high quality and valued for their form and style.

► Literature is everything written. Everything from newspaper articles to the plays of William Shakespeare or the fairy tales of the Brothers Grimm is literature. The term is also used to distinguish between well-written material and work of a lesser quality. Imaginative literature can be divided into several areas, such as DRAMA, NOVELS, POETRY and SCIENCE FICTION. Nonfiction, such as books on HISTORY, is based on events that have actually happened. The ancient Sumerians may have written the earliest literature, about 5,000 years ago. Between the 900s and 300s B.C., literature reached great heights in ancient GREECE. It included the famous poems of HOMER. With the invention of PRINTING, literature became available to almost everyone.

Lithuania (Lithuanian)

Lithuania is a republic of the U.S.S.R., bordering the Baltic Sea. Lithuania has an area of 25,097 sq. miles (65,000 sq. km). The capital is Vilnius. Lithuania was independent from 1918 to 1920.

litter 1. *n.* rubbish thrown away in a public place. 2. *vb.* all the newly born offspring of an animal. *Our cat had a litter of four kittens.*

little *adj.* not much; small or tiny.

liturgy *n.* the form of service or ritual of a church.

live (rhymes with *hive*) *adj.* living. *There are no live animals in the museum.* **lively** *adj.* full of life and energy.

live (rhymes with *give*) *vb.* 1. exist; be alive. *He lived 100 years ago.* 2. inhabit. *They live in the center of London.*

liver *n.* an organ of the body that does many jobs, including getting rid of things the body does not want and making things it needs.

A frilled lizard.

► The liver is a large important organ found in all VERTEBRATES and some INVERTEBRATES. The liver is often called the body's laboratory, as it makes and stores many vital substances. For example, it manufactures bile, a digestive fluid, urea, a waste product, and various blood proteins. The liver also stores essential materials such as PROTEINS, MINERALS, VITAMINS and glycogen.

Liverpool (Liverpudlian)

Liverpool is the third largest city in ENGLAND. More than half-a-million people live there. It is a big seaport on the River Mersey in northwest England. The city has a university and two cathedrals. Britain's longest tunnel runs under the Mersey between Liverpool and Birkenhead. Most of Liverpool was built after the INDUSTRIAL REVOLUTION.

livery *n.* 1. distinctive uniform worn by servants of a great household or city company. 2. a stable for boarding or hiring horses.

livestock *n.* farm animals.

living *adj.* alive.

living room *n.* a sitting room; the main room in a house. *They kept the TV set in the living room.*

Livingstone, David

David Livingstone (1813–73) was a Scottish doctor and missionary who explored much of southern and central AFRICA. He traveled to spread CHRISTIANITY and to help stop traders selling Africans into SLAVERY.

Livingstone made three great journeys between 1841 and 1873. He crossed Africa, discovered the VICTORIA FALLS and searched for the source of the River NILE.

In 1869, people feared that he had got lost or was dead. In 1871, an American newspaper reporter, Henry Morton Stanley, found him at Lake Tanganyika. Both men continued their explorations, but Livingstone fell ill and died as they traveled.

lizard *n.* a four-legged reptile with a tail.

► The lizard is found mainly in warm countries. Most lizards have a body covered with small overlapping scales and four limbs, but some, like the slowworm, are legless. They usually lay eggs and feed on animal matter such as insects. There are some 2,000 lizard species in the world, including the CHAMELEON, IGUANA, gecko and skink.

llama *n.* an animal of South America related to the camel family, but without a hump.

► The llama stands about 5 ft. (1.5 meters) high at the shoulder and may weigh twice as much as a man. Long, thick hair keeps it warm on the cold slopes of the Andes Mountains in South America, where it lives. All llamas come from wild ancestors who were tamed at least 4,500 years ago by the INCAS. Today, South American Indians still use llamas to

A llama from South America.

carry heavy loads. They make clothes and ropes from the llama's wool and candles from its fat.

load (rhymes with *code*) 1. *n.* something that has to be carried. *She took a load of washing to the laundromat.* 2. *vb.* fill or cover something. *They loaded the car with luggage.*
loaf 1. *n.* a complete piece of bread. *I bought two loaves from the baker.* 2. *vb.* laze about.
loan *n.* something that has been lent to you, usually money.
loathe (rhymes with *clothe*) *vb.* detest, dislike very much.
lobby *n.* entrance hall to hotel, theater, etc.
lobster *n.* a shellfish with a hard shell and 10 legs, two of which carry large claws.
► Lobsters are CRUSTACEANS. They are related to shrimps and crabs. One kind of lobster can weigh up to 44 lb. (20 kg). The lobster's body has a hard shell. It has four pairs of legs for walking and a pair of huge claws for grabbing food. When a lobster is afraid it tucks its tail under its body. This drives water forward and pushes the lobster backward to escape.
Lobsters hide among rocks on the seabed. They feed on live and dead animals. A female lobster can lay thousands of eggs.

local *adj.* belonging to a fairly small area. *This local newspaper gives news about our town.*
localize *vb.* restrict to a particular place.
locate *vb.* find exact position; establish in a particular place.
loch *n.* a Scottish lake.
lock 1. *vb.* fasten something. *n.* a fastening for a door or a box that needs a key to open it. 2. *n.* a piece of hair. 3. *n.* a section of a canal or river where the water levels can be changed by opening and shutting large gates.
► Lock and key are methods of protecting property. Simple wooden locks were developed in ancient Egypt. There are now several kinds. The Yale lock contains a series of pins and drivers, which are all raised only when the correct key is inserted. Combination locks have no key. They are worked by a dial which is turned backward and forward to release the tumblers, which hold the bolt.

locker *n.* a cupboard that can be locked.
locket *n.* a small case worn on a chain around the neck. *A locket may contain a picture.*

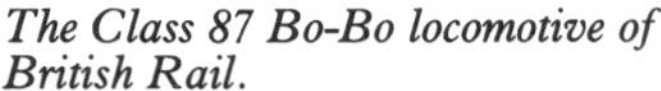

George Stephenson's "Rocket" of 1829.

A huge diesel locomotive.

Amonorail running on an overhead track.

The Class 87 Bo-Bo locomotive of British Rail.

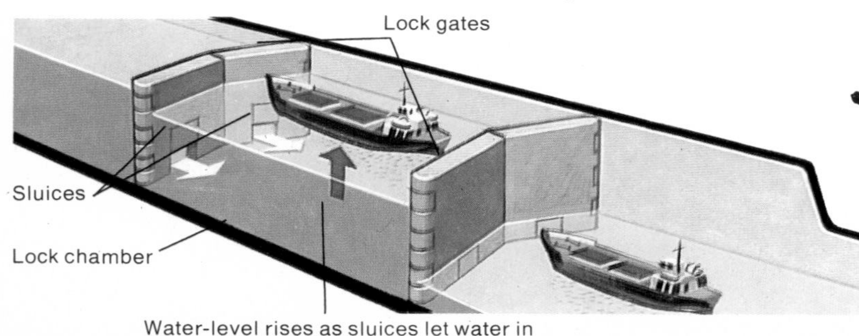

A lock is like a step. It raises or lowers barges on the canal from one level to another.

locomotive *n.* a machine on wheels that pulls trains.
► Locomotives can be powered by steam, diesel or electricity. Steam locomotives need time to build up pressure. Diesel locomotives can be quickly stopped or started, and use fuel more efficiently than steam locomotives. The most powerful diesel locomotives are diesel-electric. The ENGINE drives an electric generator and the electric power produced is fed to traction motors geared to the driving wheels. Electric locomotives stop and start quickly, and produce no smoke or exhaust fumes. They also need less maintenance. Two French electric locomotives hold the rail speed record of 206.6 mph (330.8 k/h). Most locomotives pick up the electric current from an overhead wire via a sprung arm called a *pantograph* on top of the engine body. Others pick up current from an insulated third rail.
The first steam locomotive was built in 1804 by a British inventor, Richard Trevithick (1771–1833). The first really successful one was the *Rocket*, built in 1829 by another Briton, George Stephenson (1781–1848). Electric locomotives were pioneered by the German firm

of Siemens and Halske in the late 1800s. Diesel locomotives were first used in 1912. (*see* RAILROAD).

locust *n.* an insect like a grasshopper.

► Locusts sometimes breed in huge numbers. They fly far across land and sea in vast swarms to find new feeding places. A big swarm may have millions of locusts. When they land, the locusts eat all vegetation in their path and can thus destroy vast areas of crops.

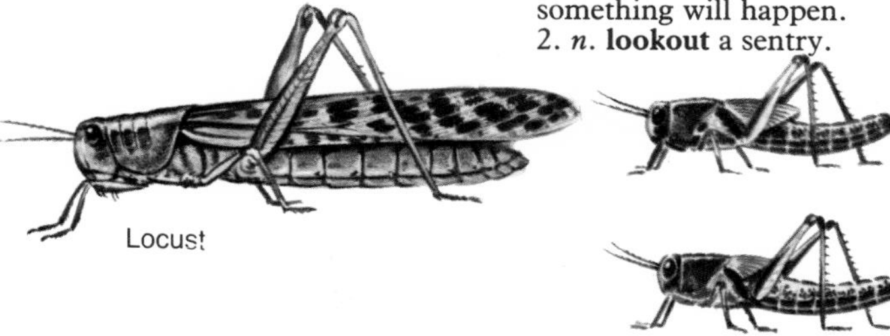

lodge 1. *n.* a small house at the gates of a large house. 2. *vb.* stay in someone's house and pay to stay there. 3. *n.* a beaver's home.
loft *n.* a room at the top of a house used for storing things; an attic.
log *n.* 1. a length of tree that has been cut down. 2. a written record of happenings, especially in a ship.
logic *n.* the science of or particular method of reasoning. **logical** *adj.* in accordance with the principles of logic.
loiter *vb.* go along very slowly; dawdle.
lollipop *n.* a candy on a stick.

London (Londoner)
The capital of the UNITED KINGDOM of GREAT BRITAIN and NORTHERN IRELAND. London is a great commercial city, standing on the River THAMES. It contains many places associated with events in British history, including the Houses of PARLIAMENT, WESTMINSTER ABBEY, the Tower of London, and so on. London was founded by the Romans. It was largely rebuilt after the Great Fire of London (1666).

lonely *adj.* 1. without friends. 2. away from other people. *They had a lonely house in the woods.*
long 1. *adj.* having a specified length. *How long is that table?* 2. *adj.* of unusually great length. *He has very long legs.* 3. *vb.* wish for very much. *I long to see you.*

Longfellow, Henry Wadsworth
Henry Wadsworth Longfellow (1807–1882) was the most famous American poet of the 1800s. His best-known poems include *The Song of Hiawatha, The Village Blacksmith* and *The Wreck of the Hesparus*.
longitude *n.* a distance measured in degrees east or west from a line on the map joining Greenwich, England, and the North and South Poles.
look *vb.* use one's eyes to see something.
look after *vb.* take care of. *Can you look after our cat while we are away?*
look forward to *vb.* think with pleasure about something that is going to happen.
looking glass *n.* a mirror.
look into *vb.* investigate.
look out 1. *vb.* watch to see whether anyone is coming, or whether something will happen. 2. *n.* **lookout** a sentry.
look up *vb.* search for an item as if in a dictionary, encyclopedia or other book. 2. improve. *The weather is looking up.*
look up to *vb.* admire someone. *I always looked up to my brother because he was so good at football.*

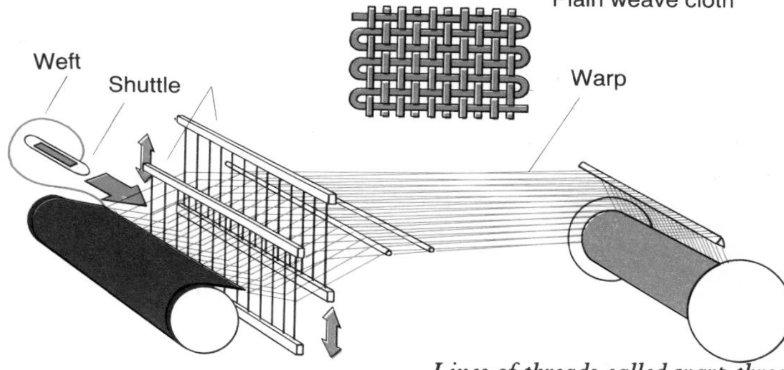

Lines of threads called warp threads move up and down in a loom. In between each movement, a shuttle pulls another thread called the weft between the warp threads.

loom 1. *n.* a machine for weaving cloth. 2. *vb.* appear in a vague or misty way; get larger. *The house loomed through the fog.*
loop *n.* a circle or part circle of wire, string or other material.
loose *adj.* not tight or firm. *One of my teeth is loose.* **loosen** *vb.* make or become loose.
loot *n.* & *vb.* plunder.
lop *vb.* cut off the ends of (especially a tree).
lord *n.* a nobleman.
lorry *n.* a big, open vehicle that carries heavy loads.

Los Angeles
Los Angeles is the second largest city in the UNITED STATES. The city lies in sunny southern CALIFORNIA. On one side of Los Angeles is the Pacific Ocean. Behind it are the San Gabriel Mountains.
There are thousands of factories and a big port in Los Angeles. Visitors go to see Disneyland and HOLLYWOOD. Los Angeles makes more movies and television films than any other city in the world.

lose *vb.* (past **lost**) 1. no longer possess. 2. go astray. 3. be beaten in a game.
lost *vb.* past part. of **lose**.
lotion (**low**-*shun*) *n.* a liquid applied to the skin for cosmetic or medicinal reasons.
loud *adj.* noisy; not quiet.
loudspeaker *n.* part of a radio or record player that changes electric waves into sound.

Louis (**French Kings**)
Eighteen French kings were called Louis.
The first was Louis I (778–840). Louis IX (1214–70) led two CRUSADES. Louis XI (1423–83) won power and land from his nobles. Louis XIII (1601–43) made the French kings very powerful. Louis XIV (1638–1715) ruled for 72 years and built a great palace at VERSAILLES. All the French nobles had to live in his palace. Louis XVI (1754–93) was beheaded after the FRENCH REVOLUTION.

Louisiana (*abbrev.* **La.**)
Louisiana is a state in the southern U.S.A. It lies on the coast of the Gulf of Mexico, at the delta of the MISSISSIPPI RIVER. Its capital is Baton Rouge, but its most famous city is New Orleans.
The state is rich in timber, oil and natural gas, and cotton and rice are grown.
Louisiana was bought from France as part of the Louisiana Purchase in 1803. New Orleans is famous for its picturesque French Quarter and for the Mardi Gras festival held each year. It is also well- known as the birthplace of jazz.

lounge 1. *vb.* sit or stand in a lazy way. 2. *n.* a sitting room.
louse *n.* (plural **lice**) a small bloodsucking insect that feeds on animals or humans.

Louvre
The world's largest art museum, the Louvre is a beautiful building in PARIS. It holds about 275,000 works of art, including the Venus de Milo and LEONARDO DA VINCI'S *Mona Lisa.* The main parts of the Louvre were built in the reign of LOUIS XIV.

love *vb.* & *n.* be very fond of someone or something.
lovely *adj.* attractive; pretty. *What a lovely room.*
low *adj.* not high; near the ground. *A low table.*
lower 1. *adj.* not as high as. 2. *vb.* make something less high.
loyal *adj.* faithful to others. *We trust him as a loyal friend.*
lubricate *vb.* use oil or grease to make a machine work smoothly by cutting down the friction between two surfaces.
lucid *adj.* clear, easy to understand.
luck *n.* chance; good fortune. *Wish me luck.*
lucky *adj.* fortunate. *How lucky you were passing by.*
ludicrous *adj.* ridiculous, absurd. *That is a ludicrous suit you are wearing.*
luggage *n.* the cases, bags and other containers that are taken on a journey.
lukewarm *adj.* tepid; slightly warm; halfhearted.
lullaby *n.* a song that is sung to send a baby to sleep. **lull** *vb.* cause to sleep; soothe.
lumbago *n.* inflammation of the muscles of the lower back.
lumber *n.* timber prepared for use.
lumberjack *n.* a person who cuts down trees, especially in North America.
lump *n.* a bump, a swelling.
lunacy *n.* foolishness; insanity.
lunar *adj.* of or about the moon. *There will be a lunar eclipse this week.*
lunatic *n.* person who is insane.
lunch *n.* the midday meal (from **luncheon**, now rare) *vb.* eat lunch.
lung *n.* your body has two lungs inside your chest, forming a single organ by which you breathe.
► Air-breathing VERTEBRATES have two lungs, usually in the upper part of the body. Air, from the nose or mouth, travels down the windpipe, through the two *bronchi* (tubes connecting the windpipe to each lung) and into the lungs. In the lung, the bronchial tube divides and redivides many times until the air is being carried by millions of tiny tubes called *bronchioles.* Each bronchiole ends in a minute balloon called an *alveoli*, or air sac. The walls of the air sac contain hair-like vessels, *capillaries*, carrying blood. Oxygen spreads, or diffuses, through the air sac walls into the capillaries; at the same time, carbon dioxide diffuses from the blood into the lungs.

lunge *vb.* & *n.* thrust at or attack suddenly.
lupin *n.* plant with flowers on a long spike.
lurk *vb.* wait unseen. *Strange creatures lurk in these woods.*
lust *n.* great desire.
lute *n.* pear-shaped plucked string instrument similar to a guitar.

Martin Luther pinning up the list of 95 arguments, setting out what he thought was wrong with the Church.

Luther, Martin
Martin Luther (1483–1546) was a German priest who quarreled with the Roman Catholic Church and started the Protestant REFORMATION.
Luther thought God looked kindly on anyone who believed in him. Luther did not like the way priests forgave people's sins in return for money. He also believed that God's teachings lay in the BIBLE. The Bible was more important to Luther than what the POPES said. Luther's followers are called Lutherans.

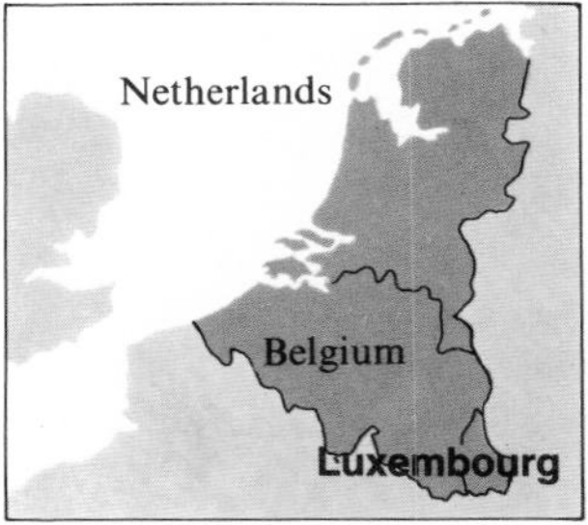

Luxembourg (Luxemburger)
Luxembourg is a Grand Duchy in Western EUROPE. French is one of the official languages, although most people speak a dialect of German. This rich nation has large iron ore reserves. Throughout the 1900s a considerable number of immigrants from Italy and other European countries have settled in the country.
AREA: 999 SQ. MILES (2,586 SQ. KM)
POPULATION: 360,000
CAPITAL: LUXEMBOURG
CURRENCY: FRANC
OFFICIAL LANGUAGES; LUXEMBURGISH, FRENCH

luxury *n.* an expensive thing that is not really needed. *Most people think that a fur coat is a luxury.* **luxurious** *adj.* very comfortable.
lynx *n.* a wildcat with a short tail and tufted ears.
► The lynx is a wild cat about 2½ ft. (75 cm) long with tufted ears and a fringe of hair on the cheeks. The lynx lives in forests where it hunts small animals by night. Lynxes run little, but are good walkers, climbers and swimmers and have exceptionally keen sight. The small lynx of North America, with a reddish-brown coat, is called a bobcat or wildcat.

Lyons
Lyons is a large city in eastern FRANCE. It stands at the point where the Rhône and Saône rivers meet. In WORLD WAR II, it was the center of the French Resistance movement. Today, its industries include textiles, chemicals and electrical equipment.

lyre *n.* a harplike instrument.
lyrebird *n.* an Australian pheasant-like bird that takes its name from the cock's tail feathers which form a fan in the shape of a lyre.

M

The towering peaks of the Himalaya Mountains

macabre *adj.* horrifying, gruesome.

Macao (Macaon)
Macao is a small Portuguese territory on the southeastern coast of CHINA. It lies at the mouth of the Canton River, and is densely populated. Nearly all the people are Chinese. Macao has been Portuguese since 1557. It was once the chief European trading center in China. However, its importance declined with the rise of HONG KONG.
AREA: 6 SQ. MILES (16 SQ. KM)
POPULATION: 333,000
CAPITAL: MACAO
CURRENCY: PATACA
OFFICIAL LANGUAGES: CHINESE, PORTUGUESE

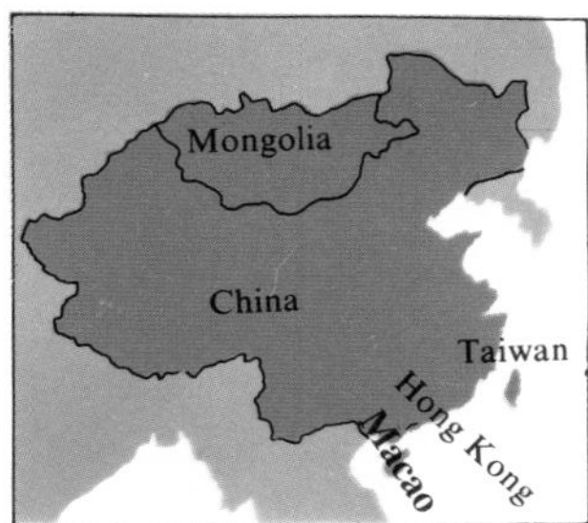

macaroni *n.* long tubes of flour paste that are cooked and eaten. *Macaroni and spaghetti are Italian dishes.*
macaroon *n.* sweet biscuit made with coconut or almonds.
macaw *n.* a large brightly colored parrot found in the tropical rainforests of Central and South America. Many species have gaudy green, blue, red or yellow feathers.

Macbeth
A king of Scotland and the main character in SHAKESPEARE's play. Macbeth succeeded Duncan I, whom he killed in 1040. Macbeth was killed in 1057 by Malcolm III.

mace *n.* 1. symbolic staff of authority. 2. spice made from outer skin of nutmeg.
machete (*ma*-**chet**-*ee*) *n.* heavy knife used for cutting vegetation and as a weapon in Central America.
machine *n.* a tool that has movable parts working together to do something.
► Machines make our jobs easier. They carry us from place to place, and make the goods we need. Until the INDUSTRIAL REVOLUTION, there were very few machines. In the Middle Ages the most powerful machines were mills and wheels driven by wind and water.

STEAM ENGINES were known to the ancient Greeks, but were used only as toys. The machine age did not begin until the 1700s. Later, in the 1800s, came other forms of power, such as the gasoline engine and the electric motor. The INTERNAL COMBUSTION ENGINE, which uses oil as fuel, has been used since the early 1900s for the AUTOMOBILE. JET ENGINES drive aircraft of today.

machine gun *n.* a gun that can fire many bullets very quickly without being reloaded.
machinery *n.* machines; the moving parts of machines.
► **Simple Machines** All the machines we see working around us are related to one or another of six simple machines. These machines were among the oldest and most important inventions.

A machine is stronger than a person. It uses a greater *force*. When a force is used to move something, we can say that *work* is done. Machines make work easier. The *wedge*, for example, helps us to split things. A wedge hammered into a small crack in a tree trunk will split the trunk in two. Chisels, knives,

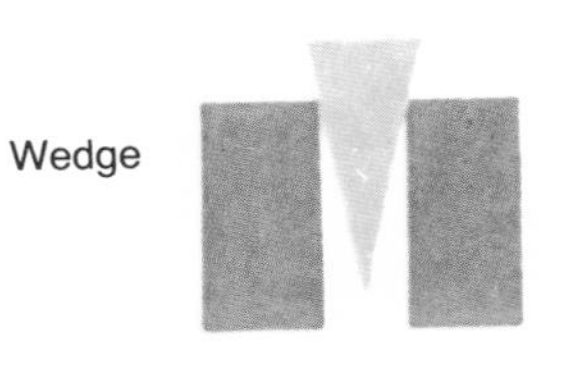

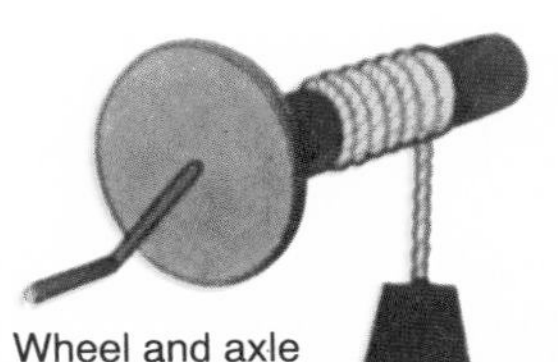

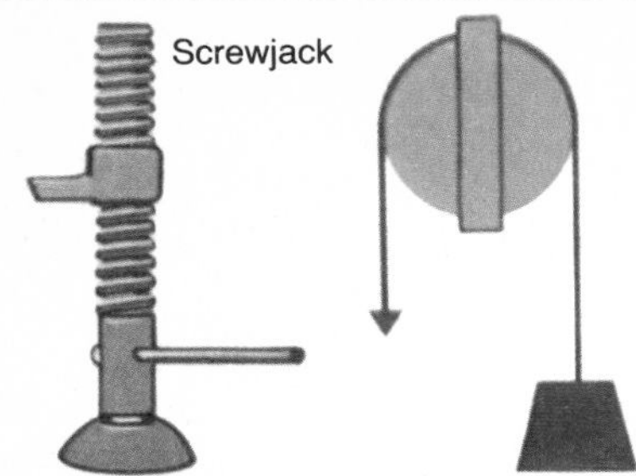

nails and axes are all different forms of wedges.

The screw can pull things together or push them apart. With a jackscrew, a man can quite easily lift a car weighing far more than himself. There are many kinds of *levers*. The simplest is a long pole, pivoted or balanced on a log and used to lift a heavy rock. The lever changes a small downward force into a bigger upward force.

The *inclined plane* makes it easier to raise heavy loads to higher levels. It is easier to pull a load up a slope than to lift it straight up. The PULLEY also makes lifting easier. A simple pulley is used in the winding mechanism that raises water from a well. A more complicated machine is the block and tackle, which has several sets of ropes and pulleys.

Probably the most important of all simple machines is the *wheel and axle*. This is used not only for moving loads, but also in all sorts of machines – such as clocks.

Mackenzie River
The Mackenzie River is Canada's longest river. It runs 1,120 miles (2,800 km) through the Northwest Territories, rising in the GREAT BEAR LAKE and emptying into the Arctic ocean.

mackerel *n*. slender, streamlined fish with a wide-forked tail, found in all the world's seas.
mackintosh *n*. a waterproof coat, raincoat.
mad *adj*. insane, crazy; angry.

Madagascar (Madagascan)
Madagascar is an island republic off the southeast coast of AFRICA. Much of the country consists of a high plateau, studded with volcanic peaks. Most people work on the land. Coffee, cloves and vanilla are exported. Oil refining is important, and there is some mining.

Madagascar is the world's fourth largest island. It was once a French colony, but achieved independence in 1960. (See map on opposite page.)
AREA: 226,670 SQ. MILES (587,041 SQ. KM)
POPULATION: 9,167,000
CAPITAL: ANTANANARIVO
CURRENCY: MALGACHE FRANC
OFFICIAL LANGUAGES: MALAGASY, FRENCH, ENGLISH

Most machines are complicated devices; but they are based on six types of simple machine: the lever; the inclined plane; the wheel and axle and the wedge (previous page) and the jackscrew and pulley (left).

madam (**mad**-*um*) *n*. polite form of addressing a woman.
madden *vb*. irritate; make mad.
made *vb*. past of **make**.

Madeira A Portuguese island off the northwest coast of Africa. It is famous for its wine.

Madonna *n*. the Virgin Mary.

Madrid
Madrid is the capital of SPAIN. It was chosen by King Philip II (1527–98) as his capital because it was in the middle of the country. Madrid is a dry, windy city; cold in winter and hot in summer. It is the center of Spanish life, and the seat of the country's parliament (the Cortes). It has many fine buildings, including the Prado, a famous museum. Madrid is the center of Spain's road and railroad network.

magazine *n*. 1. a soft-covered book of text and advertisements that comes out weekly or monthly. 2. the part of a gun that holds the bullets.

Magellan, Ferdinand
Ferdinand Magellan (1480–1521) was a Portuguese explorer and mariner, whose name in Portuguese was Fernão de Magalhães. Magellan served under Charles V of Spain. In 1519 he set out with five ships to find a western sea route to Asia. He was murdered in the PHILIPPINES, but one of his ships returned to Spain in 1522, the first to sail around the world.

people, such as witches and sorcerers, have magical powers. Magic is often closely tied up with religion. But most people today think of magic as the conjuring tricks performed by magicians on television, in the theater or at parties.

magician (*ma*-**ji**-*shun*) *n*. a person who does magic tricks.
magistrate *n*. a minor judge; a person who has the power to put the law into force.
magma *n*. molten rock which, when it solidifies, becomes igneous rock.

Magna Carta
The Magna Carta is a signed agreement, or charter, that was drawn up in the time of King JOHN of England. In those days, not even the great barons or nobles could argue with the king. This was accepted by everyone, provided the king governed the country fairly.

But King John was a bad ruler. He demanded extra taxes from the people and quarreled with the barons. In 1215 the barons compelled John to sign the Magna Carta which secured the rights of the barons and made the King answerable to the law. This document marked the beginning of a new system of government in which the king had to rule according to the law.

magnesium *n*. a light, silver-white metallic element (symbol – *Mg*).
► Magnesium burns brilliantly when set alight, so it is used in fireworks. The hydroxide of magnesium is the familiar "milk of magnesia," an antacid for stomach disorders. Most magnesium is obtained from sea water.
magnet *n*. a piece of iron or steel that can pull other pieces of iron and steel toward it. **magnetic** *adj*. acting like a magnet.
► Magnetic compasses were in use in Europe by about A.D. 1200, but

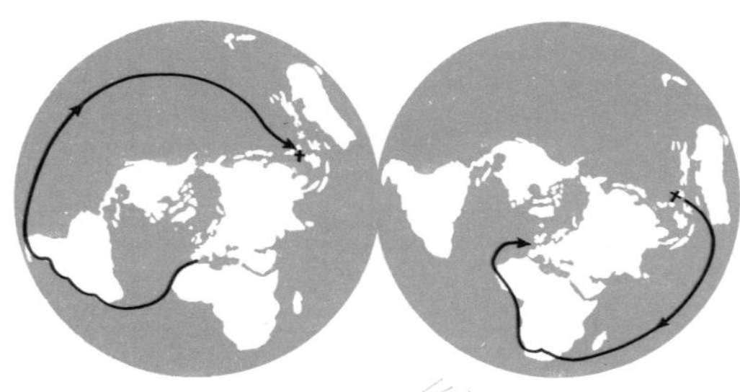

The route taken by Magellan's expedition (1519–22) – the first circumnavigation of the world. Magellan himself was killed at the spot marked x.

maggot *n*. larva, grub of a fly.
magic *adj*. & *n*. the belief that by doing or saying certain things, nature can be controlled and people can be influenced supernaturally.
► All through history people have believed that certain things or

the Chinese are believed to have noticed long before that a suspended magnet always points in the same direction. A magnet can be used as a COMPASS because the earth itself is a huge magnet that attracts the ends of any other magnet, pulling it in a

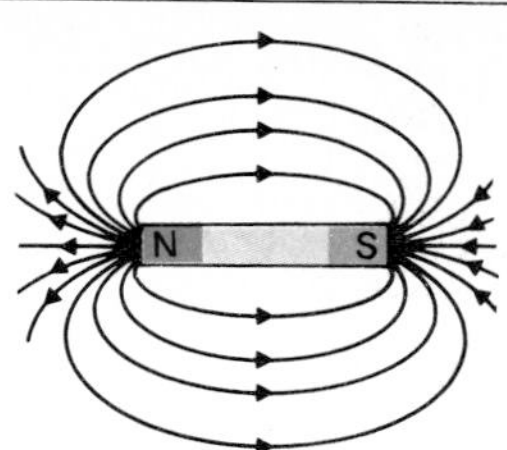

Left: *The magnetic lines around the poles of a bar magnet.*

Below left: Unlike poles attract.

Below: Like poles repel.

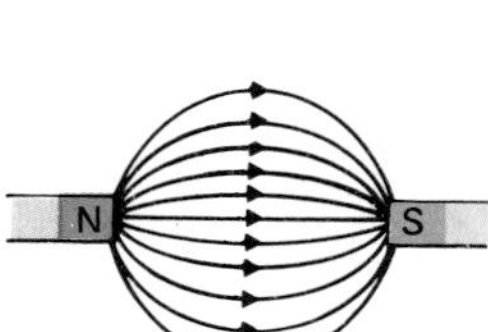

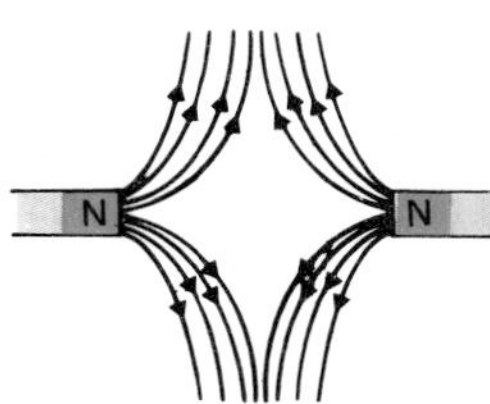

north-south direction. The end of the magnet that points north is called the north pole; the other end is the south pole. It is a basic law of magnetism that like poles repel and unlike poles attract each other, north attracts south but repels another north. IRON is the strongest magnetic metal; others are NICKEL and COBALT. These metals can be made magnetic by subjecting them to a magnetic field, either by stroking them with another magnet or by placing them inside an electric coil. Electric currents produce magnetic fields. If a wire is wound around a piece of iron and electric current is passed through the wire, the whole becomes an electromagnet. Also, when a wire is moved in a magnetic field, ELECTRICITY is generated in the wire.

magnificent *adj*. marvelous; very impressive.
magnify *vb*. make something appear bigger. *If you look through a drop of water, it will magnify things.* **magnification** *n*.
magnifying glass *n*. a lens that magnifies things.
magnolia *n*. a tree or shrub famous for its large, pale, fragrant flowers which bloom early in spring.
magpie *n*. black-and-white bird related to the crow.
Magyar *n*. & *adj*. language and people of Hungary.
mahogany *n*. a tall tree growing in tropical Africa and America whose hard, red wood is used for making furniture.
maid *n*. a girl; a female servant.
mail 1. *n*. letters and parcels sent by post. *vb*. send by post. 2. *n*. armor made of metal rings.
mailbox *n*. a receptacle for letters.
maim *n*. injure, cripple.
main *adj*. the most important; the largest. *The main road runs near our house.*

Maine (*abbrev*. **Me.**)
Maine is a rocky, wooded state in the northeast corner of the United States. It is the largest of the New England states. Maine's rocky coastline has thousands of small bays and inlets.

Four-fifths of Maine is covered by thick forests. The processing of potatoes and other foods such as lobsters, sardines and blueberries has grown in recent years. Skiing, camping and other outdoor activities are popular.

Maine is thought to have been explored by John Cabot in the 1490s. It was part of MASSACHUSETTS until 1820, when it entered the Union as a separate state. The state capital is Augusta.

mainland *n*. principal or larger land mass, without the nearby islands.
mainly *adv*. for the most part, chiefly.
maintain *vb*. 1. keep in good order. 2. support. 3. assert as true. 4. carry on.
maize *n*. a cereal crop. also called sweetcorn and Indian corn.
majesty *n*. having impressive or royal appearance; a title given to kings and queens, who are addressed as "Your Majesty." **majestic** *adj*.

Maize or corn.

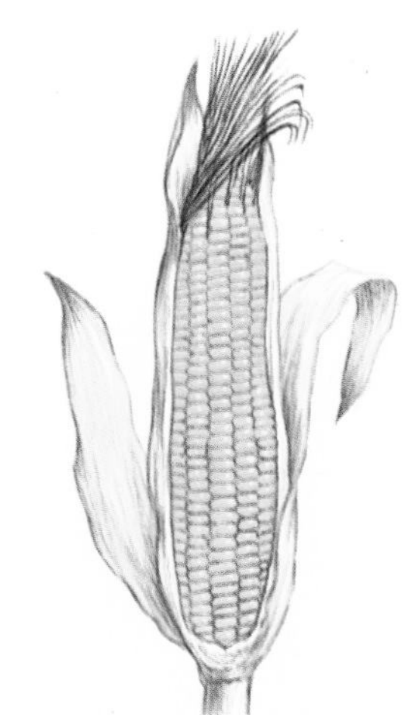

major 1. *n*. an army officer between captain and lieutenant colonel. 2. *adj*. important. *The scientist made a major new discovery.*
majority *n*. greater part of a number; more than half. *The majority of the class went swimming.*
make 1. *vb*. (past **made**) create or invent something; prepare; gain. 2. *n*. the maker's name. *What make is your car?*
makeshift *adj*. temporary substitute.
makeup *n*. the cosmetics (paints and powders) people put on their faces.
make up for *vb*. do something good after you have done something bad. *I was nasty to my sister, but I made up for it by helping her this afternoon.*
mal- *prefix* meaning bad or inadequate, e.g. **malformed** *adj*. badly formed. **maltreat** *vb*. treat badly.
malaria *n*. a disease which occurs mostly in tropical and subtropical areas. It is transmitted from infected to healthy people by the female Anopheles mosquito.

Malawi (Malawi)
Malawi is a republic in southern AFRICA. It lies alongside Lake Malawi in the East African Rift Valley. About half the people work in agriculture. The main food crop is corn. A former British colony, Malawi was called Nyasaland until independence in 1964.
AREA: 47,749 SQ. MILES (118,484 SQ. KM)
POPULATION: 6,376,000
CAPITAL: LILONGWE
CURRENCY: KWACHA
OFFICIAL LANGUAGES: ENGLISH, CHICHEWA

Malaysia (Malaysian)
Malaysia is a monarchy in Southeast ASIA. It consists of mainland Malaya and the provinces of Sabah and Sarawak in northern BORNEO. About half the people work on the land. Rice is the main food crop. Much of the country is forested, and there is an important timber industry. Malaysia has considerable mineral

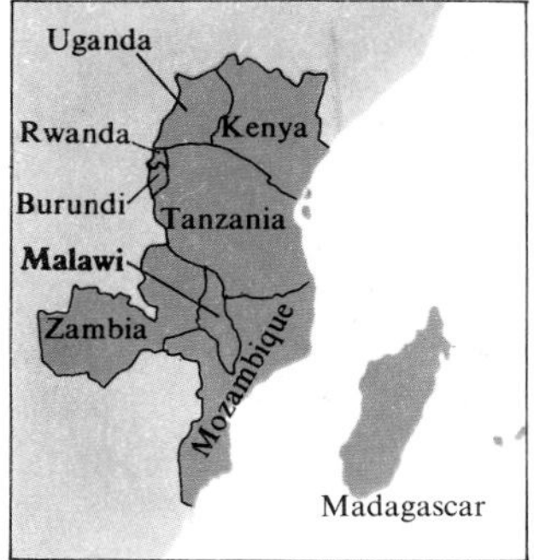

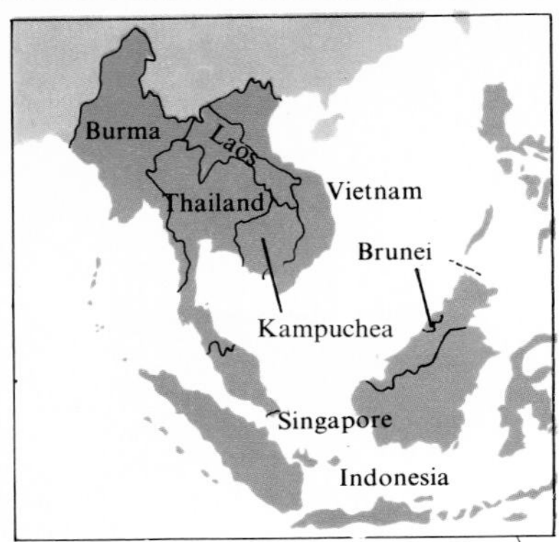

resources, and oil production is increasing.

A former British protectorate, Malaysia became independent in 1963. There followed a period of fighting with INDONESIA. SINGAPORE was originally part of Malaysia, but separated in 1965.

AREA: 127,324 SQ. MILES (329,749 SQ. KM)
POPULATION: 14,777,000
CAPITAL: KUALA LUMPUR
CURRENCY: MALAYSIAN DOLLAR
OFFICIAL LANGUAGE: MALAY

male 1. *n.* & *adj.* (of) a boy or man. 2. *n.* any creature of the sex that does not lay eggs or give birth.

Mali
Mali is a landlocked republic in northwestern AFRICA. The Niger River flows through the south of the country. Most of Mali consists of grassy plains. In the north is the SAHARA. Tuareg nomads live in the north desert, with black African farmers in the south.

Mali was formerly a French protectorate, under the name of French Sudan. It achieved full independence in 1960.

AREA: 478,793 SQ. MILES (1,240,000 SQ. KM)
POPULATION: 6,966,000
CAPITAL: BAMAKO
CURRENCY: MALI FRANC
OFFICIAL LANGUAGE: FRENCH

mallet *n.* wooden hammer; implement for hitting croquet ball.
malt *n.* barley prepared for brewing.

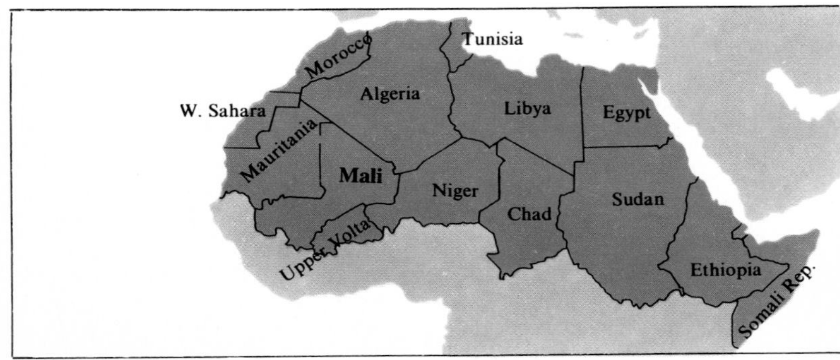

Malta (Maltese)
Malta is an island in the MEDITERRANEAN SEA. It lies south of Sicily. Since ancient times it has been a naval base, for it guards the Mediterranean trade routes to the East. For centuries Malta was ruled by the Knights of St. John, but in 1813 it became British. During World War II, Malta survived heavy bombing raids and the whole island was awarded the George Cross medal.

Since 1962 Malta has been self-governing. Today, it is a republic.

AREA: 122 SQ. MILES (316 SQ. KM)
POPULATION: 340,000
CAPITAL: VALLETTA
CURRENCY: MALTESE POUND
OFFICIAL LANGUAGES: MALTESE, ENGLISH

mammal *n.* any of the animals of which the females feed their young with milk from their bodies.
► Mammals are the most highly developed class of animals on earth and, as they have larger brains than any other living creature, they are the most intelligent. They are VERTEBRATES but differ from other backboned animals by their growth of hair and secretion of MILK. All mammals have hair – ranging from porcupine spines to sheep's wool – although some, such as the hippopotamus and humans, have very little. And all mammals feed their young on milk from the mother's body: "mammal" comes from *mamma* which means milk-secreting organ. There are three groups of mammals: *monotremes* – such as the duckbilled platypus, which lay eggs; MARSUPIALS – like KANGAROOS and KOALAS, which rear their young in pouches; and *placental* mammals, which keep their babies inside the female's body for a relatively long time. Human beings are placental mammals. The 5,000 species of mammals alive today vary in size from the giant Blue Whale to the tiny shrew.

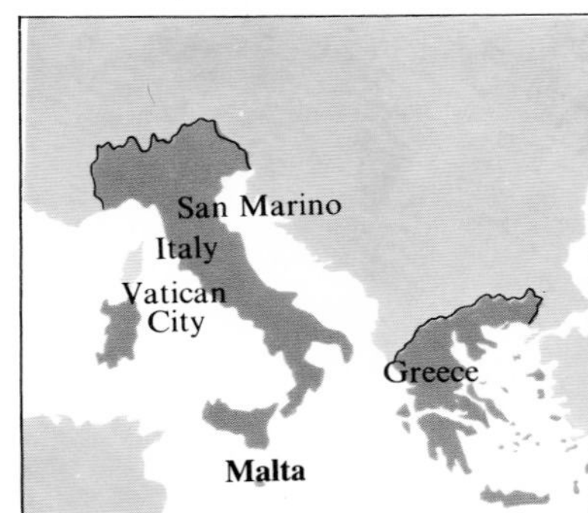

Mammals are the only vertebrates with a single bone in the lower jaw. Biologists have found fossils with this feature dating from the period of the dinosaurs, some 200 million years ago. These first mammals probably survived the changes that killed the great reptiles because they had already developed fur and warm blood. From these ancient creatures, the size of rats, a vast variety of mammals developed suited to widely varying conditions in nearly every part of the world.

All female mammals feed their young with milk from their bodies.

mammoth *n.* a large animal like an elephant, but now extinct.
► During the ICE AGES, woolly mammoths roamed the plains of Europe and North America. They looked like shaggy-haired elephants, with long curling tusks. But they lived in much colder climates than the elephants of today.

Mammoths lived together in herds, feeding on plants, grass and leaves. Their enemies included the fierce saber-toothed tiger, wolves and also cavemen, who hunted mammoths for food. Sometimes a group of hunters drove a mammoth into a pit, where it could be killed with spears.

The frozen bodies of mammoths have been dug up by scientists in the icy tundra of Siberia. Mammoth remains have also been found in tar pits in California. The last mammoths died out about 30,000 years ago.

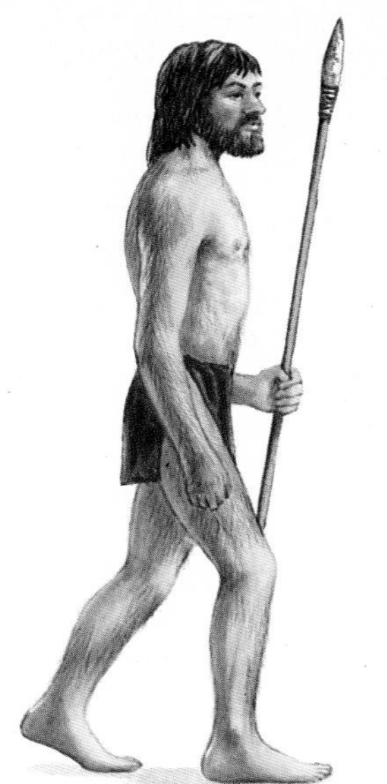

man *n.* (plural **men**) a grown-up male human; sometimes also used to mean all people, men and women (**mankind**). *vb.* supply with men; guard.

► Man – a word used for human beings in general – is a MAMMAL, but a rather clever one. He is very like his relatives, the APES. He has the same kind of bones, muscles and other things inside his body. But the main difference between man and any other animal is the size of his BRAIN. Compared to the size of his body it is enormous. Man uses his big brain to think things out, and when he has found the answer to a problem, he can talk about it with others. This is why man is the most successful animal.

All scientists are now agreed that human ancestors were apelike creatures who slowly, over millions of years, evolved (changed) into people we know today. All people today are one species, whether they are black, yellow, brown or white.

manage *vb.* 1. take charge of something. *She manages a supermarket.* 2. succeed in doing something even if it is not easy. *I can just manage to keep up with you.*

manager *n.* a person whose job is to take charge of other people at work.

mane *n.* the long hair on the neck of a horse or lion.

Manet, Edouard

Edouard Manet (1832–1883) was a famous French painter. He liked to paint everyday outdoor experiences – children, beggars, bullfights and horseraces – using strong, free brush strokes and rapid changes from light to dark. Manet founded a group of painters called the Impressionists.

maneuver (*man-***oo***-ver*) *n.* planned movement of troops; skillful plan. *vb.* guide, manipulate.

Manganese

Manganese is one of the most useful metals. Its chief use is to make steel exceptionally tough and strong, and to remove impurities from it. Without manganese, steel rails, for example, would be worn away very quickly. Manganese is a silvery white metal, with a touch of red. It is an ELEMENT with the chemical symbol Mn.

manger *n.* a box for horses or cattle to eat from in a stable.

mania *n.* a mental illness; a craze.

manicure *n.* & *vb.* care of the hands and nails. **manicurist** *n.*

manifesto *n.* statement of policy.

Manitoba

With Alberta and Saskatchewan, Manitoba is one of Canada's three "prairie provinces". It lies in central Canada and contains fertile plains in the south on which wheat, oats and barley are grown. But since the 1960s, agriculture has declined and now the manufacture of iron and steel products, railway equipment and furniture are more important. Manufacturing accounts for nearly half of Manitoba's wealth; agriculture for less than 25 percent. Winnipeg, the capital, is one of Canada's leading industrial cities. The province of Manitoba was created in 1870. It was linked by rail to the U.S. in 1878 and with eastern Canada in 1881. This caused a rapid increase in the population.

mankind *n.* all people – men, women and children – everywhere.

man-made *adj.* artificial; made by humans. *A canal is a man-made river.*

manner *n.* the way a thing is done or happens. **manners** *pl. n.* how you behave toward others. *She has very good manners.*

manor *n.* in the Middle Ages, a lord's house and the land he owned.

mansion (**man**-*shun*) *n.* a large, grand house.

manslaughter *n.* killing a person without planning to do so.

manu- *prefix* meaning hand, e.g. **manuscript** written by hand.

manual 1. *adj.* of or done with the hands. *Has your car got a manual or automatic shift?* 2. *n.* handbook, textbook.

manufacture *vb.* make things in a factory.

many *adj.* a lot; several; a large number. *A millipede has many legs.*

Maoris

The Maoris are the native people of NEW ZEALAND. These well-built, brown-skinned people came in canoes from Pacific islands to New Zealand in the 1300s. The Maoris were fierce warriors who fought with clubs made of bone or greenstone. They fought many battles against the white men who first came to New Zealand. This war did not end until 1865, and there were some outbreaks of fighting for years afterwards.

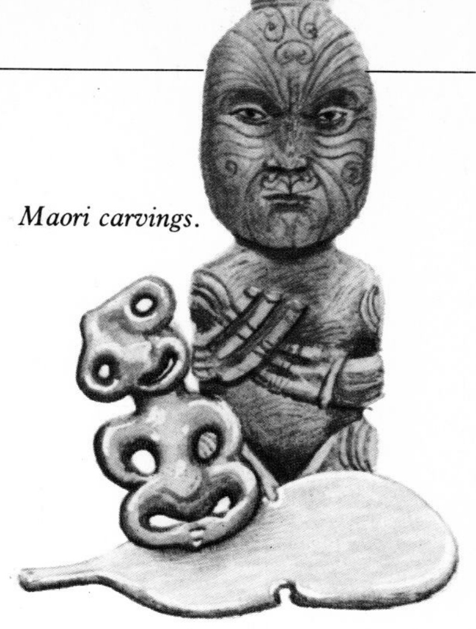

Maori carvings.

The Maoris were very skillful at weaving, dancing, and, above all, carving. Maori carving is full of decoration. They liked to cover every inch of the surface of their work with curves, scrolls and spirals. Their tools were made from greenstone, a stone rather like jade. And they carved greenstone itself to make little figure ornaments called tikis. Tattooing was also an important part of Maori art.

Today the Maoris play an important part in the life of New Zealand. They have seats in the New Zealand Parliament. Many Maoris have married white people. About one in every eight New Zealanders is a Maori.

Mao Tse-tung

Mao Tse-tung (1893–1976) was a great Chinese leader. He was the son of a farmer and trained to be a teacher. In 1921 he helped to form the Chinese Communist Party and fought against the Chinese Nationalists under Chiang Kai-shek. In 1934 he led 90,000 Communists on a 368-day march through China to escape Nationalist forces. This feat, called the Long March, was the longest military march ever. When Mao Tse-tung beat the Nationalists he became head of the Chinese government in 1949. He wanted China to become as rich as America, but many of his plans for his country did not work. He resigned from his job as head of the Chinese Communists. He had many arguments with the Russian Communists. Mao also wrote books about guerrilla warfare, as well as poetry.

map *n.* a drawing of the earth's surface or part of it, often showing things such as rivers, mountains, countries and towns. *vb.* to make a map.

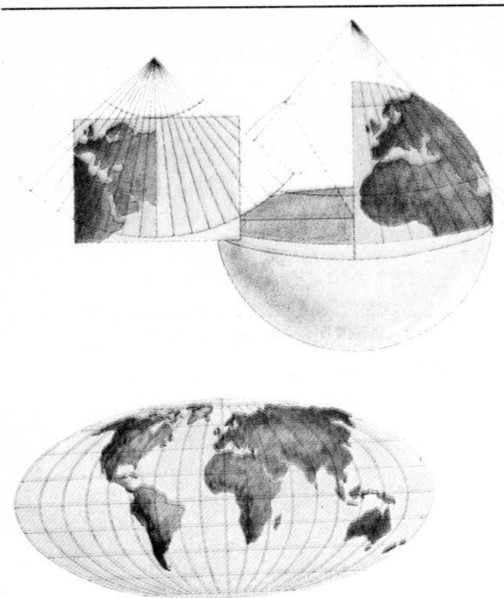

Top: Conical projections are used to make the maps in most atlases. Lines of latitude and longitude are curved. Above: In the Molleweide projection land areas appear distorted.

► Most maps are drawn to scale so that distances can be measured off them. Topographic maps are small-scale maps, showing natural and man-made features, together with the height of the land, depicted by contours. Large-scale maps are called plans. Special maps show many things, such as population distribution, weather conditions and even the incidence of diseases.

maple *n.* a deciduous tree native to the Northern Hemisphere. In autumn, its leaves turn spectacular shades of yellow, orange and red. One species, the sugar maple, is tapped for its sweet syrup. The maple leaf is the emblem of Canada.

Marat, Jean Paul
Jean Paul Marat (1743–93), a French doctor born in Switzerland, became one of the main perpetrators of the Reign of Terror in the FRENCH REVOLUTION. He was eventually murdered in his bath by Charlotte Corday, who sympathized with the moderate opponents of Marat.

marathon *n.* a very hard long-distance race of 26 miles 385 yards. It has been run in the Olympic Games since 1896.
► The Marathon is named after a Greek soldier's run from the town of Marathon to Athens in 490 B.C. to bring news of a Greek victory over the Persians. In 1908 there was a famous finish to the Olympic Marathon. At the end of the race a small Italian, Dorando Pietri, staggered into the stadium in the lead. He collapsed twice in the last 100 yards and had to be helped over the finishing line. He was disqualified because of this, but everyone remembers this as Dorando's Marathon.

marble *n.* 1. a hard stone that can be carved and polished. 2. a small glass or china ball used in games.
► Marble is a rock that is formed when LIMESTONE is squeezed and made very hot inside the earth. Pure marble is white, but most of the rock has other substances in it which give it lots of colors. If a piece of marble is broken, the broken faces sparkle like fine sugar. (The word marble means "sparkling".)
Marble has long been used for making statues as well as for building. It is easy to shape and takes a high polish. The most famous marble for sculpture comes from quarries at Carrara in Italy. It is very white and has a very fine grain.

march *vb.* walk with a regular pace like a soldier. *n.* a piece of music to which people can march.
March *n.* the third month of the year.

Marconi, Guglielmo
Guglielmo Marconi (1874–1937) was the man who, most people say, invented RADIO. His parents were rich Italians. When he was only 20 he managed to make an electric bell ring in one corner of a room with radio waves sent out from the other corner. Soon he was sending radio signals over longer and longer distances. In 1901 he sent the first message across the Atlantic. In 1924 he sent signals to Australia.

Marco Polo
Marco Polo (1254–1324) was an Italian explorer. He is famous for the long journey he made to faraway China at a time when the people of Europe knew little about the East. His father and his uncle were merchants from VENICE and they decided to take the young Marco with them when they set out for the East in 1271. They crossed Persia and the vast Gobi desert. In 1275 they reached Peking and were welcomed by KUBLAI KHAN, a great MONGOL conqueror. The Polos stayed for many years during which Marco traveled all over China in the service of the Khan. They left China in 1292 and arrived home in Venice in 1295. Later, Marco's stories of his travels were written down. *The Travels of Marco Polo* is one of the most exciting books ever written.
mare *n.* a female horse.
margarine *n.* a fat used instead of butter.
► Margarine is made from vegetable FATS and oils. VITAMINS are usually added to make it nearly as nourishing as butter. Margarine was invented in 1867 by a French chemist called Mège-Mouries. He won a prize offered by the French government for finding a cheap substitute for butter.

margin *n.* the blank space around the edge of a page of printing or writing; border.

Marie Antoinette
The wife of Louis XVI of France. Marie Antoinette (1755–93) became unpopular because of her extravagance and support of Austrian interests. She was executed in the FRENCH REVOLUTION.

marigold *n.* a garden plant belonging to the daisy family, with bright yellow or orange flowers.
marina *n.* a dock for yachts with every facility for a yachting vacation.
marine (*mu*-**reen**) *adj.* to do with the sea. *A whale is a marine animal. n.* a soldier serving on board ship.

marine life
Most scientists believe that all life began in the sea and stayed there for millions of years before moving onto the land. The oceans and seas take up nearly three-quarters of the earth's surface, and living creatures are found from the surface to the greatest depths. The animals range in size from tiny protozoans that can be seen only with a microscope, to the great Blue Whale, the biggest animal that has ever lived. Ocean plants also vary enormously in size. Some are tiny one-celled plants, others, such as the seaweed kelp, can be more than 100 feet long. Plants cannot, however, live very far below the surface. This is because they need light, and light diminishes rapidly with depth. All marine life depends on the thin layer of tiny microscopic creatures called PLANKTON that floats near the surface. The plankton serve as food for other sea creatures. It is calculated that nine-tenths of all ocean life exists to be eaten by some other form of life.

mariner *n.* an old-fashioned word for a sailor.
marionette *n.* a puppet moved by strings.
mark 1. *n.* & *vb.* a spot or pattern on something. *There is a dirty mark on your shirt.* 2. *vb.* judge quality of and correct. *The teacher will mark our homework.* 3. *n.* unit of money in Germany.
market *n.* a group of open-air shops or stalls; anywhere that goods are sold. *vb.* sell goods in a market.
marmalade *n.* a jam made from oranges and lemons.
marquis, marquess (**mar**-*kwiss*) *n.* nobleman ranking below a duke but above an earl.
marriage *n.* wedlock.
► Marriage is a contract between a man and a woman. Marriage laws are different in various countries according to the religion and customs of those countries. For example, Muslim men can have up to four

wives. In a few places it is possible for one woman to marry several men. Many countries have a religious ceremony when people are married.

In Christian weddings the bride's father usually "gives her away" to the bridegroom. The bridegroom is helped by the best man, who sees that the wedding goes smoothly. Many people nowadays get married in civil ceremonies that are not religious.

marrow *n.* 1. soft tissue containing blood vessels in the cavities of bones. 2. large fleshy vegetable of the gourd family.

marry *vb.* become husband and wife, unite in **marriage** *n.*

Mars (God)
Mars was one of the oldest and most important of the Roman GODS. He was the son of JUPITER and Juno and became the god of war. His son, Romulus, was supposed to have been the founder of ROME. The temples and festivals of Mars were important to the Romans. The month of March was named after him. It was the first month in the Roman year.

Mars (Planet)
The planet Mars is only about half the size of the earth. It takes about two years to travel around the sun. The surface of Mars has huge volcanoes and great gorges, far bigger than those on earth. Most of Mars is covered with loose rocks, scattered over a dusty red surface. This is why Mars is called the "Red Planet." It has a North Pole and a South Pole, just like our earth – both covered with snow or frost.

Seen through a telescope, the red surface of Mars is crisscrossed by thin gray lines. Some early astronomers thought that these lines were canals which had been dug by manlike creatures. They said these canals had been dug to irrigate the soil, since Mars has very little water. But space probes to Mars in 1965, 1969 and 1976 found no trace of the canals. The American *Viking* spacecraft landed on Mars and took samples of the planet's soil. But it was unable to find any kind of life on Mars.

The planet has two tiny moons – Phobos and Deimos. Phobos, the larger of the two, is only about 15 miles (24 km) across.

Because Mars has a smaller mass than the earth, things on its surface weigh only about 40 percent of what they would weigh on earth. A day on Mars is about the same length as an earth day.

Marseilles
The second city of FRANCE, Marseilles lies at the mouth of the Rhône River on the MEDITERRANEAN coast. It was founded by the Greeks in about 600 B.C. A major port and manufacturing center, Marseilles is a center for imports from North AFRICA.

marsh *n.* low-lying, wet land.

marsupial *n.* one of a group of mammals in which the females carry their young in a pouch on their bodies, like a kangaroo.

► A young marsupial is born very undeveloped and very small (a baby kangaroo is as tiny as 1 in. (2 cm) and cannot possibly look after itself. Instead, it crawls into its mother's pouch and stays there for several months, feeding off its mother's milk. The female's milk glands open into the pouch. The young animal does not leave the pouch for good until it is able to fend for itself. Except for the OPOSSUMS of North, South and Central America, all the world's marsupials live in Australia. They include KANGAROOS, wallabies and KOALAS.

martial *adj.* warlike.

martin *n.* small bird related to the swallow.

martyr *n.* someone who suffers or dies for beliefs. *There were many martyrs among the early Christians.*

marvelous *adj.* splendid; excellent. *What a marvelous view.* **marvel** *n.* wonderful happening. *vb.* be astonished.

Marx, Karl
Karl Marx (1818–83) was possibly the most influential political thinker and writer of modern times. He saw history as a series of class struggles which would end when the workers overthrew their masters. His major work, *Das Kapital*, formed the basis for the beliefs of modern COMMUNISM. He is buried in London, England.

Marxist *n.* & *adj.* of or a supporter of the thinking of Karl Marx (1818–83). **Marxism** *n.*

Maryland (*abbrev.* **Md.**)
Maryland is one of the smallest states. It lies on the Atlantic coast and is almost divided in two by Chesapeake Bay.

For a small state, Maryland is a land of contrasts, from the small tobacco farms in the southwest to the sophisticated weapons industries around Baltimore, the state's largest city. There are hills, valleys, swamps, plateaus and coastal plain, plus the long shoreline of Chesapeake Bay. Manufacturing is the state's most important industry.

Maryland was named after Henrietta Maria, wife of CHARLES I of England. The new colony was founded as a haven for persecuted Roman Catholics. Maryland was one of the original 13 states. Its capital, Annapolis, was capital of the United States from 1783 to 1784.

Mary, Queen of England
Mary I (1516–58) a devout ROMAN CATHOLIC, became queen of England in 1553. Her marriage to Philip II of Spain involved England in European wars. Her attempts to restore Roman Catholicism led to the execution of many Protestants.

Mary, Queen of Scots
Mary, Queen of Scots (1542–87) was the last ROMAN CATHOLIC ruler of Scotland. She was also heir to the Protestant ELIZABETH I of England. Until her execution, she was the center of plots to overthrow Elizabeth.

marzipan *n.* sweet paste made from almonds.

mascara *n.* coloring used on eyelashes.

mascot *n.* a person, animal or thing thought to bring good luck. *The regiment's mascot is a goat.*

masculine *adj.* male, manly; vigorous.

mash *vb.* & *n.* (to make) pulp.

mask *n.* a covering for the face; a disguise; face of a fox, dog, etc. *vb.* cover with a mask; disguise.

A Viking spacecraft on the surface of Mars.

M

mason *n.* a person who works in stone; a builder.
mass *n.* 1. a large amount. 2. the amount of material in something. 3. Eucharist or Holy Communion service.
► In physics, mass is the quantity of matter in a body. A baseball has more mass than an apple, although they look the same size. Mass should not be confused with weight. Weight is the force with which a body is attracted to the earth by gravitation. A baseball weighs more than an apple on earth. In space neither would have any weight, but the baseball would still have a greater mass. Weight varies from place to place. Mass is the amount of matter in something and does not vary.

Massachusetts (*abbrev.* **Mass.**)
Massachusetts is a state in the northeast corner of the United States, in New England. The long finger of land that juts out into the Atlantic and gives the state its strange shape is called Cape Cod.

Massachusetts was the site of the landing of the MAYFLOWER in 1620 and of the colony the Pilgrims founded. It was one of the original 13 states. BOSTON and its outlying towns were a center of revolutionary activity in the years just before the War of INDEPENDENCE. The BOSTON TEA PARTY and Boston massacre both took place in the state's capital and largest city. The battles of Lexington and Concord, which began the Revolution, took place outside Boston.

The INDUSTRIAL REVOLUTION brought manufacturing to Massachusetts, particularly the textile industry. Today electronics is an important industry in the state.

Massachusetts is also the home of many of the country's leading universities and colleges. Boston is an important cultural center; its Museum of Fine Arts and the Boston Symphony are world famous. Close by are Harvard University and the Massachusetts Institute of Technology.

massacre *vb.* & *n.* brutal killing of large numbers of people.
massage *vb.* & *n.* treatment of body by rubbing and pressing with the hands.
massive *adj.* huge and solid.
mast *n.* 1. the pole that holds a ship's sails. 2. fruit of beech and oak used as pig fodder.
master *n.* a man who has other people working for him; the captain of a merchant ship; a male schoolteacher. **masterly** *adj.* skilful. **mastery** *n.* control, authority.
masterpiece *n.* a work of art done with great skill.
mastiff *n.* large thickset dog.
mat *n.* a floor or table covering.

match 1. *n.* a game or contest. *A football match.* 2. *n.* a small thin piece of wood, with the end coated with an inflammable substance, used for lighting fires, etc. 3. *n.* equal to. *The champion boxer was more than a match for the challenger.* 4. *vb.* go with something. *Does this handbag match my shoes?*
mate 1. *n.* a companion; (usually of animals) each parent of a young one is the mate of the other parent. 2. *vb.* produce young. 3. *n.* an officer of a merchant ship, under a captain.
material *n.* any substance from which something is or can be made. *Bricks, wood and cement are all building materials.*
maternal *adj.* of or concerning a mother; motherly.
mathematics *pl. n.* (*abbrev.* **math**) the science of numbers and shapes.
matinée (*mat-n-***ay**) *n.* afternoon performance in a theater.
matrimony *n.* marriage.
matron *n.* a woman attendant, guard or superintendent in an institution; a married woman of mature age (now old-fashioned).
matt *adj.* dull, without shine. *Matt paint.*
matter 1. *n.* the stuff of which things are made. 2. *vb.* be important. *We think it matters that you are late.*
► The stuff of which everything is made is called matter – solids, liquids and gases. A vital property of matter is its MASS, and all forms of matter have gravitational attraction (*see* GRAVITY). People used to think that the total amount of matter in the universe was constant; that matter could neither be created nor destroyed. But Albert EINSTEIN showed that matter and energy could be interchanged. The mass of an object in motion is greater than its mass at rest.

mattress *n.* a cloth case stuffed with hair, feathers, or other material, often supported with springs, and placed on top of a bed for lying on.
mature *vb.* & *adj.* ripe, completely developed. **maturity** *n.*

Mauritania (Mauritanian)
Mauritania is an Islamic republic in northwestern AFRICA. Most of the country lies in the SAHARA. The main agricultural region is near the Senegal River in the south. About 80 percent of the population are of ARAB or Berber descent. Many of them are farmers. The country's chief resource is iron ore, and copper is also mined.

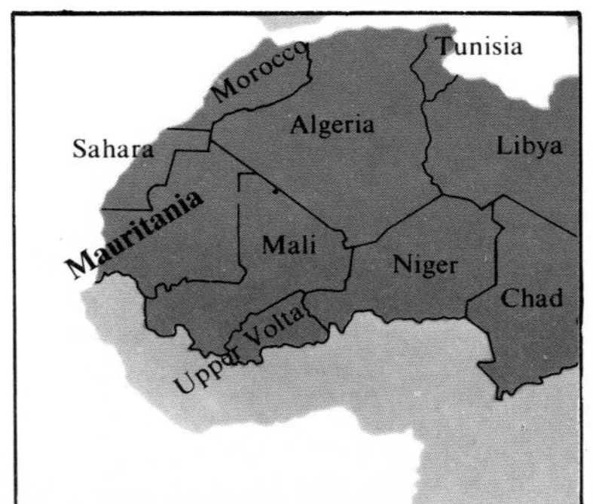

A former French colony, Mauritania became independent in 1960.

AREA: 397,977 SQ. MILES (1,030,700 SQ. KM)
POPULATION: 1,721,000
CAPITAL: NOUAKCHOTT
CURRENCY: OUGUIYA
OFFICIAL LANGUAGES: ARABIC, FRENCH

mauve (rhymes with *rove*) *n.* & *adj.* a pale purple color.
maximum *adj.* & *n.* the greatest possible. *The maximum speed in the United States is 55 miles per hour.*

MATHEMATICAL TERMS
acute angle an angle that is less than a right angle.
angle the difference in direction between two lines that are crossed.
bisect divide into two equal parts.
circumference length around a closed curve, such as a circle.
cube number we get by multiplying any number by itself twice. Also a six-sided solid figure whose sides are all squares.
factors numbers that multiply together to give a particular number; 2 and 6 are factors of 12.
fraction numbers which stand for parts of a whole such as ¼ or ½.
hexagon a plane figure having six sides
hypotenuse the side opposite the right angle in a right-angled triangle.
obtuse angle an angle that is greater than a right angle.
parallelogram a four-sided figure having two sides parallel in one direction and two sides parallel in another direction.
pentagon a plane figure having five sides.
quadrilateral a plane figure that has four sides.
rectangle a parallelogram with four right angles.
scalene triangle with no sides or angles equal.
square number we get by multiplying any number by itself; the square of 7 is 49. Also, a parallelogram whose sides are right angles and whose sides are equal.
theorem a statement in geometry that we know is true only when we have tried it out and seen that it works.
trapezium a quadrilateral having no two sides parallel.

may *vb.* something that could possibly happen. *I may be able to help you.*
May *n.* the fifth month of the year.

Maya
The Maya Indians first lived in CENTRAL AMERICA in the A.D. 400s. They grew maize and sweet potatoes and kept pet dogs. Later they built cities of stone, with richly decorated palaces, temple, pyramids and observatories. Even today, many of these wonderful buildings are still standing, hidden in the jungle. The Maya were also skilled in astronomy and mathematics, and they had an advanced kind of writing.

The Maya people did not have any metals until very late in their history. They built only with stone tools. And they had no knowledge of the wheel. Their lives were controlled by religion. They worshiped a sun god, rain gods, soil gods, and a moon goddess who looked after women.

maybe *adv.* perhaps.

Mayflower
Mayflower is the name of the small sailing ship which, in 1620, carried the first Puritan Pilgrims to America. They were looking for religious freedom in the New World. The ship set out from Plymouth, England, with 102 passengers on board. The crossing of the wild Atlantic was stormy and they nearly turned back. Finally, after 65 days at sea, they reached the American coast. The Pilgrims landed at what is now MASSACHUSETTS, at a place they called Plymouth after their home port. The Mayflower was only about 90 ft. (27 meters) long and weighed about 170 tons.

mayonnaise *n.* a cold sauce made with oil, vinegar and eggs.
mayor (rhymes with *mare*) *n.* the head of a town or city.
maze *n.* a network of winding paths from which it is difficult to find a way out.
meadow *n.* a grassy field, particularly near a river.
meager (**me**-*gur*) *adj.* lean, poor.
meal *n.* 1. food eaten at a particular time, e.g. breakfast, lunch and dinner. *When do you have your main meal?* 2. grain ground to powder; flour.
mean 1. *vb.* stand for; show. *A red flag means danger.* 2. *vb.* intend to do something. *We always mean to be good, but often we aren't.* 3. *adj.* miserly; unwilling to share with others. 4. *adj.* average.
meander *vb.* wander about.
meaning *n.* what something means. *The English meaning of the French word "chat" is "cat".*
means *pl. n.* 1. method by which something is done. 2. money.
meant *vb.* past of **mean**.
meanwhile *adv.* (or **meantime**) during the same time. *We were in the garden. Meanwhile the thieves entered the house by a front window.*
measles *n.* an infectious disease which causes red spots on the body and a fever.
measure *vb.* find the size or amount of a thing. *n.* something in which size, weight, length, etc., can be stated. *A foot is a measure of length.*
meat *n.* the flesh of cows, sheep and other animals eaten as food.

Mecca
Mecca is the Holy City of the Muslims, and MUHAMMED'S birthplace. It is in SAUDI ARABIA. In the center of Mecca is the Great Mosque, and in the mosque's courtyard is the Ka'aba, which houses the sacred "Black Stone." Muslims believe it was given to Abraham by the archangel Gabriel. This stone is kissed by pilgrims to Mecca.

mechanic *n.* a person who works with machines.
mechanical *adj.* to do with machines; worked by machinery.
mechanics *pl. n.* the branch of physics that deals with the effect of force acting on bodies.
► Mechanics is usually divided into two branches – statics and dynamics. Statics deals with stationary bodies, dynamics deals with particles and bodies in motion.

medal *n.* a flat piece of metal, often like a coin, with words or a picture on it, given as recognition for excellence or achievement.
► Medals are given as awards for distinguished service in war or peace. Medals were introduced around the 1400s. Famous medals include the Medal of Honor (U.S.A.), the Victoria Cross (Britain), the Croix de Guerre (France), the Iron Cross (Germany) and the Hero of the Soviet Union (U.S.S.R.).

meddle *vb.* interfere in.
medicine (**med**-*u-sin*) *n.* 1. the science of healing. 2. something taken to make you better when you are ill.
► Medicine is the prevention of disease, the science of healing and the relief of pain. Probably the most important part of a doctor's work is diagnosis, by which the doctor finds out a patient's illness from studying the symptoms. Medicine became a science in Europe through the work of HIPPOCRATES in ancient Greece. The writings of another Greek, Galen (A.D. 129–199) dominated medical thought until the 1500s, when the science of anatomy made great advances in our knowledge of the human body, and William HARVEY made a number of discoveries about the circulation of BLOOD. In the late 1700s, Edward JENNER performed the first vaccination against SMALLPOX. In the 1800s, the use of anesthetics (*see* ANESTHESIA), ANTISEPTICS and Louis PASTEUR'S discoveries about microorganisms in the air were major steps forward. And the 1900s have seen many more advances, including the wide use of ANTIBIOTICS, VACCINES, blood transfusions and organ transplants.

medieval (*med*-**ee**-*val*) *adj.* of the Middle Ages.
mediocre (*meed-ee*-**oh**-*kur*) *adj.* average quality, second-rate.
meditate *vb.* think deeply about. **meditation** *n.*

Mediterranean Sea
The Mediterranean is a large sea surrounded by three continents – Africa, Europe and Asia. It flows out into the Atlantic Ocean through the narrow Strait of GIBRALTAR. It is also joined to the BLACK SEA by a narrow passage.

In ancient times, the Mediterranean was more important than it is now. In fact, it was the center of the Western world for a long time. The Phoenicians were a seafaring people

Three famous decorations.

Victoria Cross (Great Britain)

Purple Heart (USA)

Order of Victory (USSR)

M

who traveled around the Mediterranean from about 2500 B.C. Then the Greeks and Romans sailed the sea. The Romans were in control of the whole Mediterranean for nearly 500 years. They even called it Mare Nostrum, which means "our sea."

The SUEZ CANAL was opened in 1869, joining the Mediterranean to the RED SEA. The canal was very useful because it shortened the distance by sea between Europe and the East.

medium (**mee**-*de-um*) *adj*. middle size. *The robber was of medium height with fair hair.*
meet *vb*. (past **met**) join or come face to face with someone. *When shall we meet again?*
meeting *n*. a coming together of two or more people.
megalith *n*. large prehistoric stone.
melancholy (**mel**-*an-co-lee*) *adj*. sad, gloomy.

A megalithic tomb from Portugal dating from about 4000 B.C.

Melbourne, Australia
Melbourne is the capital of VICTORIA state in southeastern AUSTRALIA. It is an important center of finance, commerce, industry and culture. The second largest city in Australia, Melbourne was founded in 1835. It was named after Lord Melbourne, then the English prime minister.

mellow *adj*. soft and ripe. *vb*. soften (with age or experience).
melody *n*. tune; principal part in harmonized music. **melodic** *adj*.
melon *n*. a creeping or climbing plant grown in warm climates for its large juicy fruit.
melt *vb*. turn a solid into a liquid by heating it. *The ice cream melted in the sun.*

Melville, Herman
Herman Melville (1819–91) gained a reputation as one of America's greatest writers from his masterpiece, *Moby Dick*. Surprisingly, this novel was either ignored or misunderstood in his own lifetime. The books for which Melville first became famous, such as *Typee* (1846) and *Omoo* (1847), drew on his experiences as crew member of a whaling ship in the Pacific islands, as did *Moby Dick* (1851).

member *n*. 1. a person who belongs to a group or team of people. *Winston is a member of the football team.* 2. a limb, an arm or leg.
memory *n*. the ability to remember things; what is remembered. *I have a very clear memory of being in the hospital.* **memorize** *vb*. learn by heart. **memorable** *adj*.
men *n*. plural of **man**.
menace *n*. & *vb*. threat(en).
menagerie *n*. collection of wild animals.
mend *vb*. & *n*. repair. *On the mend.* getting better.

Mendel, Gregor
Gregor Mendel (1822–84) was an Austrian priest who became famous for his work on HEREDITY. Heredity is the passing on of traits such as eye color, skin color, and mental ability from parents to their children.

Mendel grew up on a farm, where he became interested in plants. When he entered a monastery he began growing peas. He noticed that when he planted the seeds of tall pea plants, only tall pea plants grew up. Then he tried crossing tall peas with short peas by taking pollen from one and putting it in the other. He found that again he had only tall plants. But when he crossed these new mixed tall plants with each other, three-quarters of the new plants were tall and one-quarter were short. Mendel had found out that things like tallness or shortness are controlled by tiny genes, passed on from each parent. He also found out that some genes are stronger than other genes. The importance of his work was not realized until 1900.

menorah *n*. the seven-branched candlestick used in Jewish worship. The seven branches are supposed to represent the sun, moon and five planets known to antiquity.
mental *adj*. concerning the mind.
mention *vb*. refer to, remark. *n*. brief note.
menu *n*. a list of the food you can have at a meal in a restaurant.
merchant *n*. a person who makes a living by buying and selling things.

Mercury (God) In Roman MYTHOLOGY, Mercury was the messenger of the gods. He was usually shown as an athletic young man, wearing a winged cap and winged sandals, and carrying a winged staff entwined with snakes.

mercury *n*. a heavy, silver-colored liquid metal; quicksilver.
► Mercury is the only metal that is liquid at room temperature. Mercury's chemical symbol is Hg. Often called quicksilver, it is used in THERMOMETERS and BAROMETERS. It forms ALLOYS called amalgams with most metals: silver and gold amalgams are used to fill teeth. The main source of mercury is cinnabar.

Mercury (Planet)
The planet MERCURY is the smallest planet in the SOLAR SYSTEM. It is also the closest to the sun. A day on Mercury lasts for 176 of our days. During the long daylight hours it is so hot that lead would melt. During the long night it grows unbelievably cold. Little was known about Mercury's surface until the space probe *Mariner 10* passed within 500 miles (800 km) of the planet. It showed Mercury to have a thin atmosphere and big craters like those on the moon.

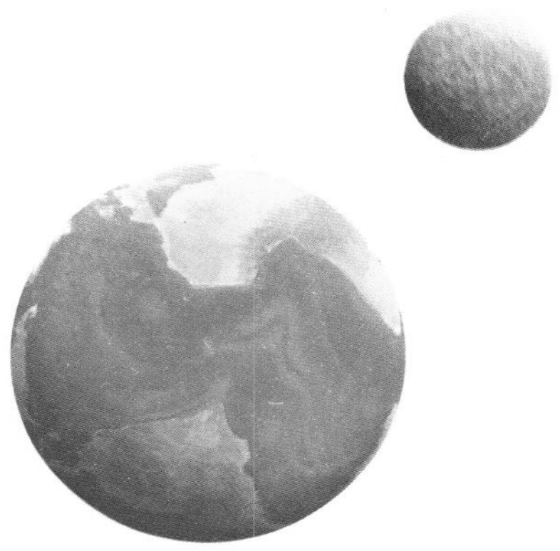

Mercury compared with our planet, earth.

Mercury travels very fast through space – at between 23 and 35 miles (37 and 56 km) per second. This great speed and its nearness to the sun give it the shortest year of all planets (the time it takes Mercury to go once around the sun). Mercury's year lasts only 88 of our earth days.

mercy *n*. readiness to forgive, compassion; a fortunate happening.
merge *vb*. blend, combine with. **merger** *n*.
meridian *n*. any line of longitude. *The prime meridian (0° longitude) passes through Greenwich Observatory in England.*
merit *vb*. deserve, be worthy of. *You merit praise for your work.*
mermaid *n*. a legendary creature with a woman's body and a fish's tail.
merry *adj*. happy and cheerful.
merry-go-round *n*. an amusement park ride with toy animals and vehicles that goes around.
mesmerize *vb*. hypnotize.

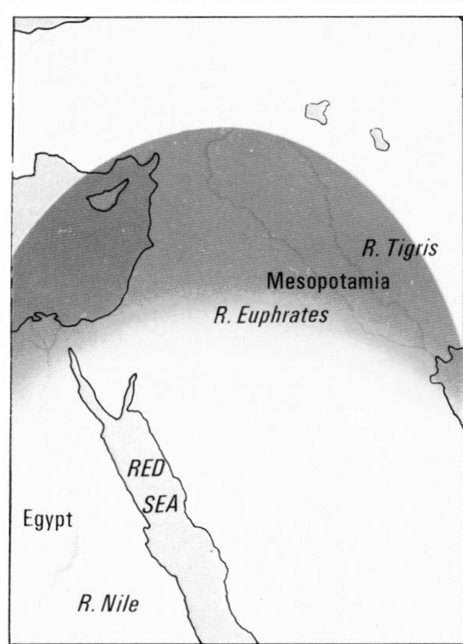

The Fertile Crescent, where farming first began, included Mesopotamia, "the land between the two rivers."

Mesopotamia
A region between the Tigris and Euphrates rivers, now mostly in Iraq. It was the center of several early civilizations, including that of the SUMERIANS.

mess *n.* 1. untidiness and dirt. 2. a place where soldiers and sailors take their meals.
message *n.* a piece of information sent to somebody.
messenger *n.* a person who carries a message.
Messrs. (**mess**-*erz*) abbreviated plural of Mr. used in the title of a company (*Messrs. Jones, Smith & Sons*) or in a list of men's names.
met *vb.* past of **meet**.
metal *n.* any sort of material like iron, steel, tin or copper.
► There are more than 100 ELEMENTS on the earth. About two-thirds of these are metals. Copper, TIN and IRON were the first metals to be used. They were made into tools and weapons. GOLD and SILVER were also known very early on. They are often made into jewelry.
Most metals are shiny. They all let heat and electricity pass through them. Copper and silver are the best for this. Nearly all metals are solid unless they are heated.
Some metals are soft. They are easy to beat into shapes, and they can be pulled into thin wires. Other metals are brittle and break easily. Some metals are very hard and so it is difficult to work with them. Metals can be mixed together to form ALLOYS. Tin and copper, which are both soft, when mixed together form BRONZE, a strong alloy, hard enough for swords and spears.

metaphor *n.* word or phrase taken from one field of experience and used to say something in another field, e.g. "*All the world's a stage.*" "*Did you land a job today?*" "*No, not a bite.*"
meteor *n.* a small solid body that rushes from outer space into the earth's atmosphere.
► Millions of meteors fall on the earth every day. Most of them burn up before they reach the ground. On clear nights you can sometimes see shooting stars. They are meteors. When a large meteor reaches the ground, it is called a meteorite. Meteorites often make large holes.

meteorite *n.* a meteor that reaches the earth without burning up.
meteorology *n.* the study of the changing conditions in the atmosphere and the causes of weather.
► One of the main jobs of a meteorologist is WEATHER FORECASTING. Scientific meteorology began with the ancient Greeks. In the 1600s, scientific instruments, such as BAROMETERS and THERMOMETERS, were developed and observations became more precise. Today meteorological stations are scattered around the world, on land and at sea. At these stations, regular measurements are made of conditions at ground level and in the upper atmosphere. Data also comes from weather SATELLITES and RADAR.

meter *n.* 1. a measure of length. *There are 100 centimeters in a meter.* 2. an instrument for measuring or recording quantities, speed, etc. *The gas meter shows how much gas we use in our house.* 3. the rhythm of a line of verse.
method *n.* a way of doing something; a system.
metric *adj.* the system of measuring based on the meter, the kilogram and the liter.
► The metric system is the decimal system of weights and measures in which the meter is the unit of length, the gram is the unit of weight, and the liter is the unit of capacity. In the decimal system each unit is 10 times as large or small as the next unit. The prefixes used to indicate magnitude are: *mega*, million; *kilo*, thousand; *hecto*, hundred; *deca*, ten; *deci*, tenth; *centi*, hundredth; and *milli*, thousandth. Most countries of the world either use or are introducing the metric system. It was developed by French scientists.

Mexico (Mexican)
Mexico is a country in NORTH AMERICA. It lies between the United States in the north and Central America in the south. To the east is the Gulf of Mexico, a big bay. On the west lies the Pacific Ocean. Much of the country is hilly with fertile uplands. The highest mountains reach over 18,000 ft. (5,700 meters). In the southeast, the low Yucatan peninsula sticks out far into the Gulf of Mexico.
Mexico is a tropical country. But most of the land is high. This makes the climate cool and dry. The north has desert in places.
The first people to live in Mexico were Indians, such as the AZTECS.
AREA: 761,646 SQ. MILES (1,972,547 SQ. KM)
POPULATION: 74,539,000
CAPITAL: MEXICO CITY
CURRENCY: PESO
OFFICIAL LANGUAGE: SPANISH

mice *n.* plural of **mouse**.

Michelangelo
Michelangelo Buonarroti (1475–1564) was a sculptor and painter of the Italian RENAISSANCE. He had a lifelong interest in the human figure. His interest was expressed in his early work, including the statue of David. His paintings include the great FRESCOES in the Sistine Chapel, in the VATICAN. He also designed the dome of St. Peter's Basilica.

Michigan (*abbrev.* **Mich.**)
The state of Michigan is touched by all of the five GREAT LAKES except Lake Ontario and has the longest shoreline of any inland state.
Michigan is the world's largest producer of automobiles. The center of the automobile industry is in Detroit, the state's largest city. It is one of the nation's leading manufacturing states and is also a center of tourism.
Michigan was an important French fur trading region during the 1700s. It became a state in 1837. Soon a number of important roads, railroads and canals were built, and the state's development was rapid. The capital is Lansing.

micro- *prefix* meaning small, minute; a millionth part of, e.g. **microfilm, microwave**.
microbe *n.* a tiny creature that can be seen only through a microscope.
microphone *n.* an instrument that picks up sound waves and turns them into electric waves for broadcasting or recording.

► Different types of microphones are used for different purposes. The most common is the microphone used in TELEPHONES. A simple microphone consists of a piece of soft iron with a coil of wire around it. This electromagnet is placed close to a thin disk of metal called a diaphragm. The diaphragm vibrates as the sound waves from your voice strike it and this causes changes in the strength of the MAGNETISM of the electromagnet. This in turn causes electric current to flow through wires joining the microphone to the recording apparatus. The current changes at the same speed as the sounds that caused it changed. At the reproducer there is another electromagnet and diaphragm. The varying current makes the receiver diaphragm vibrate in the same way as the microphone diaphragm. So it reproduces the sound that strikes the microphone.

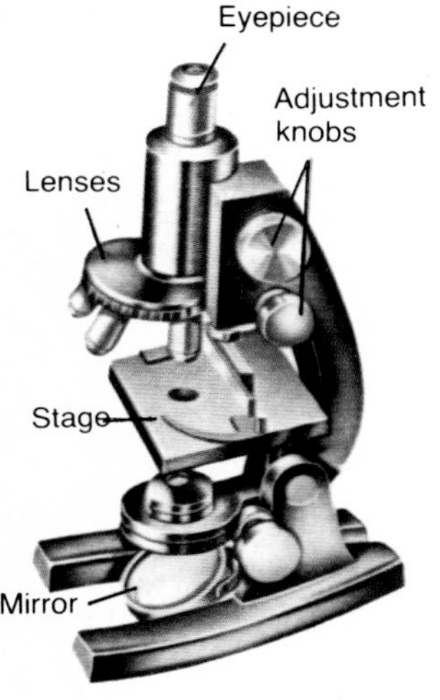

microscope *n.* an instrument for making very small things big enough to see; it magnifies them.
► If we say that the magnification of a microscope is ×100, the image is 100 times larger than the object viewed. The simplest microscope is a magnifying glass. But the microscopes used in scientific laboratories are much more complicated. They contain a number of LENSES, and tiny details of animals, plants and other objects can be seen. The highest magnification possible using glass lenses and ordinary light is about ×1,600. For higher magnifications the electron microscope is used. It uses a beam of electrons (*see* ATOM) which is focused on the object, just like LIGHT waves. Magnifications of about ×2,000,000 can be achieved.

Midas, King
Greek legend says Midas was the king of Phrygia, in Asia Minor, the land now called TURKEY.
The god Dionysus granted Midas a wish. Midas wished that everything he touched would turn to gold. At first Midas was happy. He went round his palace and touched all the things he could see. They turned into glittering gold. But then his new power began to go wrong. When his children ran in to see him, Midas hugged them. His touch turned them into little golden statues. When Midas tried to drink water or eat food, they turned into gold.
Midas was sorry that Dionysus had given him his wish. He asked Dionysus for help. The god told Midas to bathe in the Pactolus River. The waters washed away his power. Ever after, the river was famous because people kept finding gold in its sands.

middle *n.* the center part of something; a person's waist.

Middle Ages
The Middle Ages was a period of history in Europe which began when the ROMAN EMPIRE collapsed in the 400s and ended when the RENAISSANCE began in the 1400s.
During the Middle Ages, Europe was split into many tiny kingdoms and states. People lived under the feudal system. The feudal system divided everyone into groups. The king ruled the country. The nobles, or barons, had to swear loyalty to the king. In return, the king gave them land and power. The barons often lived in CASTLES. Each baron had KNIGHTS who served him. The baron gave land to the knights in return for their help. Free farmers and craftsmen lived on the baron's land. They were called yeomen. The baron also ruled people called serfs. Serfs had to work hard for the baron. They were like slaves.
Most people farmed the land. Towns were small and trade was not important. The Church was very powerful. It made its own laws and influenced the way people lived.

Middle East
The Middle East includes most of southwest ASIA. It stretches from the eastern shores of the Mediterranean Sea to the mountains of AFGHANISTAN. There are 17 countries in the Middle East. Sometimes EGYPT is included, although it lies in Africa. ARABS live in most of the Middle East.
The Middle East was the home of great civilizations of the past. Thousands of years ago, the empires of BABYLON and Assyria started in IRAQ. IRAN was once known as Persia. The Persians also had a great empire.
ISLAM, CHRISTIANITY and JUDAISM all started in the Middle East. MECCA and Medina, in Saudi Arabia, are holy cities of Islam.

midge *n.* small insect; gnat.
midget *n.* a very small person.
midnight *n.* twelve o'clock at night.

Midwestern States
These are a group of 12 states in the center and north of the United States. They are Ohio, Indiana, Michigan, Illinois, Wisconsin, Missouri, Iowa, Minnesota, Kansas, Nebraska, and North and South Dakota. The Midwestern States are the granary of the U.S. There are also rich mineral deposits. They make up nearly a fifth of the area of the United States, and have more than one-fourth of the country's population.

midwife *n.* a woman who helps at the birth of a child. **midwifery** *n.*
might 1. *vb.* past of **may**. *You might have told me earlier.* 2. *n.* power; strength.
mighty *adj.* very strong.
migraine *n.* a throbbing headache accompanied by nausea.
migrate *vb.* move from one place to another to live, as birds do in the autumn. **migration** *n.*

Long journeys made by migrating birds. From top: The swallow, wheatear and bobolink. The Arctic tern flies from the Arctic to the Antarctic and back.

► Many mammals, birds, fish, insects and other animals move from one region to another at certain times of the year and return at other times. This regular movement between two places is called migration and is usually connected either with breeding or feeding. SALMON live in the sea but swim up river to breed. In winter, when the Arctic TUNDRA is frozen, caribou move south into the forests in search of food and shelter. Swallows, breeding in North Europe, fly 7,000 miles (11,000 km) to South Africa to find winter warmth and insect food. Insects themselves are great travelers: the monarch butterfly migrates between Canada and Mexico.

Milan (Milanese)
Milan is a large industrial city in northern ITALY. It lies on the Plain of Lombardy. Its industries include printing, publishing, engineering and chemicals. Milan has a fine cathedral. The city became part of Italy in 1860.

mild *adj*. moderate; gentle; (of weather) temperate.
mildew *n*. tiny fungus on plants or on growing decaying matter.
mile *n*. a measure of distance; 1760 yards.
militant *adj*. aggressive, warlike.
military *adj*. to do with soldiers and war.
milk *n*. a food that all baby mammals live on. It comes from the breasts, or mammaries, of the baby's mother. The baby sucks the milk from its mother's nipple. *vb*. draw milk from.
► At first, the milk is pale and watery. It protects the baby from diseases and infections. Later, the milk is much richer and creamier. It contains all the food the baby needs. Milk is full of fat, sugar, starches, protein, vitamins and minerals. After a while the baby grows teeth and starts to eat other kinds of food.
People use milk from many animals. These include cows, sheep, goats, camels, and even reindeer. Milk is used to make many foods. Cream, butter, yogurt, cheese and some ice cream are all made from milk.

Milky Way
When you look at the sky on a clear, moonless night you can see a pale cloud of light. It stretches across the heavens. If you look at it through binoculars or a telescope, you can see that the cloud is really millions of stars. All these stars, and most of the other stars we see, are part of our GALAXY. It is called the Milky Way.
Astronomers think that the Milky Way has about a trillion stars like our sun. The Milky Way stretches over a distance of about 100,000 light-years.

Side and plan views of our galaxy, the Milky Way. The arrows mark the position of the sun, about 30,000 light years from the center of the galaxy.

Our own SOLAR SYSTEM is 30,000 light-years from the center of the Milky Way.
The Milky Way has a spiral shape. Its trailing arms turn slowly around the center. They take 200 million years to make a full circle. Since the time of the earth's origin, the earth and our sun together have made only 20 revolutions of the Milky Way. From earth, we see the Milky Way through the arms of the spiral.
The Milky Way is not a special galaxy. There are thousands of other galaxies with the same shape. There may be millions and millions of other galaxies in the UNIVERSE.

millennium *n*. a thousand years.
millet *n*. important cereal crop, cultivated as a basic food in the drier regions of Africa and Asia – especially in India and China.
milligram *n*. a very small measure of weight; one thousandth of a gram.
millimeter *n*. a small measure of length, shortened to *mm* (10 mm=1 centimeter).
milliner *n*. person who designs, makes, sells women's hats.
million *n*. one thousand thousand (1,000,000).
millionaire *n*. a person who has a million dollars.
millipede *n*. small wormlike animal with a tough outer skeleton, segmented body and two pairs of legs on almost every segment.
► Millipedes are slow, nocturnal creatures that feed on decaying plants. There are about 8,000 species. Most of them, when disturbed, curl up into a tight coil.

Milne, A.A.
Alexander Milne (1882–1956) was a British writer famous for his children's stories and poems. His best loved books include *Winnie-the-Pooh* and *The House at Pooh Corner*. Milne also wrote a book of poetry called *When We Were Very Young*. He wrote his stories for his son, Christopher Robin. Winnie-the-Pooh was Christopher Robin's toy bear. The stories were written in the 1920s, but many children still like to read them today.

Milton, John
John Milton (1608–74) was an English poet. His most famous poem is the great epic *Paradise Lost*, which tells of the expulsion of Adam and Eve from the Garden of Eden. After a long period of study, Milton traveled in Italy and other European countries. During the English CIVIL WAR, he supported the Parliamentary side. Later, Milton served as Latin Secretary to the new government. In 1652 he became blind. He dictated much of his greatest poetry to his daughters.

mime *vb*. & *n*. act without using words.
► Mime is the art of acting in silence. A mime artist does not speak. Instead, his movements tell the story. He uses his face, hands and body to show how he feels. Mime artists are like dancers. They must control every movement with great care so that the audience can follow the story.
Mime was popular in ancient Greece and Rome. Then it was noisy and included a lot of acrobatics and juggling. The actors wore masks. Mime was also popular in the Middle Ages. Later, entire plays were mimed without words. Mime is used a lot in dancing, especially ballet.

mimic *vb*. imitate someone. *n*. a person who mimics.
minaret *n*. a tall tower attached to a mosque from the top of which Muslims are called to prayer.
► People who follow the religion of ISLAM pray in mosques. Minarets are an important part of a mosque. They are tall, slim towers from which the criers, or muezzins, call people to prayer. From the top of the minarets, the muezzins' voices ring out across the city. Muslims are called to prayer five times a day.
Most minarets are elegant and beautiful. The tallest minaret in the world is near New Delhi in India. It was built in A.D. 1193 and is 240 ft. (73 meters) high.

mince *vb*. cut into tiny pieces. *n*. meat that is chopped up finely.
mincemeat *n*. a mixture of dried fruits and fat that is cooked in pies and tarts, especially at Christmas.

M

mind 1. *n*. that part of a person which thinks, has ideas, and remembers; the brain. 2. *vb*. look after. *Our dog minds the house when we are out*. 3. *vb*. object to something. *I do mind being left alone*.

mine 1. *pron*. belonging to me. 2. *n*. a deep hole in the ground from which coal or other minerals are taken. *vb*. take minerals from the ground. **miner** *n*. a mine worker.

► Mining means digging MINERALS out of the earth. It is one of the world's most important industries. When minerals lie in one place in large quantities they are known as ores. People mine minerals such as GOLD, SILVER, and TIN. They also mine COAL.

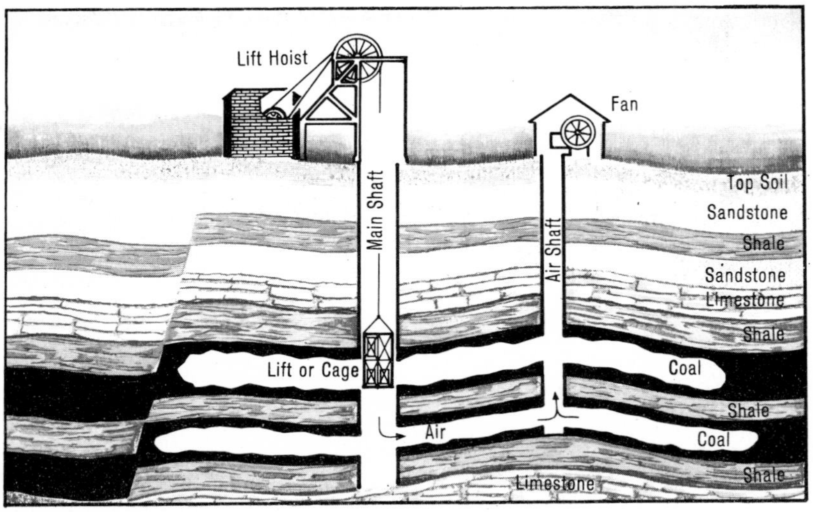

Altogether there are over 2,000 minerals. Yet most of the earth's rocks are made up of only 30 minerals. The most common mineral of all is quartz. Nearly all grains of sand are quartz.

mingle *vb*. blend, mix (with).

miniature *adj*. very small in scale.

minimize *vb*. reduce to smallest possible amount.

minimum *adj*. the least possible amount. *The minimum price of a seat was $2*.

minister *n*. 1. a clergyman; a parson. **ministry** *n*.

mink *n*. cat-sized semiaquatic mammal with a brown coat and bushy tail.

The different layers of rock that may be found between coal seams in an underground coal mine.

mineral *n*. a crystalline material that comes from the ground. *Coal, salt, and diamonds are all minerals*. *adj*. of or belonging to minerals.

► The rocks of the Earth are made up of materials called minerals. Some, such as GOLD or platinum, are made up of only one ELEMENT. Others, such as QUARTZ and SALT, consist of two or more elements. Some minerals are metallic, such as COPPER or SILVER. Other minerals are nonmetallic, like SULFUR.

Pure minerals are made up of ATOMS arranged in regular patterns, known as CRYSTALS. Minerals form crystals when they cool from hot GASES and liquids deep inside the earth. Crystals can grow very large if they cool slowly. But, large or small, crystals of the same mineral always have the same shape. The exception is CARBON. It takes one crystal shape when it is DIAMOND and another when it is graphite.

► Minks, found wild in North America and Europe, generally live in river banks and feed on small creatures such as frogs, water birds and fish. They are also bred on special farms for their valuable glossy fur.

Minnesota (*abbrev*. **Minn**.)
The state of Minnesota lies west of the Great Lakes and is full of scenic beauty. Mines produce iron, copper, nickel and taconite; farms produce large quantities of dairy products, corn, livestock, fruit and vegetables.

Most of Minnesota's people live in cities. The largest are the "Twin Cities" of Minneapolis and the capital, St. Paul. Duluth, on the shores of Lake Superior, has the nation's largest inland harbor.

The name "Minnesota" comes from two Sioux Indian words that mean "sky-tinted water." The state has more than 15,000 lakes and is home of the headwaters of the MISSISSIPPI RIVER, which rises in Lake Itasca in the northern part of the state.

Minnesota was explored by French fur traders and missionaries in the 1600s. After 1763 the territory came into British hands, and in 1812 the United States gained full control over the region. It entered the Union as a state in 1858.

minnow *n*. small freshwater fish belonging to the carp family. Most species are under six inches long.

minor *adj*. lesser or smaller, unimportant. *His car was involved in a minor accident, and was only slightly damaged*.

mint *n*. 1. a green, leafy herb used for flavoring food. 2. a place where coins are made.

minus *prep*. the mathematical sign (−) meaning take away or less than (6−4=2).

minute (**min**-*it*) *n*. a short period of time. *There are 60 minutes in one hour*.

minute (*my*-**nute**) *adj*. very tiny.

miracle *n*. a remarkable event that cannot be explained.

mirage *n*. an image of something caused by atmospheric conditions; a visual illusion.

mirror *n*. a shiny surface that reflects things; a looking glass. *vb*. reflect as a mirror.

► A mirror is made of a flat sheet of glass on the back of which is sprayed a thin layer of SILVER or ALUMINUM. A coat of paint on top of the metal layer prevents it being scratched. Light is reflected from the metal through the glass. Mirrors made of polished metal were used in the Iron Age, and the ancient Egyptians had silver and bronze mirrors about 2500 B.C.

mis- *prefix* meaning bad or wrongly. The meaning of such words can be found by referring to the main word, e.g. **misbehave, misprint, mispronounce**.

mischief *n*. naughtiness. **mischievous** *adj*.

miser *n*. a person who loves money for itself; a mean person.

miserable *adj*. very unhappy.

misery *n*. great unhappiness.

miss *vb*. 1. fail to hit, catch or see something that you want to. *If Sally does not hurry she will miss the train*. 2. be sad because someone is not with you. *When mother was in the hospital, we all missed her very much*.

Miss *n*. the title that goes before the name of an unmarried woman. *Miss Moody is the head teacher of our school*.

missile *n*. an object or weapon that is thrown or sent through the air, often by a rocket.

missing *adj*. not present; not found.

mission (**mi**-*shun*) *n*. team sent to do some special work; specific task.

missionary *adj*. & *n*. a person who goes to another country to tell people about his or her religion or to do helpful work.

Mississippi (*abbrev.* **Miss.**)
The state of Mississippi lies along the eastern shore of the river from which it gets its name, in the Deep South. Before the American CIVIL WAR Mississippi was a rich cotton state. It is now one of the leading producers of oil and natural gas. The great MISSISSIPPI RIVER deposits the rich silt which makes western Mississippi very fertile, and here cotton is still grown. Other important farm products include soybeans and dairy products.

Mississippi's capital and largest city is Jackson.

Mississippi was explored by the Spanish adventurer, Hernando de Soto, but it was the French who first settled in the region. Mississippi entered the Union as the 20th state in 1817.

Mississippi River
The Mississippi River is the longest river in the U.S.A. It rises in Minnesota in the north and flows 2,360 miles (3,780 km) southward to the Gulf of Mexico. It has 250 tributaries, small rivers which branch off from it. The waters of the Mississippi carry a lot of mud. As a result, its DELTA, where most of the mud is dumped, is growing out to sea at a rate of one mile (1.6 km) every 16 years.

Missouri (*abbrev.* **Mo.**)
The state of Missouri owes much of its success in trade and industry to its position, midway between the Atlantic and the Rocky Mountains, and to the two great rivers that form its eastern border, the MISSISSIPPI and the Missouri. St. Louis is an important industrial center and the state's largest city. Jefferson City is the capital.

Missouri was known in the 1800s as the starting point of the Santa Fé and Oregon Trails, much used by wagon trains of pioneers.

Missouri mines and quarries yield coal, clay, limestone and lead. The state is the nation's main lead producer.

Missouri territory was first visited by the French in the 1670s. In 1803 it was sold to the United States as part of the Louisiana Purchase. Missouri became a state in 1821.

mist *n.* a thin fog; water vapor in the air.

mistake *vb.* & *n.* (past **mistook** past part. **mistaken**) something you do without intending to; an error. *I made a mistake in my arithmetic.*

mister *n.* (written as Mr.) the title that goes before a man's surname. *Our teacher is called Mr. Todd.*

mistletoe *n.* an evergreen plant with shiny white berries which grows as a parasite on trees, especially apple trees; widely used as a Christmas decoration.

miter *n.* 1. headdress worn by a bishop. 2. special joint at corner of picture frame, etc.

mitten *n.* a kind of glove with one place for four fingers together and another for the thumb separately.

mix *vb.* mingle or join together. **mixer** *n.* a machine for mixing ingredients.

mixture *n.* anything made by mixing things together.

▶ When powdered iron and sand are stirred together they form a mixture. The iron can easily be separated from the sand by using a magnet. When such substances are mixed together they do not change. They can always be separated from each other. Air is a mixture of gases such as NITROGEN, OXYGEN, etc. These gases can be separated from the air. Liquids can also be mixtures. This is why medicine bottles often bear the instruction "Shake the Bottle"; if left standing, the various ingredients in the mixture separate, the densest falling to the bottom. A mixture should not be confused with a compound. A compound is formed by a chemical reaction; a mixture is not.

moan *n.* & *vb.* groan, especially with pain or unhappiness; grumble.

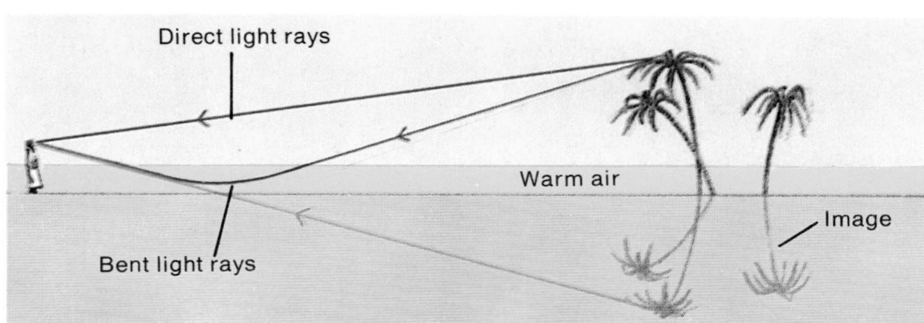

When a mirage forms, light rays from the sky or an object such as a tree bend as they pass through warm air near the ground. This happens because the air gets warmer near the hot ground and light rays bend when they pass between cooler and warmer air. The tree and sky are seen in their normal positions by light rays that come directly to the eyes. The rays that have been bent also reach the eyes, which assume that they too have come directly. An image of the tree and sky is therefore seen on the ground beneath the tree.

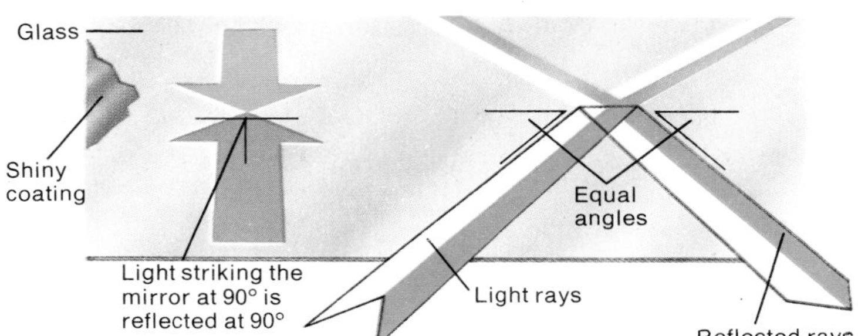

How a mirror works. Light rays pass through the glass of a mirror and are reflected from the shiny coating. But the image is always reversed. This is because light rays from the right side are reflected back on this side. So you see the object's right side to your right side.

moat *n.* a deep ditch around a castle.

mob *n.* noisy crowd, gang. *vb.* crowd around.

mobile *adj.* moving, movable. **mobility** *n.*

moccasin *n.* shoe made of deerskin or soft leather.

mock *vb.* make fun of, scoff at. **mockery** *n.*

model *n.* 1. a copy of something, usually smaller. *The architect showed us the model he had made of the new building. vb.* make a model. 2. someone who sits while an artist or photographer paints or photographs; someone whose job is to wear and show new clothes.

moderate (**mod**-*er-at*) *adj.* not extreme; of average quality.

modern *adj.* of present or recent times. *My mother likes living in a modern house, but my father would like to move to an older one.* **modernize** *vb.* (make modern) bring up to date.

M

modest *adj*. not boastful, not excessive. **modesty**. *n*.
mohair *n*. hair of the Angora goat.

Mohenjo-Daro
The first civilization in INDIA and PAKISTAN of which historians have records was in the valley of the River INDUS. The two biggest cities were called Harappa and Mohenjo-Daro. These cities were built between 2500 and 1800 B.C. Both of them had a citadel containing a bath house and a grain store. The buildings were made with bricks fired in a kiln. There were covered drains for rain and waste water. The Indus Valley civilization came to an end in about 1500 B.C. Historians believe that the cities were attacked by invading tribes.

moist *adj*. slightly wet. **moisten** *vb*. to make moist. **moisture** *n*.
mold (rhymes with *sold*) 1. *n*. a hollow container. When a hot substance is poured into a mold it cools into the shape of the container. 2. *vb*. to shape. 3. *n*. a small fungus that grows on damp decaying things.
mole *n*. 1. a small furry animal that lives in a tunnel underground. 2. a small dark mark on the skin. 3. a secret spy.
molt (rhymes with *colt*) *vb*. shed old feathers, hair, shell, or skin periodically. *Snakes molt and have new skin under the old one*.
molecule *n*. a number of atoms joined together to form a stable and definite structure.
► A molecule is the smallest part of a compound that is still the compound. WATER is a compound made up of oxygen and hydrogen atoms; each water molecule has in it two hydrogen atoms and one oxygen atom. If any of these three atoms is removed, we no longer have a water molecule. Before the identification of atoms it was thought that molecules were the smallest particles of nature.

molest (*mo*-**lest**) *vb*. annoy, pester.
mollusk *n*. one of a group of animals with soft bodies and no backbone. Most mollusks, like snails, limpets and oysters, have hard shells.
► There are about 70,000 different kinds of mollusks. After insects they are the most numerous of all animals. They are found everywhere from deserts and mountains to the depths of the sea.
Mollusks have soft bodies and no backbones. Instead, a hard outer SHELL protects their body. Some mollusks, such as squid and cuttlefish, have their shell inside their body. Certain kinds of slug have no shell at all. Some shells are only an eighth of an inch wide. Others, like the giant clam, are over a yard wide. As a mollusk grows, its shell grows with it. The shell is made of a hard limy material formed from the food the mollusk eats. Shells have many strange shapes and patterns.
The largest mollusk is the giant squid. This can grow to as much as 40 ft. (12 meters).

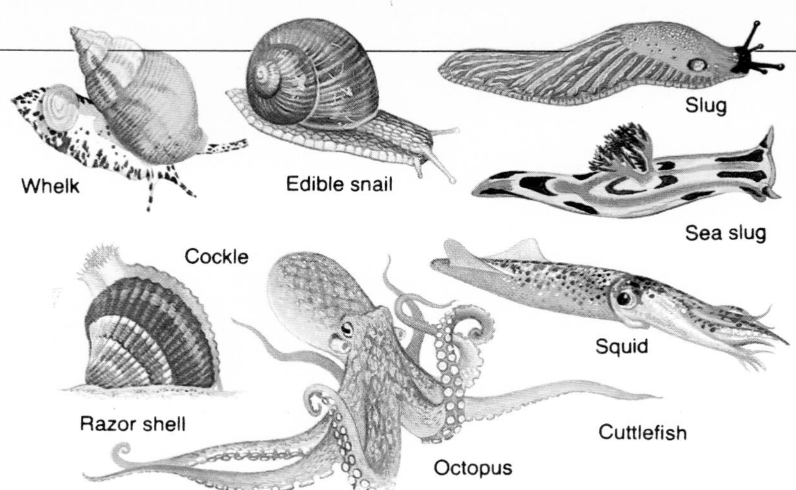

moment *n*. a very short period of time. *Wait a moment*.

Monaco (Monagesque)
Monaco is a tiny principality on the MEDITERRANEAN coast of south-eastern FRANCE. Its main sources of income are tourism and gambling. Monte Carlo is a luxury resort with a famous casino. It is also the setting for a motor racing Grand Prix, and the finish of the Monte Carlo rally (road race).
At one time Monaco belonged to an Italian family. It became fully independent in 1861. It maintains strong links with France and uses French money.
AREA: 467 ACRES (190 HECTARES)
POPULATION: 25,000
CAPITAL: MONACO
CURRENCY: FRENCH FRANC
OFFICIAL LANGUAGE: FRENCH

France
Monaco
Andorra
Corsica

monarch ("ch" like "k") *n*. a king or queen.
monastery *n*. a place where monks live and work. **monastic** *adj*.
► In monasteries monks lead a religious life and obey strict rules. Monasteries are especially important in the BUDDHIST and Christian religions.
Christian monasteries began in Egypt around A.D. 300. Hermits were religious men who lived alone. A group of hermits came together and made rules for their way of life. Soon after, communities of monks began to grow up. The monks worked as farmers, laborers and teachers, and helped the poor.
One of the most famous monks was St. Benedict. He founded the Benedictine order. Many groups of monks followed his rules for running a monastery. St. Benedict divided the day into periods of prayer, religious study and work.

Monday *n*. the second day of the week, between Sunday and Tuesday; named after the moon.
money *n*. coins or bank notes used to buy things.
► We use money every day to pay for things we buy. We pay with either coins or paper bills. This sort of money is known as cash. There is also another kind of money. It includes checks, credit cards and travelers' checks.
Almost anything can be used as money. In the past people have used shells, beads, cocoa beans, salt, grain and even cattle. But coins are much easier to use than, say, cattle. For one thing, they do not die suddenly. They are also easy to store and to carry around.

The obverse and reverse (heads and tails) of an Italian 100 lire piece.

Coins were first used in China. They were also used by the ancient Greeks as early as 600 B.C. They were valuable because they were made of either gold or silver. They were stamped with the mark of the government or the ruler of the country for which they were made. The stamp also showed how much each coin was worth.

Later, people began to use coins made of cheaper metals. The metal itself had no value, but the coins were still worth the amount stamped on them. They also started to use paper money. It no longer mattered that the money itself had no real value. It was backed by the government and BANKS, which people could trust. This is the kind of money we use today.

Monet, Claude
A French Impressionist painter. Monet (1840–1926) produced masterly landscapes showing the changing effects of light at various times of the day.

Mongolia (Mongolian)
Mongolia is a landlocked Communist republic in the heart of ASIA. It lies between the Soviet Union and CHINA. Mongolia is a high, flat country. The GOBI desert in the south covers one-third of the total area. The remainder of the country consists of rolling grassland, with mountain ranges in the west. Most of the people were formerly nomadic herdsmen. Now, all agriculture is organized into large state or collective farms. Mongolia is sometimes called Outer Mongolia to distinguish it from neighboring Inner Mongolia, a region of China.

AREA: 604,283 SQ. MILES (1,565,000 SQ. KM)
POPULATION: 1,772,000
CAPITAL: ULAN BATOR
CURRENCY: TUGRIK
OFFICIAL LANGUAGE: MONGOL

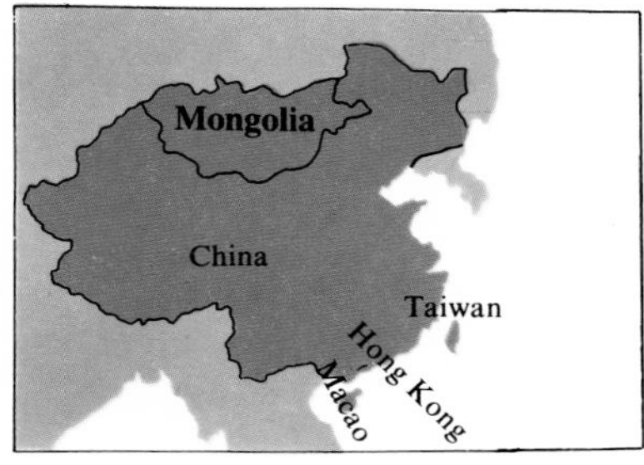

Mongols
The Mongols were NOMADS who lived on the great plains of central ASIA. They herded huge flocks of sheep, goats, cattle and horses, which they grazed on the vast grasslands of the region. They lived in tent villages that they could quickly pack up and take with them when they moved on to find new pastures.

The Mongols were superb horsemen and highly trained warriors. In the 1200s they formed a mighty army under the great GENGHIS KHAN. Very soon, swift-riding hordes of Mongols swept through China, India, Persia and as far west as Hungary.

Under GENGHIS KHAN, and later his grandson, KUBLAI KHAN, the Mongols conquered half the known world. But they were unable to hold their empire together. In less than 100 years the Mongol empire had been taken over by the Chinese.

Today more than half the Mongolian people live and work as farmers. They keep over 20 million animals in herds.

mongoose *n.* (plural **mongooses**) a small mammal of Africa and southern Asia, a relative of the weasel. It has a low body, a bushy tail and short legs. An adult mongoose is about 1½ feet long.
► Mongooses live in burrows and feed on small birds, poultry, mice and rats. Their fierceness and speed also helps them to kill dangerous snakes like the cobra.

A mongoose can pounce so quickly that a cobra has no time to strike with its fangs.

mongrel *adj.* & *n.* a dog that is a mixture of different types of dogs.

monk (rhymes with *bunk*) *n.* a member of a religious group of men who live, work and pray together in a monastery.

monkey (**mun**-*kee*) *n.* a furry animal that belongs to the same group as apes and people.
► Monkeys are MAMMALS that belong to the same group of animals as APES and MAN. Most monkeys have long tails and thick fur all over their bodies. Monkeys are usually smaller than apes. Their hands and feet are used for grasping and are very similar to those of humans.

There are about 400 different kinds of monkey. Most live in the tropics, especially in forests, in Africa, Asia and South America. South American monkeys have long tails that they use like an extra arm or leg when swinging through the branches of trees.

On the ground monkeys usually move about on all four limbs. But when they are using their hands to hold something they can stand or sit up on two legs.

Monkeys live in family groups known as troops. They spend a lot of time chattering, playing, fighting and grooming each other. Each troop of monkeys has its own special place where it lives and feeds. It will fight fiercely to defend this area against other invading groups.

mono- *prefix* meaning one, alone, e.g. **monochrome** painting in one color. **monosyllable** word with one syllable, e.g. me.

monopoly *n.* sole control of something.

monorail *n.* a railway which runs on one rail.

monsieur (*mus*-**yer**) *n.* (plural **messieurs** pronounced **may**-*s-yer*) the French for mister or sir.

monsoon *n.* a wind system in which prevailing winds blow in opposite directions in winter and summer. *In India, the well-known summer monsoon brings heavy rainfall.*

monster *n.* a large and frightening creature. **monstrous** *adj.* very large.

Montana (*abbrev.* **Mont.**)
Montana is one of the Rocky Mountain States. Its name means "mountainous" in Spanish, for the Rockies cover the western two-fifths of the state, and the high, rolling Great Plains the rest. Montana was developed for its rich mineral deposits, and much of the state's early history was bound up with mining. The capital, Helena, started as a mining camp called Last Chance Gulch.

A number of different Indian tribes lived in Montana before Europeans first visited it. In 1805 the state was explored by Lewis and Clark on their expedition to the Pacific coast. Montana was the site of the Battle of Little Bighorn (1876), popularly known as Custer's Last Stand.

month *n.* one of the 12 parts into which the year is divided. **monthly** *adv.* once a month.

Montreal
Montreal is a city on the island of the same name in QUEBEC Province, CANADA. Situated on the St. Lawrence Seaway, it is the country's chief port. It is a major industrial, transport and cultural center, and has two universities.

The site of Montreal was explored by Jacques CARTIER in 1535. The city was governed by the French until 1760, when it became British.

monument *n.* something that reminds us of a person or event. *The Tomb of the Unknown Soldiers is a monument to soldiers who died in American wars.*

mood *n.* the way you feel. **moody** *adj.* subject to changes of mood; gloomy.

moon *n.* the earth's only natural satellite and our nearest neighbor in space.

semi-abstract, but they convey pathos and tragedy. His drawings, such as those of people seeking shelter from air raids, are also impressive.

moose *n.* (plural **moose**) a large, dark brown deer found in the cold northern forests of Alaska and Canada. The male carries huge, flattened antlers. *Moose are similar to the European and Asian elk.*

mop *n.* a bundle of fibers on the end of a stick, used for cleaning floors.

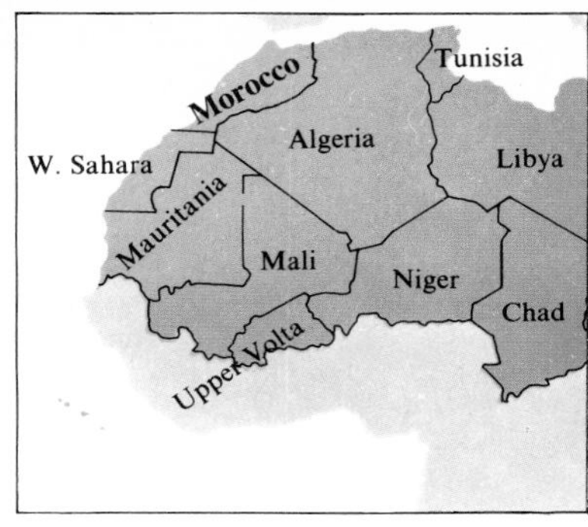

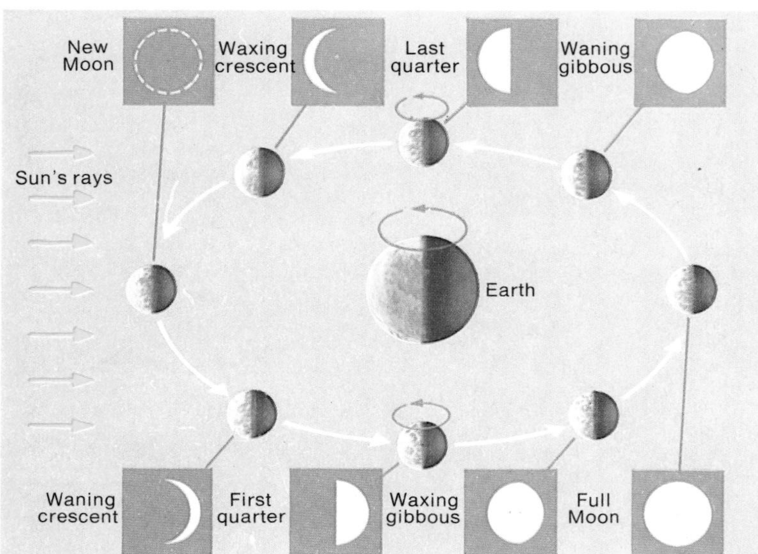

► The moon orbits the earth at an average distance of 238,900 miles (384,400 km). The month, based on a complete cycle of the moon's phases from full moon to full moon, has been a unit of time since earliest recorded history. The average time between full moons is 29½ days. The moon always turns the same face towards earth. Its surface has thousands of craters, most of which were probably formed by meteorites from outer space. On July 20, 1969, *Apollo II* astronauts Neil Armstrong and Edwin Aldrin became the first human beings to walk on the surface of the moon. Experiments carried out during this and later moon flights have taught us much about our moon. We now know that our neighbor is made up of much the same elements as are some volcanic rocks on earth, but they contain no water.

moonlight *n.* the light from the moon.

moor 1. *n.* an open boggy wasteland often covered with grasses. 2. *vb.* tie up a boat.

Moore, Henry
Henry Moore (1898—) is a British sculptor. He has worked in wood, stone and bronze. His figures are

moped (**mo**-*ped*) *n.* a kind of small motorized bicycle.

morale (*more*-**ahl**) *n.* condition of the state of mind and confidence of people. *Morale is high! We're going to win!*

morals 1. *pl. n.* rules or system of good behavior. **moral** *adj.* concerned with what is right or wrong.

moral *n.* a practical lesson. *He's in the hospital. The moral of that is, don't ride on the wrong side of the road.*

more *adj*\ a greater amount or number. *May I have some more pudding?*

Mormons
Mormons are people who belong to the Church of Jesus Christ of Latter-day Saints, a religious group founded by Joseph Smith in 1830. The name Mormon comes from the Book of Mormon, which Mormons believe is a sacred history of ancient American peoples.

The Mormons began first in New York, but were persecuted for their belief and driven out. Led by Brigham Young, they finally settled in Salt Lake Valley, Utah.

morning *n.* the early part of the day, between night and afternoon.

Morocco (Moroccan)
Morocco is a monarchy in Northwest AFRICA. It contains much of the Atlas mountain range and part of the SAHARA. Most people are farmers but much of the country's income comes from industry. The main resource is phophates, and other minerals are mined. There is also a considerable tourist industry.

The northern tip of Morocco is separated from Spain by the narrow Straits of Gibraltar.

In the 1970s, Morocco took over the Western (formerly Spanish) Sahara. Guerrilla troops resisted, and fighting continued into the 1980s.

AREA: 172,423 SQ. MILES (446,550 SQ. KM)
POPULATION: 21,280,000
CAPITAL: RABAT
CURRENCY: DIRHAM
OFFICIAL LANGUAGE: ARABIC

Morse code *n.* a system of sending messages by a series of dots and dashes for letters.

► In Morse code each letter has its own dot and dash pattern. The code was invented by Samuel Morse, an American artist, to send messages along a telegraph wire. The telegraph operator presses a key at one end to send a signal along the wire to a sounder at the other end. A short signal is a dot and a long signal is a dash. The first message was sent in 1844.

Morse code can also be signaled by lights.

A	·–	S	···
B	–···	T	–
C	–·–·	U	··–
D	–··	V	···–
E	·	W	·––
F	··–·	X	–··–
G	––·	Y	–·––
H	····	Z	––··
I	··	1	·––––
J	·–––	2	··–––
K	–·–	3	···––
L	·–··	4	····–
M	––	5	·····
N	–·	6	–····
O	–––	7	––···
P	·––·	8	–––··
Q	––·–	9	––––·
R	·–·	0	–––––

Onion domes of the Kremlin, Moscow.

mortal *adj.* that which must die; causing death. *A mortal wound. n.* a human being.

mortar *n.* 1. a mixture of cement, lime, sand and water. *Mortar is used to hold bricks together.* 2. a vessel for grinding substances in (with a **pestle**).

mortgage *n.* transfer of property as security for a sum of money borrowed. *vb.* give over by mortgage.

► A mortgage is a way of borrowing a large amount of money to buy something expensive such as a house. Mortgages usually come from banks and other businesses which arrange loans to buy homes. People usually have to save some money of their own before they can borrow enough for a house.

Until the loan is repaid, the bank still owns the house, but allows the person borrowing money to live in it. The borrower must pay back the amount first borrowed and an extra sum called interest. Mortgages are usually repaid in regular small amounts over a number of years.

mosaic *adj.* & *n.* a picture made from little bits of colored stone or glass set into cement.

► Mosaic making is an ancient art. The Sumerians made mosaics nearly 5,000 years ago. Mosaics are a very practical way of decorating floors and walls, as they can be washed without being spoiled. In ancient Rome, every villa and palace had its dazzling mosaics showing scenes from everyday life.

Mosaics were also used to make pictures of saints, angels and Jesus in churches all over Greece, Italy and Turkey.

Moscow (Muscovite)
Moscow is the capital of Russia. It is also the biggest city in the country. Nearly eight million people live there.

Moscow lies on a plain across the River Moskva. It is the largest industrial and business center in the country. Everything is made in Moscow, from cars to clothes. It is also the political and cultural center of the Soviet Union.

Moscow was first made the capital of Muscovy in 1547, during the reign of Ivan the Terrible, the first tsar (emperor) of Russia. It grew up around the KREMLIN, an ancient fort from which the Muscovy princes used to defend their country. Moscow remained the capital of the tsars until 1712 when Peter the Great moved it to St. Petersburg. The city remained very important, even after it was nearly burned down during NAPOLEON's occupation of 1812.

After the Revolution of 1917, Moscow once more became the seat of government.

Moses
In the BIBLE, Moses was a Jewish leader, lawgiver and prophet. According to the Old Testament, Moses (*c.* 13th century B.C.) led the JEWS out of captivity in Egypt so that they might find the "Promised Land" (PALESTINE). Moses received the Ten Commandments from God, and formalized the Jewish Religion (*see* JUDAISM).

Moslem see **Muslim**.

mosque (*mosk*) *n.* a building in which Muslims worship.

mosquito (*mos-***kee***-to*) *n.* (plural **mosquitoes**) small insect that sucks blood. *Some mosquitoes carry malaria and other diseases.*

► Mosquitoes are a small kind of fly. They have slender, tube-shaped bodies, three pairs of long legs and two narrow wings. There are about 1,400 different kinds. They live all over the world from the tropics to the Arctic, but must be able to get to water to lay their eggs.

Only female mosquitoes bite and suck blood. They have special piercing mouths. Males live on the juices of plants. When the female bites, she injects a substance into her victim to make the blood flow more easily. It is this that makes mosquito bites itch.

Some kinds of mosquito spread serious diseases. Malaria, yellow fever and sleeping sickness are passed on by mosquitoes.

moss *n.* small green or yellow plants that grow on damp surfaces in low, closely packed clusters.

► There are more than 12,000 different kinds of moss. They are very hardy plants and flourish everywhere, except in deserts, even as far north as the Arctic. Most mosses spread in carpets on the ground in shady forests, or over rocks and the trunks of trees.

Mosses are very simple kinds of plants. They were among the first to make their home on land. They have slender creeping stems that are covered with tiny leaves. Instead of long roots that reach down into the soil, mosses simply have a mass of tiny hairs that soak up moisture and food. Mosses do not have flowers. They reproduce by spores, like FERNS. One kind, sphagnum moss, grows in bogs and is the plant that makes peat.

most *adj., pron.* & *adv.* the greatest; the largest number.

motel *n.* a roadside hotel for people who arrive by car.

moth *n.* a winged insect, like a butterfly, that usually flies at night.

► Moths belong to one of the biggest insect groups. There are over 100,000 kinds of moth and they are found all over the world. The smallest scarcely measure $\frac{1}{8}$ in. (3 mm) across. The largest may be bigger than a person's hand. Some moths have very striking colors that warn their enemies that they are poisonous or bad tasting. Moths have a good sense of smell. They find their food by "sniffing" their way from

Common hair moss, one of several species, which forms extensive dark-green mats on moors and bogs.

M

plant to plant. A male moth can follow the scent of a female 2 miles (3 km) away.

Like butterflies, moths have a coiled, tube-like mouth, or *proboscis*, for sucking the nectar from flowers. Moth larvae, or CATERPILLARS feed mainly on leaves or plant juices. But the clothes moth larva eats wool and fur, causing the "moth holes" we often find in woolen clothing. Other harmful moth larvae include the "cutworms," which are actually caterpillars of several moths that attack root crops such as potatoes and turnips. A moth beneficial to us is the silk moth, whose larva, the silkworm, spins the silk used in clothes and fine furnishings.

Moths begin life as eggs, usually in the spring. They hatch into caterpillars. The caterpillar feeds on leaves until it is fully grown. Then it spins itself a silk cocoon. This protects the caterpillar while its body changes into a moth. A few kinds of moth do not spin cocoons, but bury themselves in the ground or in piles of leaves until they grow into moths.

mother *n.* a female parent; a woman who has children. *vb.* care for or protect.

Mother Goose

Mother Goose is the name given to the fictitious old woman who narrated nursery rhymes. She is often shown on the covers of nursery rhyme books riding through the air on the back of a goose.

The tradition of Mother Goose is over 200 years old and was first used in a book of fairy tales put together by the Frenchman Charles Perrault. Collections of rhymes that now include *Jack and Jill*, *Humpty Dumpty*, *Simple Simon*, and others began to be published in England and America in the 1700s. Many of the rhymes were not originally written for children, but came out of folklore or as comments on the political or social scene of the time.

motion *n.* 1. moving. 2. gesture. 3. formal proposition.

▶ The scientific laws applied to bodies in motion were set out by Sir Isaac NEWTON in 1687. Newton's First Law of Motion states that an object either remains still or goes on moving at a steady rate unless acted upon by another force. An example of this is the way in which passengers in a car are thrown forward if the car comes to a sudden stop.

Newton's Second Law says that the amount of force that is needed to make an object change its speed depends on the mass of the object and on how much its rate of speed is to be changed. The fact that a baseball is more difficult to stop than a tennis ball traveling at the same speed illustrates this Law.

Newton's Third Law of Motion, perhaps his most famous, says that for every action there is an equal and opposite reaction. One of the most dramatic examples of this is a rocket engine, which, as its burning gases are forced backward, pushes the rocket forward.

motion picture *n.* a sequence of photographs or drawings projected from film onto a screen in such rapid succession that it gives the illusion of moving people and things.

▶ The art of making motion pictures came from an invention called the *kinetoscope*, built by Thomas EDISON in 1891. Soon after Edison's machine became known, two French brothers, Auguste and Louis Lumière, built a similar machine of their own called a *cinematographe*. This machine projected pictures from a piece of film onto a screen. The pictures were shown one after the other, so quickly that the images on the screen appeared to move. In 1896, in Paris, the Lumière brothers gave the world's first public film show. Soon, people all over Europe and North America were making films.

These early films did not look much like the ones we are used to seeing today. They were only in black and white, the movements were very jerky and they had no sound. At first, films were made to show news and real events, but by 1902 film-makers began to make up their own stories, using actors to play the parts of imaginary people. These "movies" were very popular in France and the United States, and HOLLYWOOD became the movie-making center of the world. The first "talkie," or motion picture with sound, was shown in the United States in 1927. It was called *The Jazz Singer*.

The United States remained the leader in the film world. Huge amounts of money were spent on films that used hundreds of actors, singers and dancers, lavish costumes and specially designed "sets" or backgrounds. But Europe too produced many important films, and, after World War II, a more realistic type of film became popular, telling stories of everday life.

Today films are made all over the world, although the United States still produces most of the big feature films, using modern technology to create fantastic visual effects. Television has been a threat to the film industry since the 1960s, and there have been many experiments in recent years to develop new kinds of films. For example, films that create not only the sight and sound of what is happening in the picture but also what it feels like. And many of the big studios are cashing in on the popularity of television by producing "made for TV" films shown exclusively on television.

motive *n.* something that causes a person to take action.

motor *n.* an engine that uses electricity, gas or oil to produce a movement.

Motorboat

Boats and other small craft that are driven by internal combustion ENGINES are called motorboats. A motorboat can be anything from a dinghy with an outboard engine to a large launch or fishing boat.

Smaller motorboats generally have a gasoline engine like a car, but diesel engines are used in lifeboats, fishing boats and small warships such as minesweepers. An "inboard" engine is one that is attached inside the hull and is usually permanent; an "outboard" engine can be clamped to almost any boat and has its own propellor and shaft.

motorcycle *n.* a two-wheeled vehicle propelled by an internal combustion engine.

▶ The first motorcycle was built in 1885 by the German Gottlieb Daimler. He fitted one of his gasoline ENGINES to a wooden bicycle frame. But today's motorcycles are very complicated machines. The engine is similar to that of a car, but smaller. It is either a two-stroke or a four-stroke engine, and it may have from one to four cylinders. The engine can be cooled by either air or water. It is started by pushing down a kick-starter. This turns the engine and starts it firing. The speed is controlled by a twist-grip on the handlebars. The clutch works from a hand lever. The gears are changed by a foot lever. Another foot pedal works the brake on the back wheel. A chain connects the engine to the back wheel and drives it around.

motorist *n.* someone who drives a car.

motorize *vb.* to put a motor on something. *We motorized our boat.*

Mott, Lucretia

Lucretia Mott (1793–1880) was an American Quaker minister, abolitionist and pioneer of women's rights. Born in Nantucket and raised in the Quaker religion, she began to speak at Quaker meetings as a young woman and by 1821 had become a minister. She helped to found the American Anti-Slavery Society with William Lloyd Garrison in 1833 and was a radical among abolitionists in that she believed in immediate freedom for the slaves. She and her husband harbored runaway slaves in their Pennsylvania home. At times she antagonized more moderate Quakers with her radical views.

In 1840 Lucretia Mott was sent as a delegate to a World Anti-Slavery Convention in London, but was denied entry on the grounds of her sex. This act helped to confirm her views in favor of equality for women, and she joined Elizabeth Cady Stanton in calling the first women's rights convention in Seneca Falls, New York. This is often thought to mark the formal beginning of the women's rights crusade.

mottled *adj*. marked with spots of different colors.

Mound Builders
In archeology, a mound is any low hill or "bump" on the earth's surface that has been caused by past activities of people. A simple mound may be merely heaps of shells, refuse from the shellfish diets of early peoples. Other mounds are the remains of dwelling places that have been built, repaired, destroyed and rebuilt so many times in their history that a mound of debris has formed. Many of these can be seen in Turkey and other part of the Near and Middle East.

In the United States, the people we call the Mound Builders were prehistoric Indians who lived in various parts of the country between the Great Lakes and Mexico. They are called Mound Builders because they built different kinds of mounds of earth and stone.

The most common type of mound is the burial mound, built over the graves of the dead. These burial mounds were dome-shaped or cone-shaped and from 20 to 250 feet (6 to 76 meters) across. They could be as much as 70 feet (21 meters) high.

Other later mounds looked like flat-topped pyramids. Scientists think they may have been used as temples. Some of these mounds are huge. The Monk's Mound, near East St. Louis, Illinois, is over 1,000 feet (300 meters) long, 700 feet (210 meters) wide, and 100 feet (30 meters) high. The people who built the temple mounds are believed to have lived about the year A.D. 1000. They lived mostly in the area around the Mississippi River.

These early Indians were farmers and hunters. They made beautiful ornaments of bone, silver, copper and stone. Their weapons were made of stone, wood, and copper. And they were fine sculptors.

mount 1. *vb*. go up something; get onto a horse to ride it; rise sharply. *The cost of candy mounted after the sugar shortage*. 2. *n*. a saddle horse; small hill.

mountain *n*. a very high hill.
► A large part of the earth's surface is covered by mountains. The greatest mountain ranges are the Alps of Europe, the Rockies and the Andes of the Americas and the HIMALAYAS of Asia. The Himalayas are the greatest of them all. They have many of the world's highest peaks, including the biggest, Mount EVEREST.

"Young" mountains are, in terms of the earth's history, recently formed. These include the jagged peaks of the Rockies, Alps and Himalayas. Examples of "old" mountains can be found in the Appalachian mountain system, which stretches from Maine to Alabama. Parts of this system have been worn down by erosion and glacial action over millions of years into low, rounded mountains.

There are mountains under the sea, too. And sometimes the peaks of under-sea mountains stick up above the sea's surface as islands. The highest volcanic peaks in the world are the great mountains of lava that rise over 29,500 feet (9,000 meters) from the floor of the Pacific Ocean, forming the islands of Hawaii. Mauna Loa, one of these, is much higher than Everest.

Mountains are formed by movements in the earth's crust. Some mountains are formed when two great land masses move toward each other and squeeze up the land in between. The Alps were made in this way. Other mountains are VOLCANOES, great heaps of ash and lava that poured out when the volcano erupted. Many volcanic peaks are long *extinct* – that is, any volcanic activity stopped long ago. Others, called *active* volcanoes, still erupt from time to time. Still others are termed *dormant* volcanoes, because they have remained "quiet" for perhaps hundreds of years but are capable of erupting again.

When the height of a mountain is given, it means the height above sea level. This can be a lot more

The sun's energy that reaches the earth's surface and heats it up arrives as shortwave radiation. This is easily absorbed by the air. There is more air near the earth's surface than higher up. So the higher you go, the colder it is. The diagram shows the different types of vegetation that grow at different altitudes.

HIGH MOUNTAINS

	m	ft
Asia		
Everest (Himalaya-Nepal/Tibet)	8,848	29,028
Godwin Austen (Pakistan/India)	8,611	28,250
Kanchenjunga (Himalaya-Nepal/Sikkim	8,579	28,145
Makalu (Himalaya-Nepal/Tibet)	8,470	27,790
Dhaulagiri (Himalaya-Nepal)	8,172	26,810
Nanga Parbat (Himalaya-India	8,126	26,660
Annapurna (Himalaya-Nepal)	8,075	26,492
Gasherbrum (Karakoram-India)	8,068	26,470
Gosainthan (Himalaya-Tibet)	8,013	26,291
Nanda Devi (Himalaya-India)	7,817	25,645
South America		
Aconcagua (Andes-Argentina)	6,960	22,835
North America		
McKinley (Alaska-U.S.A.)	6,194	20,322
Africa		
Kilimanjaro (volcanic-Tanzania)	5,895	19,341
Europe		
Elbruz (Caucasus-USSR)	5,633	18,481
Mont Blanc (Alps-France)	4,810	15,781
Antarctica		
Vinson Massif	5,139	16,680
Oceania		
Wilheim (Bismarck Range-New Guinea)	4,694	15,400

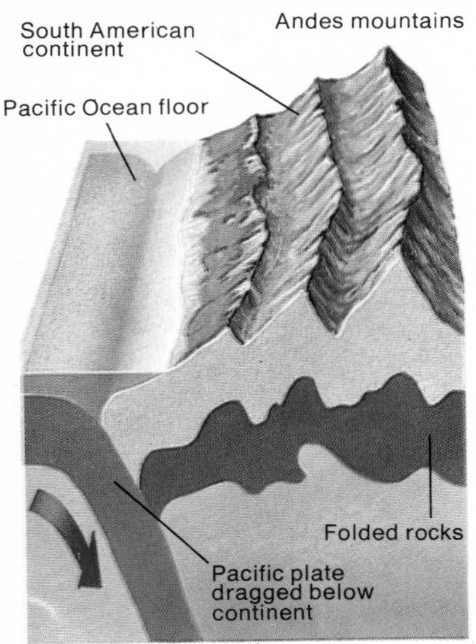

This diagram shows how the Andes are being formed. Part of the Pacific Ocean floor is being pushed under South America. Earthquakes and volcanoes result. And the rocks at the edge of South America are being folded and faulted and pushed up to form a great mountain chain.

than the height from the base.

mountaineer *n.* a person who climbs mountains.
mourning *n.* grief, great sadness after someone dies. **mourn** *vb.*
mouse *n.* (plural **mice**) a very small rodent.
► A mouse like its relative the rat is a pest to human beings. It can do a great deal of damage to stores of food, usually at night. One mouse can have 40 offspring a year, and when the young are 12 weeks old they can themselves breed. People have used cats to catch mice for thousands of years. The wood mouse, field mouse, harvest mouse, and dormouse are mice that live in the countryside.

moustache *n.* hair grown on the upper lip.

A wood mouse. It is nocturnal and very common.

mouth *n.* the opening in the face into which you put food and through which your voice comes; that part of a river where it flows into the sea.
mouth organ *n.* a small musical instrument played by blowing and sucking.
move *vb.* change position of something; change residence, location, etc.; stir, affect with emotion. *n.* e.g. a chess move. **movable** *adj.* that can be moved.
movement *n.* 1. activity; the act of moving. 2. section of a piece of music.
movie *n.* motion picture.
mow (rhymes with *toe*) *vb.* cut grass or hay. **mower** *n.* mowing machine.

Mozambique
Mozambique is a republic in south-eastern AFRICA. Most people in this poor country work on the land. Some coal is mined and there is a little industry. Formerly ruled by Portugal, Mozambique achieved independence in 1975 following a guerrilla war.
AREA: 302,346 SQ. MILES (783,030 SQ. KM
POPULATION: 10,987,000
CAPITAL: MAPUTO
CURRENCY: METICAL
OFFICIAL LANGUAGE: PORTUGUESE

Mozart, Wolfgang Amadeus
Wolfgang Amadeus Mozart (1756–91) was an Austrian and one of the greatest composers of music that the world has known. He began writing music at the age of five. Two years later he was playing at concerts all over Europe. Mozart wrote over 600 pieces of music, including many beautiful operas and symphonies. But he earned little money, and died in poverty at the age of 35.

Mr. *abbrev.* the polite title given to a man (short for Mister), e.g. *Mr. Smith.*
Mrs. *abbrev.* the polite title that goes before the surname of a married woman.
Ms. (*miz*) *n.* a polite title used before the surname of a woman. It does not show whether or not she is married.
much *adj* & *adv.* a great deal; a considerable amount. *You are making too much noise.*
muck *n.* manure, filth.
mud *n.* wet, soft earth. **muddy** *adj.* covered with mud.
muddle *n.* a confused mess. *vb.* muddy up; confuse.
muezzin *n.* Muslim who calls people to daily prayer from atop a minaret.
mug 1. *n.* a tall kind of cup without a saucer. 2. *n.* person's face or mouth. 3. *vb.* assault someone, usually in order to rob. *n.* mugger.

Muhammad
Muhammad (A.D. 570–632) was the founder and leader of the RELIGION known as ISLAM. He was born in MECCA in Saudi Arabia. At the age of 40 he believed that God asked him to preach to the ARABS. He taught that there was only one God, called Allah.

In 622 he was forced out of Mecca, and this is the year from which the Muslim calendar dates. After his death his teachings spread rapidly and a century later his followers had created an empire that stretched from Spain to India.

mule *n.* 1. a horselike animal that is the foal of a male ass and a female horse or pony (a mare). 2. kind of slipper without a back.
multi- *prefix* meaning many, e.g. **multilateral** many sided.
multiply *vb.* make something a given number of times bigger. *When you multiply by three, the answer is three times greater.* **multiplication** *n.*
mumble *vb.* mutter; talk indistinctly.
mummy *n.* the preserved body of a human or animal. *v.* **mummify**.
► Belief in a life after death has led many people to try to preserve the bodies of their dead. The body would then be ready to come back to life in the next world.

The ancient Egyptians made mummies of their dead. The bodies of PHARAOHS and rich people were treated with stuff to preserve them, covered with a kind of tar and then wrapped in linen cloths. The mummy was placed in a casket on which a face was painted. This casket was placed inside another coffin, and the coffin was sometimes put inside another, larger box. The bodies of the poor, however, were dried in salt and wrapped in coarse cloths.

mumps *n.* an illness that makes the neck and sides of the face swell.

Munich
Munich is a university city in the south of West GERMANY. It is the capital of the state of Bavaria. Its

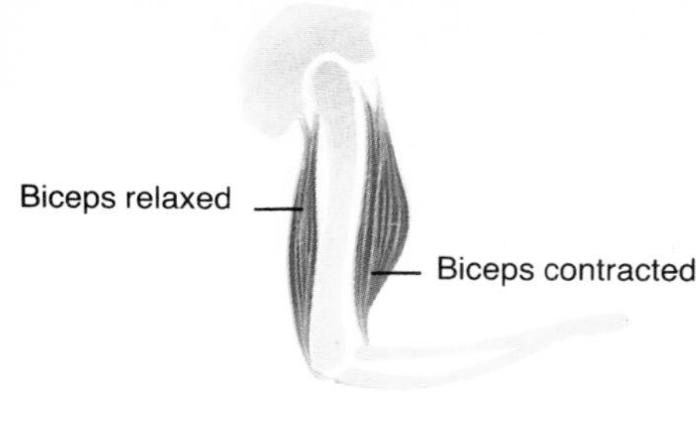

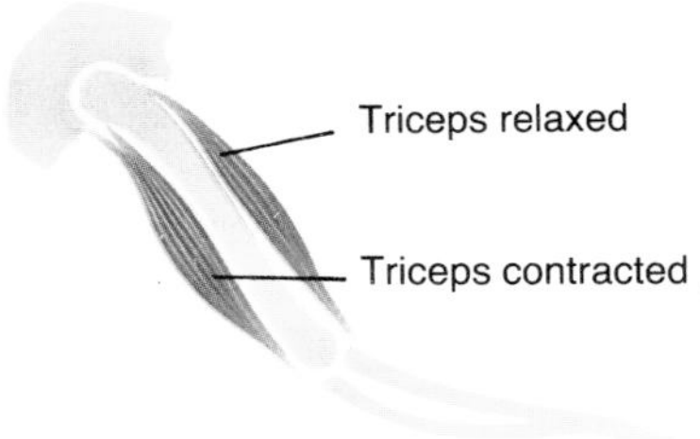

Muscles work by pulling. They are connected to the bones by tendons. The arm is bent when the biceps muscle contracts. It is straightened when the triceps contracts and the biceps relaxes.

many industries include brewing, and it is famous for its annual beer festival.

In 1923, Munich was the site of Hitler's unsuccessful attempt to take over the government of Bavaria. The city was heavily bombed by the Allies during WORLD WAR II.

You can make a spore print of a mushroom by carefully cutting the ripe caps from the stalks and laying them gills down on paper. Cover the cap for a few hours with a bowl.

mural *n.* a picture painted on a wall.
murder *n.* & *vb.* criminal killing of someone. **murderer** *n.* **murderess** *n.*
murmur *vb. n.* make a low sound; mutter. *All he could hear was the gentle murmur of the river.*

Murray-Darling System
The Murray-Darling System is an Australian river system important for irrigation and hydroelectric power. The Murray River is 1,600 miles (2,575 km) long. The Darling, a tributary, is 1,702 miles (2,740 km) long.

muscle (**mus**-*sel*) *n.* one of the fleshy parts of the body that make you move. *You make movement by tightening the right muscles.* **muscular** *adj.*
► There are two different kinds of muscle. Some work when your brain tells them to. When you pick up a chair, your brain sends signals to muscles in your arms, in your body and in your legs. All these muscles work together at the right time, and you pick up the chair. Other kinds of muscles work even when you are asleep. Your stomach muscles go on churning the food you have eaten. Your heart muscles go on pumping blood. The human body has more than 500 muscles.

museum (*mu*-**zee**-*um*) *n.* a building where interesting things from other times and places are kept and shown to the public.
► There are different kinds of museum. Some have objects connected with one subject such as nature. Others have objects from the museum's neighborhood and are of interest mostly to people who live there. Objects in museums are looked after by experts and are often kept in glass cases.

mushroom *n.* a kind of fungus that is safe to eat.
► Mushrooms grow in woods, fields and on people's lawns – almost anywhere, in fact, where it is warm enough and damp enough. Mushrooms are in the FUNGUS group of plants. They have no green coloring matter (CHLOROPHYLL), so they feed on decayed matter in the soil or on other plants. Fungi that are poisonous are often called toadstools.

music *n.* the sound made by someone who sings or who plays a musical instrument. **musical** *adj.* **musical** *n.* a play or film in which music is an essential part.
► The very earliest people probably made singing noises and beat time with pieces of wood. We know that the ancient Egyptians enjoyed their music. Paintings in the tombs of the pharaohs show musicians playing pipes, harps, and other stringed instruments. The ancient Greeks also liked stringed instruments such as the lyre. But we have no idea what this early music sounded like, because there was no way of writing it down.

By the Middle Ages, composers were writing music for groups of instruments. But it was not until the 1600s that the ORCHESTRA as we know it was born. The first orchestras were brought together by Italian composers to accompany their operas. It was at this time that violins, violas and cellos were first used.

As instruments improved, new ones were added to the orchestra. BACH and HANDEL, who were both born in 1685, used orchestras with mostly stringed instruments like the violin. But they also had flutes, oboes, trumpets and horns. Joseph HAYDN was the first man to use the orchestra as a whole. He invented the symphony. In this, all the instruments blended together so that none was more important than the others.

A new kind of music began with the German composer BEETHOVEN. He began writing music in which some of the notes clashed. This sounded rather shocking to people who listened to his music in his day. Later musicians tried all kinds of mixtures of instruments. In the 1900s new kinds of music were made by composers such as Igor Stravinsky and Arnold Schoenberg. Others since then have used tape recorders and electronic systems to produce new and off-beat sounds.

MUSICAL TERMS
allegro fast and lively.
andante at a moderate speed.
baritone low in pitch, but not as low as bass.
bass lower in pitch than a baritone.
beat the pulse of a piece of music.
chord a group of notes played at the same time.
concerto a piece of music that features a solo instrument, such as a piano, with an orchestra.
forte loud.
fortissimo very loud.
largo very slow.
movements the separate sections into which long pieces of music are divided.
octave from one note to a note of the same name, above or below.
opus a single work by a composer.
pianissimo very soft.
sonata a long work for one or two players, usually in three or four movements (sections) in contrasting rhythms and speeds.
soprano highest female voice.
symphony a large work for orchestra, usually in three or four movements.
tempo pace or speed of a piece of music.
treble generally high in pitch.
tenor high male voice.

M

But music still has three things: melody, harmony, and rhythm. The melody is the tune. Harmony is the total sound when several notes are played together. A group of notes is called a chord. Rhythm is the regular "beat" of the music.

►► **Musical Instruments** There are four kinds of musical instruments. In wind instruments, air is made to vibrate inside a tube. This vibrating air makes a musical note.

All *woodwind* instruments such as clarinets, bassoons, flutes, piccolos and recorders have holes that are covered by the fingers or by pads worked by the fingers. These holes change the length of the vibrating column of air inside the instrument. The shorter the column the higher the note. In *brass* wind instruments, the vibration of the player's lips makes the air in the instrument vibrate. By changing the pressure of the lips, the player can make different notes. Most brass instruments also have valves and pistons to change the length of the vibrating column of air, and so make different notes.

Stringed instruments work in one of two ways. The strings of the instrument are either made to vibrate by a bow, as in the violin, viola, cello and double bass; or the strings are plucked, as in the guitar, harp or banjo.

In *percussion* instruments, a tight piece of skin or a piece of wood or metal is struck to make a note. There are lots of percussion instruments – drums, cymbals, gongs, tambourines, triangles and chimes.

Electronic instruments such as the electric organ and the synthesizer make music from electronic circuits.

musician (*mu*-**zish**-*un*) *n.* a person who makes music.

musket *n.* a firearm, in use from about 1540 to about 1840. It was muzzle-loading and smooth-bored. Matchlocks, wheellocks and flintlocks were all different versions of it, as the firing mechanism was improved.

Muslim *n.* a follower of the Islamic religion.

mussel *n.* a small mollusk found mainly in the sea.

► Mussels are *bivalves*: that is, their shell is in two parts and hinged together. Like other bivalves, they feed by filtering tiny particles from the water. The best-known species is the edible mussel which lives in dense clusters on coastal rocks. Its shell is blue-black.

Mussolini, Benito

Benito Mussolini (1883–1945) was an Italian dictator. He founded the Fascist Party in 1919, was made Prime Minister in 1922, and made himself dictator from 1925. He changed many institutions, invaded Ethiopia, conquered Albania, and took Italy into WORLD WAR II on Germany's side. In 1943 he was made to resign, but was rescued by German paratroopers and set up a state in northern Italy. He was killed trying to flee the country in 1945.

Mystery plays were plays about Bible stories or the lives of the saints. They were performed outdoors in the Middle Ages.

must *auxiliary verb* (a verb which goes with and helps another verb). expressing command. *You must not walk on the grass.* expressing obligation. *I must finish this letter today.* expressing a result or deduction. *She left two hours ago. She must be nearly home by now.* expressing the obvious. *You must have heard of Henry VIII.*

mustard *n.* a hot-tasting condiment made from the mustard plant and used to flavor food; dark yellow color.

mutilate *vb.* injure, damage, disfigure.

mutiny *n.* uprising, revolt, especially by members of armed forces.

mutter *vb.* speak in a low tone, under your breath; murmur.

mutton *n.* the meat of a sheep.

muzzle 1. *n.* open end of a gun barrel. 2. *n.* animal's snout 3. *vb.* to restrain from expression.

Mycenaean Civilization

The Mycenaean Civilization was the first civilization of ancient GREECE, named after one of its great palaces at Mycenae. It was a society of warrior princes, living by trade and piracy, and speaking a form of Greek. It had links with the Minoan civilization of Crete, and flourished in about 1600–1200 B.C., but was destroyed by invaders soon after this.

mystery *n.* something that is difficult to explain or understand. **mysterious** *adj.*

myth *n.* an old story about imaginary people.

N

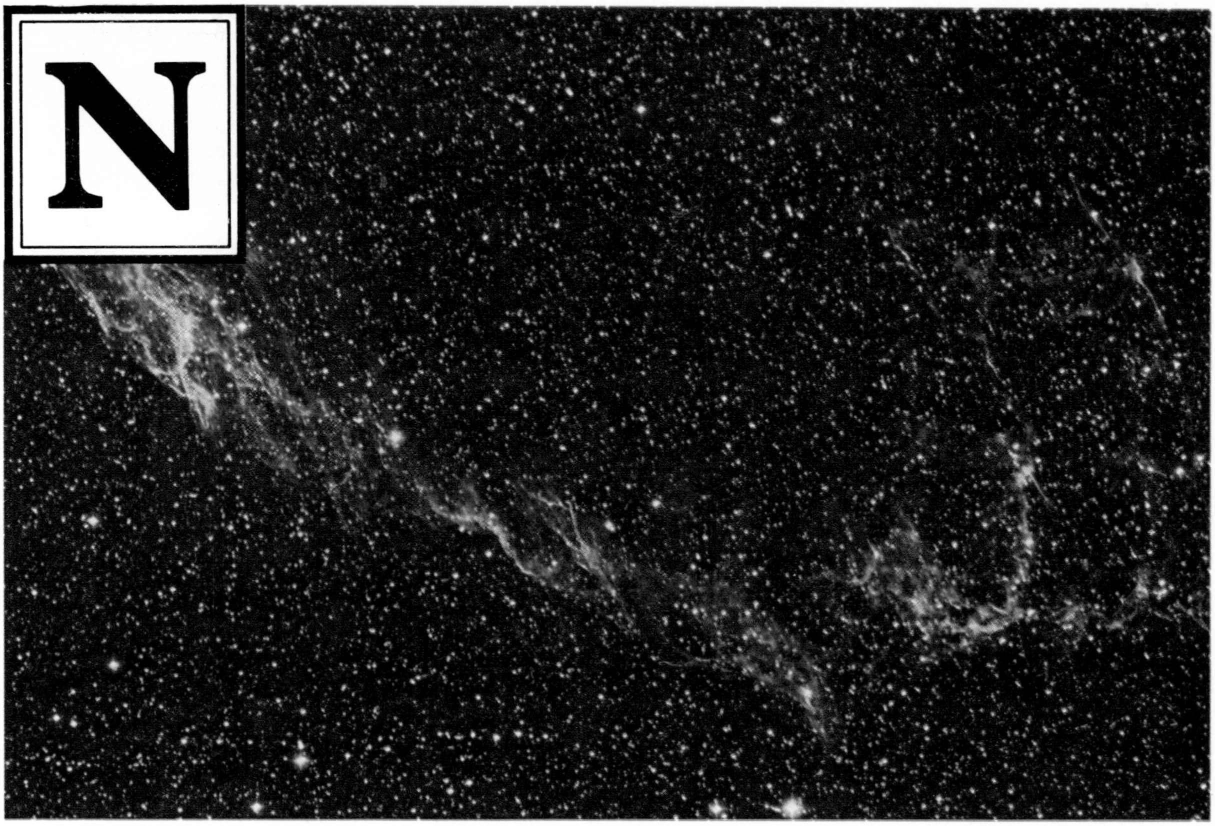

The night sky.

nag 1. *n.* a horse, usually small and of poor quality. 2. *vb.* worry and find fault with constantly; scold. **nagging** *adj.*

nail 1. *n.* thin piece of metal with a point at one end and a flat head at the other, used to fasten things together. *vb.* fasten with nails. 2. *n.* the hard layer over the outer tip of a finger or toe.

► Nails and claws are made of hard skin, like animals' horns. They grow at the end of toes and fingers. When they are broad and flat they are called nails, but if they are sharp and pointed they are claws. Human nails are of little use. But birds, mammals and reptiles use their claws to attack and to defend themselves.

A close look at an animal's claws will tell you about its way of life. Cats and birds of prey have very sharp claws. They are hooked for holding onto and tearing prey. ANTEATERS have long, strong, curved claws for tearing termites' nests apart.

naked *adj.* bare, without any clothes on; unprotected (eye).

name *n.* the word which we use for a person, animal or thing. *vb.* give a name to.

► Most people have more than one name. A first name is a personal name chosen by our parents. Our last name, or surname, is a family name. It can often tell us something about our ancestors. The names "Smith" and "Shepherd", for example, are the names of jobs. Some people have names of places as surnames, such as "Bedford". Other surnames just add "son" to the father's name, such as "Jackson" or "Johnson."

namely *adv.* that is to say.

namesake *n.* a person of the same name.

Namibia (Namibian)
Namibia is also called South West Africa. It is ruled by SOUTH AFRICA. Much of the country consists of desert (the Namib) and semi-desert (the Kalahari). The main activity is raising cattle and other livestock. Diamonds and other minerals are mined. The area was a German colony (German South West Africa) until WORLD WAR I. The UNITED NATIONS and South Africa are in dispute about the status of Namibia. A guerrilla war, begun in 1966, continued into the 1980s.
AREA: 318,278 SQ. MILES (824,292 SQ. KM)
POPULATION: 1,066,000
CAPITAL: WINDHOEK
CURRENCY: RAND
OFFICIAL LANGUAGES: AFRIKAANS, ENGLISH

nanny *n.* a child's nurse.

nanny goat *n.* a female goat.

Nansen, Fridtjof
Fridtjof Nansen (1861–1930) was a Norwegian explorer, zoologist and statesman. He made the first crossing (from east to west) of GREENLAND. He next tried to reach the North Pole. Nansen let his ship, the *Fram*, freeze in the ice, and drifted with it. He then set out for the Pole on skis and dog sleds. Although he did not reach the Pole, he got farther north than anybody before him.

Later Nansen was the Norwegian ambassador to London. He won the 1922 NOBEL Peace Prize for his humanitarian work during the aftermath of WORLD WAR I.

nap *n.* & *vb.* (take) a short sleep.

naphtha *n.* a highly flammable oil.

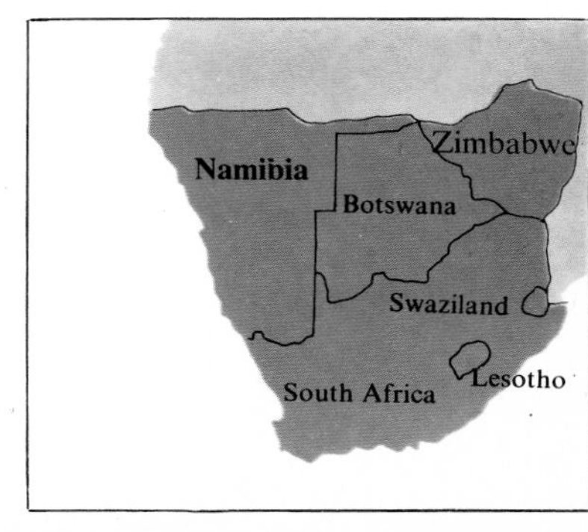

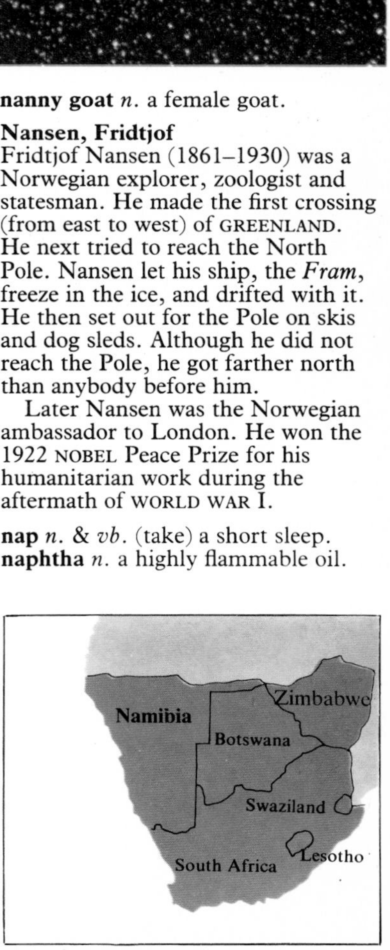

napkin *n.* a cloth for wiping fingers and lips and for protecting clothes at meals.

Naples (Neapolitan)
Naples is a major port in southern central ITALY. Overlooking the Bay of Naples, it is dominated by Mt. Vesuvius. Naples was founded in about 600 B.C. by the Greeks. Subsequently it came under Roman rule. It was later the capital of the Kingdom of the Two Sicilies (Sicily and Naples). Naples became part of Italy in 1861.

Napoleon Bonaparte
In 1789 the people of FRANCE rebelled against the unjust rule of their king and his nobles. This revolution was supported by a young man who had been born in the island of Corsica 20 years before. His name was Napoleon Bonaparte (1769–1821).

Napoleon Bonaparte

Napoleon went to the leading military school in Paris, and by 1792 he was a captain of artillery. Three years later he saved France by crushing a royalist rebellion in Paris. Soon Napoleon was head of the French army and won victories in Italy, Belgium and Austria. In 1804 he crowned himself emperor of France in the presence of the Pope. Then he crowned his wife, Josephine.

But Napoleon could not defeat Britain at sea. He tried to stop all countries from trading with England, but Russia would not cooperate. So Napoleon took a great army into Russia in the winter of 1812. This campaign ended in disaster. His troops were defeated by bitter weather.

After further defeats, Napoleon was forced to resign and was exiled to the island of Elba, off the coast of Italy. He returned to France in 1815, and marched his army into Belgium. In June he was finally beaten by the British under WELLINGTON and the Prussians under Blücher. He was made prisoner by the British on the lonely Atlantic island of St. Helena, where he died in 1821.

Napoleon was a small man. His soldiers adored him and called him "the little corporal." His speedy rise to power was helped by his first wife, the beautiful Josephine. Napoleon drew up a new French code of law. Many of his laws are still in force today.

narcissus *n.* plant similar to a daffodil; name of a mythological Greek youth who fell in love with his own reflected image and was turned into a flower.
narrate (**nare**-*rate*) *vb.* relate, give an account of. **narrative** *n.* story. **narrator** *n.* person who tells a story.
narrow *adj.* not wide, small in width; intolerant (**narrow-minded**).
narwhal *n.* a small whale, about 17 feet long, found in the Arctic Ocean. Narwhals swim together in great schools and feed mainly on cuttlefish and squid.
nasal *adj.* of the nose.
nasturtium (na-**stir**-*shum*) *n.* garden climbing plant with orange, red, or yellow flowers.
nasty *adj.* unpleasant; not nice; spiteful.

Natal
Natal is SOUTH AFRICA's smallest province. Situated on the east coast, its capital is Pietermaritzburg. The main activity is farming, but industry is also important. The Republic of Natal was established in 1838 by the Boers (Dutch settlers). It became a British colony in 1843, and joined the Union of South Africa in 1910.

nation (**nay**-*shun*) *n.* a country and the people who live in it.
national (**nash**-*u-nal*) *adj.* belonging to one country. *The national flag of the United States is the Stars and Stripes.* **nationality** *n. He has British nationality.*
national anthem *n.* official hymn or song of a nation.
nationalist *n.* a person who wants independence for his or her country or province.
nationalize *vb.* transfer industry, etc., from private ownership to control by the state.
national parks *pl. n.* special areas of land that are set aside and protected by governments.
► National Parks are usually chosen for their scenic beauty, wildlife and plant life. People can enjoy national parks by visiting them, but there are strict laws regulating hunting, fishing, building, mining, or lumbering.

The idea for national parks came when people began to realize that population growth was threatening wild areas and their plant and animal life. In many countries, over the centuries, vast areas of forest have been cut down to make more farmland, and the creatures that lived in these forests disappeared. In the United States, where land once seemed endless, settlement of the West led to the near-extinction of the BISON, shot in large numbers for their skins, meat, and just for sport. All over the world farmers killed animals that threatened their crops or livestock. Other animals died because the plants they fed on were cut down or burned to make room for crops.

A few people realized the danger as early as the 1540s, when an area where hunting was forbidden was set up in Switzerland. But widespread interest in conservation did not really begin until the 1800s. In the United States, the first national park was established in 1872. This was Yellowstone National Park, which covers 3,471 sq. miles (8,990 sq. km), most of them in WYOMING. Yellowstone is now only one of over 30 national parks. They are run by the National Park Service, which makes sure that the laws regarding the parks are obeyed, and does all it can to prevent forest fires and pollution of lakes and streams, and to protect animal and plant life in the parks.

Africa has many great parks, including the 8,000 sq. mile (20,000 sq. km) Kruger National Park in South Africa. There, visitors can see and photograph elephants, lions and many other animals roaming freely in their natural surroundings. Some Australian parks protect rare plants and such animals as the koala. A large park in New Zealand was established to prevent the notornis, a flightless bird, from becoming extinct. An Indonesian national park contains the last few surviving Java rhinoceroses.

native *n.* a person who was born in a particular place. *Angus is a native of Scotland.*
nativity *n.* being born; a birthday. *A nativity play is about the birth of Jesus.*

NATO
The North Atlantic Treaty Organization was founded in 1949. It links the countries of North America and Western Europe in a mutual defense pact, so an attack on one is an attack on all. The headquarters are in Paris, but the United States contributes most of the pact's armed forces.

natural *adj.* made by nature, not by people or machines.
natural gas *n.* a gas which occurs naturally underground and does not have to be manufactured.
► Natural gas is usually found in OIL fields, but is sometimes found on its own. When there is only a little natural gas in an oil field, it is burned off. If there is plenty, it is piped away and used for cooking, heating and producing ELECTRICITY. Today, natural gas is an important fuel.
Natural gas is found in large quantities in Russia, in Texas and Louisiana in the United States, and in the NORTH SEA oil fields. Half the world's supply of natural gas is used by the United States.

naturalist *n.* student of nature.
naturally *adv.* of course; as might be expected; without putting on airs; plain.
nature *n.* 1. the whole universe and all its life. *Nature includes everything that is not made by people or machines.* 2. essential character or quality of a person or thing. *It was not in her nature to be unkind.*
naughty *adj.* badly-behaved, wicked (usually used of children).
nausea (**naw**-*zee-ah*) *n.* urge to vomit; extreme disgust. **nauseous** *adj.* disgusting.
nautical *adj.* concerned with ships, sailors and navigation.
nautilus *n.* a sea animal with a soft body inside a hard, spiral shell. The shell is lined with a shiny substance called mother-of-pearl.
nave *n.* the main part of the church from the front porch to the altar.
navel *n.* the "belly button," a depression in the stomach left after the umbilical cord is cut.
navigate *vb.* find the way for a ship or aircraft.
navigation *n.* working out the correct route for a ship, aircraft, etc.
► Navigation at sea was originally based on watching the positions of the sun, moon and stars. Navigational aids were developed in the Middle Ages and new inventions and improvements have continued since then: the COMPASS, astrolabe, quadrant, SEXTANT, speed log, CHRONOMETER, charts and BUOYS. Today, RADIO, RADAR and other electronic aids play a big part, and in air navigation these are all-important. Space navigation is based on star observations backed by COMPUTER analysis.

navy *n.* a country's warships and all the people who sail in them. **naval** *adj.* concerning the navy and ships.

Neanderthal Man
A primitive type of human who lived 100,000 to 30,000 years ago, during the Paleolithic period. Its remains were first discovered in 1856. It was more apelike than a modern human; short and rather stooping, with very strong arms and legs, heavy brows and a low forehead. But it did use primitive flint tools.

near *adv.* & *prep.* not far in time or distance. *Tom stood near the door.*
nearly *adv.* almost. *You nearly missed the bus.*
neat *adj.* tidy, having everything in the right place.

Nebraska (*abbrev.* **Nebr.**)
Nebraska lies in the heart of the Great Plains in the center of the United States. It is one of America's great farming states. Omaha, Nebraska's largest city, is the nation's biggest meat-packing center and the second-largest cattle market in the world.
Nebraska formed part of the Louisiana Purchase of 1803. The Oregon Trail brought settlers to Nebraska, where conflict soon arose with the Sioux, Arapaho and Cheyenne Indians, who saw their hunting grounds gradually disappearing.
Nebraska became the 37th state in 1867. The capital is Lincoln.

Nebuchadnezzar
King of BABYLONIA (reigned 605–562 B.C.). He defeated the Egyptians, brought Palestine and Syria into his empire, and took many captive Jews to Babylon after they had attempted to revolt.

necessary *adv.* that which has to be done. *It is necessary to have a license to drive a car.* **necessity** *n.* something that is needed, indispensable thing.
neck *n.* the narrow part of the body between the head and the shoulders.
necklace (**neck**-*lus*) *n.* a string of beads or other ornaments worn around the neck.
nectar *n.* a sweet liquid in flowers that is collected by bees.
nectarine *n.* a type of peach. Nectarines taste like peaches but they are smaller and have a smooth skin instead of a fuzzy one.
need *vb.* require; want something urgently. *She's been working very hard and needs a vacation. n.* a want or requirement.
needle *n.* 1. a pointed instrument used for sewing or knitting. 2. a pointer in a meter or a compass. 3. leaf of fir or pine.
needlework *n.* sewing, embroidery, etc.
negative 1. *adj.* expressing denial or refusal. *He gave a negative answer by which he means no.* the opposite of positive. 2. *n.* photographic image in which light areas are dark and dark areas are light.
neglect *vb.* give little care to. *If you neglect your garden, it will become full of weeds.* **negligence** *n.*
negotiate *vb.* discuss so as to reach an agreement. *The union is negotiating with the management over working hours.* deal with, manage. **negotiation** *n.*
Negress *n.* a Negro woman or girl.
Negro *n.* a person who belongs to the black-skinned race, especially one (originating) from Africa.

Nehru, Jawaharlal
Nehru (1889–1964) was an Indian statesman. He joined GANDHI's Nationalist Movement against British rule, and was imprisoned several times. After independence in 1947, Nehru became prime minister. His daughter, Indira Gandhi became prime minister two years after his death. She was assassinated in 1984.

neigh *n.* & *vb.* a noise made by a horse.
neighbor (**nay**-*ber*) *n.* someone who lives near you.
neighborhood *n.* the area around the place where you live. **neighborly** *adj.* like a good neighbor, friendly.
neither *adj.* & *pron.* not one nor the other.

Horatio Nelson.

Nelson, Horatio
Horatio Nelson (1758–1805) was a British admiral at the time when Britain was at war with the French, led by NAPOLEON BONAPARTE.
Nelson joined the navy when he was 12 and was captain of a frigate by the time he was 20. He was made a rear-admiral in 1797. By then he had already lost an eye in battle. Soon he lost an arm too.
In 1798 he led his ships to victory against the French at Alexandria in Egypt.
Nelson's most famous battle was his last. It was fought against a French fleet led by Admiral Villeneuve. For nearly 10 months in 1805, Nelson's ships chased Villeneuve's across the Atlantic and back. Then, on October 21, they met off the Cape of Trafalgar in southern Spain. Nelson was killed on board his ship, the *Victory*.

N

Before the battle Nelson sent a message to all the ships in his fleet: "England expects every man to do his duty."

Nelson River
The Nelson and Saskatchewan rivers make up an important river system in CANADA. The Saskatchewan River rises in the Rockies and flows into Lake Winnipeg; the Nelson River flows out of the same lake carrying the outflow to Hudson Bay. The total length of the river system is 1,600 miles (2,575 km).

Neolithic
The Neolithic Period, or New Stone Age, was the most recent phase of the Stone Age. Its culture was based on farming rather than on hunting or gathering.

neon *n.* a colorless gas used in light tubes (symbol – *Ne*).

Nepal (Nepalese)
Nepal is a monarchy in southern ASIA, between CHINA and INDIA. Two-thirds of the country is mountainous. It contains some of the highest mountains in the world, including Mt. EVEREST (*see also* Himalayas). Most people work on the land, but mining and industry are increasingly important. One of the peoples of Nepal are the warlike Gurkhas, who contribute a brigade to the British, and also to the Indian Army.
AREA: 54,365 SQ. MILES (140,797 SQ. KM)
POPULATION: 14,932,000
CAPITAL: KATHMANDU (KATMANDU)

CURRENCY: RUPEE
OFFICIAL LANGUAGE: NEPALI

nephew *n.* the son of your brother or sister.

Neptune (God)
Neptune was the Roman name for the Greek god Poseidon, the god of the sea. People believed that when he was angry he sent storms and floods. He carried a three-pronged spear called a trident. The Romans believed that Neptune caused earthquakes by striking the ground with his trident, and that once when he struck the ground the first horse appeared.

Neptune (Planet)
The PLANET Neptune is named after the Roman god of the sea. It is a large planet (much bigger than earth) far out in the SOLAR SYSTEM. It is about 2,793 million miles (4,493 million km) from the SUN. Only PLUTO is farther away. It takes Neptune 165 years to circle the sun. (The earth takes 365 days.)

Being so far from the sun, Neptune is a very cold place. Scientists think its atmosphere is rather like JUPITER's, which is mostly made up of the gas HYDROGEN. Neptune has two moons, Triton and Nereid.

Early astronomers were unable to see Neptune, but they knew it had to be there. They could tell there was something affecting the orbit of the nearby planet URANUS.

In 1845 two astronomers, Adams in England and Leverrier in France, used mathematics to work out where Neptune should be. Astronomers used this information the next year, and spotted Neptune.

Left: Nereid (arrowed) is a satellite of Neptune. It is only 186 miles (300 km) across and takes almost a year to go around a very elongated orbit.

Nero
Nero (A.D. 37–68) became emperor of the ROMAN EMPIRE when he was 17. In A.D. 64, Rome was nearly destroyed by fire. Nero may have started the fire himself but he blamed the Christians, many of whom he had tortured to death. He was such a wicked ruler, he was finally forced to leave Rome. He killed himself in A.D. 68.

nerve *n.* 1. a fiber that carries sensations and messages between the body and the brain. 2. boldness and self-assurance.

nervous *adj.* easily frightened, excitable, tense; also **nervy**.

► The nervous system is the system of nerves that runs throughout the body. It consists of three main parts. First there is the *central nervous system* (CNS): BRAIN, and the great bundle of nerves leading to the brain called the spinal cord. This is the part that makes decisions. (Some emergency actions, called *reflexes*, are decided in the spinal cord and not in the brain.) Second, there are the *peripheral nerves*. These take messages to the CNS from all parts of the body, and take back the orders that control the body's actions. Third, there is the *autonomic nervous system*, which is rather separate. It governs the automatic functions of the body, like the heartbeat, that are not under complete conscious control.

nest *n.* a home that a bird or other animal makes out of twigs, grass, feathers, etc., generally as a shelter for its eggs and its young. *vb.* make or have a nest.

► Many creatures, from ANTS to APES, build nests, but the most elaborate nests in the animal kingdom are those made by BIRDS. Birds build their nests in all kinds of places, ranging from the tops of tall trees to underground holes, and use all sorts of materials, such as twigs,

The emperor Nero.

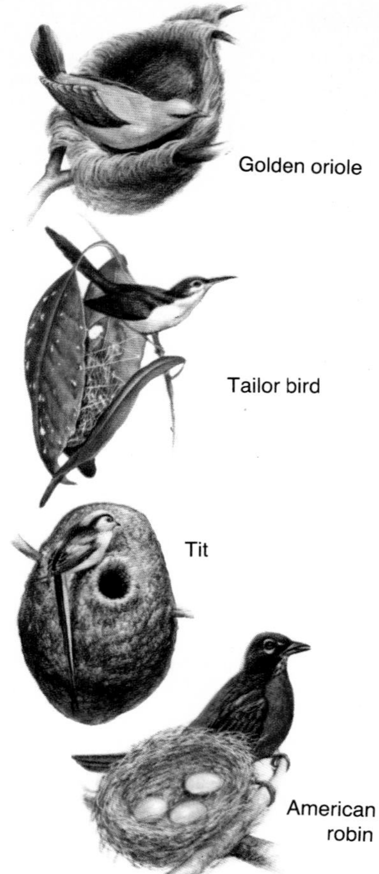

Birds' nests of different shapes.

grass, leaves, mud, moss and hair. Most nests are cup-shaped but some also have a roof to give the eggs extra protection. Birds use nests only for breeding and not as permanent homes; but some species, like storks, return every year to the same nest.

nestling *n.* a bird too young to leave the nest.
net 1. *n.* a material made of loosely woven string, thread or wire, so there are many holes between the threads. *vb.* catch or cover with a net. 2. *adj.* the price of something after discount, postal charges, etc. have been taken off. Similarly for **net weight**.

Netherlands (Dutch)
A densely populated monarchy in Western EUROPE, the Netherlands is a country which has been largely reclaimed from the sea. Nearly half of the land is below sea level. The reclaimed polders are rich farmland. Arable farming is extensive and livestock, dairy and poultry farming are especially important. But much of the nation's wealth now comes from manufacturing, although most raw materials have to be imported. The Netherlands is a member of the EUROPEAN ECONOMIC COMMUNITY.

AREA: 15,771 SQ. MILES (40,844 SQ. KM)
POPULATION: 14,324,000
CAPITAL: AMSTERDAM
SEAT OF GOVERNMENT: THE HAGUE
CURRENCY: GUILDER
OFFICIAL LANGUAGE: DUTCH

nettle 1. *n.* a common weed with stinging hairs on its leaves. 2. *vb.* irritate, provoke.
neuter (**new**-*ter*) *adj.* neither male nor female.
neutral *adj.* 1. not taking sides, especially in a war or dispute. 2. having no electrical charge.
neutron *n.* an electrically neutral atomic particle.

Nevada (*abbrev.* **Nev.**)
Nevada lies in a vast, dry area in the western United States that is mostly desert and plateau.

Nevada's farms depend heavily on irrigation, and produce sheep, cattle, hay, alfalfa seed and wheat. Mines yield copper as the major ore. By far the greatest part of Nevada's income comes from tourism. The gambling centers of Las Vegas and Reno are world famous, and Lake Tahoe, on Nevada's western border, is a popular ski resort.

Nevada became the 36th state of the U.S.A. in 1864. The state capital is Carson City.

never *adv.* not ever; at no time. *I've never seen him before.*
new *adj.* made or used for the first time; not old.

New Brunswick
New Brunswick is on the eastern coast of CANADA, just north of the U.S. border, and is one of Canada's four Atlantic provinces. It was largely settled by "Tories" – those loyal to the king of England – from the American colonies who fled to Canada after the American War of INDEPENDENCE. The province takes its name from the family name of King George III.

Most of New Brunswick is covered with forests. Timber from these forests is floated to the sea down New Brunswick's major rivers, for lumbering is one of the province's chief industries. New Brunswick's forests are also good hunting and fishing grounds, and many tourists visit the province each year.

The capital of New Brunswick is Fredericton, which lies along the St. John river in the south-central part of the province. New Brunswick became one of the original four provinces of the Dominion of Canada in 1867.

Newfoundland
Newfoundland is one of CANADA's Atlantic Provinces. It consists of the island of Newfoundland and Labrador, on the mainland. One of the world's most famous fishing areas, the Grand Banks, lies off Newfoundland.

The island of Newfoundland has a rocky coast, with many bays and deep inlets. The forests in the center of the island support a large wood-pulp and paper-making industry. Mines yield gypsum, iron ore, lead and zinc. Only a small part of the island is farmed. Labrador, on the mainland, has a colder climate; about a third of the land is covered with forests. Only about 2 percent of the province's population lives in Labrador. In the northwest lies one of the richest deposits of iron ore.

Newfoundland was Britain's oldest colony, first claimed in the 1580s. It joined Canada in 1949. The capital is St. John's.

New Guinea see **Papua New Guinea**

New Hampshire (*abbrev.* **N.H.**)
One of the New England states, New Hampshire is a small, scenic state of mountains, lakes and rivers. Its capital is Concord.

New Hampshire's soil is rocky and not suited to farming on a large scale. Instead, the state has developed a strong manufacturing industry. Factories produce leather goods, electrical equipment, and machinery.

Europeans first came to New Hampshire in the early 1600s, and permanent settlement began in 1623. The colony was originally a part of Massachusetts, but established a separate government in 1776 and was one of the original 13 states.

New Jersey (*abbrev.* **N.J.**)
New Jersey, one of the original 13 states, lies between the major cities of NEW YORK and Philadelphia, and is an important commuter base and transportation center. The capital is Trenton.

Most of New Jersey is low, flat coastal plain and is well suited to industrial development. Factories produce chemicals, machinery, food products and clothing. There are small but important farming and fishing industries.

New Jersey was settled by Europeans in the 1600s, first by the Dutch and later by the English. Because of its location, New Jersey was the scene of many important battles of the American War of INDEPENDENCE.

N

New Mexico (*abbrev.* **N.Mex.**)
New Mexico is steeped in history from its Indian and Spanish heritage. It is also in the forefront of modern America as the site of the first atomic bomb test. The state capital is Santa Fe.

New Mexico's spectacular desert landscapes are broken by high, rugged buttes (isolated steep mountains). In the north are forested mountain areas. In the river valleys, such as along the Rio Grande, fruit and vegetables are grown.

Since WORLD WAR II the state has been a leader in the field of energy research. New Mexico has nearly half of the nation's uranium reserves and large deposits of coal and natural gas. In addition, the U.S. government has financed a wide range of aerospace, nuclear, and defense projects in the state.

New Mexico was originally a Spanish colony, governed by Mexico from 1821 until the area came under U.S. control after the Mexican War. New Mexico became the 47th state in 1912.

New Orleans
City, seaport and former capital of Louisiana, it is situated on the Mississippi River about 100 miles (160 km) from the river mouth on the Gulf of Mexico. New Orleans was founded in 1718 by the French and rose to become one of the foremost cotton ports of the world. The city has been influenced by a mixed heritage that includes French, Spanish, Creole and black cultures. It is famous as a jazz center and for its annual Mardi Gras festivities, but is also an important port and industrial center.

news *n.* recent or up-to-date information; a program about recent events on TV or radio; the contents of a newspaper.

New South Wales
New South Wales has more people (over five million) than any other state in AUSTRALIA. The capital is SYDNEY, and other important cities include Newcastle and Wollongong. Sheep farming and mining (mainly at Broken Hill) are traditional occupations, but the state's prosperity is now based on manufacturing industry.

newspaper *n.* a set of printed sheets of paper containing news, and usually published either daily or weekly.

newt *n.* a lizardlike amphibian.
► Newts have similar life stories to frogs; they are born in streams and ponds, spend their adult life on land, but return to water to breed. Most species are brown with dark markings and have an orange belly with black spots.

New Testament
The New Testament forms the second part of the Christian Bible. It contains 27 books. The four Gospels (Matthew, Mark, Luke and John) tell the life story of JESUS. The New Testament also contains the Acts of the Apostles, and the Epistles (letters) of St. PAUL.

Newton, Isaac
Sir Isaac Newton (1642–1727) was an English mathematician and scientist who made some of the world's greatest discoveries. He left Cambridge University in 1665 when plague shut the University. In the 18 months before the University reopened, Newton did much of his most important work.

He invented a new kind of mathematics called calculus. Today, calculus helps designers to shape such complicated things as aircraft wings.

Newton's experiments showed that white LIGHT is a mixture of all the colors of the rainbow (the spectrum). By studying the spectrum of light from a star or other glowing object, scientists can now find out what that object is made of. Newton's studies of light also led him to build the first of all reflecting TELESCOPES.

New York City
New York City is the largest city in the United States. The city stands mainly on three islands that lie at the mouth of the Hudson River. The island of Manhattan holds the heart of New York, and many of its most famous sights. Built on Manhattan's solid rock base, some of the world's tallest skyscrapers tower above New York's streets. These include the Empire State Building, once the tallest building in the world, the Chrysler Building, and the twin towers of the World Trade Center. The area around Wall Street at the southern end of Manhattan is the home of the New York Stock Exchange and is the city's chief financial district. The UNITED NATIONS' headquarters is in New York. Fifth Avenue is a famous shopping street, and Broadway is known for its theaters. Perhaps New York's best-known sight is the Statue of Liberty, which stands on an island in New York Harbor. New York is one of the world's great business centers. Its factories produce more goods than those of any other U.S. city.

Europeans first settled there in 1624. The Dutch bought Manhattan from the Indians for a handful of cloth, beads and trinkets. The Dutch named their settlement New Amsterdam. Later, the English seized it and renamed the colony New York in honor of the Duke of York.

New York State (*abbrev.* **N.Y.**)
New York State is situated between the Atlantic coast and the Great Lakes and, with the busiest port in the United States, is a national leader in industry, finance, fashion, art and communication. In terms of population, New York is second only to California, a state with over three times its area.

In the north of New York are the wild and heavily wooded Adirondack Mountains. South of the mountains lie the Mohawk River Valley and good pasture land that supports dairy farming.

New York was first settled by the Dutch in the 1600s, when it was called New Netherlands. When the English took over in 1664, they renamed the colony New York after the Duke of York, the king's brother. New York was the scene of many battles during the American War of INDEPENDENCE. The state capital is Albany.

New Zealand
New Zealand is an independent monarchy within the Commonwealth of Nations. It lies in the South Pacific Ocean and consists of two main islands: North Island and South Island, together with various smaller islands. The most densely populated part of New Zealand is North Island, a land of rolling hills and low mountains, including three active volcanoes. Geothermal steam is used to generate electricity. South Island is mountainous, with a mostly rugged coastline.

The MAORIS, who now form 8 percent of the population, reached New Zealand in the 1300s. In 1839 a settlement was established at what is now Wellington, by the British New Zealand Company. New Zealand became a British colony in 1841. Land disputes between the settlers and the Maoris led to fighting, but after a gold rush in 1861, immigration increased quickly.

Today, 91 percent of the people are of European, mostly British, origin. In 1907 New Zealand became a self-governing dominion in the British Empire.

The people now enjoy a high standard of living. Sheep and cattle farming are the main industries and

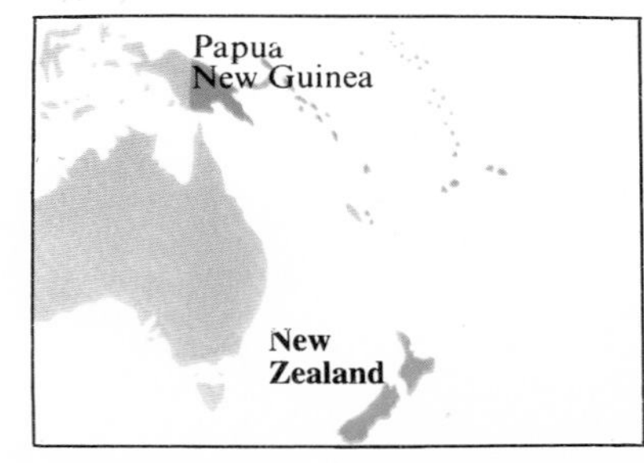

butter, cheese, meat and wool dominate the exports. But manufacturing is increasing quickly in the cities, including AUCKLAND, WELLINGTON, DUNEDIN and CHRISTCHURCH.
AREA: 103,742 SQ. MILES (268,676 SQ. KM)
POPULATION: 3,400,000
CAPITAL: WELLINGTON
CURRENCY: NEW ZEALAND DOLLAR
OFFICIAL LANGUAGE: ENGLISH

next 1. *adj.* nearby. *They live next to us.* 2. *adv.* following. *What would you like to do next?*

Niagara Falls
Niagara Falls is a large waterfall on the Niagara River, which forms part of the border between Canada and New York State. Water from most of the Great Lakes flows through this river. Each minute about 450,000 tons of water plunges about 165 feet (50 meters) from a cliff into a gorge.

Niagara Falls is divided by an island into two parts, the Horseshoe, or Canadian, Falls, and the American Falls.

A cross-section of Niagara Falls. The rock at the top is hard dolomite. The lower layers are shales, limestones and sandstones. The softer shales are gradually undercut as the water lashes against them.

nib *n.* the point of a pen.
nibble *vb.* eat in very small bites. *n.* a small bite.

Nicaragua (Nicaraguan)
Nicaragua is a republic in CENTRAL AMERICA. In the center is a highland region with active VOLCANOES. In the Pacific coastal lowlands are two huge lakes, Managua and Nicaragua. The climate is hot and humid. The main activities are farming and mining for gold, silver and copper. Formerly a Spanish colony, Nicaragua became independent in 1821.

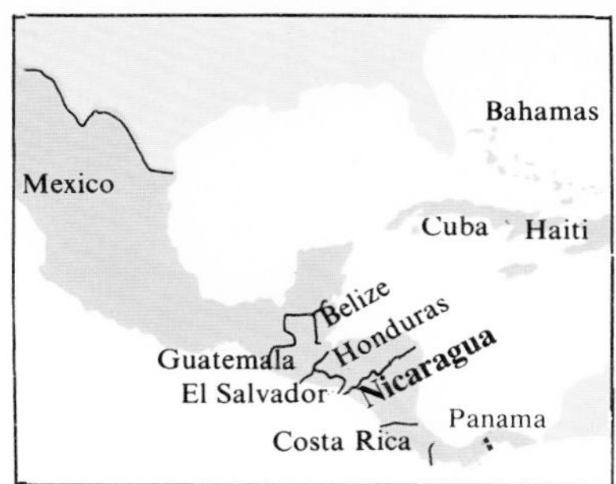

AREA: 50,196 SQ. MILES (130,000 SQ. KM)
POPULATION: 2,851,000
CAPITAL: MANAGUA
CURRENCY: CORDOBA
OFFICIAL LANGUAGE: SPANISH

nice *adj.* good or pleasant. *Have a nice time.*
nick 1. *n.* notch. 2. *n.* final critical moment. *In the nick of time.* 3. *v.* notch, cut.
nickel 1. *n.* a tough, hard, silvery-white metal element widely used in the form of plating and in alloys. It is electroplated onto metals such as steel to protect them from corrosion, and is added, with chromium, to steel to make it stainless. 2. *n.* a U.S. coin worth five cents.
nickname *n.* an extra name given to a person or place. *We call Mr. Baker by his nickname, Floury.*
niece (rhymes with *fleece*) *n.* the daughter of your brother or sister.

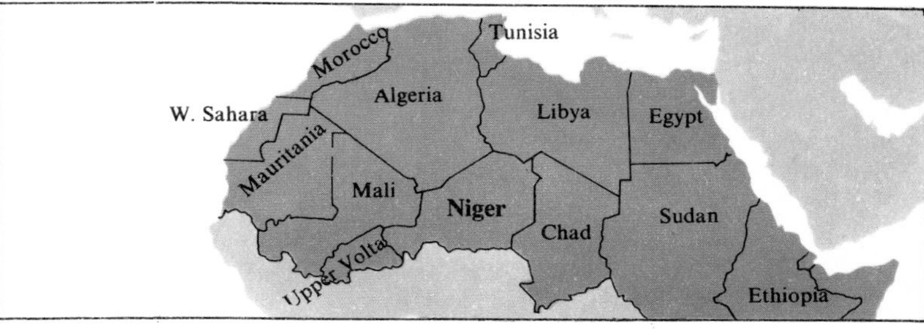

Niger (Country)
Niger is a landlocked republic in Northcentral AFRICA. It is named after the NIGER River, which flows through the southwest. In the north, Tuareg nomads live in the Sahara. Most of the people in the south are black farmers. Mining, particularly of uranium, is important. Niger was once a French colony and is one of the world's poorest countries. It gained full independence in 1960.
AREA: 489,218 SQ. MILES (1,267,000 SQ. KM)
POPULATION: 5,600,000
CAPITAL: NIAMEY
CURRENCY: FRANC
OFFICIAL LANGUAGE: FRENCH

Niger (River)
The Niger is a major river in AFRICA. It rises in GUINEA near the border with SIERRA LEONE. It then flows through MALI and NIGER and forms the border with BENIN before entering NIGERIA. It enters the sea in the Gulf of Guinea in a vast DELTA. The Niger is 2,580 miles (4,160 km) in length.

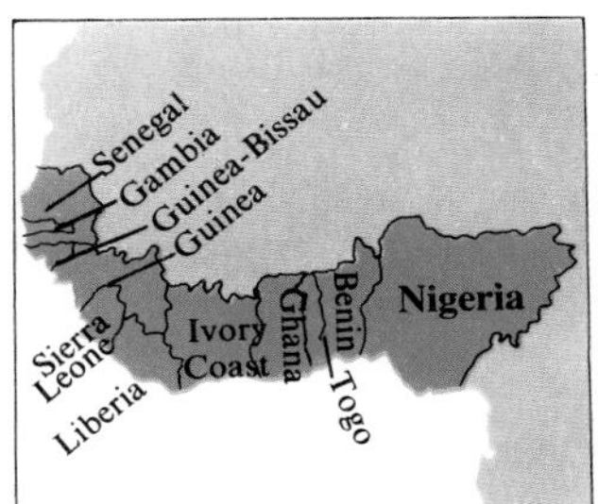

Nigeria (Nigerian)
This nation in West AFRICA is named after the NIGER River that flows through it to the Atlantic Ocean. Nigeria has more people than any other nation in Africa.

All Nigeria is hot. Dry grass and scrubby trees are scattered across much of the country. But swamps and forests line the coasts.

The four main groups of people are the Hausa and Fulani of the north, the Yoruba and Ibo of the southeast. The Yoruba and Ibo are Negro people, but the Muslim Hausa and Fulani are Hamitic, a brown-skinned people with narrow noses and thin lips.

About half the people are Muslims, and about a quarter are Christians.

Farming is Nigeria's chief industry. Important crops include cocoa, groundnuts (peanuts), palm kernels and palm oil. Tin and columbite are mined. Nigeria is one of Africa's leading oil producers.

Nigeria was the home of several African civilizations, which produced some of the finest African art. British influence in Nigeria began in the 1700s. From 1906, Britain ruled the entire country.

N

Nigeria gained independence in 1960 and became a republic in 1963.
AREA: 356,668 SQ. MILES (923,768 SQ. KM)
POPULATION: 88,847,000
CAPITAL: LAGOS
CURRENCY: NAIRA
OFFICIAL LANGUAGE: ENGLISH

night *n.* the time between evening and morning, when it is dark. **nightly** *adj.* happening or recurring every night.
nightingale *n.* a bird famous for its beautiful song which is usually heard in the late evening or early morning. Nightingales live in damp shady woodlands and feed on insects.

Nightingale, Florence
Florence Nightingale (1820–1910) founded modern NURSING. She was wealthy and could have had an easy life, but instead she chose to work for the sick. In those days countless patients died in dirty hospitals run by untrained nurses. Florence Nightingale trained as a nurse, and ran a women's hospital in London.
In 1854 she took 38 nurses to Turkey to tend British soldiers wounded in the CRIMEAN WAR. Her hospital was a dirty barracks that lacked food, medicines and bedding. She cleaned it up, found supplies, and gave the wounded every care she could and so saved hundreds of lives.

nightmare *n.* a frightening dream.
nil *n.* nothing, zero.

Nile
The Nile River in Africa may be the longest river on earth. (Some people think that the AMAZON is longer.) The Nile was once shown to measure 4,145 miles (6,670 km). It rises in BURUNDI in central Africa and flows north through EGYPT into the Mediterranean Sea. It is very important to the farmers who live around it.

nimble *adj.* quick-moving; agile.
nip *vb.* pinch like a crab.
nit *n.* the egg of the louse found in the hair.
nitrogen *n.* a colorless, tasteless gas. It is an element (symbol – *N*).
► The earth's ATMOSPHERE is nearly four-fifths nitrogen. It is essential to life for plants and animals. Plants get their nitrogen from the soil. These, in turn, get their nitrogen from the air or from fertilizers and decaying matter. Animals obtain nitrogen by eating plants or by eating other animals. The way in which nitrogen passes from the soil to plants and animals, and then back to the soil again, is an important part of the balance of nature called the *nitrogen cycle*. Nitrogen is used for making ammonia, fertilizers, explosives and plastics.

Noah
Noah was a patriarch of the Old Testament chosen by God to preserve the human race and animals from the great flood with which God proposed to drown the world as punishment for its wickedness. Noah built an ark in which he installed his family and representatives of every kind of animal found on earth.

Nobel Prizes
Alfred Nobel (1833–96) a Swedish chemist and millionaire, donated funds in his will for a series of annual awards. These awards are known as the Nobel Prizes. The five original prizes were for chemistry, physics, medicine, literature and peace. They have been awarded annually on December 10, since 1901, to individuals of any nationality, for outstanding work in these areas. A prize for economics was added in 1968. They are regarded as the highest awards in their fields.

noble *adj.* (or **nobleman** *n.*) a man of high rank, such as a duke.
nobody *n.* no one; no person. *There's nobody here.*
nocturnal *adj.* belonging to, or active in, the night.
nod *vb.* & *n.* bow the head slightly; be drowsy.
noise *n.* a sound (usually disagreeable or loud). *Don't make so much noise.* **noisy** *adj.* making a lot of noise.

Nolan, Sydney
Australian artist (1917–). His paintings show different aspects of Australian life: the deserts and its explorers and inhabitants – especially the bandit Ned Kelly.

nomad *n.* a member of a group of people who wander from place to place.
► Many people live in lands too dry to farm. Such people keep herds of animals and sleep in tents. They travel to find fresh pasture for their animals. Many nomads still live in or near the great deserts of Africa and Asia.

non- *prefix* meaning not. The sense of words with the prefix should be clear when the meaning of the main word is known, e.g. **nonsmoker** a person who does not smoke. **nonstop** without stopping.
nonsense *n.* foolish talk or behavior.
noon *n.* midday; twelve o'clock in the daytime.
noose *n.* a loop of rope. *The noose becomes tighter when one end of the rope is pulled. vb.* catch with a noose, make a noose in.
nor *conj.* and not, not either.
Nordic *adj.* of or relating to tall, blond Germanic people of northern Europe.

Norfolk
Norfolk is a seaport city and important naval base in southeastern Virginia. It is the headquarters for the Atlantic Fleet, the Second Fleet and for NATO's Supreme Allied Command, Atlantic. The city was settled in 1680. Nearby Hampton Roads was the scene of the famous battle between the ironclads *Monitor* and *Merrimack* in 1862.

norm *n.* standard of quality, etc.
normal *adj.* regular, as expected. *The normal temperature of the human body is 98.6° F.*

Norman Conquest
William of Normandy, claiming to be the rightful heir to the throne, invaded England in 1066 and defeated King Harold at the Battle of Hastings. He became William I or WILLIAM THE CONQUEROR (1066–87). Normans became the ruling class.

Normans *n. pl.* The Normans were the VIKINGS (Norsemen) who invaded northwest France and adopted French language and customs.
► The Norman rule over Normandy was acknowledged by the French king in A.D. 911. From there, in the 1000s and 1100s, they conquered England, parts of Wales and Ireland, southern Italy, Sicily and Malta. They also took an important part in the CRUSADES. Gradually they became absorbed through intermarriage with local populations, and they ceased to be a separate people after the 1200s.

Norse *n.* & *adj.* (language) of ancient Scandinavia, especially Norway.
► **Norse myths** are old North European tales about gods and heroes of long ago.
One story tells how the world was made from the body of the first giant, who was killed by three of the first god's grandsons. Another story tells how the god Odin and two other gods made the first man from an ash tree and the first woman from an elm. A third tale tells how the jealous god Loki killed Odin's son Balder the beautiful. In this tale, Balder stands for summer and his death stands for the start of winter.
Norse myths said that the gods lived in Asgard, a home in the sky, but they travelled down a rainbow to visit the earth.

north *n.* one of the points of the compass. *When you face the sunrise, north is on your left.*

North America
North America stretches north from tropical PANAMA to the cold ARCTIC Ocean, and east from the PACIFIC Ocean to the ATLANTIC Ocean. Only ASIA is larger than this continent.
North America has the world's largest island (GREENLAND), and the

NORTH AMERICA
0 500 1,000 miles
0 500 1,000 1,500 kilometers
Capital Cities
Nome
Yukon
Alaska
Fairbanks
Anchorage
Mackenzie
Great Bear L.
Whitehorse
Juneau
Great Slave L.
Greenland
Baffin Is
Hudson Bay
Churchill
CANADA
ROCKY MOUNTAINS
Edmonton
Vancouver
Calgary
Seattle
L. Winnipeg
Regina
Winnipeg
Portland
PACIFIC OCEAN
Missouri
Quebec
Halifax
L. Superior
Montreal
Ottawa
St Lawrence
Minneapolis
St Paul
L. Michigan
L. Huron
Toronto
L. Ontario
Boston
San Francisco
Salt Lake City
Milwaukee
Detroit
L. Erie
New York
Cleveland
Philadelphia
USA
Chicago
Pittsburgh
Baltimore
Denver
Indianapolis
Columbus
Washington DC
Las Vegas
Colorado
Kansas City
Los Angeles
St Louis
Santa Fe
San Diego
Phoenix
Albuquerque
Bermuda
Memphis
Red
Tucson
Mississippi
Atlanta
El Paso
Dallas
ATLANTIC OCEAN
SIERRA MADRE
Jacksonville
G. of California
San Antonio
Houston
New Orleans
Rio Grande
Gulf of Mexico
Miami
Nassau
Monterrey
BAHAMAS
MEXICO
Havana
CUBA
DOMINICAN REPUBLIC
San Juan
HAITI
Guadalajara
Port-au-Prince
Santo Domingo
PUERTO RICO
Mexico City
Kingston
JAMAICA
BARBADOS
Belmopan
BELIZE
Caribbean Sea
GUATEMALA
HONDURAS
Port-of-Spain
Guatemala City
Tegucigalpa
TRINIDAD & TOBAGO
San Salvador
EL SALVADOR
NICARAGUA
Managua
COSTA RICA
Panama Canal Zone
San José
Panama
PANAMA

N

largest freshwater lake (Lake Superior). It contains the second largest country (CANADA), the second longest mountain range (the ROCKY MOUNTAINS), and the third longest river (the MISSISSIPPI River). North America's natural wonders include NIAGARA FALLS and the GRAND CANYON (the largest gorge on land).

The cold north has long, dark, frozen winters. No trees grow here. Farther south stand huge evergreen forests. Grasslands covered most of the plains in the middle of the continent until people plowed them up. Cactuses thrive in the deserts of the southwest. Tropical trees grow quickly in the hot, wet forests of the south.

Peoples from all over the world have made their homes in North America. First came the ancestors of the AMERICAN INDIANS and ESKIMOS. Later came Europeans, who brought black slaves from Africa. Most North Americans speak English, French or Spanish, and are Christians. They live in more than 30 nations. The United States and Canada are large, powerful and rich. But many of the nations of Central America and the WEST INDIES are small and poor.

Only one person in every ten people in the world lives in North America. Yet North Americans make half the manufactured goods on earth. This is because North America's farms and mines produce huge amounts of food and minerals to feed the workers and supply materials for their factory machines.

North Carolina (*abbrev.* **N.C.**)
North Carolina is one of the South Atlantic States and one of the original 13 states of the Union. It was the site of the first English colony in the New World (Roanoke, 1585). The Wright Brothers' first powered air flight took place at Kitty Hawk, North Carolina, in 1903.

North Carolina is a farming state. It grows more tobacco than any other. Cotton, peanuts, soybeans and corn are also grown, and livestock is important. The making of textiles is the main North Carolina industry. North Carolina also ranks first in the nation as a producer of household furniture.

In the west of North Carolina stand the Blue Ridge and Smoky Mountains.

The largest cities are Charlotte, Greensboro, Winston-Salem and Raleigh, the capital.

North Dakota (*abbrev.* **N.Dak.**)
North Dakota is a farming state on the Canadian border. To the south is South Dakota. The largest city is Fargo, and Bismarck is the capital.

North Dakota is an important producer of wheat, barley, flax and sunflower seed. The most fertile land is found in the eastern part of the state; land in the west is more suitable for grazing.

The Badlands of North Dakota lie in the southwest. The area was named Badlands by the pioneers, who found them very difficult to cross. Much of this land is bare and dry. But the scenery of the Badlands is startling, with many strange buttes (isolated hills with steep sides) standing up from the plains.

North Dakota became a state in 1889.

Northern Ireland see Great Britain, Ireland, Ulster.

Northern Territory
The Northern Territory is a large area in the north of AUSTRALIA. It has a tropical climate, and much of the center and south consists of desert. Stock breeding is encouraged by the government, but most of the Territory is too dry to grow crops. Mining of iron ore, bauxite and other materials is important. The chief towns are ALICE SPRINGS in the south, and DARWIN, the capital and only seaport, in the north.

North Pole
The North Pole is the place farthest north on earth. Its LATITUDE is 90° north. The North Pole is the northern end of the earth's axis. This is an imaginary line around which the earth spins, like a wheel spinning around its axle.

The North Pole lies in the middle of the Arctic Ocean, the surface of which is always frozen. The sun does not rise in winter or set in summer.

The first person to reach the North Pole was the American Robert E. PEARY . He arrived in 1909 with sledges pulled by dogs.

North Sea
This part of the ATLANTIC OCEAN separates Great Britain from Scandinavia and other northern parts of mainland Europe. The North Sea is relatively shallow. Over the Dogger Bank, a submerged plateau between England and Denmark, depths of less than 60 feet (18 meters) occur. Winter storms often make this sea dangerous for ships.

The North Sea is an important waterway. The sea gives access to some of the world's largest and busiest ports, including London, Amsterdam, Rotterdam, Hamburg and Copenhagen. Its waters are rich in fish, and the seabed holds oil and gas.

North Star
The North Star, or Polaris, is the bright pole star that marks the North Pole. It is the brightest star in the constellation Ursa Minor – the Little Bear or Little Dipper. It can be found by continuing the imaginary line drawn through the two stars in the bowl of the Big Dipper.

Northwest Passage
This was a longed-for sea route from Europe to Asia around the top of North America. Explorers took nearly 400 years to find it. This was because ice hindered ships trying to sail through the ARCTIC Ocean north of Canada.

In 1576 Sir Martin Frobisher began 300 years of English exploration. But it was Roald AMUNDSEN of Norway whose ship first sailed the Northwest Passage in 1906. In 1969 an oil tanker broke a path through the ice. But the ice is so thick that ships may never regularly use this sea route.

Northwest Territories
Northwest Territories is a vast region of northern Canada. It has about one-third of the total land area of the country, but has only 43,000 inhabitants. Many people are Eskimos or American Indians. The discovery of uranium and the strategic importance of the area to North American defense has brought the Northwest Territories into greater prominence in recent years.

The Northwest Territories borders on the provinces of Manitoba, Saskatchewan, Alberta and British Columbia in the south. To the west lies the Yukon. It is divided into three districts: Franklin, Keewatin and Mackenzie. The capital is Yellowknife.

Norway
Norway is Europe's sixth largest country. This long, northern kingdom is wide in the south but narrow in the center and the north. Mountains with forests, bare rocks and snow cover much of Norway. Steep inlets called FIORDS pierce its rocky coast.

Summers in Norway are cool and winters long. It is very cold in the Arctic north, but the rainy west coast is kept fairly mild by the GULF STREAM.

Norwegians catch more fish than any other Europeans, and their North Sea oil wells are among Europe's richest.

AREA: 125,188 SQ. MILES (324,219 SQ. KM)
POPULATION: 4,138,000
CAPITAL: OSLO
CURRENCY: KRONE
OFFICIAL LANGUAGE: NORWEGIAN

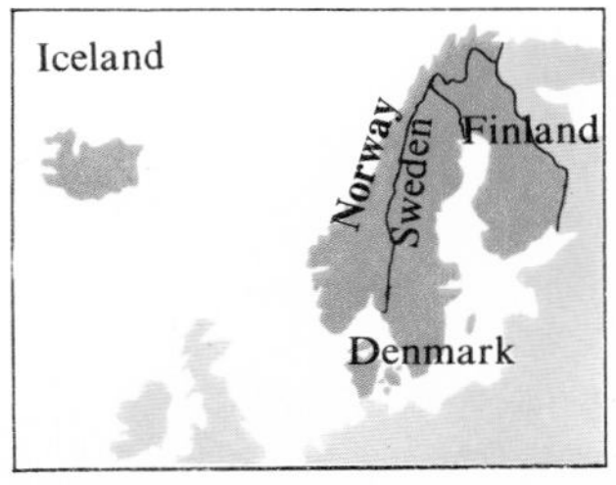

nose *n.* the organ in the middle of the face used by people and many animals for breathing and smelling.
► The nose contains two openings, the nostrils. Air is taken in through the nostrils and passes into the narrow tubes, called nasal passages, which connect with the throat. The sense of SMELL is located in the upper part of the nose. There, special nerve endings react to the vapors and scents given off by most substances.

nostalgia *n.* homesickness; a wish to return to some past period.
nostril *n.* either of the openings in the nose through which you breathe and smell.
nosy *adj.* inquisitive.
not *adv.* a word that makes a statement negative. *I do not know what you are talking about.*
note 1. *vb.* write down a few words to remind yourself or someone else about something. **notebook** 2. *n.* a short letter. 3. *n.* a single musical sound. *Catherine played one note on the piano.* 4. *n.* paper money.
noted *adj.* famous, well-known (for).
nothing *n.* not anything. *Have you nothing to say?*
notice (**no**-*tiss*) 1. *n.* something written down or shown to people to tell them something. *The notice on the door said, "KEEP OUT."* 2. *vb.* see something. *I noticed that she had a new hat.*
notify *vb.* inform, make known. **notification** *n.*
nougat (**noo**-*gut*) *n.* candy made from nuts, sugar and egg whites.
noun *n.* the name of a person, place or thing. *John, Paris and cat are all nouns.*

Nova Scotia
Nova Scotia is a long, narrow peninsula province in eastern CANADA. It is one of the Maritime Provinces and is attached to the mainland by an isthmus. One of the most colorful parts of Canada, Nova Scotia is known for its scenery and for its romantic history, including its French and Scottish heritage. The story of the forced removal of some of Nova Scotia's original French, or Acadian, settlers by the English in the 1700s was immortalized in Henry Wadsworth LONGFELLOW's long narrative poem *Evangeline*. Cape Breton Island makes up the north, and the narrow Bay of Fundy has the highest TIDES on earth. There are many lakes and forests, and important mines and orchards. The coastal waters are rich in fish, and fishing is an important industry. Halifax, capital of the province, is also a major port of Canada.

novel 1. *n.* a long written story. **novelist** *n.* writer of novels. 2. *adj.* new, strange, unknown.
► There are many kinds of novels. For instance, some are adventure tales, like *Treasure Island* by Robert Louis STEVENSON. There are horror novels like Mary Shelley's FRANKENSTEIN, SCIENCE FICTION novels, humorous novels like *Tom Sawyer* by MARK TWAIN, and satirical novels like Jonathan SWIFT's *Gulliver's Travels.* Swift slyly pokes fun at mankind. Authors like Sir Walter SCOTT wrote historical novels (novels set in the past).
Novels can be about people at any place or time. They are all meant to entertain us. But the best novels give us a new way of looking at life. Writers like Charles DICKENS showed up the harsh lives of poor people in England in the middle 1800s.
Novels grew out of short stories written in Italy in the 1300s. One of the first famous novels was the Spanish story DON QUIXOTE. Some of the first English novels with believable stories were Daniel DEFOE's.

November *n.* the eleventh month of the year.
novice (**nov**-*iss*) *n.* beginner; a person who enters a convent or monastery on a trial basis.
now *adv.* at the present moment. *You may go home now.*
nowadays *adv.* at the present time.
nowhere *adv.* not anywhere.
nozzle *n.* spout of a waterhose, etc.
nuclear *adj.* 1. to do with atomic energy. *When the nucleus of an atom is split, it produces nuclear energy.* 2. (in other sciences) to do with the central parts of larger things.

Nuclear Energy
An ATOM is a tiny particle of matter, made up of a nucleus surrounded by electrons. The nucleus is itself only a tiny part of the whole atom, yet the two parts of the nucleus, the proton and the neutron, are bound together by forces of enormous strength.
When the neutron and the proton are separated this force is released in the form of ENERGY. This is how nuclear energy is produced. The atom's nucleus can be broken apart by bombarding it with other nuclear particles in huge "atom smashers" or accelerators called *cyclotrons* and *synchrotrons*.
The atoms of certain elements can split by themselves without being bombarded in accelerators. The atoms of URANIUM, for example, can do this. Uranium-235 is an ISOTOPE uranium. If a lump of uranium-235 is larger than a certain size, all its atoms split in a fraction of a second and enormous amounts of energy are given off as an explosion. Uranium-235 is used to make ATOMIC BOMBS. But this CHAIN REACTION, as it is called, can be controlled in a nuclear reactor to give us useful nuclear energy. The center of the reactor is called the core. Here the uranium is housed inside rods. Around the rods is placed a moderator, a substance such as graphite or water that slows down the neutrons. In case the chain reaction starts to go too quickly, control rods are also placed in the core. They are made of metals such as cadmium or boron that absorb neutrons, and they can be moved in or out of the core. To remove the heat produced in the uranium rods, a liquid or gas coolant is pumped through the core. When this coolant leaves the core it goes to a heat exchanger, where it gives up its heat before returning to the core. This heat is used to drive TURBINES which in turn drive large GENERATORS.

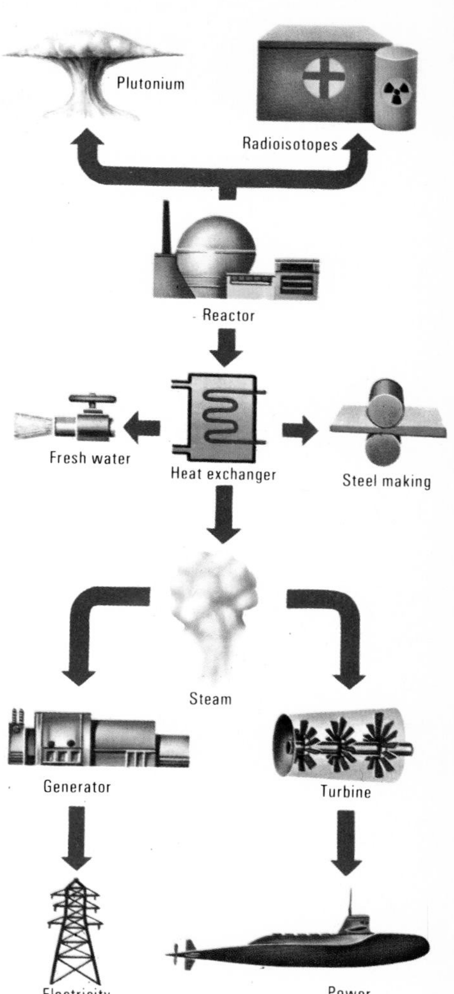

How nuclear power is used. The reactor's heat is used via a heat exchanger. The reactor can also produce plutonium or radioisotopes directly by irradiating elements with neutrons.

N

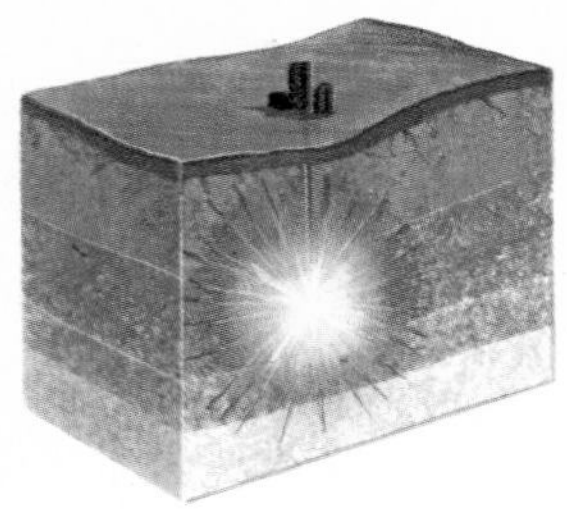

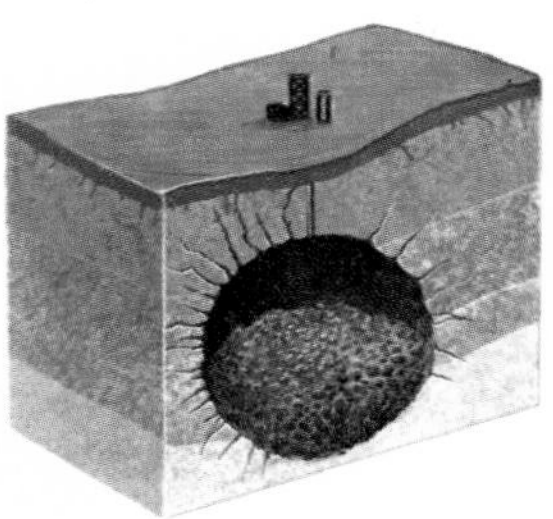

Nuclear explosions deep underground produce huge cavities of broken rock from which minerals, oil or gas could be obtained.

nucleus *n.* a central part of something, such as an atom or a cell (in biology).
nude *adj.* naked; bare; having no clothes.
nudge *vb.* & *n.* (a) push gently with the elbow to attract attention.
nugget *n.* solid lump, especially of precious metal, e.g. gold.
nuisance *n.* something or somebody that causes trouble.
numb (rhymes with *gum*) *adj.* not able to feel. *vb.* make numb.
number *n.* 1. a word or figure showing how many. *5, 37 and 6 are all numbers.* 2. a quantity or amount. *There were a large number of books left on the shelf.*
► In STONE AGE times people showed a number like 20 or 30 by making 20 or 30 separate marks. In certain caves you can still see the marks that they made.

In time people invented special signs or groups of signs to show different numbers. Such signs are called numerals. For centuries many people used Roman numerals. But these are rather clumsy. For instance, the Roman numerals for 38 are XXXVIII. Our much simpler system uses Arabic numerals that were first used in India.

numerous *adj.* great numbers of, many.
numismatic *adj.* to do with coins and medals.
nun *n.* a woman who has taken vows to live a religious life.

nurse 1. *n.* a person who is trained to look after people who are ill, very young or very old. 2. *vb.* act as a nurse; cherish. 3. suckle.
► People who are very ill, old or handicapped need nursing in their homes or in a HOSPITAL. Nursing can mean feeding, washing and giving treatment ordered by a doctor. It is hard work and needs special skills. Men and women train for years before becoming nurses. Modern nursing owes much to the example set by Florence NIGHTINGALE.

nursery *n.* 1. a room for a baby or small child. *A nursery school is for very young children.* 2. a place where young plants are grown for sale.
nut *n.* 1. the fruit of certain plants with a hard shell. 2. a piece of metal with a hole in the center that screws on to a bolt to fasten it.
► Nut is a popular name for a plant fruit which consists of a hard or leathery shell containing a kernel. Many kernels are edible, such as the ALMOND, Brazil nut and sweet CHESTNUT. In BOTANY, a nut is a plant fruit which contains only one seed and which does not open on ripening to distribute the seed.

nutmeg *n.* the hard seed of a tropical fruit used as a spice; another spice, **mace**, comes from the outer part of the nutmeg fruit.
nylon *n.* a strong, elastic, artificial (man-made) fiber.
► Nylon is a type of PLASTIC with widespread uses, especially in the form of fiber. In 1928, an American chemist called Dr. Wallace Carothers started to search for materials suitable for making synthetic fibers. Ten years later, he announced his discovery of the material now called nylon. It is made from benzene (obtained from coal), oxygen, nitrogen and hydrogen. Nylon's excellent elastic properties make it especially suitable for stockings and tights. Clothes made from nylon drip-dry quickly and resist creasing; nylon carpets are hardwearing; and nylon ropes are strong and rot-proof. An important use for rigid, molded nylon is in the manufacture of bearings and gears. Unlike metal components, these rarely require lubrication.

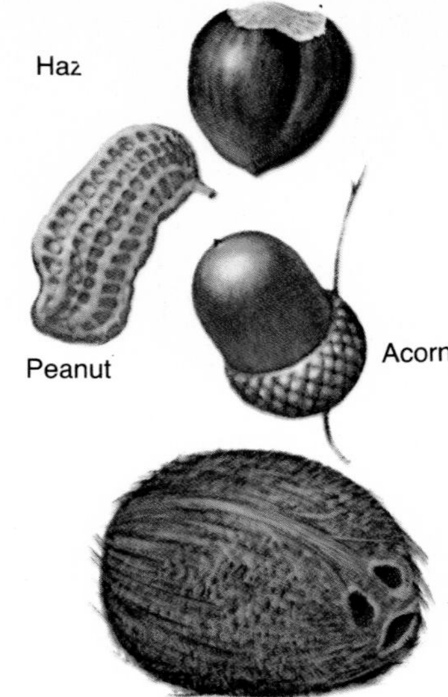

nymph *n.* 1. minor goddess of nature in ancient mythology. 2. larva of certain insects such as dragonflies.

Binary				Decimal
Ø	Ø	Ø	Ø	0
Ø	Ø	Ø	1	1
Ø	Ø	1	Ø	2
Ø	Ø	1	1	3
Ø	1	Ø	Ø	4
Ø	1	Ø	1	5
Ø	1	1	Ø	6
Ø	1	1	1	7
1	Ø	Ø	Ø	8

Above: Roman and Arabic numerals. Right: Binary numbers and their decimal equivalents.

O

Oil platforms in Lake Maracaibo, Venezuela.

oak *n.* a large tree on which acorns grow.

► Some oaks measure over 38 ft. (11 meters) around the trunk. They grow slowly and may live for 900 years. Most have leaves with deeply notched (wavy) edges. But evergreen oaks have tough, shiny, smooth-edged leaves.

Oak wood is hard and slow to rot. People used it to build sailing ships. Tannin from oak bark is used in LEATHER making. Cork comes from cork oak bark.

oar (rhymes with *sore*) *n.* a pole with a flat end for making a rowboat move through water. *Most rowboats have two oars.*

oasis (*o*-**ay**-*sis*) *n.* a fertile place in the desert.

► An oasis may be just a clump of palm trees or much larger. Egypt's Nile valley is a huge oasis. Oases are found where there is water. This can come from rivers, wells or springs. These may be fed by rain that falls on nearby mountains and seeps through rocks beneath the surface of the desert. People can make oases by drilling wells and digging IRRIGATION ditches.

oath *n.* a solemn promise.

oats *pl. n.* grain from a cereal. *Ground oats are called oatmeal and are used to make porridge.*

obedient *adj.* doing what you are told. *Our dog was very naughty as a puppy, but now he is quite obedient.*

obelisk *n.* a stone monument, in the shape of a tall pillar: four-sided, narrowing upward, and topped by a small pyramid shape. *The Washington Monument is an example of an obelisk.*

obey (*o*-**bay**) *vb.* do what you are told.

obituary *n.* an announcement of a person's death.

object (**ob**-*ject*) 1. *n.* anything that can be touched or seen.

object *vb* (*ob*-**ject**) say that you do not agree with something. *She objected to the way the people were chosen.* **objection** *n.* expression of disapproval. **objectionable** *adj.* disagreeable.

oblige *vb.* 1. make someone do something. 2. do a favor. 3. bind someone by gratitude. **obligation** *n.* duty.

oblique *adj.* slanting; roundabout; indirect.

obliterate *vb.* destroy completely. *The bombs obliterated the center of the city.* **obliteration** *n.*

oblong *n.* a rectangle; a flat figure with two parallel pairs of straight sides, two longer than the others, and four right angles.

oboe *n.* a musical instrument made of wood and played by blowing.

obscure *adj.* dim, vague, indistinct. *vb.* hide.

observe *vb.* notice; watch carefully; follow orders, instructions. **observation** *n.* observing; comment.

observatory *n.* a place from which observations are made, usually of heavenly bodies.

► Major observatories are built in places where optical sightings will be least affected by atmospheric conditions. Dry, mountainous regions are ideal. Relatively little dust is found at high altitudes. Conditions are even better in outer space, but launching and running an observatory in space would be very expensive. However, many useful observations have been made from the Russian *Salyut* and American *Skylab* general-purpose space laboratories. Fortunately, astronomers no longer have to rely on optical telescopes alone. Since the 1940s RADIO ASTRONOMY has provided a vast range of information, impossible to discover by visual means.

obsolete *adj.* no longer used, discarded.

obstacle *n.* something that gets in the way; a hindrance.

obstinate *adj.* not easily made to agree to do something. *A donkey can be very obstinate if it does not want to work.*

obstruct *vb*. block; get in the way. **obstruction** *n*.
obtain *vb*. get possession of something.
obverse *n*. front surface of a coin or medal bearing the head or main design.
obvious *adj*. easily seen or understood.
occasion *n*. a special time or event. **occasional** *adj*.
occident *n*. the West or western part of the world. **occidental** *adj*.
occupation *n*. what you do or are doing; your job.
occupy *vb*. live in or be in. *Sam will occupy the second floor of the building.* **occupant** *n*. person living in a property.
occur *vb*. (past **occurred**) happen; take place. **occurrence** *n*. happening; incident.
ocean (o-*shun*) *n*. one of the great bodies of sea water that surround the continents.
► Oceans cover nearly three-quarters of the surface of the earth. If you put all the world's water in 100 giant tanks, 97 of them would be full of water from the oceans.

The oceans are always losing water as water vapor, drawn up into the air by the sun's heat. But most returns as RAIN.

Rainwater running off the land takes salts and other MINERALS to the oceans. For instance, enough sea water to fill a 1-mile square tank would hold 16 million tons of MAGNESIUM. Water from the world's oceans supplies most of the magnesium we use.

There are four oceans. The largest and deepest is the PACIFIC OCEAN (70 million sq. miles/181 million sq. km). The second largest is the ATLANTIC OCEAN (41 million sq. miles/106 million sq. km). The INDIAN OCEAN (28 million sq. miles/ 73,490,000 sq. km) is smaller but deeper than the Atlantic Ocean. The Arctic Ocean (5,500,000 sq. miles/ 14,350,000 sq. km) is the smallest and shallowest ocean.

The oceans are never still. Winds crinkle their surface into waves. Winds also drive the GULF STREAM and other currents that flow like rivers through the oceans. Every day the ocean surface falls and rises with the TIDES. In winter, polar sea water freezes over. ICEBERGS from polar seas may drift hundreds of miles through the oceans.

Oceans are home to countless living things. The minerals in sea water help to nourish tiny plants drifting at the surface. The plants are food for tiny animals. These animals and plants are called PLANKTON. Fish and some whales eat plankton. In turn, small fish are eaten by larger hunters.

Oceania
Oceania sprawls over an enormous area of the Pacific Ocean but its total land mass makes it the smallest of the continents. It covers 3,286,000 sq. miles (8,510,000 sq. km) and its population is 24.5 million.

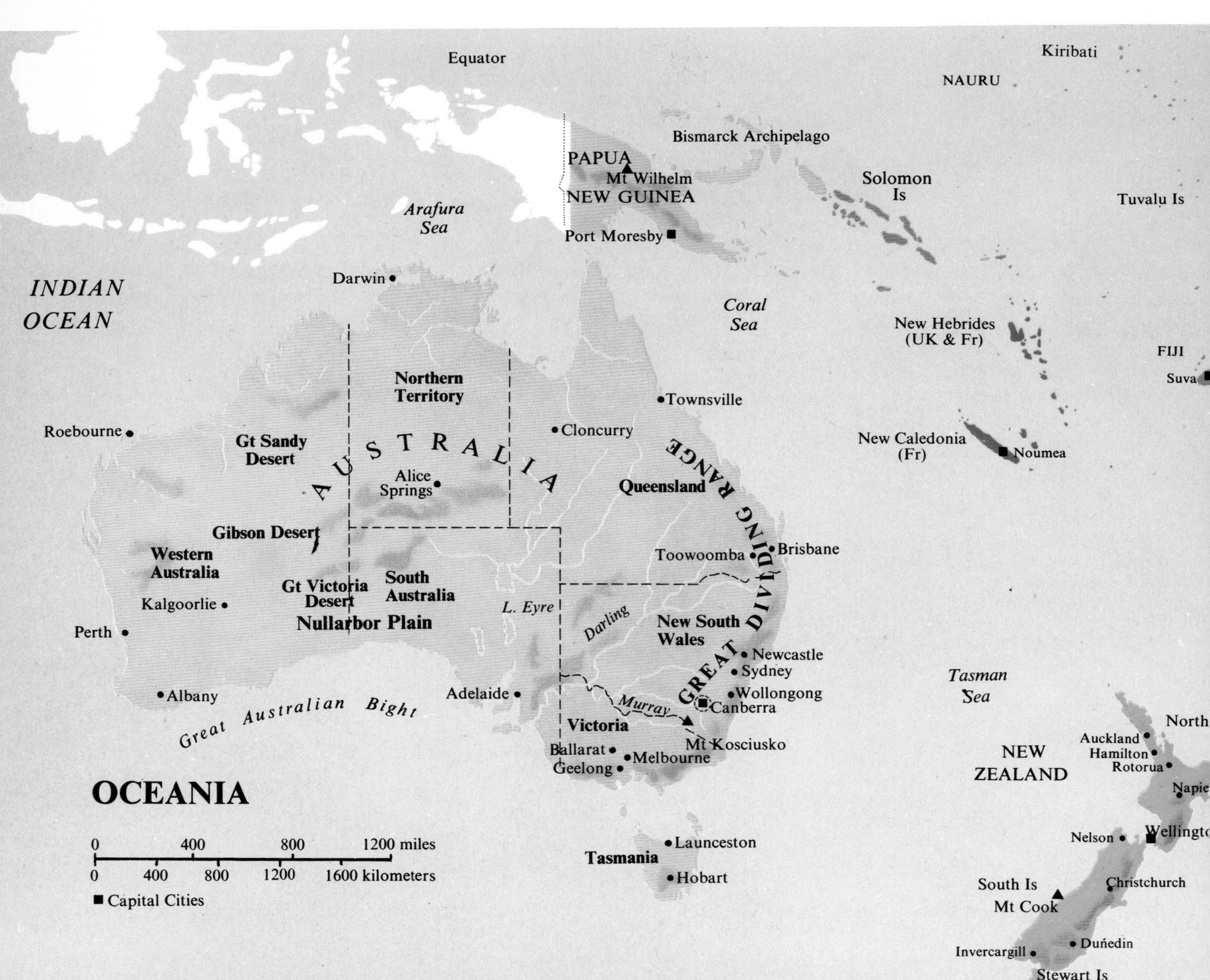

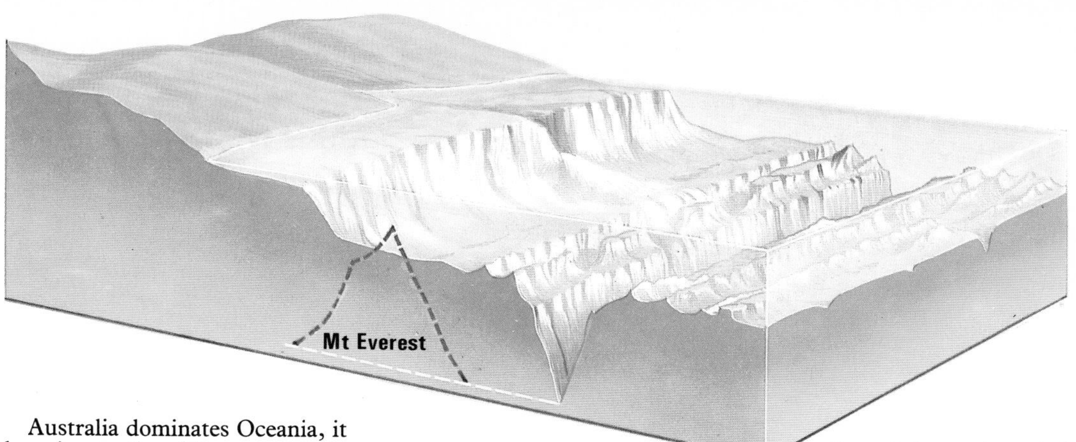

Beyond the continental shelf the seabed slopes down steeply. The deepest ocean trench would cover Mount Everest.

Australia dominates Oceania, it has nine-tenths of its area, and three-fifths of its population. Oceania also includes New Zealand, Papua New Guinea and about 3,000 or so Pacific Islands. Some islands, such as Fiji and Western Samoa, are fairly thickly populated, but others are uninhabited.

o'clock *n.* the hour of the day. *We start school at nine o'clock.*
octagon *n.* a flat figure with eight equal sides. **octagonal** *adj.*

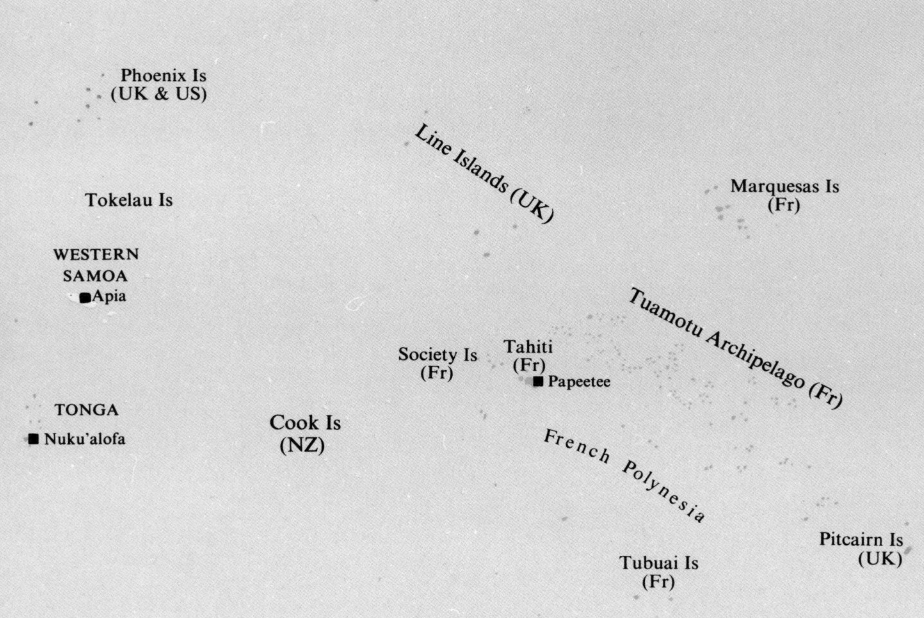

octave *n.* (in music) eight notes of a scale, e.g., C, D, E, F, G, A, B, C.

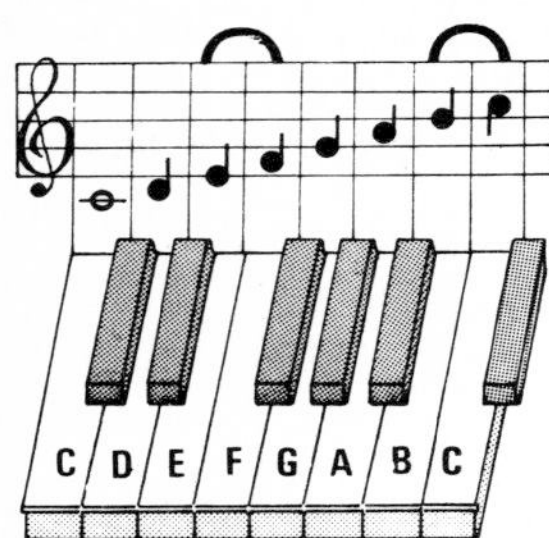

An octave on a piano. Above the keys is written the scale of C major, played on white notes only.

October *n.* the 10th month of the year.

octopus *n.* a sea animal with a soft body and eight arms.

► There are about 50 kinds of octopus. They are MOLLUSKS that live in the sea. Octopus means "eight feet", but the eight tentacles of an octopus are usually called arms. The largest octopus has arms about 30 ft. (9 meters) across, but most octopuses are no larger than a man's fist. Suckers on the tentacles grip crabs, shellfish or other prey. An octopus's tentacles pull its victim toward its mouth. This is hard and pointed, like the beak of a bird.

The octopus hides in an underwater cave or crevice. It creeps around the seabed searching for food. Its two large eyes keep a watch for enemies. If danger threatens, the octopus may confuse its enemy by squirting an inky liquid. The ink hangs in the water like a cloud. An octopus can also dart forward by squirting water backward.

odd *adj.* 1. peculiar, strange. 2. a number that cannot be divided exactly by two. *3, 27, and 101 are odd numbers.*

oddments *n. pl.* odds and ends; scraps; bits and pieces.

odor *n.* smell.

Odyssey
An epic poem by the Greek poet HOMER. It tells the story of the wanderings of Ulysses (Odysseus), a Greek hero, as he tries to return home to his kingdom of Ithaca after the Trojan War. The word is now also used to describe any long journey, or story of such a journey.

Oedipus
Legendary Greek king of Thebes. He unintentionally killed his father and married his mother – as an oracle had predicted. Sophocles wrote two famous tragedies on the subject.

off *prep.* from; away from. *Stephen fell off his bicycle.*

offend *vb.* cause dislike, anger, etc. *I am sorry if I have offended you.* **offense** *n.*

offer *vb.* 1. say that you will do something for someone. *I thanked him for offering to help me clean the room.* 2. hold out something to someone. *Sean offered me a bag of candy. n.* a price proposed, usually by a buyer.

office *n.* a place where people work whose business needs writing and recording.

officer *n.* a senior person in the army, air force or navy; president, treasurer, etc., of a society.

offspring *n.* the child or children of a family; plants or young animals.

often *adv.* many times; frequently.

ogre (**o**-*ger*) *n.* a cruel giant in stories.

Ohio (*abbrev.* **O.**)
Ohio is a Midwestern state bordering Lake Erie on the north. Its southern boundary is the Ohio River. Ohio is a great industrial state, producing large quantities of iron and steel. It is also well-known for its mining and agriculture.

The state has a large population – some 11 million – and more than three-quarters of Ohio's people live in city areas. The biggest cities are Cleveland, Columbus, the capital, Cincinnati and Toledo.

Before the Civil War, Ohio was a leading anti-slavery state. Many Ohioans joined the Union army. Ohio became the 17th state in 1803.

oil *n.* kinds of liquid that do not mix with water and usually burn easily. *vb.* apply oil; lubricate.

► Oil is a greasy chemical compound which dissolves in ether, but not in water. Usually the term refers to substances that are liquid at normal room temperatures; solids are referred to as fats. Oils are obtained from various animal, vegetable or mineral sources.

Some layers of the earth's crust consist of waterproof rock (brown in diagram). In others the rock is porous like a sponge (blue). Oil or gas gets trapped in folds and held in by the waterproof rock.

Fixed oils, which do not evaporate easily, are obtained mostly by squeezing animal or vegetable substances, such as fish or seeds. Such oils vary greatly in their drying properties. Some, called "drying oils", form a hard surface film when left in contact with the air. This makes them suitable for use in paints or varnishes.

Volatile oils evaporate quickly. Some, such as lavender, have a pleasant smell and are used in soaps and scents. Others, such as clove, are used to flavor food and medicines. Animal and vegetable oils have widespread uses, but our most important source of oils is the mineral petroleum.

Scientists think that petroleum was formed from the decayed remains of tiny plants and animals that lived in the sea millions of years ago. Many petroleum regions have since become land masses owing to movements in the earth's crust. Petroleum is extracted by drilling wells to great depths. The crude oil obtained is a black mixture so valuable to us that it is sometimes called "black gold". Refineries separate it into gasoline, diesel oil, fuel oil, lubricants, asphalt and many other substances. Other industries use petrochemicals (chemicals made from petroleum) for numerous products including plastics, drugs, antiseptics, cosmetics, fertilizers and detergents.

ointment *n.* a medicine made in a paste or cream.

Oklahoma (*abbrev.* **Okla.**)
Oklahoma is a South Central state with a warm climate and short, mild winters. It has almost three million people, more than half of whom live in city areas. The capital is Oklahoma City.

Oklahoma is an agricultural state, most of its cash revenue coming from cattle.

The Red River is Oklahoma's southern border; the Arkansas River flows through the state's northeast.

Indian tribes used to hunt buffalo across the land that is now Oklahoma. Among these tribes were the Wichita, Quapaw, Plains Apache, and the Osage. The first Europeans to visit the area were Spanish explorers. Most of Oklahoma was part of the Louisiana Territory which the United States bought from France in 1803. For many years the state was a vast Indian reservation. About 3 percent of the population is of Indian descent.

Oklahoma became the 46th state in 1907.

old *adj.* having lived for a long time; out-of-date.

old-fashioned *adj*. out-of-date, not worn or used nowadays.

olive *n*. a small oval fruit with a hard stone and bitter, oily flesh. *adj*. dullish green color (color of an olive).

► Olives grow on trees with slim gray-green leaves and twisted trunks. Farmers pick olives when they are green and unripe, or when ripe they hit the trees with sticks to knock the olives onto sheets spread on the ground. People eat olives and cook food in olive oil made from crushed olives.

Most olives come from Italy, Spain and other countries by the Mediterranean Sea.

Olympic Games
The original Games were held in ancient Greece, in Olympia. They took place every four years, from before 776 B.C. to A.D. 396. At first they were just foot races, but later there was boxing, wrestling and chariot and horse races. The modern Games have been held every four years since 1896 (except in wartime) and in a different country each time. They are supervised by the International Olympic Committee, and there are many more events (team sports, water sports, weapon sports). The Winter Olympics are held in the same Olympic year (since 1924), and feature snow and ice sports. All Olympic competitors have to be amateur.

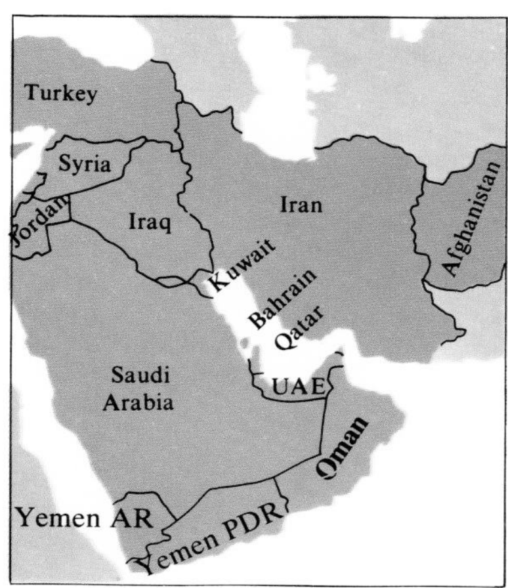

Oman
Oman is a sultanate (monarchy) in the southeast corner of ARABIA. The interior is mainly dry and barren, although there are some fertile areas, particularly near the coast. Most of the people are farmers or fishermen, but oil production is the main source of wealth.

AREA: 82,035 SQ. MILES (212,457 SQ. KM)
POPULATION: 950,000
CAPITAL: MUSCAT
CURRENCY: OMANI RIYAL
OFFICIAL LANGUAGE: ARABIC

Omar Khayyám
Omar Khayyám (*c*. 1050–*c*. 1122) was a Persian poet, astronomer and mathematician. Having written a book on algebra, he became royal astronomer and produced a new Persian calendar. Today, he is best known for his long poem the *Rubáiyát*. This was freely translated into English by Edward Fitzgerald and published in 1859. Fitzgerald's translation has become a minor literary classic in its own right.

omelet, omelette *n*. a kind of pancake made of fried beaten eggs, often with a meat, vegetable or cheese filling.

omen *n*. sign of good or evil to come. **ominous** *adj*. threatening.

omit *vb*. leave out; fail to put in. **omission** *n*.

omni- *prefix* meaning all, e.g. **omnipotent** all powerful. **omnivorous** feeding on all kinds of food.

once *adv*. 1. at one time only. *I have only been to Venice once*. 2. at a time in the past. *She once lived in Africa*.

onion *n*. a strong-tasting bulb eaten as a vegetable or used to add flavor to other foods.

► Most kinds of onion have a BULB made up of tightly packed layers of leaves. This is the part we eat. The leaves contain a special kind of oil. When you peel an onion a vapor from the oil makes your eyes water.

onlooker *n*. spectator.

only *adv*. & *adj*. a single one; no one or nothing else. *He was the only person to give the right answer*.

Ontario
Ontario is a province in the center of CANADA. It has more people than any other Canadian province – a third of the country's population. It is also the richest, producing almost half of all Canada's manufactured goods. The main industry is the making of cars. But Ontario is not only an industrial province. Its farmers produce a third of Canada's farm products. The capital and largest city is Toronto. Ontario's beautiful lake regions make it a favorite vacationland.

onyx (**on**-*iks*) *n*. semiprecious stone with layers of different colors.

opal *n*. a precious stone, a form of quartz much prized for its rainbow play of colors.

opaque (*o*-**pake**) *adj*. not letting the light through; unintelligible.

open *adj*. & *adv*. not closed. *Leave the door open*. *vb*. make or become open.

openly *adv*. in public; frankly.

opera *n*. a play in which the words are sung.

► The music in opera is usually thought to be more important than the words and acting. Some operas also use dance and spectacular stage effects. Opera started in Italy in the late 1500s, and rapidly became a popular form of entertainment. Since then the greatest operas have come from Austria (MOZART), Germany (Wagner) and Italy itself (Verdi). There is also light opera, which is humorous, and combines songs and speech.

operate *vb*. 1. work. *Do you know how to operate the machine?* 2. carry out a surgical operation.

operation (*op-per-***ay***-shun*) *n*. 1. a treatment by a doctor in which the patient's body is cut. 2. a carefully planned action.

operator *n*. a person who works a machine, e.g. a telephone switchboard.

opinion *n*. what someone thinks; an idea with which not everyone agrees. **opinionated** *adj*. stubborn in one's opinions.

opossum *n*. a marsupial mammal that lives in North and South America.

► Some opossums look like rats, others look like mice. The Virginian opossum is as big as a cat. This is

O

North America's only MARSUPIAL. It can climb trees and can cling on with its tail. A female has up to 18 young, each no larger than a honeybee. If danger threatens, the Virginia opossum pretends to be dead. If a person pretends to be hurt, we say he is "playing possum".

opponent *n.* someone who opposes something; a foe.
opportune *adj.* suitable, convenient.
opportunity *n.* a good chance to do something. *While the children were out, their mother took the opportunity to clean their rooms.*
oppose *vb.* resist; be against. *I oppose the plan to rebuild the bus station.*
opposite 1. *n.* the reverse of something. *Fat is the opposite of thin.* 2. *adj.* on the other side. *The house on the opposite side of the road is painted blue.*
opt *vb.* make a choice.
optician (*op*-**tish**-*un*) *n.* a person who makes or sells glasses. **optic** *adj.* concerning the eyes or sight.
optimism *n.* belief that the best will happen. **optimist** *n.*
or *conj.* a connecting word introducing the second of two choices. *Coffee or tea?*
oral *adj.* spoken; concerning the mouth.
orange 1. *n.* round juicy fruit with a thick skin. 2. *n.* & *adj.* a color like an orange.
► The orange is a popular citrus fruit grown in most subtropical countries. It is round with tart, juicy flesh divided into segments. There are two main types of orange: the sweet orange which is eaten raw or squeezed for its juices; and the bitter, or Seville, orange, which is used for making marmalade. The orange tree is evergreen and has fragrant white flowers.

Orange Free State
The Orange Free State is a province of the Republic of SOUTH AFRICA. It lies between the Vaal and Orange rivers. Primarily a farming province, the Orange Free State has important gold mines. Other minerals include diamonds and coal. The province was settled by Boers (Dutch farmers) in the 1800s. Later, it was taken over by the British. It became a province of the Union of South Africa in 1910.

orangutan *n.* a reddish-brown ape that lives in the forests of Indonesia.
► The name orangutan comes from Malay words meaning "man of the woods." A male is as heavy as a man, but not as tall. Orangutans use their long arms to swing through the branches of trees as they hunt for fruit and leaves to eat. Each night they make a nest high up in the trees. A leafy roof keeps out rain.
Human beings are the orangutan's main enemy. Hunters kill mothers to catch their young to sell them to zoos. Orangutans are already scarce. They could become extinct.

orator *n.* an eloquent public speaker.
oratorio *n.* musical work for choir and orchestra often on a religious subject and without action or scenery.
orb *n.* sphere or globe.
orbit *n.* the path followed by any body in space around another body. *vb.* travel in an orbit.
► Planets move in orbits around the sun, and the moon and numerous artificial satellites orbit the earth. The shape of these orbits is *elliptical*, like a squashed circle. The *perigee* is a body's closest distance and the *apogee* its farthest distance from the body it orbits. In atoms, one or more electrons orbit a nucleus.

orchard *n.* a piece of ground where fruit trees are grown.
orchestra (**ork**-*estra*) *n.* a group of musicians who play together. **orchestral** *adj.*

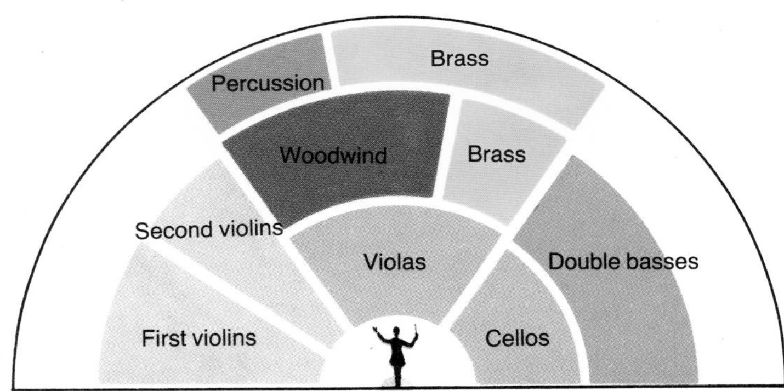

One way in which the instruments of an orchestra are arranged in a semicircle around the conductor.

► The word orchestra once meant "dancing place". In ancient Greek theaters, dancers and musicians performed on a space between the audience and stage. When Italy invented opera, Italian theaters arranged their musicians in the same way. Soon people used the word orchestra to describe the group of musicians, and not the place where they performed.
The modern orchestra owes much to HAYDN. He arranged its musical instruments into four main groups: string, woodwind, brass and percussion.

orchid *n.* one of a family of showy perennial flowering plants.
► The orchid is a fascinating flower. An orchid bloom consists of six petal-like segments; one segment, called the lip, is much larger than the others and has a special color or shape. Most orchids are found in the tropics.

order 1. *vb.* command somebody to do something. *The officer ordered the troops to advance.* 2. *n.* a list of things that you want. *The waiter took our order for lunch.* 3. *n.* a succession of events. 4. *n.* tidiness. 5. *n.* a religious community. *These monks belong to the Order of Saint Benedict.*
orderly 1. *adj.* tidy. 2. *n.* a soldier who looks after an officer; hospital employee who does routine work.
ordinary *adj.* normal; usual; not strange or interesting.
ore *n.* rock or earth from which metal can be taken.
► Some ores are simply heated until the molten metal runs out. Gold, silver and copper can be obtained in this way. In other ores, the metals exist as COMPOUNDS, being chemically combined with other elements, such as oxygen or sulfur. Iron, for example, is found as iron oxide, and copper is often found as copper sulfide. The pure metals are obtained from compound ores like these by chemical treatment or by electrolysis.

Oregon (*abbrev.* **Oreg.**)
Oregon is a Pacific Coast state. The Cascade Mountains run north and south to divide the state into two main regions. The area west of the mountains has plenty of rain. To the east of the Cascades the climate is dry. Most of the state's 2.5 million people live in the Willamette Valley between the low Coastal Mountain range and the Cascades. The state's largest cities are Portland, Eugene and Salem, the capital.
Nearly half of Oregon is covered with forest, so it is the nation's leading lumber state. Oregon has many rivers. Great dams and hydroelectric plants provide a large part of the state's power.
In the 1840s Oregon was the end of the route that settlers from the East traveled to reach the west coast – the Oregon Trail. Great numbers of settlers poured in during this period, and fought many fierce wars with the Indians.

When Oregon became a territory in 1848, it included what is now the state of Washington. Then, Washington became a separate state. In 1859, Oregon became the 33rd state.

organ *n*. 1. any part of an animal's body that has a particular job to do. *The heart is the organ that pumps blood around the body*. 2. a musical instrument with a keyboard and pipes. **organist** *n*. organ player.
► The largest organ has more than 30,000 pipes. Each pipe makes a special sound as air flows through it. An organist plays an organ by pressing keys arranged in rows called *manuals*. Each manual controls a different set of pipes. Levers or knobs called *stops* allow the organist to combine different groups of pipes. Electronic organs sound similar, but have no pipes.

organism *n*. a living animal or plant.
organization *n*. an organized group.
organize *vb*. make arrangements for something to happen; give orderly structure to.
orient *n*. the East or eastern part of the world. **oriental** *adj*.
origami *n*. Japanese art of folding paper into intricate shapes.
origin *n*. beginning, source; starting point. **originate** *vb*. create, come into being; spring from.
original *adj*. the earliest or first; new, not copied. *n*. thing from which another is copied.

Orkney Islands
The Orkneys are a group of islands off the north coast of SCOTLAND. There are nearly one hundred islands, most of which are uninhabited. The largest island is Mainland (Pomona). The Orkneys are rich in prehistoric remains.
The discovery of oil in the NORTH SEA threatens the traditional way of life of the people. The Orkneys are a separate administrative area of the United Kingdom. The chief town is Kirkwall.

ornament *n*. something which is used as a decoration. *vb*. adorn. **ornamental** *adj*.
ornithology *n*. study of birds. **ornithologist** *n*.
orphan *n*. a person whose parents are dead. *adj*. **orphanage** *n*. an institution for orphans.
orthodox *adj*. holding correct or acceptable opinion; not heretical; conventional. **orthodoxy** *n*.

Osaka
Osaka is the second largest city in JAPAN. A major port on the island of Honshu, it has a large shipbuilding industry. Other industries include textiles, steel manufacture, electrical equipment and chemicals.

Oslo
Oslo is the capital and largest city of NORWAY. It stands at the head of Oslo Fiord, on the southeastern coast of the country. An ice-free port, it handles timber and many other products. The city was destroyed by fire in 1624. It was rebuilt by the Danes who called it Christiania. The name was changed back to Oslo in 1925.

osmosis *n*. the process by which liquids pass through a porous membrane (skin) until the fluids on both sides of the membrane have been equalized in some way.
osprey *n*. a large fish-eating bird of prey found in most parts of the world. It is brown with a white head and underparts.
ostrich *n*. a very large bird that lives in southern Africa. Ostriches cannot fly, but are very fast runners.
► This is the largest living bird. An ostrich may weigh twice as much as a man and stand more than 7ft. (2 meters) high. Ostriches cannot fly. If an enemy attacks, an ostrich can run away or kick hard enough to rip a lion open.
Ostriches roam in herds, led by a male. The females lay large, white eggs in a nest dug in the sand. Ostriches can live for over 50 years.
other *adj*. one of two; different; alternative.

Ostriches run very fast on two long toes that help to lengthen their stride.

otherwise *adv*. 1. in another way. 2. if not, or else. *You'd better hurry, otherwise we'll go without you*.

Otis, James
James Otis (1725–1783) was an American patriot, writer and lawyer. He graduated from Harvard in 1743 and later practiced law in Boston. He took a stand against the Writs of Assistance (which gave the British the right to search any house for smuggled goods) by appearing in court for a group of Boston merchants. Otis was the author of several pamphlets arguing the rights and stating the grievances of the colonists.

The otter lives mainly near rivers or seas.

Ottawa
Ottawa is the capital of CANADA, and it is the third largest city. Ottawa is in the province of ONTARIO in southeast Canada. The Ottawa and Rideau rivers flow through the city.
Ottawa's best known buildings are the Parliament buildings, which stand on a hill above the Ottawa River. They include the tall Peace Tower which contains 53 bells. Ottawa also has universities and museums.
British settlers began building Ottawa in 1826. They named it after the nearby Outawouais Indians. More than one citizen in three is French-speaking.

otter *n*. a flesh-eating water animal that lives in many parts of the world.
► Otters are large relatives of the WEASEL. They have long, low bodies and short legs. An otter hunts in water for fish and frogs. Thick fur keeps its body dry. It can swim nimbly by waggling its tail and body like an eel.
Otters are wanderers. By night they hunt up and down a river, or roam over land to find new fishing grounds. They love to play by sliding down a bank of snow or mud.

Ottoman Empire
The Ottoman Empire was a Turkish Muslim empire that took its name from Osman in the 1200s. By the 1600s it covered much of eastern Europe, North Africa and the Middle East, including Iran.
In 1453 the Ottoman Turks captured the city of Constantinople (modern Istanbul). This completed

O

their conquest of the BYZANTINE EMPIRE. The Ottoman Empire reached its peak under Suleiman the Magnificent (1530–66) who almost succeeded in capturing Vienna. However, the empire received a serious setback when its fleet was destroyed in the great naval battle of Lepanto in 1571.

During the 1700s, Russia began to take over part of the empire to the north of the Black Sea. Later, there was a whole series of revolts among the subject peoples of the empire. By 1913, it had lost nearly all its territory in Europe. WORLD WAR I finally caused the breakup of the empire. Out of the ruins of the Ottoman Empire emerged modern TURKEY under the leadership of Kemal ATATURK.

ought auxiliary or helping *vb.* expressing duty, probability, etc. *We ought to help those in need. She ought to have been home by now.*
ounce *n.* small measure of weight. *There are 16 ounces in one pound.*
our *pron.* & *adj.* belonging to us. *Come to our house.*
oust *vb.* drive away, get rid of.
out- *prefix* meaning more, longer, outside, beyond.
out *adv.* not in; away from somewhere or something. *I'm afraid Mr. Jones is out this afternoon.*
outback *n.* the interior of Australia; the bush.
outboard motor *n.* a motor for driving a small boat. It is hung over the stern (back) of the craft.
outbreak *n.* a start; a breaking out; an epidemic.
outdoors *adv.* outside a house or other building.
outfit *n.* all the clothes needed for a special purpose.
outgrew past of **outgrow**.
outgrow *vb.* become too large for something. *Robert will soon outgrow his gray pants.*
outing *n.* a day's holiday.
outlaw *n.* a person who has broken the law; a bandit. *vb.* declare a person an outlaw.
outlay *n.* money spent on something.
outline *n.* the outside shape of something, a drawing that shows only the shape of something; the main facts about something.
outright *adv.* on the spot; completely.
outside *n.* & *adv.* the opposite of inside; the outer surface of something; the outdoors.
outskirts *n.* the edges of a town.
outspoken *adj.* frank, plain, factual.
outwit *vb.* be too clever for.
oval *n.* & *adj.* an egg-shaped figure.
ovation *n.* warm applause.
oven *n.* the enclosed part of a stove where food is baked or roasted.
over 1. *adj.* above. 2. *adv.* finished. 3. *prefix* (**over-**) excessive, beyond, further than. Words prefixed with **over-** are usually self-explanatory, if the main word is known.
overalls *n.* a piece of clothing worn over others to keep them clean.
overboard *adv.* having fallen into the water from a ship or boat. *"Man overboard."*
overcome *vb.* conquer.
overdraft *n.* a bank loan in which a customer's account shows that there are insufficient funds to meet checks. The bank charges interest on the amount outstanding.
overflow *vb.* flood, spill out. *I left my bath running and it overflowed all over the floor.*
overhang *n.* & *vb.* hang out over something.
overhaul *vb.* 1. examine thoroughly and repair if necessary. 2. overtake.
overhead *n.* the running costs of a business such as administrative and advertising costs not directly related to production.
overlap *vb.* cover one thing partly with another; partly coincide.
oversee *vb.* supervise, superintend.
overtake *vb.* pass another moving thing, particularly a vehicle.
overtime *n.* time spent working after the usual hours; extra wages paid for such work.
overture *n.* 1. musical introduction. 2. opening of negotiations.
owe (rhymes with *low*) *vb.* need to pay money back to someone.
owl *n.* a bird of prey that usually hunts by night.
► Owls have soft feathers that make no sound as they fly. Their large eyes help them to see in the dimmest light. Owls also have keen ears. Some owls can catch mice in pitch darkness by listening to the sounds they make. An owl can turn its head right around to look backwards.

When an owl eats a mouse or bird, it swallows it complete with bones and fur or feathers. Later, the owl spits out the remains as pellets which we sometimes find on the ground.

There are over 500 kinds of owls. Some of the largest and smallest owls live in North America. The great gray owl of the north is as long as a man's arm. The elf owl of the south is shorter than a sparrow. The screech owl, known for its mournful wail, is the only common small species with ears. The burrowing owl nests in abandoned rabbit or prairie dog burrows.

own *vb.* possess or have. *Father owns that field.* **owner** *n.* someone who owns something. *My father is the owner of that field.*
ox *n.* (plural **oxen**) a domestic animal of the cattle family.
► Oxen are a group of big, heavy animals that include domestic (farm) cattle, BISON, wild and tame BUFFALO, and the yak. Oxen have split hoofs and a pair of curved horns. They eat grass. The heaviest domestic cattle can weigh two tons.

Many of us use the word ox only for domestic cattle, especially the kinds that are kept for meat or for pulling carts or plows. People probably began to domesticate cattle 9,000 years ago in Greece.

Oxford
Oxford is a famous university city in central southern England. It lies at the point where the River THAMES (locally called the Isis) joins the River Cherwell.

The university dates from about 1167. University College, the oldest college, was founded in 1249. There are many other fine old college buildings.

oxygen *n.* one of the gases of the air.
► Oxygen is the life supporting gas making up one-fifth of the AIR by volume. Humans and other land animals absorb oxygen from the air they breathe. Fishes absorb dissolved oxygen from the water. Oxygen is a chemical element obtained commercially by separation from liquid air. Substances burn by combining with oxygen. Extremely hot flames are produced in welding torches by burning other gases with pure oxygen.

oyster *n.* a shellfish that is highly prized as a table delicacy.
► Oysters are mollusks with a soft body protected by a broad hinged shell. This is rough on the outside. The inside of a pearl oyster's shell is smooth, shiny mother-of-pearl. Pearl oysters make PEARLS.

Several kinds of oysters are eaten as food. People farm oysters in shallow coastal water. Oysters cling to empty shells, rocks or wooden posts on the seabed. When they grow large enough they are harvested.

Oystercatcher
The oystercatcher is a coastal bird related to the plover and found on shores and islands all around the world. It has a long, thin, red bill and red legs; its plumage is black and white, or black.

Oystercatchers forage for burrowing worms, crustaceans and mollusks. It is unlikely that they feed on oysters, though they can open some bivalves with their strong bills.

ozone *n.* a form of oxygen in which each molecule contains three atoms instead of the usual two.
► Ozone is formed from normal oxygen by electrical sparking, and is responsible for the characteristic smell sometimes noticed near electric motors. Ozone is used as a sterilizing agent and bleach. An ozone layer in the atmosphere absorbs much of the sun's harmful ultraviolet radiation.

P

A painting of the Plain of Crau by Vincent Van Gogh.

pace *n.* a single step; speed or way of walking. *vb.* walk slowly and regularly. *He paced up and down the room.*

Pacific Ocean
This is the largest and deepest of all the OCEANS. Its waters cover more than one third of the world. All the CONTINENTS would fit inside the Pacific Ocean with room to spare. Its deepest part is deep enough to drown the world's highest mountain.

The Pacific Ocean lies west of the Americas, and east of Australia and Asia. It stretches from the frozen far north to the frozen far south. There are thousands of tiny islands in the Pacific. Most were formed when VOLCANOES grew up from the seabed. Sometimes earthquakes shake the seabed and send out huge TIDAL WAVES.

pacify *vb.* make calm, peaceful.
pack 1. *vb.* put things into a bag or other container ready for a journey. *n.* a holder for carrying things on a journey. 2. *n.* a group of animals that hunt together.
package *n.* a parcel or bundle of things packed together.
packet *n.* a small parcel.
pack ice *n.* large pieces of floating ice in the ocean.
pact *n.* a solemn agreement.
pad 1. *vb.* walk along softly. 2. *n.* a kind of small cushion used to protect something from rubbing. 3. *n.* sheets of paper joined together at one edge.
paddle *n.* a short oar for making a canoe move through water. *vb.* propel with paddle; move hands or feet about in shallow water.
paddock *n.* small enclosed field for horses.
paddy *n.* 1. wet field where rice is grown. 2. the growing rice itself.
padlock *n.* a removable lock.
pagan *n.* & *adj.* a person who is not a member of one of the world's major religions; a heathen; a person of no religion.
page *n.* 1. a leaf or sheet of paper, particularly in a book. 2. a boy working as messenger in a hotel, attending the bride at a wedding, etc.
pageant *n.* an open-air show or display, often celebrating an historical event.
pagoda *n.* an Asian temple, usually in the form of a tower with many stories and several roofs.
paid *vb.* past of **pay**.
pail *n.* another word for bucket.
pain *n.* an unpleasant feeling in the body; suffering.
► Pain is a warning that something is wrong somewhere in your body. You feel pain if something burns or presses hard on the ends of certain NERVES. Those parts of the body with the most nerve endings feel pain most easily.

Sometimes pain is useful. It teaches you to avoid what caused it. If you prick yourself with a pin you learn not to do it again. But headaches and toothaches serve no useful purpose. Chemists have invented anesthetic drugs and other painkillers to deaden pain caused by disease and injury.

painful *adj.* feeling or causing pain.
painstaking *adj.* careful.
paint *n.* colored liquid, which can be used for decorating and protecting walls or other surfaces, or for making pictures. *vb.* cover with paint; create a picture with paint.
► Paint is made up of a *pigment*, which gives it its color; a *binder* (such as oil, latex or resin) which dries on contact with air; and a *solvent* (water or spirit) to make it flow.

painting *n.* a painted picture.
► Painting is an art that dates back to the paintings of animals done by prehistoric people on the walls of caves. Some paintings in fact are still done directly on walls (these are called murals or frescoes). But most are painted on canvases – pieces of fabric stretched tight on wooden supports. The type of paint normally used is oil paint. This was developed in the Netherlands in the 1400s. Other paints include WATER COLORS and synthetic acrylic paints. A painter may choose any subject, including scenes from history,

P

"The Marriage Contract" by the British artist William Hogarth in the National Gallery, London.

Above right: A self-portrait by the Dutch artist Rembrandt.
Right: A painting by the French primitive artist Henri Rousseau.

religion and mythology; individual people (portraits); landscapes and seascapes; animals; scenes from everyday life; still lifes (flowers, bowls of fruit, etc.); and abstract patterns of shapes and colors. A painting can be built up gradually, with successive layers of paint – the traditional technique. Or it can be created more directly, as if the painter is "drawing" with the paint. In either case, color, texture and design are used to create an effect.

pair *n.* two of the same kind. *Look at that pair of doves sitting on my windowsill.*
pajamas *n.* a loose jacket and pants worn in bed.

Pakistan (Pakistani)
Pakistan is a Muslim nation in southern ASIA. The north and west are mountainous. Most people are farmers who live in river valleys, such as that of the INDUS. From 1947, when it became independent, to 1971, Pakistan included BANGLADESH (then East Pakistan). But a bitter civil war led to the breakup of the country.
AREA: 310,421 SQ. MILES (803,943 SQ. KM)
POPULATION: 85,558,000
CAPITAL: ISLAMABAD
CURRENCY: RUPEE
OFFICIAL LANGUAGE: URDU

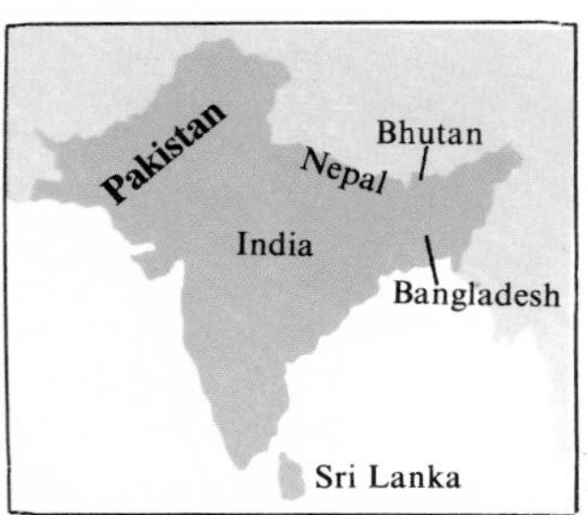

pal *n.* a close friend.
palace *n.* the home of a ruler, such as a king, queen, or bishop.
palate *n.* the roof of the mouth.
pale *adj.* not having much color.
pallor *n.* lack of color.

Palestine
Palestine is the Biblical Holy Land; it now belongs mostly to ISRAEL. The Romans took Palestine in 63 B.C. and, in the A.D. 70s, they crushed Jewish opposition and many JEWS emigrated. The area came under Muslim Arab rule in the 600s. In 1882 a group of Zionist pioneers settled in Palestine and Israel was established in 1948. Parts of Palestine in neighboring Arab nations were taken by Israel during Arab-Israeli wars.

palette *n.* board with a thumbhole on which an artist mixes paints.
palindrome *n.* word or sentence, etc., that can be read the same backward or forward. *Able was I ere I saw Elba.*
palisade *n.* a fence made of stakes.

Palladio
Andrea Palladio (1508–80) was one of Italy's greatest and most influential architects. He re-created in his designs the beauty and balance of ancient Roman architecture. His buildings included palaces and villas in Vicenza, such as the Villa Rotonda, and beautiful churches in Venice.

palm *n.* 1. the inner surface of the hand. 2. a tree with no branches but many large leaves near the top.
► A palm tree has leaves that sprout straight out of the top of its trunk, rather like the fingers of an outspread hand. There are more than 1,000 kinds of palm. Not all are trees. Some are shrubs and others are vines. Most grow in warm climates.
Palms are useful plants. People make mats and baskets from their leaves. We eat the fruits of some palms, such as coconuts.

pampas *n.* vast grass-covered plain of South America.
pamper *vb.* spoil.
pamphlet (**pamf**-*let*) *n.* a leaflet.
pan 1. *n.* a wide, flat vessel or saucepan, especially one used for frying food. 2. *prefix* meaning of or all. *Pan-American means all states of North and South America.*

Panama Canal
The Panama Canal crosses PANAMA in CENTRAL AMERICA. Ships use it as a short cut between the Atlantic and

Pacific Oceans. It is 50.72 miles (81.63 km) long. Before it was finished in 1914, ships from the United States' east coast had to sail right around South America to reach the west coast. Sets of locks on the CANAL raise and lower ships as they cross the mountainous countryside of Panama.

Panama (Panamanian)
Panama is a narrow republic in CENTRAL AMERICA. It lies between COSTA RICA and COLOMBIA. Behind the coastal plains the land is mountainous. The PANAMA CANAL, situated at the narrowest point of the country, joins the ATLANTIC and PACIFIC oceans. The Canal Zone was formerly controlled by the U.S.A., but reverted to Panama in 1979. However, the United States retains control over the canal itself.

Only a small proportion of the land is cultivated. Bananas, rice and sugarcane are important crops. Panama also has reserves of copper. But Panama's chief resource is the Canal. It became independent from Spain in 1819 as part of Colombia. Panama became a separate nation in 1914.

AREA: 29,210 SQ. MILES (75,650 SQ. KM)
POPULATION: 2,012,000
CAPITAL: PANAMA CITY

Bahamas
Cuba
Haiti
Jamaica
Belize
Honduras
Guatemala
El Salvador
Nicaragua
Costa Rica
Panama

CURRENCY: BALBOA
OFFICIAL LANGUAGE: SPANISH

pancake *n.* a flat cake made from batter cooked in a frying pan.
pancreas *n.* a gland near the stomach which helps the digestion.
panda *n.* a bearlike animal from Asia.
► The panda is an Asian MAMMAL related to a raccoon. There are two kinds of panda. One, the Red Panda, is the size of a large cat and lives in the Himalayas. It has a thick black and red coat and spends most of its time in trees; it is active at night and feeds on bamboo, fruit and nuts. The other, the Giant Panda, is a bigger, bear-like animal found in the bamboo forests of western China. It has white fur, with black legs, shoulders, ears and eye patches. The Giant Panda moves slowly; it rests by day and shuffles around at night eating bamboo shoots, small mammals and fish. Pandas are now protected as a rare species.

pane *n.* a single sheet of glass in a window.
panel *n.* 1. a division of a surface such as in a door. 2. a group of experts, entertainers, etc.
panic *n.* a sudden fear or terror which may lead people to act unthinkingly. *vb.* be affected by panic. **panicky** *adj.*
panorama *n.* a wide, all-around view. **panoramic** *adj.*
pansy *n.* a garden flower of the violet family, usually purple, yellow or white in color.
pant *vb.* breathe in and out quickly.
panther *n.* a leopard.
pantomime *n.* a kind of play with music and dancing; a performance that uses only facial and bodily gestures.
pantry *n.* a room or large cupboard where food, cutlery, crockery, etc. are kept.
pants *pl. n.* trousers.
papal *adj.* of or relating to the Pope.
paper *n.* thin, flat sheets of material for writing or printing on. *vb.* stick paper on walls.
► Paper was invented in China in A.D. 105, and reached Europe via the Arabs. Paper is made from vegetable fibers (usually wood). Wood pulp comes from the United States, Canada, Scandinavia and the U.S.S.R. The fibers are mixed with water and reduced to a pulp. The pulp goes into a mesh mold and is then pressed and dried to form a sheet. Most paper is treated to prevent it from being too absorbent – that is, so ink does not spread when it is written on. This is called *sizing*. The paper may also be dyed, or *watermarked*, whereby patterns or markings are pressed into the paper while it is still wet.

In 1799 Louis Robert invented a machine to produce a continuous reel of paper. Some modern machines can make 250 tons of paper a day. Handmade papers are still produced for high quality purposes.

paperback *n.* book bound in a paper cover.

papier-mâché (*pa-per-mu-***shay**) *n.* pulped paper used for modeling.
papoose *n.* North American Indian baby.
paprika *n.* a mild, sweet red pepper.

Papua New Guinea
Papua New Guinea is a country in the southwestern PACIFIC ocean. It consists of the eastern half of New Guinea (the western part belongs to INDONESIA) and a number of smaller islands. New Guinea contains forested mountain ranges, and broad, swampy river valleys. Numerous tribal languages are spoken. The main resource is copper. Other major products are coffee, cocoa, timber and fish.

New Guinea has been ruled by the Netherlands, Germany, Britain and Australia. The country achieved full independence within the COMMONWEALTH in 1975.

AREA: 178,270 SQ. MILES (461,691 SQ. KM)
POPULATION: 3,221,000
CAPITAL: PORT MORESBY
CURRENCY: KINA
OFFICIAL LANGUAGE: ENGLISH

papyrus (*pap-i-rus*) *n.* a kind of paper made from the papyrus reed in ancient Egypt.
par *n.* equality, normal amount.
parable *n.* a story that teaches a simple lesson.
parachute *n.* an umbrellalike apparatus used for floating down from an aircraft. *vb.* descend by parachute.
► Parachutes slow down objects traveling through air. A person wearing a parachute can jump from a plane high in the sky and float safely down to earth. Parachutists called skydivers use special parachutes that they can steer to land just where they want. Some racing cars and planes use parachutes as extra brakes.

parade 1. *n.* a procession. 2. *n.* soldiers gathered for inspection. *vb.* assemble; display.
paradox *n.* a statement which seems contradictory but is nonetheless true.
paragraph *n.* several sentences grouped together because they deal with one main idea.

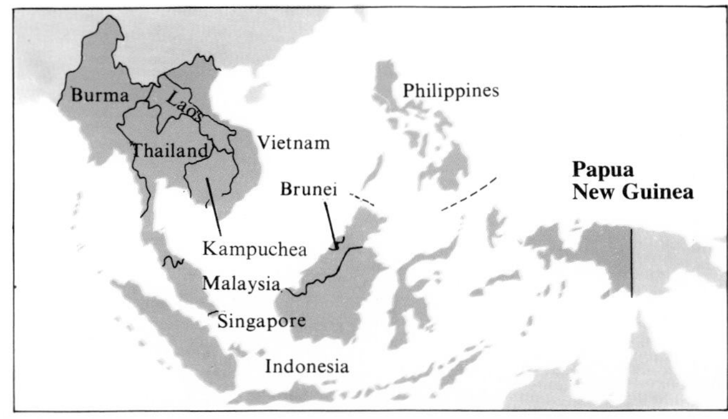

Paraguay (Paraguayan)
Paraguay is a landlocked, subtropical country in the center of SOUTH AMERICA. Its main river is also called the Paraguay. Most people work on the land, and cattle rearing is important. Cotton and soybeans are major crops, and forestry is another traditional industry. Since it declared itself independent of SPAIN in 1811, Paraguay has been involved in several wars with neighboring countries.

AREA: 157,057 SQ. MILES (406,752 SQ. KM)
POPULATION: 3,254,000
CAPITAL: ASUNCIÓN
CURRENCY: GUARANI
OFFICIAL LANGUAGE: SPANISH

parakeet *n.* small, long-tailed parrot.
parallel *vb.* & *adj.* lines that are the same distance from each other along their entire length. *The tracks of a railway are parallel.*
paralysis *n.* **paralyze** *vb.* (make) helpless.
paralyzed *adj.* unable to move or feel.
paramount *adj.* supreme.
parapet *n.* low wall along edge of roof, etc.
paraplegia *n.* paralysis of the legs and lower part of the body.
parasite *n.* an animal or plant that lives in or on another living animal or plant. **parasitic** *adj.*
► Parasites usually weaken and sometimes kill their "host." Some animal parasites live inside the host's body: the tapeworm, for example, attaches itself to the host's intestines and steals the digested food. Others, such as the FLEA, hang on to the skin and live by sucking blood. There are also two kinds of plant parasite. Those such as the MISTLETOE have leaves but no roots; they only take water from the host and use it to make their own food. But other plants have no roots and no leaves – just flowers – and these depend entirely on their host for nourishment.

parasol *n.* a sunshade similar to an umbrella.
parcel *n.* a package that has been wrapped up in paper, usually for sending through the mail.
parchment *n.* the skin of a sheep or goat, specially dried and prepared, and used in former times for writing on. *Parchment was used for books and documents before the introduction of paper.*
pardon *vb.* forgive someone. *n.* forgiveness.
parent *n.* a mother or father.
parental *adj.* of parents.

Paris (Parisian)
Paris is the capital of FRANCE, and France's largest city. The river SEINE divides the city into the left bank and the right bank.

If you gaze down on Paris from the Eiffel Tower you will see many parks and gardens, fine squares and tree-lined avenues. Other famous landmarks are the cathedral of Nôtre Dame, the basilica of the Sacre Coeur, the Arc de Triomphe and the Louvre Palace, now a famous museum.

Paris is a major cultural center, with an ancient university, and many fine art galleries, theaters and museums.

Paris is famous for its women's fashions, jewelry and perfume. Another important industry is car manufacturing.

parish *n.* 1. the district that surrounds and belongs to a church. 2. a local Protestant church community.
park 1. *n.* a public garden. 2. *vb.* stop one's car in a parking place. **parking lot** *n.* a place where people can leave their cars.
parliament *n.* the group of people who are elected to make the laws of a country.
► A parliament is a meeting of people held to make a nation's laws. One of the first parliaments was Iceland's *Althing*, which was founded more than 1,000 years ago.

In Great Britain, the HOUSES OF PARLIAMENT stand by the river THAMES in LONDON. Members of Parliament chosen by the people sit in the House of Commons. Certain (unelected) noblemen and churchmen sit in the House of Lords. The British Parliament was started in 1265. It grew gradually out of a meeting of nobles who advised the king. In the 1300s it was divided into the two Houses, and by the 1700s Parliament had become more powerful than the king.

parody *n.* piece of music or literature in which an artist's style is imitated in order to amuse or ridicule; satirical imitation.
parole *n* & *vb.* a release of a prisoner before his or her prison sentence is finished.
parrot *n.* a brightly colored tropical bird with a hooked beak.
► The parrot is found mainly in Southeast Asia, Australia and South America. There are about 500 species; many of them are good mimics, able to copy other sounds, especially human voices. Parrots generally inhabit trees and feed on fruit and nuts; they can live for 50 years.

parsley *n.* an herb grown in temperate lands. Its fine, curly leaves are used either fresh to decorate foods, or fresh or dried as a flavoring.
parsnip *n.* a sweet root vegetable.
part 1. *n.* a piece of something; not the whole thing; a role in a play. 2. *vb.* divide into parts; leave one another's company.

Parthenon
The Parthenon is the famous temple in ATHENS, built 447–438 B.C. It was so called because it was dedicated to the goddess Athena Parthenos (meaning "the Virgin"). It was reduced to ruins in 1687, when the Venetians bombarded Athens (then held by the Turks). Part of the Parthenon's beautiful sculptured frieze was acquired by Lord Elgin and is now in the British Museum.

participate *vb.* take part in; share.
participle *n.* an adjective formed from a verb, e.g. a going concern.
particle *n.* a very small part of something.
particular *adj.* one rather than another. *This particular book is very interesting.* **particularly** *adv. I particularly like this book.*
partition 1. *n.* a temporary wall or screen. 2. *vb.* separate into parts. *India was partitioned into two countries – India and Pakistan.*
partly *adj.* to some extent; not all. *The pedestrian was partly to blame for the accident.*
partner *n.* & *vb.* a person who does something with someone else. *Alice is my tennis partner.* **partnership** *n.*
partridge *n.* common game bird, related to the pheasant, found in Europe, Africa and Asia. Most species live on the ground.
party *n.* a group of people who come together to enjoy themselves; an

The African gray parrot can imitate almost any sound.

organized group that tries to get certain people elected.
pass 1. *vb.* go by. *You have to pass the school to reach the park.* 2. *vb.* give something to someone who cannot reach it. *Please will you pass me the butter.* 3. *vb.* satisfy examiners. *I passed all my exams.* 4. *n.* a piece of paper that allows you to go somewhere or do something. *My grandma has a pass that allows her to go free on the buses.* 5. *n.* a narrow passage through mountains.
passage *n.* a narrow way between buildings or through a building.
passenger *n.* a person being taken in a motor vehicle, ship or aircraft.
passerine *n.* & *adj.* (in zoology) a very large order of perching birds.
passion *n.* strong emotion; enthusiasm.
Passover *n.* an important Jewish religious festival, lasting eight days and held in springtime. It commemorates the escape from Egypt under Moses. There is a ritual meal in the home on the first evening.
passport *n.* a document that travelers show when going from one country to another.
password *n.* a secret word that helps one to be recognized by a sentry.
past 1. *n.* the time before the present time. *The Sumerians lived in the distant past.* 2. *adv.* up to and farther than something. *You go past the school to get to the hospital.*
pasta *n.* Italian dish made from cooked flour paste in various shapes, e.g. macaroni, spaghetti, etc.
paste *n.* any thick, semi-liquid substance, such as toothpaste; a kind of glue used for sticking paper. *vb.* stick things together with paste.
pastel *n.* a crayon. *adj.* soft, pale (color).
pastern *n.* the part of a horse's foot between fetlock and hoof – the "ankle."

Pasteur, Louis
Louis Pasteur was a French scientist (1822–95) who discovered some of the important roles played by micro-organisms (minute living organisms). He thus founded the science of microbiology. Pasteur found out how tiny YEAST cells cause the fermentation of sugars to alcohol. He also discovered that similar processes turn wine to vinegar and make milk go sour. To prevent foods from being spoiled in this way, Pasteur devised the heating process now called *pasteurization.*

pasteurize *vb.* kill germs by heating, especially milk. The way to do this was discovered by Louis Pasteur.
pastime *n.* a game, a hobby; anything done to pass the time in a pleasant way.
pastor *n.* a clergyman.
pastry *n.* baked goods made of a mixture of flour, fat, and water.
pasture *n.* a field or piece of land for grazing livestock.
pat *vb.* & *n.* tap with the flat of the hand. *She patted the dog, which wagged its tail.*
patch 1. *n.* a small piece of ground or color. *There was a small patch of grass in the playground.* 2. *n.* a small piece of material sewn on to clothing to cover a hole. 3. *vb.* mend with a patch.
patchwork *n.* bits of material sewn together in a pattern.
patella *n.* the kneecap.
patent 1. *n.* document giving an inventor the exclusive right to make and profit from his invention for a certain number of years. 2. *adj.* obvious; unconcealed.

The Jewish Passover ceremony. It celebrates the deliverance of the Jewish people from slavery under the Egyptians. On the first night of Passover families gather together for a ritual meal called the Seder.

paternal *adj.* of or relating to a father, fatherly.
path *n.* a narrow track or footway.
pathetic *adj.* moving one to pity or contempt.
patience (**pay**-*shunce*) *n.* be able to wait calmly without complaining.
patient (**pay**-*shent*) 1. *n.* someone who is looked after by a doctor. 2. *adj.* able to wait a long time without getting cross.
patio *n.* courtyard near a house.
patriarch *n.* father or founder of a tribe. *Abraham was a patriarch of Old Testament times.*
patriot *n.* a person who loves his country and all it stands for. **patriotism.** *n.*
patrol 1. *vb.* & *n.* go around a place to see that everything is correct. *His job is to patrol the factory at night.* 2. *n.* a small group of soldiers, aircraft or ships carrying out a special task in wartime. 3. *n.* a small group in the Scout movement.
pattern *n.* 1. a design that is repeated on something to decorate it. *I have a dress with a pattern of flowers on it.* 2. anything that is copied to make something else. *Mother used my dress as a pattern to make a dress for my sister.* 3. a repeating feature in mathematics.

Paul, St.
St. Paul was a great missionary (messenger) of the early Christian Church. He was born in Tarsus of Jewish parents who called him Saul. A Roman citizen, he at first persecuted Christians. The NEW TESTAMENT tells how he was converted to Christianity by a vision he saw on the road to DAMASCUS. Under his new name, he traveled widely in the countries around the eastern Mediterranean.

The New Testament contains 13 of his *epistles* (letters). Tradition says that Paul was executed for his beliefs in Rome in about A.D. 64.

pause (*paws*) *n.* stopping for a short time. *vb.* stop temporarily; hesitate.
pave *vb.* cover the ground with flat stones or concrete.
pavement *n.* an artificially covered path at the side of a road.

Pavlov, Ivan
Russian researcher into physiology (1849–1936). He won a NOBEL PRIZE in 1904 for work on digestion. But he is mainly remembered for his work with animals which revealed an unconscious process of "learning by association." This greatly influenced modern psychology.

paw *n.* the foot of some kinds of animal, such as dogs and cats.
pawn 1. *n.* a chessman of least value. 2. *vb.* hand over something of value as security for money borrowed.
pay 1. *n.* money for doing a job, particularly when given weekly or monthly. 2. *vb.* hand over money in exchange for something.
pea *n.* climbing plant cultivated for its seeds which are eaten as a vegetable. The round seeds – peas – are contained in a long pod and picked when they are unripe and green.
peace *n.* freedom from war or violence; calm.
peach *n.* a sweet, roundish, juicy kind of fruit with a hard stone and yellow-red, fuzzy skin.
peacock *n.* a large ornamental kind of pheasant, the male peafowl.
► Peafowl, found wild from INDIA through to INDONESIA, live in jungle lands near water. The peacock is a

The peacock's train spreads like a giant fan.

brilliant blue with a long train of feathers that spreads out into a magnificent fan; the peahen (female) has no train. Peafowl have been domesticated for centuries. Once bred for food, they are now kept for ornament in gardens and parks.

peak *n.* the top of a mountain; highest point (on a graph, etc.).
peal *n.* a loud ringing of bells.
peanut *n.* a groundnut; a nut that grows in a pod under the ground.
► The peanut is an important crop grown in warm parts of the world. Peanuts are covered by a red, papery skin and contained in wrinkled, yellowish pods. The nuts are full of PROTEIN and are either eaten raw or turned into peanut butter. They also produce oil, used for manufacturing margarine and soap, and they can be made into cattlefeed.

pear *n.* a sweet, juicy fruit that is narrow at one end.
pearl *n.* a silver-white gem found in some oysters (a kind of shellfish).
► Many pearls look like tiny silvery balls. They are made of *nacre*. This is the same substance that forms mother-of-pearl, the shiny lining inside an oyster shell.

If a grain of sand gets inside the shell the oyster covers the grain with layers of nacre. In time these layers form a pearl. People often put beads in oysters to persuade them to make pearls. Such *cultured* pearls come mainly from Japan. Most natural pearls are found in the Persian Gulf.

Pearl Harbor
Pearl Harbor is a U.S. naval base on the island of Oahu in HAWAII. It is famous as the scene of a surprise attack on the United States Pacific Fleet by the Japanese in World War II. As the Japanese had not previously declared war, the attack, which took place on December 7, 1941, took the United States by surprise.

Japanese carrier-based aircraft bombed the U.S. warships and sank or crippled 18 of them. This event led directly to the United States' entry into the war. The U.S.A. first established a naval base at Pearl Harbor in 1900.

Peary, Robert
Robert Peary (1856–1920) was an American explorer. In 1886 he made an expedition to GREENLAND and proved that it was an island. After two unsuccessful attempts, he finally reached the North Pole in 1909. A rival explorer, Frederick Cook, claimed to have gotten to the Pole a year earlier. However, the U.S. Congress officially recognized Peary's claim to be the first person to reach the North Pole. Since then, some doubts have been cast on Peary's achievement.

peasant *n.* (obsolete) a person who works on the land.
peat *n.* a kind of turf which can be used as a fuel instead of coal.
pebble *n.* a small, rounded stone.
peccary *n.* a wild pig of Central and South America.
peck *vb.* strike or pierce repeatedly with the bill or beak.
peculiar *adj.* very strange or unusual. *The man was wearing a peculiar hat with green feathers all over it.*
pedal *n.* a part that is pressed by the foot to make something work. *The pedals of a bicycle turn the wheel. vb.* press pedals.
pedestal *n.* base of a column.
pedestrian *n.* a person walking. *adj.* of walking; dull, uninspired, commonplace.
pedigree *n.* & *adj.* a record of the members of a family who have lived up to now. *Our dog has a pedigree that shows even her great-grandparents.*
peel *vb.* remove the skin of a fruit or vegetable. *n.* a piece of fruit or vegetable skin. *Don't throw orange peel onto the pavement.*
peep *vb.* look at something quickly, or through a small hole or space. *n.* a glance.
peer 1. *vb.* look at closely, as if unable to see properly. 2. *n.* an equal. 3. *n.* a lord (fem. **peeress**).
peg 1. *n.* a small piece of wood or other material, used for hanging things on. *Hang your coat on that peg.* 2. *n.* & *vb.* (place in) a definite category.
Pekinese *vb.* small breed of dog with a snub-nose and long, silky hair.

Peking (Beijing)
Peking is the capital of CHINA. The city stands on a sandy plain in the eastern part of the country. Many people work in factories making things like machinery, clothes and flour.

Peking is 3,000 years old and has some beautiful and ancient buildings. These date from the time when Peking had two parts, called the Inner City and the Outer City.

The Chinese emperor used to live in a palace in the Forbidden City. This was inside the Inner City. No one except the royal family was allowed inside. Peking's palaces are now museums.

pelican *n.* a large, brown or white water bird.
► Pelicans are found near estuaries and swamps in warm regions. They have a small head, short legs, massive body, long neck and a giant beak with a big pouch. The beak and pouch act as a fishing net. Although pelicans are clumsy on land, they are superb swimmers and fliers.

pelt 1. *vb.* hurl or strike repeatedly. 2. *n.* an animal's skin or fur.
pen *n.* 1. a small fenced place for animals. 2. a tool for writing that uses ink. 3. a female swan.
penalize *vb.* give a penalty to, or put at a disadvantage.
penalty *n.* fine or punishment.

Penang
Penang is the name of an island off MALAYSIA, in Southeast ASIA. The state of Penang consists of the island and Province Wellesley, a coastal strip on the Malayan mainland. Formerly ruled by Britain, Penang became a state of Malaysia in 1963.

pencil *n.* a writing instrument consisting of graphite ("lead") encased in wood. *You can usually rub out marks made with a pencil.*
pendant *n.* an ornament that hangs down on a chain.
pendulum *n.* a weighted rod that is hung so that it can swing back and forth, as on some clocks.

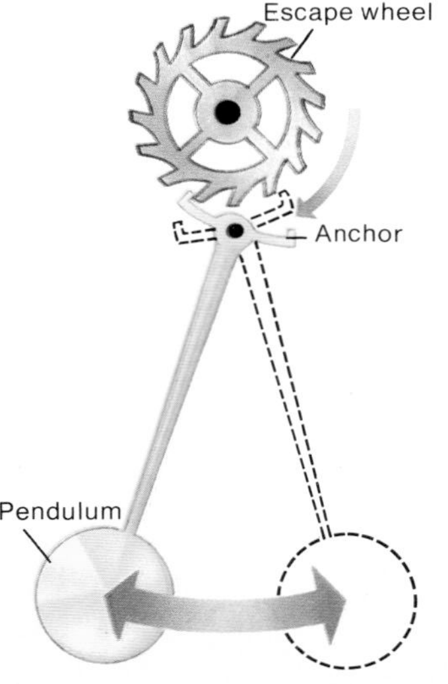

▶ When the weight of a pendulum is pulled to one side and then released, GRAVITY sets it swinging to and fro in a curved path called an *arc*. Each swing takes the same amount of time, no matter whether the swing is big or small. This makes pendulums useful for keeping time in CLOCKS. After a while a pendulum stops. But a pendulum clock keeps its pendulum swinging with a device called an escapement. This makes the "tick-tock" sound.

penetrate *vb.* pierce, pass into. **penetrating** *adj.* discerning.
penguin *n.* a flightless, fish-eating sea bird, found in the Southern Hemisphere, especially the Antarctic.
▶ There are 17 species of penguin, ranging in size from the little Blue Penguin of Australia (20 in./50 cm tall) to the great Emperor Penguin of Antarctica (over 3 ft./1 meter tall). All species have gray or black backs and white fronts. Their paddlelike wings are used for swimming; on land, they have an upright waddling walk.

Penguins nest in large breeding grounds on the shoreline. Some build simple nests; others lay their eggs directly onto the ground.

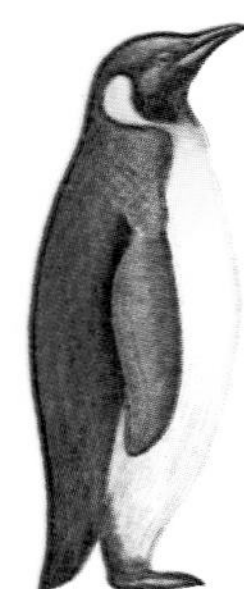

The King Penguin. Penguins are found in the colder regions of the Southern Hemisphere.

penicillin *n.* a substance used in medicine to kill bacteria.
▶ Penicillin can be given in a pill or by injection. It is a natural substance, extracted from certain molds (FUNGI). It was discovered by Sir Alexander FLEMING in 1928.

peninsula *n.* a piece of land almost surrounded by sea. *Italy is a peninsula.* **peninsular** *adj.*
penis *n.* male organ of reproduction in humans and mammals.
penknife (**pen**-*nife*) *n.* a small knife that shuts into itself.

Pennsylvania (*abbrev.* **Pa.**)
Pennsylvania is called the Keystone State because it was in the center of the original 13 American colonies. It is a great manufacturing, mining and farming state, with a large population.

The Appalachian Mountains cross the state from east to west. West of the mountains lie plateaus that rise to more than 2,000 ft. Plains lie in the southeast. The main rivers are the Susquehanna and the Delaware. The capital is Harrisburg.

The colony of Pennsylvania was started by the English Quaker William Penn. Pennsylvania played a big part in the American War of INDEPENDENCE. In 1774, the first Continental Congress met in PHILADELPHIA, and the Declaration of INDEPENDENCE was adopted there in 1776.

In the Civil War, Pennsylvania was invaded by General Robert E. LEE. He was beaten back at the Battle of Gettysburg.

pen pal *n.* someone who writes to you and to whom you write although you have not met.
pension (**pen**-*shun*) *n.* money paid regularly to someone who has retired from work. *vb.* give a pension.
penta- *prefix* meaning five, e.g. **pentagon** *n.* a five-sided figure.

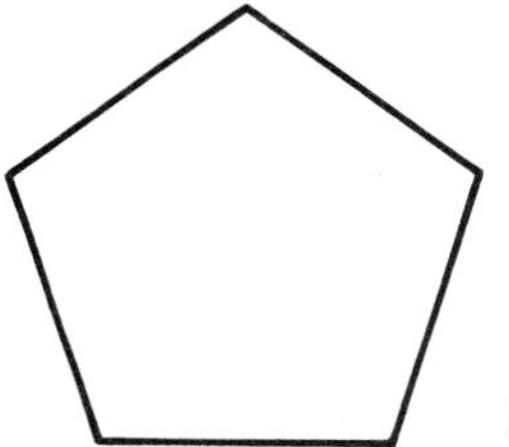

Pentagon

Pentecost *n.* Jewish harvest festival. Christian Whitsun.
penultimate *adj.* next to last.
people (**pee**-*pl*) *n.* men, women and children; human beings; race. *All the people on our street came to the party.* *vb.* populate.

Peoples Democratic Republic of Yemen see **Yemen P.D.R.**

pepper *n.* a hot-tasting powder made from dried berries of various tropical plants. *Pepper is used to flavor food.*
peppermint *n.* kind of mint grown for its oils.

Pepys, Samuel
Samuel Pepys (1633–1703) was an English government official who wrote a famous diary. This gives us a lively idea of what life was like in London in the reign of CHARLES II. Pepys wrote about the fire that burned down much of London. He set down gossip about the king, described family quarrels, and told of visits to the theater.

per *prep.* by, through, by means of, for each, e.g. **percent** for each hundred, a fraction written as part of 100. *50 percent is 50 parts in 100, or ½; 10 percent is 10 parts in 100, or 1/10. Percent is usually written* %
perceive (*pur*-**seeve**) *vb.* become aware of. **perception** *n.* understanding; acute awareness.
perch 1. *n.* a resting place for a bird. *vb.* rest on a perch. 2. *n.* a common freshwater fish.
percussion instrument *n.* a musical instrument that is struck or shaken. *Drums, tambourines and triangles are percussion instruments.*
perennial *n.* & *adj.* lasting for a long time; for more than a year. *Roses and lilies-of-the-valley are perennial flowers.*
perfect *adj.* so good that it cannot be made better. *vb.* make perfect.
perforate *vb.* make holes in.
perform *vb.* do something in front of other people. *We performed our play in front of the whole school.* do something; carry out. *I am sure that he will perform the task perfectly.* **performer** *n.*
performance *n.* something that is done so that other people can see or hear it.
perfume (**purr**-*fyoom*) 1. *n.* a scent, a sweet-smelling liquid. (*purr*-**fyoom**) 2. *vb.* spread a sweet scent around.
▶ Perfume, or scent, is used to give a pleasant scent to the body. The ancient Egyptians made perfume by soaking fragrant wood in water and oil, and then rubbing the liquid on their bodies. Today, expensive perfumes are still made from plant and animal oils, but cheaper ones usually have synthetic ingredients (mainly coal tar products). Traditional plant oils include rose, jasmine and lavender, though there are many more. Animal oils include musk, produced by scent glands in certain animals such as the musk deer, civet and beaver.

perhaps *adv.* maybe; possibly. *Perhaps they have forgotten to come.*
peril *n.* danger, risk of danger.
perimeter (*per*-**rim**-*e-ter*) *n.* the distance around the outside of an area.
period *n.* 1. a length of time. 2. occurrence of menstruation. **periodic** *adj.*
periodical *n.* publication which appears at regular intervals.
periscope *n.* an instrument like a tube with mirrors in it that lets someone see over something. *We used a periscope to see over the heads of the crowd.*
perish *vb.* become destroyed, come to end, die. **perishable** *adj.* not long-lasting. *Salads are highly perishable.*
permafrost *n.* a term used for layers of soil or rock that are permanently frozen.
permanent *adj.* unchanging; not expected to change. *This is now our permanent address.* **permanence** *n.*
permission *n.* being allowed to do something. *The teacher gave us permission to go home early.*
permit (**purr**-*mit*) *n.* writing license stating that something is allowed. (*pur*-**mit**) *vb.* allow.

P

perpendicular *adj.* upright, at right angles to the horizon.
perpetual *adj.* lasting forever.

Persia see **Iran**

persist *vb.* go on resolutely, stubbornly; take a firm stand.
person *n.* any man, woman or child. *Did a person in a brown hat come in here?*
personality *n.* special characteristics that distinguish a person; a character; a well-known personality.
perspective *n.* a method of representing in two dimensions the optical effect of distance in three dimensions.
persuade (*per*-**swade**) *vb.* make or try to make someone change his or her mind; influence, convince. **persuasion** *n.*

Peru (Peruvian)
Peru is the third largest nation in SOUTH AMERICA. It touches five other countries. Western Peru is washed by the Pacific Ocean. The sharp snowy peaks of the high Andes Mountains cross Peru from north to south like a giant backbone. Between the mountains and the ocean lies a thin strip of desert. East of the mountains hot, steamy forests stretch around the AMAZON.

Many Peruvians are Indians, or descended from Spanish settlers, or a mixture of the two. Peruvians grow sugar cane and coffee. The sheep and LLAMAS in the mountains produce wool. Peru mines copper, iron and silver. Its ocean fishing grounds usually hold more fish than those of any other nation in the world.

People have been building towns in Peru for several thousand years. The most famous people were the INCAS who ran a city empire high in the Andes mountains. But in the 1530s a small Spanish force under Francisco Pizarro captured the Inca emperor, Atahualpa, whose empire was eventually destroyed. Ruins of this early civilization can be seen in Peru today. Peru became a Spanish colony until it was finally granted its independence in the 1820s.

AREA: 492,252 SQ. MILES (1,285,216 SQ. KM)
POPULATION: 18,786,000
CAPITAL: LIMA
CURRENCY: SOL
OFFICIAL LANGUAGE: SPANISH

pessimism *n.* a belief that everything will turn out badly; the opposite of optimism. **pessimist** *n.*
pest *n.* plant or animal that is harmful or causes trouble. *Rats are pests on a farm because they eat grain.*
pester *vb.* annoy continually; keep asking questions.
pestle *n.* implement for pounding substances (in a mortar).
pet *n.* a tame animal kept for fun. *vb.* treat as a pet; fondle.
petal *n.* one of the leaflike parts of the flower of a plant.
peter out *vb.* come gradually to an end.

Peter the Great
Tsar of Russia (born 1672, reigned 1682–1725). He was anxious that Russia should become a modern nation along Western European lines, and carried out many important changes. He founded the Russian navy, and sent expeditions to the Pacific to look for gold and establish trading stations. During his reign, Russia went to war with Turkey (1694–1700), and then with Sweden (1700–1721) for control of the Baltic. Peter the Great built St. Petersburg (Leningrad) as the new capital of Russia.

petrify *vb.* (literally) turn into stone; terrify.
petticoat *n.* a kind of underskirt worn by girls and women, usually a little shorter than the outer clothes.
petty *adj.* small, unimportant, trivial. **petty cash** *n.* cash kept for small items.
pew (rhymes with *few*) *n.* a bench in a church.
pewter (**pyou**-*ter*) a dull gray metal which is an alloy (mixture) of lead and tin.
pharaoh (**fair**-*oh*) *n.* a king of ancient Egypt.
► We use the word *pharaoh* to mean "king" when we talk of the kings of ancient EGYPT. (The ancient Egyptians gave their kings other titles as well). "Pharaoh" comes from *peraa*, which means "great house."

Egyptians believed that each pharaoh was the same god in the shape of a different man. He lived in certain ways said to have been fixed by the gods. The pharaoh was said to look after all the needs of his people. He was supposed to rule everything and everyone in Egypt. He owned all the land. All of Egypt's nobles, priests and soldiers were supposed to obey him. But in fact the priests and nobles became largely responsible for running the country.

phase *n.* a stage in the development of something; one of the various stages of the moon's monthly journey around the earth. *vb.* carry out by phases.

pheasant *n.* a long-tailed game bird common in many parts of the world.
►The male pheasant's plumage has bright metallic colors. Pheasants spend most of their time on the ground, scratching the earth for seeds and insects.

phenomenon (*fe*-**nom**-*enon*) *n.* a remarkable person, happening or thing. **phenomenal** *adj.* amazing.
phi (*fie*) *n.* the 21st letter of the Greek alphabet (φ) which is shown in English spelling as *ph*. All words beginning with *ph* in English come from Greek words and are pronounced with the sound of **f**, e.g. **phone** (*fone*).

Phidias
Greek sculptor and architect (*c.* 500–432 B.C.) who built the Parthenon in Athens.

Philadelphia
Philadelphia is a historic city in Pennsylvania. In 1682 William Penn started a Quaker settlement there. The Declaration of INDEPENDENCE was signed in Independence Hall, the home of the famous LIBERTY BELL. Philadelphia was the colonial capital from 1777–1788, and capital of the new United States (1790–1800).

philharmonic *n.* symphony orchestra.

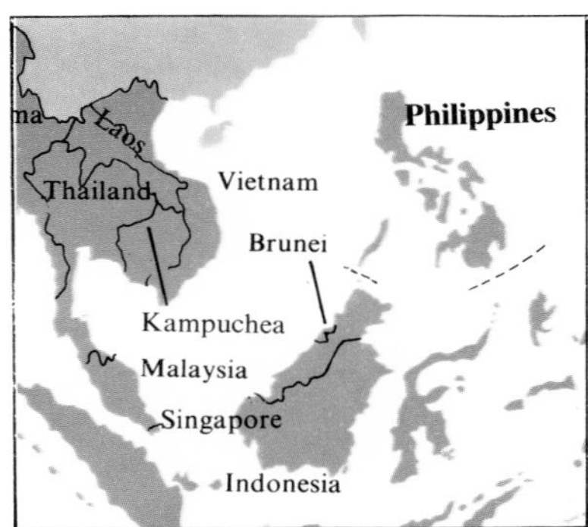

Philippines (Filipino)
The Republic of the Philippines consists of over 7,000 islands in Southeast ASIA. Most of the islands are small and uninhabited. The two largest are Luzon in the north and Mindanao in the south. The country is mountainous and contains active volcanoes. Earthquakes and *typhoons* (tropical storms) are common. Industry is taking over from agriculture as the main occupation. The country's mineral wealth includes gold, silver and copper. Tourism is also important. The islands were discovered by MAGELLAN in 1521, and later colonized by SPAIN. This fact explains why today most Filipinos are Roman Catholics. The United States took over the islands in 1898 after the Spanish-American

war. The country became independent in 1946.
AREA: 115,837 SQ. MILES (300,000 SQ. KM)
POPULATION: 50,697,000
CAPITAL: MANILA
CURRENCY: PESO
OFFICIAL LANGUAGE: PHILIPINO

philosophy *n.* the search for understanding; the study of ideas. **philosopher** *n.*
phobia *n.* strong fear, dislike of.

Phoenicians
The Phoenicians were a people who lived in the coastal lands of Lebanon from about 3000 B.C. They were organized into city states, such as Tyre and Sidon, and were skilled seamen. From the 1100s B.C. they began to trade all over the Mediterranean and beyond, and founded colonies such as CARTHAGE. They also invented the first ALPHABET.

phoenix *n.* a mythical Arabian bird which was supposed to burn itself to death every 500 years and then be miraculously reborn from its own ashes.
phone *n.* & *vb.* short for **telephone**.
phonetics *pl. n.* the branch of the study of languages that deals with pronunciation and which uses special **phonetic alphabets** to cover all the different sounds that languages use. **phonetic** *adj.*
phoney (**fo**-*ney*) *adj.* sham, not genuine.
phosphorus *n.* a nonmetallic element that occurs in various physical forms (symbol – *P*).
► White or yellow phosphorus is a waxy, poisonous, inflammable solid. It catches fire spontaneously in air, so is usually kept under water. When heated, it changes to red phosphorus. This form is nonpoisonous and does not ignite spontaneously. Under extreme pressure, white phosphorus changes to a black form. Phosphorus is essential to life and occurs in bones as calcium phosphate. Phosphorus was used to make matches, and phosphorus compounds are used as detergents and fertilizers.

photography *n.* the process or art of taking pictures with a camera.
► The word *photography* comes from Greek words that mean "drawing with light." When you take a photograph, rays of LIGHT produce a picture on the film of your CAMERA.
What happens is this. First you look through a viewfinder at the subject you want to photograph. You may have to adjust the camera to focus on the subject and to make allowances for the amount of light available. Then you press a button that lets light from the subject enter the camera. The light passes a LENS that produces an image of your subject on a film in the camera. But the image shows up only when the film is developed (treated with chemicals). A developed film is called a *negative*. This shows black things white, and white things black. From negatives you can print *positives*, the final photos.

photostat *vb.* & *n.* a copy of writing or pictures made by a special machine.
photosynthesis *n.* a process by which green plants turn carbon dioxide and water into carbohydrates.
► In photosynthesis, carbon dioxide enters the plant through its LEAVES and the water is taken in by the roots. Photosynthesis, which means "building with light," only happens in the presence of sunlight and a special green coloring matter, called CHLOROPHYLL. The chlorophyll absorbs light energy from the sun and uses it to power various chemical reactions that convert the carbon dioxide and water into sugar. During the process, oxygen is given off. Photosynthesis mostly takes place in the leaves.

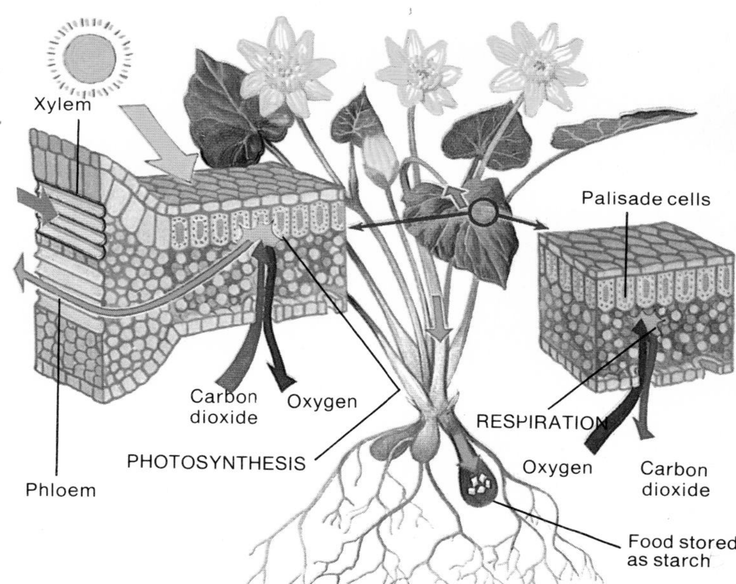

A green pigment called chlorophyll in the upper layer of cells in each leaf converts light energy into chemical energy. This fuels photosynthesis.

phrase *n.* a group of words linked together to form part of a sentence. *"Part of a sentence" is a phrase in the last sentence.*
physical *adj.* 1. having to do with the body. 2. (of a map) showing features like high and low ground and rivers.
physics *n.* the study of light, heat, sound and energy.
► The science of physics can be split into various branches. MECHANICS deals with objects and forces, and is subdivided into *statics* (stationary objects) and *dynamics* (moving objects). Other branches of physics are HEAT, LIGHT, SOUND, and ELECTRICITY and MAGNETISM. Nuclear physics is the study of the physical properties of ATOMS and their constituent particles.

piano *n.* a musical stringed instrument with a keyboard. **pianist** *n.* a person who plays the piano.
► A piano has keys that connect with padded hammers that strike wires inside. The first design was built in 1709 (forerunners were the virginals and clavichord). There are two types: the upright piano, with vertical strings; and the concert or grand piano, with horizontal strings.

Picasso, Pablo
Pablo Picasso (1881–1973) was the most famous artist of this century. He was born in Spain but lived mostly in France.
People said Picasso could draw before he learned to talk. Early on he painted poor people and circus performers. He disliked paintings that looked like photographs, and admired the curving shapes of African sculpture. Picasso began painting people as simple shapes like cubes, and as if they could be seen from several sides at once. Picasso did hundreds of paintings, as well as sculpture and pottery.

Piccard, Auguste
Auguste Piccard (1884–1962) was a Swiss inventor who explored the

P

atmosphere and the ocean depths. In 1932 he floated 53,000 ft. (16,000 meters) high inside an airtight metal ball hung from a huge balloon. He also designed a bathyscaphe. In 1960 this took men deeper down into the ocean than anyone had ever been before.

piccolo *n.* a small musical wind instrument which produces very high notes.

pick 1. *vb.* select or choose something. 2. *vb.* dig at something (with your fingers). 3. *n.* a sharp tool for digging.

picket *n.* & *vb.* 1. a person posted by a union during a strike, who may try to prevent from working those who want to work. 2. a pointed stake driven into the ground.

pickle *vb.* preserve vegetables or other food in vinegar, brine, etc. **pickle** *n.*

pick up *vb.* 1. lift something up with your hand. *Pick up your pencils when I say now.* 2. give someone a ride in your car. *I picked up old Mr. Brown and took him to the library.*

picnic *n.* & *vb.* a meal eaten out of doors in the countryside. *This field will be just right for our picnic.* (past **picnicked**).

picture *n.* a drawing, painting, photograph or other illustration. *vb.* describe; imagine.

pie *n.* food in a pastry crust.

piebald *adj.* & *n.* (color of) horse with patches of black and white.

piece *n.* a part of something; a fragment; a musical or literary composition. *vb.* put together, mend.

pier (*peer*) *n.* a structure built out over water. *A pier is a place for ships to stop at.*

pierce *vb.* bore through, make a hole in, perforate.

pig *n.* swine; a farm animal whose meat provides pork and bacon.
► Pigs are bred throughout the world. They have stout, heavy bodies covered with rough, bristly hair. People have kept pigs for about 5,000 years. They provide meat, and their fat, skin and hair are used to make products like lard, leather and brushes.

pigeon (**pid**-*jun*) *n.* a medium-sized bird found all over the world. *Many pigeons live in towns and cities.*
► Pigeons and doves are birds that eat seeds or fruit. Many make soft cooing sounds. Pigeons are larger than doves. The crowned pigeon is bigger than a chicken, but the diamond dove is almost as small as a lark.

Tame pigeons all come from rock doves, which nest on cliffs. Homing pigeons will fly great distances to return home. A bird once flew 800 miles (1,300 km) in one day.

piglet *n.* a young pig.

pigment *n.* substance that gives color, e.g. to paints, plastics, etc.
► The skin contains a pigment called *melanin*. The more melanin there is, the darker the skin's color.

pigmy see **pygmy**.

pigsty *n.* a building for pigs.

pigtail *n.* a tight braid or plait of hair.

pike *n.* 1. a kind of spear used in former times. 2. a fierce freshwater fish.
► Pike live in the Northern Hemisphere. They are yellowish-green and measure up to 5 ft. (1.5 meters) in length. They are greedy, vicious creatures and will attack and eat fish as large as themselves.

pilchard *n.* small fish of the herring family.

pile 1. *n.* a heap of things on top of each other. *vb.* throw in a pile. 2. *n.* (atomic pile) nuclear reactor.

pilgrim *n.* a person who travels to visit a holy place. **pilgrimage** *n.* a pilgrim's journey.

Pilgrim Fathers
The Pilgrim Fathers were a group of Puritans who originally lived in the English county of Nottinghamshire. They lived in fear of persecution for their religious beliefs. Finally, they decided to emigrate to North America to achieve religious freedom. After various setbacks, they sailed from Plymouth in the MAYFLOWER in September 1620. After a stormy crossing of the ATLANTIC which took 65 days, they landed at what is now Plymouth, MASSACHUSETTS. The following year they gathered in their first harvest. This event is still celebrated throughout the United States as THANKSGIVING DAY.

On November 21, 1620, the Pilgrim Fathers dropped anchor at Plymouth, Massachusetts after a long, stormy voyage.

pill *n.* a small ball of medicine.

pillar *n.* a post, often made of stone, for supporting a building.

pillbox *n.* a box to keep pills in.

pillion *n.* a saddle for a passenger on a motorcycle or bicycle.

pillow *n.* a kind of cushion on a bed for supporting the head.

pillowcase *n.* removable washable cover for a pillow.

pilot *n.* a person qualified to fly an aircraft; a person who is trained to take a ship through difficult waters. *vb.* guide, act as pilot of. *adj.* experimental.

pimple *n.* small inflamed swelling on the skin.

pin *n.* a small, thin piece of metal like a tiny nail, sharp at one end, and used for fastening things together. *vb.* fasten with pins.

pinafore *n.* a kind of apron worn over a dress. *She wears a pinafore to keep her dress clean.*

pincer *n.* 1. claw of a crab, lobster, etc. 2. **pincers**. *pl.* a tool for gripping things, especially for pulling out nails.

pinch *vb.* 1. grip between a finger and a thumb; hurt by squeezing. 2. (*slang*) steal.

Evergreen pine needles.

pine *n.* an evergreen coniferous (cone-bearing) tree with needlelike leaves. **pine cone** *n.* fruit of the pine.
► There are about 200 species of pine, all growing in the cooler parts of the Northern Hemisphere. Pine is a valuable timber tree. Its pale wood is mostly used for furniture, construction work and paper pulp. Some species are also tapped for resin from which turpentine is obtained.

pineapple *n.* a large, sweet, juicy tropical fruit with a prickly covering.

pinion *n.* bird's wing, especially the outer joint.

pink 1. *n.* & *adj.* a pale red color. 2. *n.* a kind of garden flower.

pint *n.* a measure for liquids, etc. *There are eight pints in one gallon.*

pioneer *n.* a person who goes to a new place or country to settle; someone who is the first to do something.
pious *adj.* holy, devout.
pip *n.* the seed of a fruit.
pipe *n.* 1. a tube along which water, etc., can flow. 2. a device, usually wooden, for smoking tobacco.
pipedream *n.* a fantastic plan or hope.
pipeline *n.* pipe with pumps for conveying gases, liquids, etc.
piper *n.* person who plays pipes.
piranha *n.* savage freshwater fish from tropical South America.
► Piranhas, about 1 ft. (30 cm) long, are carnivorous. With their strong jaws and sharp teeth, they attack and tear the flesh off other fishes and mammals – even human beings.

pirate *n.* a sea robber.
► Pirates were common from ancient times until the 1800s, and survived until recently in the China Seas. But the 1600s and 1700s were the great age of piracy. Arab pirates from North Africa patrolled the "Barbary Coast" along the Mediterranean and the eastern Atlantic, while Englishmen such as Henry Morgan and Captain Kidd raided Spanish shipping in the West Indies. They stole cargoes and often killed or captured the crews of the vessels they attacked.

pirouette *n.* & *vb.* (in ballet) a spin on one leg.

Pisa
Pisa is a city near the west coast of ITALY, on the River Arno. It has many tourists who come to see the famous Leaning Tower. This is the belltower of Pisa Cathedral. Completed in 1350, it has continued to lean over very slowly as the ground beneath it has sunk. GALILEO was born in Pisa. Legend says that he used the Leaning Tower for some of his experiments.

pistil *n.* the seed-producing part of a flower.
pistol *n.* a small gun that is held in one hand.
pit *n.* 1. a deep hole with steep sides. 2. a mine.
pitch 1. *n.* a distillation of tars, resin. 2. *vb.* throw something. 3. *n.* a sticky black material like tar. 4. *vb.* put up a tent. *They will pitch the tent out of the wind.* 5. *n.* the sound of a musical note, i.e. whether it is higher or lower than another.
pitcher *n.* 1. container for holding and pouring liquids. 2. a person who throws (**pitches**) the ball to the batter in baseball.
pitchfork *n.* a long-handled fork used for lifting hay.
pitfall *n.* a covered pit acting as an animal trap; an unknown danger.
pity *vb.* & *n.* a feeling of sadness for someone's troubles.

placard *n.* a notice or poster in a public place.
place *n.* a particular area or location. *vb.* put something in position.
placid *adj.* calm; not easily upset.
plagiarize *vb.* use someone else's ideas or writings and pass them off as one's own.
plague (*playg*) *n.* a dangerous illness which is very quick to spread. *vb.* pester, bother.
plain 1. *adj.* simple; ordinary; with no pattern on it. *Her dress was plain blue with a lace collar.* 2. *n.* a large flat area of country, usually treeless.
plaintiff *n.* person who brings a suit or action in a court of law.
plait (rhymes with *ate*) *n.* & *vb.* weave three or more strips together.
plan 1. *n.* a drawing that shows where things are. 2. *vb.* decide what you are going to do. *Shall we plan a hike this weekend?*
plane 1. *n.* short for airplane. 2. *n.* & *vb.* a tool for making wood smooth. 3. *n.* a tall tree with large leaves and bark that peels.
planet *n.* one of the bodies that move around a star.

The nine planets of the solar system. Mercury is the smallest and Jupiter the largest. Planets do not give out light. They reflect light from the sun.

► The word planet comes from a Greek word meaning wanderer. Long ago, skywatchers gave this name to "stars" that seemed to move instead of keeping still like the rest. We now know that planets are not STARS but objects that travel around stars.
The EARTH and other planets of our SOLAR SYSTEM travel around the star we call the SUN. Each planet travels in its own ORBIT. But they all move in the same direction, and, except for Mercury and Pluto, they lie at about the same level.
Astronomers think the planets came from a band of gas and dust that once whirled around the sun. They think that GRAVITY pulled parts of this band together as blobs that became planets.
The nine planets in the solar system are MERCURY, VENUS, EARTH, MARS, JUPITER, SATURN, URANUS, NEPTUNE, and PLUTO.

planetarium *n.* a big room or building, with a domed ceiling, for reproducing the movement of planets and other heavenly bodies.
► Early planetariums, called *orreries*, were small mechanical models of the SOLAR SYSTEM. The modern planetarium is a domed building containing a complex assembly of optical projectors. These throw images of the stars and planets onto the inside of the curved ceiling, which represents the sky. The images can be moved to show the seasonal changes in the night sky or to simulate the crash of a meteorite.

plank *n.* a long flat piece of wood.
plankton *n.* tiny plants and animals that drift in the sea.
► Most plankton are so small they can only be seen with a microscope.
Planktonic plants are called *phytoplankton*. They live near the surface, where they find the light they need. Some tiny plants swim by lashing the water with little whips. Others have spiky shells that look like glass.
Planktonic animals are called *zooplankton*. Some live deep down and rise at night to feed. Zooplankton includes tiny one-celled creatures, and baby crabs and fish.

P

The plant kingdom is divided into a number of groups. The Angiosperms or flowering plants (1) include broad-leaved trees and most flowers (dicotyledons) as well as such plants as lilies and grasses (monocotyledons); Gymnosperms (2) include conifers; Ferns (3), mosses (4), fungi (5) and algae (6) make up the other groups.

All sea creatures either depend directly on plankton for food or else on other animals that feed on plankton.

plant 1. *n.* any living thing (particularly a flower) that is not an animal. *vb.* put a plant in the ground. *We have just planted several trees.* 2. *n.* a factory or any other industrial building or machinery.

► Life on earth consists of plants and animals. Although most animals are able to do many more things than plants – such as moving, seeing and hearing – there is one very important thing they cannot do; animals cannot make food, while some plants – green plants – can. (By PHOTOSYNTHESIS green plants use the sun's energy to turn carbon dioxide and water into sugar). Because of this, animals need plants to survive. They either feed directly on plants or on other animals that have themselves eaten plants. Plants are therefore a vital part of the living world.

There are over 350,000 kinds of plants. They can be divided into two main groups: plants that bear seeds and those that do not. The seed-bearing group is the largest and consists mainly of CONIFERS and flowering plants. Seed-bearing plants have well-developed roots, stem and LEAVES and produce FRUITS which contain the seeds. Plants without seeds are much simpler. In some, like FUNGI, the plant body is not separated into root, stem and leaf; others, like MOSSES, have stems and leaves, but no true root system to penetrate the soil.

plaster *n.* a coating put on walls and ceilings, to give a surface for decoration. It is made from certain cement powders, mixed with water and sand. *vb.* smear with plaster.

plastic 1. *n.* a light, strong material that is manufactured. 2. *adj.* pliable, malleable; made of plastic.

► A great many plastics are in common use, each with different properties. All plastics can be shaped easily when heated, and they all have long-chain MOLECULES – molecules made up of a chain of repeated small units. Such substances are called *polymers*, and most of them are made from petroleum products. Plastics react to heat in one of two ways. Some soften and melt, and only return to a solid state when they cool. These are called *thermoplastics* and are used to make things like bowls and buckets. Others remain quite rigid when reheated after they are formed; these are *thermosetting* plastics. They remain rigid because their long molecule chains are criss-crossed.

Most plastic products are made by molding. In *injection molding*, thermoplastic chips are heated until they melt; then the melted plastic is forced into a water-cooled mold under pressure. This method of making things from plastic is very widely used. In *blow molding*, air is blown into a blob of molten plastic inside a hollow mold, forcing it against the walls of the mold. Thermoplastics can also be shaped by *extrusion*. In extrusion, molten plastic is forced through a shaped hole or "die." Fibers for man-made TEXTILES and sheet plastic may be made in this way.

Thermosetting plastic products can be made by *compression molding*. Thermosetting powder, the molecules of which have not yet crisscrossed into a rigid plastic, is placed in the lower half of a mold. The mold is heated and the plastic powder molecules start to crisscross. Before this reaction is complete the top half of the mold is forced down onto the lower one and the plastic is pushed into shape between the two halves.

plate *n.* a flat, round piece of crockery from which food is eaten.

plateau (*plat*-**oh**) *n.* (plural **plateaus**, **plateaux**) level land higher than the land around it.

platform *n.* a small raised stage; the raised place beside the railway lines where people wait at a station.

platinum *n.* silvery, valuable metal.

platitude *n.* a dull, stale, commonplace remark, e.g. *Long time no see.*

Plato

Plato was a Greek philosopher (*c.* 428-*c.* 348 B.C.). As a follower of SOCRATES, Plato took over and developed his philosophy. He wrote 30 surviving "dialogues," including the *Symposium* (on love), the *Phaedo* (on the immortality of the soul) and the *Republic* (on politics). He also founded a school of philosophy in ATHENS.

platypus *n.* an odd-looking, dark-brown furry aquatic mammal with a bill (beak).

► The platypus is found only in AUSTRALIA and TASMANIA. It is about 18 in. (45 cm) long and has short legs, webbed feet and a wide, flat bill. The platypus is the world's most primitive MAMMAL. It has a very simple brain and, unlike any other mammal except the spiny anteater, it lays eggs; but because the platypus feeds its young on milk, it is a true mammal. The platypus lives in burrows in the banks of streams and pools, and eats small water creatures.

play 1. *vb.* have fun and not work; perform on a musical instrument; take part in or play a game. 2. *n.* a story that is told by people acting and talking to each other, usually on a stage; a dramatic piece.

playground *n.* an area for children to play in.
playtime *n.* a period when children can stop working and amuse themselves; break time.
playwright *n.* a person who writes plays; a dramatist.
plead *vb.* present a case in a law court; urge.
pleasant *adj.* nice; good or agreeable.
please 1. *vb.* make someone happy. 2. *adv.* a word to show politeness or emphasis in a request. *Please shut the door.*
pleasure *n.* feeling of being happy.
pleat *n.* a fold in cloth or paper. *vb.* make a pleat.
plebiscite (**pleb**-*iss-ite*) *n.* direct voting by all electors on a particular question or issue.
plectrum *n.* an implement made of horn, plastic, or metal for plucking the strings of a guitar, zither, etc.
pledge *n.* security; something pawned; word of honor. *vb.* promise, give one's word.
plenty *n.* much; a lot. *We have plenty of time.* **plentiful** *adj.* in large numbers or quantities.
pleurisy *n.* painful inflammation of the delicate surface lining (pleura) of the lung.
plod *vb.* trudge; walk or work with effort.
plot 1. *n.* a secret agreement to do something, usually bad. *The police discovered a plot to rob the bank. vb.* scheme. 2. *n.* a small piece of ground. 3. *n.* the main things that happen in a story.
plow (rhymes with *how*) *n.* & *vb.* a machine used to cut and turn over land to prepare it for planting.

The platypus is a primitive mammal. It lays eggs but feeds its young with milk from its body.

pluck 1. *vb.* pull feathers off a bird; gather; pick at strings on a guitar, violin, etc. 2. *n.* courage. **plucky** *adj.*
plug 1. *n.* a piece of wood, rubber or other material used to fill a hole. 2. *n.* a device for joining electrical equipment to the electricity supply. 3. *vb.* stop up with a plug.
plum *n.* a sweet round fruit with juicy flesh and a hard central stone.
plumage *n.* the entire clothing of feathers of a bird.
plumber (**plum**-*mer*) *n.* a person who fits and repairs water pipes in a building.
plump *adj.* rounded. *vb.* make plump. *She plumped up the cushions.*
plunder *vb.* rob violently, especially in war. *n.* things stolen by force; loot.
plunge *vb.* jump or fall into. *The man plunged into the canal after the drowning child.*
plural *adj.* a word which shows that there are more than one. *Cats, kittens and children are all plural nouns.*
plus *prep.* & *adj.* and, added to. *Four plus six equals 10.*

Pluto (God)
Pluto, in Roman mythology, is the god of the dead, and brother of Neptune and Jupiter. Most of the stories about him are borrowed from the Greek god Hades.

Pluto (Planet)
The planet Pluto is named after the god who ruled the world of the dead. Pluto must be bitterly cold as it is the farthest PLANET from the sun. It is almost 40 times farther from the sun than the EARTH.

Pluto spins and moves around the sun much more slowly than the earth. A day on Pluto may equal nearly a week on earth. One year on Pluto lasts almost 248 of our years.

Pluto is only half as wide as the earth, and weighs one-sixth as much.

p.m. *abbr.* after midday, from the Latin words *post meridiem.*
pneumatic (*new*-**matt**-*ik*) *adj.* worked by air under pressure; filled with air.
pneumonia (*new*-**moan**-*ya*) *n.* a serious illness of the lungs.
poach *vb.* 1. cook by simmering in water, e.g. poached eggs. 2. take game or fish illegally. **poacher** *n.*
pocket *n.* a bag sewn into a garment for carrying things; receptacle for balls in billiards, etc.; a cavity or deposit (of gold, etc.). *vb.* put into one's pocket; take illegally.
pod *n.* a long seed holder on some plants. *Peas grow in a pod.*

Poe, Edgar Allan
Edgar Allan Poe (1809–49) was an American poet and writer of short stories. He is regarded as the writer of the first modern detective story with *The Murders in the Rue Morgue.* Many of his other tales, such as *The Pit and the Pendulum*, are horror stories.

poem (**po**-*em*) *n.* a piece of writing with a special rhythm. *Poems are often written in short lines with the last word in one line rhyming with the last word of another line.*
poet (**po**-*et*) *n.* a person who writes poems.
poetry (**po**-*etry*) *n.* poems; verse.
► Poetry is LITERATURE in which special techniques have been used to give an exciting and rhythmic effect. Almost all poetry uses *meter* (regular patterns or rhythm), and much of it uses rhyme. Other important techniques are *alliteration* (words beginning with the same letter) and *assonance* (words with the same vowel sounds, although they do not actually rhyme). The main kinds of poetry are lyric (which deals with personal emotion), dramatic (as in plays), and narrative (as in ballads and epics).

point 1. *n.* the sharp end of something, such as a needle or pencil. 2. *vb.* stick out a finger in the direction of something. 3. *n.* the main idea. *Do you see the point of what has just been said?*
poison *n.* & *vb.* a substance that makes people become ill or die. **poisonous** *adj.*
► Some poisons get into the body through the skin. Some are swallowed. Poisonous gases are harmful if someone breathes them in with air.

Different poisons work in different ways. Strong ACIDS or alkalis "burn." Nerve poisons can stop the heart. Some other poisons can make the body bleed inside.

DRUGS called antidotes can cure people who are suffering from certain poisons.
►► **Poisonous Plants** Many plants are poisonous to animals and human beings. This helps to protect the

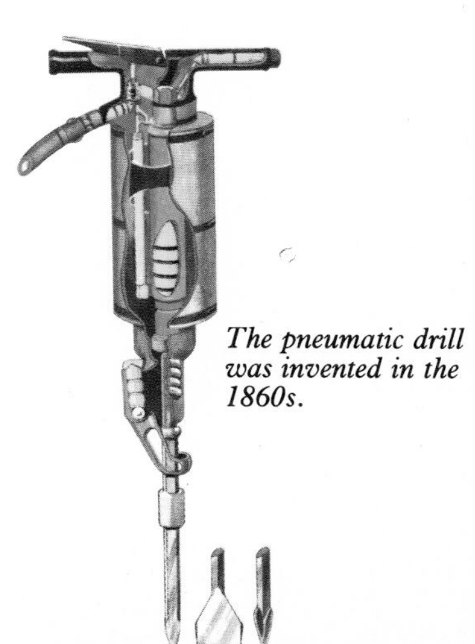

The pneumatic drill was invented in the 1860s.

plants from being eaten or damaged by animals.

Certain plants are deadly if eaten. Many people have died after eating a poisonous FUNGUS they mistook for a mushroom. Deadly nightshade, monkshood, and cassava are all deadly flowering plants. But people can eat tapioca, made from cassava that has been washed to get rid of its poison.

poke *vb.* push with a stick, finger, etc. **poker** *n.* instrument for stirring a fire.

poker *n.* a card game in which the player bets that the value of his hand is higher than those of the other players.

Poland (Polish, Pole)
This is the seventh largest country in EUROPE. Poland lies in Eastern Europe, south of the Baltic Sea. Most of Poland is low farmland although forests sprawl across the Carpathian Mountains in the south. Poland's largest river is the Vistula. This rises in the mountains and flows into the Baltic Sea. Rivers often freeze in Poland's cold, snowy winters.

Many Poles are Roman Catholics. Poland grows more flax and potatoes than almost any other nation. Only three other countries mine more coal than Poland. Its factories make machinery and ships.

Poland's frontiers have changed many times, and it has often been invaded. In the late 1700s it disappeared from the map. After WORLD WAR II, a Communist government was set up. Dissatisfaction with the pro-Russian government led to strikes and riots in the 1970s and 1980s. A national trade union – Solidarity – was formed, but its leaders were arrested in 1981 when a military government took power.

AREA: 120,732 SQ MILES (312,677 SQ KM)
POPULATION: 36,300,000
CAPITAL: WARSAW
CURRENCY: ZLOTY
OFFICIAL LANGUAGE: POLISH

polar *adj.* of or near the North or South Poles. *Polar bears live near the North Pole.*

pole *n.* 1. either the most northerly point of the earth (the North Pole) or the most southerly point (the South Pole). 2. one of the ends of a magnet. 3. a long, thin piece of wood or metal; a post.

A French traffic policeman.

police *n.* the people who help to keep the law and catch criminals. *vb.* control, provide with police.

► Police work for a government to keep law and order in their country. Their main task is to see that everyone obeys their country's laws. Part of this job is protecting people's lives and property. Police also help to control crowds and traffic. They help people hurt in accidents, and they take charge of lost children. Computers help police trace stolen property and criminal records.

Policemen try to prevent crime, and track down and capture criminals. This can be dangerous and sometimes they are killed.

policy *n.* a considered method of action carried out by a government, etc.

polish *vb.* make something smooth and glossy. *n.* smoothness; substance used to polish a surface.

polite *adj.* well-mannered.

politics *pl. n.* the science or art of government. **politician** *n.* a person taking part in politics.

poll (rhymes with *coal*) *n.* voting, number of votes. *Opinion poll.*

Polar bears are the only bears with white fur. They spend much of their life on ice floes hunting fish and seals.

pollen *n.* a fine powder on flowers which fertilizes other flowers. **pollinate** *vb.* fertilize with pollen.

► Each kind of flowering plant has pollen grains of a special shape and size. Some are so small that 6,000 would make a row no longer than a person's thumb.

Pollen grains contain male CELLS. When these meet *ovules* (female cells) on the same flower or another flower they produce SEEDS. But to do this the pollen grains must first reach the *stigma*. When pollen reaches the stigma, it grows down inside a stalk to reach the ovule. This process is called *pollination*.

Some flowers are pollinated by the wind, others by insects.

pollution *n.* the spoiling of air, soil, water or the environment by poisonous wastes. **pollute** *vb.*

► Until now, most of the wastes produced by living things have been removed by other living things. But today, people produce more wastes than nature can cope with.

Cars and factories pour smoke and fumes into the air. Chemical FERTILIZER and pesticides can kill off wild plants and animals. Poor SEWAGE DISPOSAL and oil spills make seas and rivers filthy.

polo *n.* a game similar to hockey and played on horseback.

poltergeist *n.* a noisy ghost. *The poltergeist made strange noises in the attic at night.*

poly- *prefix* meaning many, e.g. **polyandry** having more than one husband. **polysyllable** a word with more than one syllable.

Polynesia (Polynesian)
The word *Polynesia* means "many islands." It is one of the three main divisions of islands in the PACIFIC Ocean. The other two are Melanesia and Micronesia. Polynesia is the most easterly division. It includes HAWAII, Easter Island and Samoa.

Scientists believe that the Polynesian people originally sailed to the islands from the mainland of ASIA. Polynesians are tall, powerful people, the lightest skinned of the Pacific Islanders.

polytechnic (*poll-i-***tek***-nik*) *n.* a school giving instruction in many technical subjects.

pomegranate *n.* a fruit with a red rind whose flesh is full of seeds.

pomp *n.* splendor and ceremony.

Pompeii
Two thousand years ago, Pompeii was a small Roman city in southern Italy. A sudden disaster killed many of its citizens and drove out the rest. But the same disaster preserved the streets and buildings. Today, visitors to Pompeii can learn a great deal about what life was like inside a Roman city.

Plaster casts of two people overtaken by the rain of ash and cinders that blanketed Pompeii on August 24 A.D. 79.

In A.D. 79 the nearby volcano VESUVIUS erupted and showered Pompeii with volcanic ash and cinders. Poisonous gases swirled through the streets. About one citizen in every 10 was poisoned by fumes or burned to death by hot ash. The rest escaped. Ash and cinders soon covered up the buildings. In time the people living in the surrounding countryside forgot that Pompeii had ever been there.

For centuries Pompeii's thick coat of ash protected it from the weather. At last, in the 1700s, people began to dig it out. The digging has gone on until today. Archeologists discovered buildings, streets, tools, and statues. They even found hollows left in the ash by the decayed bodies of people and dogs killed by the eruption. The archeologists poured plaster in these hollows. They let the plaster harden, then they cleared away the ash. They found that the plaster had formed life-size models of the dead bodies.

pond *n.* a small area of water; a tiny lake which may be natural or artificial.

► **Pond life**: A pond may seem empty but it is a living world of plants and animals.

Tall plants such as reeds and arrowheads grow around the rim. Shallow water near the edge holds underwater plants like hornwort, Canadian pondweed and waterlilies.

Millions of algae and other tiny plants, as well as tiny animals like water fleas, make up the PLANKTON drifting in the water.

Pond life is most plentiful where plants grow thickly just below the water's edge. Countless tiny CRUSTACEANS, INSECT larvae, worms and MOLLUSKS find food and shelter here. Frogs and newts lay eggs in spring. Here, too, water birds browse on water plants or hunt for small fish. Larger fish live in the deeper water farther out. Dead plants and animals sink to the bottom where worms and other creatures eat them.

pony *n.* (plural **ponies**) a small horse.

poodle *n.* small lively dog with a black or white curly coat; the coat is often clipped. Poodles were originally Russian gundogs.

pool *n.* 1. a small, deep area of water; a pond. 2. a game like billiards.

poor 1. *adj.* & *n.* having little or no money. 2. *adj.* deserving pity. *The poor old lady has been ill for many years.* 3. *adj.* not good. *Tom's exam results were very poor.*

pop 1. *n.* a small bang. 2. *abbr.* short for popular, as in pop music and pop art.

pope *n.* the head of the Roman Catholic Church.

► The Pope is accepted by all Catholics as the representative of JESUS CHRIST on earth. He lives and rules in the VATICAN CITY, a small area within the city of Rome. Pope means "father" and was the name originally taken by the bishops of Rome. There have been Popes for over 1,900 years, ever since the time of St. Peter, the first bishop of Rome.

poplar *n.* slender, quick-growing tree of the willow family.

pop music *n.* short for popular music.

► Modern pop music has strong, lively rhythms, and simple, often catchy, tunes. Most pop tunes are songs. A pop group usually has one or more singers with musicians who play such instruments as electronic guitars, synthesizers, and electronic organs.

Famous pop groups like the BEATLES, Rolling Stones, and Abba have attracted huge audiences.

Poppy

The poppy has gray-green leaves and showy white, orange, red or purple flowers. Two well-known kinds are the corn poppy, which colors the summer fields with scarlet, and the opium poppy, which produces the drug opium.

popular *adj.* liked by a lot of people. *I think Andrew is the most popular boy in our class.* **popularity** *n.* being generally liked. **popularize** *vb.* make popular.

population *n.* all the people living in a place, city, country or the world. **populate** *vb.* fill with people.

► In the STONE AGE, the whole world held only a few million people. Their numbers were kept down by lack of food, injury and disease. As people have solved these problems, the human population has increased.

Between A.D. 1 and 1650 the world's population doubled. It doubled again in only 150 years after 1650. Since then it has risen even faster. In 1930 the world had two billion people. By 1980 there were over twice that many. The world's population is still growing too quickly.

porcelain *n.* fine china.

► The Chinese developed the art of making porcelain using *kaolin*, a pure form of clay that remained white when fired; and *petuntse*, which helped the clay turn hard and glass-like at a low temperature. Porcelain is hard and does not absorb water like earthenware. It became known in Europe only in the late 17th century.

porch *n.* a covered entrance to a building.

porcupine *n.* a large rodent covered with pointed spines.

► Porcupines are named from Latin words for "spiny pig." A porcupine is really a RODENT with many hairs shaped as long, sharp spines or quills. If a porcupine is attacked it backs toward its enemy and lashes its tail. Some of the spines stick into its enemy and cause painful wounds or even death.

American porcupines are a different group from that of Asia, Africa and Europe.

A porcupine.

pore *n.* a tiny opening in the skin. **porous** *adj.* having pores and so allowing liquid through.

pork *n.* the flesh of a pig.

porpoise *n.* a small sea animal of the whale family.

porridge *n.* soft food made of grains boiled in milk or water.

port 1. *n.* a harbor; a town by the sea with a harbor. 2. *n.* & *adj.* the left side of the ship or aircraft as you are facing forward. 3. *n.* airport: buildings, runways, etc., for airplanes and passengers. 4. *n.* the name of a Portuguese wine.

► A harbor may be no more than a sheltered piece of water with an entrance wide and deep enough to take ships. A port is a harbor with DOCKS that make it easy for ships to load and unload.

Certain countries have fine natural harbors. These include SAN FRANCISCO in the United States and

BOMBAY in western India. NEW YORK CITY and LONDON are ports built near or at the mouths of rivers.

Many harbors have been at least partly made by man. For example, engineers build breakwaters out into the sea to keep out big waves. Then, too, many harbors need DREDGING to keep their water deep enough to take big oceangoing ships. Sometimes harbors are made far inland on rivers. Manchester in England has one, and so does HOUSTON, Texas.

portable *adj.* capable of being carried, especially by hand. *A portable typewriter.*
portcullis *n.* a grating lowered to protect a gateway in a castle.
porter *n.* a person who is employed to carry things; doorkeeper, especially of large buildings.
porthole *n.* a round window in a ship.
portray *vb.* make a picture of.
portrait *n.* a picture of a person.

Portugal (Portuguese)
This is a narrow, oblong country in southwest EUROPE. It is sandwiched between the Atlantic Ocean and Spain, a country four times the size of Portugal.

Much of Portugal is mountainous. Rivers flow from the mountains through valleys and across plains to the sea. Portugal's mild winters and warm summers help its people to grow olives, oranges and rice. Its grapes produce port, a wine named after the Portuguese city of Oporto. Portugal's woods yield more CORK than those of any other nation. Its fishermen catch sardines and other sea fish. Portugal has mines and factories. The Portuguese language is similar to Spanish.
AREA: 35,555 SQ MILES (92,082 SQ KM)
POPULATION: 10,390,000
CAPITAL: LISBON
CURRENCY: ESCUDO
OFFICIAL LANGUAGE: PORTUGUESE

Portuguese man-of-war *n.* a kind of jellyfish.
► This big JELLYFISH lives in warm seas. Its large, gas-filled float sticks up above the water like the sail of an old-fashioned wooden warship. Beneath the float hangs a whole collection of animals that live together as a colony.

The longest animals have stringy tentacles. Some trail 35 ft. (10.5 metres). Each tentacle is armed with stinging cells, whose poison is said to be as deadly as a cobra's. If a fish brushes against them it becomes paralyzed. The tentacles seize their prey and then pull it up beneath the float.

pose *vb.* 1. arrange or place. 2. behave in an affected way; show off. 3. put (a question or problem).
position *n.* the place taken by somebody or something. *When you are all in position, the race will begin.* *vb.* place in position.
positive 1. *adj.* not negative; clear, confident, undoubted. 2. *n.* photographic print.
possess *vb.* have or own. *Do you possess any money?* **possession** *n.* thing owned. **possessive** *adj.* unwilling to share.
possible *adj.* & *n.* that which can happen, exist or be achieved.
possum *n.* (phalanger) the name given to a group of Australian marsupials.
► Phalangers all live in trees and have thick furry coats. They are commonly called possums because they look rather similar to the American OPOSSUM.

post- *prefix* meaning behind or after, e.g. **postmortem** examination after death.
post 1. *n.* the mail. *vb.* send a letter. 2. *n.* a thick upright pole, such as a goalpost. 3. *n.* a job or position.
postcard *n.* a card, often with a picture on one side, which you can write a message on and send through the post. *A postcard does not need an envelope.*
poster *n.* a picture, usually with writing, which goes on a wall to advertise something.
post office *n.* a building or room in which postal business is carried out.
► The post office is a government organization that brings the letters we receive and takes the letters that we send. Many towns and villages have a building called a post office, where postal work is done.

To send a letter you must first address its envelope, then add a stamp bought from a post office. The stamp is to pay for what happens after you have put the letter in a mailbox for collection.

Letters collected by local mailmen are cancelled (marked so the stamps cannot be used again). Then they are sorted according to the towns they are to go to. The sorted letters travel quickly overland by train or plane. Overseas letters usually go by plane.

When letters reach the end of their journey, they are sorted according to streets and house numbers. A mailman then delivers them.

The Portuguese man-of-war is a colony of polyps that floats on the surface of the sea. It has tentacles 35 feet (10.5 meters) long lined with stinging cells.

postpone *vb.* put off until a later time, defer. **postponement** *n.*
pot *n.* round vessel for holding liquids, etc. *vb.* plant in a flowerpot.
potassium *n.* an extremely reactive metallic element (symbol – *K*).
► When placed in water, potassium reacts violently and bursts into

A potter at his wheel.

flames. Because it reacts so quickly with oxygen or water, it is stored under oil. Potassium compounds are used in medicine, photography, explosives, soaps and dyes, and as fertilizers.

potato *n.* (plural **potatoes**) the edible tuber of the potato plant, widely eaten as a vegetable.
► Potatoes are rich in STARCHES and contain PROTEINS and different VITAMINS. Potatoes must be cooked to give nourishment that we can use.
Potato plants are related to tomatoes. Each plant is low and bushy with a soft stem. Each potato grows on a root as a kind of swelling called a tuber. When its tubers have grown, the plant dies. But new plants spring up from the tubers.
Potatoes were first grown by South American Indians. Spanish explorers brought potatoes to Europe. Today most are grown in Europe and Asia.

potter *n.* a person who makes pottery.

Potter, Beatrix

Beatrix Potter (1866–1943) was a British writer who wrote the words and painted the pictures in a series of books for young children. The most famous one is probably *The Tale of Peter Rabbit*, but she wrote many others about different animals too.

pottery *n.* pots and other things made of baked clay; a place where pottery is made.
► People have been making pottery for thousands of years. Early pots were thick, drab and gritty. They leaked, and they cracked if heated. In time people learned to make pottery that was more useful and more beautiful. Today, there are two main kinds of pottery. These are *porcelain* and *stoneware*. PORCELAIN is fine pottery made with white China clay. Thin porcelain lets the light show through. Stoneware (also called earthenware) is often made of blue, brown, gray, red or yellow clay. Stoneware is usually thicker than porcelain and it does not let the light show through.
To make a pot, a potter puts a lump of moist clay on a spinning disk rather like a record turntable. She or he uses thumbs and fingers to shape the clay into a pot and leaves this pot to dry. Next the pot may be coated with a wet mixture called a glaze. Then the pot is fired (heated) with others in an oven called a kiln. Firing makes the pots rock hard and turns their glaze into a smooth, hard, shiny coat. This makes pots leakproof. It also decorates them. Different glazes produce different colors.

pouch *n.* small bag; the receptacle in which marsupials – kangaroos, etc. – carry their young.

poultry *n.* hens, ducks, geese, turkeys and any other domestic fowl.
► All birds kept for meat or eggs are known as poultry. To most people, poultry means chickens, DUCKS, geese and TURKEYS. But guinea fowl, OSTRICHES, partridges, PEACOCKS, pheasants, and PIGEONS can be kept as poultry too.
Chickens outnumber other kinds of poultry. There are probably more chickens than people, and they lay enough eggs to give everyone on earth several hundred eggs each year. Chickens also produce meat more cheaply than sheep or cattle. This is because it costs less in food to produce a pound of chicken meat than it costs to make a pound of beef or lamb or mutton.

pounce *vb.* make a sudden attack. *The cat pounced on the mouse.*
pound 1. *n.* a measure of weight. *There are 16 ounces in one pound.* 2. *n.* a British unit of money. *There are 100 pence in a pound.* 3. *vb.* hit heavily and often.
pour *vb.* cause liquid to flow in a continuous stream, e.g. from a bottle.
poverty *n.* the lack of money.
powder *n.* fine dry particles; cosmetics or medicine in this form. *vb.* sprinkle with powder.
power *n.* the strength or ability to do something; a country with great influence.
powerful *adj.* very strong or important or influential.
power station *n.* a building for generating and distributing electricity.
► Power stations are places where the ENERGY in heat or in flowing water is changed into electrical energy for use in homes and factories. Most power stations obtain their energy from a FUEL which makes steam that works a GENERATOR or a group of generators.
These produce electric current that often travels overland through wires slung between tall metal towers called pylons. First, the current may pass through a transformer. This raises the pressure of the current and so reduces the amount that leaks away as the current flows.
The world's largest power station has 12 generators worked by water from the Yenisey river in Siberia. This power station could heat six million one-bar electric heaters.

practicable *adj.* capable of being done or used.
practical *adj.* able to do useful things.
practice *n.* something you do often to get better at it. *My piano practice lasts for an hour every day.* action not theory; professional business of doctor, lawyer, etc.
practice *vb.* do something often so that you can do it well. *I practice the piano every day.*

Prague

Prague is the capital of CZECHOSLOVAKIA. It lies on the river Vltava, not far from the border with East GERMANY. Today it is one of Eastern Europe's main commercial, industrial and communications centers. In the Middle Ages, Prague was the capital of Bohemia. It became the capital of Czechoslovakia when the country was formed in 1918, after World War I.

prairie *n.* a wide plain with very few trees, especially in North America.

Prairie dog

The prairie dog is a medium-sized rodent of the western United States. It is a ground squirrel, about a foot (30 cm) long and with a short tail. The prairie dog is a social mammal, living in "dog towns" — underground burrows with vertical shafts to the surface. Prairie dogs communicate danger to one another by short "whistles" that send them quickly to safety in their burrows.

praise *n.* & *vb.* say good things about someone or something.
prank *n.* practical or mischievous joke.
prawn *n.* a small sea animal with a thin shell and five pairs of legs. *Prawns look like large shrimps and can be eaten as food.*
pray *vb.* talk to God.
prayer *n.* what is said when talking to God.
pre- *prefix* meaning beforehand, e.g. **prehistoric** before history was written.
preach *vb.* give a sermon; give advice. **preacher** *n.*
prearrange *vb.* arrange ahead of time.
precaution *n.* care or action taken beforehand to prevent harm or bring about good results.
precious (**press**-*shuss*) *adj.* very valuable, costly.
precipice *n.* the steep side of a mountain or high cliff.
précis (**pray**-*see*) *n.* summary of essential facts.
precise *adj.* exact, very accurate. *Give me the precise details of what happened.*
predator *n.* an animal that hunts other animals. *A tiger is a predator in the jungle.*
predict *vb.* say what is likely to happen in the future; forecast.
preen *vb.* (of birds) cleaning feathers with the beak; groom oneself.
preface *n.* an introduction to a book.
prefer *vb.* like one thing rather than another. *I prefer skiing to jogging.*
pregnant *adj.* to be going to have a baby.

prehistoric *adj*. things that happened before written history.

► *Prehistoric animals* are those that lived before history began, about 5,000 years ago. We know about them from their FOSSILS found in rocks. Different kinds of creature lived at different times. Many scientists think that each kind came from another by a process known as EVOLUTION.

The first prehistoric animals probably looked like little blobs of jelly. They lived in seas perhaps a billion years ago. Larger animals without backbones came later. By 600 million years ago there were jellyfish and sponges much like those alive today. There were also strange beasts with jointed bodies. From these, much later, came crabs, insects, millipedes and spiders.

The first backboned animals were strange, armored fishes that lived about 500 million years ago. In time there were some fishes that could breathe dry air and crawl around on land on stumpy fins. These fishes gave rise to prehistoric AMPHIBIANS. Some looked like SALAMANDERS the size of crocodiles. From amphibians came early REPTILES, and all the other backboned animals.

About 200 million years ago began the Age of DINOSAURS. Some dinosaurs may have weighed 250 tons and were as long as several buses. They were the largest land animals ever. Above them flew the first BIRDS. There were also

Life first became abundant on the earth during the Cambrian Period (1). Trilobites and brachiopods were among the most common animals. During the Ordovician Period (2) squid-like animals called nautiloids were very common in the seas. The Silurian Period (3) saw the appearance of many more kinds of fishes and also the first land-living plants. The Devonian Period (4) is also known as the Age of Fishes because there were so many kinds. Large trees and fernlike plants appeared during the Carboniferous Period (5) and formed huge forests. In the swamps lobe-finned fishes were gradually changing into the first amphibians. The first reptiles evolved from the amphibians toward the end of the Carboniferous Period.

Many kinds of reptiles made their appearance during the Permian Period (6), including some with strange sail-like structures on their backs. It was from this group of reptiles that the first mammals appeared toward the end of the Triassic Period (7). The Triassic marks the beginning of the Age of Reptiles. Many reptiles roamed the land during the Triassic times, among them the ancestors of the great dinosaurs. The first big dinosaurs appeared during the Jurassic Period (8). The largest of them, such as Brachiosaurus, *were plant eaters.* Stegosaurus *was heavily armored with bony plates to protect it from the flesh-eating dinosaurs. Some reptiles called pterosaurs evolved wings and began to fly through the air, while another group of reptiles produced* Archaeopteryx, *the first true bird. The Cretaceous Period (9) saw many more dinosaurs on the land. The largest of the flesh-eating dinosaurs was* Tyrannosaurus rex. *Many of the plant-eating species were protected by strange bony horns and collars. Flowering plants made their first appearance. The Tertiary Period (10) is sometimes known as the Age of Mammals. The dinosaurs had become extinct and the mammals rapidly evolved to take their place. The Quaternary Period (11), which began only about two million years ago, saw the emergence of man* (Homo sapiens), *while the Northern Hemisphere suffered a series of severe glaciations or Ice Ages. Mammoths were able to survive the cold because of their woolly coats, but they could not survive the attacks by early men.*

PTERODACTYLS, strange furry beasts with wings like bats. One kind was the largest animal that ever flew. Meanwhile big reptiles with limbs shaped like paddles hunted fishes in the seas.

About 65 million years ago the dinosaurs, pterodactyls, and strange sea reptiles died out. The new masters of the land were prehistoric birds and MAMMALS. Some gave rise to the birds and mammals of today.

►► **Prehistoric humans** lived long ago before there were any written records of history. We know about these early times from the tools, weapons and bodies of ancient people, which are dug out of the ground. Prehistory is divided into the STONE AGE, the BRONZE AGE and the Iron Age. The ages are named after the materials that people used to make their tools and weapons.

The Stone Age lasted for a long time. It began around 2½ to 3

P

million years ago when, many scientists believe, humanlike creatures began to appear on the earth. They were different from the apelike animals which lived at the same time. They had larger brains, used stone tools and could walk upright. They lived by hunting animals and collecting plants.

Around 800,000 years ago, a more humanlike creature appeared. Scientists call this kind of early human *Homo erectus*. This means "upright man." *Homo erectus* is probably the ancestor of more advanced types of humans, called *Homo sapiens*. This means "intelligent man." One kind of *Homo sapiens* was Neanderthal Man, who appeared about 100,000 years ago. Neanderthal Man finally died out and was replaced by modern man, who is called *Homo sapiens sapiens*. Modern man first appeared in Europe and Asia around 35,000 years ago.

Toward the end of the long Stone Age, prehistoric people first began to use metals. The first metal they used was copper. They made copper tools about 10,000 years ago. About 5,000 years ago, people invented bronze. Bronze is a hard ALLOY of copper and tin. This was the start of the Bronze Age, when the earliest civilizations began. The Bronze Age ended about 3,300 years ago, when people learned how to make iron tools. Iron is much harder than bronze. With iron tools, people could develop farming and cities more quickly than ever before. The start of the Iron Age marks the beginning of modern times.

prejudice *n*. biased or one-sided opinion.
preliminary *adj*. introductory; before the main business.
première (*prem*-**yair**) *n*. first showing of a film or performance of a play.
premium *n*. the regular payment for an insurance policy; a bonus.
prepare *vb*. get ready. **preparation** *n*.
Presbyterian *n*. a member of the Presbyterian church.
► The Presbyterian Church is a Protestant church of British origins, and based on the teachings of John CALVIN, the French reformer and lawyer. Its European counterpart is the Reformed Church. The Presbyterian Church is the national church of Scotland.

prescription *n*. a doctor's order for medicine. **prescribe** *vb*. advise use of.
presence *n*. being in a place; the bearing or appearance of a person.
present (**prez**-*ent*) 1. *n*. something that is given to somebody, a gift. 2. *n*. this time; now. *At present there are 20 children in my class*. 3. *adv*. being in the place spoken about. *Who was present at the meeting last night?*
present (*pree*-**zent**) *vb*. 1. give someone something in public. *The mayor presented prizes at our school assembly*. 2. show or perform. *Our class presented a play for our parents*. **presentable** *adj*. fit to be shown.
presently *adv*. soon; now.
preserve *vb*. keep safe from harm; make something last a long time. *The ancient Egyptians preserved their dead pharaohs as mummies*.
president *n*. the (usually) elected head of a country or organization.
► The President of the UNITED STATES is the world's most powerful elected person. He is head of state, like the Queen or King of Britain. He is also head of the government, like a PRIME MINISTER. The president is also the commander-in-chief of the army, navy and air force. The president is elected for a four-year term and may serve two terms. Since 1789 the United States has had 40 presidents. The first was George WASHINGTON. Other famous presidents of the past include Thomas Jefferson, Abraham Lincoln, and John F. Kennedy.

press 1. *vb*. push on something. *The boys pressed their noses against the window of the cake shop*. 2. *vb*. press something flat by pushing hard on it. *Father presses his trousers*. 3. *n*. a printing machine. 4. *n*. newspapers.
pressure (rhymes with *thresher*) *n*. how much one thing is pressing on another or against the walls of a container; urgency.
prestige *n*. having a good reputation; having influence.
presume *vb*. take for granted; suppose to be true. **presumption** *n*. 1. having reason to think something probable. 2. impudence.
pretend *vb*. give the impression that something is the case when it is not. *Let's pretend we're asleep*.
pretext *n*. false excuse.

Pretoria
Pretoria is the administrative capital of South Africa and the residence of the president and chief Ministers. Parliamentary sessions take place in Cape Town. Pretoria, which is in the TRANSVAAL, was founded in 1855.

pretty *adj*. attractive; nice-looking. *Victoria wore a pretty dress to the party*. *adv*. fairly, moderately.
prevail *vb*. triumph over; get one's own way.
prevalent *adj*. common, widespread.
prevent *vb*. stop something from happening. *The rain prevented us from going out*. **prevention** *n*.
preview *n*. an advance showing or performance of a film, play, etc., before it is seen by the public.
previous *adj*. former, coming before. **previously** *adv*.
prey (rhymes with *ray*) *n*. an animal that is hunted by another animal as food. *Rabbits and mice are the prey of owls*.
price *n*. the sum of money that is paid for something. *vb*. fix a price; find out the price of. *I priced the ring*.
priceless *adj*. 1. too valuable to have a price. 2. funny.
prick *vb*. make a mark with a small sharp point.
prickle *n*. a sharp point in the stem of a plant, a fine thorn.
pride *n*. the feeling of being proud; sense of one's own worth. *vb*. be proud of; flatter oneself.
priest (rhymes with *least*) *n*. a person who is trained to perform religious rites.

Priestley, Joseph
Joseph Priestley (1733–1804) was an English chemist and Unitarian minister remembered as the discoverer of OXYGEN. He had a keen interest in experiment, though no scientific training. Harassed in England for his pro-American and French sympathies, he emigrated to the U.S.A., founding the first Unitarian Church there, in 1796.

prim *adj*. neat; prudish, stiff.
primary *adj*. first in time or importance. *The primary colors are blue, red and yellow*.
prima donna *n*. principal female singer in an opera; a vain person.
primate *n*. 1. (biology) member of the highest order of mammals that includes lemurs, monkeys, apes and humans. 2. (ecclesiastical) an archbishop.
prime minister *n*. a head of government (especially in the British Commonwealth).
► Britain and many other countries – especially in the Commonwealth – have a prime minister. The prime minister is usually the leader of the political party (or group of parties) with the greatest number of seats in PARLIAMENT. The prime minister chooses a group of people to help in the running of the government. These people are called *ministers*. The group is called a *cabinet*.

primitive *adj*. undeveloped, simple, rough; old-fashioned.
primrose *n*. a spring flower with usually yellow petals.
prince *n*. the son of a king or queen.

Prince Edward Island
Prince Edward Island, in the Gulf of St. Lawrence, is the smallest province of CANADA. Much of the island forms part of Prince Edward Island National Park. Fishing and food processing are two of the most important industries. The capital is Charlottetown.

The island was discovered by Jacques CARTIER in 1534, and later became a French colony. Britain took it over in 1758, during the

French and Indian War. It was renamed after a son of King George III. Prince Edward Island became part of Canada in 1873.

princess *n.* the daughter of a king or queen.

principal *adj.* the most important. *n.* head of a school.

principle *n.* an important rule; law of nature. *Always telling the truth is a good principle to follow.*

print 1. *n.* letters that you do not join together. 2. *vb.* use a machine to put letters or pictures onto paper. *This book has been printed on a hand press.*

printer *n.* a person or company that prints books, magazines, newspapers, etc.

printing *n.* a way of reproducing words and pictures by pressing an inked pattern on paper, fabric or metal.

► The chief methods of printing are *letterpress*, *lithography* and *photogravure*. Letterpress is the oldest and began in Europe in the 1400s with Johann GUTENBERG. (However, this kind of printing was known in Japan as early as A.D. 770). Each letter or piece of "type" is set on a small stick of metal which carries a line of type. A number of these lines are then locked together into a frame. For more than 400 years, *typesetters* placed the bits of type in position by hand. Then they inked it and pressed paper on top. Modern Typesetting is done by machines, either linotype or monotype. More recently computers have begun to be used.

Three basic printing processes. Letterpress is done from a raised surface. Lithography, or offset printing, is done from flat plates, chemically treated so that only parts with the image accept ink. In gravure the design is cut into the plate.

Most illustrations today are produced by the "half-tone" process. The image is photographed through a mesh screen which turns it into a pattern of tiny dots that can be transferred to the printing plate, showing up as areas of light and dark when printed.

printout *n.* printed sheets produced by a computer.

Sunlight shining through a prism splits up into the colors of a rainbow.

prior 1. *adj.* earlier. *A prior engagement.* 2. *adv.* before. *Prior to your arrival.* 3. *n.* head of a religious house called a **priory** (*n.*).

prism *n.* a solid block of transparent material used in various instruments to disperse (split up) or reflect light or other rays.

prison *n.* a secure building in which people who break the law may be kept.

prisoner *n.* a person who is kept in prison.

private *adj.* not open to the public; belonging to only one person or to a few people.

privilege *n.* a right given as a special advantage or favor.

prize *n.* something that is given to someone as a reward. *I won a prize in the competition.* *vb.* value highly.

probably *adv.* likely to happen, but not certain. *We will probably go to the country next week.*

probation *n.* 1. period of testing a person's suitability. 2. suspending a prisoner's sentence and allowing him or her freedom under supervision.

probe *vb.* explore or examine closely.

problem *n.* a question for which an answer is needed; a difficulty that needs to be solved. *We are having a problem with our roof.*

procedure *n.* method of doing things.

process *n.* a way of making something. *The process of making paper is a complicated one.*

procession *n.* a number of people and vehicles moving along together; a parade. **proceed** *vb.* go forward; continue; resume.

proclaim *vb.* announce publicly; declare. **proclamation** *n.*

procrastinate *vb.* delay, put off.

prodigal *adj.* wasteful, extravagant *n.* person who spends recklessly. *Jesus told the parable of the prodigal son.*

produce (**prod**-*yous*) *n.* things that are made or grown. (*pro*-**dyous**) *vb.* 1. make. 2. bring something out to show it. *The magician produced a rabbit from his hat.*

producer *n.* 1. someone who makes or grows something. 2. person who directs production of a play, etc.

product *n.* something that is produced. *The product of that factory is ice cream.*

profess *vb.* declare, admit openly (beliefs, etc.); have as a **profession** or occupation. **professional** *n.* & *adj.*

profit *n.* the difference between the cost of making something and the price it is sold at.

profound *adj.* deep; having great depth of knowledge; difficult to understand.

program *n.* 1. a set of instructions to a computer. 2. a list of events or things that are going to happen.

progress (**proh**-*gress*) *n.* advance, improvement. *vb.* (*proh*-**gress**) improve; move on.

progressive *adj.* moving forward, advancing. *n.* a person who favors social advances and reforms.

prohibit *vb.* forbid.

project (**proj**-*ekt*) *n.* a plan to be worked on. *Our class is working on a project to start a vegetable garden.* *vb.* (*proh*-**jekt**) make plans for; throw, jut out.

projectile *n.* a rocket.

projector *n.* machine for showing (projecting) motion or still pictures on a screen.

prolong *vb.* cause to continue, make longer.

promenade *n.* (place made for) leisurely walking in public.

prominent *adj.* outstanding, noticeable, distinguished. *He is a prominent member of the club.*

promise *vb.* pledge that you will do something. *n.* What you have promised to do. *I promised to tidy my room, but I did not keep my promise.* **promising** *adj.* likely to turn out well.

promote *vb.* raise to a higher position or office; encourage. *We should like to promote a good atmosphere in the school.* **promotion** *n.* **promotional** *adj.*

prompt 1. *adj.* on time; without delay. 2. *vb.* urge; incite; help actor by saying words he or she has forgotten.

prone *adj.* 1. lying face down. 2. liable, disposed to. *He was prone to lie.*

prong *n.* one of the sharp ends of a fork.

pronghorn *n.* shy antelopelike animal of North America. It is about 3 feet tall.

pronoun *n.* a word used for a noun, like he, she, it, they, him, our.

► A pronoun is a word mainly used

P

as an alternative to a NOUN. By using pronouns, we can refer to ouselves, other people and things without having to repeat their names all the time. Instead of saying Mr. Smith, the pronoun *he* or *him* can be used.

pronounce *vb*. make the sound of a word. **pronunciation** *n*.

proof *n*. 1. something that shows that what is said is true, evidence. *I need some proof before I will believe it.* 2. impression of type that can be corrected before final printing. **proofreader** *n*. a person who corrects printers' proofs.

prop *n*. & *vb*. support, lean against something. *The ladder was propped against the wall.*

propaganda *n*. spreading of ideas or information and the information so spread.

propel *vb*. send forward.

propeller *n*. two or more blades that spin around.

► A propeller is used to drive ships and airplanes. It moves something forward by pushing air or water backward. A propeller is made of two or more blades, which are mounted on a hub. The blades are twisted, so that the angle at which the water or air strikes the blades gives the greatest possible thrust. The movement of a propeller is like that of a screw passing through wood.

The first hand-cranked propeller was made in 1776 for a submarine. The first aircraft to use a propeller was a French airship which flew in 1852. This propeller was turned by a steam engine. The propellers used by the American WRIGHT BROTHERS on their aircraft in 1903 were turned by a gasoline engine. HELICOPTERS have huge propellers which lift them and make them fly.

As the blades of a propeller turn, they speed up the movement of the water passing through them. The speeded-up water drives the ship forward.

proper *adj*. right, suitable. *She was not wearing the proper clothes for a party.*

properly *adv*. factually correct. *We were not properly informed.*

property *n*. things owned.

prophet *n*. 1. a person who tells what is going to happen in the future. 2. in the Bible, a person who speaks for God. **prophesy** *vb*. speak as a prophet; foretell.

proportion *n*. part of; a ratio. *The proportion of people who use hearing aids has increased.*

propose *vb*. suggest, put forward an idea; intend to; offer marriage. **proposal** *n*.

proprietor *n*. owner of a business.

prosaic *adj*. ordinary, not very interesting.

prose *n*. written language without meter; not poetry.

prosecute *vb*. take to court; start legal action. **prosecution** *n*.

prosper *vb*. flourish, grow rich, be successful. **prosperity** *n*. **prosperous** *adj*.

protect *vb*. keep safe from danger, guard. **protection** *n*. that which protects.

protein (**pro**-*teen*) *n*. a body-building material in some foods, like eggs, meat and milk.

► Proteins are chemical compounds forming an essential part of every CELL in plants and animals. Proteins perform a wide range of important tasks. For example, most HORMONES and all enzymes are proteins that control chemical processes in living organisms. Proteins from one organism sometimes enter an animal's body and cause illness. But the foreign proteins, or *antigens*, stimulate the formation of other proteins called *antibodies*. These combine chemically with the antigens, making them harmless. Weakened antigens of certain diseases are used in vaccination. Our bodies obtain protein from foods such as meat, milk, eggs, fish, soybeans and nuts. In the process of DIGESTION, these are broken down into substances called *amino acids*. The body then builds up other proteins from these acids.

protest (*proh*-**test**) *vb*. say or show how you think something is wrong; object to. *We had to protest about the new school rules.* (**proh**-*test*) *n*. an objection.

Protestant *n*. a member of any Christian church which resulted from the protest against and separation from the Roman Catholic Church.

► Protestants are Christians who do not belong to the Roman Catholic or the Eastern Orthodox churches. Protestants believe that the things written in the BIBLE are more important than any rules made by church leaders. There are some passages in the Bible which can be explained in different ways. Protestants believe that people should make up their own minds about what these mean.

Protestantism began with the REFORMATION, when Martin LUTHER led a movement to change the ROMAN CATHOLIC CHURCH. In 1529, the Roman Catholic Church in Germany tried to stop people from following Luther's ideas. Luther's followers protested against this and were then called Protestants. Early Protestant groups included the Lutherans, Calvinists (PRESBYTERIANS) and to some extent Anglicans. Later groups included the Baptists, Congregationalists, Methodists and QUAKERS.

proto- *prefix* meaning first, e.g. **prototype** the first model of something before general production.

proud *adj*. 1. thinking that you are better than others. 2. pleased that someone else has done well. *Mother was very proud when I won a prize.*

prove *vb*. show that something is true. *Can you prove that you saw a ghost?*

proverb *n*. a short saying that gives a warning or advice.

► The BIBLE contains a book called *Proverbs*. Proverbs are often easy to remember. One famous proverb is "A stitch in time saves nine." All peoples have proverbs. Many African languages are rich in them. Typical African proverbs are: "He who takes his time does not fall" (Somalia); "The dog you did not feed will not hear your call" (Zaire).

provide *vb*. give sustenance or support; supply for use. *Our teacher provided us with new pencils.*

province 1. *n*. a large area of a country with its own government; 2. *pl*. *n*. the whole country outside the capital. **provincial** *adj*.

provision *n*. what is provided. **provisions** *pl*. *n*. food and drink. **provisional** *adj*. temporary.

provoke *vb*. stir up feeling; irritate. **provocation** *n*.

prow *n.* the bow of a ship; the forepart.
prowl *vb.* go about silently and secretly.
prudish *adj.* prim, affected modesty. **prude** *n.*
prune 1. *n.* a dried plum. 2. *vb.* cut away parts of a plant to control the way it grows.
pry *vb.* look into; interfere inquisitively.
psalm (*sahm*) *n.* a sacred song in the Book of Psalms in the Old Testament in the Bible.
psycho- (**sye**-*co*) *prefix* meaning of the mind.
psychology (*sye*-**koll**-*o-jee*) *n.* the study of the mind and how it works.
► Psychology comes from the Greek word *psyche*, meaning mind or soul. Psychology deals with the way people and animals learn, think and react to what their senses tell them. It also examines the way we reason and make decisions. Psychologists may work as researchers and study the way messages are carried to and from the BRAIN. They may also work as teachers or in clinics where they see and treat patients. Others carry out large-scale studies of hundreds of people to find out their attitudes, their reactions and the way they behave in certain situations. An important branch of psychology deals with the behavior of animals.

psychopath (**sye**-*kuh-path*) *n.* mentally ill or unstable person.
ptarmigan (**tar**-*mig-an*) *n.* a bird of the grouse family whose plumage changes from brown and white in summer to grey and white in winter.
pterodactyl (*tero*-**dack**-*til*) *n.* prehistoric flying reptile.
► Pterodactyls lived between 195 and 65 million years ago, when dinosaurs roamed the earth. Our knowledge of them comes from studies of their FOSSILS.

There were about 20 kinds of pterodactyl. Some were tiny, no larger than sparrows. But some had wing spans of over 20 ft. (6 meters), and one fossil had a wing span of 51 ft. (15.5 meters). They had small, compact bodies. Even the largest probably weighed no more than 35 lb. (16 kg). The wings were flaps of leathery skin. The skin stretched between the body and the long arms, rather like modern bats.

Pterodactyls were not true fliers. It is thought they glided over the sea, catching insects and fish in their toothed beaks. They had short legs and were probably clumsy on land.

Ptolemy, Claudius
A famous Greek-Egyptian scientist (*c.* A.D. 100–170) who lived in Alexandria in Egypt. From his astronomical studies he concluded that the earth was the center of the universe, and that the sky was a sphere within which hung the sun, moon, stars and planets.

pub *n.* saloon, bar.
puberty *n.* period when boys and girls mature and become men and women capable of producing children.
public 1. *adj.* known to everyone; belonging to everyone. 2. *n.* the people; the community as a whole.
publication *n.* a work that is published.
publicity *n.* making known publicly by means of advertisements, etc.
publish *vb.* have a book, newspaper or magazine printed for sale or to be given away; make known generally. **publisher** *n.*
pudding *n.* a food made of flour and other ingredients, often boiled; a soft, thick, creamy dessert.
puddle *n.* a very small pool of water, usually dirty and temporary.

Puerto Rico (Puerto Rican)
Puerto Rico is an island in the West Indies. It is a U.S. Commonwealth and is self-governing. The scenery and tropical climate attract many tourists. The chief product is sugar cane, but light industry is also important. Christopher COLUMBUS discovered the island in 1493 and it was ruled by SPAIN until 1898. It became a U.S. possession following the Spanish-American War. Many Puerto Ricans have emigrated to the United States.
AREA: 3,435 SQ. MILES (8,897 SQ. KM)
POPULATION: 3,187,600
CAPITAL: SAN JUAN
OFFICIAL LANGUAGES: SPANISH, ENGLISH

puffin *n.* a bird of the auk family.
► The Atlantic puffin lives in the North Atlantic Ocean. It is a black and white bird, with orange feet and an odd, flattened, orange bill. It breeds in summer. In winter it goes far out to sea, feeding on fish. Puffins swim well under water.

pug *n.* small breed of dog with a snub-nose and tightly curled tail.
pull *vb.* heave something toward yourself.
pull down *vb.* (of buildings) take them down, destroy.
pulley *n.* a wheel with a rope around it, used to lift or move heavy things more easily.
► A pulley is a simple MACHINE. It consists of a wheel on a fixed axle. A rope or belt passed over the wheel is tied to a load. When the rope is pulled, the load is raised. Such pulleys raise loads that are too heavy or difficult to lift otherwise.

A *movable pulley* runs along a rope. One end of the rope is fixed to a support. The load hangs from the pulley itself. When the other end of the rope is pulled, the pulley moves the load along the rope. Pulleys are used in machines such as cranes.

pull off *vb.* succeed with something.
pullover *n.* a jersey or sweater.

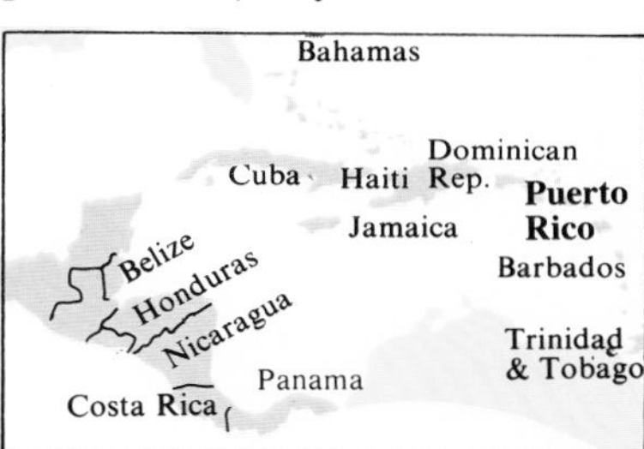

The pterodactyls or pterosaurs were related to the dinosaurs. At one extreme the group included tiny specimens the size of a sparrow; at the other, giants like the pteranodon (right) whose wingspan was nearly 23 ft. (7 meters).

P

pulp 1. *n.* soft part of a fruit. 2. *n.* soft mass of dried vegetable matter, especially wood, for making paper. *vb.* destroy shape and hardness by beating something, often with water.

pulpit *n.* a raised structure in a church from which the priest or minister talks.

pulse *n.* the throbbing of your heart that you can feel in your wrist; rhythmical beat. **pulsate** *vb.*

► The pulse is a beating or throbbing in the body's ARTERIES. These are BLOOD vessels that carry blood away from the HEART. A pulse beat occurs as the heart contracts and pumps blood into the arteries. This makes a wave of pressure that stretches the artery walls.

Doctors measure pulse rates to find out if the heart is beating normally. They usually feel the *radial artery* in the wrist. But the pulse can be felt wherever an artery passes over a bone. The normal pulse rate for men is 72 beats per minute. For women it is 76 to 80 beats. But pulse rates between 50 and 85 are considered normal. Children have faster pulses.

puma *n.* large member of the cat family from America; cougar.

pump *vb.* push liquid or air through pipes. *The heart pumps blood around our bodies by contracting. n.* a machine or apparatus that does this.

► Pumps are machines for moving fluids (liquids or gases). *Reciprocating pumps* have a piston moving back and forth in a cylinder. Devices called valves control the flow so that the fluid moves in one direction only, not back-and-forth. In *rotary pumps*, fast-turning propellerlike blades make the fluid flow. *Centrifugal pumps* contain turning vanes that make the fluid rotate. CENTRIFUGAL FORCE causes the moving fluid to pass along an outlet pipe.

pumpkin *n.* a large, usually round, orange-colored vegetable which grows on the ground in many warm parts of the world.

punch 1. *vb.* hit someone with the fist. *n.* a blow with the fist. 2. *n.* a tool for cutting holes. 3. *n.* a mixture of wine, lemon, hot water, spices, etc.

punctual *adj.* on time.

punctuation *n.* the marks used in writing like the period (.) the comma (,) the semicolon (;) the colon (:) the question mark (?) and exclamation mark (!) **punctuate** *vb.*

puncture *vb.* & *n.* pierce; make a hole in something; a hole.

Punic Wars
Three Punic Wars were fought by CARTHAGE and Rome for the control of the Western Mediterranean, between 264 B.C. and 146 B.C. The Romans won, though at great cost, and totally destroyed Carthage in revenge, razing it to the ground.

punish *vb.* do something to someone who has done wrong so that he or she will not want to do it again. **punishment** *n.*

punt 1. *n.* long flat-bottomed boat propelled by a pole. 2. *n.* & *vb.* kick a ball.

puny *adj.* small.

pupa *n.* (plural **pupae**) the chrysalis stage in an insect's development.

pupil *n.* 1. a person who is learning from a teacher; a student. 2. the round dark opening in the colored part (the **iris**) of the eye.

puppet *n.* a kind of doll that can be made to move by pulling strings, fitting it onto the hand, etc.

► Puppets are miniature human or animal figures that are usually hand-held. Glove puppets are slipped over the hand and worked by moving the fingers. Puppets can also be worked by strings from above, or by rods from below. The most famous of all puppets are the couple, Punch and Judy.

puppy *n.* a young dog.

purchase *vb.* & *n.* buy; something that is bought.

pure *adj.* not mixed with anything; clean.

purple *adj.* & *n.* a dark, red-blue color.

purpose *n.* intention, object.

purr *vb.* the low vibrating sound made by a contented cat.

purse 1. *n.* an object used for carrying money. 2. *vb.* pucker your lips.

pursue *vb.* chase after. *The crowd pursued the thief.* **pursuit** *n.*

pus *n.* yellowish fluid around an inflamed part of the skin.

push *vb.* press against forcefully; shove something away without striking it.

put *vb.* place something somewhere.

put aside *vb.* keep something to use it later; save. *I put aside some of my money every week for my vacation.*

put off *vb.* 1. decide to do something later than planned. *We had the flu so we put off the party until next week.* 2. feel badly about something you dislike. *I was quite put off by the way she spoke to me.*

putty *n.* a grayish paste which hardens when dry and is used for fixing glass into window frames.

put up *vb.* accommodate for a short time. *I can put you up for the night.*

put up with *vb.* not to complain about something even though you do not like it; tolerate. *It's not a very nice place, but my brother likes it, so I will just have to put up with it.*

puzzle *n.* a difficult problem. *vb.* perplex.

Pygmy *n.* small, dark-skinned people who live in the hot equatorial forests of Africa. The men are seldom taller than five feet and the women are even smaller.

The Great Pyramid of Cheops.

pyjamas see **pajamas**.

pylon *n.* tall metal tower supporting electric cables.

pyramid *n.* a structure with a square (or other) base and sloping sides that meet at the top.

► The Egyptians built pyramids as royal tombs. The first was built in about 2650 B.C. at Sakkara. It is 204 ft. (62 meters) high. The three most famous pyramids are near Giza. The Great Pyramid, built in the 2600s B.C.by the PHARAOH Khufu, is 449.5 ft. (137 meters) high. Khafre, who ruled soon after Khufu, built the second pyramid. It is 447.5 ft. (136.4 meters) high. The third, built by Khafre's successor Menkaure, is 240 ft. (73.1 meters) high. About 80 pyramids still stand in Egypt.

Central and South American Indians also built pyramids as temples from the A.D. 100s to 500s. One huge pyramid is at Cholula, southeast of Mexico City. It is about 177 ft. (54 meters) high.

Pyrenees
The Pyrenees is a mountain range which runs along the French-Spanish border. The highest peak is Pico de Aneto, 11,168 ft. (3,404 meters) above sea level. The small state of ANDORRA nestles in the Pyrenees.

Pythagoras
A Greek mathematician of the 6th century B.C. who laid the roots of modern GEOMETRY. He was one of the first to believe that the earth was a sphere.

python *n.* a large kind of snake.

► Pythons can grow to 30 ft. (9 meters) long. They are not poisonous. Pythons are found in Africa, Asia and Australia. Most species have brown and yellow patterns. Pythons are very strong and kill their prey – all kinds of animals – by encircling them and squeezing them until they are asphyxiated.

Qatar
Qatar is an Arab Emirate on the Persian Gulf. It occupies a peninsula consisting mainly of desert, and most people live in the coastal regions. Oil production dominates the economy. The state declared its independence from Britain in 1971.

AREA: 4,247 SQ. MILES
(11,000 SQ. KM)
POPULATION: 294,000
CAPITAL: DOHA
CURRENCY: QATAR RIYAL
OFFICIAL LANGUAGE: ARABIC

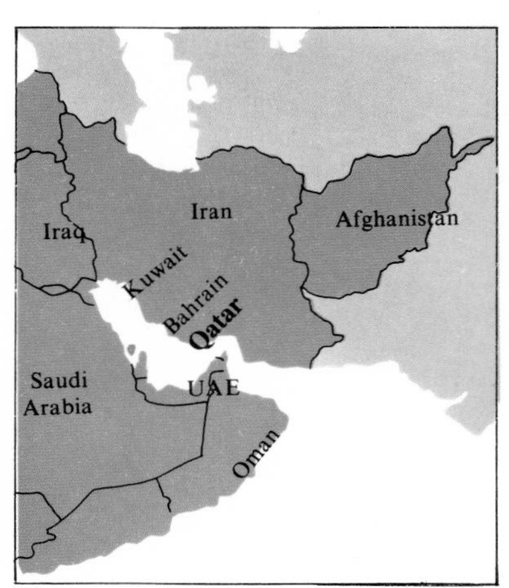

quack 1. *vb.* make a noise like a duck. 2. *n.* a person who pretends to be a doctor, but is not properly qualified.

A slate quarry in Wales.

quadrangle *n.* a four-sided courtyard.
quadrant *n.* 1. an instrument for measuring vertical angles. 2. one-quarter of a circle.
quadruped *n.* a four-footed animal. *A horse is a quadruped.*
quadruplet *n.* one of four babies born at the same time to the same mother.
quail *n.* a small game bird, related to the partridge and found in most parts of the world.
quaint *adj.* odd but pleasant; old-fashioned. *We spent our holiday in a quaint little fishing village in New England.*
quake *vb.* tremble, e.g. with fear.

Quakers
The Quakers are also known as the Society of Friends. They are a PROTESTANT group that was founded by George Fox in England during the 1650s.

They were called Quakers because some of them shook with emotion at their meetings. Early Quakers were often badly treated because of their belief that religion and government should not be mixed. Quakers have simple religious meetings and many do not have ministers.

qualification *n.* 1. knowledge or skill making person fit for a post. 2. modification.

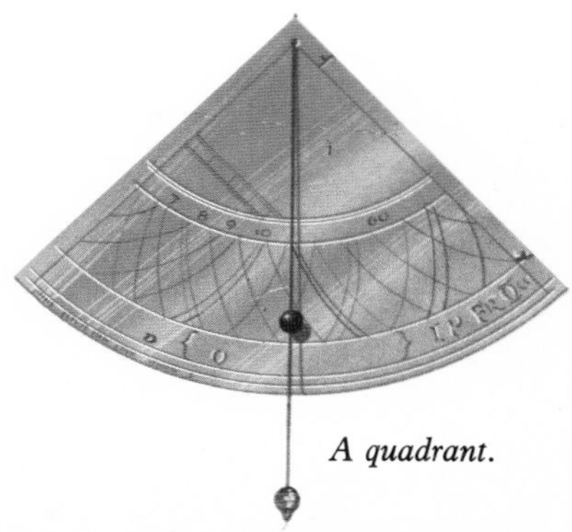

A quadrant.

Q

qualify *vb.* 1. become fit for a post. 2. limit the meaning of a statement so that it is less general.
quality *n.* how good or bad a thing is. *We want the best quality of carpet.*
quantity *n.* how much; the size, weight, or number of anything. *What quantity of cement do you need?*
quarantine (**kwar**-*ant-een*) *n.* a period when someone who has a disease is kept away from other people so that they cannot catch it.
quarrel *vb.* & *n.* argue angrily. **quarrelsome** *adj.*
quarry *n.* 1. a place where stone for building and other purposes is taken out of the ground. 2. an animal that is hunted, prey.
► Unlike mines, quarries are always open to the sky. They are huge pits where rocks are cut or blasted out of the ground.

As long ago as prehistoric times, people had quarries where they dug up FLINT to make into tools and weapons. They used bones as picks and shovels.

Nowadays, rock is quarried in enormous amounts. Explosives blast loose thousands of tons. This is scooped up by bulldozers and diggers, and taken to crushers. The rock is ground into stones for use in roads, railroads, concrete and cement. Not all rock is removed in this way. Stone such as marble and granite that is used in building and paving is cut out of the ground rather than blasted. Electric cutters, wire saws and drills are used to cut the rock.

quart (*kwort*) *n.* a measure of liquids (1.14 liters). *There are two pints in a quart.*
quarter *n.* 1. one of four equal parts of a whole; ¼. 2. a district. *The Latin Quarter of Paris.*
quarterly *adj.* due every quarter of the year, i.e., every three months. *n.* publication issued every quarter.
quartet *n.* four people doing something together, especially making music.
quartz *n.* a common, hard mineral.
► Quartz consists of crystalline silica (silicon dioxide). Its purest form, known as rock crystal, is colorless and clear. But most quartz is white and opaque. Varieties colored by impurities include rose quartz, smoky quartz, citrine (yellow), and amethyst (purple or violet). These and other varieties are used in jewelry. Being harder than steel, quartz is a useful abrasive. Slices of quartz tend to vibrate at fixed frequencies when suitable electrical signals are applied to them. Because of this, quartz crystals are used to regulate electronic watches and clocks.

quasar *n.* small brilliant object that emits radio waves far out in space.
quash *vb.* suppress, declare as not valid.
quasi- *prefix* meaning seemingly or almost.
quaver 1. *vb.* tremble; trill (of singing voice). 2. *n.* a very short note in music.
quay (*key*) *n.* a landing place for ships.

Quebec
Quebec is the largest province in CANADA. Over five million people live there. It stretches from the United States in the south, up into the Arctic. The ST. LAWRENCE RIVER lies in south Quebec. This great river runs from the GREAT LAKES to the Atlantic Ocean.

The far east is hilly. The mountains here are the northernmost finger of the Appalachian range. Northern Quebec is a vast wilderness of lakes and forests. It is part of a plateau of ancient rock called the Canadian Shield.

Most people live in towns and cities along the St. Lawrence valley. Much of Quebec's farmland is found here. The largest city, MONTREAL, is also the second biggest French-speaking city in the world. Quebec was first settled as a colony of France from the early 1600s to 1763. Afterwards it was taken over by the English. Quebec city, the capital of the province, is an important sea-port. It was founded in 1608 and is unique in North America as the only fortified town.

Quebec (city)
An inland Canadian seaport and capital of QUEBEC province. It is a center for manufacturing (paper, leather, clothing) and distribution.

A historic city, Quebec was founded by Samuel de Champlain (1608). In the struggle between French and English for control of Canada, it was captured by the British under Gen. WOLFE in a famous battle of the French and Indian War.

Smoky quartz

Tiger's eye

queen *n.* 1. the female ruler of a country or the wife of a king. 2. the most powerful piece at chess.
queer *adj.* strange and peculiar. *This soup tastes very queer.*
quell *vb.* overcome, subdue, crush.
quench *vb.* satisfy thirst; put out fire.
query *n.* a question. *vb.* ask a question.
quest *n.* a search.
question *n.* & *vb.* something that you ask when you want to find out something and get an answer. *n.* subject being discussed.
question mark *n.* a punctuation mark, like this (?). It goes at the end of written questions.
queue (rhymes with *dew*) *n.* a line of people waiting for something.
quiche (*keesh*) *n.* a pastry shell filled with beaten egg and milk and savory ingredients.
quick *adj.* fast; speedy.
quickly *adv.* to do something fast and without delay. *Come quickly.*
quicksand *n.* a kind of swampy ground consisting of sand and water which will suck down a person or animal that tries to walk on it.
quicksilver *n.* another name for mercury (metal).
quiet *adj.* not noisy; calm.
quill *n.* large feather used as a pen or plectrum.
quilt *n.* padded bed covering.
quince *n.* a tree and its acid pear-shaped fruit.
quinine *n.* a strong, bitter-tasting substance made from the bark of the cinchona tree, used as a medicine to treat malaria.
quintet *n.* a group of five, usually musicians.
quintuplet *n.* one of five babies born at the same time to the same mother.
quit *vb.* leave; give up.
quite *adv.* 1. completely, wholly, entirely. *You are quite right.* 2. to a considerable extent. *He dives quite well, but he's a poor swimmer.*
quiver 1. *vb.* tremble slightly and rapidly; 2. *n.* a case for holding arrows.
quiz *n.* a set of questions asked to find out how much people know, usually as a competition.
quotation marks *pl. n.* punctuation marks like this ("......") or this ('......'). They are used in writing mainly to show spoken words.
quote *vb.* repeat someone else's words.

R

Rome – the forum.

rabbi *n.* a teacher of Jewish law; the leader of a synagogue.
rabbit *n.* a small mammal with long ears and a very short tail.
► Rabbits originally came from Europe. Today they are found all over the world. Rabbits live in burrows in the ground. Each one is the home of a single family. A group of burrows is known as a warren. Rabbits leave their burrows at dusk to feed on grass and other plants. They can be a pest to farmers.

rabble *n.* a mob, disorganized crowd of people.
rabid *adj.* infected with rabies; mad.
rabies *n.* a usually fatal disease of the nervous system which is caught by being bitten by a rabid animal.
raccoon *n.* a tree-dwelling American mammal with long, grayish fur.
► In North America, raccoons are common creatures of the wild. They have a short pointed nose and a bushy tail ringed with black. They may grow to as much as 3 ft. (90 cm) long.

Raccoons live in forests. They make their homes in tree holes and are good climbers. At night, they leave their hollows to hunt for food. They will eat almost anything.

The raccoon is an intelligent animal which swims and climbs trees.

race 1. *n.* a group of people of common ancestry who are alike and have the same skin color. 2. *vb.* compete with others to find out who is fastest. *n.* a contest of speed.
racial *adj.*
► The **human race** is a term that refers to all people on the earth. But race also means any group of people who look alike in certain ways.

Nobody knows for sure how and when the different races came into being, but the three main ones in the world are the Mongoloid, the Caucasian and the Negroid.

The first is known for straight dark hair, yellow-brown skin and almond-shaped eyes. The second has hair color ranging from blond and red to black, is fair-skinned and round-eyed. The third has dark, tightly curling hair and dark brown skin color. In addition to these three main races, there are also a number of minor ones.

racialist *n.* 1. a person who believes that the races are fundamentally different. 2. someone who supports or stirs up racist conflicts.
rack *n.* 1. framework or stand for holding objects. 2. a medieval instrument of torture.
racket *n.* 1. a lot of noise, a din. 2. a light bat used to hit balls in tennis, badminton or squash. 3. an unlawful means of making a living.
radar *n.* an instrument that sends out radio waves. These waves are reflected back off objects like aircraft or ships, and the reflection shows where the object is.
► Radar is a term standing for Radio Detection And Ranging. It is a system for locating distant objects by transmitting RADIO signals and detecting their reflections. The reflected signals are displayed as images on the screen of a cathode-ray tube. Sea and air navigators use radar to study their surroundings, especially when visibility is bad. And flight controllers use it to observe the planes they guide in and out of

A radar station transmits radio signals. These signals are reflected back from the airplane and displayed as an image on a screen. From this the position of the airplane can be worked out.

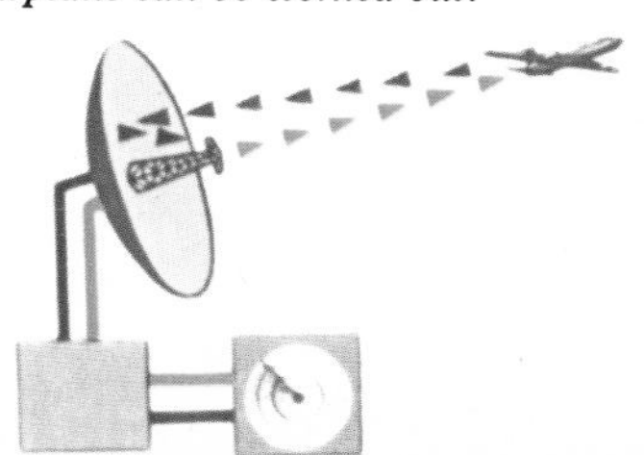

R

airports. Some airplanes use radar altimeters for direct measurement of their height above the ground. Radar also plays an important military role in watching for enemy missiles and aircraft in early-warning systems.

radiate *vb*. 1. give out heat and light. 2. be arranged like spokes.
radiator *n*. 1. a device that sends out heat. 2. the part of a car that keeps the cooling water at the correct temperature.
radical *adj*. fundamental, going to the root; (in politics) in favor of reforms and social change.
radio *n*. an instrument that receives radio waves and uses them to produce sounds which you can hear. *vb*. transmit by radio.

► Radio is the use of certain ELECTROMAGNETIC WAVES to carry information, such as MORSE CODE, speech, or music. Radio waves are also used in TELEVISION to carry sound and vision signals.

The idea of transmitting radio waves was first thought of by the Scottish scientist James Clerk Maxwell in 1865. He thought that there must be some way of making an alternating (back-and-forth) electric current produce electromagnetic waves. But it was the German scientist Heinrich Hertz who discovered how to do it. In 1887, Hertz made a spark jump the gap between the ends of two metal rods. When this happened, another spark jumped the gap in a nearby metal ring. Energy had been transmitted to the ring in the form of radio waves.

Among those to hear of Hertz's simple, but important experiment was a young Italian student called Guglielmo MARCONI. Using the ideas of Hertz and others, Marconi built a simple transmitter and receiver. When he switched on the transmitter, a bell rang in the receiver. The year was 1894, and the range of this simple equipment was only about 13 ft. (4 meters). But, within two years, Marconi had increased the range to about 2 miles (3 km). And, in 1901, he succeeded in transmitting signals across the Atlantic.

By this time, wireless TELEGRAPHY, the use of radio for sending Morse Code signals, had become a rival to the electric telegraph. And wireless telephony, the transmission of speech by radio, was soon to become an alternative to the TELEPHONE. This important development was made possible by Lee De Forest's invention of the *triode valve* in 1906. With the new valve, circuits were designed to enable speech, or other sounds, to be superimposed on a radio wave. Sets for receiving the signals ranged from simple crystal sets with headphones to much more complex and sensitive sets with several large, glowing valves.

Besides its use as an alternative to the telephone, radio had much more to offer. For it provided an excellent means of communicating with and entertaining the public at large. So, in the 1920s, radio broadcasting stations started to spring up. Since those days, amazing changes have taken place in the field of radio. The development of the TRANSISTOR in the 1940s made it possible for the size and cost of equipment to be greatly reduced.

►► **Radioactivity** The nuclei of certain ISOTOPES (*see* ATOM) are unstable and tend to disintegrate (break up) to form different nuclei. In this process, charged alpha particles or beta particles are emitted and a new element is formed. Substances that undergo such changes are said to be radioactive, and the process of change is called radioactive decay. The time taken for half the atoms in any quantity of a radioactive substance to decay is called the half-life of the substance. In some cases, this is less than half a second, while, for one radium isotope, it is 1,620 years. When a substance undergoes radioactive decay, it changes into another element. Thorium, for example, gradually decays to form lead. The radiation emitted by radioactive substances can be harmful to us. But small doses are used in some forms of medical treatment.

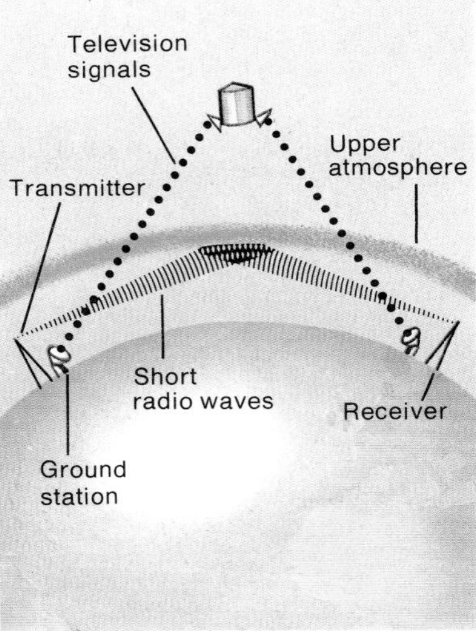

The illustration shows how radio and television waves can travel around the curve of the earth by being bounced off orbiting communications satellites.

►►► **Radio Astronomy** A heavenly body, such as a STAR, does not only give off LIGHT waves. It sends out many kinds of radio waves too. Radio astronomers explore the UNIVERSE by "listening" to the radio signals that reach earth from outer space. These signals are not made by other forms of life. They come from natural events, such as exploding stars or heated clouds of gases.

Radio telescopes have giant aerials – often dish-shaped. They pick up faint signals that have come from places much deeper in space than anything ever seen by ordinary TELESCOPES. The first large radio telescopes were built after World War II. The biggest in the world is at Arecibo in Puerto Rico. Its huge receiving dish is 1,000 ft. (305 meters) wide.

►►►► **Radiocarbon Dating** is a technique for estimating the age of ancient objects that were once alive, such as wood.

A living tree acquires a radioactive

A radio telescope usually has a large hollow or concave dish which reflects the signals from space onto the radio receiver.

isotope (*see* ATOM) that decays at a known rate after the tree has been cut down (*see* RADIOACTIVITY). So, by measuring the amount of radioactive isotope present, the age of the wood can be estimated.

radio waves *pl. n.* invisible waves sent out by a transmitter and traveling very fast.

radish *n.* a small roundish root with a strong peppery taste.

radium *n.* a rare, radioactive metal.

▶ Radium is an ELEMENT. It is found only in URANIUM ore and was first discovered by Marie CURIE. She was examining some uranium and realized that it had much more radioactivity than it should have had. Radium is very radioactive, and is dangerous to handle.

In its pure form, radium is a whitish metal. About five tons of uranium ore have to be mined to make just one gram of radium. Each year, less than 2.64 oz. (75 grams) are produced in the entire world. Most comes from Canada and Zaire.

Radium is used in medicine to treat cancer. COMPOUNDS of it are also used to make luminous dials.

radius *n.* (plural **radii**) a straight line from the center of a circle to its edge or circumference.

raffia *n.* a fiber from an African palm tree, used for weaving and matting, etc.

raffle *n.* & *vb.* a lottery; dispose of by lottery.

raft *n.* logs fastened together to make a sort of boat without sides.

rafter *n.* one of the crossbars of wood in a roof.

rag *n.* a piece of torn clothing or material.

rage *n.* great anger. *vb.* rave, be violent.

raid *n.* & *vb.* a surprise attack.

rail *n.* 1. a long bar or rod. 2. one of the long metal strips that form a railroad track.

railing *n.* a fence made of metal bars.

railroad *n.* the organization that controls a system of tracks, and the trains that run on them.

▶ Railroads have been in use since the 1500s. At first, rails were made of wood and wagons were pulled by horses. These railroads were used to haul carts in metal mines. Railroads are useful because heavy loads can be pulled along them very easily and smoothly.

Steam LOCOMOTIVES came into use in the early 1800s. In 1825, the first steam engine to be used on a public railroad began to run between Stockton and Darlington in England. The engine, called the *Rocket*, was built by George STEPHENSON. A few years later, the *Rocket* was hauling 20-ton loads over a 35 mile (56 km) run in under two hours. The age of steam locomotion had begun.

In the railroad building boom that followed, tens of thousands of miles of track were laid down by the 1850s. Today, there are about 785,000 miles (1,250,000 km) of railroad lines in the world. The longest railroad in the world is the Trans-Siberian line in Russia. It runs from Moscow to Nakhodka, a distance of 5,799 miles (9,334 km). The trains make 97 stops.

For many years STEAM ENGINES remained the most important kind of power unit. But since the 1930s they have been largely replaced by DIESEL ENGINES and electric locomotives. These can accelerate faster, are cleaner, quieter, and easier to refuel and to maintain. But they are not that much faster than steam engines. The world record for steam, 126 mph (202 k/h), was set in 1938. Few diesels can yet better this speed. However, a new generation of TURBINE-powered supertrains are now being built that are able to run much faster. The Hokaido of Japan can reach speeds of 160 mph (256 k/h).

Railroads changed the lives of everyone. As the railroads spread, they brought new industry and people to many towns and villages. Railroads were largely responsible for opening up the American West. Many towns in the United States became large and prosperous because the railroad passed through them.

rain *n.* drops of water falling from the sky. *vb.* fall or send down as rain.

▶ When rain pours down, it is only the sky returning the same water to earth that originally evaporated from the land and sea.

Rain forms when water vapor in the air starts to cool. As the vapor cools it turns first of all into tiny droplets, which form wispy CLOUDS. The droplets grow and the clouds thicken and turn a dull gray. At last the drops become so heavy that they start to fall. Depending on how cold it is, the drops hit the ground as either rain or SNOW.

The amount of rain that falls is widely different from place to place.

The first "wagonways" were used in mines. The Newcastle coal "chaldron" (left) dates from 1773.

An early version of road-rail in France. The coach was lifted off its wheels and loaded onto the wagon.

Below: First Class carriages on the Liverpool and Manchester Railway in England in 1830.

R

In the Atacama Desert in Chile, less than 1 in. (25 mm) of rain falls in 20 years. But in eastern India, monsoon rains drop 1,080 in. (2,743 cm) a year.

rainbow *n.* an arch of color in the sky. A rainbow is caused by sun shining on rain or mist.
► The gorgeous colors of a rainbow are formed by sunlight shining on drops of rain. The best time for rainbows is right after a shower, when the clouds break and sunlight streams through.

Rainbows can only be seen when the sun is behind you and low over the horizon. When the sun's rays strike the raindrops, each drop acts as a prism and splits the LIGHT into a spectrum of colors ranging from red to violet.

raincoat *n.* a waterproof overcoat.
rainfall *n.* the amount of rain that falls in a period of time.
raise *vb.* lift up; make higher.
raisin *n.* a dried grape.
rake *n.* a tool like a comb on a long handle. *vb.* use a rake.

Raleigh, Walter
Sir Walter Raleigh (1552–1618) was an English knight at the court of ELIZABETH I. He was a soldier, explorer, historian and poet. He tried unsuccessfully to set up a colony in Virginia, in the newly discovered land of North America. He introduced potatoes and tobacco smoking to the English. But his boldness and dashing way of life made him many enemies, and he was executed for treason during the reign of JAMES I (VI of Scotland).

rally *vb.* come together, arouse, recover from illness. *n.* meeting, competitive event.
ram 1. *n.* a male sheep. 2. *vb.* strike against violently. *The ship rammed the submarine.*
ramble 1. *vb.* wander about without purpose. 2. *vb.* talk in a disconnected way. 3. *n.* a walk for pleasure.
ramp *n.* a sloping floor, path, etc., leading from one level to another.
rampart *n.* fortified mound of earth.
ramshackle *adj.* broken down; derelict.
ran *vb.* past of **run**.
ranch *n.* a large farm with a lot of land for grazing.
rancid *adj.* smelling and tasting foul, especially fats. *The butter was rancid.*
random *adj.* (at random) without purpose; haphazard.
rang *vb.* past of **ring**.
range 1. *n.* a row of mountains. 2. *n.* the distance over which a gun can fire a bullet. 3. *n.* a large area of open country. 4. *n.* stove with oven and burner. 5. *vb.* place in rows.
ranger *n.* 1. keeper of a forest or national park. 2. specially trained soldier. 3. mounted policeman. 4. senior guide or scout.
rank *n.* 1. a title or place that shows how important someone is. *General is a very high rank in the army.* 2. row, a line.
ransack *vb.* search thoroughly; plunder.
ransom *n.* money paid to a kidnapper to make him or her release a prisoner. *vb.* buy freedom.
rap *n.* & *vb.* the sound of knocking, especially on a door.
rape *n.* & *vb.* forcing a woman to have sexual intercourse.

"The Betrothal of the Virgin" by Raphael, painted in oil in about 1504.

Raphael
Raffaello Sanzio (1483–1520), usually called Raphael, was an Italian artist of the RENAISSANCE. He was taught by Perugino, before going to FLORENCE to study the work of the great masters, such as LEONARDO DA VINCI. In 1508, the Pope invited Raphael to come to ROME, where he decorated some of the rooms in the VATICAN. The best known of these *frescoes* (wall paintings) is the School of Athens. Raphael was also an architect, and designed beautiful tapestries. Although he died at 37, he is regarded as one of the greatest painters of all time.

rapid 1. *adj.* swift; fast. 2. *n.* part of a river with fast current, usually with rocks or obstructions (also **rapids**).
rapid transit *n.* rapid passenger transportation in cities, e.g. subway.
rapier *n.* a kind of sword with a slim blade, used for thrusting.
rare *adj.* unusual; not often found.

R

rascal *n.* a worthless fellow; a naughty person.

rash 1. *n.* lots of red spots on the skin. 2. *adj.* reckless, hasty.

raspberry *n.* a small red berry which is good to eat.

► The raspberry is a fruit that is closely related to the blackberry, and made up of a number of tiny round parts called drupelets that are red or yellow-white in color.

rat *n.* a rodent (gnawing animal) found in large numbers all over the world. *vb.* betray friends.

► Rats often live in towns and cities. They are well adapted to scavenging on human litter, and thrive wherever there are people. Rats spread diseases including the dreaded bubonic PLAGUE that succeeded in wiping out a quarter of Europe's population in the 1300s.

rate 1. *n.* charge or payment, according to some standard. *My rate for cleaning windows is $2 an hour.* 2. *n.* speed over a given distance. 3. *vb.* estimate, regard. *How do you rate her chances of winning?*

rather 1. *adj.* somewhat. *Our friend is rather late.* 2. *adv.* preferably. *I would rather stay at home than go out this evening.*

ratio *n.* the relationship in amount or size between two or more things. *The ratio of text to pictures in this book is about 2 columns (of text) to 1 (picture).*

ration *n.* a fixed portion, especially of bob. *During the war the sugar ration was four ounces a week.*

rattle 1. *vb.* make a clattering noise. 2. *n.* a baby's toy which makes a rattling noise when shaken.

rattlesnake *n.* a poisonous snake.

► There are 30 different kinds of rattlesnake, which are found from Canada to Argentina. Their name comes from the rattle at the tip of their tail. It is made of loose, horny bits of skin that make a whirring noise when the snake shakes its tail. This sound can be heard up to 100 ft. (30 meters) away.

A bite from any rattlesnake will cause a painful wound and sometimes even death. The largest type is the eastern diamondback, which lives in the southern coastal region of the United States. It may reach as much as 8 ft. (2.4 meters) in length.

rave *vb.* talk wildly without making sense; speak with great enthusiasm. *She raved about his bushy beard.*

raven *n.* a large, black bird of the crow family.

► Ravens grow up to 25 in. (64 cm) in length. They feed on carrion and small animals and live as long as 26 years. They can be recognized by their hoarse croaking cry.

ravine *n.* a deep valley or gorge.

raw *adj.* 1. uncooked. *It can be dangerous to eat raw meat.* 2. without experience. *Many of the soldiers were raw recruits.* 3. sensitive to touch.

ray *n.* 1. line or beam of light, heat or some kind of energy. 2. a flat kind of fish.

rayon *n.* the name given to various man-made textile fibers containing cellulose, a substance found in the walls of plant cells.

razor *n.* an instrument for shaving hair from the skin.

re- 1. *prep.* concerning *Re the book you lent me.* 2. *prefix* meaning again, repeated. By knowing the meaning of the main word the sense of the prefixed word should, in most cases, be obvious, e.g. **reintroduce**, **rethink**.

reach *vb.* get or grab hold of something; arrive at.

react *vb.* respond to; change chemically.

reactor *n.* an apparatus in which atomic energy is produced.

read *vb.* look at, and understand, writing or printing.

ready *adv.* prepared. *Are you ready yet?* In a fit state; willing.

real *adj.* actual; alive; correct; genuine.

realize *vb.* come to understand. *Judy realized that she must have seen a ghost.*

really *adv.* truly; correctly. *Do you really mean that?*

realm (*relm*) *n.* another word for kingdom.

reap *vb.* cut and collect a crop, especially a cereal, such as wheat.

rear 1. *n.* & *adj.* the back part; at the back. *I like to sit at the rear of the classroom.* 2. *vb.* look after young creatures as they grow up. 3. *vb.* (of a horse) stand up on the back legs.

reason *n.* anything that explains why or how something has happened; power of mind to think. *vb.* try to reach conclusions by thinking. **reasonable** *adj.* having good judgment; moderate; fair.

rebel (**reb**-*el*) *n.* someone who revolts against a government; someone who refuses to obey orders. (*ri*-**bell**) *vb.* revolt, organize a **rebellion** *n.*

rebuke *n.* & *vb.* speak severely to, reprimand.

recall *vb.* 1. remember; bring back to mind. 2. call someone back.

recede *vb.* move back, withdraw. **recession.** *n.* decline in activity or prosperity.

receipt (*re*-**seet**) *n.* an official piece of paper stating that a bill has been paid.

receive (*re*-**seeve**) *vb.* get something that has been given to you or sent to you; accept.

recent *adj.* not long ago.

receptacle *n.* container.

recital *n.* a performance, usually of music. *A piano recital.*

recite *vb.* say aloud from memory.

The safety razor was invented in 1880 by King C. Gillette.

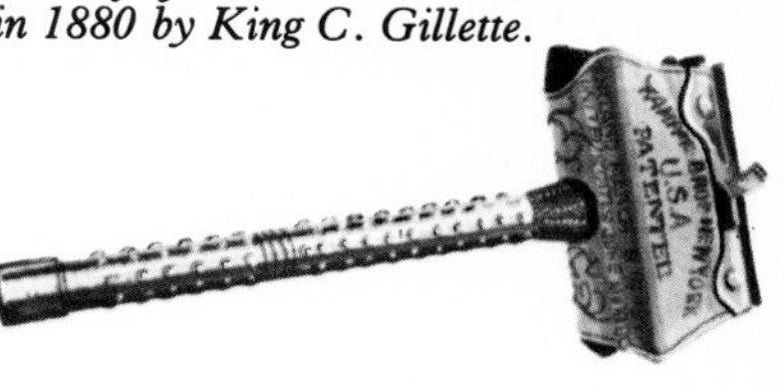

Paul can recite a poem by heart.

reckless *adj.* careless, rash, wild.

reckon *vb.* calculate, count; estimate; suppose, think.

reclaim *vb.* 1. restore poor or abandoned land to agricultural use. 2. get back something you are entitled to.

recline *vb.* lean; lie.

recognize *vb.* 1. know that you have seen somebody or something before. *I wonder if she will recognize me after all those years?* 2. acknowledge.

recommend *vb.* advise; speak or write favorably of. *I recommend this book to you.*

reconcile *vb.* 1. make friends again after a quarrel. 2. resign oneself to.

record (**reck**-*ord*) 1. *n.* a flat disk which makes sounds when it is turned on a record player. 2. *n.* & *adj.* the best performance known. *She scored a record number of goals.*

record (*ree*-**kord**) *vb.* 1. write something down so that it will be remembered. 2. put sounds on a record or tape.

► Making a record is a complicated process. First, a microphone turns the voices and music into electronic signals. These are made stronger, amplified, so as to make a sapphire "chisel" vibrate as it cuts a very fine groove into a smooth disc. This is the master disc.

A metal copy in reverse is made from the master disc so that the grooves stand out as ridges on the copy. Next, metal stampers are made. The records are made of a plastic material that is heated to soften it before it is pressed between two stampers.

recorder *n.* a musical instrument made of wood or plastic, played by blowing into one end.

recording see **record.**

record player *n.* phonograph, a machine for playing records.

recover *vb.* 1. get something back. *He recovered his boot from the mud.* 2. get better. *I am glad you have recovered from your fall.* **recovery** *n.*

recreation *n.* enjoyable exercise, refreshment of mind and body.

recruit *n.* a newly enlisted or drafted member of the armed forces. *vb.* enlist someone.

rectangle *n.* a four-sided figure in which the opposite sides are equal to each other and all four angles are right angles.

R

recuperate *vb.* get better after an illness; regain, recover.
recur *vb.* (past **recurred**) occur again. **recurrence** *n.*
red *n.* & *adj.* the color of blood. *Red is one of the primary colors.*

Red Cross
The Red Cross is an international organization that helps the sick, the hungry and the suffering. It has its headquarters at Geneva in Switzerland. Its symbol is a red cross on a white flag.

The Red Cross was founded by Henri Dunant in 1863 after he had seen the terrible suffering of wounded soldiers. The organization helps the wounded of all armies – it does not take sides. Today it is based in more than 70 countries and cares for soldiers and civilians all over the world. The American Red Cross was founded by Clara Barton in 1881.

Red Sea
The Red Sea is a narrow arm of the Indian Ocean. It stretches for 1,200 miles (1,900 km), dividing Arabia from northeast Africa. It has an area of about 170,000 sq. miles (440,300 sq. km). At its northern end it is linked to the MEDITERRANEAN SEA by the SUEZ CANAL. Its southern end is guarded by the narrow straits of Bab el Mandeb.

The Red Sea is quite a shallow body of water. As there are no major currents which flow through it, it is also very warm and salty. It is full of CORAL reefs and islands.

reduce *vb.* make less. *If you reduce the price I will buy it.*
redundant *adj.* exceeding what is needed, superfluous; needlessly repetitive. **redundancy** *n.*
reed *n.* tall, firm-stemmed grass that grows near water.
reef *n.* a ridge of rock or sand near the surface of the sea.
reel 1. *n.* device for winding, e.g. fishing line; length of film on a spool. 2. *n.* Scottish dance. 3. *vb.* sway, be giddy.
refectory *n.* a dining room in a convent, monastery or some schools.
referee *vb.* & *n.* a person who controls a football or boxing match. **ref** (*abbrev.*).
reference book *n.* a book that is used to find particular pieces of information. You do not usually read through the whole book. *Dictionaries and encyclopedias are reference books.*
referendum *n.* voting on a particular issue by all voters; a plebiscite.
refine *vb.* remove impurities. **refinery** *n.* a building or equipment where oil, sugar, or metal is refined.
reflect *vb.* send back light, heat, sound or radio waves from any object.

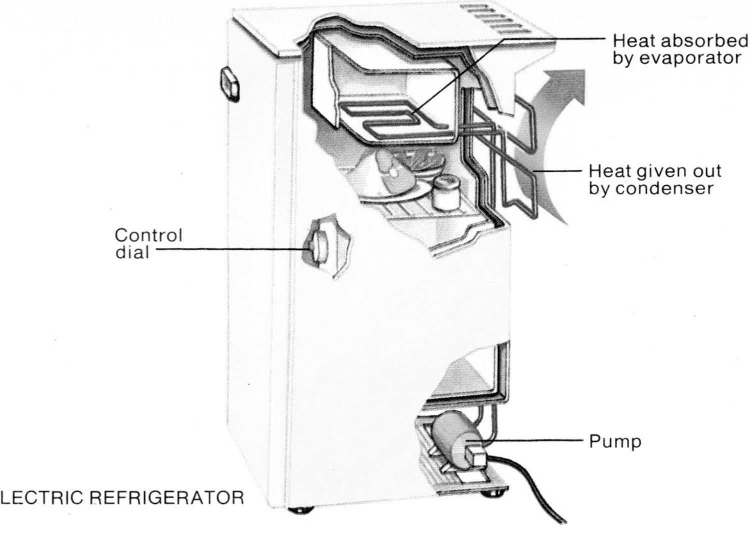

ELECTRIC REFRIGERATOR

An electric refrigerator has a special gas which is compressed to turn it into a liquid. The cold fluid is pumped through the pipes of the refrigerator to carry heat away from the food.

reflection *n.* the picture you see in a mirror or in calm water.
reform *vb.* make a great political or social change; improve. **reformation** *n.*
► The Reformation is the name given to the period of great religious upheaval that began in Europe in the 1500s.

At that time, a revolt occurred in the ROMAN CATHOLIC CHURCH. Groups of people broke away to set up their own churches. These people became known as PROTESTANTS.

The Catholic Church of the time had a lot of political power. Some of its members felt it had too much. These people protested and the revolt that followed led to much violence and bloodshed.

What many Protestants wanted was a simpler, more basic form of CHRISTIANITY, and one that allowed them greater freedom to worship as they chose. As the Protestant movement grew, many kings and rulers saw the new religion as a chance to widen their power. They were happy to support the Protestant cause because in many ways the religious protest also helped them to gain more influence.

refraction *n.* the bending of light when it passes from one medium to another.
► Light is refracted when, for example, it passes from air to water, or vice versa. Light passing into an optically denser medium is bent towards the normal – a line perpendicular to the surface of the material. LENSES and PRISMS both bend light by the process of refraction.

refrain 1. *vb.* curb, restrain, keep oneself from doing. 2. *n.* regularly recurring phrase or verse at the end of stanzas of a poem.
refresh *vb.* give new energy to.

refrigerator *n.* a cabinet or room in which food is kept very cold so that it does not spoil.
► Refrigerators are really just boxes, with an electric motor running a cooling system. They are insulated to keep the inside of the refrigerator cold for some time, even when the motor is not running. The average temperature is kept at 35 to 45°F (2 to 7°C).

The cooling system has a special gas in it. This gas is first compressed (squeezed) to turn it into a liquid. The liquid then flows through hollow tubes inside the refrigerator into an *evaporator*, which turns it back into gas. This gas is pumped around the system. As it goes around the inside of the refrigerator it draws out any heat from the inside.

When it is pumped outside the refrigerator the gas is compressed again. This turns it back into a liquid and it gives out the heat it picked up on the inside. The liquid is pumped round and round, turning from liquid to gas and back again. As this goes on, the air inside the refrigerator becomes colder and the heat is taken to the outside. The process works like a sort of heat sponge.

refuge *n.* a shelter from danger. **refugee** *n.* person escaping danger and seeking shelter.
refund *n.* & *vb.* return money.
refuse (*re-***fyuze**) *vb.* say that you will not do something that you are asked to do. **refusal** *n.*
refuse (**ref**-*yuse*) *n.* rubbish, things that are thrown away.

regal *adj*. concerning kings and queens, royal; magnificent.
regalia *n*. emblems and symbols of royalty, e.g. crown, scepter, etc.
regard *vb*. look at; take into consideration; hold in high esteem. *n*. gaze, concern. **regards** *pl. n*. respectful friendly feelings. *I send you my regards.*
regarding *prep*. concerning.
regatta *n*. a race meeting for boats and yachts.
regent *n*. a person who takes the place of a monarch if the monarch is too young or too ill to rule.
reggae (**reg**-*ay*) *n*. West Indian music with a strong beat.
regime (*ray*-**zheem**) *n*. a system of government; a period of rule.
regiment *n*. a large army unit.

Regina
The provincial capital of Saskatchewan, Canada, Regina is an agricultural center and supply center for the oil fields and mines of southern Saskatchewan.

region (**ree**-*jun*) *n*. an area of the world or of a country with no particular border. *Evergreens grow mainly in the colder regions of the world.* **regional** *adj*.
register 1. *n*. a book in which lists of things or other information is kept. 2. *vb*. record; put in writing. *I wish to register a complaint.*
regret *n*. & *vb*. be sorry for something that has been done.
regular *adj*. happening in the same way or at the same time again and again. *There is a regular bus service between most big cities.*
regulate *vb*. 1. govern or control according to rules. 2. adjust (a watch, etc.).
rehearse *vb*. practice, particularly for a play or concert. **rehearsal** *n*. a practice performance of a play.
reign (rhymes with *pain*) *vb*. & *n*. period of rule (as a king or queen).
reindeer *n*. a kind of large deer that lives in cold regions.
► In North America reindeer are also known as caribou. Reindeer are large MAMMALS with brown coats and white belly markings. Both males and females have great branches of antlers.
Reindeer live in large herds. In their summer breeding grounds on the open tundra (treeless plains), they feed on grasses and other vegetation.
At the end of the summer there is a huge MIGRATION farther south where they spend the winter. Reindeer are hunted by ESKIMOS for their skin, meat and antlers. The Lapps of northern Scandinavia keep large reindeer herds.

reins (rhymes with *canes*) *pl. n*. straps fastened to a bridle to control a horse.
reject *vb*. refuse to accept or keep something because it is not good enough.
rejoice *vb*. to be happy.
relapse *vb*. & *n*. slip or fall back into a former worse state.
relative *n*. someone who belongs to the same family as you. *Your aunt and uncle are your relatives.*

Relativity
In 1905, Albert EINSTEIN's Special Theory of Relativity appeared to show that the physical laws established by Isaac NEWTON could not be applied to bodies moving at speeds approaching that of light. For, said Einstein, length, mass and time all change according to a body's VELOCITY. In fact, at the velocity of light, a body would have no length and infinite mass. And, for that body, time would stand still. Many scientific observations made since this theory was published have confirmed Einstein's predictions. In 1916, Einstein published his *General Theory of Relativity*, dealing with accelerating bodies and gravitational fields. This theory suggests that gravitation is a property of space – a "curvature" caused by the presence of matter.

relax *vb*. become less tight; loosen. *If you relax your muscles you will feel better.*
relay race *n*. a race in which each person in a team goes part of the distance.
release *vb*. set free, liberate; put into circulation. *The film was released first in Scotland.*
relevant *adj*. relating to or connected with the subject being discussed.
reliable *adj*. can be trusted and depended upon. *She is a reliable dentist.*
relic *n*. something that survives destruction; something belonging to a holy person kept by others as an object of reverence.
relief (*re*-**leaf**) *n*. 1. removal or lessening of pain. 2. help given to refugees, etc. 3. carving in which the designs stand out from the surface.
relief map *n*. a map that shows where high and low areas of land are.
relieve *vb*. free; give aid to.
religion *n*. a belief that there is a god who created and controls the universe. **religious** *adj*.
► People have many different ideas about God and the ways in which they should show their beliefs. But all religions are basically about one main thing – God and the way in which people believe in him.
The greatest religions of today are Buddhism (based on the teachings of the BUDDHA), CHRISTIANITY, Hinduism (followed by HINDUS), ISLAM and JUDAISM. All are very ancient. The most recent is Islam, which was founded about 1,300 years ago. The smallest of the world's major religions is Judaism with about 15 million followers. The largest, Christianity, has well over 100 million followers, scattered all over the world.

A statue of Baal, one of the supreme gods of the Canaanites at the time when the Israelites were conquering the area. Strange rites connected with the worship of Baal included human sacrifice.

Like ancient peoples, the primitive peoples of today may worship many gods and spirits. Often these gods are part of nature. They may be rocks, trees and lakes. Certain forces of nature such as wind, rain and thunder may also be thought to be holy. And so too are certain kinds of animals.
The religions of today are very different from the primitive religions. Most are very grand, with magnificent shrines and temples as places of worship. Statues and works of art showing religious figures are common. Specially trained priests and holy men say prayers and lead religious ceremonies. They also study the laws and teachings of the religion. These are often written down in holy books, which have been passed down from one generation to the next.

relish 1. *n*. enjoyment of food. 2. *n*. a sauce. 3. *vb*. get pleasure from.
reluctant *adj*. unwilling, hesitating. **reluctance** *n*.
rely *vb*. depend on. *I rely on you to give me a lift tomorrow.*
remain 1. *vb*. stay after others. *Sue remained in the house when the others went out.* 2. *vb*. be left over after some has been taken away. *You can have the few candies that remain.* 3. **remains** *pl. n*. what is left after some amount has been taken away; a dead body.
remainder *n*. what is left over when a part has gone or been taken away.

R

remark *vb.* & *n.* comment, observe.
remarkable *adj.* worth noticing; extraordinary.

Rembrandt
Rembrandt, Harmens van Rijn (1606–69) is one of the most famous of all Dutch painters. He and his helpers produced many paintings. Over 700 exist today. He also produced thousands of drawings.

Rembrandt is best known for his portraits of the wealthy townspeople of Holland. Unlike many painters, he became very successful while he was still alive. However, later in life, many of the rich people no longer bought his pictures because they did not like the way his painting had changed. Although he became very poor, this was the time when he painted some of his best works.

remedy *n.* medicine or treatment for a disease. *vb.* put right.
remember *vb.* keep something in mind; recall, or bring something to mind; not to forget. *Remember to telephone me when you arrive.*
remind *vb.* make or help someone remember. *Sarah reminded everyone about her birthday.*
remote *adj.* far away from other places, times, or relations. *We spent our honeymoon on a remote island.*
remove *vb.* take away.
Renaissance *n.* a French word meaning "rebirth" and describing the great revival in learning, art, etc., that took place in Europe from the 14th to 16th century.

► Since the times of the ancient Greeks and Romans there had been little interest in art, science, architecture and literature. Then, during the 1300s, Italian scholars began to take an interest in the past. They also looked for new scientific explanations of the mysteries of the world and the universe. During the Renaissance, a great number of painters, sculptors and architects were at work in Italy. The works of art of LEONARDO DA VINCI and MICHELANGELO are among the most famous products of this time. From Italy, the ideas of the Renaissance quickly spread to the rest of Europe.

At the same time, there was a great growth in trade. Later, there were voyages to explore Africa and India, and in 1492 America was discovered by Christopher COLUMBUS.

rendezvous (**ron**-*day-voo*) *n.* an appointed meeting place. *vb.* meet at an appointed place.

Renoir, Pierre Auguste
A French painter (1841–1919) of the Impressionist school. Renoir was born the son of a poor tailor and his first job was painting designs on porcelain to pay his way to art school. His paintings are loved for their joy and gaiety.

rent 1. *n.* a regular payment made for the use of a house or other place or thing. 2. *vb.* have the use of something you pay a rent for.

repair *vb.* make something that is broken whole again; mend.
repeat *vb.* say or do again.
repeatedly *adv.* again and again.
repel *vb.* drive back, turn away.
repellent *adj.* unattractive.
repent *vb.* feel sorrow or regret for the wrong one has done.
replace *vb.* put back where it came from. *Please replace the book on the right shelf.*
replica *n.* an exact copy of something.
reply *vb.* answer someone. *n.* an answer.
report 1. *vb.* tell of something; give an account of (for publication). *n.* the account itself, spoken or written. 2. *n.* a bang.
reporter *n.* a person who obtains and writes about news for a newspaper, TV, etc.
represent *vb.* act or speak for other people.
reprimand *vb.* speak sharply to, scold. *n.* official rebuke.
reproduce *vb.* 1. make something happen again; copy. *The concert was recorded on tape and reproduced the next day.* 2. give birth.
reproduction *n.*
► Reproduction is the ability of all living things, whether plants or animals, to produce more life like themselves. Humans give birth to babies, chickens lay EGGS and flowers produce SEEDS and POLLEN. The most usual way among higher animals is for the male to produce sperm and the female to produce an egg; the

Saint Peter's basilica in Rome – a fine example of the Renaissance throwback to classical architecture. The dome is built to precise mathematical precision – typical of Greek and Roman buildings.

Above: A self portrait by Leonardo da Vinci (1452–1519). Possibly the greatest man of the Renaissance, he was both a scientific genius and a brilliant painter. Probably his best known painting is the "Mona Lisa" (left) painted in oil in about 1504.

The komodo dragon is the largest lizard in the world. It can measure over 10 ft. (3 meters) long.

Above: The Marine iguana is a lizard and like most reptiles has scaly skin and lays hard-shelled eggs on land.

R

two must combine before new life is formed.

reptile *n.* a cold-blooded vertebrate animal that creeps or crawls. *Crocodiles, snakes and tortoises are all reptiles.*

► Reptiles are the most advanced of all cold-blooded animals. They live on land and in the sea. In all, there are about 6,000 different types of reptile.

Except for the North and South poles, reptiles live in all parts of the world. Most, however, live in warm regions. This is because they are cold-blooded and must therefore get their warmth from their surroundings.

When it is cold they become very sleepy and cannot move fast enough to catch food or escape enemies. Most reptiles that live in cold places spend the winter in HIBERNATION.

Reptiles played a very important part in the EVOLUTION of the earth. It is thought that about 200 million years ago, the first reptiles left the water and began to roam over the land. They soon became the strongest form of life on earth. They ruled the planet for close to 100 million years. One group of reptiles, the DINOSAURS, were the most spectacular creatures ever to walk the land.

Reptiles are still well-suited for life on land. They have thick, leathery skins that stop their bodies from drying up in hot weather. Those that eat meat have powerful jaws and sharp teeth, and some have poison fangs for killing their prey. Most reptiles lay eggs. The eggs have hard shells or tough leathery skins to protect them. A few reptiles, such as some sea snakes and lizards, give birth to live young.

Today, there are four main groups of reptiles: ALLIGATORS and CROCODILES, LIZARDS and SNAKES, TORTOISES and TURTLES, and the rare tuatara. The biggest reptiles are the alligators and crocodiles. The estuarine crocodile of South-East Asia grows to 20 ft. (6 meters) in length, and is the biggest reptile of them all.

There are over 5,000 kinds of lizards and snakes. They live everywhere, from deserts to jungles and faraway ocean islands. Some have poisonous bites with which they kill their prey.

Tortoises and turtles are well protected by their hard shells. Tortoises live mostly on land. The biggest are the lumbering giants of the Pacific and Indian Ocean islands. They may live as long as 150 years and reach 500 lb. (225 kg) in weight.

One of the strangest reptiles of all is the tuatara, which looks rather like an IGUANA. It is a living FOSSIL and so is put in a group all by itself. It was common about 150 million years ago. Today, only a few live on the islands off the coast of New Zealand. It is one of the very few reptiles that can live happily in a cool climate.

republic *n.* a country that elects its head of state, usually a president, and does not have a king or queen.

► A republic is a form of government by which the people rule themselves. Usually they hold ELECTIONS to choose their leaders. Many republics have been formed to take over powers from kings who ruled unfairly.

But few republics really give the power to rule to the people. The first republics were in ancient Greece and Rome, but many of the people in these countries were slaves. Today, some so-called republics are run by people who have not been elected.

reputation *n.* a person's qualities or character as seen and judged by others.

request *vb.* & *n.* ask for something. *He requested this tape.*

require *vb.* 1. need. *She requires some help with the costumes.* 2. insist on.

rescue *vb.* take from danger; set free. *The knight will rescue the princess from the dragon. n.* being rescued.

research (*re-***surch**) *vb.* investigate, look into, carefully. (**ree-***surch*) *n.* inquiry, scientific study.

resemble *vb.* be or look like something or somebody else. *Alan resembles his grandfather.* **resemblance** *n.*

reserve 1. *vb.* keep back to use later. *Shall I reserve a chair for you if you are late? n.* a place kept for a special purpose. *You can see some very rare birds at the bird reserve.* 2. *n.* a player who does not play for the team unless someone else is unable to play. **reserved** *adj.* shy.

reservoir *n.* a place where a large amount of water is stored, often in an artificial lake.

resident *n.* someone who lives in a particular place, a permanent inhabitant. **reside** *vb.*

resign (*re-***zine**) *vb.* give up, especially to give up a job. **resignation** *n.*

resin *n.* a sticky gum that oozes (leaks slowly) from trees; rosin, the best known, comes from pines.

resist *vb.* oppose; go against. **resistance** *n.*

resources *pl. n.* the useful things that a person or country has. *Oil is one of our country's greatest resources.*

respect *vb.* & *n.* (have) a high opinion of; esteem. **respectable** *adj.* decent; of good solid behavior.

resort (*ri-***zort**) 1. *vb.* turn to. *He was so unhappy he resorted to overeating.* 2. *n.* vacation area.

re-sort (*ree-***sort**) *vb.* sort again.

resolve *vb.* decide, be determined to. *I resolve to get to work on time in the future.*

responsible *adj.* in charge of something. *I am responsible for the paint cupboard.* **responsibility** *n.*

rest 1. *vb.* lie down; relax. 2. *n.* the remainder. *What has happened to the rest of our group?* **restful** *adj.* quiet, soothing.

restaurant *n.* a place where you can buy and eat food.

restore *vb.* put back as it was before; repair. *Sue restores old furniture.*

restrict *vb.* keep within bounds, limit. **restriction** *n.*

result 1. *n.* & *vb.* something that happens because of some action or happening. *Joe's injury was the result of a kick at football.* 2. *n.* the final score in a game.

resume *vb.* begin again, take back. *After the interval the concert resumed.*

resurrect *vb.* bring back to life. **Resurrection** *n.* the rising of Jesus Christ from the tomb.

retail *vb.* sell goods in a shop. *See* **wholesale**).

retain *vb.* hold back, keep.

retina *n.* coating at the back of the eyeball which is sensitive to light.

retire *vb.* 1. give up work, usually because one is old. 2. go back;

R

withdraw. *The rain was so heavy, we had to retire to the pavilion.*
retreat *vb.* go back from.
return *vb.* 1. give something back. *Could you please return my pen.* 2. go back, come back again. *When do you return from your holiday?*
reunion *n.* being reunited, a coming together again.
reveal *vb.* uncover; make known. *I can now reveal the secret.*
revenue *n.* the money that a government receives from taxation, etc.
revere *vb.* show respect, honor for.

Revere, Paul
Paul Revere (1735–1818) was a well-known silversmith and engraver. But he is best remembered for his heroic ride on the night of April 18, 1775, when he was sent to warn American patriots that British troops were advancing from Boston to seize the Americans' supply depot in Concord. The battles at Lexington and Concord began the American War of INDEPENDENCE.

reverse 1. *vb.* go backward, particularly in a vehicle. 2. *n.* the opposite of something.
reversible *adj.* able to be reversed.
review 1. *n.* published opinion of a book, play, etc. *vb.* examine, criticize. 2. *vb.* & *n.* inspect troops.
revise *vb.* look over again in order to correct or improve. **revision** *n.*
revive *vb.* bring back to life or consciousness; make active again. *The Olympic Games were revived in modern times.*
revolution *n.* 1. a time when a government is changed by force, not by an election; a time when ideas and the way people live are changed by new ideas or actions, as in the *Industrial Revolution.* 2. a full turn of a wheel. **revolve** *vb.*

Revolutionary War, U.S. *see* **Independence, American War of.**

revolver *n.* a handgun with its ammunition held in a revolving cylinder.
reward *n.* a present given to someone for what has been done. *We were given a reward for helping to catch the thief. vb.* give reward.
rheumatism *n.* the name given to a group of diseases which cause pain in the muscles and joints and make them stiff and hard to move.

Rhine
The Rhine is the main waterway of Europe. It is linked by canals with the Danube, Elbe and Rhône rivers. This makes it possible to sail from the Black Sea to the North Sea and the Baltic Sea.

The Rhine begins in the Swiss Alps and it empties into the sea near Rotterdam in Holland. Large ships up to 2,000 tons can sail right up the Rhine to Strasbourg in the heart of Europe.

The Rhine valley has the heaviest population in West GERMANY. Major cities, such as Essen, Dusseldorf and Cologne lie along its banks, or along rivers that flow into it.

Between Bonn and Mainz, two ancient German cities, the Rhine flows through a beautiful narrow gorge. This is the area where much of Germany's wine is made. Ancient castles dot the cliff tops by the river. In the Middle Ages, the lords who commanded these castles made trading vessels pay a fee to use the river.

rhinoceros *n.* a large African or Asian animal with a very thick skin and one or two horns on the snout.

Rhinoceros

► The rhinoceros is one of the largest and strongest of all land animals. A full-grown male can weigh as much as 3.5 tons.

This massive beast has a tough, leathery skin and sprouts one or two horns on its snout. These may grow as long as 50 in. (127 cm).

The rhinoceros lives in Africa and in southeastern Asia. There it feeds on leafy twigs, shrubs and grasses. (It is, surprisingly, a vegetarian.)

Although an adult rhino has no natural enemies, it is so widely hunted for its horns that it has become a dying species. When ground into a powder, its horns are believed to be a powerful medicine. However, the rhino's ability to charge swiftly over short distances makes it a very dangerous animal to hunt.

Rhode Island (*abbrev.* **R.I.**)
Rhode Island, in New England, is the smallest state in the U.S.A. It is not an island, though it includes many islands that lie in Narragansett Bay. Rhode Island was once an important producer of textiles. Today, many new industries have come to the state, and jewelry and silverware are the state's leading manufactured products.

Rhode Island was founded by refugees from Puritan-controlled Massachusetts. One of these, Roger Williams, established Providence, now the capital, in 1636. From its infancy, Rhode Island gained a reputation as a haven for those seeking religious or political freedom. Rhode Island became the 13th state in 1790.

rhubarb *n.* a leafy plant the stalks of which are often cooked and eaten.
rhyme *n.* & *vb.* use a word that sounds like another word. *"Egg" and "beg" rhyme with each other.*
rhythm (**rith**-*em*) *n.* the pattern of beats in music and poetry.
rib *n.* one of the curved bones of the chest.
ribbon *n.* a narrow piece of material used as an ornament or for tying things, as well as in typewriters.
rice *n.* a cereal grass that is widely grown for food. It grows in wet parts of India and China and in most warm climates.
► Rice is a member of the GRASS family. Its grains are one of the most important CEREAL crops in the world. It is the main food of most Asian people.

Young shoots of rice are planted in flooded fields called paddies. Here they grow in 2–4 in. (5–10 cm) of water, until they are ready to be harvested. Young rice has long narrow leaves and fine clusters of flowers that turn into the grains that we eat.

rich *adj.* 1. having a great deal of money; wealthy. 2. (of food) containing a great deal of fat, cream, etc.

A 13th-century tile depicting Richard I of England (1189–1199). Richard led the Crusades to the Holy Land with great success, earning himself the name the Lionhearted.

Richard I
Richard I (reigned 1189–99) was a king of England, who spent only six months of his 10-year reign in that country.

Richard was crowned in Westminster in 1189 and set off at once to take part in the CRUSADES. In

The four gaits or paces of a horse.

1187 the armies of ISLAM, led by Saladin, had retaken Jerusalem. In 1189 a new crusade was called to drive them out.

Richard I, known as the Lion-Hearted because of his courage and ferocity in battle, first sailed to Cyprus. After taking the island he went on to the Holy Land, where he and his allies, the French, took the city of Acre. In 1192 they tried to take Jerusalem but failed. On the trip home, Richard was taken prisoner and was freed only in 1194. The last years of his reign were spent mainly in France fighting his former allies, and he was killed there in 1199.

rickshaw *n.* small, oriental two-wheeled passenger vehicle drawn by a man on foot or bicycle.
rid (get rid of) *vb.* throw away something that is not wanted.
riddle *n.* a puzzling question. *"What goes up when the rain comes down?" is a riddle. (The answer: "an umbrella".)*

Winchester carbine, USA, 1886

ride *vb.* (past **rode** past part **ridden**) travel on something, particularly a horse or bicycle.
► Horses were one of the earliest forms of transport, but today, most people ride them for pleasure. It takes a great deal of skill to ride a horse well. Some people test their skill in competitions in jumping and cross-country events, and in various sports such as polo. But many people ride just for enjoyment.

One of the most important things a rider must learn is how to tell a horse what to do. There are two kinds of signals used for this. The first, known as *natural aids*, are given by hand, leg and voice commands. The second uses *artificial aids*. These include riding sticks and spurs.

Command signals must be given smoothly and correctly, otherwise the horse will become confused about what its rider wants it to do. A horse must be taught exactly what each signal means and it must learn to obey these signals promptly.

Making a horse walk forward is not very difficult to do. To begin moving, squeeze the horse's sides with your lower legs. When moving to a *trot*, increase your leg pressure on the sides of the horse. Tighten up the reins so that the bit sits more firmly in its mouth, then ease off. Keep up a steady leg pressure. When the horse is trotting keep sitting up straight.

To go to a *canter* from a trot, increase your leg pressure once again. Stay closely seated in the saddle and do not lean too far forward as this upsets the rhythm of the horse. The canter is the hardest of all paces; it takes a lot of practice.

When a horse is *galloping*, bring your weight forward and lean on your knees and the stirrups. It is important to stay in control so that the horse can be slowed and guided without difficulty.

rider *n.* a person who rides, particularly on horseback.
ridge *n.* a long narrow part higher than what is on either side.
ridiculous *adj.* silly enough to be laughed at. **ridicule** *vb.* make fun of.
rifle *n.* a gun that is held against the shoulder when it is fired.
►The ancestor of the modern rifle was the matchlock, which became popular in the 1500s. Today all armies use rifles. Most are automatic. They fire in the same way as machine guns and can empty a magazine of bullets in a single long burst of fire. Rifles can fire up to 1,200 shots a minute.

The inside of a rifle barrel has a spiral groove, called rifling, first introduced in the early 1800s. This makes the bullet spin around as it leaves the barrel. A spinning bullet flies straight, and more accurately, to its target.

rift *n.* a split, opening; chasm.
rig *n.* 1. arrangement of ships' sails. 2. equipment for drilling oil wells.
rigid *adj.* stiff; unbending; strict.
right 1. *n.* & *adj.* the opposite of left. 2. *adj.* correct; accurate; good. *Do you have the right time?*
rim *n.* 1. the edge of a container. 2. *n.* the outside edge of a circle.
rind *n.* the thick, tough skin of some fruits and vegetables, of cheese and bacon, and of a tree.
ring *n.* 1. a circle, such as the ring in a circus. 2. a circular band of gold or other material worn on a finger as an ornament. 3. the sound made by a bell.
rink *n.* a place for skating.
rinse *vb.* wash out in clean water.

Rio de Janeiro
Rio de Janeiro is a city on the south-east coast of BRAZIL, and is that country's main seaport. It lies in a magnificent mountain setting on the western side of the Bay of Guanabara. It is a major commercial, industrial and cultural center. Rio de Janeiro was the capital of Brazil until 1960, when its place was taken by the new city of BRASILIA in the interior of the country.

riot *n.* a noisy and violent disturbance by a crowd. *vb.* take part in a riot.
rip *vb.* tear something.
ripe *adj.* (of fruit) ready to be eaten. **ripen** *vb.* grow ripe.
ripple *n.* small movement on the surface of water.
rise *vb.* come or go up; get up.
risk *n.* the chance of danger or loss. *vb.* expose to risk. **risky** *adj.*

This illustration shows how a river can change the landscape by erosion and by depositing the eroded material farther downstream.

LONGEST RIVERS

	mi	km
Nile (Africa)	4,145	6,670
Amazon (S. America)	4,000	6,437
Mississippi-Missouri-Red Rock (N. America)	3,872	6,231
Yangtze (China)	3,400	5,470
Ob-Irtysh (U.S.S.R.)	3,200	5,150
Zaire* (Africa)	3,000	4,828
Lena (U.S.S.R.)	3,000	4,828
Amur (Asia)	2,800	4,506
Yenisey (U.S.S.R.)	2,800	4,506
Hwang Ho (China)	2,700	4,345
Mekong (SE. Asia)	2,600	4,184
Niger (Africa)	2,486	4,000

*Formerly Congo River

rite *n.* the set words and actions of a (religious) ceremony. **ritual** *adj.* & *n.* concerned with rites; the rite itself.
ritzy *adj.* in fashion, snobby. *She wore a ritzy hat to show off to her friends.*
rival *n.* a competitor; an opponent. *vb.* compete with.
river *n.* a large stream of water that flows from higher to lower ground and into another river, a lake or sea.
► Rivers are one of the most important geographical features in the world. They range in size from little more than swollen streams to mighty waterways that flow thousands of miles.

The greatest rivers in the world are the AMAZON, the MISSISSIPPI and the NILE. They all drain huge areas of land. The basin of the Amazon for example, stretches over an area larger than all of western Europe.

Some rivers serve as roads that allow ocean-going ships to sail far inland. In tropical jungles they are often the only ways to travel. Rivers with DAMS supply us with electric power. They are also tapped for water to irrigate farmland.

rivet *n.* a bolt for joining metal plates together. *vb.* join with rivets; hold the attention.
roach *n.* silvery freshwater fish.
road *n.* a wide path or highway for cars and other vehicles.
► Early roads were built soon after the invention of the WHEEL, but the Romans were the first great road builders. Some of their long, straight roads still survive. The Romans made roads of gravel and stones. The surface paving stones were arched in the middle so that rain ran off into ditches.

Modern road building began during the INDUSTRIAL REVOLUTION. In the early 1800s, a Scottish engineer, John McAdam, became the pioneer of modern road making. But the stony surfaces of his roads were not good for vehicles with rubber tires. Later, macadamized roads were built. They are covered with tar or asphalt to make them smooth.

roam *vb.* wander; go here and there.
roar *n.* & *vb.* loud, deep sound like the noise a lion makes.
roast *vb.* cook food in an oven.
rob *vb.* take or steal things. **robber** *n.* a person who steals; a thief. **robbery** *n.* theft.

robe *n.* a long, loose dress or gown, sometimes worn as part of a national or ceremonial costume. *vb.* put on robes.
robin *n.* a small bird of the thrush family with rusty-orange feathers on its throat and breast. *Robins often make their homes in town gardens.*

Robin Hood
Robin Hood is the legendary hero of many English ballads. He was a daring and gallant outlaw who robbed from the rich to give to the poor. He is said to have lived in Sherwood Forest in Nottinghamshire at the end of the 1100s.

robot *n.* a machine that can be made to do things that people do.
► The word robot is a modern one coming from the Czech for "forced labor". Robots are being used more and more in industry and science to do tasks that are dangerous or repetitive. Robots may handle hot or radioactive devices. These are simply a pair of arms and fingers operated by a human. Other robots are programmed to do jobs such as welding cars on assembly lines. They are operated by computers. In science fiction films and stories, robots often look like humans and are able to talk and think.

rock 1. *n.* a large stone. 2. *n.* a type of popular music with a strong beat. 3. *vb.* move back and forth.
► Rock is the substance that forms the earth's crust. It is made up of mixtures of MINERALS. Rocks are divided into three main types: *igneous*, *sedimentary*, and *metamorphic*. Igneous rocks are formed when molten lava from volcanic eruptions turns solid. Granite, obsidian, basalt and pumice are igneous rocks. Igneous rocks make up about four-fifths of the earth's crust.

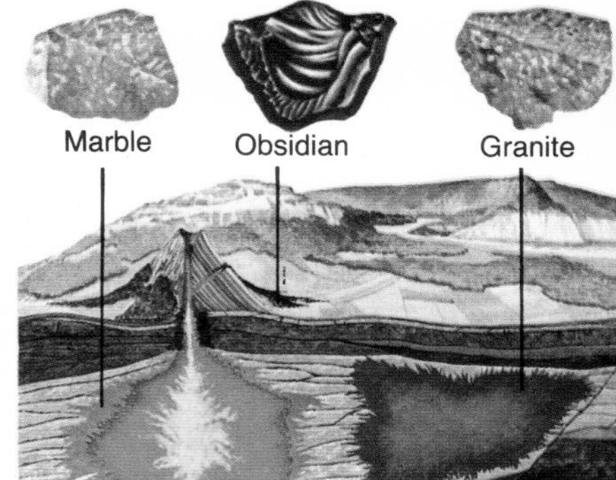

Sedimentary rocks are formed when mud and small stones (sediment) harden. Limestone is formed from line mud. Pebbles are pressed into conglomerates. Granite and obsidian are igneous rocks and were once hot and molten.

Sedimentary rocks are igneous rocks that have been worn away by rivers, seas, wind and rain. The worn-away particles of these rocks are carried away and deposited, for instance, at the bottom of the sea. After millions of years these particles are compressed to form sedimentary rocks. Sandstone and limestone are sedimentary rocks.

The third main kind of rock, metamorphic rock, is formed by the action of great heat and pressure on igneous and sedimentary rocks inside the earth's crust. Marble is a metamorphic rock formed from limestone.

rocket *n*. 1. a firework that shoots up into the sky. 2. a device for sending missiles and spacecraft into space.
► The first rockets were used in warfare by the Chinese in the 1200s. Like the rockets now used as fireworks, these missiles were propelled by GUNPOWDER. Gases produced by the fast-burning chemicals were forced from the back of the rockets, causing them to be propelled upward. In the same way, if you stand on a wagon and throw bricks from it, the wagon will move in the opposite direction. The action of throwing the bricks produces an equal and opposite reaction force that thrusts the wagon forward. The important difference between the rocket and the jet engine is that the rocket does not take in air (*see* JET PROPULSION). This enables it to operate in outer space, where a jet would cease to function. In fact, rockets are the only known means of propelling space vehicles. Spacecraft are usually launched by a three-stage rocket. A large *booster rocket* provides power for liftoff. After burning out, the booster separates and drops away, leaving a smaller, *second-stage rocket* to take over. This too drops away after use. Then an even smaller, *third-stage rocket* gives the spacecraft the final boost it needs to enter space. During later stages of the mission, small rocket engines control the spacecraft.

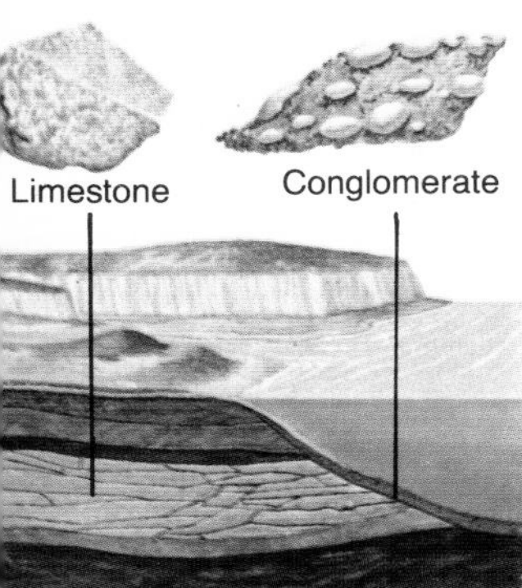

Rocky Mountains
The Rockies, as they are usually called, form the main mountain system of North America. The Rockies run down the western side of North America from Alaska to New Mexico. They are part of the enormous Cordilleran chain that extends from the Arctic Circle to Cape Horn.

The highest peak is Mount McKinley 20,320 ft. (6,195 meters). In Mexico the chain is called Sierra Madre, and from Panama southward through South America it is known as the *Andes*.

rod *n*. a long, straight stick.
rode *vb*. past of **ride**.
rodent *n*. one of a group of fairly small mammals that gnaw things. *Rats, mice and squirrels are all rodents*.
► Rodents have large, sharp front teeth that grow all the time. The animals wear down these teeth by gnawing their food. They also use their teeth to dig burrows in the ground for their homes and nests. BEAVERS even cut down trees with their teeth.

The 2,000 or so rodents also include MICE, RATS, PORCUPINES and SQUIRRELS. The South American capybara is the largest rodent. It looks like a giant GUINEA PIG. It grows to a length of 4 ft. (1.25 meters) and weighs over 100 lb. (45 kg). The smallest rodent is the European harvest mouse. It grows only about 5.3 in. (135 mm) long.

rodeo *n*. performance by American cowboys of riding and other skills.
► In bareback riding, a cowboy rides a bronco (a half-wild or bad-tempered horse). In saddle-bronco riding, the cowboy rides one-handed, using one rein, a saddle and a halter. Bull riding and calf roping are other events. In steer wrestling, the cowboy chases a young bull, or steer, on horseback, grabs its head and pulls the steer down. A comic contest is catching a greased pig. The first recorded rodeo was held in 1869.

rogue *n*. a bad man; a rascal.
roll 1. *vb*. turn over and over. 2. *n*. make something into a shape like a tube. 3. *vb*. flatten with roller. 4. *n*. a small loaf of bread.
rollerskates *pl. n*. set of wheels attached to a boot for skating on the ground.
rolling pin *n*. a long tube used for rolling out pastry to flatten it.
Roman Catholic *n*. a Christian who accepts the pope as the head of the church.

Roman Catholic Church
The Roman Catholic Church is the original Christian Church and is still by far the largest. Its leader is the POPE who lives in the VATICAN in Rome. The church traces its history back to the APOSTLES of the 1st century A.D.. Catholics view their Church as the authority that enshrines the teachings of JESUS CHRIST. (*See* CHRISTIANITY; REFORMATION.)

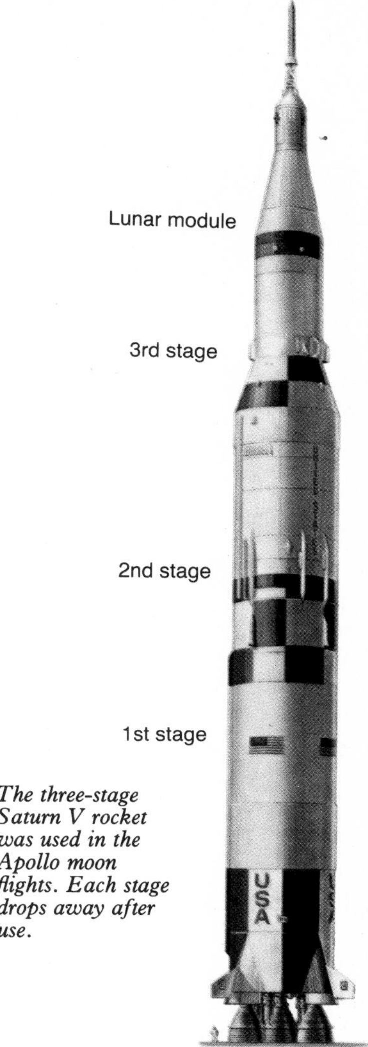

The three-stage Saturn V rocket was used in the Apollo moon flights. Each stage drops away after use.

romance *n*. medieval tale of chivalry; a love story. *vb*. exaggerate. **Romance** *adj*. languages based on Latin. **romantic** *adj*. imaginative, remote, mysterious.

Roman Empire
The ancient Romans built up a vast empire around the Mediterranean Sea. ROME was the center of the empire. Legend says that Rome was founded in 753 B.C.. In the 500s B.C., it was ruled by the ETRUSCANS. It was not until 509 B.C. that Rome began to rule itself. Then it was run by officials, called consuls, and magistrates. They were patricians

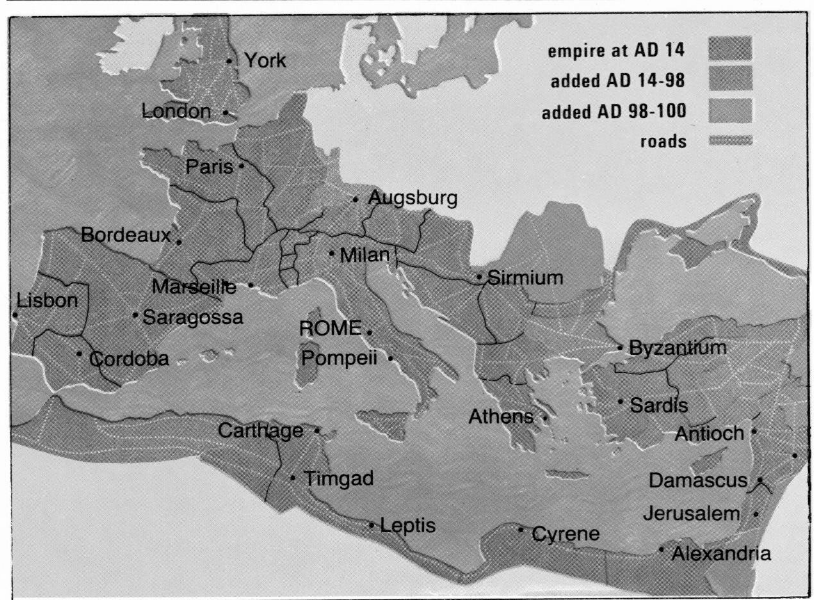

(rich people). The consuls shared power with the Senate, a council of men from rich families. Many years passed before the plebeians (poor people) won the right to become officials.

In the 200s B.C. the power of Rome began to reach out to all Italy. It took over the island of Sicily from the powerful city of Carthage, and in 146 B.C. Rome completely destroyed Carthage. Roman power spread in all directions. But the Romans quarreled with each other and fought civil wars between 133 and 27 B.C.. In 49 B.C., Julius CAESAR became dictator. He ruled Rome until he was murdered in 44 B.C. Another civil war followed, then Caesar's adopted son, Octavian, became the first Roman emperor. He was renamed Augustus, and made peace throughout the empire.

In the early days of Roman rule, many Christians were killed. But in A.D. 313, Emperor Constantine gave Christians freedom of worship. He also set up the city of Byzantium, or Constantinople, in the east of the empire (*see* ISTANBUL). In 395, the empire was split into two. The western half had its capital at Rome, and Byzantium was the capital of the eastern half. In the 400s, the western empire was attacked by tribes from the north. It collapsed and was split into small kingdoms. The eastern empire lasted until the Turks took it in 1453. But Roman architecture, art, engineering, law and literature greatly influenced European ideas.

Right: Every Roman legion carried a standard topped by an eagle.
Below: Hadrian's Wall in Britain, northern boundary of the Roman Empire.

Romania (Romanian)
Romania is a communist republic in southeastern EUROPE. Farming is important, but manufactured goods are the main exports. Romania was created in 1861 from a union of Moldavia and Walachia. After World War II, a Communist government took power. However, Romania became increasingly independent of the U.S.S.R. in the 1970s.

AREA: 91,704 SQ. MILES
(237,500 SQ. KM)
POPULATION: 22,653,000
CAPITAL: BUCHAREST
CURRENCY: LEU
OFFICIAL LANGUAGE: ROMANIAN.

romanticism *n.* a late 18th- and early 19th-century artistic movement.

Rome
Today the capital of ITALY, Rome was once the center of a great empire. It is believed to have been founded in 753 B.C., on the east bank of the River Tiber. After Julius Caesar's death in 44 B.C., his adopted son Augustus established the Roman Empire and made himself its first emperor.

The city flourished and the golden age of Roman culture began. Riches and tributes poured into the city and a great number of magnificent buildings and monuments were erected, the ruins of which still stand today.

With the collapse of the empire in A.D. 476, the city declined. It was sacked during the wars of the Germans and the Byzantines, but regained its importance at the end of the A.D. 400s when it became established as the center of Christianity.

Romulus
According to legend Romulus was the founder and first king of Rome.

roof *n.* the top covering of a building. *vb.* cover with a roof.
rook 1. *n.* a bird belonging to the crow family. 2. *n.* a castle-shaped chess piece. 3. *vb.* defraud.
room *n.* a space; a compartment in a building, such as a living room or bedroom.

Roosevelt, Franklin Delano
Franklin Delano Roosevelt (1882–1945) was elected to four terms as president, the longest any U.S. president has served.

When Roosevelt, as Democratic candidate, was elected president in 1932, the country was in the grip of the worst economic depression ever. Roosevelt instituted many reforms known as the "New Deal". Special agencies were set up to revive the economy.

Roosevelt at first kept the United States out of World War II. He supported the Allies through the Lend-Lease Plan. But in 1941 the Japanese attacked PEARL HARBOR, and Congress declared war on Japan and later on Germany and Italy. With Winston CHURCHILL and Joseph STALIN, Roosevelt was one of the three great Allied leaders. Roosevelt died suddenly on April 12, 1945, just before the Allies won the war in Europe.

Roosevelt, Theodore
Theodore Roosevelt (1858–1919) served as 26th president of the United States, from 1901–09. He was elected Republican vice-president in 1900, and took office as president when President McKinley was assassinated.

Theodore ("Teddy") Roosevelt led an exciting life before becoming president. He was a big game hunter and rancher. In 1898 he commanded the Rough Riders in the Spanish-American War in Cuba. As president, Roosevelt worked hard for many major reforms. He was a dedicated supporter of conservation. In foreign affairs, Roosevelt believed that America should "walk softly and carry a big stick".

roost *n.* & *vb.* a resting place for birds; a perch.
root *n.* the part of a plant that grows under the ground.
rope *n.* thick strong cord. **ropy** *adj.* like rope.
rose *vb.* past of **rise**.
rose *n.* a prickly shrub with showy flowers. *adj.* deep pink.
► There are thousands of different roses. Many have been bred from the wild sweetbrier and the dog rose. Some roses flower only in early summer, but most garden roses now flower for many months. Their colors include red, pink, yellow and white.

rosemary *n.* an evergreen shrub used in cooking and making perfume.
Rosh Hashanah *n.* the festival of the Jewish New Year.
rot *vb.* go bad; decay.
rotate *vb.* go around and around. **rotation** *n.*
► **Rotation of crops**. A system of planting different crops which are grown in rotation in the same field. Crops that take one type of nutrient from the soil are alternated with crops that either restore that nutrient or take a different one. This allows the soil to rest and be restored so that it can remain in use and give high yields.

rotor *n.* the rotating blades on top of a helicopter which serve as both the propellers and wings of a fixed wing aircraft. They provide both **thrust** and **lift**.
rotten *adj.* to be soft or bad. *Wasps like to eat rotten apples.*

Rotterdam
Europe's busiest port and a major manufacturing city in the NETHERLANDS. Rotterdam has 1,023,000 people, including its suburbs. A canal links it to the NORTH SEA.

rough (rhymes with *cuff*) *adj.* 1. not smooth. *My dog has a rough coat.* 2. not gentle. 3. done quickly and not meant to be exact. *Can you draw me a rough plan of the town in which you live?*
round *adj.* shaped like a circle or a ball.
round trip *n.* a trip taken to a place and then back again. *It costs less money to buy a round trip ticket.*
round up *v.* to bring together, usually cattle. **roundup** *n.*
rouse *vb.* wake up; stir, excite.
route (rhymes with *boot*) *n.* the road or direction taken to get somewhere.
routine (*root*-**een**) *n.* set way of doing things.
row (rhymes with *cow*) *n.* & *vb.* noise, quarrel.
row (rhymes with *go*) 1. *vb.* use oars to make a boat move through water. 2. *n.* a line. *She planted a row of beans in her garden.*
rowdy *adj.* noisy and disorderly.

royal *adj.* to do with kings and queens. *When a king is married he has a royal wedding.* **royalty** *n.* being royal; a percentage paid to an author, etc., according to sales.
rub *vb.* 1. slide or press something against something else; polish. 2. rub out, remove marks etc. on paper, blackboard, etc.
rubber *n.* 1. a strong, elastic material made from the sap of a rubber tree. 2. a piece of rubber, or plastic, used for wiping out pencil marks.
► Most natural rubber comes from the rubber tree. When the bark of the tree is cut, a white juice called latex oozes out. The juice is collected and then treated with acid to produce crude rubber. Today, most natural rubber comes from Malaysia and Indonesia.

Scientists found ways of making synthetic rubber during World War I. Synthetic rubber is made from oil and coal. More synthetic rubber is now made each year than natural rubber.

rubbish *n.* waste matter that is thrown away.
rubble *n.* debris; pieces of stone, brick, from a building.

Rubens, Peter Paul
Peter Paul rubens (1577–1640) a Flemish painter who worked on huge canvases that were full of light and color. He studied in Italy and did many paintings for the Spanish and French courts. He traveled to many countries as a diplomat, and was knighted in London by Charles I in recognition of his talents.

ruby *n.* a red, crystalline precious stone.
rucksack *n.* a bag that can be strapped on your back for carrying.
rudder *n.* a flat, upright, movable wood or metal piece at the back of a boat or aircraft used for steering.
ruddy *adj.* a healthy reddish color. *He had a ruddy complexion.*
rude *adj.* 1. bad-mannered; impolite. 2. crude or simple (old-fashioned).
rug *n.* thick, heavy fabric used as floor covering; a mat or small carpet.

Ruhr
The Ruhr in West GERMANY is an industrial and coal-mining region around the valley of the River Ruhr, tributary of the RHINE. The Ruhr includes the cities of Essen, Dortmund and Duisberg. It became important in the mid-1800s, during the INDUSTRIAL REVOLUTION.

ruin (**roo**-*in*) 1. *vb.* spoil completely. 2. *n.* (usually used in plural) the remains of an old building. *We visited the* **ruins** *of an abbey on our school outing.*
rule 1. *n.* a law; something that must be obeyed. 2 *vb.* be in charge of a

R

country, keep under control, govern. *William the Conqueror ruled England after 1066.*

ruler *n.* 1. a straight strip marked in units (inches, etc.) used for drawing lines or measuring. 2. a person who rules a country.

rum 1. *n.* an alcoholic liquor distilled from the fermented products of the sugar cane.

Rumania see **Romania**

rumble *vb.* & *n.* deep sound like that of distant thunder.

ruminant *n.* animal such as cow and deer which chews the cud.

rummage *vb.* search through a confused pile of things.

rumor *n.* a story that is passed around, but may not be true; hearsay. *There is a rumor that a spacecraft has landed in China.*

rump *n.* buttocks; back part of a mammal.

rumple *vb.* wrinkle, crease.

run *vb.* (past **ran**) go very fast (of a person or animal); go smoothly; control. *She runs the office.*

run across *vb.* meet someone by chance. also **run into**.

rung *vb.* past of **ring**.

rung *n.* one step of a ladder.

runner *n.* messenger; person who runs in a race; the part on which a sled slides.

runway *n.* the hard surface on which an aircraft takes off and lands.

rural *adj.* of or about the countryside.

rush 1. *vb.* move very fast. 2. *n.* a kind of strong grass that grows near water.

rusk *n.* piece of bread rebaked until it is crisp.

Russia *see* **U.S.S.R.**

Russian Revolution

The Russian Revolution was one of the most important events of this century. In the early 1900s, Russia was ruled by emperors called tsars. Many of the people were *serfs* (poor peasants who were little better than slaves). In many ways the country was still living under a feudal system little changed from that of the Middle Ages.

Increasingly, ordinary Russians began to complain about the way they were treated by the ruling class. The first revolution took place in 1905, but the tsar's forces finally suppressed the revolutionaries. In 1914, WORLD WAR I broke out, and the country suffered enormous casualties and food shortages. Another revolution took place in 1917. This time, the tsar was forced to abdicate (resign) and a Provisional Government was set up under Alexander Kerensky. However, LENIN and other Bolshevik (Communist) leaders had by now returned from exile. Lenin quickly took over the government of the country. One of the first acts was to sign a peace treaty with GERMANY, in order to take Russia out of the fighting. After a period of civil war, the Communists gained complete control of the country. In 1922, Russia established the U.S.S.R. (Union of Soviet Socialist Republics).

The Russian Revolution of 1917. Bolsheviks in Petrograd (formerly St. Petersburg and now Leningrad).

rust *n.* the reddish-brown crust that forms on iron and some other metals when they become damp. *vb.* become covered with rust.

► As rust forms, the surface of the metal is eaten away. Rusting is speeded up near the sea, where the air contains salt, or in cities where air POLLUTION is severe.

To prevent rusting, iron and steel may be coated with such metals as tin or zinc. Grease, oil and paint also protect the metal. Stainless steels are ALLOYS made of iron and rust-resistant metals, such as nickel and chromium.

rustic *adj.* to do with the country.

rustle 1. *n.* & *vb.* crisp sound of dry leaves. 2. *vb.* steal livestock.

rusty *adj.* rusted; out of practice. *My piano playing is rusty.*

rut *n.* a furrow in a road made by wheels. *The track was full of ruts and potholes.*

Rutherford, Ernest

Ernest Rutherford (1871–1937) was the famous New Zealand scientist who helped to lay the foundation of modern nuclear PHYSICS. He developed the theory that explains the shape of ATOMS and their orbiting particles called electrons. He was awarded the NOBEL PRIZE for CHEMISTRY in 1914.

ruthless *adj.* having no pity.

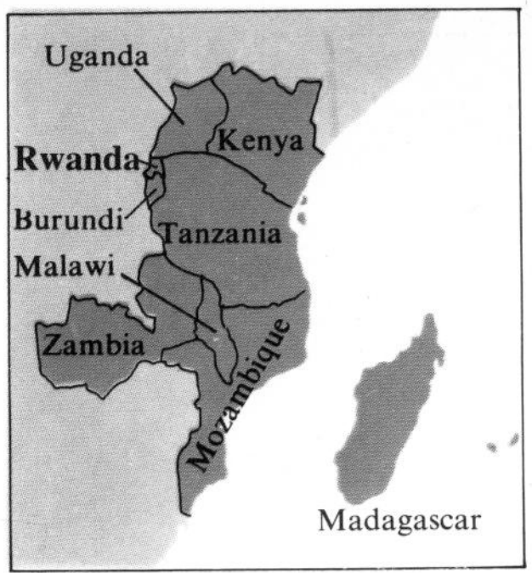

Rwanda

Rwanda (pronounced Rue-and-a) is a small landlocked country in east-central AFRICA. The climate is equatorial, but is cooler in the highlands. Most of the people work on the land. The main cash crop is coffee. Rwanda was once part of German East Africa, but was occupied by Belgium in 1916. It became a fully independent republic in 1962.

AREA: 10,170 SQ. MILES (26,338 SQ. KM)
POPULATION: 5,067,000
CAPITAL: KIGALI
CURRENCY: RWANDA FRANC
OFFICIAL LANGUAGE: KINYARWANDA, FRENCH.

rye *n.* a cereal grain that, with barley, is one of the hardiest grown. It is used to make flour as well as alcoholic drinks such as whisky, gin, vodka and kvass.

S

A cable car climbing a steep hill in San Francisco.

sabbath *n.* a weekly religious day of rest. The sabbath is Saturday for Jews, and Sunday for Christians.
saber (**say**-*ber*) *n.* a sword with a curved blade.
saber-toothed tiger *n.* prehistoric carnivorous mammal. In its largest form it was bigger than a modern lion, and had two canine teeth eight inches long in its upper jaw, for slashing at its prey.
sable *n.* a small, carnivorous mammal of the weasel family, valued for its dark fur.
sabotage (**sabb**-*oh-tazh*) *vb.* & *n.* damage something on purpose.
saccharin (**sack**-*er-in*) *n.* white crystalline substance, 300 times as sweet as sugar, discovered in 1879. It is used in the diets of diabetics and dieters.
sack 1. *n.* a large bag made of strong material. 2. *vb.* dismiss someone from a job. 3. *vb.* destroy a town captured in war.
sacred *adj.* to do with religion and worship. *The Bible and the Koran are sacred books.*
sacrifice *vb.* give away something precious, often to God. *n.* the thing that is given away.
sad *adj.* unhappy; sorrowful. **sadden** *vb.*
saddle *n.* the rider's seat used on a bicycle or a horse. *vb.* put a saddle on; burden someone with a task or person.

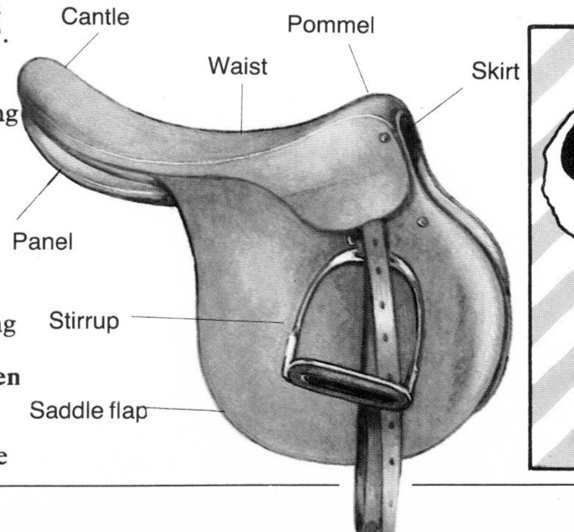

safari (*sa*-**far**-*ee*) *n.* an expedition, usually in a hot country, at one time for the purpose of hunting animals, but today for observing and photographing them.
safe 1. *adj.* protected from danger. 2. *n.* a special strong, locked cabinet where money and other valuable things can be kept.
safeguard *vb.* protect *n.* something that prevents injury.
safety *n.* being safe from loss or injury. *The cattle were moved from the flooded fields to a place of safety.*
safety pin *n.* a pin that locks its sharp point into itself by means of a clasp.
saffron *n.* a type of crocus, the stigmas of whose flowers give us the powder called saffron which is used as a flavoring in food and as a yellow dye.
sag *vb.* droop, bend, hang down (especially in the middle).
saga (**sah**-*gah*) *n.* an old story, especially one that tells of the ancient Norse heroes of Scandinavia.
sage 1. *n.* perennial herb belonging to the mint family, the leaves of which are used in cooking as a seasoning. 2. *adj.* & *n.* wise; a wise person.

Sahara
The Sahara is the world's largest hot DESERT. It covers about 3.5 million sq. miles (8.5 million sq. km) in North AFRICA. It extends from the

The extent of the Sahara.

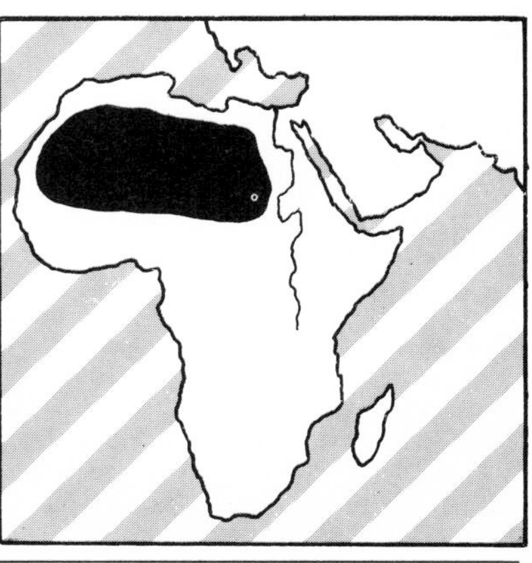

S

Atlantic Ocean in the west to the Red Sea in the east. In the north, it stretches to the MEDITERRANEAN coast in LIBYA and in EGYPT. In the south, it becomes a dry region with a few small plants. Recently, the lands south of the Sahara have had very little rain. Because of this the desert is slowly spreading southward.

About a third of the Sahara is covered by sand. Other parts are covered by gravel and stones, or by bare rock. The Sahara is one of the hottest places on earth. The world's highest air temperature in the shade, 136.4°F (57.7°C), was recorded there.

The people are mostly ARABS or Berbers. Some are NOMADS. They travel between OASES (water holes) with their CAMELS. The people cover their faces with veils to protect them against wind-blown sand and dust. Other people live in villages around the larger oases. The greatest number live in the fertile NILE valley in Egypt. The Sahara has become an important area because it has a lot of OIL and NATURAL GAS.

said *vb.* past of **say**.

sail *vb.* travel across water in a ship or boat, especially when the travel is powered by wind.

► Sailing is the use of the wind to propel a boat. Once the chief form of power at sea, today it is mainly a sport. *Fore-and-aft rigging* is almost universal: triangular sails mounted on booms and gaffs, in line with the boat's keel. (Many old types of vessel used square rigging: square sails hanging from spars at right angles to the keel.) This has affected many sailing techniques. With fore-and-aft sails, careful trimming (adjustment of the angle of the sails) allows sailing across the wind (reaching) to be faster than sailing with it (running). Also the maneuver of tacking into the wind becomes possible.

sailor *n.* a person who goes to sea in a ship, or who sails a boat; a member of a ship's crew.

saint *n.* an extremely good person, particularly one who has been recognized as holy by the church.

► Christian saints are people who have been *canonized* (named as saints) by the ROMAN CATHOLIC CHURCH or the Eastern Orthodox churches. Most saints are canonized long after their deaths.

When someone is being made a saint, the church looks at the person's life to see if he or she was very good. The saint must also have taken part in a miracle.

Countries and even trades may have their own saints. These are called patron saints. For example, the patron saint of Ireland is St. Patrick; of sailors, St. Christopher; of musicians, St. Cecilia.

St. John's

St. John's is the capital, chief port and industrial center of the Canadian province of Newfoundland. It is one of the oldest continuously occupied cities of North America. John Cabot is believed to have discovered the harbor in 1497.

St. Lawrence River

The St. Lawrence River in QUEBEC in Canada flows from Lake Ontario into the ATLANTIC Ocean. It is the final part of the St Lawrence Seaway, which is a system of canals and locks joining the river to the GREAT LAKES. This allows seagoing ships to sail as far inland as Lake Superior.

sake *n.* end; benefit; purpose. *For the sake of discussion, we will say it is true.*

salaam *n.* an Arabic word meaning peace, and a form of greeting in the East.

salad *n.* a mixture of uncooked vegetables such as lettuce, tomato, or cold cooked dish, served with dressing.

Saladin Saladin (1138–93) was a sultan of Egypt. He conquered Syria and took Jerusalem from the Christians. During the Third Crusade, the Christians failed to recapture Jerusalem and their leader, Richard the Lion Hearted, of England, was forced to make peace with Saladin.

PATRON SAINTS

St. Agatha	Nurses
St. Andrew	Scotland (November 30)
St. Anthony	Gravediggers
St. Benedict	Speleologists
St. Cecilia	Musicians
St. Christopher	Sailors
St. Crispin	Shoemakers
St. David	Wales (March 1)
St. Dunstan	Goldsmiths and silversmiths
St. George	England (April 23)
St. Hubert	Hunters
St. Jerome	Librarians
St. Joseph	Carpenters
St. Lawrence	Cooks
St. Luke	Physicians
St. Matthew	Tax collectors
St. Michael	Policemen
St. Nicholas	The original Santa Claus
St. Patrick	Ireland (March 17)
St. Paul	Carpet-weavers and tent-makers
St. Peter	Blacksmiths and fishermen
St. Valentine	Sweethearts
St. Vitus	Dancers and comedians
St. William	Hatters

salamander *n.* a small amphibian with a lizardlike body.

► Salamanders are often brightly colored. Most salamanders are about 6 in. (15 cm) long. They lay eggs in ponds or springs. When they are fully grown, salamanders leave the water and spend most of their lives on land. They live in damp places. Salamanders eat insects and snails. If they lose their tail or a leg, they grow a new one.

Scientists use the name salamander for a group of European salamanders. But the name is also given to other amphibians with tails. The giant salamander of Japan is 5 ft. (1.5 meters) long. Another salamander, the axolotl of North America, stays in water all its life.

salary *n.* the money paid to someone for work performed.

sale *n.* 1. the act of selling. 2. the selling of goods cheaply.

saliva (*sal*-**eye**-*va*) *n.* spit; the liquid in your mouth.

salmon *n.* (plural same) a kind of fish that is highly prized as food.

► The salmon hatches in freshwater streams, makes its way to the sea, and remains there for about three years before migrating back upstream to its birthplace to breed. This difficult upstream migration can involve journeys of up to 3,000 miles (5,000 km) and spectacular leaping of rocks and small waterfalls.

salt *n.* a chemical compound formed, with water, when a metal or other substance reacts with an acid; common table salt, or sodium chloride. *You add salt to season or preserve food. adj.* having a **salty** taste. *adj.* containing salt. *It is easier to float in salt water than in fresh water.*

► Common salt, or sodium chloride (*NaCl*), is a harmless compound of the metal sodium (*Na*) and the green, poisonous gas chlorine (*Cl*). It is very important in the human diet and as a food preservative and is universally used as a flavoring. It is obtained from sea water and from deposits in rocks.

Salts are chemical substances that are compounds of an ACID and a base. For example, hydrochloric acid and caustic soda unite to give *sodium chloride* and water. Salts formed from hydrochloric acid are called chlorates; from sulfuric acid, sulfates; from nitric acid, nitrates; and so on. The earth's crust contains many salts of natural origin. Salts are among the most important of chemical compounds, widely used in industry and agriculture.

salute *vb.* & *n.* raise your stiffened hand to your forehead or hat as a form of greeting or honor.

salvage *vb.* save from loss or destruction.
salvation *n.* rescue, saving the soul.

Salvation Army
A Protestant body involved with social and religious work among the poor. Founded as the Christian Mission, it was given its present name soon after, in 1878. It is organized on military lines, with ranks and uniforms, and holds outdoor services. It has about 1.5 million members throughout the world.

salvo *n.* the firing of several guns at the same time.
same *adj.* similar to, or identical with something. *Sally and I go to the same school.*
samovar *n.* a Russian tea urn.
sampan *n.* a kind of Chinese boat.
sample *n.* an example of something, which can be used to show what the others are like. *vb.* judge quality of.
samurai *n.* a Japanese warrior of former times.
► At first only the emperor's guards were called Samurai. But from the 1100s to 1867, all the military people in Japan were called Samurai. They included warriors, lords, and Japan's military ruler, the *shogun.*
The Samurai wore very decorative armor and headdresses, and carried two swords. They believed in a way of life called *Bushido,* which means "the way of the warrior." Samurai had to be very brave. They fought for honor, in much the same way as the knights of Europe. They did not like trade and profit-making. If a Samurai did something dishonorable, he had to kill himself with his own sword. This was called *hara-kiri.*
The Samurai lost their power at the end of the 1800s. Changes in Japan meant that they were not so important any more. Even their name was changed. But today, many people in Japan and around the world are interested in the Samurai.

A Samurai — a knight of medieval Japan.

sanction *n.* & *vb.* allow, authorize.
sanctuary *n.* a safe place for people, or for birds and animals. *In a bird sanctuary it is against the law to hunt or kill the birds.*
sand *n.* tiny grains of minerals, mainly quartz, formed by the erosion of rocks, and often forming beaches.
► Grains of sand are smaller than those in gravel, but larger than those in silt or mud. Sand piles up on coasts. Inland, in dry places, it forms hills called DUNES. The main mineral in sand is QUARTZ. Layers of sand may be pressed together in the ground to form a hard rock called sandstone.

sandal *n.* a kind of open shoe, attached to the foot by straps.
sandstone *n.* a rock consisting of grains of sand, mostly quartz, which have been compressed.
sandwich *n.* a kind of food, consisting of meat or other filling between two slices of bread.
sane *adj.* sensible, normal, sound in mind. **sanity** *n.*

San Francisco
San Francisco is one of the most colorful cities in the United States and is its chief PACIFIC port. The city lies along a large bay about halfway down the CALIFORNIA coast. The Golden Gate Bridge, one of the world's longest suspension bridges, crosses the entrance to the bay. San Francisco is known for the cable cars that run up and down its steep hills. Nearly destroyed by an earthquake in 1906, San Francisco today is a busy center for commerce, education and the arts.

sang *vb.* past of **sing.**
sanitary *adj.* of or concerning health, especially relating to cleanliness.
sank *vb.* past of **sink.**

San Marino
San Marino is the world's smallest independent republic. It is situated south of Rimini in ITALY, which completely encloses it. San Marino occupies a picturesque site on the triple peaks of Mt. Titano in the Apennines. It is said to date from the 300s A.D. Tourism is the principal industry.
AREA: 24 SQ. MILES (61 SQ. KM)
POPULATION; 21,000
CAPITAL: SAN MARINO
CURRENCY: ITALIAN LIRA
OFFICIAL LANGUAGE: ITALIAN.

Sanskrit *n.* & *adj.* a language of ancient India.
sap *n.* the juice in the stems of plants.
sapling *n.* a young tree.
sapphire *n.* transparent blue stone, valued as a gem; the hardest mineral known apart from diamond.

Saracen
Originally the Greek and Roman name for the people of northwest Arabia. In medieval Europe it was used to describe MUSLIMS, whether Arabs, Moors or Turks.

Sarawak
Sarawak is a state of MALAYSIA in Southeast ASIA. It lies in the north-west of the island of BORNEO. The interior of Sarawak is mountainous and forested, and its chief products include timber and rubber. Sarawak was once ruled by white rajahs (the Brooke family). It became a British Crown Colony in 1946, and part of Malaysia in 1963.

sarcasm *n.* a bitter remark of contempt or scorn, often ironical. **sarcastic** *adj.*
sarcophagus (*sar*-**kof**-*a-gus*) *n.* a stone coffin.
sardine *n.* a small fish of the herring family.
► Sardines are a popular food, and are usually sold in cans. Their oil is used in various industries. Dried and powdered, they are used as a chicken feed and as a FERTILIZER. Sardines were named after the Italian island of Sardinia. They are now caught throughout the Mediterranean Sea and off western Europe and North America.

Sardinia
Sardinia is a mountainous island in the MEDITERRANEAN. It belongs to ITALY. Its Italian name is Sardegna.
Most of its people are farmers and fishermen (the sardine gets its name from Sardinia). A number of metals and other minerals are mined, including gold, silver, zinc and lead. Tourism is also important. There are many prehistoric remains on Sardinia, which was also a trading

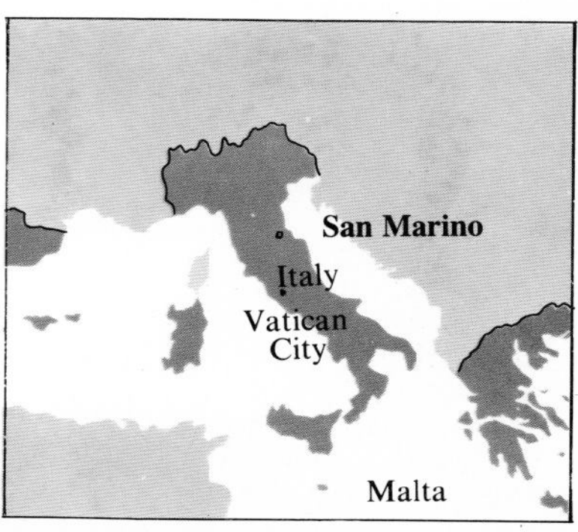

center for the PHOENICIANS, GREEKS and CARTHAGINIANS. Sardinia became a kingdom in 1720, and part of ITALY in 1861.

Sargasso Sea
The Sargasso Sea is an area of the North Atlantic Ocean, between the WEST INDIES and the AZORES, which is covered by seaweed. Its name comes from the Portuguese *sargaco* (seaweed).

sari *n.* a length of cloth draped around the body as a dress, and worn mainly by Indian women.
sash *n.* 1. a band or scarf, worn across the shoulder or around the waist. 2. the frame and glass of a movable window.

Saskatchewan
Saskatchewan is one of Canada's three "Prairie Provinces". The southern part of the province consists of miles of farmland, broken only by tall grain elevators scattered along the railroad lines. Wheat is the province's chief crop – enough is grown to supply about two-thirds of Canada's needs.

Northern Saskatchewan is rocky, forested and rich in minerals. Copper, uranium, and some gold and silver are mined here. Today, oil refining is Saskatchewan's chief industry. The two largest refineries are in Regina, the capital.

Saskatchewan became a Canadian province in 1905.

sat *vb.* past of **sit**.
satan *n.* the devil; the evil one in many religions.
satchel *n.* a small bag, usually of leather or canvas.
satellite *n.* 1. a moon. 2. an artificial object put into orbit around the earth.
► A body that moves in ORBIT around another body is called a satellite. The moon, for example, is the earth's natural satellite. But most satellites are man-made devices launched into space by powerful ROCKETS. Manned spacecraft may become temporary satellites during space missions, but most artificial satellites are unmanned. Some carry scientific instruments for studying the stars and planets. Others send back information about the world's weather. Communications satellites enable radio, television and telephone signals to be transmitted around the curvature of the earth. Signals beamed from one part of the earth are received by the satellite and retransmitted to a receiving station on another part of the earth.

satin *n.* cloth with a shiny face and a dull back.
satire *n.* a form of comedy in which sarcasm and wit are used to ridicule people's follies.

Indian women wearing saris.

satisfactory *adj.* adequate; all right, or good enough.
satisfied *vb.* past of **satisfy**.
satisfy *vb.* please, make someone contented. *He wanted to satisfy his teacher, so he did his homework carefully.* fulfill; comply with.
saturate *vb.* fill something, e.g. a sponge, so completely that no more can be absorbed.

The Mercury spacecraft was the first American satellite to carry a man.

Saturday *n.* the seventh day of the week, between Friday and Sunday; named after Saturn, Roman god of harvests.

Saturn (Planet)
Saturn is the second largest PLANET in the SOLAR SYSTEM after Jupiter. It is about 75,000 miles (120,700 km) across. Saturn is famous for the rings that circle it. These rings are made of billions of icy particles. The rings are more than 170,000 miles (273,600 km) across, but they are very thin. The particles in the rings may be the remains of a moon which drifted too close to Saturn and broke up.

To the naked eye, Saturn looks like a bright star. The planet is actually mostly made up of light gases, and it is less dense than water. But scientists think that it may have a solid core. Saturn has 10 SATELLITES. The largest is Titan. It measures about 3,000 miles (4,800 km) across – about the size of Mercury. Titan is the only known satellite to have an atmosphere – a layer of gases surrounding it.

sauce *n.* a liquid mixture served with some foods for added flavor.
saucepan *n.* a metal cooking pot with a handle and sometimes a lid.
saucer *n.* a small curved plate on which a cup stands.
saucy *adj.* cheeky, impudent. **sauciness** *n.*

Saudi Arabia
Saudi Arabia is an oil-rich desert kingdom in southwest ASIA. It occupies most of the peninsula of ARABIA. Ninety percent of the country consists of plateaus, including the Nafud Desert in the north and the "Empty Quarter" in the south. Most Saudis are Muslim ARABS. Mecca and Medina, both in Saudi Arabia, are the two holiest places of ISLAM.

Saturn's ring system. The second ring is about 17,400 miles (28,000 km) wide.

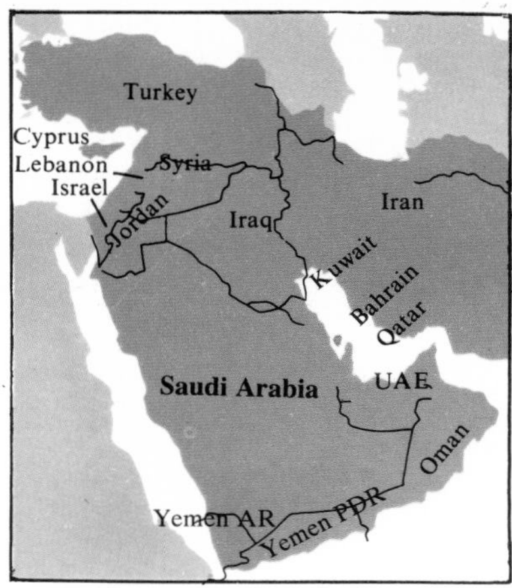

Today, the Saudi economy is entirely dominated by oil, which was first discovered in 1938. In 1980, only the U.S.S.R. and the U.S.A. produced more oil than Saudi Arabia.

The country formed part of the OTTOMAN EMPIRE from 1517–1916. Modern Saudi Arabia was founded in 1927 by Ibn Saud, its first king.

AREA: 830,045 SQ. MILES (2,149,690 SQ. KM)
POPULATION: 9,418,000
CAPITAL: RIYADH
CURRENCY: RIYAL
OFFICIAL LANGUAGE: ARABIC

sauna (**saw**-*na*) *n*. a kind of hot steam bath, of Finnish origin.

saunter *vb*. stroll, walk in a leisurely way.

sausage *n*. a chopped meat mixture which is made into a tube-shape inside a skin.

savage *adj*. wild and fierce; uncivilized. *vb*. attack and bite (of animals).

savanna *n*. large areas of grassy African plains. The *llanos* and *campos* of South America are other examples of savanna vegetation.

save *vb*. 1. rescue. *The crew of the sinking ship were all saved*. 2. build up a reserve of money. *We are saving up for our summer holiday*. 3. keep for future use. 4. bring about spiritual salvation.

savings *pl. n*. the money someone has saved, often kept in a bank.

savior *n*. someone who saves you from danger. *Jesus Christ is often called the Savior*.

saw 1. *n*. a sharp tool with teeth for cutting wood. 2. *vb*. cut something with a saw. *How long will it take to saw those planks in half?* 3. *vb*. past of **see**.

sawdust *n*. dust of wood, made by sawing.

Saxons

The Saxons were a group of barbarian tribes, originally from north Germany. Their name may have come from a short sword, the *seax*, which was their national weapon. In the 200s and 300s A.D. they spread south, and eventually invaded Roman territory. They often raided the coast of England, and in about A.D. 450 they invaded it, together with the Angles and Jutes. They beat the Roman-British CELTS, and by A.D. 500 most of England was in ANGLO-SAXON hands (with the Saxons mainly in the south – Essex, Sussex and "Wessex"). Their various local kingdoms lasted until the Danish (VIKING) invasions. Meanwhile on the Continent, Saxons had settled as far south as the coast of Gaul. But later, in A.D. 772–804, CHARLEMAGNE made a series of expeditions that broke the power of the Continental Saxons and incorporated them into his empire.

saxophone *n*. a metal woodwind musical instrument, played by blowing into it, used mainly in jazz bands.

say *vb*. speak; tell or announce something.

saying *n*. a well-known phrase or proverb. *"Too many cooks spoil the broth" is a saying*.

scab *n*. the dry protective crust that grows over a wound

scaffolding *n*. a structure of tubes and planks used when a building is being put up or repaired.

scald *vb*. & *n*. burn with hot liquid or steam.

scale 1. *n*. one of the thin pieces of hard skin that covers the bodies of fish and reptiles. 2. *n*. a series of measuring marks on an instrument such as a ruler or thermometer. 3. *n*. a set of musical tones arranged in order. 4. *vb*. climb something.

scalene *adj*. something with unequal sides and angles.

scales *n*. an instrument for measuring how much things weigh.

scalp *n*. the skin and hair on your head.

scalpel *n*. a small knife used by surgeons.

scan *vb*. 1. read over quickly. 2. pass a beam of light over (in television and radar). 3. (in poetry) have the correct rhythm.

A village of wooden houses of the type built by the Anglo-Saxons in the 500s.

scandal *n*. a disgraceful fact or event which causes outrage. **scandalize** *vb*. shock.

Scandinavia *n*. term used to include Denmark, Finland, Iceland, Norway and Sweden.

► Scandinavia is the name given to the peninsula in northern EUROPE which contains NORWAY and SWEDEN. The term is often loosely used to include DENMARK, FINLAND, ICELAND and the FAROES. However, the *Nordic Countries* is a more accurate name for the whole group.

Scandinavia has a ridge of mountains running down the western side like a spine.

The coast of NORWAY, on the west, contains many *fiords* (inlets of the sea). In Sweden, to the east, the mountains slope down more gently to the sea. The north of the region lies within the ARCTIC Circle.

All the Scandinavian countries have quite small populations. The standard of living in each country is high.

scar *n*. the mark left on skin from a wound, after it has healed. *vb*. mark with scars.

scarab *n*. a type of dung beetle, considered sacred by the ancient Egyptians.

scarce *adj*. rare, uncommon, in short supply. *Because of the fuel shortage, oil is very scarce*. **scarcity** *n*. being scarce, in short supply.

scare *vb*. frighten.

scarecrow *n*. figure of person dressed in old clothes set up in a field to frighten birds away from crops.

scarf *n*. (plural **scarves**) a piece of cloth, generally used to cover the head or shoulders.

scarlet *n*. & *adj*. bright red.

scatter *vb*. go off in different directions, to throw something so that it spreads out. *Jilly scattered crumbs on the bird table*.

scavenge *vb*. feed on carrion or garbage. **scavenger** *n*. *Dogs are terrible scavengers*.

S

scene (*seen*) *n*. 1. the place where something happens. *Luckily, there was a policeman at the scene of the accident.* 2. a section of a stage play; place represented on the stage.
scenery (**seen**-*ery*) *n*. 1. the natural features of a place, such as hills, fields and trees. 2. the painted curtains and screen used to make a theater stage look like a real place.
scent (*sent*) *n*. a smell, usually a pleasant one; a perfume; odor of an animal. *vb*. detect.
sceptic (**skep**-*tic*) *n*. a person who doubts the truth (of religion, etc.). **sceptical** *adj*.
schedule (**sked**-*ule*) *vb*. & *n*. a timetable, a plan, a scheme.
scheme (*skeem*) *n*. & *vb*. plot, plan.
schism (**siz**-*um*) *n*. a break or split in a political party or religious group.
scholar *n*. a student; a clever person who has studied hard and knows a great deal; a person who has won a scholarship (prize) at a school or college. **scholarly** *adj*. learned.
scholarship *n*. money won by someone in an exam to pay school or university fees.
school *n*. 1. a place where children are educated; its building. 2. a group of fish swimming together.
► In most countries, children must go to school for a certain number of years, such as between the ages of five and 16. But some poor countries do not have enough schools or teachers. However, they try to make sure that all children go to school long enough to learn how to read, write and use numbers.

schooner *n*. a fast sailing ship, generally with two masts.
► Schooners were once used for trading, and were developed in the American colonies in the 1700s. They had specially streamlined hulls, and all their sails were of fore-and-aft rigging.

Schubert, Franz Peter
Franz Schubert (1797–1828) was an Austrian composer who wrote a great variety of music. He is perhaps best known for his songs, called *lieder*.

Schumann, Robert
Robert Schumann (1810–1856) was a German composer. He wrote many well-known pieces for the piano, two symphonies and over a humdred songs.

science *n*. 1. knowledge gotten by studying, watching and testing. 2. study of physical world, e.g. physics, biology or astronomy. **scientific** *adj*.
► The main branches of science are ASTRONOMY, BIOLOGY, CHEMISTRY, GEOLOGY, MEDICINE, PHYSICS and MATHEMATICS. All scientists try to find reasons for the observations they make. Having found a possible reason for some phenomenon, experiments are performed to test the theory. As a result, the theory may be rejected or may become established as a law of science. This is known as *scientific method*.
However, even so-called laws may after a while be disproved or refined when new evidence is discovered. For example, we now know that NEWTON's laws of motion are not quite true. Although they are quite satisfactory for most purposes, they do not apply to bodies moving at extremely high speeds. EINSTEIN's *Special Theory of* RELATIVITY, published in 1905, showed that changes were needed in Newton's laws for fast-moving bodies.
Established scientific laws should not, therefore, be regarded as the absolute truth. They are merely the best available explanation of observed events and may be changed later if the need arises.

science fiction *n*. stories that are based on imagined scientific events.
► Writers of science fiction often use new scientific discoveries (or discoveries not yet made!) in their stories. They imagine how these discoveries might change the world in the future. Many of the stories are about space travel and time travel, and meetings between creatures from different planets. Some writers describe life in the future to show how many things they think are wrong in the world today.
Jules Verne (1828–1905) and H.G. Wells (1866–1946) were two of the first great science fiction writers. Recent writers include Isaac Asimov, Ray Bradbury and Arthur C. Clarke.

scientist *n*. a person who studies a scientific subject.
scissors *pl. n*. a tool with two blades joined together, which cut when they meet.
scoff *vb*. mock; make fun of.
scold *vb*. speak crossly to someone about what they have done or not done. *The teacher scolded them for being late for school.*
scone (*skon*) *n*. a small, flat round plain cake.
scoop 1. *n*. ladle or large spoon; *vb*. to spoon. 2. *n*. an important news story found in only one newspaper.
scooter *n*. 1. a vehicle with two wheels, a base, and a handlebar. 2. a motorscooter is a light kind of motorbike with a small engine.
scorch *vb*. darken the surface of something by burning it slightly. *n*. a slight burn.
score 1. *n*. a result in a game. *At the final whistle the score was two goals to one.* *vb*. gain points in a game. 2. *vb*. scratch or mark something. 3. *n*. an old-fashioned word for 20.4. *vb*. & *n*. copy of music showing all vocal and instrumental parts.

The white diagonal cross of St. Andrew on a blue background is the national flag of Scotland.

scorn *n*. & *vb*. feel or show contempt; despise.
scorpion *n*. a small creature of the spider family, with a poisonous sting in its tail.
Scotch *n*. & *adj*. whiskey and tweed from Scotland.
scot-free *adj*. without punishment.

Scotland (Scottish; a Scot)
Scotland is part of the UNITED KINGDOM of GREAT BRITAIN and NORTHERN IRELAND. Scotland has three main regions: the highlands in the north; the central lowlands, a wide fertile region; and the southern uplands. There are also many islands, including the Hebrides (well-known for Harris tweed), Orkneys and Shetland Islands. Manufacturing and mining are the most valuable sectors of the economy. Scotland's largest city, GLASGOW, stands on the River Clyde. Scotland united with England and Wales in 1707. But the Scots have retained their own traditions and culture – notably their own legal system and established church. The country's capital is EDINBURGH.

Scotland Yard
Scotland Yard is the headquarters of the Metropolitan POLICE in London, England. It is also the national base of the Criminal Investigation Department (CID), and keeps criminal records and fingerprints. The name comes from the street in London where this famous center once stood.

Scott, Robert Falcon
Captain Robert Falcon Scott (1868–1912) was a British naval officer and an explorer of the ANTARCTIC. His first expedition was in 1901–04. With four companions, he began the march to the SOUTH

The scorpion uses the sting in its "tail" to kill its prey.

POLE in 1911. After suffering great hardships, he reached the Pole on January 17, 1912. But he was disappointed to find that the Norwegian, Roald AMUNDSEN, had been there a month earlier. Scott and his companions, drained of energy, started back to base but perished in a snowstorm. Ironically, they were only a short distance from a supply base where they would have been safe.

Scott, Walter
Walter Scott (1771–1832) was a Scottish poet and novelist. After early success as a poet, he wrote the long *Waverley* series of historical novels (*Waverley, Rob Roy, The Heart of Midlothian*, etc.). These gave him a reputation throughout Europe as a leader of the Romantic movement in literature.

scoundrel *n.* rogue, a person without principles.
scour *vb.* 1. clean thoroughly. 2. rush about looking for something.
scout *n.* 1. someone who is sent out ahead of the group to look for difficulties or dangers. 2. a member of the Boy Scouts or Girl Scouts.
scowl *n.* a cross look. *vb.* frown at.
scramble *vb.* 1. rush in confusion. *We managed to scramble to the top of the hill.* 2. mix up, as in *scrambled eggs.*
scrap 1. *n.* a small piece of food; a fragment. 2. *vb.* get rid of something. 3. *n.* old cars or other metal objects that have been thrown away. 4. *n.* a fight.
scrapbook *n.* a book in which to save pictures, newspaper clippings and other papers.
scrape *vb.* 1. scratch; slide along. *Our dad scraped his car on the gate-post.* 2. only just succeed. *Bill barely scraped through his exam.*
scratch *vb.* drag a sharp point, such as a needle or fingernail, over something; rub with fingernails to relieve itching.
scrawl *vb.* & *n.* scribble; hasty or bad handwriting.
scream *n.* a high-pitched yell, usually of pain or fright. *vb.* give a sudden, harsh cry.
screen 1. *n.* a partition; a frame covered with wood or cloth, and used to hide something. *They put a screen around my bed in the hospital when the doctor came.* 2. *n.* upright surface on which films, etc., are projected; part of television or radar on which picture appears. 3. *vb.* protect someone. 4. *vb.* show on screen. 5. *vb.* investigate a person's life and character for reliability.
screw *n.* a nail with a spiral groove called the thread which pulls the screw into the wood. *vb.* fasten with a screw.
screwdriver *n.* a tool for driving screws into walls and other things.

scribble *vb.* scrawl, write carelessly; make untidy patterns with a pen or pencil. *Our teacher scolded me for scribbling in my book.*
scripture *n.* holy writings, especially the Bible.
scroll (rhymes with *hole*) *n.* a roll of paper with writing or pictures on it.
scrub 1. *vb.* clean by rubbing with a wet brush. 2. *n.* ground covered with shrubs, brushwood, etc.
scruff *n.* the back of the neck.
scruple *n.* a doubt because of what one's conscience says.
scull *vb.* row with small light oars called **sculls**.
sculptor *n.* a person who makes statues or carvings. **sculpt** *v.*
sculpture *n.* the art of making things from wood, stone or other hard materials; the product itself.
► Sculpture is the making of three-dimensional shapes as works of art. Traditionally, sculptors carved their work out of stone or (especially in tribal societies) out of wood. They usually chose living things as their subjects: human beings, animals, or gods and goddesses. Almost all the ancient civilizations produced sculpture of this kind. In Europe the tradition began in Greece, and continued in Rome and RENAISSANCE Italy. In the 1900s there have been a number of new developments. Sculptors have been influenced by "primitive" art from Africa and the South Pacific. They have tried new materials: metal, glass, plastic, and even pieces of discarded "junk." And, influenced by *Abstract Art*, some sculptors have concentrated on making abstract shapes, such as *mobiles* – hanging collections of shapes that move in the wind. Important sculptors of the 1900s include Jacob Epstein, Barbara Hepworth, Henry MOORE, Ossip Zadkine and Louise Nevelson.

scum *n.* impurities that float to the surface of a liquid.
scurf *n.* flakes of dead skin on the scalp.

Three styles of sculpture: The classical Venus de Milo (left); Bronze woman and child (below) by Renoir (1841–1919); and (above) an abstract sculpture by the British Henry Moore.

S

scythe ("sc" like "s") *n.* a tool with a curved blade for cutting grass or corn.

sea *n.* the big areas of salt water which cover most of the earth; the oceans.

► Seas influence the climates and the ways of life of people in coastal regions. This is partly because the sea heats and cools more slowly than the land or the air. Hence, coastal regions generally have fairly mild climates. Currents in seas also transport relatively warm water to cool regions and relatively cold water to warm regions. Onshore winds are warmed or cooled by the seawater and their effects are felt on land.

About 3.5 percent of seawater consists of dissolved ELEMENTS. By far the commonest of these elements are sodium and chlorine, which together form salt. Because of the salt content of seawater, it is easier to swim in a sea than in a freshwater lake.

sea anemone *n.* a soft-bodied, tube-like sea animal.

► Sea anemones are closely related to CORALS, but they do not build a hard cup around themselves as corals do.

Sea anemones cling to rocks. Many live on or near the seashore. They look like flowers. This is because they have one or more rings of petal-like tentacles around their mouths. The tentacles have stinging CELLS, and trap small fish and other tiny animals that float by. The sea anemone then pulls the food into its stomach through its mouth, and digests it.

sea gull *n.* a bird that lives near the sea and eats fish.

sea horse *n.* a small fish with a horse-shaped head.

► Sea horses are strange fishes with delicate bony bodies. Most are between 6 and 10 in. (15 and 25 cm) long. Sea horses swim by waving their back fin. They often cling to seaweed with their tails. The males look after the eggs. They keep them in a pouch on their bellies until the eggs hatch. Sea horses are found in seas in tropical and warm areas.

seal 1. *n.* a smoothly furred mammal which lives in or near the sea. 2. *vb.* close something by sticking its edges together. *We sealed the letter with glue.* 3. *n.* an impression stamped on to something to show that it is genuine. *The letter was stamped with the king's seal.*

► Seals are large sea MAMMALS. Many of them live in the icy waters of the far north. They spend most of their time in the sea, but often come ashore to lie in the sun. They also have their young, called pups, on land. Seals have streamlined bodies and legs shaped like flippers for swimming. They can swim as fast as 10 mph (16 km/h). They also have a thick layer of fat, or *blubber*, under their skin to protect them from the cold. Seals eat fish and other sea creatures, including birds. Some kinds of seal are hunted for their skins. The culling of seal populations has caused controversy in recent years.

sea level *n.* land that is at the same level as the sea. It is used to measure the height of all other land. *The hill was 40 feet above sea level.*

sea lion *n.* a sea mammal that is very similar to the seal but which has small ears on the outside.

seam *n.* the line where two pieces of cloth are sewn together.

search *vb.* look for thoroughly. *n.* the act of searching, an investigation.

seashell *n.* the hard covering of a sea creature, especially a mollusk.

seashore *n.* the seacoast; the land closest to the sea.

► The shores surrounding earth's seas and oceans are shaped by water. Along some shores, fierce waves hammer at rocks and carry away loads of stones and earth. Along others, the waves and tides bring in pebbles and sand and dump them. All over the world, shores are being changed by restless waves and by the constant rise and fall of TIDES.

There are several kinds of seashore. They can be rock, sand, mud, pebble or a mixture. All shores are home for a great variety of living things.

Limpets, winkles, whelks, barnacles, SEA ANEMONES and SPONGES are some of the creatures found on rocky shores. All these animals cling to rocks and eat tiny pieces of food that float by in the water. Others, such as cockles, razor shells, clams and CRABS, like sandy and muddy beaches.

Seashores have their own plants. Many of these plants are SEAWEEDS. But other plants have learned to grow in these wet, salty places. Most shore plants and animals are able to live in and out of water. When the tide is in, they are often underwater, but when the tide is out, they are left on land.

Many birds live along the seashore. Some shore birds use their long beaks to dig for worms and insects in the mud. Others catch fish in the sea.

seaside *n.* the seashore; the district bordering the sea. *We are spending a week at the seaside.*

season *n.* a time period, one of the four divisions of the year called spring, summer, fall and winter.

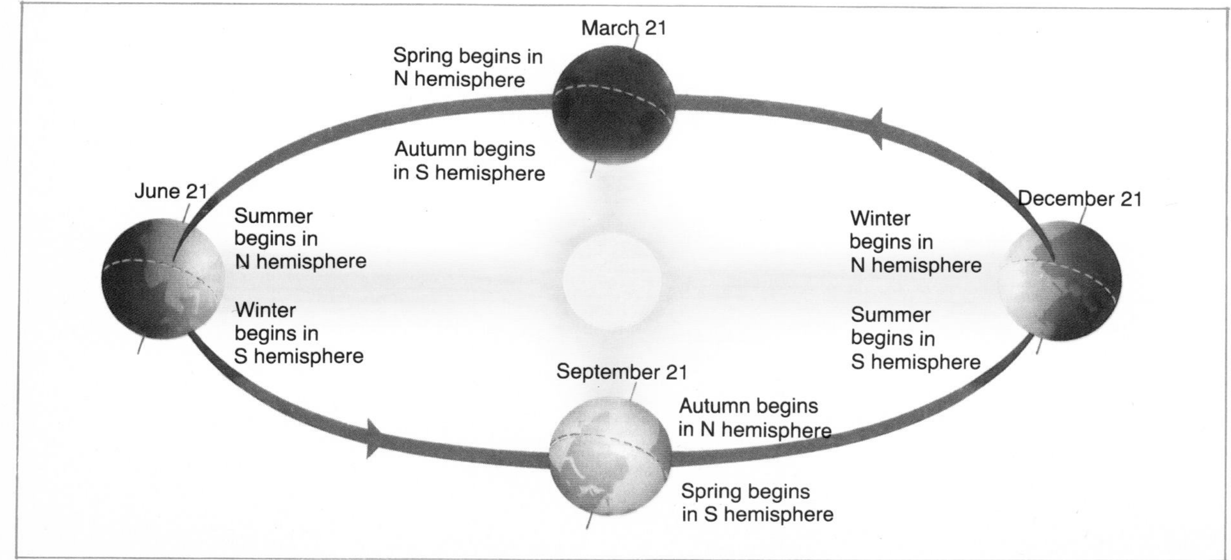

► Seasons happen because the EARTH is tilted on its *axis* (a line through the center of the planet between the NORTH and SOUTH POLES). As the earth travels around the SUN, first one pole, then the other, leans toward the sun. When the North Pole tips toward the sun, it is summer in the northern half of the world and winter in the southern half. Six months later, it is the South Pole's turn to lean sunward, making it summer in southern lands and winter in northern ones. Spring and autumn, the half-way seasons between summer and winter, happen when the earth is sideways on to the sun.

At the poles, there are only two seasons: summer and winter. During the polar winter the sun never rises and days are dark. In the summers the sun shines all the time and there are no real nights.

Away from the poles, toward the middle parts of the world, days become longer in summer and shorter in winter. Farthest from the poles, at the EQUATOR, the earth's tilt has no effect. The sun is always high in the sky and the four seasons of spring, summer, autumn and winter do not exist.

seasoning *n.* flavoring added to food. **season** *vb.*

seat *n.* a piece of furniture for sitting on.

sea urchin *n.* a small spiny creature that lives on the seabed.

► The sea urchin's body is protected by a hard, round case covered with stiff spines. Between the spines it has tube feet ending in suckers. Its mouth lies under the body and has five teeth that are so sharp they can cut through a steel plate nearly a half-inch thick. Urchins eat tiny plants and animals from the seabed. People eat sea urchins in Mediterranean countries.

seaweed *n.* a large group of plants that grow in or near the sea.

► Instead of roots, seaweeds have *holdfasts* that glue them to rocks, shells and other objects. Most seaweeds are a kind of algae.

Seaweeds that live near the surface are green. Lower down, they are brown and, in really deep water, red. Like most plants, seaweeds need sunlight to make food. As the sun's rays do not reach deeper than 600 ft. (180 meters), there are no seaweeds below this depth. A jelly made from seaweed is used in many foods and drugs such as ice cream and aspirin. In some countries, such as Japan, people eat seaweeds as a vegetable.

seaworthy *adj.* a ship that is in a fit state to go to sea.

secateurs *pl.n.* pruning clippers.

second 1. *adj.* the one after the first. *He came in second in the race.* 2. *n.* one-sixtieth of a minute. 3. *n.* the assistant to a boxer or duelist. 4. *vb.* give one's support to; endorse. *I second that idea.*

secondhand *adj.* already used, not new. *We bought my bike secondhand from a neighbor.*

secret *n.* a piece of information that is kept hidden, confidential.

secretary *n.* 1. an office worker who types letters and makes arrangements for other people. 2. company officer who keeps records of a company.

sect *n.* a group of people who have beliefs (especially religious) in common.

section *n.* one of the parts into which something can be divided. *The apple was cut up and I got a section of it.*

sector *n.* any part of a circle between two radii and the circumference.

secure 1. *adj.* safe, out of danger. 2. *vb.* fix something so that it is safe. *The guard made sure the door lock was secure.*

seduce *vb.* tempt or lead astray. **seduction** *n.* **seductive** *adj.*

see *vb.* (past **saw** past part. **seen**) 1. observe with the eyes. *Can you see that star?* 2. understand. *Now I see what you mean.*

see about *vb.* make arrangements for something to happen. *I'll see about ordering a Christmas tree.*

Dandelion, ash and sycamore seeds are scattered by the wind. The spikes of burdock seeds stick to passing animals.

seed *n.* a tiny part of a plant from which a new plant may grow.

► At the center of a seed is a tiny embryo of a new plant, complete with root, shoot, and one or more special leaves. Around this there is usually a stock of food cells for the embryo – the *endosperm*. Then there is the hard outside – the *testa*. Seeds are spread in many different ways: by the wind, by sticking to animals, by being eaten by birds, etc. But

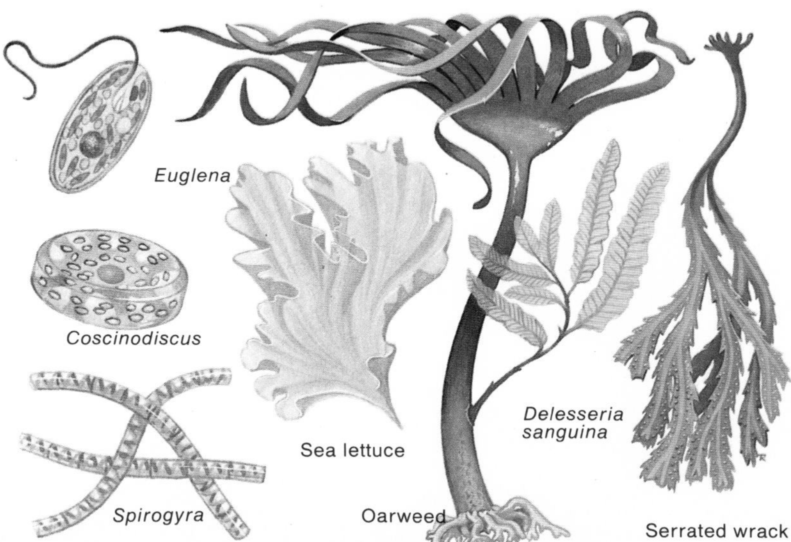

Seaweeds belong to a plant group called algae.

S

they need good conditions of soil, moisture and temperature before they will begin to grow (*germinate*). (*see* PLANTS)

seek *vb*. (past **sought**) look for; try to obtain.
seem *vb*. appear to be. *He seems honest enough, but you can never be sure*. **seeming** *adj*. apparent but not real.
see off *vb*. go with someone to the place where they start a journey.
seesaw *n*. a long plank balanced on a central support, which rocks up and down when people sit on the ends.
seethe *vb*. cook by boiling.
segment *n*. one separate part of something. *Oranges can be divided into separate segments with your fingers*.
segregate *vb*. keep apart or set away from others. **segregation** *n*.

Seine, River
The Seine is a river in northern FRANCE. It rises in Burgundy in the east and flows northwest through Champagne. The best-known stretch of the Seine lies in the heart of PARIS. From Paris the river flows through Normandy to enter the English Channel near Le Havre. Large ships can use the Seine as far as Rouen, while smaller boats and barges can reach Paris. The Seine is linked by canal to many other important rivers, including the RHINE.

seize (rhymes with *sneeze*) *vb*. grab something firmly, or by force; snatch. *The mugger seized the woman's handbag*.
seldom *adj*. not often.
select *vb*. choose from a group as best or most suitable. *Ben was selected from his class for the team*. **selection** *n*. what is selected; things from which to select.
self- *prefix* meaning by oneself or itself, automatic, independent.
self *n*. (plural **selves**) a person's individuality, most often used in pronouns such as myself, yourself, etc.
self-defense *n*. protecting yourself against attack.
selfish *adj*. caring too much about yourself and what you want, rather than about other people.
self-service *n*. a restaurant, shop, etc., set up so that the customers can serve themselves.
sell *vb*. (past **sold**) exchange something for money.
semaphore *n*. a system of sending messages with flags which you hold in the air.
semi- *prefix* meaning half, e.g. **semicircle**, **semidetached**.

Senate (U.S.)
The Senate is the upper house of CONGRESS, the lawmaking body of the U.S.A. Each state elects two senators, each of whom serves for six years. About one-third of the Senate is elected every two years.
The first senate was the governing body of ancient ROME. There were usually about 600 senators. Each was chosen for life.

send *vb*. (past **sent**) cause something or someone to go to a particular place; dispatch.
send off for *vb*. write asking for something you want to be sent to you. *I am going to send off for that record*.

Senegal
Senegal is a low-lying republic in West AFRICA. Most people work on the land, and the main cash crop is peanuts. Fishing and mining are also important. Dakar, the capital, is West Africa's most industrialized city. Formerly a French colony, Senegal became fully independent in 1960. In 1982, Senegal set up a confederation with neighboring

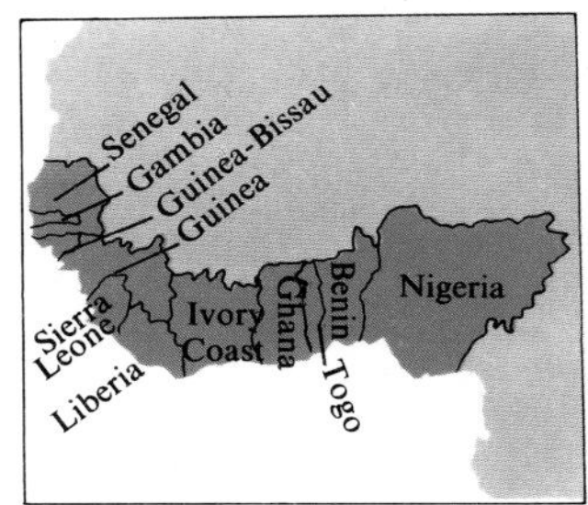

GAMBIA called Senegambia. Both countries have, however, retained their sovereignty.
AREA: 75,754 SQ. MILES (196,192 SQ. KM)
POPULATION: 5,967,000
CAPITAL: DAKAR
CURRENCY: FRANC
OFFICIAL LANGUAGE: FRENCH

senile *adj*. old and feebleminded.
senior *adj*. older in years, or more important than others.
señor *n*. the Spanish word for Mr. or Sir.
señora *n*. the Spanish word for Mrs. or Madam.
señorita *n*. the Spanish word for Miss.

The semaphore code is a system of flag signals. Each letter, from A (top left) to Z (bottom right) has a different signal.

sensation *n.* being aware through the senses; feeling; a thrilling event. *The first space flight was a sensation.* **sensational** *adj.*
sense 1. *n.* one of the ways your body has to tell you what is happening around you: sight, hearing, touch, smell and taste. 2. *n.* the meaning of something. *I can't make sense of what he is saying because he is talking too fast.*
sensible *adj.* behaving in an intelligent way. **sense** *n.* such behavior.
sensitive *adj.* affected by external stimulation, e.g. light. *The film is very sensitive to color.* easily hurt; delicate.
sent *vb.* past of **send**.
sentence 1. *n.* a group of words that make sense together. 2. *n.* a punishment given to a criminal by a law court. *The burglar got a sentence of two years in prison. vb.* pronounce sentence on.
sentimental *adj.* full of feelings (sentiments), especially soft, romantic ones; overly emotional.
sentry *n.* someone whose job is to guard something at a gate, etc.
sepal *n.* a kind of leaf that forms the outside part of a flower.
separate 1. *adj.* divided, not joined together. *The jigsaw came in 100 separate pieces.* 2. *vb.* divide up, sort out. *She asked me to separate the peas from the beans.* **separation** *n.*
September *n.* the ninth month of the year.
sequel *n.* the next part, continuation or installment of a story, etc.
sequence *n.* order of things coming after one another. *A sequence of events.*
sequoia *n.* one of a family of North American *conifers* (cone-bearing trees).
► There are two kinds of sequoia, the redwood and the giant sequoia. Redwoods, over 330 ft. (100 meters) high, are among the world's tallest trees. Giant sequoias are not as tall, but their trunks are much larger.
The world's largest tree is a giant sequoia named "General Sherman". This huge tree has enough wood to build 40 houses. Many sequoias can be seen in Sequoia National Park in California.

serene *adj.* calm, unruffled.
serf *n.* a person in history who belonged to the place where he lived, and to the lord who owned the land. *A serf was a kind of slave.*
sergeant *n.* a noncommissioned rank in the army, air force, or marines.
serial *n.* a story that is told in parts, instead of all at one time. *We watch the serial on TV every Sunday night.*
series *n.* a number of things that happen one after the other, and which belong together in some way. *Peter had a series of colds last winter.*
serious *adj.* thoughtful, not funny; important because of possible danger.
sermon *n.* a religious speech, lecture delivered from a pulpit.
serpent *n.* an old-fashioned word for a snake.
serrated *adj.* having teeth or notches on the edge. *A serrated knife.*
servant *n.* a person who is paid to work in the house of another person.
serve *vb.* 1. work for someone. 2. sell things in a shop. 3. give out the food at a meal.
service 1. *n.* occupation of a servant. 2. *pl. n.* the armed forces. 3. *n.* a set of utensils etc. *A dinner service containing 12 plates etc.* 4. *n.* supplying what is necessary. *Water, gas and electricity are essential services.* 5. *n.* a religious ceremony. 6. *n.* (in tennis etc.) the act of serving a ball. 7. *vb.* maintenance (of a car etc.).
sesame *n.* an herb that is used for flavoring. The seeds are also used to make oil.
session *n.* a meeting or series of meetings in court to do business, etc.
set 1. *n.* a group of people or things that belong together. *We bought a set of table mats for our brother.* 2. *vb.* become hard. *The jelly was left to set overnight.* 3. *vb.* arrange things in a certain way. *Will you set the table for dinner, please?*
set about *vb.* begin to do something.
set eyes on *vb.* catch sight of something.
set in motion *vb.* start something off.
set sail *vb.* begin a voyage.
set off *vb.* start out on a journey.
settee *n.* a sofa, a long soft seat.
settle *vb.* 1. go to a place and stay there. *My uncle went to Canada to settle.* 2. decide something. *We couldn't agree which of us should eat the cake, so we asked Dad to settle the argument for us.* 3. pay a bill.
settlement *n.* 1. a place to where people have moved, built houses and decided to live. 2. terms of an agreement.
set upon *vb.* attack someone.

Seven Wonders of the World
The Seven Wonders of the World were seven outstanding objects that were built in ancient times. Only one of these Wonders, the PYRAMIDS, exists today. The others were:
The Hanging Gardens of BABYLON, which seem to have been built high up on the walls of temples. They were probably a gift from King Nebuchadnezzar II to one of his wives.
The Temple of Artemis, at Ephesus (in Turkey) This temple was one of the largest in the ancient world.
The Statue of ZEUS at Olympia, Greece, showed the king of the gods on his throne.
The tomb at Halicarnassus (now in Turkey) was a massive tomb built for Mausolus, a ruler in Persia. It became so famous that all large tombs are now called *mausoleums*.
The Colossus of Rhodes, in Greece, was a huge, bronze statue of the sun god, Helios. It stood over the harbor entrance.
The Pharos of Alexandria, in Egypt, was the first modern LIGHTHOUSE. It was built in 270 B.C. on the island of Pharos outside Alexandria harbor.

Seven Years War
The Seven Years War was the name given to the war of 1756–63 with Britain and Prussia fighting France, Austria and Russia. It was caused by colonial rivalry between Britain and France, and the European rivalry between Prussia and Austria. The North American part of this struggle became known as the French and Indian War. The victories of Wolfe at Quebec and Clive at Plassey resulted in the British conquest of CANADA and the founding of her Indian empire. The success of Prussia under Frederick II made Prussia the dominant power in central Europe.

sever *vb.* cut or break; separate.
several *adj.* some, usually three or more, but not many. *There were several coats left in the hall.*
severe *adj.* strict or harsh, not gentle. *The weather was very severe.*

Severn River
The Severn River is Britain's longest river. It rises in westcentral Wales and flows for 210 miles (335 km) along a semi-circular course to drain into the Bristol Channel. The Severn Road Bridge, linking London with South Wales, was opened in 1966.

sew *vb.* (past **sewed** past part. **sewn**) join pieces of material together with a needle and thread. **sewing** *n.*
sewage *n.* human waste carried through drains by water.
► Sewage is led through underground sewers to *filters*, where it is treated to remove BACTERIA. The purified sewage can be made into fertilizer, but it is usually just piped into rivers or into the sea. In some countries (e.g. China) human sewage is saved for use as manure on the land.

sewer *n.* a large drain for taking away sewage and waste water.
sewing machine *n.* a machine for sewing cloth, leather, etc.
► The sewing machine was popularized by the American, Isaac Singer (1811–75). There are home

S

and industrial versions. Many are now powered by an electric motor, rather than by hand or treadle (foot pedal).

sex *n.* being male or female. **sexual** (*adj.*) desires.
► Some very simple creatures reproduce by splitting in two (like the amoeba) or by growing a bud that develops into a new adult. But most living things use sexual reproduction. This means that an offspring can only be made by uniting male and female CELLS. Sometimes male and female cells come from different parts of the same adult – as with many plants (*see* BIOLOGY). But usually they are made by different male and female adults – as with men and women. From ADOLESCENCE, men begin to produce male cells (sperm) in their *testes*, and women begin to produce female cells (ova) in their *ovaries*. When a man and a woman make love, in sexual intercourse, the sperm flow through the man's penis into the woman's body. If one of the sperm unites with an ovum, the resulting combination of cells begins to grow into a new human being inside the woman. She is then said to be *pregnant*, and if all goes well she gives birth to a baby nine months later.

sextant *n.* an instrument to measure angles. used in navigation.
► Sextants are used by sailors to find the position of their ship when land is out of sight. A sextant works by measuring the ANGLE of the sun or, at night, of a star to the horizon to find its *altitude*. By measuring the altitude and direction of the sun or stars, and by noting the exact time of the observations, the sailor can work out the position of his ship.

Seychelles
This republic consists of about 90 islands in the Indian Ocean, north-east of MADAGASCAR. Victoria, the capital, is situated on Mahe, which is the largest island. Most of the people are of mixed French and African origin. The main activities are farming and tourism. The first settlers on the islands were French, but Britain ruled the Seychelles from 1810 until independence in 1976.
AREA: 108 SQ. MILES (280 SQ. KM)
POPULATION: 70,000
CAPITAL: VICTORIA
CURRENCY: RUPEE
OFFICIAL LANGUAGES: ENGLISH, FRENCH

A ship's sextant.

shabby *adj.* worn-out; thin and faded. *He always wore a shabby old suit to the office.*
shack *n.* a hut, especially a roughly built one.
shade *n.* 1. out of direct sunlight. *The dog sat in the shade where it was cool.* 2. something which protects against strong light or heat. *The lampshade was made from paper.* 3. how dark or light a color is. *My shirt is a darker shade of green than yours.* *vb.* screen from light.
shadow 1. *n.* the dark shape cast by an object when it is in a strong light. 2. *vb.* follow someone closely, as a shadow does.
shady *adj.* shaded; uncertain; dishonest.
shaft *n.* 1. a long handle, such as the one on a spear. 2. a narrow, deep hole that leads to a mine or pit.
shaggy *adj.* having tangled hair.
shake *vb.* (past **shook** past part. **shaken**) move vigorously from side to side, or up and down. *In some countries, people shake hands with friends every time they meet.* tremble, vibrate. **shaky** *adj.* unsteady, trembling.

Shakespeare, William
William Shakespeare is the greatest English dramatist (1564–1616). Born in Stratford-on-Avon, he married Anne Hathaway in 1582. He is said to have joined a group of actors, and from 1589 was an established playwright in London. He wrote a great number of plays including comedies (*Much Ado About Nothing* and *As You Like It*); tragedies (*Macbeth, Hamlet, King Lear*); English histories (*Henry IV, Richard III*); classical histories (*Anthony and Cleopatra*) and the "last plays" (*The Tempest, A Winter's Tale*). He also wrote poems, including *Venus and Adonis* and the *Sonnets*.

shall *auxiliary vb.* a word that indicates determination, or that something will happen in the future. *I shall get up early tomorrow morning.*
shallow *adj.* not deep. *The water was shallow and only covered my feet.*
shalom *interj.* a Jewish greeting.
shame 1. *n.* feeling sorry and regretful for having done something wrong; guilty feeling. 2. *n.* (*casual*) a regrettable thing. *What a shame you couldn't come.* 3. *vb.* make ashamed.
shampoo *n.* liquid for washing your hair. *vb.* wash your hair.
shamrock *n.* the name for some kinds of clover.
► St. Patrick was supposed to have used a shamrock in his preachings, to illustrate the doctrine of the Holy Trinity. Because of this, it has become the badge of Ireland and symbol of St. Patrick's Day.

Shanghai
Shanghai is the greatest Chinese port, handling about 50 percent of her overseas trade, and CHINA's largest city. Shanghai is near the Yangtze-kiang estuary. It was first developed by European powers, when they began trading with China in the 1800s.

Shangri-la *n.* an imaginary place where everything is almost perfect.

shan't *vb.* abbr. of **shall not**.
shanty *n.* 1. crudely built hut or dwelling, usually of wood. *This area is known as shantytown.*
shape *n.* the outline of something; what appearance it has. *The soap was made in the shape of a bear.* *vb.* give shape to. **shapely** *adj.* **shapeless** *adj.*
share *vb.* divide and distribute something among a group. *Annie shared her candy with us.*
shark *n.* a family of large, fierce fish.
► Sharks have a wedge-shaped head, long body and a triangular back fin that often sticks out of the water. The skeletons are made of rubbery gristle, not bone. Most sharks live in warm seas. They vary greatly in size. The dogfish, one of the smallest sharks, is only 2 ft. (60 cm) long. The largest ocean fish, the whale shark, measures over 50 ft. (15 meters) – as long as two buses.
The whale shark is harmless to humans and other animals, as it lives on PLANKTON. But many sharks are cruel killers, with rows of razor-sharp teeth. Several are man-eaters. The greediest monster, the great white shark, swallows its prey whole. The remains of big animals, such as horses, seals and other sharks, have been found in its stomach.
Other man-eaters are the blue shark, the tiger shark, and the leopard shark, which has leopard-like spots. The smell of blood in water drives sharks crazy so that they attack anything near, even other sharks. Along the beaches of Australia and South Africa, swimmers are protected from sharks by nets, electric barriers and lookouts. Some kinds of shark lay eggs, but most sharks have live offspring.

sharp 1. *adj*. having a pointed end or fine edge that cuts things easily. 2. *adj*. sudden or quick. *There was a sharp bend in the road*. 3. *n*. a musical note raised by a semitone. **sharpen** *vb*. make sharp.
shatter *vb*. break into small pieces.
shave *vb*. & *n*. cut hair off parts close to the skin. *Most men shave their chin every day*. **shaving** *n*.
shawl *n*. a cloth worn about the shoulders for warmth or for decoration.
sheaf *n*. (plural **sheaves**) a bundle of grain stalks tied together after they have been harvested.
shear *vb*. cut the wool from a sheep.
shears *pl. n*. a pair of scissors with large blades, used for cutting heavy fabrics, shearing sheep etc.
sheath *n*. a cover for a sword or a knife. **sheathe** *vb*.
shed 1. *n*. a small hut. 2. *vb*. let things fall off or drop away. *Some trees shed their leaves in the fall*.
sheen *n*. glossiness, brightness.
sheep *n*. (plural **sheep**) a common farm animal with a woolly coat.
► Sheep have been part of human life for thousands of years. At first, sheep were kept for their milk and skins. Milk can be made into cheese and the skins were used for clothing. Then, people discovered that the animals' thick coats could be *sheared* (shaved off) and the wool woven into cloth. Today, sheep are kept mostly for wool and for meat (*mutton* or *lamb*). But, parts of sheep are also used for making glue, and FERTILIZER. The *gut* strings on violins and tennis rackets also come from sheep.

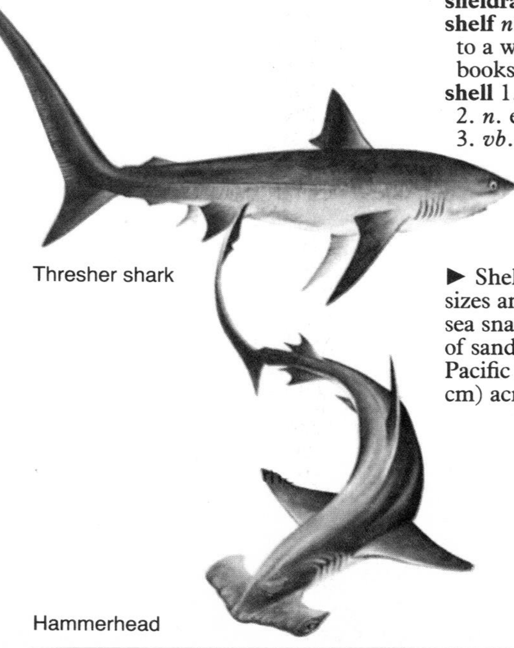

Thresher shark

Hammerhead

All sheep are related to goats. Wild sheep, found mostly in Asia, look very like goats. They have large horns and do not have woolly coats. Female sheep are called *ewes* and males are *rams*.

sheepdog *n*. a dog used to herd or guard sheep.
sheer *adj*. 1. very steep, like the side of a cliff. 2. of fine material, can be seen through.
sheet *n*. a thin, flat, rectangular piece of metal, paper or fabric; bed covering of linen, cotton, etc.
sheik (*sheak*) *n*. an Arab chief.
shekel *n*. the main unit of currency of Israel.
sheldrake *n*. a European wild duck.
shelf *n*. (plural **shelves**) a plank fixed to a wall, etc., on which to keep books or other articles.
shell 1. *n*. a thin hard outer covering. 2. *n*. explosive artillery projectile. 3. *vb*. remove shell from.

► Shells are usually hard and are all sizes and colors. The shells of some sea snails are no bigger than a grain of sand but the giant clam of the Pacific Ocean has a shell 4 ft. (120 cm) across.

Some land animals such as SNAILS and TORTOISES have shells, but most creatures with shells belong in the sea. Shelled sea animals include MOLLUSKS and CRUSTACEANS. Some of these, like OYSTERS, scallops, shrimps and LOBSTERS, can be eaten. These are often called shellfish although they are not really fish at all. Shellfish have been an important food for thousands of years. In some places, prehistoric kitchen remains have been found that are just enormous mounds of shells, as high as a three-story house.

Shells are often used as decorations and for jewelry. In former times some shells, especially cowrie shells, were used as money.

shellfish *n*. a soft-bodied water animal that lives inside a shell for protection.
shelter *n*. a place that protects you, e.g. from unpleasant weather. *vb*. serve as a shelter; take shelter.
shepherd *vb*. & *n*. a person who looks after sheep for a living. **shepherdess** *n. fem*.
sheriff *n*. a law officer.

Sherman, William Tecumseh
William Tecumseh Sherman (1820–1891) was one of the great Union generals of the Civil War. He is best remembered for his march of 400 miles across GEORGIA, "from Atlanta to the sea," in which he destroyed everything that could be of use to the enemy. After a rest at Savannah, Georgia, Sherman turned north, but before he could reach Richmond, the Confederate capital, the Confederacy had collapsed.

Sherman commanded the army for 23 years.

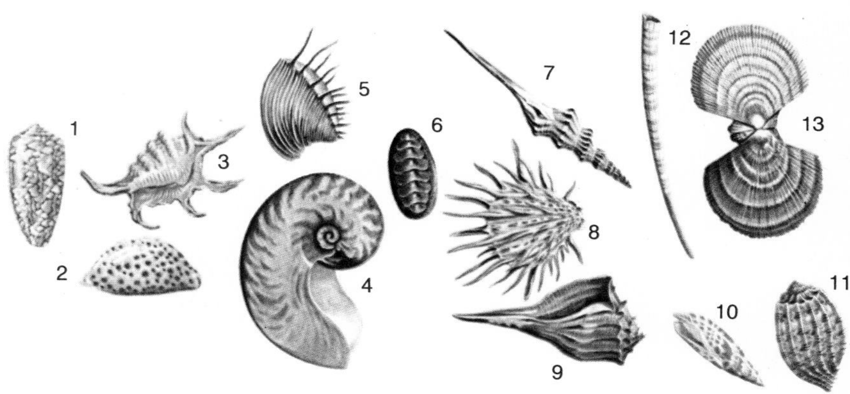

Types of shell:
1. Textile cone shell 2. Tiger cowrie 3. Scorpion shell 4. Nautilus 5. Royal comb Venus 6. Chiton 7. Spindle shell 8. Thorny oyster 9. Left-handed whelk 10. Bishop's mitre 11. Harp shell 12. Elephant's tusk 13. Northern scallop.

S

shield 1. *n.* a large piece of metal, leather, etc., used to protect the person who carries it against attack. 2. *vb.* cover or protect something. *He used his hand to shield his eyes from the glare.*
shift *vb.* change the position of something. *Graham wants to shift the table into the corner of the room.*
shilling *n.* a coin used in several countries before decimal currency. A British shilling was worth five new pence, and there were 20 shillings in a pound (£1).
shin *n.* the front of the leg between the knee and the ankle.
shine *vb.* (past **shone**) give out a steady beam of light. **shiny** *adj.*
shingle *n.* slate or wood part for roofs and house sides.
ship *n.* a large seagoing boat. *vb.* take or send by carrier.
► Today, most ships are cargo vessels. They are usually built for a certain type of cargo. *Tankers* carry liquids such as oil or wine. Some oil tankers are so long that the crew can ride bicycles around the decks. *Bulk carriers* take dry cargoes like coal and wheat that can be loaded loosely. *Container ships* carry all kinds of goods packed in large boxes called containers. *Refrigerator ships* are for carrying fresh food like fruit and meat.

Planes have replaced most passenger ships, but there are still a few liners such as the *Queen Elizabeth 2* crossing the oceans. And there are many ferries, which take people and cars across smaller stretches of water.

►► **Shipbuilding** The world's first ship was probably a log. In time, people learned to build CANOES by hollowing out logs. They also learned to tie logs, or reeds, together to make a raft. These early boats were all driven by wooden paddles and oars.

About 5,000 years ago, the ancient Egyptians invented sails and discovered how to build boats out of planks of wood. This meant that ships became big enough and powerful enough to cross the seas and oceans. For thousands of years, ships used both oars and sails. But finally, sails took over. By 1400, sea-going ships were all sailing ships. Two famous kinds of sailing ships were GALLEONS in the 1500s and CLIPPERS in the 1800s.

The age of the sail came to an end with the invention of steam engines and iron *hulls*. Steam engines, running on wood and coal, worked paddle wheels at the sides of ships. Later, paddle wheels were replaced by propellers at the stern. The world's first steamboat, the *Clermont*, started work on the Hudson River (New York) in 1807. A few years later, the first all-iron ship, the *Vulcan*, was launched. The most spectacular iron ship ever built was the *Great Eastern*, a huge vessel 690 ft. (210 meters) long with room for 4,000 passengers. More changes came with the 1900s. Ships are now built of steel, not iron, and are powered by oil or even nuclear fuel instead of coal.

shipwreck *n.* an accident in which a ship is sunk or badly damaged at sea; a wrecked ship.
shipyard *n.* a place where ships are built or repaired out of the water.
shire *n.* 1. a county. 2. large horse once used for pulling heavy loads.
shirk *vb.* run away from, avoid doing. *She shirked her responsibilities.*
shirt *n.* an article of clothing for the top half of the body, with sleeves and a collar.
shiver *vb.* shake with cold or fear.
shoal *n.* a group of fish swimming together.
shock *n.* an unpleasant surprise. **shocking** *adj.* scandalous, very bad.

LINER LENGTHS COMPARED

Great Western (1837) 212 ft. (64.6 m)

Great Eastern (1858) 692 ft. (210.3 m)

Mauretania (1906) 787 ft. (239.9 m)

Queen Mary (1934) 1,000 ft. (305 m)

Normandie (1932) 1029 ft. (313.6 m)

United States (1952) 990 ft. (301.8 m)

France (1962) 1035 ft. (315.5 m)

Queen Elizabeth (1968) 963 ft. (293.5 m)

NAUTICAL TERMS

abeam across the ship, at right angles to its length.
aft at or near the stern.
amidships in the middle of the ship.
astern backwards – behind the stern.
beam width of ship at its widest point.
bow the front of the ship.
bowsprit long projection from the bow that supports rigging and possibly a jib or spritsail.
bridge raised deck from which a ship is navigated.
bulkhead wall dividing up the inside of a ship.
capstan a small winch (lift).
crow's nest look-out position at the top of a mast.
deck the planked or plated-over "floor" across a ship's hull. A small vessel has only one deck; an ocean liner may have many.
draft depth of a ship below water.
fathom unit of length used for measuring the depth of water, equal to six feet.
fore nearest to the bows.
forecastle or **Fo'c'sle** raised deck in the bows.
galley a ship's kitchen.
gunwale upper edge of the side of a ship.
helm steering control of a ship.
hold space below deck for cargo.
hull the body of a ship.
jib triangular sail between the foremast and bowsprit.
keel the main piece of steel or wood along a ship's bottom from stem to stern.
knot a measure of speed – one nautical mile an hour.
leeward direction toward which the wind blows. The lee side of a ship is therefore the sheltered side, away from the wind.
nautical mile a measure of distance, equal to 1/60 of a degree of latitude, or 6,080 ft.
poop a raised deck at the stern.
port the left-hand side looking forward.
screw underwater propeller used to move a ship.
sheet rope or cable attached to the end of a yard.
spar metal or wooden pole used as mast, yard, boom, etc.
spritsail square sail on yard suspended from the bowsprit.
SS steamship.
starboard The right-hand side of a ship looking forward.
stern the back of a ship.
wake or **wash** the waves and foam caused by a moving ship.
watch a spell of duty for a seaman.
windward direction from which the wind blows. The windward side is therefore the one exposed to the wind.
yard length of timber, generally horizontal, and pivoted to a mast, from which a sail is suspended.

shoe *n.* a protective covering for the foot.
► At first shoes were just pieces of leather wrapped around the feet. Later, sandals and boots were made. For a long time, all shoes were made by hand, with thick leather soles and softer leather upper parts. Leather is still used, but most shoes today are made in factories. Some shoes are made of plastic, and many have plastic or rubber soles. Clogs are shoes made of wood.

shone *vb.* past of **shine**.
shook *vb.* past of **shake**.
shoot 1. *vb.* use a gun, or a bow and arrow; wound with gun. 2. *vb.* go quickly. 3. *vb.* photograph with a camera. 4. *n.* the tip of a growing plant. 5. *vb.* kick for a goal at soccer.
shop 1. *n.* a room or building where goods are sold. 2. *vb.* buy things from a shop. **shopper** *n.*
shopkeeper *n.* a person who owns or looks after a shop.
shoplifter *n.* a person who steals from a shop.
shop steward *n.* a spokesperson elected by workers.
shore *n.* the land along the edge of a sea or lake.
short 1. *adj.* the opposite of long or tall. *Both his parents are very short.* **shorten**. *vb.* make or become short in length or time. 2. *adv.* to be lacking in something. *I am running short of envelopes.* **shortage** *n.*
shortbread *n.* thick cookie made of flour, sugar and shortening.
shortcoming *n.* a failing, defect.
shorthand *n.* a way of writing quickly by means of symbols.
shortly *adv.* soon, before long.
shorts *pl. n.* short trousers that end above your knees.
shortsighted *adj.* 1. condition of someone who can see clearly when things are close, but cannot see things farther away; nearsighted. 2. lacking foresight.
shot *vb.* past of **shoot**.
shot *n.* 1. the firing of a gun. *We heard a shot in the distance.* 2. an attempt to do something. 3. injection of a drug. 4. lead pellets in the cartridge of a shotgun.
shot put *n.* an Olympic event which involves throwing a heavy metal ball as far as possible with one hand. The ball weighs 16 pounds for men, eight pounds 13 ounces for women.
should *vb.* a word meaning "ought to." *I should apologize to her.*
shoulder *n.* the part of your body from your neck to your arm. *vb.* push with shoulder; assume responsibility. *She shouldered the job of bringing up her brother's children.*
shout *vb.* & *n.* call out or speak loudly; a loud cry. *My grandfather is a bit deaf, so you'll need to shout.*
shove *vb.* & *n.* push.

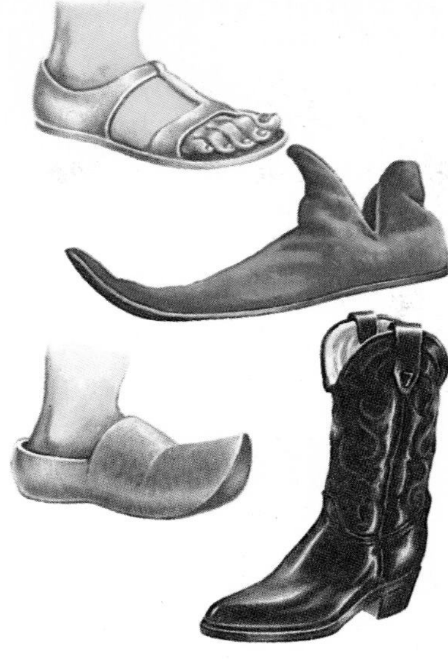

Sandals were made first of woven grass and later of leather. Leather has always been the commonest material for making shoes, though clogs are made of wood.

shovel *n.* a large spade with a curved blade to lift and toss material. *vb.* use a shovel.
show 1. *vb.* (past part. **shown**) let something be seen. *Show me what you have written.* 2. *n.* a play or other entertainment. *The artist arranged a show of his paintings.*
shower *n.* 1. a short period of light rain. 2. a special device for sprinkling water over oneself as a form of bathing.
show off *vb.* display proudly; try to make people think you do something very well.
show up *vb.* 1. expose. 2. arrive.
shrapnel *n.* fragments from a bomb, etc.
shred *vb.* tear or cut into pieces. *n.* a narrow, torn-off piece.
shriek *n.* & *vb.* a high-pitched scream.
shrill *adj.* high and loud (of a sound).
shrimp *n.* a small edible shellfish with a long tail.
► Shrimps are close relations of lobsters, crayfish and crabs. They are all CRUSTACEANS. They have long feelers and a jointed shell on the abdomen. Shrimps can be of several colors and some change color to match their surroundings. They can be anywhere from an inch to 18 inches long. The larger shrimps are often called *prawns.*
The shrimp catch in the United states exceeds that of any other shellfish.

shrink *vb.* (past **shrank**) get or make smaller. *Wool often shrinks in hot water.*
shrub *n.* a bushy plant, like a small tree.
shrug *vb.* raise or lift the shoulders. *n.* a symbol of indifference.
shrug off *vb.* brush aside; take no notice of.
shrunk *vb.* past part. of **shrink**.
shudder *vb.* & *n.* tremble convulsively with cold or fear.
shuffle 1. *vb.* mix cards so that they are not in any special order.
shun *vb.* avoid, keep away from.
shut *vb.* close. *Shut that door.*
shutter *n.* 1. a cover for a window. 2. part of a camera.
shuttle *n.* an instrument used in weaving for carrying thread back and forth.
shuttlecock *n.* a cork filled with feathers that is hit back and forth in the game of badminton.
shuttle service *n.* an aircraft or train that travels regularly between two places.
shy 1. *adj.* not liking to meet other people. 2. *vb.* turn away in sudden fear. *Horses sometimes shy away from strange objects.*

Siberia
Siberia is part of the U.S.S.R. It lies in ASIA. Siberia stretches over 5.2 million sq. miles (13,486,000 sq. km). It reaches from the ARCTIC in the north to the border of MONGOLIA in the south, and from the Ural Mountains in the west to the Pacific Ocean in the east.
Siberia has been part of Russia since the 1600s. Before the 1950s it had few industries. Since then, mines for gold, diamonds and other minerals have been opened, and oil and gas fields have been found. But there are still people in the north of Siberia who live in a traditional way, hunting and herding reindeer.
A famous railroad, the Trans-Siberian, runs across the area. Parts of Siberia have great forests which are used for timber. Most people are farmers, producing cattle, wheat, rye and potatoes.

Sicily
Sicily is the largest island in the MEDITERRANEAN. It lies off the south-western tip of ITALY, separated from the mainland by the Strait of Messina. Sicily is a mountainous island and contains Mt. Etna, the highest active volcano in Europe. Fishing, farming and tourism are important activities. The island is still dominated by an illegal secret society known as the *Mafia.* Many Sicilians have been forced by high unemployment to emigrate, especially to the U.S.A. Sicily has been invaded many times and ruled by many different countries. At one period it formed part of the Kingdom of the Two Sicilies (the other being the republic of NAPLES). It was captured by the Italian patriot GARIBALDI and became part of a united Italy in 1860.

S

sick 1. *adj.* ill, not well. *Feeling sick to your stomach means you feel like you will vomit.* **sicken** *vb.* begin to feel ill; feel loathing. **sickening** *adj.* nauseating. **sickness** *n.* ill health; a disease.
sickle *n.* a reaping tool with a curved blade and short handle.

side *n.* 1. the edge, wall or boundary of something. 2. the part of your body between the armpit and the hip. 3. a team in a game, or a country in wartime.
sideways *adj.* with one side first. *Crabs move sideways along the ground.*
siege ("ie" as in "ee") *n.* a time when an army surrounds (besieges) a town or building so that people cannot get in or out.

Sierra Leone
Sierra Leone is a republic in West AFRICA. Its name means "Lion Mountain" in Portuguese. Most of the people are Black Africans, and the climate is tropical. Rice is the main food crop. Coffee, cocoa and palm kernels are the main cash crops. Diamonds and bauxite are the most important exports. The capital, Freetown, is so called because it was founded as a settlement for freed slaves. A former British protectorate, Sierra Leone achieved full independence in 1961.
AREA: 27,700 SQ. MILES (71,740 SQ. KM)
POPULATION: 3,643,000
CAPITAL: FREETOWN
CURRENCY: LEONE
OFFICIAL LANGUAGE: ENGLISH

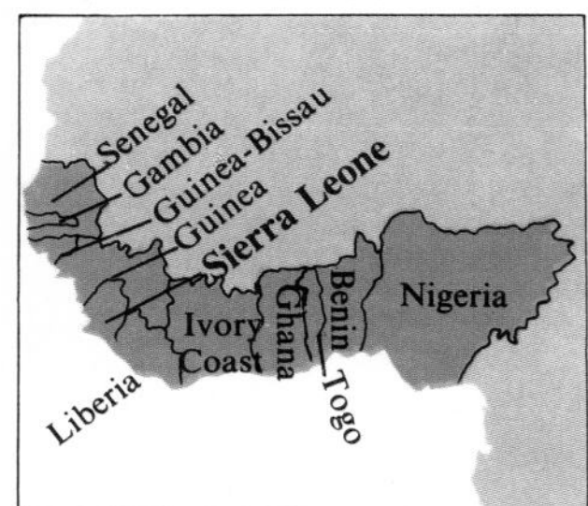

siesta (*see*-**yes**-*ta*) *n.* an afternoon nap.
sieve (rhymes with *give*) *n.* a frame with a stiff net, used to separate small things from larger ones or to drain off liquid.*vb.* use a sieve.

sift *vb.* put through a sieve.
sigh (rhymes with *die*) *vb.* & *n.* breathe out loudly, usually to show that you are tired, bored or sad.
sight *n.* 1. the ability to see. *Sight is one of the five senses.* 2. something that is seen by someone. *We saw a very strange sight on the beach.*
sign 1. *n.* board with words or pictures to give information to people. *The sign said "danger."* 2. *vb.* write your own name on something. 3. *n.* a mark or clue that has a special meaning. *The footprints were a sign that someone had been to the house.*
signal 1. *n.* a sound or movement that has a special meaning, especially from a distance. *Car drivers have to signal before they turn.* 2. *vb.* send a message. *He used semaphore to signal the news.*
signature *n.* someone's name written in his or her own writing.
significance *n.* the importance of; the meaning of. *What is the significance of a dog wagging its tail?*
signor *n.* (plural **signori**) the Italian word for Mr. or Sir.
signora *n.* (plural **signore**) the Italian word for Mrs. or Madam.
signorina *n.* the Italian word for Miss.
signpost *n.* a post bearing a sign that tell travelers the direction and distance of places.
silage ("i" rhymes with "eye") *n.* animal fodder made from green crops and preserved in a silo.
silence *n.* a time of complete stillness. *vb.* make silent.
silent *adj.* without any sound.
silhouette *n.* the outline or shape of something.
silicon *n.* after oxygen the most common element in the Earth's crust. It is found in quartz.
► Silicon chips are tiny pieces of the ELEMENT silicon. They can be made to carry very small electrical circuits, called microcircuits. These are used in transistor radios, digital watches, electronic calculators and computers. Because the chips are so small, the objects they are used in can be small too.

silk *n.* a natural fiber from the cocoon of the silkworm moth. **silky** *adj.* like silk.
► Silkworms, which are really CATERPILLARS, are kept in special containers and fed on mulberry leaves for about four weeks. At the end of this time they spin their cocoons and start to turn into moths. Then they are killed and each cocoon is unwound as a long thread between 2,000 to 3,000 ft. (600 and 900 meters) long. There are several varieties of silk moths, some produce white silk and some yellow silk. Most of them pass through several generations each year.
Two-thirds of the world output of raw silk is produced in Japan.
Silk was first used in Asia centuries ago, especially in China and Japan. Silk WEAVING in Europe began in the 1400s. Silk makes a very fine, soft material and can be dyed beautiful colors.
sill *n.* the ledge along the bottom of a window.
silly *adj.* stupid, foolish; frivolous.
silt *n.* deposit of fine soil left by a river. *vb.* become choked with silt.
silver 1. *n.* a valuable, whitish, shiny metal (symbol – *Ag*); coins made from metal of the same color. 2. *n.* & *adj.* a color that looks like the metal.
► Silver bends very easily, and can be beaten into many shapes and patterns. Like gold, it can be hammered out into thin sheets. It is used to make useful and decorative things, such as spoons and forks, bowls, and jewelry. Sometimes it is used as a coating on cheaper metals such as copper or nickel, to make them look like silver. It can also be mixed with another metal (usually copper), and then it is called *sterling* silver.
Silver used to be made into coins, but "silver" coins are usually made of a mixture of copper and nickel. "Silver" paper is not silver at all, but aluminum.
Silver carries electricity well and is used for this in industry. Some chemicals made from silver react to light and are used in photography. Another chemical, silver nitrate, is painted on the back of glass to make mirrors.
Silver is often found in the first state in the ground, but much silver comes from the sulfide ore argentite.
The leading producers of mined silver are Mexico, Canada, the United States, the U.S.S.R., Peru and Australia.

silver screen *n.* a screen on which to show motion pictures.
similar *adj.* like something else, but not exactly the same; of the same kind. *Robyn has a dress similar to mine, but hers has red bows instead of blue ones.*
simmer *vb.* cook in a liquid just below boiling point.
simple *adj.* 1. easy; not difficult. *This game is simple.* 2. basic; not complicated. *A screw is a simple machine.* **simplify** *vb.* make simple.
sin *n.* breaking a religious law, or doing something that is known to be wrong. *vb.* commit a sin.
since 1. *prep.* from a time past. *We haven't met since we were little.* 2. *adv.* because. *I often meet John, since we live in the same street.*
sincere *adj.* honest, true.
sing *vb.* (past **sang** past part. **sung**) use the voice to make musical sounds.

Singapore
Singapore is a small country in Southeast ASIA, off the southern end of the Malay peninsula. Three-fourths of the population are Chinese, but people from all over the world live there.

The capital city, also called Singapore, has one of the busiest ports in the world and trades with many countries. For a short time Singapore was part of Malaysia but now it has its own government.

AREA: 224 SQ. MILES (581 SQ. KM)
POPULATION: 2,476,000
CAPITAL: SINGAPORE
CURRENCY: SINGAPORE DOLLAR
OFFICIAL LANGUAGES: MALAY, CHINESE, TAMIL, ENGLISH

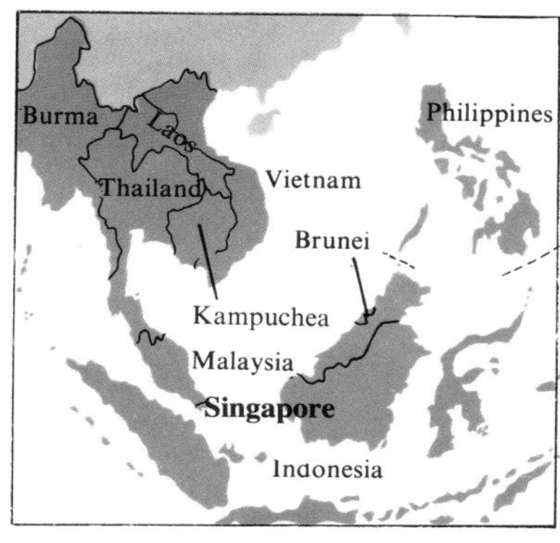

singe *vb.* burn something slightly at the edges.
singer *n.* a person who sings, earns money by singing, etc.
single *adj.* 1. just one. *You have only a single chance in this game.* 2. *adj.* unmarried.
singular *n.* & *adj.* 1. one person or thing, not plural. 2. *adj.* exceptional.
sinister *adj.* frightening, something that seems evil.
sink 1. *vb.* (past **sank** past part. **sunk**) drop down; decline. *A stone will sink to the bottom of a pool.* 2. *n.* a basin with drain and water supply, for washing things in.
sip *vb.* drink in small quantities.
siphon *n.* tube for transferring liquid from one vessel to a lower one; once it is full of liquid, the difference in pressure at the ends of the tube ensures a continuous flow. *vb.* draw through a siphon.
Sir *n.* the title placed before the name of a knight or baronet. *Sir John Smith.* a polite way of addressing a man.
siren *n.* an instrument for making a loud warning signal, like a police siren.
sister *n.* a daughter of the same parents as someone; a nun.
sit *vb.* (past **sat**) rest on your bottom.
site *n.* a place for structures. *There was a bulldozer on the building site.* *vb.* locate or place.
situate *vb.* place, locate.
situation *n.* a place or position; a temporary state or condition. *The situation is serious.* a set of circumstances.
size *n.* measurement, showing how large or small something is.
skate *n.* a steel blade fixed to a boot for fast movement on ice. *vb.* glide on skates.
► Roller skating and ice skating are both popular sports. Roller skates have four wheels made of steel and rubber. Ice skates have a thin steel blade.

There are two main kinds of ice skating. Figure skating and ice-dancing to music are OLYMPIC sports. Speed skaters race against each other.

The first ice skates had runners, or blades, of bone. Today, figure skates have jagged teeth at the front to help grip the ice when starting and stopping. Speed skates have longer blades.

Other sportsmen who use skates include ice hockey players.

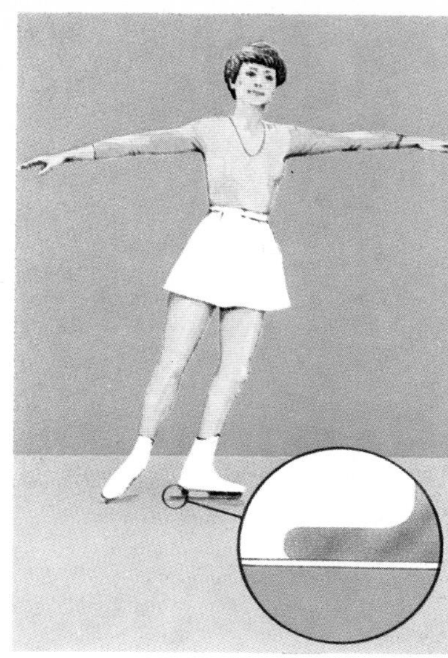

Ice hockey skate

The pressure of an ice skater's weight causes the ice to melt beneath the skates so that the skater slides on a film of water between the skates and the ice. The film immediately freezes again.

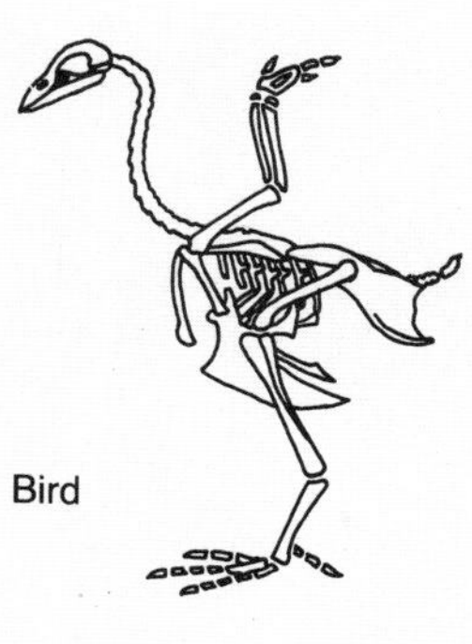

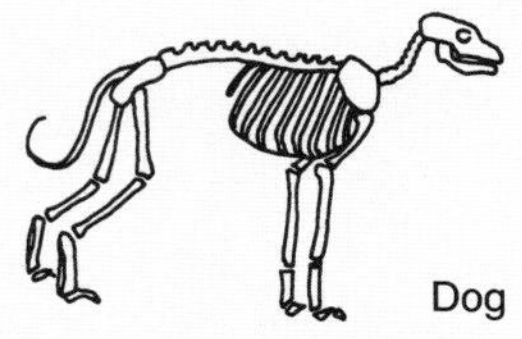

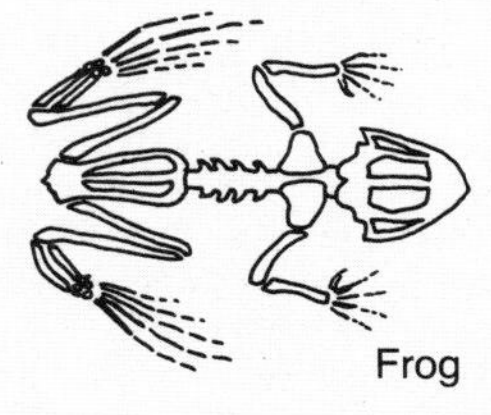

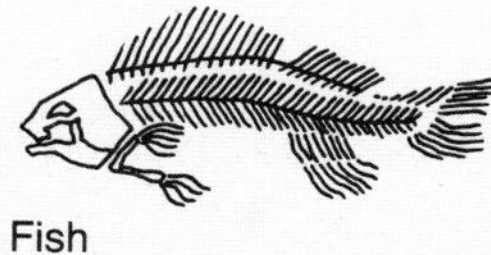

The skeletons of four quite different vertebrates (animals with backbones): fish, amphibian, mammal and bird.

skeleton *n.* the framework of bones in the body of an animal.
► If we did not have a skeleton, our bodies would be shapeless blobs. The skeleton protects our vital organs, such as the heart, liver and lungs. It is also an anchor for our MUSCLES.

In humans and other animals with backbones (VERTEBRATES), the skeleton is inside the body, covered by the flesh and skin. In other animals, such as INSECTS and SPIDERS, the skeleton is like a hard crust on the outside of the body. It is called an *exoskeleton*. Some animals, such as the jellyfish and octopus, do not have a skeleton. Their bodies are supported by the water they live in.

There are more than 200 bones in the human skeleton. These include the bones of the spine, skull (which protects the brain), ribs, pelvis, breastbone and limbs. Joints are

S

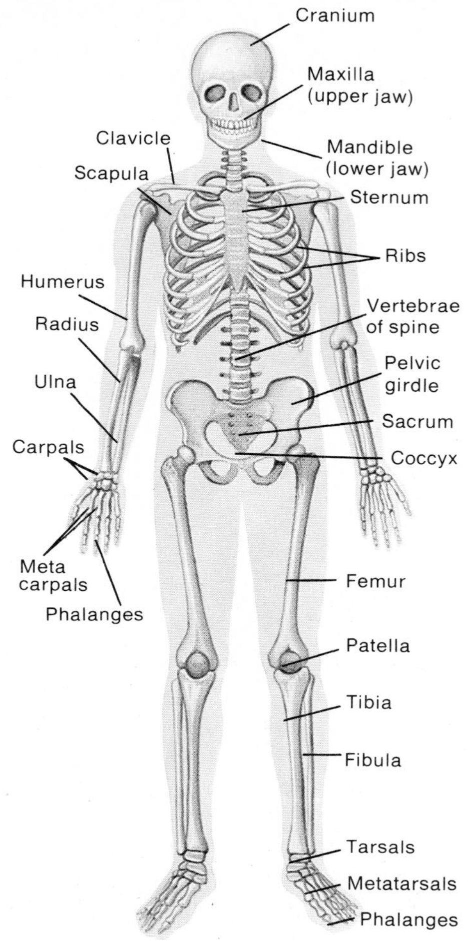

places where bones meet. Some joints (like those in the skull) do not move. Others, like those in the shoulders and hips, help us to move about. Muscles across the joints tighten, or *contract*, to move the bones.

sketch *vb.* & *n.* draw quickly and roughly; an outline.
skewbald *n.* & *adj.* (a horse) marked in white and patches of color other than black.
ski *n.* long strips of wood or other material fixed to boots for fast movement over snow. *vb.* travel on skis.
► Skiing probably started around 3000 B.C. The oldest skis ever found date back to 2500 B.C., and we know that the VIKINGS used skis. Today, skiing is a popular sport and is part of the Winter OLYMPIC GAMES.
There are four main kinds of skiing: *cross-country, slalom* (obstacle course), *downhill* and *ski jumping*. Downhill skiing is especially popular. In recent years the trend has been toward shorter skis.

skid *vb.* slip out of control. *Cars often skid on icy roads.*
skill *n.* the ability to do something very well. **skillful** *adj.*
skim *vb.* 1. remove scum from the surface of a liquid. 2. pass lightly over.
skimp *vb.* give too little attention to; use too little of.
skin 1. *n.* the covering on the outside of the body. 2. *vb.* remove the skin of an animal; strip or peel off.
► The skin acts as a barrier to infection, and prevents the body from losing water and heat too rapidly. It has two layers. The outer part (*epidermis*) is a protective layer of dead cells. It is constantly being rubbed away and replaced from beneath. The inner part of the epdermis contains the pigment that gives skin its color.
The inner part (*dermis*) contains blood and lymph vessels, nerve ends, hair roots, sweat glands and sebaceous (fat) glands.

skin diving *vb.* going underwater without a full diving suit and breathing line.
► Strictly speaking a skin diver uses just a face mask, fins, and a snorkel tube and must come back to the surface to breathe. But the term is also used for *scuba* divers, who carry a self-contained breathing apparatus working from compressed air tanks.

skinny *adj.* thin, lean.
skip *vb.* hop or jump, as over a jump rope.
skipper *n.* the captain of a ship or boat.
skirt *n.* a piece of clothing worn by women around the lower half of the body, and not divided like trousers. *vb.* go around edge or border of.
skull *n.* the bony frame of the head.
skunk *n.* a North American mammal, related to the weasel and badger, which secretes a foul odor.
► There are three kinds of skunk: the *hognosed*, the *spotted* and the *striped skunk*. They all live in North America. The best known is the striped skunk, which is black with white markings on its back. All skunks are able to drive enemies away by squirting a stinking liquid from a gland under their tails. If another animal is hit by this liquid, the smell will cling to its fur for days.
Skunks eat many things, including insects, rats, mice, birds, eggs and plants. They feed at night and sleep in burrows during the day.

The skin is waterproof and prevents water from escaping. Sweating through the pores helps to cool you down. The skin also protects the body from damage and germs.

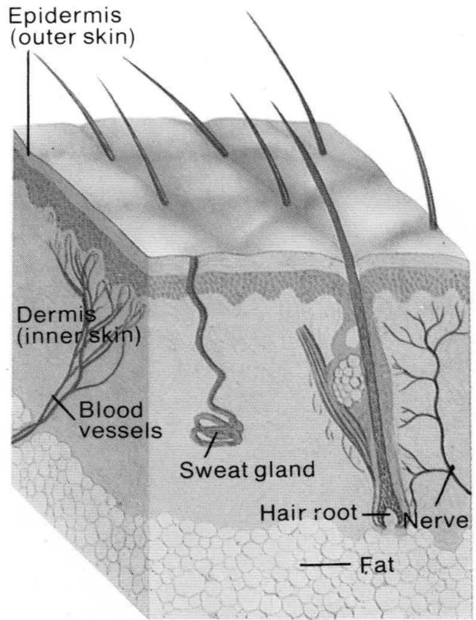

sky *n.* the dome of the heavens overhead.
► What we see when we look up is a section of the earth's ATMOSPHERE, with the immensity of space beyond. The blue color is due to the atmosphere, which splits up the sun's light like a SPECTRUM, and scatters the blue part of the light more than the rest. Without an atmosphere, the sky would look black, except for the sun, moon and stars.

skydiving *n.* a form of parachute jumping.
► Skydiving started in the 1940s, and now it is a popular sport. Skydivers jump from an airplane and fall a long way before they open their parachutes. They have to fall in a special direction to land on their target on the ground.

skylight *n.* a window in the roof of a building.
skyline *n.* the silhouette or outline of things against the sky.
skyscraper *n.* a very tall building with many floors.
► The first skyscraper was built in 1884 in CHICAGO. It was designed by William Le Baron Jenney.
All the early skyscrapers were built in NEW YORK and Chicago. Now they are built all over the world. For many years, the tallest skyscraper was the Empire State Building in New York – 102 stories high. Now there are two taller ones – the Sears Tower in Chicago and the World Trade Center in New York, both 110 stories.

slab *n.* a thick slice. *This slab of marble is too heavy to carry.*
slack *adj.* 1. loose. *That rope is too slack.* 2. careless; lazy. **slacken** *vb.* make or become slack.
slain *vb.* past of **slay**.
slam *vb.* & *n.* shut (a door) very hard and noisily; the noise made by slamming.
slander *n.* & *vb.* damage a person's character by spreading lies. **slanderous** *adj.*
slang *n.* a way of using words that is thought to be less correct than other ways. *"Cop" is slang for police officer.*
slant *vb.* & *n.* a slope, like the one a ladder makes when it is up against a wall; attitude; bias.
slap *vb.* hit something with the flat of the hand. *n.* a blow.
slash *vb.* make long cuts in something. *n.* a slashing cut.
slate 1. *n.* a grayish kind of rock, which can be split into thin sheets for use as a roofing material. 2. *n.* a writing tablet, made of slate, formerly used in schools.
slaughter *vb.* kill, usually when many animals or people are killed at once. *n.* killing of animals for food.
slave *n.* a person who is owned by someone else, and has to work without pay, doing exactly what the owner wants. **slavery** *n.*
► In ancient civilizations, prisoners captured in war were often made into slaves, and poor people sometimes sold their children as slaves.
From the 1500s, the Spanish took people from Africa as slaves for their colonies in America. By the 1770s, British ships were carrying slaves to America. Hundreds were packed tightly into ships. Conditions were terrible, and many slaves died on the way. Public opinion became hostile and slave trading was made illegal in 1807. In 1834 all slaves in the British Empire were freed. Slavery was ended in the U.S.A. in 1865, after the CIVIL WAR.

Slavs
Slavs are the most numerous ethnic and linguistic group of people in Europe. The Slavs were a tribe that migrated from Asia in the 2nd and 3rd centuries B.C. Today, they are mostly found in eastern and southeastern Europe. They speak many different, but related tongues. Those nationalities of Slavic origin include Russian, Ukrainian, Polish, Czech, Slovak, Serb, Bulgarian, Macedonian and Croat.

Slaves on a treadmill in a West Indies plantation. The first slaves were taken from Africa to the New World in 1562 by Sir John Hawkins.

slay *vb.* kill violently.
sled *n.* a small vehicle used for traveling over snow or ice. *A sled has runners made from strips of wood or metal instead of wheels.*
sleep *n.* the time when you are unconscious and resting. *I average eight hours' sleep a night. vb.* be or fall asleep.
► People and other animals need sleep to stay healthy. Without it, people become short-tempered and after a long time they may start having *hallucinations* – seeing things that are not there.
There are four different stages of sleep. At each stage the electrical waves given off by the BRAIN change. When we are deeply asleep, these waves are slow and large. When we are only lightly asleep the waves are faster. This is the time when we – and all mammals – dream and eyes move rapidly.

sleeping bag *n.* a padded bag for sleeping in, often used when camping.
sleepy *adj.* tired; full of sleep; ready for bed.
sleet *n.* a mixture of rain and snow which falls very hard.
sleeve *n.* 1. the part of an article of clothing that covers the arm. 2. a tubular cover that fits over a machine part.
sleigh (rhymes with *ray*) *n.* a large vehicle used for traveling over snow or ice. Some sleighs have engines, others are pulled by animals.
slender *adj.* thin, narrow.
slept *vb.* past of **sleep**.
slew *vb.* past of **slay**.
slice 1. *n.* a thin piece cut from something, such as a loaf of bread. 2. *vb.* cut something into slices.
slick *n.* patch of oil on water.
slide 1. *vb.* move smoothly over something. *It's fun to slide on the ice in winter.* 2. *n.* a slippery chute, often in a park, on which children climb and slide. 3. *n.* a piece of glass, film, etc., for use in a microscope or projector.

Slide rule
A slide rule is a device for making rapid calculations to a high degree of approximation. It has two scales on which numbers are represented by their logarithms, one scale being made to slide against the other.

slight 1. *adj.* small, not important. *Belinda made a slight mistake.* 2. *vb.* ignore; treat with contempt.
slim *adj.* thin, slender. *vb.* to become thinner.

S

slime *n.* unpleasantly wet, slippery substance. **slimy** *adj.*
sling 1. *n.* a piece of cloth used to support an injured arm. 2. a loop of leather used for throwing stones, sometimes also called a slingshot. 3. *vb.* hurl. 4. *vb.* hang or suspend from something.
slink *vb.* move away slowly and quietly (in fear or shame).
slip *vb.* miss your footing; slide.
slipper *n.* a soft shoe worn in the house.
slippery *adj.* easy to slip or slide on, such as an icy or oily surface.
slit 1. *n.* a long, narrow hole. 2. *vb.* make a cut in something.
slope *vb.* & *n.* a slanting place, an incline, especially on a hill.
sloppy *adj.* messy, untidy; over-sentimental.
slot *n.* a narrow opening in something that smaller things can be pushed through. *Some front doors have slots for letters.*
sloth (rhymes with *cloth*) *n.* 1. a tree-dwelling mammal found in tropical America. 2. laziness.

► Sloths move very slowly, usually at night. They spend most of their lives hanging upside down in trees. They eat leaves, buds and twigs. Their fur is often covered with masses of tiny green plants, called algae. This makes the sloth hard to see among the leaves. A sloth's grip is so secure that it can even fall asleep without letting go of the branch it is hanging from.

There are two mains kinds of sloth, the two-toed and the three-toed. In prehistoric times there were huge giant sloths that were about 20 ft. (6 meters) tall.

Two-toed sloth

slow *adj.* moving at a sluggish pace; not fast; taking a long time to do; (of clocks) behind correct time.
slug *n.* a crawling land mollusk, related to the snail, but with little or no shell.
slum *n.* an overcrowded area with old, poor-quality houses.
slump *vb.* & *n.* fall suddenly or heavily; a decline in trade.
sly *adj.* clever at tricking people in secret; cunning.
smack *vb.* hit hard with the flat part of your hand. *n.* a slap; the sound of a smack.
small *adj.* little; tiny; not large.
smallpox *n.* a very contagious disease.

► Smallpox, one of the world's most dreaded diseases, can be spread to other people very easily. It starts like a cold, but soon the body is covered with spots that turn into blisters. These can leave scars if the person gets better, but many people who catch smallpox die from it.

Smallpox can be prevented by vaccination. There have been no new outbreaks of smallpox in the world for several years. It may have been wiped out. Smallpox vaccine was first made in 1796 by Edward JENNER.

smart 1. *adj.* clever. 2. *adj.* well-dressed, neat. 3. *n.* & *vb.* (cause or have) a sharp, stinging pain.
smash *vb.* break something to pieces.
smear *vb.* & *n.* daub; spread grease or paint roughly over a surface.
smell 1. *n.* the sense which tells you what scent something has. 2. *vb.* use your sense of smell; to sniff. 3. *n.* a scent, often unpleasant.

► Smell is one of the five human senses. Like TASTE, it uses nerve endings that respond to chemicals (rather than to pressure, heat or light). But while taste responds to solid and liquid chemicals, smell responds to gases and vapors. In higher animals the smell receptors (*olfactory nerves*) are set in mucous membrane in the NOSE. Some animals use smell to find food and avoid enemies, and to recognize their own home territory. In some moths, the males can smell the chemicals released by females at a distance of several miles. The human sense of smell is much weaker, but it can still detect tiny quantities of a scent, and identify over 10,000 different odors.

smelly *adj.* having an unpleasant odor.
smelt 1. *vb.* separate a metal from its ore by heating to a high temperature. 2. *n.* a kind of fish.
smile *vb.* turn up the corners of the mouth as a sign of pleasure or amusement; grin. *n.*
smith *n.* someone who makes things from metal. *A goldsmith makes jewelry and ornaments from gold.*
smog *n.* heavily polluted, smoky air. *The word "smog" is made up from "smoke" and "fog."*

► There are two kinds of smog. One is a very thick, smelly mixture of smoke and FOG. It used to be very common in London. In the winter of 1952, there was a very bad smog and about 4,000 people died of chest diseases. Since then, laws have been passed to make sure there is less smoke in London and no more smogs.

The other kind of smog is caused by air POLLUTION from fumes from refineries, car exhausts, factories, etc. These fumes are changed by sunlight into a white mist that hangs over cities. Smog of this sort can be dangerous to the people who live in cities. It can hold chemicals that are harmful.

smoke 1. *n.* the greyish vapor given off by a fire. 2. *vb.* smoke cigarettes or other kinds of tobacco; emit smoke. *The chimney smokes.* **smoker** *n.* a person who smokes tobacco.
smolder *vb.* burn very slowly, without a flame.
smooth *adj.* even or slippery; gentle to the touch. *That floor has a very smooth surface now that it has been sanded and polished.* *vb.* make smooth.
smother *vb.* deprive of air; stifle by covering with a blanket, etc.
smudge *n.* dirty mark, blur, stain.
smug *adj.* highly self-satisfied.
smuggle *vb.* take things into a country secretly by hiding them. *Smuggling is against the law.*
snack *n.* a small, quick meal.
snaffle *n.* a kind of bit in the harness of a horse.
snag *n.* an unexpected difficulty.
snail *n.* a small mollusk with a soft body and a hard protective shell.

► Snails are MOLLUSKS with a coiled shell on their back. There are more than 80,000 kinds in the world. Some live on land, some in fresh water and some in the sea. They are eaten by fishes and birds, and some kinds are used as food for humans.

Most snails are very small. But one of the largest, the giant land snail, is about 8 in. (20 cm) long.

snake *n.* a long, thin reptile without legs or eyelids. *Some snakes are poisonous.*

► A snake's body is covered with a scaly skin which it sheds several times a year. Snakes move by wriggling along the ground or swinging their body in loops. They

Boa constrictor

Grass snake
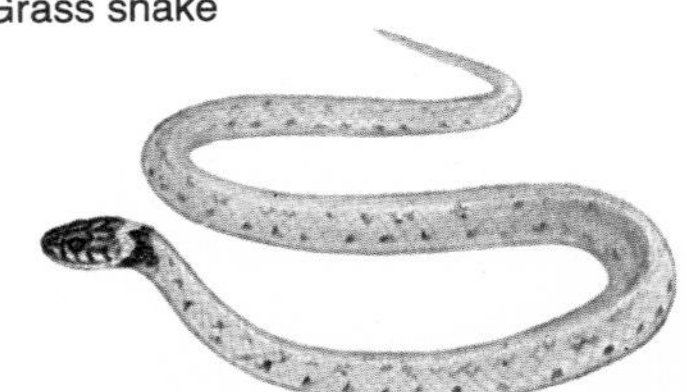

swallow their food whole – small mammals, lizards, birds, eggs, insects and fish. Some have poison glands which release deadly venom into hollow or grooved fangs which they inject into their victims when they bite. The biggest snakes grow to some 33 ft. (10 meters) in length. Snakes live all over the world, except for the polar regions, New Zealand, Hawaii and Ireland, where, it is said, Saint PATRICK drove them out.

There are four kinds of poisonous snakes in the United States: rattlesnakes, the water mocassin or cottonmouth, the copperhead, and two species of coral snakes. Copperheads, mocassins and rattlesnakes are pit vipers. They have vertical pupils in their eyes, just like cats. Pit vipers also have a deep pit on either side of the head between the nostril and the eye. Coral snakes can only be identified by their color patterns.

snap 1. *vb*. break suddenly. 2. *vb*. bite at someone suddenly. *Dogs sometimes snap at unfriendly people*. 3. **snap**(**shot**) *n*. a photograph.
snare *n*. & *vb*. a trap for animals.
snarl *vb*. growl and show teeth, as an angry dog does.
snatch *vb*. take away quickly. *The cat tried to snatch the fish from the plate*. *n*. a sudden grab.
sneak *vb*. to move stealthily, quietly, furtively. *He sneaked away*. *n*. an underhanded person.
sneer *vb*. (at) scoff, show contempt. *n*. a scornful smile, etc.
sneeze *n*. & *vb*. a sudden rush of air through the nose, caused by an irritation of the mucous membrane.
sniff *vb*. draw in air quickly and audibly through your nose. *n*. act of sniffing.
snippet *n*. a small piece. *He read a snippet from the newspaper*.
snob *n*. someone who admires people only if they are rich or important. **snobbish** *adj*.
snooker *n*. a game played on a billiard table, using balls and a cue.
► Snooker is played with 15 red balls, six colored balls and a white cue ball. The object of the game is to sink the balls into the table's pockets in a certain order so as to score points.

snooze *vb*. & *n*. (take) a short sleep; nap.
snore *vb*. & *n*. (make) a noise through the nose or mouth when asleep.
snorkel *n*. a tube for breathing air through when you are under the water.
snort *vb*. & *n*. noise made by forcing air violently through the nose.
snout *n*. an animal's nose.
snow *n*. & *vb*. flakes of frozen water that fall from the sky in very cold weather.
► Snow is made up of ice CRYSTALS. Snow falls when the weather is very cold. Only about one third of the earth's surface ever has snow. It falls all year around in the polar regions at the far north and south of the world, and in winter in places near them. It also falls on the peaks of high mountains.

Snow crystals are always six sided, though each crystal is different from all others. If snow falls in large amounts it can cause problems by blocking roads, railroads and airports. But there are plenty of people who like snow, especially if they enjoy winter sports such as skiing and tobogganing.

snowball 1. *n*. a ball of compressed snow. *The children were having great fun throwing snowballs at each other*. 2. *vb*. grow or increase rapidly.
snowdrop *n*. a green and white flower that grows in early spring.
snowstorm *n*. a heavy fall of snow with a high wind; a blizzard.
snug *adj*. warm and cozy.
soak *vb*. leave something in liquid for a very long time.
soap *n*. a substance made from oil or fat and used for cleaning things. *vb*. lather with soap.
► Soap and detergents are chemical compounds used to remove dirt and grease. When dissolved in water, soaps and detergents form chains of ATOMS. One end of each chain attaches readily to dirt or grease particles, making them relatively easy to remove. Soaps form insoluble gray scum when dissolved in hard water. But this problem has been largely overcome in modern detergents.

soar (rhymes with *door*) *vb*. fly high in the sky.
sob *vb*. cry noisily.
sober *adj*. sensible, levelheaded; not drunk.
soccer *n*. a ball game played between two teams, each with 11 players.
social *adj*. 1. living together in groups. *Ants are social insects*. 2. to do with people and how they live. *My aunt works in the social services office in our town*.

A single snowflake may be made up of thousands of tiny ice crystals.

socialism *n*. a politicial doctrine which places the means of production and distribution in the hands of all the people.
society *n*. all the people who live in a group or country, and the way they live and meet.
sock *n*. an article of clothing worn on the foot, beneath a shoe; a short stocking.
socket *n*. a hole into which something fits. *Jack put the bulb into the electric light socket*.

Socrates
Socrates was a Greek philosopher (*c*. 470–399 B.C.) who laid the foundations of much of Western thinking. His method was to take nothing for granted but to ask endless questions in the search for the truth. His teachings were unacceptable to the people of Athens, and he was sentenced to death by drinking the poison hemlock.

soda *n*. washing soda (*sodium carbonate*), baking soda (*sodium bicarbonate*), caustic soda (*sodium hydroxide*).
sodium *n*. a silvery-gray metal (symbol – *Na*) that is so soft that it can be cut with a knife.
► Sodium is the sixth most abundant ELEMENT in the earth's crust. One of the most widespread sodium compounds is the chloride, common salt. Sodium belongs to the group of alkali metals, so-called because they react with water to form hydroxides which are strong alkalis. The bicarbonate is an ingredient of baking powder, and the hydroxide is used in the making of soaps, detergents, aluminum and textiles.

sofa *n*. an upholstered soft seat for two or more people.
soft *adj*. not hard; having a shape that is easily changed; comfortable. **soften** *vb*. make soft.
soil 1. *n*. the earth in which plants live and grow. 2. *vb*. stain with dirt.
► Soil is a layer of small MINERAL particles on the surface of the earth. It covers the rocks the earth is made of and is sometimes quite thick. Soil may be sand or clay, and may contain the rotted remains of plants, called *humus*.

If soil particles are very fine, it is called *clay*. If they are coarser, it is *silt*, and if they are very coarse, it is called *sand*. Good soil is a mixture of all of these, with plenty of humus. People often add animal manure or chemical FERTILIZERS to poor soil. This makes the soil richer and can also put in extra minerals which some plants need.

solar *adj*. to do with the sun. *Some people heat water with solar energy*.
► **Solar energy** is energy radiated by the sun, which can be collected and

Roman centurion

Crusader knight

French sailor (WW1)

Australian infrantryman (WW2)

U.S. marine (present day)

put to use. It can be converted to electricity by photoelectric cells. Artificial satellites use this technique to provide the electricity they require. Solar energy is also used for domestic heating. Usually the radiant energy is made to heat water, which is then stored in an insulated tank. The heat is released, when required, through a system of hot-water radiators.

►► The **solar system** consists of the SUN and the PLANETS and other bodies orbiting around it. These include the COMETS and ASTEROIDS. All the orbiting bodies in the solar system move in nearly the same plane. This is why the sun, moon and planets all appear to move across the same part of the sky. This zone, called the zodiac, is divided into 12 regions, which are named after CONSTELLATIONS.

sold *vb*. past of **sell**.

solder *n*. an alloy, usually of tin and lead, having a low melting point, used for joining (**soldering**) certain metals. *vb*. join using solder.

soldier *n*. a member of an army.

sole 1. *n*. the flat part underneath your foot or your shoe. 2. *n*. a flat sea fish. 3. *adj*. just one thing or person. *He was the sole member of the class to fail the test.*

solemn *adj*. serious, thoughtful.

solid 1. *n*. anything that can be touched, and is not a liquid or a gas. 2. *adj*. not hollow, with no space inside. *The ball was made of solid rubber.* **solidify** *vb*. make or become solid.

solitary *adj*. alone, lonely.

solo *adj*. on your own. *Jane gave a solo performance on her guitar.*

Solomon Islands

The Solomon Islands make up an island nation in the southwestern Pacific. It lies east of New Guinea, and Papua New Guinea includes the two most northern islands, Bougainville and Buka. The largest island is Guadalcanal. Full independence from Britain was achieved in 1978.

soluble *adj*. capable of dissolving.

solve *vb*. find the answer to a problem or puzzle. **solution** *n*. the answer.

Somali Republic

The Somali Republic is situated on the Horn of AFRICA. The Gulf of Aden lies to the north and the Indian Ocean to the east. The country is hot throughout the year, and much of it consists of semi-desert. Most of the people are NOMADS, herding sheep, camels and cattle. The country is made up of areas formerly ruled by Britain and Italy. It became an independent republic in 1960. In the 1970s, a flood of Somali-speaking refugees poured into the country from neighboring ETHIOPIA. A state of emergency was declared in 1980.

AREA: 246,214 SQ. MILES (637,657 SQ. KM)

POPULATION: 4,125,000

CAPITAL: MOGADISCIO (MOGADISHU)

CURRENCY: SOMALI SHILLING

OFFICIAL LANGUAGES: SOMALI, ARABIC

somber *adj*. gloomy.

some *pron*. & *adj*. part of something; not all; not everyone; an unspecified amount.

somebody *n*. a person, particularly when you are not sure who it is. *Somebody has stolen my purse.*

someplace *adv*. somewhere.

somersault *vb*. & *n*. turn head over heels.

something *n*. anything; any object. *I've got something in my eye.*

sometime *adv*. at an unknown time in the future. *I hope we meet again sometime.*

sometimes *adv*. occasionally; from time to time; not often. *I sometimes play tennis on weekends.*

somewhere *adv*. at some place. *I've left my pen somewhere but I can't remember where.*

son *n*. someone's male child.

sonar *n*. an apparatus that uses sounds and their echoes to locate objects in deep water.

► Sonar is an abbreviation for SOund NAvigation and Ranging, equipment using sound waves to detect submerged objects or find the depth of water under a ship. Sounds are transmitted from the bottom of a ship and are reflected back by objects under the water. The echoes are picked up and displayed on the

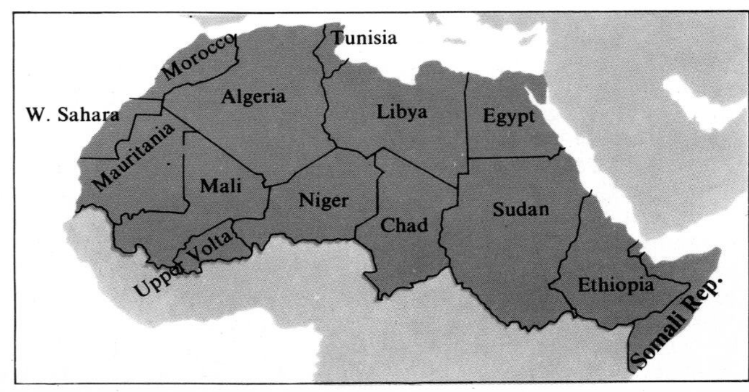

screen of a cathode-ray tube. The images produced indicate the time taken for the sound echoes to bounce back, and so the depth of the objects or the sea bottom.

sonata *n.* musical composition, especially for piano, generally having three movements.
song *n.* a short poem set to music and sung.
sonic boom *n.* disturbing bang, like an explosion, heard on the ground when an aircraft flies faster than the speed of sound; caused by shock waves set up by the aircraft.
sonnet *n.* a poem of 14 lines with a fixed rhyme scheme, e.g. ababcdcdefefgg.
soon *adv.* in a short time. *I'll have to go soon.*
soot *n.* black flakes or powder left behind, particularly in a chimney, after a fire.
soothe *vb.* make someone calm when he or she is upset or angry. **soothing** *adj.*
sophomore *n.* second-year student.

Sophocles
Sophocles (*c.* 496–*c.* 406 B.C.) was one of the greatest of the ancient Greek playwrights. He wrote over 100 plays, but only seven complete tragedies survive. These include *Antigone* and *Oedipus Rex.* His plays paint a dark picture of the struggle of individuals against their fate. Sophocles pioneered a number of technical changes in Greek drama, such as the introduction of scenery.

sorcerer (**sors**-*er-er*) *n.* a magician; someone who can cast magic spells.
sore *adj.* & *n.* something that hurts when it is touched, like a bruise; painful.
sorrow *adj.* sadness, grief.
sorry *adj.* regretful. *I'm sorry I'm late.*
sort 1. *n.* things grouped by a common feature; kind. *What sort of person is he?* 2. *vb.* arrange things according to class or kind; classify. *Please sort the laundry by color.*
sought *vb.* past of **seek**.
soul (rhymes with *hole*) *n.* the part of a person that is thought to live forever, especially by religious people.
sound *n.* anything that you can hear.
► Sound is a sensation experienced when certain vibrations are received by the EAR. Sounds are produced by vibrating objects, such as guitar strings, the column of air in an organ pipe, bells or a shattering pane of glass. When a body vibrates, it compresses and stretches the surrounding air. The pressure variations produced pass through the air in wavelike fashion, rather like vibrations passing along a long, slack spiral spring. Each part of the air (or spring) moves back and forth, transmitting the vibrations to the next part. The frequency of a sound, expressed in hertz (Hz), is the number of waves produced each second. Sound frequencies range from about 20 Hz to about 20,000 Hz. The wavelength of a sound is the distance between the tops of adjacent waves. Sound travels at a velocity of 1,120 ft. (332 meters) per second in air at 32°F (0°C).
►► **Sound reproduction** In radios, record players and tape recorders, sound is reproduced on loudspeakers. They convert electrical signals, matching the SOUND waves, into physical vibrations. These vibrations resemble those produced by the objects that made the original sounds. Hi-fidelity equipment can reproduce sound with lifelike clarity.

sound barrier *n.* the speed of sound. *When a plane travels faster than sound, it goes through the sound barrier.*
soup (rhymes with *loop*) *n.* a liquid food made from meat or vegetables cooked in water, milk, etc.
sour *adj.* sharp-tasting like lemons, not sweet; bad tempered.
source *n.* the starting point, the beginning. *This river's source is in that mountain.*
south *n.* the direction opposite north on a compass.

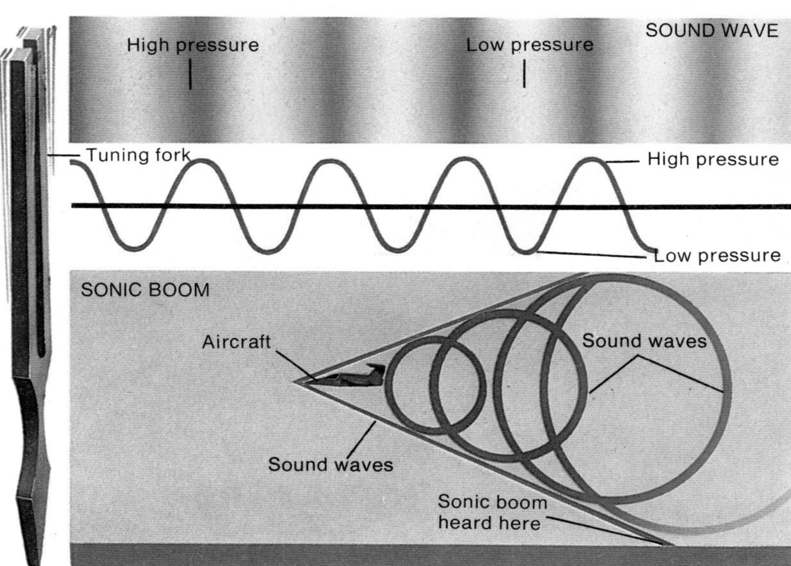

Sound is a form of energy which moves in waves. Through air it travels one mile in five seconds. As the bands of pressure caused by the waves hit your eardrums they make them vibrate. This causes signals to travel to your brain.

The speed of sound is known as Mach 1. Twice the speed of sound is Mach 2, and so on. The diagram shows how a sonic boom is made by a supersonic aircraft.

South Africa
South Africa is a republic in southern AFRICA, in which black Africans form 70.2 percent of the population; Europeans, 17.5 percent; Coloreds, 9.4 percent; and Asians, 2.9 per cent. The Europeans control the political and business life of the nation and the government operates a controversial racial policy, called "separate development" or *apartheid.* This involves allocating 13 percent of the country for black African occupation, while the Europeans retain the rest.

Farming is important and there are vast mineral deposits, but manufacturing is the leading activity. The first European settlement was established in 1652. Modern South Africa came into being in 1910 when the four provinces, Cape Province, Natal, Orange Free State and Transvaal were united.
AREA: 471,471 SQ. MILES (1,221,037 SQ. KM)
POPULATION: 30,844,000
CAPITAL: PRETORIA (SEAT OF GOVERNMENT) CAPE TOWN (SEAT OF LEGISLATURE)
CURRENCY: RAND
OFFICIAL LANGUAGES: AFRIKAANS, ENGLISH

SOUTH AMERICA
Barranquilla
Maracaibo
Caracas
Orinoco
VENEZUELA
Georgetown
Paramaribo
Cayenne
GUYANA
SURINAM
FRENCH GUIANA
Medellín
Llanos
Bogotá
Cali
COLOMBIA
Equator
Quito
Galapagos Is
ECUADOR
Guayaquil
Amazon
Belém
Manáus
Fortaleza
Selvas
PERU
BRAZIL
Chiclayo
Trujillo
Recife
São Francisco
ANDES MOUNTAINS
Callão
Lima
Cuzco
Salvador
BOLIVIA
Brasília
La Paz
Cochabamba
Oruro
Sucre
Brazilian Highlands
PACIFIC OCEAN
Paraná
PARAGUAY
Atacama Desert
Rio de Janeiro
São Paulo
Gran Chaco
Asunción
CHILE
Pôrto Alegre
Córdoba
Mt Aconcagua
Rosario
URUGUAY
Valparaíso
Santiago
Buenos Aires
Montevideo
ARGENTINA
La Plata
Pampas
Bahía Blanca
Colorado
ATLANTIC OCEAN
Chubut
Patagonia
0 500 1000 miles
0 500 1000 1500 kilometers
Capital Cities
Falkland Is
Tierra del Fuego
Cape Horn

S

South America
South America is the world's fourth largest continent. Lying between the Atlantic and Pacific oceans, it stretches from the EQUATOR in the north to the ANTARCTIC in the south, from the Andes mountains in the west, to the wide AMAZON delta in the east.

The Andes are the longest mountain range in the world. They run along the Pacific coast for 5,000 miles (8,000 km). They are also the starting point of one of the world's greatest rivers, the Amazon. This huge waterway travels 4,000 miles (6,437 km) across South America and empties 26 million gallons (118 million liters) of water into the ocean every second. The huge area drained by the Amazon is thick with jungle.

Two other great rivers are the Orinoco in the north and the Plate in the south. The land south of the Amazon jungle has swamps, lakes, grasslands and, near the continent's tip, the Patagonian desert.

In most of South America, the climate is warm and sunny. It is very hot and wet in Amazonia and icy cold in the high Andes.

There are 13 countries in South America. The largest, BRAZIL, takes up half the continent. Most South Americans speak Spanish. But in Brazil they speak Portuguese, in Guyana they speak English, in French Guiana, French, and in Surinam, Dutch. These different languages are the leftovers of history. South America was explored by the Spanish and Portuguese in the 1500s. Then Spain, Portugal and other European countries set up colonies. In the 1800s, most of these colonies won their independence.

The first people of South America were Indians. Most of them, including the INCAS, were killed by the conquerors. Later, the Europeans brought in African slaves. Today, most South Americans come from European and African ancestors. There are still some Indians in the Andes and Amazonia.

South America is very rich. The rocks of the Andes are full of minerals. There is silver in Peru, tin in Bolivia and copper in Chile. There are also huge amounts of oil in Venezuela in the north. The open grasslands of Argentina, Uruguay and Paraguay provide food for millions of sheep and cattle. Brazil's farmers produce a third of the coffee in the world. Peru's fishermen catch a fifth of the world's fish.

So far this wealth has not been used properly. Most South Americans are poor. Many people still scrape a living from the land. They grow potatoes and oats in mountain areas and rice and bananas in the low regions.

The biggest city in South America is Buenos Aires which is in Argentina.

South Australia
South Australia is a state in the central Australian continent. The climate of most of the state is dry, and the northwest consists mainly of desert. Most of the state's agriculture takes place near the coast, where the climate is milder. More than half of the population live in ADELAIDE, which is a major industrial center.

South Carolina (*abbrev.* **S.C.**)
South Carolina is a triangular state on the southeastern coast of the United States. It is best known in history as the place where the CIVIL WAR began in 1861. As one of the original 13 colonies, South Carolina is rich in historic sites. Charleston, once a wealthy port for the export of rice and indigo, still has a number of mansions dating from before the Civil War. Much of the state is forested, especially in the western highlands. Along the east coast are swamps, pine forests and rich farmlands. The capital is Columbia.

South Carolina was named for King Charles I of England. The *South* was added in 1730 when North and South Carolina became separate colonies.

South Carolina's nickname is the Palmetto State. It became the eighth state of the Union in 1788.

South Dakota (*abbrev.* **S.Dak.**)
The state of South Dakota is rich in landmarks of the Old West. It is the home of the famous "Badlands", a region of canyons and towering pinnacles of rock that rise out of a desert landscape. The state was also the last outpost of the Sioux Indian nation, which controlled the area until 1876.

South Dakota is named for the Sioux Indians, who called themselves Lacota or Dakota, meaning "friends." The state's nickname is the Sunshine State.

Most of the people of South Dakota are farmers, raising cattle, pigs, wheat, corn and hay. Pierre is the capital.

South Dakota was part of the Louisiana Purchase of 1803. Gold was discovered there in 1874, though fur trading had begun in the 1700s. The state was admitted to the Union with North Dakota in 1889.

Southeast Asia Treaty Organization
The southeast Asia Treaty Organization (SEATO) was formed to prevent the spread of Communism in Southeast Asia. The treaty was signed in 1954 by representatives of the United States, the United Kingdom, France, Australia, New Zealand, Pakistan, Thailand and the Philippines. The permanent headquarters of the organization are in Bangkok, Thailand.

SEATO did not develop into a strong military alliance because countries such as India, Japan and Indonesia did not join.

South Pole
The South Pole is the point on the map that marks the southern end of the EARTH's axis. The NORTH POLE marks the northern end. The South Pole lies among high, frozen mountains in the middle of ANTARCTICA. The first person to journey to the pole was the Norwegian explorer, Roald AMUNDSEN, in December 1911. The British explorer Captain SCOTT reached the pole one month later.

South West Africa *see* **Namibia**

souvenir *n.* something that you keep to remind you of a place, person, or an event.
sovereign *n.* a king or queen; supreme ruler.
sow (rhymes with *how*) *n.* a female pig.
sow (rhymes with *so*) *vb.* (past **sowed** past part **sown**) put seeds in the ground so that they grow.
soybean *n.* a bushy plant, native to Asia, grown for its seeds (beans) which are rich in protein.
► The soybean is one of our oldest crops. It comes from China, where it has been grown for over 5,000 years. During the 1900s, the soybean spread to other places. It is now an important crop in many countries, especially the U.S.A., U.S.S.R. and Brazil.

Most soybeans are grown for oil and meal. The oil is used for salads, cooking and to make margarine. Soy meal is a nourishing food for animals and people. Both oil and meal are also used to make paint, ink and soap.

space *n.* 1. the distance between things. *How much space did you leave on the bookshelf?* 2. the blank area between written words on lines. 3. the region beyond the earth's atmosphere. *The sun, moon and stars are all in space.*
spacecraft *n.* a vehicle that orbits the earth, or travels in space, away from earth.
► The first spacecraft were launched in the late 1950s. There were two types: SATELLITES and probes. Satellites go into ORBIT around the earth. Probes zoom away from earth to explore other planets. These first spacecraft had no crew. Probes and most satellites are still unmanned, but there are now some manned spacecraft.

All spacecraft are thrust into space by huge, powerful ROCKETS. These rockets are in three parts or stages.

Satellites and probes are full of scientific equipment such as measuring instruments, cameras, tape recorders and radio transmitters. This equipment runs on electricity made from sunlight. The information collected is radioed back to earth, where scientists study it.

Manned spacecraft are far more complicated. As well as scientific equipment, they carry other special equipment to keep their ASTRONAUTS alive and well.

►► **Space Exploration** On October 4, 1957, the Russians sent the first artificial satellite into orbit around the earth. Called *Sputnik I*, it measured only 23 in. (58 cm) in diameter, and weighed a mere 184 lb. (84 kg). America's first satellite, launched the following year, was smaller still.

The first space traveler to orbit the earth was a dog called Laika. It was launched in the Soviet satellite *Sputnik II* only a month after the flight of *Sputnik I*. Information from instruments connected to the dog was transmitted back to earth. This enabled scientists to see how the animal stood up to the stresses of launching and the weightless conditions in space. Experiments like this paved the way for the first manned satellite. On April 12, 1961, the Soviet Yuri Gagarin became the first person to orbit the earth. His spacecraft, *Vostok I*, returned safely after making one complete circuit. The first American in orbit was John Glenn, who made three circuits in his *Friendship* 7 spacecraft on February 20, 1962.

During the next few years both the Soviets and Americans launched numerous manned and unmanned earth satellites. And unmanned craft called space probes were sent to investigate the moon, Mars and Venus. Early moon probes were designed to crash onto the moon, sending back close-up pictures during descent.

By 1966, the United States and the Soviet Union had both developed techniques for soft landing probes on the lunar surface. For the first time, pictures and other information were transmitted directly from the moon. And other probes were sent into orbit around the moon to photograph the side which is always hidden from us on earth.

In July 1969, the U.S. astronaut Neil Armstrong became the first person to walk on the moon. This historic achievement was watched by about 600 million television viewers. On the moon, Armstrong and fellow astronaut Edwin Aldrin carried out various scientific experiments and collected samples of rock and soil for analysis back on earth. The Soviets obtained samples from the moon too, but achieved this using unmanned probes.

In 1976, two American *Viking* probes soft-landed on Mars. Experiments were carried out on soil samples and radioed back to earth. Scientists had hoped to discover if any form of life was present, but the results were inconclusive. However, it seems likely that somewhere beyond our solar system, some form of life – even highly intelligent life – must exist.

A space shuttle is launched attached to two booster rockets and a huge fuel tank (which is the only part that is not reusable). One of the shuttle's important uses is to carry Skylab into orbit. A spacelab is a portable workshop or lab. Different teams will equip their own spacelab, and book a flight.

spade *n.* 1. a tool for digging the ground. 2. a playing card of the suit called spades.

spaghetti *pl. n.* long thin rods of pasta (dried paste made of wheat flour).

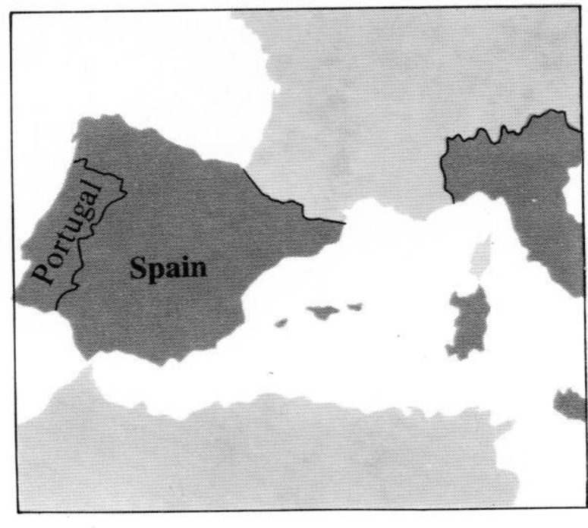

Spain (Spanish, Spaniard)
Spain is a monarchy which occupies most of the Iberian peninsula in southwestern EUROPE. It also includes the Balearic islands in the Mediterranean and the Canary Islands in the Atlantic. Mainland Spain consists mostly of a tableland, between 2,000–3,000 ft. (600 and 900 meters) above sea level. Mountain ranges include the Sierra Nevada and the PYRENEES.

Farming is the chief industry. Barley, fruits, grapes, olives, potatoes, wheat and vegetables are grown. Livestock, especially sheep, cattle, pigs and goats, are also important. Coal, iron, zinc and other minerals are mined. Manufacturing is important in the cities, such as MADRID and Barcelona. Tourism is a major industry, and every year 30 million visitors enjoy Spain's sunny climate, beaches, beautiful cities and ancient castles.

Spanish (Castilian) is the official language. There are also three other important languages: Catalan, BASQUE, and Galician. Many people who speak these languages want a greater degree of independence for their regions.

Spain has been conquered many times by such peoples as the Carthaginians, Phoenicians, Romans, Visigoths and Moors. Christian rule was restored in Spain in the 1200s. In the 1500s Spain became the world's most powerful nation. It acquired a great overseas empire, which it lost in the 1800s and 1900s. Spain suffered a bitter civil war in the 1930s and it became a dictatorship led by General Francisco Franco (1892–1975). However, after Franco's death, a constitutional monarchy was established, with Juan Carlos I as king.

AREA: 194, 908 SQ. MILES (504,782 SQ. KM)
POPULATION: 38,671,000
CAPITAL: MADRID
CURRENCY: PESETA
OFFICIAL LANGUAGE: SPANISH

span *vb*. extend from one side of something to the other. *The bridge had to span a very wide river. n.* distance between piers of bridge.
spaniel *n*. any of a number of kinds of dogs having feathered tail and legs and large drooping ears.
spank *vb*. hit, usually on someone's bottom, as a punishment.
spar *vb*. to take part in a practice bout of boxing.
spare *adj*. extra to what is needed. *You can use my spare pen. vb.* do without. *I can spare you the afternoon.*
spark *n*. a tiny glowing bit from a fire; a flash of light.
sparkle *vb*. flash with light, send out sparks, glitter.
sparrow *n*. a small seed-eating bird.
► Sparrows are noisy, bold, and have a quick, darting flight. There are three kinds, the house sparrow, the tree sparrow and the hedge sparrow.

Sparta
The capital of Laconia in ancient GREECE, founded in the 9th century B.C. Sparta was a city dedicated to the military arts. Its ruling class forged it into a powerful state which rivaled Athens, but its power declined when ALEXANDER THE GREAT conquered all of Greece.

spasm *n*. involuntary and abnormal muscle contractions.
spat *vb*. past of **spit**.
spawn *n*. the eggs of fish and other water animals, such as frogs. *vb*. produce or deposit eggs.
speak *vb*. (past **spoke** past part. **spoken**) talk; communicate aloud by using words.
spear *n*. a weapon made from a long pole with a sharp point on the end. *vb*. pierce with a spear.
special *adj*. different from others, and usually better than them, exceptional. *My birthday is a very special day for me.*
speciality *n*. 1. something a person is especially good at. *Tina's speciality was cooking*. 2. a special or distinctive product.
specialize *vb*. study and become an expert in one subject, etc. *This college specializes in science.*
species *n*. a group of animals or plants that are alike in some way. *Mice are a species of rodent, and so are rats.*
specific gravity *n*. the density of a substance compared with the density of water at 39°F (4°C). If, for example, a substance is twice as dense as water, then it has a specific gravity (S.G.) of two.
specify *vb*. name or state in detail. **specification** *n*. detailed description of an item or of work that needs to be done.
specimen *n*. a sample, a small amount or an example of something that shows what the rest are like.
speck *n*. a tiny amount of something, usually dust.

Cocker spaniel

Brittany spaniel

Springer spaniel

The sphinx at Giza in Egypt.

spectacles *pl. n*. a pair of eyeglasses worn to help you see better.
spectator *n*. someone watching a game or other entertainment, an onlooker. *The spectators cheered when Kevin scored a goal.*
spectrum *n*. when a ray of light passes through certain materials, especially glass, it splits into bands of colors called a spectrum, which looks like a rainbow.
► The whole range of electromagnetic waves is known as the electromagnetic spectrum. And any mixture of electromagnetic waves can be separated into a spectrum of its component frequencies. White light, for example, can be split up by a PRISM to form separate colored bands. Rainbows are seen when raindrops split up sunlight.

speculate *vb*. 1. ponder. 2. buy or sell shares of property or stock in the hope of making a profit.
speech *n*. 1. speaking. 2. a talk given to a group of people.
speed *n*. how fast something or someone moves. *vb*. go fast.
► Speed is how fast something moves. It is usually measured by the distance moved in a certain time. A car's speed is measured in miles per hour. An LP record makes 33 complete turns every minute. LIGHT travels at 186,000 miles (300,000 km) per second.

speedometer *n*. an instrument for measuring how fast a vehicle is moving.
spell 1. *vb*. indicate letters of a word in the correct order. 2. *n*. magic words that are supposed to make something happen in a strange way. *The witch's spell turned the prince into a frog*. 3. *n*. a period of time. *A spell of fine weather.*
spend *vb*. (past **spent**) 1. use money to buy things. *How much do you spend on bus fares each week?* 2. stay a period of time. 3. use a period of time for some activity.
spew *vb*. throw up, vomit.
sphere *n*. a round object, e.g. a ball.
sphinx *n*. in mythology, the sphinx was a fabulous monster of the ancient world with a winged lion's body and a human or animal head.
► Sphinx statues have been found in Egypt, Greece, Crete and Turkey. The Egyptian sphinx heads were usually images of gods or kings. Those in Greece were of young women. The Greek sphinx sat by the

S

wayside, it was told, asking riddles of travelers, whom she devoured if they could not answer correctly.

spice *n*. vegetable products used to flavor and preserve food. *vb*. flavor with spice.
► Spices have a strong taste and smell. They are made from the dried parts of plants, usually ground into a powder. Most spice plants grow in hot countries, such as Africa, India and Indonesia. Pepper, ginger, cloves, cinnamon and nutmeg are common spices.

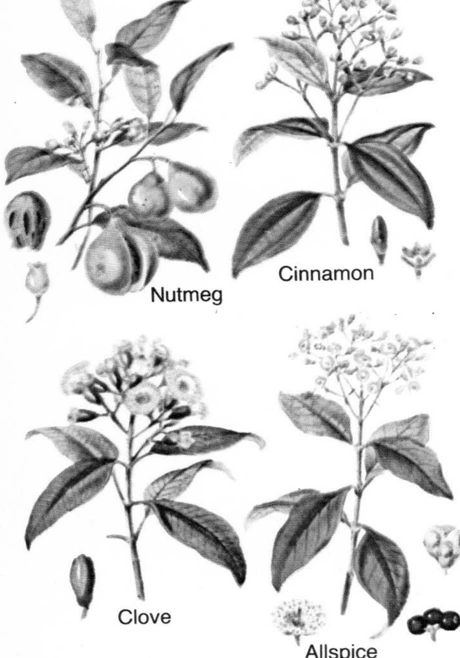

Some of the many spices that were grown and brought back by medieval merchants from the East to the West where they fetched huge prices.

spider *n*. a small animal with eight legs. *Some spiders make webs to catch insects.*
► Although spiders look like insects, they are not. Insects have feelers and wings, spiders do not. Insect bodies have three parts, spiders' bodies have two.

All spiders spin silk threads. Many of them use the threads to make a sticky web for catching insects. Not all spiders trap their food in webs. Some are hunters and chase their prey; others lie in wait, then pounce. When a spider catches something, it stuns or kills it with a poisonous bite. All spiders have poison, but in most cases it does not hurt people.

There are about 30,000 kinds of spider. They are all sizes. The comb-footed spider is no bigger than a pinhead, but some bird-eating spiders can be 10 in. (25 cm) across.

spied *vb*. past of **spy**.
spies *n*. plural of **spy**.
spike *n*. a long thin object with a sharp point; a large headless nail. *vb*. fix with spikes.
spill *vb*. let something fall out of its container. *Did you spill the salt on the table?*
spilled *vb*. past of **spill**.
spin *vb*. (past **span** past part. **spun**) 1. turn around quickly in one place like a top. 2. make thread by twisting fibers together; make a web.
spinach *n*. a leafy green vegetable with a high iron and vitamin A and C content.
spinal column *n*. see **spine**.
spine *n*. the long line of bones down the middle of your back, the backbone; spinal column. **spineless** *adj*. lacking character.
► Human beings and all other VERTEBRATES have a spinal column. It is the main part of the SKELETON. It supports the body and protects the spinal cord.

The spinal column is made up of a number of small bones. These bones called vertebrae are held together by strands of strong tissue called ligaments. In between each bone is a small disk of springy cushions which keep the bones from rubbing against each other. A child has 33 vertebrae, but as he or she grows older some of the vertebrae grow together, so that an adult has only 26. Different animals have different numbers of vertebrae. A swan has 25 just in its neck. Some anteaters have as many as 49 in their tails.

The spinal cord is part of the BRAIN. It is made from the same material but stretched into a cable. It runs down the spine along the spinal canal, a tube through the backbone. NERVES branch off the cord and spread all over the body.

spiral *vb*. & *n*. the shape a line makes when it circles around, like the thread of a screw.
spire *n*. the tall pointed part of a church or other building; steeple.
spirit *n*. 1. a soul. 2. a ghost. 3. courage. 4. *pl. n*. alcohol.
spit *vb*. (past **spat**) throw out saliva from mouth.

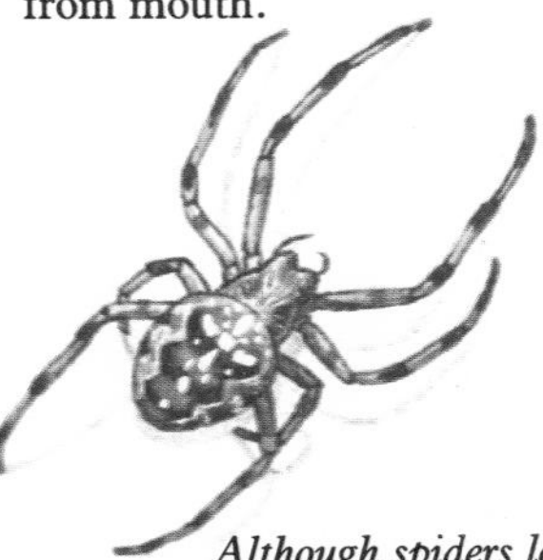

Although spiders look like insects they are not. Insects have six legs. Spiders have eight.

splash *vb*. throw water about. *n*. the sound of splashing; a patch of color.
splashdown *n*. the landing of a spacecraft in the sea on completion of a mission.
splendid *adj*. very good; very impressive in some way; magnificent. *We saw a splendid castle when we visited Mexico.*
splinter *n*. a small, sharp piece of wood or other material. *vb*. break into splinters.
split *vb*. break something into parts. *The class split up and went off in different directions*. *n*. a splitting.
spoil *vb*. 1. impair. *That pole spoils the view*. 2. treat a child or other person indulgently. *The old man tended to spoil his grandchildren.*
spoke *vb*. past of **speak**.
spoke *n*. radiating bar connecting the hub and rim of a wheel.
sponge *n*. 1. a sea animal with a very light, soft body. 2. a soft object used for washing, once made from the sea animal, but today usually made of plastic. *vb*. wipe with a sponge.
► A sponge is a simple water animal. Most sponges belong to warm seas and oceans, but some live in cold seas. A few are freshwater creatures. A sponge's body is a mass of jellylike flesh full of tiny canals, which end in holes on the body's surface. Water, carrying oxygen and food pieces, goes in through the holes and travels along the canals. This is how the animal breathes and feeds. Wastes are taken away through other canals.

When the sponge dies, the skeleton is left behind. Some of these skeletons are soft and flexible, and these are the kind we use for cleaning.

sponsor *n*. 1. a godfather or godmother. 2. a person or company paying for radio or TV advertising; a person or company who supports financially an athlete, etc.
spoon *n*. a device with a handle and bowl for eating liquids and other food.
spore *n*. the tiny dustlike cell from which some plants grow. *Ferns and mushrooms have spores instead of seeds.*
sport *n*. activity, pleasurable games. *Football, tennis and baseball are all sports.*
spot 1. *n*. a small area. *This is a pleasant spot*. 2. *vb*. pick out someone or something. *Can you spot your friend in the crowd*? 3. *n*. a blob. 4. *n*. a spot light.
spotlight *n*. a strong beam of light that can be moved around.
spouse *n*. husband or wife.
spout 1. *n*. the part of something, such as a teapot, where the liquid comes out. 2. *vb*. gush. *Whales spout when they get to the surface to get rid of stale air*. 3. *vb*. (*casual*) go

on speaking. *He could spout poetry for hours.*

sprain *vb.* damage a joint, such as your ankle, by tearing or straining the ligaments. *James sprained his ankle roller skating. n.* such injury.

sprang *vb.* past of **spring**.

sprawl *vb.* & *n.* spread out carelessly. *Adrian's books are sprawled all over the office.*

spray *vb.* & *n.* (squirt) a liquid in a fine mist.

spread *vb.* & *n.* extend; cover something. *There's no need to spread the butter so thickly on your toast.*

sprightly *adj.* light and lively. *Grandma is a sprightly woman for her age.*

spring 1. *vb.* move suddenly upward. *The tiger springs quickly at the goat.* 2. *n.* one of the seasons of the year, when plants begin to grow again after winter. 3. *n.* a place where water comes out of the ground. 4. *n.* a piece of metal able to return to its original shape or position after being forced into another.

► Springs are mechanical devices, usually metal, that store energy when distorted. In clocks and watches, a spiral spring stores energy when wound up. This energy is used to turn the mechanism, when the spring slowly unwinds. In some vehicles, springs separate the body from the wheels. On passing over a bump, energy that would otherwise give the body a severe jolt is absorbed by the springs, thus ensuring a smoother ride.

sprinkle *vb.* scatter or pour out in particles or small drops. *He sprinkled salt over his food.*

sprint *vb.* & *n.* run at top speed, especially for a short distance. *He won the 5,000-meter race by putting in a very fast sprint at the finish.*

sprout *vb.* start to grow.

spruce 1. *n.* a tree belonging to the pine family.

► Spruce trees grow as far north as the Arctic Circle. They are evergreens and have cones that hang downward. There are about 40 kinds of spruce. One kind, the Norway spruce, is the traditional Christmas tree. Spruce trees are grown for timber and wood pulp. Spruce timber is strong and light and is used for ladders, masts, boxes and violins. Most of the world's newspapers are printed on paper made from spruce pulp. Seven species of spruce are native to North American forests.

sprung *vb.* past part. of **spring**.

spun *vb.* past of **spin**.

spur 1. *n.* a sharp device worn on a rider's boot and used to prod the horse into going faster. 2. *vb.* prod or encourage someone. *I hope my advice will spur you into immediate action.*

spurt 1. *n.* a sudden, brief burst of effort, particularly in a race. 2. *vb.* gush or spout.

spy *vb.* find out something by secret methods. *n.* (plural **spies**) a person who does that, usually for a government.

squad *n.* a small group of soldiers or people working together; a football team plus reserves.

squalor *n.* filth, dirt. **squalid** *adj.*

squander *vb.* spend wastefully. *She squandered a week's wages on a lot of worthless rubbish.*

square *n.* an area with four equal sides and four right angles; an open space enclosed by houses. *adj.* in the shape of a square. *vb.* & *n.* multiply a number by itself; the result of such multiplication. *4, 9, 16 and 25 are all squares.*

squash 1. *vb.* press something so that its shape flattens out. 2. *n.* a game played by two players on a special court with a small, black rubber ball and racket.

squat *vb.* 1. crouch on the ground with your knees bent. 2. settle in an unoccupied building.

squaw *n.* an American Indian name for a wife or woman.

squeak *vb.* make a high-pitched noise like a mouse. *I must oil that door to stop it from squeaking. n.* a short shrill cry.

squeal *vb.* & *n.* a long shrill sound.

squeeze *n.* & *vb.* press something tightly, compress.

squid *n.* a 10-armed sea mollusk related to the octopus.

► The squid has a slender body and a square-shaped head and ten long "arms." Squids move through the water by jet propulsion. They take in water through their gills and squirt it out through a forward pointing funnel, so that they glide through the sea backwards. If frightened, they shoot a cloud of inky liquid into the water. The giant squid of the Atlantic Ocean may grow up to 50 ft. (15 meters) and is said to have attacked ships.

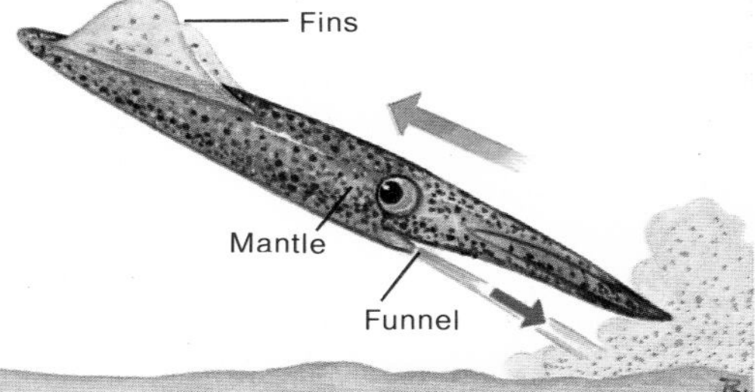

A squid swims by using jet propulsion. It squirts water out of its funnel and can move very fast.

squint *vb.* & *n.* look with eyes partly closed.

squirrel *n.* a small gray or red rodent with a bushy tail and long hind legs.

► Tree squirrels have sharp claws for climbing and a long, bushy tail that helps them to steer and keep their balance. Tree squirrels can leap 10 ft. (3 meters) to reach one tree from another.

Flying squirrels jump 10 times farther than that. These little creatures have flaps of skin between their front and back legs. The flaps form a parachute when a flying squirrel jumps and spreads its limbs. Tree squirrels and flying squirrels feed on leaves, twigs or seeds.

Ground squirrels live in burrows under the ground. They include the chipmunks, prairie dogs and woodchucks.

squirt *vb.* shoot out from a narrow opening. *The toothpaste squirted out of the tube.*

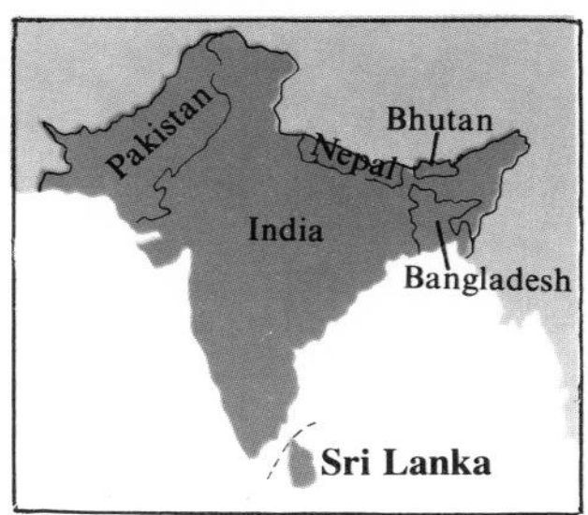

Sri Lanka

Sri Lanka is an island country off the southern tip of INDIA. Until recently, Sri Lanka was called Ceylon. The island is near the equator, and so the climate is tropical. Most of the tropical trees and shrubs have been cleared away to make room for crops, but there are still bamboo and palm trees. Animals such as elephants, leopards, monkeys, snakes and colorful birds live in the wilder areas.

Over half of the people of Sri Lanka are Sinhalese, who are Buddhists. Other groups include the Tamils, who are Hindus, the Moors who are Muslims and the Burghers, who are Christian descendants of Dutch and Portuguese settlers. From time to time there has been strife between Sinhalese and Tamils.

AREA: 25,334 SQ. MILES (65,610 SQ. KM)
POPULATION: 15,398,000
CAPITAL: COLOMBO
CURRENCY: RUPEE
OFFICIAL LANGUAGE: SINHALA

S

St. 1. an abbreviation for saint. *St. Francis of Assisi.* 2. an abbreviation for street. *Chestnut St.*

stab *vb.* wound someone with a knife or another sharp weapon. *n.* a wound.

stable 1. *n.* a building for horses and cattle. 2. *adj.* steady, firmly fixed.

stack *n.* & *vb.* arrange things on top of each other in an orderly pile.

stadium *n.* a large roofless building with tiers of seats surrounding a field or track, where people gather to play or watch sports, such as football, baseball, etc.

staff *n.* 1. a group of people who work together. *There are four teachers on the staff of this school.* 2. a long, thick stick.

stag *n.* a male deer.

stage 1. *n.* the raised platform in a theater on which people perform plays. *vb.* put on a play. 2. *n.* a point in the development of something. *What stage have you reached with your project?*

stagecoach *n.* a horse-drawn passenger vehicle running regularly between established stops.

► Before RAILROADS were invented, many people traveled in stagecoaches. A stagecoach was rather like a big box on wheels. Up to eight passengers climbed in through doors and sat on two rows of facing seats, like the seats in the compartment of a modern railroad car. The seats were often hard. Traveling became easier when stagecoaches were given springs and cushions.

The driver of the stagecoach sat on an open seat outside to drive the team of horses that pulled the coach. Often there were hard seats on the outside for extra passengers. As many as six horses were used to pull a stagecoach. Every 20 miles (32 km) or so, the driver had to stop to get fresh horses. Even a fresh team took an hour to cover 10 miles (16 km).

stagger *vb.* walk unsteadily.

stagnant *adj.* water that is standing still and is therefore not fresh. **stagnate** *vb.*

stain 1. *n.* a mark or colored patch on something. *The teacher had an egg stain on his tie.* 2. *vb.* mark; change the color of something; dye.

► **Stained glass** is a colored sheet of glass. Pieces of glass of different colors are put together to create a picture. In the MIDDLE AGES craftsmen made stained glass windows for churches. The windows showed scenes from Bible stories. When sunlight shines in through stained glass windows, the pictures glow with rich colors – especially red, blue and green.

Craftsmen still make stained glass. They color it by adding chemicals to the molten (melted) GLASS as it is being made. Artists also use enamel paint to paint details on the glass. The glass is then baked so that the enamel melts into the surface of the glass. Then the pieces of glass are fitted together to make the picture. Strips of lead hold all the pieces in place.

staircase *n.* a set of stairs, complete with banisters, etc.

Part of a stained glass window in Norwich Cathedral, England. It shows St. Benedict, founder of the Benedictine Order, surrounded by some of his monks.

stairs *pl. n.* a series of steps in a staircase.

stalactite *n.* an icicle-shaped stone structure hanging from the roof of a cave. **Stalagmites** are similar but grow upward from the floor.

► Stalactites and stalagmites are found in caves hollowed out of limestone rock. They get their names from Greek works that mean "dripping." This is because both are made by water dripping from the ceilings of caves. The water may hold tiny particles of a mineral called calcite. As the water dries up, it leaves a little calcite behind. After a long time, this grows into stalactites and stalagmites.

stale *adj.* not fresh; old.

Stalingrad, Battle of
The Battle of Stalingrad was one of the most important battles of World War II. It lasted for five months in 1942 and ended in the defeat of the Germans by the Soviet forces. When the German army failed to capture the city of Stalingrad (now Volgograd), it was forced to retreat with the loss of more than 300,000 men. Bitter cold and lack of supplies took a heavy toll on the Germans.

Stalin, Joseph
Joseph Stalin (1879–1953) was the head of the Communist Party and the leader of the Soviet Union for a quarter of a century until his death. He was infamous for the ruthless way he ran the country, but was successful at defeating Germany in World War II and made his nation a major world power. (*see* COMMUNISM)

stalk (rhymes with *walk*) 1. *adj.* the stem of a plant. 2. *n.* & *vb.* follow or pursue something or someone secretly.

stall 1. *n.* a table or a stand in a marketplace. 2. *n.* a division of a barn or stable for one animal. 3. *vb.* stopping a car engine by mistake.

stallion *n.* a male horse.

stamen *n.* the male part of the flower that holds the pollen.

stamina *n.* staying power, endurance.

stammer *n.* a speech fault in which the person repeats the sound at the beginning of words. *"I c-c-can't s-s-see."* *vb.* speak with a stammer.

stamp 1. *vb.* bang your foot on the ground. 2. *n.* a small label bought at a post office, which has to go on letters and parcels.

► A stamp can be a special mark, or a piece of printed paper with a sticky back. A PASSPORT and many other kinds of document must bear the correct government stamp. Postage stamps are stuck on letters and parcels to be carried by the post office. Each nation has its own

The penny black of 1840 was the first postage stamp with a sticky back.

A 19th-century stagecoach. It could travel about 10 miles (16 kilometers) an hour along good roads.

postage stamps. Millions of people collect postage stamps. Some kinds are scarce and valuable.

Postage stamps werer first issued in Britain in 1840. They were the idea of a man called Rowland Hill.

stand 1. *vb.* (past **stood**) be upright, in place. *The statue stands in the middle of the square.* 2. *n.* something on which things can be displayed, like a small, high table.
standard *n.* 1. something by which things can be compared or measured. *This ruler is not the standard size. It's much too short.* 2. a flag on a pole, usually raised to show loyalty to a country or its government.
stand-in *n.* someone who acts for another person when that person cannot be there. **stand in** *vb.*
stand out *vb.* be conspicuous.
stand up to *vb.* defend oneself against.
stank *vb.* past of **stink**.
stanza *n.* a division of a poem, a group of lines.
star *n.* 1. one of the tiny shining lights you see in the sky at night. Stars are really very large, and all except our sun are many millions of miles away. 2. a famous singer or actor.
► Stars are heavenly bodies giving off vast amounts of light or other radiant energy produced by nuclear fusion reactions. Some stars are millions of times larger than the earth. The sun is a relatively small star called a dwarf. *Binary stars* consist of two separate stars orbiting around a common point. *Pulsars* are stars that emit pulses of energy.

starboard *n.* & *adj.* the right side of a ship when you are facing toward the front, or bow.
starch *n.* an important food substance formed in plants. *vb.* stiffen with starch.
► Starches are a group of white powders produced by green plants. Each plant makes its own type of starch. But all starch is made of carbon, oxygen and hydrogen, the same ingredients found in SUGAR. Starches and sugars are foods called *carbohydrates*. Carbohydrates give plants energy for growth. Plants store energy as starch in their leaves, stems or roots.

CEREALS and POTATOES are rich in starch. If we eat these foods, their starches change to sugars that give our bodies energy.

stare *vb.* & *n.* look hard or searchingly for a long time.
starfish *n.* a creature of the seabed with a disk-shaped body and five or more arms.
► Starfish do not have backbones. But they have a SKELETON made up of bony plates. They creep about on tiny tube feet arranged along the underside of their arms.
Seawater that enters the starfish's body is squeezed down into these tubes. As the water is sucked back up into the body, the tips of the feet form suckers that will cling to solid objects.

Many starfish have tiny spines on their upper sides, which they use to protect themselves. If one arm of a starfish is cut off, the creature can grow a new one to replace it.

A starfish can open and eat a cockle. It uses its tube feet to grip both halves of the cockle's shell. Then it pulls the shell open. The starfish pushes part of its stomach out of its mouth, which is under the middle of its body. The stomach slips inside the cockle shell and digests the cockle's soft body.

starlight *n.* light from the stars.
starling *n.* a common bird with glossy black, brown-spotted feathers.
Stars and Stripes *n.* the U.S. flag.
start 1. *n.* the beginning of something. 2. *vb.* begin. 3. *vb.* turn a motor on. *He was unable to start his car.*
startle *vb.* surprise someone.
starve *vb.* grow ill from not having enough food, or from not having any at all. **starvation** *n.*
state 1. *n.* how something or someone is. *The garden is in an untidy state.* 2. *n.* a country, or division of a country. *There are 50 states in the United States of America.* 3. *vb.* say in words something. *This book states that the king is dead.*
stately *adj.* dignified, grand.
statement *n.* a formal description or detailed account of something.
station *n.* 1. a place with platforms and buildings where trains stop to pick up and drop off passengers. 2. a place that provides a public service, e.g. a fire station.
stationary *adj.* standing still, not moving.
stationery *n.* the paper, pens, pencils, ink and other materials used for writing.
statistics *pl. n.* the science of collecting figures, studying them and drawing conclusions about their meaning. For example, a bus company might count how many people travel by bus to work each day to help decide what kind of buses and how many to run on its routes.
statue *n.* a model in stone or metal of an animal, person, etc.
stay *vb.* remain; live somewhere for a time. *n.* a period of staying.
steady *adj.* firmly positioned; well-balanced. *vb.* make steady, stable.
steak (rhymes with *make*) *n.* a thick slice of meat or fish.
steal *vb.* (past **stole** past part. **stolen**) take something that does not belong to you by theft.
steam *n.* & *vb.* water so hot it has turned into water vapor, or gas.
steam engine *n.* an engine or locomotive powered by steam.
► Boiling water turns into steam. Steam will fill 1,700 times more space than the water that it came from. So if you squash steam into a small container it presses hard against the sides. If one side is free to move, the steam pressure will push it outward.

In the 1700s British inventors began to use this fact to build engines powered by steam. Early steam engines worked with a simple back and forth motion. In Thomas Newcomen's engine a furnace heated water in a boiler. The water gave off steam that pushed a piston up inside a cylinder. When the steam cooled and turned back to water, air pressed

Below: A steam locomotive. The steam is made in the boiler. When the driver opens the regulator valve, steam under high pressure passes from the boiler to the valves in the cylinders and pushes the pistons which drive the wheels.

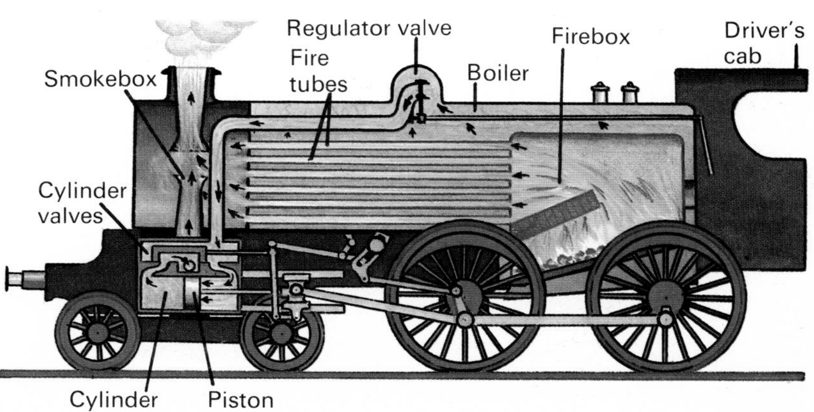

S

the piston down again. Newcomen's engine was used to pump water from flooded mines.

James WATT built a more powerful engine where steam pushed the piston first one way and then the other. Rods from the piston spun a wheel. By the early 1800s, such engines were moving heavy loads faster than people or horses could. Yet, unlike people and horses, steam engines never tired.

Steam engines powered factory machines that made the INDUSTRIAL REVOLUTION possible. They also powered LOCOMOTIVES and steamships. For the first time, people traveled faster than horses or the wind.

The INTERNAL COMBUSTION ENGINE has largely taken the place of steam engines. But many ships' propellers and power station GENERATORS are worked by steam which spins wheels called TURBINES.

steamer *n.* a boat driven by the power of a steam engine.
steel *n.* a strong metal made from iron in a furnace.
► Steel is iron with a carbon content of up to about 1.5 percent. The carbon is present in the form of a compound called *cementite* (iron carbide). Adding carbon to iron increases the strength and hardness of the metal, and these qualities are adjusted by a heating process called *tempering*. Steel is made by first removing carbon and other impurities from molten iron or scrap steel and then adding an accurately measured amount of carbon. Stainless steel and other steel ALLOYS are made by adding carbon and metals such as chromium, manganese and tungsten.

steep *adj.* sloping sharply.
steeple *n.* a tall pointed tower on a church or other building.
steer *vb.* control the direction of a vehicle, ship, etc.
stem *n.* the stalk of a plant, the part that grows up from the ground.
stench *n.* unpleasant smell.
stencil *n.* a flat sheet of metal, plastic or special paper into which words, patterns, etc., are cut. They can be copied by passing ink or paint through the holes onto paper or other materials. *vb.* use a stencil.
step 1. one of the movements you make when you walk, run or dance. 2. one of the flat parts of a stairway or ladder, where you put your feet when you climb them. 3. a stage in a process.
step- *prefix* indicating a relationship through remarriage, e.g. **stepchild, stepdaughter, stepfather,** etc.

Stephenson, George
George Stephenson (1781–1848) was a British engineer and inventor. He began work as a mining engineer, and built a locomotive to pull coal cars. In 1825 he drove his engine, *Locomotive*, on the Stockton-to-Darlington railway line. This was the first public passenger train. His most famous locomotive, the *Rocket*, was built in 1829.

stereo or **stereophonic sound** *n.* sound that is put through two or more loudspeakers.
sterilize *vb.* destroy all germs with heat or strong antiseptic. **sterile** *n.* free of germs; unable to bear offspring.
sterling *n.* the money of Great Britain. *adj.* made of sterling silver.
stern 1. *adj.* strict or severe. 2. *n.* the back end of a boat or ship.
stethoscope *n.* an instrument used to listen to people's heartbeats and the sound of their breathing.
► Stethoscopes means roughly, "chest watchers." Stethoscopes magnify (make louder) the sounds inside the body, and so help doctors to listen to the lungs and heart. A modern stethoscope has two earpieces joined by rubber tubes to a disk or bell-shaped end, which the doctor places on the patient's chest.

Stethoscopes were invented in the early 1800s by the French doctor Rene Laënnec. He got the idea after watching a child tap one end of a log while another child listened at the other end. Laënnec's stethoscope was just a wooden tube.

Stevenson, Robert Louis
Robert Louis Stevenson (1850–94) was a Scottish author of adventure stories such as *Treasure Island*, an exciting tale about a hunt for pirate treasure. *Kidnapped* is an adventure story set in the wilds of Scotland in the 1700s. Stevenson also described his own travels, and wrote *A Child's Garden of Verses*.

stew *n.* & *vb.* a meat and vegetable mixture, usually boiled slowly for a long time.
steward *n.* a man who looks after people, often on a train or plane.
stewardess *n.* a woman who looks after people, often on a train or plane.
stick 1. *n.* a wooden rod or twig. 2. *vb.* glue or fix things together.
sticker *n.* an adhesive label.
stick up for *vb.* support someone who is in trouble. *I knew it wasn't Ted's fault so I tried to stick up for him when the others blamed him.*
stiff *adj.* not easily bent, rigid.
still 1. *adj.* motionless; soundless. *Please keep still.* 2. *adv.* even so, however. *I can still hear them walking.* 3. *n.* apparatus used in distilling alcohol.

stilts *pl. n.* a pair of poles on which you can stand and walk above the ground. **stilted** *adj.* stiff, pompous.
stimulus *n.* something that makes you active or energetic; an incentive. **stimulate** *vb.*
stinger *n.* a sharp organ of some plants and animals to protect themselves. *Wasp stings hurt. vb.* wound by pricking.
stingy *adj.* not generous, mean.
stink *vb.* & *n.* smell bad.
stir *vb.* 1. move liquid around with a utensil. *Steve forgot to stir the soup, and it burned.* 2. rouse.
stirrup *n.* a metal support that hangs on each side of a horse's saddle, into which the rider puts his or her feet.
stitch *n.* (plural **stitches**) one of the loops of thread made in cloth when you are sewing or in yarn when you are knitting. *vb.* sew.
stoat *n.* a small, slim mammal of the weasel family with a black-tipped tail and reddish brown fur.
► Stoats live in the countries of northern Europe. The stoat's body, including its tail, is about 12 in. (30 cm) long. It eats rabbits and smaller animals, such as rats and mice. In the far north its fur turns white in winter, and is known as *ermine*. But it keeps the black tip on its tail.

stock *n.* 1. goods kept to be used or sold. *I keep a large stock of paper in that closet.* 2. a share in a company.

Stock Exchange
A stock exchange is a place where people called stockbrokers buy and sell *stocks* and *shares*. These are pieces of paper that show that someone owns a share in a business company. A company's stock tends to cost more if the company does well, and gets cheaper if it does badly. People buy stock hoping to sell it at a higher price later. Meanwhile they expect to get *dividends* – shares of the money the company makes.

As business grew after the Middle Ages, people needed a market place for buying and selling stock. In 1531 Antwerp opened Europe's first stock exchange. Now, many cities have stock exchanges. Millions of stocks change hands each day in the exchanges of New York, London and Tokyo.

Stockholm
Stockholm is the capital of SWEDEN. It stands on a group of islands on the BALTIC Sea coast. It is a handsome city with wide streets and attractive parks. Stockholm is a commercial, industrial and cultural center. It was founded in the 1200s, and became the capital of Sweden in 1436. The Royal Palace contains many art treasures.

stocking *n.* a covering for the leg; a long sock.

Stonehenge at sunset.

stole *vb.* past of **steal**.
stomach *n.* organ in the middle part of your body, into which food goes after it is swallowed and where digestion begins. *vb.* endure, tolerate, put up with.
► In human beings, the stomach is a pear-shaped sac. At one end it is connected by the *esophagus* to the mouth. The other end is joined to the small intestine. The stomach breaks down food by kneading it with digestive juices. It turns it into a semi-fluid mass called *chyme*.

stone *n.* 1. a kind of rock. *The statue was made from stone.* 2. a small piece of rock. *I've got a stone in my shoe.* 3. the hard seed of some fruits, e.g. plums, cherries. 4. a gem, a precious stone. 5. a measure of weight, the same as 14 pounds.

Stone Age
The Stone Age was the great span of time before people learned how to make metal tools. Stone Age people used stone, wood and bone instead of metal. The Stone Age probably began more than three million years ago. It ended in Iraq and EGYPT when the BRONZE AGE began there about 5,000 years ago. But some Australian ABORIGINES and forest tribes in New Guinea still live largely Stone Age lives.

The Stone Age had three parts: *Old*, *Middle* and *New*. The Old Stone Age lasted until 10,000 years ago in the Middle East. When it began, hunters could scarcely chip a pebble well enough to sharpen it. When the Old Stone Age ended, people had learned to chip flint into delicate spearheads, knives and scrapers.

In the Middle Stone Age, hunters used tiny flakes of flint in arrows and harpoons.

The New Stone Age began in the Middle East about 9,000 years ago. New Stone Age peoples made smooth ax heads of ground stone. Farming replaced hunting in the New Stone Age.

Stonehenge
Stonehenge is a huge prehistoric temple on Salisbury Plain in southern England. The main part is a great circle of standing stones. Each is more than twice as tall as a person and weighs nearly 30 tons. Flat stones were laid across the tops of the standing stones to form a ring. Inside the ring stood smaller stones and a great block that may have been an altar. The big stones were raised 3,500 years ago. Other parts are older.

stood *vb.* past of **stand**.
stool *n.* a seat or chair without a back or arms.
stoop *vb.* bend the body; condescend *n.* a habitual bend in the back. *My grandfather has a slight stoop.*
stop *vb.* 1. come to a halt. *The car stopped at the traffic lights.* 2. prevent. *n.* a halt, pause.
store 1. *n.* a large shop. 2. *vb.* keep things until they are needed. *Squirrels store nuts.*
stork *n.* a tall white bird with a long beak and legs, and wide wings.
► Storks can wade in swamps and capture fish and frogs. But some kinds prefer feeding on dead animals. There are more than a dozen kinds of stork living in warm parts of the world.

The white stork is the best known kind. In the summer, white storks nest in Europe and central Asia. In the fall, they fly south. Flapping their wings soon makes storks tired. They prefer to soar and glide.

storm *n.* a very strong wind with rain, hail, snow, thunder, etc.
story *n.* (plural **stories**) 1. one floor of a building. *My bedroom is on the third story.* 2. a fictional narrative. *Please tell me a story.*
stout *adj.* thick and heavy.
stove *n.* an apparatus used for cooking food or heating.
stowaway *n.* someone who hides in a ship, aircraft or some other form of transport, in order to travel in secret or without paying.
straight 1. *adj.* not bent or crooked. *You can draw a straight line with a ruler.* 2. *adv.* directly. *Did you come straight home from school?*
straightaway *adv.* immediately. *n.* section of road having no curves.
straighten *vb.* make something right, correct or straight. *Henry asked me to help him straighten the carpet.*
strain *vb.* 1. push, stretch or try too hard; injure by overusing. *n.* 2. drain liquid from a solid through a cloth or net of small holes.
strait *n.* a narrow channel of water connecting two larger bodies of water.
strand *n.* a thread.
strange *adj.* odd; unusual.
stranger *n.* someone you don't know.
strangle *vb.* kill by pressing hard on the throat, choke. **strangulation** *n.*
strap *n.* a strip of leather or some other material used to fasten or hold things. *vb.* fasten with straps.

In many parts of Europe storks nest on chimneys.

S

strategy *n.* the art of planning a military campaign, political or economic policy, etc.

Stratosphere
The stratosphere is a layer of the earth's atmosphere that starts between six and 10 miles (10 and 16 km) up. It extends to a height of about 30 miles (50 km). Airplanes climb into the stratosphere, where there is very little wind.

stratum *n.* (plural **strata**) a layer (of rock, clouds, etc.)

Strauss, Richard
Richard Strauss (1864–1949) was a German composer who could play the piano well at the age of four. He is known chiefly for his tone poems such as *Don Juan, Till Eulenspiegel* and *Don Quixote*. He also wrote several operas, among them *Salome* and *Der Rosenkavalier*. He was also a famous conductor.

Stravinsky, Igor
Igor Stravinsky (1882–1971) was an American composer who was born in Russia. He is best known for his ballet music, *The Firebird, Petrouchka* and *The Rite of Spring*. In these he collaborated with the great ballet manager Sergei Diaghilev.

straw *n.* 1. dry stalks of grain. 2. a thin tube for drinking through.
strawberry *n.* a small plant belonging to the rose family, with white flowers and red fruit.
► Strawberries grow on low, bushy plants. They can be grown outside in countries around the world, including southern Canada, central Europe and Japan. There are also many strawberry farms in the United States.
Strawberries contain a lot of sugar. They also have large amounts of VITAMIN C – even more than oranges and lemons.

stray *vb.* wander away. *The fence was broken and so the cows could stray onto the road.*
streak 1. *n.* irregular band of color. *The white marble is streaked with red.* 2. *vb.* rush past.
stream *n.* 1. a brook; a small river. 2. a flow of anything.
streamline *vb.* design (a vehicle, etc.) with a smooth shape to cut down wind resistance.
► Ships that are built with smooth, curving sides move through the water faster and more easily than any other. This is because there is nothing to get in the way of the water or stop it from moving quickly around the ship. This sort of ship design is called *streamlined.*
Other things are also designed in a streamlined way. Airplanes with smooth tapering wings and bodies allow the air to pass around the plane easily, and not slow it down. River bridges with smooth curves create fewer waves and whirlpools around them, and so they are safer. Automobiles, too, are usually streamlined.

street *n.* a road lined with buildings, particularly in a town.
strength *n.* how strong something or someone is. *Walter did not have the strength to lift the barrel by himself.* **strengthen** *vb.* make or become stronger.
stress 1. *n.* tension, strain. 2. (in mechanics) pressure or force exerted on a body. 3. *vb.* & *n.* emphasis. *I cannot stress too much the importance of a good diet.*
stretch 1. *vb.* pull something out so as to make it bigger. 2. *n.* a length of time or a distance. *Janet could see a long stretch of road ahead of the car.*
stretcher *n.* a movable bed for carrying sick or injured people.
strict *adj.* stern; exact; inflexible.
stride *vb.* (past **strode**) walk with long steps. *n.* a long step; a pace.
strife *n.* conflict, struggle.
strike 1. *n.* hit hard. 2. *vb.* stop work as a protest against the people who employ you. *n.* when people strike. *The workers have been on strike for six weeks now.*
string *n.* thin cord or rope.
strip 1. *n.* a long narrow piece of material. 2. *vb.* take off all your clothes; deprive; tear off.
stripe *n.* a band of color, especially on clothing and other fabric. **striped** *adj.*
strive *vb.* (past **strove**) try hard. *You must strive to do better.*
strode *vb.* past of **stride**.
stroke 1. *vb.* move your hand gently over something. *Carol liked to stroke her cat's soft fur.* 2. *n.* a serious illness which can result in paralysis (being unable to move all or part of the body.)
stroll (rhymes with *pole*) *vb.* & *n.* walk along slowly.
strong *adj.* powerful; having great strength; difficult to break.
stronghold *n.* a castle, fortified place.
strong point *n.* what a person is particularly good at doing.
struck *vb.* past of **strike**.
structure *n.* anything that has been built. *A house is a structure, and so is a table.*
struggle *n.* hard contest. *vb.* strive; violent effort; fight, usually using your whole body. *Jenny had to struggle to free herself from the rope.*
strum *vb.* play a musical instrument lightly with the fingers.
strut *n.* a wooden or iron bar which strengthens a framework.

Stuarts
The House of Stuart was a royal family that ruled Scotland from 1371 to 1603 and England and Scotland from 1603 to 1715.
As royal rulers, the Stuarts were unlucky. Out of 14 who were crowned, six were killed, and seven became king or queen before they were old enough to rule for themselves.
MARY, QUEEN OF SCOTS was put to death by ELIZABETH I, who feared that Mary might replace her as the Queen of England. Mary's grandfather had been married to the daughter of an English king. So when Elizabeth died without leaving a child to inherit her throne, the crown went to Mary's son James. He ruled as JAMES I of England and as James VI of Scotland.
The Stuart kings of England claimed so much power that they became unpopular. CHARLES I was executed in the English CIVIL WAR, and CHARLES II's brother JAMES II was forced to leave the country. The throne went to his eldest daughter and her husband WILLIAM OF ORANGE, then to James's youngest daughter Anne. Under Anne, England and Scotland were united as Great Britain. Anne was the last Stuart ruler. She died in 1715.
Stuart supporters called Jacobites led two revolts to win back the throne for James's descendants. In 1715 they fought for his son, James Edward. In 1745 they fought for Charles Edward, James Edward's son "BONNIE PRINCE CHARLIE." Both revolts failed.

Engraved portrait of Charles Edward Stuart — "Bonnie Prince Charlie".

stub 1. *n.* short piece left after the main part has been used or removed. *A cigarette stub. vb.* extinguish (put out) by crushing. 2. *vb.* bump. *Donald stubbed his toe on the rock.*
stubborn *adj.* not willing to change, or to do what other people want.
student *n.* someone who is studying, usually at a school or a college.
studio *n.* an artist's workroom; a place for recording, broadcasting, or making films.
study 1. *vb.* read and learn; to look at something carefully. *He had to study the map for a long time before he*

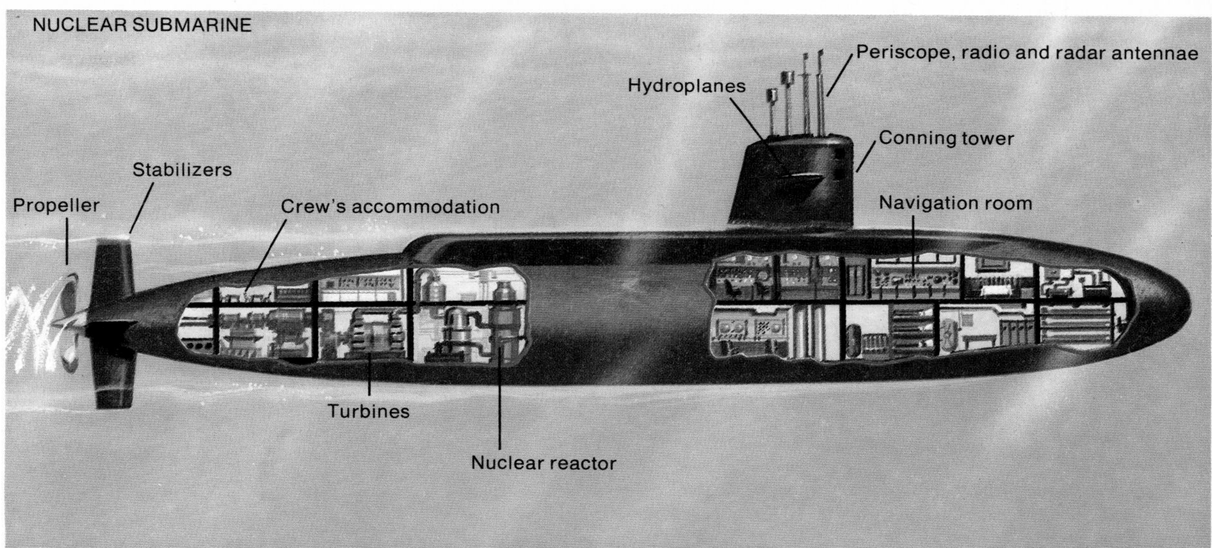

made the journey. 2. *n*. a room devoted to study or literary work.

stuff 1. *vb*. fill something with some kind of material. *My teddy bear is stuffed with wool.* 2. *n*. anything you don't know the name of. *What's the stuff your Dad mended the cup with?*

stuffy *adj*. having no fresh air, smelling stale and airless.

stumble *vb*. miss one's footing; come close to falling.

stump *n*. the short, stubby remains of something, such as the part of a tree that is left in the ground after the rest of it has been cut down.

stun *vb*. 1. make senseless with a blow on the head. 2. astonish.

stung *vb*. past of **sting**.

stunk *vb*. past part. of **stink**.

stunt 1. *vb*. stop the growth of. 2. *n*. a difficult feat, a showy performance (often for publicity).

stupid *adj*. slow of mind; dull.

sturdy *adj*. strong, well built.

sturgeon *n*. a toothless, sharklike fish valued for its roe (eggs) which are sold as a delicacy under the name of caviar.

► There are about 25 species of fresh- and saltwater sturgeon. The sturgeon has a long, slim body protected by rows of bony plates. Most kinds live in seas and swim up rivers to lay their eggs.

The largest sturgeon is the beluga, found in Russian waters. Belugas can grow to 26 ft. (8 meters) and weigh a ton. Sometimes they eat young seals.

stutter *vb*. stammer.

sty *n*. 1. a painful red swelling on the eyelid. 2. a pen in which pigs are kept; a pigsty.

style *n*. the way something is done or made. *Tim's shirt is the latest style, but he doesn't like it.* **stylish** *adj*. fashionable; having a good sense of style.

stylus *n*. a fine point used for playing records, etc.

sub- *prefix* meaning under, inferior, lower, e.g. **subhuman, subnormal, subsoil.**

subject *n*. 1. the thing that is being talked about or written about. *John is the subject of everyone's interest.* 2. someone who is ruled by a government, or by a king or queen.

submarine *n*. a kind of boat that can move under the water instead of on the surface. *adj*. under the sea.

► To make a submarine dive, the crew has to make the submarine heavier than the amount of water needed to fill the space taken up by the submarine. To rise, the crew makes it lighter than that amount of water. When water and submarine both weigh the same, the boat stays at the same level under the surface.

Ordinary submarines use battery-powered electric motors while they are underwater and diesel engines when cruising on the surface. Nuclear subs use heat from a nuclear reactor on board to drive a steam turbine. So nuclear subs can remain submerged for a long time.

In the 1870s an English clergyman invented a submarine powered by a steam engine. But each time it dived the crew had to pull down its chimney and put out the fire that heated water to produce steam.

By 1900 the American inventor John P. Holland had produced a much better underwater boat. Gasoline engines drove it on the surface. But gasoline needs air to burn. Under water the boat ran on

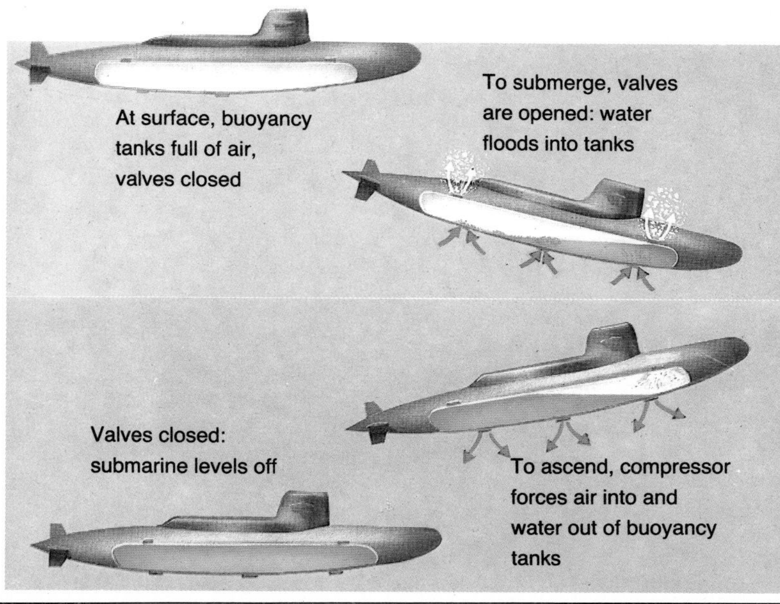

S

battery-driven motors that did not need air.

Submarines equipped with guns and TORPEDOES were used very effectively as weapons in both World War I and II. They destroyed thousands of tons of ships.

In 1955 came the first nuclear-powered submarine. Such boats can travel around the world without having to come up for air. Nuclear-powered submarines are warships. Today, people use the bathyscaphe and other underwater craft to explore the seabed. Small underwater boats called *submersibles* are used to carry out underwater work.

submerge *vb*. plunge, go or put under water.
subscribe *vb*. contribute, sign one's name to. **subscription** *n*.
subside *vb*. settle, sink back to normal. *The flood gradually subsided.*
subsidy *n*. financial help from a government to industry, farming, etc., to keep prices down.
subsidize *vb*. pay a subsidy to.
substance *n*. anything that can be seen or touched. **substantial** *adj*. solid, considerable.
substitute 1. *vb*. put in place of something else. *Peter substituted oil for butter when he cooked the onions.* 2. *n*. a player in a game who joins in for someone else. *Paul was only a substitute but he scored the winning goal.*
subtle *adj*. delicate, refined; difficult to understand or distinguish.
subtract *vb*. take away an amount from a total. **subtraction** *n*.
suburb *n*. the outlying parts of a town, usually where people live. **suburban** *adj*.
subway *n*. an underground tunnel, particularly one for pedestrians; an underground railway.
succeed *vb*. 1. achieve something you set out to do. 2. come after (a king or other important person.) *He succeeded his father as Duke of Dorset.* **success** *n*. achievement, a good outcome.
successful *adj*. able to do what you want to do or try to do.
such *adj*. of that kind. *How can you believe such stories?*
suck *vb*. pull into the mouth through suction. *Baby sucks his thumb.*
suckle *vb*. feed young at the breast; draw milk from the breast or udder.

Sudan (Sudanese)
This is the largest country in AFRICA. It is more than three times the size of Texas.

Sudan is a hot country in north-east Africa. Desert sprawls across the north. There are flat grasslands in the middle. The south has forests and a huge swamp.

Sudanese people include Arabs and Negroes. Most live near the NILE, which flows north across the country. The Sudanese raise cattle, grow crops like sugar cane, or work in cities.

AREA: 967, 553 SQ. MILES (2,505,813 SQ. KM)
POPULATION: 19,373,000
CAPITAL: KHARTOUM
CURRENCY: SUDANESE POUND
OFFICIAL LANGUAGE: ARABIC

sudden *adj*. happening quickly and without warning. *A sudden idea struck her.* **suddenly** *adv*.
sue *vb*. seek justice by legal action.
suede (*swade*) *n*. leather made from skin of a young goat (kid), cowhide, etc., with flesh side out.
suet *n*. fat that protects kidneys of cattle and sheep, used in cooking.

Suez Canal
The Suez Canal crosses Egypt between Port Said (pronounced *side*) on the Mediterranea Sea and the Suez on the Red Sea. It is the world's longest CANAL that can be used by big ships. It measures 100 miles (160 km) from end to end and 197 ft. (60 meters) across its bed. Ships use it as a short cut on voyages between Europe and Asia. This saves them sailing 6,000 miles (9,650 km) around southern Africa.

The canal was begun in 1859 by a French company run by the engineer Ferdinand de Lesseps. More than 8,000 men and hundreds of camels worked on it for 10 years. France and Britain operated the canal until Egypt took it over in 1956.

Sunken ships blocked the canal for eight years after Egypt's war with Israel in 1967. But DREDGING has now made it much wider and deeper than it was a century ago.

suffer *vb*. experience pain or unhappiness. **suffering** *n*.
sufficient *adj*. enough to meet one's needs; adequate; not too much.
suffix *n*. syllable(s) added at the end of a word to make another word, e.g. host host**ess**, red redd**ish**, king king**dom**.
suffocate *vb*. die from being unable to breathe. **suffocation** *n*.
sugar *n*. a sweet food.

► Sugar is one of a group of CARBOHYDRATES usually having a sweet taste. Sugars are important to plants (*see* PHOTOSYNTHESIS), and are vital to human life as they are easily digestible and provide an immediate source of energy (*see* GLUCOSE). The form of sugar commonly used as a foodstuff comes mostly from sugar cane, a tall grasslike plant grown in the tropics, and from sugar beet.

suggest *vb*. put forward an idea indirectly; hint.
suggestion *n*. plan, thought.
suicide *n*. die by killing yourself on purpose. **suicidal** *adj*.
suit 1. *n*. a jacket with trousers or skirt that are made to be worn together. 2. *vb*. be right for a certain purpose, convenient, appropriate. *It will suit me to go now, because I am not busy.* 3. *n*. a legal process. 4. one of the four sets in a pack of cards.
suitable *adj*. correct, right for what is needed. *That dress will be very suitable for traveling.*
suitcase *n*. a large bag or case for carrying clothes, etc., on a journey.
suite *n*. a set of rooms or matched furniture. *A three-room suite.*
sulfur *n*. a nonmetallic element often found in the form of yellow crystals (symbol – *S*).

► Sulfur is found as yellow crystalline rock in the region of VOLCANOES and hot springs. Plastic sulfur is formed by pouring molten sulfur into cold water. Flowers of sulfur is a fine powder made by condensing sulfur vapor. Sulfur is used to make drugs, gunpowder, SULFURIC ACID and numerous chemical products.

Most sulfur is made into sulfuric acid, the most important of all industrial chemicals. The largest use of the acid is in the production of fertilizers such as ammonium sulfate. Vast quantities are used in metal refining, electroplating and making artificial fibers.

The United States is the world's largest sulfur producer. Much of it is mined underground by an ingenious method. It is melted by steam and then pumped while molten to the surface.

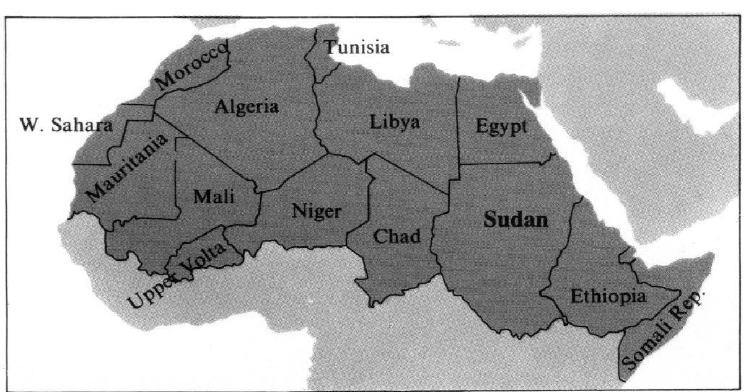

sulfuric acid *n*. an extremely corrosive, colorless, oily acid widely used in the chemical industry.
sulk *vb*. be in a bad temper. **sulky** *adj*.
sullen *adj*. silently bad-tempered.
sultan *n*. a king or sovereign of a Muslim state.
sultana *n*. a light-colored seedless grape grown for raisins and wines; a sultan's wife.
sum *n*. 1. the whole amount. 2. the result of added numbers.

Sumerians
A civilization that flourished in the southern part of BABYLON some 5,000 years ago. From about 3000 B.C. to 1900 B.C. the Sumerians were the most important nation of the Middle East. They were the first people to write down their language, in a script known as *cuneiform*. They wrote on clay tablets that were baked to harden, and were kept in libraries.

summarize *vb*. give a short account, sum up. **summary** *n*. a brief account of the main facts.
summer *n*. the warmest season of the year, between spring and fall.
summit *n*. top, highest point, peak.
summon *vb*. call together.
sum up *vb*. state concisely.
sun *n*. The sun is the central body in the solar system and the nearest star to the earth.
► Compared with other stars, the sun is relatively small and dim. Astronomers describe it as a yellow dwarf. But because it is only 93 million miles (150 million kilometers) away from us, the sun appears large and bright. Heat, light and other forms of electromagnetic waves are produced by nuclear reactions in the sun's core. A little of this energy reaches the earth, thus making life possible on our planet. At its core, the sun's temperature is about 27,000,000°F (15,000,000°C) while its surface temperature is a relatively cool 11,000°F (6,000°C). Roughly round in shape, the sun has a diameter of about 865,000 miles (1,392,000 km). It consists of gases, mostly hydrogen (90 percent) and helium (8 percent).

sunburn *n*. red or brown coloring of the skin caused by over exposure to sunlight.
Sunday *n*. the first day of the week; the Christian day of worship; named after the sun.
sundial *n*. a kind of clock that shows the time by a shadow the sun makes on a dial.
► Sundials are probably the oldest tool for measuring time. People may have used some kind of sundial in Egypt, 3,000 years ago. But they can be used only when the sun is shining.
Most sundials have a flat metal dial, with the edge marked off in hours. A pointed piece of metal, called a *gnomen*, sticks up in the middle of the dial. When the sun shines, the shadow of the gnomen falls across the dial. The edge of the shadow marks the time of day. It moves around with the sun.

sunflower *n*. a tall plant with a large, flat flower edged with yellow petals.
► The sunflower grows on a stem that carries big, broad leaves. The flowers try to twist around to keep facing the sun.
Garden sunflowers live less than a year. But in that time one seed once produced a plant about 23 ft. (7 meters) high.
People cook food in the oil that comes from crushed sunflower seeds. The crushed seeds themselves make a useful food for cattle.

sung *vb*. past part. of **sing**.
sunk *vb*. past part. of **sink**.
sunlight *n*. the light of the sun.
sunny *adj*. bright with sunshine.
sunrise *n*. dawn, morning, the time when the sun comes up.
sunset *n*. dusk, evening, the time when the sun goes down (**sundown**).
sunshine *n*. direct rays from the sun.
sunspots *pl. n*. dark patches that appear from time to time on the surface of the sun.
► Sunspots may last for months or disappear within a few hours. Sunspots appear dark because their temperature is about 3,600°F (2,000°C) lower than the surrounding temperature. The cause of sunspots is unknown, but their occurrence reaches a peak every 11 years and is associated with eruptions on the surface of the sun called flares and prominences.

super- *prefix* meaning above, over, more than, on top (of).
superb *adj*. excellent, magnificent.
superficial *adj*. on the surface.
superior *adj*. higher; better.
superlative *adj*. the best.
supermarket *n*. a large self-service shop where customers can buy food and many other goods.

supernatural *adj*. something that does not have an ordinary explanation.
supersede *vb*. take the place of.
supersonic *adj*. faster than the speed of sound.
► **Supersonic flight**. At sea level, the speed of sound is about 760 miles (1,220 km) per hour. At higher altitudes, the air is thinner and the speed of sound decreases. Supersonic speeds are often expressed in terms of a Mach number; i.e. the speed in relation to the local speed of sound. A rocket traveling at Mach 3, for example, is moving at three times the local speed of sound. When an aircraft flies at supersonic speed, shock waves build up and are heard as "sonic booms" on the ground. These sometimes break windows and cause other damage. Aircraft designed for supersonic flight have a pointed nose and sweptback wings to reduce problems that are associated with shock waves.

superstitious *adj*. believing in luck, chance and magic happenings. **superstition** *n*.
supervise *vb*. oversee, watch over, control. **supervision** *n*.
supper *n*. a meal eaten at the end of the day.
supple *adj*. easy to bend; not stiff. *Athletes have to be supple*.
supply *vb*. **supplied** *past*. 1. give

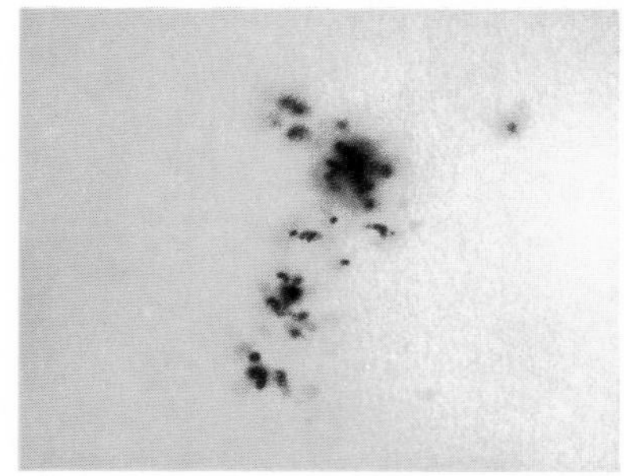

what is needed. *I will supply you with a book*. 2. *n*. things that are kept to be used later. *We have a large supply of pencils*.
support *vb*. hold up; help; supply with a home and food; regularly watch or attend, e.g. football. **supporter** *n*.
suppose *vb*. think that something is so, although it may not be. *Let's suppose that it will take us two hours*.
suppress *vb*. put down, crush; (of information) conceal. *The enemy suppressed the news of the defeat*.
supreme *adj*. the greatest; most excellent, reliable, etc.
sure *adj*. certain. *Are you sure that is true*? **surely** *adv*.
surf *n*. waves breaking on the shore of a beach.
surface *n*. outer or upper part of something. *The astronauts landed on*

the surface of the moon. vb. bring or come to the surface. *The truth will surface.*

Surface tension
Surface tension is the force that makes the surfaces of liquids behave in certain ways. It is surface tension that makes drops of water form into a ball, because a sphere has the smallest possible area for the enclosed volume of water. It also allows a needle to be floated on the surface of clean water. It is just as if there were a thin skin covering the surface.

An important effect of surface tension is called *capillarity*. This causes liquids to rise in tubes of small size. If a narrow tube is dipped into a glass of water, the water will rise in the tube to a height perhaps several inches above the level of the water in the glass.

surgeon *n.* a doctor who operates on people.

surgery *n.* treating disease or injuries by operating.
► Surgery is a branch of medicine that deals with injury and disease mainly by operating on the body with instruments. Surgeons can cut away diseased parts, remove objects that have lodged themselves in the body and repair broken tissues. Early surgeons dealt mainly with blood-letting, the lancing of infections and the removal of limbs. They made no use of painkillers. Today surgeons can replace kidneys, transplant hearts, repair bone with metal or plastic pins, remove organs, graft skin and carry out many other operations.

Surinam
Surinam is a republic in north-eastern SOUTH AMERICA. It was formerly called Dutch Guiana. The climate is tropical and rainfall is heavy. Farming and forestry are important, but bauxite is the most valuable resource. Britain founded a colony in Surinam in 1650. However, the area was ruled by the Dutch for most of the period until full independence was granted in 1975.
AREA: 63,040 SQ. MILES (163,265 SQ. KM)
POPULATION: 404,000
CAPITAL: PARAMARIBO
CURRENCY: GUILDER
OFFICIAL LANGUAGES: DUTCH, ENGLISH

surly *adj.* bad-tempered, sullen.
surname *n.* your family name. *My name is Anne Bell, so my surname is Bell.*
surpass *vb.* do better than; go beyond.
surplus *adj.* & *n.* what is left over when need or use is satisfied.
surprise *n.* something that happens unexpectedly. *The party was a lovely surprise. vb.* attack or come upon suddenly; astonish. **surprising** *adj.*
surrender *vb.* give in. *The soldiers had to surrender when they lost the battle.* to give up possession of.
surround *vb.* enclose, or be all around. *Flower gardens surround our house.* **surroundings.** *pl. n.*
survey *vb.* 1. take a look at a view. 2. look carefully at a house or other building before it is sold, to check that there is nothing wrong with it. 3. measure an area of land. **surveying** *n.* the measurement and mapping of parts of the earth's surface.
► Surveys are used to locate and define features such as rivers, lakes and coastlines, and to show the height of land areas. Surveying is also used in marking out property boundaries.

Surveyors use measuring instruments and work out certain sums to find the exact positions of places on the earth's surface. This kind of information makes it possible for people to make maps and charts and to build bridges, roads and so on.

Photographs taken from an airplane are a modern way of making maps. The photographs are taken in strips, each picture slightly overlapping the one next to it. Special instruments can then turn the photographs into a map of the area covered.

survive *vb.* remain alive, especially through changes or difficult times. **survivor** *n.* a person who survives.
suspect (*su*-**spekt**) *vb.* have a feeling that something is true, although you are not sure; doubt. *I suspect that someone has worn my bathing suit because it seems damp.* (**sus**-*pekt*) *n.* a person who is suspected of having done something (usually bad.)
suspend *vb.* 1. hang something up. 2. stop, cancel or postpone something.
suspense *n.* state of anxiety or excitement while waiting for something to happen.
suspicion *n.* mistrust, a feeling that something is wrong.
sustain *vb.* 1. hold up, support. 2. suffer (an injury, etc.).
swallow 1. *vb.* make food go down your throat. 2. *n.* a small bird with long, slim wings and a forked tail.
► This fast, agile flier opens its short beak wide to catch insects in the air. Swallows have short legs. They perch better than they walk. They build nests of mud and straw on or inside buildings. Swallows that nest in northern lands fly south to warmer countries for the winter.

swam *vb.* past of **swim**.
swamp 1. *n.* a bog or marsh. 2. *vb.* overwhelm by an excess; flood.
swan *n.* a graceful long-necked water bird with paddling feet.
► Swans are among the heaviest birds able to fly. In order to take off, they need a long, clear stretch of water.

Swans swim with webbed feet, lowering their necks to feed on underwater plants. They build bulky nests by pools or rivers. Their young are known as *cygnets*.

Some kinds of swan fly south in spring and fall. They fly in V-shaped flocks.

swank *vb.* & *n.* (a) show off.
swap *vb.* exchange one thing for something else. *Will you swap your lunch for mine?*
swarm *n.* a large group of bees or other insects. *vb.* form a swarm.
swastika *n.* two kinds of cross, one the symbol of the Nazis in Germany, the other a religious symbol in India.
sway *vb.* swing slowly back and forth.

Swaziland
Swaziland is a landlocked kingdom

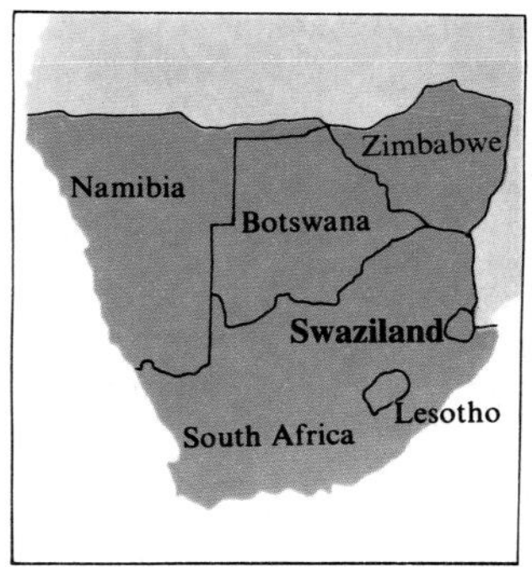

in southern AFRICA. It lies between SOUTH AFRICA and MOZAMBIQUE. Most people work on the land, but mining is also important. Britain ruled the area from 1902 until full independence was granted to Swaziland in 1968.
AREA: 6,704 SQ. MILES (17,363 SQ. KM)
POPULATION: 581,000
CAPITAL: MBABANE
CURRENCY: LILANGENI
OFFICIAL LANGUAGE: ENGLISH

swear *vb.* 1. use bad language, words that many people do not think right. 2. make a solemn promise, vow. *The knight had to swear to obey his king.*
sweat (rhymes with *wet*) *vb.* & *n.* the liquid that comes out of your skin when you are hot or nervous.

sweater *n.* a knitted or crocheted garment for the top of your body.

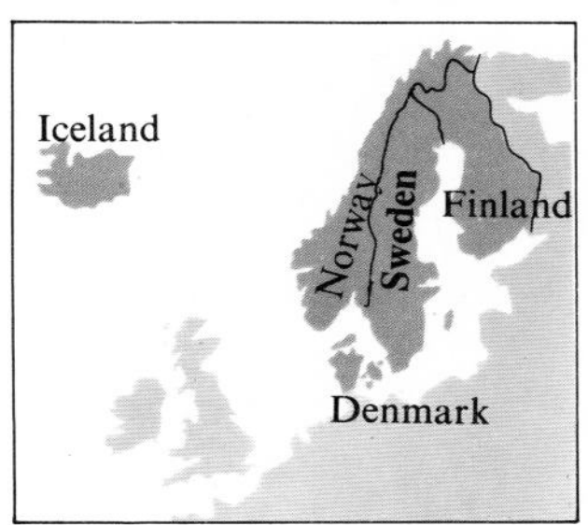

Sweden (Swedish *adj.*, the Swedes)
Sweden is a monarchy in northwest EUROPE. It is a mountainous and thinly populated country. However, it is prosperous and its people enjoy one of the world's highest standards of living.

The cold north lies above the ARCTIC Circle and includes part of the region called LAPLAND. The most important place in the north is the region around the towns of Gällivare and Kiruna, where rich deposits of iron ore are mined. Mining and manufacturing are Sweden's leading industries. Shipbuilding, machinery and steel products are all important. Industrial centers include STOCKHOLM, Gothenburg and Malmö. Sweden lacks coal and most electricity comes from HYDROELECTRIC POWER stations. Forestry is another major industry, but farming is confined to the south, which has warm summers.

The country is known for its many scientists and inventors. One of them, Alfred Nobel (1833–96) founded the NOBEL PRIZES. Sweden has been politically neutral for over 150 years. Political stability has enabled its governments to introduce an advanced system of social welfare. Neutral Sweden plays an important part in international affairs.

AREA: 173,742 SQ. MILES (449,964 SQ. KM)
POPULATION: 8,347,000
CAPITAL: STOCKHOLM
CURRENCY: KRONA
OFFICIAL LANGUAGE: SWEDISH.

sweep *vb.* (past **swept**) 1. clean with a brush. 2. glide majestically.
sweeping *adj.* extensive, wide. *The government took sweeping measures to improve the economy.*
sweet 1. *adj.* having a sugary taste. 2. *n.* a candy such as a toffee or chocolate. 3. *adj.* charming. **sweeten** *vb.* make sweet.
swell *vb.* get bigger, increase. **swelling** *n.*
swept *vb.* past of **sweep**.
swerve *vb.* & *n.* (make) a sudden violent turn; a swerving motion. *The driver had to swerve to avoid hitting a dog.*
swift 1. *adj.* fast, quick. **swiftness** *n.* 2. *n.* a fast-flying bird with long wings.

Swift, Jonathan
Jonathan Swift was an Irish-born writer, poet, churchman and political journalist (1667–1745). He became the dean of Saint Patrick's Cathedral in Dublin. In 1726, he published his most famous book, *Gulliver's Travels.* In it, he poked fun at many human weaknesses.

swig *vb. n.* drink in long drafts.
swill 1. *n.* part-liquid food for swine. 2. *vb.* drench; guzzle or gobble.

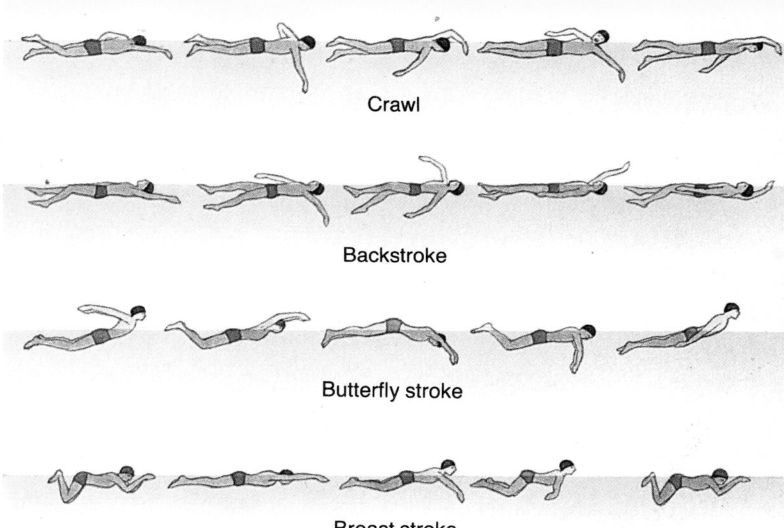

Four popular styles of swimming. The crawl, developed in Australia early in the 20th century, is the most efficient and fastest way of traveling through water.

swim *n.* & *vb.* (past **swam** past part. **swum**) move yourself along while afloat in water.
► Swimming is healthy exercise, and being able to swim may save your life if you fall into water by accident. Many animals know how to swim from birth. But people have to learn, usually with help from a trained instructor.

Swimmers usually use one or more of five main kinds of stroke. These are called breaststroke, butterfly stroke, backstroke, sidestroke, and crawl.

swine *n.* a collective word for pigs; (casual) unpleasant person.
swindle *vb.* cheat. *n.* fraud.
swing *vb.* (past **swung**) move yourself or something else backward and forward along an arc. *The monkey was swinging from branch to branch. n.* a seat slung by ropes.

switch 1. *n.* a device for turning lights and other electrical appliances on and off. *vb.* switch on, switch off. 2. *vb.* change from one thing to another.

Switzerland (Swiss)
A federal republic in southcentral EUROPE, Switzerland is divided into 25 small cantons (states). The powers of government are split between the cantons and the national goverment. The ALPS and the Jura mountains cover about two-thirds of the country. There are superb waterfalls, deep valleys and beautiful lakes. Lakes cover about one-fifth of the land. Farming is limited by the rugged nature of the land, but cheese, butter, sugar and meat are all important products. Switzerland lacks minerals and many raw materials are imported. The nation is best known for its skilled craftsmen, who make scientific instruments, watches and so on. Chemicals and textiles are other important industries. Banking and tourism are also important. About 6 percent of the workforce is employed in agriculture. Industry and services have 47 percent each.

There are three main languages. German is spoken by 74.5 percent of Swiss nationals; French by 20.1

S

percent; and Italian by 4 percent. Romansch, a language related to ancient Latin, is spoken by about 1 percent. In the past the Swiss fought many wars to maintain their independence. Switzerland has been neutral for over 100 years. It does not belong to the United Nations, although it has joined some of the UN's specialized agencies.

AREA: 15,942 SQ. MILES (41,288 SQ. KM)
POPULATION: 6,350,000
CAPITAL: BERN
CURRENCY: SWISS FRANC
OFFICIAL LANGUAGES; FRENCH, GERMAN, ITALIAN, ROMANSCH

swivel *n.* a device joining two parts which enables either one or both parts to turn freely. *vb.* pivot, turn on a swivel.
swollen *vb.* past part. of **swell**.
swoop *n.* & *vb.* rush down (out of the sky.) *The eagle swooped on its prey.*
sword *n.* a hand weapon with a long blade.
► Swords were once important weapons used by foot soldiers in hand-to-hand fighting. Later, men fought duels with swords. Early swords were made of bronze. Then came swords made of iron and steel.
Different peoples developed various kinds of swords. The Romans used a short sword with a sharp point and two sharp edges. Arabs and Turks fought with a *scimitar* – a curved sword with one cutting edge. In the 1500s, swordsmen used *rapiers*. These were long, narrow, two-edged, and pointed. In time, swords were replaced by firearms.

swordfish *n.* a big tropical fish, with a sword-shaped bony snout.
► The swordfish's sword is half as long again as the rest of its body. It is strong enough to pierce the planks of a boat. A swordfish can be as much as 20 ft. (6 meters) long, and can weigh up to 1,000 lb. (450 kg).

swore *vb.* past of **swear**.
swum *vb.* past part. **swim**.
swung *vb.* past of **swing**.
sycamore *n.* a tree belonging to the maple family.

Sydney
Sydney is the largest city in AUSTRALIA, and the capital of NEW SOUTH WALES. More than three million people live in Sydney. It stands on a fine natural harbor (Port Jackson) crossed by a famous steel-arch bridge. Sydney makes chemicals, machinery and ships and is an important port. It was founded in 1788 as a settlement for convicts sent out from England. Sydney is the seat of both Anglican and Roman Catholic archbishops and has a university, founded in 1850.

syllable *n.* one section or part of a word, which can be said by itself. *Ambulance has three syllables: am-bu-lance.*
syllabus *n.* a course of studies.
symbol *n.* a sign. *In arithmetic the symbol + means "add."* **symbolize** *vb.*
symmetrical *adj.* having the same shape and size on both sides of a central line. *All these capital letters are symmetrical, even the second one: A E H M O T X.* **symmetry** *n.*
sympathy *n.* a feeling for another person's distress or unhappiness; to be in tune with another person. **sympathize** *vb.*
symphony (**sim**-*fon-ee*) *n.* a form of long musical composition for a full orchestra, usually consisting of three or four movements.
symptom *n.* some indication, sign or mark on the body, e.g. a rash or high temperature, pointing to a disease.
synagogue *n.* a meeting place for Jewish religious worship and teaching.
synod *n.* a meeting or council of clergy (and laity) of a church.
synonym *n.* a word that has the same meaning as another word. *Looking glass is a synonym for mirror.*
synopsis *n.* a summary, especially of a story or play.
synthetic *adj.* & *n.* made artificially.

Syria (Syrian)
This Arab country lies just east of the Mediterranean Sea. Much of Syria is covered by dry plains that are hot in summer and chilly in winter. NOMADS drive flocks of sheep and goats over the dry lands. Farmers grow grains, grapes and apricots, where rivers or rain provide water.
Most Syrian towns grew up on the roads used by merchants long ago to bring goods from the East. DAMASCUS is the oldest capital anywhere. People have lived there for 4,500 years.

syringe *n.* an instrument for sucking a liquid in, and forcing it out again, in a thin stream.
syrup *n.* a sticky, sweet, thick liquid, made from sugar and water.
system *n.* a group of items forming as a unified whole; an organized procedure. *Filing system.* organs that together perform a function. *Digestive system.* **systematic** *adj.* methodical.

The synagogue (a word meaning "to bring together") is a Jewish place of worship. It contains an everburning lamp and a closet, called the holy ark, which holds the Scrolls of the Law.

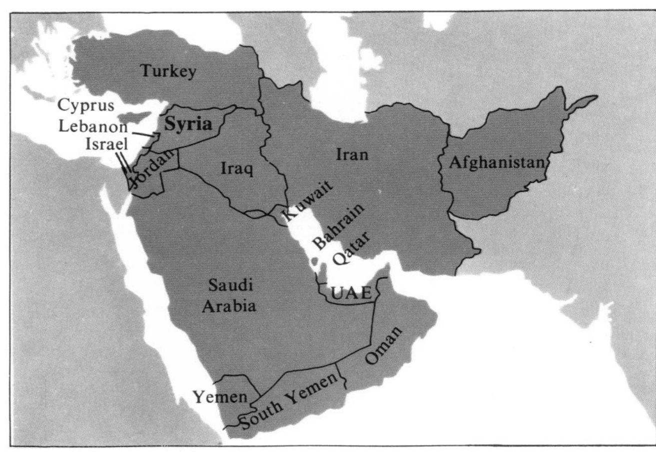

AREA: 71,502 SQ. MILES (185,180 SQ. KM)
POPULATION: 9,227,000
CAPITAL: DAMASCUS
CURRENCY: SYRIAN POUND
OFFICIAL LANGUAGE: ARABIC

T

Trees in their fall colors.

tabby *n.* a domestic cat.
tabernacle *n.* a tent used by the Jews in Biblical times; a place of worship; a receptacle for consecrated hosts.
table *n.* 1. a piece of furniture with a flat top supported by legs. 2. a way of arranging figures, such as a multiplication table.
tablespoon *n.* a large spoon used for serving food. *A tablespoon is often used to measure amounts in cooking.*
tablet *n.* round, compressed drug or medicine; sheets of paper glued together at one edge.
table tennis *n.* a game played on a table, using paddles and a celluloid ball.
► The table on which this game is played measures 9 ft. by 5 ft. (2.7 meters by 1.5 meters), using a net, a celluloid ball and solid bats with rubber faces. Each player tries to keep hitting the ball back across the net, so that it bounces on the table on the opponent's side.

tabloid *n.* small-sized newspaper that contains news, etc., in a condensed form and which has many photographs.
taboo *n* & *adj.* something that must not be talked about, touched, etc.; set apart.
tack 1. *n.* a small flat-headed nail. 2. *vb.* sew with long loose stitches. 3. *vb* & *n.* sail a boat into the wind. 4. *n.* a zig-zag course on land.
tackle 1. *n.* equipment for a sport or some other activity. *Dad keeps his fishing tackle in the garage.* 2. *vb.* start work on a problem. *John decided to tackle the washing alone.* 3. *vb.* throw down or stop an opponent, especially in football.
tact *n.* knowing what to say or do to avoid offense. **tactless** *adj.* **tactful** *adj.*
tactics *pl. n.* the science of using military forces in a war. **tactical** *adj.*
tadpole *n.* a young frog or toad, at the stage between the egg and the adult.

Taft, William Howard
William Taft (1857–1930) was the 27th president. He continued many of the policies of Theodore Roosevelt.

tag *n.* 1. a small label. 2. a game in which one person chases the others, and catches them by touching or "tagging" them.
tail *n.* a projection at the back of many kinds of animal. *Some monkeys use their tails as a fifth limb.* *vb.* follow close behind.
tailor *n.* a person who makes or alters suits, coats, etc.

Taiwan (Taiwanese)
Taiwan is an island republic off the coast of CHINA. When the Communists took over China in 1949, their Nationalist opponents set up a government in Taiwan (previously called Formosa). Taiwan represented China in the UNITED NATIONS until 1971, when Communist China was admitted.

Taiwan is a mountainous country, with fertile plains to the west. The climate is tropical. Most of the people are Chinese. Rice, sugar cane, sweet potatoes and tea are major crops. The economy is dominated by manufacturing industry, and textiles, electronic goods and many other items are exported to the West.

Taiwan became Chinese in the 1860s. It was ruled by JAPAN from 1895 to 1945.

AREA: 13,885 SQ. MILES (35,961 SQ. KM)
POPULATION: 17,100,000
CAPITAL: TAIPEI
CURRENCY: TAIWAN DOLLAR
OFFICIAL LANGUAGE: CHINESE

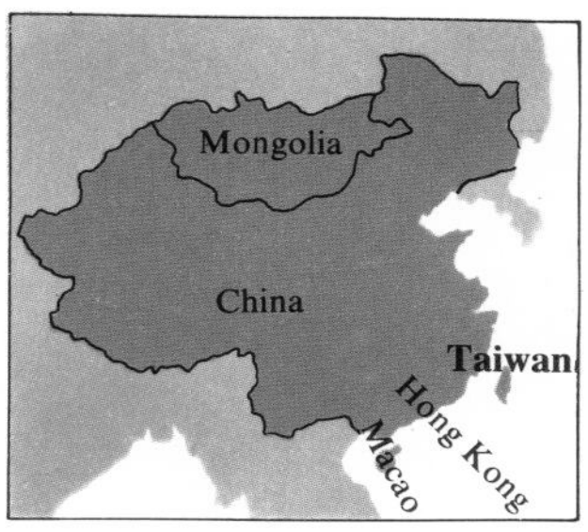

Taj Mahal
This is a beautiful tomb which stands on the Jumna river at Agra in north INDIA. The emperor, Shah Jahan,

T

The Taj Mahal.

built it for his favorite wife, Mumtaz Mahal, who died in 1631. The shah planned to build an exact copy in black marble for himself on the other side of the river. His son prevented this and so when the shah died he was buried with his wife in her tomb.

take *vb*. (past **took** past part. **taken**) get possession of something; catch or gain.

take after *vb*. resemble. *Doesn't Tina take after her mother?*

take in *vb*. 1. be tricked. *I was taken in by what he said, but it was really a lie*. 2. bring someone into your house. *The hotel was full, so the manager found a motel to take us in.* 3. understand. *I'm sorry but I didn't quite take in what you said.* 4. make something narrower. *The skirt was too big, but I took it in at the waist.*

takeoff *n*. 1. take to the air (of an aircraft). **take off** *vb*. 2. a parody, humorous mimicry.

take over *vb*. assume control of. **takeover** *n*.

take up *vb*. start doing something which is new to you. *My father has decided to take up pottery.*

talc *n*. a mineral with a soapy feel which is ground to a powder to make talcum powder for dusting the body after a bath.

tale *n*. a story; mischievous gossip.

talent *n*. an ability to do something well. *Nell has a natural talent for skating.*

talk (*tawk*) *vb*. speak. *n*. a short lecture. **talkative** *adj*.

tall *adj*. having greater than average height, often said of people and buildings. *Simon is not as tall as his brother.*

Talmud *n*. book of Jewish tradition.

talon *n*. the long claw of a bird of prey, such as a hawk.

tambourine *n*. a musical instrument shaped like a shallow drum, with disks around it. It is shaken, and beaten with the hand.

tame *adj*. an animal that is not wild, and is used to being with humans; uninteresting. *vb*. make tame.

tamper *vb*. meddle with.

tan 1. *n*. a light brown color. *vb*. turn brown in the sun. 2. *vb*. make animal skins into leather.

tandem *n*. a bicycle with two seats.

tang *n*. a sharp taste or smell.

tangerine *n*. a small loose-skinned kind of orange.

tangled *adj*. disordered. **tangle** *vb*. & *n*. twisted interwoven strands.

tango *n*. & *vb*. Latin American dance; music for this dance.

tank *n*. 1. large container for liquids. 2. an armored fighting vehicle with guns, which moves on treads instead of wheels; a jail cell used for receiving prisoners.

► A tank is completely enclosed and heavily armored, and runs on caterpillar tracks. It is armed with a large gun firing shells, fitted to a revolving turret, plus usually one or more machine guns. The crew is normally four or five. Tanks were first used in World War I (from 1916), but their full potential was not realized until the success of the German tankborne invasion of France in World War II.

The first tank was used by the British in the Battle of the Somme in 1916. Among German tanks of World War II was the Panther (below) whose heavy armor was nearly 5 inches think. A British tank of today is the Chieftain 2 (above).

tankard *n*. drinking vessel with a handle.

tanker *n*. a ship used to carry oil or other liquids.

tantrum *n*. a sudden fit of bad temper.

Tanzania (Tanzanian)
Tanzania is a republic in East AFRICA. It consists of Tanganyika on the mainland and the islands of Zanzibar and Pemba. Lake Victoria lies in the northwest of the country. Tanzania also has Africa's highest peak, Mt. KILIMANJARO. Most people work on the land: coffee, cotton, cashew nuts and sisal are major crops. Minerals include gold, diamonds and tin. The country contains several famous NATIONAL PARKS.

Tanganyika was formerly part of German East Africa, while Zanzibar was a British protectorate. Britain occupied Tanganyika during World War I. It became independent in 1961. Zanzibar joined with Tanganyika in 1964.

AREA: 364,920 SQ. MILES (945,087 SQ. KM)
POPULATION: 19,388,000
CAPITAL: DODOMA
CURRENCY: TANZIAN SHILLING
OFFICIAL LANGUAGES: ENGLISH, SWAHILI

tap 1. *n*. a device for turning on and off the flow of water into a sink, bath, etc., 2. *vb*. knock gently but repeatedly. 3. *vb*. take water, information, etc. from a source. *I think that my telephone has been tapped.*

tape 1. *n*. a narrow length of material used for tying or in dressmaking. 2. *n*. a strip of plastic which is used to record sound. *vb*. record on magnetic tape.

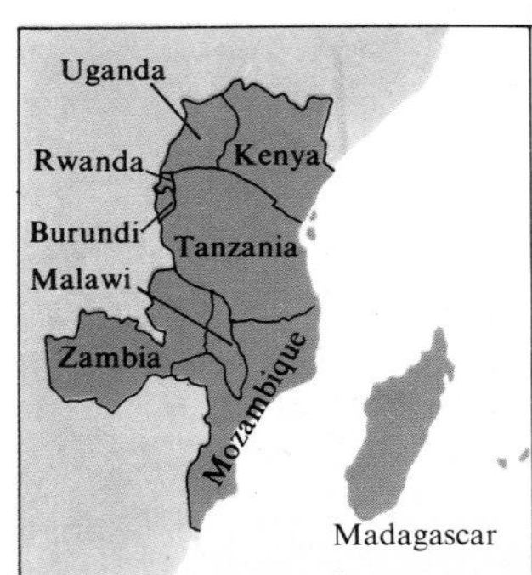

taper 1. *n.* long thin candle used for lighting lamps, etc. 2. *vb.* make or become smaller toward the end. *A church spire tapers.*

tape recorder *n.* an instrument for recording sounds on tape and playing the sound back again.

tapestry *n.* a picture on cloth, made by sewing or weaving in colored threads.

► Tapestries are made by WEAVING colored silk thread across closely packed rows of strong linen or wool threads, held in a frame. Sometimes real gold or silver threads are used.

The design for the tapestry is drawn onto the linen threads with ink. The weaver works from the back of the tapestry. A mirror placed in front of the work shows how the design is going.

tapir *n.* a nocturnal animal of tropical America, Malaya and Sumatra which is related to the horse.

tar *n.* a dark, thick, sticky substance obtained from wood, coal, etc.

tarantula *n.* large, black, south European spider, named after the town of Taranto in Italy; it has a slightly poisonous bite.

► In the Middle Ages, people thought the tarantula's bite was very dangerous; its victim was supposed to die of melancholy – unless cured by music. Musicians played a series of lively tunes – tarantellas – to tempt the victim to get up and dance and so sweat out the poison.

target *n.* anything that has an object shot or thrown at it. *An archery target is usually made of straw covered with canvas.*

tariff *n.* price list; list of custom duties.

tarmac *n.* a road surface of broken stones mixed with tar (short for tarmacadam).

tarpaulin *n.* waterproof cloth, originally of tarred canvas.

Tarsier
The tarsier is a small animal with huge eyes, big ears and a long tail. it has long hind legs and short front legs that help it to jump among the trees in which it lives. The tarsier lives in the East Indies and the Philippines.

tart 1. *adj.* sharp- or sour-tasting. 2. *n.* a pie with pastry underneath the filling but not on top of it.

tartan *n.* a traditional Scottish woolen cloth, woven in one of a variety of square patterns.

► Tartans were adopted by the Highlanders of Scotland. Each Scottish *clan* (large family group) has its own tartan. Some have two: a dull-colored one for hunting and a more brightly colored one for special occasions.

At first, the tartan cloth was worn in one long piece. Part of it was wrapped around the body to make a skirt and the rest was worn over the shoulder. At night, it could be taken off and used as a blanket. The separate, pleated kilt was not worn until the 1880s.

task *n.* a job, a piece of work. *It was her task to make the beds in the morning.*

Tasman, Abel Janszoon
Abel Janszoon Tasman (1603–59) was a Dutch explorer and nagivator. In 1642, he was sent by the Dutch East India Company to explore the coasts of AUSTRALIA and New Guinea (see PAPUA NEW GUINEA). Tasman discovered TASMANIA, which he named Van Diemen's Land in honor of the governor of the Dutch East Indies. He also discovered New Zealand and many islands in the PACIFIC Ocean.

Tasmania (Tasmanian)
The island of Tasmania is the smallest state of AUSTRALIA. It lies off the south coast of VICTORIA, separated from the mainland by the Bass Strait. Tasmania is mountainous and heavily forested, with a mild climate. Sheep rearing and dairy farming are important occupations.

Tasmanian devil
The Tasmanian devil is an animal that looks somewhat like a small bear. It has black fur with white spots and lives in the island of TASMANIA. It is a MARSUPIAL that comes out at night to hunt other animals such as sheep.

tassel *n.* a bunch of hanging threads used as an ornament.

taste 1. *n.* the sense by which you can tell the flavor of food and drink; the flavor itself. *vb.* try food or drink to see if you like it. 2. *n.* good or bad judgment in art, clothing, etc. *I admire her taste in clothes.*

► We can taste food because we have taste buds on our tongues. The TONGUE is covered in tiny bumps. The taste buds are buried in the sides of these bumps. There are clusters of buds on the back, tip and sides of the tongue. NERVES, running from the buds to the brain, tell you whether the food you are eating is sweet, sour, bitter or salty.

Taste is not the same as flavor. Flavor is a mixture of the taste and the SMELL of food. If you have a bad cold and your nose is blocked, food hardly tastes of anything.

Two types of tartan.

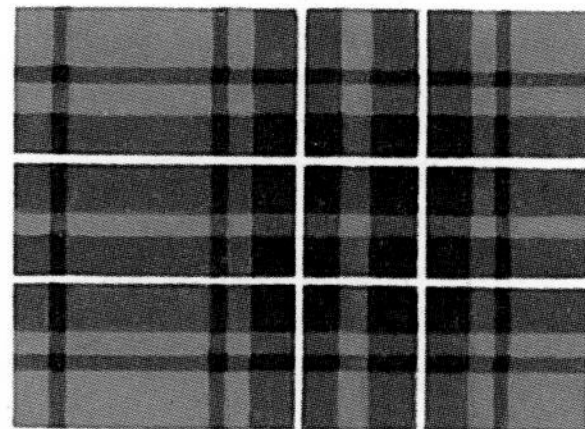

tattoo *vb* & *n.* mark or color the skin with patterns.

taught *vb.* (*tawt*) past of **teach**.

taut (*tawt*) *adj.* when something has been stretched so that it is firm. *Pull that rope until it is taut.* **tauten** *vb.*

tavern *n.* an inn or pub where food and drink are served to patrons; saloon; bar.

tawny *adj.* yellowish-brown color.

tax *n.* (plural **taxes**) money paid to the government by people and organizations.

taxi 1. *n.* a car with a driver that can be hired for short journeys. 2. *vb.* the long run an aircraft makes to or from the runway.

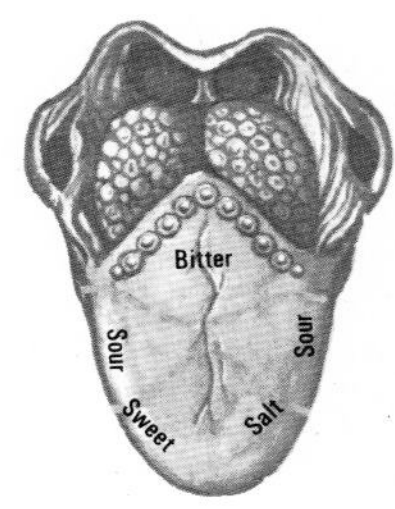

The four main kinds of taste bud are distributed over the tongue so that different areas taste different flavors.

Taylor, Zachary
Zachary Taylor (1794–1850) was the 12th president of the United States. He served as a major in the War of 1912 against Great Britain and later he led his troops to victories in the Mexican War. He was nominated by the Whig Party as its candidate for president in 1848. Taylor won, but he had a great deal to learn about being president. He leaned heavily on others for advice. President Taylor was a slaveowner, but he did not oppose the admission of California and New Mexico to the Union as free states. The South would not agree to the admission without other slavery problems being settled. Taylor died before this argument could be settled.

Tchaikovsky, Peter Ilyich
Tchaikovsky (1840–93) is probably the best known of all the great Russian composers. His work includes operas, concertos,

symphonies, ballet music and many other pieces. Among the music for ballets he wrote *Swan Lake*, *The Sleeping Beauty*, and *The Nutcracker*.

Tchaikovsky originally studied law, and worked in the Russian Ministry of Justice. At the age of 23 he left his job to study music. His marriage, in 1877, was a disaster. Later he was given financial assistance by a wealthy widow on condition that they never meet.

tea *n.* the dried leaves of an evergreen shrub. The leaves are soaked in boiling water to make the drink called tea.

► The tea bush is grown chiefly in China, northern India, Sri Lanka and Japan. The pickings are dried, heated, and may be fermented. Tea reached Europe in 1610. At first it was brewed and stored in barrels like beer. It is the world's most widely used beverage.

Tea contains *caffeine*, a mild stimulant, and *tannin*. Young leaves make the best tea.

teach *vb.* instruct other people; give them knowledge and encourage them to think for themselves. **teaching** *n.* the act or profession of a teacher.

teacher *n.* a person who instructs (teaches) other people, usually in a school or college.

teak *n.* an evergreen tree with very hard wood grown in India, Burma, and Thailand.

team *n.* 1. a group of people in a game or sport who are all on the same side. *There are 11 players on a football team.* 2. a group of people who join together to do a particular job.

teapot *n.* a vessel with a curved handle and spout for making and pouring out tea.

tear (*tare*) *vb.* (past **tore** past part. **torn**) rip something such as cloth or paper, pull apart by force; move or act with great violence, force or speed.

tears (*teers*) *pl. n.* drops of salt water which fall from your eyes when you cry.

tease (*teeze*) *vb.* make fun of someone, often unkindly.

technical *adj.* to do with machinery or how things work.

technology *n.* the study of technical ideas.

tedious *adj.* boring; tiresome because of its length or dullness.

tee *n.* place from which a golfer drives the ball at the beginning of each hole; small peg on which the golf ball is placed to drive off.

teenager *n.* a young person between the ages of thir*teen* and nine*teen*.

tee shirt *n.* (also **T-shirt**) a short-sleeved collarless, cotton undershirt; also a pullover knit sport shirt of the same style.

teeth *n.* plural of **tooth**.

► Teeth are hard, bonelike structures attached to the jaws of most VERTEBRATES except birds. There are usually two rows of teeth, one in the upper jaw and one in the lower jaw. Teeth are basically used for biting, tearing and chewing food. An animal's teeth are adapted to its diet. Gnawing creatures such as RATS have sharp pointed teeth; grazing creatures, such as HORSES, have flat grinding teeth. Teeth are not only used for eating. Some CARNIVORES, such as HYENAS, use their teeth to catch prey. BEAVERS use their teeth to fell trees, and ELEPHANTS use two of their teeth – grown out as long tusks – for digging and fighting.

teethe *vb.* cut (grow) new teeth. **teething** *n.*

teetotal *adj.* never drinking alcohol.

Tehran

Tehran (or Teheran) has been the capital of IRAN (Persia) since 1788. It is also the capital of the province of the same name in northern Iran, whose northern border is the Elburz Mountains. Tehran is one of the most important commercial and industrial cities in the Middle East. It has been largely modernized and rebuilt since 1925.

telecommunications *pl. n.* long-distance signals by telephone, radio, telegraph, and television.

telegram *n.* a word message sent by telegraph or radio.

telegraph *n.* a system for sending long-distance messages by electric current. **telegraphy** *n.*

► Before the 1800s, visual or audible signals were used for conveying messages between distant points. Electric telegraph systems were introduced in the 1800s. Samuel Morse devised a method of sending messages using long and short pulses of electricity to represent letters and numbers (*see* MORSE CODE). Radiotelegraphy is the transmission of telegraph signals by means of RADIO.

telephone *n.* an instrument for talking to people over long distances by turning speech into electrical impulses, which travel along wires. *vb.* use the telephone.

► The first practical telephone, patented by Alexander Graham BELL in 1876, represented a major breakthrough in communications. But Bell's instrument produced only a weak signal that was difficult to hear over long distances. However, others were quick to improve on the system, and the telephone soon became a commercial success in the United States. At first, telephones were used mainly by lawyers, bankers and large firms,

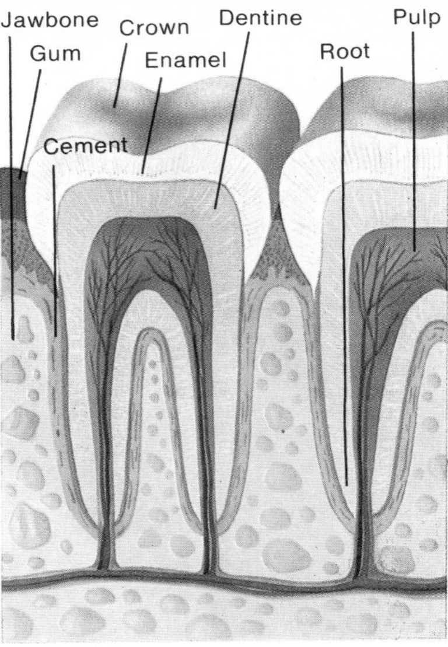

The parts of a tooth. The enamel is the hardest substance in the body. Below the enamel is a layer of dentine which also forms the root. The pulp at the core of the tooth contains nerve fibers and blood vessels.

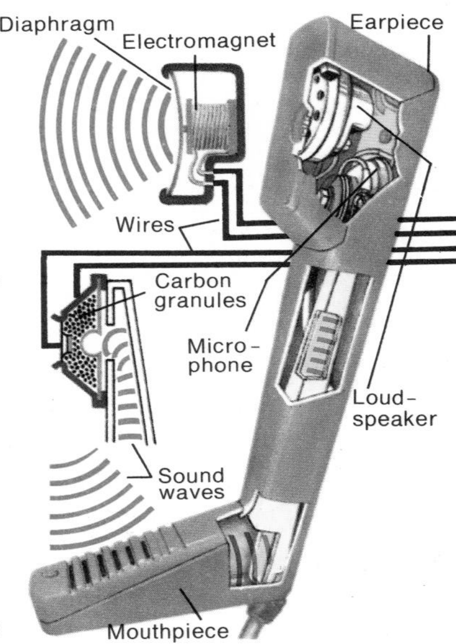

How a telephone works. An electric signal travels from the mouthpiece along the wires to the other telephone where it enters a small loudspeaker in the earpiece. This contains an electromagnet which causes a diaphragm to vibrate as the incoming current varies. This produces the sound of your voice.

often for communication only between different departments of the same organization. Users called a switchboard operator who made the required connection. But, as more and more firms became subscribers, exchanges were established to interconnect them. The first automatic exchange was patented by Almon Strowger in 1889. Callers selected other subscribers by pressing three keys. Dial telephones were introduced in 1896. Since then, worldwide telephone networks have been established using landlines and communication SATELLITE links. (*see* MICROPHONE).

telescope *n.* a tube-like instrument with special lenses, which makes distant things appear clearer and larger.
► A Dutch optician called Hans Lippershey invented the telescope in 1608. Hearing of this useful device, the Italian inventor Galileo Galilei built one for himself the following year. Although a crude instrument by today's standards, Galileo used it to make many important discoveries in ASTRONOMY. His telescope was of the refracting type – that is, it used lenses to bend light and thus produce a magnified image (*see* LENS). This type of telescope suffered from a defect called chromatic aberration. Colored fringes could be seen around the images, and the problem became worse as the magnification was increased. Isaac NEWTON invented the reflecting telescope to overcome this defect. By replacing the main (*objective*) lens with a curved mirror, Newton managed to eliminate the unwanted coloration. Modern high-quality telescopes may be of the refracting or reflecting type. Today's refracting telescopes use compound lenses, made from elements of different types of glass cemented together, to prevent chromatic aberration. Large optical telescopes are usually of the reflecting type using a mirror, as huge lenses would tend to distort under their own weight. Another kind of telescope is the radio telescope (*see* RADIO ASTRONOMY).

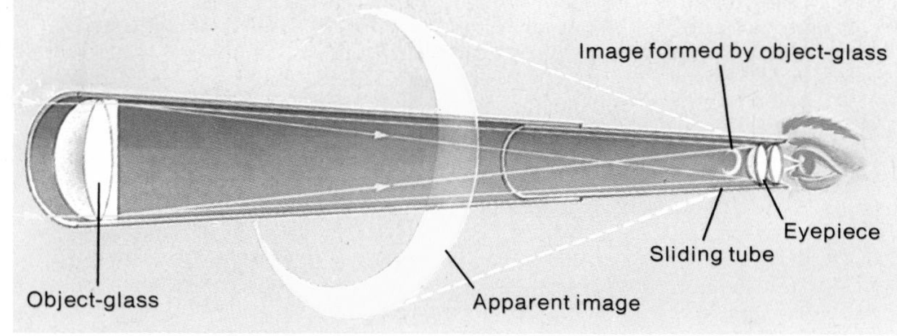

Above: A refracting telescope in which a lens (the object glass) forms a small image of the object inside the tube. The eyepiece (a much smaller lens) magnifies the image.

Below: Two types of reflecting telescopes. Both have a special mirror with a slightly hollow or concave surface to form its image. A Newtonian telescope has a small flat mirror to reflect the image through the side of the tube. The Cassegrain sends the light back through a small hole in the main mirror. Most amateurs use Newtonian telescopes, since they are cheaper.

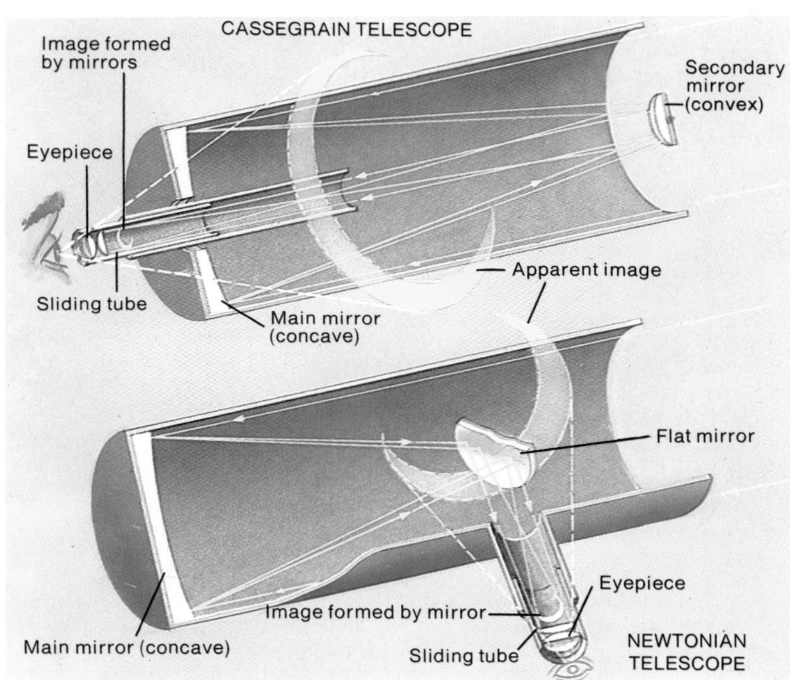

television *n.* a way of sending and receiving pictures and sounds by radio waves. **TV** *abbr.* **televise** *vb.*
► The basic theory of television was developed in the 1800s, but many years passed before practical television became possible.

In 1880, the English scientists Ayrton and Perry put forward an idea called electric vision. They proposed using a number of photoelectric cells to convert each part of an image into an electric signal. The idea was that the signals would be sent over wires and used to light an array of tiny lamps at the far end. In this way, variations in brightness in the original image would be reproduced. One problem was that the system required hundreds of wires between the transmitting and receiving equipment.

German scientist Paul Nipkow overcame this difficulty by devising a mechanical scanning system. Using a rotating perforated disk, he arranged for each part of the image to fall, in turn, on a single photoelectric cell. Only one pair of wires would be required to convey the signal, and one lamp and a scanning disk would be used to reconstruct the image. Unfortunately, there was a major problem. The signal produced by a photoelectric cell was too weak to light a lamp. So real progress in television had to wait for the invention of an amplifying device – the triode tube – in 1907. This enabled the weak signal from a photoelectric cell to be strengthened sufficiently to light a neon lamp.

Using Nipkow's mechanical scanning system, and tubes for amplification, Scotsman John Logie

T

Baird developed a practical television system in the 1920s. By this time, radio broadcasting services were being established, and some organizations started experimenting with television transmissions. In 1936, the British Broadcasting Corporation started the world's first regular broadcasts of scheduled television programs. Besides using the Baird system, the BBC also tried another technique – electronic scanning, using specially designed CATHODE RAY TUBES. This proved vastly superior, and the Baird system was soon abandoned.

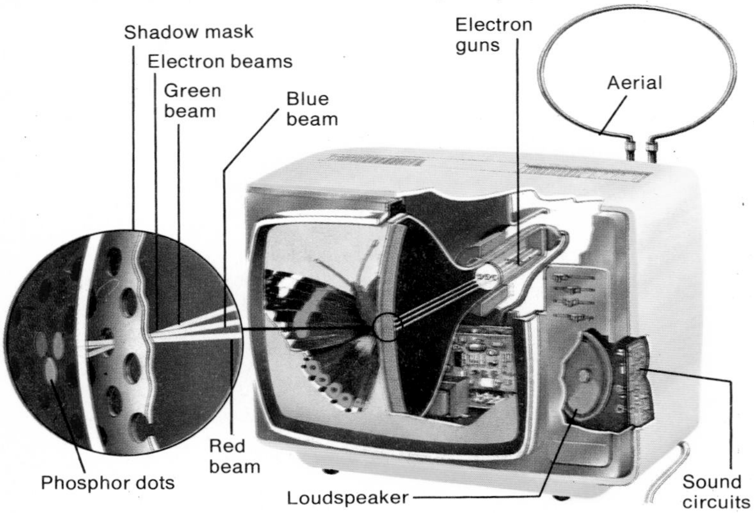

The television camera changes light waves into electrical "vision" signals. These are sent out on radio waves. The antenna picks up these signals, which go to a tube inside the set. There, an electronic gun fires electrons (tiny electric particles) in lines across the screen. The screen lights up in lines that make up a picture. In a color set three electron beams scan the screen – red, green and blue, which when mixed together give a full-color picture.

All modern television systems use electronic scanning systems to analyse and reconstruct the pictures. In the television camera, a LENS forms an image of the studio scene on a camera tube. A beam of electrons (*see* ATOM) rapidly scans this image, line by line, and is made to vary in strength according to image brightness. The varying flow, or current, of electrons produced is called the vision signal. Sound and vision signals from the studio are transmitted together. In the receiver, a beam of electrons scans the screen of a picture tube, tracing a series of lines across it. The vision signal is used to vary the brightness along the lines and thus reproduce the original scene. As scanning occurs so quickly, the viewer has the illusion of seeing a complete picture, although it is actually constructed bit by bit. In color television, separate signals corresponding to the three primary colors of light are used to form a full-color image on the screen of a specially designed picture tube.

tell *vb.* give information to somebody. *Tell me about your trip.*
temper 1. *n.* your mood (usually when bad). *Gareth was in a bad temper because his parents refused to let him watch TV.* 2. *vb.* make a metal harder and more pliable by heating it and then cooling it rapidly.
temperament *n.* a person's character and way of feeling, thinking and behaving. *She has a gentle temperament.*
temperamental *adj.* sudden changes of mood.
temperate *adj.* a climate that is neither too hot nor very cold; moderate; avoiding excesses. *New Zealand has a temperate climate.*
temperature *n.* degree of hotness or coldness. *Temperature can be measured with a thermometer.*
► Temperature is measured on a scale marked on a THERMOMETER. Many people today use the Celsius or CENTIGRADE SCALE. A Fahrenheit scale is also used, for example, to measure body temperature.

Some animals, such as mammals like people, are warm-blooded. Their temperature stays much the same. Humans can stand quite a wide range of body temperature. The normal body temperature of a healthy person is 98.6°F (37°C). The temperature of a person who is ill might go up to 106°F (41°C) or more.

Other animals, such as snakes, lizards and frogs, are cold-blooded. Their body temperature goes up and down with the temperature of their surroundings. These animals can survive until their body temperature drops almost to freezing point.

tempest *n.* violent storm.
temple *n.* 1. a building used for meeting and worship in some religions. 2. flat part of the side of the head between ear and forehead.
tempo *n.* the speed at which a piece of music is played.
temporary *adj.* lasting for a limited time, not permanent. *We had a temporary power failure today.*
tempt *vb.* try to persuade someone to do something they ought not to; entice.
tenant *n.* a person who rents and occupies someone else's property.
tend *vb.* 1. be likely to do something. *This car tends to steer to the left.* 2. look after. *Shepherds tend their sheep in the fields.*
tender 1. *adj.* delicate, soft, easily hurt. 2. *vb.* offer. *The minister tendered his resignation.* 3. *n.* a small boat in which you get to a larger one.
tendon *n.* tough fibrous tissue that connects muscle to bone.

Tennessee (*abbrev.* **Tenn.**)
Tennessee is in the eastern central part of the United States. It spreads from the Appalachian Mountains in the east, to the MISSISSIPPI River in the west. It is a very narrow state and is bordered by eight others.

The name comes from the Cherokee Indians, who called their main settlement and the nearby river "Tennese." Both the British and the French were interested in the land, and it was not until the late 1700s that the British gained control.

The state was once almost entirely a farming one, but now it is mostly industrial. Chemicals, textiles, food, and metal products are among the most important things manufactured there. Tennessee also has enormous HYDROELECTRIC stations, which were built in the 1930s by the Tennessee Valley Authority.

Tennessee is also famous for two of its cities, Memphis and Nashville.

tennis *n.* a ball and racket game for two or four people, which is played on a specially marked court.
► A tennis court is divided in half by a net 3 ft. (90 cm) high in the center. If two people play it is called a singles match. If four people play it is called a doubles match.

Tennis balls must be about 2 in. (50 mm) in diameter and weigh about 2 ounces (56.7 grams). They must bounce between 53 in. (1.35 meters) and 58 in. (1.47 meters) when dropped from a height of 100 in. (2.5 meters) onto concrete. A tennis racket can be any size.

A tennis match is divided into sets. Usually women play three sets and men play five. Each set has at least six games. To win a game, one player must score at least four points. Modern tennis is a simple version of an old French game called *real* tennis or royal tennis.

tenon *n*. piece of wood which fits into a hole (a *mortise*) to join two parts of a piece of furniture, etc.
tenor *n*. & *adj*. highest natural adult male singing voice.
tense *adj*. taut; showing mental or physical strain.

Two of the many different shelters of the North American Indians: a bark tepee built by Creee Indians, and a Creek Indian house of branches.

tent *n*. a shelter made from waterproof material, such as canvas, stretched over a frame of metal poles, and held up with ropes.
► Tents were originally made of animal skins or bark and have been used by wandering nomadic tribes since prehistoric times. Now mostly used for camping, modern tents may have plastic windows, built-in floors and zip doors.

tentacle *n*. a long, thin, snakelike "arm" of animals such as the octopus.
tepee *n*. American Indian tent.
tepid *adj*. slightly warm.
term *n*. 1. a set period of time. *The spring term lasts for 10 weeks.* 2. word or expression which is used to describe particular ideas in different professions, e.g. medical terms. 3. *pl. n.* conditions.
terminal 1. *n*. a building where some form of transportation ends. 2. *adj*. the end; final, particularly of an illness which someone will not survive.
terminate *vb*. bring to an end.
terminus *n*. an end station on a bus, train or air route.
termite *n*. an insect like an ant that builds large hills of earth and mud.
► All termites live in large groups called colonies. Each colony has a queen, her king, soldiers and workers. Most termites are workers. They are small, blind and wingless. They dig the tunnels or build the mound and find food for the rest of the colony.
Soldier termites have large strong heads, and are also blind and wingless. They defend the colony from attack. The queen is three times as large as the other termites and does nothing but lay eggs. She is kept in a chamber in the middle of the colony, with her king. The workers feed her and look after the eggs until they hatch.

tern *n*. a seabird.
terrace *n*. a level area cut out of a slope; a row of houses built as a single block.
terra-cotta *n*. brownish-red baked clay used for statues, pottery and tiles and as a covering material on buildings.
terrapin *n*. a name for a small kind of turtle.
► Terrapins live in ponds, lakes and rivers. The female is slightly larger than the male, but never grows much bigger than a human hand. Terrapins spend most of their lives in water, coming ashore only to lay their eggs. They eat crabs and snails, other small water animals and plants. Some people like to eat terrapin meat.

terrible *adj*. very bad, frightening, dreadful.
terrier *n*. one of various kinds of small dog that can dig out or drive out small game animals.
terrific *adj*. terrifying; excellent. *We had a terrific time in Norway.*
terrify *vb*. make someone very frightened.
territory *n*. an area of land.
terror *n*. great fear. (*casual*) a tiresome person.
terse (*turs*) *adj*. brief, concise.
test 1. *vb*. try out something. *I want to test the car before I buy it.* 2. *n*. a set of questions to be answered; a kind of small exam.
testes *pl. n.* (singular **testis**) also **testicle** egg-shaped glands contained in the scrotum, a bag hanging behind the penis in male mammals. The testes produce sperm.
testify *vb*. give evidence under oath. *n*. **testimony**.
tetanus *n*. a dangerous disease in which the muscles become rigid.
tether *n*. a rope for fastening an animal so that it can only move within a set radius.

Giant nests like this are built by tiny termites.

The common tern.

Teuton *n*. a member of the Germanic race.
text *n*. the main part of a printed book.

Texas (*abbrev.* **Tex.**)
Texas is the second largest state in the U.S.A. It produces more oil, natural gas and cotton than any other state, and is important in electrical power and fishing too. Texas is a farming state as well.
The vast area of Texas is centered along the southern border of the main part of the United States. The name comes from a small tribe of Indians, who lived in the eastern part near the Sabine River. They were called the tejas.
The inhabitants have a rich heritage, for six different nations have claimed the land at various times, including Spain, France and Mexico. Many settlers went there during the 1800s, when the cattle industry developed and the railroad opened up the land. In 1901 an enormous oil field was discovered near Beaumont. Oil has since been found in about 80 percent of the land.
Although Austin is the state capital, Houston is the biggest city and is important for industry and shipping.

textbook *n*. a book giving information for study in a school or college.
textile *n*. woven cloth of any sort.
► Traditionally a textile is a woven fabric (*see* WEAVING), but today all fabrics are classed as textiles (including knitted fabrics, felts and lace). The traditional materials used for textiles are WOOL, LINEN and SILK, and COTTON. But today many artificial fibers are made – some from wood pulp and cotton (e.g. rayon and acetate), but most chemically from coal and oil (e.g. NYLON and polyester). Sometimes natural and artificial fibers are mixed in a fabric, to get the best of both. The output, quality and variety of textiles has been greatly increased by the mechanization of spinning and weaving. Other new developments include treatments to make fabrics flame resistant and easy to care for.

texture *n.* how the surface of something feels when you touch it.

Thailand (Thai)
Thailand is a country in Southeast ASIA. It sits in the middle of BURMA, LAOS and KAMPUCHEA. The south coast opens onto the Gulf of Thailand, which is part of the South China Sea. In the southwest corner a long, thin PENINSULA stretches down to Malaysia. One part of it is only 10 miles (16 km) across.

Thailand is bigger than California. Most of the people live in the middle. Many rivers flow through this part of the country, making it very fertile. Most people are farmers. Rice is the most important crop but cotton, tobacco, corn, coconuts and bananas are also grown. Some farmers rear pigs, and buffalo to plow the rice fields. In the north, across the border with Burma, there are large forests of teak, which is an important export. The peninsula is covered in mountains and jungles. It is very rich in minerals, especially tin.

Thailand used to be called Siam. In 1939, the name was changed. Thai means "free," so Thailand means the land of the free. During WORLD WAR II, the Japanese took over and ruled Thailand, but now it is independent. There is a king, but the country is ruled by an elected government.
AREA: 198,467 SQ. MILES (514,000 SQ. KM)
POPULATION: 49,414,000
CAPITAL: BANGKOK
CURRENCY: BAHT
OFFICIAL LANGUAGE: THAI

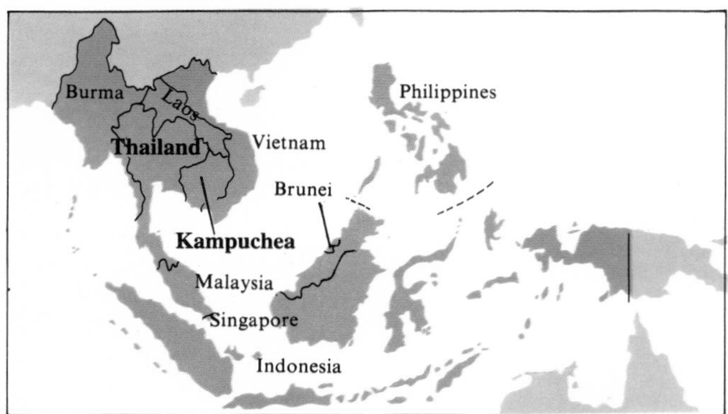

Thames River
The Thames River is the longest and most important river in ENGLAND. It begins in the Cotswold Hills and flows eastward, until it reaches the North Sea. The Thames flows through the middle of London, which was once the most important port in Europe. Now the docks that once stretched 35 miles (56 km) along the riverside, are closed and ships stop lower down the river.

A Greek theater with a stage and circular orchestra for the chorus. The actors were men who wore masks to show the part they were playing.

Not very long ago, the Thames around London was one of the dirtiest rivers in the world. Now it has been cleaned so thoroughly that fish are coming back to live in it.

than *conj.* introducing second part of a comparison. *Jill is taller than Jack.*
thank *vb.* tell someone that you are grateful to them. *Thank you for the lovely party.*

Thanksgiving Day
Thanksgiving Day was first celebrated in America by the PILGRIM FATHERS. They were PROTESTANTS who sailed to North America in 1620 so that they could follow their religious beliefs in peace. After their first year there, they held a feast to give thanks to God because they had survived. Today, Americans celebrate Thanksgiving Day on the fourth Thursday of November. The festival meal includes turkey and pumpkin pie.
thatch *n.* a roof covering made from layers of straw or reeds.
thaw *vb.* melt (of ice or snow).
theater *n.* 1. a place where plays are performed by actors and watched by an audience. 2. an operating room where medical students may watch surgical operations performed.
theatrical *adj.*
► The earliest theaters we know about were in Greece. They were simply flattened patches of ground on a hillside. The audience sat in rows on the hill above so that they could all see the "stage." When the Greeks built their theaters they followed this plan. They cut a half-moon or horseshoe shape in the hillside and lined it with rows of stone seats, looking down on a round, flat stage.

The Romans copied the Greek pattern, but they built most of their theaters on flat ground. The rows of seats were held up by a wall. The Romans built a theater in nearly every large town in the empire.

In Britain, there were no theater buildings before the 1500s. Troops of actors went around the country performing plays outside churches or in market places. They used their traveling carts as stages. Later, they began to put on plays in the great halls of rich people's houses and in the courtyards of inns. The first theaters to be built were made of wood, and looked very much like inns. The stage jutted out into a large yard. Galleries of seats ran all around the sides. These theaters had no roofs. When it rained, the groundlings — the poor people who stood in the yard around the stage — got wet. SHAKESPEARE's plays were performed in theaters like this.

Later, theaters had roofs. The stage was moved back and the audience sat in straight rows directly in front of it. Most theaters today look like this. But many people are interested in going back to the Greek plan.

theft *n.* stealing.
their *pron.* belonging to them.
theme *n.* the main subject. *The theme of the book is love.*
then *adv.* at that time. *I didn't know you so well then.* after that; next.

theology *n*. the study of religion.
▶ Theology tries to deal with the nature of God and of our relationship with him. Christian theology deals with the study of the BIBLE, the doctrines of the church, the nature of "right" and "wrong," the different paths to God, the forms of public worship, and the defense of Christian beliefs against criticism. There is also comparative religion, which studies different religious beliefs throughout the world.

theory *n*. an idea to explain something. *I have a theory about why he ran away.*

there *adv*. in or to that place. *Put the box down there.*

therefore *adv*. for that reason; and so.

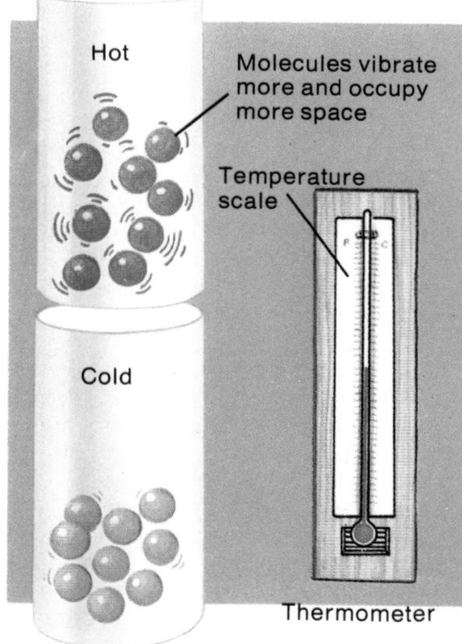

The tube of a thermometer contains a liquid (silver is mercury, red or blue is colored alcohol). When the thermometer gets warm the liquid expands and force some of the liquid up the tube. If it gets colder, the liquid contracts and falls.

thermometer *n*. an instrument for measuring temperature.
▶ A thermometer usually consists of a glass tube marked with a scale. Inside is another, thinner glass tube, which ends in a bulb containing liquid MERCURY. When the temperature goes up, the mercury gets warm and expands (grows bigger). It rises up the tube. When it stops, you can read the temperature on the marked scale. When it gets cold, the mercury contracts (grows smaller) and sinks down the tube. Most thermometers measure temperatures between the boiling and freezing points of water. This is between 32° and 212° on the Fahrenheit scale or 0° and 100° on the CENTIGRADE SCALE.

Medical thermometers, which are small enough to go in your mouth, measure your blood heat. This is usually 98.6°F (37°C). Household thermometers tell you how warm or cold the air around your house is.

thermos *n*. a vacuum container for keeping beverages or foods at a constant temperature.

thermostat *n*. an instrument that automatically controls a heating system or sprinkler system.
▶ The thermostat in many electrical appliances, such as electric blankets and irons, is a simple switch, the moving part being a *bimetallic* strip. It consists of two strips of metal that expand at different rates when heated. As the strips are bonded together, the uneven expansion causes bending. This movement switches off the electric current when the temperature rises beyond a certain point. After a short period of cooling the bimetallic strip returns to its original position and switches the current on again. The thermostat's automatic switching action ensures that the temperature of the appliance is kept within certain limits.

thesaurus *n*. a book like a dictionary, but without definitions, and with words of similar meaning listed together in groups.

thick *adj*. wide; not thin or slender. *The walls of the ancient castle were several feet thick.* 2. (of a liquid) flows more slowly. 3. an impolite word meaning "stupid."

thicket *n*. a dense growth of small trees and shrubs.

thief *n*. (plural **thieves**) a person who steals.

thigh (rhymes with *my*) *n*. the part of your leg between your hip and your knee.

thimble *n*. a small covering, often made of metal, worn on the finger to avoid pricking it when sewing.

thin *adj*. lean, slim; not thick.

think *vb*. 1. use your brain to work out a problem; consider, reflect. 2. believe. *I think that's the right direction, but I'm not absolutely sure.*

think over *vb*. consider.

third 1. *adj*. next after second. 2. *n*. one of three pieces that make the whole thing. *There were three of us, so we each had one third of the cake.*

Third World
The Third World is a phrase used to describe the poorer nations in our world. The first two "worlds" are the rich and powerful nations of the East, led by the Communist countries of the U.S.S.R and CHINA; and the Western countries, of which the most powerful is the UNITED STATES.

The Third World countries are in ASIA, AFRICA and SOUTH AMERICA. Many of them supply the rest of the world with cheap food, minerals, timber and fibers, as well as cheap labor.

thirst 1. *n*. (a dry feeling caused by) the need to drink. 2. *vb*. want something to drink. **thirsty** *adj*.

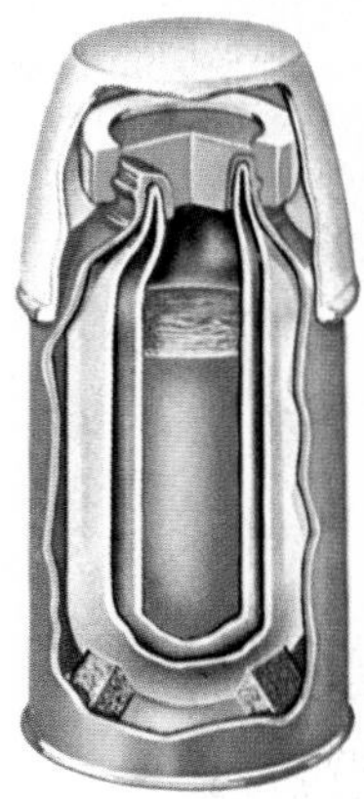

A thermos or vacuum bottle has double walls. Between them is a vacuum to keep the heat in.

Thirty Years War
The Thirty Years War in Germany (1618–48) was between the Catholic HAPSBURG emperors and the Protestant princes. It was a power struggle as much as a religious war. The princes were aided by, in turn, Denmark, Sweden and France. In the end the Hapsburgs lost any real authority over the local princes, but the population and countryside had been devastated by the conflicting armies of paid mercenary soldiers.

this *pron*. & *adj*. (plural **these**) the one here, not a different one.

thistle (**this**-*sel*) *n*. one of a family of plants with prickly leaves. *The thistle is the national emblem of Scotland.*

thorax *n*. part of an insect that bears the wings and legs; (in humans) the chest.

thorn *n*. a sharp spiky projection on some kinds of plant, such as the rose.

thorough (**thur**-*o*) *adj*. proper and careful. *Fred gave his room a thorough cleaning.*

thoroughbred *n*. a pure breed of horse.

thoroughfare *n*. a public main road or street.

though (*tho*) *conj*. even so; even if; although.

thought *vb*. past and past part. of **think**.

thought (*thawt*) *n*. an idea or an opinion; meditation. **thoughtless** *adj*. unthinking, inconsiderate. **thoughtful** *adj*. absorbed in thought; considering other people.

thousand *n*. the figure 1,000; 10 hundreds.

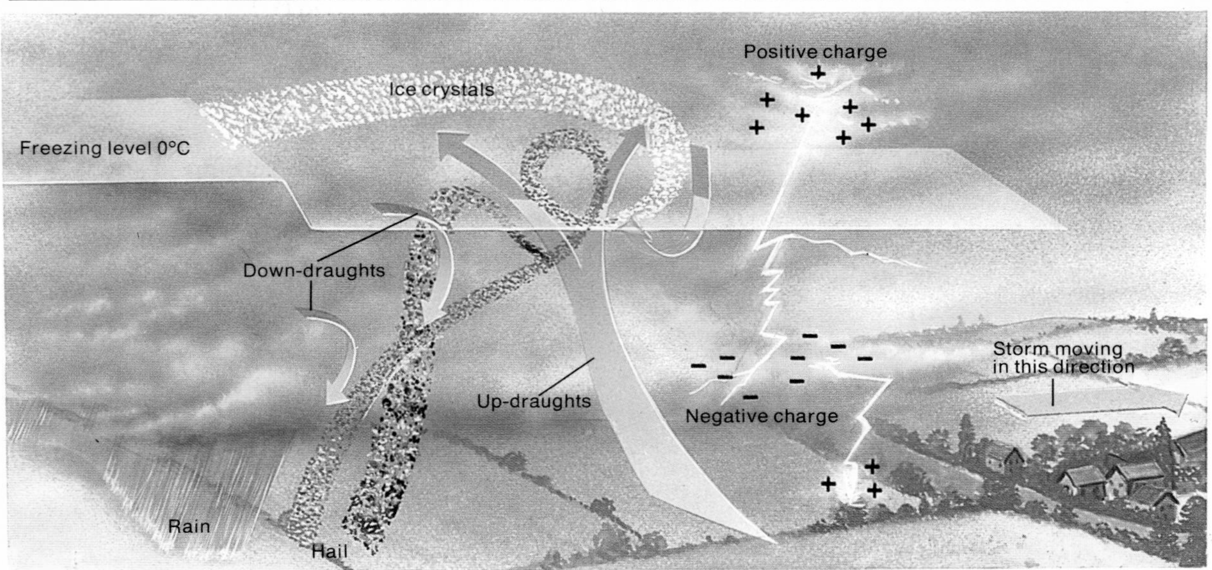

thrash *vb.* beat; defeat.
thread (rhymes with *bed*) *n.* a length of spun fiber. *vb.* put a thread through a hole, such as the eye of a needle. **threadbare** *adj.* with the threads showing, shabby.
threaten *vb.* warn that you will do something bad. *Michael tried to threaten his sister with a punch.* **threat** *n.*
thresh *vb.* beat the seeds from stalks of grain.
threw *vb.* past of **throw**.
thrift *n.* manage one's money carefully; not being extravagant. **thrifty** *adj.* economical.
thrill *vb.* make someone excited. **thriller** *n.* a novel or play with a lot of suspense and intrigue, usually about crime.
throat *n.* the front of your neck, and the tubes inside that take food and air into your body.
throb *vb.* beat strongly and rhythmically like the heart.
thrombosis *n.* a blood clot in the heart or a blood vessel.
throne *n.* a special chair for a king or queen, or some other important person.
throttle 1. *vb.* choke, strangle. 2. *n.* a device for controlling the flow of fuel in a car, etc.
through (*thru*) *prep.* from one side to another. *The stone went right through the glass.*
throw *vb.* (past **threw** past part. **thrown**) fling or hurl an object, such as a ball.
throw up *vb.* be sick, vomit.
thrush *n.* 1. member of a family of small songbirds. 2. a disease affecting animals' feet.
thrust *vb.* push, force, shove; pierce. *They thrust their way through the crowd. n.* a stab. *A sword thrust.*
thug *n.* a gangster, cutthroat or ruffian.

thumb (*thum*) 1. *n.* the short, thick finger on each hand. 2. *vb.* flick through the pages of a book or magazine. *John thumbed through the magazine.*
thunder *n.* the noise that follows lightning in a storm.
thunderstorm *n.* a rainstorm with thunder and lightning.
► Thunderstorms are caused by ELECTRICITY in the air. Different electrical charges build up inside big rain clouds. When the charges are strong enough, a spark leaps from one charged part of the cloud to another. Sometimes the spark jumps from the cloud to the ground. We see the spark as LIGHTNING. Lightning heats up the air. The air expands (gets bigger) so quickly that it explodes, making the crashing noise we call thunder.

Since sound travels much slower than LIGHT, you always hear thunder after you see lightning. It takes thunder about five seconds to travel one mile. To find out how many miles away the storm is, count the seconds between seeing the lightning and hearing the thunder, and divide the number by five.

Thursday *n.* the fifth day of the week, between Wednesday and Friday; named after Thor, Norse god of thunder.
thus *conj.* and so.
thyme (*time*) *n.* an herb, of the mint family, used in cooking.
thyroid *n.* an important gland in the neck near the larynx.
► The thyroid makes a hormone that helps growth and stimulates the body's *metabolism* (its rate of working). If the thyroid is too active it may enlarge, swelling the neck (goiter). If it is under-active it may cause a type of mental deficiency (cretinism).

Thunder is the sound made when lightening heats up the molecules of air along its path. The heated molecules expand and collide with colder molecules and so set up sound waves. Thunder travels at about 12 miles a minute while lightning travels at about 186,000 miles per second.

tiara *n.* a jeweled head ornament worn by women.

Tibet (Tibetan)
Tibet is a region of China. It occupies a high windswept plateau in southcentral ASIA. Tibet was part of China in the 1700s and 1800s, but it became virtually independent in the 1900s. In 1950 China occupied Tibet. After putting down a revolt in 1959, the Chinese made Tibet an autonomous region in 1969.

tick 1. *vb.* make a light, repeated sound like a clock. 2. *n.* a small insect that burrows into the skin of animals and sucks their blood.
ticket *n.* a piece of printed card or paper that allows you to enter somewhere, such as a cinema, or travel on public transport. *Tom had to pay his bus fare again because he'd lost his ticket.*
tickle *vb.* touch someone lightly. *I tickled the baby's feet and made her laugh. n.* sensation of tickling.
tide *n.* the regular rise and fall of the sea. **tidal** *adj.*
► The highest, spring tides, occur when the earth, moon and sun are in a straight line. The combined gravitational pull of the moon and sun makes high tides higher and low tides lower. The lowest, neap, tides occur when the moon, earth and sun form a right angle (*see* GRAVITY).
In the Bay of Fundy the tidal range can be as much as 50 feet (15 meters).

►► **Tidal waves** have nothing to do with tides. They are nearly always caused by an EARTHQUAKE under the sea. Sometimes they can be caused by very strong winds. Tidal waves can travel very fast – up to 500 mph (800 k/h) – and can easily destroy whole towns. One of the worst tidal waves happened in 1883. A VOLCANO on the island of Krakatoa in the East Indies exploded. The tidal wave caused by the explosion killed more than 20,000 people.

One strange thing about tidal waves is that people at sea may never notice them. This is because the patch of sea that is suddenly raised or lowered is so large, and the ships on it so small in comparison, the people on board do not feel the movement.

Another name for tidal wave is *tsunami* (pronounced *sue-na-me*).

tidy *adj*. neat, in order. *vb*. make tidy.

tie 1. *vb*. fasten something with string or rope. 2. *n*. a thin piece of cloth worn knotted around the neck of a shirt.

tier (rhymes with *ear*) *n*. two or more ranks or layers placed above one another. *The wedding cake had four tiers.*

tiff *n*. a minor quarrel.

tiger *n*. a large, striped animal belonging to the cat family.

► Tigers live in Asia and have an orange coat striped with black. They lie quiet during the heat of the day and hunt by night, usually alone. They kill and eat all kinds of animals, from monkeys to buffaloes, even people. Tigers are good swimmers, but poor climbers; yet they can spring up to a branch 20 ft. (6 meters) high.

At Full Moon and New Moon, when the sun and moon are pulling in the same direction, we get spring tides with higher high tides and lower low tides. When the sun and moon are pulling at right angles, we get neap tides.

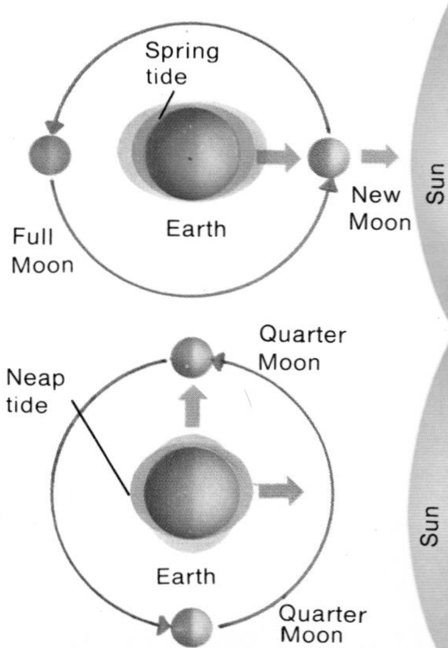

tight *adj*. 1. close-fitting; difficult to remove. 2. (*slang*) drunk.

tights *pl.n*. a close-fitting piece of clothing that covers your feet, legs and body up to your waist.

tigress *n*. a female tiger.

tile *n*. a flat piece of hard material used to cover floors, walls or roofs.

till 1. *n*. a machine used for adding and storing money in a shop. 2. *vb*. dig the land. 3. *prep*. up to, as late as.

tiller *n*. the handle or lever for turning a boat's rudder from side to side.

tilt *vb*. make something slope or slant. *n*. a sloping surface.

timber *n*. growing trees or their wood; wood suitable for carpentry or building.

Through over-hunting tigers have become rare and are now protected.

time *n*. seconds, minutes, hours, days, months and years are all ways of measuring time. *vb*. record time of; choose the right time.

► Our system of keeping time is based on periods determined by the movements of the earth and moon. The rotation of the earth on its axis gives us the length of each day. The movement of the moon around the earth gives rise to the moon's changing appearance, known as its phases. These repeat every *lunar* (moon) month. And the earth's period of rotation around the sun determines the length of the year. For convenience, we have modified our CALENDAR so that each year contains exactly 12 months and exactly 365 days, or 366 days in LEAP YEARS.

As primitive people became more civilized, their life became more complicated. In order to plan their activities, they invented various timekeeping devices. These early clocks included the sundial, water clock, sandglass and marked candle. Mechanical clocks appeared in the 1300s. These had only an hour hand, for it was not until the late 1600s that clocks were accurate enough to warrant having a minute hand. Today, extreme accuracy can be attained. Wrist watches regulated by tiny vibrating crystals remain accurate to within a few seconds over a period of several weeks.

timetable *n*. a list of times at which certain things will happen. *The timetable showed us when our train would depart.*

timid *adj*. shy, not brave.

tin 1. *n*. a soft, pale metal which is mixed with other metals, or sometimes used to coat metal objects. 2. *n*. a container for food, a can. 3. *adj*. made of tin.

► Tin is one of the oldest METALS known to us. People were mining tin before IRON was discovered. Tin was mixed with copper to make BRONZE.

Tin was mined in CORNWALL in England, long before the birth of Christ. The Phoenicians sailed from the Mediterranean to trade cloth and precious stones for it. Tin mining went on in Cornwall until 1928. Then large amounts of tin were discovered in MALAYSIA and other countries.

Tin cans are made from sheets of steel that have been coated with tin. Tin does not rust.

tinge *vb*. give a slight color to; tint.

tingle *vb*. a sensation like "pins and needles."

tinker *n*. a person who goes from place to place mending things, such as pots and pans.

tinkle *n*. a short ringing sound like a bell.

tinsel *n*. glittering and sparkling material used for decorations.

tint *vb*. & *n*. a slight or pale color.

tiny *adj*. very small.

tip 1. *n*. the point or end of something. *You can only see the tip of an iceberg above the sea.* 2. *vb*. knock over or spill something. 3. *n*. & *vb*. give someone, such as a waiter, reward for service.

tipsy *adj*. slightly drunk.

tiptoe *n*. the end of your toe. *vb*. walk on tiptoe. *She tiptoed out of the room.*

tire *vb*. become weary. **tireless** *adj*. seemingly incapable of becoming tired.

tissue *n*. 1. any kind of very fine fabric or material. 2. a paper handkerchief. 3. the mass of cells that make up the body of an animal or plant.

T

tit or **titmouse** *n.* any of a variety of small, active birds, e.g. blue tit.
titanium *n.* a silvery metallic element found in various ores and used mainly as an alloy. (symbol – *Ti*).

Titian
Titian was an Italian painter (c. 1487–1576). His real name was Tiziano Vecellio. He is famous for royal portraits of the HAPSBURGS Charles V and Philip II of Spain; for religious paintings such as the *Entombment of Christ*; and for mythological pictures such as *Venus and Adonis*. He also introduced new approaches to composition and use of color. He was the greatest of the Venetian painters of the Renaissance.

title *n.* 1. the name of a book, play, film, etc. 2. the words used to show a person's rank, such as "Doctor."
titter *vb.* & *n.* a nervous giggle.
toad *n.* a froglike amphibian that has a rough warty skin. It lives mainly on land.
► Toads are AMPHIBIANS. They have no teeth, a rough and warty skin and are usually fatter and clumsier than frogs. They spend less time in the water than frogs, but most of them mate and lay their eggs in water, and spend the first part of their lives as tadpoles.
Toads eat slugs, snails, caterpillars, insects and other small animals. They flick out their long sticky tongues to catch food. If attacked, toads can produce poison from the two bumps behind their eyes. This poison covers their skin,

The male midwife toad carries the eggs in strings wrapped round his legs.

and makes the toads harmful to most of their animal enemies.

toadstool *n.* a kind of fungus like a mushroom, many varieties of which are poisonous.
toast *vb.* & *n.* 1. a slice of bread browned on both sides by grilling. 2. drink to someone's health, success or happiness. *We drank a toast to Rob on his birthday.*
tobacco *n.* the plant or leaves of the plant nicotiana which are dried and used in cigarettes, pipes, and cigars.
toboggan *n.* a long, flat sled for sliding down snowy hills. *vb.* travel by toboggan.
► The North American Indians first made and used toboggans to bring home their winter catch.
Most toboggans are used for fun. On the famous Cresta Run in Switzerland, big toboggans are ridden by teams of competitors and can go as fast as 90 mph (145 k/h).

today *n.* this day; the present time.
to-do *n.* unnecessary fuss.
toe *n.* one of the five digits on the foot.
toffee *n.* a sticky kind of candy made from sugar and butter.
toga *n.* a flowing garment worn by men in ancient Rome, made of a large circular piece of woolen cloth.
together *adv.* in company with someone or something.

Togo
Togo is a small republic in West AFRICA, sandwiched between BENIN in the east and GHANA to the west. The climate is tropical. Farming is the main activity, and cocoa and coffee are the most important crops. Phosphates are the chief export.
Formerly a German protectorate, Togo was partitioned between Britain and France during WORLD WAR I. In 1957 the British section joined Ghana. French Togo became fully independent in 1960.
AREA: 21,623 SQ. MILES (56,000 SQ. KM)
POPULATION: 2,693,000
CAPITAL: LOME

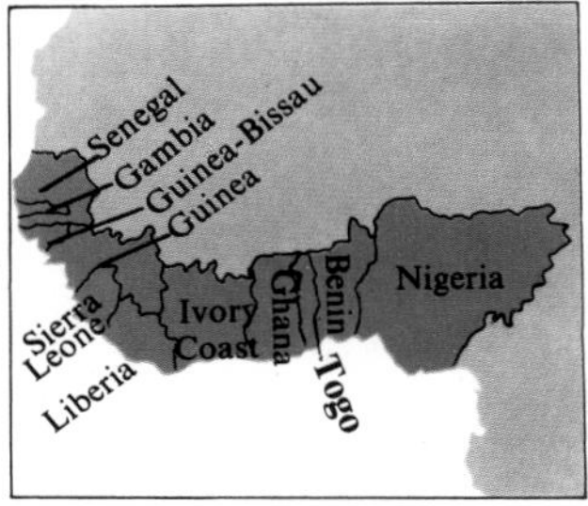

CURRENCY: FRANC
OFFICIAL LANGUAGE: FRENCH

toil *vb.* & *n.* work very hard. *She toiled all day for little pay.*
toilet *n.* a lavatory, or the room in which the lavatory is.
token *n.* a symbol; a coin or other item used to represent something else.

Tokyo
Tokyo is the capital of JAPAN. Nearly 12 million people live there, twice as many people as live in the whole of Finland. Tokyo is on the southeast coast of Honshu, the main island of Japan.
Almost every kind of work goes on in this enormous city. There are factories which make paper, electrical goods, automobiles and motorbikes. There are also huge shipyards and oil refineries on the coast. So many people work in Tokyo that some have to spend four hours a day going to and from their places of work.
Much of the city was destroyed by an earthquake in 1923. What was left was badly bombed in WORLD WAR II. Since then the city has been almost entirely rebuilt, but a number of beautiful old buildings remain. The Imperial Palace is an old shogun castle, and there are many ancient temples and shrines.

The toga (right) was a flowing garment worn by Roman men. It was made of a large circular piece of woolen cloth. Women wore a stola (left).

told *vb.* past of **tell**.
tolerate *vb.* allow to happen; endure or put up with. *I will not tolerate bad manners.*
toll (rhymes with *coal*) 1. *n.* money paid in some places for crossing a bridge or for using a road. 2. *n.* & *vb.* ring or sound (of) a large, heavy bell, especially one used for funerals.

Tolstoy, Count Leo Nikolaevich
Tolstoy (1828–1910) was a Russian nobleman who is considered to be one of the world's greatest writers. His masterpiece is *War and Peace*, an immensely long book about Russian life during the Napoleonic Wars. *Anna Karenina* is the title of another famous novel by Tolstoy.

tomahawk *n.* an Indian war hatchet.
tomato *n.* (plural **tomatoes**) a round, red, juicy fruit eaten as a vegetable.
► Tomatoes contain a very good supply of vitamins A and C. They were first grown in South America. They were being grown in the Andes mountains thousands of years ago. In 1596 the Spanish brought them to Europe. But at first, no one there would eat them because they were thought to be poisonous. Tomatoes were kept as ornamental plants. For a long time, they were called "love apples", or "golden apples."
In hot countries such as Spain and Italy tomatoes are grown in the open. In cool countries, such as Holland, they are grown in greenhouses. When they are ripe they can be eaten fresh in salads. Otherwise they are canned whole, or made into sauce, paste or juice for cooking.

tomb (rhymes with *room*) *n.* a place where dead bodies are buried.
tomcat *n.* a male cat.
tome *n.* a large, heavy, scholarly book.
tom-tom *n.* a small drum, usually played with the hands.
tomorrow *n.* & *adv.* the day after today.
ton *n.* measure of great weight. *A "short" ton is 2,000 pounds.*
tone 1. *n.* the musical quality of a sound. 2. *vb.* tint (of colors, etc.).
► A tone in MUSIC is the sound of any one note. A tone may be a long or a short sound, or soft or loud. Tone can also describe colors. Deep tones are dark colors such as navy blue. Warm tones are colors like red and orange.

Tonga (Tongan)
Tonga is an island kingdom in the South PACIFIC. It consists of 169 islands and islets. There are both coral and volcanic islands. Coconuts and bananas are leading products. Most of the people are Polynesians. Tonga was formerly known as the Friendly Islands, and was a British protectorate from 1900 until it was granted its independence in 1970.
AREA: 270 SQ. MILES (699 SQ. KM)
POPULATION: 99,000
CAPITAL: NUKU'ALOFA
CURRENCY: PA'ANGA
LANGUAGE: ENGLISH

tongs *pl. n.* (a pair of) an implement similar to pincers for grasping and holding objects, especially hot ones, e.g. *coal tongs.*
tongue *n.* the flap of muscle inside the mouth that we use for tasting, swallowing and speaking.
► The human tongue is made up of muscle which is covered by a mucous membrane. It contains many nerves and *taste buds*. Flavors such as sweet, sour and salty go from the taste buds through nerves to the brain. We then notice a taste sensation. The tongue's movement directs food towards the teeth or the throat, and also changes the shape of the mouth to help give the different sounds used in speaking. The letters "t" and "g," for example, cannot be pronounced without using the tongue in a certain way.
Only VERTEBRATES have tongues. In toads, the tongue is fixed to the front of the mouth. Snakes have forked or split tongues which can "smell" the air. Cats' tongues are covered in tiny hooks of flesh which they can use like combs to clean their fur.

tonight *n.* the night of this day.
tonsils *pl. n.* a pair of glands at the back of the throat, one on each side.
► Tonsils help to protect the body from GERMS coming in through the mouth.
Children have very large tonsils. These gradually shrink as they grow older. Sometimes, tonsils can become infected. They swell up and are very painful (*tonsillitis*). The tonsils may have to be taken out in a hospital.

too *adv.* as well as; also; in addition to something. *May I come, too?*
took *vb.* past of **take**.
tool *n.* a device such as a hammer or screwdriver that helps you do a job; an implement.
tooth *n.* one of the hard, bony parts in your mouth which are used for chewing food. **toothache** *n.* a pain in one or more teeth.
top 1. *n.* the highest point of something, summit. 2. *n.* a spinning toy. *adj.* at the top, uppermost.
topaz *n.* a semiprecious usually crystalline stone of yellow, white, blue or pink.
topic *n.* a subject of conversation, etc. **topical** *adj.* relating to what is of interest at the moment.
topple *vb.* overturn, fall headlong.
topsy-turvy *adv.* & *adj.* upside down; totally disordered.
torah *n.* the scroll of the first five books of the Bible – the Pentateuch – used in a synagogue for religious purposes.
torch *n.* a burning stick used to give light or flame.
tore *vb.* past of **tear**.
torment *n.* & *vb.* tease, annoy, cause distress.
torn *vb.* past part. of **tear**.
tornado *n.* (plural **tornadoes**) a violent storm with heavy rain.
► Tornadoes mostly happen in the Americas. While hurricanes are strong winds that build up over the sea, tornadoes build up over land. They happen when large masses of cloud meet. The clouds begin to whirl around each other. Gradually, these whirling clouds join together to make a gigantic, twisting funnel. When this touches the ground, it sucks up anything in its path – trees, houses, animals, trains or people.

Toronto
Toronto is the capital of the Ontario province in CANADA. It has a good harbor, sheltered by islands, and this has made it an excellent port for the GREAT LAKES. Toronto handles a lot of the ocean shipping that comes through the St. Lawrence Seaway.
Toronto is the second largest city in Canada. It has many factories and businesses which produce goods such as timber, machines, clothing, electrical parts, aircraft and furniture. It is also the center of book publishing in Canada. Canada's largest university is in Toronto.
In 1749, the French set up a trading post on the site. There had been an Indian village there called Toronto, which means "the place of meeting." The British chose Toronto as their capital of the province in 1794.

torpedo *n.* a cigar-shaped explosive weapon used against ships.
► A torpedo is propelled by an electric motor or engine. Its nose contains devices that guide it to its target. The warhead, behind the nose, has a device which makes the torpedo explode. Some torpedoes explode near a ship's hull. Others explode when they hit the ship. Surface vessels such as motor torpedo boats and destroyers use torpedoes. So do submarines and aircraft. ROCKETS can carry them to distant targets.
Motor torpedo boats are used to defend coastal waters. Because of their speed, which can be over 50 knots, they are also used as commando raiders.

torrent *n.* 1. a rushing stream. 2. a heavy flow of something.

Torricelli, Evangelista
Evangelista Torricelli (1608–1647) was an Italian scientist who helped GALILEO with his work in Florence. Torricelli is remembered chiefly for his invention of the barometer. The vacuum formed at the top of the tube of a mercury barometer is still called a "Torricellian vacuum." He also made a microscope and some of the best telescopes of his day.

torso *n.* the trunk of a body or statue (without head or limbs).

A tornado moving across a Texas city.

T

tortoise *n.* a slow-moving land reptile with a hard shell.
▶ Tortoises can walk only about 15 ft. (4.5 meters) in a minute. When frightened, they pull their heads and legs inside their domed shells. The 40 or so kinds of tortoise live on land in warm parts of the world. They are similar to TURTLES and TERRAPINS, but these reptiles live in water.
Giant tortoises live in the Galapagos Islands and islands in the Indian Ocean. They can weigh up to 496 lb. (225 kg) and be 6 ft. (1.8 meters) long. Some large tortoises live for over 150 years – that is far longer than any other animal.

torture *n.* & *vb.* treating someone very cruelly on purpose.
toss *vb.* throw lightly into the air.
total 1. *adj.* complete, all of something. 2. *n.* the answer when a series of numbers is added together.
totem *n.* an emblem or symbol of a clan or family. *A* **totem pole** *is carved with emblems that tell a story.*
▶ Totem poles are long, wooden poles, which contain several carved symbols, one on top of another. The totems are often birds, fish or other animals. Totem poles stand outside the homes of North American Indians of the Pacific Coast.

toucan *n.*, a large bird with an enormous orange beak.
▶ A toucan's beak is very large, but it is also very light. It uses its beak to feed and probably also to attract a mate. Its plumage color varies according to species. It is usually a mixture of black and yellow, orange, red, blue, green or white. Toucans belong to the forests of tropical America, live in flocks and feed mostly on fruit. They make a harsh, ugly noise.

touch 1. *vb.* feel something. *I reached out until I could just touch the wall.* 2. *n.* the sense of feeling.
touching 1. *vb.* having surfaces in contact with one another. 2. *adj.* feeling of tenderness. *The film had a very touching ending.*
tough (*tuff*) *adj.* not easily cut, strong and rough.
tour *n.* & *vb.* a journey on which a number of places are visited.
tournament *n.* a series of games in which the skills of the competitors are tested.
tow *vb.* pull a vehicle, boat, etc., behind another. *Our car's broken down. Can you tow us to the nearest garage?*
toward *prep.* in the direction of something. *The car was coming toward us much too fast.*
towel *n.* absorbent cloth for drying or wiping off wetness.
tower *n.* a kind of tall building, or the tall part of a building such as a church.

An African leopard tortoise.

town *n.* a large group of houses and other buildings that is larger than a village but smaller than a city.
toy *n.* a child's plaything.
▶ The first toys date back to early times. The ancient Egyptians made toys from clay and wood. Some wooden toy crocodiles made by them had movable jaws. Toys made between the 1500s and 1800s were often works of art and are prized by collectors.

trace 1. *vb.* copy something by covering it with very thin paper and drawing around the outline that shows through. **traceable** *adj.* 2. *n.* a small sign, mark or amount left by something.

This painted thunderbird is part of a totem pole carved by the Kwakiutl, an American Indian tribe of Canada.

trachea (**tray**-*keya*) *n.* the windpipe.
track 1. *n.* a series of marks left by an animal or a vehicle. *vb.* follow something by watching for the signs, or tracks, it has left behind. 2. *n.* a railway line. 3. *n.* very strong chains of steel which are used instead of wheels on tanks and some kinds of tractor. 4. *n.* section of a recording.
tract *n.* 1. a stretch of land. 2. a pamphlet or leaflet.
tractor *n.* a strong motor vehicle used to pull farm machinery.

trade *vb.* buy and sell; exchange.
▶ Trade also includes barter, which is the exchange of one type of goods for goods of a different kind. Domestic trade is trade that takes place within one country.
Companies that buy goods in large quantities from factories or farms, store them and then sell them to stores are called *wholesalers*. Companies that sell the goods to the general public are called *retailers*.
International trade is trade between countries. Imports are things that a country buys. Exports are things that a country sells. Some imports and exports are said to be *visible*. These include raw materials, such as iron ore, and farm products, such as food. They also include factory-made goods, ranging from pencils to jets. Other imports and exports are *invisible*. These include banking and INSURANCE, transport services and money spent by tourists.
Nearly every country now depends on trade. For example, poor countries import factory-made goods, because they lack industries of their own. To do this, they export the raw materials and food they produce.
Trade gives us a wider choice of things to buy. But it also makes countries depend on each other. If one country's trade slows down, its trading partners feel the effects.

trademark *n.* a special mark or sign used to show who made something and prevent illegal copying.
trade union *n.* an organization of people who work in the same sort of job; a **labor union**.

The new (above) and older type of railroad track.

► The main aim of trade unions is to get better wages for their members and better working conditions. Some unions look after their members and their families in times of trouble. If a trade union has a serious disagreement with an employer, it may stop its members from working. This is called a *strike*.

Modern trade unions were formed in the early days of the INDUSTRIAL REVOLUTION. They were first made legal in the 1870s. Since then, unions have gradually increased their power. Today, trade unions play an important part in the affairs of many countries.

tradition *n.* beliefs, customs, etc., which are handed down from one generation to another.

traffic *n.* vehicles such as cars and trucks, or people, traveling along roads. *The traffic is very heavy today, because lots of people are driving out into the countryside.*

traffic jam *n.* a situation when the traffic has come to a standstill or slowed down to a crawl.

traffic light *n.* a crossing signal of colored lights on a pole, which tells drivers when to go, slow down, and stop.

tragedy *n.* (plural **tragedies**) 1. a kind of play, usually with a sad ending. 2. any very sad event. *His death at such an early age was a terrible tragedy for his parents.* **tragic** *adj.*

► A tragedy is a type of play (DRAMA) in which the hero (or heroine) is caught in a situation or course of action from which there is no honorable escape. It usually ends with the hero's death. Great tragedies were written in the 400s B.C. in Athens (by AESCHYLUS, Sophocles and Euripides); in Renaissance England (by SHAKESPEARE and MARLOWE) and in France in the 1600s (by Corneille and Racine).

trail 1. *n.* a series of marks that show the way to somewhere; track. 2. *vb.* pull something along behind you. 3. *vb.* (of plant) grow along or hang down to the ground.

trailer *n.* a vehicle that is towed along behind another one.

train 1. *n.* a group of carriages or wagons joined together and pulled along the track by an engine. 2. *vb.* prepare for a test of skill. *The team trains three times a week.*

traitor *n.* someone who betrays country or friends.

tramp 1. *vb.* walk heavily. 2. *n.* a long walk, a hike. 3. *n.* a homeless person who wanders, or tramps, from place to place.

trample *vb.* tread heavily on something, thus crush or destroy.

tranquil (**tran**-*kwill*) *adj.* calm, peaceful. **tranquillizer** *n.* a calming drug.

trans- *prefix* meaning across or beyond, e.g. **Trans-Continental Railroad.**

transaction *n.* business that is carried out.

transfer *vb.* move from one job or place to another.

Transformer

A transformer is an electrical device that increases or decreases the voltage in a circuit. It has two separate coils of wire, placed near each other. The coils are usually wound on iron formers. An alternating voltage in one coil causes an alternating voltage in the other coil. If the *primary* coil has fewer turns of wire than the *secondary* coil, the voltage is greater in the secondary coil. If the primary coil has more turns than the secondary coil, the voltage is less in the secondary coil. Transformers are used in generating stations and in electronic equipment.

transistor *n.* a very small electronic device that is used in radios and other electrical equipment; a radio that uses transistors.

► A transistor is used to *amplify* (strengthen) signals in electronic equipment, such as radio receivers and television sets. Practical transistors were developed by American scientists William Shockley, Walter Brattain and John Bardeen in the late 1940s. When it became possible to mass produce reliable transistors, they were used instead of tubes in all kinds of electronic equipment. Transistors are much smaller than tubes, more efficient and cheaper generally to produce.

Today, complex circuits containing thousands of transistors can be constructed cheaply on chips of silicon only a quarter of an inch square. This development has revolutionized electronics.

translate *vb.* change from one language into another. *Pam had to translate a poem from Italian into English.* **translator** *n.*

transmission *n.* the passage of radio waves from the transmitting to the receiving station.

transmit *vb.* pass on, send out; broadcast.

transparent *adj.* something that is clear enough to see through.

transplant *vb.* move a plant from one bit of soil to another; move an organ, such as a heart or kidney, from one person's body to another.

transport (*trans*-**port**) *vb.* carry people or goods from one place to another. (**trans**-*port*) *n.* the vehicles in which people are carried.

transpose *vb.* change the order of.

Transvaal

The Transvaal lies in the northeast of SOUTH AFRICA. It is mainly dry and arid, and farming relies heavily on irrigation. The province contains Pretoria, the country's administrative capital, and Johannesburg, its largest city.

The Transvaal contains the world's richest goldfield. Much of its industry consists of processing and manufacturing connected with its mineral wealth.

trap *n.* & *vb.* a device for catching animals.

trapdoor *n.* a door covering an opening in the floor.

trapeze *n.* a bar hung on ropes far above the ground, and from which acrobats can swing.

trapezoid *n.* a four-sided figure with no sides parallel.

trash *n.* rubbish.

travel *n.* & *vb.* (past **traveled**) go from one place to another, make a journey.

trawler *n.* a fishing boat that drags (or trawls) nets along the bottom of

A mountain railroad. To prevent the locomotive slipping backward, a third, toothed, rail is laid in the center of the track, between the other two rails. Under the train are extra wheels called pinion wheels, the cogs of which mesh with the teeth of the center rail.

the sea to catch fish. **trawl** *n.* a large net. *vb.* to fish with a trawl.
► Trawling is fishing with a large bag-shaped net (trawl), dragged along the sea bottom. It is used to catch white fish such as haddock and cod. Modern trawlers are 100–170 ft. (31–52 meters) long, and some have equipment for automatically processing the catch.

tray *n.* a flat object for carrying dishes, etc.
treachery *n.* betraying the trust a person has in one.
treacle *n.* a dark kind of syrup, produced as a by-product of sugar refining.
tread 1. *vb.* (past **trod** past part. **trodden**) put your feet down on the ground. 2. *n.* the rubber and its raised pattern on the outside of a tire. 3. *n.* top surface of a step.
treason *n.* trying to overthrow a government or to kill or injure its leader.
treasure 1. *n.* a store of valuable things, such as gold and jewels. 2. *vb.* value something very highly. *Alan treasures signed photos of several stars.* **treasury** *n.* a place where valuable things are kept; the funds of a state.
treat 1. *vb.* behave toward someone in a certain way. *Caroline treats her baby brother very kindly.* 2. *vb.* use something to improve or change. *You can treat this stain with salt.* **treatment** *n.* 3. *n.* something that gives you special pleasure. *My aunt took us to the play for a treat.*
treaty *n.* a written and signed agreement between countries relating to alliance, commerce, etc.
tree *n.* the tallest kind of plant with only one thick central stem or trunk.
► Most trees grow to more than 25 ft. (7.6 meters) high. The biggest tree is a type of sequoia. These giants can grow to over 360 ft. (100 meters) high, and can be 80 ft. (25 meters) around. Trees can also live a long time. One bristlecone pine in California is nearly 5,000 years old.
Above the ground is the *crown* of the tree. This is made up of the trunk, branches, twigs and leaves. The *roots* are below the ground. They are the fastest growing part of the tree. They support the crown like a giant anchor. The roots take in water from the soil. The water is drawn up through the trunk to the leaves. A fully grown apple tree takes in about 79 gallons (360 liters) of water a day.

There are two main kinds of trees. CONIFERS are trees with needlelike leaves, such as PINES and SPRUCES. In place of flowers, they produce their seeds in cones. Most conifers are evergreens. This means they do not lose their leaves in the fall. Conifers grow in cold or dry regions.

The other kind of tree is the flowering, or broad-leaved, tree. Many of them, such as ELMS and OAKS, are *deciduous*, that is, they lose their leaves in the fall. But some broad-leaved trees, such as holly and many tropical forest trees, are evergreen. Broad-leaved trees have flowers which develop into FRUITS that completely surround the seeds. These trees are often called hardwoods, because of their tough, hard wood. It is harder than that of the softwood conifers.

Wild Apple

Yew

Walnut

tremble *vb.* shake gently all over.
tremendous *adj.* of great size or power; excellent.
trench *n.* a ditch, often used in warfare to protect troops.
trend *n.* the general direction or course.
trendy *adj.* following the latest fashions.
trespass *vb.* go on somebody else's land or property unlawfully. **trespasser** *n.* person who trespasses.
tri- *prefix* meaning three or threefold, e.g. **tricolor** having three colors.
trial *n.* 1. an examination in a court of law. 2. a test of something to see how good it is. *We watched the trial of the new helicopter.* 3. a hardship, affliction.
triangle *n.* 1. a flat shape with three sides. **triangular** *adj.* 2. a musical instrument made of metal, that is hit with a small metal rod.

► In mathematics a triangle is a plane figure bounded by three straight lines with the sum of the interior angles totalling 180°. The points of intersection are called *vertices*. The lines between the vertices are called sides; altitude is the perpendicular distance from the base (any side) to the opposite vertex. The area of a triangle equals one half the product of a base and its corresponding altitude.

tribe *n.* a group of people who have the same customs and language. **tribal** *adj.*
tributary *n.* a small stream or river that flows into a larger one.
trick 1. *n.* a joke or prank; a deceitful act or scheme. *vb.* deceive, cheat. 2. *n.* a piece of "magic" done by a conjuror. 3. *n.* a round played in some card games, such as bridge and whist.
trickle *vb.* flow in a thin stream.
tricolor *n.* a three-colored flag, especially the blue, white and red flag of France.
tricycle *n.* a three-wheeled cycle.
tried *vb.* past of **try**.
trifle *n.* 1. an unimportant or small thing. 2. a sweet pudding made from cake, custard, fruit, wine and cream. **trifling** *adj.* of small importance.
trigger *n.* the lever on a gun that is used to fire it.
trigonometry *n.* a branch of mathematics concerned with the properties of triangles.

► It was originally developed to help astronomers and navigators with calculations involving angles and distances. Trigonometry is also used by today's scientists and engineers in problems involving repetitive changes or movements, such as vibrations.

trim 1. *adj.* neat and tidy. 2. *vb.* cut something so as to make it neat and tidy. *Please trim my hair.* 3. *vb.* & *n.* (adorn with) small ornaments.

Trinidad and Tobago
This West Indian republic lies off the coast of VENEZUELA in SOUTH AMERICA. It consists of the island of Trinidad and the much smaller island of Tobago. Both are hilly and have a tropical climate. Citrus fruit, cocoa, coffee and sugar cane are grown. However, the main sources of wealth are oil, and asphalt from the Trinidad Pitch Lake. Tourism is also important.

The islands were discovered by Christopher COLUMBUS in 1498.

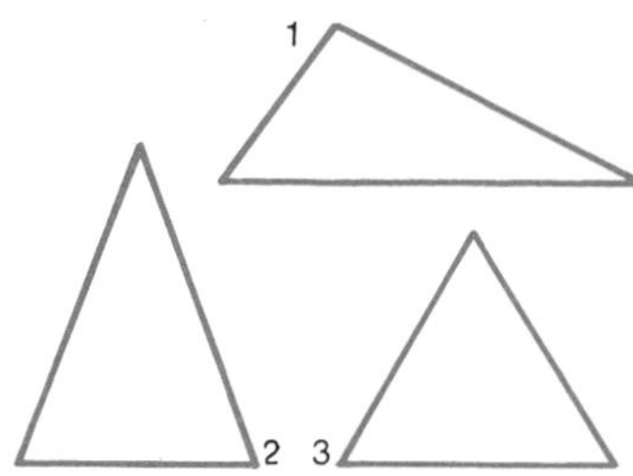

Three kinds of triangle: 1. Scalene 2. Isosceles 3. Equilateral.

Later, they passed into British hands. Full independence was achieved by the islands in 1962.
AREA: 1,981 SQ. MILES (5,130 SQ. KM)
POPULATION: 1,193,000
CAPITAL: PORT-OF-SPAIN
CURRENCY: TRINIDAD DOLLAR
OFFICIAL LANGUAGE: ENGLISH

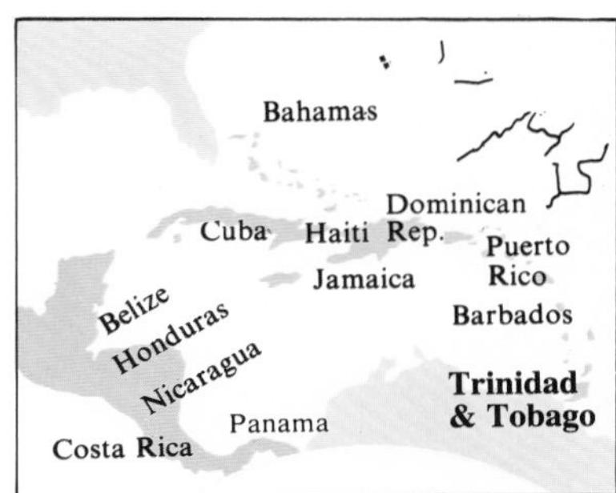

trinity *n.* a group of three.
trinket *n.* a small ornament or jewelry of little value.
trio *n.* three people working together, especially musicians.
trip 1. *n.* & *vb.* catch your foot on something and fall over. 2. *n.* a journey. *Have a good trip.*
tripe *n.* 1. the stomach of a cow eaten as food. 2. rubbish, worthless stuff.
triple *adj.* made of three parts. *vb.* make or become three times as great or as many.
triplet *n.* one of three babies born to the same mother at the same time.
triumph *n.* great victory or achievement. *vb.* rejoice in victory. **triumphal** *adj.*

T

troika *n.* Russian vehicle drawn by three horses abreast.

Trojan War
The Trojan War was fought in about 1200 B.C. between the Trojans of TROY and the Greeks. It lasted for 10 years. The poet Homer, in his poem the *Iliad*, tells the story of only a few days of the war. We know the rest of the story from other writings.

Paris was a prince of Troy. He fell in love with Helen, the wife of King Menelaus of Sparta in Greece. Paris took Helen to Troy, and Menelaus with other Greek kings and soldiers went to get her back. They besieged Troy for years. In the end they won by tricking the Trojans with a huge wooden horse, filled with Greek soldiers. (*See* TROY).

troll *n.* a goblin or dwarf, usually evil, in Scandinavian legends.
trolley *n.* an electric car for passengers that runs on tracks.
trombone *n.* a musical wind instrument made of brass.
► A trombone is a long tube that is bent twice to make it easier to hold. At one end is a mouthpiece; at the other a bell like that on a trumpet. Part of the tube is a sliding section. The player changes notes with his or her lips, and by moving the sliding section back and forth while blowing.

troops *pl.n.* a body of soldiers, armed forces in general.
trophy *n.* something taken in victory especially when kept as a memorial; a prize; a memento.
tropical fish *pl.n.* fish that live in the warm seas of tropical regions, often along the edges of coral reefs.
► Many small, brightly colored freshwater tropical fish are popular AQUARIUM pets. Marine fish can also be kept, but they are more expensive and difficult to look after. They have to have saltwater containing just the right amount of salt to live in. Many kinds of marine tropical fish can be seen in public aquariums.

Tropical fish live in warm water. Most tanks have a heater to keep the water at around 75°F (24°C). The exact temperature depends on the type of fish. A cover on the tank holds the heat in and stops the water from evaporating (drying up). Electric light bulbs in the cover light the tank and also heat the water. Most aquariums have air pumps that add OXYGEN to the water and filter it to keep it clear. Water plants also provide oxygen.

The most common tropical freshwater fish is the guppy. Its young are born alive, though they are often eaten by their parents. Other common kinds of tropical fish are angelfish, barbs and neon tetras.

tropics *pl.n.* the areas of land around the equator. **tropical** *adj*.

trot *vb.* & *n.* run with short steps like the slow run of a horse.
trouble *n.* problem; difficulty; disgrace or punishment. *Jerry got into trouble for breaking a window. vb.* disturb; put to inconvenience.
trough (*troff*) *n.* a long shallow container for the drinking water or feed of animals.
troupe *n.* a group of performers.
trousers *pl.n.* an article of clothing for the lower half of the body, divided into two sections, one for each leg; pants.
trout *n.* (plural **trout**) a silvery-brown, speckled freshwater fish belonging to the salmon family.
trowel *n.* 1. a garden tool like a small spade. 2. a flat-bladed tool for spreading mortar.

Troy
Troy was an ancient city sited on the coast of modern Turkey. HOMER's epic poem, the *Iliad*, tells how it was besieged by the Greeks for 10 years, and how it finally fell through a trick (the gift of a huge wooden horse with soldiers hidden inside). The story of Troy was thought to be imaginary until a German amateur archaeologist, Heinrich Schliemann, discovered the site of the city in 1871–94. (*See* TROJAN WAR).

truant *n.* a child who stays away from school when he or she is supposed to be there. **truancy** *n.*
truce *n.* a period when two sides in a war or quarrel agree to be at peace.
truck *n.* a motor vehicle used to carry big or heavy loads.

trudge *vb.* plod; walk steadily with great effort.
true *adj.* correct; accurate; not false; genuine. *I hope what you say is true.*
truffle *n.* 1. edible fungus that grows underground. 2. soft candy made of a chocolate mixture.
► Truffles have been cultivated in many parts of Europe and are a popular food. Because truffles grow underground, farmers use pigs to find them. The pigs are able to locate the fungi by smelling them. They then dig them out with their snouts.

Truman, Harry S.
Harry S. Truman was the 33rd president of the United States. He became president in 1945, at the end of WORLD WAR II when President Roosevelt died.

The years after the war were difficult ones for the president and for the country. When Truman stood as the Democratic candidate in 1948, many people thought he would lose. Some newspapers even printed their headlines ahead of time, saying Truman had been beaten. But Truman won and went on to become a respected leader who did a lot for world peace.

trumpet *n.* a brass wind musical instrument, played by pressing valves. *vb.* proclaim.
► Trumpets are one of our oldest instruments, dating from over 4,000 years ago. Modern trumpets consist

A male Siamese fighting fish.

of a coiled brass tube. The tube has a mouthpiece at one end and a flared bell at the other. To make different notes, the player changes the shape of his lips and blows harder or softer. He also presses down on stalklike valves to alter the length of tube being used. These valves were first added in the 1800s.

Brass sections of ORCHESTRAS contain trumpets. The trumpet is often used as a solo instrument in brass, jazz and military bands.

trump up *vb*. invent, fabricate.
trunk *n*. 1. the main stem of a tree. 2. the body of an animal apart from the head or limbs. 3. a large box. 4. the long nose of an elephant. 5. the luggage compartment of a car.
truss *vb*. tie up tightly; bind.
trust *vb*. believe that something or somebody is good, or will tell the truth. *n*. confidence in a person.
truth *n*. correctness, accuracy; something that is true. *I'm telling you the truth*.
try 1. *vb*. attempt to do something. **trying** *adj*. exhausting, difficult to bear. *He is a trying person*.
tsar (*zar*) *n*. (variant spelling of **czar**) the emperor of Russia until 1917.
tsetse (**tet**-*si*) *n*. brownish fly found in tropical Africa.
► Using a piercing-sucking mouthpiece, the tsetse feeds on the blood of animals, including humans. Testse flies are deadly pests, as they carry and transmit fatal diseases, such as sleeping sickness in humans and nagana in cattle.

Tuatara
The tuatara is the most primitive reptile alive today. It spends the day in a burrow and comes out at night to search for insects and other animal food. Often, instead of digging its own burrow, the tuatara shares the home of a petrel or other seabird.

tub *n*. 1. a small barrel. 2. a bath (bathtub). 3. an old, slow and clumsy ship or boat.
tuba *n*. a large musical wind instrument that gives a low note.
tubby *adj*. short and fat.
tube *n*. a long, hollow cylinder, especially for conveying liquids.
tuber *n*. the large part of an underground stem from which new plants grow. *A potato grows from a tuber*.
tuberculosis *n*. a disease caused by bacterial infection.
► One form of tuberculosis is carried in infected milk, and attacks the bones and joints of young people. The other is spread by bacteria in the air, and usually attacks the lungs. Both have now almost disappeared in developed countries.

tuck *n*. & *vb*. fold under. *Sheets are tucked under the mattress*.

Tudors
The House of Tudor was an English royal family which ruled England from 1485 to 1603. The first Tudor king was HENRY VII. He was a grandson of a Welsh squire, Owen Tudor, who had married Henry V's widow. Henry VII came to the throne after defeating Richard III at the Battle of Bosworth (1483). This ended the WAR OF THE ROSES (1455–85) between the houses of Lancaster and York. To join the houses, Henry VII, who belonged to a branch of Lancaster, married Elizabeth of York.

Henry VII was succeeded by his son, HENRY VIII. During the reign of Henry VIII (1509–47) the arts flourished in England. The king used PARLIAMENT to pass laws which broke all ties between England and the Roman Catholic Church.

Henry VIII was succeeded first by his son EDWARD VI, then by his daughters, Mary I and ELIZABETH I. When Elizabeth died in 1603, the crown went to King James VI of Scotland, the first of the Stuart kings.

The Tudors were strong rulers. During their time, England became richer and more powerful, especially at sea. The voyages of England's daring seamen led to more trade and new colonies. SHAKESPEARE wrote his plays during the reign of Elizabeth I.

Tuesday *n*. the third day of the week, between Monday and Wednesday; named after Tiw, Norse god of war.
tuft *n*. a small bunch, cluster or clump. *A tuft of hair or grass*.
tug 1. *vb*. pull hard.
tugboat *n*. a small, powerful boat that tows larger ships in and out of port.
tulip *n*. a brightly colored, spring garden flower which grows from a bulb.
tumble *vb*. fall down suddenly.
tumbling *n*. skill or practice of gymnastic feats, e.g. handsprings, flips, without use of any apparatus. *vb*. **tumble**.

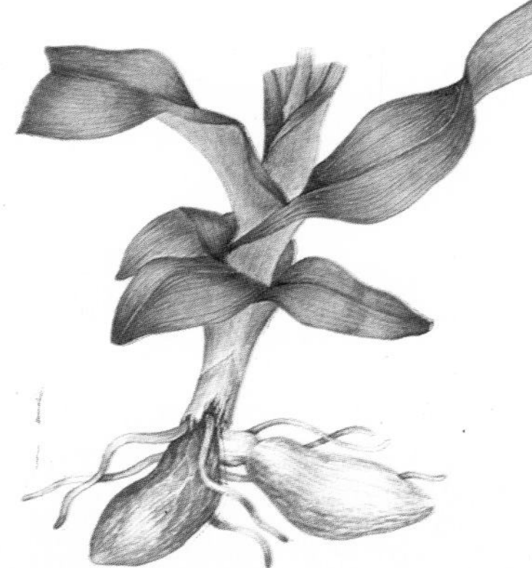

Tubers (wild orchids)

tumbler *n*. 1. a large glass without a stem. 2. an acrobat.
tummy *n*. (*casual*) stomach.
tumor *n*. a lump or swelling in the body made up of abnormal cells.
► Some tumors are malignant; they spread into the normal body cells and can travel to new parts of the body. These are called CANCERS and are highly dangerous.

The medal issued by Elizabeth I, the last of the Tudors, to celebrate the defeat of the Spanish Armada in 1488.

tuna *n*. a large fish, of the mackerel family.
► Tuna fishing is a big industry in many parts of the world. The tuna's flesh is rich in PROTEINS and VITAMINS. Most tuna live in warm seas, but they may swim into northern waters in summer. Different kinds of tuna include the bluefin, which may be 10 ft. (3 meters) long, and the albacore. Tuna are the only fish whose body temperature is higher than that of the water around them.

tundra *n*. the cold, treeless plains in the arctic and subarctic regions.
► In the tundra, the temperature never rises above freezing point except for about two months in the summer, when there is continual daylight.

tune *n*. a musical melody, especially the music that goes with a song. *He hummed a cheerful tune*.
tungsten *n*. (also called *wolfram*), a hard, heavy, gray-white metallic element (symbol – *W*).
► Tungsten is resistant to corrosion and has a high melting point. Tungsten is found in the minerals wolframite and scheelite. The metal is used to make electric light bulb filaments and is also used in various ALLOYS.

tunic *n*. a long, close-fitting jacket, often part of a uniform.

Tunisia (Tunisian)
Tunisia is a sunny country in North AFRICA. Its beaches attract many tourists from Europe. The north is rugged and has the most rain. The south is part of the dry SAHARA. Farming is the main industry in this small nation. But oil and phosphates are important exports. Most of the people are Muslims.

Near the capital, also called Tunis, are the ruins of Carthage. Carthage was a great Mediterranean Sea power until it was destroyed by the ROMAN EMPIRE in 146 B.C..

AREA: 63,174 SQ. MILES (163,610 SQ. KM)
POPULATION: 6,625,000
CAPITAL: TUNIS
CURRENCY: TUNISIAN DINAR
OFFICIAL LANGUAGE: ARABIC

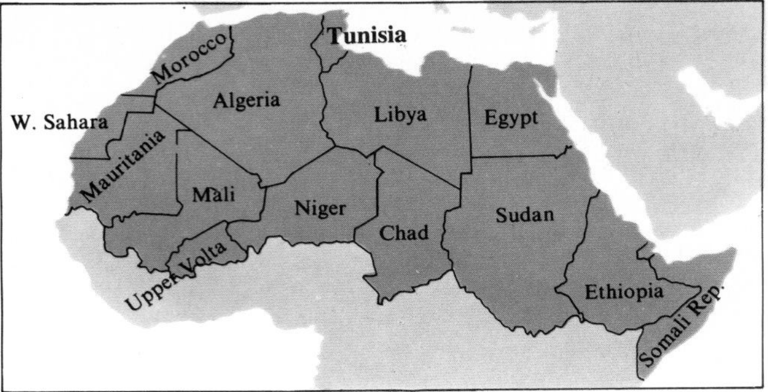

tunnel *n.* an underground passage. *vb.* dig under the ground.

▶ Tunneling is important in MINING, transportation and WATER SUPPLY. The Romans built tunnels to carry water. Today, the world's longest tunnel brings water to NEW YORK CITY. It is 105 miles (169 km) long.

The most famous tunnels are for roads and railroads. Tunnels must have a supply of fresh air, because car fumes are poisonous. But they can be used in all weather, whereas roads that wind over mountains may be blocked by snow. Railroad tunnels also run through mountains. Many large cities have underground railroads called subways.

Different methods are used to build tunnels. In hard rock, the tunnel is blasted out with explosives. Cutting machines, like those used to drill oil wells, are used in softer rock. In the softest rocks, tunnel shields are used. These are giant steel tubes, the same size as the intended tunnel. The front edge of the shield is sharp and is pushed into the earth. The earth is dug out and the tunnel behind the shield is lined to stop it from caving in.

Some underwater tunnels are built by lowering sections of tunnel into the river. Divers join them together. When the tunnel is complete, the water is pumped out. Subways can be built in deep trenches. When they are finished, they are covered over.

turban *n.* a head covering consisting of a long strip of cloth wound around and around a cap. Turbans are traditionally worn in some Eastern countries, often for religious reasons.

turbine *n.* an engine with a driving wheel (or screw) which is turned by water, steam or air.

▶ Water wheels and WINDMILLS are simple turbines.

Water turbines are used at hydroelectric power stations. These stations are next to dams or waterfalls. The force of water carried through a pipe in a dam turns the turbine. As the turbine spins it drives a GENERATOR, which produces the electricity. Some turbines are wheels or drums, with blades like screws or PROPELLERS.

Steam turbines are operated by jets of steam. They have many uses. They are used to produce electricity, to propel ships and to operate PUMPS. Gas turbines are turned by fast-moving jets of gas. The gases are produced by burning fuels such as oil. Gas turbines are used to turn the propellers of airplanes.

turbojet *adj.* & *n.* a type of gas turbine in which hot gases produced by the burning of fuel turn the blades of a fan whose shaft works the blades of a compressor which sucks in air and forces it into the combustion chamber.

Tunneling machines called moles are like huge drills that bore a shaft through the ground. The rotating cutters at the head of the mole dig out the earth, which is carried away on a conveyor belt.

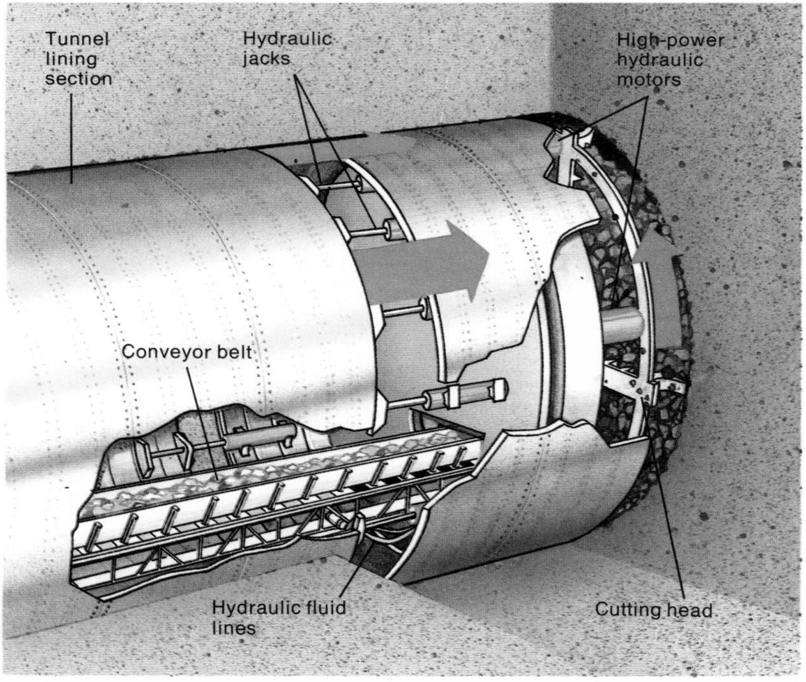

turbot *n.* a large flat fish.

tureen *n.* a large deep bowl for serving soup, etc.

turf *n.* 1. grass-covered ground. *"The turf" is an expression sometimes used to mean "horse-racing."* 2. a piece of earth with grass attached to it, cut from the ground.

▶ Turf is the top layer of soil. It is bound together by the roots of grass and other plants. Turf is also another name for peat. Peat forms in swampy ground from the remains of partly rotted plants. When cut and dried, peat is used as a fuel, and in the chemical industry.

Turin
Turin is a city on the Po River in northern ITALY. Today it is an important manufacturing center, and is the home of the Italian motor industry. In the 1860s, Turin briefly became the first capital of a united Italy. It was badly damaged during

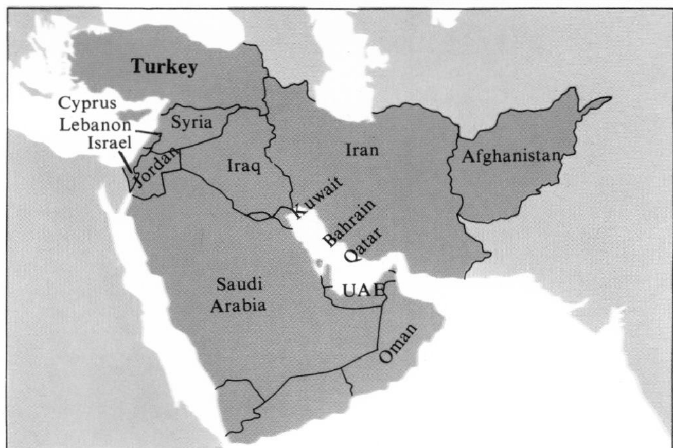

World War II, but many fine buildings remain.

Turkey (Turkish, Turk)
Turkey is a republic which is divided between ASIA and EUROPE. Asian Turkey (also called Asia Minor) covers 97 percent of the country. It consists mainly of plateaus and rugged mountains, bordered by broad coastal plains. The largest city, ISTANBUL, stands on the BOSPORUS, which forms part of the channel which links the MEDITERRANEAN and Black seas and separates Asian from European Turkey.

The Turks once ruled the great OTTOMAN empire. This empire collapsed in World War I and Turkey was modernized in the 1920s and 1930s by its first president, Kemal ATTATURK (1881–1938). Most of the people are farmers, but mining, especially for chrome ore, is important.

AREA: 301,399 SQ. MILES (780,576 SQ. KM)
POPULATION: 47,633,000
CAPITAL: ANKARA
CURRENCY: TURKISH LIRA
OFFICIAL LANGUAGE: TURKISH

turkey *n.* a large American bird of the pheasant family, bred in many parts of the world for its delicate meat.
► Wild turkeys live in small flocks in the forests of North and Central America. The first people to keep turkey for food were the AZTECS of Mexico, then they were brought to Europe by the Spanish CONQUISTADORS. Turkey is traditionally eaten at Christmas in various countries and on Thanksgiving Day in the U.S.

turn 1. *vb.* revolve; go around. 2. *vb.* change direction; face the other way. 3. your place in a scheduled order. *n. It's my turn.*

turn down *vb.* refuse an offer or ideas. *I wanted to turn down the job, but I needed the money, so I agreed to do it.*

Turner, J.M.W.
J.M.W. Turner was an English painter (1775–1851). He is best known for the almost abstract paintings of his later life, which captured dazzling effects of light, weather and water (e.g. in the railway painting *Rain, Steam and Speed*). Turner's work greatly influenced IMPRESSIONISM.

The Fighting Téméraire by J.M.W. Turner. (National Gallery London).

turnip *n.* a plant grown for its roundish, white, edible root, which is cooked and eaten as a vegetable.

turnout *n.* 1. the number of people attending a function. *There was a big turnout for the president's visit.*

turn up *vb.* 1. arrive, usually unexpectedly. *Emma turned up just before dinner.* 2. increase something by using a control. *That knob on the radio turns up the sound.*

turquoise *n.* a blue or green semi-precious stone.

turret *n.* 1. a small tower, usually in a larger building. 2. a revolving part of a warship, tank, etc., that holds a gun.

turtle *n.* a reptile that can pull its head and limbs inside its shell.
► The name turtle is usually used for those shelled reptiles that live in water. The shells of turtles are similar to those of tortoises. These are both made of bony "plates" which are covered by large horny scales. Small turtles that live in fresh water, rather than seawater, are called terrapins.

Marine, or sea, turtles spend most of their lives in warm seas. They swim great distances to find food, and many of them have webbed toes, or flipperlike legs, to help them swim well. They eat water plants, such as seaweed, and some small sea animals. Turtles often swim under water, but they come up to the surface to gulp air into their lungs.

The snapping turtle is a meateater

Turtles go ashore to lay their eggs which they bury in sand, or hide among weeds. Both these places help to keep the eggs warm, and safe from animals that would eat them.

Baby turtles hatch on their own. They then dig themselves out

T

of their nest and head for the sea. This journey is treacherous, because their shells have not yet hardened. Crabs, snakes and birds are waiting to snap them up, before they reach the water.

tusk *n.* a long, large, pointed tooth on an elephant, walrus, etc.

The gold mask of Tutankhamen. He died in 1352 B.C. having reigned for about eight years.

Tutankhamen
Tutankhamen was a PHARAOH of ancient EGYPT. His tomb was discovered in 1922 by a British archaeologist, Howard Carter (1873–1939). Carter, with the Earl of Caernarvon, was digging in the Valley of the Kings, in Egypt. The discovery was an exciting one, because Carter had found the only tomb of a pharaoh that had not already been robbed of its treasures. In the tomb were a golden throne, caskets, statues, precious stones and furniture. There were four gold shrines, one inside another, in the burial chamber. The *sarcophagus* (coffin) contained the mummified body of the pharoah. These magnificent treasures can now be seen in a museum in Cairo.

Tutankhamen became pharaoh when he was about 11 years old. He probably became ruler because, as a child, he had married the daughter of Pharaoh Akhenaton. Akhenaton had made everyone worship the sun god Aton and had set up a new capital at Amarna. Tutankhamen brought back the old religion and moved the capital back to Thebes. He died in 1352 B.C., having ruled for about eight years.

tutor *n.* a private teacher; a person who gives individual instruction to students.

tutu *n.* the short frilly skirt worn by a ballerina.

Twain, Mark
Mark Twain (1835–1910) was a great American storyteller and humorist. His best known novels are *The Adventures of Tom Sawyer* (1876) and *The Adventures of Huckleberry Finn* (1885). These books were written from his memories as a boy in Missouri and his life as a boat pilot on the MISSISSIPPI. Twain's real name was Samuel Langhorne Clemens. He took his penname from an expression used by river pilots to indicate two fathoms of water.

twice *adv.* two times.
twig *n.* a small branch on a tree or bush.
twilight *n.* the dim light between sunset and nighttime.
twin *n.* one of two children born to the same mother at the same time.
twinge *n.* a sharp, shooting pain.
twinkle *vb.* send out little flashes of light.
twirl *vb.* spin, turn around and around.
twist *vb.* wind around, turn and curve.
tycoon *n.* a very rich businessman.

Tyler, John
John Tyler (1790–1862) was the 10th president of the United States. He was vice-president when William Harrison died in office. Tyler inherited a political situation that he could not support, so his term as president was one long battle with his own Whig Party. The annexation of Texas was the chief issue during the latter half of Tyler's term, but Texas did not become a state until 1845, when James Polk was president. On Tyler's last day of office, he signed a bill admitting Florida to the Union.

type 1. *n.* a kind, a sort. *Tulips are a type of flower.* 2. *vb.* use a typewriter. 3. *n.* the letters used to print words.
typewriter *n.* a machine that prints letters.
► Typewriters produce letters and figures, which look like lines of type in a book. When you strike a key on a typewriter keyboard, it moves a metal bar. A raised letter on the end of this bar is pressed against an inked ribbon. This marks an inked image of the letter onto a sheet of paper which is held around a roller.

The first practical typewriter was invented in 1867 by an American, Christopher Latham Sholes (1819–90). Mark TWAIN used a Sholes machine to write his *Life on the Mississippi* (1883). He was the first author to write his story on a typewriter.

There are now many kinds of typewriter, including electric ones and even machines that produce BRAILLE lettering.

typhoid fever *n.* an infectious disease in which the intestines become inflamed.
typhoon *n.* a tropical cyclone (windstorm) that often brings rain.
► Typhoons occur in eastern Asia. These storms hit the PHILIPPINES and the southern coasts of China. They can cause enormous destruction.

typhus *n.* a severe feverish disease marked by eruptions on the skin.
typical *adj.* a good example of its kind.
typist *n.* a person who uses a typewriter.
tyrannosaurus *n.* a huge, flesh-eating dinosaur that lived more than 70 million years ago.
► Tyrannosaurus was the largest meat-eating animal that has ever lived on earth. Tyrannosaurus stood about 20 ft. (6 meters) high on its two powerful legs and was up to 50 ft. (15 meters) long. It had two short forelimbs and sharp, daggerlike teeth, which were 6 in. (15 cm) long. Its eye sockets were big enough to hold a human head. The name comes from two Greek words, meaning "terrible lizard".

tyranny *n.* oppressive and cruel use of power.
tyrant *n.* a cruel, unfair ruler.

How a typewriter works. The keys are marked with letters, numbers and signs. When the key is struck a type bar connected to the key strikes an inked ribbon which marks the paper, held around a cylinder. A spring pulls the cylinder, so moving the paper to the next position. In electric typewriters, an electric motor moves the type bars and cylinder.

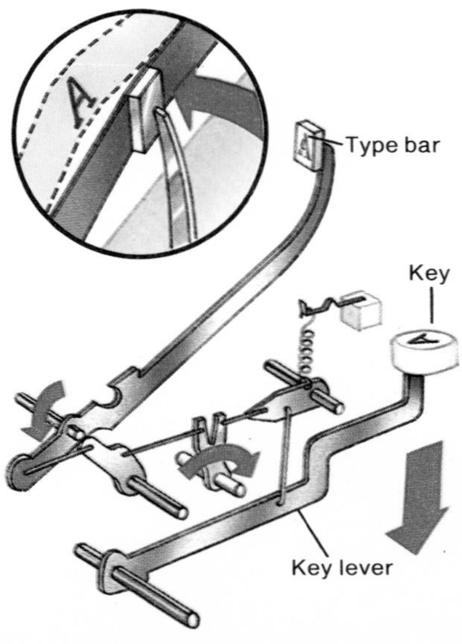

U

A U.S.S.R. spectacular – the annual May Day procession through Moscow's Red Square.

U-boat *n.* German submarine in both world wars.

udder *n.* the bag-like part of a female mammal, such as a cow, from which milk comes.

UFO

Unidentified Flying Objects are more often called UFOs. They are unknown objects that people see in the sky. Reports of UFOs go back thousands of years. Some may be METEORS or air BALLOONS. Others could be tricks of the light, and some are probably just jokes or mistakes.

But some reports of UFOs seen by several people or tracked by RADAR have never been explained. Some people think that these may be alien spacecraft. They are often called "flying saucers," because some are supposed to look like upturned saucers. No one really knows if they exist.

Uganda

Uganda is a small republic in the middle of East AFRICA. It was ruled by Britain until 1962, when it became independent. General Idi Amin seized power in 1971. He was a brutal dictator and many people were murdered under his rule. But in 1979, Ugandans and Tanzanian soldiers took over Uganda and Amin fled.

Part of Africa's largest lake, Lake Victoria, lies in Uganda. Most Ugandans are farmers. The most important crops are coffee, tea and cotton.

AREA: 91,139 SQ. MILES (236,036 SQ. KM)
POPULATION: 13,983,000
CAPITAL: KAMPALA
CURRENCY: UGANDAN SHILLING
OFFICIAL LANGUAGE: ENGLISH

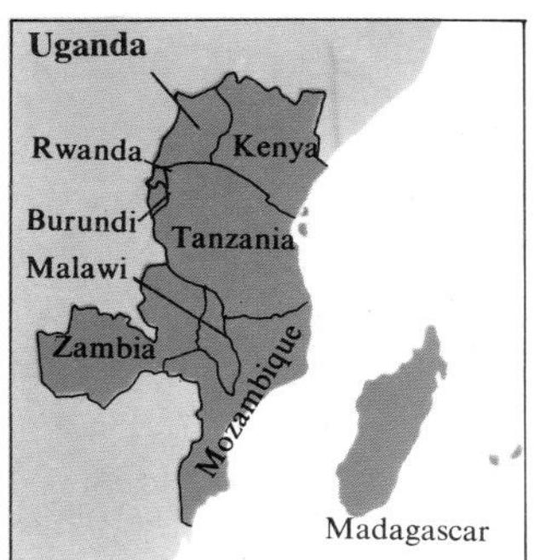

ugh *inter.* an expression of disgust.

ugly *adj.* unpleasant to look at; not beautiful or handsome. **ugliness** *n.*

Ukraine

A region in southwest U.S.S.R., the Ukrainian Soviet Socialist Republic is the U.S.S.R.'s chief farming area. It also has great reserves of coal and various metals, and manufacturing is very important. The Ukraine has 50 million people (1977) and an area of 233,089 sq. miles (603,700 sq. km). Its capital is Kiev.

ukulele (*you-ka-***lay***-lee*) *n.* a small guitar with four strings.

ulcer *n.* an open sore, usually with a flow of pus (infected fluid).

► An ulcer can be on the skin or in the digestive tract (e.g. in the mouth or stomach). An ulcer is usually due to infection or irritation. Gastric ulcers (in the stomach) are caused by irritation from the digestive juices, and must be treated by a very mild diet.

ulna *n.* the inner of the two bones of the forearm.

Ulster

Ulster was once one of the four ancient kingdoms of IRELAND. (The others were Munster, Leinster and Connaught). Later, under British rule, Ulster was a province consisting of nine counties: Antrim, Armagh, Cavan, Coleraine (later called Londonderry), Down, Donegal, Fermanagh, Monaghan and Tyrone. When the Republic of Ireland became independent, six counties chose to remain in the UNITED

KINGDOM. Cavan, Donegal and Monaghan joined the Republic, and became known as Ulster Province. However, the name Ulster is today most often used to mean the six counties of Northern Ireland.

ultimate *adj*. last, final, eventual. *Our ultimate aim is to be successful.*
ultraviolet radiation *n*. light beyond the visible spectrum.

► If LIGHT from the sun shines through a prism it splits up into a rainbow of colors, called a spectrum. Red is at one end of the spectrum and violet at the other. Ultraviolet light lies just beyond the violet end of the spectrum. We cannot see it, but it will blacken photographic film and make some chemicals glow. Most ultraviolet light from the sun is lost in the atmosphere. But enough rays reach earth to give us suntans. If more rays reached us, they would be very harmful.
Many kinds of disease-causing bacteria can be killed by exposure to ultraviolet rays. The rays can purify the air and sterilize surgical instruments.

Ulysses
Ulysses is the Roman name for a brave and cunning Greek hero, called Odysseus. His famous adventures are told in HOMER's poem the *Odyssey*. It tells how Ulysses took 10 years to return home after the TROJAN WAR.

On his journey he was captured by a cyclops, a one-eyed, man-eating giant. A witch called Circe changed his men into pigs. Later, sirens (sea maidens) lured his men to their deaths. When he finally reached home, his wife, Penelope, was surrounded by suitors. She had agreed to marry any man who could shoot an arrow from Ulysses' bow through 12 rings. Ulysses, in disguise, was the only man who proved able to do this. He then killed all the suitors.

umbilicus *n*. the cord connecting the developing fetus with the mother's placenta and through which the fetus is fed. When the child is born the cord is cut, leaving the "belly button." **umbilical** *adj*. of the navel.
umbrella *n*. a fabric shade, supported by a wire frame with a handle which people carry to keep the rain off. *You can fold up an umbrella when you're not using it.*
umpire *n*. the person who sees that the rules are obeyed in certain games. *Important tennis matches have an umpire to oversee them.* *vb*. act as umpire.
un- *prefix* expressing negation, lack of, etc., used before adjectives, adverbs and verbs. If the meaning of the main word is known then the sense of the word with the added prefix should usually be clear, e.g. **unaccompanied** not escorted or accompanied. **unbalanced** not balanced. **unchristian** not in accordance with Christian beliefs or practices.
unadulterated *adj*. pure; unmixed with any other material.
unanimous (*you*-**nan**-*i-mus*) *adj*. when everyone agrees.
uncanny *adj*. strange, mysterious.
uncivil *adj*. rude, impolite.
uncle *n*. the brother of your mother or father.
uncompromising *adj*. unyielding; stubborn.
unconscious *adj*. not conscious, not knowing what is happening around you, unaware of.
uncouth *adj*. clumsy and awkward in manners and language.
uncover *vb*. take the cover off something, or show it.
undemonstrative *adj*. reserved. *A person who does not show feelings openly is undemonstrative.*
under *adj*., *adv*. & *prep*. beneath.
under- *prefix* meaning below, beneath, less than, lacking in. When the meaning of the main word is known, the sense of the prefixed word should in many cases be clear, e.g. **underweight, understate**.
undercover *adj*. not in the open, secret.
underdog *n*. a loser or someone who will almost certainly lose in any fight or contest.
undergraduate *n*. a student at a university who has not yet earned a degree.
undergo *vb*. suffer, experience.
underground railroad *n*. a railroad which runs mainly below ground.

► Underground electric trains can carry passengers across cities much faster than buses, which drive slowly through the busy streets above. Most underground RAILROADS, called subways, run through TUNNELS driven through the rock beneath a city. Elevators and escalators carry passengers from the surface to the stations deep underground.

The first underground railroad opened in London in 1863. Today the world has over 60 subway systems. Some of these are vast. London's system employs enough workers to people a town. Its 480 trains run on 250 miles (400 km) of track. New York City's track is almost as long. This is the busiest subway system of all. About a billion people travel on it every year.

New York has almost 500 stations. But the largest subway stations are in Moscow. Their huge platforms were also built to serve as giant air-raid shelters.

underline *vb*. 1. draw a line under words on a page to make them stand out, e.g. Danger. 2. emphasize, stress.
underneath *adv*. & *prep*. beneath. *The mechanic was lying underneath the car he was repairing.*
underpass *n*. a place where one road passes under another one.
understand *vb*. (past **understood**) grasp the meaning of something with your mind; know. *Did you understand what the teacher was saying?* **understanding** *n*. the ability to know; an agreement.
understanding *adj*. gentle, kind.
understudy *n*. an actor who takes over from the usual performer of a part in an emergency.
undertake *vb*. agree to do; be responsible for. *John undertook to look after the herb garden.*
undertaker *n*. a person who arranges funerals.
underwrite *vb*. (in insurance) accepting the risk or liability for what is insured.

Baker Street station in London on the Metropolitan subway.

undo *vb*. 1. untie (a knot); unbutton; remove. 2. reverse; bring to nothing. *This government says it is going to undo the damage caused by the last government.*
undress *vb*. take clothes off.
undue *adj*. too much, excessive. *They gave him undue praise.*
undulate *vb*. rise and fall like waves.
unearth *vb*. dig up or discover something. *Granny managed to unearth some old family photos from her desk.*
unemployed *adj*. without a paid job; out of work; not being used.
unemployment *n*. the state of being unemployed.
unequal *adj*. not the same; not equal.
unfair *adj*. not just or according to the rules.
unfortunate *adj*. unlucky.
unfounded *adj*. not based on fact. *Your doubts about my honesty are unfounded.*
unfrock *vb*. remove a person from being a priest.
unfurl *vb*. unfold and display. *The flag was unfurled.*
ungainly *adj*. awkward, clumsy.
unhappy *adj*. miserable; not happy; unfortunate.
uni- *prefix* meaning one, e.g. **unicellular** having only one cell.
unicorn *n*. an animal in stories and legends that has a body like a horse and a single horn in the middle of its forehead.
► The word *unicorn* means "one horn". According to legend, the unicorn's horn is long and straight with a spiral twist.

The first picture of a unicorn was carved on stone more than 2,500 years ago. Later, tales of the unicorn were told in lands as far apart as China and Italy. A Greek writer who lived about 2,400 years ago thought that a unicorn was white with a purple head and a red, white and black horn. He wrote that drinking from the horn could save people from poison.

In the MIDDLE AGES, rich people who were afraid of being poisoned used to drink from what they thought were unicorn horns. In fact, these were really rhinoceros horns.

uniform 1. *n*. matching clothes worn by all the members of a group of people, such as a school or an army. 2. *adj*. unvarying, constant; to one standard. *The books are of uniform size.*
union *n*. joining together of a number of things or people. *The American colonies formed a union in 1789.*
unique (*yoo*-**neek**) *adj*. the only one of its kind; having no equal.
unit *n*. a single thing, or a group of things that are thought of as being one thing.

Uniforms help us to identify people doing a particular job. And firemen, for instance, also wear uniforms that are designed to protect them. Some uniforms help to give authority to the person doing the job. Most people behave better when they see a policeman or policewoman in the distance.

Zoologists think that the idea of the unicorn may have arisen when someone saw an oryx at a distance. From far away, this big desert antelope sometimes seems to have one long horn instead of two.

Uniforms worn during the War of Austrian Succession (1740–48) which involved most of the states of Europe. Although each state tended to follow one particular style of uniform for each branch of its army, each regiment's dress still varied considerably.

U

unite *vb.* join together, combine.
unity *n.*

United Arab Emirates
This oil-rich group of seven emirates (kingdoms) lies in the Arabian peninsula on the Persian Gulf. It was formerly called the Trucial States. The Emirates are: Abu Dhabi, Ajman, Dubai, Fujairah, Ras al Khaimah, Sharjah and Umm al Qaiwain. The UAR is a flat, hot desert country. The states entered into treaties with Britain from 1820. British forces withdrew from the area in 1971. The states then joined an independent federation.
AREA: 32,280 SQ. MILES (83,600 SQ. KM)
POPULATION: 1,040,000
CAPITAL: ABU DHABI
CURRENCY: DIRHAM
OFFICIAL LANGUAGE: ARABIC

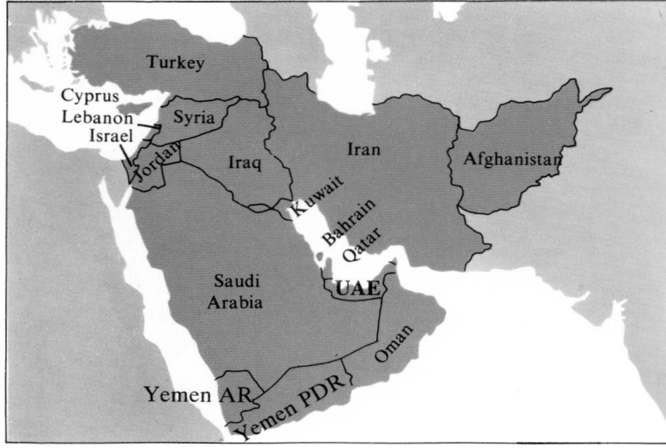

United Kingdom
The full title of the U.K., as it is often called, is the United Kingdom of Great Britain and Northern Ireland. (GREAT BRITAIN consists of England, Scotland, and Wales).

Scotland has three main land regions. The highlands are divided by Glen More into the rugged north-western highlands and the Grampians, which include Ben Nevis. The main island groups are the Orkney and Shetland Islands to the north and the Hebrides to the west. The central lowlands are the most densely populated region, with coalfields, the leading cities and much farmland. Scotland's southern uplands are a mainly farming region.

Northern **England** contains the Cumbrian Mts. (or the Lake District), where England's highest peak, Scafell Pike, 3,209 ft. (978 m) is situated, and the Pennines which run north-south. Coalfields near the edge of the Pennines have stimulated growth of major industrial regions. England's other highland region Exmoor and Dartmoor is in the southwest. Lowland England contains many fertile plains crossed by ranges of low hills, such as the Cotswolds, Chilterns and the North and South Downs in the southeast.

Wales is a mainly highland country, rising to Snowdon, 3,560 ft. (1,085 m). South Wales contains a large coalfield on which a major industrial region has been built.

Northern Ireland contains uplands and plains. In the east Lough Neagh, the U.K.'s largest lake, covers 153 sq. miles (396 sq. km). The U.K.'s longest rivers are the Severn and the Thames, on which the capital London stands.

The U.K. has a moist, temperate climate, moderated by the warm North Atlantic Drift (Gulf Stream). Average temperatures seldom exceed 64°F (18°C) in summer or fall below 37°F (3°C) in winter.

The U.K. is highly urbanized: 91 percent of the population lived in urban areas in 1980. In 1978 agriculture employed only 2 percent of the working population, industry 43 percent and services 55 percent.

Farming is highly efficient but food is imported.

The U.K.'s industrial economy was originally based on its abundant coal and iron ore resources. Coalmining has declined although the economy has recently been boosted by the discovery of oil and natural gas in the North Sea.

Manufacturing is extremely varied. Invisible earnings from banking, insurance, tourism and other services make a vital contribution to the economy.

In the late 1700s the U.K. was the first nation to change from an agricultural to an industrial society. Wealth from trade and industry made the U.K. one of the world's greatest nations in the 1800s. It played a major role in World War I, but this sapped its resources. After the war, southern Ireland broke away to become the Irish Free State (*see* IRELAND).

World War II proved an even greater drain on the U.K.'s economy than World War I. The U.K. transformed its empire into the Commonwealth, which has given it a greater voice in world affairs. The U.K. joined the EEC in 1973, but it suffered from the world recession in the early 1980s. Its many problems include increasing competition for its manufacturing products in world markets, and violent conflict in Northern Ireland.
AREA: 94,232 SQ. MILES (244,046 SQ. KM) NOT INCLUDING THE ISLE OF MAN AND CHANNEL ISLANDS
POPULATION: 55,670,000
CAPITAL: LONDON
CURRENCY: POUND STERLING
OFFICIAL LANGUAGE: ENGLISH (WELSH AND GAELIC ARE ALSO SPOKEN)

Top: The red St George's cross of England can be seen flying from church towers.

Center: The flag of Wales does not form part of the Union Flag. It was officially recognized in 1959. It is the red dragon of Cadwallader, Prince of Gwynedd.

Above: The white St Andrew's cross of Scotland.

Below: The so-called cross of St Patrick was incorporated into the Union Flag in 1801.

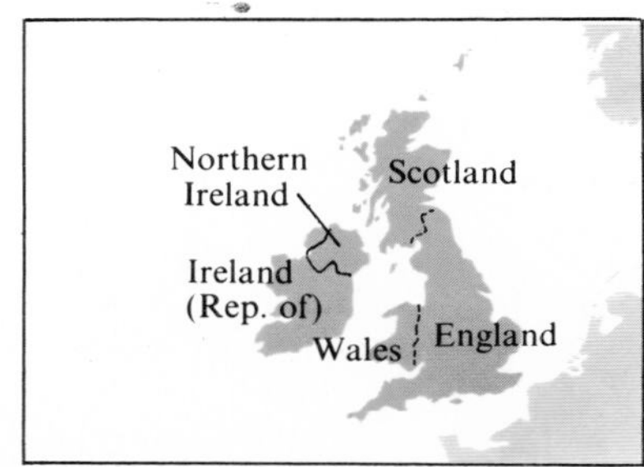

UNITED NATIONS: MEMBER COUNTRIES

Country	Joined*	Country	Joined	Country	Joined	Country	Joined
Afghanistan	1946	Dominica	1978	Lebanon	1945	Sào Tome & Principe	1975
Albania	1955	Dominican Republic	1945	Lesotho	1966	Saudi Arabia	1945
Algeria	1962	Ecuador	1945	Liberia	1945	Senegal	1960
Angola	1976	Egypt	1945	Libya	1955	Seychelles	1976
Antigua and Barbuda	1981	El Salvador	1945	Luxembourg	1945	Sierra Leone	1961
Argentina	1945	Equatorial Guinea	1968	Madagascar	1960	Singapore	1965
Australia	1945	Ethiopia	1945	Malawi	1964	Solomon Islands	1978
Austria	1955	Fiji	1970	Malaysia	1957	Somali Republic	1960
Bahamas	1973	Finland	1955	Maldives, Rep. of	1965	South Africa	1945
Bahrain	1971	France	1945	Mali	1960	Spain	1955
Bangladesh	1974	Gabon	1960	Malta	1964	Sri Lanka	1955
Barbados	1966	Gambia	1965	Mauritania	1961	Sudan	1956
Belgium	1945	Germany, East	1973	Mauritius	1968	Surinam	1975
Belize	1981	Germany, West	1973	Mexico	1945	Swaziland	1968
Benin	1960	Ghana	1957	Mongolian PR	1961	Sweden	1946
Bhutan	1971	Greece	1945	Morocco	1956	Syria	1945
Bolivia	1945	Grenada	1974	Mozambique	1975	Tanzania	1961
Botswana	1966	Guatemala	1945	Nepal	1955	Thailand	1946
Brazil	1945	Guinea	1958	Netherlands	1945	Togo	1960
Bulgaria	1955	Guinea-Bissau	1974	New Zealand	1945	Trinidad & Tobago	1962
Burma	1948	Guyana	1966	Nicaragua	1945	Tunisia	1956
Burundi	1962	Haiti	1945	Niger	1960	Turkey	1945
Byelorussian SSR	1945	Honduras	1945	Nigeria	1960	Uganda	1962
Cameroon	1960	Hungary	1955	Norway	1945	Ukrainian SSR	1945
Canada	1945	Iceland	1946	Oman	1971	USSR	1945
Cape Verde	1975	India	1945	Pakistan	1947	United Arab Emirates	1971
Central African		Indonesia	1950	Panama	1945	United Kingdom	1945
Republic	1960	Iran	1945	Papua New Guinea	1975	United States	1945
Chad	1960	Iraq	1945	Paraguay	1945	Upper Volta	1960
Chile	1945	Ireland, Rep. of	1955	Peru	1945	Uruguay	1945
China†	1945	Israel	1949	Philippines	1945	Vanuatu	1981
Colombia	1945	Italy	1955	Poland	1945	Venezuela	1945
Comoros	1975	Ivory Coast	1960	Portugal	1955	Vietnam	1976
Congo	1960	Jamaica	1962	Qatar	1971	Yemen Arab Republic	1947
Costa Rica	1945	Japan	1956	Romania	1955	Yemen PDR	1967
Cuba	1945	Jordan	1955	Rwanda	1962	Yugoslavia	1945
Cyprus	1960	Kampuchea	1955	St. Lucia	1979	Zaire	1960
Czechoslovakia	1945	Kenya	1963	St. Vincent &		Zambia	1964
Denmark	1945	Kuwait	1963	the Grenadines	1980	Zimbabwe	1980
Djibouti	1977	Laos	1955	Samoa	1976		

* The UN came into existence in 1945.
† in 1971 the UN voted for the expulsion of Nationalist China and the admittance of Communist China in its place.

The United Nations Organization came into existence in 1945, in an attempt to maintain peace throughout the world and foster co-operation between different nations. Its charter was signed by 50 countries. All member states were to be treated as equals, to maintain peace, and to settle disputes amicably. Its headquarters is in New York and all members sit in the General Assembly.

United Nations
The United Nations is the international organization which works for peace and security throughout the world. The U.N. also has specialized agencies which deal with other matters, such as food and agriculture, health, labor, etc. The UN was set up in 1945 by 51 nations. By the start of 1984 its membership had grown to 157.

The main organs of the U.N., based in New York City, are the *General Assembly*, the *Security Council* and the *Secretariat*. The General Assembly consists of delegates from all member nations. It discusses international problems and each nation has one vote. The Security Council, with 15 members, is concerned mainly with keeping the peace. The Secretariat services the U.N. Its head, the secretary-general, is also a diplomat who can act on his own to solve problems, without having to refer them to the other organs of the U.N.

The symbol of the United Nations, a map of the world inside olive branches, for peace.

United States of America
(American)
The United States is the world's fourth largest nation. The U.S.S.R., CANADA and CHINA are bigger in area, and more people live in China, INDIA and the U.S.S.R. The United States has 226.5 million people. About 87 percent of them are white and 12 percent black. Two-thirds of the population is Protestant, a quarter Roman Catholic and about 3 percent Jewish. Three-fourths of the people live in cities or their suburbs.

There are 50 states in the United States. Forty-eight are in the same part of NORTH AMERICA. The other two are ALASKA in the north, and the Pacific islands of HAWAII in the south.

The mainland United States stretches from the ATLANTIC to the PACIFIC. On the Atlantic coast there is a narrow plain with heavily populated areas. The Appalachian mountain chain borders the coastal plain from the top of ALABAMA north to MAINE and on into Canada. West of the Appalachians there is the vast interior plain of the United States. This great plain stretches, almost

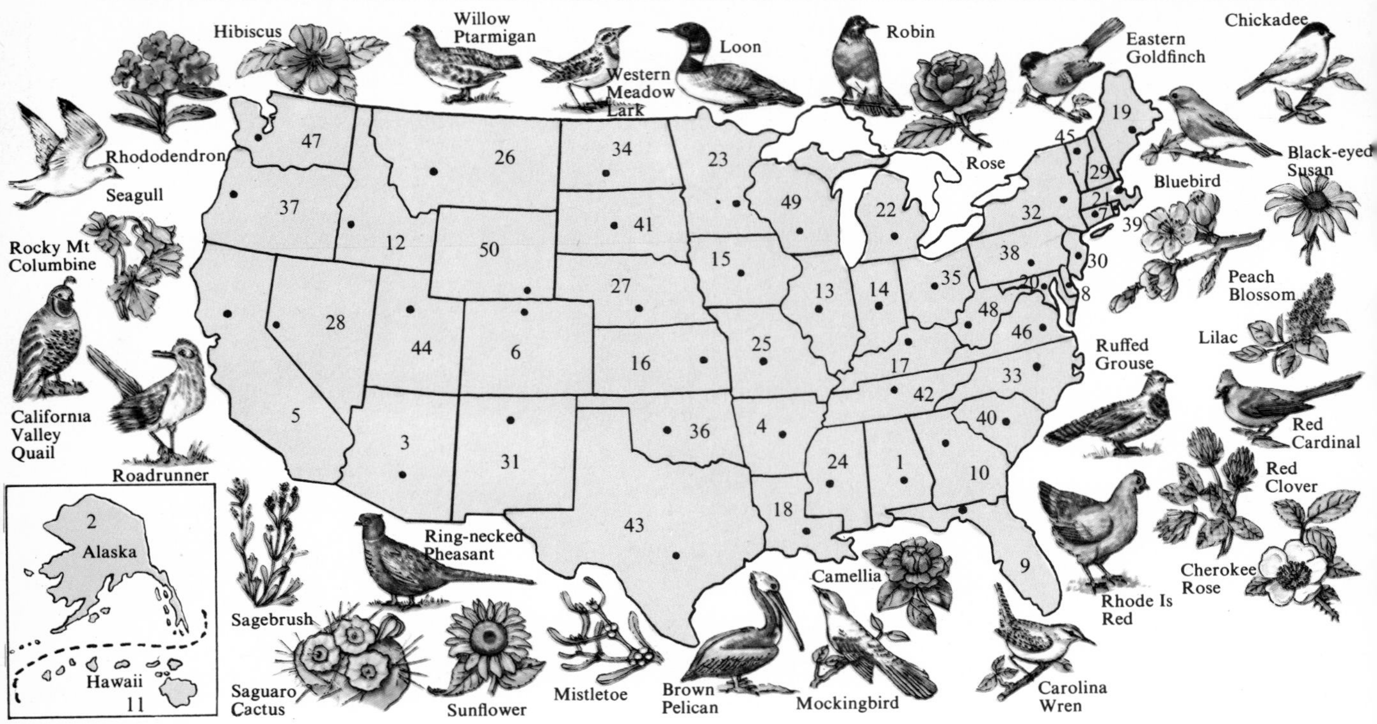

The national symbol of the U.S.A.

unbroken, to the Rockies. Great rivers flow through the plains. The Ohio and the Wabash rivers are in the east. The Missouri and Mississippi in the west drain into the Gulf of Mexico.

From the Rockies to the Pacific coast, the land changes completely. There are great mountain ranges, deep gorges such as the Grand Canyon, fertile plateaus, and the great desert areas of the southwest. Between the Rockies and the Pacific coast are the Sierra Nevada and Cascades ranges.

The United States is the richest nation in the world. Most of the land is ideal for farming and the grazing of livestock. There are vast supplies of oil, natural gas, coal, timber and metals and minerals. But the United States is now using so much oil, it has to buy extra supplies from abroad.

The United States is a young country. The original 13 colonies declared their independence from England in 1776 and the War of INDEPENDENCE broke out. The fighting ended in 1781, but a peace treaty was not signed until 1783. George WASHINGTON was elected the first president in 1789.

In 1785, the most important men in the new country met to work out a CONSTITUTION. The federal system they worked out is still the basis of the United States government.

By the mid 1800s, explorers had added new land to the original colonies, and the country stretched as far as the Pacific.

From 1861 to 1865 the country was torn apart by the CIVIL WAR. The Northern anti-slavery forces won and slavery was abolished.

Between 1870 and 1900 millions of Europeans came and settled in the United States. The population doubled in 30 years. The United States became a world power.

When WORLD WAR I broke out in 1914, the United States did not want to become involved. But attacks by German submarines on American ships helped to bring the United States into the war in 1917. More than two million men were sent to Europe in 1917 and 1918. American industry mobilized for war and played a large part in ending the conflict.

After the war, President Woodrow Wilson wanted the United States to join the new League of Nations, but the Senate turned him down. Once again, America thought she could live in isolation from the rest of the world.

The 1920s was a period of prosperity. It was also the period of Prohibition – the banning of alcoholic drinks – and "bootleggers" and gangsters who sprang up largely because of Prohibition. But the prosperity ended in 1929 when the stock market crashed and the Great Depression began. President Franklin D. ROOSEVELT began a New Deal policy. He enacted a record number of bills aimed at giving relief to the nation, to cut unemployment and speed up recovery.

During Roosevelt's time in office, Adolf HITLER came to power in Germany and Benito MUSSOLINI in Italy. As war clouds began to form over Europe, most Americans still hoped to stand apart from any foreign conflict. But when Hitler plunged Europe into war in 1939, the United States sent vital supplies to Britain and France.

As WORLD WAR II went on, the American people began to think of themselves as being on the side of the Allies.

America entered the war when the Japanese attacked PEARL HARBOR,

State	Capital	Population (1980)
1 Alabama	Montgomery	3,890,061
2 Alaska	Juneau	400,481
3 Arizona	Phoenix	2,717,866
4 Arkansas	Little Rock	2,285,513
5 California	Sacramento	23,668,562
6 Colorado	Denver	2,888,834
7 Connecticut	Hartford	3,107,576
8 Delaware	Dover	595,225
9 Florida	Tallahassee	9,739,992
10 Georgia	Atlanta	5,464,265
11 Hawaii	Honolulu	965,000
12 Idaho	Boise	943,935
13 Illinois	Springfield	11,418,461
14 Indiana	Indianapolis	5,490,179
15 Iowa	Des Moines	2,913,387
16 Kansas	Topeka	2,363,208
17 Kentucky	Frankfort	3,661,433
18 Louisiana	Baton Rouge	4,203,972
19 Maine	Augusta	1,124,660
20 Maryland	Annapolis	4,216,446
21 Massachusetts	Boston	5,737,037
22 Michigan	Lansing	9,258,344
23 Minnesota	St Paul	4,077,148
24 Mississippi	Jackson	2,520,638
25 Missouri	Jefferson City	4,917,444
26 Montana	Helena	786,690
27 Nebraska	Lincoln	1,570,006
28 Nevada	Carson City	799,184
29 New Hampshire	Concord	920,610
30 New Jersey	Trenton	7,364,158
31 New Mexico	Santa Fe	1,299,968
32 New York	Albany	17,557,288
33 North Carolina	Raleigh	5,874,429
34 North Dakota	Bismarck	652,695
35 Ohio	Columbus	10,797,419
36 Oklahoma	Oklahoma City	3,025,266
37 Oregon	Salem	2,632,663
38 Pennsylvania	Harrisburg	11,866,728
39 Rhode Island	Providence	947,154
40 South Carolina	Columbia	3,119,208
41 South Dakota	Pierre	690,178
42 Tennessee	Nashville	4,590,750
43 Texas	Austin	14,228,383
44 Utah	Salt Lake City	1,461,037
45 Vermont	Montpelier	511,456
46 Virginia	Richmond	5,346,279
47 Washington	Olympia	4,130,163
48 West Virginia	Charleston	1,949,644
49 Wisconsin	Madison	4,705,335
50 Wyoming	Cheyenne	470,816

Hawaii, in December 1941. America was now the leading power of the Western world. Roosevelt died as the war was ending. Vice-president TRUMAN was elected and it was he who gave the order to drop the first atomic bombs on Japan.

After the war, the Cold War between the United States and the U.S.S.R. began. Both countries had fearful nuclear weapons. But neither country wanted to start a full-scale war.

From 1950 to 1953 American troops fought to repel a Communist North Korean invasion of South Korea. During the 1950s and 1960s the United States became involved in a similar struggle against Communist forces in Vietnam.

AREA: 3,615,319 SQ. MILES (9,363,123 SQ. KM)
POPULATION: 226,500,000
CAPITAL: WASHINGTON D.C.
CURRENCY: U.S. DOLLAR
OFFICIAL LANGUAGE: ENGLISH

universal *adj. n.* general, common, done by most people. *Art and music are universal.*

universe *n.* everything in existence; all space; the cosmos.

► Our most powerful telescopes have revealed that the universe contains at least 10 billion star systems, or GALAXIES. Most scientists think that the universe was created in a gigantic explosion called the Big Bang. Others think that matter is being created all the time. All are agreed that the universe is expanding, as astronomical observations clearly indicate that the galaxies are getting farther apart all the time. It is possible that this expansion will be followed by a period of contraction, and that the whole process will then repeat.

university *n.* a place where people go on studying after they have left high school; an institute of higher education (college) with the authority to award degrees.

► At school people are taught a little about many subjects. But at a university, students often study just one or two subjects. They go to talks called *lectures*, and smaller study groups known as *tutorials* or *seminars*. They write essays and maybe carry out experiments in a laboratory. University students use libraries to find out much of what they need to know from books.

After three years or so students take their final examinations. If they pass they are given a degree, usually a bachelor of arts (B.A.) or a bachelor of science (B.S.). If they continue their studies they can earn higher degrees. A master's degree takes one or two more years and a doctorate degree can take as long as seven years. A university degree often helps people find better jobs. All doctors, lawyers and teachers have degrees.

Arab peoples had universities more than 1,000 years ago. Europe's first university grew up in the 1000s at Bologna in Italy. Soon after, universities were founded at Paris in France, Salamanca in Spain and Oxford in England. Today most countries have universities.

unkempt *adj.* untidy in appearance.

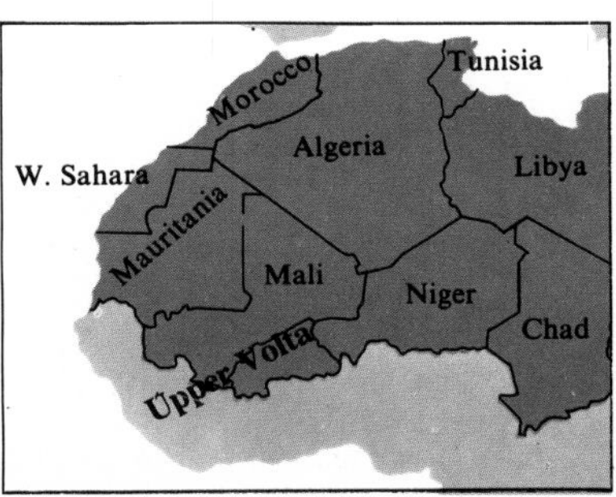

unkind *adj.* not kind; treating others badly. **unkindness** *n.*

unknown *adj. n.* not known; unexplored.

unless *conj.* except. *I'm not coming unless you come too.*

unload *vb.* empty a load from something, such as a ship or truck; remove ammunition from gun.

unlucky *adj.* not lucky; unfortunate. *Anne played so well that her team was unlucky not to win.*

unnecessary *adj.* not necessary; something that can be prevented.

unpack *vb.* remove things from a container, particularly a suitcase.

unpleasant *adj.* not pleasant; nasty or disagreeable.

unsavory *adj.* offensive, disagreeable.

unscathed *adj.* unharmed.

unseemly *adj.* not suitable for the time and place; improper.

unsightly *adj.* ugly.

untidy *adj.* not tidy, nor orderly; leaving things in a mess. *Adrian's bedroom was incredibly untidy.*

until *prep.* & *conj.* till; before; till such time as. *The dentist cannot give you an appointment until next week.*

untold *adj.* too many to be counted.

unusual *adj.* not usual; strange or peculiar, remarkable. *Caroline was wearing a most unusual dress.*

unwell *adj.* ill; sick; not well.

unwieldy *adj.* awkward to handle.

unwitting *adj.* unaware of; not knowing.

unwrap *vb.* take the wrapping off something, such as a parcel or present.

up *adv.* & *prep.* in, to a higher place, level, etc.

upheaval *n.* great disorder, change.

uphill 1. *adv.* going up a hill or slope. *Riding a bicycle uphill can get very tiring.* 2. *adj.* difficult. *Life can sometimes be an uphill struggle.*

upholstery *n.* the padding and covering of chairs and sofas. **upholsterer** *n.*

upkeep *n.* cost of keeping in good repair.

upon *prep.* on; on top of.

upper *adj.* above, in a higher place.

Upper Volta (Burkina Faso)
Upper Volta is a landlocked republic in West AFRICA. Its climate is tropical. Most of the people are poor, and farmers. Cattle, sheep and goats are reared. Cotton and other cash crops are grown in the south and south-west. Food, textiles and metal products are the main manufactures. Upper Volta is a former province of French West Africa. It became independent in 1960.

AREA: 105,875 SQ. MILES (274,200 SQ. KM)
POPULATION: 5,917,000
CAPITAL: OUAGADOUGOU
CURRENCY: FRANC
OFFICIAL LANGUAGE: FRENCH

U

upright *adj*. 1. vertical, standing straight. *We put the pole upright in the sand*. 2. honest. *She is an upright woman*.

uproar *n*. a violent disturbance, commotion.

upset *vb*. (past **upset**) 1. knock something over. *Mark upset the milk*. 2. make someone unhappy. *The bad news upset Jan*.

upshot *n*. the outcome, final result. *The upshot of the argument was that we agreed to do nothing*.

upside down *adv*. the "wrong" way up. *Sloths spend most of their time hanging upside down from branches of trees*. In total disorder.

upstage *adv*. back of the stage away from the footlights.

upstairs *adv*. *adj*. & *n*. above the ground floor of a building. *Go upstairs to your bedroom*.

upstart *n*. a person who has risen suddenly to a position of power or wealth.

upstream *adv*. & *adj*. in the direction opposite to the flow of the stream or river, higher up the river.

uptight *adj*. nervous, annoyed.

Ur

An ancient city in MESOPOTAMIA. In the Bible it is called Ur of the Chaldees, and is named as the home of ABRAHAM. Its site was discovered in the 19th century. Excavations by Sir Leonard Woolley showed that it had been inhabited from about 3500 B.C. At one time it seems to have experienced a great flood, and this may have given rise to the Bible legend.

uranium *n*. a hard, heavy silvery, metallic element that is radioactive (symbol – *U*).

► This metal is one of the heaviest of all known ELEMENTS. It was named after the planet URANUS. Uranium gives off RADIOACTIVITY. As it loses atomic particles it decays, and after millions of years, ends up as LEAD. People working with uranium often need protective clothing to shield their bodies from radiation damage.

Uranium is the fuel used to make ATOMIC ENERGY in atomic bombs and nuclear power stations. It is mined in many countries. Most of the Western world's uranium comes from the United States and Canada.

Uranus

The PLANET Uranus is 19 times farther away from the sun than the earth is. We cannot see Uranus with our eyes alone. It was the first planet discovered with the help of a TELESCOPE. Uranus looks like a greenish-yellow disk, with faint markings that may be clouds.

Uranus is unlike our earth in many ways. For one thing, it is much larger. You could fit 52 planets the size of earth inside Uranus. The distance through the middle of Uranus is about four times the distance through the middle of the earth.

Unlike our planet, Uranus is made up mainly of gases. Its whole surface is far colder than the coldest place on earth.

Uranus spins so fast that one day lasts less than 11 hours. But Uranus takes so long to ORBIT the sun that one of its years lasts 84 of ours. Five small moons travel around Uranus. Astronomers have also found that the planet is circled by five thin rings.

urban *adj*. to do with cities. *A city is an urban area*.

urchin *n*. a mischievous, shabbily dressed boy.

urge *vb*. encourage, drive on. *n*. strong force or desire.

urgent *adj*. so important that it needs to be attended to at once. **urgency** *n*.

urine *n*. amber-colored liquid waste that is excreted.

► Urine is made in the KIDNEYS from water and waste products filtered out of the blood. Humans excrete about 1.75 pt. (1 liter) a day.

urn *n*. a vase or container for storing the ashes of the dead; large vessel with a tap for holding hot drinks.

Uruguay (Uruguayan)

Uruguay is one of the smallest countries in SOUTH AMERICA, but it is wealthier than most of the others. It lies in the southeast, between the Atlantic Ocean and its two big neighbors, ARGENTINA and BRAZIL.

Low, grassy hills and lowlands cover most of Uruguay. Many rivers flow into the big Uruguay River or into the wide river mouth called the Plate River. Uruguay has mild winters and warm summers.

Most Uruguayans are descended from Spanish or Italian settlers. Uruguayans speak Spanish. More than one in three of them live in the capital Montevideo. Its factories make clothing, furniture and other goods. But most Uruguayans work in meat-packing plants, wool warehouses or on country ranches. Millions of sheep and cattle graze on these ranches.

Uruguay sells large amounts of meat, leather and wool to other countries. But it imports more than it exports.

More than half of the people are Roman Catholics and most are of European origin.

AREA: 68,041 SQ. MILES (176,215 SQ. KM)
POPULATION: 2,934,000
CAPITAL: MONTEVIDEO
CURRENCY: PESO
OFFICIAL LANGUAGE: SPANISH

usage *n*. customary practice or manner of doing things.

use (rhymes with *views*) 1. *vb*. employ something for a particular purpose. *You use a saw for cutting wood*. 2. *n*. (rhymes with *juice*) the way in which something is used. *Plastics have many different uses*.

used *adj*. not new; secondhand.

used to *vb*. 1. know some experience well because it has often happened. *We are used to waiting a long time for the bus*. 2. referring to the past. *Her parents used to live in Australia but then they moved to New York*.

useful *adj*. helpful, valuable.

useless *adj*. of no use; no good to anyone. *A broken watch is useless*.

U.S.S.R. (Soviet)

The Union of Soviet Socialist Republics, usually called the U.S.S.R. or the Soviet Union, is the largest country in the world. It extends nearly halfway around the world and is larger than all of South America. Over 60 languages are spoken within its boundaries. Because of its diverse population, the U.S.S.R. is divided into 15 republics, the largest of which is the Russian Soviet Federal Socialist Republic (RSFSR), which is called simply Russia.

The European part of the U.S.S.R., west of the Ural Mountains and the Caspian Sea, covers only about one-quarter of the nation. But over 70 percent of the people live there. European U.S.S.R. has much fertile farmland, especially in the UKRAINE. It also contains most of the nation's great industrial and mining centers, together with the two largest cities, MOSCOW and LENINGRAD. Asian U.S.S.R. is less developed and vast areas are too cold or too dry to support large numbers of people.

The U.S.S.R. has enormous natural resources. It leads the world in producing chromium, iron, lead and manganese, and is second only to the U.S.A. in coal, oil, and natural gas production. The principal industrial areas are the Ukraine, Moscow, Gorki and Leningrad.

The country was ruled as an empire from the 1500s to 1917 when the tsar, Nicholas II, was overthrown. Imperial Russia was

The hammer and sickle – an emblem of the union of peasants and industrial workers.

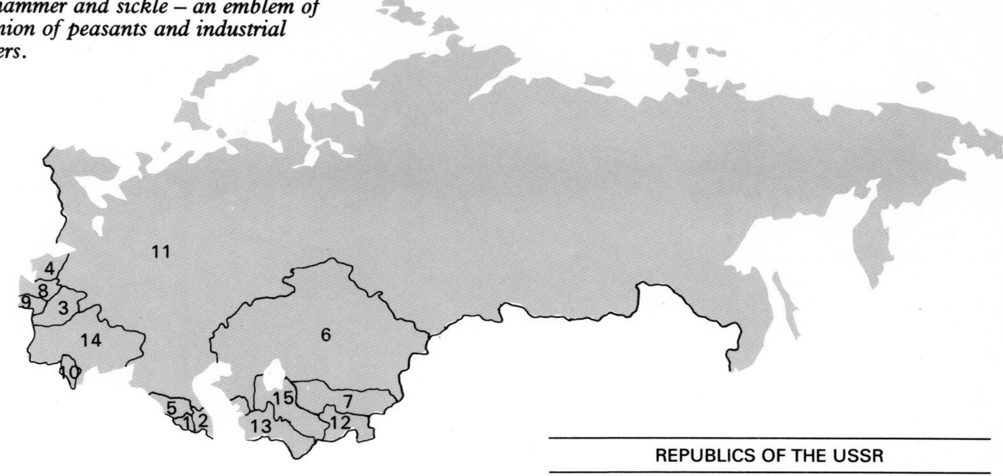

REPUBLICS OF THE USSR

	Population 1980	Capital
1. Armenia	3,100,000	Yerevan
2. Azerbaijan	6,200,000	Baku
3. Byelorussia	9,600,000	Minsk
4. Estonia	1,500,000	Tallinn
5. Georgia	5,000,000	Tbilisi
6. Kazakhstan	15,000,000	Alma-Ata
7. Kirgizia	3,600,000	Frunze
8. Latvia	2,500,000	Riga
9. Lithuania	3,400,000	Vilnius
10. Moldavia	4,000,000	Kishinev
11. Russian SFSR	138,400,000	Moscow
12. Tadzhikistan	4,000,000	Dushanbe
13. Turkmenistan	3,000,000	Ashkhabad
14. Ukraine	50,000,000	Kiev
15. Uzbekistan	15,800,000	Tashkent

renowned for its great literature, music, ballet, and so on.

In 1917, the Bolshevik communists, under Vladimir Ilyich LENIN (1870–1924), seized power. Despite the destruction caused by World War I, the revolution and subsequent civil war, and by World War II, the Communists have made the U.S.S.R. one of the world's super-powers. Progress has been especially marked in the state-owned manufacturing industries and in technology. The U.S.S.R. was the first nation to enter the Space Age, when *Sputnik I*, an artificial satellite, was launched into orbit around the earth on October 4, 1957. The development of agriculture has been less successful. (*see* COMMUNISM)
AREA: 8,650,010 SQ. MILES (22,402,200 SQ. KM)
POPULATION: 268,800,000
CAPITAL: MOSCOW
CURRENCY: RUBLE
OFFICIAL LANGUAGE: RUSSIAN [60 other languages are also spoken]

usual *adj*. the normal way in which something happens, or is done; most of the time. *Dan wore his usual clothes to the party.*

usually *adv*. in an ordinary or a normal way. *We usually go to school together.*

usurp *vb*. seize or take possession of by force or illegally (especially authority or power).

usury *n*. money-lending at a very high rate of interest. **usurer** *n*. a person who practises usury.

Utah (*abbrev*. **UT.**)
Utah is a mineral-rich state in the ROCKY Mountains area of the U.S.A. It is divided down the middle by the Wasatch Range of the Rocky Mountains. West of the Wasatch is the Great Basin and Great Salt Lake. The Great Salt Lake Desert lies south and west of the lake. The capital and largest city is Salt Lake City.

When we think of Utah we think of the MORMONS, who were its first settlers. Salt Lake City became the center of the Mormon religion and their Church of Jesus Christ of Latter-day Saints.

One of Utah's main industries is mining. Large amounts of copper, coal, uranium and oil are produced.

There is also a Sea Gull Monument in Salt Lake City. It commemorates the time when seagulls saved Utah's crops in 1848 by eating up a plague of crickets. Bingham Canyon, near Salt Lake City, has the world's largest open-pit copper mine. Bonneville Salt Flats are used as a great automobile speedway. The Dinosaur National Monument, near Jensen is littered with ancient reptile fossils.

utensil *n*. a tool or instrument, especially one that is used in cooking. *An egg whisk is a very handy utensil.*

A 13th-century monastery at Novgorod, an ancient and once important city of Russia.

uterus (**yoo**-*ter-us*) *n*. the womb, the organ in which an unborn mammal is carried.

utilize *vb*. make use of.

Utopia *n*. an imaginary and perfect place. **utopian** *adj*.

utter 1. *adj*. complete or total, especially something bad. *The room was an utter mess.* 2. *vb*. say something, make a sound. *The kitten tried to utter a faint mew.*

utterance *n*. words spoken.

U-turn *n*. when a vehicle changes direction through 180° by turning on a U-shaped course; a complete change of policy.

V

A volcanic island – White Island – which lies off the coast of North Island, New Zealand.

vacant *adj*. empty; not filled. **vacancy** *n*. being vacant; unoccupied property or job. *There is a vacancy in the post office*.
vacate *vb*. give up, make empty, leave. *Customers are asked to vacate the premises as soon as they have finished their business*.
vacation *n*. holiday; time when courts, schools, etc. are closed.
vaccinate (**vak**-*sin-ate*) *vb*. inoculate against a disease, notably smallpox. **vaccination** *n*. **vaccine** *n*.
► Vaccine is a substance to make a person immune to a specific disease. Most are injected, but some are given by mouth. They work by stimulating the body's natural resistance. Routine childhood vaccinations are given against a number of diseases, including poliomyelitis, diphtheria and whooping cough.

vacuum 1. *n*. an absolutely empty space. 2. *vb*. clean by suction, using a *vacuum cleaner*.
► A vacuum gets its name from *vacuus*, the Latin word for empty. When you try to empty a container by pumping out the air, some air always stays behind. This partly empty space is called a partial vacuum. New air always rushes in to fill the space. This is how your LUNGS work. When you breathe out, you make a partial vacuum in your lungs. Air rushes to fill the space, making you breathe in.
vagabond *n*. a person without a fixed home.
vague *adj*. not clear, indefinite, indistinct. **vagueness** *n*.
vain *adj*. 1. showing too much pride. 2. futile, unsuccessful. *They searched for the dog in vain*. **vanity** *n*.
vale *n*. a valley.
valence (**vay**-*lence*) *n*. (also called **valency**) the number of chemical bonds with which an atom or a radical (group containing different atoms) can link with other atoms.
► Chlorine, for example has a valence of one, while zinc has a valence of two. For this reason, each MOLECULE of the compound zinc chloride (S—$ZnCl_2$) contains one zinc atom linked by its bonds to two chlorine atoms, as its formula shows. Iron and some other elements have more than one valence – that is, atoms of these elements may join with different numbers of other elements.

Valentine
Valentine is the name of two Roman saints. Valentine of Rome was a priest and doctor. Valentine of Terni was a bishop. According to legend, both were beheaded during a period of religious persecution. St. Valentine's Day is celebrated on February 14 each year. There is nothing in either Valentine legend to account for the custom of choosing a partner of the opposite sex and sending "valentines" on this day. It may have had its origin in the pagan Roman festival of Lupercalia.

valet *n*. a man who looks after the personal needs of his employer, hotel guests, etc.
valiant *adj*. brave, courageous.
valid *adj*. legally acceptable. *Is your driving license valid for all countries?*
valley *n*. a hollow between hills; a U-shaped or V-shaped depression in the earth's surface.
► Most valleys were made by rivers wearing away the land as they flowed to the sea. Mountain valleys are often narrow with steep sides and a sharply sloping floor. Gorges are very narrow valleys with towering cliffs on either side. Valleys grow wider and shallower as they come down the mountains to meet the plains. During the ICE AGES many valleys filled with huge GLACIERS. These inched slowly down the valleys,

making them deeper and wider.

Rift valleys occur when a block of land sinks between roughly parallel faults in the earth's surface. The best known of these is the Great Rift Valley in East Africa.

center. Its exports include timber and timber products, grain and fish. The area was explored in 1792 by the British navigator Captain George Vancouver, who also gave his name to nearby Vancouver Island.

Horn (peaked point)
Arete (sharp ridge)
Hanging valley
Glaciated valley

Ice scooped out this glaciated valley and shortened ridges and valleys that ran in from the sides. This created hanging valleys above the main one.

valuable *adj*. of great value or worth.
value 1. *n*. the amount of money that something is worth. 2. *vb*. estimate value of; think highly of.
valve *n*. 1. a device that controls the flow of liquid, allowing it to go in one direction only. 2. one half of a hinged shell.
vampire *n*. 1. a dead person in old stories who is supposed to suck the blood of living people. 2. a small bat found in the forests of Central and South America.

► According to legend, vampires leave their graves at night to suck the blood of their living victims. Day by day their victims grow paler and weaker until they die. Then they become vampires themselves.

Vampires cannot come out of their graves while the sun is up. Garlic and the sign of the cross are supposed to keep them away. But the only way to kill them is to drive a wooden stake through their heart.

►► Unlike vampires, the **vampire bat** really exists. Despite its name, only one species of vampire feeds entirely on the blood of other animals. It attacks its victims at night while they are asleep. With its sharp teeth, the bat cuts the skin and then laps up the blood. Other species live on insects and fruit.

van *n*. a covered vehicle for carrying things.

Vancouver

Vancouver, in British Columbia, is Canada's third largest city and its chief Pacific Port. Vancouver is an important industrial and cultural

vandal *n*. a person who destroys or damages things for no obvious reason. **vandalism** *n*.
vane *n*. a device that revolves in the wind and indicates wind direction. *Vanes are often put at the top of buildings*.

Van Gogh, Vincent

This Dutch painter (1853–90) became a friend of GAUGUIN and was a leading Post-Impressionist artist (*see* IMPRESSIONISM). He was born in Branant in the Netherlands, but spent most of his life in France. He painted very quickly, using bold brush strokes and bright colors to create an immediate impact. During a period of insanity he cut off one of his ears. In the end he committed suicide.

vanilla *n*. & *adj*. the pod of a tropical climbing plant used to flavor ice cream and other foods.

► Vanilla comes from a climbing plant, which belongs to the same family as ORCHIDS. Each plant grows up a tree, clinging on with little roots that sprout on the stem. Vanilla was first grown in Mexico. Now, most vanilla comes from tropical islands such as Tahiti, in the Pacific, and Madagascar.

Vanilla plants make their seeds in pods. The name vanilla is Spanish for "little pod". The pods are picked before they are ripe. Then they are dried. After that, they are chopped up and soaked in alcohol and water to make vanilla essence.

vanish *vb*. disappear suddenly.

vanquish (**van**-*kwish*) *vb*. defeat, conquer.
vapor *n*. a substance such as gas, mist or smoke. *Steam is water vapor*.
variety *n*. 1. a number of different things or kinds of. *You can buy this blouse in a variety of colors*. 2. a form of popular entertainment, involving comedians, singers, dancers, etc.
various *adj*. having different varieties; several. *Michael has worked at various jobs since he left school*.
varnish *n*. a liquid made from chemicals like resins which is used like paint and, when dry, is hard, shiny, and transparent. *vb*. coat with varnish.
vary *vb*. change, become different.
vase *n*. a glass, china or pottery container, deeper than it is tall, often used to hold flowers.
vast *adj*. very large in size, amount, etc. *The circus tent was vast*.
vat *n*. a large, usually uncovered container for holding liquids.

Vatican City State

The Vatican City is the home of the Pope and the headquarters of the ROMAN CATHOLIC CHURCH. It stands on Vatican Hill in ROME, and is the smallest independent country in the world. It is only the size of a small farm but it has its own flag, radio station and railroad. It also issues its own stamps.

The Vatican City is surrounded by

The Vatican flag with its symbol of triple tiara and crossed keys.

walls and contains many famous buildings. These include the Vatican Palace, which has more than 1,000 rooms; the Sistine Chapel, decorated by MICHELANGELO; and St. Peter's Basilica.

AREA: 108.7 ACRES (44 HECTARES)
POPULATION: ABOUT 1,000
CURRENCY: ITALIAN LIRA
OFFICIAL LANGUAGES: ITALIAN, LATIN

vault 1. *vb*. jump with your hands resting on something for support. *Denise tried to vault over the fence*. 2. *n*. an underground room, often used to store valuable things. 3. *n*. an arched roof.
veal *n*. the meat of a young calf.
veer *vb*. change direction, especially of the wind; change one's mind.
vegetable *n*. a plant, especially one grown for food. *Vegetables taste less sweet than most fruits*.

► Usually, only part of a vegetable is eaten, either the root, stem, leaf, seed or fruit. Onions and carrots are root vegetables, but asparagus is a stem vegetable. Members of the cabbage family, such as sprouts and kale, are all leaf vegetables. PEAS and BEANS are seed vegetables while CUCUMBERS and TOMATOES are fruit vegetables.

vegetarian *n.* a person who does not eat meat or fish. *Some vegetarians do not eat milk or eggs either.*

vegetation *n.* all the plants that grow in a certain area.

vehement (**vee**-*a-ment*) *adj.* violent, energetic.

vehicle *n.* anything that is used to transport people or things from one place to another. *Trains, cars and carts are all vehicles.*

veil *n.* a covering for the head, and especially the face, in some Eastern countries.

vein (rhymes with *lane*) *n.* 1. one of the blood vessels that takes blood back to the heart from various parts of the body. 2. a layer or streak of mineral.

► Most veins carry blood that has no oxygen left in it, but the veins leading from the LUNGS to the heart carry blood that is again rich in oxygen. Veins have thin walls, and valves to help the blood overcome the pull of gravity. The blood's flow back to the heart is helped by the squeezing action of muscles.

Varicose veins are veins on the surface of the skin that are swollen and sore. They usually occur on the inside of the legs, and may need surgery. Varicose veins appear more often in people who are overweight and those whose work involves a lot of standing.

Velasquez, Diego Rodriguez De Silva Y

Velasquez (1599–1660) was a Spanish painter who in 1623 became court painter to Philip IV of Spain, and completed many royal portraits. He is best known for *Las Meninas* (a court group study) and the *Rokeby Venus*.

velocity *n.* the speed of a body measured in a given direction.

► A vehicle traveling due north at a given speed would have the same velocity in that direction. But, while traveling at the same constant speed, it could be said to have a smaller velocity in the northeasterly direction, and zero velocity in the easterly direction.

velvet *n.* a fabric with a thick, soft pile of short, raised threads all over its surface. *Velvet is used largely for curtains and furnishings.*

vendetta *n.* an Italian word meaning a feud or violent hostilities, especially between families.

veneer *n.* a thin layer of good quality wood covering wood of poorer quality; superficial appearance.

Venezuela (Venezuelan)

Venezuela is a large country on the north coast of SOUTH AMERICA. Most of southern Venezuela is covered by flat-topped mountains. Angel Falls, the highest waterfall in the world, is in Venezuela. A grassy plain stretches across the middle of the country on either side of the Orinoco River.

Venezuela grows coffee, cotton and cocoa. But its minerals, especially oil, make it the richest country on the continent.

AREA: 352,164 SQ. MILES (912,050 SQ. KM)
POPULATION: 15,920,000
CAPITAL: CARACAS
CURRENCY: BOLIVAR
OFFICIAL LANGUAGE: SPANISH

vengeance *n.* punishment inflicted on someone to pay back harm or wrong done; revenge.

Venice (Venetian)

Venice is a beautiful city in ITALY, on the Adriatic Sea. It is built on a cluster of low, mud islands. There are more than 100 of them. The houses are built on wooden posts driven into the mud. Instead of roads, Venice has canals. Sometimes the sea floods the city, which is slowly sinking into the mud at about ⅛ in. (2 mm) a year.

For hundreds of years, Venice was the most important center for trade between Europe and the empires of the east. The city became very rich and is full of palaces and fine houses built by merchants.

venison *n.* the meat of a deer.

venom *n.* the poison of certain snakes and other poisonous animals, injected by biting or stinging.

vent *n.* an outlet or opening through which gas, etc., can escape. *He gave vent to his feelings.*

ventilate *vb.* circulate air to freshen (a room); discuss something openly and freely.

ventriloquist *n.* someone who can make the voice seem to come from somewhere else.

► Ancient peoples used to think that a ventriloquist's voice came from his belly. The word ventriloquist comes from Latin words that roughly mean "belly speaker".

In fact, a ventriloquist speaks in the same way as everyone else, but with some differences. He leaves his mouth slightly open and tries to keep his lips still. He takes a deep breath and slowly lets it out as he "talks." The ventriloquist makes the sounds of different words by using his throat muscles, the roof of his mouth, and the tip of his tongue. Because he does not use his lips, the letters, "p" and "b" often sound like "k" or "g."

venture *vb.* & *n.* risk, dare to. *"Nothing ventured nothing gained," as the proverb says.*

venue *n.* a meeting place.

Venus (Goddess)

Venus was the Roman goddess of love, grace and beauty. The Greeks had a similar goddess called Aphrodite. Many of the stories about Venus began as tales about Aphrodite.

Most stories say that Venus was born in the sea foam near the Greek island of Cythera. Although she was the most beautiful goddess, she married the ugliest god. He was Vulcan, the god of fire. But Venus also fell in love with other gods and with men. Venus and the war god, Mars, had a son called Cupid, the god of love. She also loved a Greek king called Anchises, and they had a son called Aeneas. The Romans believed that Aeneas helped to start the city of Rome.

Venus liked to help lovers. She started the TROJAN WAR by making Helen of Troy fall in love with Paris.

The marble statue of the Venus de Milo, discovered on the Greek island of Melos in 1820.

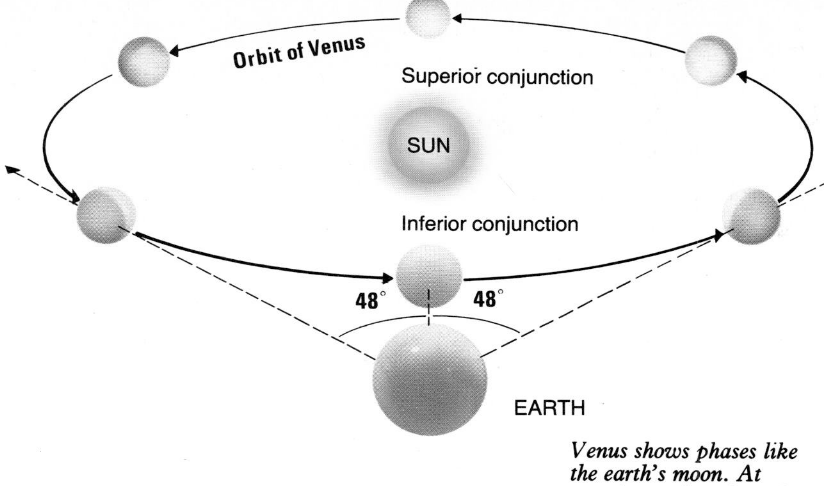

Venus shows phases like the earth's moon. At superior conjunction, the sunlit hemisphere is turned directly towards the earth. At inferior conjunction we can see only the dark side.

Venus (Planet)
The PLANET Venus is named after the Roman goddess of beauty and love. Venus is the brightest planet in the SOLAR SYSTEM. We see it as the morning star or the evening star, depending on where it is on its journey around the sun.

Venus takes only 225 days to go round the sun. So more than three years pass on Venus for every two on earth. But Venus itself spins so slowly that one day on Venus lasts for 243 days on earth. It is the only planet to spin in the opposite way to the direction of its ORBIT.

Venus is about the same size as earth, but weighs a little less. It is also much hotter, because it is much closer to the sun. The surface of Venus is hidden under a dazzling white cloak of cloud. This may be made of tiny drops of sulfuric acid. The atmosphere on Venus is mainly CARBON DIOXIDE. This acts rather like a greenhouse roof, trapping the sun's heat. The rocks on Venus are hotter than boiling water.

veranda, verandah *n.* a covered patio or terrace on the ground floor of a house.

verb *n.* a word for something that is done, or happens. *In "the cat ate the rat," the verb is "ate."*

verdict *n.* the decision of a judge. *The verdict was "not guilty."*

vermin *n.* (plural **vermin**) any animals, from insects to rats, which cause harm to crops, etc., or which spread disease.

Vermont (*abbrev.* **Vt.**)
Vermont is a small new England state in the northeastern corner of the United States on the Canadian border.

Burlington, Vermont's largest city, overlooks Lake Champlain, which forms the state's western border. The capital is Montpelier.

Vermont is famous for its beautiful scenery, peaceful villages, white churches and rolling hills. Maple sugar and syrup, asbestos and the country's finest marble are among the state's main products.

Vermont's history began with the arrival of French explorers, but the English took control at the end of the French and Indian War in 1763. In 1777 Vermont became an independent republic and outlawed slavery. Vermont was the first state to be added to the original 13 – in 1791.

Versailles
Versailles is a palace in France which stands in a city, also called Versailles, just outside Paris.

Versailles palace was begun by LOUIS XIV in 1661, for the king and his court. It was built on the site of a hunting lodge. The most famous architects, sculptors and gardeners of the time worked on the palace and its magnificent park.

The palace is built of pink and cream stone. It is more than half-a-mile (800 meters) long. Inside are hundreds of beautiful rooms. The most famous is the Hall of Mirrors. It is lined with 483 enormous mirrors, and is full of paintings.

Louis XIV spent enormous sums of money on the palace. The great expense and luxury of the Versailles palace was one of the causes of the FRENCH REVOLUTION.

versatile *adj.* having ability in different skills.

verse *n.* one section or part of a song or poem.

version *n.* one form or variant of an original book, incident, etc. *That is your version of what happened. My version is totally different.*

versus *prep.* in contest against. It is shortened to *v.* in sports, e.g. Jets *v.* Cowboys, and in lawsuits, e.g. Jones *v.* Smith.

vertebra *n.* (plural **vertebrae**) the small bones of the spine.

vertebrate *n.* an animal with a backbone, or spinal column.

► The name *vertebrate* comes from a Latin word that means "to turn." The backbone is made up of a number of short bones called *vertebrae*. Most vertebrates can bend and straighten their backbones by slightly turning their vertebrae. Many things make vertebrates different from other animals. Most have a bony case to protect their BRAIN, a set of ribs to protect their HEART, LUNGS and other delicate parts, and one or two pairs of limbs.

Louis XIV of France. The magnificence in which he lived in his new palace at Versailles earned the nickname of "Le Grand Monarque" ("The Great Monarch").

And most vertebrates have a SKELETON made of bone.

vertical *adj.* straight up and down, upright, perpendicular.

Vespucci, Amerigo
Amerigo Vespucci (1454–1512) was an Italian explorer. He made several

V

expeditions to Central and South America on behalf of the Spanish and Portuguese. He was not in command of the expeditions, but served as navigator. Unlike Christopher COLUMBUS, who had discovered the West Indies a few years earlier, Vespucci realized that the Americas were a new continent. (Columbus thought he had sailed to ASIA.) America was named in honor of Amerigo Vespucci.

vespers *n.* an evening church service.
vessel *n.* 1. a hollow utensil, especially one for holding liquids. 2. a ship or boat.
vest *n.* a sleeveless garment, usually V-necked, worn over a shirt.
vestige *n.* a slight trace or evidence of something that once existed.
vestment *n.* an official robe or gown worn for services and rites.
vestry *n.* a room in a church where vestments are kept.

Vesuvius
Vesuvius is one of the world's most famous VOLCANOES. The mountain rises over the Bay of Naples in southern Italy. It is about 4,000 ft. (1,200 meters) high, but gets shorter every time it erupts.

The first eruption we know about happened in A.D. 79. Vesuvius threw out ash and lava that between them buried the Roman cities of POMPEII and Herculaneum. There have been nine bad eruptions in the last 200 years.

vet *n.* an abbreviation for veterinarian.
veteran *n.* someone with a lot of experience.
veterinarian *n.* a doctor for animals.
► Veterinary medicine deals with the diseases of animals. The training of veterinarians is similar to that of doctors, involving a university course. Although veterinary medicine is still largely concerned with farm animals, it now embraces the study and care of dogs, cats, birds and laboratory animals. Veterinary science plays an essential part in the control of diseases in food animals.

veto *n.* (plural **vetoes**) the power to forbid or prohibit something. *vb.* refuse to agree to.
vex *vb.* annoy or irritate someone.
via (**vie**-*a*, **vee**-*a*) *prep.* by way of. *Today the train went via Oxford instead of Reading.*
viable *adj.* workable.
viaduct *n.* a long bridge that is built to carry a railway, road, or canal across a valley.
vibrate *vb.* move very quickly back and forth, quiver.
vicar *n.* a clergyman in charge of a church and parish.
vice 1. *n.* a very bad habit or immoral conduct. 2. *n.* a tool that holds things steady and in one place so they can be worked on.
3. *prefix* (**vice**-) in place of, next in rank to, e.g. Vice-President of the United States.
► The United States Constitution says that if the president dies or is unable to perform his duties, the vice-president shall become president.

Because the vice-president may have to become president, the qualifications for the office are the same as those for a presidential candidate. The vice-president is elected at the same time and in the same way as the president, also for four years.

The vice-president's chief duty is to preside over the SENATE. In the case of a tie vote, he casts the deciding vote.

vicinity *n.* neighborhood. *If you are ever in the vicinity, do drop in.*
vicious (rhymes with **wish**-*us*) *adj.* fierce, violent, savage.
victim *n.* someone who suffers harm or danger.
victor *n.* one who defeats an enemy or opponent; winner.

Victoria, Austalia
Victoria is a beautiful and prosperous Australian state. It has an area of 87,884 sq. miles (227,618 sq. km). The capital is MELBOURNE. The MURRAY River forms the state's northern boundary. About 75 percent of the land is farmed. Various crops are grown and cattle and sheep are reared. But manufacturing is now the most important industry. Victoria became a separate British colony in 1851.

Victoria, Canada
Victoria is the capital of BRITISH COLUMBIA. It is a busy port handling Pacific Ocean shipping.

Victoria Cross
The VC is the highest British decoration for bravery, founded by Queen VICTORIA in 1856. The medal is bronze with a crimson ribbon. Originally all the crosses were made from the metal of Russian cannons captured at Sevastopol in the CRIMEAN WAR.

Victoria Falls
This great waterfall stands on the Zambezi river, which flows between Zambia and Zimbabwe in southern Africa. About halfway along its course, the river plunges down for about 350 ft. (100 meters), into a narrow gorge. The falls are the second largest in Africa. Only the Stanley Falls, in Zaïre, produce more water.

Victoria Falls were discovered by the Scottish explorer David LIVINGSTONE in 1855 during his second expedition. He named the falls after Queen Victoria.

Victoria became Queen in 1837 at the age of 18. She reigned for 64 years. This portrait was painted in the early years of her reign.

Victoria, Queen
Queen Victoria (1819–1901) ruled Great Britain for 64 years, longer than any other British monarch. During her reign, the nation grew richer and its empire larger than ever before. She was the queen of many countries, including Australia, New Zealand, Canada and South Africa, and was the empress of India.

Victoria was the daughter of Edward, Duke of Kent. GEORGE III was her grandfather. She was just 18 when she inherited the throne from her uncle, William IV. Two years later, she married her German cousin, Prince Albert. They had four sons and five daughters. Prince Albert died of typhoid fever in 1861.

Victoria was very popular with her people. In 1887, she had been queen for 50 years. All over the British Empire there were huge parades and parties to celebrate this Golden Jubilee. In 1897, there were more celebrations, this time for her Diamond Jubilee.

Victorian *adj.* belonging to the reign of Queen Victoria.
victory *n.* success, winning. **victorious** *adj.*
vicuna *n.* a small South American camel without a hump.
► The vicuna stands only about 3 ft. (90 cm), at the shoulder. It ranges from the north of Peru to northern Chile and is seldom found at less than 14,000 ft. (4,000 meters) above sea level. The vicuna lives in herds of a few females and their young, with one male.

Vicunas have finer fleeces than any other wool-bearing animal. The coat is light brown to reddish yellow.

Because the wool is so highly prized, the vicuna has been greatly reduced in numbers. The government of Peru protects the animal and controls the sale of its fleece.

The ancient Incas hunted the vicuna only once every four years. They used its wool to make robes for their rulers.

videotape *n.* a magnetic tape used for recording the pictures and sounds from or for television movies and programs.

► A videotape is like the tape used in a tape recorder, but wider. The pictures the camera takes are turned into magnetic signals on the tape. When the tape is played back through a special machine, the signals are turned back into pictures.

vie *vb.* compete with someone.

Vienna (Viennese)
Vienna is the capital city of AUSTRIA. More than one-and-a-half million people live there. Until the end of World War I it was the home of the powerful HAPSBURG family.

Vienna stands on the DANUBE river. It is a very ancient site. CELTS settled there more than 2,000 years ago. Then the Romans built a city called Vindobona. Many buildings from the MIDDLE AGES still stand in Vienna. The most famous is St. Stephen's Cathedral.

Vienna has always been popular with artists and musicians. BEETHOVEN and MOZART lived there.

Vietnam (Vietnamese)
Vietnam is a country in Southeast ASIA. It is just a bit larger than New Mexico and only 40 miles (55 km) wide in some parts. Vietnam is a hot damp country.

Vietnam used to be divided into two countries, North Vietnam and South Vietnam. Hanoi was the main city in the north and Saigon (now called Ho Chi Minh City) in the south. From the 1950s until 1975, the two countries were at war. South Vietnam was supported by the United States. North Vietnam was Communist. Now the whole country is Communist.

AREA: 127,249 SQ. MILES (329,556 SQ. KM)
POPULATION: 51,742,000
CAPITAL: HANOI
CURRENCY: DONG
OFFICIAL LANGUAGE: VIETNAMESE

view 1. *n.* act of seeing; what is seen. 2. *n.* opinion. *Have you any views on this topic?* 3. *vb.* look at.

viewfinder *n.* device to help photographer aim the camera, indicating the part of the scene that will appear on the film.

Vikings *n. pl.* Scandinavian seafarers who raided and plundered many parts of Europe between the 700s and 1100s.

► The Vikings lived in Norway, Sweden and Denmark. A great number of Vikings left their homes to raid villages and build settlements in northern Europe. They settled in England, Ireland and France. Vikings also traveled to Russia, and even to the great city of CONSTANTINOPLE. Many settled in Iceland, and from there, some went to Greenland.

A scene from the Bayeux Tapestry showing the Normans crossing the Channel in longboats to invade England. The battle that followed put a "Viking" king on the English throne.

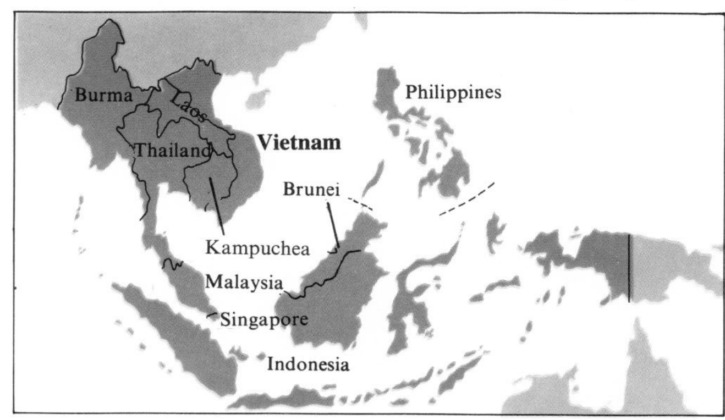

The Vikings sailed in long ships, which were faster than any others at that time. Ships were very important to the Vikings. They sometimes buried their kings and chiefs in large ships. These "tombs" were then buried or burned.

The Vikings were the first European people to discover North America. They sailed there from Greenland, but they did not settle there.

vile *adj.* horrible, unpleasant.

villa *n.* a country house in Roman times; a small house in a suburban or residential district.

village *n.* a group of houses and other buildings that is smaller than a town and usually has a church.

villain *n.* a wicked or evil person.

Vinci, Leonardo Da see LEONARDO DA VINCI

vine *n.* a climbing or creeping plant.

vineyard *n.* a place where grapevines are grown.

vinegar *n.* an acid liquid used for flavoring and preserving food.

► Vinegar is a weak mixture of acetic acid and water, used for flavoring food and also for preserving food by pickling (soaking in vinegar). It is traditionally made from wine (wine vinegar), beer (malt vinegar) or cider (cider vinegar). Some cheap modern vinegar is made chemically.

viola *n.* a stringed musical instrument that looks like a large violin.

V

violence *n.* great physical force.
violent *adj.*
violet 1. *n.* & *adj.* a color, like a mixture of blue and purple. 2. *n.* a small plant with violet-colored or white flowers.
violin *n.* a stringed musical instrument played with a bow.
violinist *n.* player of a violin.
► A violin is a curved wooden box, shaped rather like a figure eight. A long neck is fixed to one end of the box. Four strings, made of gut or nylon, are stretched from the top of the neck to the bottom end of the box.

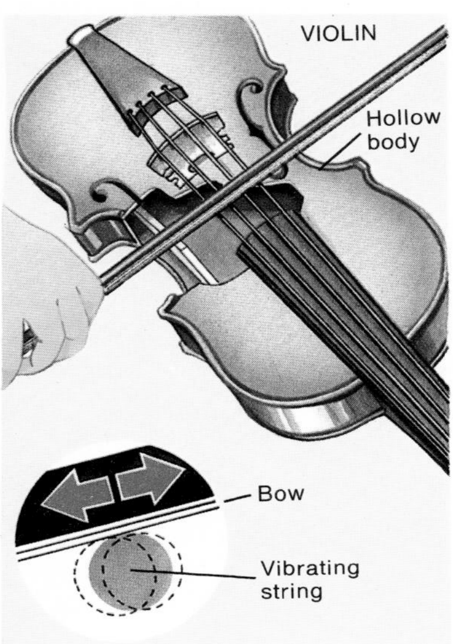

When a bow is moved across a string, the rough surface of the hairs in the bow keeps it vibrating. Pushing the bow down makes the vibration stronger and the sound louder. The vibrating string sets the hollow body of the violin vibrating too, making the sound louder.

The violin is played with a bow made from horsehair. When this is drawn across the strings they vibrate to make sounds. The strings can also be plucked with the fingers.

A violin is usually the smallest stringed instrument in an ORCHESTRA. Violins are normally made of maple at the front and pine wood at the back.

viper *n.* one of a group of poisonous snakes.

Virginia (*abbrev.* **Va.**)
Virginia is a southern state named after Queen ELIZABETH I of England, the "Virgin Queen." This historic state was the site of more battles in both the American War of INDEPENDENCE and the CIVIL WAR than any other. It is famous for its historic buildings and stately homes. The first permanent English settlement in North America was at Jamestown in 1607.

Williamsburg was the capital of Virginia from 1699 to 1799. Part of the town has been rebuilt to look as it did when Virginia was an English colony.

Tobacco is Virginia's leading crop and is exported to many parts of the world. Leading manufactures are chemicals and textiles.

The largest cities are Norfolk, Richmond, the capital, and Virginia Beach.

virtue *n.* goodness; morality; merit.
virtuoso *n.* a highly skilled persons especially in playing a musical instrument.
virus *n.* a tiny living particle that can carry and cause diseases.
► A virus is a minute organism – much smaller than BACTERIA – that can only be seen with an electron microscope.

Viruses can only grow and reproduce inside living CELLS. Some viruses use animal cells, others use plant cells. The virus makes the "host" cell produce virus material instead of normal cell material. As a result, the host cell is damaged, perhaps fatally, and this eventually causes illness in the animal or plant. Many diseases that attack human beings are caused by viruses. They include smallpox, measles and the common cold. Doctors try to protect people from viral diseases by vaccination. The VACCINE itself is made from viruses.

visa *n.* a stamp on a passport

VITAMINS

Vitamin	Chief Source	Needed for
Vitamin A	Carotene (which body can convert to Vit. A) in carrots, egg yolks, butter, yellow or orange fruits, vegetables	growth, prevention of dry skin; formation of visual purple, which aids vision in dim light; lack of Vit. A can lead to atrophy of white of eye
Vitamin B_1 (thiamine)	wheat germ, bread, pork, liver, potatoes, milk	prevention of beri-beri
Vitamin B_2 (riboflavin)	milk, eggs, liver	lack may result in skin disorders, inflammation of tongue, and cracked lips
Biotin	liver, yeast, milk, butter	probably concerned with healthy skin
Folic acid	many green vegetables, liver, yeast, mushrooms	prevention of one form of anemia
Nicotinic acid (niacin)	yeast, liver, bread, wheat germ, kidney, milk	prevention of pellagra
Pantothenic acid	many foods, but abundant in liver, yeast, and eggs	lack may play part in skin disorders
Vitamin B_6 (pyridoxine)	meat, fish, milk, yeast	lack can lead to convulsions in babies or anemia in adults
Vitamin B_{12} (cyanocobalamin)	liver, kidney, eggs, fish	formation of red blood cells, healthy nerve tissue
Vitamin C	fresh fruit and vegetables	prevention of scurvy
Vitamin D	margarine, fish, oils, eggs, butter, also formed in skin exposed to sunlight	formation of bones; lack causes rickets in children
Vitamin E	most foods	little known but may affect fertility and aging
Vitamin K	green vegetables; also formed by bacteria in intestine	blood clotting

allowing a person to enter a particular country.

viscount (**vie**-*count*) *n.* title of a nobleman (peer) ranking between an earl and baron.

viscountess *n.* the wife of a viscount.

visible *adj.* capable of being seen. *The ship was still just visible on the horizon.*

vision *n.* 1. the power of seeing, eyesight. 2. something seen in a dream, etc. 3. great power of imagination.

visit *vb.* pay a call on someone; go to see a place; stay with or at. *n.* a journey made in order to visit a place or person.

visitor *n.* a person who comes to see or stay with someone; a traveler who is staying in a place for a short time only.

visor *n.* the part of a helmet, usually movable, that covers the eyes; a shade, such as the flap inside a car window that protects your eyes from the sun.

visual *adj.* concerned with sight and seeing. **visualize** *vb.* imagine, form a picture. *She tried to visualize what the dress would be like without pleats.*

vital *adj.* 1. of great importance. 2. lively, energetic.

vitamin *n.* one of a group of chemical substances that our body needs in order to stay healthy.

► Vitamins are found in different kinds of food. There are six kinds of vitamin. Scientists call them A, B, C, D, E and K. Vitamin B is really a group of vitamins.

The first people to realize that certain kinds of food were important to health were sailors. On long voyages they got a disease called *scurvy* if they could not eat fresh fruit and vegetables. These contain vitamin C. From the 1700s, English sailors were given limes to eat to prevent scurvy. This is why they were nicknamed "limeys" by the Americans.

No food has all the vitamins we need. That is why it is important to eat a mixture of things. Some people take their vitamins in pills. No one really needs pills if they eat well. Very old people, young babies and women expecting babies all need more vitamins than usual.

Vivaldi, Antonio

Antonio Vivaldi (1675–1741) was an Italian composer whose highly ornamental music is elaborate but clear. His best known composition is a group of concertos, *The Four Seasons.*

vivid *adj.* lively; bright and clear. *Dickens wrote vivid descriptions of London life.*

vixen *n.* a female fox.

vocabulary *n.* all the words known or used in a certain language.

vocal *adj.* to do with the voice.

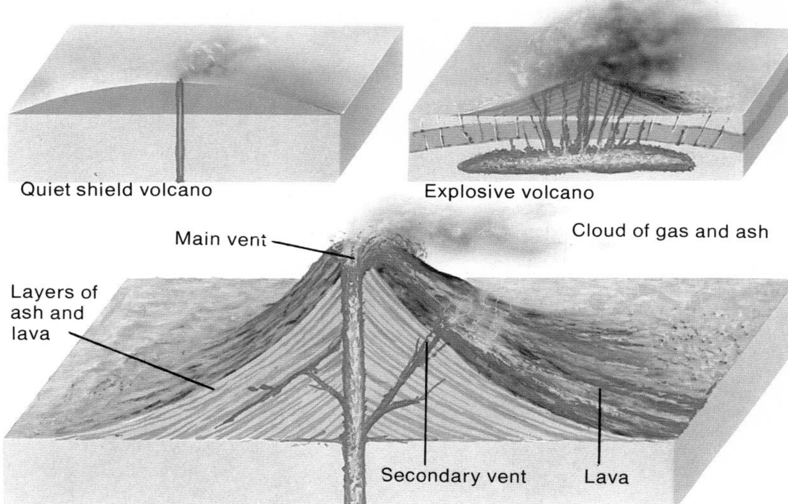

Volcanoes can be active, dormant (sleeping) or extinct. Active volcanoes vary in shape depending largely on the thickness of the lava. Really thick lava, for instance, hardly flows at all. It is squeezed out of the volcano like toothpaste. Such lava may form a volcanic plug. Gases build up inside and may eventually make the whole volcano explode.

vocation *n.* a calling (by God) to do special work; a career or profession.

vodka *n.* type of alcohol made in the Soviet Union and Poland – a strong mash liquor which has no color and little flavor.

vogue *n.* the fashion at a particular time. *Hats are again in vogue.*

voice *n.* the sound produced when you speak or sing; your ability to make such a sound.

► The sound of the human voice is made by air passing over the vocal chords (which are two folds of mucous membrane in the larynx). Movements of the TONGUE and lips change the sound into words, and the resulting sounds are strengthened by resonating in the hollow sinuses of the skull. Use of the voice is controlled by the brain, which is why brain damage can cause loss of speech.

Vivaldi

void *adj.* 1. containing nothing; vacant. 2. having no legal force; not valid.

volcano *n.* (plural **volcanoes**) an opening in the surface of the earth from which magma (molten rock), gas and steam are forced out; a mountain formed from hardened magma. **volcanic** *adj.*

► In ancient Greek stories, volcanoes were the chimneys of the underground forge of the fire god. The Roman name for this god was Vulcan. Volcanoes are named after him.

Some volcanoes are gently sloping mountains with cracks, or *fissures,* in them. Hot liquid rock called *lava* flows out through the fissures. Other volcanoes are steep-sided mountains with a large hole at the top. These are called cone volcanoes. They are the kind that *erupt* (explode).

Erupting volcanoes can do a lot of damage. The city of POMPEII was destroyed by VESUVIUS in A.D. 79. In 1883 Krakatoa, a volcano in Indonesia, erupted causing a TIDAL WAVE that killed 36,000 people. Volcanoes can also make new land. An island called Surtsey, south of Iceland, was made by a volcano which erupted under the sea in 1963.

There are about 455 active volcanoes on land, with another 80 or so beneath the oceans. There are many more that are now extinct.

vole *n.* a small rodent that looks like a mouse.

► Voles are closely related to

V

LEMMINGS. They are about 4 in. (10 cm) long, and live in all the cooler countries of the world.

The bank vole lives in shallow burrows. Sometimes it shares tunnels made by MOLES. Bank voles dig out storerooms and bedrooms from the burrows and line them with chewed grass.

The meadow vole lives in rough fields and on moors. Many meadow voles now live on the grassy slopes along highways. They sit up and eat with their "hands" like squirrels.

Water voles are often called "water rats." They live in river banks, where they dig deep burrows. Water voles are good swimmers. They eat only leaves, grass, roots and berries, which they store in their river bank burrows in autumn. "Ratty" in Kenneth Grahame's famous book *The Wind in the Willows* is a water vole.

A short-tailed vole.

Volga River

The Volga is the greatest river in the U.S.S.R. It starts in the Valday Hills southeast of Leningrad, and flows southeastward to the Caspian Sea. Here it spreads out into a DELTA with more than 200 channels. From November to March each year nearly the whole river is frozen over.

The Volga has always been important to Russia. In 1522, IVAN THE TERRIBLE and his army sailed down it. On the way, they built fortress towns to guard the new "road" to the sea. The river was used to transport logs from the north and send back grain.

Today, CANALS link the Volga to the Baltic Sea, the Black Sea, Moscow and the River Don. Oil, steel, coal, timber and bricks are carried on the waterway.

volley *n*. 1. flight or return of a ball before it has hit the ground. *vb*. 2. a number of missiles, e.g. arrows, fired at the same time.
volt *n*. a unit for measuring electrical pressure or electromotive force.

Volta, Count Alessandro

Count Alessandro Volta (1745–1827), an Italian physicist, is famous for his work on electricity. He made many inventions, including the voltaic pile and the voltaic cell. The unit of potential difference, the volt, is named after him.

Voltaire

Voltaire is the pseudonym of the French philosopher and author François Marie Arouet (1694–1778). One of the earliest contributors to Diderot's *Encyclopedie*, he was a dedicated opponent of civil restraints and organized religion. His best known work, *Candide*, is a satirical, philosophical novel.

volume *n*. 1. the amount of space something takes up. 2. a single book, particularly one of a set. 3. loudness. *I can't hear the radio properly; could you please turn up the volume?*

► You can work out the volume of an object by measuring its height, width and depth and multiplying the figures together. So a brick with equal sides, each 4 in. (10 cm) long, has a volume of 64 cubic in. (1,000 cubic cm) that is 4 in. × 4 in. × 4 in.

It is easy to find out the volume of boxes or bricks or anything with straight edges. Measuring the volume of something with irregular sides is more difficult. A method was discovered by ARCHIMEDES, the Greek scientist. A story told about him says that he was getting into his bath, which was full to the brim, and water spilled over the side. He suddenly realized that the volume of water that spilled over was exactly the same as the volume of his body. This means that any irregularly shaped object can be measured by plunging it into water and measuring the rise of the water level.

voluntary *adj*. doing without being asked or forced to; done without payment or obligation.
volunteer *n*. a person who offers to do something without being asked; a serviceman who joins up from his own choice. *vb*. offer one's services. *Jim volunteered to mow the lawn.*

The French philosopher Voltaire as an old man.

vomit *vb*. throw up food from your stomach through your mouth; be sick.
vote *vb*. show what you want from a group of choices by supporting one of them; ballot.
voucher *n*. a coupon; a certificate.
vow *vb*. & *n*. (make) a solemn promise.
vowel *n*. one of the sounds represented by the letters A, E, I, O, U and sometimes Y.

► Vowels are pronounced with the mouth open. What they sound like depends on the position of your TONGUE in the mouth. The shape your lips make is also important.

Because the tongue and the lips can shape themselves in hundreds of different ways, there are hundreds of different vowel sounds. Sometimes two or three vowel sounds are run together to make another sound. The vowel sounds in one language are often very difficult for speakers of another language to learn.

voyage *n*. a journey, particularly by sea.
vulgar *adj*. crude, coarse, in bad taste.
vulnerable *adj*. unprotected and easily wounded; open to attack and liable to have feelings hurt.

Egyptian vulture

vulture *n*. one of a family of large birds of prey which feed largely on dead animals.

► Vultures live in the hot, dry parts of the world. The largest land bird in North America is a type of vulture. This is the California condor. When its wings are spread out, it measures up to 10 ft. (3 meters).

Sometimes, vultures have to wait for their dinner until a large hunter such as a lion has made a kill. When the lion has eaten its fill, wild dogs and hyenas gorge on the remains. Then it is the vulture's turn.

Most vultures have bald heads and necks. This prevents their feathers from getting messy when they plunge their heads into large carcasses. They have very good eyesight and can spot dead or dying animals from far away.

W

A waterway market in Thailand.

waddle *n.* & *vb.* walk in a clumsy way like a duck.
wade *vb.* walk through water; move with some difficulty, progress slowly. *The river was just shallow enough for us to wade across.*
wadi *n.* an Arabic word meaning the dry bed of a river.
wafer *n.* a thin crisp biscuit; material sliced very thin.
waffle 1. *n.* a small, crisp kind of pancake. 2. *n.* & *vb.* talk or write nonsense.
wag *vb.* quick jerky movements up and down or from side to side. *A dog wags its tail when it is pleased.*
wage *vb.* carry on, take part in. *They waged war for five years. n.* the money you get for working, usually paid weekly.
► Wages used to be paid according to the amount of work done – the weight of coal mined or the number of shirts made. Today, most wages are paid for the length of time people spend working. Overtime, or time worked in addition to normal hours, is paid at a much higher rate. TRADE UNIONS were formed to see that their members were paid fair wages and given reasonable working conditions.

waggle *vb.* wave or wag; wobble. *The pilot waggled the wings of his aircraft to show he had seen us.*

Wagner, Wilhelm Richard
Richard Wagner (1813–83) was a German Romantic composer. Most of his musical output consists of opera, for which he wrote both the words and the music. He had the Festival Opera at Bayreuth specially built to stage his productions. His best-known works include *The Flying Dutchman* (1843), *Tannhauser* (1845) and the four-part *Ring of the Nibelungs*(1851–74).

wagon *n.* an open cart with four wheels; delivery truck.

wagtail *n.* one of a family of small birds with sharp beaks and long tails.
► Wagtails eat flies and other insects and are often found near water. As they run along the ground in search of food their heads bob fast and their tails wag up and down. There are yellow wagtails as well as pied wagtails.

waif *n.* a homeless, abandoned child.
wail *n.* a mournful cry, usually loud and shrill. *vb.* cry in wails, lament.
waist *n.* the narrow part of the body between the chest and the hips.
waistcoat *n.* a sleeveless jacket, sometimes worn as part of a suit.

A wagon train of pioneers makes it way westward through the Rocky Mountains – a fearful barrier across the routes to the rich farmlands of the West Coast.

W

wait *vb.* stay in one place, expecting something to happen. *We will wait here until you come back.*
waiter *n.* a man who serves food in a restaurant.
waitress *n.* (plural **waitresses**) a woman who serves food in a restaurant.
wake 1. *vb.* (past **woke** past part. **woken**) stop sleeping; rouse from sleep. 2. *n.* the track left in water by a ship.

Wales (Welsh)
Wales is part of the UNITED KINGDOM of Great Britain and Northern Ireland. It consists mostly of beautiful mountains and plateaus. River valleys and fertile coastal plains cover about one-third of the land. The most important regions are the coalmining and metal-manufacturing areas in southeastern Wales. Another small coalfield is in the northeast. Farming is also important.

England conquered Wales in 1282 and the two countries were united in 1536. But the Welsh people have retained their own individual culture.

walk *vb.* & *n.* (of a person or animal) move along at a steady pace, travel on foot, advance by steps.
walkie-talkie *n.* a portable radio telephone.
Walkman *n.* a small portable cassette tape player with headphones.
walkover *n.* an easy victory.
wall *n.* a barrier made of brick or stone surrounding a piece of land; the side of a room or building. *vb.* (**in**) protect with a wall.
wallaby *n.* a kind of marsupial, smaller than a kangaroo.
► Wallabies live in AUSTRALIA, NEW ZEALAND and parts of New Guinea. There are many different kinds of wallaby. Most are about the size of hares, though the biggest is roughly 3 ft. (1 meter) long with a 24 in. (60 cm) tail.

Wallabies feed mostly on grass. They also make good food for people and other animals. Some breeds are hunted for their valuable fur.

wallet *n.* a folding purse in which money or papers are kept.
wallow *vb.* splash about in mud; take delight in; be helpless. *They were left to wallow in ignorance.*
walnut *n.* deciduous tree belonging to the Northern Hemisphere, grown for its fine wood and its edible nut of the same name.
walrus *n.* (plural **walruses**) a large sea animal with long tusks, which lives in the Arctic.
► The walrus belongs to the SEAL family. Its enormous canine teeth form two tusks. The walrus uses them to scrape up the clams and shellfish it eats. It also uses its tusks to fight, and even polar bears keep away from fully grown walruses.

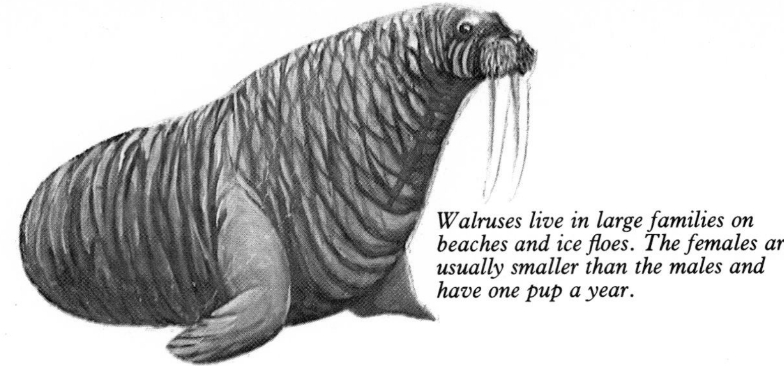

Walruses live in large families on beaches and ice floes. The females are usually smaller than the males and have one pup a year.

The Atlantic and the Pacific walrus both live in the ARCTIC. The male Atlantic walrus measures up to 13 ft. (4 meters) and weighs as much as 3,970 lb. (1,800 kg).

In the 1930s walruses almost disappeared through being hunted for their tusks and skins. Now there are laws to protect them, and their numbers are slowly increasing.

waltz (rhymes with *false*) *n.* a dance in three-quarter time. *vb.* dance a waltz; have easy success.
wand *n.* a slender stick used by fairies and magicians in stories to cause magic spells.
wander *n.* go from place to place without having a plan or a purpose. **wanderer** *n.*
wane *vb.* become smaller. *The moon is waning.*
wangle *vb.* get something by cunning; finagle. *Fred wangled a free ticket to the show.*
want 1. *vb.* wish for or strongly desire something; need. 2. *n.* lack of something; need (of).
wanted *adj.* sought (especially by the police).
war *n.* armed conflict between two or more countries or groups of people.

War of 1812
The War of 1812 was a war between the United States and Great Britain. It was an offshoot of the Napoleonic Wars. Both Britain and France wanted to draw the U.S. to its side, and each tried to stop American trade with the other. Britain blockaded all ports controlled by France and many U.S. sailors were seized to serve on British ships. President James Madison sent a message to Congress recommending war. This was declared on June 18, 1812. The British captured and burned Washington, D.C., but were halted at Fort McHenry, Maryland. Troops led by Andrew Jackson defeated a British force at New Orleans and the war ended in 1815 with the Treaty of Ghent.

ward *n.* 1. a room in a hospital where sick people needing similar care stay. 2. administrative division of a town. 3. *vb.* keep watch over, guard.
warden *n.* a guard in charge of prisoners in a jail.
ward off *vb.* prevent something happening.
wardrobe *n.* a cupboard where clothes are hung and stored.
warehouse *n.* a large building where goods of all sorts are kept. *vb.* store in a warehouse.
warfare *n.* the state of war.
warm *adj.* slightly hot; affectionate.
warn *vb.* tell people of danger. **warning** *n.* something that tells you of danger. *There was a warning light by the bridge, so we stopped.*
warp 1. *vb.* become twisted or bent. 2. *n.* the vertical threads on a loom, used for weaving.
warren *n.* a place where a group of rabbits live together in burrows.
warrior *n.* a fighter.
warship *n.* a military ship, especially one armed for combat.

Warsaw
Warsaw is the capital of POLAND, and is also its largest city. It is a major transport and communications center, with a variety of heavy industries. Warsaw has a fine Gothic cathedral and a medieval castle. It was occupied by German troops in both World Wars and was largely rebuilt after being badly damaged in World War II.

Wars of the Roses
The Wars of the Roses is the name given to the civil wars fought in England between 1455 and 1487. For 30 years the houses of York and Lancaster, both descendants of EDWARD III, fought against each other for the throne. The white rose was the emblem of York and the red rose the emblem of Lancaster.

The struggle ended in 1485 at the Battle of Bosworth, when the Lancastrian Henry Tudor defeated and killed Richard III. Henry was crowned HENRY VII, the first TUDOR king. He married a Yorkist princess and killed his rivals.

wart *n.* a small, hard lump on the skin.

During the Franco-Prussian War Paris was besieged for over four months.

W

Wart hog
The wart hog is a wild swine found in the open plains of Africa. It is a very ugly animal that reaches a height of about 2.5 ft. (75 cm) and, except for a bristly mane along the back, it has no hair. It has a large head with small eyes and two pairs of wartlike growths. It also has large tusks. It is closely related to the pig.

wash *vb.* clean something by soaking it in water.

MAJOR WARS

Date	Name	Won by	Against
431–404BC	Peloponnesian War	Peloponnesian League, led by Sparta, Corinth	Delian League, led by Athens
264–146BC	Punic Wars	Rome	Carthage
1337–1453	Hundred Years War	France	England
1455–1485	War of the Roses	House of Lancaster	House of York
1618–1648	English Civil War	Parliament	Charles I
1701–1713	War of the Spanish Succession	England, Austria, Prussia, Netherlands	France, Bavaria, Cologne, Mantua, Savoy
1740–1748	War of the Austrian Succession	Austria, Hungary, Britain, Holland	Bavaria, France, Poland, Prussia, Sardinia, Saxony, Spain
1756–1763	Seven Years War	Britain, Prussia, Hanover	Austria, France, Russia, Sweden
1775–1783	American War of Independence	Thirteen Colonies	Britain
1792–1815	Napoleonic Wars	Austria, Britain, Prussia, Russia, Spain, Sweden	France
1812–1814	War of 1812	United States	Britain
1846–1848	Mexican-American War	United States	Mexico
1854–1856	Crimean War	Britain, France, Sardinia, Turkey	Russia
1861–1865	American Civil War	23 Northern States (the Union)	11 Southern States (the Confederacy)
1870–1871	Franco-Prussian War	Prussia and other German states	France
1894–1895	Chinese-Japanese War (1st)	Japan	China
1898	Spanish-American War	United States	Spain
1899–1902	Boer (South African) War	Britain	Boer Republics
1904–1905	Russo-Japanese War	Japan	Russia
1914–1918	World War I	Belgium, Britain and Empire, France, Italy, Japan, Russia, Serbia, United States	Austria, Hungary, Bulgaria, Germany, Ottoman-Empire
1931–1933	Chinese-Japanese War (2nd)	Japan	China
1935–1936	Abyssinian War	Italy	Abyssinia (Ethopia)
1936–1939	Spanish Civil War	Junta de Defensa Nacional (Fascists)	Republican government
1937–1945	Chinese-Japanese War (3rd)	China	Japan
1939–1945	World War II	Australia, Belgium, Britain, Canada, China, Denmark, France, Greece, Netherlands, New Zealand, Norway, Poland, South Africa, Soviet Union, United States, Yugoslavia	Bulgaria, Finland, Germany, Hungary, Italy, Japan, Romania
1950–1953	Korean War	South Korea and United Nations forces	North Korea and Chinese forces
1957–1979	Vietnam War	North Vietnam	South Vietnam, United States
1967	Six-Day War	Israel	Egypt, Syria, Jordan, Iraq
1967–1970	Nigerian Civil War	Federal Government	Biafra
1971	Pakistani Civil War	East Pakistan (Bangladesh) and India	West Pakistan
1973	Yom Kippur War	Ceasefire arranged by United Nations; fought by Israel against Egypt, Syria, Iraq, Jordan, Sudan, Saudia Arabia, Lebanon	

washer *n*. a small flat ring used to make a joint tight, such as on a tap.

Washington (*abbrev*. **Wash.**)
Washington state lies on the Canadian border and the PACIFIC OCEAN. The Cascade Mountains, running north and south, divide the state in two. The eastern part of the state is dry and covered mainly by the great Columbia Plateau. West of the Cascades the state is green and often rainy.

The largest cities are Seattle, Spokane and Tacoma. Olympia is the capital.

Washington state produces apples, wheat and hops. Livestock and fishing are important. Mineral production includes uranium, silver and gold. The state's main industries are aircraft production and timber. Washington is called the "Evergreen State" because of its vast forests.

The first Americans came to Washington in 1805. They were led by Lewis and Clark, the famous explorers. In 1846, Washington state became part of the newly created Oregon Territory. In 1889 it became the 42nd state of the U.S.A.

Washington, D.C.
Washington, D.C., is the capital of the United States. It is named after the first president, George WASHINGTON, who chose its site on the Potomac River between Maryland and Virginia. It stands on a piece of land called the District of Columbia (hence the name D.C.).

Washington is the seat of Congress and the Supreme Court. The president's residence, the WHITE HOUSE, is there. So is the Capitol, with its white dome, and the Lincoln Memorial.

George Washington, who became the first president of the United States of America.

Washington, George
George Washington (1732–99) was the first president of the United States. He led the colonists to victory during the American War of INDEPENDENCE.

In 1787, he helped to write the Constitution of the United States. On the first election day, everyone voted for General Washington as president. He served two terms as president, from 1789 until 1797.

George Washington was buried at Mount Vernon. His birthday is a national holiday in the United States.

wasp *n*. a flying insect with a striped body and a sting in its tail. **waspish** *adj*. snappy, irritable.
► There are many different kinds, or species of this insect. Some wasps are called social insects because they live together in large groups. These wasps have different jobs to do for the group. A few of them are queens, and lay eggs. Others are workers who build the nests and collect the food. But most wasps are solitary insects that live alone, build their own nests, lay their own eggs and collect their own food.

Some wasps build nests in hollow trees, or in the roofs of houses. Others use holes in the ground, or hang nests from the branches of trees.

Wasps have a very powerful sting, which they use to stun their prey or to defend themselves.

waste *vb*. use more than you need of something, or throw something away although you could have used it. *n*. unwanted material. **wasteful** *adj*. extravagant.

watch 1. *vb*. look on. *Did you watch the football game?* 2. *n*. a timepiece, usually worn on the wrist.

watch for *vb*. be on the alert for.

watch over *vb*. guard, protect.

water 1. *n*. the most common of all liquids, formed from two gases: oxygen and hydrogen. 2. *vb*. sprinkle with water; apply water to; dilute.
► Just over 70 percent of the earth's surface is covered with water, on which all life depends. Most of this water is in the OCEANS, from which it evaporates to fall later as rain, snow or hail. Water that falls on land eventually evaporates or drains into the rivers and flows back into the seas and oceans. This continuing process is called the *water cycle*. Besides supporting life, water helps to shape the land, wearing away valleys and depositing material elsewhere. Chemically, pure water is known as hydrogen oxide (H_2O). It is unusual in that, on cooling, it contracts to reach maximum density at 39°F (4°C), and then expands on freezing at 32°F (0°C). This

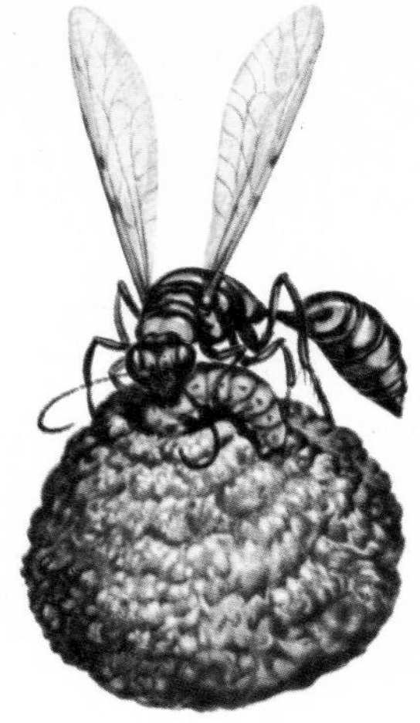

A potter wasp makes a clay cell and stocks it with caterpillars. She then lays her eggs in it.

expansion causes water pipes to burst in cold weather.

water boatman *n*. a water bug with long and powerful hind legs.
► Water boatmen use their hind legs like oars when swimming. They have a pouch under their shells, where they can carry air for breathing under water. Many of them are CARNIVORES and live on small fishes, tadpoles and other insects from which they suck the blood with a pointed beak.

water buffalo *n*. a large kind of ox, used as a beast of burden in many Eastern countries.
► The water buffalo of Asia is one of the largest of all wild cattle. The males can weigh as much as a ton, and can be almost 6 ft. (2 meters) in height. Their horns may spread over 10 ft. (3 meters) from tip to tip.

The Indian buffalo is a useful animal on farms, especially in the rice fields. Water buffaloes are also kept for their milk. These powerful, stocky animals suffer if they have too much hot sun. They must be allowed to bathe regularly, or wallow in the mud.

watercolor *n*. a painting done with paint that dissolves in water.
► The water in watercolor paint gives it a light, delicate color. The paint does not completely cover the surface it is put on. Sometimes the paper or cardboard shines through the paint as a sort of background color. Watercolor paint is often used for landscape and flower paintings.

water cycle *n*. the continuous movement of water from lakes and seas via the atmosphere to land areas and back again.
► Tiny drops of water are constantly separating from the surface of the

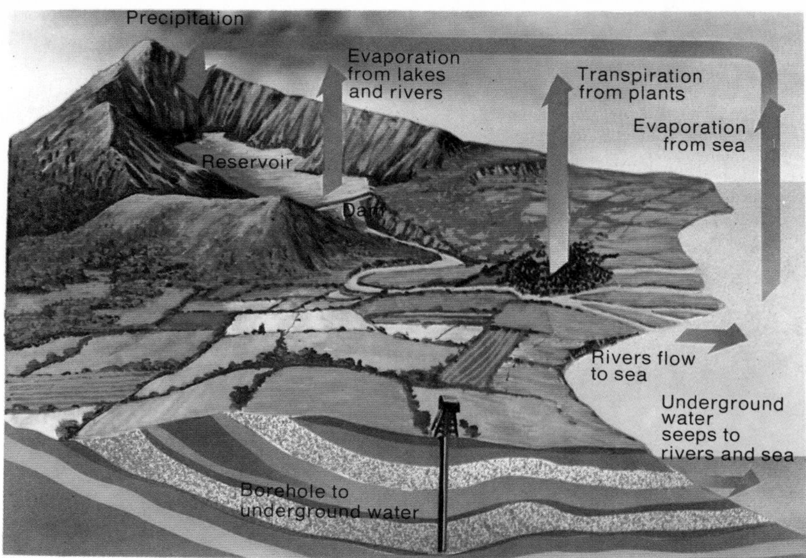

The water cycle. Rain or snow falls on the land and flows off in rivers or soaks in as underground water. Eventually the water reaches the sea. Water is evaporated from the sea and forms clouds from which rain falls to the earth.

earth's oceans, lakes, rivers and streams. These tiny drops are in the form of a gas called water vapor. There is always water vapor in the air and more water evaporates in warm weather than in cold.

The water vapor from the oceans and rivers rises and, when it reaches cold air high above us, it condenses to form water droplets which we see as clouds. The tiny droplets of water in a cloud bump into each other. As they bump together they join up and form larger droplets. As this goes on, the droplets grow larger and larger until they form a raindrop. When the raindrops are heavy enough they fall out of the clouds. And if the air is cold enough, they fall as snowflakes or hailstones.

When rain falls on the earth it runs into streams. The streams run into rivers and lakes. Some of the rain soaks into the ground and is taken up by plants. All this water evaporates once more and the water cycle goes on and on. The total amount of water on the earth and in the atmosphere around it never changes; it only moves around and around.

waterfall *n.* a rush of water which falls from a high place in a river or stream.

► Waterfalls are made by the water slowly wearing away the rock of the riverbed it flows over. Some sorts of rock are softer than others, and get worn away faster. The soft rock is worn away, leaving a cliff of hard rock, over which the river's water pours.

The most famous waterfalls are NIAGARA FALLS, between the U.S.A. and Canada, and the VICTORIA FALLS in the Zambezi River, Africa. The highest waterfall in the world is Angel Falls in Venezuela. It is 3,212 ft. (979 meters) high. The highest waterfall in the United States is Ribbon Falls in the Yosemite National Park, with a drop of 1,612 ft. (490 meters).

Waterfalls are not only scenic attractions. They are often harnessed for electric power. Part or all of a fall may be diverted from its course and made to turn a turbine, thus giving energy.

Waterloo, Battle of

The Battle of Waterloo was fought on June 18 1815, between the French, on one side, and the Prussians, British, Germans, Dutch and Belgians on the other side. The French lost the battle.

It was an important battle because NAPOLEON BONAPARTE led the French army. He had escaped from his prison island to become emperor of France again.

The battle was fought near a Belgian village called Waterloo. Napoleon's army had already attacked the Prussians two days before, and the Prussians had retreated. Then Napoleon decided to attack the rest of the mixed army, led by the British Duke of WELLINGTON. Wellington kept in contact with the Prussian army leader, Blücher, hoping the Prussians could join the battle and help against the French.

The ground was thick with mud making it difficult to move the heavy guns. Napoleon waited to attack until the sun dried the ground. That gave Blücher time to get his army across to help Wellington.

Both sides fought with great bravery, but the arrival of the Prussians in the late afternoon turned the tide. The French army was decisively defeated.

waterlogged *adj.* so soaked with water as to be unable to float.

watermark *n.* a special design impressed onto paper which can be seen when held up to the light.

water polo *n.* a game played in water with a large inflated ball and two teams of seven swimmers. The ball is thrown from one swimmer to another, and each team tries to score goals.

water power *n.* mechanical force derived from weight or motion of water.

After his defeat at the battle of Waterloo, Napoleon was exiled to St. Helena, in the South Atlantic, where he died in 1821.

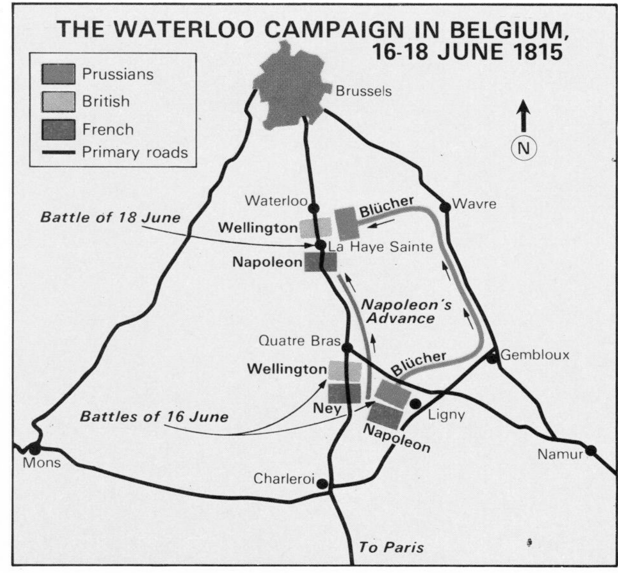

► Since Roman times, people have used the water wheel to obtain useful energy from the water flowing in rivers. At first, buckets were fitted to the rim of a vertically mounted wheel that dipped into the water. The wheel turned as the moving water pushed against the buckets. Later water wheels had wooden paddles instead of buckets. Water wheels were still commonly used in the 1800s. Many flour mills, saws, pumps and other machines were driven by water power. Today hydroelectric power stations use the energy of flowing water to drive TURBINES. These are linked to GENERATORS that produce electricity. In some areas, electricity is generated using the energy of waves and tides.

waterproof *n.* & *adj.* a material that does not let water pass through it.
water skiing *n.* skiing on water, in which the person is towed along by a motor boat. As a competition, water skiing includes slalom (steering around markers), distance jumping and figure skiing.
water supply *n.* the source or means of distributing water to people, including reservoirs, tunnels, etc.
► All humans need water for drinking as well as for washing and sanitation. Industries and agriculture use enormous amounts of water. This means that people need to have constant and safe supplies of water.

Lakes and reservoirs are often used for this. The water can be pumped through pipes to the houses and factories where it is needed. Sometimes natural lakes can supply water. Sometimes DAMS have to be built across river valleys, to flood them and turn them into lakes. In other places deep wells are sunk into the ground, to get at underground water. These are called *artesian wells.*

When no water can be found above or below the ground, people have to use sea water. It is treated in a distillation plant, which takes out the salt. This is a very expensive way to produce water, but in some parts of the world it is the only way.

Drinking water has to be clean. Diseases can be caught from dirty water. Before water is pumped to houses it is put through filters which remove germs and dirt. Sometimes a few chemicals are added, to make the water really safe.

water table *n.* the level below which the earth is saturated with water.
watertight *adj.* something that water cannot get into or out of without the thing breaking; leakproof.
waterwheel *n.* a wheel that uses the force of falling water to run machinery.
► Water, from a lake or river, runs down a chute onto the wheel. As the water rushes out of the chute, it hits blades fixed to the wheel's rim and makes the wheel turn. GEARS connect the turning wheel to machinery.

Waterwheels were invented about 2,000 years ago and were the first machines not worked by animals or people.

watt *n.* a unit of electric power.
► One watt is used when work is done, or energy consumed, at the rate of one *joule* per second. The watt is also equal to the power used when an electric current of one AMPERE flows through a conductor across which a potential difference of one volt is maintained. One horsepower is equal to 745.7 watts.

Watt, James
James Watt (1736–1819) was a Scottish engineer who spent much of his life developing STEAM ENGINES. In early steam engines, steam was heated and cooled inside a cylinder. Watt designed a model where steam escaped from the cylinder and cooled outside. This made the engine much more powerful.

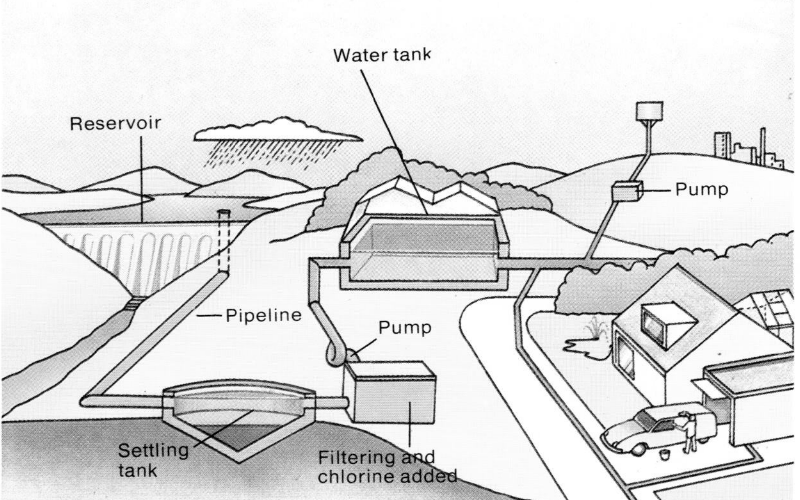

Our water usually comes from a large reservoir fed by a river and rain. Water from the reservoir goes to the water works to be purified. The pure water is then pumped to water tanks or water towers. It then flows through pipes to homes by gravity, or it is pumped.

wattle *n.* a plant found in Australia belonging to the acacia family, which produces branches suitable for interwoven (wattle) roofs and fencing. Its golden flower is Australia's national emblem.
wave 1. *n.* a moving ridge on the surface of the sea. 2. *n.* a curve or curl in your hair. 3. *vb.* signal to someone by moving your hand.
► When the wind blows over the sea it disturbs the water's surface. A light breeze causes gentle ripples, but a storm gale can whip up waves higher than a house.

Although ripples and waves move across the sea, the water itself does not travel with them. Instead, each passing wave just lifts the water up and down. This explains why floating objects like seabirds and bottles bob up and down on waves but do not travel with them.

Most sea waves are caused by the wind. But the most dangerous waves are set off by underwater earthquakes and volcanoes. These giant waves, often called TIDAL WAVES, sometimes flood coast lands and drown many people.

Sea waves carry energy, usually energy from the wind. Some other forms of energy travel in waves. LIGHT, SOUND and RADIO, for example, all move from one place to another in waves. Just as sea waves travel without taking the water with them so a sound wave crosses a room without actually moving the air along.

waver *vb.* hesitate, be undecided.
wax *n.* a soft, yellowish material often used for making things waterproof.
► Wax is obtained from various animal, plant and mineral sources (eg. beeswax, the wax in the ear, paraffin wax, sealing wax). All are solids, do not dissolve in water, and melt at low temperatures.

way *n.* 1. a method. *Can you show me the right way to do this problem?* 2. a path. 3. direction. *Do you know your way home?*
weak *adj.* fragile, easy to break, not strong. **weaken** *vb.* make (or become) weak.

wealth *n.* a great amount of money or property. **wealthy.** *adj.* rich.
wean *vb.* change a baby animal from drinking its mother's milk to eating other foods; free gradually from a habit.
weapon *n.* an object, such as a gun or sword, used for fighting.
wear (*ware*) *vb.* 1. be dressed in, have on your body. *Penny wanted to wear her new dress and her pearl necklace to the party.* 2. become less good through being used. *The car brakes have begun to wear quite a lot.*
weary (**weer**-*i*) *adj.* tired; tired (of).
weasel *n.* a small meat-eating animal related to the badger and the otter.
► The weasel is the world's smallest carnivore (meat-eater). It has a long, thin body with short legs, and red-brown fur. In the far north, its fur turns white in winter to match the snow. Weasels are fierce hunters and can chase small creatures, such as voles and mice, down narrow burrows. The stoat is very similar, but is larger and has a black tip on its tail.

weather 1. *n.* conditions in the atmosphere, which may be wet or dry, hot or cold, etc. 2. *vb.* come safely through (a storm).

► The weather – sunshine, fog, rain, cloud, wind, heat, cold – is always changing in most parts of the world. Today may be hot and dry, tomorrow cool and wet. These changes are caused by what happens in the atmosphere, the layer of air above the earth.

The atmosphere is always moving, driven by the sun's heat. Near the equator the sun's strong rays heat the air. At the North and South poles the sun's rays are weaker and the air is colder. This uneven heating means the atmosphere is never still. Huge masses of warm and cold air flow around and around between the tropics and the polar regions. As these wandering air masses meet, rise and fall, heat and cool, they cause weather.

When cold and warm masses meet, the air whirls inwards in a giant spiral called a depression. Depressions bring cloud, wind, rain and summer THUNDERSTORMS. They can also cause violent TORNADOES and hurricanes.

The meeting line between two air masses is called a front. When cold air pushes up behind warm air, it forms a cold front; when a warm air mass catches up with a cold mass, it creates a warm front. Fronts usually bring changes in the weather.

Increasing power of destruction: from crossbow (top) to the Gatling machine gun to Minuteman III missile in its underground silo.

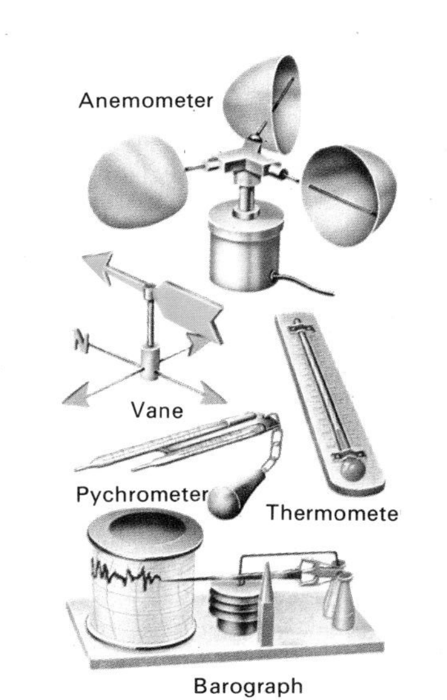

Weather forecasters use instruments to measure windspeed, air pressure and temperature.

►► **Weather Forecasting**
Throughout the world, meteorologists at weather stations record information, such as atmospheric pressure, temperature, rainfall and wind speed. This information is transmitted to forecast centers, where it is used to compile weather charts. Lines called isobars are drawn on maps to show places of equal atmospheric pressure. From such maps, forecasters can predict how the weather will change. Television pictures transmitted from weather SATELLITES to ground stations enable meteorologists to observe cloud patterns in the region.

weather vane *n.* a device for determining wind direction.
weave *vb.* (past **wove**; past part. **woven**) make cloth on a loom with a pattern of threads.
► The oldest fabric we know of was woven nearly 8,000 years ago in what is now Turkey. These first weavers learned to make LINEN from flax. By 2000 B.C. the Chinese were weaving cloth from silk. In India, people learned to use fibers from the cotton plant. Meanwhile NOMADS from the deserts and mountains of Asia discovered how to weave wool.

W

First, the fibers were drawn out and twisted into a long thread. This process is known as spinning. Then, rows of threads were stretched lengthwise, side by side, on a frame called a loom. These threads made up the *warp*. A crosswise thread, the *weft*, was then passed through from one side of the loom to the other, going over and under the warp threads. A *shuttle*, like a large needle, was used to feed the weft through the warp.

Spinning wheels and looms were worked by hand until the 1700s. Then, machines were invented for spinning and weaving. As these machines worked far faster than hand looms, cloth became cheap and plentiful.

web *n.* a loose set of threads. *A spider makes a web with threads from its body.*

Some spiders build shapeless webs – like the cobwebs of the house spider. Others, such as the garden spider, build beautiful cartwheel-like webs.

web foot *n.* a foot, like the ones on ducks and frogs, which has skin joining the toes together.
wedding *n.* a marriage ceremony. **wed** *vb.*
Wednesday *n.* the fourth day of the week, between Tuesday and Thursday; named after Woden, Anglo-Saxon god of war.
wee *adj.* a little bit; tiny.
weed *n.* a wild plant that grows where it is not wanted, such as in a flower bed. *vb.* remove weeds **weedy** *adj.* full of weeds; (*casual*) lean and scrawny.

► On farms and in gardens, weeds damage crops and flowers by taking a large share of water, minerals and sunlight. They usually grow very quickly. In places where weeds grow thickly, cultivated plants do not develop properly; they may produce only a few flowers, small seeds, unhealthy leaves or weak roots.

There are several ways of controlling weeds. In gardens, people break up the soil with a hoe. This disturbs the weed roots and stops growth. They also pull the weeds out of the ground: this is called weeding. On farms, the soil is broken up by plowing and harrowing. Farmers also spray their field with weedkiller. Most weedkillers are selective – the chemicals in them only affect certain plants: they destroy weeds without harming crops.

Weeds are only a nuisance when they interfere with cultivated plants. In woods and fields, away from gardens and farms, weeds are useful plants. Weeds are food for many insects, birds and mammals. Butterflies suck the nectar from nettle flowers. Goldfinches eat seeds from teasels. Donkeys feast on thistles.

week *n.* the sequence of seven days from Sunday to Saturday; any seven-day period.
weekday *n.* a day other than Sunday or Saturday.
weekend *n.* the period between the end of one working week and the beginning of the next, usually Saturday and Sunday. A long weekend might include Friday and Monday.
weekly *adj.* & *adv.* every week.
weep *vb.* cry with tears coming from your eyes.
weevil *n.* type of beetle distinguished by its long snout.

► Weevils, with over 60,000 species, form the largest family in the animal kingdom and are found all over the world. In general, each species feeds on a particular plant and many do great damage to crops.

weft *n.* the horizontal threads on a loom, used for weaving.
weigh *vb.* measure the heaviness of something by using scales.
weight *n.* 1. how much something weighs. *What is the weight of that parcel?* 2. a heavy piece of metal or other substance. *A deep-sea diver has lead weights on the diving suit to help descend more quickly.*

► **Weights** and **measures** are used to work out the size of things. The two main kinds of measurement are weight and length. They answer the questions "How heavy?" and "How long?". Length is also used to find area and volume. There are several systems of weights and measures. The most common is the metric system.

►► **Weightlessness** GRAVITY is the force that pulls everything on earth downward. It keeps objects on the earth's surface and stops them from floating away. This force of gravity gives objects, including our bodies, weight.

The pull of gravity becomes weaker with distance. Out in space, earth's gravity has very little effect. Also, the pull of gravity from other planets is very weak because they, too, are far away. This means objects in space weigh nothing.

Weightlessness makes life difficult for an astronaut in a spacecraft. If he tries to take a step, his feet leave the cabin floor and he floats about. If he pours a drink into a glass, the liquid bounces out and drifts around. If he lets go of a tool in midair, it hangs there instead of falling. Also, weeks of weightlessness can affect the way in which his body works. Special gadgets help astronauts live with weightlessness.

weight lifting *n.* one of the sports included in the Olympic Games in which competitors lift very heavy weights from the floor to above their heads.

► Weight lifters, like boxers, are divided into classes according to their own body weight. Champion weight-lifters can lift over 550 lb. (250 kg).

Many other athletes, such as swimmers and football players, do weight-lifting as an exercise to strengthen their muscles and improve their breathing.

weird *adj.* strange; peculiar; odd.
welcome *n.* & *vb.* do or say things which show you are pleased when someone arrives.
weld *vb.* join metals by heating or pressure or a combination of both. *n.* a welded joint.

► When a piece of metal is welded onto another, the two pieces of metal are heated until they melt together. When they cool they form just one piece of metal. A join made by welding is very strong.

Welders work with gas or electricity. In gas welding a very hot flame from a gas torch melts the metal. In electric welding, an electric CURRENT jumps from an electric welding rod to the metals and melts them. Sometimes a filler metal is added to bridge the join. Common melting techniques use a gas flame or an electric arc, or feed electricity into the metal.

welfare *n.* people's health and happiness.
well 1. *adj.* healthy. 2. *adv.* to do something in a good or successful way. *Emma swims very well.* 3. *n.* a deep hole for underground water.

Wellington
Wellington is the capital of NEW ZEALAND, and is situated on the south coast of North Island. It is one of New Zealand's busiest ports. MAORIS once lived around the harbor. The first European settlement was set up in 1839.

Wellington, Duke of
Arthur Wellesley, the Duke of Wellington (1769–1852), was a British soldier and statesman. In 1803 he led the troops whose victories put India firmly under British rule. In 1808 he began to drive NAPOLEON's French troops out of Portugal and Spain. In 1815 his British troops helped to defeat Napoleon at the great Battle of WATERLOO in Belgium.
Wellington later held important jobs in the British government. He was made commander-in-chief of the army in 1827 and served as prime minister from 1828 to 1830.

Wells, H.G.
H.G. (Herbert George) Wells (1866–1946) was an English writer who trained as a scientist, and became famous for the first modern science fiction in English (*The Time Machine*, *The War of the Worlds*). He later turned to comic realism (*Kipps*, *The History of Mr. Polly*) and theories of social progress (*The Outline of History*).

Welsh *adj*. & *n*. of Wales; the people and language of Wales.
went *vb*. past of **go**.
wept *vb*. past and past part. of **weep**.

Wesley Brothers
John Wesley (1703–91) was an English religious leader who founded Methodism. With his brother Charles (1707–88), he started out at the "Holy Club" at Oxford, England, in 1729. In 1735 the brothers went as missionaries to the colony of GEORGIA in America.
Charles Wesley wrote over 6,000 hymns, many of which are still popular today.

west *adj*., *adv*. & *n*. one of the points on a compass; the direction in which the sun sets.

West, The
The West is a region of the United States, generally considered to include the Rocky Mountain States and the three Pacific Coast States.
Fur trading stimulated the first movement west; then Christian missionaries followed to work with the Indians. The Texas fight for independence lured many settlers and the West began to open up. Large-scale migration began in 1843. The Gold Rush of 1849 created the need for transcontinental railroads. The joining of the Central and the Union Pacific railroads at Promontory Point, Utah, in 1869 formed the first railroad link with the West.
The Homestead Act of 1862 led to a marked increase in the West's population after the Civil War.

western 1. *adj*. of Western (i.e. West European and American) countries; belonging to, or coming from, the west. 2. *n*. a film or book about the American Wild West. **westernize** *vb*.

Western Australia
The largest AUSTRALIAN state, Western Australia has an area of 975,920 sq. miles (2,527,621 sq. km). The capital is PERTH. Large areas are desert or semi-desert. But crop farming is important in the south-west and livestock are reared in parts of the interior and north. Mining is especially important, because western Australia has huge reserves of iron ore and other minerals.

Western Samoa
Western Samoa is an island nation in the PACIFIC. The largest islands are Savai'i and Upolu, where the capital is situated. The people are mostly Polynesians. Bananas, cocoa and coconuts are among the chief crops. Western Samoa was a German colony before World War I. NEW ZEALAND ruled the islands from 1920–61. They became independent in 1962.
AREA: 1,097 SQ. MILES (2,842 SQ. KM)
POPULATION: 164,000
CAPITAL: APIA
CURRENCY: TALA
OFFICIAL LANGUAGES: ENGLISH, SAMOAN.

West Indies
The West Indies is an island chain separating the Caribbean Sea from the Atlantic Ocean. The largest islands are CUBA, Hispaniola (divided between the Dominican Republic and Haiti), JAMAICA and Puerto Rico (a self-governing Commonwealth of the U.S.A.). The tropical islands of the West Indies are mainly agricultural and sugar cane is the chief crop, together with fruits and tobacco. Tourism is increasing, especially during the warm winters. Most of the islands are volcanic.
In 1492 Christopher COLUMBUS thought that he had reached Asia and so the islands were, wrongly, named the Indies. Spain first controlled the area, but later France, the Netherlands and Britain established colonies and African slaves were imported to work on the European plantations. Today most people are of Negro, European or mixed ancestry. English, French and Spanish are the main languages of the islands.

Westminster Abbey
Westminster Abbey is a church consecrated in 1065 in England. It was gradually rebuilt (1245–1528) and later added to by Christopher WREN in 1740. All the English monarchs, except one, have been crowned there. It is also the traditional burial place of famous people, such as statesmen and writers.

West Virginia (*abbrev*. **W.Va.**)
West Virginia is a state in the south-east of the U.S.A. It is bordered on the west by the Ohio River, and on the south by Virginia. It is a rugged state, covered for the most part by mountains. Mining is very important. Only Kentucky produces more coal.
West Virginia was part of Virginia until the Civil War. When the war began in 1861, the north-western counties declared their independence from Virginia and sided with the Union. After the war, the West Virginians refused to join with the rest of Virginia. In 1863 West Virginia became the 35th state of the United States.
West Virginia's largest cities are Huntington and Charleston, the capital.

wet *adj*. consisting of, or soaked with, liquid; rainy. *vb*. make wet.
whale *n*. a very large sea animal that looks like a fish. *vb*. hunt whales.
► Whales are big sea MAMMALS well built for living in the water. A thick layer of fat called blubber keeps out the cold. A whale's body is shaped for easy swimming. Its front limbs are shaped as flippers. It also has a broad tail flattened from top to bottom, not from side to side like a fish tail.
Being mammals, whales must swim to the surface to breathe. They take in air through a blowhole, or two slits, on top of the head. Baby whales are born in water. As soon as they are born they swim up to the surface to breathe.
There are two groups of whales. Toothed whales like the DOLPHIN mostly eat fish. But killer whales are toothed whales that attack seals, penguins and other whales.
Baleen whales are the other main group of whales. Baleen whales include the blue whale, the largest mammal that has ever lived. They catch tiny shrimplike creatures with a special sieve made of a horny

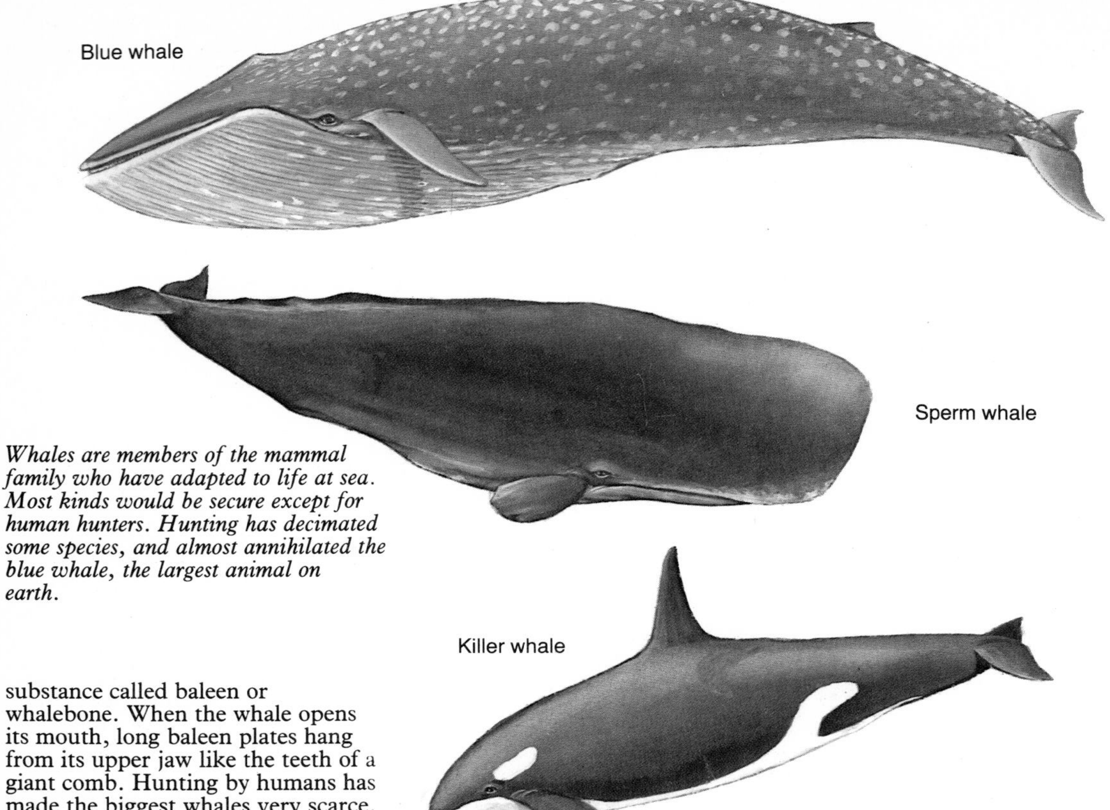

Whales are members of the mammal family who have adapted to life at sea. Most kinds would be secure except for human hunters. Hunting has decimated some species, and almost annihilated the blue whale, the largest animal on earth.

substance called baleen or whalebone. When the whale opens its mouth, long baleen plates hang from its upper jaw like the teeth of a giant comb. Hunting by humans has made the biggest whales very scarce.

wharf *n.* a place where ships are loaded and unloaded.
what *interrogative adj.* used in questions which ask for a selection from an indefinite number or quantity. *What do you want?*
whatever *pron.* no matter what. *Whatever he may say, I still don't believe him.*
wheat *n.* the grain from which most flour is made.
► Grains of wheat are seeds produced by a certain kind of grass. Mills grind the seeds into flour. Wheat is mostly made of energy-giving STARCHES. It also contains body-building PROTEIN, as well as FATS, MINERALS and bran.

Wheat grows best in dry, mild climates. The seed is sown in winter or spring and harvested when the grain is dry and hard. Most wheat comes from the United States, the U.S.S.R., China and India.

After wheat is harvested, it is usually trucked to storage bins, called *grain elevators*. There it can be stored for a long time.

wheel *n.* a circular structure that is revolveable around an axle.
vb. push or pull a bicycle, cart, etc.
► Wheels are one of the most useful inventions. This is because a wheel turning on an axle is a good way to move loads. It is easier to move a heavy load with wheels than it is to lift the load or drag it on the ground.

STONE AGE people may have learnt to roll loads along on logs. But BRONZE AGE people first invented the wheel about 5,000 years ago. The oldest known wheels looked like slices cut across a log.

Later, people learned that a wheel with spokes was just as strong as a solid wheel, but much lighter. Today the wheels of cars and planes have hollow rubber tires filled with air to make them springy.

Ball bearings keep wheel hubs turning easily on their axles. Wheels with notched edges turn one another in the GEARS that help to work all kinds of machinery.

Wheat is probably the world's most important food crop.

wheelbarrow *n.* a small garden cart with one wheel in front, pushed by holding two handles.

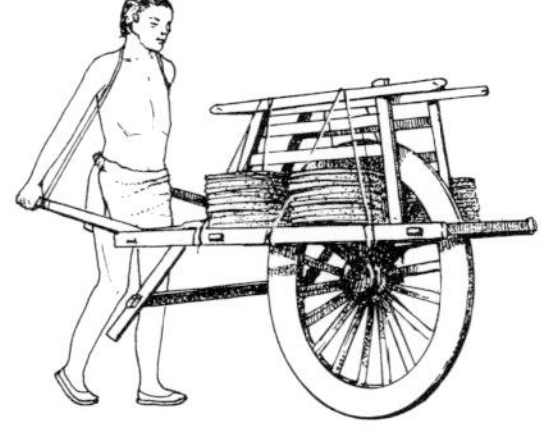

The wheelbarrow was invented in China in the 3rd century A.D.

wheeze *vb.* breathe with difficulty and making a hissing sound.
when *adv.* & *conj.* at the time that; at what time. *When is our next meeting?*
whenever *conj.* at every time; at any time. *Come whenever you like.*
where *adv.* & *conj.* in such a place; in which place? *Where did you leave your case?*
wherever *adv.* & *conj.* in whatever place. *I shall find him, wherever he is hiding.*
whether *conj.* if. *Do you know whether we are late?*

which 1. *interrogative adj.* used in questions that ask for a selection from a limited number or quantity. 2. *relative pronoun* that stands for a previous noun.
while 1. *n.* a period of time. *I've been waiting all this while.* 2. *conj.* during the time when. *Did anyone phone while I was out?* 3. *vb.* pass away the time. *Joan whiled away the time by reading a book.*
whim *n.* a sudden idea, fancy. *He went to the circus on a whim.*
whine *vb.* 1. make a high-pitched unhappy or distressed cry. 2. complain in a whining voice.
whip 1. *n.* a long rope or strip of leather joined to a handle, usually used to hit animals. 2. *vb.* beat cream, eggs, etc., until they thicken.
whirl *vb.* turn around fast in circles; rush along.
whirlpool *n.* a place in a river or ocean where the water spins around.
whirlwind *n.* a fierce wind that blows in circles, small rotating windstorm.
whisk 1. *vb.* beat eggs with a whisk. 2. *n.* go or carry off quickly. *The waiter whisked our plates away.*
whiskers *pl. n.* hair that grows on the face.
whiskey *n.* distilled liquor made from grain.
whisper *n.* & *vb.* talk in a low voice, without vibrating the vocal cords.
whist *n.* a card game for four players using all 52 cards and a trump suit.
whistle 1. *n.* & *vb.* make a shrill sound by blowing through your tightened lips. 2. *n.* an instrument for blowing through to make a whistling sound. *vb.* to blow a whistle.
white *n.* & *adj.* the color of snow.
white elephant *n.* a possession that is more trouble than it is worth.
White House *n.* residence of the president of the U.S.
whiting *n.* a small sea fish.

Whitman, Walt
Walt Whitman (1819–1892) is thought by many people to be the greatest American poet. In 1855 Whitman published, at his own expense, a book of 12 poems called *Leaves of Grass*. For the rest of his life he went on publishing expansions and revisions of this work. Whitman wrote about America, and no poet has done it better or on a grander scale.

Whitney, Eli
Eli Whitney (1765–1825) was the American who invented the cotton gin (engine). The cotton gin is a machine which separates cotton fibers from the seeds. Before Whitney invented the gin, this job had to be done by hand by slaves.

Whitsun *n.* short for "Whitsunday"; a Christian festival held on the seventh Sunday after Easter. Also known as Pentecost, it celebrates the day when Christians believe the Holy Spirit comforted the apostles.
who 1. *interrogative adj.* which person. *Who did that?* 2. *pron.* the person that. *I know who was speaking to you.*
whoever 1. *interrogative adj.* what person. *Whoever would have thought it?* 2. *pron.* any person. *Ask whoever you like to the party.*
whole (rhymes with *mole*) *adj.* all of something, a complete thing; uninjured.
wholesale *n.* & *adj.* selling things in large quantities, usually to be sold again. *vb.* sell wholesale. *see* **retail**.
whooping cough *n.* an infectious disease marked by terrible coughing.
► Whooping cough used to kill many babies and young children. People catch it by breathing in bacteria from someone suffering from the disease. Victims of the disease cough with a whooping noise as they take a breath. Drugs can help to cure whooping cough. Most children can be protected by INOCULATION.

whose *interrogative adj.* of whom. *Whose book is this?*
why *interrogative adv.* for what reason. *Why are you looking at me like that?*
wick *n.* the thread or material put into a candle or lamp which burns when ignited.
wicked *adj.* bad, evil.
wide *adj.* broad; having the sides far apart.
widow *n.* a woman whose husband is dead and who has not married again.
widower *n.* a man whose wife is dead and who has not married again.
width *n.* how broad something is; the distance from one side to the other.
wield *vb.* 1. use with the hands. 2. exercise authority, etc.
wife *n.* (plural **wives**) the woman to whom a man is married.
wig *n.* false hair to cover a bald head or to cover one's own hair with different hair.
► People have been wearing wigs since Bronze Age times. In ancient Egypt a wig helped to show a person's rank. Fashionable Roman women wore extra pieces of hair taken from blonde Germans.

In the 1600s French nobles started a fashion for big, heavy wigs of hair curled into ringlets. In the 1700s fashionable men wore short wigs powdered white.

Nowadays, people may wear small hairpieces to cover bald patches. Some women wear wigs to match fashions. Actors wear wigs to help them look like the different characters.

wigwam *n.* a hut used by North American Indians, made of a frame of poles covered with bark or skin.
► Some wigwams were shaped like an upside-down bowl. Others had upright sides and a sloping roof like that of a house.

Tents with round floors and pointed tops are tepees. Tepees were made by American Indians who lived on the grassy plains. They arranged poles into a cone. Then they stretched buffalo hide over the poles. Smoke from the fire inside escaped from a hole at the top. The plains Indians were nomads, who moved from place to place following the herds of buffalo (bison). Their tepees could be easily taken down and carried with them.

wild *adj.* not tame; original or natural state; living in a natural way; out of control, uncontrolled.
wilderness *n.* an uninhabited and uncultivated area of land.
wilding *n.* wild plant or animal.
will 1. *vb.* a form of the verb "to be," indicating determination or future action. *What will you do next?* 2. *n.* intention, determination, desire. 3. *n.* a document that says what will happen to someone's property when he or she dies.

William the Conqueror
William the Conqueror (reigned 1066–87) was William I of England, and England's first Norman king. Before that he was Duke of Normandy in northern France. (Normandy was named after the Normans or Northmen, also called VIKINGS).

He defeated HAROLD at the Battle of HASTINGS in 1066.

In the 17th and 18th centuries wigs were very popular. Today they are mostly worn by people with little hair and by actors who need to change their appearance.

W

William II
William II (reigned 1087–1100) became king of England when his father WILLIAM THE CONQUEROR died in 1087. William II was called William Rufus because of his red complexion (Rufus means red).

William II
William II (1859–1941) was the last German kaiser and king of Prussia. Early in his reign he dismissed the chancellor Bismarck. From that time William governed as he wished and chose advisers who would not interfere. William's international ambitions helped start World War I.

William of Orange
William of Orange (reigned 1689–1702) was a PROTESTANT ruler of the Netherlands, who became King William III of England, Scotland and Ireland.

In 1677 he married his Protestant cousin, Mary. In 1688 the English invited William and Mary to rule them in place of Mary's unpopular father, the Catholic JAMES II. James fled when William landed with his army. No one was killed in this so-called "Glorious Revolution," and William defeated James in Ireland in 1690.

Williams, Tennesee
Tennesee Williams (1911–1983) is the pen name of Thomas Lanier Williams, the American playwright. He was born and raised in Mississippi, and his best writing is about the Southern society. Williams is best known for the plays, *The Glass Menagerie, A Streetcar Named Desire* and *Cat on a Hot Tin Roof*.

Williamsburg
Williamsburg, Virginia, is a historic city and a famous tourist attraction. Much of it has been kept as it was in colonial times.

The English established Williamsburg in 1633. They called it Middle Plantation, but in 1699 they renamed it Willliamsburg in honor of King William III of England. It was then that the capital of the Virginia colony was shifted from Jamestown to Williamsburg.

willing *adj*. ready to do what is wanted or needed.

Willkie, Wendell Lewis
Wendell Willkie (1892–1944) was the Republican candidate for president when Franklin D. Roosevelt ran for a third term. Willkie was defeated, but when the United States entered World War II, he organized a program of national unity. Roosevelt sent him to several countries as his envoy.

willow *n*. one of a family of deciduous trees found in many parts of the world, generally near water.

► There are about 300 kinds of willow. Some grow 100 ft. (30 meters) high. But Arctic willows are so tiny that you can step on them.

Willows bear catkins, and most have slim, pointed leaves. Some have long, springy twigs. People cut these and weave them together to make baskets. Willow wood has many other uses.

Wilson, Woodrow
Woodrow Wilson (1856–1924), the 28th president of the United States, came to office in 1913, just before WORLD WAR I. Wilson led the country into the war in 1917.

In 1918 Wilson produced a plan for an association of nations working for peace. This association became known as the League of Nations. To Wilson's bitter disappointment, the U.S. Senate would not allow the United States to join the League. They thought it would mean U.S. interference in European affairs.

But after WORLD WAR II, the U.S. people were finally convinced that a worldwide peace-keeping organization was necessary. The United Nations came into being in 1946.

wilt *vb*. 1. droop like a plant without water, become limp. 2. become weak.

win *vb*. gain victory in a contest or game; succeed. *n*. victory in a game. **winner** *n*.

wince *vb*. & *n*. shrink back as if in pain.

wind (rhymes with *kind*) *vb*. 1. turn the spring of a clock so that it will work. 2. wrap thread, wool, etc., around something.

wind (rhymes with *sinned*) *n*. the movement of large masses of air. **windy** *adj*.

► Wind blows because some air masses become warmer than others. In warm air, the tiny particles of air spread out. So a mass of warm air is lighter than a mass of cold air that fills the same amount of space. Because warm air is light it rises. As warm air rises, cool air flows in to take its place. This causes the steady trade winds that blow over tropical oceans. CLIMATE and WEATHER largely depend on the wind.

A scale of wind speeds was worked out in 1805 by Admiral Sir Francis Beaufort. It is called the Beaufort Scale. In it the force of the wind is shown by numbers from 0 to 12. The number 0 shows that there is a calm in which smoke rises straight up. At 1 smoke drifts slowly. By the time we get to 4 we have a breeze in which small branches are moving and flags flap. At force 7 whole trees are moving and it is difficult to walk against the wind. Force 12 is something few of us will ever see. It is a full hurricane, with terrible damage to ships at sea and houses on land.

wind instrument *n*. a musical instrument that is played by blowing into it.

windmill *n*. a mill powered by the action of the wind on "arms" called *sails*.

► Windmills were used in Asia as early as the A.D. 600s and came to Europe in the 1100s.

In early windmills a wheel with long sails was fixed to a tower. The whole tower could often turn to face the wind. As the wind turned the sails, the turning wheel moved machinery inside the mill. This machinery was used to do useful work such as turning heavy stone wheels to grind corn.

Westerlies are mixed warm and cold air. Trade winds are warm winds and polar easterlies are cold polar winds.

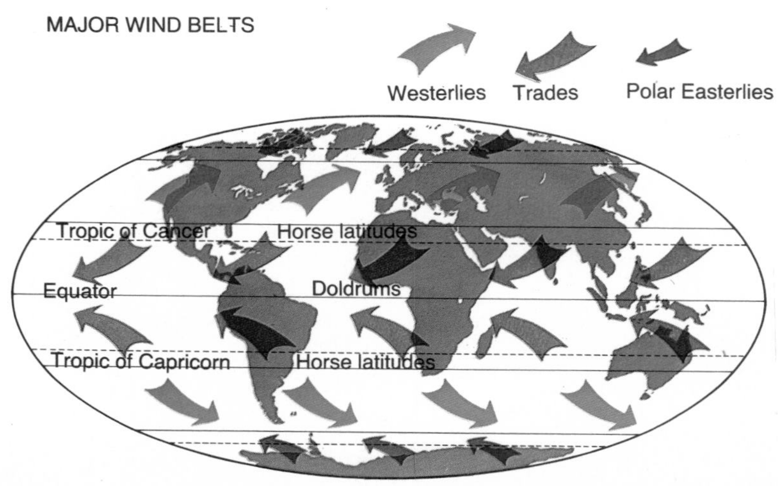

A windpower generator at Gedser, Denmark.

Nowadays, people are trying to make better windmills as a way of generating electricity. These windmills are usually on a tower made of steel girders. Some have sails like airplane propellers which turn at a high speed when the wind blows. The propellers turn a generator which makes electricity.

window *n.* an opening, usually covered by glass, in the wall of a building to let in light and sometimes air.

windshield *n.* the front window of a car.

Wind tunnel

A wind tunnel is a chamber in which scale models, or sometimes full-size, airplanes and automobiles are placed in an artificial wind. This allows engineers to find out how the planes and cars will behave in most situations before the airplane or car itself is built. Though it is impossible to ensure that a new airplane will fly perfectly on its first flight, wind tunnels have greatly reduced the chance of mistake.

wine *n.* an alcoholic drink made from the fermented juice of grapes.

► A YEAST organism found on the skin of grapes turns the fruit sugar into alcohol by a process known as fermentation. Wine can be white or red (depending on the grapes it is made from) and sweet or dry (depending on whether fermentation is allowed to continue until all the fruit sugar has gone). France is the country most famous for its wines, but Italy produces more wine than any other country.

wing *n.* 1. the part of a bird or insect used for flying. 2. one "arm" of an aircraft that provides lift. 3. side extension of a building.

wink *vb.* close one eye briefly, perhaps as a signal to someone.

Winnipeg

Winnipeg is the capital of Manitoba province of CANADA. It is the main commercial center of the "Prairie Provinces," and has one of the largest grain markets in the world. Winnipeg was founded in 1812 by the British Hudson Bay Company. It came under Canadian rule in 1870.

Winnipeg, Lake

Lake Winnipeg is the third largest lake in CANADA. Its area is 9,094 sq. miles (23,533 sq. km). It drains into HUDSON BAY through the Nelson River. Lake Winnipeg was discovered in 1733. It was used as a waterway by fur trappers and explorers.

winter *n.* the coldest season of the year, between autumn and spring. *vb.* spend the winter in, at, etc.

wipe *vb.* rub something clean or dry.

wipe out *vb.* destroy completely. *A bad earthquake can wipe out a whole village.* **wipeout** *n.*

wire *n.* a long thread of metal that can be bent and twisted.

► Wire has many uses. Barbed wire fences keep sheep and cows in fields. Wires twisted together form cables strong enough to hold up some of the world's largest bridges. Wires also carry electric current. Electric cords and telephone and telegraph lines use wires.

Metals used for making wire include copper, iron, aluminum and silver. Heavy blocks of metal are heated, and then passed through rollers that squeeze them into long narrow rods. These are pulled through narrow holes to make them still longer and thinner. Then the wire is wound onto a turning drum. Lastly, the wire is heated in a furnace. This makes it softer and less brittle.

Freshly picked grapes being emptied into vats. They will then be pressed. From the colorless grape juice wine is made.

Wisconsin (*abbrev.* **Wis.**)

Wisconsin is a Midwestern state bordering the Great Lakes. It is best known as the leading dairy state.

Wisconsin's largest cities are Milwaukee, Madison, the capital, and Racine. Although Milwaukee is near the center of the North American continent, it is a busy port. Ships reach it from the Atlantic Ocean by sailing up the St. Lawrence River to the GREAT LAKES.

The first Europeans to reach the Wisconsin area were French. In 1836, Wisconsin Territory was organized, with the first capital at Belmont. But the legislature chose Madison as the site of the new capital. In 1848, Wisconsin became the 30th state of the U.S.A.

wisdom *n.* accumulated knowledge and understanding.

wise *adj.* able to understand many things.

wish *vb.* & *n.* want or desire something. *I wish it wasn't raining.*

wishbone *n.* a small bone (the *furcula*) in front of a bird's breastbone. *People sometimes break a chicken's wishbone between them. The person with the bigger piece gets a wish.*

wisteria *n.* an ornamental climbing plant with purple flowers.

wit *n.* intelligence; humor.

witch *n.* (plural **witches**) a woman in stories who uses magic to make things happen.

witchcraft *n.* the skills of a witch; use of magic or sorcery.

► **Witchcraft** is the supposed ability to work magical spells, with the help of evil spirits or the devil. Up to the Middle Ages there were many "wise women" who had a wide knowledge of herbs and healing. But fear of these women or "witches" became general in western Europe from the 1400s to the 1600s and led people to believe that their knowledge was evil. Many harmless women were executed as a result.

►► **Witch Doctor** In many countries there are special priests who are thought to have magic power over illness. These priests, called witch doctors, cast spells over sick people. They also use magic to try to cure sick animals or to make the crops grow. Sometimes they use magic against their enemies.

Some witch doctors pretend to remove things from people's bodies. But many people still believe that witch doctors can cure them.

W

with *prep*. connected to; possessing; in the company of. *Robin was playing with his little sister*.
withdraw *vb*. (past **withdrew** past part. **withdrawn**) pull back from something, or take back. *Sally is going to withdraw from the match*.
wither *vb*. become dry, shrivel.
withers *pl. n*. the ridge between the shoulder bones of a horse.
withhold *vb*. keep back, refuse to give.
without *prep*. not having something. *James came to school without his books*.
withstand *vb*. still keep one's position, oppose, resist.
witness *n*. & *vb*. a person who sees something happen, particularly a crime.
wizard *n*. a man in stories who uses magic to make things happen.
wobble *vb*. rock unsteadily from side to side; waver.
woke *vb*. past of **wake**.
wolf *n*. (plural **wolves**) a wild animal of the dog family. *vb*. eat greedily.
► These CARNIVORES include the red wolf of South America, and the gray, or timber, wolf of the world's northern forests. Gray wolves have thick fur, long legs, and powerful jaws. A pack of wolves can chase and kill a sick or injured deer much larger than themselves. When gray wolves are hunting, they howl to signal to each other where they are. Each spring the female wolf has four to six pups.

Wolfe, James
James Wolfe (1729–59) was a British soldier. As a young officer, he fought against the forces of Bonnie Prince Charlie at the Battle of Culloden. Promoted to major-general, he fought against the French in North America during the SEVEN YEARS WAR. Wolfe won the Battle of Quebec by an attack from the ST. LAWRENCE River. His plan involved scaling cliffs known as the Heights of Abraham. Both Wolfe and Montcalm, the French commander, were killed in the battle. As a result of the battle, CANADA became a British possession.

woman *n*. a grown-up female human.
womb *n*. the organ in which the young of mammals is carried and developed until it is born; the uterus.
wombat *n*. a burrowing marsupial (pouched mammal) related to the koala, and found in the wild only in Australia.
won *vb*. past of **win**.
wonder *vb*. ask yourself something; feel surprised.
wonderful *adj*. a happening that is so good it surprises you.
won't *abbrev*. for **will not**.
wood *n*. 1. a number of trees growing together in one place, a small forest. 2. the trunk and branches of trees cut up and used to make things, lumber, timber.
wooden *adj*. made of wood.
► Wood is the tough, inner part of TREES and shrubs. A tree trunk consists of tubes carrying water and food, and strong fibers. As the tree gets older, it grows more tubes and fibers and the trunk becomes thicker and thicker. The older tubes (no longer carrying food or water) and fibers are compressed in the center of the trunk. They form the heartwood. Heartwood is very hard and solid. The rest of the trunk, full of working tubes, forms the sapwood. Sapwood is softer and less durable than heartwood. There are two types of wood: softwood and hardwood. Softwood comes mostly from CONIFERS. Much of it is turned into pulp which is used for making paper, rayon, plastics and cellophane. Hardwood comes from broad-leaved trees and is mainly used for furniture and construction work.
►► **Wood carving** is often done as a hobby, but many people have also carved wood for a living. In prehistoric times, people used stone tools to shape tree trunks and limbs into weapons and ornaments. Gradually they became more skilled in carving.

Some wood carving is now done by machine. But before this was possible, wood carvers were important and well-paid people. In the MIDDLE AGES, and until the 1700s, wood carving was used a lot in buildings. Roof beams, walls and doors were decorated with shapes and figures. Pictures were carved on screens and panels. Churches had altars and statues carved from wood. Delicately carved furniture was made for rich nobles and merchants.

woodcut *n*. a picture printed from a carved wooden block.
► The picture is drawn on the block of wood and the background is then cut away, leaving the original lines of the drawing on a raised surface. This surface is covered with ink and then pressed onto paper. It is the oldest known form of PRINTING and was used by the Chinese in the 200s B.C.

wooden *adj*. made of wood.
woodpecker *n*. one of a family of tree-climbing birds found in most parts of the world.

Timber wolves. The wolf is clearly a direct ancestor of the dog.

► There are about 200 kinds of woodpecker. Woodpeckers have sharp, powerful bills with which they

Green woodpecker

drill holes through the bark of trees. They reach in with their long tongues to fish out the insects that live there.

Most woodpeckers have bright colors and markings, especially on their heads.

woodwind *n.* a family of musical instruments, played by blowing through a mouthpiece and into a hollow tube. Different notes are made by opening and closing holes in the instrument.

woodwork *n.* making things out of wood; the things that are made.

wool *n.* the natural hairy undercoat of sheep.

► Sheep's wool is a modified type of hair. It was probably the first fiber to be made into cloth by spinning and WEAVING. It can be turned into smooth (worsted) or "hairy" (woolen) material, and is used for blankets, carpets, tweed clothes, and knitted articles.

woolen *adj.* & *n.* (cloth or yarn) made from wool.

word *n.* a unit of written or spoken speech, made up of a number of letters. *We leave spaces between words when we write them down.*

word processor *n.* automated typewriter system that displays written words on a screen so that the composition can be edited before it is printed.

wore *vb.* past of **wear**.

work 1. *n.* anything that requires effort; a job. 2. *vb.* do a job.

worker *n.* someone who works for a living.

workshop *n.* a place where things are made or mended.

world *n.* the earth and universe.

World War I

The 1914–18 war between the Allied Powers (led by Britain, France and Russia) and the Central European Powers (led by Germany, Austria-Hungary and Turkey) was caused by territorial rivalries. (The immediate trigger was the assassination in the Balkans of the heir to the Austrian throne.) The struggle in western Europe quickly bogged down in opposing lines of trenches. These scarcely moved for the rest of the war, despite appalling loss of life (about 10 million deaths). On other fronts, Russian losses were heavy and sparked the Russian Revolution; the German fleet avoided battle (apart from Jutland in 1916), but her submarines sank many merchant ships and almost starved Britain into surrender; and Lawrence of Arabia led an Arab revolt against the Turks. After her allies had dropped out, and the U.S.A. had joined the Allies on April 2, 1917, Germany was forced to capitulate by the growth of revolutionary movements in her own cities and general exhaustion. The Treaty of Versailles in 1919 forced her to pay enormous war damages that led in part to World War II.

World War II

The 1939–45 war was between the Allies (led by Britain, America and the U.S.S.R.) and the Axis Powers (HITLER's Germany, MUSSOLINI's Italy, and Japan). Before it began there were many invasions and annexations (seizures of land) by the Axis Powers, culminating in Germany's invasion of Poland in September 1939. This was followed in 1940 by the German conquest of Denmark, Norway, the Netherlands, Belgium and France, then the air battle for an invasion of Britain. Here Germany failed, but in 1941 invaded the Balkans, North Africa and the U.S.S.R. In 1942 came the turning point: German armies were defeated in the Soviet Union (Stalingrad) and North Africa (by the British at Alamein). Also, Japan's attack on the U.S. navy at PEARL HARBOR brought the United States into the war. In 1943 the Allies invaded Italy while the Soviets drove the Germans back from the east. The Allied invasion of France (D-Day) in 1944 led to the liberation of France, Belgium and the Netherlands. This and the Soviet advance brought the invasion and surrender of Germany in 1945. Meanwhile in the Pacific the U.S. had advanced steadily. The dropping of two atomic bombs in 1945 rapidly brought an end to the war.

Above: In World War I both armies became bogged down in trenches. Millions of soldiers died trying to gain a few yards of muddy ground.

Below: American troops manning an anti-tank gun during World War II

W

worm *n.* the common name for a large group of animals with long, thin, limbless bodies.
▶ There are many different groups of worms. Some are very primitive, such as flatworms and roundworms; these live as PARASITES inside other animals or plants. Others are more complex and have bodies built up of segments. Segmented worms are called *annelids*. The earthworm is an annelid.

worn *vb.* past part. of **wear**.
worry *vb.* be upset or anxious about something or someone.
worse *adj.* not as good as.
worsen *vb.* make or become worse.
worship *n.* & *vb.* praise God.
worst *adj.* the least good.
worth *n.* the value of something.
worthless *adj.* having no value; useless; lacking worth.
would *vb.* a word that implies both possibility and the desire to do something. *I would like to help you.*
wound 1. *n.* an injury or a cut. *vb.* inflict a wound. 2. *vb.* past of **wind**.
wrap *vb.* cover something by enfolding; make a parcel. *n.* a loose garment such as a shawl.
wreath *n.* an arrangement of flowers or leaves tied together in a circle.
wreck *vb.* damage something so badly that it cannot be used again. *n.* a ship or building that has been badly damaged.
wren *n.* one of a family of insect-eating songbirds that are found in most parts of the world.
▶ Wrens are small birds, usually no more than a few inches long. They have short tails, and thin pointed beaks with which they catch and eat insects.

Wrens usually have dull markings to help them hide in hedges and on the ground. In tropical countries some wrens have long tails and beaks.

Wren, Christopher
Sir Christopher Wren (1632–1723) was an English architect. He began life as a scientist, but the Great Fire of London (1666) gave him his opportunity as an architect. His plan for the complete rebuilding of the city was not used, but he did have the chance to design many new London churches including St. Paul's Cathedral, his masterpiece. His other buildings include the Royal Exchange, Royal Naval College and Marlborough House in London and in the Sheldonian Theater, Oxford.

wrench *n.* & *vb.* pull or twist violently.
wrestle *vb.* fight using your body as a weapon.
wretched *adj.* very miserable or sad.
wriggle *vb.* twist and turn your body, squirm.

Earthworms leave "casts" of soil on the surface. They feed on tiny bits of plant left in the soil.

Wright Brothers
The Wright brothers, Orville (1871–1948) and Wilbur (1867–1912) were the American pioneers of flying. While running a cycle repair business they made a wind tunnel for aeronautic research. Experiments in making a glider soon began. They chose Kitty Hawk, North Carolina, where the weather conditions were most suitable to test their ideas. Having achieved success with their glider, the brothers became determined to make a powered machine. They completed their airplane in 1903 and fitted it with a gasoline-powered engine. On December 17, 1903, the plane, piloted by Orville Wright, made a short but successful flight. This was the first controlled flight in a heavier-than-air machine.

During the next few years, the Wrights made many flights, which gradually became longer. But the brothers were not taken seriously by the United States government until 1908, when they were offered a contract to supply airplanes to the War Department.

In 1912, Wilbur Wright died of typhoid fever, and Orville continued the experiments alone, spending many years contributing to the development of aviation.

The Wright Flyer was airborne for 12 seconds and flew about 120 ft. (40 meters).

wring *vb.* squeeze liquid out of clothing, etc., by twisting.

wrinkle *n.* a crease on skin, cloth or other flat surfaces. *vb.* become marked with wrinkles.
wrist *n.* the joint between your arm and your hand.
wristwatch *n.* a watch that is worn around the wrist.
write *vb.* (past **wrote** past part. **written**) put down words on paper.
▶ **Writing** is written speech developed over thousands of years. Take the sentence "Man kills tiger." At first, a picture of a man killing a tiger was used. Then symbols were used: one for man, one meaning kill, and one for tiger. Later the pictures became associated with the sound of the words, which meant they could be used to make up other words (just as you might draw a picture of an eye to mean "I"). This led to ALPHABETS of sounds, but still without any vowels: "Mn klls tgr." Finally the Greeks added vowels, for a complete alphabet as used today.

written past part. of **write**.
wrong 1. *adj.* incorrect. *You gave the wrong answer*. 2. *n.* an old-fashioned word meaning evil or wickedness.
wrote *vb.* past of **write**.

wrung *vb.* past of **wring**.

Wyoming (*abbrev.* **WY**)
Wyoming is a Rocky Mountain State. It is one of the largest states in size, and one of the smallest in population.

The most important industry in the state is mining. Oil, coal, uranium and iron ore are produced in large quantities. More than three-fourths of the state is used for sheep and cattle grazing.

Tourists to Wyoming visit the state's beautiful national parks, national forests and wildlife refuges. YELLOWSTONE NATIONAL PARK in northwestern Wyoming is the nation's largest national park. It has the world's largest geyser area, breathtaking waterfalls and canyons and a large population of bears.

There are only two cities of any size, Cheyenne, the capital, and Casper.

X

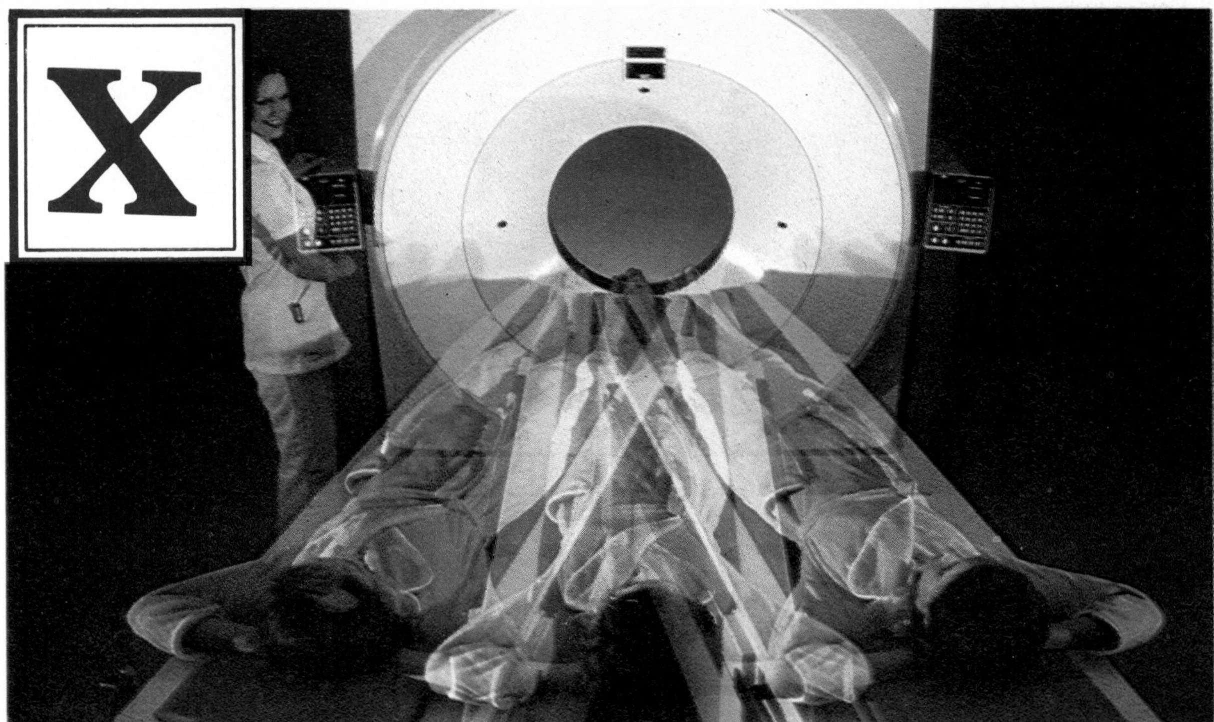

The X-ray scanner can take detailed pictures of a part of the body from different angles. The patient lies on a couch which moves automatically into the scanner "tunnel."

Xavier, Saint Francis
Saint Francis Xavier (1506–52) was a Spanish missionary who is sometimes called the "Apostle of the Indies." With Saint Ignatius Loyola, he was one of the founders of the Society of Jesus (JESUITS). After a period of working as a priest in Rome, he traveled to India, Japan, China and many other countries in the Far East. Xavier made thousands of converts to Christianity.

xenophobia (*zen-o-***foab***-ya*) *n.* a great dislike of foreigners.

Xenophon
Xenophon (430?–354? B.C.) was a Greek historian and soldier and a disciple of Socrates. In command of 10,000 Greek soldiers stranded in Persia by the defeat of their Persian allies, he led them for 1,500 miles to the Bosporus and safety.

xerography (*zeer-***og***-ra-fee*) *n.* a process for photocopying documents, widely used in offices.
► When a document is copied in this way, a metal plate is coated with selium, a substance that conducts electricity when exposed to light. The copy is projected through a lens, and a positively charged hidden image is stored on the plate. The plate is dusted with negative black powder which clings to the image. Paper is rolled on the plate and given a positive charge which attracts the powder to the paper. The paper is heated to melt the powder and forms a permanent image on the paper.

X ray *n.* a form of electromagnetic waves which can pass into or through most living things.
► X-rays were discovered in 1895 by William Röntgen. He produced the rays by accident when passing electricity through a gas at extremely low pressure. Röntgen found that the waves passed through the human body and would record its bone patterns on a photographic plate. This technique is now widely used in hospitals for studying patients' bones and internal organs.

xylophone (**zy**-*lo-fone*) *n.* a musical instrument made up of rows of wooden or metal bars that are struck with hammers.
► The xylophone produces a crisp, bell-like sound when struck. Each bar is of different length and produces a different sound when struck. An electric version of the xylophone, called a vibraphone, is sometimes used.

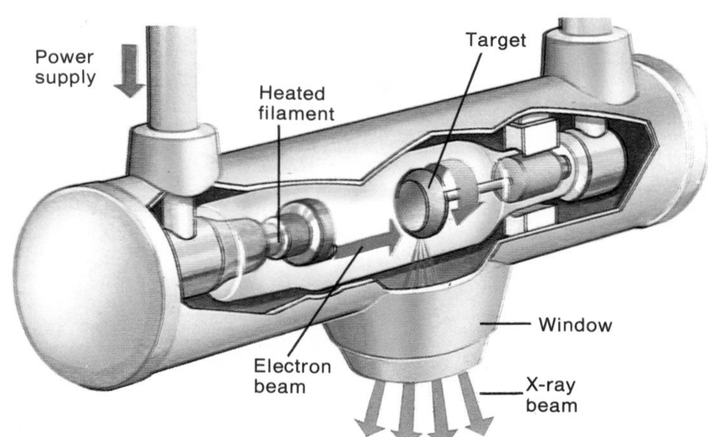

How an X-ray machine works. A high voltage supply accelerates electrons in a beam toward a metal target. As they hit the target the electrons give out X-rays which leave the machine through a window and pass through the patient's body to a photographic plate.

Y

Yachts in the Keil races in West Germany.

yacht *n.* a light sailing boat.
yak *n.* a large kind of ox, with a shaggy black coat and long horns.
► Yaks live on the cold, high plateaus of central Asia and have long been domesticated. They are kept as beasts of burden and also for their milk, meat and hides. Yaks are among the largest wild cattle, yet they climb nimbly up mountains.

yam *n.* the edible root of various tropical climbing plants.

Yangtze
The Yangtze is the longest river in China. From its source high in the mountains of Tibet, it flows 3,420 miles (5,470 km) across the center of China, pouring into the Yellow Sea near Shanghai.

The river takes its name from the ancient kingdom of Yang, which grew up along its banks 3,000 years ago. Today, the Yangtze is still one of the main trade routes in China. Big ships can sail up it as far as Hankow, nearly 700 miles (1,125 km) inland.

Millions of people live and work on the Yangtze. Some live on the river itself in sailing boats called junks.

yank 1. *vb.* & *n.* pull suddenly. 2. *n.* British nickname for U.S. American. Also **Yankee**.
yap *vb.* & *n.* a short shrill bark, like the sounds small dogs make.
yard *n.* 1. a measurement of length (3 feet or 36 inches). 2. an open space surrounded by walls and buildings. 3. a spar slung from a mast to support a sail.
yardstick *n.* a yard measure; a standard of comparison.
yarn *n.* 1. fibrous strand used in knitting and weaving. 2. a tale.
yashmak *n.* veil worn by Muslim women over the face.
yawn *vb.* open your mouth wide when you are bored or sleepy. *n.* the act of yawning.
ye *pron.* an old-fashioned word for you.
year *n.* the amount of time it takes the earth to travel around the sun; the period from January 1 to December 31; any period of 12 months.
► The earth takes 365¼ days to orbit the sun. However, a calendar year is only 365 days long. This is why every four years, the extra quarter days are lumped together to make a "leap" year of 366 days.

yearly *adj.* every year; once a year.
yeast *n.* a substance used to make bread and beer rise.
► Yeast is very useful because it turns sugar into alcohol and carbon dioxide gas. This process is called *fermentation.* Today, yeast is grown in huge vats. It is then pressed into cakes or small pellets, ready to be sold.

There are over 150 different kinds of yeast. The most important are brewer's yeast and baker's yeast which are used to make beer and bread.

In wine- and beer-making, yeast turns the sugar in grapes or malted barley into alcohol, while most of the gas bubbles away. In bread-making, the carbon dioxide gas forms bubbles, which makes the bread dough rise.

yell *vb.* shout loudly. *n.* a loud cry.
yellow *n.* & *adj.* the color of a lemon. *Yellow is one of the primary colors.* *vb.* turn yellow.

Yellowstone National Park
Yellowstone National Park is the oldest and the largest national park in the U.S.A. Most of the park lies on a volcanic plateau in northwest WYOMING. The remainder is in IDAHO and MONTANA. It has about 10,000 hot springs. The most famous of these is Old Faithful, a geyser that erupts about once an hour. Yellowstone contains magnificent mountains and lakes, rivers and gorges, as well as many kinds of wildlife. It was established in 1872.

Yemen Arab Republic
The Yemen Arab Republic is a hot, dry country in Arabia. The land rises from a narrow coastal plain to a high plateau dotted with mountain peaks. The highlands contain Arabia's best farmland, and most of the people work in agriculture. Before World War 1, Yemen was part of the OTTOMAN EMPIRE. In 1962 the *imam* (king) was overthrown and a republic was proclaimed.
AREA: 75,204 SQ. MILES (195,000 SQ. KM)
POPULATION: 6,142,000
CAPITAL: SAN'A
CURRENCY: RIAL
OFFICIAL LANGUAGE: ARABIC

Yemen, People's Democratic Republic
The People's Democratic Republic of Yemen occupies the southern part of the Arabian peninsula. It also includes various offshore islands. Inland, the country has mountains,

fertile valleys and large deserts. The chief occupations are farming and fishing, but Aden, the capital, has an oil refinery. Aden was once an important British naval base. The British left in 1967, and the country became known as the Southern Yemen People's Republic. Later, a

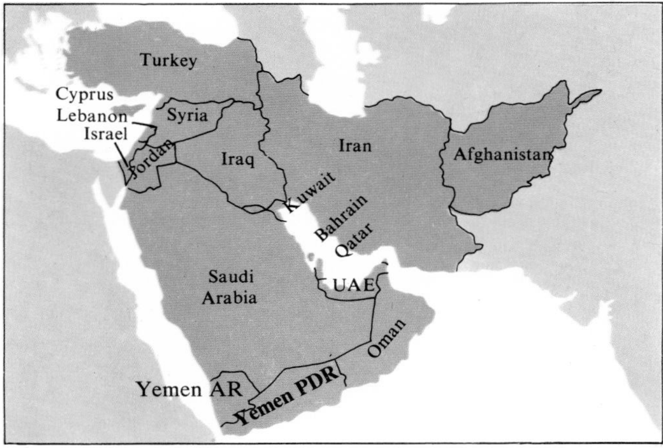

Communist government took over and gave the country its present name.
AREA: 128,567 SQ. MILES (332,968 SQ. KM)
POPULATION: 1,905,000
CAPITAL: ADEN
CURRENCY: DINAR
OFFICIAL LANGUAGE: ARABIC

yen *n.* the currency unit of Japan.
yesterday *n.* & *adv.* the day before today.
yet 1. *adv.* up to the present time. *Have you finished your work yet?* 2. *conj.* nevertheless.
yew *n.* an evergreen conifer often planted in churchyards.
Yiddish *n.* the international language used by Jewish people.
► Yiddish developed in medieval times, based on German with added words from Hebrew, Russian and Polish. Yiddish literature grew from folk songs and fables, to include poetry, novels, and more recently, newspapers.

yield 1. *vb.* give in, give up. 2. *n.* the amount of grain or fruit on a plant or within an area of a farm. *We got a good yield of plums from that tree.*
yodel *vb.* & *n.* sing(ing) in the manner of Swiss mountaineers, the voice going from normal to falsetto.
yoga *n.* a Hindu spiritual system of meditation. *The form of yoga popular in Western countries uses special postures and breathing exercises to give control of mind and body.*
► Yoga is an ancient word that means union. People who follow yoga believe that their soul can be united with a World Soul. To get ready for this meeting they must train their bodies and their minds. They do special exercises to get their bodies fit. They also do "mind" exercises, called meditation.

yogurt or **yoghurt** *n.* milk fermented by a bacterium.
► Yoghurt is a Turkish word for fermented milk. It is made by adding special BACTERIA to fresh cow's or goat's milk. The bacteria sours the milk and makes it thicken.
Yoghurt first came from the Balkans. People in Iran, Bulgaria, Greece and Turkey have eaten yoghurt for hundreds of years. It is rich in vitamin B.

yoke *n.* a wooden harness which joins a pair of oxen at the neck for working together. *vb.* link together.
yolk (rhymes with *soak*) *n.* the yellow part inside an egg.
Yom Kippur *n.* the Day of Atonement, a Jewish feast marking 10 days of penitence and abstinence at the start of the Jewish New Year (mid-September).
Yorkshire pudding *n.* a batter of eggs, flour and milk cooked in drippings and traditionally eaten with roast beef.

Yosemite National Park
Yosemite National Park is a wilderness in California, about 200 miles (320 km) east of San Francisco. It covers a vast area in the center of the Sierra Nevada mountains and is one of the most spectacular and beautiful areas in the United States. There are hundreds of species of birds and animals, and groves of the famous giant sequoia trees. Yosemite Valley in the center of the park contains much of the national park's finest scenery.
There are many spectacular waterfalls.

you *pronoun* used for the second person singular and plural. *Could you please lend me your pen, John?* or *Can you all hear me?*
young 1. *adj.* not old. 2. *n.* baby animals. *Mammals feed their young on milk.* **youngster** *n.* a young girl or boy.
your *pronoun* & *adj.* belonging to you.
youth *n.* (plural **youths**) the time when one is young; a young man or woman; (collective) young people. *The youth of today will deplore the youth of tomorrow.*
Yo-yo *n.* a toy that consists of a reel or disc that winds and unwinds from a string held in the hand.

Yugoslavia (Yugoslavian, Yugoslav)
Yugoslavia is a Communist republic on the Mediterranean Sea. The coast is an attractive tourist area. Inland, there are barren mountains, but fertile plains cover the northeast. Yugoslavia was created in 1918. A Communist government took over in 1945, but it has remained independent of the Soviet Union and China. About a third of the population belongs to the Orthodox Church and a quarter of the people are Roman Catholics. The chief river is the DANUBE, with its tributaries. In addition to Belgrade, the largest cities are Zagreb, Skopje and Sarajevo.

AREA: 98,772 SQ. MILES (255,804 SQ. KM)
POPULATION: 22,745,000
CAPITAL: BELGRADE
CURRENCY: DINAR
OFFICIAL LANGUAGES: SERBO-CROAT, SLOVENE, MACEDONIAN.

Yukon River
The Yukon rises in northwestern CANADA and flows through ALASKA through a huge DELTA into the Bering Sea. It is about 2,300 miles (3,680 km) long, and it is the fourth largest waterway in North America. Most of the river is navigable during the summer months.

Yukon Territory
The Yukon Territory is a region of northwestern CANADA, on the border with ALASKA. The climate is cold and the area is thinly populated. The main activity is mining for gold, silver, copper, zinc and other minerals. Whitehorse is the capital. The largest rivers are the YUKON and Mackenzie. The region was explored by the Hudson Bay Company in the 1840s. The discovery of gold led to a gold rush in 1896.

Z

The ruins of the Ziggurat at Ur, one of the leading cities of ancient Sumeria.

Zaïre
Zaïre is a huge country that sprawls across the heart of Africa. It includes most of the vast Zaïre River. The Zaïre, once called the Congo, flows 3,000 miles (4,800 km) from its source to the Atlantic Ocean.

Zaïre is a hot, rainy country and much of it is covered with jungle. There are lakes and highlands in the east and south. Copper, cobalt and diamonds are mined here. These minerals make Zaïre a wealthy country. Most of the people are farmers growing tea, coffee, cocoa and cotton.

Zaïre once belonged to Belgium. It became the Republic of Zaïre in 1971.

AREA: 905,617 SQ. MILES (2,345,409 SQ. KM)
POPULATION: 29,826,000
CAPITAL: KINSHASA
CURRENCY: ZAIRE
OFFICIAL LANGUAGE: FRENCH

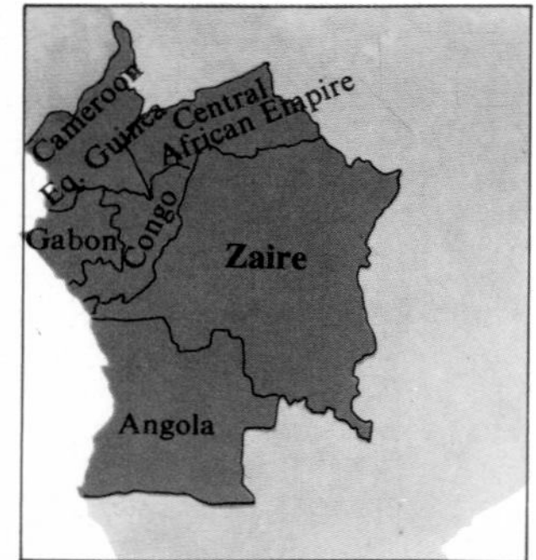

Zaïre River
The Zaïre River in Central Africa was formerly called the Congo. It rises in southern Zaïre and flows about 3,000 miles (4,800 km) to the Atlantic Ocean. Its course is interrupted by many waterfalls and steep rapids, and it has great potential as a source of hydroelectric power. The Zaïre is Africa's second longest river, the longest being the NILE.

Zambezi River
The Zambezi is Africa's fourth longest river. It flows about 1,600 miles (2,575 km) across southern Africa before emptying into the Indian Ocean. The Kariba Dam, Lake Kariba, the Cabora Bassa dam and the magnificent VICTORIA FALLS are on the Zambezi.

Zambia (Zambian)
Zambia is a country in southern Africa. It is entirely surrounded by land. Zaïre, Tanzania, Malawi, Mozambique, Botswana, Zimbabwe and Angola all share borders with Zambia.

The name Zambia comes from the ZAMBEZI river. Much of the country is rolling, highland plains. Most Zambians are poor and farmers. Nearly all of the country's wealth comes from its copper mines. Almost a quarter of the world's copper is mined there.

AREA: 290,602 SQ. MILES (752,614 SQ. KM)
POPULATION: 5,992,000
CAPITAL: LUSAKA
CURRENCY: KWACHA
OFFICIAL LANGUAGE: ENGLISH

zany (**zay**-*nee*) *adj.* absurd, eccentric; strangely funny.

Zanzibar
Zanzibar is an island in the Indian Ocean, just off the east coast of Africa. It forms part of TANZANIA. The soil is fertile and the island is famous for its cloves. In the past, Zanzibar has been ruled by the Arabs, Portuguese and the British. It was once the center of the slave trade. Many famous African explorers of the 1800s began their expeditions at Zanzibar.

zeal *n.* an old-fashioned word meaning enthusiasm or eagerness.

zebra *n.* an African animal related to the horse, with dark stripes on a light body.

► Zebras belong to the horse family. They live in the open grasslands of Africa to the south of the Sahara. Each animal has its own special pattern of stripes.

Zebras live in herds. Although they can run very fast, they are often

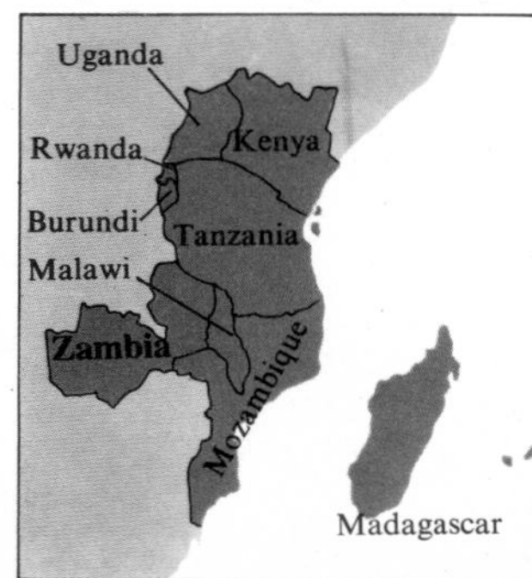

No two zebras have the same stripe pattern.

hunted by lions, leopards and hyenas. The zebra's stripes seem to make it conspicuous, but in fact they help to camouflage the animal, breaking up its outline against a varied background.

zebu (**zee**-*boo*) *n.* a humped ox of Asia and Africa.

Zen *n.* a sect of Buddhism that originated in Japan.

zenith *n.* point of the sky directly overhead; highest point; acme.

Zeppelin, Count von
Count Ferdinand von Zeppelin (1838–1917) was a German army officer who invented the first rigid airship, named zeppelin after him. He made his first ascent in a balloon while acting as an observer with the Union Army during the Civil War. On retiring from the army he began to design and manufacture airships.

During WORLD WAR I, zeppelins were used in bombing raids over London. However, they proved too vulnerable to attack and were replaced by airplanes. A series of disasters between the two World Wars marked the end of the airship's development, although recently there has been renewed interest in the idea of the airship as a freight carrier.

zero *n.* nothing; the figure 0.

zest *n.* enthusiasm, lively enjoyment; gusto.

Zeus
According to the myths and legends of the ancient Greeks, Zeus was a ruler of all the gods. He lived on Mt. Olympus and was married to Hera. He was the father of the gods Apollo, Dionysus and Athene. He often came to earth disguised as an animal. At one time he turned himself into a swan to attract Leda, the queen of Sparta. She bore him twin sons, Castor and Pollux.

Zeus was the son of the ancient god Kronos. The stories say that Zeus and his brothers, Poseidon and Hades, killed Kronos and took over his throne. Poseidon took the sea, Hades took the underworld and Zeus took the world and the sky.

ziggurat *n.* a type of pyramid built in ancient Babylonia, the sides of which were built in huge "steps," each story set in from the one below. Ziggurats were used as temples and observatories.

zigzag *adj.* & *n.* going one way and then another, like the letter Z. *vb.* move in a zigzag way.

Zimbabwe (Ancient)
Zimbabwe is a ruined city in southern Africa. The name Zimbabwe comes from an African word meaning "home of a chief" and it is possible that the city was once the capital of a great African empire.

Explorers first found the ruins in 1868, but archaeologists did not begin to dig there until the 1940s. They discovered temples, towers and massive walls all built of huge stone slabs mostly fitted together without mortar. The most spectacular ruin is the Elliptical Building. It has curved walls over 275 yards (250 meters) long and as high as a house. A long eerie passage separates these outer walls from similar inner walls. Inside the building stands a tall, tapering tower.

Finds at Zimbabwe show that people were living there 1700 years ago. They were probably farmers. But it seems that the city was later abandoned. People returned to live in Zimbabwe about A.D. 1000 and the oldest stone ruins date from this time. From then until the early 1800s, Zimbabwe appears to have been a busy city and was perhaps the center of an important gold trade. Nobody yet knows how and why the city of Zimbabwe came to an end.

Zimbabwe (Country)
Zimbabwe used to be called Rhodesia. It is a small country in southern Africa, and lies inland, about 150 miles (240 km) from the Indian Ocean. About 97 percent are Black Africans; most of the others are English-speaking Whites.

Zeus, shown here on a coin, was the chief of all the Greek gods. He was known as Jupiter or Jove by the Romans.

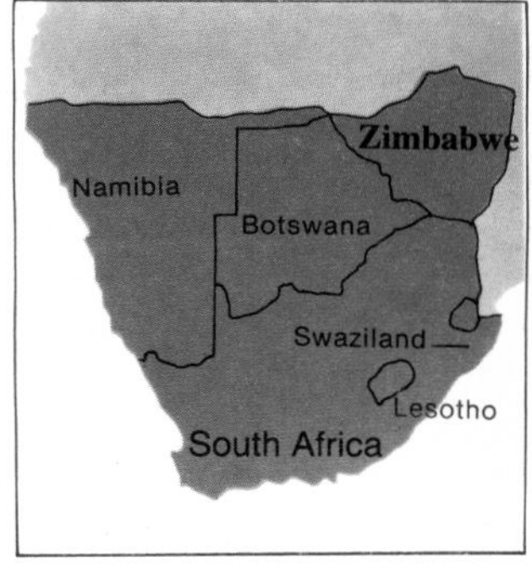

Zimbabwe is bordered by the Zambezi river in the north. The Zambezi is famous for the VICTORIA FALLS and the Kariba Dam. The Kariba Dam is a great hydroelectric scheme that supplies power to both Zimbabwe and its neighbor Zambia.

Until 1965, Zimbabwe was a British colony. In that year, it declared itself independent. Britain, however, did not recognize the new nation's existence. During the next 15 years, growing unrest and guerrilla warfare finally forced Zimbabwe to turn to Britain again to help solve its problems. In 1980 the country became independent.

AREA: 150,812 SQ. MILES (390,580 SQ. KM)
POPULATION: 7,878,000
CAPITAL: HARARE
CURRENCY: ZIMBABWE DOLLAR
OFFICIAL LANGUAGE: ENGLISH

zinc *n.* a hard, bluish-white metal element (symbol – *Zn*).

► Zinc has been mined since ancient times and has been used in making brass for over 2,000 years. Brass is an ALLOY of zinc and copper.

A large share of the world's zinc comes from Canada, Australia and the Soviet Union. Zinc mines usually contain other metals such as copper, gold, lead and silver.

Most zinc is used to *galvanize* steel. Galvanizing is putting a thin coat of zinc on steel to protect it. Zinc is also used to make cells in electric batteries. Brass as well as Zinc forms part of many other alloys including nickel and bronze.

zipper *n.* a fastener with two sets of teeth that lock together. *vb.* fasten with a zipper.

zither *n.* a many-stringed musical instrument having a shallow horizontal body and played with picks and by plucking.

zloty *n.* principal money unit of Poland. The word means golden.

zodiac *n.* a name given by ancient astrologers to the band of sky through which the sun, moon, and all the planets except Pluto appear to move.

► The first people to study the Zodiac, over 4,000 years ago, were the astronomers of ancient BABYLON. They divided it into 12 sections, with a group of stars in each section. The sections get their names, called signs, from the shapes of the star groups. The 12 signs of the Zodiac are Aries (Ram), Taurus (Bull), Gemini (Twins), Cancer (Crab), Leo (Lion), Virgo (Virgin), Libra (Scales), Scorpio (Scorpion), Sagittarius (Archer), Capricornus (Goat), Aquarius (Water-carrier), and Pisces (Fish). Each Zodiac sign is linked to part of the year. Pisces, for example, covers the period February 19 to March 20. Astrologers use the Zodiac signs to discover people's characters and to foretell the future.

zombie *n.* a corpse said to be brought back to life by witchcraft; a will-less person, someone who behaves like a robot.

zone *n.* & *vb.* part of a town or larger area that is set off as distinct.

zoo *n.* a place where captive wild animals are kept for public display (short for zoological gardens).

► There are more than 330 zoos in the world today. The first zoos were in ancient Egypt. Queen Hatshepsut kept a zoo in 1500 B.C. More than 3,000 years ago the emperors of China kept animals, birds and fish in natural gardens where they could feel at home. In the Middle Ages in Europe, kings gave each other presents of apes, peacocks and lions. Private collections of animals were called menageries.

Since the 1700s, scientists have been interested in the study of animals. They began to sort animals into groups and give them Latin names so that the same animal would have the same name wherever it lived. Their work led directly to the building of the first public zoos. The very first zoo was London Zoo, built in 1829.

Modern zoos have natural settings for their animals such as moats, ditches and hedges. This means that the animals have room to walk about, and can stay indoors or go out according to the weather.

Zoos are important for the care and breeding of rare or endangered kinds of animals. For instance, the Hawaiian goose and Père David's deer would not exist today if zoos had not saved them.

zoology *n.* the study of animals.

zoom 1. *n.* sharp upward movement. 2. *n.* a loud low hum. 3. *vb.* focus a camera quickly from long-shot to close-up by use of a special lens.

A Zulu. The Zulus were a brave and powerful tribe in the 1800s. More than half a million now live in Zululand in Natal, South Africa.

Zulu

The Zulus are a Black African people of the BANTU family, noted for their massive physique. Originally cattle-herders, they were formed into a warrior nation by their great king Shaka, in about 1820. With the help of a new short stabbing spear called an *assegai*, they conquered a wide area, but in the late 1800s were beaten by the Boers and British. About three million are left today, as laborers in South Africa.

Zurich

Zurich is the largest city in SWITZERLAND. It lies in the north of the country by the Lake of Zurich in the foothills of the Alps. Zurich is the commercial center of Switzerland, and is famous for its banking and finance houses. It is also a cultural center, having Switzerland's largest university.